encyclopedia of social theory

edited by
austin harrington
barbara l. marshall
hans-peter müller

Routledge
Taylor & Francis Group

LONDON AND NEW YORK

Published 2006 by Routledge
2 Park Square, Milton Park, Abingdon, Oxon OX14 4RN

Simultaneously published in the USA and Canada
By Routledge
711 Third Avenue, New York, NY 10017

First issued in paperback 2015

Routledge is an imprint of the Taylor & Francis Group, an informa business

© 2006 Routledge

Typeset in Bembo and Helvetica by Taylor & Francis Books

British Library Cataloguing in Publication Data
A catalogue record for this book is available from the British Library

Library of Congress Cataloging in Publication Data
A catalog record for this book has been requested

ISBN 13: 978-0-415-75393-7 (pbk)
ISBN 13: 978-0-415-29046-3 (hbk)

encyclopedia of social theory

Social theory ... he central terrain of ideas that links rese... h in sociology to key problems in the ... iosophy of the human sciences. At the ... t of the twentieth century, social theory v... s the body of thought that sought to grou... d sociology as an independent discipline. At the start of the twenty-first century, ... cial theory is the dynamic nexus of con... pts and ideas that informs sociology's di... ogue with a protean variety of approache... in neighbouring disciplines. In recent yeal... social theory has stood at the forefront of ... most exciting debates in fields ranging ... cross sociology and anthropology, politi... l theory and political economy, media ... d cultural studies, feminist theory and p... -colonial studies.

The *Encycl... edia of Social Theory* provides a unique re... ce source for students and academics, ... acing all major aspects of the field. V... ...n by more than 200 internationally distinguished scholars, almost 500 entries cover core contemporary topics,

concepts, schools, debates, and personalities in the history of the discipline. Special attention is paid to leading schools and debates, with shorter entries reserved for biographies of key theorists and definitions of key terms. Entries are fully cross-referenced and contain concise listings for further reading. A comprehensive index guides the reader to further divisions of content.

Austin Harrington is Lecturer in Sociology at the University of Leeds, UK, and Research Fellow at the Max Weber Centre for Advanced Study at the University of Erfurt, Germany.

Barbara L. Marshall is Professor of Sociology and Women's Studies at Trent University, Canada.

Hans–Peter Müller is Professor of Sociology at the Humboldt University of Berlin, Germany.

contents

introduction

The Routledge *Encyclopedia of Social Theory* contains 479 entries, each in varying length categories ranging from approximately 300 to 2,500 words. Though a sizeable figure, this total permits us to make only a limited selection from the vast range of topics, themes, concepts, debates, schools and authors that today pass by the broad and open-ended name of 'social theory'. Social theory is, by definition, an interdisciplinary undertaking, composing a large nexus of domains in the humanities and social sciences. Social theory gravitates around the discipline of sociology but also pulls into its orbit a veritable galaxy of fields ranging from history, philosophy, economics and political science to anthropology, geography, cultural studies, media studies, women's studies and area studies. This encyclopedia cannot possibly do justice to the full panoply of links between sociology and these other fields. Nor can it compete with the many other reference works available today for more specialised domains such as social policy, feminist theory, post-colonial studies, religious studies or psychoanalytic theory—even though each of these named areas intersects with social theory in key ways. Nevertheless, we believe the present encyclopedia offers a spread of entries that reflects this rich conjunction of ideas as judiciously and comprehensively as it can within the constraints of a single volume.

In this brief Introduction we want to underline a few general considerations underlying our difficult decisions about which kinds of material to include in the volume and which to leave out.

1. This encyclopedia caters chiefly to topics in social *theory*, rather than to topics in empirical sociology or empirical social research. Topics consisting of a relatively large component of empirical information and a relatively small component of theoretical analysis receive less treatment in this work. We have determined entry headwords according to the extent to which they are driven specifically by a theory or by the extent to which they raise issues that are specifically conceptual, epistemological or methodological in character.

2. This is an encyclopedia primarily of *social* rather than *political* theory. Social theory and political theory relate to and depend on one another very closely, and the present work naturally covers a range of key concepts in political thought, such as democracy, equality, liberty, liberalism, socialism, anarchism, communitarianism, and several others. However, we must emphasise that this encyclopedia is aimed primarily at the social or sociological end of the spectrum of the field, rather than at the normative political end.

3. The emphasis of this encyclopedia falls on concepts, themes, debates and

schools of thought, rather than on intellectual personalities. Entries for names of individual theorists have been confined to brief overviews of no more than about 300 words. The purpose of this policy has been to release space for lengthier treatments of the principal ideas, theses and arguments for which these theorists are chiefly celebrated or criticised. Our aim has been to exploit the advantages of the format of an encyclopedia both in dividing material into analytically distinct elements and in linking these elements together by thematically guided *cross-references*. This format, we believe, is particularly well-suited to a concentration on conceptual analysis and synthesis, rather than on intellectual biography.

4. The encyclopedia contains 106 entries on the work of individual theorists. This roster will inevitably be open to criticism. There are some names we could not possibly have excluded; but there are many other figures we could not have included without raising virtually endless and intractable issues of relative parity of importance. Our necessarily rather pragmatic selection is based on considerations of canonical influence, originality and critical depth, but is in no way meant to imply a roll-call of the 'greatest of the great'.

5. Lengths of entries for concepts, themes and schools have been determined by relative scope and complexity of the topic, by relative disciplinary centrality, and by relative modernity and contemporaneity. By 'modernity' and 'contemporaneity' we mean social thought and analysis from around the eighteenth and nineteenth centuries onwards, but mostly in the twentieth and twenty-first centuries. Short entries are conceived simply as definitions of terms.

Longer entries aim to provide concise overviews of substantive fields of research and debate.

6. Our policy in this one-volume work has been to commission a large number of succinct but tightly cross-referenced entries, rather than a smaller number of longer entries under less discriminate headwords. Headwords aim to reflect technical differences between terms as closely as possibly, more after the fashion of a dictionary than a compendium of themed areas such as a handbook. The entry for 'stratification', for example, may be read in conjunction with 'inequality', 'class', 'status', 'gender', 'elites', 'caste', 'prestige', 'cultural capital', 'poverty', 'underclass', and 'social inclusion and social exclusion'. We use cross-references both to divide material into units and to link these units together by 'family resemblance', in Wittgenstein's celebrated phrase.

7. The encyclopedia includes one large entry for 'religion' and three separate entries for Christianity, Judaism and Islam, but omits entries for all other world religions. We include the three Western monotheistic religions because these have historically featured not only as *objects* but also as dimensions in the formation of the *concepts* of modern Western social thought, whereas, at least until recently, religions such as Hinduism, Buddhism or Confucianism have featured in social theory at most as distant objects of research. We do not here imply that social theory is an exclusively Western enterprise. If social theory was an exclusively Western enterprise in the past, it is no longer so today. Nevertheless, with respect to the study of world religions and civilizations, the present encyclopedia must defer to better equipped reference works available

today in such fields as global cultural studies, religious studies and area studies.

8. Similarly, we include two entries for 'Europe' and 'America' but omit entries for other world regions. We do so not because we subscribe to a Eurocentric or Western-centred view of world culture. We do so because adequate treatment of non-Western regional contexts is well beyond our available resources; and because Europe and America (qua the USA) are the initial historical sites of the emergence of social theory as a scientific institution; and because Europe and America have been profoundly complex signifiers for numerous influential names in modern cultural criticism, from Alexis de Tocqueville to Jean Baudrillard.

9. The encyclopedia addresses a range of concepts, themes and debates in feminist theory and in feminist responses to main- or 'malestream' social theory. However, it cannot be as compre- hensive in its coverage of these issues as works devoted specially to women's studies, such as the Routledge *Encyclopedia of Feminist Theory* edited by Lorraine Code, among others.

10. Some headwords are marked in the listing of entries by their synonyms or near-synonyms. For 'labour', we write '*see* Work'. For 'ethics', we write '*see* Morality'. For terms such as 'sanction', 'discipline', 'punishment' and 'surveillance', we write '*see* Social control'. For all other synonyms or near-synonyms, for other overlapping terms or for words included under more encompassing terms, please see the index at the end of this volume. Note that in the List of Entries 'change' appears as 'social change', 'justice' as 'social justice', 'reproduction' as 'social reproduction', and 'system' as 'social system'.

Austin Harrington
Barbara L. Marshall
Hans-Peter Müller

acknowledgements

The volume editors thank the Directorate of the Institute of Social Sciences at the Humboldt University of Berlin for funds made available for the services of research assistants at the Lehrstuhl für Allgemeine Soziologie, 2003–4. The volume editors particularly thank Il-Tschung Lim for vital assistance in the tasks of assigning, collecting and coordinating entries from the contributing authors and reporting to the management team at Routledge Reference. The volume editors also thank Ingar Abels, Julia Behne, and Andreas Weiß for key editorial assistance in the preparation of the final manuscript.

contributors

Christopher Adair-Toteff
Mississippi State University

Robert Adcock
University of California, Berkeley

Lisa Adkins
University of Manchester

Brian Alleyne
Goldsmith's College, University of London

Robert J. Antonio
University of Kansas

Caroline Arni
University of Berne

Roland Axtmann
University of Wales, Swansea

Feyzi Baban
Trent University, Ontario

Maurizio Bach
University of Passau

Veit Bader
University of Amsterdam

Dirk Baecker
University of Witten/Herdecke

Patrick Baert
University of Cambridge

Gideon Baker
University of Salford

Sekhar Bandyopadhyay
Victoria University of Wellington

Jack Barbalet
University of Leicester

Benjamin Barber
University of Maryland

Andrew Barry
Goldsmith's College, University of London

Rainer Bauböck
Austrian Academy of Sciences, Vienna

Ulrich Beck
Ludwig Maximilian University of Munich

Johannes Berger
University of Mannheim

Tony Blackshaw
Sheffield Hallam University

James Bohman
Saint Louis University

Cornelia Bohn
University of Trier

Craig Brandist
University of Sheffield

Jens Brockmeier
New School University, New York

Hauke Brunkhorst
University of Flensburg

Christian Brütt
Humboldt University of Berlin

Sonja Buckel
University of Frankfurt

Lars Bullmann
Ruhr University of Bochum

Günter Burkart
University of Lüneburg

Joan Busfield
University of Essex

Tim Butler
King's College, University of London

Philip Catton
University of Canterbury

Robin Celikates
University of Erfurt

Naomi Choi
University of California, Berkeley

Kevin Christiano
Notre Dame University

Karen S. Cook
Stanford University

Nick Crossley
University of Manchester

Charles Crothers
Auckland University of Technology

Jens Dangschat
Technical University of Vienna

Gerard Delanty
University of Liverpool

Eoin Devereux
University of Limerick

Göran Djurfeldt
Lund University

Klaus Eder
Humboldt University of Berlin

Klaus-Dieter Eichler
University of Mainz

Stuart Elden
University of Durham

Christoph Fehige
University of Constance

Ralph Fevre
Cardiff University

Beate Fietze
Humboldt University of Berlin

Robert Fine
University of Warwick

Karsten Fischer
Humboldt University of Berlin

Günter Frankenberg
University of Frankfurt

Susanne Fuchs
Wissenschaftszentrum Berlin

Jan A. Fuhse
University of Stuttgart

Steve Fuller
University of Warwick

Matthew Gandy
University College London

Heiner Ganßmann
Free University of Berlin

Vincent Geoghegan
Queen's University, Belfast

Alexandra Gerbasi
Stanford University

Ute Gerhard
University of Frankfurt

Uta Gerhardt
University of Heidelberg

Nigel Gibson
Harvard University

Bernhard Giesen
University of Constance

Emily Gilbert
University of Toronto

Graeme Gilloch
University of Salford

Gert-Joachim Glaeßner
Humboldt University of Berlin

Jukka Gronow
University of Uppsala

Steven Grosby
Clemson University

Matthias Gross
UFZ Centre for Environmental Research, Leipzig

Peter Hägel
Humboldt University of Berlin

Lawrence Hamilton
University of KwaZulu-Natal

Philip Hancock
Warwick Business School

xvi

Rom Harré
University of Oxford

Austin Harrington
University of Leeds

Anke Hassel
Max Planck Institute, Cologne

Pierre Hassner
Sciences Po, Paris

Mark Haugaard
National University of Ireland

Wilhelm Heitmeyer
University of Bielefeld

Rosemary Hennessy
State University of New York at Albany

Andreas Hess
University College Dublin

Myra Hird
Queen's University, Ontario

Trevor Hogan
La Trobe University

John Holmwood
University of Sussex

Alan How
University College Worcester

David Howarth
University of Essex

Jason Hughes
University of Leicester

James D. Ingram
New School University, New York

Engin F. Isin
York University, Toronto

Stevi Jackson
University of York Heslington

Søren Jagd
University of Roskilde

Lynn Jamieson
University of Edinburgh

David Jary
University of Birmingham

Guillermina Jasso
New York University

Richard Jenkins
University of Sheffield

Fabien Jobard
CNRS, Paris

Danielle Juteau
University of Montreal

Stephen Kalberg
Boston University

Stephen Katz
Trent University, Ontario

Suzanne Keller
Princeton University

Duncan Kelly
University of Sheffield

Rachel Kerr
King's College, University of London

Thomas Khurana
University of Potsdam

Richard Kilminster
University of Leeds

Barbara Kinach
University of Maryland, Baltimore

Sascha Kneip
University of Heidelberg

Helmut Kuzmics
University of Graz

Raymond M. Lee
Royal Holloway College, University of London

Thomas Lemke
University of Frankfurt

Il-Tschung Lim
University of Mannheim

Bodo Lippl
Humboldt University of Berlin

Marcus Llanque
Humboldt University of Berlin

Tim Lockley
University of Warwick

David Lyon
Queen's University, Ontario

Jürgen Mackert
Humboldt University of Berlin

Kirk Mann
University of Leeds

Oliver Marchart
University of Basel

Barbara L. Marshall
Trent University, Ontario

Steffen Mau
University of Bremen

Vanessa May
University of Leeds

Jim McGuigan
University of Loughborough

Volker Meja
Memorial University of Newfoundland

Wolfgang Merkel
Wissenschaftszentrum Berlin

Peter-Ulrich Merz-Benz
University of Zürich

Lukas Meyer
University of Bremen

Murray Milner
University of Virginia

Barbara Misztal
University of Leicester

Virág Molnár
Princeton University

Catherine A. Morgan
University of Leeds

Raymond A. Morrow
University of Alberta

Charlotte Müller
University of Bern

Hans-Peter Müller
Humboldt University of Berlin

Armin Nassehi
Ludwig Maximilian University of Munich

Friedhelm Neidhardt
Wissenschaftszentrum Berlin

Carlos Novas
London School of Economics

Gertrud Nunner-Winkler
Max Planck Institute, Munich

Darren O'Byrne
Roehampton University

Brian O'Connor
University College Dublin

Patrick O'Mahony
University College Cork

Thomas Osborne
University of Bristol

David Owen
University of Southampton

Frank Pearce
Queen's University, Ontario

Anton Pelinka
University of Innsbruck

Mary Pickering
San Jose State University

Gary Pollock
Manchester Metropolitan University

Annie Potts
University of Canterbury

Christine Pries
Frankfurter Rundschau

Momin Rahman
University of Strathclyde

William Ramp
University of Lethbridge

Werner Raub
University of Utrecht

Andreas Reckwitz
University of Hamburg

Karl-Siegbert Rehberg
Technical University of Dresden

Tilman Reitz
University of Jena

Martin Riesebrodt
University of Chicago

Derek Robbins
University of East London

Ralf Rogowski
University of Warwick

Frank Ruda
Ruhr University of Bochum

Thomas Sablowski
Wissenschaftszentrum Berlin

Barry Sandywell
University of York

Bobby Sayyid
University of Leeds

Uwe Schimank
University of Hagen

Christian Schmidt-Wellenburg
Humboldt University of Berlin

Thomas Schneider
University of Erfurt

Wolfgang Ludwig Schneider
University of Gießen

Ralph Schroeder
Oxford Internet Institute

Alan Scott
University of Innsbruck

Wes Sharrock
University of Manchester

Martin Shaw
University of Sussex

Alison Sheldon
University of Leeds

Steffen Sigmund
University of Heidelberg

Don Slater
London School of Economics

Laureen Snider
Queen's University, Ontario

Urs Stäheli
University of Bern

Helmut Staubmann
University of Innsbruck

Elaine Stavro
Trent University, Ontario

Nico Stehr
University of British Columbia

Jochen Steinbicker
Humboldt University of Berlin

Heinz Steinert
University of Frankfurt

Nick Stevenson
University of Nottingham

Rudolf Stichweh
University of Lucerne

Piet Strydom
University College Cork

Daniel Šuber
University of Constance

Richard Swedberg
Cornell University

Arpad Szakolczai
University College Cork

Keith Tester
University of Portsmouth

Bjørn Thomassen
American University of Rome

Jacob Torfing
University of Roskilde

Keith Tribe
King's School Worcester

Jonathan Turner
University of California, Riverside

Stephen P. Turner
University of South Florida

Ralf E. Ulrich
University of Bielefeld

John Veit-Wilson
University of Newcastle

Michael Vester
University of Hannover

Thomas Voss
University of Leipzig

Gerhard Wagner
University of Frankfurt

Peter Wagner
European University Institute, Florence

Tony Walter
University of Reading

Frank Webster
City University London

Bernd Wegener
Humboldt University of Berlin

Siegfried Weichlein
Humboldt University of Berlin

Johannes Weiss
University of Kassel

Harald Wenzel
Free University of Berlin

Ulla Wessels
University of Leipzig

Sam Whimster
London Metropolitan University

Andrew Whitworth
University of Leeds

Iain Wilkinson
University of Kent at Canterbury

Malcolm Williams
University of Plymouth

Monika Wohlrab-Sahr
University of Leipzig

Michaela Wünsch
Humboldt University Berlin

Anna Yeatman
University of Alberta

Karine Zbinden
University of Sheffield

Reinhard Zintl
University of Bamberg

Phil Zuckerman
Pitzer College, California

list of entries

A

ACTION

Action is the realization of the power of a person or thing to effect change in itself and its environment. To act or to actualize is to make real the potential or power that an actor possesses. In the language of Aristotle's three modalities of possibility, necessity and actuality, action is the movement from 'I can' to 'I do', or from 'I must' to 'I do'. I cannot act if I lack the power or possibility to do so; though sometimes I *must* act, even if I lack the power to do so. To make actual or become actual thus is to move from a state of possibility to a state of reality, or from a state of the future ('not yet') to a state of the present ('now').

Most languages distinguish between (1) action as process or performance and (2) action as completed phase, unit, result or end-state of a course of acting. Thus English distinguishes 'acting' and 'act'; French distinguishes *agir* and *action*, German distinguishes *Handeln* and *Handlung*, and so on. The result of acting is the deed, *fait* or *Tat*, and so on. An act of law, or an act of war, or an act in the theatre, is the completed bounded phase or result or record of a process of acting, deliberating, playing or conspiring, and so on.

Action in social theory usually contrasts with the term **structure**. Structure is classically thought of as limiting or constraining action negatively, by reducing the range of possibilities available to an actor or by pre-determining the actor's possibilities and deeds beyond the actor's free choice. But structure also shapes, moulds or articulates action in some sense and thus 'enables' it to a certain extent. The idea that action is 'enabled' by structure is sometimes referred to by the term 'structuration' (see **structuration school**). Structure is then said to be bound up with the **agency** of the actor, where agency is defined as the ability of actors to act freely within the limits of a medium of some kind.

Action is usually distinguished by philosophers and social theorists from non-intentional behaviour, where 'intentional' denotes representation of desires in the form of goals or purposes of action. It was in this sense that Max **Weber** defined action in the opening paragraph of *Economy and Society* as 'behaviour to which the actor attaches a subjectively intended meaning' (Weber 1968: 4). I do not truly act, Weber argued, if I am only induced or stimulated to behaving in a certain way by something that is external to me and that I cannot recognize as my own *reason* for acting – for example, by hypnotism or by a sudden noise that makes me jump in fright. To attach a subjectively intended meaning to my behaviour implies that I can account for, and be responsible, for my conduct, in the sense of my **autonomy** and moral responsibility as an individual. According to Kantian philosophy, I am at once a creature of nature, bound to the laws of nature which determine my impulses, and, at the same time, a free being capable of determining

1

my own courses of action (see **Kantianism and Neo-Kantianism**). This implies that when I act, the causes of my acting can be my *reasons for acting*. The theme of reasons as causes of action was explored later in the twentieth century by analytical philosophers of language, notably by Donald Davidson (1980), in opposition to earlier standpoints of **behaviourism** and **positivism** that had sought to reduce or 'bracket off' all reference to a subject's inner mental states in favour of strictly observable physical processes (see also **reductionism** and **causality**).

In addition, Weber distinguished between intentional action in a narrow sense of action consciously oriented to ends by deliberate calculation of appropriate means and a wider, more diffuse range of types of action guided by feelings and **emotion**, by longstanding social customs and **tradition**, and by 'values', especially 'ultimate values' expressed in **religion**, **ritual** and **myth**. Intentional action, in the narrow sense, Weber termed 'purposive-rational action' (*zweckrationales Handeln*). Purposive-rational action implies an ability to convert knowledge of an objective causal relation between two states of affairs into a subjective teleological relation: I know that fire causes water to boil; I want to boil water; therefore I light a fire. But perfectly purposive-rational action of this kind is rarely found in social reality in any interesting and complex sense. For example, in the stock exchange traders invariably fall short of this ideal, and a large part of their action is determined by emotions of fear or euphoria. Today, theorists of **rational choice** demonstrate at length the manifold ways in which actors seeking rational strategies in pursuit of their interests may also deviate from the most effective courses of action. Weber therefore defined three other types of action: 'affectual action', motivated by emotion, passion or impulse; 'traditional action', motivated by conformity to social precedent; and 'value-rational action', motivated by rational pursuit of an end, but where the end in question cannot itself function as a means because it is, for the actor, the ultimate end in life, represented as 'salvation', 'election to the kingdom of God', or 'happiness'. Thus the concluding thesis of Weber's study of the **Protestant ethic** and its relation to the 'spirit of capitalism' in early modern Europe was that over the courses of processes of **industrialization** and bureaucratization, the Puritan's value-rational beliefs that had once given spiritual sense to the entrepreneur's purposive-rational calculations were now defunct: where purposive-rational action had once been *embedded* in value-rational action, now such action was left to spin around in its own moral void, like an 'iron cage' of meaningless compulsions.

Besides 'action' in general, the concept of 'social action' in particular is foundational for social theory. Social action in a strict sense should be distinguished from generally socially conditioned action. Clearly all action by an individual is socially conditioned in a general sense: I cannot act privately, keep secrets, lie to others, surprise, manipulate, or dominate others, without the existence of others. But some actions I can perform predominantly only in solitude, while other actions I can perform predominantly only in concert with others. I can pray or urinate alone, and I can die alone; I need not perform any of these actions with another person, though my performance of these actions – even the ultimate borderline case of death – is always socially structured, just as my every act of speech, even when I talk to myself or think alone, is socially structured. However, only action *in concert with others* counts as 'social action' in the strict sense. Here again the canonical definition is provided by Weber when he writes that 'social action is action which on account its subjective meaning is oriented in its course by the action of another' (Weber 1968: 4). Social action occurs only when I 'orient' or 'relate' my action to the action of another, who must exist in some more or less definite spatio-temporal relation to me, though he or she or they may not be known to me personally, indeed may be wholly anonymous to me.

A further requirement for Weber is that interaction must be informed by norms, rules or conventions of some kind. A collision between two cyclists is social action only to the extent that the two cyclists fail to fulfill a prevalent **convention** to avoid one another by riding on alternate sides or to the extent that they swear at each other or argue about the collision's causes. The crashing of the two vehicles is not in itself social action but only a physical event. Similarly, it follows that a panic reaction in a crowd of people in which each individual is caused to react by the stimulus of others without a chance to communicate or to deliberate with them also fails to count as social action in the strict sense of intentionally mediated, symbolically structured interaction. Crowd behaviour thus stands on the borderline between collective intentional action and mass affection or mass stimulus-and-response. Social action may issue in **conflict** or non-cooperation, possibly even in **war and militarism**; or it may be dominated by the egoistic or tyrannical action of one party in relation to another; but all such action is social if and only if it is produced with a shared orientation to a code or body of norms – for example, rules of engagement in a battle – even if the code or the rules are violated in some way.

The specifically social character of human action in general was poorly understood by the movements of eighteenth- and nineteenth-century **political economy** and **utilitarianism**, although these movements achieved spectacular results in applying putative psychological laws about the springs of human motivation to economic and strategic behaviour. The primary conceptual innovation of Marx's critique of classical political economy was to demonstrate that human beings are not atoms of economic action competing in a social vacuum, in the image of *homo oeconomicus*, but vitally interdependent members of definite social **groups**. It followed that altruistic behaviour could not be explained solely by strategic mitigation of self-regarding **interests**, as when I concede some short-term profit to myself for the sake of a longer-term security or when I elect to support my family, kin and friends to the extent that I see them as supporting my sphere of power. Later positivist thinking, culminating in the work of **Pareto**, sought to explain such behaviour by reference to a category of 'irrational' or 'non-rational' factors, covering the influence of religion, custom and tradition. The inadequacies of such thinking were exposed in the middle decades of the twentieth century by three schools of thought, each of them paralleling the example set by Weber. These were (1) Alfred **Schutz**'s project of a **phenomenology** of the social world; (2) George Herbert **Mead**'s psychology of social behaviour oriented to human **interaction**; and (3) Talcott **Parsons**'s framework of sociological **functionalism**.

Drawing on Henri Bergson's conception of the flow of time as a process of lived 'duration' and on Edmund Husserl's theory of 'internal time-consciousness', Schutz emphasized two aspects of the quality of action in society: first, the always unfinished processual character of courses of acting relative to ends-in-view that can be continually revised and altered in the light of experience; second, the essentially socially constituted character of the actor's ends. Similar considerations underlay Mead's analysis of the relationship between children and parents and other elementary bonds of primary interdependence. Parsons's magnum opus of 1937 *The Structure of Social Action* incorporated this focus on the elementary particles of action – the 'action frame of reference', as he called it – into analysis of the total structures of social order prevailing over and above the consciousness of any one individual. Human societies consist both of multiple 'unit acts' by individuals acting in multitudinous relations to one another and of *systems* that integrate, order and structure these acts into coherent patterns (see **social system**). Parsons thereby sought to reconcile the aspect of free will that is essential to human agency (see **voluntarism**) with the observation that actors choose ends typically in contexts of pre-structured expectation and not at random.

In the 1960s Parsons's approach came under fire from a number of directions. Two pertinent criticisms were, firstly, that the concept of action tended to be swallowed up in his work into the concept of system, and, secondly, that the concept of action in his work appeared resistant to definite empirical application. There followed a renaissance of interactionist approaches in the spirit of the **Chicago School** of sociologists, including the **dramaturgical school** led by **Goffman** and the programme of **ethnomethology** formulated by **Garkinkel**. In Europe Ludwig **Wittgenstein**'s linguistic analyses led to a theory 'speech–acts' and **performatives** propounded by the philosophers John Austin and John Searle, emphasizing that language-in-use not only describes the world but actively constructs the world. In different ways these ideas fed into Jürgen **Habermas**'s theory of 'communicative action' (see **communication**) and into Jacques **Derrida**'s conception of **deconstruction**. For other theorists, including notably Niklas **Luhmann** and Gilles **Deleuze**, the concepts of action, consciousness and intentionality were redundant artifices of **metaphysical** thinking that had to be abandoned in favour of the terminology of **systems theory** and **cybernetics**.

References and further reading

Coleman, J.S. (1990) *Foundations of Social Theory*. Cambridge, Mass.: Harvard University Press.

Davidon, D. (1980) *Essays on Actions and Events*. Oxford: Oxford University Press.

Joas, H. (1996) *The Creativity of Action*. Cambridge, UK: Polity Press.

Mead, G.H. (1934) *Mind, Self, and Society*. Chicago: University of Chicago Press.

Moya, C.J. (1990) *The Philosophy of Action: An Introduction*. Cambridge: Polity Press.

Parsons, T. (1937) *The Structure of Social Action*. New York: The Free Press.

Schutz, A. ([1932] 1967) *The Phenomenology of the Social World*. Evanston: Northwestern University Press.

Weber, M. ([1922] 1968) *Economy and Society*. Berkeley: University of California Press.

AUSTIN HARRINGTON

ACTOR–NETWORK THEORY

Many of the key ideas of what came to be known as actor-network theory (ANT) were first formulated in a 1981 paper by Michel Callon and Bruno **Latour**. Their work, along with that of John Law, has been closely identified with the approach. Although ANT can be understood as a quite general approach to social theory, it has been particularly influential in **social studies of science**, although in recent years there has been increasing interest in ANT in political sociology, social geography, media studies, social anthropology and other fields.

The idea of the actor-network derives some inspiration from **semiotics**. An actor (*actant*) in this account is not an individual agent with a given **identity**, but rather an entity whose identity is formed through its shifting **network** of relations with other actors. In addition, as in semiotics, actors can be either humans or non-humans. In this way, ANT poses a radical challenge to social theory in arguing that sociology should be as much concerned with the **agency** and identity of non-humans as of humans. In conceiving of the identity of actors as relational rather than essential, ANT has much in common with **post-structuralist** approaches to social theory such as those associated with the philosophy of Michel **Foucault**, Michel Serres and Gilles **Deleuze**.

While the central claims of ANT parallel arguments in philosophy, the approach has been best developed through detailed empirical studies. Indeed, ANT draws some inspiration from micro-sociological and ethnographic work, such as that of Erving **Goffman**. There are also connections between ANT and the sociology and philosophy of Gabriel Tarde. For Tarde, as for ANT, society is not conceived of as a structure or a system but as a multiplicity of **associations** between human and non-human actors.

References and further reading

Callon, M. and Latour, B. (1981) 'Unscrewing the Big Leviathan: How Actors Macrostructure Reality and How Scientists Help Them Do So', in K. Knorr-Cetina and A. Cicourel (eds), *Advances in Social Theory and Methodology*. London: Routledge & Kegan Paul.

Callon, M., Law, J. and Rip, A. (eds) (1986) *Mapping the Dynamics of Science and Technology*. London: Macmillan.

Latour, B. (1993) *We Have Never Been Modern*. Hemel Hempstead: Harvester Wheatsheaf.

Latour, B. (2002) 'Gabriel Tarde and the End of the Social', in P. Joyce (ed.), *The Social in Question*. London: Routledge.

Law, J. (1994) *Organizing Modernity*. Oxford: Blackwell.

Law, J. and Hassard, J. (eds) (1999) *Actor–Network Theory and After*. Oxford: Blackwell.

Law, J. and Hassard, J. (2002) *Aircraft Stories: Decentering the Object in Technoscience*. Durham, NC: Duke University Press.

ANDREW BARRY

ADORNO, THEODOR WIESENGRUND (1903–1969)

German theorist

A member of the **Frankfurt School**, Adorno constantly engaged in polemical disputes with what he termed 'positivist sociology', arguing that it lacks methodological self-reflection and falls short of a dialectical self-consciousness (see **dialectical**). **Positivism** takes society as it is given, and thereby fails to recognize the influence of the exchange structure on all social phenomena. Positivist sociology serves to perpetuate the notion of society as an aggregate of indivualized atoms. Adorno's writings on **art and aesthetics**, literature and music in relation to material social structures seek to validate the thesis of **critical theory** that society is not the sum of its 'appearances', and that is not an unalterable given. Adorno's aesthetic studies also seek to reveal the 'mimetic' operations of the social in artworks. His theoretical work can be understood in terms of a project to reveal the variety of ways in which experience has been diminished by modern forms of capitalist **rationality and rationalization and instrumental reason**.

Major works

([1947] 1972) (with Max Horkheimer) *Dialectic of Enlightenment*. New York: Herder and Herder.

([1949] 1973) *Philosophy of Modern Music*. London: Sheed & Ward.

([1951] 1974) *Minima Moralia*. London: NLB.

([1956] 1982) *Against Epistemology: A Metacritique*. Oxford: Blackwell.

([1966] 1973) *Negative Dialectics*. London: Routledge.

([1970] 1997) *Aesthetic Theory*. Minneapolis, MN: University of Minnesota Press.

Further reading

Cook, D. (2004) *Adorno, Habermas and the Search for a Rational Society*. London: Routledge.

Jarvis, S. (1998) *Adorno: A Critical Introduction*. Cambridge: Polity.

O'Connor, B. (2004) *Adorno's Negative Dialectic*. Cambridge, MA: MIT Press.

BRIAN O'CONNOR

AGE

Age is one of the most important and diverse yet least theorized principles of social organization and **stratification**, spanning macro-structural and micro-experiential dimensions of social life. As a principle of social organization, age can be broken down into the four major analytical categories of life course, **generation**, cohort and population. Beginning in the early twentieth century, the nascent sciences of pediatrics, geriatrics and gerontology claimed that the age groups of childhood, adolescence, adulthood and old age were distinguishable by their unique developmental characteristics. As earlier stages of life became associated with maturation and socialization, later stages of life were problematized and cast in terms of decline and role-loss. The psychologist G. Stanley Hall pioneered age studies with his two influential books, *Adolescence* (1904), and *Senescence* (1922), and later Erik Erikson theorized eight stages of development with each marked by specific identity crises and resolutions based on life course transitions. Others followed who theorized the life course as a complex interplay between social, psychological and physiological factors.

In the late twentieth century, social critics pointed to the connection between research on the life course and the bureaucratic standardization of age hierarchies in legal, educational, military, industrial and economic systems (Katz 1996). In the 1980s, critical age studies emerged to highlight further problems with life course thinking, in particular, the life course as a socially constructed universalizing model based on white, masculine, heterosexual and middle-class cultural patterns and regimes of **embodiment**. In reality, life course politics is an arena of struggle whereby race, gender, sexual, and class divisions intersect with those based on age, while social order and power are constituted through a plurality of life course structures and experiences. For example, Dannefer links the lives and life courses of Third World child laborers, American youth gangs, 'trendy' Amazonian shamans and Western consumer groups to the production, environmental and labor networks of global commodity capitalism (2003).

Generation is a second organizational component of age, introduced into social thought by Karl **Mannheim** in his essay 'The Problem of Generations', which broadened the idea of generation to include factors of identity, consciousness, history and location (1952). Today culturally formed generations such as 'Generation X' or the 'Woodstock Generation' would fit well in Mannheim's perspective. Especially innovative in Mannheim's work was the focus on the relationship between generation and class, and their combined role in the intergenerational transmission of culture (Edmunds and Turner 2002). In the last quarter of the twentieth century a new political image of generations emerged, depicting a competition between shrinking younger and growing older generations for limited social provisions. Labelled by critics an 'apocalyptic demography' (Gee and Gutman 2000), this image of intergenerational conflict has proved to be an unkind ideological manifestation of the collapse of welfare governments, the privatization of support services and increasing employment insecurity for younger generations. Research demonstrates that more intergenerational interdependence and cooperation exists than antagonism, and that older generations, whose needs are far from jeopardizing the stability of Western economies, believe in sustaining the viability of pan-generational welfare institutions.

The concept of generation is related to theories of age *cohorts*, a key idea found in ethnographic research on age groups that captures how individual biographies and socio-structural events are intertwined. Cohort is a static category signifying a point in time whereby wars, technological innovations, revolutions, economic fluctuations or other forms of social change define certain age groups and characterize their outlook. Cohort is also part of a qualitative methodological approach to aging that looks at the subjective expressions of social change within the chronological memories and narratives of specific groups, and historicizes the taken-for-granted norms and meanings associated with age. Both the categorical and methodological aspects of cohort analysis provide an understanding of how individual lives lived within specific periods of time collectively structure the experience of aging. A seminal cohort study is Glen Elder Jr.'s *Children of the Great Depression* (1974).

Life course, generation and cohort are clustered into *populations*. Populations appear to be naturally and statistically calculable aggregations of age groups. The young, the middle-aged and the old are represented and measured in demographic discourses where terms such as median age, fertility and mortality rates, dependency ratios, migration and immigration and life expectancy characterize collective life. Graphic 'age pyramids' portray the resulting shape of changing historical relationships between age groups as some grow larger and others decline. Three important demographic trends in Western societies today are the growth of aging populations, the decline in fertility rates and the longevity gap between women and men. These have important future political and economic implications; for example, women, because they outlive their spouses, are often more alone, unsupported, marginalized and poor.

When populations are examined from a more critical theoretical perspective, however, they can be seen as the political basis for the historical division of peoples into governable and knowable sectors, as **Foucault** demonstrates in his work on the 'bio-politics of the population' (1980). In this sense, one can genealogically trace each age population and the state provisions created for it to the modern political concerns about health, wealth, security, productivity and the regulation of the social sphere. In today's 'risk society', as conceptualized by Ulrich **Beck**, the public agenda to govern dependent populations has shifted to a neo-liberal emphasis on individual responsibility and risk management (see **risk**). Hence, vaguely specified age groups such as 'youth' have been reinvented as risk categories, just

as 'seniors' are idealized as lifestyle specialists whose social acceptability relies on their wise investment choices and programs of self-care.

Age, along with race, class, gender and disability, often organizes social relations on the basis of social **inequality**, where age groups are stratified chronologically and structurally defined by their productive and reproductive relationships to capitalist economies. Critical literature in **exchange theory** and **political economy** examines how 'interlocking systems of oppression' (Estes 2001) are created from the conjunction of the capitalist division of laboring age groups, ageist policy biases favoring privileged classes, the devaluation of domestic and care work and the inequitable distribution of resources among different ages. Complementing such literature, **feminist** research tackles the social processes whereby **gender** and age create a 'double jeopardy' of oppression at each transitional point in the female life course, thus bringing to the study of age a focus on the body, sexuality and the exploitation of the private sphere, especially where the family is a site of gender and age conflict. Feminists who study young (Driscoll 2002), middle-aged (Woodward 1999) or older groups of women (Calasanti and Slevin 2001), have contributed incisive critiques of the patriarchal configurations of feminine identities, such as girlhood, daughterhood, motherhood and widowhood. Critical theoretical perspectives on age, gender and inequality also stress the agency of groups who, based on their socially inscribed age identities, lobby the state for social security, pension and healthcare reforms.

Finally, cultural and postmodern studies of age caution that in the late twentieth and early twenty-first centuries, the temporal and generational boundaries that had set apart childhood, middle age and old age in the past, are now blurred and indeterminate. New labour and retirement structures, the importance of leisure and consumerism on a global scale and the medical, pharma-cological and commercial stretching of middle age into later life have created the paradoxical imperative to grow older without aging (Gilleard and Higgs 2000). Newly identified age groups such as 'boomers' and 'third agers' are celebrated for pursuing personal and bodily lifestyle experiments with timelessness, as age as a barrier to suc-cessful living disappears from commercial portrayals of permanently mature consumer citizens, whether young or old. Thus, cri-tical anti-ageism is confused with cultural anti-aging, as the concept of age in con-sumer capitalism becomes a fascinating problem of identity across the life-course and between generations, cohorts and populations.

References and further reading

Calasanti, T. and Slevin, K. F. (2001) *Gender, Social Inequalities and Aging*. Walnut Creek, CA: Altamira.

Dannefer, D. (2003) 'Whose Life Course Is It, Anyway?', in R.A Settersten, Jr. (ed.), *Invitation to the Life Course*. Amityville, NY: Baywood.

Driscoll, C. (2002) *Girls*. New York: Columbia University Press.

Edmunds, J. and Turner, B. S. (2002) *Genera-tions, Culture and Society*. Buckingham: Open University Press.

Elder, G. H. Jr. (1974) *Children of the Great Depression*. Chicago: University of Chicago Press.

Estes, C. L. and Associates (2001) *Social Policy and Aging*. Thousand Oaks, CA: Sage.

Foucault, M. (1980) *The History of Sexuality*. New York: Vintage.

Gee, E. M. and Gutman, G. M. (eds) (2000) *The Overselling of Population Aging*. Don Mills, ON: Oxford University Press.

Gilleard, C. and Higgs, P. (2000) *Cultures of Ageing*. Harlow: Prentice Hall.

Katz, S. (1996) *Disciplining Old Age*. Charlottes-ville, VA: University Press of Virginia.

Mannheim, K. (1952) *Essays on the Sociology of Knowledge*. London: Routledge & Kegan Paul.

Woodward, K. (ed.) (1999) *Figuring Age*. Bloo-mington, IN: Indiana University Press.

STEPHEN KATZ

AGENCY

Referring usually to human agency, the term 'agency' typically conveys the voli-tional, purposive, and intentional aspects of human activity as opposed to its more constrained and determined elements. A general condition for agency ('doing something') is that the agent possesses a degree of **autonomy**. A second idea is an associated **reflexivity**.

The term 'agency' is far from being the only or main term referring to these aspects of human activity. What is central to agency is often dealt with under other terms. Thus agency can be synonymous with, or closely related to **action** and 'performativity' (see **performative**). A capacity for agency is usually part of what is central in conceptions of **self**, **person and personality**, **identity**, **sub-ject and subjectivity** – although it should be noted that unlike the term 'agency', 'sub-ject' contains a central ambiguity between active agency and passive subjection. There is also a relation to **embodiment**, in that a degree of 'continuity' between self-identity and the body is usually assumed, although the implications of this relation raise com-plex questions about the nature of desire, rationality, imagination and **emotion**.

The primary use of the term, which has a long ancestry in philosophy, refers to the capacity possessed by an individual social actor, or by collectivities of social actors, to choose between options and to affect out-comes, whether physical or social. In this sense, human agency is regarded in terms of 'causal power'.

Debates about the nature and scope of human agency touch especially on debates about **structure**, and they relate centrally to issues of **determinism** and **voluntarism**. While in some sociological theories (e.g. **symbolic interactionism** and **ethnomethodology**) human agency is central, for others (e.g. **functionalism** and **structuralism**) structural determination is uppermost. In structuralist and post-structuralist approaches, the claim is often made for a wholesale 'decentring' and a dissolution of the subject, and the concept of the self and agency can seem to dissolve in the determining or fragmenting **power** of discursive processes and structures (see **discourse**).

In the work of the **structuration school**, the relation between agency and structure is a central topic, with various proposals for a resolution in terms of an interaction between agency and structure. Structure is here seen as both constituted by human agency and at the same time as the very medium of this constitution. While classical and modern sociological theorists are often presented as one-sidedly emphasizing either 'agency' (e.g. **Weber**, **Mead**) or 'structure' (e.g. **Durkheim**), most approaches have in practice involved a subtle interrelation of the two.

Concerning issues of interpretation and **explanation** associated with agency, Von Wright (1971) distinguishes between Aristotelian teleological understanding and Galilean causal explanation. For R. G. Collingwood, conceptions of **causality** are seen as deriving historically from the idea of human active powers. For Von Wright, while usually modern scientific explanation is arrived at by asserting a nomological connection between cause-factor and effect-factors, a form of teleological social explanation involves no reference to laws but explains or understands human action by reference to actors' beliefs and reasons.

For Max **Weber**, meaningful interpretation was to be seen as at the same time a form of causal explanation. For Weber, a commitment to interpretive adequacy in an account was not inconsistent with a wider exploration of how and why particular events occur or their wider – including 'unintended' – implications.

For **Giddens** (1984) it is axiomatic that individual agency as the capacity to intervene in the world or to refrain from **action** involves 'causal power'. This does not rule out conceptions of agency as the property of **social movements**, collectivities or societies,

but it expresses these in the context of what Giddens calls a 'duality of structure'. In contexts of **domination** and dependency, there usually exists a 'dialectic of control' in which the subordinated can exercise at least some control. For example, even prisoners exercise a small degree of agncy in relation to prison officers. This is a viewpoint reflected in the way that agency reappears in post-structuralist and postmodernist discourse, with such concepts as 'localized agency'. For Giddens, three levels of motivation exist: (1) what he calls 'discursive consciousness'; (2) 'practical consciousness' (what actors do but do not usually put into words); and (3) the unconscious. Rationalizations and repressed motives, deep structural analyses of meanings and 'unintended consequences' can also be potentially accommodated within such a framework.

The concept of agency as involving relatively autonomous, potentially 'transformative' causal active powers is especially central to realist social theory and the realist philosophy of social science (see **realism**). It is particularly present in the work of Harré (1979), Bhaskar (1979) and Archer (2000), who advance a strong critique of **reductionism**, including agency-denying theories, such as **behaviourism** and some versions of Marxian theories of **ideology**. For Bhaskar, as for Giddens, social structures do not exist independently of the conditions they govern; and society is both the ever present condition and the continually reproduced outcome of human agency. On the other hand, neither do individuals shape social action or construct social institutions in conditions entirely of their own making.

For Bhaskar and Archer, human agency implies ontological realism. Human beings continually sustain relations with three orders of reality: the natural, the practical and the social. 'Reality claims' are a precondition for human activity. As Archer puts it, whereas some theorists maximize the distinction between social-scientific and natural-scientific analysis, others seek to minimize it. For Hollis and Smith (1994) – who maximize difference – the 'stuff of social worlds' consists either of rules and meanings which are subjectively apprehended and meaningfully understood, or of an independent environment objectively apprehended and causally explained. But for realist theorists, causal powers are held as generative mechanisms in both physical and social spheres, notwithstanding some differences between the social and physical sciences. They can be potentially interrelated within a single account in which hermeneutic understanding and scientific causal explanation provide an overall account of the 'causal efficacy of people'. The conditions and consequences of action span both domains.

A final dimension of agency requiring discussion concerns its relation to 'emancipatory' knowledge and action (see **emancipation**). As expressed by Archer, human agency involves 'cares, concerns, commitments, and rectifying goals'. In some respects, this looks back to a **Marxism** that is neither purely humanistic nor purely structuralist. Compared with conceptions of Marxism in which actors are merely 'supports for structures' or versions of structural-functionalism where actors figure only as 'cultural dopes', conceptions of praxis in which actors make a difference are involved. A more general emphasis in sociology on human agency and human interests can place the individual at the centre of any analysis and connect with issues of moral choice, political capacity and social change. One example is **Habermas's** (1972) version of **critical theory**. For Giddens, the goal is a reworking of social democracy via new areas of agency associated with new social movements. More generally, differences in the agency of the powerful compared with the less powerful – revolving around class, ethnicity, age, gender and sexuality – are central in the more substantive exploration of agency.

References and further reading

Archer, M. (2000) *Being Human: The Problem of Agency*. Cambridge: Cambridge University Press.

Barnes, B. (2000) *Understanding Agency*. London: Sage.

Bhaskar, R. (1979) *The Possibility of Naturalism*. Brighton: Harvester.

Castoriadis, C. (1989) *The Imaginary Institution of Society*. Cambridge, MA: MIT Press.

Giddens, A. (1984) *The Constitution of Society*. Cambridge: Polity.

Habermas, J. (1972) *Knowledge and Human Interests*. London: Heinemann.

Harré, R. (1979) *Social Being*. Oxford: Blackwell.

Hollis, M. and Smith, S. (1994) 'Two Stories about Structure and Agency', *Review of International Studies*, 20: 245–50.

McNay, L. (2000) *Gender and Agency*. Cambridge: Polity.

Von Wright, G. (1971) *Explanation and Understanding*. London: Blackwell.

Winch, P. (1963) *The Idea of a Social Science*. London: Routledge.

DAVID JARY

ALEXANDER, JEFFREY C. (1947–)
US sociologist

Alexander's contributions have shaped the theoretical development of American sociology and its historiography, standing for an amalgamation of the history of sociology with sociological theory building. Following the early project of **Talcott Parsons**, Alexander strove for a synthesis of classic and contemporary accounts of sociology which resulted in his four-volume series of works, *Theoretical Logic in Sociology* (1982–83). Alexander links the approaches of **Marx** and **Durkheim** and the interpretive approach, embodied in **Weber**, to **structural functionalism**. He has pursued a path towards a 'postpositivist' theory via systematic synthetic reappraisals of classic themes concerning the relationship of **structure** and **agency** and **culture**. Since his efforts in the late 1980s Alexander has been emphatically engaged in the project of a 'strong programme' of cultural sociology, stimulated by the late work of Durkheim.

Major works

(1982–83) *Theoretical Logic in Sociology.* Berkeley: University of California Press.
(1985) *Neofunctionalism.* Beverley Hills: Sage.
(1987) *The Micro–Macro Link.* Berkeley: University of California Press.
(1988) *Action and its Environments: Toward a New Synthesis.* New York: Columbia University Press.
(1989) *Structure and Meaning: Relinking Classical Sociology.* New York: Columbia University Press.
(1998) *Neofunctionalism and After.* Oxford: Blackwell.
(2003) *The Meanings of Social Life: A Cultural Sociology.* New York: Oxford University Press.

Further reading

Joas, H. (1988) 'The Antinomies of Neofunctionalism. A Critical Essay on Jeffrey Alexander', *Inquiry*, 31(4): 471–94.

BERNHARD GIESEN
DANIEL ŠUBER

ALIENATION

In the writings of Karl **Marx**, the historical process through which human beings have become estranged from non-human **nature** and from the products of their activity (productive forces, capital, social institutions and **culture**) is termed 'alienation'. The cumulative results of the human productive capacity confront subsequent generations as an independent, objectified force, i.e. as an alienated reality. Marx focused in particular on the alienating effects of the **labour** undertaken in large-scale, capitalist, industrial factories. The concept is also used in the sociology of **mass culture and mass society** and **urbanism** to convey a cluster of experiences, including depersonalization, powerlessness and lack of cohesion in people's lives, particularly in industrial societies.

In the 1920s and 1930s the predicament of humankind in modern secular societies was widely discussed by existentialist philosophers, psychoanalysts, theologians and Marxists as the problem of alienation. The debate was further fuelled by the publication for the first time in 1932 of Marx's analysis of alienation in his *Economic and Philosophic Manuscripts* of 1844. The term is often linked with **reification**, which was not used by Marx but by Georg **Lukács** in his influential book *History and Class Consciousness* of 1923, which anticipated the theme of human 'objectification' discussed in the *Manuscripts*. For Lukács, reification is the extremity of the alienation of humans from their products which arises from the phenomenon of commodity fetishism, through which social reality is experienced as a tissue of images and illusions (see **commodity and commodification**.

For Marx, alienated labour occurs when workers are alienated from: (1) their product, which does not belong to them; (2) work itself, because it is only a means of survival, something forced on them in order to live; (3) themselves, because their activity was not their own, resulting in feelings of self-estrangement; and (4) from other people in the factory because each sells his or her labour power individually as a commodity.

Economic egoism for Marx was a result of alienated labour, as was private **property**. Egoism did not express an enduring characteristic of human beings but was a product of class societies in the capitalist phase. The abolition of alienated labour meant that labour would acquire its true collective, 'species' character and egoism in the above sense would be superseded. For Marx, the organization of large-scale commodity production and the individualistic wage labour contract of the early capitalist factories of his time constituted a travesty of the species character that labour *should* have if it were organized in a way truly congruent with the assumed nature of man. In Marx's work, alienation is thus a 'critical' concept, to be used as a measuring rod for calibrating the human costs of capitalist civilization (see **critical theory**).

Hegelian philosophy had already described, in a metaphysical framework, human history as a process of alienation through which humans have been increasingly transformed from creative subjects into passive objects of social processes (see **Hegelianism and Neo-Hegelianism**). Marx insisted that liberation from alienation had to be achieved in practice by real people and not apparently solely in the realm of consciousness or self-awareness, as in Hegel. Marx's secular **humanism** relied heavily on Ludwig Feuerbach's materialist theory of religion in which he claimed that human beings have projected their own essence and potentialities into God, who then confronts them in an alienated form (see **materialism**). In the *Manuscripts*, Marx argued that religious alienation was only one aspect of the propensity of human beings to alienate themselves from their own creations, which could be explained as aspects of the economic alienation arising out of the capitalist productive process.

This analysis was fused with the politics of **communism**, as the future society into which Marx projected the 'complete return of man himself as a social (i.e. human) being – a return become conscious, and accomplished within the entire wealth of previous development' (Marx 1844: 95). History is thus the simultaneous loss of human beings in their own products and their subsequent recovery of themselves, a real process of alienation that Hegel had perceived in a mystified manner. In Marx's theory of history, the developing forces of production progressively outgrow their relations in a series of historical **modes of production** as the realization of this process. With the social formation of capitalism 'the pre-history of human society accordingly closes' (Marx 1859: 22).

Two problems have dominated the debate about alienation. First, the model of human beings at the heart of the theory is controversial. Marx's conception of *homo laborans* takes labour from the dominant experience of factory work of his time and places it as the central, defining human characteristic. Around this idea are then hung a number of further contestable assumptions about human sociability, freedom and control, self-realization and collective labour as its own reward, derived from Rousseau and the French socialists.

Second, existentialists have suggested that while alienation may be exacerbated under capitalist production, in its basic form it is symptomatic of something perennial in the human condition. Eliminating alienation at the point of production through workers' self-management would leave the spheres of distribution and exchange untouched, thus perpetuating further sources of alienation. Since Marx thought that economic alienation was the basis of all other aspects, the supersession of private property would mark the end of expropriation by capitalists and hence the end of all alienation. But Marx did not foresee the emergence of new forms of expropriation and the exploitation of people by each other and, hence, further forms of alienation (Axelos 1976).

Robert Blauner (1964) separated Marx's concept into the four testable dimensions of powerlessness, meaninglessness, isolation and self-estrangement in the workplace. In a study of various industrial settings in the USA, he found that alienation was at its greatest in mass production and at its least in craft production. Some have argued that this kind of empirical approach misses the critical-philosophical intention of Marx's concept, while others have argued that it is the only way to give precision to a concept which is quasi-metaphysical and inherently indeterminate.

References and further reading

Axelos, K. (1976) *Alienation, Praxis and Techne in the Thought of Karl Marx*. Austin, TX: University of Texas Press.

Blauner, R. (1964) *Alienation and Freedom*. Chicago: University of Chicago Press.

Lukács, G. ([1923] 1971) *History and Class Consciousness*. London: Merlin Press.

Marx, K. ([1844] 1967) *Economic and Philosophic Manuscripts*. Trans. M. Milligan. Moscow: Progress Publishers.

Marx, K. ([1845] 1968) *The German Ideology*. London: Lawrence & Wishart.

Marx, K. ([1859] 1971) *A Contribution to the Critique of Political Economy*. London: Lawrence & Wishart.

Meszaros, I. (1970) *Marx's Theory of Alienation*. London: Merlin Press.

RICHARD KILMINSTER

ALTHUSSER, LOUIS (1918–1990)

French theorist

Taught philosophy at L'École normale supérieure. Well versed in **Hegel** and, of course, **Marx**, Althusser repudiated any conflation of **Hegelianism** and **Marxism** (see **Hegelianism and Neo-Hegelianism**). Althusser rendered explicit Marx's implicit strategy of reading classical economics, to uncover the presence of more than one discourse in the same text. Althusser illustrated how such 'symptomatic readings' went beyond conventional dogmatic, or, even, immanent critiques. Althusser argued that Marx's mature work differed radically from his early work, locating an 'epistemological break' in Marx's thought as evidenced by the emergence, by the late 1850s, of a radically new *set* of concepts produced and organized around a new 'problematic'. The humanist notion of a founding individual or collective subject and of society as its (imperfect) expression, was analytically displaced, primacy was assigned instead to structured sets of social/material relations. Modes of production, of reproduction and exploitation, for example, are articulated through relations of production connections and productive forces connections; these in turn have conditions of existence constituted by relatively autonomous economic, political and ideological practices (see **modes of production**). Ideological

practices constitute and reconstitute subjects by interpellating them within particular social relations. These latter are often – but by no means necessarily – functionally integrated with each other. Althusser's later 'aleatory materialism' emphasized the necessity of examining both the nature of different practices and their articulation with each other, to *discover* which process is 'determinant in the last instance'. Tragically, in 1980, in a psychotic episode, Althusser killed his wife, Hélène Legotien. Institutionalized, but then released, he ceased to publicly participate in French intellectual life although some of his unpublished works, including anguished autobiographical writings, have become available posthumously.

Major works

([1965] 1969) *For Marx*. London: New Left Books.

([1968] 1970) (with Étienne Balibar) *Reading Capital*. London: New Left Books.

(1971) *Lenin and Philosophy*. London: New Left Books.

Further reading

Warren, M. (2003) *Louis Althusser*. London: Palgrave.

FRANK PEARCE

AMERICA

America has fascinated since the time it was first 'discovered' and named after the Italian-Spanish seafarer and discoverer, Amerigo Vespucci. Since the conquest of the two continents of the Americas by Europeans, encounters between the Old and the New World have generated wide-ranging ideas about America's **symbolic** identity. Yet America's cultural history prior to its 'discovery' has only recently become an issue of public debate, notably in the framework of **post-colonial theory**.

As Tzvetan Todorow (1984) notes, for the European discoverers, America and its original inhabitants came to signify an idea of otherness. Confronted with this **Other**, European reactions ranged from sheer ignorance and negative reactions (Columbus), to brutal conquest (Cortes), to affection and religious conversion or assimilation (Las Casas). Confrontations were not limited to the experience of first-wave European forces encountering native Americans. Over the course of centuries of **colonization**, settlement and later independence in which original colonists and natives would eventually become nearly indistinguishable, two different Americas finally emerged, divided by **language**. Yet, as Seymour Martin **Lipset** (1963) emphasized, language was not the only **difference**. The religious division of Catholicism in South and Central America and Protestantism in the North (with the exception of Québec) proved to be decisive influences. And as with language and religious orientation, the different **cultures**, customs and political experiences of the original European countries proved to be equally important. Influenced by English culture and customs, the North American settlers subscribed to ideas of the rule of law, **freedom** and administration of the **community**. Driven by a commercial spirit, they learned to trade, farm and reap the fruits of the new environment. The inhabitants of New England entertained ideas of **progress**, **education** and scientific inquiry, while the Spanish and Portuguese colonies remained dominated by the legacies of absolute **monarchy** and feudalism, and by poorly developed agrarian economies. As Frederick Pike (1992) observes, such differences would eventually lead to a division, one which historians of ideas have described in terms of a dichotomoy between a hegemonic North America symbolizing **civilization** and material progress and a Latin America representing backwardness and primitivism.

At present, the US largely monopolizes definitions of the symbolic meaning of America. And not least an account of the USA's rise to a position of near-global political, economic and military **hegemony**, anti-Americanism is now a widespread ideological currency, particularly among European, Latin American and Arab **intellectuals** but by no means limited to these.

As James W. Ceaser (1997) emphasizes, this contrasts with the predominantly optimistic tradition of thinking about America inaugurated in the nineteenth century by Alexis de **Toqueville**. The development of a US intellectual **elite** in the late eighteenth and nineteenth centuries proved decisive in generating a range of intellectual building blocks and political concepts that include in particular the concept of 'American exceptionalism', as discussed in such documents as the *Federalist Papers*, the frontier thesis of Fredrick Jackson Turner, as well as Tocqueville's *Democracy in America*. It has produced a distinct kind of political theology, as well as re-inventing the tradition of classical **republican** political thought, as discussed by Hannah **Arendt** and J. G. A. Pocock among others. It has articulated a newly defined **liberalism** – discussed by Louis Hartz, Judith N. Shklar, and Stephen Holmes among others – and is closely associated with the distinctively American tradition of philosophical pragmatism, from C. S. Peirce to William James, John Dewey and G. H. **Mead**.

Later twentieth-century social and political thinkers in the USA have since made entensive contributions to our understanding of the nature of **power**, **democracy**, justice, **pluralism**, **multiculturalism**, **civil society** and the task and role of intellectuals in a democratic society. Among some of the most influential authors in public debates and diverse academic fields have been W. E. B. **Du Bois**, Talcott **Parsons**, Robert **Merton**, Barrington **Moore**, C. Wright **Mills**, Robert A. Dahl, Sheldon Wolin, John **Rawls**, Michael **Walzer**, and Ronald Dworkin, Nathan Glazer, Anthony Appiah, Henry Louis Gates, Jeffrey C. Goldfarb, and Jeffrey C. **Alexander**.

Yet as Richard Hofstadter (1963) pointed out in the 1960s, the development of political and social thought in the US has been accompanied by a strong force of anti-intellectualism in the wider American society. More recently, the debates surrounding the attacks of September 11, 2001, and subsequent US foreign policy indicate an intellectual environment that has fought hard to sustain itself in the face of far-reaching threats to civil liberties and powerful nationalist sentiments in the US **media and mass media**.

References and further reading

Ceaser, J. W. (1997) *Reconstructing America: The Symbol of America in Modern Thought*. New Haven, CT: Yale University Press.

Hess, A. (2001) *American Social and Political Thought: A Concise Introduction*. New York: New York University Press.

Hofstadter, R. (1963) *Anti-Intellectualism in American Life*. New York: Vintage Books.

Lieven, A. (2004) *America Right or Wrong: An Anatomy of American Nationalism*. Oxford: Oxford University Press.

Lipset, S. M. (1963) *The First New Nation: The United States in Historical and Comparative Perspective*. New York: Penguin.

Mann, M. (2003) *Incoherent Empire*. Cambridge: Cambridge University Press.

Pike, F. B. (1992) *The United States and Latin America: Myths and Stereotypes of Civilization and Nature*. Austin, TX: University of Texas Press.

Shklar, J. (1998) *Redeeming American Political Thought*. Chicago: University of Chicago Press.

Todorow, T. (1984) *The Discovery of America: The Question of the Other*. New York: HarperCollins.

ANDREAS HESS

ANARCHISM

For some social and political theorists, anarchism is an overly **idealist** philosophy which may have some moral validity but is unrealistic or dangerous when put into practice. However, it can be argued that anarchism is a theory – or a loose family of theories – with continuing application. It addresses a central problem of **democracy**: how can **organizations** coordinate action while preserving individual **autonomy**? In particular, anarchism addresses the question of how action can be coordinated without the emergence of leaders or *hierarchy*. Its core belief is that autonomy is sacrosanct and cannot be legitimately delegated to representatives or to a state (Wolff 1970). This need not result in all social controls being dismantled: controls are legitimate if agreed to by those subject to them. Determining the scope and nature of these controls without eradicating autonomy requires a firm commitment to democracy and mutual support. Thus rather than denoting chaos, ideal anarchy denotes order – but an order arising only with the full consent and active participation of all its members.

Anarchist thought developed particularly in the nineteenth century. Where Social **Darwinism** held that humanity was inherently bestial and that life was a struggle in which only the 'fittest' survived, Kropotkin (1902) argued that in both nature and society 'fitness' depended on collaboration, not competition. In his thesis, spontaneous autonomous organization for mutual benefit was a natural and common occurrence. Over time, however, this impulse to collaborate had been corrupted. Unproductive castes, such as priesthoods, used charismatic or traditional **authority** to command resources (see **domination** and **authority**). **Stratification** and hierarchy were the abstract consequences, while **church** and **state** were the practical results. The appropriation of resources (as taxes and tithes) by these hierarchies and their control over education, government, and the military not only deprived most people of autonomy but also provoked active conflict between rulers and ruled. To maintain an unjust system, **elites** could not extend the people's autonomy, but controlled and ultimately eradicated it via the modern **bureaucratic** state and corporate organizations.

Anarchists hold that society should be comprised not of hierarchical organizations but of **networks** which emerge sponta- neously and evolve dynamically, and in which people participate voluntarily. The domination of bureaucracies has condi- tioned people to the idea that hierarchies and leaders are 'natural'. It is assumed that without them there can be no effective action, and that outbreaks of uncontrolled, spontaneous action are inherently danger- ous. Against this assumption, anarchists hold that this is precisely the form that 'outbreaks of democracy' often take when **social control** breaks down and people act and organize spontaneously to address democratic deficits and reassert their autonomy (Blaug 1999).

Anarchism is a practice more than it is an ideology or dogma. There are many anar- chisms, each developed by its practitioners, and the family of associated theories con- tinues to evolve. Critiques are now as likely to be focused not only on organized reli- gion and the state but also on **capitalism** and its corporations; on **patriarchy**; or on human relationships with the non-human world, as discussed by theorists of **ecology and environmentalism**.

Like many radical philosophies, anar- chism is confronted with problems of infighting over tactics and orthodoxy. This is particularly evident in the debate between Bookchin (1995), on the one hand, and Zerzan (1999) and Watson (1996), on the other. Bookchin observes that without a commitment to democracy and mutual respect, anarchism can decay into ineffectiveness, or into forms of extreme economic libertarianism, especially if private property is considered sacrosanct. But unlike some other idealistic philosophies, contemporary anarchism is constantly tested and developed in the 'laboratories' of worker co-operatives, anti-road camps, pirate radio stations and other locations for social activism (Merrick 1996; Ferrell 2001). These exist not only for specific political ends but also to stimulate new forms of organizing.

Anarchist networks are fragile and often ephemeral, but this can be attributed as much to repression as to tensions within them. During the Spanish Civil War – which saw a significant flowering of anarchist practices – the anarchist militias were per- secuted by both royalists and communists (c.f. Orwell 1951). Today, even apparently democratic elites may pass and enforce laws designed to repress or diffuse democratic outbreaks. But anarchist movements always remain a possibility because self-organizing networks are an inherent feature of com- plex systems, including social systems.

References and further reading

Blaug, R. (1999) 'Outbreaks of Democracy', in L. Panitch and C. Leys (eds), *Socialist Register 2000*. Rendlesham: Merlin.

Bookchin, M. (1995) *Social Anarchism or Lifestyle Anarchism*. Edinburgh: AK.

Do or Die, journal issues 1–10 (first published 1992). Brighton: Do or Die.

Edwards, S. (ed.) (1970) *Selected Writings of Pierre-Joseph Proudhon*. London: Macmillan.

Ferrell, J. (2001) *Tearing Down the Streets: Adventures in Urban Anarchy*. New York: Pal- grave.

Kropotkin, P. (1902) *Mutual Aid: A Factor of Evolution*. London: Heinemann.

Merrick (1996) *Battle for the Trees*. Leeds: God- haven Ink.

Orwell, G. (1951) *Homage to Catalonia*. London: Secker & Warburg.

Watson, D. (1996) *Beyond Bookchin: Preface for a Future Social Ecology*. New York: Autonomedia.

Wolff, R. P. (1970) *In Defense of Anarchism*. New York: Harper & Row.

Woodcock, G. (ed.) (1977) *The Anarchist Reader*. Brighton: Harvester.

Zerzan, J. (1999) *Elements of Refusal*. Columbia, MO: Columbia Alternative Library.

ANDREW WHITWORTH

ANOMIE

In Emile **Durkheim**'s study *Suicide* (1897) and other writings, loss of the effectiveness of the moral framework that regulates people's lives is termed 'anomie'. Anomie literally means lacking a moral law (*nomos*). When the framework of norms which keeps people's expectations, goals and desires within realistic and manageable limits breaks down, they begin to desire the unattainable. This condition produces continuous unhappiness, one symptom of which is a rise in the suicide rate. Anomie is likely when **industrialization** or commercialization happen quickly in a formerly traditional **society**. Expectations are raised and people experience boundless opportunities for pleasure and excitement, causing uncertainty about **values** and goals. The concept was used by Durkheim to diagnose the social malaise of modern societies where the economic system was one of contract, exchange and economic individualism (see **Individualism and Individualization**).

Durkheim distinguished two kinds of anomie: acute and chronic. Acute anomie arises typically from a sudden economic boom, when aspirations rise and desires and appetites generally increase. An economic slump can also result in anomie. As people are suddenly forced into a lower standard of living, they experience new and unaccustomed limits to their desires and goals, for which their moral code has not adequately prepared them.

Chronic anomie refers to the endemic condition of discontent generated by industrial **capitalism**, which continually raises expectations and desires. Limitless possibilities arise which cannot be attained by all and a thirst for novelties produces new sensations which quickly lose their savour. People want more and more in continuous cycles of dissatisfaction and discontent. Neither a sense of community nor established **religion** can provide robust moral codes for regulating desires and goals within achievable limits, nor a solid moral foundation generally. For Durkheim, chronic anomie describes the modern social condition of everyone.

At the individual level, experiences associated with anomie, particularly the acute kind, must not be understood as simply vague feelings of unease or apprehension. In Durkheim's usage there are affinities with later existentialist discussions of human experience. At stake are profound feelings that have been described in terms of horror, fear of absence and sickly dread. If the normal assumptions governing people's lives at a fundamental level disappear, an uncanny feeling of unreality arises. Anomie occurs not only in economic life but also in, for example, divorce or separation, which Durkheim refers to as 'domestic or conjugal anomie'. Here individuals can experience existential anxiety, groundlessness and loss of meaning. This kind of loss of grounding, or non-being, can also occur in, say, bereavement or the experience of being a refugee (see **death and mortality**).

Robert K. **Merton**'s theory of **deviance** embodied a reformulation of the concept inspired by Durkheim's conception of chronic anomie. He argued that in industrial societies the legitimate means of achieving the cultural goal of economic success are unevenly distributed due to inequalities of access to them. American society was anomic because the cultural goal of success is unattainable for many people: there is a perennial disjuncture between the goal and access to the legitimate means of achieving it. Most people conform, but others adapt in various ways by finding alternative, illegitimate, means to achieve the same goal. Various critics have seen in Merton's influential formulation of anomie a loss of the concept's original moral and critical cutting edge.

Controversy over two further issues has continued. First, in *Suicide*, Durkheim did not systematically analyze the separate effects of the two related phenomena of anomie and egoism, which correspond to the two spheres of moral regulation and social integration. He only offered instances where both conditions occurred together. If the two concepts refer only to one social state, as he implied, then the independent explanatory status of both, including anomie, becomes problematic. Second, the model of human nature implied in Durkheim's work generally and in the concept of anomie in particular, is that of *homo duplex*, which posits a dualism in humans between reason and passion. It is a model classically associated with **conservatism**, although in the case of Durkheim, this association has been contested in view of his liberal and socialist leanings. The current Durkheimian revival in sociology has given new credence to Durkheim's model of human nature, which has also helped to bring the concept of anomie back onto the centre stage of social science.

References and further reading

Alexander, J. C. (ed.) (1988) *Durkheimian Sociology: Cultural Studies*. Cambridge: Cambridge University Press.

Durkheim, E. ([1897] 1970) *Suicide: A Study in Sociology*. Trans. J. A. Spaulding and G. Simpson. London: Routledge.

Mellor, P. (2004) *Religion, Realism and Social Theory: Making Sense of Society*. London: Sage.

Merton, R. K. (1968) 'Social Structure and Anomie', in *Social Theory and Social Structure*, rev. edn, London: Collier Macmillan.

Mestrovic, S. (1991) *The Coming Fin-de-siècle: An Application of Durkheim's Sociology to Modernity and Postmodernity*. London: Routledge.

Orru, M. (1987) *Anomie: History and Meanings*. London: Allen Lane.

Shilling, C. and Mellor, P. (1998) 'Durkheim, Morality and Modernity: Collective Effervescence, *Homo Duplex* and the Sources of Modern Action', *British Journal of Sociology*, 49(2): 193–209.

RICHARD KILMINSTER

ARENDT, HANNAH (1906–1975)

German-born theorist

A Jewish émigré, Arendt spent most of her intellectual career in the USA. In *Origins of Totalitarianism* (1979), she offers a profound understanding of **totalitarianism** and of the elements of modern political life that made it possible. These include secular anti-Semitism, imperialist **violence**, **national** exclusivity in anti-imperial movements, and broadly the rise of European nihilism (see **imperialism**). Unlike conventional theorists Arendt saw the deficiencies of liberal democracy as implicated in the origins of totalitarianism. Her intellectual project, however, was not only to avert its repetition but to understand **freedom** as the *raison d'être* of political life. In *The Human Condition* she focuses on the importance of the **public sphere** for modern political life. Her controversial *Eichmann in Jerusalem* questions the nature of evil in modernity and the role of international criminal law in combating it. *On Revolution*, examines three streams of the modern revolutionary tradition: French, American and its 'lost treasure' – participatory **democracy**. She explores why freedom was denied and speculates on how the revolutionary tradition might be reconfigured. *Between Past and Future*, explores how teleological conceptions of historical progress annul the freedom of the present. In *Life of the Mind* she addresses divisions between thinking, willing and judging that beset modern consciousness, and the threat to the activity of understanding that the modern age poses. Arendt was critical of social scientists for their failure to face up to the evils of the modern age, but her determination to uncover human experience makes her work more like a social theory of political life than a political theory as such.

Major works

(1979) *The Origins of Totalitarianism*. New York: Harcourt Brace.

(1958) *The Human Condition*. Chicago: University of Chicago Press.

(1963) *Eichmann in Jerusalem*. London: Faber and Faber.

(1961) *Between Past and Future*. London: Faber and Faber.

(1978) *Life of the Mind*. Secker and Warburg.

Further reading

Baehr, P. (2002) 'Identifying the Unprecedented: Hannah Arendt, Totalitarianism, and the Critique of Sociology', *American Sociological Review*, 67: 804–31.

Canovan, M. (1992) *Hannah Arendt: A Reinterpretation of her Political Thought*. Cambridge: Cambridge University Press.

Fine, R. (2001) 'Understanding Evil: Arendt and the Final Solution', in M. P. Lara (ed.) *Rethinking Evil: Contemporary Perspectives*. Berkeley, CA: University of California Press.

ROBERT FINE

ARISTOCRACY

Literally meaning 'the rule of the best' in classical Greek, the phenomenon of aristocracy has a variegated history. Today we can distinguish three aspects: (1) a social stratum, generalizable across diverse cultural contexts after a certain level of social development; (2) European aristocracy; and (3) decline among European aristocracies in the wake of state-formation, **democratization** and **industrialization**.

Aristocracy is a form of 'nobility', defined through hereditary rank, relatively closed against the more 'common' members of clans or **tribes**. Aristocracy begins to be institutionalized at the level of agrarian societies. With the establishment of chiefdoms, positions of nobility come to be inherited rather than obtained directly through prowess in battle. The wealthier and more differentiated planter-societies become, the more they develop powerful leading groups (for example, the Maya). In agrarian societies, the limitation of available land prevents lower strata from wandering away in discontent, thus facilitating their subjugation (Harris and Johnson 1999). A food-producing **peasantry** develops as chiefs turn into **monarchs**, and chiefdoms into **states** and empires, all in long-term unintentional chains of action. The distance between aristocracy and 'the people' increases and reaches a maximum in absolutist monarchies (Lenski 1966). Only industrialization leads gradually to a more egalitarian form of **stratification**. The power dimensions of aristocracies may be either physical (as with warriors) or administrative (as with bureaucrats) or religious (as with priests) or economic (as with patrician merchants in city-republics).

In Europe in the Middle Ages the combination of military power and landed property of vassals led to the rise of a feudal aristocracy (see **feudalism**). According to Max **Weber**, this seigneurial **class** acquires a specific kind of **charisma**, transmitted through the bonds of blood. In this context 'hereditary charisma' of noble families means an objectification of an originally purely personal gift of grace which becomes relevant for the political structuring of states, as clan-states, feudal, patrimonial or even bureaucratic states (Weber 1978: 250). An aristocracy may also function as a military service class in an eastern absolutism of Russian coinage (c.f. Anderson 1974). Most often, aristocracy is tied to the institution of **monarchy** with a prince or king as *primus inter pares*, or it forms a dominating class operating in an oligarchic or city-patrician framework, electing its leaders as doge or consul. In ancient Greece, the delicate and fragile relationship between aristocracy, timocracy, democracy, anarchy and tyranny was considered in terms of an ongoing circular process of transition from one stage to the other.

The decline of the European aristocracy as a military nobility began in the late Middle Ages and became irreversible with the rise of early modern states and their standing armies. In France, this development gave rise to a nursed and tamed court aristocracy (c.f. **Elias** 1983), complemented by a new 'noblesse de robe' of bourgeois bureaucrats joining the old 'noblesse d'épée'. Hermetic closure against the lower ranks had always been only theoretical, and stages of closure have been regularly followed by relative openness. Early modern England saw a commercially based, titled and untitled nobility becoming bourgeois, and the eighteenth century in England became – somewhat paradoxically after civil war and revolution – the great era of aristocracy and gentry. In the German case, the eastern class of Junkers retained a much more militarized position and mentality and thus was able partially to 'feudalize' the rising **bourgeoisie**. In Central Europe, aristocracies retained much of their political influence by occupying the pillars of the army and state **bureaucracy** until 1914, thus underlining the '*ständischen*' (estate) character of these offices. But also in England, we find an overrepresentation of aristocrats in government far into the twentieth century. Even as late as 1922, half the members of the British Cabinet were of noble origin (Cannadine 1990: 711).

Although financial and industrial **capital** since the twentieth century has greatly reduced the social significance of aristocracy in all European societies, aristocracy retains its influence in the formation of mentalities and in matters of taste. In France since the nineteenth century, this has been achieved through the establishment of 'grandes écoles' that seamlessly fuse bourgeois and aristocratic codes to a **habitus** of fine distinctions (see, especially, the work of Pierre **Bourdieu**). England in the nineteenth century experienced an amalgamation of the gentlemen's code of the landed property with the utilitarian Christian reformism of the **middle class**. Formulated as the ideal of 'muscular Christianity', it became one of the motors of colonial missionary movement. In Germany after 1871, the merging of the aristocracy and the bourgeoisie led to a new 'good society' of duelling fraternities (Elias 1996). Even the ideas and origins of the European **welfare state** are not understandable without tracing its ethos to an aristocratic legacy that provides 'protection' and 'care' in exchange for deference and loyalty (Sorenson 1997).

References and further reading

Anderson, P. (1974) *Lineages of the Absolutist State*. London: NLB.

Bourdieu, P. (1989) *La Noblesse d'État*. Paris: Edition de Minuit.

Cannadine, D. (1990) *The Decline and Fall of the British Aristocracy*. New Haven, CT: Yale University Press.

Elias, N. ([1969] 1983) *The Court Society*. Oxford: Blackwell.

Elias, N. ([1989] 1996) *The Germans*. Oxford: Blackwell.

Harris, M. and Johnson, O. (1999) *Cultural Anthropology*. Boston: Allyn and Bacon.

Lenski, G. (1966) *Power and Privilege*. New York: McGraw-Hill.

Sorenson, A. (1997) 'On Kings, Pietism and Rent-Seeking in Scandinavian Welfare States', *Acta Sociologica*, 41: 363–75.

Stone, L. (1965) *The Crisis of the Aristocracy 1558–1641*. Oxford: Clarendon Press.

Weber, M. ([1922] 1978) *Economy and Society*. Berkeley, CA: University of California Press.

HELMUT KUZMICS

ARON, RAYMOND (1905–1983)
French theorist

Aron's early work dealt with the **epistemology** of historical research and with German sociology. He introduced Max **Weber** to France. Throughout his career, he fought to overcome the gap between sociology, philosophy and politics, reinterpreting Montesquieu, **Tocqueville** and **Marx** in this light. After World War II, his main interest turned to the interpretation of twentieth century society. He investigated the links between **industrial society**, social struggles and political regimes and between war, **revolution** and **totalitarianism**. He was a central figure in French ideological discussions, an outspoken critic of Jean-Paul **Sartres** Marxism, and the most prominent critic of 'secular religions' (a term he coined) and of Marxism. But above all, he was France's main international relations theorist, as well as its most famous and respected commentator on international affairs. His diagnosis of the Cold War in terms of 'peace impossible, war improbable' remained valid until 1989. His major treatise *Peace and War* (1967), and his monumental study on Clausewitz provide an intellectual framework of lasting value (see **War and militarism**).

Major works

(1954) *The Century of Total War.* London: Verschoyle.
(1958) *War and Industrial Society.* London: Weidenfeld & Nicolson.
(1961a) *The Dawn of Universal History.* London: Weidenfeld & Nicolson.
(1961b) *Introduction to the Philosophy of History: An Essay on the Limits of Historical Objectivity.* London: Weidenfeld & Nicolson.
(1965) *Main Currents in Sociological Thought.* New York: Basic Books.
(1967) *Peace and War. A Theory of International Relations.* London: Weidenfeld & Nicolson.
(1968) *Progress and Disillusion.* London: Pall Mall Press.
(1983) *Clausewitz, Philosopher of War.* London: Routledge & Kegan Paul.

PIERRE HASSNER

ART AND AESTHETICS

A central issue for social theorists and philosophers of the arts is the question of whether art consists in any universally recognizable perceptual qualities or whether the word 'art' must be understood to refer simply to the practices, attitudes and outlooks of different cultural institutions that elect to classify objects in the world in particular ways (see **classification**). Proponents of 'institutional theories' of art argue that insofar as it possible for one object to be accounted a work of art and another physically indistinguishable object not to be accounted a work of art, the only factor capable of distinguishing art from non-art is the social fact of the decision of a particular cultural institution – the 'art world' – to confer *status* on certain objects (Danto 1964; Dickie 1974). One of the most frequently discussed cases in this connection has been Marcel Duchamp's Dadaist 'ready-made' *Fountain* at New York's

Museum of Modern Art, consisting of a ceramic men's toilet bowl, which appears to be materially indistinguishable from a toilet bowl in any men's cloakroom.

Institutional theories of the arts gain support from the observations by anthropologists that societies that do not possess a formal institution or concept of art cannot necessarily be understood as producing art. It seems clear that not all societies can be understood as producing art in the sense in which art has been understood in Western culture since Renaissance and the Enlightenment in Europe. Certainly few societies have seen art in terms of a special, quasi-sacred domain of expressive activity pursued for its own sake, without regard to utility or practical purpose, aiming at an ideal of autonomous aesthetic plenitude – an ideal famously enshrined in the nineteenth-century French slogan 'art for art's sake', or *l'art pour l'art*.

However, one general difficulty with institutional theories that strive for 'value-neutral' understandings of art, is that 'art' is not only a classificatory term; it is also, intrinsically, a value-laden honorific term. It is for this reason that sociological studies of the arts cannot be dissociated from the discipline of aesthetics, defined as the study of grounds for declarations of pleasure in perceptual experience. To understand something as a work of art is to understand it as embodying value of some kind; this value rests on perceptually significant sensory qualities that illuminate the spectator's experience in some way (Wollheim 1980). It is in this sense that experiencing an object as an art object is not reducible merely to recognizing it as an instance of a prevailing cultural and institutional fact, convention or code of perception.

Evaluative appreciation of art need not preclude a rigorous sociological consciousness of the relativity of ideas of art and aesthetic value to changing material contexts of cultural production and consumption. Sociological studies of the arts that emphasize the

21

imbrication of aesthetic value with political values of democracy and equality of access to cultural acclamation are sharply critical of, but not ultimately incompatible with, traditional humanistic ideas of art as intrinsically valuable sources of humane self-understanding and self-flourishing (see **humanism**).

Marxist approaches are represented by social historians of art such as Arnold Hauser and Lucien Goldmann and by the Hegelian-Marxist thinkers Georg **Lukács**, Ernst **Bloch**, Walter **Benjamin**, Siegfried **Kracauer**, Theodor **Adorno**, Max **Horkheimer** and Herbert **Marcuse**. These authors emphasize correlations between forms and contents of works of art and social **class** relations, especially insofar as these revolve around the artist's relation to a patron, or the market, or the state or any other source of economic subsistence. Much of this work draws on the Marxian vision of aesthetic forms as both vehicles of **ideology** that may function to legitimate existing relations of class domination and as utopian intimations or 'fore-images' of a future communistic society (see **utopia**).

More recent approaches in post-Marxist cultural studies criticize the older writers' concentration on class relations at the expense of differences of **gender** and **ethnicity** in the production of culture (Chadwick 1990), as well as their neglect of the receptive activity of audiences in constructing and recombining the contents of cultural products, including the contents of commercial media images. Particular objection has been taken to the **Frankfurt School**'s unsympathetic attitude to **mass culture and mass society** and to its excessively bleak view of the 'culture industry'. Adorno's normative attachment to the **modernist** aesthetic form has been seen as undervaluing the subversive and communicative resources of some kinds of **popular culture** – an issue discussed among others by Fredric **Jameson** in relation to the emergence of a **postmodernist** turn in the cultural practices of late capitalist modernity (see also Huyssen 1986).

Contemporary French sociological studies of the arts are greatly influenced by Pierre **Bourdieu**'s analyses of audience responses to works of art in terms of differential cultural, educational and socio-economic backgrounds (Bourdieu 1984; 1996). These and other approaches continue to take their lead from **Durkheim**'s ideas about cultural **classification** systems, as well as from Max **Weber's** conception of the emergence of the aesthetic sphere as a relatively autonomous field of cultural validity in the rationalization processes of modern societies.

References and further reading

Becker, H. (1982) *Art Worlds*. Berkeley, CA: University of California Press.

Bourdieu, P. (1984) *Distinction: A Social Critique of the Judgement of Taste*. London: Routledge.

Bourdieu, P. (1996) *The Rules of Art*. Cambridge: Polity Press.

Chadwick, W. (1990) *Women, Art and Society*. London: Thames and Hudson.

Danto, A. (1964) 'The Artworld', *Journal of Philosophy*, 61(19): 571–84.

Dickie, G. (1974) *Art and the Aesthetic*. Ithaca, NY: Cornell University Press.

DiMaggio, P. (1987) 'Classification in Art', *American Sociological Review*, 52: 440–55.

Geertz, C. (1983) 'Art as a Cultural System', in *Local Knowledge*. New York: Basic Books.

Gell, A. (1998) *Art and Agency*. Oxford: Oxford University Press.

Harrington, A. (2004) *Art and Social Theory: Sociological Arguments in Aesthetics*. Cambridge: Polity Press.

Huyssen, A. (1986) *After the Great Divide: Modernism, Mass Culture, and Postmodernism*. Bloomington, IN: Indiana University Press.

Witkin, R. (1996) *Art and Social Structure*. Cambridge: Polity Press.

Wollheim, R. (1980) 'The Institutional Theory of Art', in *Art and its Objects*, 2nd edn. Cambridge: Cambridge University Press.

Zollberg, V. (1990) *Constructing a Sociology of the Arts*. Cambridge: Cambridge University Press.

AUSTIN HARRINGTON

ASSOCIATIONS

Associations refer to the formation of people for a common purpose in a free and voluntary manner. Associations are thus the organized correlates of human sociability. They vary wildly in size and scope as well as in forms: from business associations to unions to **social movements**, co-operatives and citizens' action groups in **civil society**. Analytically speaking, associations belong to the space between social groups on the one hand (see **group**) and formal organizations on the other hand (see **organization**). Social groups such as the family as a primary group are based upon **intimacy**, continuous contact, face-to-face-interaction and obligatory membership – one belongs to one's family whether one likes it or not (see **family and household**). Formal organizations are collectivities made up of formal, voluntary and finite membership. A white-collar worker in a large corporation applies for a job, is successful, and with the job comes a set of occupational **role** expectations and positional rights and obligations. Either retirement or 'firing' finish the relationship between the individual and the organization.

In classical social theory, associations were conceptualized as a 'bridge' between individual and society. **Tocqueville**, for instance, focused his analysis of modern society upon different forms of *voluntary associations*, at the level of the community in his celebrated work *Democracy in America*. The American spirit of **voluntarism** leads to the spontaneous uniting of social forces in order to tackle a problem collectively, no matter how big or small. He contrasted this American **mentality** of self-reliance with the European reluctance to get organized and instead to rely on the action of the state (see **state and nation-state**). Emile **Durkheim** followed in the footsteps of Tocqueville when he proposed the institutionalization of occupational associations in France during the Third Republic. According to his analysis, the demise of all intermediary corporations after the Revolution and the prohibition of **trade unions** in the wake of the Parisian Commune left French society in a situation where a centralized state was confronted by a mass of unorganized individuals. In his view, this lack of societal organization with a powerful central state, on the one hand, and disconnected individuals, on the other, provided a true 'sociological monstrosity' and was largely responsible for the crisis of **anomie** in France at the time.

In German classical social theory it was not the historical-empirical lack of intermediate associations but rather the complexity and plurality of organizational forms in modern society that inspired sociological reflection. Ferdinand **Tönnies** tried to capture the main thrust of the transition from **tradition** to **modernity** by the distinction between **Gemeinschaft and Gesellschaft** which was somewhat misleadingly translated as *community and association* by C. P. Loomis in 1955. For him, modern social relationships were based primarily upon social contracts echoing the distinction by Henry Sumner Maine between **status** and **contract**.

Georg **Simmel** was, above all, interested in the social forms of life. Social life is based upon **exchange** which he conceptualizes as 'soziale Wechselwirkungen' or as it was translated by Simmel's American student, Albion Small, as social **interaction**. These social interactions give rise to different 'Formen der Wechselwirkungen' or forms of association (see also **form and forms**). Simmel distinguishes, among others, social **conflict**, competition, **power** and **domination**, the cross-cutting of social circles and the web of **group** affiliations. This approach to deciphering the forms of associations in a pure and abstract way was later called *formal sociology* by Simmel's successors Leopold von Wiese and Alfred Vierkandt. This type of reasoning became the foundation for contemporary **network** theory and also shows similarities with French **structuralism**.

Max **Weber** chose quite a different path in order to delineate the associational structure of modern society. In *Economy and Society*,

Weber sets out with the concept of 'social action', moves on to 'social relationships' and terminates his conceptual reflections with the concept of order. Action, relationship and order define the **micro-, meso- and macro-levels** of social reality and it is within these realms that forms of association can be distinguished. Weber does so by a host of definitions and distinctions between open and closed relationships, voluntary and compulsory association, enterprise and formal organization, communal and associative relationships, political and hierocratic organizations, types of order and domination. Starting from this analytical grid Weber was able to develop a series of important conceptual distinctions which we still employ today: for instance, the triad of **class**, **status** (or rather, *Stand* **or estate) and party** as different types of communal relationships; the distinction between **church** and **sect** within the realm of religion and hierocratic organization; or the distinction between household and enterprise which stood at the cradle of the birth of the modern economy.

Classical social theory shows why association today means at least two things. Associations in the wider sense are almost coterminous with **society** as they comprise all forms of human sociability. Associations in the narrower sense refer to the meso-level of social life, and thus are located between the individual on the micro-level and the state on the macro-level. In this sense they refer to all kinds of voluntary mobilization of social forces between intimate groups and formal organizations.

References and further reading

Durkheim, E. (1893) *De la division du travail social*. Paris: Alcan.

Durkheim, E. (1950) *Leçons de sociologie: Physique des mœurs et du droit*. Paris: Presses Universitaires de France.

Simmel, G. (1908) *Soziologie*. Berlin: Duncker & Humblot.

Tocqueville, A. de (1835, 1840) *De la démocratie en Amérique*. Paris: Gallimard.

Tönnies, F. ([1887] 1979) *Gemeinschaft und Gesellschaft*. Darmstadt: Wissenschaftliche Buchgesellschaft.

Weber, M. (1921) *Wirtschaft und Gesellschaft*. Tübingen: Mohr-Siebeck.

HANS-PETER MÜLLER

AUTHORITY

In general, authority is a relational form of **power** that is exercised over social agents by actors in positions of leadership, where the source of compliance is either legitimacy or some other form of consent (see **legitimacy and legitimization**). While authority may entail command and obedience, it is to be distinguished from forms of **domination** based purely upon coercion. Conversely, while entailing consent, authority is also distinct from influence where compliance is derived from persuasion or argument.

As argued by Arendt (1958), in classical Greece, authority was a right to command derived from true knowledge. Plato argued that authority entailed knowledge of the 'forms'. In Thomas Aquinas, the classical view became transformed into the authority of the **church** as the interpreter of God's law.

During the **Enlightenment**, the association between authority and the dictates of **religion** led to a reversal of the classical view. Authority represented the absence of truth and reason. This is exemplified by **Kant** in his essay, 'What is Enlightenment?', in which he argued that enlightenment is the courage to think without dependence on external authority. This interpretation lies at the heart of the distinction between authority and influence. In conservative political thought, the opposition between reason and authority takes the form of an association between authority and tradition. Consequently, thinkers like Edmund Burke argued that legitimate government and authority should be based upon tradition, not on unconstrained reason. Conversely, but from the same premises, radicals such as Saint-Simon and Bakhunin saw the creation of a just and rational society in terms of an overthrow of both tradition and authority.

In the seventeenth century, Thomas Hobbes developed an essentially pragmatic view of authority. In his thesis, in order to overcome the inconvenience of the 'state of nature', individuals agree by social **contract** to give their personal powers to a sovereign who, in effect, becomes 'author' of their actions. Consequently, the scope of sovereign authority becomes virtually unlimited.

In classical sociology, Max **Weber** (1978) is central to the debate on authority. Weber's German term *Herrschaft* implies both authority and domination through coercion. Since Weber distinguished between coercive and legitimate *Herrschaft*, most sociologists have followed **Parsons**'s interpretation of authority as 'legitimate domination'. However, there are exceptions to this approach. For example, Wrong (1995) argues for the concept of 'coercive authority'. Wrong's theoretical reason is that Weber would never have lost sight of the fact that most actual political authority is partly derived from coercion, even if only historically so. However, as these terms are **ideal types** for Weber, it can be argued that such actual empirical cases are not pure forms of authority and, furthermore, that power may move from one source to another. Over time, power that was once derived from coercion may become based upon legitimacy – coercive domination can become authority.

Weber viewed legitimacy as entailing consent based upon rules, practices and beliefs, shared by ruler and followers (Beetham 1991; Raz 1990). These have four sources: (1) *purposively rational* action, oriented towards means – ends efficiency and legality; (2) *value rational* action, justified in terms of ultimate values; (3) *affectual action*, derived from emotions; (4) *traditional action*, based upon age-old rules and customs. Bureaucratic legal authority derives its legitimacy from purposively rational action and is associated with modernity. Traditional authority derives legitimacy from traditional action and is typical of traditional societies. Weber's perception of traditional authority is influenced by the Kantian view of traditional authority as irrational, whereas bureaucratic authority is seen as rational. Both these forms of authority are routine and stable.

Weber's third form of authority, based on **charisma**, is unstable, exceptional and also 'irrational'. According to Weber, this form of authority derives legitimacy from affectual action. Leaders endowed with exceptional qualities such as Moses and Jesus gain legitimacy through the emotions of their followers. Because charismatic authority is destabilizing to other forms of authority, it is a source of **social change**. But as it is exceptional, it rarely lasts beyond the lifetime of a charismatic leader: to be perpetuated, it has to be routinized as traditional or legal bureaucratic authority. In modern democracies Weber considered parliament as an important source of social change because it provides leaders with the chance to display charisma.

Curiously, Weber did not develop a fourth type of authority corresponding to 'value rationality'. Willer (1967) suggests this form should be called 'ideological authority' and should derive its basis from adherence to a system of value, for instance, religious movements, nationalism and, in its initial phases (before becoming routine), democracy. Like charismatic authority, this is an exceptional and dynamic authority, lasting only as long as ideological fervour is sustained (see **nationalism**).

Developing Weber's analysis, Parsons (1958) argued that in social systems the economy and polity should be considered as working in parallel. On the one hand, the economy enables systems to adapt to the environment and, on the other, the polity facilitates system goals. Within the economy, money is a circulating medium that is based upon **trust** and consent and, analogously, the polity contains authoritative power which derives its legitimacy from trust in the capacity of political leaders to realize collective goals.

While Parsonian structural **functionalism** has fallen out of favour, the comparison (and contrast) between money and power is suggestive. An actor in authority effectively 'has' power in much the same way as the wealthy 'have' money. However, money can be spent in a number of ways, while those in authority can use power only for specific purposes. What is at issue is not the quantity of power (the equivalent of not being able to afford something) but the use to which power can be put. The President of the USA has the authority to declare war on millions (a large amount of power), yet does not have the power to have a single political opponent assassinated (smaller quantity of power). When actors use their authoritative power appropriately, it is not 'spent' or 'used up' like money, but rather, if it is exercised effectively, it increases through use. It is only through illegitimate use that authority is 'spent'. However, while confined in scope, authority is distinct from 'delegation' where power is confined to specified decisions. Authority entails the power to pursue collective goals, although there is some flexibility concerning the means. It is this quality which enables effective leaders to increase their legitimacy and hence their authority.

In contrast to Parsons, Marxist sociologists tend not to take the legitimacy of authority at face value. It becomes theorized as 'false consciousness', or as rationalizations (justifications used by **elites**), or as **hegemony** (consensus as a manifestation of bourgeois control over knowledge). One other view, defended by **Dahrendorf** (1957), is that modern forms of social organization entail distribution of authority among social roles that define expectations of subjection and domination, thus creating two distinct sets of positions or types of persons in constant conflict.

Echoing both Marx and Weber, **Giddens** (1981) argues that history should be interpreted in terms of the twin evolution of two types of resources. Allocative resources (Marx) entail the control of material things, including raw materials, means of production and produced artefacts. Authoritative resources (Weber) involve control over people, including their positioning in time and space and control over their lives and life chances. In this view, the industrial revolution not only presupposed mechanical advancements but equally the creation of a disciplined workforce. Capitalists need labour which they have the authority to situate in an exact position in space (next to a machine) for a specified length of time (working day). The industrial revolution is premised upon the steam engine *and* the clock, on both allocative and authoritative resources.

The work of **Beck** and Giddens (1991) on late modernity suggests the emergence of another authority type. As **risk** society develops, actors continually seek assessment of risk based upon 'expert authority'. This applies both to global issues (where environmentalists and their opponents appeal to the authority of experts) and in everyday life (where actors routinely defer to them). This idea of authority appears to represent a return to the classical view of authority as legitimacy derived from knowledge.

References and further reading

Arendt, H. (1958) 'Authority', *Nomos*, I.

Beetham, D. (1991) *The Legitimation of Power*. London: Macmillan.

Dahrendorf, R. (1957) *Class and Class Conflict in an Industrial Society*. London: Routledge.

Giddens, A. (1981) *A Contemporary Critique of Historical Materialism*. London: Macmillan.

Giddens, A. (1991) *The Consequences of Modernity*. Cambridge: Polity.

Lukes, S. (1978) 'Power and Authority', in T. Bottomore and R. Nisbet (eds), *A History of Sociological Analysis*. London: Heinemann.

Lukes, S. (1987) 'Perspectives on Authority', *Nomos*, XXIX.

Parsons, T. (1958) 'Authority, Legitimation and Political Action', *Nomos*, I.

Raz, J. (ed.) (1990) *Authority*. New York: New York University Press.

Weber, M. (1978) *Economy and Society*. Berkeley, CA: University of California Press.

Willer, D. (1967) 'Max Weber's Missing Authority Type', *Sociological Inquiry*, 37: 231–39.

Wrong, D. (1995) *Power: Its Forms, Bases, and Uses*. London: Transaction.

MARK HAUGAARD

AUTONOMY

Autonomy means self-determination. It refers to the right of states or institutions to regulate their affairs, or to the ability of individuals to direct their lives by free will and according to reason. On a first level, autonomy entails the **freedom** to do as one wants. This freedom can be restricted by external or internal barriers. For example, young children, lacking the ability of cognitive and affective self-distancing, are in the grip of their immediate sensations or desires. On a second level, autonomy implies being able to want as one wants. This presupposes meta-cognitive and meta-volitional abilities: individuals take a stance towards their spontaneous (first order) desires and decide with reasons which ones they want to determine their will (second-order volition) (Frankfurt 1988). Autonomy fails if the action is not motivated by reasons but determined by chance or by non-willed causes. This may occur under the influence of uncontrolled drives, addictions, unconsidered needs for conformity, or, more broadly, by forms of **social control**, coercion or 'manipulation'. Another way of putting this is to say that moral behaviour is first determined by immediate desires, then by a second-order desire to follow a norm which, in turn, is supported by reason. According to **Kantian** philosophy, autonomy is no longer justified by God's commands or natural law but by the rational will of all concerned.

References and further reading

Elster, J. (1979) *Ulysses and the Sirens*. Cambridge: Cambridge University Press.

Frankfurt, H. G. (1988) *The Importance of What We Care About*. Cambridge: Cambridge University Press.

Habermas, J. ([1968] 1971) *Knowledge and Human Interests*. Boston: Beacon Press.

Kant, I. ([1784] 1970) 'An answer to the Question: What is Enlightenment?' in *Kant's Political Writings*. Cambridge: Cambridge University Press.

GERTRUD NUNNER-WINKLER

B

BAKHTIN CIRCLE

The Bakhtin Circle refers to a multi-disciplinary group of Soviet scholars including the cultural theorist Mikhail Bakhtin (1895–1975), the linguist Valentin Vološinov (1895–1936) and the literary scholar Pavel Medvedev (1891–1938). The group combined **Kantian philosophy**, **phenomenology**, **Hegelian philosophy** and **Marxism** to develop a theory of language centred on an idea of dialogue. This involved an account of literary history based on a dialectic of novelistic (critical) and poetic genres, and a theory of critical culture as derived from a communally experienced festive laughter, carnival.

The language theory was chiefly developed by Vološinov in *Marxism and the Philosophy of Language* ([1929] 1973) in which dialogue emerges as the discursive embodiment of intersubjective relationships (see **intersubjectivity**). In the 1930s and 1940s Bakhtin developed this idea according to idealist and juridical principles to argue that all languages are equally (in)capable of approaching the 'thing in itself', that all discursive forms have generic features, and that the individual is responsible for his or her discursive acts. 'Dialogism' becomes the means by which spurious truth claims are unmasked and their authoritarian (monologic) motivations exposed. Laughter is held to be the bearer of the critical spirit, structuring dialogic engagements with authoritarian discourses. Drawing on ideas developed by a number of Soviet scholars of the time, Bakhtin claims that this principle derives from the collective spirit of pre-class society and, as such, challenges social inequities. Discernible in Renaissance carnivals, the principle permeates prose literature in the form of certain folkloric and 'carnivalistic' semantic clusters. The works of writers such as Rabelais and Cervantes are held to be particularly rich in such features.

In Bakhtin's final works, monologism and dialogism are explicitly linked to the methods of the natural and human sciences respectively.

References and further reading

Brandist, C. (2002) *The Bakhtin Circle: Philosophy, Culture and Politics*. London: Pluto Press.
Brandist, C. *et al.* (eds) (2004) *The Bakhtin Circle: In the Master's Absence*. Manchester: Manchester University Press.
Hirschkop, K. (1999) *Mikhail Bakhtin: An Aesthetic for Democracy*. Oxford: Oxford University Press.
Vološinov, V. N. ([1929] 1973) *Marxism and the Philosophy of Language*. Cambridge, MA: Harvard University Press.

CRAIG BRANDIST

BARTHES, ROLAND (1915–1980)
French theorist

Barthes was the author of numerous works in literary theory and criticism and *semiotics*, today recognized as cornerstones in the discipline of cultural studies. His most famous work, *Mythologies* (1993) is a series of short vignettes debunking as so many 'myths' the petty-bourgeois **ideology** that can be conveyed through **popular culture** and the **media and the mass media** in various forms of coding. Taking his cue from the structural linguistics of Ferdinand de Saussure and structuralist theory, Barthes analyzed social structures on the model of relations between linguistic elements in texts (see **structuralism**). He also developed a theory of the sign based on the distinction between 'denotation' and 'connotation' formulated by the Danish linguist Louis Hjelmslev (1899–1963). In his major work *Elements of Semiology* (1964), Barthes examines the social significance of material objects with the aid of the Saussurean definition of the sign, the 'signifier' and the 'signified'.

Among some of his most illuminating exercises are his analyses of fashion, dress code and eating etiquette. In other works, including notably *S/Z* (1974), Barthes presents the text as a self-constituting entity actualized in the reading process, thematizing the 'writerly' text, as opposed to the 'readerly' text which forecloses meaning by conforming to established literary conventions. Barthes is best known for his conception of the 'death of the author', where the author is polemically seen as no more than a function of discursive structures and conventions, rather than as a unique creative individual. This conception became of central concern to other French thinkers loosely associated with post-structuralism, including Jacques **Derrida**, Michel **Foucault** and Julia Kristeva.

Major works

(1964) *Elements of Semiology*. New York: Hill and Wang.
(1974) *S/Z*. Trans. R. Howard. Oxford: Blackwell.
(1993) *Mythologies*. Trans. A. Lavers, London: Vintage.

Further reading

Sontag, S. (ed.) (1993) *A Barthes Reader*. London: Vintage.

KARINE ZBINDEN

BATAILLE, GEORGES (1897–1962)
French theorist, librarian, philosopher, critic, and novelist

Bataille's perennial concern – expressed in all his life and works – was with an asymmetrical dialectic encompassing the immanent development of the anguished individual and his or her changing relations with different modalities of the awe-inspiring sacred power of collectivities. His earliest work embraced the full range and potential excesses of individual and interpersonal experiences, emphasizing the totality of emotions and bodily functions. He began a life-long relationship with a Kojèvean Hegelian Marxism and at the same time, jointly with dissident Surrealists, began to develop a radical Maussian Durkheimianism. Bataille argued that 'society ... combining organisms at the highest level, makes them into something other than their sum', and that transgression transcends and completes an interdiction, thereby enhancing the transgressive experience. Bataille reinterpreted the categories of the **sacred** and profane to refer to the socially heterogeneous, where is found 'expenditure without reserve', and the socially homogeneous, the loci of utilitarian calculation. His later work explored the nature of, and the limits of the knowledge of, allegedly bounded integral systems, such as identities, conceptual systems, structures, societies and historical development. These produce an unacknowledged excess, inexplicable within their own terms of reference. In seeking to maintain themselves against potential disruption often associated with their own internal logics, such systems need loss through excessive expenditure. All are 'restricted economies' locatable in 'general economies' which cannot be adequately conceptualized or controlled. Indeed, the sacred is now seen as the totality of the world and the profane as abstractive practices *vis-à-vis* this totality. His ideas influenced **Derrida**, **Foucault**, **Deleuze**, **Lyotard** and **Baudrillard**.

Major works

(1999) *Visions of Excess: Selected Writings 1937–1939*, Allan Stoekl (ed., tr.,) Minneapolis, MN: University of Minnesota Press.
([1943] 1988) *Inner Experience*. Albany, NY: SUNY Press.
([1947] 1988) *The Accursed Share*. New York: Zone Books.
([1957] 1962) *Erotism: Death and Sensuality*. San Francisco: City Lights.

Further reading

Surya, M. ([1992] 2002) *Georges Bataille: An Intellectual Biography*. London: Verso.

FRANK PEARCE

BAUDRILLARD, JEAN (1929–)

French theorist Baudrillard has contributed to a wide range of issues in philosophy, social theory, media analysis and cultural criticism. In a number of diverse and often intellectually disparate texts, he has theorized the present as a global consumer society of simulation and simulacra shaped by the media and **mass media** and new information technologies (see **simulacrum**). Baudrillard's early writings are in the **Marxist** tradition of the critique of capitalism, the theory of **everyday** life (influenced by Henri **Lefebvre**), and the 'society of the spectacle' perspective associated with Guy Debord. In *Symbolic Exchange and Death* (1993) he fuses a Marxist analysis of contemporary capitalism with a critical semiotics of everyday life. The society of consumer capitalism is seen as inaugurating a new era of **capitalism**, dominated by an ever-expanding logic of sign values where

signs are displaced by media-generated simulacra (see **consumption**). Like the Italian semiologist, Umberto Eco, Baudrillard's later thought is devoted to problems generated by the transition from industrial societies dominated by production, exchange-value, and political economy to a civilization characterized by hyper-real sign-values, the mass production of culture, and generalized communications technologies. Baudrillard writes about a modern universe of hyper-communication in which signifiers are totally 'emancipated' from the signified and the referential. Baudrillard's work has had a wide-ranging impact upon debates in postmodern theory and politics, media analysis, cultural studies, sociology, and contemporary aesthetic theory (see **postmodernism and postmodernity**).

Major works

([1972] 1981) *For a Critique of the Political Economy of the Sign*. St Louis, MO: Telos.
([1973] 1975) *The Mirror of Production*. St Louis, MO: Telos.
([1976] 1993) *Symbolic Exchange and Death*. London: Sage.
([1981] 1983) *Simulations*. New York: Semiotext(e).
([1990] 1993) *The Transparency of Evil*. London: Verso.

Further reading

Kellner, D. (ed.) (1994) *Baudrillard: A Critical Reader*. Oxford: Blackwell.
Sandywell, B. (1995) 'Forget Baudrillard', *Theory, Culture & Society*, 12: 125–52.

BARRY SANDYWELL

BAUMAN, ZYGMUNT (1925–)

Polish-born theorist resident in Britain. Bauman's work is a **hermeneutics** of the relationship between **praxis** and **social structures**. Bauman's commitment to praxis as the striving for **utopia** means that his work is a version of **critical theory**, drawing on the early **Marx**, as well as **Gramsci**, **Simmel**, **Bloch** and Polish sociological **humanism** (particularly Ossowski). He also draws on European literature and poetry, and because of this it is perhaps better to identify Bauman as a practitioner of the sociological imagination than as an orthodox sociologist. Bauman argues that praxis is utopian because it points towards a world of autonomous human self-creation, but the insecurity that is associated with **autonomy** leads to reified social structures that promise security and which are underpinned by **power** (as both coercion and consent). In **modernity**, **security** was established through ordering designs (i.e. Nazism and notions of 'purity') or through notions of a perfect future (**communism**, particularly its Stalinist form), and in **postmodernity** it is established through consumerism (see **postmodernism and postmodernity**). Bauman seeks to recover the utopian possibilities of praxis, which he links to an ethics of being for the **Other**, irrespective of the demands of reified social structures and power. Bauman initially identified this as a 'postmodern ethics', but it also motivates his discussions of **globalization** and 'liquid modernity'. Bauman's work has had a major impact on debates about the **Holocaust**, modernity, postmodernity, **morality**, and consumerism.

Major works

(1973) *Culture as Praxis*. London: Routledge & Kegan Paul.
(1989) *Modernity and the Holocaust*. Cambridge: Polity.
(1993) *Postmodern Ethics*. Cambridge: Polity.
(2000) *Liquid Modernity*. Cambridge: Polity.

Further reading

Beilharz, P. (2000) *Zygmunt Bauman: Dialectics of Modernity*. London: Sage.
Smith, D. (1999) *Zygmunt Bauman: Prophet of Postmodernity*. Cambridge: Polity.

Tester, K. (2004) *The Social Thought of Zygmunt Bauman*. Basingstoke: Palgrave Macmillan.

KEITH TESTER

BEAUVOIR, SIMONE DE (1908–1986)
French novelist, essayist and philosopher

Drawing on **Sartre**'s existentialism and Husserl and **Merleau-Ponty**'s **phenomenology** of the body, de Beauvoir has made important contributions to **feminism**. *The Second Sex* (1949) is reputed to have inspired second-wave feminism and initiated the **sex/gender distinction**. Her infamous statement, 'Woman is not born but becomes one', sees gender as a social and cultural process (**social constructionism**) rather than mandated by sexed differences. Since woman's inferiority has been coupled with her biological weaknesses and the inexorable logic of reproduction, this distinction provides an antidote to the fear that biology is destiny. As a phenomenologist, de Beauvoir describes the phenomenon *woman* – analyzing the multiple meanings involved in this reality. This includes problematizing our existing ideas of femininity, women's subordination, sexuality, **embodiment**, self – other relations. This is not a turn to the subject, or only in so far as it sees the subject in relation to objects, processes and events in which it is enmeshed. De Beauvoir explores the myriad situations (political, social, cultural and psychological) in which women are constituted as **Other** to men – reduced to an object rather than subject. Radical cultural feminists believed de Beauvoir diminished women's achievements and endorsed masculine activity as a goal for liberated women. The French differential post-structuralists (Irigaray, Kristeva) believed her attention to **equality** involved the inclusion of women in existing masculine institutions and practices rather than forging a new feminine symbolic order. In the **cultural turn**, de Beauvoir has been dismissed as an Enlightenment humanist –

overly optimistic about changing social reality through reason and revolution (see **humanism**). Her notion of the lived and situated body saves her from these charges, for she manages to appreciate the significance of everyday culture, the non-rational and history in the process of becoming woman.

Major works

([1949] 1989) *The Second Sex*. Trans. H. M. Parshley, New York: Vintage.
(1976) *The Ethics of Ambiguity*. Trans. B. Frechtman, New York: Citadel.

ELAINE STAVRO

BECK, ULRICH (1944–)

German theorist

Beck is known primarily for his ground breaking thesis on **risk** society. In this work he argues that a fundamental break is taking place within the social history of modernity as we move away from an older 'industrial society' towards a new 'risk society'. He claims that where it was largely the case that earlier generations were blind to the ecological hazards of modernization, in the emergent risk society, a social consciousness of large-scale industrial hazards (particularly in relation to chemical pollutants, nuclear technologies and genetic engineering) has a great bearing upon people's cultural attitudes and social behaviours. As a result, we are reaching the point where politics is more likely to be conducted as a response to collective anxieties, risk, **recognition**, public dialogue and **social inclusion** than as a means to resolve age-old concerns of material scarcity. At this point, Beck discerns a 'second' or a new 'radicalized' modernity guided by the ideals of 'ecological enlightenment'. He explores the possibilities that exist within contemporary societies for humanity to respond to the threat of global disaster with **social movements** to radically reform the technologies

and science of modernization so as to secure planetary survival. This thesis is elaborated in relation to matters of **reflexivity**, 'reflexive modernization', **individualism and individualization**, **globalization** and a new cosmopolitan perspective on international politics and law (see **cosmopolitanism**).

Major works

(1992) *Risk Society: Towards a New Modernity*. London: Sage.
(1995a) *Ecological Politics in an Age of Risk*. Cambridge: Polity.
(1995b) *Ecological Enlightenment*. Buffalo, NY: Prometheus.
(1995c) *The Normal Chaos of Love* (with E. Beck-Gernsheim). Cambridge: Polity.
(1997) *The Reinvention of Politics*. Cambridge: Polity.
(1998) *Democracy Without Enemies*. Cambridge: Polity.
(1999) *World Risk Society*. Cambridge: Polity.
(2000a) *What is Globalization?* Cambridge: Polity.
(2000b) *The Brave New World of Work*. Cambridge: Polity.
(2002) *Individualization* (with E. Beck-Gernsheim). London: Sage.

Further reading

Beck, U. and Willms, J. (2004) *Conversations with Ulrich Beck*. Cambridge: Polity.
Mythen, G. (2004) *Ulrich Beck: A Critical Introduction to the Risk Society*. Andover: Pluto Press.

IAIN WILKINSON

BEHAVIOURISM

Behaviourism is the name of a philosophical and scientific doctrine, according to which **knowledge** of human conduct can be obtained only if the concepts of mind and consciousness are jettisoned in favour of exclusive focus on externally observable behaviour. In its methodological version, behaviourism advocates bracketing of consciousness for purposes of the objective study of behaviour and is therefore close to **empiricism**. As a **metaphysical** position, it denies consciousness completely and is thus a variant of **materialism**. This objectivist and even reductionist doctrine made its first appearance in American psychology but then spread to the wider social sciences, leading to their renaming as 'behavioural sciences'. Having met resistance in Europe, it gained currency largely in the American sphere of influence. Here, however, the diffusion of behaviourism was severely curtailed by the cognitive revolution and the emergence of the cognitive sciences, including cognitive sociology (see **cognitivism**). Consequently, behavioural sociology's heyday came to an end in the 1970s. Some commentators discover the roots of behaviourism in ancient Greece and in early modern Britain and France, but it is more strictly an early twentieth-century movement. Behaviourism is most closely associated with the names of the American scientists John B. Watson, Burrhus F. Skinner and George C. **Homans**.

The immediate impetus to behaviourism came from the Russian physiologist, Pavlov, whose experiments on the salivary reflex in dogs led to the central concept of 'conditioned reflex'. The intellectual background against which Watson founded behaviourism was broader, however. Stimulated positively by Pavlov, behaviourism was an extreme reaction to the widely held introspective philosophy of the late nineteenth century, particularly the introspective school of psychology represented by Wilhelm Wundt in Germany and E. B. Titchener in the United States.

In the 1930s, Skinner introduced 'radical behaviourism' as a transformation of Watson's classical stimulus-response model. Instead of simple reflex or 'respondent behaviour' in the sense of inherited responses to particular, pre-given stimuli such as food or bright light, Skinner shifted the emphasis to voluntary, learned or 'operant behaviour' which is elicited by

environmental events, such as speech or classroom teaching, and then influenced by the ensuing consequences.

Emerging in the early 1960s from this notion of a set of relations linking behaviour and environment, behavioural sociology represented by Homans, Richard Emerson and others focused, within the context of dyads and **groups**, on how the consequences of behaviour, such as rewards and punishment, systematically modify its subsequent execution (see **exchange theory**). In Homans's (1961) view, sociology is the study of individual behaviour and **interaction** rather than of **institutions** or social **structures**, yet at this level its focus is not consciousness but the patterns of reinforcement or the history of rewards and costs leading people to do what they do.

Whereas the widespread hostile reception of Skinner's *Beyond Freedom and Dignity* (1971) signalled the decline of behaviourism, inroads against the doctrine had already been made by the cognitive revolution of the late 1950s, particularly but not only by the displacement of behavioural psychology by cognitive psychology. George Herbert **Mead** (1962), the major influence behind **symbolic interactionism** who in the 1920s borrowed the emphasis on the actor from Watson and even presented his own work from what he called 'a behavioristic point of view', vehemently disagreed with Watson's rejection of mind and consciousness. Mead insisted, by contrast, that perception, attention, memory, imagination, reasoning and **emotion** should be included as part of the act and that the act itself should be located in a broad social context, for only then would a creative and dynamic concept of the actor be possible (see **action**).

This early criticism found clear formulation in the vociferous arguments against behaviourism put forward by proponents of cognitivism. In the 1960s, Jean **Piaget** (1970) criticized 'the myth of the sensory origin of scientific knowledge' from the standpoint of the 'construction' (see **social constructionism**) of knowledge. Central to this for Piaget was the internal, unobservable organizing principle that he called the 'schema' (see **framing**). Similarly Noam **Chomsky** (1968) attacked behaviourism in general, and Skinner in particular, for adopting a narrow perspective that occludes the cognitive system of knowledge and belief acquired through **socialization** which generates the kinds of behaviour we observe. Today, vestiges of behaviourism survive in empiricist, **rational choice** and micro-economic approaches.

References and further reading

Chomsky, N. (1968) *Language and Mind*. New York: Harcourt, Brace & World.

Guerin, B. (1994) *Analyzing Social Behavior*. Reno: Context Press.

Homans, G. C. (1961) *Social Behavior*. New York: Harcourt, Brace & World.

Mead, G. H. ([1934] 1962) *Mind, Self and Society*. Chicago: University of Chicago Press.

Piaget, J. (1970) *Psychology and Epistemology*. Harmondsworth: Penguin.

Skinner, B. F. (1953) *Science and Human Behavior*. New York: Free Press.

Skinner, B. F. (1971) *Beyond Freedom and Dignity*. New York: Knopf.

Watson, J. B. ([1924] 1970) *Behaviorism*. New York: W. W. Norton.

PIET STRYDOM

BELL, DANIEL (1919–)

US sociologist

Bell conceives of society as analytically differentiated into three relatively autonomous spheres: politics, **social structure** and **culture**.

In *The End of Ideology* (1960), Bell argues that party politics are no longer governed by the **ideologies** of the left and the right. Instead, a consensus shared by all the major parties has emerged, which acknowledges the necessity and desirability of **democracy**, a mixed **economy**, and the **welfare** state, but which also creates the possibility of new **conflict**, particularly through a discontented young generation of intellectuals. In *The Cultural Contradictions of Capitalism* (1976) Bell analyzes developments in American culture. His main thesis is that due to rising mass **consumption**, hedonism and self-indulgence are spreading, standing in stark contrast to the requirements of the overall economic system, and creating a contradiction which questions the integrity of the culture. In *The Coming of Post-industrial Society* (1973) Bell identifies and analyzes the change in social structure from industrial to **post-industrial society**, characterized by two central dimensions: the shift from manufacturing to services as the main economic sector, and the centrality and codification of knowledge as the new axial principle of social structure (see **knowledge and knowledge society**).

Major works

(1960) *The End of Ideology*. Glencoe, IL: Free Press.

(1973) *The Coming of Post-Industrial Society: A Venture in Social Forecasting*. New York: Basic Books.

(1976) *The Cultural Contradictions of Capitalism*. New York: Basic Books.

Further reading

Waters, M. (1996) *Daniel Bell*. London: Routledge.

JOCHEN STEINBICKER

BENDIX, REINHARD (1916–1991)

German sociologist

Influenced by **Weber**, Bendix's widely read *Max Weber: An Intellectual Portrait* (1960) still remains one of the best expositions of Weber's substantive ideas. Bendix's own intellectual legacy rests on his comparative studies of the **state**, **authority** and **society**. *Class, Status and Power* (1953), a reader jointly edited with Seymour Martin **Lipset**, established **stratification** and **power** as a central concern of sociology at a time when **Parsonian** normative consensus was the orthodoxy. *Work and Authority in Industry* (1956) compared the ideological justification of managers in four different societal settings. *Nation-Building and Citizenship* (1964) and *Kings and People* (1978) started a golden age in historical informed accounts of the development of power structures and legitimacy in Western and non-Western societies (see **legitimacy and legitimation**). In modern societies, power can no longer rest on status inequality – an observation Bendix credited to **Tocqueville**. The organization of **work** requires forms of managerial ideology, and nation–states require forms of democratic legitimacy (see **state and nation-state**). The content of these forms in particular societies will draw upon specific cultural traditions and contingencies of nationhood. Bendix's address in 1970 as President of the American Sociological Association deftly charted some of the better places for sociology to position itself, across the axes of scientific distance versus engagement, and hard-nosed scientism versus naïve humanism (Bendix and Roth 1971).

Major works

(1956) *Work and Authority in Industry: Ideologies of Management in the Course of Industrialization.* Berkeley, CA: University of California Press.

(1960) *Max Weber: An Intellectual Portrait.* New York: Doubleday.

(1964) *Nation-Building and Citizenship.* New York: John Wiley & Sons.

(1971) (with G. Roth) *Scholarship and Partisanship: Essays on Max Weber.* Berkeley, CA: University of California Press.

(1978) *Kings or People: Power and the Mandate to Rule.* Berkeley, CA: University of California Press.

(1984) *Force, Fate, and Freedom: On Historical Sociology.* Berkeley, CA: University of California Press.

Skocpol, T. (ed.) (1985) *Vision and Method in Historical Sociology.* Cambridge: Cambridge University Press.

SAM WHIMSTER

BENJAMIN, WALTER (1893–1940)
German–Jewish theorist

Closely associated with the **critical theory** of the **Frankfurt School**, Benjamin drew on motifs from **Marxism**, **Judaism** and literary **modernism**. He pioneered an idiosyncratic revolutionary politics of redemption embracing a wide range of contemporary cultural forms, including film and photography. His abiding concern with recovering the critical potential of marginal and anachronistic cultural phenomena brought him little recognition in his own lifetime. The incomprehension which greeted his post-doctoral *Habilitationsschrift*, *The Origin of German Tragic Drama* ([1928] 1985) ended his hopes of an academic career. Benjamin lived an impecunious existence as a freelance writer in Berlin, Frankfurt, and, from 1932, in exile in Paris. Some of his most important contributions to social and cultural theory were developed as part of his ultimately unfinished study of mid-nineteenth-century Paris, *The Arcades Project* (1999). This Surrealist-inspired 'prehistory' of modernity was to explore the 'dreamworld' of **consumption** formed by the city's shopping arcades and fetishized commodity culture. Benjamin came to focus on the writings of Charles Baudelaire, reading poetry and prose as expressions of modern metropolitan experience (embodied in the *flâneur*) and the commodification of art. Benjamin's essays on photography (*A Small History of Photography* 1931) and film (*The Work of Art in the Age of Mechanical Reproduction* 1935) argue for the radical potential of these media in overcoming the traditional power or 'aura' of the original artwork. His *Theses on the Concept of History* (1940) challenged 'historicist' and Marxist readings of historical **progress** and sketched a redemptive politics based on the 'dialectical image'. Unable to escape occupied France in 1940, Benjamin committed suicide on the Spanish border.

Major works

([1928] 1985) *The Origin of German Tragic Drama*. London: Verso.
([1931] 1985) 'A Small History of Photography', in *One Way Street*. London: Verso.
([1935] 1973) 'The Work of Art in the Age of Mechanical Reproduction', in *Illuminations*. London: Collins.
(1986) 'Theses on the Philosophy of History', in A. Hazard and L. Searle (eds) *Critical Theory Since 1965*. Tallahassee, Florida: Florida State University Press.
(1983) *Charles Baudelaire: A Lyric Poet in the Era of High Capitalism*. London: Verso.
(1999) *The Arcades Project*. Cambridge, MA: Belknap.

Further reading

Buck-Morss, S. (1991) *Dialectics of Seeing*. Cambridge, MA: MIT Press.
Leslie, E. (2000) *Walter Benjamin*. London: Pluto.
Gilloch, G. (2002) *Walter Benjamin*. Cambridge: Polity.

GRAEME GILLOCH

BERGER, PETER AND LUCKMANN, THOMAS

Peter L. Berger and Thomas Luckmann's celebrated book, *The Social Construction of Reality* (1996), draws upon European sociology (**Marx**, **Weber**, **Durkheim**) and philosophical anthropology (Plessner, **Gehlen**). Concepts from those traditions are blended with American social-psychology (**Mead**, Cooley, **Parsons**). The inspiration of Alfred **Schutz** is also prominent in the book, evidenced by the centrality of concepts such as *Lebenswelt*, natural attitude, finite provinces of meaning and methodological 'bracketing' (see **lifeworld**). In particular, the text draws upon the 'genetic

phenomenology' of the later Schutz, which had attempted to correct for the egoism and tacit solipsism of classical **phenomenology**. The resulting synthesis claims to be a reorientation of the classical *Wissensoziologie* of Karl **Mannheim** away from 'higher' ideas and ideologies towards the social situations of everyday life, where taken-for-granted knowledge had more importance for ordinary people.

The book describes the basic parameters of the process whereby objective social reality comes to be confronted by a human subject. The relationship between humans as producers and the social world, their product, plays itself out in an ongoing social dialectic of three 'moments' (derived from Hegel and the young Marx): externalization, objectivation and internalization. Humans externalized themselves to create social institutions and a stable environment, which 'kept chaos at bay'. In the course of the **socialization** process, this objectivated world is internalized, thus completing the cycle. Hence, society is seen as both objectified subjectivity (hence analyzable as social facts as Durkheim specified); and subjectified objectivity (hence meaningful, as the phenomenologists maintained).

The authors take for granted the 'protosociological' (Luckmann) status of their theoretical propositions. These are held to be non-empirical, universal structures, not a description of any specific society. The 'transcendental' character of the book is not, however, always appreciated by commentators who have frequently criticized it for not dealing with **power**, **domination** and **inequality** in specific societies, when this was never its purpose. But the charges of **rationalism**, latent **functionalism**, **positivism** and **conservatism** are arguably better founded.

Major work

(1996) *The Social Construction of Reality: A Treatise in the Sociology of Knowledge*. New York: Doubleday and Co.

Further reading

Lafferty, W. (1977) 'Externalization and Dialectics: Taking the Brackets off Berger and Luckmann's Sociology of Knowledge', *Cultural Hermeneutics*, 4(2): 139–161.

RICHARD KILMINSTER

BINARY

'Binary' is a term used to describe pairs of opposed elements which organize cultural categories in **myth** and **ritual**; associated with **structuralist** analyses of myths and folktales by **Lévi-Strauss** and Propp. It can be traced back to **Durkheim**'s claim that a sacred/profane duality is central to religious life; to Hertz's work on left/right binaries; and to the **semiotic** theory of de Saussure, Jakobson and Troubetskoy. Lévi-Strauss proposed that myths articulate systems of **classification** in which binary categories are combined according to specific rules (e.g., of exchange), producing a repertoire of culturally specific variations. For example, culinary and alimentary systems can be analyzed as variations on fundamental dualities such as raw/cooked or clean/unclean. Lévi-Strauss claimed that the binary cognitive and semiotic organization of human culture reflects universals of human thought. Edmund Leach proposed that binaries find a source in the 'imperfect' symmetry of the human body. An emphasis on binaries does not rule out the possibility of triadic classifications (as in Dumézil's analyses of Indo-European mythology, or Lévi-Strauss's own raw/cooked/rotten triad), or even of quaternary distinctions composed of binary pairs. Analysis of binaries has been fruitfully extended to **popular culture** and **media**, and to critiques of 'modern' distinctions (e.g., culture/nature, civilization/barbarity, **normal/pathological**, Occidental/Oriental), but the idea that binaries might indicate cultural or mental universals has been criticized. **Derrida** claimed that a tendency in Western thought to absolutize binaries is evident – despite Lévi-Strauss's attempts at ethnological distancing – in an 'ethic of nostalgia for origins' governing the latter's treatment of the 'culture/nature' distinction.

References and further reading

Derrida, J. (1978) 'Structure, Sign and Play in the Human Sciences', in *Writing and Difference*. Chicago: University of Chicago Press.
Douglas, M. (2002) *Purity and Danger: An Analysis of the Concepts of Pollution and Taboo*. London: Routledge.
Fiske, J. (1990) *Introduction to Communication Studies*. London: Routledge.
Leach, E. (1989) *Claude Lévi-Strauss*. Chicago: University of Chicago Press.
Lévi-Strauss, C. ([1949] 1971) *The Elementary Structures of Kinship*. Boston: Beacon.
Lévi-Strauss, C. ([1964] 1983) *The Raw and the Cooked*. Chicago: University of Chicago Press.
Said, E. (1979) *Orientalism*. New York: Vintage Books.
Segal, R. A. (1996) *Structuralism in Myth: Lévi-Strauss, Barthes, Dumézil and Propp*. New York: Garland Publishers.
Turner, V. (1970) *Forest of Symbols: Aspects of Ndembu Culture*. Ithaca, NY: Cornell University Press.

WILLIAM RAMP

BLOCH, ERNST (1885–1977)
German theorist

Bloch's central concern was to validate the concept of **utopia** in modern social theory and philosophy. His early work, culminating in *The Spirit of Utopia* (1918), combined Expressionist aesthetics, messianic religious thinking, and radical social theory. Bloch sought to analyze the malaise of contemporary culture and the imagery of a transformed capitalist world. Early theoretical influences were **Hegel** and **Marx**, **Simmel** and **Lukács**. With time, Bloch became more self-consciously Marxist, though, unlike most of the **humanist** Marxists, he aligned himself politically (until the late 1950s) with Soviet **commun-**

ism. For the rest of his life he sought to develop and refine a dynamic future-orientated conception of the natural and social world. The universe in this conception is seen as unfinished; it is 'not-yet', and its future is decisively in the hands of an active humanity. His undoubted masterpiece, *The Principle of Hope* (1959) is an account of the interrelationship between 'objective hope', the concrete possibilities of a particular time, and 'subjective hope', embodied in simple daydreams, mass culture and consumerism, as well as in the complex visions of works of art and music. With a great encyclopedic sweep, Bloch charts the presence of utopian yearning in culture, **religion**, **philosophy** and **science**, **society** and **nature**. Much of his work displays similarities with the tradition of the **Frankfurt School** and **critical theory**.

Major works

([1918] 2000) *The Spirit of Utopia*. Stanford, CA: Stanford University Press.
([1935] 1991) *Heritage of Our Times*. Oxford: Polity.
([1959] 1986) *The Principle of Hope*. Oxford: Blackwell.

Further reading

Geoghegan, V. (1996) *Ernst Bloch*. London: Routledge.
Hudson. W. (1982) *The Marxist Philosophy of Ernst Bloch*. London: Macmillan.

VINCENT GEOGHEGAN

BLUMER, HERBERT (1900–1987)

US theorist

Blumer is regarded as the founder of the approach known as **symbolic interactionism**, which has been closely associated with the work of the **Chicago School** of sociologists. Blumer's conception of symbolic interactionism grew out of the legacy of the American pragmatist philosophers, including John Dewey and especially George Herbert **Mead** (see **pragmatism**).

Blumer's conceptual contribution is mainly set out in one book, *Symbolic Interactionism: Perspective and Method* ([1969] 1986). Here he argues for the centrality of the process of 'interpretation' to sociological understanding. Human beings react to situations and to each other as they perceive or interpret them. Sociological theories and methodological devices often falsely exclude interpretation from explicit attention, and therefore assign to many social phenomena both a givenness and a permanence that, on closer inspection, they prove not to possess. Society as 'symbolic interaction' is a huge complex assembled through the formation and reciprocal articulation of the lines of **action** of many individuals. The corresponding methodological imperative is for inspection of the process of interpretation in its course, of the ways in which people in **interaction**, through their actions and responses, shape and manifest the interpretations that guide their conduct. Blumer also conducted several substantive studies of cinema audiences, drug users, racial prejudices and the impact of **industrialization** (often with an interest in policy questions).

Major work

([1969] 1986) *Symbolic Interactionism: Perspective and Method*. Berkeley, CA: University of California Press.

WES SHARROCK

BODY

See: embodiment

BOURDIEU, PIERRE (1930–2002)

French sociologist

Bourdieu began his career under the influence of **phenomenology** and French philosophers of science. He was conscripted to the army in Algeria in 1956. During the War of Independence he sought to carry out a phenomenological analysis of cultural adaptation (what he called 'Fieldwork in philosophy'. In France in the 1960s and under the influence of **Lévi-Strauss**, he first presented his work as social anthropology, but then established himself as a sociologist of **education** and of **culture**. During this time he developed the concepts of **habitus**, **cultural capital**, and **social reproduction**.

Bourdieu sought to reconcile **ontology** and **epistemology**, social **practices** and social theory, **agency** and **structure**, subjective **lifeworld** experience and scientific objectivity. His goal was to outline a theory of practice which commended sociological **reflexivity**. This meant that social theories and concepts have to be analyzed as components of the social situation which they try to explain. A politically engaged intellectual, Bourdieu sought to democratize scientific intervention. His work has had a major impact on the study of **class**, **status**, **stratification** and social **inequality**.

Major works

([1972] 1977) *Outline of a Theory of Practice*. Cambridge: Cambridge University Press.
([1979] 1986) *Distinction: A Social Critique of the Judgement of Taste*. London: Routledge.
([1980] 1990) *The Logic of Practice*. Cambridge: Polity.
([1984] 1988) *Homo Academicus*. Cambridge: Polity.
(1992) (with L. J. D. Wacquant) *An Invitation to Reflexive Sociology*. Cambridge: Polity.

Further reading

Robbins, D. M. (2000a) *Bourdieu and Culture*. London: Sage.
Robbins, D. M. (ed.) (2000b) *Pierre Bourdieu*, 4 vols. London: Sage.

DEREK ROBBINS

BOURGEOISIE

The concept of bourgeoisie, originally a title for the free inhabitants of the late medieval city, designates a major force in modern history: the owners of means of production, the wealthy and the educated, or generally a **middle class** between the **aristocracy** and the **working class**. Conflicting as these definitions may be, they all share the problem of accounting for the collective agent they name. This problem is essentially the question of what makes the bourgeoisie a unity, a '**class**'.

When the fall of feudal absolutism left open the discursive space of the ruling group, the bourgeois was not much more than one among other members of the third estate; at best, in Rousseau's view or **Hegel**'s definition, any persons privately enjoying the benefits of political society. The young **Marx** (1848) adopted this conceptual tradition – with one crucial turn: in his eyes, it was the logic of private life, namely that of a privatized economy, which dominated political life. A second conceptual turn emerged when early nineteenth-century French socialists identified the bourgeoisie as the specific group owning and making **capital**. At this point, Marx (1876) and his followers could precisely say who governed society through economy: the owners and controllers of industrial **production**, accumulating capital by exploiting those who must work for wages.

Some predictions implicit in or associated with this description have proved misguided. Instead of a growing polarization between bourgeoisie and **proletariat**, western societies have seen the emergence of new technocratic, state-bureaucratic and managerial classes whose 'bourgeois' character is at least questionable. Yet the non-Marxist paradigms have also raised questions: should the bourgeoisie be defined by work ethic (Weber [1903] 1976), by certain cultural distinctions, or social ideals? As long as there are privileged and ruling groups in capitalism, this matter remains to be solved.

References and further reading

Marx, K. ([1844] 1975) 'The Jewish Question', in *Marx and Engels Collected Works*. New York: International Publishers.

Marx, K. (1876) *Capital I*, in *Marx and Engels Collected Works*, vol. 35. New York: International Publishers.

Wallerstein, I. (1995) 'Bourgeoisie', in W. F. Haug (ed.) *Historisch-Kritisches Wörterbuch des Marxismus*. Hamburg: Argument.

Weber, M. ([1903] 1976) *The Protestant Ethic and the Spirit of Capitalism*. New York: Scribner.

TILMAN REITZ

BRICOLAGE

'Bricolage' means literally the cobbling together of disparate elements. It is a term used by **Lévi-Strauss** (1966) to describe a characteristic procedure of mythical thought in which heterogeneous items from different cultural or practical contexts are re-used and juxtaposed in ways that give them new meaning. Bricolage illustrates the limitations as well as the creativity of **myth**, which trades on existing cultural repertoires and re-uses them in novel ways. The re-ordering of cultural elements is 'pre-constrained' by their 'original' meanings, but also displaces those meanings. Lévi-Strauss employed the term in studies of myth in so-called 'primitive' societies, but did so to propose the existence of a basic and universal procedure of human thought. His argument thus resembles the discussion of 'elementary' social forms by **Durkheim** and **Mauss**, but Lévi-Strauss referred to a capacity of mind rather than to forms of social organization. In its application to contemporary life, the term now has a broader range of meaning, referring to the assembly of existing cultural material into new styles or fashions, e.g., in **postmodern** architecture, but also in **popular culture**: musical styles, video and film, and material on the World Wide Web. In each of these instances, available cultural items are re-contextualized in relation to each other to produce an ensemble that, with repetition and variation, becomes recognizable as a new style, or **identity**, in its own right. These uses of bricolage imply a degree of unconventionality or resistance to a dominant culture (as in youth culture or **queer** culture), and often the subversion or de-centring of **essentialist** claims to historical necessity, universality, or primacy. Though used by Lévi-Strauss to describe basic, universal procedures of thought, the term is now often linked to **deconstructionist** or **postcolonial** social or cultural theories.

References and further reading

Chandler, D. (2004) *Semiotics: The Basics*. London: Routledge.

De Certeau, M. (2002) *The Practice of Everyday Life*. Berkeley, CA: University of California Press.

Dyer, R. (1987) *Heavenly Bodies: Film Stars and Desire*. Basingstoke: Palgrave Macmillan.

Hebdige, D. (1981) *Subculture: The Meaning of Style*. London: Routledge.

Lévi-Strauss, C. (1966) *The Savage Mind*. Chicago: University of Chicago Press.

Segal, R. A. (1996) *Structuralism in Myth: Lévi-Strauss, Barthes, Dumézil and Propp*. New York: Garland Publishers.

Willis, P. (1990) *Common Culture*. Milton Keynes: Open University Press.

WILLIAM RAMP

BUREAUCRACY

Bureaucracy commonly refers to a hierarchical system of management or administration. Reputedly coined by the seventeenth-century French Administrator of Commerce, Jean Claude Marie Vincent de Gournay with somewhat sarcastic overtones, the term has its modern origins in the combination of the French *bureau* and the Greek *kratia*. While it has long suffered from negative cultural associations – inefficiency and an irrational obsession with rules and regulation – its organizational origins are to be found in a largely progressive attempt to overcome such administrative problems. That is, bureaucracy emerged as a mode of predominantly rational, impartial practice, integral to the modern aspiration for a more efficient organizational order.

Our contemporary understanding of bureaucracy is that largely bequeathed by the historical and sociological work of Max **Weber** (1978). Central to Weber's conception is his proposition that a bureaucracy, in its ideal form, establishes a structural context for the exercise of legal-rational authority embedded within a relationship between officials and their subordinates premised upon the following elements: **rights** and responsibilities enshrined in written rules and **regulations**; the systematic structuring of **authority** relations; appointment and promotion based upon **contract** and formalized procedures; technical or academic qualifications as conditions of appointment; monetary payment as salaried; differentiation of the incumbent official from the office held; and establishment of the **work** of the incumbent as a full-time occupation (see also **profession and professionalization**).

While Weber judged the bureaucracy to characterize the most technically superior means by which the most advanced institutions and activities of both the **market** and **state** could be administered, he nevertheless displayed a marked ambivalence to what he considered to be the inevitable expansion of bureaucracy as an organizing principle concomitant with a more general process of social **rationalization** (see **rationality and rationalization**). On the one hand, he considered its greatest virtue to be that it provided an institutional means by which general rules could be applied to specific cases, thereby ensuring fair and predictable treatment of the individual by government and associated institutions. On the other hand, Weber was deeply pessimistic about the deleterious effect that bureaucracy's *iron cage* would have on the spiritual and creative aspects of human life, creating a world of 'specialists without spirit, sensualists without heart' (Weber 1930).

Weber's analysis of bureaucracy in terms of an **ideal type** of rational administration led subsequent sociologists to interpret it as a benchmark by which the efficiency, of organizational administration can be judged. During the 1950s and 1960s the concept of bureaucratic efficiency came under particular scrutiny. Robert **Merton** (1949) indicated what he considered to be potential dysfunctions arising from the bureaucratic model. Most notable was the tendency of bureaucratic officials to follow rules and procedures in an uncritical and inflexible manner, leading not only to a lack of overall organizational creativity but also to a situation where adherence to regulations came to take priority over the pursuit of organizational goals in themselves. Studies by Peter Blau (1955), among others, recognized, however, that such inertia was only one possible outcome of the bureaucratic form. Of equal prevalence was the tendency of officials to ignore or circumvent regulations by establishing their own informal procedures for dealing with the demands of the job in a more responsive and often more satisfying manner.

Such a focus on the presence of informal **practices** in the formalized structure of bureaucracy led to a number of studies of possible variations in the type of bureaucracy that might operate in differing settings. Alvin Gouldner's (1954) study of an American gypsum mine provided a notable example of the ways in which degrees of bureaucratization differed across operations in the plant. Most notable was the initial lack of bureaucratic formality among miners who operated in a far more uncertain environment and who were dependent on both individual initiative and mutual support and cooperation. This, and the modes of practice associated with it, then became a source of tension and ultimately dispute when new management attempted to impose the more formal bureaucratic norms associated with the administrative dimension of the operation. More systematic typologies emerged in the work of Burns and Stalker (1961), Pugh *et al.* (1963), and, in particular, Henry Mintzberg

(1983) who popularized the idea of the 'adhocracy' – or 'rule of ad hoc' – which he derived from Toffler. Mintzberg characterizes this as a reversal of the bureaucratic form of **organization** and administration based upon the informality of project work and decentralization of formal hierarchies.

The idea of the adhocracy is particularly pertinent in the face of a range of recent assaults on bureaucratic principles in an age of global markets, advanced information and production technology and an ever more demanding consumer public. In the wake of the idea of a post-bureaucratic mode of administration (Nonet and Selznick 1978) and a series of popular managerial texts such as Peters and Waterman's (1982) *In Search of Excellence*, an increasing emphasis in organizational thinking has been placed on the value of radical decentralization. Great weight has been placed on the creation of flatter administrative structures, erosion of status differentials, and use of performance-based rewards to encourage operational flexibility and increased procedural **autonomy**.

Yet despite much of the evangelical rhetoric surrounding the demise of bureaucracy, several studies suggest that assumptions of the disappearance of hierarchical structures associated with bureaucracy and their concomitant status differentials are premature. Within many public and private sector organizations, increasing state regulation has resulted in a consolidation of formal procedure and the universal enforcement of codified frameworks of practices. These, combined with the pervasive influence of culture management technologies, have arguably served to further rationalize organizational activity in line with the underlying principles of bureaucratic command control.

According to George Ritzer (1996), bureaucracy is not only alive and well but is increasingly ubiquitous in the form of 'McDonaldization'. While not entirely reducible to the logic of bureaucracy,

McDonaldization – as a manifestation of societal rationalization processes – exhibits many of its key characteristics, predominantly the pursuit of efficiency through the standardization of practice and procedure, and the limitation of creativity and ingenuity. Ritzer here re-visits the iron cage metaphor deployed by Weber, charting its relevance for contemporary consumer relations.

In an age in which bureaucracy has been challenged both for its alleged inadequacies as a mode of organizing in a flexible globalized economy and for its potentially dehumanizing consequences, it has, however, remained strikingly resilient. Certainly there has been little serious questioning of the principle that organizations cannot operate adequately without at least some degree of bureaucratic input in the form of codified procedures, hierarchical management structures and the like. And while the label 'bureaucrat' may continue to carry pejorative connotations – for example, in Licence refer to the European Union, there is little sign of a credible alternative to the role played by bureaucrats in the foreseeable future. Indeed, there has recently emerged a revalorization of the bureaucratic ethos, as a governing principle of public service organizations. One author, Paul Du Gay (2000), defends the value of public administration based upon principles such as the **equality** and universality (see **universalism**) of treatment and the role of the bureaucrat as impartial agent of the democratic state in the face of continuing calls for greater flexibility and entrepreneurialism.

References and further reading

Blau, P. M. (1955) *The Dynamics of Bureaucracy*. Chicago: University of Chicago Press.

Burns, T. and Stalker, G. M. (1961) *The Management of Innovation*. London: Tavistock.

Du Gay, P. (2000) *In Praise of Bureaucracy*. London: Sage.

Gouldner, A. (1954) *Patterns of Industrial Bureaucracy*. New York: Free Press.

Merton, R. (1949) *Social Theory and Social Structure*. New York: Free Press.

Mintzberg, H. (1983) *Structure in Fives*. Englewood Cliffs, NJ: Prentice Hall.

Nonet, P. and Selznick, P. (1978) *Law and Society in Transition*. New York: Harper Colophon.

Peters, T. and Waterman, R. (1982) *In Search of Excellence*. New York: Random House.

Pugh, D. S. *et al.* (1963) 'A Conceptual Schema for Organizational Analysis', *Administrative Science Quarterly*, 8(3): 289–315.

Ritzer, G. (1996) *The McDonaldization of Society*. Thousand Oaks, CA: Pine Forge.

Weber, M. ([1904] 1930) *The Protestant Ethic and the Spirit of Capitalism*. New York: Charles Scribner's Sons.

Weber, M. ([1922] 1978) *Economy and Society*. Berkeley, CA: University of California Press.

PHILIP HANCOCK

BUTLER, JUDITH (1956–)

American cultural theorist, Professor at University of Berkeley, CA. Her work is influenced by **Derrida**, **Foucault** and **Lacan**. She has had a major impact on debates about **power**, **gender**, **sexuality** and **identity**. In *Gender Trouble* (1990), her most influential book, she criticized feminists for **essentialism**, assuming that women had stable attributes and common interests and hence perpetuating existing binary gender relations (male and female). This denied differences and unwittingly contributed to compulsory heterosexuality. Since gender is an achievement – **performative** – she calls for women to refuse stable gender identities and invent new ones. Calling for the transgression of dominant heterosexist norms, Butler was among the first to propose **queer theory**. Following Foucault, she uncoupled the connections between sex, gender and desire, challenging the feminist focus on reproduction and ahistorical biological differences. She does not deny biological differences, but rather is interested in the discursive and institutional conditions under which biological facts become salient. Hence biology is discourse-dependent. The voluntarist implications of her work have troubled materialist, realist and psychoanalytic feminists. Butler stresses the importance of using the media to disseminate alternative queer images and symbols. Many of the traditional left are critical of her version of cultural politics which, they claim, has both fragmented and diluted left political strategies. Turning away from analyzing socio-economic issues she has focused on representational issues instead. Butler contests this formulation of the problem and argues that the **cultural turn** is not merely cultural.

Major works

(1990) *Gender Trouble: Feminism and the Subversion of Identity*. London: Routledge.

(1993) *Bodies that Matter*. London: Routledge.

(1997a) *Excitable Speech: A Politics of the Performative*. London: Routledge.

(1997b) *The Psychic Life of Power*. Stanford, CA: Stanford University Press.

(1998) 'Merely Cultural', *New Left Review*, 33–44: 227.

(2000) *Antigone's Claim: Kinship between Life and Death*. New York: Columbia University Press.

ELAINE STAVRO

C

CAPITALISM

Capitalism is a mode of organizing economic life dominated by the profit-oriented use of wealth. Its precondition is a monetary economy, since only **money** as abstract **wealth** drives the desire for continuous and unlimited gain typical of capitalism. However, the use of money is only a necessary, not a sufficient condition for capitalism. As **Marx** (1967) pointed out, typical transaction chains in a simple monetary economy can be described as C-M-C, that is, exchanging a commodity C for money M in order to attain a different, more useful commodity (see **commodity and commodification**). By contrast, the typical capitalist transaction chain is M-C-M, using money to buy commodities in order to sell them for more money, or making a profit. But again, the drive for maximizing profits is only a necessary, not a sufficient condition for modern capitalism, the form that has revolutionized economic life since the seventeenth century. Capitalist traders and venture capitalists maximizing profits already existed in antiquity. In contrast, occidental capitalism, as Max **Weber** (1978) called it, started only once the M-C-M transaction was applied not only to trade and credit, but also to **production**. Industrial capitalists spend money to buy means of production and to hire workers. Their combined efforts result in products which can be sold with a profit. In Marx's terms: the owner of M become capitalists as soon

as they buy the means of production and labour power, organize a production process and sell the resulting products for a profit (see **mode of production**). This mode of organizing production became dominant with the industrial revolution (see **industrialization**). Its major precondition in terms of social structure was the availability of **labour** power as a commodity; in other words, the creation of a labour market. For this to happen, on the one hand, workers must not be able to produce their means of subsistence on their own; they must be separated them from the land. On the other hand, workers must be able to form **contracts** as legally fully recognized persons, even though their only property is their ability to work.

Whereas Marx emphasized this social structural condition of workers being 'free in a double sense', Max **Weber**'s emphasized the gains in rationality achieved by capitalist organization and made possible by precise monetary calculation. The ability to abstract from concrete products and needs that underlies the evaluation of goods and services in terms of money is the major cultural precondition of capitalism and its specific 'formal rationality'. A quantity of money defines the starting point of the capitalist enterprise. Its success is measured periodically by comparing the returns in terms of the money gained in sales to the initial outlay. Such a calculation is possible as a sustained and rational operation only under the condition – external to the individual enterprise – that trade on **markets** and the use of money are widespread and effective prices are generated for the most important goods and services. The formation of effective prices presupposes a competitive struggle that moves traders away from purely subjective and arbitrary evaluations to socially objective evaluations. This condition of rationality – external to the individual enterprise – is complemented by an internal condition, namely that **work** in the factory is subject to the discipline required to make wage costs calculable. In both Marx's and Weber's view, this discipline is achieved, on the one hand, by the threat of dismissal, of non-renewal of the labour contract which leaves workers without means of subsistence, and on the other, by **domination**, that is, by hierarchical organization and top-down control of work performance (cf. Tilly 1998).

Competition, reproduction and growth

Competition is important not only because of the formation of the effective prices that underpin precise calculation. Capitalist firms produce for exchange, and thereby also compete to attract buyers who hold money to spend when and on what they choose. This competition operates in two basic ways: one can offer prices lower than those for similar products, or one can offer better or new products. In both ways, the capitalist system puts a premium on innovation, either in terms of process or product innovations. This arrangement results in the uniquely dynamic properties of capitalist economies. Striving for maximum profits induces a constant search for new ways to produce things, be it new means of production or new forms of organizing production, and a constant search for new things to produce. Joseph **Schumpeter** famously spoke in this connection of 'creative destruction'. The competitive pressure on the capitalist to keep costs low is translated

into pressures on workers to work as much as possible for as little pay as possible.

This constellation resulted in widespread **poverty** among the **working classes** in early capitalism until workers started to organize to better resist such pressures. Both the organization of labour unions (see **trade unions**) and the introduction of universal suffrage helped to secure better legal and bargaining positions of workers. Nonetheless, it remains a characteristic feature of the capitalist mode of production that it involves **conflict** both over working conditions and the distribution of the net product or *surplus* (the proceeds of the production process minus the outlays for means of production). Typically, these conflicts are softened during periods of strong growth and become harsher during periods of recession, their strength thus varying with economic cycles typical of capitalist development.

The three classes of landowners, capitalists and workers receive money incomes – rents, profits and wages – which enable them to buy their share of the surplus. The resulting circular flow turns the capitalist economy into a self-reproducing system to the extent that it produces its own inputs as outputs. Self-reproduction implies (1) that means of production expended are replaced, and (2) the revenues of the three classes induce their members to reappear continuously in sufficient numbers on the respective markets. These conditions mean that both real and monetary magnitudes, products and prices, have to fulfil complex requirements of proportionality. To determine these conditions of reproduction was one of the major problems of classical **political economy** since Quesnay, culminating in Sraffa's (1960) demonstration that the prices enabling reproduction cannot be determined independently of distribution. This implies that the capitalist economy is not only a self-reproducing, but also a self-referential system: its decisive rules and norms of operation cannot be derived from the physical world.

Growth, that is, expanded reproduction, comes about insofar as part of the surplus is not consumed but used to expand the productive apparatus. In monetary terms, those individuals or households able to save parts of their current income face competing attractions: either spend on **consumption** now or increase future income by saving and accumulating **wealth**. In the early phases of capitalism, the drive to accumulate at the cost of current consumption was supported by the religious beliefs emerging from the Protestant Reformation, as Weber demonstrated in his study of the **Protestant ethic**. But Weber, as well as Marx, observed that once the capitalist system stands on its own feet, maximizing money income turns into a general propensity which replaces the habit of seeing money income merely as a means to consumption. This subjective response to money as the 'absolute means', in Georg **Simmel**'s phrase corresponds to a systemic property of a capitalist economy insofar as firms continuously strive to improve their market position by expansion. As most investment is financed by the incomes of the wealthy, the trade-off between profits and wages in a dynamic perspective turns into a trade-off between current and future consumption. If wages are too high, investments will be depressed so that current high wages translate into lower growth, thus into lower future income for all. However, depressed investments imply declining employment. Since workers' bargaining power is inversely related to **unemployment**, wages will decline. The resulting increases in profits will feed higher investments which, in turn, imply increasing employment. The workers' bargaining position improves again – and the whole cycle can start again (Goodwin 1967). This type of argument demonstrates that the processes of capitalist reproduction and growth involve complicated balancing conditions which, in a self-regulated system with decentralized decision-making, can be fulfilled only at the cost of periodically returning **crises**.

Finance capital and globalization

A major change in the development from early industrial to contemporary capitalism came about through two related institutional innovations: the evolution of the banking and credit system, and the establishment of the modern **corporation**. Both involved not only a change in the nature of money, but also the crowding out of industrial capital from centre stage by finance capital (see **post-industrial society**). On the one hand, practically all savings were channelled into the banking system by offering interest payments to savers. On the other hand, any actor could turn to the banking system for financing additional consumption or an investment. Most importantly, capitalist entrepreneurs no longer had to rely solely on their own financial resources but could, in theory, be as propertyless as the worker, as long as they could convince a money-holder or a financial intermediary, most likely a bank, to lend them the money required to build or extend an enterprise.

The possibility of financing an investment by borrowing implies a historically new and crucial role of the rate of interest: the rate of interest now becomes the benchmark for the minimum returns on any investment. Profits come to be defined as the excess of such returns over the interest due on the capital borrowed. Since the nation–state competes with private investors for funds, and lending to the state, with its power to tax, becomes the lowest risk investment, the rate of interest on the public debt becomes a parameter for money holders deciding what assets to hold (see **state and nation–state**). Financial markets thus offer a choice between a range of assets so that perceived risks and expected returns come to be proportional (see **risk**). At the same time, the volatility of financial markets due to the speculative element involved in calculating risks implies a premium on liquidity: the more money-like an asset is, the quicker the possibility to adjust to perceived market changes, and the lower the chance of being locked into a bad asset or missing the opportunity to reap windfall profits.

The modern corporation emerged in the context of financial markets. It is built on the separation of ownership and management. Any money-holder can become an owner by buying shares in the corporation. The entrepreneurial function is taken over by managers who are paid for their performance. While firms can satisfy their needs for funding by offering shares, money-holders can invest in such shares without excessive risks. Their liabilities are limited so that, in the case of bankruptcy, the value of their shares will be annihilated but no further obligations result. Expected returns on capital in relation to the rate of interest drive the price of shares. Such expectations are speculative since they have to be formed in an environment with limited and asymmetric information.

Despite this speculative component, share prices today have become the major indicator of a firm's performance, implying that management is more and more pre-occupied with the way the firm is observed by financial markets, observations which are not necessarily tightly coupled to the firm's actual performance. As **Keynes** (1936) and Kalecki (1943, 1954) argued, this constellation implies a hierarchy of markets different from industrial capitalism where product markets took centre stage. Now, financial markets, governed by the interests of wealth owners and firms competing for their funds, are dominant. The rates of interest generated in these markets determine which investments in production are feasible. Such investments in turn are linked to the demand on product markets in a self-referential manner so that, as Kalecki put it, 'Capitalists earn what they spend while workers spend what they earn.' Thus the employment generated by a modern capitalist economy is a residual. Financial markets dominate product markets which dominate labour markets.

The dominant role of financial markets has been further enhanced since the last decades of the twentieth century by **globalization** and the associated public emphasis on so-called shareholder values. The withering away of socialist economic systems has been accompanied by a world-wide opening of markets, increasing the mobility chances of capital, and above all, of financial capital. The ease of investing abroad in turn increases the credibility of the exit threat used by firms in their bargaining both with employees and with states. As a consequence, capital has reaffirmed its decisive role not only in economic matters but also in the sense of stronger selective effects on culture and politics. Globalization therefore has been interpreted as driving the convergence of historically quite different, nation–state-based capitalist economies towards a uniform system governed more and more by market relations only.

However, research on *varieties of capitalism* demonstrates that, mostly, capitalist firms have remained embedded in institutional frameworks shaped by the political and cultural traditions associated with societies defined by nation–states (see **embedding and disembedding**). This is because, in their business strategies, firms try to make use of 'comparative institutional advantages' (Hall and Soskice 2001), thereby at least partially strengthening rather than abolishing institutional differences. Since nation–states, cultures and most of the people involved in them remain relatively locality-bound and immobile compared to the supranational coordinating capacities of markets and the mobility of capital, the tensions between capitalist economies and their social environment remain as relevant as ever. But equally as relevant remain attempts to instrumentalize capitalist economies, with their innovative and disciplining capacities, for the well-being of all, whether with the help of **welfare states** (Esping-Andersen 1990) or not.

References and further reading

Albert, M. (1993) *Capitalism vs. Capitalism*. New York: Four Walls Eight Windows.

Dobb, M. (1963) *Studies in the Development of Capitalism*. London: Routledge.

Esping-Andersen, G. (1990) *The Three Worlds of Welfare Capitalism*. Cambridge: Cambridge University Press.

Goodwin, R. (1967) 'A Growth Cycle', in C. H. Feinstein (ed.) *Socialism, Capitalism and Economic Growth*. Cambridge: Cambridge University Press, pp. 54–8.

Hall, P. A. and Soskice, D. (eds) (2001) *Varieties of Capitalism*. Oxford: Oxford University Press.

Kalecki, M. (1943) 'Political Aspects of Full Employment', in E. K. Hunt and J. G. Schwartz (1972), *A Critique of Economic Theory*. Harmondsworth: Penguin, pp. 420–30.

Kalecki, M. (1954) *The Theory of Economic Dynamics*. London: George Allen & Unwin.

Keynes, J. M. (1936) *The General Theory of Employment, Interest and Money*. London: Macmillan.

Marx, K. ([1867] 1967) *Capital*, vols 1–3. New York: International Publishers.

Schumpeter, J. A. (1942) *Capitalism, Socialism and Democracy*. New York: Harper.

Soskice, D. (1999) 'Divergent Production Regimes: Coordinated and Uncoordinated Market Economies in the 1980s and 1990s', in H. Kitschelt, P. Lange, G. Marks, and J. D. Stephens (eds) *Continuity and Change in Contemporary Capitalism*. Cambridge: Cambridge University Press, pp. 101–34.

Sraffa, P. (1960) *Production of Commodities by Means of Commodities: Prelude to a Critique of Economic Theory*. Cambridge: Cambridge University Press.

Tilly, C. (1998) *Work Under Capitalism*. Boulder, CO: Westview Press.

Weber, M. ([1904/5] 1958) *The Protestant Ethic and the Spirit of Capitalism*. New York: Scribner.

Weber, M. ([1920] 1978) *Economy and Society*. Berkeley, CA: University of California Press.

HEINER GANßMANN

CASTE

The word caste, derived from the Portuguese word *castas*, was used by Western observers to identify the social units among the Indian Hindus. However, the nature of this social formation has changed significantly over time and currently varies so widely in different parts of India that it is difficult to think of a universal definition.

The ancient Indian society since about 1000 BC was divided into four *varnas* defined in terms of occupational specialization, i.e., the Brahmanas or the priests, the Kshatriyas or the warriors, the Vaisyas or the farmers, traders and producers of wealth, and the Sudras or the people who served these three higher groups. Eventually, towards the fifth century CE, people outside these four **groups** came to be considered untouchables, constituting a fifth category, known variously as Panchamas, Ati-Sudras or Chandalas.

However, the *varna* system subsequently lost its relevance and provided only a civilizational model to conceptualize social rank across the **regions**. In the real world, more important were the *jatis*, or localized occupational groups, which were often further subdivided according to professional specialization. These groups were developing alongside the *varnas* and social historians and sociologists commonly refer to them as castes. The *jatis* are occupational groups, whose membership is defined by birth, and whose exclusiveness is maintained by stringent rules of endogamy and restrictions on commensality. Each and every caste is ascribed a ritual rank, which places its members in an elaborate hierarchy that encompasses the entire Hindu **society**, and at the bottom of this **structure** are located the untouchables. However, given the cultural diversities of India, this 'book-view' of caste may not be found everywhere. And because of this localized nature of caste, most of these groups still prefer to express their rank by identifying with one of the broader civilizational categories of *varna*.

What determines the rank of a caste is a matter of intense controversy among sociologists. Louis Dumont (1972) thought that in Indian society where the **sacred** supposedly encompasses the secular, making the Brahmana priest more powerful than the Kshatriya king, the religious notions of purity and pollution determine the ritual rank of a caste. The Brahmana, as the supreme embodiment of purity, remains at the top of the hierarchy, while the untouchable, being totally impure, occupies the bottom, and in the middle there are groups with varied grades of purity and impurity. Such cultural notions of caste ranking have been questioned by others like Nicholas Dirks (1987), who has pointed out that caste was integrally connected to **power** relations in pre-colonial society. The king was not subordinate to the priest; the crown was never as hollow as it was made out to be by the western colonial observers. On the contrary, caste ranking was determined by distance from the crown, legitimated by royal **authority** and associated notions of honour. In other words, there was and always has been a positive correlation between caste rank, **wealth** and **power**.

Each caste in this social order is assigned a *jati dharma* or a moral code of conduct, the performance or non-performance of which, or their *karma*, supposedly determines their caste **status** in the next life. The temporal power of the king in tandem with the spiritual authority of the priest maintained social discipline in this caste society, which is often thought to be a rather rigid social hierarchy. But in reality, there were powerful **social movements** from the fifteenth century onwards, which effectively interrogated the ideological **hegemony** of the caste system. The rigours and rigidity of caste society therefore vary significantly from region to region.

Being associated with a hereditary occupation, caste has also been functionally significant, indicating some sort of a social **division of labour**. But being a closed group, caste is different from **class**, and the functional specialization is organically linked to hierarchy (see **status**). In other words, it is a system of gradation, with 'a

great deal of ambiguity in the middle region', where various peasant castes vie for superiority of status (Beteille 1991: 43) (see **peasantry**). **Modernity** and economic development have further weakened the link between caste and hereditary occupation, leading to limited social mobility. But such discrepancies between caste-irrelevant roles and caste-ascribed status are gradually resolved, as the system tolerates limited positional readjustments in order to maintain its hierarchical structure. In modern India, however, the hierarchical notions of caste have lost legitimacy in the public domain. But in private spheres, castes are at the same time 'substantialized' as groups with cultural distinctiveness, which has evaluative meaning (Fuller 1996). Thus, while castes have become more differentiated internally because of social mobility, the cultural assertion of their distinctiveness as signifier of status has prevented the demise of the caste system. But these are reinvented ethnicized castes, often the focal points for political mobilization and demands for **social justice**, having little relevance to the religious notions of purity and pollution (see **ethnicity**).

References and further reading

Bandyopadhyay, S. (2004) *Caste, Culture, and Hegemony: Social Domination in Colonial Bengal*. New Delhi: Sage.

Beteille, A. (1991) *Society and Politics in India: Essays in Comparative Perspective*. London: Athlone Press.

Dirks, N. (1987) *The Hollow Crown: Ethnohistory of an Indian Kingdom*. Cambridge: Cambridge University Press.

Dirks, N. (2001) *Castes of Mind*. Princeton, NJ: Princeton University Press.

Dumont, L. (1972) *Homo Hierarchicau*. London: Paladin.

Fuller, C. J. (ed.) (1996) *Caste Today*. Delhi: Oxford University Press.

Gupta, D. (2000) *Interrogating Caste: Understanding Hierarchy and Difference in Indian Society*. New Delhi: Penguin.

SEKHAR BANDYOPADHYAY

CASTORIADIS, CORNELIUS (1922–1997)

Greek-born French theorist

Co-founder of the French political group and journal *Socialisme ou Barbarie*, Castoriadis advanced an internal critique of **Marxism** together with a critique of **bureaucracy** in both **socialism** and **capitalism**. In his later writings, Castoriadis develops a theory of the 'imaginary institution of society'. Rather than being determined by a transcendent ground, every **society** autonomously institutes its unity by way of creating a relatively coherent set of imaginary significations irreducible to the 'rational' or the 'real' (see **institution and neo-institutionalism**). The role of these significations is to provide answers to fundamental questions concerning the nature and purpose of social life allowing society to constitute an **identity** for itself. At the same time, society's **institutions** are constantly subverted by processes of creative self-alteration. Politics is the conscious attempt to alter society's institutions, an attempt that is ontologically based on society's transformative potential which Castoriadis terms the 'radical imaginary'. Castoriadis's political project may be described as a form of libertarian **socialism** oriented towards popular **autonomy** and direct **democracy** (see **democracy and democratization**). His writings from the *Socialisme ou Barbarie* period (1949–65) exerted considerable influence on the French student movement of May 1968.

Major works

([1975] 1987) *The Imaginary Institution of Society.* Cambridge, MA: MIT Press.
(1988–93) *Political and Social Writings,* 3 vols. Minneapolis, MN: University of Minnesota Press.
(1991) *Philosophy, Politics, Autonomy.* New York: Oxford University Press.
(1997a) *World in Fragments.* Stanford, CA: Stanford University Press.
(1997b) *The Castoriadis Reader.* Oxford: Blackwell.

Further reading

Busino, G. (ed.) (1989) *Autonomie et auto-transformation de la société: La philosophie militante de Cornelius Castoriadis.* Geneva: Droz.
Curtis, D. A. (1992) 'Cornelius Castoriadis', in P. Beilharz (ed.) *Social Theory: A Guide to Central Thinkers.* North Sydney: Allen and Unwin.

OLIVER MARCHART

CAUSALITY

There are many models of causal reasoning in social theory, drawn from a variety of sources such as natural science, the **law**, **statistics**, and the model of intentional **action**, along with more specific analogies to such things as organisms and feedback mechanisms, as well as to underlying forces. In 1900, the term 'social causation' usually referred to underlying defining forces in **society**, and there were many candidates – earth, hunger, energeticism, and libido.

Human action itself provides another model of causal **explanation**. We might think of this as the intervention model, since actions are made or not made, performed or not performed, in the context of some ongoing state of causal activity into which individual acts intervene to shift it in one direction or another. One curious causal concept, the idea of an omission as a cause, figures in connection with legal responsibility and is also systematically applied to historical responsibility. If I fail to put on the brake on my car and it rolls down the hill, I have caused the car to roll down the hill, though my only action was to omit a normal action.

Causality is important in social theory because of the difficulty of constructing suitable in-filling or connecting mechanisms between supposed causes and effects. The situation of the social theorist contrasts with the commonplace situation in the natural sciences, where broad well-established correlations, such as between cancer and smoking, can eventually be accounted for in terms of causal mechanisms that directly connect the fact of smoking to the outcome of cancer. If we consider, for example, the rise of science and the rise of **democracy**, we might come up with a theory which explained why democratic regimes, though initially less likely to provide the circumstances for achievement in science, eventually became part of the conditions for the advancement of science as a major publicly funded activity of the kind it is today. To answer such questions would require some sort of mechanism connecting these large facts about democracy with science.

One kind of answer would be to appeal to a general law stating a causal relationship, on the model of physics, but generally speaking, such appeals have not succeeded – there are no plausible, non-tautological laws; and those which seem to be candidates for law status require a considerable amount of additional **knowledge** to apply. Usually this knowledge, the pragmatics, is insufficient to do the work of the explanation on its own.

Why is this so? In constructing such a connection, what one has to work with is a mass of historical material, much of which is a record of decisions made by democratic and aristocratic politicians and citizens under very complex circumstances and in terms of a wide variety of beliefs about science, along with a great many individual facts about particular scientists and scientific institutions and their funding, which will not reduce to a simple pattern. While one can, as in this case, describe what appears to be a causal relationship, it is not a relationship that seems explicable in terms of a single common mechanism describable by a law. This is characteristic of large-scale historical and social processes. On the level of individual action and circumstance, the mechanisms appear to be governed by a wide degree of **contingency**, and there are often exceptions. The fact of **complexity** leads social theorists to posit intermediary mechanisms of abstract kinds which are not

law-like and are assumed to operate behind the façade of ordinary decision-making and human **action** and to account for connections between large-scale observed facts. This produces an ongoing problem about the nature of the relationship between these explanatory constructions, notions such as 'class consciousness', for example, and the mass of known, understandable and causal knowledge of actions, decisions and beliefs that are part of the intentional world of historical actors, as well as a problem about the status of these kinds of explanations.

There is a notion of causality that has played an especially important role in the statistical social sciences as well as in the conception of the social as a medium of causation. The concept was introduced initially by G. Udny Yule (1895, 1896) who accounted for variations in **poverty** in the UK under different welfare regimes. Yule suspected that generous welfare measures had the effects of disinclining people to **work**, thus increasing poverty. The data available for these hypotheses, however, were, as is typical in social science cases, entangled with a large number of other variables which might themselves have produced the observed differences, such as differences in the relative well-being of the regions in question.

The problem was to remove the effect of all of these possible confounding variables and determine what effects of welfare regimes remained. This leads to a concept of causality as effect that persists after other causes are corrected for. This is not a primary conception of causality since the causal relationship that remains is itself understood as the other effect, as a correlational relationship which can be understood in terms of some sort of mechanism.

References and further reading

Hempel, C. (1965) 'The Function of General Laws in History', in *Aspects of Scientific Explanation and Other Essays in the Philosophy of Science*. New York: Free Press.

51

McIver, R. M. ([1942] 1964) *Social Causation.* New York: Harper & Row.

Weber, M. ([1905] 1949) 'Critical Studies in the Logic of the Cultural Sciences', in *The Methodology of the Social Sciences.* New York: Free Press.

Yule, G. U. (1895, 1896) 'On the Correlation of Total Pauperism with Proportion of Out-relief', *Economic Journal*, 5: 603–11 and *Economic Journal*, 6: 614–23.

STEPHEN P. TURNER

CENTRE AND PERIPHERY

Asymmetrical relationships in social theory are expressed in two ways: on a **vertical** dimension and on a **horizontal** dimension. Vertically, social difference is understood as **inequality**, in the image of a hierarchy. This is the typical image of **class** analysis, **gender** analysis and social **stratification**. White collar and blue collar, **bourgeoisie** and **proletariat**, men and women, upper and middle class, are examples. Horizontally, it is possible to speak of 'centre' and 'periphery'. Here, some theoretical approaches treat horizontal social differences also as inequalities, while others do not. It they do not and instead consider differences as heterogeneity, we are confronted with what was once called **consensus** theory in the 1950s and the 1960s. Edward Shils (1975) used a Weberian frame of reference in a Durkheimian vein and saw the centre as the seedbed of action, values, symbols and ideals of society. It is typically the centre where economic, political and cultural developments take off while in one way or the other the periphery, lagging behind, profits from the centre. If, however, social differences are regarded as social inequality, we face **conflict** theory. Here the **power** asymmetry between centre and periphery is stressed. Most notably, Immanuel **Wallerstein** (1974) demonstrates that core capitalist countries since the seventeenth century such as Britain, the Netherlands, France, Germany, the USA or Japan, systematically exploit the periphery in the capitalist world

system (see **world systems theory**). This useful distinction is widely applicable and our contemporary world knows many centres and peripheries (see **classification**).

References and further reading

Blau, P. M. (1977) *Inequality and Heterogeneity.* New York: Free Press.

Greenfeld, L. and Martin, M. (eds) (1988) *Center: Ideas and Institutions.* Chicago: University of Chicago Press.

Kreckel, R. (1992) *Politische Soziologie der sozialen Ungleichheit.* Frankfurt am Main: Campus.

Müller, H.-P. (1992) *Sozialstruktur und Lebensstile.* Frankfurt am Main: Suhrkamp.

Shils, E. (1975) *Center and Periphery.* Chicago: University of Chicago Press.

Wallerstein, I. (1974) *The Modern World System.* New York: Academic Press.

HANS-PETER MÜLLER

CHARISMA

The term 'charisma' was introduced into sociology by Max **Weber**. Literally it denotes 'the gift of grace'. According to Weber, it implies 'a certain quality of an individual personality by virtue of which [one] is considered extraordinary and treated as endowed with supernatural, superhuman, or at least specifically exceptional powers or qualities' (Weber 1978: 216, 241; see also **Eisenstadt** 1968; Sennett 1975). The term was taken from the theology of the New Testament, denoting the gifts of the Holy Spirit. It is derived from Greek *charis*, a term looking back to the archaic social network of gift exchanges (Meier 1987).

In Weber's sociology, charisma forms one of the three 'pure' or 'ideal' types of legitimate **domination** or **authority** (Weber 1978: 212–16). However, in Weber's work, charisma also plays a much wider role, connecting the three main typologies of social action, legitimate order and legitimate domination. While preserving some of its theological affinities, Weber gave the term a different twist. Charisma is best manifested by individuals who successfully resolve extraordinary situations that threaten a **community**. The two main types of such situations are threats posed by other human communities and natural disasters such as floods, droughts, storms or earthquakes. The two main charismatic types are thus the hero and the magician.

While charismatic qualities appear in extraordinary situations, with things returning to normality after the emergency has passed, there is a tendency for temporary arrangements to become transformed into a permanent office, or what Weber called the 'routinization' of charisma. This leads to the emergence of ritualized, sacrificial **religion** (see also **ritual**), on the one hand, and centralized rule over territories, on the other.

Charisma, however, might return even in the context of large entities, and this is where the concept becomes interesting for Weber. In the context of priestly religion, the reappearance of charisma is associated with the figure of the prophet. It is in this connection that Weber speaks of the 'great process' of demagification or disenchantment and the rise of the modern world (see **secularization**). In the context of secular rule, charisma is fundamental for the rise of politics in Greece, as embodied in the person of Pericles as the law-giver. Here Weber's concept of prophetic charisma in ancient Israel can be compared with Michel **Foucault**'s interest in political and philosophical *parrhesia* in classical Greece (Szakolczai 2003).

Weber connects the rise of the modern capitalist market economy and democratic politics to the further routinization of charismatic renewals, in the direction of legalization and rationalization (see **rationality and rationalization**). However, he leaves open the possible return of charisma in religion or politics. While being cautious about the possible appearance of new prophets, Weber assigns an important role to charismatic leadership in democratic mass politics

(Weber 1976: 182) Given that the popular vote is cast for persons and not for parties or movements, the charismatic qualities of politicians play a dominant role in contemporary politics, and are emphasized by the **media and mass media**.

It is here that some problems with Weber's concept appear. Weber takes for granted the link between mobilizing appeal and the ability to solve problems. Yet widespread attractiveness can be gained by political personalities of quite questionable, even sinister, character. The application of the term 'charismatic' to political leaders such as Lenin, Stalin, Mussolini and Hitler creates more confusion than clarity. In order to discriminate between various types of political leaders with non-rational and non-traditional appeal, it has been suggested that charisma as a type should be complemented by and contrasted with the figure of the 'trickster', as studied by anthropologists and mythologists (Radin 1972; Horvath 1998).

This problem becomes especially serious when combined with another shortcoming. Weber assumes that **crisis** situations calling for charismatic action are derived from external threats when there is clear consensus about the desirable outcome. However, the model does not work for internal dissolutions of order, when the entire community is divided, and when furthermore the opportunities for divisive, demagogic, 'trickster'-type politicians are particularly ripe. Here the model should be complemented by approaches such as René Girard's theoretization of the 'sacrificial crisis' and the 'scapegoating mechanism' (Girard 1989; see Szakolczai 2003: 18–22).

Weber offered a series of important clarifications of the concept of charisma. He made a distinction between primary or natural charisma, due simply to personal characteristics, and artificial charisma, induced by ascetic techniques or possibly by drugs (Weber 1978: 400). He furthermore differentiated between the source of charisma in individual qualities, and the eventual recognition of charisma by the followers or the general public, considered decisive for the validity of charismatic authority (ibid.: 242). A closely related distinction is between charismatic people and charismatic communities, elaborated especially in Weber's 'Ancient Judaism' and further developed by Norbert **Elias** as 'group charisma'.

References and further reading

Eisenstadt, S. N. (ed.) (1968) *Max Weber on Charisma and Institution Building.* Chicago: University of Chicago Press.

Girard, R. ([1982] 1989) *The Scapegoat.* Baltimore, MD: Johns Hopkins University Press.

Horvath, A. (1998) 'Tricking into the Position of the Outcast', *Political Psychology*, 19(2): 331–47.

Meier, C. (1987) *La politique et la grâce.* Paris: Seuil.

Radin, P. (1972) *The Trickster: A Study in American Indian Mythology.* New York: Schocken.

Sennett, R. (1975) 'Charismatic De-legitimation: A Case Study', *Theory and Society*, 2(2): 171–181.

Szakolczai, A. (2003) *The Genesis of Modernity.* London: Routledge.

Weber, M. ([1904–5] 1976) *The Protestant Ethic and the Spirit of Capitalism.* London: Allen and Unwin.

Weber, M. ([1921–22] 1978) *Economy and Society.* Berkeley, CA: University of California Press.

ARPAD SZAKOLCZAI

CHICAGO SCHOOL

The Department of Sociology at the University of Chicago was a pioneering host for American sociology. After the founding of the department in 1892, the 'Chicago School' received considerable impetus with Robert E. Park's career relocation from journalism to academic life after 1913. Encouraged by W. I. Thomas, who contributed the concept of the 'definition of the situation' to sociological discourse, Park sought to make sense of the social consequences of the rapid transformation experienced by the city of Chicago through **industrialization** and through urbanization of a rapidly expanding immigrant population (see **urbanism and urbanisation**). The potential for **conflict** and exploitation in this situation showed that policy innovation was needed and that this was to be based on scientifically sound research. The aim was not to rise above the tensions, inequalities and conflicts constitutive of the transforming city but to engage with them through direct research into the situation and experience of those who were subordinated and marginalized within the processes of change. One necessity was to disseminate an awareness of the diversity of viewpoints brought into co-existence and contact within the same urban space, and to understand the dynamics of their interrelationships with a view to understanding the ways in which potential conflicts between them could be minimized. This was not undertaken as a matter of the dispassionately technical management of **social change**, but from the point of view of attaining greater **social justice**.

The approach taken to research was not at first methodologically self-conscious, and it readily used data materials of all kind. But it was marked by an emphasis (owing much to journalistic traditions of finding out by first-hand investigation) on fieldwork-style investigations in which researchers sought to get close to those living the lives they were investigating – often concealing the fact that they were researchers. A large number of studies of different **groups** were produced, collectively pioneering the idea of 'understanding the actor's point of view'. It is a persistent idea in sociology that documenting the way in which members of society themselves experience their social world and respond to it is a primary task. W. I. Thomas, together with Florian Znaniecki, produced a monumental body of papers drawing on personal documentation such as letters and on the archives of Polish newspapers in order to capture and record the often dislocating experience of Polish Peasants. Their study *The Polish Peasant in Europe and America* (1918–21) analysed **migration** from the **culture** of a traditional peasant society into the alien environment of American **values** and the American city. Other notable studies explored the lives of homeless hobos, of members of boys' gangs and of criminal delinquency, as well as of young women who worked as dancers for hire (see **crime** and **deviance**).

The orientation of these studies was toward identifying the points of view which would be largely unknown to middle-class academic constituencies. They sought to criticize the perception of these ways of life as merely symptomatic of social disorganization and moral breakdown. The aim of the studies was to challenge such judgements, to emphasize, first of all, the way in which the circumstances one finds oneself in alter the way in which one perceives things and impose a set of practical necessities to which adaptation must be made. Thus, seen in context, the behaviour of disparaged types would no longer appear as manifestations of the waywardness of individuals, but as an embodiment of a collective response, expressive of the culture to which the individual belonged, with the culture itself having been formed in response and adjustment to the conditions under which its bearers must live.

Much of Chicago's sociology both during the heyday of the School and after can be understood as reacting against the idea of 'social disorganization' which had been a powerful idea in American social and political thought. It concentrated on distinguishing between the lives of independent communities, such that the standards of one should not be made the a priori standards imposed as a framework for the understanding or moral evaluation of the other. The empirical studies repeatedly showed that the lives of the under-privileged and the deviant (see **deviance**) were not literally disorganized but were conducted according to their own

codes and **practices**, that they were organized on the same sociological bases as more eminent and respectable communities (see **community**).

The heyday of the Chicago School extended from the 1910s through to the 1930s. After this period, research was motivated and practised in much the same way, and was equally attentive to the lives of subordinate and marginalized group. However, it did so under the influence of a changed set of sociological ideas, particularly those elaborated from the teachings of the Chicago-based philosopher G. H. **Mead** by the sociologist Herbert **Blumer**. These ideas became known as **symbolic interactionism**. The development of this tradition from the late 1930s into the 1960s occasions talk of a 'second Chicago School'. This second phase also focused on the actor's point of view to highlight how courses of action which might otherwise seem irrational and ineffective may instead be rational in relation to circumstances. The later phase of the Chicago School is associated with the work of Anselm Strauss, Howard Becker, Tamotsu Shibutani and others.

References and further reading

Bulmer, M. (1984) *The Chicago School of Sociology*. Chicago: University of Chicago Press.
Fine, G. A. (ed.) (1995) *A Second Chicago School?* Chicago: University of Chicago Press.

WES SHARROCK

CHOMSKY, NOAM (1928–)
US theorist

Chomsky redefined linguistics as a naturalistic and science-oriented theory of a biologically endowed 'language faculty', postulating a 'universal grammar' that manifests itself in the development of more specific transformational grammars (see **language**). This led to a paradigm shift, away from **behaviourism**, and was highly influential for psychology and cognitive science. Chomsky considered his enterprise to be part of the **rationalist** tradition following a Cartesian idea of innate mental structures. In this view, language acquisition is the unfolding of a biologically endowed mental propensity, triggered once the child (or perhaps more precisely, the brain) is exposed to 'linguistic experience'. Chomsky has often revised his theory, but has always held some key convictions: a focus on syntax, strictly separated from semantics, pragmatics, and any functional considerations of social language use or **discourse**, which he excluded from the scientific study of language; and an individualist, mentalist, and internalist understanding of language. As a consequence, only 'I-languages', i.e., languages that are part of a speaker's individual mental make-up, are a proper object of study, rather than public 'E(xternal)-languages' used by social groups. An outspoken critic of imperialist US foreign policies from Vietnam to Iraq, Chomsky is an ardent proponent of the rights of the public **intellectual** to intervene in the field of politics and the **media and mass media**. Yet curiously, his ideas of the scientific study of language and the mind seem to have been untouched by his social activism.

Major works

(1957) *Syntactic Structures*. Hague: Mouton and Co.
(1965) *Aspects of the Theory of Syntax*. Cambridge: MIT.
(1966) *Cartesian Linguistics*. NY: Harper and Row.
(1968) *Language and the Mind*. NY: Harcourt Brace.
(1980) *Rules and Representations*. Columbia University Press.
(1981) *Lectures on Government and Binding*. Dordrecht, Netherlands: Foris Publishers.
(1995) *The Minimalist Program*. Cambridge: MIT.

Further reading

McGilvray, J. (ed.) (2005) *The Cambridge Companion to Chomsky*. Cambridge: Cambridge University Press.

JENS BROCKMEIER

CHRISTIANITY

In tracing the historic origins of Christianity, we depend largely on scriptures written by early Christian believers. According to the New Testament, Christianity started with a group of men gathering around a charismatic leader (see **charisma**) named Jesus, who was wandering through Galilee during the Roman occupation preaching and healing (Theissen [1977] 1978; **Weber** [1919] 1978). Originally, Jesus' message was directed exclusively to the Jews. He referred positively to the framework of **Judaism** (see **Judaism**). Convinced however, that the end of time was close, he taught his disciples to cut their bonds with their families and occupations and to follow him. The charismatic group of disciples gained financial support from a wider assembly, among them several women who were closely related to Jesus until his death. The social context of the charismatic group, the expectation of the imminent end of time, and the contents of his teachings led to an egalitarian structure among his followers, who ignored differences in **status** and **gender**.

After Jesus' crucifixion, the movement spread into the Hellenistic world through proselytizing, notably through the organizational agency of Paul. In the second and third centuries, the hierarchical structure of a **church** with professional clerics and a monarchical episcopate developed. This organizational structure is distinctively different from other religions. After a period of persecution, Christians were tolerated by the Roman Empire. In the fourth century, Christianity finally became the state religion of the already weakened empire.

During the Middle Ages, church and state were closely linked, supported by the universalistic ideal of a homogeneous Christian kingdom and culture in which both powers – church and state – worked together as the 'two swords of Christianity'. The other side of this ideal was the harsh consequences for those who seemed to threaten it. This led to persecutions of heretics, but also to the medieval Crusades, originally motivated to defend Jerusalem against Muslim invaders. In 1054, the profound differences between Eastern and Western Christianity resulted in a schism. Both developed separately with strong differences that continue even today, making social scientists talk of different civilizations (**Eisenstadt** 1982; Huntington 1996). Christian Orthodoxy up to the present has been less influenced by **Enlightenment** ideas, with consequences for the use of the Bible and the understanding of the priest's office.

In the sixteenth century Martin Luther's theology of 'sola fide, sola gratia, sola scriptura', emphasized the individuality of every persons relationship to God, inaugurating the Protestant Reformation. His teaching must be considered an early expression of modern **subjectivity** and Enlightenment. His concept of the two reigns of god became important as an early theory of the distinction between church and state and of the differentiation of religious and political **roles**. With reference to Calvin's theology and its impact on Ascetic Protestant sects, Max Weber developed his influential **Protestant ethic** thesis ([1904–5] 1930) about the religious foundation of the 'spirit' of modern **capitalism**. Max Weber also pointed out the specific development of Western Christianity as compared to other civilizations. In this thesiss, it was only the **Occident** where the combination of several rational developments – in religion, science, **bureaucracy**, **economy**, the **law** and other areas – enabled the differentiation of value spheres and enforced a general process of rationalization (see **rationality and rationalization**). He was convinced that Christianity – especially ascetic Protestantism – was the major factor in this process.

Similarly, his close colleague Ernst Troeltsch argued in *The Social Teachings of the Christian Churches* (1912) that Protestantism, closely followed by religious toleration and religious pluralism in parts of Western Europe and North America, were the decisive factors in the shaping of a modern culture of **individualism and individualization**. Troeltsch also argued that before the rise of of the Protestant sects, Christianity had remained an essentially conservative social force, resigned to compromise and acquiescence in the dominance of the secular ruling powers of the monarch and the emperor. Against the Marxist view of Karl Kautsky, Troeltsch argued that Christianity from its earliest inception until the seventeenth century was never an instrument of any class struggle and never generated any social **emancipation** movement, despite its early association with the revolt of the slaves against Roman oppression. This thesis was for the most part confirmed by Karl **Mannheim** in his work *Ideology and Utopia* of 1929, although it was contested by Ernst **Bloch** in his work of 1918 *Geist der Utopie*, a portrait of Thomas Münzer and the peasants' revolt in sixteenth century Germany. Most classical sociological analyses of Christianity thus alternate between positions that stress either (1) its affinity tp individualism, liberalism and conservatism (Weber, Troeltsch), or (2) its immanent normative relationship to fraternity, community, collective liberation and **social justice**. The latter diagnosis was particularly important to Georg Lukács in *History and Class Consciousness* (1922), which built on Hegel's dialectic of master and slave (see **master–slave dialectic**) and the early philosophical Marx of the *Theses on Feuerbach*, thematizing Feuerbach's conception of the self-**alienation** of man in God that turned the relationship between creature and creator on its head. This world-view also remains central today to Liberation Theology in Latin America and was fundamental to the struggle against **slavery** among African Americans in the nineteenth century.

With respect to functional differentiation between politics and religion, the investiture contest in the eleventh and early twelfth century over the emperor's right to install bishops was of relevance (Blumenthal

1991). But it was only in the early twentieth century that most of the European nations truly separated church and state. Some – like France and Switzerland – did it in the strict way of *laïcité*. Others – like Germany – maintained close relations between state and church, but abolished the system of a state church. In the Scandinavian countries and in England, this system survived much longer, with the consequence that Swedish citizens were automatically members of the Church of Sweden by birth. It was particularly the philosophical **Enlightenment** movement that questioned the strong position of Christian churches in Europe. In France, after the Revolution this eventually led to the French system of *laïcité*: the strict separation of church and state. For the emerging European **nation–states** in nineteenth-century Europe, it was the French Revolution as well as the Christian heritage that served as material for the construction of national myths. For this reason, historians have considered the European nation–states as daughters of religion *and* of revolution.

In the nineteenth and twentieth centuries the Christian churches in many Western European countries faced severe processes of **secularization** (Bruce 1999), defined as separation between church and state as well as the decline in individual participation in church activities and church membership. This process was more thorough-going in countries with a predominantly Protestant population, but since the 1960s it has also affected the Catholic Church in many European countries (Martin 1978). Secularization had the least effect in Poland and Ireland where national **identity** is closely linked to Catholicism. But the population of the United States of America also has maintained high levels of subjective religiosity. Among American sociologists of religion, this has been interpreted as the result of a combination of church–state separation and high religious plurality, which has emphasized the competition between different religious agents in a vital religious market. The situation

in the United States is also different in another respect. Due to the religious and cultural mixing in the course of immigration, the institutional shape of Christianity was – unlike Europe – not dominated by the major confessions and churches of Catholicism or Lutheran and Reformed Protestantism, but rather by smaller denominations with characteristic entrepreneur-like activities in local churches.

The secularization process that has distinctly changed the ideological landscape in Western Europe, as well as the politically enforced secularization processes in many Eastern European countries, has resulted in a situation in which Europe – at least in statistical terms – is no longer the heartland of Christianity. Today, South America and Asia, especially Korea, are the most dynamic regions of Christianity, and they are developing their own kind of Christianity, which in many respects differs from the European variety.

References and further reading

Bloch, E. (1918) *Geist der Utopie*.

Blumenthal, U. (1991) *The Investiture Controversy: Church and Monarchy from the Ninth to the Twelfth Century*. Philadelphia, PA: University of Pennsylvania.

Bruce, S. (ed.) (1999) *Religion and Modernization: Sociologists and Historians Debate the Secularization Thesis*. Oxford: Clarendon Press.

Eisenstadt, S. N. (1982) 'The Axial Age: The Emergence of Transcendental Visions and the Rise of Clerics', *European Journal of Sociology*, 23: 294–314.

Hamilton, M. (1998) *Sociology and the World's Religions*. New York: St. Martin's Press.

Huntington, S. (1996) *The Clash of Civilizations*. New York: Simon & Schuster.

Lukács, G. ([1923]) 1971) *History and Class Consciousness*. Cambridge, MA: MIT Press.

Mannheim, K. (1929) *Ideology and Utopia*. New York: Harcourt Brace.

Martin, D. (1978) *A General Theory of Secularisation*. Oxford: Blackwell.

Marx, K. (1845) *Theses on Feuerbach*.

Stark, R. (1996) *The Rise of Christianity: A Sociologist Reconsiders History*. Princeton, NJ: Princeton University Press.

Theissen, G. ([1977] 1978) *The First Followers of Jesus: A Sociological Analysis of the Earliest Christianity*. London: SCM.

Troeltsch, E. ([1912] 1931) *The Social Teachings of the Christian Churches*. New York: Macmillan.

Weber, M. ([1904–5] 1930) *The Protestant Ethic and the Spirit of Capitalism*. London: Allen & Unwin.

Weber, M. ([1919] 1978) *Economy and Society*. Berkeley, CA: University of California Press.

Wuthnow, R. (1985) 'State Structures and Ideological Outcomes', *American Sociological Review*, 50: 799–821.

MONIKA WOHLRAB-SAHR

CHURCH

The term 'church' has at least three different dimensions: (1) a *communal* dimension inasmuch as it refers to the gathering of religious (see **religion**) – usually Christian – communities; (2) a *religious* dimension inasmuch as it refers to a specific self-understanding of such communities with more or less explicit eschatological connotations; and (3) an *institutional* (see **institution**) and *organizational* (see **organization**) dimension inasmuch as it refers to a specific social form that religious communities have taken. From the sociological perspective a church is mainly looked upon as a type of religious organization – although the other two meanings of the term come into play as well. When the organizational aspect of the church is too prominent, the other dimensions may lead to conflicts in which members stress the importance of lived face-to-face meetings and an orientation towards religious instead of organizational matters, and vice versa.

Looking at the church as an organization, two perspectives are of relevance: (1) How are religious communities transformed into church organizations and with what consequences?; (2) How does the organizational type of the church differ from other possible types of organization, within and outside **Christianity**?

As organizations, churches develop in the course of the institutionalization of religious communities that have gathered around a charismatic leader. This process was analyzed by Max **Weber** ([1919] 1978) in terms of the routinization of **charisma**. In order to survive the founder's death and the succession of different leaders, the charisma which was originally attached to the person of the founder needs to be associated with the church as an institution and especially with the office held by its representatives. Weber called this *Amtscharisma*. The latter is of specific importance for the Catholic Church which continues to the present day to justify the exclusion of women from priesthood with the charisma of the priest's office. Priests are thought to stand in direct succession to the original apostles. According to this logic, male priests need to follow male apostles.

Weber proposed that a church develops when a hierocracy turns into a regulated profession of priests; when the hierocracy's expectations towards possible followers become universal, irrespective of ethnic and national ties; when dogma and ritual practice are rationalized, written down, commented and taught in a systematic way; and when all of this is enclosed in an institutionalized community. Referring to Weber, Thomas O'Dea (1961) and others (Yinger 1961) started a discussion about certain dilemmas that arise in the process of institutionalization. Such dilemmas may cause conflicts in churches and, in the long run, may lead to schisms and to the formation of **sects** which stress the 'original' religious purpose as opposed to 'secondary' organizational matters.

Niklas **Luhmann** (1972) underlined the complex relationship between different types of church membership. In his analysis, a large group of members is mainly interested in the continuation of the church and give it general support (and money). These members do not necessarily seek to fulfil religious needs there, yet they depend on members whose religious activities symbolize the continuation of the church as a religious organization. The relationship between general support and active religious involvement appears to be of specific relevance for the remarkable differences between churches in Europe and North America.

Ernst Troeltsch ([1912] 1931) and Max Weber distinguished between the church and the sect as different organizational types. In contrast to the sect-type, the church is seen as a community that people are usually born into, rather than becoming members voluntarily; which is inclusive rather than exclusive in its religious offerings and demands; and in which charisma is associated with religious offices rather than with personalities. In addition, churches, in contrast to sects, usually behave much more in accordance with the values of the society and with the state (see **state and nation-state**). Troeltsch thought of *mysticism* as a third religious form, which focuses on personal religious sentiments and is critical of organization-building.

This church–sect typology has, however, been regarded as an inadequate account of the North American situation. Richard Niebuhr (1929) first elaborated the term 'denominationalism'. In this analysis, denominations are voluntary **associations**, but, unlike sects, they are much more inclusive, as well as bureaucratic, and they accept the values of the secular society and the state (Wilson 1959).

Weber in his typological approach also used the term 'church' for Islamic and some Buddhist institutions (see **Islam**). However, the organizational type of the church has developed most clearly within Christianity. In countries with a predominately Christian population, churches have been the key complementary and legitimizing **institution** of the state. But churches have also served as the organizational 'address' to which the state turns in order to deal with religious matters. For this reason, in some European countries it has become necessary for other religions such as Islam, to develop church-like institutions which can negotiate with state representatives over religious issues such as religious education in schools and burial rites.

References and further reading

Coser, L. (1967) 'Greedy Organizations', *Archives européennes sociologique*, VIII: 196–215.

Demerath, N. J. III, Hall, P. D., Schmitt, T. and Williams, R. H. (eds) (1998) *Sacred Companies: Organizational Aspects of Religion and Religious Aspects of Organization*. Oxford: Oxford University Press.

Luhmann, N. (1972) 'Die Organisierbarkeit von Religionen und Kirchen', in J. Wössner (ed.) *Religion im Umbruch*. Stuttgart: Enke.

Niebuhr, H. R. (1929) *The Social Sources of Denominationalism*. New York: World Publishing.

O'Dea, T. F. (1961) 'Five Dilemmas in the Institutionalization of Religion', *Journal for the Scientific Study of Religion*, October: 207–13.

Troeltsch, E. ([1912] 1931) *The Social Teachings of the Christian Churches*. Louisville, KY: Westminster John Knox.

Weber, M. ([1919] 1978) *Economy and Society*. Berkeley, CA: University of California Press.

Wilson, B. R. (1959) 'An Analysis of Sect Development', *American Sociological Review*, 24. 3–15.

Yinger, M. (1961) 'Comment', *Journal for the Scientific Study of Religion*, October; 40–4.

MONIKA WOHLRAB-SAHR

CITIZENSHIP

Citizenship is a complex political, legal, social and cultural **institution** that governs both *who* are to be considered members or citizens of a particular polity, who are to be considered quasi-members (strangers, outsiders) and non-members (aliens) and *how* these people are to conduct themselves and each other in a given polity. Being a citizen almost always means not only being a member of the polity but also involves mastery of modes and forms of conduct appropriate to being a member (see **civic education**). Just what constitutes membership and its appropriate modes and forms of conduct are always objects of struggle among subjects with claims to citizenship. It is through these claims to citizenship that citizenship becomes a locus of **rights** and obligations. These claims and the combination of rights and obligations that define it have worked themselves out very differently in different moments of history.

The ancient Greeks are credited with inventing the institution of citizenship roughly around the eighth century BC by giving a certain new meaning to the **city**: the idea of the *polis* (Manville 1990). Until then, the city, it is said, was governed by god-kings and, after that, by the citizens. What happened at that particular moment? It seems that a new figure entered the stage of history who was a male and a warrior and who owned **property** (not the least of which included the means of warfare). Those who were not male and did not own property such as women, slaves, merchants, craftsmen, or sailors found themselves cast as the **Others** of that figure. The male figure had the right to govern his city (belonging) and to bequeath that right to his son (blood). By governing himself by the laws of his city, the citizen also governed the strangers, outsiders, and aliens of the city.

The figure of the Roman citizen played itself out under quite different conditions. Being a Roman citizen meant being a member of an empire that stretched beyond the city of Rome (Gardner 1993; Sherwin-White 1973). Yet being male, a warrior and owning property were still the elements that differentiated a Roman citizen from strangers, outsiders, and aliens. These elements persisted well into the age of the **state** and **nation–state**. It is possible to hold, with Max **Weber**, that a change occurred during the twelfth to fifteenth centuries in **Europe** when being a citizen gradually ceased to be associated with prowess in war and military virtue. Yet still at this time, being a citizen involved owning property and being male. Therefore, arguably the most significant feature of citizenship occurred in the late eighteenth and early nineteenth centuries

when citizenship became associated with *nationality* and was understood as membership of the state rather than the city. It was then that the principles of *jus sanguinis* (by blood) and *ius soli* (by territory) were rearticulated through the state and reinscribed in the nation (Brubaker 1992) (see **nationalism**).

If each of these historical moments articulated the figure of the citizen rather differently, what explains the ostensible unity of this concept? The answer lies partly in the fact that every dominant group reinscribed and reinvested itself in that original figure as the real foundation of its symbolic and imaginary constitution. It also lies in the fact that the original elements of citizenship – property, war and masculinity – remained the foundational elements that differentiated citizens from strangers, outsiders, and aliens (Smith 1997) (see **stranger**). But the future may well remember the twentieth century for having dismantled the foundational elements of citizenship. It was in this particular century that property was no longer tied to citizenship, while women became at least formal if not substantive claimants to it, and the nature of war and warriorship was fundamentally altered by being fought by special kinds of mercenaries and technological weaponry (Janoski 1998). Moreover, it was in the twentieth century that the universal figure of the citizen was shown to be predominantly made up of attributes of a particular social group: Christian, heterosexual, male, white and adult (Young 1989).

Does this realization mean the end of citizenship today? Judging by the seemingly inexorable rise of another figure – namely, the consumer – it may appear to us as though citizenship has come to some kind of an end. This, however, need not imply the end of citizenship as a normative idea capable of continuous reconstruction. What is at least clear is that the gradual spread of civil rights in the eighteenth century, towards political rights in the nineteenth century, was consolidated in the twentieth century by the establishment of *social rights*, as T. H. **Marshall** (1992) notably argued. Today, while we witness the dismantling of the traditional elements of citizenship (property, warriorship, masculinity), we also observe the emergence of a new kind of citizen figure. New historical narratives are being told about citizenship that make it appear less a bastion of property, warriorship and masculinity and more about the struggles of redistribution and **recognition** by those who formerly were its strangers, outsiders and aliens (Kymlicka 1995; Isin and Wood 1999).

References and further reading

Beiner, R. (ed.) (1995) *Theorizing Citizenship*. Albany, NY: State University of New York.
Brubaker, R. (1992) *Citizenship and Nationhood in France and Germany*. Cambridge, MA: Harvard University Press.
Gardner, J. F. (1993) *Being a Roman Citizen*. London: Routledge.
Heater, D. B. (1990) *Citizenship: The Civic Ideal in World History, Politics, and Education*. London: Longman Group.
Isin, E. F. (2002) *Being Political: Genealogies of Citizenship*. Minneapolis, MN: University of Minnesota Press.
Isin, E. F. and Wood, P. K. (1999) *Citizenship and Identity*. London: Sage.
Isin, E. F. and Turner, B. S. (2002) *Handbook of Citizenship Studies*. London: Sage.
Janoski, T. (1998) *Citizenship and Civil Society: A Framework of Rights and Obligations in Liberal, Traditional, and Social Democratic Regimes*. Cambridge: Cambridge University Press.
Kymlicka, W. (1995) *Multicultural Citizenship*. Oxford: Oxford University Press.
Manville, P. B. (1990) *The Origins of Citizenship in Ancient Athens*. Princeton, NJ: Princeton University Press.
Marshall, T. H. ([1950] 1992) *Citizenship and Social Class*. London: Pluto.
Sherwin-White, A. N. (1973) *The Roman Citizenship*, 2nd edn. Oxford: Oxford University Press.
Smith, R. M. (1997) *Civic Ideals: Conflicting Visions of Citizenship in U.S. History*. New Haven, CT: Yale University Press.
Young, I. M. (1989) 'Polity and Group Difference: A Critique of the Ideal of Universal Citizenship', *Ethics*, 99, January: 250–74.

ENGIN F. ISIN

CITY

See: Urbanism and urbanization

CIVIC EDUCATION

Civic education is as old as the Greco-Roman ideal of the democratic citizen and hence as old as **democracy** itself. From the time of the ancients when democracy was understood to rest on the participation of the educated *cives*, democratic advocates argued that citizens were made rather than born, and had to be educated into the responsibilities of civic participation. Plato's argument in *The Republic* for Philosopher Kings can be understood as an aristocratic version of this position (only the learned can rule), while the Greek ideal of *padaeia* (like the later concepts of *Bildung* in German and *Formation* in French) linked **education** to the virtues of **autonomy**, self-government and the well-ordered commonwealth.

Modern democratic philosophy, beginning with social **contract** theory, forges vital links between democratic constitutionalism, competent **citizenship** and civic education. It presupposes John Locke's modern doctrine of knowledge as a function of experience rooted in the interaction of a 'blank tablet' mind with a sensory worldly environment. When knowledge is the story experience writes on character, character and behavior can be seen as vulnerable to manipulation, modification and education. Locke's *Second Treatise of Government* (1976) and his *Letter on Education* both depend on his *Essay Concerning Human Understanding* ([1690] 2000) with its empiricist rational psychology, just as Rousseau's *The Social Contract* (1993a) finds a companion piece in his educational tract *Emile* (1993b).

In both the English and the French **Enlightenment** traditions, it is posited that while *homo oeconomicus* (the autonomous, interest-pursuing individual) may forge the social contract, only citizens are capable of sustaining the democratic constitutions the social contract yields (see **constitution**).

Natural men and natural women are endowed with natural **rights**, but citizenship is artificial rather than natural. Given that human nature is acquired rather than innate, citizenship must be learned and earned.

The American founding fathers predicated the success of the new American Constitution on the development of a citizenry capable of enacting and defending in practice the 'natural rights' whose protection that constitution guaranteed in theory. John Adams in Massachusetts argued in the 1780s for institutions of public schooling that would afford all who were to be citizens an education that was, in the first instance, civic. Thomas Jefferson made clear in his epitaph that his founding of the University of Virginia was part and parcel of his authorship of the Declaration of Independence and the Virginia Bill of Religious Freedom, giving clear expression to the indissoluble linkage between rights and the educated citizen.

Nineteenth-century common schools and land grant colleges were conceived with civic education among their primary missions, and America's public education system has always gained an important part of its legitimacy from its devotion to integrating immigrants into American life and teaching practicing that 'apprenticeship of liberty' which for **Tocqueville** was the most necessary if most 'arduous of all apprenticeships'. To a degree, civic education has, as a result, become an 'American' idea. John Dewey's pragmatist insistence at the beginning of the twentieth century on the ties between education and democracy gave its American character vital impetus (see **pragmatism**). Celebrating the experiential character of all knowledge and the affinities between 'problem solving' in politics and in thought, Dewey's *Democracy and Education* argued that democracy was first of all about the education of citizens, and that education was about the sustaining of democracy.

Only following World War II with the emergence of a new political science focused on elections rather than participation and more interested in voters than in citizens, in individual interests than in common ground, did the social science preoccupation with civic education lose some of its vibrancy. Even as it became more important in post-war Europe and Asia where the founding of new democracies in the rubble of German **fascism** and Japanese **imperialism** focused on civic training and re-education, it was hobbled by notions of the professionalization and vocationalization of schooling in America. The earlier triumph of the German model of the Research University (first practiced at Johns Hopkins at the end of the nineteenth century) gradually displaced the model of the liberal arts college (the liberal arts understood as the 'arts of liberty' by which free men and women acquired the skills and competences of liberty) and helped erode the idea of a 'civic mission' for education.

Nevertheless, both in historical political theory and in American history, there has been a close connection between the robustness of democratic practices and the devotion to civic education. The weak or thin representative system is less concerned with civic education, with a tendency to assume that voters are little more than private political consumers expressing private political preferences. Those wedded to a more participatory or deliberative approach mirroring strong democratic arrangements are compelled to argue for a strong civic education curriculum in which the responsibilities of active citizenship (far more than voting) are diligently acquired.

References and further reading

Boyer, E. (1983) *A Nation at Risk*. Washington: National Committee on Excellence in Education.

Dewey, J. ([1916] 2000) *Democracy and Education: An Introduction to the Philosophy of Education*. Bristol: Thoemmes.

Friedman, M. ([1962] 2000) *Capitalism and Freedom*. Chicago: University of Chicago Press.

Locke, J. (1976) *The Second Treatise of Government: (An Essay Concerning the True Original, Extent and End of Civil Government) and A Letter Concerning Toleration*. Oxford: Blackwell.

Locke, J. ([1690] 2000) *Essay Concerning Human Understanding*. London: Routledge.

Locke, J. ([1693] 2001) *Some Thoughts Concerning Education*. Oxford: Clarendon Press.

Moe, T. M. and Chubb, J. E. (1990) *Politics, Markets and America's Schools*. Washington, DC: Brookings Institution.

National Commission on Excellence in Education (1984) *A Nation at Risk: The Full Account*. Cambridge, MA: USA Research.

Rousseau, J. J. (1993a) *The Social Contract and Discourses*. London: Dent.

Rousseau, J. J. (1993b) *Emile*. London: Dent.

BENJAMIN R. BARBER

CIVIL RELIGION

Civil religion has been defined by Robert Bellah (1975: 3) as 'that religious dimension, found ... in the life of every people, through which it interprets its historical experience in the light of transcendent reality'. The concept of civil religion refers to a unique relationship between **religion** and politics, typically in reference to the nation (see **state and nation-state**). For example, we might see it in the use of biblical quotations in presidential addresses or in religious jeremiads directed at government policies. The interplay between civil religion and the nation – state has been seen as contributing to the pacification of civil strife and **conflict**, and hence as an important mechanism of social **integration** in modern secular societies. Normally, it includes secular **symbols** and **rituals** that provide some sense of belonging and **solidarity**, especially a 'myth of origin' which relates or reconstructs the nation's history, 'purpose' or 'destiny' in the world. Civil religion may also function to define legitimate membership of a nation, indicating **taboos** that define the national society's external boundaries and differentiating it from others. Civil religion confers **legitimacy** on social order by evoking commitment and **consensus**.

Originally used by Jean-Jacques Rousseau, Robert Bellah gave this concept its central sociological meaning, especially (but not only) with reference to the USA. Bellah identified three key dimensions. First, biblical themes are compatible with national traditions and national churches (see **church**). It in this perspective that ideas of America as 'God's new Israel' are rooted. Second, there is a relevant aspect of a process of **secularization** and a tendency towards religious **individualism** and privatism. Third, there is the more institutional aspect of the American Puritans' commitment to religious liberty and toleration of religious pluralism.

Other studies have indicated ways in which this concept by no means need be limited in its application to the USA. **Durkheim**'s analysis of religion, secular education and civic **humanism** suggests universal possibilities of civil religion. Many societies express their political unity in religious-political terms. As a result, we find many studies of civil religion over a wide range of national contexts. Many of these concentrate on matters of symbolic action and rituals, rather than on the more institutional structures of the nation–state. It is also necessary, however, to attend to the role of organizational constraints, resources, and interest **groups**. Social cleavages often determine the relations between state and religion. Civil religion in the context of secularized nation–states becomes an increasingly important ideological factor of national mobilization processes, an important part of the 'imagined **community**' of social entities (see **nationalism**).

References and further reading

Bellah, R. (1967) 'Civil Religion in America', *Daedalus: Journal of the American Academy of Arts and Science*, 96: 1000–21.

Bellah, R. (1975) *The Broken Covenant: American Civil Religion in a Time of Trial*. New York: Seabury.

Bellah, R. and Hammond, P. (eds) (1980) *Varieties of Civil Religion*. San Francisco: Harper & Row.

Dobbelare, K. (1986) 'Civil Religion and the Integration of Society: A Theoretical Reflection and an Application', *Japanese Journal of Religious Studies*, 13(2–3): 127–45.

Müller, H.-P. (1988) 'Social Structure and Civil Religion: Legitimation Crisis in a Later Durkheimian Perspective', in J. Alexander (ed.) *Durkheimian Sociology*, Cambridge: Cambridge University Press. pp. 129–59.

Richey, R. and Jones, D. (eds) (1974) *American Civil Religion*. New York: Harper & Row.

Wuthnow, R. (1998) *The Restructuring of American Religion and Faith since World War II*. Princeton, NJ: Princeton University Press.

STEFFEN SIGMUND

CIVIL SOCIETY

Civil society is a modern concept that has various origins and incarnations. In the early modern period in Europe between the 1650s and 1770s, it corresponded to all intermediary **institutions** such as guilds, associations, organizations, cities and corporate bodies such as universities and churches that stood between the increasingly centralizing **state** and the isolated individual. The primary focus of the concept was the suspect if not seditious nature of these intermediary institutions in the eyes of the state. The consolidation of the state meant usurpation and abolition of the special privileges of these institutions and the centralization of their administration and jurisdiction. The state increasingly came to see itself as the guarantor, superior and governor of such institutions, and those that resisted such consolidation were deemed 'seditious'. As such, civil society and the institutions that made up its character were by and .large understood to be opposed to the state.

From approximately the 1770s onwards, civil society was increasingly understood as a sphere independent from the state. The institutions that made up such an independent or autonomous (see **autonomy**) sphere were not understood in the same way as in the preceding period. They were now deemed to be free from the encroachment of the state, and they included institutions such as private businesses. If the early modern conception of civil society was an attack on the positive liberties of intermediary institutions that had been built over a long time since the twelfth century, the modern conception of civil society was articulated in terms of negative liberties over against the state. The emerging modern conception of civil society understood the older intermediary institutions as vestiges and fragments of the past where special privileges hindered the capacities of bourgeois citizens and their relationship to the state. Civil society in the eighteenth century was increasingly constituted as being made up not of intermediary institutions but of bourgeois citizens engaged in activities beyond the regulatory institutions of the state. Civil society stood for relatively autonomous spheres of economic, political and social activities of citizens of a state. However, because the French state became the most centralized and consolidated in Europe, French thought and practice also sensed the dangers of conceiving civil society only as negative liberties of citizens from the state. From Jean-Jacques Rousseau and Montesquieu to Alexis de **Tocqueville** a strand of thought emerged that, while emphasizing civil society as a relatively autonomous sphere of the activities of citizens, was also aware of some of its limitations. This new strand of thought articulated the need for positive liberties of intermediary institutions such as associations, cities, organizations, societies and unions. In the late nineteenth century, Otto von Gierke (1866) and Emile **Durkheim** (1984; 1992) became the most significant social theorists of civil society by urging the necessity of intermediary institutions to mediate between the citizen and the state.

Since the 1990s the concept of civil society has re-emerged as a mantra to describe numerous practices in diverse societies. The initial impetus for its renewed currency was the democratic revolutions in Eastern Europe and the former member states of the Warsaw Pact. Many writers argued that under the communist regimes there were almost no intermediary and relatively autonomous institutions and spheres left between the communist subject and the state. The result of the rise of civil societies in these states after communism was an unmistakable connection made between the importance of civil society and **democracy** (Keane 1998).

In recent years, civil society has also become an operative concept in the emerging democracies in Latin America, Africa, the Middle East and Asia. Here it is understood as referring primarily to intermediary institutions that resist non-democratic tendencies of states and multinational business corporations. In this picture, the democratization of previously authoritarian states (see **authority**) and the neo-liberal opening of **markets** have been seen as proceeding hand in hand in a process of resistance to the centralizing tendencies of states and business monopolies (Alvarez *et al.* 1998; Sajoo 2002; Schak and Hudson 2003).

But the rise of civil society institutions and discourses has not been limited to developments *within* sovereign states. Also evident is the rise of various intermediary institutions such as non-governmental organizations, associations, aid groups and numerous other groups that operate *across* various states, leading some commentators to talk of the emergence of a 'global civil society' and its limits (Keane 2003; Laxer and Halperin 2003). Since there is no global state and global governance is made up of a multitude of intersecting, overlapping and transversing jurisdictions, organizations and movements, it is perhaps improper to consider the emerging spheres as acting against the state as such. Nevertheless, the actions of some transnational global organizations, such as Médecins Sans Frontières, Amnesty International, Human Rights Watch to Greenpeace, have been crucial in fostering democratizing tendencies in the policies and practices of some states.

References and further reading

Alvarez, S. E., Dagnino, E. and Escobar, A. (eds) (1998) *Cultures of Politics/Politics of Cultures: Revisioning Latin American Social Movements.* Boulder, CO: Westview Press.

Black, A. (1984) *Guilds and Civil Society in European Political Thought from the Twelfth Century to the Present.* Ithaca, NY: Cornell University Press.

Cohen, J. L. and Arato, A. (1992) *Civil Society and Political Theory.* Cambridge, MA: MIT Press.

Durkheim, E. ([1890] 1992) *Professional Ethics and Civic Morals.* London: Routledge.

Durkheim, E. ([1894] 1984) *The Division of Labor in Society.* New York: Free Press.

Ehrenberg, J. (1999) *Civil Society: The Critical History of an Idea.* New York: New York University Press.

Hall, J. A. (ed.) (1995) *Civil Society: Theory, History, Comparison.* Cambridge: Polity.

Kaviraj, S. and Khilnani, S. (eds) (2001) *Civil Society: History and Possibilities.* Cambridge: Cambridge University Press.

Keane, J. (ed.) (1988a) *Civil Society and the State: New European Perspectives.* London: Verso.

Keane, J. (1988b) *Democracy and Civil Society.* London: Verso.

Keane, J. (1998) *Civil Society: Old Images, New Visions.* Stanford, CA: Stanford University Press.

Keane, J. (2003) *Global Civil Society?* Cambridge: Cambridge University Press.

Laxer, G. and Halperin, S. (2003) *Global Civil Society and Its Limits.* New York: Macmillan.

Sajoo, A. B. (ed.) (2002) *Civil Society in the Muslim World: Contemporary Perspectives.* London: I. B. Tauris.

Schak, D. C. and Hudson, W. (eds) (2003) *Civil Society in Asia.* Aldershot: Ashgate.

Von Gierke, O. F. (1866) *Das Deutsche Genossenschaftsrecht.* Berlin: Weidmann.

ENGIN F. ISIN

CIVILIZATION

'Civilization' is clearly a heavily value-laden term, imbued with problematic notions of **'progress'** and cultural superiority. In academic sociology, however, the term has acquired a more scientific and relatively value-neutral mode of application, notably due to the influential work of Norbert

Elias. Elias published his magnum opus *The Civilizing Process* ([1939] 2000), on the eve of the Second World War. The title of this work appears profoundly at odds with the events that were then unfolding. In fact, however Elias saw its origins in what he called 'the crisis and transformation' of Western 'civilizations', and the quest to understand 'why we actually torment ourselves in this way' (ibid.: 368). For Elias, the term 'civilization' pointed neither to the progressive triumph of rationality, nor necessarily to a doomed form of human existence. Instead, it denoted a set of long-term social processes that could be studied both theoretically and empirically.

There are parallels in Elias's work with the ways in which anthropologists and sociologists have come to deploy the term '**culture**' – also a highly value-laden term in lay usage. Significantly, Elias starts *The Civilizing Process* by considering the '*sociogenesis*' or social generation of the terms *Zivilisation* and *Kultur*. He traces the emergence of the former term to members of the French court in the early modern era who originally used it to express distinction and refinement. He traces the latter to the German **bourgeoisie** during the same period who used this term to stress their uniqueness and difference from other European powers. Thus for Elias, 'civilization' is a term that over time has come to express the self-consciousness of Western **Europe**. While the word's '-ization' component signals a process, most lay uses of the term tend to imply a state or a 'final destination', a fully 'developed society'. It is important to distinguish, therefore, between 'civilization' as a normative term and Elias's technical concept of 'civilizing processes'. In Elias's account, it refers to processes in which certain groups *come to understand themselves* as 'civilized' and 'others' as 'uncivilized'.

Through studying processes of civilization, one of Elias's central objectives was to build an understanding of the link between long-term shifts in patterns of social relationships,

or what he called human **figurations**, and processes of change in the structure of human affects and personality (see **person and personality**). In order to study this link between *sociogenesis* and *psychogenesis*, Elias studied long-term shifts in codes of etiquette expressed in books or good manners. Texts such as Erasmus's *De civilitate morum puerilium* ('On Civility in Boys') contained advice and guidance intended for children and young adults of the secular upper classes on everything from how to behave at the dinner table to how one should approach and curb emotions and bodily functions. Examining such evidence, Elias constructs a picture of social life in the Middle Ages that later came to be regarded as 'vulgar', 'distasteful' or 'uncivilized', such as urination and defecation in public. Elias showed how it was normal for people in the Middle Ages to eat from a common dish with unwashed hands, or to spit on to the floor, or to break wind at the table (ibid.: 72–109). In stipulating what one should not do, the Renaissance manners texts gave a strong indication of what was commonplace. For example, it was recommended that one should not use the tablecloth to blow one's nose (ibid.: 122). Elias was able to demonstrate that the restraints on behaviour, which we today take for granted as self-constraints, have emerged gradually over time.

Elias's analysis reveals an overall direction of change in the development of Western societies, namely a set of civilizing processes involving an increasing 'social constraint towards self-restraint'. His work illustrates how a growing range and number of aspects of human behaviour have come to be regarded as distasteful and pushed 'behind the scenes of social life'. In indissoluble relation to this shift, Elias argues, people have increasingly come to experience an advancing threshold of shame and repugnance in relation to their bodily functions. Social constraints towards self-restraint become 'internalized' as 'second nature', so that in certain contexts we feel embarrassment and nausea.

Some critics have argued that Elias ignores examples of people with seemingly highly-developed 'civilized controls' during the very earliest stages of the period he examines. In fact, Elias was well aware of such cases, discussing extreme forms of asceticism and renunciation in certain sectors of medieval society. However, he noted that these stood in contrast to equally extreme forms of behaviour involving the indulgence of pleasure. For Elias, therefore, processes of civilization involve a *gradual stabilization* of human behaviour, processes characterized by 'diminishing contrasts and increasing varieties' (ibid.: 382). They are particularly related to the rise of *stable power monopolies*, notably through the rise of centralized nation–states and unified national cultures (see **state and nation–state**).

In his later work Elias examined the causes of what he called 'de-civilizing processes', particularly with respect to the case of Nazi Germany (1994). Since Elias's death, several sociologists have developed forms of comparative 'civilizational analysis' influenced by his approach, including notably Shmuel **Eisenstadt**.

The idea of civilization and its relation to **violence**, control and self-control, desire, sublimation and **sexuality**, was also a central theme for **Freud** (in *Civilization and its Discontents* (1930)), for **Marucse** (in *Eros and Civilization* (1955)), for Talcott **Parsons**, and for many other theorists of the **socialization** process.

References and further reading

Elias, N. ([1939] 2000) *The Civilizing Process*, rev. edn. Oxford: Blackwell.
Elias, N. (1994) *The Germans*. Oxford: Blackwell.
Mennell, S. (1998) *Norbert Elias: An Introduction*. Dublin: University College Dublin Press.
Loyal, S. and Quilley, S. (2004) *The Sociology of Norbert Elias*. Cambridge: Cambridge University Press.
Van Krieken, R. (1998) *Norbert Elias: Key Sociologist*. London: Routledge.

JASON HUGHES

CLASS

Social class denotes divisions by unequal distribution of **power**, and life chances in society, intersecting with divisions by **gender**, **status**, **age**, and **ethnicity**. Class divisions also correspond to different ways of life and visions of society.

First used for taxation in ancient Rome, the term is especially used for societies based on rational **capitalist** market economies. In Western Europe, since the late eighteenth century, it replaced the terms 'estates', 'ranks' and 'orders', as a consequence of the French political revolution and the English industrial revolution. During this transition, the dominant power of the estates of **aristocracy** and clergy, based on inherited rank, was contested by a 'third estate' of the 'people', based on productive functions in the **division of labour**. After the 1790s, this 'productive class' (so named by Saint Simon) came to be further divided into the **bourgeoisie** and **working class**. This gave rise to the concept of three conflicting classes, elaborated by Ricardo in 1817 and dominating social thought from **Marx** to **Weber**: the old upper class of the landed aristocracy, living from rent; the new 'middle class' of the industrial bourgeoisie, living from capital returns; and the working class, living from manual **labour**. In the twentieth century, new structural shifts motivated deep controversies, often against the background of the Marxist antagonism of bourgeoisie and **proletariat**. Today, less strongly antagonistic concepts of class are more prominent. Common terms have been social milieu (**Durkheim**), 'stratum' (Geiger), 'social divisions', or 'institutionalized class conflict' (**Dahrendorf**), as distinct from 'naked' or 'deregulated' class conflict (Esping-Andersen 1999).

Since the origins of sociology in the late nineteenth century, there has been much dispute about whether class distinctions and identities can unequivocally be deduced from a single causal source. Marx, in particular, has been regarded as placing exclusive emphasis on the economic causes of class. In reality, however, the classical thinkers all employed *relational* or *field* ways of thinking, aiming at the complex historical whole. Max Weber's approach is exemplary. Weber divided the phenomena of class into three levels, all linked in different ways to the distribution of power. He distinguished: (1) 'classes', placed within the economic order; (2) 'estates' (narrowly translated as '**status** group'), placed within an order of social 'honour'; and (3) 'political 'parties', struggling for domination in the political order (see **party**). All three orders influence each other but act in 'relative autonomy' from one another.

Subsequent theories have further elaborated these three levels of (1) socio-economic *class situation*; (2) socio-cultural *class behaviour*; and (3) socio-political *struggle for rights and domination*. Prominent contributors have been Geiger, Parkin, **Bourdieu** and **Giddens**, among others. How class 'in itself' translates from a mere nominal entity into social identities and actions ('class for itself') is especially answered on the non-economic levels.

Max Weber on class

Weber defines class primarily as a group of persons sharing the same 'class situation' (*Lage*) or the same 'life chances'. These comprise typical chances of access to goods as well as external standing (*Stellung*) and internal life experiences (*Lebensschicksal*). Weber distinguishes different types of classes by the *means* by which a class situation is reached; that is, by the kind and extent of control over goods by work qualifications and by the respective returns from a given economic order. Weber distinguishes

'property classes' (living from rent) and two types of 'acquisition classes' living from the productive utilization either of capital (bourgeoisie) or of work (working class), in commodity and labour markets. Using the term 'chance', Weber insists that although defined by common class situations, classes are not communities but merely represent possible bases for communal action. Common class situations may result in ways of acting which need not necessarily take the form of rational representation of **interests** (such as through **associations**) but may be reactive and amorphous.

In Weber's definition, 'class situations' primarily depend on market positions, in contrast to a pre-modern 'estate-based society' (*ständische Gesellschaft*) where social situations primarily depend on distributions of social 'honour' by *conventions of conduct* and by *juridical privilege*. However, the market-based propertied classes themselves adopt estate-like strategies 'with extraordinary regularity' to control access to their privileged class situation. This may occur either (1) through intermarriage and social intercourse, largely limited to those who conform to the conventions of honour and to a distinct way of 'life conduct' (*Lebensführung*); or (2) through striving to secure their life chances through legal privilege. Both mechanisms of 'closure' against newcomers support 'monopolies' over specific material or non-material goods and chances, including the regulation of property and higher education.

In his chapters on classes and on religion in *Economy and Society*, Weber (1968) denies any unequivocal determination of conduct and beliefs by class situation, but admits that a common economic situation implies a probability for typical behaviour. In his analysis of this correspondence between class situation and cultural conduct of life, Weber filled a gap left by Marx. Durkheim's work has also helped to fill this gap. According to Durkheim's concept of *milieu*, lasting **solidarity** is not produced by commodity exchange but by the moral ties developed in the elementary subdivisions of society. These include the familial, territorial and occupational milieus, which distinguish themselves by slowly developing a 'corpus of moral rules' that are internalized in individuals' moral **habitus**. Weber and Durkheim have since prompted many scholars, especially Geiger (1932), Bourdieu (1984) and their followers, to seek consistent relations between occupational clusters and habitus types.

Weber's two basic concepts have been elaborated further with regard to the complex socio-political struggles of classes and groups. A party, describing any political faction struggling for influence or domination in planned ways, *may* represent and mobilize the interests of 'classes' or 'estates', but often does not do so. Many political sociologists underline ways in which modern party politics intersects not only with class but also with regional, ideological and religious cleavages (Lepsius 1993). The concept of *closure* explains the politics of juridical distribution of power, life chances and educational chances among classes. It also includes new and countervailing powers in the corporate negotiation system which contest established privileges – most notably **trade unions**.

On all three Weberian levels, the twentieth century has seen deep changes. Debates pointed especially to three types of problems: first, structural **differentiations**, including increasing class depolarization, deindustrialization, **education** and skill standards; second, increasing autonomies of life conduct, including in some cases outright decoupling from class structuration; and third, the return or renewed rise to prominence of non-class cleavages based on gender, age, ethnicity and **religion**. Debates have oscillated between abandoning class concepts and developing more complex paradigms. They have also considered the role played by different national paths and by the spread of industrial and service structures

to developing countries (see especially **Bendix** and **Lipset** [1953] 1966; Joyce 1995; Grusky 2001; Crompton 1998).

Class transformations

In the early twentieth century, scholars discussed the decline of the *old middle estate* of small owners which, contrary to Marx's expectations, did not join the ranks of the proletariat but formed a *new middle estate* of service employees, retaining conservative attitudes (Geiger 1932). Debates then shifted from private to *manager capitalism*. Some expected a 'regime of managers' replacing old dominant classes in capitalist as well as **communist** countries. Others understood this as a 'horizontal' modernization of class fractions (Bourdieu), expressing the functional differentiation between ownership and control of capital (Geiger, Dahrendorf). Together with higher professionals, administrators and officials, the dominating class transformed into what Goldthorpe (1980) grouped together as the *upper service class* (see **middle class**).

From the 1940s to the 1960s, horizontal shifts accelerated. The rise of communist and fascist regimes had shown the risks of intensified class conflicts. Thus in the advanced Western societies of the post-war period, changes came to be embedded into new societal models of institutional regulation of class situations, designed to direct the working-class majority towards improved life chances (sometimes described as 'deproletarization'). This operated on all three of Weber's levels (see especially Geiger 1949; Esping-Andersen 1999). Growing productivity radically decreased agrarian and, partly, industrial employment, leading to rapidly expanding skilled service occupations. The remaining working class divided into skilled, semi-skilled and unskilled fractions. To contain the risks unleashed by these transformations, social-democratic and conservative **welfare states** extended institutional guarantees, social **security**, health and educational opportunities to the middle and working classes, including an extension of civil, political and social **citizenship** and improved employment rights – notably examined by T. H. **Marshall**. Collective bargaining or 'institutionalized class conflict' allowed for the historic rise of mass income and **consumption**. As a consequence of opening options, the importance of life style and 'postmaterialist values' increased.

This rise of a broadly integrated middle class together with the discrediting of (Eastern) Marxism supported the 'orthodox consensus' of harmonistic theories of **stratification** defended by **Parsons** and others, as well as the conception of an industrial class society with open chances in a plurality of contexts defended by **Dahrendorf** and others. However, in opposition to this liberal consensus (and to dogmatic Marxist positions), more open class concepts were developed by other theorists, notably by Bendix and Lipset ([1953] 1966) who revisited elements in the thinking of Weber, Marx and Durkheim (see **Bendix**). In Britain the early pioneers of what came to be known as Cultural Studies – Raymond Williams, Richard Hoggart, E. P. Thompson, Paul Willis – re-discovered the working-class life through its active cultural practices (see **culture and cultural turn**). John Goldthorpe (1980) examined the new 'affluent workers', developing a concept of occupational classes in the Weberian tradition and confirming the persistence of vertical inequalities. Goldthorpe's statistical analyses confirmed a substantial absolute rise of material and educational standards, but revealed a strikingly disproportionate difference in the *relative* chances of working-class children to move up into the service class.

The more 'horizontal' differentiations of class have been discussed in the context of post-industrial and **postmodern** theories of *restructuring* or *destructuring* of class (see **post-industrial society**). These have been influential in part as a reaction to the short-lived structuralist-Marxist class schemes of the 1970s proposed by **Althusser** and Poulantzas. Postindustrial theories refer to horizontal shifts from industrial to a 'service society' or 'knowledge society' (see **knowledge and knowledge society**), with the optimistic vision of decreasing constraints of class domination and alienation at work and of the weakening of property **elites** by a rising knowledge elite (see Daniel **Bell**). Educational degrees and training certificates were seen as 'new forms of property' that would give rise to **intellectuals** as a 'new class' (Gouldner).

Postmodernist theories have pushed the argument about weakening class identities still further. Structural differentiation has been seen as encouraging cross-cutting or **bricolage** identities (Hall; Pakulsky and Waters). **Identity** has been seen as becoming independent ('decoupled') from the structural constraints of **need**, class domination and milieu ties, allowing a reflexive choice of lifestyle and milieu. These theories of 'individualization' and 'reflective modernization' have been formulated notably by Ulrich **Beck** and Anthony Giddens. Political action has been seen by some as no longer predominantly concerned with material redistribution but instead with 'post-materialist' values, such as the rights of citizens, women, ethnic groups and **ecology and environmentalism**.

Class reproduction

Post-materialist theories of class refer to important real increases of personal autonomy, reflexivity, education and differentiation in present-day society. However, while they are not compatible with monolithic class concepts, the 'horizontal' changes and movements they identify should be seen as going together with more open and complex concepts of vertical class divisions. 'Heterogeneity' is obvious in large employment aggregates (such as those of Goldthorpe) which embrace many subgroups, but when analysis touches on elementary subgroups, there is ample evidence of more consistent experiences and mentalities. Grusky and Sörensen found a return of 'occupational habitus', as did Geiger in the 1930s. In the 1970s Bourdieu (1984) developed a complete panorama of class fractions in France, confirming a significant correspondence between occupation, life style and class habitus, reproduced by the mechanisms of distinction operating to reinforce intergenerational continuity of class privileges and chances (for the German case, see also Vester 2001). This parallels Goldthorpe's notion of the intergenerational 'demographic continuity' of class, as privileges impede meritocratic competition for life chances.

Many theories have seen education as the principal cultural mechanism sorting individuals into occupational and class contexts. But exactly how this happens is open to debate. For some authors, human capital *replaces* economic capital as the principal stratifying force today. But, for Bourdieu, **cultural capital** only supports bourgeois privileges, insofar as it transmits economic, cultural and social capital accumulated by former generations and relies on social selection in the education system. Similarly, Hartmann (2004) finds that, internationally, the self-recruitment of business elites has not changed. More open identities of the new fractions of the 'bourgeois' or 'service class' have been found by Savage *et al.* (1992) who distinguish public sector professionals, managers and government bureaucrats in Britain.

In studying class *reproduction*, the concept of *closure*, helps to identify the mechanisms of juridical, institutional and cultural privileging of life chances. This allows sociologists to focus on those fractions of the dominant class who do not directly reproduce by 'property' (see **property and property rights**), 'exploitation' or 'domination' and 'authority' over employees, but instead rely on institutional privilege – as with the *nomenklatura* in the former communist states and the holders of professional credential advantages in capitalist societies.

In the study of social class change, the *institutional theory of stratification* of Esping-Andersen (1999) is helpful, as it includes all the complex interrelations of Weber's levels. Institutional regulations are here seen to follow different national 'paths' in the social-democratic (Scandinavian), liberal (Anglo-Saxon) and conservative (Continental European) and other welfare states. All these models are challenged by new developments, resulting from rising productivity and world market deregulation. The shift towards services, re-skilling and new technologies has not produced an expected decline of **inequality**. Instead, it has produced decline in the *middle* ground, as services now expand both into higher skilled technical-professional jobs and into low-skilled low-end services – with both segments showing a substantial increase in female membership. Contemporary debates have centred on retarded economic growth, **social inclusion and social exclusion**, precariousness and **unemployment** as well as pressures on the well-qualified middle groups. Findings confirm that concepts of **social justice** have not disappeared. Although they no longer follow direct class lines, they crystallize around socio-political 'camps' that are still oriented towards basic welfare concepts – liberal, conservative and social-democratic (Lepsius 1993; Vester 2001).

References and further reading

Bendix, R. and Lipset, S. M. (eds) (1966) *Class, Status and Power: Social Stratification in Comparative Perspective*. New York: Free Press.

Bourdieu, P. ([1979] 1984) *Distinction: A Social Critique of the Judgement of Taste*. Cambridge, MA: Harvard University Press.

Crompton, R. (1993) *Class and Stratification: An Introduction to Current Debates*. Cambridge: Polity.

Durkheim, E. ([1893/1902] 1933) *The Division of Labor in Society*. New York: Macmillan.

Esping-Andersen, G. (1999) *Social Foundations of Postindustrial Economies*. Oxford: Oxford University Press.

Geiger, T. (1932) *Die soziale Schichtung des deutschen Volkes*. Stuttgart: Enke.

Geiger, T. (1949) *Die Klassengesellschaft im Schmelztiegel*. Cologne: Kiepenheuer.

Goldthorpe, J. (1980) *Social Mobility and Class Structure*. Oxford: Clarendon Press.

Grusky, D. B. (ed.) (2001) *Social Stratification: Class, Race and Gender in Sociological Perspective*. Boulder, CO: Westview Press.

Hartmann, M. (2004) *Elitesoziologie*. Frankfurt am Main: Campus.

Joyce, P. (ed.) (1995) *Class*. Oxford: Oxford University Press.

Lepsius, M. R. ([1966] 1993) 'Parteiensystem und Sozialstruktur', in M. R. Lepsius, *Demokratie in Deutschland*. Göttingen: Vandenhoek & Ruprecht.

Savage, M., Barlow, J., Dickens, P. and Fielding, T. (1992) *Property, Bureaucracy and Culture: Middle-Class Formation in Contemporary Britain*. London: Routledge.

Savage, M. (2000) *Class Analysis and Social Transformation*. London: Sage.

Vester, M. (2001) 'The Transformation of Social Classes: From "Deproletarianization" to "Individualization"?', in G. Van Gyes and H. de Witte (eds) *Can Class Still Unite?* Aldershot: Ashgate, pp. 37–78.

Weber, M. ([1922] 1968) *Economy and Society*. Berkeley, CA: University of California Press.

MICHAEL VESTER

CLASSICS

Classics are those earlier texts or authors that have gained exemplary status within contemporary sociology. Collectively, the works of **Weber**, **Marx** and **Durkheim**, sometimes along with those of **Simmel**, **Mead** and **Parsons**, form a canon of classics through which sociology understands itself. The concepts developed by these authors provide verbal shorthand for communicating and developing ideas, while also serving to integrate an often bewilderingly varied discipline. However, beyond this function they have a privileged position because current sociologists often find in them insights that illuminate present situations.

Interest in recent years has focused on the justification for having classics. Sociology's early positivist aspirations suggested the discipline had no need of them as it would proceed scientifically, verifying or falsifying hypotheses (see **positivism**). The work of the founders would be of no greater value than of any other empirically testable material. However, sociology has not developed along positivist lines but has become primarily a discursive discipline, proceeding on the basis of reasoned argument from evidence, rather than prediction from causal connections. This is because the sociologist is invariably faced with evidence that is both empirical and normative, so that factual description and interpretive evaluation are bound up together. When sociologists use concepts such as **rationalization**, **commodity** fetishism or **patriarchy**, they necessarily imply an evaluation of the material to which these concepts refer. Moreover, such terms entail reference to the states of mind of the actors and sociologists involved and thereby to the discursively contestable nature of these ideas in **everyday** life.

More recently, the challenge to classic texts has come from a post-positivist, social constructionist quarter (see **social constructionism**). On the basis that classic texts, no less than other artifacts, are a product of the ideological conditions from which they emerged, they deserve no special respect. To assume they are beyond the effects of history is to bestow on them a quasi-sacred status akin to that attributed to texts in a religious canon. Connell (1997) argues that the work of the European founders of sociology, written between 1840 and 1920, reveals elements of **ideology** in its distinctions between pre-modern and modern societies, tacitly valorizing the latter and naïvely celebrating colonial Europe's own sense of **progress**.

The drive to debunk the **authority** of classics has also, sometimes contradictorily, been accompanied by a desire to extend the canon. If it is restricted to the work of a few dead white European males, its intellectual possibilities are limited, as is its relevance to a contemporary audience. The role of institutional life in the creation of classics has been considerable. The influence of **Parsons**'s work and his preference for Durkheim and Weber over Simmel and Marx shaped how the discipline was conceived during the 1950s and the 1960s. More recently and in opposition to this exclusionary impulse, Parker (1997) argues for a more **multicultural** canon that would include W. E. B. **Du Bois**, while Deegan (2003) has made a case for the importance of nineteenth-century feminist, Harriet **Martineau**.

There is, however, a distinction to be made between the role of historical and institutional life in the creation of a canon and the nature of 'classic-ness' itself. The usual criticism levelled against advocates of the classic is that they mistakenly believe its greatness is inherent and thus wrongly think its insights are supra-historical. However, in *Truth and Method* (1989), **Gadamer** argues that it is precisely the ability of a classic text to resist efforts at explaining it solely in terms of context that draws us back to it again and again. The reason that classic texts persist is because the claims they make on us continue to reverberate in the present. He is not arguing that classic texts are 'above' history, but that their eminence springs from history; it is history that allows us to see ourselves more clearly in the classic. The apparent timelessness of a classic text is, as he puts it, 'its mode of historical being'. It appears timeless only because history permits us to see its contemporary significance. History, in Gadamer's account, is not a linear sequence of events but an ongoing fusion of the horizons of past and present. The classic text shines out because it renders that relationship clear, allowing us to see how much we continue to share with the past.

References and further reading

Alexander, J. (1987) 'On the Centrality of the Classics', in A. Giddens and S. Turner (eds), *Social Theory Today*. Cambridge: Polity.

Baehr, P. (2002) *Founders, Classics, Canons*. London: Transatlantic.

Campbell, C. (1989) *The Romantic Ethic and the Spirit of Consumerism*. Oxford: Basil Blackwell.

Connell, R. (1997) 'Why Is Classical Theory Classical?', *American Journal of Sociology*, 102: 1511–57.

Deegan, M. J. (2003) 'Textbooks, the History of Sociology and the Sociological Stock of Knowledge', *Sociological Theory* 21: 298–305.

Gadamer, H. G. (1989) *Truth and Method*. London: Sheed and Ward.

Guillory, J. (1993) *Cultural Capital*. Chicago: University of Chicago Press.

How, A. (1998) 'That's Classic! A Gadamerian Defence of the Classic Text in Sociology', *Sociological Review*, 46: 828–48.

Parker, D. (1997) 'Viewpoint: Why Bother with Durkheim?', *Sociological Review*, 45: 122–46.

ALAN HOW

CLASSIFICATION

Classification refers to the sorting of objects, people, events, **emotions**, **actions** and tasks into categories based on their perceived similarities and differences. Humans have a strong propensity to classify, as classifying promises to bring order in social life and reduce social **complexity**. Social theorists have at the same time asserted that the resulting classifications are themselves rooted in the social and moral order of society. To borrow a phrase of Pierre **Bourdieu**, this premise implies that classifying 'classifies the classifier' (Bourdieu 1984: 6). Students of classification have set out to map the relationship between social organization, symbolic **representations** and conceptual systems. Their theories have focused on exploring classification as the symbolic inscription of **social relations**, on the construction of boundaries between classificatory categories, the cognitive aspects of classification, and the analysis of large-scale classification systems.

The origins of research on classification can be traced back to the work of Emile **Durkheim**, who in his seminal writing, *The Elementary Forms of Religious Life* and *Primitive Classification* (with Marcel **Mauss**), expounded the idea that classification is socially determined. Anthropologists such as Mary **Douglas**, Claude **Lévi-Strauss** and the sociolinguist Basil Bernstein built on Durkheim's initial insights to expand the analysis of the structured and categorical nature of social reality. They argued that classification generally proceeds through the construction of **binary** oppositions, such as **sacred** and profane, purity and impurity, good and evil, light and dark, home and work, that correspond to underlying social distinctions.

A growing body of literature has placed the definition and construction of boundaries between classificatory categories, that is 'boundary work', at the centre of sociological analysis (see Lamont and Molnár 2002, for a review of this literature). These studies have moved beyond the rigid **structuralism** of Durkheim and his followers that assumed a perfect homology between social structure and classification schemes; they have shown that the correspondence results from more contingent, contentious and complex social and symbolic processes. They have pointed out that classification systems not only mirror social relations but also are instrumental in constituting them. This approach has also emphasized that the study of classification is central to understanding a broad range of social phenomena in modern societies, from identification processes (Jenkins 1997) and **knowledge** production (Gieryn 1999) to the symbolic reproduction of social inequalities (Bourdieu 1984; Lamont 2000) (see **inequality**).

Another strand of research has examined classification from a cognitive perspective. It argues that the cognitive processes that underlie the emergence of classificatory categories are themselves neither simply personal nor 'logical', but **intersubjective** (Zerubavel 1991). Though classification may be a human universal, the nature of the constructed categories varies significantly across **groups** and locales. In addition, this approach investigates various properties of classificatory boundaries such as their salience, permeability, or degree of naturalization.

The study of large-scale classification systems, made up of interrelated sets of categories exemplified by the census, racial, disease, and occupational classifications, has revolved around three themes: the politics of classification, the communicative function of classification, and the discrepancies between official and **everyday** classification schemes. Classification schemes appear to have a putatively functional or scientific quality, despite being socially and politically constructed (**Foucault** [1966] 1994). The **state** and dominant social actors have the power to construct and impose categories on other social groups, thereby shaping, reinforcing, and even obscuring social hierarchies (Bourdieu 1984). In fact, systems of classification, including the very logics of such systems, constitute an important stake in **power** struggles between social groups. While acknowledging that classification always reflects ethical and political choices and institutionalizes **difference**, others stress that classification systems are important interfaces enabling communication across communities (Bowker and Star 2000). They constitute an important communication infrastructure that helps to develop and maintain coherence across social worlds; for instance, through standardization. Finally, researchers point to the incongruity between official classifications and 'folk taxonomies' (D'Andrade 1995). They argue that ordinary people have room to manoeuvre in using highly institutionalized categories. They can deploy these categories strategically and infuse them with informal meanings. They may also develop alternative classification schemes that can be mobilized to subvert official categories.

The diverse theoretical traditions reviewed here betray the profoundly dialectical nature of classification: classificatory categories are the product of social relations, historical, cultural and structural constraints, but simultaneously, people use them to construct society, to make and remake, to reinforce but also to contest prevailing social realities.

References and further reading

Bourdieu, P. (1984) *Distinction: A Social Critique of the Judgement of Taste*. Cambridge, MA: Harvard University Press.

Bowker, G. C. and Star, S. L. (2000) *Sorting Things Out: Classification and Its Consequences*. Cambridge, MA: MIT Press.

D'Andrade, R. G. (1995) *The Development of Cognitive Anthropology*. Cambridge: Cambridge University Press.

Foucault, M. ([1966] 1994) *The Order of Things*. New York: Vintage Books.

Gieryn, T. F. (1999) *Cultural Boundaries of Science: Credibility on the Line*. Chicago: University of Chicago Press.

Jenkins, R. (1997) *Rethinking Ethnicity*. London: Sage.

Lamont, M. (2000) *The Dignity of Working Men: Morality and the Boundaries of Race, Class, and Immigration*. Cambridge, MA: Harvard University Press.

Lamont, M. and Molnár, V. (2002) 'The Study of Boundaries in the Social Sciences', *Annual Review of Sociology*, 28: 167–95.

Zerubavel, E. (1991) *The Fine Line: Making Distinctions in Everyday Life*. New York: Free Press.

VIRÁG MOLNÁR

COGNITIVISM

Cognitivism is the concern with processes of knowing, their structuring and outcomes, including the production, organization and use of **knowledge**. While traditionally understood as involving mental phenomena and thus associated with philosophy and psychology, this area is also a serious social scientific concern. Here it is dealt with as linking the individual, institutional and cultural levels. The modern cognitive lineage is traceable to **Kantian** philosophy, but only since the culmination of twentieth-century developments in cognitive science have social scientists embraced it. Previously, **realism, empiricism, positivism** and **behaviourism** provided bases for opposition against cognitivism, as they partially still do. In sociology, leading theorists such as Peter **Berger**, Harold **Garfinkel**, Erving **Goffman**, Alain **Touraine**, Jürgen **Habermas**, Pierre **Bourdieu**, Niklas **Luhmann** and Anthony **Giddens** cleared the way for the approach, which is most strongly associated with the work of Aaron Cicourel (1973), Ron Eyerman and Andrew Jamison (1991), and Eviatar Zerubavel (1997).

Kant's writings on 'schematism' founded a tradition that has provided a basis for developments in **epistemology**, psychology, neuroscience and linguistics, making possible the so-called 'cognitive revolution' of the 1950s. Until the 1980s, the cognitive sciences matured on the basis of the information processing model which took cognition as analogous to the computer. However, following criticisms, an alternative connectionist model of parallel distributed processing gained currency. This broadening of cognitive science in the early 1980s was followed by a further step towards the environment of cognition, resulting in cognition being regarded as embodied activity situated in real-world contexts. Here anthropology and sociology began to exert a remarkable impact on cognitive science theory and methodology. A link was also established with dynamical theory, so that cognition became understood as a complex process of dynamic interaction within a situation among different cognitive systems borne by individuals and **groups** in mutual communication. In relating to objects and tools, such individuals and groups are seen as drawing different cognitive orders or models of reality from the available cultural repertoire and as thematizing them through different **media**, thus contributing to the constant transformation of the relational complex to which they belong.

Well before cognitive science emerged in reaction to behaviourism, the early impulses signalled by Kant, Hegel, Peirce and their followers were incorporated into different strands of social theory which both anticipated and supported the new departure. Karl **Mannheim** significantly introduced the sociology of knowledge, while the cognitive dimension was clearly present in early **critical theory**. It was more explicitly treated, however, by Alfred **Schutz** and George Herbert **Mead** through their phenomenological and pragmatist concerns with culturally structured social knowledge, **action**-oriented cognition, socio-cognitive processes and expectation structures. **Phenomenology**, **social constructionism**, **symbolic interactionism**, and **ethnomethodology** a became established in the 1960s against the background of the critique and decline of positivism and **functionalism**, and coincided with an increasing interest in the cognitive revolution in the context of the growing importance of communication. It was at this time that cognitive sociology gained a distinct profile. This occurred most explicitly in the work of Cicourel (1973) and Helga Nowotny (1973). In 1981, Knorr-Cetina and Cicourel could speak of a 'cognitive turn' in sociology. While the cognitive concern resonates strongest with interpretative and critical traditions, there are both some interpretative social scientists who reject it as a reductive scientific enterprise, on the one hand, and, on the other, strong naturalists (Turner 2002) who seek to base social theory on neural processes.

Thus far, cognitive sociology has passed through four phases. Initially, it focused on the organization of experience and **social relations** with a view to decomposing reified or abstract concepts of social **structure**, **culture**, **language** and knowledge by appealing to cognitive processes and communication. Second, conversation analysis and **discourse** analysis emerged, concentrating in different ways on **everyday**, scientific and cultural knowledge and associated cognitive and communicative processes. Meanwhile, schema theory made strides in cognitive science, with Goffman and Touraine introducing the equivalent concepts of 'frame' (see **framing**) and 'cultural model', yet the analysis of cognitive processes in these terms at **group** and sociocultural levels had to await the third phase in the late 1980s. Here a cognitivist concept of culture, replacing the traditional unitary one, advanced the analysis of the **structuration** of such processes. Yet differences remain among the respective currents founded by William Gamson and Habermas, as well as American repertoire theory and French pragmatic sociology. Simultaneously, the shift in cognitive science from 'computationalism' to 'connectionism' made available the concept of '**network**' for the analysis of higher-order collective agents and cognitive systems. Since the late 1990s, the focus has been on how cultural schemas dynamically relate to action, social structure, physical objects and external forms in social processes.

References and further reading

Cicourel, A. V. (1973) *Cognitive Sociology*. New York: Free Press.

DiMaggio, P. (1997) 'Culture and Cognition', *Annual Review of Sociology*, 23: 263–87.

Eyerman, R. and Jamison, A. (1991) *Social Movements: A Cognitive Approach*. Cambridge: Polity.

Knorr-Cetina, K. and Cicourel, A. V. (eds) (1981) *Advances in Social Theory and Methodology*. London: Routledge & Kegan Paul.

Nowotny, H. (1973) 'On the Feasibility of a Cognitive Approach to Science', *Zeitschrift für Soziologie*, 2(3): 282–96.

Strydom, P. (2000) *Discourse and Knowledge*. Liverpool: Liverpool University Press.

Turner, S. P. (2002) *Brains/Practices/Relativism: Social Theory after Cognitive Science*. Chicago: University of Chicago Press.

Zerubavel, E. (1997) *Social Mindscapes: An Invitation to Cognitive Sociology*. Cambridge, MA: Harvard University Press.

PIET STRYDOM

COLEMAN, JAMES S. (1926–1995)
US theorist

Coleman was a student of **Merton**, **Lipset**, and Paul Lazarsfeld. His main fields of substantive social research have covered **education**, the **family and household**, **stratification**, mass communication, political sociology, and **organizations**. His pioneering contribution to the development of mathematical sociology aims to provide tools to generate theoretical insights based on a rigorous form of methodological individualism (see **methods and methodology**). The derivation of policy implications from theory and empirical research is a characteristic feature of his work. Coleman's research strategy attempts a synthesis of **Durkheim**'s programme of studying social structures and **Weber**'s programme of studying macro-level social outcomes of individual action. Coleman thus focuses on macro-micro-macro transitions, using **rational choice** assumptions as a micro-theory of **action** (see **micro-, meso- and macro-levels**). Coleman shaped an approach to sociology that aims at the systematic integration of theory, empirical research, and statistical methods. In his work, theory is regarded not as a system of concepts without empirical content but as an empirically informed system of propositions implying testable hypotheses and statistical models.

Major works

(1961) *The Adolescent Society*. New York: Free Press.
(1964) *Introduction to Mathematical Sociology*. New York: Free Press.
(1966) *Equality of Educational Opportunity*. Washington, DC: Government Printing Office.
(1982) (with T. Hoffer and S. Kilgore) *High School Achievement*. New York: Basic Books.
(1990) *Foundations of Social Theory*. Cambridge, MA: Belknap.

Further reading

Clark, J. (ed.) (1996) *James S. Coleman*. London: Falmer.

Lindenberg, S. (2000) 'James Coleman', in G. Ritzer (ed.) *Blackwell Companion to Major Social Theorists*. Malden, MA: Blackwell.
Marsden, P. U. (2005) 'The Sociology of James Coleman', *Annual Review of Sociology*, 31: 1–24.
Sorensen, A. and Spilerman, S. (eds) (1993) *Social Theory and Social Policy: Essays in Honor of James S. Coleman*. Westport, CT: Praeger.

WERNER RAUB

COLLECTIVISM

Collectivism is a doctrine stressing the significance of macro-level concepts thus giving priority to **groups**, **institutions**, and **structures**, rather than to the individual or individual dispositions and conduct (see **micro-, meso- and macro-levels**). It appears in different forms: (1) an ontological version, for which reality consists essentially of collective social phenomena; and (2) a methodological version accepting that collective phenomena possess **authority** over the individual but denying that such phenomena preclude the importance of the individual. Early social thinkers such as Vico and Montesquieu defended forms of collectivism, while idealist philosophers such as Hegel stimulated its subsequent development. Collectivism is typically associated with authors such as **Comte**, **Marx**, **Durkheim**, and **Lukács**. O'Neill (1973) documents the vehement opposition of 'methodological **individualism**' against collectivism, particularly as represented by Hayek, **Popper** and Watkins, inspired by Max **Weber**. In the late twentieth and early twenty-first centuries, Jon Elster, James **Coleman**, Colin Campbell and Stephen Turner have continued this criticism in some form or another (see **individualism and individualization**). Older attempts to resolve the issue of the relation between collectivism and individualism by overcoming the limitations of both, for example, the attempts of **Simmel** and Cooley, have been followed by new proposals such as 'relational sociology' (Bhaskar 1979), 'structuration theory' (**Giddens** 1984) and 'methodological situationalism' (e.g. Knorr-Cetina 1988).

References and further reading

Bhaskar, R. (1979) *The Possibility of Naturalism.* London: Harvester.

Domingues, J. M. (1995) *Sociological Theory and Collective Subjectivity.* London: Macmillan.

Giddens, A. (1984) *The Constitution of Society.* Cambridge: Polity.

Knorr-Cetina, K. (1988) 'The Micro-Social Order: A Reconsideration', in N. G. Fielding (ed.) *Actions and Structure.* London: Sage.

O'Neill, J. (ed.) (1973) *Modes of Individualism and Collectivism.* London: Heinemann.

PIET STRYDOM

COLONIZATION

See: post-colonial theory

COMMODITY AND COMMODIFICATION

The idea that commodities and commodification are important to our understanding of modern society originates in **Marx**'s conception of the capitalist **mode of production**. His *Capital* ([1867] 1959) begins with an analysis of the social form of commodity (see **capitalism**). The products of **labour** take on this specific form whenever they are produced for exchange, meaning that labour ceases to be social in itself and henceforth is only social when mediated through exchange. Labour's products no longer have any use value to their producers, but henceforth only to the anonymous representatives of the **market**. Therefore, in a capitalist economy, social riches appear as a huge collection of commodities. The commodity is the key to the understanding of the entire capitalist society in which social relations between human beings take the form of relations between things, or are reified (see **reification**). To emphasize the strangeness of this state of affairs Marx speaks of the fetish character of commodities

which makes social relations mysterious, like the religious fantasy worlds of primitive people who accord magical powers to things.

From the value form of the commodity Marx further deduced the form of **money** and capital forms. By showing that the wage labourer sells not his labour *per se* but more precisely his labour **power**, Marx revealed the source of surplus value and the secret of capitalist exploitation. As a result of the inner dynamics of capital accumulation, capitalist relations gradually expand and take over new fields and areas of production, trade and service, thus leading to increasing commodification and reification of **social relations**.

Today, economic theorists have reservations about Marx's analysis of the inner contradictions and dynamics of capitalism, but many cultural theorists and critics still appeal to his ideas of commodification and reification in relation to late modern or postmodern **culture**. These interpretations begin from **Lukács**'s seminal work *History and Class Consciousness* ([1923] 1971) which combines **Weber**'s theory of rationalization with Marx's idea of reification. Lukács's thinking had a strong influence on the critical theory of the **Frankfurt School** both in their more specific analyses of the impact of capitalist mass production on works of **art and aesthetics** and, more generally, in their interpretations of capitalist **modernity and modernization** as one-dimensional processes, and as a betrayal of real human reason (see **mass culture and mass society**).

Haug's ([1973] 1986) analysis of commodity aesthetics and advertising was a systematic effort to develop the basic ideas of Marx's theory of commodity exchange. As Haug argued, one result of the basic distinction between the use value and exchange value is the development of a third form of value in late capitalism, the illusory value of consumer appeal which founds the entire realm of marketing and advertising, based on the creation of cultural

79

signs and symbols (see **consumption**). **Baudrillard**'s ([1972] 1981) argument here was that Marx's critique of commodity production was based on a nineteenth century idea of universal objective human needs which failed to grasp adequately the role of signs and symbols in the construction of consumer desires.

Examples of cultural analyses today employing the concept of commodification are Zukin's (1995) studies of the importance of cultural symbols in city landscapes, Ritzer's (1996) thesis of McDonaldization, and Kellner's (2003) analyses of **media** and commodity spectacles, as well as **Bauman**'s (2000) reflections on the effects of modern **consumption** on postmodern **identities**. Similarly, **Jameson**'s (1991) diagnosis of the fragmented nature of **postmodernism** has its roots in his understanding of the role of commodity relations in late capitalism.

References and further reading

Baudrillard, J. ([1972] 1981) *For a Political Economy of a Sign*. St. Louis, MO: Telos.
Bauman, Z. (2000) *Liquid Modernity*. Cambridge: Polity.
Haug, W. F. ([1973] 1986) *Critique of Commodity Aesthetics*. Cambridge: Polity.
Jameson, F. (1991) *Postmodernism, or the Cultural Logic of Late Capitalism*. London: Verso.
Kellner, D. (2003) *Media Spectacle*. London: Routledge.
Lukács, G. ([1923] 1971) *History and Class Consciousness: Studies in Marxist Dialectics*. London: Merlin.
Marx, K. ([1867] 1959) *Capital: A Critique of Political Economy*. Moscow: Progress Publishers.
Ritzer, G. (1996) *The McDonaldization of Society*. London: Sage.
Zukin, S. (1995) *The Cultures of Cities*. Oxford: Blackwell.

JUKKA GRONOW

COMMUNICATION

The concept of communication as a term of generalized thematic importance in social theory has two leading contemporary exponents: Jürgen **Habermas** and Niklas **Luhmann**. In addition, it is possible to speak of a distinct kind of **postmodernist** attitude to communication, reflecting ideas in the **deconstructive** and anti-consensualist thinking of French theorists such as **Derrida** and Jean-François **Lyotard** (1988). A multitude of more concrete analyses of communication appears in contemporary theories of the **media and mass media**. These in turn adopt and adapt strands of thought in philosophies of **language**, in theories of linguistic pragmatics (see also **pragmatism**), semantics and **semiotics**, **discourse** analysis, conversation analysis, social psychology, **ethnomethodology**, socio-linguistics, theories of the nature of **meaning** and **symbols**, and ancient ideas about rhetoric and oratory since Plato, Aristotle and Cicero.

Habermas's major theoretical project of the 1970s and the 1980s, published as *The Theory of Communicative Action* (1984, 1987), elaborates ideas about language, **socialization**, **rationality and rationalization**, **morality** and cognitive development in the writings of G. H. **Mead**, **Durkheim**, **Chomsky**, **Piaget**, Lawrence Kohlberg and Anglo-American analytical philosophy. Habermas's key starting-point is J. L. Austin's and John Searle's theory of 'speech-acts', building on the later **Wittgenstein**'s understanding of linguistic meaning in terms of practical *use*. According to Austin (1962) and Searle (1969), speech is active or **performative** in the sense that it consists not only of propositional contents that purport to describe states of affairs in the world but also of a variety of pragmatic moments which have no semantic valency (and hence no 'truth conditions') but which nevertheless imply definite conditions of correct or 'successful' usage. Austin observed that the utterance 'I promise to pay you ten dollars tomorrow' is 'felicitous' (even if the speaker in fact defaults on the promise) in a way that the utterance 'I promise you that it will rain tomorrow' cannot be (unless, say, we imagine that the speaker is God). Habermas interprets this and other similar observations as demonstrating that speech and language carry certain rational rules of adequate and appropriate construction. The 'communicative competence' that every speaker of language begins to acquire from the earliest days of childhood consists of abilities to generate well-formed syntactic structures (as in Chomsky's 'linguistic competence') capable of eliciting assent or dissent from an interlocutor. Even radical disagreements between speakers presuppose bedrock norms of discursive **intersubjectivity**, in the absence of which the speakers would not even be able to recognize themselves as disagreeing with each other. Habermas sees this structure of rational mutual expectation between speakers as revealing a basic resource of communicative rationality in the everyday **lifeworld** of ordinary people which can and should be drawn upon in the forging of open, inclusive, uncoerced and unmanipulated consensuses in the decision-making processes of **civil society** and the **public sphere**. Speakers are normatively motivated to give reasons or arguments for the validity-claims they routinely attach to their utterances – whether these be theoretical truth-claims (typical of scientific communication) or practical rightness-claims (typical of moral communication) or expressive authenticity claims (typical of aesthetic communication) (see also Brandom 1994).

Communication, for Habermas, demonstrates that social actors are necessarily *'interested in reason'* (a phrase he adopts from **Kant**'s moral and political philosophy) and are therefore necessarily predisposed to **Enlightenment** and to **emancipatory** social projects that strive to remove **domination**, **violence** and **ideology** from the spaces of public and private life. Habermas also argues that the earlier members of the **Frankfurt School** failed sufficiently to appreciate this specifically dialogical

moment of social life, seeing only a tragic '**dialectic** of enlightenment' in which a highly emasculated order of **instrumental reason** carried by capitalism and technocracy comes to objectify or reify the tissues of sociality.

In a very different direction, Niklas Luhmann (1995) sees the concept of communication as pertaining not only to intentional, linguistically mediated interaction between individuals but also, and especially, to relationships between abstract **social systems**. Luhmann contends that meaning in Edmund Husserl's **phenomenological** sense of noetic acts of consciousness is best thought of simply in terms of properties of relations of **differentiation** and **integration** between two or more social systems and their functionally subservient 'sub-systems' – whether these are personality systems (individuals) or complex economic systems (markets), eco-systems, political systems (states, polities and their laws), or cultural systems (e.g. religious belief systems, education systems). Systems communicate with one another in a **cybernetic** sense by transmitting **information** to one another in a binary code of 'yes'/'no' reactions. For example, an overheating economy 'communicates' with the state or the political system insofar as it sends a signal to the finance minister or the head of the national bank to raise interest rates. Following **Parsons**, Luhmann here sees **money** and **power** as belonging among the foremost 'communication media' of social systems. In Luhmann's work, the concept of communication is deployed in an essentially **functionalist** sense, very different from the strongly normative use of the term advocated by Habermas.

Postmodernist ideas about communication typically begin from Jacques **Derrida**'s interventions in speech-act theory. Crucial for Derrida (1978) is the insight (emphasized by Wittgenstein) that language is misconceived when it is thought of merely as an instrument for the transmission of mental contents from one speaker to another (as in John Locke's seventeenth-century 'representationalist' theory of language). Insofar as language is a *medium* and not simply a *means* of communication, any utterance is liable to signify something different from what a speaker may intend it to signify. Even when a speech-act is well formed, or 'felicitous' in Austin's sense, it may always fail to elicit an expected type of response from the hearer. Therefore communication qua transmission of intentional contents is never guaranteed: communication is always susceptible to ambiguity, instability or excess or chronic deferral of sense, exemplified by irony or sarcasm and or by many other kinds of quotational 'iteration'. Derrida here writes famously of **différance** or **difference**. Similar ways of thinking appear in Jean-François Lyotard's (1988) reflections on failures of communication across 'language-games', as well as in Michel **Foucault**'s reflections on regimes of discursive power in definite social and historical worlds.

References and further reading

Austin, J. L. (1962) *How to Do Things with Words*. Oxford: Oxford University Press.

Brandom, R. (1994) *Making It Explicit: Reasoning, Representing and Discursive Commitment.* Cambridge, MA: Harvard University Press.

Derrida, J. (1978) 'Structure, Sign and Play in the Discourse of the Human Sciences', in *Writing and Difference*. London: Routledge.

Habermas, J. (1984) *The Theory of Communicative Action,* vol. I: *Reason and the Rationalization of Society.* Cambridge: Polity Press.

Habermas, J. (1987) *The Theory of Communicative Action,* vol. II: *Lifeworld and System.* Cambridge: Polity Press.

Luhmann, N. (1995*) Social Systems.* Stanford, CA: Stanford University Press.

Lyotard, J.-F. (1988) *The Differend: Phrases in Dispute.* Minneapolis, MN: University of Minnesota Press.

Searle, J. (1969) *Speech Acts.* Cambridge: Cambridge University Press.

AUSTIN HARRINGTON

COMMUNISM

The term communism refers to an egalitarian **society** built on voluntary **association** and on the basis of communally held rather than private property (see **property and property rights**). The idea implies that goods should be distributed to people according to their need, not according to **class** position or the blind forces of the **market**. In so-called state communism, the ideal of communal property was supposedly realized in the form of public ownership of the means of production and central state planning. While ill-fated state communism came into existence in the twentieth century, the term communism as such has a strong utopian underpinning (see **utopia**). For the early **Marx**, following in the footsteps of both **Hegelian** philosophy and early **socialism**, communism describes a society in which man's subjection to the system of the division of labour and man's **alienation** from his natural 'essence' will eventually be transcended. This implies the ideal of a harmonious **community** in which not only **poverty** but all forms of disharmony, such as **crime**, **conflict**, **inequality**, and **nationalism**, will be eradicated. In particular, it implies the 'withering away' of the state, which is seen as guaranteeing private property and class rule (see **state and nation–state**).

Marx and Engels used 'communist' as a term of self-designation after 1845, most famously in their *Communist Manifesto* written for the League of Communists in 1848. Yet the term was not coined by them. In circulation since the beginning of the 1840s, it was ascribed to the programmes of François Noël Babeuf (1760–97) and Étienne Cabet (1788–1856), who both advocated the collectivization of property. In his novel *Voyage en Icarie* (1840), Cabet outlined the life and institutions of an industrialized communist utopia, an idea that won a large number of followers, some of whom tried to establish 'Icarien' model communities in the United States. While Cabet argued for a peaceful transition to communism, Babeuf's politics directly connected to the Jacobin tradition of the French **Revolution**, instigating a revolutionary rather than what later would be called a 'reformist' tradition. Although his own 'conspiracy of equals' failed, his method of conspirational insurrection was kept alive by other communists, most prominently Louis-Auguste Blanqui (1805–81), the arch-revolutionary of nineteenth-century France who, next to Marx, was one of the main early propagators of the idea of the **proletariat** as the **subject** of social transformation.

While the question concerning the exact nature of the passage from **capitalism** to communism became decisive in later debates between 'revolutionaries' and 'reformists', in the nineteenth century, the terms socialism and communism were most often used interchangeably. Marx himself introduced a difference when referring to communism as the realm of man's **freedom**, and to socialism as the name for the transitional period leading to communism. Nonetheless, the differentiation became politically relevant only in the aftermath of World War I when revolutionary-oriented communist parties were established in opposition to the more reformist socialist parties. This differentiation was prefigured in a split in Russian social democracy in 1903 between Bolsheviks and Mensheviks, as the former, led by Lenin, argued for the model of an avant-garde **party** of professional revolutionaries, while the latter opted for the open model of a mass party. After the October Revolution of 1917 and the subsequent establishment of a 'communist' Soviet state, the passage towards communism came to be conceived along the lines of the Marxian model of a transitional yet necessary 'dictatorship of the proletariat', a concept originally coined by Blanqui. However, rather than approaching the ideal of a classless society, state communism brought about the emergence of state **bureaucracy** as the new ruling class. In this sense, state communism realized in an ironic way Engels's utopian ideal of a society in which rule over men was replaced by the 'administration of things' (an expression borrowed from the utopian socialist Saint-Simon), only that the latter turned out to be just another form of rule over men.

In the years after World War II, western European communist parties turned towards so-called 'Eurocommunism', a term associated with the leader of the Italian Communist Party Palmiro Togliatti (1893–1964) who drew significantly on the political and intellectual heritage of **Gramsci**. Communism was now defined as a nationally specific and, in Togliatti's words, 'polycentric' project (rather than a project oriented towards the Soviet Union). From the 1950s onwards, Western communist parties came to accept liberal institutions and the parliamentary system and entered political alliances with other democratic parties – with sometimes significant electoral success. Yet the dissolution of the Soviet Union and the subsequent world-wide **hegemony** of the Western liberal model of **democracy** seem to have signalled, for the time being, the end of communism as a political or intellectual force to be reckoned with.

References and further reading

Cabet, E. ([1840] 2003) *Travels in Icaria*. New York: Syracuse University Press.
Cole, G. D. H. (1953–60) *A History of Socialist Thought*, 5 vols. London: Macmillan.
Johnson, C. H. (1974) *Utopian Communism in France: Cabet and the Icariens, 1839–1851*. Ithaca, NY: Cornell University Press.
Lichtheim, C. (1961) *Marxism*. London: Routledge & Kegan Paul.
Pierson, C. (ed.) (1996) *The Marx Reader*. Oxford: Polity.

OLIVER MARCHART

COMMUNITARIANISM

Communitarianism as a current of moral, social and political thought emerged in the early 1980s as a critical reaction to John **Rawls**'s *A Theory of Justice* ([1971] 1999). It is associated with the work of Alasdair MacIntyre (1981), Michael Walzer (1983), Michael Sandel (1982) and Charles **Taylor** (1995), although there are some important differences between these authors. Inspired by Aristotle, Rousseau and Hegel, these authors' philosophical writings should also be distinguished from the political movement promoted by Amitai Etzioni and journals like *The Responsive Community*, which found some sociological support in the research conducted by Robert Bellah and others.

The different theories referred to as 'communitarian' share at least one assumption: that contrary to the liberal understanding of society as a voluntary **association** of individuals, **community** is the central reference point for any viable political, moral and social theory. This claim has implications on several levels.

First, ontologically, communitarians argue against the 'atomism' and **individualism** of liberal theory and its underlying conception of the person. They stress the social nature of individuals and their identities. The 'unencumbered self' (Sandel) which precedes its social **roles** and **values** presupposed by liberal theory does not exist.

Second, methodologically, communitarianism stresses the importance of historical and social contexts in explanation and justification. This contextualism leads to a critique of the liberal claim to neutrality and universality which communitarians regard as concealing a deep individualist bias. Differences in culturally mediated interpretive schemes preclude the possibility of neutrally justified and universally valid norms, in the sense of Kantian universalistic concepts of political thought. The content of norms is indissolubly linked to their particular and local contexts. This affects the possibility of social criticism: to be politically effective, normative content has to be internally rooted in the concrete

values and **traditions** of a particular community, not in abstract principles (Walzer). The related methodological claim of holism or **collectivism** is that communities and other collective social entities are not reducible to individual actors.

Third, normatively, communitarianism stresses the intrinsic value of community and of communal commitments, obligations and allegiances that come with membership and are not individually chosen. This evaluative background supports a critique of the disintegrating and delegitimizing effects of liberal individualism, which is seen as eroding the moral resources on which modern societies are depending. **Alienation** and the erosion of values and social bonds are often seen by communitarians as social pathologies that result from the premium placed on individual freedom and rights in Western societies. From this diagnosis they infer that social **integration** is dependent on shared **emotions**, beliefs, ideals, values and histories. Setting contextualism and particularism against universal norms and procedures means that principles of justice can only be justified with reference to particular historical communities and their specific self-understandings which are embodied in **institutions** and practices as a distinct 'way of life'.

Liberalism tends to emphasize individual **rationality**, **freedom** of choice and **autonomy** and sees the protection and enforcement of individual rights as the primary aim of the state, while relegating questions of the good life to the private domain for fear of paternalism. Communitarianism, on the other hand, understands the individual as a socially embedded agent, whose values are not purely private not merely matters of individual taste or preference – but shaped by the community. Accordingly, the primary aim of the state should be the promotion of the common good and a shared identity, a particular and substantive vision of how a community wants to live. The emphasis has shifted from rights, justice and procedures to duties, responsibilities and a vision of the good which is guiding individual and collective choice. Communitarianism takes up the older republican ideal of positive freedom and **civil society**, according to which the participation of citizens in the political life of the community is a good in itself. It should be clear that one can hold a communitarian position on one of these levels without necessarily being committed to any of the others.

Liberal counter-critiques of communitarianism have primarily attacked the validity of the communitarian conception of 'community'. They have argued that the boundaries of the 'We' invoked by communitarians are essentially contestable. The limits and the character of most communities are not easily defined. The ideal of **Gemeinschaft** (as opposed to *Gesellschaft*) is no longer a viable option for modern complex and heterogeneous societies under conditions of cultural and religious **pluralism**. In emphasizing the importance of belonging and recognition, the reaction of communitarians to multiculturalism tends to vacillate between a certain acceptance of difference and a longing for lost cultural homogeneity. Communitarians also have problems adopting a clear stance towards illiberal or authoritarian communities. They seem to be trapped in an inherently conservative and relativist position which precludes the possibility of cross-cultural critique.

Today there is less of a strict dividing line between hard-boiled liberals and traditionalist communitarians. Considerable agreement now prevails between the two camps; but key differences and disagreements still remain.

References and further reading

Avineri, S. and De-Shalit, A. (eds) (1992) *Communitarianism and Individualism*. Oxford: Oxford University Press.

Forst, R. (2002) *Contexts of Justice*. Berkeley, CA: University of California Press.

Kymlicka, W. (2001) *Contemporary Political Philosophy*. Oxford: Oxford University Press.

MacIntyre, A. ([1981] 1985) *After Virtue*. London: Duckworth.

Mulhall, S. and Swift, A. (1992) *Liberals and Communitarians*. Oxford: Blackwell.

Rawls, J. ([1971] 1999) *A Theory of Justice*. Cambridge, MA: Harvard University Press.

Sandel, M. (1982) *Liberalism and the Limits of Justice*. Cambridge: Cambridge University Press.

Taylor, C. (1995) *Philosophical Arguments*. Cambridge, MA: Harvard University Press.

Walzer, M. (1983) *Spheres of Justice*. New York: Basic Books.

ROBIN CELIKATES

COMMUNITY

Community, which derives from the Latin word *com* (meaning 'with' or 'together') and *unus* (the number one), is a widely used term, but is also a contested one. It features in sociological, anthropological and philosophical works, often with quite different meanings. The idea of community has witnessed a revival in recent years, with several new books bearing the title 'community'. Where the older literature on community was predominantly within classical sociology, the recent revival of community has largely stemmed from developments in other disciplines, such as anthropology and philosophy. With this recent **cultural turn** in theories of community comes a new emphasis on 'imagined communities' and 'symbolic communities'.

Ferdinand **Tönnies**'s *Gemeinschaft und Gesellschaft* (1887) is the classic account of community in sociological theory. In this theory, community is based on face-to-face relations but is in decline and replaced by **individualism** in a societal move that can be characterized as one from **status** to **contract**, from the village to the city, from **tradition** to **modernity and modernization**. One of the main themes in mid-twentieth-century sociology concerned the survival of community under the conditions of **industrialization** and **urbanism and** urbanization. Later sociological theories of community, such as those of the **Chicago School**, have generally focused on the small **group**, such as neighbourhoods or the small town. For sociologists, community usually designates social **interaction** in local contexts. Within sociology, especially British sociology, the subfield of community studies has made some important contributions to the study of community in terms of notions such as community regeneration and community health. Most sociologists no longer accept Tönnies's characterization of community as a settled world of tradition. Community can be the basis of political **action** and can be enabled rather than eroded by **individualism and individualization**.

Anthropological approaches stress the cultural nature of social groups. In an influential book, Cohen (1985) argued that community is a symbolic construction based on boundaries which define the relation of **self** to **other**. For Cohen, community is a cluster of symbolic and ideological map references with which the individual is socially oriented. This largely cultural approach to community also appears in Benedict Anderson's (1983) idea of 'imagined communities'. The idea of community has also figured in political philosophy and in particular in **communitarianism**. In this tradition, community designates **citizenship**. The rise of communitarianism, which is based on a political philosophy of community, is to be understood in the context of criticisms of **liberalism** and could be described as a move from contract back to community. With communitarianism a conception of community as **social capital** has also come to the fore: community is seen as an essential dimension of the working of democratic society based on public virtues such as **voluntarism**.

The new interest in community can also be explained by **globalization** and **postmodernism**. Globalization has opened up new conceptions of community beyond locality, such as cosmopolitan community and global community (see **cosmopolitanism**). With the Internet have come new ideas of virtual or cyber-community. Postmodernism has introduced the idea of community beyond unity. A postmodern community is not based on a common 'we' but on the desire for belonging and, moreover, such expressions of community are not based on secure reference points. Typically a postmodern community refers to life-style communities, to **sects**, New Age communities and various kinds of alternative communities.

Some of the main debates in social theory today on community concern three issues. The first is the relationship of community to tradition and modernity. In this context a central question concerns the nature of post-traditional community. A matter of some importance is the relation of individualism to community and the possibility of communities of dissent.

The second issue is the symbolic nature of community. Are communities real or imagined? According to some critics, the idea of community being constructed in the symbolization of boundaries leads to an overemphasis on the need for exclusion as a condition of community. The reality of most societies is some degree of **multiculturalism**, with the result that few communities are entirely homogenous.

The third issue is the rise of notions of 'community beyond propinquity' leading to debates about how important locality is for community and belonging and whether it is possible to sustain community without a shared sense of place. The tendency in the recent literature is to stress **networks** as the basis of community, leading to notions of personalized communities and communication communities. Some critics, on the other hand, argue against such conceptions of community, claiming that they never express what community is really about, namely, belonging in everyday situations.

While there is much disagreement as to whether community is rooted, bounded and territorial, there is general agreement that community can take post-traditional forms and is not endangered by individualism.

References and further reading

Amit, V. (ed.) (2002) *Realizing Community: Concepts, Social Relationships and Sentiments.* London: Routledge.
Amit, V. and Rapport, R. (eds) (2002) *The Trouble with Community: Anthropological Reflections on Movement, Identity and Collectivity.* London: Pluto.
Anderson, B. (1983) *Imagined Communities: Reflections on the Origin and Spread of Nationalism.* London: Verso.
Cohen, A. (1985) *The Symbolic Construction of Community.* London: Routledge.
Delanty, G. (2003) *Community.* London: Routledge.
Keller, S. (2003) *Community: Pursuing the Dream, Living the Reality.* Princeton, NJ: Princeton University Press.
Mayo, M. (2000) *Cultures, Communities, Identities.* London: Palgrave.

GERARD DELANTY

COMPARATIVE METHODS

With comparative methods, researchers interpret and explain the empirical variation of social phenomena over time (diachronic comparison) or at points in time (synchronic comparison). If a case study indicates that X causes Y, comparisons can discern whether and why this holds true more generally. While nearly all social science employs some form of diachronic comparison of cases over time, comparative methods principally stand for macrosocial research across **societies** and **states** in relatively simultaneous periods of time. Since **Tocqueville**'s study of the social prerequisites and effects of **democracy** in **America**, which he contrasted with socio-political orders in **Europe**, comparative methods have continuously been refined and advanced.

Debates in the **philosophy of social science**, concerning **epistemology** and **methods and methodology** have also raised questions of comparative methods, though mostly these have been pursued within the frameworks of (neo-)**positivism** or scientific **realism**. Comparative methods vary in the degree to which they rest on **explanation** or on **Verstehen** and on the degree to which they involve 'middle-range' theories or 'grand theory'. Their main aim is to establish and test statements about **causality** in macro-social affairs (see **micro-, meso- and macro-levels**). A central question is which cases to compare. Especially in comparisons with few cases, selection biases can lead to flawed conclusions. Biases can be minimized by comparing 'most similar' or 'most different' cases that share either many or few properties, which controls the sample selection (Przeworski and Teune 1970). Since the 1950s, a division between variable-oriented and case-oriented strategies has dominated comparative inquiry, with methodological divergences referring to the different approaches of **Durkheim** and **Weber** (**Smelser** 1976).

The methods of variable-oriented comparative research attempt to examine causal relations quantitatively among a limited number of variables across a large number of cases. They measure the effects of independent variables on dependent variables through statistical analysis and control. As few robust macrosocial correlations have been found, many quantitative comparisons focus on testing theoretical arguments and producing statements like 'X and Y correlate with an average probability of N per cent'. On the other hand, some powerful statistical correlations appear to exist; for example, between economic **development** and democracy (**Lipset** 1959), or between democracy and **peace** (Ray 1998). Strong correlations indicate causal effects without proving them. They constitute veto positions that need further explanation and tend to spur lively debates. Key problems of variable-oriented comparisons concern the **measurement** and the comparability of data across macrosocial units and over time (Ragin 1987: 57–68).

The methods of case-oriented comparative research try to investigate similarities and differences of historical outcomes qualitatively across a small number of cases, frequently leading to typification (see **type and typification**). Barrington **Moore**'s (1967) landmark study, for example, demonstrates comprehensively why and how **modernization** led to three different outcomes – democracy, fascist and communist dictatorships – in eight major countries. Case-oriented comparisons are affiliated with **historical sociology** and the major works of **Eisenstadt**, **Skocpol**, **Tilly**, **Bendix** and **Mann**. While the latter two are highly sceptical about general arguments, many researchers advocate that qualitative comparison should be oriented towards causal accounts and theory (King *et al.* 1994; Kiser and Hechter 1991). Often, J. S. **Mill**'s deductive-nomological methods of agreement and difference guide case-oriented comparative research (Ragin 1987: 36–44). These researchers propose searching for an explanatory variable that is the only common element across several different instances of a comparable social phenomenon. Thus, if two similar revolutions share no prior condition except agrarian poverty, then this has to be their cause. Or, if one state turns democratic and not the other, and the only different prior condition in the first case is industrialization, then this has to cause democratization. These methods are highly problematic because multiple causation is ignored and it is impracticable to consider all potential explanatory variables. Therefore, Mill's methods serve merely as preliminary means to facilitate the identification of possible routes of explanation. As they cannot establish a link between cause and effect, they have to be supplemented by efforts to examine social mechanisms through historical processes.

While variable-oriented quantitative methods have been associated with deductive explanations and general theory, and case-oriented qualitative methods with inductive interpretation and context-sensitive arguments, no method is intrinsically superior. Depending on research subject and objectives, both approaches offer distinct and sometimes complementary advantages. Whereas an investigation of social mechanisms across a few cases will profit from qualitative methods, quantitative methods are better for a focus on social effects across many cases. Frequently, combinations of both approaches tend to improve the quality of comparative social research (Ragin 1987; Rueschemeyer *et al.* 1992).

References and further reading

King, G., Keohane, R. O. and Verba, S. (1994) *Designing Social Inquiry*. Princeton, NJ: Princeton University Press.

Kiser, E. and Hechter, M. (1991) 'The Role of General Theory in Comparative-Historical Sociology', *American Journal of Sociology*, 97(1): 1–30.

Lipset, S. M. (1959) 'Some Social Requisites of Democracy: Economic Development and Political Legitimacy', *American Political Science Review*, 53(1): 69–105.

Mahoney, J. and Rueschemeyer, D. (eds) (2003) *Comparative Historical Analysis in the Social Sciences*. Cambridge: Cambridge University Press.

Moore, B. (1967) *Social Origins of Dictatorship and Democracy*. Boston: Beacon.

Perry, W. D. and Robertson, J. D. (2002) *Comparative Analysis of Nations: Quantitative Approaches*. Boulder, CO: Westview Press.

Przeworski, A. and Teune, H. (1970) *The Logic of Comparative Social Inquiry*. New York: Wiley-Interscience.

Ragin, C. (1987) *The Comparative Method*. Berkeley, CA: University of California Press.

Ray, J. L. (1998) 'Does Democracy Cause Peace?', *Annual Review of Political Science*, 1: 27–46.

Rueschemeyer, D., Stephens, E. and Stephens, J. (1992) *Capitalist Development and Democracy*. Chicago: University of Chicago Press.

Smelser, N. (1976) *Comparative Methods in the Social Sciences*. Englewood Cliffs, NJ: Prentice Hall.

PETER HÄGEL

COMPLEXITY

Complexity is one of the most distinctive constructs of scientific discourse in the twentieth century. It refers to a consciousness of the constitutive overtaxing of observers in the observation of something. In the face of complexity, social theory and other forms of theory seek ways in which observation can proceed and cope with complexity aiming at the reduction or management of its scope.

Scientific epistemology attributes complexity not to the observer but to the phenomenon observed. Complex phenomena consisting of many – i.e. of more than three or four – organized heterogeneous elements defy both causality and statistics (Weaver 1948). Complexity may be measured in terms of the number of heterogeneous elements, the number of possible relations between these elements, and the variation of these relations depending on context and time. Yet the outcome of this measure is a description that at any time will appear to fall short of its mark. Another way of putting this is to say that observers lack sufficient variability in their perceptual tools, language, or terminology to account for the actual variety of phenomena. Observers have to switch from understanding to *control*, and in order to compensate for the shortcomings of control, from error-control to information-control. They have to rely on a form of 'operational research' (Ashby 1958), which consists of comparing acceptable with non-acceptable results, in seeking to observe what occurs without giving reasons for what occurs; in never collecting more information than necessary for the task in hand; and always assuming that the system may change, and hence accepting that the only problems that can be solved are problems of the moment.

In the face of complexity, attention is focused on the selection of options of **action** and default, not on attempts to provide comprehensive accounts of phenomena.

The biological and social idea of control through information suggests a double principle of the operation of memory in dealing with complexity. Complexity theory realizes that constraints on selection bear on both sides of the relationship that produces knowledge: on the part of the phenomenon observed and on the part of the observer observing. The observer is as complex as the phenomenon under observation; yet while the observer lacks the requisite variety of observational apparatus to comprehend the complex phenomenon, the observer nevertheless attempts to deal with it (von Hayek 1967; Morin 1974). Observers are inherently selective in their choice of elements of perception, language and terminology, just as the phenomenon itself is inherently selective in its choice of elements and relations. Control by information defines the quality of information as a selected message from a set of possible other messages (Shannon and Weaver [1949] 1963). All selections are considered reductions, as much on the part of the observer as on the part of the phenomenon, and all reductions are considered with respect to their scope. The question of scope refers to the observer's ability to account for complexity while having to reduce it in order to select action and default.

Where complexity in scientific theory deals with the description of phenomena 'at the edge of chaos' (Waldrop 1992), complexity in social theory suggests research into the production and handling of selection, **contingency** and **risk** via the introduction of delay, ambivalence and oscillation (Leach 1976). Complexity forces meanings to assume forms that can account for both selection and the space of possible other selections. Social theory therefore looks for operations in **communication** and **culture** that are able not only to indicate by *distinction* but also to turn attention to the two sides of the distinction that is thereby produced (**Luhmann** 1984). Social theory dealing with complexity learns to include the fact of exclusion produced by distinctions, both with respect to phenomena under observation and with respect to theoretical architecture.

References and further reading

Ashby, W. R. (1958) 'Requisite Variety and its Implications for the Control of Complex Systems', *Cybernetica*, 1: 83–99.

Burke, K. ([1945] 1969) *A Grammar of Motives*. Berkeley, CA: University of California Press.

Leach, E. (1976) *Culture and Communication: The Logic by which Symbols are Connected*. Cambridge: Cambridge University Press.

Luhmann, N. ([1984] 1995) *Social Systems*. Stanford, CA: Stanford University Press.

Morin, E. (1974) 'Complexity', *International Social Science Journal*, 26: 555–82.

Shannon, C. E. and Weaver, W. ([1949] 1963) *The Mathematical Theory of Communication*. Urbana, IL: Illinois University Press.

von Hayek, F. A. (1967) 'The Theory of Complex Phenomena', in *Studies in Philosophy, Politics and Economics*. London: Routledge.

Waldrop, M. M. (1992) *Complexity: The Emerging Science at the Edge of Order and Chaos*. New York: Simon & Schuster.

Weaver, W. (1948) 'Science and Complexity', *American Scientist*, 36: 536–44.

DIRK BAECKER

COMTE, AUGUSTE (1798–1857)
French theorist

Comte is the founder of the terms 'sociology' and '**positivism**'. Tormented by the turmoil emanating from the French **Revolution** and the Napoleonic era, Comte sought to create a new, harmonious **society** by unifying people's beliefs and **emotions**. He designed positive philosophy – 'positivism' – to establish an intellectual **consensus**. Rejecting explanations based on God, first causes, and **metaphysical** essences, such as **Nature**, positivism embraced scientific **knowledge** based on empirical observations of concrete phenomena (see **science**). Outlined in the *Cours de philosophie positive* (1830–42), positivism included mathematics, astronomy, physics, chemistry, biology, and the new

science of society, which Comte dubbed 'sociology' in 1839. Comte's main sociological principle, the Law of Three Stages, expressed his belief that there were three eras of history: the theological, the metaphysical, and the positive. Divided into social statics (the study of order) and social dynamics (the study of **progress**), sociology was the keystone of the positivist system because it made all the sciences focus on the idea of Humanity (see **progress**). In the *Système de politique positive* (1851–54), Comte introduced a new secular **religion** to orient feelings toward the worship of Humanity. He called this the 'Religion of Humanity'. He devised a Positivist Calendar, new sacraments, and a cult of Woman to cultivate a religious culture that would help spread 'altruism' (a word he also coined), consolidate society, and usher in the new positive era. With followers in France, England, the United States, and Latin America, Comte influenced politics, sociology, the history of science, literature, philosophy, and historiography.

Major works

([1851–54] 1875–77) *System of Positive Polity*. London: Longmans & Green.

([1853] 1896) *The Positive Philosophy of Auguste Comte*. Ed. H. Martineau, 2 vols. London: Bell.

Further reading

Pickering, M. (1993) *Auguste Comte*. Cambridge: Cambridge University Press.

Scharf, R. (1995) *Comte after Positivism*. Cambridge: Cambridge University Press.

Wernick, A. (2001) *Auguste Comte and the Religion of Humanity*. Cambridge: Cambridge University Press.

MARY PICKERING

CONFLICT

Conflict is a crucial feature of all societies. It can be defined as struggle over power, scarce resources or values in which conflicting parties seek to realize their **interests**. The size of the parties involved in conflicts may range from two persons or more to **groups** or whole nations. Conflicts may range from latent oppositional interests to manifest conflicts like war (see **war and militarism**), where actors are collectively organized. Far from being an exclusively negative or destructive factor for **social relations**, conflicts are an essential feature of all kinds of social relations and may contribute to social **integration**. In modern societies this positive function can be seen as an effect of the institutionalization of violent social conflicts.

In pre-modern societies social conflicts were perceived as illegitimate, as they threatened a divine order of societal arrangements. However, **secularization** after the Renaissance decoupled human conduct from religious and moral demands, transforming the idea of social conflict. This process finds its expression in the works of early modern thinkers such as Niccolò Macchiavelli and Thomas Hobbes, as well as Charles Darwin in the nineteenth century. In the sixteenth century, Macchiavelli interpreted politics and war as rational enterprises that had to be decoupled from religious and moral demands. In *The Prince* ([1513] 1968) he defined conflict as a social medium governed by strategic rationality. Conflicts were conceptualized in terms of strategic games between rational actors. Writing against the background of violent civil war in seventeenth-century England, Thomas Hobbes identified the origin of conflict in human nature. In *Leviathan*, Hobbes held that in a state of nature man is a wolf to man since human beings seek to fulfil their own interests. In order to bring an end to war and devastating conflict, a theory of social **contract** must be devised. Individuals are to concede their right to violence to the sovereign, whose duty is to protect them and guarantee their survival. The sovereign's laws and decisions are to channel conflicts by establishing binding rules for all individuals and to enable them to live in peace. In the nineteenth century, Darwin's *The Origin of Species* (1897) was an important step towards a modern idea of conflict. In Social Darwinism the evolutionary notion of a 'survival of the fittest' was applied to human history and society. As conflict and competition were seen as driving forces of **social change**, bourgeois society appeared to be characterized by anarchic *laissez-faire* **markets**. It seemed that individual human survival depended on the realization of individual interests in conflictual relationships through the market.

With the advent of advanced industrial societies conflict becomes a chronic feature of everyday social life. From their inception, modern societies are inherently conflictual insofar as they emerge from revolutionary transformations. The industrial revolution radically transformed premodern society. The loosening of feudal bonds and the beginnings of **industrialization** set free huge numbers of peasants who then formed the ranks of the industrial **proletariat**. According to classical **Marxism**, early **capitalism** revolved around forms of deprivation and exploitation that generated class struggles between **bourgeoisie** and proletariat. Conflict between capital and labour still fundamentally characterizes capitalist societies today, though class conflict has for the most part been institutionalized in the economic and the political spheres.

While the industrial revolution triggered fierce social struggles, the French Revolution of the late eighteenth century put an end to the conflicts between **aristocracy** and an emerging bourgeoisie in the period of the rule of absolute monarchy. The struggle for political participation led to the institutionalization of both the **rights** of man and the rights of the citizen. However, as a civil, national, democratic and state-building revolution, the French Revolution also institutionalized some of the crucial cleavages in modern societies, such as those between citizens and non-citizens.

The conflictual nature of modern society is central to the ideas of the founding fathers of modern social theory. In the *Communist Manifesto*, **Marx** saw history as a history of class struggles, affirming the central precept of historical **materialism** that structural contradictions of a certain **mode of production** translate into class struggles that lead to a revolutionary transformation of society: social conflicts are thus conceptualized as the driving forces of history. In *Economy and Society* ([1921] 1978), Max **Weber** introduced conflict (*Kampf*) as a basic sociological term. Not only class struggle but also a variety of conflicts in different value spheres and societal terrains make conflict between classes, status groups, parties or communal groups a crucial feature of Weber's class theory and of his sociology of **authority**. Further, Weber's conception of open and closed social relations allowed for ways to analyze struggles over the monopolization of resources of social groups through the exclusion of others. This was seen by Weber as the driving mechanism of **stratification**.

While Marx and Weber analyzed social conflicts and their effects as inevitable aspects of society, **Durkheim** and **Simmel** focused on positive or negative *functions* of conflicts for society. For Durkheim, conflicts are a pathological phenomenon, a certain sickness of the social body resulting from unregulated spheres of society, thus posing a threat to its normative **integration**. In *The Division of Labor in Society* ([1902] 1977), Durkheim analyzed both class struggle and the conflicts between employers and employees in the capitalist enterprise as two abnormal forms of the division of labour (see **normal and pathological**).

In contrast, Simmel in *Conflict* ([1908] 1955) stresses the positive functions of conflict and their social productivity; that is, the way groups construct oppositional perspectives and the way conflict generates identities among members of the groups involved. Simmel saw conflict as a form of sociation, stressing that 'a certain amount of discord, inner divergence and outer controversy, is organically tied up with the very elements that ultimately hold the group together' (ibid.: 17–18). Simmel argued, first that conflict creates social relations where no relations existed before, thus itself being a kind of social relation and second, that conflict generates rules and norms arising out of the expectations that each party forms of the other's actions.

These contrasting interpretations of the functions of social conflict divided modern social theory in the twentieth century. In *The Social System* ([1951] 1991) Talcott **Parsons** followed the Durkheimian perspective stressing the significance of institutionalized values and norms upheld by socialized actors who are motivated to live according to certain role requirements, thus securing the consensual operation of the social system. Ralf **Dahrendorf** criticized Parsons for stressing **consensus** as an effect of the normative integration of modern society (Dahrendorf 1961). In opposition to consensus theory, Dahrendorf developed a middle-range theory that allowed a way to analyze all kinds of social conflicts as essential for the survival of societies. He argued that social life is inherently conflictual, that conflicts are not only necessary but are essential for society and are the driving forces of **social change**.

Lewis A. Coser criticized both Parsons and Dahrendorf for their one-sided conceptions of social conflicts. Coser (1956) was concerned with the role played by conflict for social stability. In *The Functions of Social Conflict* he reinterpreted Simmel's approach in a functionalist perspective in order to detect the productive effects of conflicts in the triggering of structural change, or the interplay of social change and stability.

The end of the Cold War and the demise of the Soviet Union did not mean the end of conflict in history. Since the last decade of the twentieth century, fierce racial, ethnic and religious conflicts have led to ethnic cleansing and genocide. New conflicts and **wars** have been triggered by strategic and geopolitical interests at the beginning of the twenty-first century, as disruptive conflicts for the distribution of natural resources have only just begun. To understand and explain these new conflicts of both interests and values and to find institutional arrangements for their solution is today's task for conflict sociology.

References and further reading

Collins, R. (1975) *Conflict Sociology: Toward an Explanatory Science*. London: Academic Press.
Coser, L. A. (1956) *The Functions of Social Conflict*. Glencoe, IL: Free Press.
Dahrendorf, R. (1961) 'Elemente einer Theorie des sozialen Konflikts', in R. Dahrendorf, *Gesellschaft und Freiheit*. München: Piper, pp. 197–235.
Darwin, C. (1897) *The Origin of Species: By Means of Natural Selection, or the Preservation of Favoured Races in the Struggle for Life*. London: John Murray.
Durkheim, E. ([1902] 1977) *The Division of Labor in Society*. New York: Free Press.
Hobbes, T. ([1651] 1997) *Leviathan: The Matter, Form and Power of a Commonwealth, Ecclesiasticall and Civill*. New York: W. W. Norton.
Huntington, S. P. (1996) *The Clash of Civilizations and the Remaking of World Order*. New York: Simon & Schuster.
Macchiavelli, N. ([1513] 1968) *The Prince*. New York: Da Capo.
Marx, K. and Engels, F. ([1848] 1998) *The Communist Manifesto*. New York: Verso.
Parsons T. ([1951] 1991) *The Social System*. London: Routledge.
Simmel, G. ([1908] 1955) *Conflict and the Web of Group Affiliations*. Glencoe, IL: Free Press.
Weber, M. ([1921] 1978) *Economy and Society*. Berkeley, CA: University of California Press.

JÜRGEN MACKERT

CONSENSUS

'Consensus' in sociology refers to a condition of active or passive agreement between several parties. Its antonyms are dissent and **conflict**. Proponents of the 'conflict model'

in American sociology, who regard conflict as the organizing principle of social reality, typically associate the concept of consensus with **structural-functionalist** thinking, which they see as representing a 'consensus model'. However, like 'conflict', 'consensus' is a mostly descriptive term, and therefore cannot be considered an organizing principle or ultimate explanation of reality. Conflict and consensus represent the two ends of a continuum along which human relations may be seen as varying at all times. But the postulation of one or the other end as dominant at any moment, even if empirically accurate, only describes the situation; it does not explain it.

The most detailed treatment of the idea of consensus is to be found in the writings of Edward Shils. According to Shils (1975), consensus is agreement in regard to the beliefs constitutive of the value centre of a **society** and propagated by its institutional centre. It is a necessary element of social integration and therefore a salient characteristic of any existing society. Only complete disintegration of a social entity can be characterized exclusively by dissent, and only in a society in the process of disintegration may dissent or conflict predominate over consensus. Consensus, however, is rarely complete, constant or fully articulated or involving the entire membership of the society in question. Rather, it is partial, intermittent, vague, and uneven across different social **groups**. It is most developed and uniform in modern societies whose members have a clear sense of nationality (see **nationalism**). Indeed, according to Shils, inclusive national **identity** or 'the sense of unity', is both a precondition and an essential component of consensus. In contrast, 'underdeveloped countries' are characterized by 'consensual underdevelopment', and their 'dissensual state' is attributed to the lack of 'a bond constituted by their residence in the larger bounded territory', and to the fact that at best only **elites** have 'a sense of common nationality'. Shils's structural-functionalist orientation is relevant here insofar as he explains the low level of national consciousness in underdeveloped societies by reference to lack of 'ecological integration', and a lack of 'commonly held body of culture', sponsored by an effective centralized **state**.This account can be compared to some extent to the work of Karl Deutsch and Ernest **Gellner** on nationalism

Structural functionalism is also evident in Shils's account of the processes by which consensus is formed, and hence in his account of **social change** in general. But there are also some affinities between his structural-functionalist approach and Marxian historical **materialism**.

From this angle, consensus is a function of the structure of opportunities and material interests underpinning them, making it comparable to ideological superstructure, although it lacks the rigorously coherent pattern of explicitly held and systematically espoused beliefs characteristic of ideology in a specific sense.

At the same time, when Shils writes that 'consensus maintains public order. . .by fostering of a readiness to accept peaceful modes of adjudicating disagreements among those who have a sense of their mutual affinity or identity', it appears that he is depicting what **Durkheim** referred to as 'pre-contractual elements'. In agreement with Durkheim, Shils regards modern societies as better integrated than traditional ones. However, for Shils, the stronger integration of modern societies is a function of their greater consensuality, i.e. of the degree of agreement in regard to central beliefs, whereas for Durkheim, such consensuality – the uniformity of the *conscience collective* – is the characteristic of traditional societies, reflected in the mechanical nature of their **solidarity** based on the **integration** of more or less identical segments. The differences between the two theorists and their concepts here rests on the fact that where Durkheim emphasizes the nature of

ideas on which integration is based, Shils stresses the measurable, quantitative aspect of their combination, relationship, or **structure** – the degree of their uniformity.

References and further reading

Durkheim, E. ([1902] 1977) *The Division of Labor in Society*. New York: Free Press.

Giegel, H. -J. (ed.) (1992) *Kommunikation und Konsens in modernen Gesellschaften*. Frankfurt am Main: Suhrkamp

Parsons, T. and Shils, E. A. (eds) (1951) *Toward a General Theory of Action*. Cambridge, MA: Harvard University Press.

Shils, E. (1975) 'Introduction' and 'Consensus', in E. Shils, *Center and Periphery: Essays in Macrosociology*. Chicago: University of Chicago.

Weber, M. ([1921] 1978) *Economy and Society*. Berkeley, CA: University of California Press.

THOMAS SCHNEIDER

CONSERVATISM

Outwardly conservative writers typically suggest that conservatism is nothing as vulgar as a political **ideology**. Conservatism is often outlined as a particular disposition that favours what is known and trusted, over and above that which is unknown. Central to any political and social understanding of conservatism, therefore, is a concern with managing political change, though it would be incorrect to say that conservatism opposes change itself. Equally central to this assumption, as various authors have noted, is an understanding of the extra-human origins of the social order. Traditionalist conservatism has often distilled this through the lens of a God-given hierarchy, which could, on the one hand, justify obedience to earthly powers because by so doing, one was really obeying the biblical injunction that earthly obedience will lead to heavenly reward (see **tradition**). Such arguments about hierarchy have often also been couched in more **naturalist** terms, effecting comparisons between the hierarchies of the natural world and the position of a particular class of heroic leaders or governors, capable of knowing or representing the interests of society at large.

Within these broad schemas sits an account not only of natural **inequality**, but also a more strongly focused assessment that human beings are both imperfect and imperfectible. This lends itself to what Anthony Quinton (1982) termed a conservative concern with the politics of imperfection. A corollary of this is the often-noted hostility to rationalism and rationalist planning within conservatism. This should not be confused with the argument that conservatism is irrational; on the contrary, it is often the case that conservatism tends to view other political ideologies as themselves irrational, for neglecting the fundamental relationship between change, hierarchy and imperfection. One can therefore delineate particular strands within conservatism that have been important in terms of thinking about a genealogy of this set of ideas.

The most elementary forms of conservatism discuss the religious basis of the social and political order. Developing and modifying a Christian argument about the corrupted soul after the fall from paradise, a profoundly pessimistic view of the human condition can be derived from a basis in original sin, which lends itself to the idea that humans stand in need of a redeemer. Alone we are weak and corrupted. The corruption and degradation of humans in society, rather than in one's properly natural state, were themes noticeably developed by Rousseau, whose own work contained, among other themes, Stoic and Augustinian elements. But when one sees how politics develops when underpinned by such a set of beliefs, it is clear that political activity will tend to try to reconcile the hugely divergent **interests** of the human **community**. Rousseau's solution to this was the social **contract**. It is precisely such a type of politics that conservatism suggests can never be achieved. The idea

that politics can be rationally planned and can overcome irreconcilable conflicts of interests is, on this reading, nothing more than a chimera. This is why many writers who have been interpreted as conservative are portrayed as reactionary, because often one finds in such writers' work a relatively backward-looking social philosophy that paints an idealized picture of the past as something to be longed for.

According to most conservatives, there is no end state, however desirous or otherwise, whether behind us or in the future, that is capable of being achieved or being reinstated. Here, the classical metaphor of the ship of state is usually discussed to suggest that all that politics and government should be concerned with is keeping the ship afloat; there is no final destination. Michael Oakeshott, typically understood as a major British conservative philosopher, outlined this famously in an essay entitled, 'On Being Conservative' (Oakshott, 1991). His own position, however, was more subtle than this, and he is probably best thought of as a sceptic in politics, rather than a conservative. Similarly, a critique of rationalist political planning played a major part in the writings of Edmund Burke, typically portrayed as the founding father of modern conservatism for his coruscating polemic against the French **Revolution**. Yet Burke was a Whig, interested in the relationship between **property**, **democracy** and liberty. In much the same way as many French liberals after the Revolution, Burke questioned the validity of applying an 'ancient' model of politics alongside a distinctly 'modern' model of a commercial and economical society. Only a few years before, he had been a keen supporter of the American colonists in their struggle for independence. What this means is that the genealogy of conservatism is more complex than the attribution of overly simplified positions to many of its apparent advocates.

What is typically understood by conservatism is a clear opposition to **liberalism**, which writers from Joseph de Maistre and Thomas Carlyle to Carl **Schmitt** have decried for its apparent **individualism** and political promiscuities. What is needed in this variation of conservatism is, instead, a strong leader, typically a monarch, capable of maintaining traditional hierarchies. Nevertheless, although writers such as de Maistre were hostile to the idea that a political **constitution** could be created *a priori*, many of the touchstones of liberal political philosophy, such as the rule of law, separation of **powers**, political independence, defence of private property, and individual and **group rights**, are similarly foundational to conservatism. Where writers such as de Maistre differed from Burke was in the providential interpretation of the French Revolution, and the subsequent descent into terror conceived of as divine retribution.

Conservative or 'aristocratic' liberals, by contrast, tend to highlight the dangers of the development of political **equality** under a modern liberal society in particular, and it is this wariness that has made students of J. S. **Mill** and Alexis de **Tocqueville**, in particular, think about the relationship between conservatism and liberalism in more subtle terms than a binary opposition (see **binary**). But binary oppositions have tended to structure the nature of modern political debate between conservatism and liberalism since the French Revolution. As Albert Hirschman (1992) has noted, political rhetoric since 1789 can be analyzed in terms of rhetorics of intransigence, which pit broadly conservative and reactionary politics against progressive movements for change. Reactionary rhetoric, according to Hirschman, comprises three distinct elements. First, the futility thesis suggests that to attempt to undertake political change is futile because it neglects the natural order of social life. Second, the jeopardy thesis, which fears change because of its dangers; and third, the perversity thesis, which states that change will always lead to unanticipated and most likely unfavourable situations.

Counter-posed to these **ideal types**, Hirschman suggests that progressive political thinkers have opposed conservatism by simply pursuing a politics based on the necessity, desirability and possibility of reform.

One of the key differences between liberalism and certain variants of conservatism, however, and which represents another major strand of conservative thinking, is a focus on the organic unity of political society. In some ways, one can trace this organicism through the more recent debates between liberalism and **communitarianism**, where the legacy of **Hegelianism and Neo-Hegelianism** is particularly important. In the conservative tradition, organicism is associated with writers such as Samuel Taylor Coleridge, who perceived the idea of a natural social balance maintained by a national educated **class**, which was itself underpinned by an organic idea of the constitution of a nation that grows and develops according to the dictates of reason. Similarly, in Burke's focus on the natural relationships between the dead, the living and the not yet born, one finds other important organicist assessments. As Noël O'Sullivan (1976) has suggested, such organicism remained a profoundly important legacy for conservatism as it developed through various Romantic writers (see romanticism). In the British tradition, conservatism has mainly presented itself as a pragmatic, sceptical and (most unconvincingly) as a non-ideological mode of thinking about modern politics.

References and further reading

Burke, E. ([1789] 1982) *Reflections on the Revolution in France.* London: Penguin.

Carlyle, T. ([1837] 1868) *The French Revolution.* London: Everyman.

Coleridge, S. T. ([1830] 1976) *On the Constitution of Church and State.* Princeton, NJ: Princeton University Press.

De Maistre, J. ([1797] 1994) *Considerations on France.* Cambridge: Cambridge University Press.

Femia, J. (2001) *Against the Masses*. Oxford: Oxford University Press.

Freeden, M. (1997) *Ideologies and Political Theory*. Oxford: Oxford University Press.

Hirschman, A. (1992) *The Rhetoric of Reaction*. Cambridge, MA: Harvard University Press.

Mannheim, K. ([1925] 1986) *Conservatism: A Contribution to the Sociology of Knowledge*. London: Routledge.

Muller, J. Z. (1997) *Conservatism*. Princeton, NJ: Princeton University Press.

Oakeshott, M. (1991) *Rationalism in Politics*. Indianapolis: Liberty Fund.

O'Sullivan, N. (1976) *Conservatism*. London: Dent.

Quinton, A. (1982) *The Politics of Imperfection: The Religious and Secular Traditions of Conservative Thought in England from Hooker to Oakeshott*. London: Faber and Faber.

Vincent, A. (1994) 'British Conservatism and the Problem of Ideology', *Political Studies*, 42(2): 204–27.

DUNCAN KELLY

CONSTITUTION

The concept of a 'constitution' in Western civilization dates back 2500 years, initially referring to the divine legal order, which contained not only political institutions and powers but also social and economic structures including basic ethical norms. The historical variety of constitutions as 'lex fundamentalis', 'status' and 'res publica', still present in Montesquieu's *Spirit of the Laws* (1748), come to be narrowed down under the conditions of **modernity** to the basic legal order of a **polity**. Since the introduction of written constitutions in the era of the democratic **revolutions** of the USA and France, the concept has been limited to its legal connotations: the formation and organization of the **state** or government, the distribution and balance of powers, and the guarantee of fundamental human and civic **rights** of individuals. The turn of the nineteenth century marks the beginning of modern constitutionalism. Since then constitutions have developed and proliferated as a widely copied and varied pattern for societies to design and

identify their polity according to republican and democratic principles based on the rule of law (see **republic**; **democracy**).

Historically four constitutional archetypes can be distinguished: constitutions as (1) contract, (2) manifesto, (3) programme, and (4) law.

With respect to constitutions as **contract**, one must distinguish between the social compact as a virtual social union and establishment of government in the realm of political philosophy (notably Hobbes, Locke, and Rousseau), on the one hand, and 'real contracts' structuring the *pouvoir constituant* as a legal relationship between the different contracting parties ('We, the Undersigned'), such as states, on the other hand. While philosophical contractualism focuses on constitutional rights and principles, real (federal) contracts tend to regulate the institutional modalities of government and the distribution of powers between the member states and their union, such as the Constitution of the United States (without its amendments) or the German Imperial Constitution of 1871.

With respect to constitutions as *manifesto* political manifestos, such as the French Declaration of Rights of 1789, strictly speaking, do not qualify as constitutions because according to the understanding of their authors, they are not meant to constitute something new, but rather solemnly declare an established truth ('That all men are by nature equally free and independent, and have certain inherent rights') or they assert an assumed **consensus** about civil and political rights, basic common values or a form of government. Compared to other constitutions, the normative speech act of a constitutional manifesto is limited to declaring common values and principles, rather than specific laws. Constitutions as *programme* or *plan* are germane to the socialist world of the former communist states. Constitutions were linked to the laws of scientific socialism and functioned as reflections of the socio–economic and political development at a given developmental stage and, therefore, had to be revised according to the imperatives of political ideology. Programmatic socialist constitutions can be described as semantic concessions to modern constitutionalism and contained catalogues of rights devoid of any meaningful function as guarantees of freedom and limitations of state power.

Finally, constitutions as *law* or supreme law of the land has come to dominate modern constitutional history. Constitutions as law must be considered the superior archetype because they can easily be integrated into a legal order and may integrate elements of the other three archetypes – notably manifesto speech acts, as embodied especially in preambles, and programmatic norms such as the promotion of gender equality or the protection of the natural environment. As a matter of rule, the constitutional elites invoke the People as *pouvoir constituant* (e.g. 'We the People') and the constitution-making process anticipates the republican-democratic body of legislative rules which it seeks to constitute, thus trying to solve the paradox of a 'creatio ex nihilo'.

With regard to their structure, modern constitutions follow a similar format, which is designed to address the essential problems of social coexistence and self-government in and through a nationally organized political system. First, bills of rights, complemented by rule of law principles and procedures, answer questions of justice by establishing equal freedom for individual and collective self-determination and by limiting the legitimate powers of government. Second, constitutional values and duties respond to the question of the good life in society, thus delineating the always contested contours of a commonweal or shared public interest. Third, provisions for political organization usually constitute the dominant structural element. They answer the central question of practical political wisdom concerning how to establish, run

and control the democratic state, its institutions, personnel and decision-making procedures. Fourth, the constructive element of modern constitutions refers to those provisions which relate to the amendment and revision of constitutions and to their validity, including the constitutional review of laws and the judicial redress of constitutional grievances. With these provisions constitutions refer to themselves as authoritative texts, thus establishing the reflexivity and modernity of constitutions, the relative sanctity of their text in a secularized cultural environment, and the potential prestige of constitutional courts.

References and further reading

Arendt, H. (1963) *On Revolution*. New York: Viking.

Frankenberg, G. (1996) *Die Verfassung der Republik*. Baden–Baden: Nomos.

Gough, J. W. (1955) *Fundamental Law in English Constitutional History*. Oxford: Clarendon Press.

Grimm, D. (1990) 'Verfassung II', in: O. Brunner, W. Conze and R. Koselleck (eds), *Geschichtliche Grundbegriffe: Historisches Lexikon zur politisch-sozialen Sprache in Deutschland vol. 1 VI*. Stuttgart: Klett-Gotta.

Preuß, U. K. (ed.) (1994) *Zum Begriff der Verfassung: Die Ordnung des Politischen*. Frankfurt am Main: Suhrkamp.

Schmitt, C. (1928) *Verfassungslehre*. München/ Leipzig: Duncker & Humblot.

Van Caenegem, R.C (1995). *A Historical Introduction to Western Constitutional Law*. Cambridge: Cambridge University Press.

GÜNTER FRANKENBERG

CONSTRUCTIVISM

Constructivism is not a clear-cut but a rather unspecific and variegated concept. Strictly speaking, all sociological thinking has a constructivistic nucleus. Insofar as sociology always underlines the importance of cultural and historical relativity and is concerned in a general sense with dismantling normative ideas of the autonomous subject, then social reality is always conceptualized in sociology as a constructed reality. In a narrower sense, however, constructivism represents a way of thinking which explicitly thematizes cognitive operations and social practices as processes of construction (see also **social constructionism**).

One of the most widespread versions of social constructivism stems from Peter Berger's and Thomas Luckmann's *The Social Construction of Reality* (1966)(see Berger and Luckmann). The thesis of the book is that all social reality is to be regarded as a construct of everyday practices and routines. Berger and Luckmann explain how a social order that is manifestly constructed by human practices can be experienced as an objective, external, and in some sense 'natural' reality. Central notions for Berger and Luckmann are processes of **institutionalization**, **objectivation** and **legitimation**.

Epistemological constructivism refers to different sources. One thread starts from the Kantian idea of reality as a cognitive process and cognitive construction. Ernst von Glaserfeld's (1987, 1995) 'radical constructivism' emphasizes this Kantian theme that we cannot observe any reality empirically without cognitively salient acts of observation. Another extension of this approach is Jean **Piaget**'s empirical cognitive psychology. A further thread leads to biological theories of autopoiesis (Maturana and Varela 1980) in **cybernetics** (von Foerster 1981) and to **systems theory** (**Luhmann** 1995). The connecting theme of these approaches is the idea of cognitive closure as taking into account the position of the observer. Cognitive or operative closure means that any contact with reality in cognitively operating units such as brains, consciousness, organisms, or **social systems** is cognitive contact. Epistemological constructivism in this regard does not reject the idea of the independence of reality but it questions the idea of the accessibility of reality. The main subject of this thinking is the position of observers, who construct reality through observation, even as they react to changes in their environment.

Since Karl **Mannheim**'s reconstruction of different types of knowledge as being conditioned by the class positions or interests of different actors, the sociology of knowledge has been attacking the idea of knowledge as something independent of social processes of knowledge formation. Whereas the sociology of knowledge focused at first on political attitudes or on everyday knowledge in the tradition of Alfred **Schutz**, more recent interests have been directed towards scientific knowledge. The sociology of scientific knowledge has shown empirically how science not only produces its own subjective perspectives, but also produces the objects of observation in measuring devices, oscillographs or in the modelling of theories. Therefore the main subject of this research is the laboratory as a social reality in which a scientific reality comes to be constructed (Knorr–Cetina 1981, 1999; Latour and Woolgar 1986)(see **science** and **social studies of science**).

The most ambitious challenge of constructivism for social theory is the problem of self-application. If all knowledge is to be regarded as an effect of the observer, this must also be true of the sociological observer. Therefore, social theory must consider that the sociological apparatus of observation produces the very reality it deals with.

References and further reading

Berger, P. and Luckmann, T. (1966) *The Social Construction of Reality*. Garden City, NY: Doubleday.

Foerster, H. von (1981) *Observing Systems*. Seaside, CA: Intersystems.

Knorr–Cetina, K. D. (1981) *The Manufacture of Knowledge: An Essay on the Constructivist and Contextual Nature of Science*. Oxford: Pergamon Press.

Knorr–Cetina, K. D. (1999) *Epistemic Cultures: How the Sciences Make Knowledge*. Cambridge, MA: Harvard University Press.

Latour, B. and Woolgar, S. (1986) *Laboratory Life: The Construction of Scientific Facts*, 2nd edn. Princeton, NJ: Princeton University Press.

Luhmann, N. ([1984] 1995) *Social Systems*. Stanford, CA: Stanford University Press.

Maturana, H. R. and Varela, F. J. (1980) *Autopoiesis and Cognition*. Dordrecht: D. Reidel.

Von Glasersfeld, E. (1987) *The Construction of Knowledge: Contributions to Conceptual Semantics*. Seaside, CA: Intersystems.

Von Glasersfeld, E. (1995) *Radical Constructivism: A Way of Knowing and Learning*. London: Falmer Press.

ARMIN NASSEHI

CONSUMPTION

While consumption has featured significantly in modern Western thought since at least the eighteenth century, it is only in the past few decades that it has been regarded as a socially consequential object of study. Contemporary interest in consumption rests on three broad premises, each of which places **culture** at the centre of social processes, and in ways that have made consumption studies almost paradigmatic of the **cultural turn** in social thought.

First, consumption is central to social and cultural reproduction (see **social reproduction**). All acts of consumption are profoundly cultural. Even ostensibly 'natural' and mundane processes such as eating invoke, mediate and reproduce those structures of **meaning** and practice through which social identities are formed and through which **social relations** and **institutions** are maintained and changed over time (see **identity**).

The second premise has been a concern with the 'consumer culture' as a characterization of the modern **market** society (Slater 1997; Slater and Tonkiss 2001), and more specifically as an increasingly central feature of what has come to be known as the postmodern (Featherstone 1991) (see **postmodernism and postmodernity**). Consumption as a cultural process may be central to all human society, but only the

modern West came to define itself as a consumer culture or consumer society. The underlying claim here is that, as a result of **modernization**, involving processes such as marketization, the decline of traditional status systems and the rise of cultural and political pluralism, private market-based choice has become increasingly central to social life (see **market**).

Third, it is partly through the study of consumption that we have come to better understand the role of culture in the constitution of economic processes and institutions. Consumption is not a cultural endpoint or addition to 'truly' economic processes of production or formally modelled **market** exchange, nor can it be reduced to quantitative measures of 'demand'. On the contrary, the study of consumption cultures leads us to examine the construction of objects, exchanges and relationships across a wide range of interconnected sites and processes.

Today, consumption has come to represent the site at which culture and economy most dramatically converge. Historically, however, consumption has marked a central point of division between economy and culture – indeed, the critical stalemate that stymied thinking about consumption until quite recently was structured by an opposition between economy and culture. On the one hand, liberal traditions (including neoclassical economics) assumed the autonomy of consumption processes from economic ones. On the other, critical traditions – of both the right and left – have tended to regard consumption as the site of major incursions of economic processes into culture and everyday life. For them, modern consumer culture marks the dominance of market exchange and industrial process over human life and meanings, apparently rendering them inauthentic. In such perspectives, the market drives a wedge through the previously organic relation between **production** and consumption, and monetary values become the only ones that now adjudicate social worth and distribute social goods.

The most commanding formulation of market-mediated culture as **alienation** is undoubtedly that of Marx's analysis of 'commodity fetishism' (see **commodity and commodification**). A critique or elaboration of the processes of commodification, fetishism has grounded much of the subsequent work on consumption. This is obvious in the case of the theme of **reification** in western Marxism – for example in **Lukács**'s or **Adorno**'s conception of the social landscape appearing to individuals as a consumable spectacle, rather than as an historical product of human action. Less obviously related to commodity fetishism are more recent postmodern approaches, such as that of **Baudrillard**, in which consumption appears as a spectacle of signs detached from other social relations and processes.

Post-Fordism represents another mode of articulating and stabilizing the relation between economy and culture, production and consumption. The idea of post-Fordism converges with broader characterizations of socio-economic change in the direction of increasing 'dematerialization' in which commodities are defined, produced and distributed more in relation to their signification than their materiality. The upshot is the increasing centrality of cultural processes and logics within both production and consumption and their articulation.

The contemporary research agenda that is explicitly concerned with cultures of consumption has drawn on traditions and methodologies for thinking about how meaningful goods play a part in the reproduction of **everyday** life. Three major traditions are important here. First, the various schools of **semiotics** provided a methodology for treating all objects as signs within a social circulation of meaning, and ones capable of bearing significations that were irreducible to the functionality of goods.

Second, in the tradition of material culture studies in anthropology, function is only one aspect of the meaning of goods. Rather, goods and their uses reflect, communicate and are instrumental in reproducing cosmologies (Douglas 1979). Third, we might point to the tradition of cultural studies, in many respects a development of both semiotics and of the anthropological notion of culture as the meaningful patterning of a whole way of life.

Consumption is therefore always an active cultural process. It was Thorstein Veblen ([1899] 1953) who pointed out the strategic role of consumption practices in establishing social distinction. For Veblen, the entire point of a status symbol was that it was a pure sign, serving no function other than to indicate one's wealth (see **status**). As often noted (e.g. Miller 1987) this argument is reflected in the work of **Bourdieu**, in which battles to legitimate particular criteria and hierarchies of cultural value and taste are central to the exercise of power. Bourdieu, however, treats cultural consumption as part of the *constitution* of **class** and **power** difference, not just as reflecting existing class structures rooted in economics.

For Baudrillard, as for Veblen and Bourdieu, the crucial aspect of consumption is the object as sign and hence as a marker of social distinction. 'Function' itself becomes just another sign, rather than the location of the object's authenticity. Ultimately what we really buy into in any act of consumption is not the object and its uses but rather the overall system of **representations** and our position in the matrix of differences it maps out and signals to others. Baudrillard might be interpreted as fitting in well within the older traditions of mass culture critique, as in the end it points to the complete dominance of a totalistic 'spectacle'.

Whatever contemporary consumption studies might owe Baudrillard, they have tended to develop in a different direction, treating the 'aestheticization of everyday life', the fragmentation of **identity** and apparently decreasing relevance of older social divisions as the opportunity to treat consumer culture as a kind of ironic and hedonistic playground. **Bauman** (1990) and Maffesoli (1996), for example, emphasize the neo-tribalism of consumer culture in which densely meaningful goods are like costumes in which people dress up in order to enact their current elective but flexible social memberships and allegiances. The very profusion and motility of signs have more generally been taken to suggest the opening of spaces for consumer creativity, or resistance and rebellion. Consumption is an always active process of assimilation, hence also one that is unpredictable and undetermined.

Contemporary work on global consumer cultures has developed new conceptualiza tions and agendas. Early arguments about a global consumer culture echoed the structure of mass consumption/mass culture theories, often in the form of 'Americanization' theses, which were concerned with homogenized global culture. Like earlier arguments about mass consumption, some assumed the existence of 'authentic' indigenous cultures existing before the intrusion of consumer culture. More recent work has emphasized that **globalization** of consumer culture is often heterogeneous and uneven, and that supposedly pristine consumption cultures are always entangled in wider social **networks**. The older image of American **domination** has given way to a concern with competition between regional blocs (for example, the power of Asian production and consumption) and conflict directly provoked by consumerism as a value system (see e.g. Castells 1997, on the resurrection of traditionalist identities). Appadurai (1990) offers a complex attempt to map the different economic, social, political and cultural flows that generate this unevenness. Finally, contemporary approaches to the globalization of consumption

have been marked by a more general stress on the enculturation of the economy and on notions of the **information** or **network** society.

It has been accepted, that consumption is a significant issue of cultural, social and economic reproduction, not to be treated as private, trivial or natural. Contemporary research on consumption displays an increasing concern with consumption as habitual, routine and embedded in the practical reproduction of everyday life, and has renewed concern with the relationship between consumption and persistent social structures of **power** and **inequality**.

Having asserted consumption as a significant social instance in its own right, particularly against the 'productivist bias' in much previous social thought, the research tendency is now to reconnect consumption and production, focusing on continuities and interconnections, not least through more integrated accounts of markets and market behaviours (e.g. du Gay 1997; Slater and Tonkiss 2001). This tendency has been given a considerable impetus by the rise of the Internet and e-commerce which evidences blurred boundaries between production and consumption as well as an ever more globalized reach for both.

References and further reading

Appadurai, A. (1990) 'Disjuncture and Difference in the Global Cultural Economy', *Theory, Culture & Society*, 7: 295–310.

Baudrillard, J. (1981) *For a Critique of the Political Economy of the Sign*. St Louis, MO: Telos.

Bauman, Z. (1990) *Thinking Sociologically*. Oxford: Blackwell.

Bourdieu, P. (1984) *Distinction: A Social Critique of the Judgement of Taste*. Cambridge, MA: Harvard University Press.

Castells, M. (1997) *The Power of Identity*. Oxford: Blackwell.

Douglas, M. (1979) *The World of Goods: Towards an Anthropology of Consumption* (with Baron Isherwood). New York: Basic Books.

du Gay, P. (ed.) (1997) *Production of Culture, Cultures of Production*. London: Sage.

Featherstone, M. (1991) *Consumer Culture and Postmodernism*. London: Sage.

Maffesoli, M. (1996) *The Time of the Tribes*. London: Sage.

Miller, D. (1987) *Material Culture and Mass Consumption*. Oxford: Blackwell.

Slater, D. R. (1997) *Consumer Culture and Modernity*. Cambridge: Polity Press.

Slater, D. R. and Tonkiss, F. (2001) *Market Society: Markets and Modern Social Thought*. Cambridge: Polity Press.

Veblen, T. ([1899] 1953) *The Theory of the Leisure Class: An Economic Study of Institutions*. New York: Mentor.

DON SLATER

CONTINGENCY

The concept of contingency was established in social theory as a concept for the dependency of variables on other variables and the dependency of actions on other actions. Cross-tabulations were often called contingency tables. In 1951, Talcott **Parsons** added the concept of 'double contingency'. This meant that satisfaction in **interaction** depends on one actor's choice from alternatives which again depends on another actor's complementary choice from alternatives. Through this, the possibility of indeterminacy – of a reciprocal blockade of action – was introduced into social theory. Parsons sought to resolve this indeterminacy by postulating common symbols or a common normative orientation of ego and alter.

The concept of double contingency was renewed by Niklas **Luhmann** (1976, 1984) who challenged the solution via normative commonalities. Instead he postulated that, in a situation of indeterminacy from any minimal event or minimal **action**, the beginnings of a process of system formation may arise. Norms and **symbols** are a late result of such a process of system formation.

There is also a second decisive shift in Luhmann's concept of contingency. He dissolves the affinity of contingency and dependency and introduces from the theory of modalities germane to scholastic philosophy a different understanding of contingency. Contingency then means the double negation of randomness and necessity. To call something contingent means that it is neither necessary or accidental. Such an understanding of contingency may qualify as a substantial self-understanding of **modernity** and Luhmann consequently postulated (1992) that contingency is the distinguishing feature or *Eigenwert* of modern society.

References and further reading

Luhmann, N. (1976) 'Generalized Media and the Problem of Contingency', in J. J. Loubser *et al.* (eds) *Explorations in General Theory in Social Science*. New York: Free Press.

Luhmann, N. (1984) 'Doppelte Kontingenz', in N. Luhmann, *Soziale Systeme*. Frankfurt am Main: Suhrkamp.

Luhmann, N. (1992) 'Kontingenz als Eigenwert der modernen Gesellschaft', in N. Luhmann, *Beobachtungen der Moderne*. Opladen: Westdeutscher Verlag.

Parsons, T. and Shils, E. (1951) *Toward a General Theory of Action*. Cambridge, MA: Harvard University Press.

RUDOLF STICHWEH

CONTRACT

Debates in the history of modern social and political thought about contracts or contractual relationships between members of a social group begin with the advent of theories of natural **rights** in seventeenth-century **Europe**. With differing nuances, Hugo Grotius, Samuel Pufendorf, Thomas Hobbes and John Locke all sought to account for the bases of political obligation to **sovereign** powers in ways that dispensed with traditional medieval teachings about the divinely ordained authority of monarchs. The conception of a contract, or 'covenant', was held to describe the reasons of individuals for surrendering their power to preserve and protect their own life and **liberty** to a constituted sovereign agency. Hobbes

103

famously wrote of a 'state of nature' marked by a 'war of all against all' from which individuals depart once they recognize the superior efficiency of a unified sovereign power in protecting their own life and liberty against external threats.

The seventeenth-century natural rights theorists all wrote against the background of threats to social order posed by religious factions claiming ultimate divine warrant for acts of seizure of political power (Tuck 1979). But where Hobbes's solution to what later became known as the problem of the separation of **church** and **state** was implicitly authoritarian, Locke's doctrine of religious toleration involved the implicitly libertarian proviso that a people's or **nation**'s contract with its sovereign could be legitimately broken by rebellion on grounds of interference with the private rights of individuals to freedom of conscience. Jean-Jacques Rousseau famously radicalized Locke's proto-typical political **liberalism** in a more **collectivist** direction by speaking of a 'social contract' that expresses not merely the sum of the private interests of individuals (the 'will of all') but the 'general will' of the people, based on a collectively affirmed **consensus**. This consensus was to be reached through the active participation of citizens in a common polity (see **citizenship**), thereby giving direct democratic warrant to executive power without any intermediary stratum of political representatives (see **democracy and democratization**).

Rousseau's and the natural rights theorists' contractarianism underlies much of the exercises in normative liberal political philosophy undertaken by American political and legal theorists since the early 1970s, most notably John **Rawls**, Robert Nozick and Ronald Dworkin. From around the middle of the eighteenth century, however, a range of intellectual movements began to suggest less openly normative ways of understanding the social meaning of contracts. David Hume's historical scepticism suggested

an understanding of contracts in terms of simple **conventions** by which individuals come to coordinate their actions and purposes (in his *Treatise of Human Nature*, Hume wrote of the labour of coordination needed by two men rowing a boat). Montesquieu's *Spirit of the Laws* pointed to the salience of contingent historical customs in the framing of beliefs in original contracts. The later eighteenth- and nineteenth-century movements of **political economy** and **utilitarianism** presaged an essentially sociological understanding of contracts in terms of functional agreements serving the satisfaction of individual **interests** and **needs**, especially through the economic exchange system of the **market**. Sir Henry Maine's *Ancient Law* of 1861 saw **laws** and legal arrangements in societies as evolving from relations of 'status', based on received customary sources of authority, to relations of 'contract', based on formal codified rights and responsibilities between contracting partners. This narrative was paralleled in many respects by Ferdinand **Tönnies**'s dichotomy of **Gemeinschaft and Gesellschaft**) and by **Marx**'s conception of the system of contractually obligated 'wage-slaves' with which **capitalist** relations replace **feudal** relations of personal bondage to the lord.

Today, however, the single most compelling sociological analysis of contractual relations continues to be **Durkheim**'s discussion in *The Division of Labour in Society* of 1893. Durkheim's key criticism of Maine and of all previous accounts in the French and British **positivist** traditions was that contractual relations cannot be explained solely by one individual's readiness to cooperate with another for the sake of satisfying of his or her own self-interest. One individual's willingness to cooperate depends on the **trust** of another, and trust cannot itself be explained in contractual terms without an infinite logical regress. Trust in contracts is possible, Durkheim argued, only to the extent that it is 'underwritten by the moral force of society'. Contracts only crystallize in the form of strategic attitudes a more primordial bond of moral **solidarity** between contracting parties as holders of a common *conscience collective*. Durkheim's sociological thinking here preserved the **Kantian** normative precept that a conditional 'hypothetical imperative' (I must respect others as means to my ends) presupposes a more basic unconditional 'categorical imperative' (I must respect others as ends in themselves). In this way, Durkheim demonstrated that self-interest can at most explain specific contingent contracts between individuals but not the binding obligatory force of contracts in general.

It in this sense that the return of the normative contents of natural rights theories in the contemporary neo-Kantian political and legal thought of Rawls and Dworkin marks a more intelligent understanding of the nature of contracts than that offered by the neo-utilitarian approaches of **rational choice** theory and **game theory**. The latter paradigms run aground in attempting to explain contracts by recourse purely to the interests of a 'rational egoist' in cooperating with another – because the reasons that make such interests 'rational' are not ones that can be understood in purely instrumental terms. Analysis of contractual relationships in other spheres of life beyond the economy and the formal **polity** brings this shortfall of understanding into even sharper relief. In the sphere of **intimacy**, for example, ideas of contract and consent raise a question of the deeper reserves of moral trust and **love** that give reason to parties to bind themselves to others in ways that, by definition, exceed the possibility of definite negotiation and prediction or calculation of consequences. The case of marriage in modern society (see **marriage and divorce**) is here only one instance of a type of social relation whose symbolic meaning exceeds explanation in terms of an instrumental contract because it owes its historical origins to the religious institution of a 'sacrament'. Generalizing from this case, it may be observed that the very concept of a contract is itself a product of cultural and intellectual **secularization** – just as the seventeenth-century natural rights theories originally began life as secularized transformations of the medieval Judaeo-Christian theological conception of 'natural law'.

References and further reading

Darwall, S. (ed.) (2003) *Contractarianism, Contractualism*. Oxford: Blackwell.
Pateman, C. (1988) *The Sexual Contract*. Stanford, CA: Stanford University Press.
Scanlon, T. M. (2003) *The Difficulty of Tolerance*. Cambridge: Cambridge University Press.
Tuck, R. (1979) *Natural Rights Theories*. Cambridge: Cambridge University Press.

AUSTIN HARRINGTON

CONVENTION

The concept of convention refers to an agreement or to a social regularity such as a usage, custom or rule of conduct. For David Hume ([1740] 1978) a convention is based on the anticipation of reciprocity of behaviour between individuals. A convention is an instrumental agreement with the function of coordinating interaction between two or more parties. For Max **Weber** (1978), a convention is not followed spontaneously but rather on account of the existence of social sanctions of disapproval following non-respect of the convention. The concept of convention was reintroduced into social theory in the 1960s by the philosopher David Lewis (1969). Following Lewis, the concept has been widely applied in evolutionary **game theory**, highlighting the importance of collective factors such as tradition for individual rationality. An institutional perspective on conventions was introduced by the French economists Favereau and Lazega (2002). Three characteristics of conventions are stressed by these authors. First, conventions are arbitrary, and usually carry implicit, rather than explicit, sanctions. Second, conventions may operate at the level of representations, where they function as repertoires of evaluation. Third, above the level of representations, they may also operate at the level of rules, where they form rules of conduct.

References and further reading

Favereau, F. and Lazega, E. (2002) *Conventions and Structures in Economic Organization*. Cheltenham: Edward Elgar.
Hume, D. ([1740] 1978) *A Treatise on Human Nature*. Oxford: Oxford University Press.
Lewis, D. K. (1969) *Convention: A Philosophical Study*. Cambridge, MA: Harvard University Press.
Weber, M. (1978) *Economy and Society: An Outline of Interpretive Sociology*. Berkeley, CA: University of California Press.

SØREN JAGD

COOPERATION

Cooperation means that actors contribute to a common goal or good. The common good that can be produced via cooperation may be context-specific: social order or **solidarity** within a society, **group** solidarity in intentional communities and **organizations**, **trust** and reciprocity in economic and social exchange.

Modern analyses of cooperation are inspired by **rational choice** and game theoretic ideas. In terms of **game theory**, cooperation is problematic if rational agents have incentives to choose **actions** or strategies in such a way that an inefficient or suboptimal outcome is realized. Efficiency or optimality is meant in **Pareto**'s sense as an outcome that cannot be improved without decreasing the payoffs of at least one participant. The Prisoner's Dilemma game (Axelrod 1984), where each of two players is given the option of cooperating or defecting, is a case in point. Mutual

cooperation in a Prisoner's Dilemma yields pay-offs that are superior to the pay-offs of mutual defection. The dilemma results from the fact that every actor has an incentive to unilaterally deviate from cooperation. This gives the deviating agent the highest pay-off. Besides the Prisoner's Dilemma, many other problematic situations or 'social dilemmas' share the characteristic that individually rational action produces a suboptimal social outcome (Raub and Voss 1986). These dilemmas may comprise two-person **interactions** but also interactions among more than two participants. A prominent example of a multi-person cooperation problem is public goods production which is relevant in the research on collective action (Olson 1965).

Many different mechanisms are prone to generate cooperation in problematic social dilemma situations. First, the social dilemma can be repeated indefinitely among the same participants. Then it can be rational to cooperate if one assumes that today's cooperation may induce others' cooperation in future interactions. This is because defection can be punished if interactions are repeated. Consider, for example, Rapoport's celebrated 'tit for tat' strategy in the iterated Prisoner's Dilemma (Axelrod 1984) where a participant may respond in once instance with the strategy used by the other in a previous round. Thus, 'tit for tat' may be 'friendly' (cooperates in the first round) and 'provokable' because of eventual defection. Second, in addition to repeated interactions, multilateral reputation via social **networks** is a structural condition that fosters cooperation (Greif 1994). This mechanism can be effective if information about a partner's defection spreads to third actors (potential partners). Third, many social institutions provide solutions to cooperation problems. **Coleman** (1990) argues that actors sometimes construct institutional arrangements which change their incentive structure and reduce the temptation to deviate from joint cooperation.

To illustrate, rational actors who take a hostage may create a credible commitment to cooperate even under conditions of a one-shot dilemma situation (Raub and Keren 1993). Other institutions such as informal social norms also create incentives to cooperate. Cooperation norms are based on threats to punish deviant behaviour directly and not merely indirectly by refusing future cooperation (Voss 2001).

Work on cooperation also focuses on the evolution of other-regarding **preferences**. Altruistic preferences imply that an agent's utility increases with increases in the welfare (or utility) of other actors. Clearly, altruists can be motivated to cooperate in a one-shot Prisoner's Dilemma. Another type of preference that accounts for one-shot cooperation is the aversion to **inequality** (fairness). Fairness preferences are closely related to 'altruistic reciprocity'. Positive reciprocity is the tendency to respond cooperatively towards expected or actual cooperation. This may explain conditional cooperation. Negative reciprocity means the punishment of defections with retributive sanctions. Notice that negative reciprocity occurs even under the condition of costly ('altruistic') punishments. Empirical evidence on altruistic reciprocity (Fehr and Gächter 2000; Diekmann 2004) suggests that cooperation and the enforcement of cooperation norms are not only based on social structural conditions such as repeated interactions and networks but also on 'internalized' preferences to cooperate conditionally. Ideas from **evolutionary theory** (Sober and Wilson 1998) imply that group segregation, selective mating and similar structural conditions may in the long run favour biological or cultural 'group selection' processes that shape 'altruistic' preferences among populations of egoists.

References and further reading

Axelrod, R. (1984) *The Evolution of Cooperation*. New York: Basic Books.

Coleman, J. S. (1990) *Foundations of Social Theory*. Cambridge, MA: Belknap.
Diekmann, A. (2004) 'The Power of Reciprocity', *Journal of Conflict Resolution*, 48: 487–505.
Fehr, E. and Gächter, S. (2000) 'Cooperation and Punishment in Public Goods Experiments', *American Economic Review*, 90: 980–94.
Greif, A. (1994) 'Cultural Beliefs and the Organization of Society', *Journal of Political Economy*, 102: 912–50.
Olson, M. (1965) *The Logic of Collective Action*. Cambridge, MA: Harvard University Press.
Raub, W. and Keren, G. (1993) 'Hostages as a Commitment Device', *Journal of Economic Behavior and Organization*, 21: 43–67.
Raub, W. and Voss, T. (1986) 'Conditions of Cooperation in Problematic Social Situations', in Diekmann, A. and P. Mitter (eds) *Paradoxical Effects of Social Behavior: Essays in Honor of Anatol Rapoport*. Vienna: Physica.
Sober, E. and Wilson, D. S. (1999) *Unto Others: The Evolution and Psychology of Unselfish Behavior*. Cambridge, MA: Harvard University Press.
Voss, T. (2001) 'Game Theoretical Perspectives on the Emergence of Social Norms', in M. Hechter and K.-D. Opp (eds) *Social Norms*. New York: Russell Sage.

THOMAS VOSS

CORPORATION

'Corporation' refers to a form of public or private **organization** endowed with legal rights and responsibilities akin to those ascribed to the individual **subject** or citizen. Corporations possess legal standing separate from their owners. Unlike traditional partnerships, which they have in large part supplanted in most areas of commerce and trade, corporations are generally characterized by the separation of ownership and management, the latter function being carried out by salaried professionals. After 'incorporation', the identity and legal status of the corporation are not dependent on a continuation of any particular memberships or share holdings.

Corporations are generally constituted either (1) as private limited liability companies, which protect those individuals who constitute its management or hold shares in it from being personally liable in the event of the corporation being sued; or (2) as public corporations. Public corporations are generally – though not exclusively – owned and funded by the state, their status being enshrined in statute. In the UK, the BBC is one such corporation which, while managed by its Board of Governors, is financed by the television licence fee which is collected by the Treasury and is ultimately answerable to Parliament for its activities. In general, the arrangements by which corporations are governed and the relationship between the **state**, shareholders and principal representatives of corporations are often determined by national legal and other institutional arrangements, although moves towards international standards are increasingly impacting on such arrangements.

Modern commercial corporations emerged historically during the seventeenth century, most notably in Britain with the formation of the East India Company. Originally a trade association acting as an umbrella for merchants, and thus non-profit in character, it quickly evolved over the course of the century into the first commercial corporation generating profit for what was to become its shareholders. By the end of the century, however, corporations were banned by English law due to the activities of those agents then known as *jobbers*, who sold stocks and shares at the coffee houses of London. After the collapse of the South Sea Company in 1720 which led to the ruination of the majority of its investors, the British government passed the Bubble Act, which outlawed corporations that may harm the public wealth, as well as the speculative selling and buying of shares which were to be limited to those actively taking part in the company's affairs.

By 1825 the Bubble Act had been repealed, however. Henceforth, commercial corporations increasingly came to be viewed as vital to the expansion of industrial enterprise around the globe. In parti-

cular, it was the expansion of the railways across the USA and **Europe** that fuelled the growth in corporate activity as the need for ever increasing levels of capital investment caused a significant expansion in the numbers of middle-class share owners. In the mid to late nineteenth century the final obstacle to corporate dominance of the economy was lifted with the gradual introduction of limited liability, by which shareholders could only be legally held liable to third parties to the limit of their shareholding.

Today, the global economy is dominated by transnational or multinational corporations operating in more than one country. Around 63,000 multinational corporations currently operate in the global **market**, accounting for approximately two-thirds of global trade. Some of them generate economic outputs larger than many small and some medium-sized countries. In many instances, such corporations are effectively able to negotiate with national governments the terms on which they are prepared to invest in a nation's economy.

Such dominance has led to a degree of public uncertainty about corporate **power**, spawning a number of high profile publications, media events and protests opposed to the perceived lack of democratic accountability (see Bakan 2004) (see **governance and governmentality**). Often these have linked corporate behaviour to environmental damage or to sweatshop labour conditions, especially in developing countries. There is also an increasing number of legal challenges to the supposed immunity of corporations from prosecution for criminal acts, the most prominent of these being corporate manslaughter.

References and further reading

Bakan, J. (2004) *The Corporation*. London: Constable and Robinson.
Chandler, A. D. (1977) *The Visible Hand*. Cambridge, MA: Harvard University Press.

Kanter, R. M. (1977) *Men and Women of the Corporation*. New York: Basic Books.
Supple, B. E. (1992) *The Rise of Big Business*. Brookfield, VT: E. Elgar.

PHILIP HANCOCK

COSMOPOLITANISM

In its broadest meaning, cosmopolitanism stands for an orientation or aspiration. Being cosmopolitan means to orient or aspire toward an ideal that transcends the immediate boundaries of being and belonging somewhere. According to **Derrida** (2001) such transcendence involves a double movement of hospitality: being hospitable to the other while urging the other to aspire to the same hospitality.

While cosmopolitanism is often contrasted to **citizenship**, understood as being and belonging somewhere, cosmopolitanism does not necessarily mean being or belonging nowhere. Citizenship has always embodied cosmopolitan aspirations in the sense that it has been oriented toward transcending the immediate boundaries of social entities such as tribes, villages or clans (Heater 1990; 2002). That citizenship itself became trapped in the boundaries of first the city, then the empire, then the state, and then the **nation** reminds us of its inherent yet unfulfilled aspiration of cosmopolitanism.

We receive images of cosmopolitanism from various sources. If one source is the Stoic ideal of the Hellenic world of waning cities (Schofield 1991), Confucianism and Buddhism also provided images of such hospitality (Irigaray 2002). The aspirations of cosmopolitanism have been articulated in diverse ways by Zeno of Citium, Dante of Florence, Rousseau of Geneva, **Kant** of Königsberg and today Derrida of Paris. In each case, these voices remind citizens how a citizenship of limits may harden into limits of citizenship.

Today the urgency of the idea of cosmopolitanism consists in its reminding us of how far citizenship has fallen short of its aspirations (Dallmayr 2003). Whether articulated as a hope for a cosmopolitan democratic order (Held 1995) or a plea for the state of the dispossessed (Nyers 2003), it remains a crucial component of our normative political life.

References and further reading

Dallmayr, F. (2003) 'Cosmopolitanism: Moral and Political', *Political Theory*, 31(3): 421–42.
Derrida, J. (2001) 'On Cosmopolitanism', in *On Cosmopolitanism and Forgiveness*. London: Routledge.
Heater, D. B. (1990) *Citizenship: The Civic Ideal in World History, Politics, and Education*. London: Longman Group.
Heater, D. B. (2002) *World Citizenship: Cosmopolitan Thinking and Its Opponents*. London: Continuum.
Held, D. (1995) *Democracy and the Global Order: From the Modern State to Cosmopolitan Governance*. Stanford, CA: Stanford University Press.
Irigaray, L. ([1999] 2002) *Between East and West: From Singularity to Community*. Trans. S. Pluhacek. New York: Columbia University Press.
Linklater, A. (1998) *The Transformation of Political Community: Ethical Foundations of the Post-Westphalian Era*. Cambridge: Polity Press.
Moellendorf, D. (2002) *Cosmopolitan Justice*. Boulder, CO: Westview Press.
Nyers, P. (2003) 'Abject Cosmopolitanism: The Politics of Protection in the Anti-Deportation Movements', *Third World Quarterly*, 24(6): 1069–93.
Schofield, M. (1991) *The Stoic Idea of the City*. Cambridge: Cambridge University Press.

ENGIN F. ISIN

CRIME

Crime can be defined as behaviour that violates criminal law, which is liable to public prosecution and punishment (Sacco and Kennedy 1994: 9). It is governmental **social control**, law backed by coercive (state) power. Although crime is a narrower concept than **deviance** (despite overlaps, much criminal behaviour is seen as deviant and vice versa), there are significant differences. First, the consequences for the individual thus designated can include state-sanctioned lifetime incarceration or legally prescribed death (see **death and mortality**). Second, by labelling an act a crime, the **state** makes a key public statement: it declares the designated act harmful to all citizens. This is why the state initiates action against the offender, regardless of the wishes of those it names 'victim' and 'offender'. Third, while all societies distinguish deviant from normative behaviour in the project of social control, only those with state systems have crime.

Behaviours proscribed as crime vary across **time**, by **culture** and **nation–state**. Early concepts were heavily influenced by religious doctrines which ascribed evil to supernatural forces. Those who practiced witchcraft, for example, were allied with the devil or possessed by demons. With the advent of **modernity**, states sought explanations through science, and the discipline of criminology emerged. Its goal, to understand, predict and control criminal behaviour, was first sought (and thought) through the discipline of medicine, particularly psychiatric theories of pathology and insanity. Today clinical psychology dominates sciences which examine crime at the level of the individual. Sociological concepts see crime as a social and legal construction (see **constructionism**). Within sociological thought, positivist schools look for traits that distinguish criminals from 'law-abiding' individuals. Interpretive and critical schools ask how social conditions and institutions produce crime and criminals, and how **power** is implicated in the definitional process.

Of the positivist founding fathers of sociology, Emile **Durkheim** ([1893] 1964) paid most sustained attention to deviance and crime. Durkheim saw crime as an offence against a society's fundamental, sacred values, a threat to moral **authority** and social **solidarity**. A collective response,

punishment, was required to mend the breach and restore equilibrium. Punishment did not have to be vengeful – in fact, Durkheim thought retributive sanctions characterized non-industrial societies whose solidarity depended on the similarity of their members (*mechanical solidarity*). Complex, industrialized societies, bound through interdependence in multifaceted divisions of labour (*organic solidarity*), would focus on restitution. Although Durkheim's prediction was wrong – developed societies with substantial **inequality** are more punitive than simpler societies, and levels of punishment have been increasing in recent decades (Garland 2001) – his contribution endures.

In 1938 Robert **Merton**'s theory of **anomie** or strain theory applied Durkheimian concepts to devise a sociological explanation of crime in **America**. Crime was seen as a rational response to socially induced strain caused by restricted access to legitimate opportunity structures. American **society**, Merton argued, promised success (wealth) for all. However, the socially approved means to obtain success – good schools, membership of prestigious clubs, executive positions – were unavailable to lower-class youth. Four adaptations were possible: innovation, retreatism, ritualism and rebellion. Innovators devise illegitimate means to attain culturally approved goals. During Prohibition, for example, first generation immigrants succeeded through innovative means such as racketeering. Retreatists reject both goals and means (hobos and drug addicts), ritualists accept means but not goals (petty bureaucrats who rigidly follow rules), rebels reject existing goals and means, and substitute new ones. The theory was subsequently altered to accommodate discoveries that access to *illegitimate* opportunity structures also varies by neighbourhood, **ethnicity** and **class** (Cloward and Ohlin 1960).

Control theory shifts focus from societal defects, back onto the individual. Control theories start with the assumption that people will break rules if it is in their interests to do so, and that crime is a pleasurable short-cut to achieving human desires. Conformity, then, becomes problematic: why do most people obey the law? Travis Hirschi (1969) argued that criminal acts occur when an individual's bond with society is weak or absent. People are bonded to their society through attachment, commitment, involvement and belief. Crime is less likely when individuals are emotionally *attached* to others, and care about their opinions and judgments. *Committed* individuals have a stake in conventional activities, and something to lose through criminality. Non-criminal, conforming people are more likely to be *involved* in conventional activities at the behavioural level. Finally, the more people *believe* in conventional **values and norms**, the less likely they are to engage in crime.

The assumption that crime is a rational choice has spawned new studies, industries and policies. If criminals are rational beings always seeking opportunities to offend, cities must be redesigned to create 'defensible' space. Robbery rates can be cut by switching to exact fares on buses, and fitting park benches with rigid armrests to prevent homeless people from sleeping on them. Houses in affluent suburbs, deserted all day by owners commuting to jobs in the distant city, need Neighbourhood Watch programmes, surveillance, and all manner of private **security**. Citizens must constantly monitor **risk**. A later version of control theory argues that criminals cannot defer gratification, due to inadequate training, discipline or nurturing. Lacking in self-control, they are 'impulsive, insensitive, physical...risk-takers, short-sighted and non-verbal' (Gottfredson and Hirschi 1990: 90).

Critical definitions of crime have been less influential in recent decades. In the 1970s New or Radical Criminology (Taylor *et al.* 1973) argued that **capitalism** is essentially criminogenic: the labour of the

working class (**proletariat**) is appropriated by the upper classes (**bourgeoisie**) to maximize profits. Crime occurs when the oppressed strike back against those who exploit them, and is repressed by the state to preserve class rule. This reworking of Marx explains the over-representation of the poor in prisons, and state preoccupation with crimes of the powerless at the expense of white-collar and corporate crime. In the 1980s radical criminology was criticized for romanticizing crime and ignoring victims. Moreover, surveys revealed that victims were more likely to be the girlfriend, Pakistani immigrant, or local pensioner than the privileged classes. In response, Left Realism took crime seriously. Its studies of policing showed police priorities skewed by **class**, **gender** and **race** bias. Working-class *offenders* were targeted for coercive control while working-class *victims*, especially women and visible minorities, were ignored.

Interpretive approaches were also more important in earlier decades than today. Labelling theory, rooted in **symbolic interactionism**, argues that the imposition of a criminal label increases the likelihood of criminal behaviour. Criminal justice processing or 'signification by Leviathan' (Matza 1969) sets a process in motion where 'criminal' becomes a person's master **status** or **identity**. For example, people charged as thieves come to see themselves this way when significant others and prospective employers expect and reinforce thief-like traits, thereby making conforming behaviours more difficult for the 'thief' to display. Processes of exclusion may lead to membership in a deviant **subculture** which transmits this identity, and associated skills and techniques, to new recruits.

Feminist theories have corrected patriarchal concepts which saw female crime in terms of sexuality, and female criminals as hormonal black holes (see **feminist theory**). Feminist arguments for amelioration and empowerment have been ignored, while arguments which increased punishment through redesigned legislation on domestic and sexual assault have produced policy change (Snider 2003). Critical **post-structuralist** theories, influenced by **Foucault** (1977), problematize criminology itself, situating claims to knowledge in relations of power. They examine how criminology and other **discourses** constitute the modern human subject, who constantly monitors, regulates and disciplines him/herself, and the mechanisms of the surveillant state.

Positivist, modernist concepts of crime dominate Anglo-American criminology today. Where strain theories located the causes of crime in structural, societal deficiencies, and critical perspectives question power–knowledge linkages and the role of race, gender and class, control theories have popularized the criminal as rational predator, flawed in **morality**, in **socialization**, or in the ability to defer gratification. This resonated with neo-liberal state agendas in the 1980s and the 1990s, justifying cutbacks in social programmes and dramatic increases in **inequality**.

References and further reading

Cloward, R. and Ohlin, L. (1960) *Delinquency and Opportunity: A Theory of Delinquent Gangs.* New York: Free Press.

Durkheim, E. ([1893] 1964) *The Division of Labour in Society.* New York: Free Press.

Foucault, M. (1977) *Discipline and Punish.* New York: Vintage Press.

Garland, D. (2001) *The Culture of Control.* Chicago: University of Chicago Press.

Gottfredson, M. and Hirschi, T. (1990) *A General Theory of Crime.* Stanford, CA: Stanford University Press.

Hirschi, T. (1969) *Causes of Delinquency.* Berkeley, CA: University of California Press.

Matza, D. (1969) *Becoming Deviant.* Englewood Cliffs, NJ: Prentice Hall.

Merton, R. (1938) 'Social Structure and Anomie', *American Sociological Review*, 3:672–82.

Morrison, W. (1995) *Theoretical Criminology: From Modernity to Post-Modernism.* London: Cavendish Press.

Sacco, V. and Kennedy, L. (1994) *The Criminal Event.* Scarborough, ON: Nelson.

Snider, L. (2003) 'Constituting the Punishable Woman', *British Journal of Criminology*, 43: 354–78.

Taylor, I., Walton, P. and Young, J. (1973) *The New Criminology.* London: Verso.

LAUREEN SNIDER

CRISIS

Crisis refers to a time of danger and suspense, a turning-point. In medical contexts crisis denotes the stage in an illness when a patient may either live or die. Some see sociology as a crisis science insofar as it arose amidst the dissolution of traditional society and the emergence of its modern successor. Epistemologically, crisis creates conditions in which social scientists are able to discern trends more clearly. An idea of crisis was first used to refer to the French **Revolution**, by de Bonald in a negative sense, and by Saint-Simon in a positive sense (see Koselleck [1973] 1988). Later it was applied to the consequences of **capitalism**. The classical sociologists all employed the concept, but **Marx** more emphatically than either **Durkheim**, whose concept of 'anomie' was related to it, or **Weber** who kept it at arm's length. Marx focused on the possibility that the periodic economic crisis cycle would eventually spiral into a 'universal crisis' ending capitalism.

In contemporary social theory Niklas **Luhmann** comes closest to Weber in tireless warning against over-use of the concept of crisis, although Luhmann does emphasize the vulnerability of modern social systems. Jürgen **Habermas** (1976) captured this vulnerability by analyzing a chain of 'crisis tendencies' potentially leading to the loss or transformation of social **identity**. What Habermas called the 'legitimation crisis', his neo-conservative counterparts reinterpreted as the crisis of the **welfare state** culminating in 'ungovernability' (Offe 1984). Since the 1980s uncertainty about macro-processes and their outcomes has strengthened, with the **ecology** crisis symbolizing this anxiety.

Consequently, **risk** has become the focus of conflicting interpretations of this developing crisis consciousness, as theorized by authors such as **Beck** (1999) and **Giddens** (1999).

References and further reading

Beck, U. (1999) *World Risk Society*. Cambridge: Polity.

Giddens, A. (1999) *Runaway World*. London: Profile.

Habermas, J. ([1973] 1976) *Legitimation Crisis*. London: Heinemann.

Kosolleck, R. ([1973] 1988) *Critique and Crisis: Enlightenment and the Pathogenesis of Modern Society*. Cambridge, MA: MIT Press.

Offe, C. (1984) 'Ungovernability', in C. Offe, *Contradictions of the Welfare State*. London: Hutchinson.

Strydom, P. (2000) *Discourse and Knowledge: The Making of Enlightenment Sociology*. Liverpool: Liverpool University Press.

PIET STRYDOM

CRITICAL THEORY

Critical theory can refer broadly to theoretical approaches on art or literary criticism, or to any theory that aims at the criticism of **society**. In social theory, however, it is most often applied to the **Frankfurt School**. Critical theory began in inter-war Germany as an unorthodox effort to renew **Marxism** by integrating philosophical reflection with empirical social **science**. Its key features derive from this moment: the attempt to forge a self-reflexive, interdisciplinary, materialist theory of society oriented towards human **emancipation**. It is now common to speak of three generations of critical theory: the first (from the 1930s to the 1960s) centering on Max **Horkheimer** and Theodor **Adorno**, but also including Friedrich Pollock, Walter **Benjamin**, Herbert **Marcuse**, and Erich Fromm, among others; the second (from the 1960s to the 1990s) identified with Jürgen **Habermas**; and a third (emerging since the 1980s) associated with the work of Axel Honneth and some other theorists.

Critical theory's original programme was set out in essays by Horkheimer and Marcuse after Horkheimer took the helm of the Institute for Social Research in 1930. The notion of 'critical theory' was developed in distinction to 'traditional theory'. Modeling itself on natural science, traditional theory seeks **knowledge** about specific social phenomena in the form of law-like, explanatory, predictive generalizations. It reflects the modern reduction of reason to a subjective standpoint and to technical, means–ends **rationality**. Against this, critical theory is guided by a substantive conception of reason that includes reflection on the ends of social development and the possibility of a more rational society (see **rationality and rationalization**). Questioning its presuppositions and considering the social and historical conditions of knowledge, it critically examines how categories and ideas emerge from and support the social order. Above all, it is guided by the goal of social transformation, whose obstacles and possibilities it seeks to discover with the help of the social sciences. Critical theory thus inherits from Marxism the aim of overcoming the division between theory and practice (see **praxis and practices**).

Like other varieties of Western Marxism, critical theory's central questions in the 1930s were posed by the workers' failure to overthrow **capitalism** and the rise of Stalinist and Nazi **totalitarianism**. In interdisciplinary fashion, the Frankfurt School undertook investigations ranging from the economy and politics to **culture** and the psyche. Combining the insights of **Marx**, **Weber**, and **Freud**, it tried to establish connections between capitalist exploitation, the reduction of reason to **instrumental reason**, and the effects of psychic repression. Noting parallel developments in the Soviet Union, Nazi Germany, and the liberal-capitalist West, Friedrich Pollock, Franz Neumann, and Otto Kirchheimer suggested that the **state** and the economy were fusing into a single system, a centrally-planned

113

'state capitalism' that overcame the crisis tendencies observed by Marx through ever more efficient and subtle mechanisms of social **integration**. Adorno and Benjamin argued that culture no longer provided a point of resistance to **social control** and a locus for the development of autonomous forms of individuality and sociality. In the age of **mass culture and mass society**, it instead became what Horkheimer and Adorno described as a manipulative, affirmative 'culture industry'. And as they, Marcuse and Fromm sought to show, the decline of the paternalistic bourgeois **family** led to a weakening of the **personality**, producing conformist individuals who were increasingly vulnerable to the appeal of authoritarianism (Adorno *et al.* 1950; Marcuse 1964)(see **authority**).

As the political situation darkened in the 1930s and 1940s, so did Horkheimer and Adorno's diagnosis of **modernity**. Their best-known work, the *Dialectic of Enlightenment* (1944), written during the war in exile in Los Angeles, turned increasingly to the philosophy of history. Locating the roots of the **Enlightenment** in ancient Greece, they argue that the liberatory potential of reason had been betrayed as it was used to dominate nature, others, and the **self**. Reason is reduced to instrumental reason; Enlightenment becomes its opposite, **myth** and heteronomy. This bleak assessment carried over into their post-war return to Frankfurt. The later Adorno saw the only possibilities of escape from an 'administered society' in modernist **art** and dialectical, non-identificatory thinking against reason's oppressive tendency to **totality** (*Negative Dialectics* 1966).

The Institute nevertheless contributed to the development of German social science by encouraging interdisciplinary research. In the 'positivism dispute' of the 1960s, it defended a reflective, self-critical conception of sociology, drawing on a theoretical account of the whole of society (see **positivism**). Adorno and Horkheimer also

played a major role as critical **intellectuals** opposing the repression of the past in the conservative climate of post-war Germany. Beyond this, writers who had broken with the School in the 1940s, most notably Marcuse, continued to maintain the possibility of social transformation through a 'libinal revolution', anticipating the protest movements of the late 1960s.

In the early 1960s Jürgen Habermas, then Adorno's assistant, emerged as the most important theorist of what came to be called second-generation critical theory. Beginning with the *Structural Transformation of the Public Sphere* (1962), which traces the emergence of the ideal of free and rational discussion in bourgeois **civil society**, Habermas's work constituted a break not only with the 'pessimism' but also with the basic methodological and substantial premises of the first generation. His aim has been to elaborate a broader, universalist conception of reason opposed both to positivism and to Adorno and Horkheimer's focus on instrumental rationality. In *Knowledge and Human Interests* (1968), he argues that science is always based on knowledge-constitutive interests, whether they are technical, practical or emancipatory. Rooting critical theory in the latter, Habermas finds its normative bases in the rational potential of intersubjective **communication**.

The implications of this 'communicative turn' are elaborated in his magnum opus, the two-volume *Theory of Communicative Action* (1981). Linking a reconstruction of **Durkheim**, Weber and **Parsons** with more contemporary approaches from **pragmatism** to speech-act theory, Habermas distinguishes between two fundamental modes of **action** and rationality: instrumental or strategic rationality and communicative **rationality**, the latter characterized by agents' orientation towards understanding and **consensus**. Habermas argues that all genuine **communication** presupposes a domination-free speech situation as a counterfactual ideal. This ideal then serves as a normative standard to criticize actual social relations. Using this distinction to develop a two-level theory of society, Habermas grants to **systems theory** that modern societies reproduce themselves through relatively autonomous economic and administrative systems, but insists that the **legitimacy** of the social order has to be grounded in the communicative interactions of a shared **lifeworld**, the social world seen from the participants' perspective. Under late capitalism, this lifeworld is increasingly colonized by systems, with destructive effects on social **integration** and personal **identity**.

Habermas's later work develops the practical implications of this conception. His neo-Kantian discourse ethics appeals to the idea of the ideal speech situation to assert the priority of the morally right, consisting in a procedure of universalization, over competing definitions of the good. In *Between Facts and Norms* (1992), communication forms the basis for an internal connection between law and **democracy** in the modern constitutional state: citizens must be able to understand themselves as the authors as well as the subjects of the law, with civil society constituting the indispensable link between lifeworld and political system (see **law and legality**). The idea of rational consensus formation is then further developed into a model of deliberative democracy appropriate to conditions of modern **pluralism**.

Habermas's apparent reconciliation with capitalism and the liberal state, as well as his relative neglect of social and psychic pathologies, has set the stage for an emerging third generation of critical theory. Critical theory today is not a unified movement but a range of different approaches situating themselves in the Frankfurt School tradition. In Germany, Axel Honneth reformulates critical theory as a theory of **recognition**. He seeks to identify those forms of recognition – **love**, legal and moral respect and social esteem – that constitute the conditions of individual flourishing and non-distorted social relationships. In the United States, critical theory has been taken up by theorists influenced by **feminist theory**, notably Seyla Benhabib and Nancy Fraser. Their aim is a social theory that is more sensitive to issues of identity-formation, cultural and **gender** differences, **power** and **equality**.

Approaches in the Frankfurt School tradition are not, however, the only ones that understand themselves as critical theories. Two especially fruitful alternatives are represented by Michel **Foucault** and Pierre **Bourdieu**. Whereas the former focuses on the interrelations of power and **discourse** which produce the modern notions of reason, the **subject** and well-ordered societies, the latter has elaborated a self-reflexive theory of the reproduction of social inequalities in different social fields.

Although in its traditional Frankfurt School mode critical theory may belong to the twentieth century, the expansion of global capitalism, the **crisis** of the **welfare state** and questions of new **media**, **technology** and **identity** suggest that its original tasks will continue to be taken up by approaches that define themselves as critical in the twenty-first century.

References and further reading

Adorno, T. *et al.* (1950) *The Authoritarian Personality*.New York: Harper and Row.
Adorno, T. W. ([1966] 1973) *Negative Dialectics*. New York: Seabury.
Benhabib, S. (1986) *Critique, Norm, and Utopia*. New York: Columbia University Press.
Geuss, R. (1981) *The Idea of a Critical Theory*. Cambridge: Cambridge University Press.
Habermas, J. ([1968] 1971) *Knowledge and Human Interests*. Boston: Beacon.
Habermas, J. ([1981] 1984/1987) *Theory of Communicative Action*, 2 vols. Cambridge, MA: MIT Press.
Held, D. (1980) *Introduction to Critical Theory*. Berkeley, CA: University of California Press.
Honneth, A. ([1992] 1996) *The Struggle for Recognition*. Cambridge: Polity.
Horkheimer, M. and Adorno, T. ([1947] 1972) *Dialectic of Enlightenment*. New York: Herder.

Ingram, D. and Ingram, J.-S. (eds) (1992) *Critical Theory: Essential Readings*. St. Paul, MN: Paragon.

Jay, M. (1973) *The Dialectical Imagination*. Berkeley, CA: University of California Press.

Marcuse, H. (1964) *One-Dimensional Man*. Boston: Beacon.

Wiggershaus, R. ([1986] 1994) *The Frankfurt School*. Cambridge, MA: MIT Press.

ROBIN CELIKATES
JAMES INGRAM

CULTURAL CAPITAL

Cultural capital is one of the nexus of concepts developed by Pierre **Bourdieu**. There are some social and cultural dispositions which we inherit and these constitute our **habitus**, but there are also cultural commodities which are not integral parts of our background. These are tokens which operate as currency in our position-taking society. Markets of cultural goods assign value and actors buy and sell in these markets to gain social distinction. The concept was first developed in the educational context to explain the processes of **exclusion** within the schooling system. It challenged the notion of 'giftedness' or innate intellectual superiority and questioned the assumptions of 'meritocratic' procedures. Although Bourdieu appropriated economic discourse, he was insistent that the acquisition and deployment of cultural capital are part of the strategic behaviour of all social agents. He opposed *human capital* **discourse** because it encouraged managerial control and governmental manipulation. He also extended the concept of cultural capital to include **social capital**. Bourdieu's concept of social capital is distinctive and demonstrates his different approach to the function of social science, apparent in the debate with James **Coleman** at the end of the 1980s.

References and further reading

Bourdieu, P. ([1964] 1979) *The Inheritors*. Chicago: University of Chicago Press.

Bourdieu, P. (1979) 'Les trois états du capital culturel', *Actes de la recherche en sciences sociales*, 30: 3–6.

Bourdieu, P. (1980) 'Le capital social: Notes provisoires', *Actes de la recherche en sciences sociales*, 31: 2–3.

Bourdieu, P. and Coleman, J.S. (eds) (1989) *Social Theory for a Changing Society*. Boulder, CO: Westview Press.

Martin, B. and Szelenyi, I. (2000) 'Beyond Cultural Capital: Toward a Theory of Symbolic Domination', in D. M. Robbins (ed.) *Pierre Bourdieu*, vol. I. London: Sage.

DEREK ROBBINS

CULTURAL TURN

As an event in intellectual history, the cultural turn took place in the 1960s and 1970s, both in social theory and in disciplines ranging from sociology to anthropology and history. It followed in the wake of a **'linguistic turn'** in the philosophy of science and embraced an 'interpretative turn' in scientific analysis. Against the background of diverse theoretical strands such as **structuralism, semiotics, post-structuralism, hermeneutics, pragmatism** and **Wittgensteinian** linguistic philosophy, the turn to culture contributed to an understanding of social life as fundamentally dependent on structures of **meaning** and symbolic orders (see **symbol**). From an anti-universalist, 'historicist' point of view, these cultural codes and their discourses and social practices are regarded as localized and historically specific, and thus as expressions of **contingency** (see **discourses**). In **epistemology** and the historiography of science, the cultural turn has sought to undermine positivist approaches and to interpret intellectual and scientific activities themselves as contingent social practices (see **praxis and practices**) working against a background of 'paradigms' (Kuhn 1962). In connection with the debate on postmodernism and **postmodernity**, cultural theories have contributed to scepticism towards linear theories of **modernity and modernization**, pointing out immanent cultural differences and heterogeneous paths within modernity itself. In the 1960s and 1970s, the cultural turn was closely linked to anti-bourgeois socio-political movements, including those of **gender** and **post-colonialism**, as well as to neo-avant-garde and postmodernist aesthetics. Since the 1990s, the debates on cultural **globalization** and theories of new communication **media** have given a new impulse to the turn towards **culture**.

References and further reading

Bonnell, V. and Hunt, L. (eds) (1999) *Beyond the Cultural Turn*. Berkeley, CA: University of California Press.

Foucault, M. ([1966] 1970) *The Order of Things*. London: Tavistock.

Giddens, A. (1976) *New Rules of Sociological Method*. London: Hutchinson.

Hall, S. (ed.) (1997) *Representations*. London: Sage.

Kuhn, T. (1962) *The Structure of Scientific Revolutions*. Chicago: University of Chicago Press.

Lyotard, J. F. ([1979] 1984) *The Postmodern Condition*. Minneapolis, MN: University of Minnesota Press.

Rabinow, P. and Sullivan, W. (eds) (1979) *Interpretive Social Science*. Berkeley, CA: University of California Press.

Rorty, R. (1989) *Contingency, Irony, and Solidarity*. Cambridge: Cambridge University Press.

ANDREAS RECKWITZ

CULTURE

Since the **cultural turn** of social theory and sociology in the 1970s, culture has developed into a key concept of social inquiry. It has transformed the sociological conceptions of **action**, **social structure** and **modernity**. Cultural theories understand the social in its core as a complex of **symbolic** forms and structures of **meaning**, anchored in schemes, discourses and practices (see **praxis and practices**). Cultural theories regard both the social and the natural sciences as themselves interpretative activities, and they analyze 'modernity' in terms of a non-linear sequence of conflicts between powerful cultural codes. Thus 'culture' in these theories is not a limited object of study but a general conceptual perspective which has transformed a number of empirical fields of study. Culture from this perspective has challenged traditional sociological concepts of the social as a pre-cultural structure or material basis, together with positivist self-images of science and narratives of modernity in classical (see **classics**) functionalist and classical Marxist

In the context of **Enlightenment** thought and in **bourgeois** theories of culture of the nineteenth century (for example, in Matthew Arnold's *Culture and Anarchy*), culture was primarily defined as the normative ideal of a moral and educated form of life, a universalist model partly based on the binary opposition prevalent in Germany between *Kultur* as expressive artistic uniqueness and authenticity and *zivilisation* as technological industrial progress. Romantic thought, prominently in J. G. Herder, developed a particularistic conception of 'cultures' in the plural, presenting cultures as locally and historically distinct groups sharing common customs. At the end of the nineteenth century, the new discipline of cultural anthropology extended this idea of the distinct **traditions** and patterns of behaviour of 'a people'. In contrast **structural functionalism** in the twentieth century narrowed down the meaning of culture, reducing it to a specific subsystem of modern society which contains 'cultural' institutions such as **art**, the **church** or universities. This notion of institutionalized culture as a discrete field of study found a supportive audience in post-war sociology and its conception of a 'sociology of culture'.

Since the 1960s and the 1970s a broad and heterogeneous field of influential theories has emerged in social theory which has given culture a strong explanatory status in the form of theories of meaning and of the symbolic, understood as the very precondition of social life. It includes figures such as Roland **Barthes**, Pierre **Bourdieu**,

Jacques **Derrida**, Mary **Douglas**, Michel **Foucault**, Hans-Georg **Gadamer**, Clifford **Geertz**, Harold **Garfinkel**, Erving **Goffman**, Stuart Hall, Jacques **Lacan**, Claude **Lévi-Strauss**, Paul **Ricoeur**, Alfred **Schutz**, Charles **Taylor** and others. In different ways, all these authors endeavour to provide a culturalist alternative to traditional vocabularies in the social sciences. They seek to avoid the reduction of the symbolic and the meaningful to a residual category, typical of some materialist theories of structural sociology and **functionalism** and typified by the utilitarian concept of homo oeconomicus.

In **neo**-**Kantian** and **neo**-**Hegelian** thought – for instance, in the work of Max **Weber**, Wilhelm **Dilthey** and Ernst Cassirer – we find early attempts to sketch a theory of culture as basis of the social sciences and the humanities. However, culturalist theory-building and culturalist empirical analyses from the 1960s until the first decade of the twenty-first century are largely not situated in this context. For the most part, they are anchored in two bodies of thought that are products of twentieth-century **intellectual** development: **structuralism** and **semiotics**, on the one hand, **phenomenology** and **hermeneutics**, on the other.

Culture in structuralism and hermeneutics

The first influential theoretical background of contemporary cultural theory is to be found in structuralism and semiotics. Ferdinand de Saussure's *Course in General Linguistics* outlines key concepts of a structuralist theory of **language** which were transferred to a structuralist and semiotic theory of culture, notably in the work of Lévi-Strauss and Barthes. Like language, culture forms an immanently structured system of codes that determine which utterances and actions are possible. The structure of culture thus takes effect beyond

individual control and therefore 'decentres the subject'. Like language, culture forms a system of differences in which any single item receives its identity as a carrier of meaning only in its difference from other items of the system. These systems of differences are 'arbitrary'; they are social conventions, which do not reflect an intrinsic order of things but provide contingent representations according to an immanent logic.

Since the 1970s, the structuralist concept of culture has influentially been transformed by post-structuralist authors. Michel Foucault ([1969] 1972) detects cultural codes not in categories of mind but in historically specific **discourses**, i.e. in systems of regulation in utterances and texts. Foucault regards these discourses as productive carriers of social **power** which mould the shape of the person or subject (see **subject and subjectivity**). Jacques Derrida temporalizes and destabilizes the idea of cultural codes by turning systems of differences into the incalculable sequences of *différance*. For Pierre Bourdieu ([1972] 1977), cultural codes reside in social practices, i.e. in bodily patterns of behaviour, which depend on the incorporated schemes of disposition called **habitus** and 'practical sense'. A further branch of cultural theory, developed by Laclau and Mouffe (1985), and by British Cultural Studies, seeks to tie post-structuralism to a neo-Marxist theory of **domination**, revitalizing the concepts of **ideology** and **hegemony**. Similarly, large parts of contemporary **gender** theory – such as in the work of Judith **Butler** – and **postcolonial theory** – such as in the work of Edward **Said** and Stuart Hall – develop elements of post-structuralist culturalism, analyzing 'gender' and '**race**' as contingent products of specific discursive systems of differences.

A second influential branch of culturalist theorizing can be found in the 'interpretative' tradition (see Rabinow and Sullivan 1979), originating in phenomenology and hermeneutics, together with **Wittgensteinian** linguistic philosophy. Rather than viewing culture as a subject-transcending structure of codes, culture in this tradition is seen as referring to the meaning-ascribing activity of subjects in their **everyday** taken-for-granted world. Influenced primarily by Edmund Husserl's phenomenological theory of consciousness and of the **lifeworld** and by Martin **Heidegger**'s ontological hermeneutics, the interpretative perspective regards specific acts of understanding and interpreting the world as mobilizing sources of tacit taken-for-granted **knowledge** and as thus making up core elements of the human world of culture. Scientific understanding turns out to be only a specific case of understanding in general (see **Verstehen**). Erving Goffman analyzes the interpretative work necessary 'to make sense of' everyday situations, above all in social interactions. Harold Garfinkel's **ethnomethodology** motivates reconstruction of context-sensitive everyday understanding and practical know-how, embedded in the skilful accomplishment of social practices, a theoretical idea which in recent discussion has been further elaborated by Luc Boltanski and Laurent Thévenot's (1991) theory of situative fields of action.

This dichotomy between post-structuralist and hermeneutic theories of culture in some way copies the classical distinction between '**structure**'-orientated and '**agency**'-orientated approaches. Consequently, a number of attempts have been developed to create a specific 'structure–agency link' for cultural theory, such as in the work of Bourdieu, Boltanski and Thévenot or Jeffrey **Alexander** (see also Silverman 1997). This problem of how to conceptualize meaning both as a socio-historical product of systems of differences and as an agent's tool to interpret specific situations of action is linked to the issue of how to combine the 'structuralist' determining force of cultural codes with the 'post-structuralist' incalculabilities of cultural shifts, variations, contexts and subversions.

An issue that has emerged independently of the distinction between structuralism and interpretative approaches concerns the exact status or 'place' of culture: in mind, in discourse and texts or in practices (see also Reckwitz 2000). Both classical structuralism and phenomenology used to treat meaning structures as mental schemes, a model which seems to have been outmoded since the 1970s. The two most prominent alternatives are textualist and praxiological theories of culture, which transcend the distinction between the two theoretical camps: approaches such as discourse analysis, semiotics, text hermeneutics, 'new historicism' (Greenblatt) or a 'culture as text' – approaches (Geertz 1973) that situate symbolic forms on the level of textual units, from conversation to visual surfaces. Versions of a '**practice** theory' – from Bourdieu and late Foucault to Garfinkel and Theodor Schatzki – situate structures of meaning in bodily patterns of behaviour and their background of a culturally coded tacit knowledge. Culture is here seen in terms of routinized **performative** activities and implicit stocks of knowledge which are carried by 'material' units: by bodies and artefacts. Thus, in cultural theory since the 1990s, the relation between cultural codes and their incorporation in the **body**, on the one hand, and the relation between codes and the materiality of technical artefacts on the other, have been the key focus of conceptual work. The issue of the relation between culturalism and **materialism** here arises in new ways.

Culture and post-modernity

Cultural theories offer new perspectives on classical (or less classical) phenomena of modern societies. Social classes now are analyzed as communities of life-style and of implicitly shared dispositions and schemes. Economic **organizations** are seen as depending on variable 'organizational cultures' while modern politics is seen as revolving around political discourses and specific techniques of '**governmentality**'. Both **work** and **consumption** are seen to presuppose a specific culturally moulded subject of work and a specific subject of consumption. Science has been reconstructed as an ensemble of ethno-methods in the laboratory and of particular discursive regimes. The mass media have been theorized as sequences of **signs** which in turn depend on the audience's everyday knowledge. Gender and **sexuality** have been analyzed as products of historically-specific systems of differences and their incorporation.

In addition to these applications, cultural theories also offer basic general perspectives on modernity as a whole, and very frequently these perspectives have been linked to the debate on **postmodernity** sine the 1980s. Here attention has been focused on the historical local **contingency** of seemingly universalizing structures of modern societies, which in fact depend on highly specific cultural codes (cf. Richard **Rorty** (1989)). Modernity in these perspectives turns out not to evolve around a structural unity, but to be a playing field of cultural **difference**. Whereas classical sociological modernization theories used to regard modernity as the unfolding process of the rationality of certain basic structural principles – **capitalism** or functional differentiation, industrialism or **democracy** – from the angle of culture, here a number of conflicting, open-ended cultural codes, manifest in discourses and practices, are at work which are produced in a non-linear fashion in historical time and heterogeneously distributed in space. Consequently, **time** and **space**, history and globality, are dimensions which aid a cultural analysis of modernity, demonstrating its contingency and its cultural differences. An early attempt at such an approach can be found in the work of Max Weber, in his historicization and contextualization of capitalism. Culturalist analysis of time and history since the 1970s have been primarily

illustrated by the archaeological and genealogical approach of Michel Foucault ([1976] 1978) which has inspired a number of works across the social sciences and humanities on the historical contingency of cultural codes. Post-colonial theories of space and theories of cultural **globalization** have begun to work out the cultural multiplicity of paths into modernity and the **hybrid** relationship between Western and Eastern, Northern and Southern structures of meaning. Finally, analyses of complex conflictual relations between bourgeois ('high') culture and popular culture, hegemonic cultures and **subcultures**, cultures of work and of consumption, cultures of rationality and of aesthetization, reveal the antagonistic forms in which the modern subject is constructed and produced.

References and further reading

Alexander, J. and Seidman, S. (ed.) (1990) *Culture and Society*. Cambridge: Cambridge University Press.

Boltanski, L. and Théverot, L. (1991) *De la justification: les économies de la grandeur*. Paris: Gallimard.

Bourdieu, P. ([1972] 1977) *Outline of a Theory of Practice*. Cambridge: Cambridge University Press.

Butler, J. (1990) *Gender Trouble*. London: Routledge.

Foucault, M. ([1969] 1972) *Archaeology of Knowledge*. London: Tavistock.

Foucault, M. ([1976] 1978) *The History of Sexuality*, vol. 1. London: Penguin.

Gadamer, H. G. ([1960] 1975) *Truth and Method*. London: Sheed and Ward.

Geertz, C. (1973) *The Interpretation of Cultures*. New York: Basic Books.

Grossberg, L. (ed.) (1992) *Cultural Studies*. New York/London: Routledge.

Hall, S. (ed.) (1997) *Representations: Cultural Representations and Signifying Practices*. London: Sage.

Laclau, E. and Mouffe, C. (1985) *Hegemony and Socialist Strategy*. London: Verso.

Rabinow, P. and Sullivan, W. M. (eds) (1979) *Interpretive Social Science*. Berkeley, CA: University of California Press.

Reckwitz, A. (2000) *Die Transformation der Kulturtheorien*. Weilerswist: Velbrueck.

Rorty, R. (1989) *Contingency, Irony, and Solidarity*. Cambridge: Cambridge University Press.

Silverman, H. J. (1997) *Inscriptions: After Phenomenology and Structuralism*. Evanston, IL: Northwestern University Press.

Taylor, C. (1989) *Sources of the Self*. Cambridge: Cambridge University Press.

Williams, R. (1958) *Culture and Society, 1780–1950*. Harmondsworth: Penguin.

ANDREAS RECKWITZ

CYBERNETICS

The term cybernetics, coined by Norbert Wiener ([1948] 1961), derives from the Greek word for 'pilot'. The main subject of cybernetics is the problem of how systems are steered and internally governed and how feedback loops produce special forms of reactions and practices in complex systems. The best-known example is a thermostat which both controls and is controlled by its environment, such as a heated room.

The more technical application of 'first-order cybernetics' was followed by 'second-order cybernetics' beginning in the 1970s (von Foerster 1981). In the words of von Foerster, first-order cybernetics addresses 'observed systems', whereas second-order cybernetics is interested in 'observing systems'. This means that the self-observation of systems constitutes the basic form of self-steering and self-reproduction. The idea of self-observation is useful for sociology because all **social systems** use their capacity for self-observation in self-reproduction. It is significant that all basic terms of second-order cybernetics used by sociology are formed with the prefix 'self' (from the Greek *auto*), further implying that social systems are ruled by themselves or alternatively by the results of their own practices and processes. In this sense, second-order cybernetics is mainly concerned with what are called 'operationally closed systems'.

In sociology, cybernetic approaches were influential for Talcott **Parsons**, who used the idea of first-order cybernetics to support his own notion of a 'cybernetic hierarchy of control'. Second-order cybernetics had an explicit impact on subsequent formations of sociological **systems theory**, especially on Niklas **Luhmann**'s application of the theory of autopoietic systems and the discourse of 'sociocybernetics'.

References and further reading

Ashby, W. R. (1956) *Introduction to Cybernetics*. London: Wiley.

Geyer, R. F. and van der Zouwen, J. (eds) (1986) *Sociocybernetic Paradoxes: Observation, Control and Evolution of Self-Steering Systems*. London: Sage.

von Foerster, H. (1981) *Observing Systems*. Seaside, CA: Intersystems.

Wiener, N. ([1948] 1961) *Cybernetics, or Control and Communication in the Animal and the Machine*. Cambridge, MA: MIT Press.

ARMIN NASSEHI

CYBORGS

According to popular citation, the term 'cyborg' was first coined by Manfred E. Clynes and Nathan S. Kline to refer to a human – machine hybrid that would not require conscious self-regulation (Hables Gray 1995: 31). In other words, this entity would incorporate exterior components into its own body in order to better adapt to new and changing environments. Since the 1960s, the cyborg has captured the public imagination in science fantasy novels and films almost as much as it has increasingly featured in bio-technology research and social scientific analyses. The latter focuses on the potential impact of cyborgs on aspects of the social world, including the military, reproductive processes, medical uses, disability and transgender, and **post-colonialism** among others. However, perhaps the most discussed topic is the increased use of cyberspace and the ways in which the human/computer forms a particular hybrid (see **hybridity**).

One of the most important discussions girding these analyses is the extent to which the cyborg undermines the (lingering) understanding of the body as a distinct and autonomous entity. Discussions often assume that cyborgs are a 'new' invention. But at a basic level, life is, and has always been, 'technological' in the very real sense that living matter incorporates external structural materials. Hybridizations, whether organic, non-organic or a combination of the two, are indigenous to all networking systems. Thus, while the cyborg has certainly caught the contemporary imagination, biologically speaking, it has been around for literally millions of years.

References and further reading

Balsamo, A. (1995) *Technologies of the Gendered Body*. Durham, NC: Duke University Press.

Hables Gray, C. (ed.) (1995) *The Cyborg Handbook*. London: Routledge.

Haraway, D. (1991) *Simians, Cyborgs, and Women: The Reinvention of Nature*. London: Routledge.

Kirkup, J., Janes, L. and Woodward, K. (eds) (1999) *The Gendered Cyborg: A Reader*. London: Routledge.

MYRA HIRD

D

DAHRENDORF, RALF GUSTAV (1929–)

German-born sociologist resident in Britain. Dahrendorf was notable for his attack on **Parsons**'s 'utopian' model of social integration, arguing for the centrality of social **conflict** as played out across the stages of **class**, **law** and **polity**. As such, Dahrendorf bore the influence of **Weber**'s critique of **Marx**, identifying different types of conflict, defined in terms of **interest** and **authority** rather than solely in terms of ownership of **property**. He later modified this position, arguing that conflict occurs primarily over the distribution of 'life chances'. By the 1980s, Dahrendorf had moved away from a focus on class to examine general violations of law and lack of order as the key social problem and contradiction of **modernity**. Dahrendorf also made a major contribution to the debate on social **role**, critically exploring (and rejecting) in his influential essay *Homo Sociologicus* (1958) the proposition that individual behaviour can be explained as conformity to role expectations. Since the 1990s, Dahrendorf has concentrated much of his attention on a long-standing interest in the conditions of liberal democracy and **citizenship** in European societies and how they may be used to mitigate the conflict of interests and effects of **power** that inhibit individual **freedom**.

Major works

(1959) *Class and Class Conflict in Industrial Society*. London: Routledge & Kegan Paul.

(1968) *Essays in the Theory of Society*. London: Routledge & Kegan Paul.
(1975) *The New Liberty*. London: Routledge & Kegan Paul.
(1979) *Life Chances*. London: Weidenfeld & Nicolson.
(1988) *The Modern Social Conflict*. London: Weidenfeld & Nicolson.

Further reading

Peisert, H. and Zapf, W. (eds) (1994) *Gesellschaft, Demokratie und Lebenschancen*. Stuttgart: Deutsche Verlags-Anstalt.

CATHERINE A. MORGAN

DARWINISM

See: evolutionary theory.

DEATH AND MORTALITY

Since we all die, mortality – unlike variables such as **class**, **gender**, or **age** – does not, by itself, differentiate one person from another. But how **groups** and **institutions** respond to the death of a member varies, as do death rates, and the pushing of death further into old age, has profound social consequences.

The death of an individual can threaten group stability if the group is small (as in many traditional societies), or if the individual has great **power** (such as the death of a serving American president). **Durkheim** ([1912] 1965) showed how, through religious **ritual**, groups re-constitute themselves after a member's death; social **representation** and the collective conscience are classically displayed in mourning rites. In this view, death is, paradoxically, a major root of social **solidarity**. Holst-Warhaft (2000), however, shows how, under certain conditions, the passion of grief can drive mourners to **insurrection**, subverting rather than affirming the existing social order. Others argue that **religions** can create power for themselves by exacerbating fear of death, so death becomes a socially constructed fear rather than a given that generates social solutions.

Concerning the death of the ordinary individual in large-scale, secular modern societies, Ariès (1981), Mellor and Shilling (1993) and others argue that modern institutions and the fragmentation of social groupings sequester death, together with sexuality and mental illness, leaving people without social and ideological support in the face of death. Rather than solidifying social bonds, mourners are left alone in the face of the unmentionable. One negative perception is that modern medicine abandons the dying, while the mass **media** typically favour youth and health (see **health and illness**), creating a death–denying society. Another, more positive perception is that medicine, **science** and **technology** contribute to the deferral of death, while mass media representations of both famous and ordinary deaths bolster the quality of cultural life in the face of death (Seale 1998; Walter 2004). Here we see an echo of the debate about religion in traditional societies: do medicine and the media assist or fail people in the face of death? And does death itself challenge or support these institutions?

Only since the second half of the nineteenth century has the adult death rate decreased significantly in modern Western societies; and only since the early twentieth century has the infant mortality rate dramatically declined. In less than two centuries, life expectancy at birth has moved from where it has been since the origin of *homo sapiens* – somewhere between 30 and, in unusually healthy groups, 40 – to nearly 80. The consequences of this new **demography** are significant (Blauner 1966; Goldscheider 1971). First, the elderly no longer possess rarity value, and their great numbers may be perceived as a 'burden' by the working population, though their numbers also contain the potential to become a major political force. Second, birth rates have dropped dramatically as parents no longer need to rear many children to reproduce the population; children are no longer valued workers but emotional treasures and a major reason for **consumption**. Socially expected mourning for a deceased child now greatly exceeds that for an elderly person, whereas traditionally the death of a child required little formal marking. Third, with an expectation today of 65 years between puberty and death, all kinds of new social formations become possible. **Education** of people until their mid-twenties becomes a rational investment in human capital, while women can plan their lives as well as, or instead of, bearing and rearing children. It is only in low-mortality societies that higher **education** and feminism become mass possibilities. Meanwhile many marriages end not in death but in divorce, as couples face the strains of longevity unknown to most couples in pre-modern societies (see **marriage and divorce**).

Death and mortality, though highly significant for society, have played curiously little role in sociological theory. Archaeologists, however, if they are to infer anything at all about pre-historic **social structure**, **stratification**, **power** relationships and **elites** often have to rely for data on exhumed burial artefacts, human remains, and techniques for determining age and cause of death (Parker-Pearson 1999). The relationship between death, burial rites and society has therefore played a major role in social theorizing by archaeologists.

References and further reading

Ariès, P. (1981) *The Hour of Our Death*. London: Allen Lane.

Blauner, R. (1966) 'Death and Social Structure', *Psychiatry*, 29: 378–94.

Durkheim, E. ([1912] 1965) *The Elementary Forms of the Religious Life*. New York: Free Press.

Goldscheider, C. (1971) 'The Mortality Revolution', in C. Goldscheider (ed.) *Population, Modernization and Social Structure*. Boston: Little, Brown.

Holst-Warhaft, G. (2000) *The Cue for Passion*. Cambridge, MA: Harvard University Press.

Mellor, P. and Shilling, C. (1993) 'Modernity, Self-Identity and the Sequestration of Death', *Sociology*, 27(3): 411–32.

Parker-Pearson, M. (1999) *The Archaeology of Death and Burial*. Stroud: Sutton.

Seale, C. (1998) *Constructing Death: The Sociology of Dying and Bereavement*. Cambridge: Cambridge University Press.

Walter, C. (2004) 'Disaster, Modernity, and the Media', in K. Garces-Foley (ed.) *Death and Religion in a Changing World*. Armonk, NY: M. E. Sharpe.

TONY WALTER

DECONSTRUCTION

Deconstruction is a term primarily used to name a critical approach to Western metaphysics introduced by Jacques **Derrida**. A key feature of this approach is that it does not see its critique as external to the object of that critique, but instead as operating from within the tradition of the object. Deconstruction is 'affirmative' in the sense that it does not aim at simple destruction of a system of thought, but tries instead to conceive that which remains unthought in it. This approach demands procedures which need to be determined historically and strategically but which cannot be formalized as a method (Derrida 1991). Aimed at the distinctive condition of thought that Derrida terms **logocentrism**, deconstruction aspires to reverse and re-inscribe the hierarchical **binary** oppositions constitutive of traditional metaphysics (see **metaphysical**). These include such oppositions as speech versus writing, presence versus absence, origin versus supplement (Derrida 1974, 1981). Whatever its concrete object, deconstruction always attempts to reveal certain infrastructures already at work in the analyzed texts, practices or institutions. Such infrastructures, the most notable of which Derrida terms iterability and *différance* (see **difference**), have an inherently double and aporetic character: they form the necessary conditions of our discursive practices while at the same time subverting them. Deconstruction thus seeks to expose a structural element of self-subversion or auto-deconstruction, that is at work in everyday **language** and **communication**.

References and further reading

Culler, J. (1982) *On Deconstruction*. Ithaca, NY: Cornell University Press.

Derrida, J. ([1967] 1974) *Of Grammatology*. Baltimore, MD: Johns Hopkins University Press.

Derrida, J. ([1972] 1981) *Positions*. Chicago: University of Chicago.

Derrida, J. ([1987] 1991) 'Letter to a Japanese Friend', in P. Kamuf (ed.) *A Derrida Reader*. New York: Harvester Wheatsheaf.

Gasché, R. (1986) *The Tain of the Mirror*. Cambridge, MA: Harvard University Press.

THOMAS KHURANA

DELEUZE, GILLES (1925–1995)
French theorist

Deleuze is best known as a member of the **post-structuralist** current of French philosophy which includes **Derrida, Foucault**, Kristeva, and **Baudrillard**. He is the author of a number of important studies of philosophers, notably of Spinoza, **Kant**, Nietzsche and Bergson. He has also written extensively on literary figures (Proust, Kafka and Beckett), painters (Francis Bacon) and cinema. Deleuze's main themes are derived from his critique of **identity** thinking in philosophy and the development of perspectives based on **difference** and forms of non-oppositional multiplicity. The latter has given rise to a concern with post-foundational experiments in 'rhizomic thinking'. Deleuze is co-author, with Félix Guattari, of *Anti-Oedipus: Capitalism and Schizophrenia* (1972) which criticizes the 'Oedipal paradigm' of repression and sexual identity in classical Freudian theory and proposes an alternative theory of the functions of **difference** and schizophrenia in capitalist society (see **psychoanalysis**). In rejecting the Freudian Oedipal mythology as a methodology of **social control** and regulation, they commend a view of the 'deterritorialized subject' as both desire-machine and subject-in-transition. This follows from Deleuze's view of philosophizing as a creative work of conceptual construction (1991). Like his contemporary, Michel Foucault, Deleuze's contributions to modern social thought ultimately derive from suggesting new objects for thought, engaging in experimental thinking and generating creative paths of philosophizing.

Major works

([1969a] 1989) *The Logic of Sense*. London: Athlone.
([1969b] 1994) *Difference and Repetition*. New York: Columbia University Press.
([1972] 1984) (with F. Guattari) *Anti-Oedipus: Capitalism and Schizophrenia*. London: Athlone.
([1991] 1994) (with F. Guattari) *What is Philosophy?* London: Verso.

Further reading

Ansell-Pearson, K. (ed.) (1997) *Deleuze and Philosophy: The Difference Engineer*. London: Routledge.
Hardt, M. (1993) *Gilles Deleuze: An Apprenticeship in Philosophy*. Minneapolis, MN: University of Minnesota Press.

BARRY SANDYWELL

DEMOCRACY AND DEMOCRATIZATION

Democracy is not a modern invention. This holds true for the theory of democracy as well as for the numerous attempts to realize democracy through the last two millennia

(Held 1987; Schmidt 2000). Given the multitude of normative foundations with which democratic theory has been attributed and the various concrete forms democracy constitutes, a conceptual clarification of the term 'democracy' is necessary.

The term *demokratia*, consisting of two components *demos* (people) and *kratein* (govern/rule), has existed since the middle of the fifth century BC. *Demos* meant 'all' as well as 'the many'. The term *demos* defines the people politically and not ethnically (*ethnos*). Drawing on the political definition, the question of who belongs to the people (see also citizenship) has found various answers up to the twentieth century. In Athenian democracy, only the male citizens of the *polis* were included. In the course of the eighteenth and nineteenth centuries, more advanced industrial countries included all male citizens who complied with certain requirements. Only in the course of the twentieth century did women become a part of the *demos*: Austria (1902), Germany (1918), Great Britain (1928), France (1946), and Switzerland (1971).

In ancient Greece, the term 'democracy' referred to the small, contained 'city–state', which was more of a city than a **state** (Sartori 1992: 274). The Athenian democracy was also highly 'exclusive'. It excluded slaves, immigrant residents (*metoikoi*), and women from political participation. Only male citizens were entitled to political participation in the community. Due to its exclusive nature and because it was only implemented in small city–states, ancient democracy was able to operate as a direct democracy, in which political participation and political decisions were not separated by intermediary, representative bodies and **institutions**. The legislature and the executive were united in the people's assembly, open to all citizens. The governors were to be the governed in a process of self-government. It was not until the nineteenth and twentieth centuries that 'democracy' lost its exclusive character through the extension of the right to vote. Even in Abraham Lincoln's famous Gettysburg Address (1863), in which democracy is defined as 'government of the people, by the people and for the people', the notion of democracy was still based on an exclusive understanding of people that included the male black population, but excluded women and non-taxpayers. After 1918, universal suffrage was introduced in many western industrial countries. Only thereafter can we speak of modern and inclusive democracies.

A discussion of the historical implementation of democracy in North America and Europe (see Dunn 1992; Schmidt 2000) and its theoretical and conceptual development from John Locke to Rousseau, Montesquieu, **Tocqueville**, John Stuart **Mill**, Joseph **Schumpeter**, Robert Dahl, or Jürgen **Habermas** is beyond the scope of this entry (see Held 1987). However, this short list of outstanding theorists of democracy hints at the spectrum of different concepts and models subsumed under the term. Furthermore, there remains an ongoing debate about the normative foundations and the realizability of strong and weak, direct and indirect, elitist and participative, procedural and substantial models of democracy.

The most influential model in democratic theory in the past 50 years has been Robert Dahl's concept of polyarchy. From a minimalist perspective, the American scholar states two elementary and intertwined defining characteristics: there must be open competition for public offices and **power** and, at the same time, sufficient choice and space for political participation by all citizens. Dahl frames this succinctly as 'public contestation and the right to participate' (Dahl 1971: 5). To guarantee the necessary degree of accountability of the government towards the preferences of equal citizens in a democratic community, citizens must be given three fundamental choices: (1) the opportunity to formulate their preferences; (2) the opportunity to signify their preferences to their fellow citizens and the government by individual and collective **action**; and (3) the opportunity to have their preferences weighted equally by the government in disregard of their contents and sources.

Dahl himself points out that these are only 'necessary' but not 'sufficient' conditions for a democracy. Hence, they themselves must be secured through eight institutional guarantees (ibid.: 3):

1. Freedom to form and join organizations.
2. Freedom of expression.
3. Right to vote.
4. Eligibility for public office.
5. Right of political leaders to compete for votes and support.
6. Alternative sources of information.
7. Free and fair elections.
8. Institutions for making government policies depend on votes and other expressions of preference.

It is remarkable that the separation of powers, first discussed by John Locke and further elaborated by Montesquieu is not explicit in Dahl's minimalist concept of democracy. It is only implicitly comprised in point 8. Later, Dahl (1971) completely eliminated the horizontal accountability dimension from his concept of polyarchy. Hence, Dahl represents a lean concept of polyarchy that, with its Schumpeterian minimalism, clearly distinguishes itself from the maximalism of deliberative models of democracy (Fishkin 1991; Elster 1998; Gutman and Thompson 2004).

Modern liberal democratic systems include various institutional arrangements regarding the horizontal and vertical accountability, as well as a mixture of elements of direct democracy and representative decision-making procedures. All, however, share one common characteristic: the indeterminacy of the results of political decisions. The American political scientist, Adam Przeworski, consequently defines democracy as 'a system of ruled open-endedness or organized

127

uncertainty' (1991: 13). Hence democracy is an institutionalized system of rules to solve **conflicts** in society, in which a single constitutional power, a single institution, or a single actor cannot determine or control the results of political decisions. Results of political decisions in democracies are therefore not ex-ante determined, as in authoritarian or totalitarian systems, but are only the contingent outcome of competing political actors and their actions (see **totalitarianism**).

Placing political regimes on a continuum that reaches from ideal democracy to perfect totalitarianism, one can plot more accurately the three basic types of political regimes: democracy, authoritarian, and totalitarian systems. Democracy itself can be further differentiated into three sub-types along this axis: ideal democracy, polyarchy, and defective democracy. *Ideal democracy* remains a utopian **ideal type**, as does, incidentally, perfect totalitarianism. *Polyarchy*, following Dahl literally meaning 'rule of the many', captures the average type of existing democracies.

Defective democracies must be separated from polyarchy (Merkel 2004). They fall in the grey area between autocratic and democratic regimes, but usually at a minimum represent electoral democracies, permitting meaningful free and fair elections. In 2001, Freedom House counted 120 electoral democracies world-wide. More than half of these electoral democracies display a defective rule of **law**, limitations of civil **rights**, or violations of horizontal accountability. These are by no means merely transitional regimes but tend to stabilize themselves in the long run. Thus the concept of 'defective democracy' fills a conceptual gap in democratic theory, as well as in empirical democracy research. At the beginning of the twenty-first century, there are more defective than liberal democracies world-wide.

The concept of *democratization* is best understood under the wider umbrella concept of 'regime transformation'. In general, a regime transformation or a regime change (Merkel 1999) can be defined as the interval between an old and a new system (O'Donnell and Schmitter 1986: 6ff.). It comprises the dissolution of the old and the establishment of the new regime. Basic **structures**, functions, legitimacies, and patterns of **integration** of the old regime are replaced.

System transformations can occur in two directions: from autocracy to democracy and vice versa. The end of an autocratic regime can have different causes. Systematically, internal and external causes can be distinguished. The most important of the internal causes leads to the final breakdown of legitimacy. The legitimacy of an autocratic regime wanes when economic inefficiency rises so high that the material goods intended to compensate for the deprivation (see **deprivation and relative deprivation**) of democratic rights to participate can no longer be delivered. However, both *economic inefficiency* as well as *economic efficiency*, can lead autocratic regimes into a substantial crisis. **Modernization** theory (**Lipset** 1981: 469) has convincing arguments to explain why economic development changes the social **structure**, generates a **middle class**, raises the **education** level, and evokes demands for political participation that challenge the political monopoly of the autocratic **elites**. The transformations in East Asia provide impressive empirical evidence. The most important external causes include: defeats in **wars** (1945), the withdrawal or granting of essential support from outside powers, and regional domino effects, as in Eastern Europe after 1989 (Huntington 1991).

The central step to a democracy is the transfer of political **power** from one person or a **group** of persons to a set of institutionalized rules, which are equally valid for both the ruling and the ruled (Przeworski 1991: 14). The phase of institutionalizing democracy ends when the first free elections (founding elections) are held and the new **constitution** is passed. The founding elections and the establishment of the main democratic institutions, such as the executive, the legislature, and the judiciary, do not imply that the new regime is stable or consolidated. The consolidation of democracy takes much longer than its institutionalization.

Even more contested than the beginning is the end of democratic consolidation. Minimalist positions (Di Palma 1990; Przeworski 1991) compete with more demanding concepts (Gunther *et al.* 1995; Pridham 1995). The strongest analytical differentiation to the concept of democratic consolidation was added by Linz and Stepan (1996) and later by Merkel (1998). Merkel distinguishes four levels of a political system that must be consolidated for meaningful and sustainable democratic consolidation: (1) constitutional consolidation, involving the central institutions of government, parliament, judiciary, the electoral system; (2) representational consolidation, involving parties, interest groups, and associations; (3) behavioural consolidation, involving military, large landowners, capital, radical movements, or guerrillas (4) consolidation of **civil society** (Almond and Verba 1963; Keane 1988). The consolidation of civil society forms the indispensable foundation of a functioning democracy and completes democratic consolidation. It can take decades and is often only sealed through a generational change, as we know from the comparative political culture research on the second democratization wave in Italy, Germany, Austria, and Japan. A consolidated democracy is a largely crisis-resistant democracy whose existence is not drawn into question by short-term economic, social, or political turbulences.

References and further reading

Almond, G. and Verba, S. (1963) *The Civic Culture*. Princeton, NJ: Princeton University Press.

Dahl, R. A. (1971) *Polyarchy: Participation and Opposition*. New Haven, CT: Yale University Press.

Di Palma, G. (1990) *To Craft Democracies: An Essay on Democratic Transitions*. Berkeley, CA: University of California Press.

Dunn, J. (1992) *Democracy: The Unfinished Journey*. Oxford: Oxford University Press.

Elster, J. (1998) *Deliberative Democracy*. Cambridge: Cambridge University Press.

Fishkin, J. S. (1991) *Democracy and Deliberation: New Directions for Democratic Reform*. New Haven, CT: Yale University Press.

Gunther, R., Diamandouros, N. K. and Puhle, H.-J. (eds) (1995) *The Politics of Democratic Consolidation: Southern Europe in Comparative Perspective*. Baltimore, MD: Johns Hopkins University Press.

Gutman, A. and Thompson, D. (2004) *Why Deliberative Democracy?* Princeton, NJ: Princeton University Press.

Held, D. (1987) *Models of Democracy*. Stanford, CA: Stanford University Press.

Huntington, S. P. (1991) *The Third Wave: Democratization in the Late Twentieth Century*. Norman, OK: University of Oklahoma Press.

Keane, J. (1988) *Democracy and Civil Society*. London: Verso.

Linz, J. J. and Stepan, A. (1996) *Problems of Democratic Transition and Consolidation: Southern Europe, South America and Post-Communist Europe*. Baltimore, MD: Johns Hopkins University Press.

Lipset, S. M. (1981) *Political Man: The Social Basis of Politics*. Baltimore, MD: Johns Hopkins University Press.

Merkel, W. (1998) 'The Consolidation of Post-autocratic Regimes: A Multilevel Model', *Democratization*, 3: 33–65.

Merkel, W. (1999) *Systemtransformation: Eine Einführung in die Theorie und Empirie der Transformationsforschung*. Opladen: Leske und Budrich.

Merkel, W. (2004) 'Embedded and Defective Democracies', in A. Croissant and W. Merkel (eds) 'Consolidated or Defective Democracy? Problems of Regime Change', special issue of *Democratization*, 11(5): 33–58.

O'Donnell, G. and Schmitter, P. C. (1986) *Transition from Authoritarian Rule: Tentative Conclusions about Uncertain Democracies*. Baltimore, MD: Johns Hopkins University Press.

Pridham, G. (1995) 'The International Context of Democratic Consolidation: Southern Europe in Comparative Perspective', in R. Gunther, N. P. Diamandouros and H.-J. Puhle (eds) *The Politics of Democratic Consolidation: Southern Europe in Comparative Perspective*. Baltimore, MD: Johns Hopkins University Press.

Przeworski, A. (1991) *Democracy and the Market: Political and Economic Reforms in Eastern Europe and Latin America*. Cambridge: Cambridge University Press.

Sartori, G. (1992) *Demokratietheorie*. Darmstadt: Wissenschaftliche Buchgesellschaft.

Schmidt, M. G. (2000) *Demokratietheorien: Eine Einführung.* Opladen: Leske and Budrich.

WOLFGANG MERKEL

DEMOGRAPHY

Demography is the scientific study of human population dynamics. It deals with changes in size, structure and distribution of populations according to diverse criteria, such as **age**, **sex**, marital status, educational attainment, and ethnic origin. The main research areas of demography are the determinants of population dynamics: fertility, mortality and **migration** and related processes such as **marriage and divorce**. The term 'demography' was first used by Achille Guillard, a Belgian statistician, in 1855. Population counts for taxation or military purposes were conducted in ancient Egypt, Babylonia, China and Rome. But census taking is well documented for European countries from around the fifteenth century. John Graunt (1620–74), Johann Peter Süssmilch (1707–67) and Thomas Robert Malthus (1766–1834) can be considered the intellectual founders of demography.

Demographic data are generated by census and by population registers of marriage, birth, death and place of residence. In addition, demography uses sample surveys, like the Demographic and Health Surveys (DHS) in many developing countries, which have no reliable birth and death registers. Problems researched by demographers are important topics for other disciplines, such as fertility for sociologists and mortality for epidemiologists. In many cases, the use of specific methods defines the unique approach of demography to these problems. Substantial progress in the development of demographic estimation methods for countries with incomplete or deficient statistics was achieved in the 1950s and 1960s. One of the basic methods and concepts of demography is the life (actuarial) table, which goes back to John Graunt's *Natural and Political Observations Made Upon the Bills of Mortality* in 1662. This is the basis for life insurance calculations and is applied to many other areas inside and outside of demography.

Demographic research has always tried to extrapolate insights from past and current population dynamics to the future. Thomas Robert Malthus concluded from his analysis at the end of the eighteenth century that population growth would follow an exponential pattern, while food production would grow only linearly. His *Essay on the Principle of Population*, published in 1798, made him the intellectual father of concepts of over-population. However, his prediction did not materialize. Although England and other European countries experienced a phase of population growth from the eighteenth century to the twentieth century, this proved to be only a temporary phenomenon. Demographers such as Frank W. Notestein explained in retrospect how, for a period of time termed the *demographic transition*, mortality started to decline while fertility remained on a high level. For this period the opening gap between birth rate and death rate induced population growth. However, in a later stage of this process fertility started to decline too and the gap closed. The concept of demographic transition helped to explain the temporary nature of the accelerating growth of the world population induced in developing countries during the mid-twentieth century. Experiences from the past three decades in Latin America, Asia and partly in Africa have verified this.

However, another aspect of the concept of demographic transition has required modification. Originally, demographers expected the demographic transition to lead from a pre-modern equilibrium of births and deaths through a transition process to a modern equilibrium of births and deaths. Since the 1970s it has become clearer that for many developed societies birth rates have fallen below the level of death rates, resulting in a negative natural growth rate of population. This has been called the 'second' demographic transition. Initially in most countries immigration more than compensated for the birth deficit. However, current population projections show the scope of the birth deficit as increasing. This will result in accelerated demographic ageing and further population decline in the developed world (see **age**). Until the end of the twentieth century, demography focused predominantly on population growth, mostly in developing countries. Although the growth of world population will continue for decades to come, demography in the twenty-first century is focusing increasingly on problems related to ageing and population decline.

References and further reading

Pressat, R. (1985) *The Dictionary of Demography*. Ed. Christopher Wilson. Oxford: Blackwell Reference.

Rowland, D. T. (2003) *Demographic Methods and Concepts*. Oxford: Oxford University Press.

Siegel, J. S. and Swanson, D. A. (2004) *The Methods and Materials of Demography*, 2nd edn. San Diego, CA: Elsevier Academic Press.

Walle, E. von de (1982) *IUSSP: Multilingual Demographic Dictionary, English Section*, 2nd edn. Adapted from the French Section. Ed. Louis Henry. Liège: Ordina.

RALF E. ULRICH

DEPRIVATION AND RELATIVE DEPRIVATION

The term deprivation is generally used to signal a condition of not having something which a person reasonably could expect to have. The social sciences distinguish – by analogy with the narrower concept of **poverty** – between absolute and relative deprivation. In an *absolute* interpretation of the concept, people are viewed as deprived when they cannot participate in social activities and live under social conditions and amenities which are not standard in the society to which they belong. The term *relative deprivation* refers to an experienced lack of socially perceived necessities, when individuals compare themselves with others. The experienced sense of relative deprivation therefore involves: (1) the perception of one's own situation, those of others or of the society, together with (2) comparison processes; and (3) is usually defined in subjective terms; and (4) can shape attitudes or activate behaviour.

The concept of relative deprivation was introduced and coined by Stouffer *et al.* (1949) to make sense of a puzzling empirical result. They found that the US Military Police were more satisfied with their career chances than soldiers in the Air Corps, even though the Military Police in fact had fewer opportunities to be promoted. The researchers explained this paradox with the feeling of 'relative deprivation'. Because a greater number of soldiers in the Air Corps were being promoted, the perceptions of soldiers who were *not* promoted were dominated by those who *succeeded* in getting promoted, which resulted in a feeling of deprivation. In contrast, the majority of promoted military police who had not been promoted compared themselves more with those who were also not being promoted and therefore they felt greater satisfaction with their career. In this study the main aspects of the concept of relative deprivation were identified, although they were not systematically developed. Further steps were taken by **Merton** and Rossi (1968) pointing out the kinship of the concept of relative deprivation to other sociological concepts such as 'social frame of reference', 'patterns of expectations' or the 'definition of the situation'. In particular, the importance of comparison processes of one's own situation with that of others, especially that of *reference groups*, was underlined.

The most elaborate theoretical notion of relative deprivation was worked out by W. G. Runciman in his influential study *Relative Deprivation and Social Justice* (1966). He was interested in the connection of subjective perceptions and evaluations of social **inequality** with actual inequality, especially in terms of the objective conditions of social inequality under which subjective feelings of being disadvantaged or being treated unjustly emerge or induce revolt against social conditions. An individual A is relatively deprived of X, if:

(1) A does not have X,
(2) but others, with whom A compares him or herself, are assumed to have X (whether or not this is in fact the case),
(3) A wants X and
(4) A sees a realistic possibility of getting X.

(ibid.: 10)

Runciman here uses the theory of reference groups to further develop the idea of relative deprivation via social comparisons. He extends this theory by differentiating between three reference groups: (1) the 'comparative reference group', with which an individual compares him or herself directly; (2) the 'normative reference group', from which the standards for comparisons are to be derived; and the (3) 'membership reference group' to which the individual feels he or she belongs. The type of reference group is decisive in determining whether an individual feels directly deprived. 'Egoistic deprivation' is present if an individual is dissatisfied with his or her own position within the 'membership reference group', while 'fraternalistic deprivation' occurs if an individual is dissatisfied with the group position within the social order.

These early considerations of the concept of relative deprivation and its emergence have continued to energize research in different disciplines and contexts. Social psychologists, in particular, have developed numerous theoretical models to measure and explain relative deprivation. They also point out the importance of social perception processes, which have been largely neglected in more recent sociological approaches. While theoretical considerations about relative deprivation can be applied in principle to many contexts, the term plays a particularly important role in the study of social **inequality**, poverty, **social justice** and **social movements**.

References and further reading

Davis, J. A. (1959) 'A Formal Interpretation of the Theory of Relative Deprivation', *Sociometry*, 22(4): 280–96.

Kosaka, K. (1986) 'A Model of Relative Deprivation', *Journal of Mathematical Sociology*, 12(1): 35–48.

Merton, R. K. and Rossi, A. S. ([1949] 1968) 'Contributions to the Theory of Reference Group Behavior', in R. K. Merton, *Social Theory and Social Structure*. New York: Free Press, pp. 279–334.

Olson, J. M., Herman, C. P. and Zanna, M. P. (eds) (1986) *Relative Deprivation and Social Comparison*. Hillsdale, NJ: Erlbaum.

Runciman, W. G. (1966) *Relative Deprivation and Social Justice: A Study of Attitudes to Social Inequality in Twentieth-Century England*. London: Routledge & Kegan Paul.

Stouffer, S. A., Suchman, E. A., DeVinney, L. C., Star, S. A. and Williams, R. M. Jr. (1949) *The American Soldier: Adjustment During Army Life*, vol. 1. Princeton, NJ: Princeton University Press.

Townsend, P. (1987) 'Deprivation', *Journal of Social Policy*, 16(2): 125–46.

Walker, I. and Smith, H. J. (eds) (2002) *Relative Deprivation: Specification, Development, and Integration*. Cambridge: Cambridge University Press.

BODO LIPPL

DERRIDA, JACQUES (1930–2004)

French theorist

Derrida is widely known for three major works published in 1967: *Speech and Phenomena*, *Of Grammatology*, and *Writing and Difference*. In these and subsequent writings Derrida characterized Western philosophical thought, beginning with Plato, as a 'metaphysics of presence' dependent upon a system of hierarchical oppositions, such as presence and absence, **identity** and **difference**, and interiority and exteriority. According to this 'post-structuralist' thesis, it is not possible to escape from metaphysical thought in any immediate way (see

post-structuralism). The only way to transgress it is to develop a practice of **deconstruction** or immanent dismantling of ideas, revealing a hidden aporetic logic in the **discourses** analyzed. After the late 1980s, Derrida's work underwent a change which has been generally considered to be an 'ethical turn', but might more appropriately be characterized as a change in emphasis, highlighting possible resources for social theory. This includes: (1) a conception of the irreducibility of our being-with-others and the **autonomy** of **communication** (Derrida 1988); (2) a critique of an economy of exchange (Derrida 1992); (3) an ethics of otherness linked to a specific concept of **justice** (Derrida 1990); and (4) the idea of a democracy 'to-come' (Derrida 1997).

Major works

([1967a] 1973) *Speech and Phenomena*. Evanston, IL: Northwestern University Press.

([1967b] 1974) *Of Grammatology*. Baltimore, MD: Johns Hopkins University Press.

([1967c] 1978) *Writing and Difference*. Chicago: University of Chicago Press.

(1988) *Limited Inc*. Evanston, IL: Northwestern University Press.

(1990) 'Force of Law', *Cardozo Law Review*, 11(5–6): 919–1045.

([1991] 1992) *Given Time*. Chicago: University of Chicago Press.

([1994] 1997) *Politics of Friendship*. London: Verso.

Further reading

Bennington, G. and Derrida, J. (1992) *Jacques Derrida*. Chicago: University of Chicago Press.

THOMAS KHURANA

DETERMINISM

Determinism has a complex history in social theory. Various doctrines of determinism have been reflected in political terms such as **progress** or **development** implying that progress or development occurs on a predetermined track, though not necessarily that progress or development *will* occur. Determinisms of different kinds have originated in theology, philosophy, and have been buttressed by scientific **naturalism**, particularly the idea that human **action** is ultimately physical and therefore governed by physical laws.

The most controversial and mysterious, yet potent, determinisms in social theory are what might be called 'in the last instance' determinisms, which are predictions about what must ultimately occur, given certain features of the world, humanity, or history. These features are often telic – that is, features about human purposes that are, on the aggregate historical level, casually deterministic about ultimate outcomes. Condorcet's and **Kant**'s ([1784] 1980) 'universal history' ideas and **Marx**'s ([1848] 1990) predictions of the historical process are both of this general type. Though these writers qualified their claims in complex ways that make it difficult to pin them down, they each operated by showing that the pre-existing purposive properties of individuals lead inevitably to certain collective outcomes, which can be understood as the hidden purpose of the process. Sometimes these take the form of a ratchet effect, where once something has happened, no return to the former situation is possible.

References and further reading

Condorcet, M. de ([1795] 1955) *Sketch of an Historical View of the Progress of the Human Mind*. London: Weidenfeld & Nicolson.

Kant, I. ([1784] 1980) 'Idea for a Universal History from a Cosmopolitan Point of View', in L. W. Beck (ed.) *On History: Immanuel Kant*. Indianapolis, IN: Bobbs Merrill.

Marx, K. ([1848] 1990) 'The Communist Manifesto', in D. McLellan (ed.) *Karl Marx: Selected Writings*. Oxford: Oxford University Press.

STEPHEN P. TURNER

DEVELOPMENT

From the French word *développer*, meaning 'to lay open', the term 'development' was used in the beginning of the modern era to denote the act of arguing by decomposing or dissecting phenomena. In the course of applications to all kinds of natural and cultural phenomena, the meaning of the term changed from a passive sense of unravelling to an active sense of unfolding. A given object came to be understood as an effect or sequence in the process of unfolding.

Development denotes irreversible changes prevailing over long periods that result either from an increase in quantity leading to a change in quality or from a shift from low to high quality. In both cases a direction of change is specified and an explanation is given by recourse to one or more of four basic models.

The *first* model denotes layers which form an ordered **stratification** and accommodates change in terms of the adding of new layers. The *second* model distinguishes at least three states – an initial, a middle and an end state. A process of transition is conceptualized in terms of qualitative changes; for example, in Marx's use of the concept of **modes of production**, leading to revolutionary overthrow as a theory of societal development. The *third* model describes development along a continuum between two ideal states, from **tradition** to **modernity**, where change is understood as a continuous process. The *fourth* model identifies increases in certain specific features that capture qualitative change. The concept of **differentiation**, first formulated by **Spencer**, is one of the most prominent instances of this.

In all these concepts, progression and regression are understood as temporal occurrences in the line of development. In defining a driving force of development, models of **social change** put the explanatory emphasis either on individuals and their **action** or on the structural constraints and contradictions. Concepts of development deal with the paradox of change by binding the identical with the non-identical into one grand entity, by melting historically distinctive states into one master unit, into the idea of 'universal history'.

The idea of development is closely linked to the rise of modernity and **industrialization**, and to accompanying changes in **social structure** and the **economy**. When **Kant** (1784) strictly distinguished between natural and cultural development, the way was opened for a historical, cultural and social scientific explanation of social change. From then onwards, two main lines of thought can be distinguished: on the one hand. an idealistic view, centred around the idea of the perfection of the mind and reason, represented in different ways by Hegel (see **Hegelianism and Neo-Hegelianism**) and **Comte**; on the other, a materialistic view most prominently put forward by **Marx**. Both approaches can be characterized as deterministic, since the development of the material base or the realm of ideas determines the social structure and all future development. Both understand development as **progress**, as change from lower to higher levels, which are defined by normative standards. Both are teleological, since the end-state of societal development is at least anticipated, if not known. Both draw heavily on analogies between society and the organism and can essentially be understood as evolutionist in orientation, akin to **evolutionary theory**.

At the beginning of the twentieth century, evolutionist accounts of development lost ground. Instead, historical-comparative approaches represented by **Weber**'s account of the rise of **capitalism** in the West gained importance. Weber combined idealistic and materialistic views, understanding development in terms of processes of **rationalization**, immanent potentially to all societies and cultural circles, and thus implying a multi-linear perspective (see **Occident** and **rationality and rationalization**).

In the mid-twentieth century **Parsons** joined the insights of Weber with the explicitly evolutionary thought of Spencer. Establishing a functionalist approach, Parsons's approach conceives the development of societies in terms of the effect of transitions from one state of equilibrium to another by a process of differentiation. The society in the new equilibrium is more complex and autonomous: it has improved its generalized adaptive capacity. Parsons singles out certain structural innovations which allow for this process of adaptive upgrading. He sees these as evolutionary universals by which a universal scale of development is established.

In the 1950s **functionalism** and evolutionism were seen as shedding valuable light on the problems of so-called Third World countries when compared to communist (Second World) and capitalist (First World) industrialized nations. Modernization theory became the dominant explanation for social and economic development. As Rostow (1990) points out, there was a dominant assumption of processes of rationalization in technology, social structure just distributions of wealth in society. These ideas informed many of the post-war policies in the industrialized West and were used by decision-makers world-wide in their efforts to combat underdevelopment.

However, at the end of the twentieth century the idea of development came under attack from **post-colonial theorists** (e.g. Hall 1996). Drawing on **post-structuralism**, **postmodernism** and cultural studies, these theorists have criticized the concept of modernization and linear development as Eurocentric and epistemologically naïve. Since the beginning of the twenty-first century, ideas of irreversible unilinear development have given way to explanations of adaptation drawing on teleonomic and selectionist mechanisms, leading to context-bound and open-ended pictures of the processes of development.

References and further reading

Hall, S. (1996) 'The West and the Rest: Discourse and Power', in S. Hall, D. Held, D. Hubert, K. Thompson (eds) *Modernity: An Introduction to Modern Societies*. Oxford: Blackwell.
Kant, I. ([1784] 1968) 'Idee zu einer allgemeinen Geschichte in weltbürgerlicher Absicht', in I. Kant, *Kants Werke. Akademie-Ausgabe*, vol. 8. Berlin: de Gruyter.
Nisbet, R. A. (1969) *Social Change and History: Aspects of the Western Theory of Development*. New York: Oxford University Press.
Rostow, W. W. ([1960] 1990) *Stages of Economic Growth: A Non-Communist Manifesto*. New York: Cambridge University Press.
Schelke, W., Krauth, W.-H., Kohli, M., and Elwert, G. (2000), *Paradigms of Social Change: Modernization, Development, Transformation, Evolution*. Frankfurt am Main: Campus.
Schluchter, W. (1985) *The Rise of Western Rationalism: Max Weber's Developmental History*. Berkeley, CA: University of California Press.
Weber, M. ([1920] 1988) 'Vorbemerkung', in M. Weber, *Gesammelte Aufsätze zur Religionssoziologie*, vol. I. Tübingen: Mohr.

CHRISTIAN SCHMIDT-WELLENBURG

DEVIANCE

Deviance is a contested term within and outside academe, whose meaning varies historically, by discipline and by school. Definitions of deviance stem from different epistemological and metaphysical assumptions about human nature and social order. **Consensus** or functionalist schools define deviance as acts that violate societal norms or offend against the *conscience collective* (**Durkheim** [1895] 1964) (see **functionalism**). Proponents argue that all societies have a core set of shared values that specify desirable and undesirable attitudes, behaviours and conditions. Indeed, to endure as stable social orders, they must have. **Conflict** or **Marxist** perspectives define deviance as behaviour that has been labelled as problematic, immoral or harmful. Here **power**, not consensus, determines what is deviant. Deviance becomes an attempt (successful or unsuccessful) at **social control**, a mechanism that legitimates exclusion. Sociological studies of deviance today incorporate insights from **postmodern**, **feminist** and **social construction** perspectives, shifting focus away from the deviant actor, onto the deviance-defining process.

Deviance developed from the nascent discipline of sociology through the attempts of nineteenth-century European scholars to grapple with the key question of **modernity**: how could social control be achieved, and order maintained, under democratic rule? With **industrialization** and science challenging traditional and religious belief systems, urbanization and immigration creating mobility, and bureaucratization transforming **work** and **authority**, what would provide meaning, maintain deference, and limit desire? **Inequality** was accepted as inevitable (or desirable), but control through force, the ancient coercive power of sovereign and **state**, was economically, socially and politically problematic in democratic regimes bound to deliver egalitarian **justice**. Deviance, then, provided the necessary conceptual space between the normative (the 'good') and the criminal (the 'bad').

In the past, theories derived from functionalism, **Marx**, and from **symbolic interactionism** were dominant. Functionalist or consensus traditions see deviance as an integral part of all healthy societies. It is critical to the process of forming norms and marking boundaries. Its occurrence demonstrates the limits of the acceptable, providing guidance and validation to everyone in that society. Moreover, a collective, public response to deviance, expressed through sanctions ranging from disapproval to decapitation, maintains cohesion and reinforces social **solidarity**. In *The Rules of Sociological Method* ([1895]/1964), Durkheim argued that, in a society of saints, the smallest transgression of thought, word or deed would *necessarily* be magnified and punished. A distinctive American version of this perspective, known as the theory of **anomie**, was developed by Robert **Merton** (1938). Treating **crime** as synonymous with deviance, Merton explained it as a rational response to stress induced by the disjunction between societal goals and legitimate means. The American Dream promised success (wealth) to all. However, the socially approved means to achieve success – elite schools, clubs and executive jobs – were only available to upper-middle-class Anglo-Americans. Merton hypothesized four possible responses to strain: innovation, retreatism, ritualism and rebellion. Innovation, the most interesting response to Merton and his followers, results from accepting success goals while rejecting the prescribed means of obtaining them. Bootlegging or racketeering, for example, are innovations that allow lower-class individuals to attain culturally prescribed goals through the invention of alternate, though illegitimate, means. Retreatists are seen as rejecting both goals and means (tramps, hobos and drug addicts), ritualists as accepting legitimate means but not goals (the petty bureaucrat to whom procedure is everything), while rebels reject existing goals and means and substitute new ones.

Marxist-oriented conflict theories (also called new or radical criminology) locate the causes of deviant behaviour (law-breaking) in **class conflict** and exploitation. Although Marx dismissed criminals as a *Lumpenproletiat*, an easily bribed, reactionary tool of the bourgeoisie, radical criminologists in the 1970s argued that capitalism is essentially criminogenic: the labour of the poor or **proletariat** is exploited by the rich or the **bourgeoisie** to maximize profits. Crime occurs when the alienated, oppressed **working class** refuse to accept their exploitation. It is repressed by the state, to preserve class rule. This explains the over-representation of the poor in prisons, and state preoccupation with crimes of the powerless at the expense of white-collar and corporate crime. Studies such as Paul Willis's *Learning to Labour* (1977) argued that bourgeois institutions, especially schools, sustain inequality by streaming working-class youth into dead-end jobs. Later studies examined the role of **media** in demonizing lower-class minorities (the Birmingham School).

In the 1960s labelling theory, rooted in symbolic interactionism, shifted attention onto those who impose the deviant label, questioning assumptions that deviance was a characteristic of the individual. As early as 1951, Edwin Lemert pointed out that, while everyone engages in rule-breaking behaviour (primary deviance), it is unlikely to produce secondary deviance unless noticed. Being pronounced deviant, by socially accredited officials such as the police, teachers and parents, sets in motion a process where the labelled take on the behaviour and attitudes they are expected to display.

Howard Becker in *Outsiders* (1963) showed that secondary deviance happens when the label becomes a master **status**. When reinforced in subsequent interactions by significant others, who communicate to the labelled person that deviance is henceforth expected, the deviant label becomes the person's **identity**. He/she learns to play a deviant role, which may lead to membership in a deviant **subculture**. If this happens, deviance gets built into group membership, and is passed onto successive recruits. David Matza's *Becoming Deviant*, (1969) showed how people charged as thieves come to see themselves this way. As relatives, friends and prospective employers treat them as though they are *really* 'nothing but a thief', conforming identities and behaviours become more difficult for the labelled to display, and more difficult for others to notice when displayed. Similar studies showed how staff in mental hospitals 'teach' new patients to play the role of the mental patient, and how those with a deviant identity manage the associated stigma by controlling their presentation of self, their contacts and visibility.

Dominant perspectives today build on traditional approaches in different ways. Social construction combines Weberian conflict theory, which locates power in authority relations between elite and non-elite groups, with labelling theory. Scholars ask how deviant identities and careers are maintained, and examine the characteristics and consequences of gang formation and similar deviant subcultures.

Power is the defining characteristic of deviance studies in **postmodern** perspectives grounded in the studies of Michel **Foucault**. Theorists ask how norms that define deviance are brought into being, by whom, and under which social and historical conditions. They deconstruct organized systems of knowledge that shape meaning and frame (see **framing**) experience to reveal underlying relations of power. Postmodern studies of **sexuality**, for example, trace the development of **binary** categories which classified all humans as exclusively heterosexual or homosexual, the effects of these claims, and resistance to them.

Feminist perspectives first entered deviance studies as critiques pointing out that all pre-1975 theories of deviance focused exclusively on men. Merton's theory of anomie, for example, locates deviance in the tension between prescribed success goals and restricted means, ignoring the fact that dominant goals for women in the 1950s were marriage and motherhood. Similarly, labelling theories either ignored women or presented them from the view of the male subject, 'the old lady' who shackled the free-spirited bohemian. Radical criminology seems to have assumed women were not exploited by **capitalism**, since they were never discussed. This is not true today. Scholars have now examined the differential labelling and control of women, the emphasis on the female body, the cultural obsession with female sexuality, the implications of woman as prostitute, bad mother, anorexic, or drug addict (Smart 1989).

All concepts of deviance assume the validity of the social. Deviance is a collective phenomenon, stemming from collective (social) conditions (Sumner 2004). Such beliefs are challenged by postmodern assertions that 'society' is a totalizing, essentialist category (see **postmodernism and postmodernity**). Can deviance as a concept have meaning in an individualistic age, with Internet interactions replacing face-to-face? Are neo-liberal **globalization** scripts destroying the basis of collective categorizations and judgments? Such complexities increasingly preoccupy those who study and define deviance today.

References and further reading

Becker, H. (1963) *Outsiders*. New York: Free Press.

Durkheim, E. ([1895] 1964) *The Rules of Sociological Method*. New York: Free Press.

Lemert, E. (1951) *Social Pathology*. New York: Free Press.

Matza, D. (1969) *Becoming Deviant*. Englewood Cliffs, NJ: Prentice Hall.

Merton, R. (1938) 'Social Structure and Anomie', *American Sociological Review*, 3: 672–82.

Smart, C. (1989) *Feminism and the Power of Law*. London: Routledge.

Sumner, C. (2004) 'The Social Nature of Crime and Deviance', in *The Blackwell Companion to Criminology*. Oxford: Blackwell.

Willis, P. (1977) *Learning to Labour: How Working Class Kids get Working Class Jobs*. Farnborough: Saxon House.

LAUREEN SNIDER

DIALECTIC

The philosophical concept of 'dialectic' first emerged in Plato's *Dialogues*, in which the main character, Socrates, engages in disputations with respected individuals on the definition of various ideas through a process of testing (and generally rejecting) a series of hypotheses. The rejection may lead the interlocutors in the discussion to new insights into how their analysis needs to develop. Hence dialectic is part of Plato's *maieutic* method (philosophical 'midwifery'). However, in Plato's *Dialogues* this dialectical procedure is not necessarily positive: if a concept cannot be adequately determined, it must remain inconclusive. This negative dynamic of dialectic was thematized by Aristotle who, in *On Sophistical Refutations*, described dialectical arguments as 'those which, starting from generally accepted opinions, reason to establish a contradiction'.

Immanuel Kant gave the term a pejorative significance, as he associated it with reasoning which is (1) inherently faulty, and (2) seeks to adduce untested truths about the nature of reality. For Kant, dialectic was the wanton application of logic beyond the conditions of experience.

Fully conscious of Kant's rejection of the practice of dialectical argument, G. W. F. Hegel attempted to rescue the idea of dialectic, seeing it as an essential element of any validly acquired knowledge (see **Hegelianism and neo-Hegelianism**). Dialectic for Hegel involves testing hypotheses against themselves: their **rationality** – and thereby their acceptability – are assessed in terms of their success in encapsulating the reality they seek to describe. In the *Phenomenology of Spirit*, Hegel argues that experience – a process in which we move from partial to complete knowledge – has a discernible rational structure: he calls it 'the dialectical movement of consciousness'. Elsewhere, Hegel specifies that dialectical thought is a necessary succeeding second moment of thought to the apparently 'fixed determinations' established by the abstractive understanding in the first grasp of knowing. For this reason Hegel also terms dialectic 'the negatively rational' as it is that moment of thought that recognizes the limitation of the first moment of thought, obliging us, through the force of our own rationality, to realize that the concept applied to that concept in fact contradicts the **object**. (The idea that dialectic is a process of thesis – antithesis – synthesis is a crude representation of Hegel's position.)

According to Hegel, history too can be understood as the testing of various forms of political arrangement, a process that strives to reach completion in the form of a free **civil society** reconciled with the state: this development implies a graduation through a series of increasingly adequate expressions or manifestations of **freedom**. The dialectic of history, however, is not undertaken by any human agent: it is undergone by *Geist* (Spirit or Mind) as it strives towards the realization of political freedom: each stage must be undergone, but is inevitably replaced, by the stages that follow. But the earlier stages are carried along – *aufgehoben* (sublated), as Hegel puts it – as part of the final account of the phenomenon (see **idealism**).

Karl **Marx** agreed with Hegel that history exhibits a dialectical structure. However, he disagreed both with Hegel's account of what pushed that process forward – *Geist* – and, indeed, that it had yet reached its conclusion. For Marx, dialectic was the logic of the dictum that the 'history of all hitherto existing **society** is the history of **class** struggles'. Marx elaborates by arguing that the balance between the forces of **production** and the relations of production is inherently unstable, containing an inherent 'dialectic' with the potential to lead to the overcoming of these relations. Using this materialist economic account of history, Marx believed that dialectic could have a 'scientific' application (see **materialism**). That is, if history could be understood as a dialectic of the tensions between the forces and relations of production, then it should be possible to predict the future of those relations, as they would fall within a necessary dialectic leading inevitably to their collapse. Thus dialectic acquired a predictive capacity. In this regard the Russian anarchist intellectual Alexander Herzen referred to dialectic as 'the algebra of revolution'. The scientificity of social theory was a central element of revolutionary **Marxism**, and the notion of dialectic was freely employed in the writings of Lenin and Trotsky.

The failure of scientific Marxism to predict any historical developments discredited the very idea of dialectic to its opponents. Karl **Popper** (1940) wrote an excoriating critique of dialectic which was aimed at the pseudo-scientificity of the concept; a critique that was to remind us that philosophy must not be a basis for any sort of scientific system. Even among radical theorists the notion of dialectic has come to seem less than useful as a tool of sociological analysis. However, in so far as dialectic names the moment of contradiction

between what is given and what is rational, it is a fundamental term of sociological analysis in the **Frankfurt School** of social theory, and is also a prominent associated theme in **deconstruction**'s 'logic of difference'.

References and further reading

Adorno, T. (1973) *Negative Dialectics*. London: Routledge.
Bubner, R. (1990) *Dialektik als Topik*. Frankfurt am Main: Suhrkamp.
Gadamer, H. J. (1976) *Hegel's Dialectic*. New Haven, CT: Yale University Press.
Gadamer, H.-J. (1980) *Dialogue and Dialectic*. New Haven, CT: Yale University Press.
Hegel, G. W. F. ([1807] 1975) *Phenomenology of Spirit*. Oxford: Oxford University Press.
Marcuse, H. (1955) *Reason and Revolution*. London: Routledge.
Marx, K. ([1857–58] 1973) *Grundrisse: Foundations of the Critique of Political Economy*. Harmondsworth: Penguin.
Popper, K. (1940) 'What is Dialectic?', *Mind*, XLIV: 403–26.

BRIAN O'CONNOR

DIFFERENCE

In social theory, the term difference tends to be associated with forms of theorizing which have critiqued the universalizing and normalizing pretensions in Enlightenment-influenced thinking. In particular, the term 'difference' tends to be associated with critiques of mainstream social theory enacted by **feminist theory**, critical **race** studies, **post-colonial theory** and **sexuality** studies, because such critiques operate via a logic of questioning the universal via the particular. Early feminist critiques of sociological and socio-theoretical **discourse** are exemplary of this kind of critique, especially in its illumination of a normative masculine subject and the exclusion of women from the field of the social. Such critiques opened up an empirical claim that social theory has excluded the **interests** of a variety of **groups** of people and societies (non-white people, women, non-heterosexual people, colonized people and post–colonial societies) from its key object – the social. The claim is that social science has a normalizing impulse, whereby white European male subjects are defined as normative actors in social worlds, an impulse that tends to exclude, silence and expel any differences from this norm. Crucially, within this mode of critique difference tends to be empirically imagined. 'Difference' is designated to those groups and individuals who are unlike (the also often empirically imagined) normative actor in social theory. A key strategy which emerged to counter the exclusionary impulses of social theory and sociology was the insertion of previously excluded groups into the domain of the social. Feminist social theorists and sociologists, for example, sought to insert 'women' into the domain of the social via specifically sociological research projects focused on women and extended socio-theoretical discourses to this previously excluded group.

At least two issues are important to note about this strategy. First, difference tends to be understood as an *exclusion from* a norm, which assumes that these differences would (to some extent at least) be minimized via inclusion (see **inclusion and exclusion**). Second, in this strategy (and in positive social science understandings of difference more generally), difference tends to be attributed to and associated with particular groups of people. Difference is assumed to be a property of certain groups of human beings.

These assumptions have been put into doubt by a definition of difference associated with deconstructive modes of theorizing (see **deconstruction**). A number of social and cultural theorists, especially Jacques **Derrida** (1982), have examined how the discourses of western metaphysics – including social theoretical discourses – operate not via a strategy of the exclusion of difference from a norm, but with repressed or hidden notions of difference. Derrida calls this *différance*, and argues it is crucial for the process

of meaning-making in such discourses, because even though suppressed, *différance* is *constitutive* of the meaning of dominant terms and tropes. The term 'masculine', for instance, depends for its meaning on the term 'feminine' – even though the latter may not be explicitly invoked. Thus, while ostensibly we may read, for example, classical social theory as concerning a narrative of the emergence (and triumph) of the European masculine subject within modernity, and as concerning the erasure and exclusion of difference, a deconstructive reading may suggest that the meaning of this narrative relies upon a whole range of repressed terms – including the feminine, the non-European, the non-modern, and so on – terms which always threaten to destabilize the dominant meaning of the narrative. Rather than the solid, unitary centre of classical social theory, the European masculine subject therefore emerges as unstable, dispersed and ambiguous. A deconstructive reading of social theory would reveal, in other words, not a series of exclusions which result in the stability and unitary nature of the European masculine subject, but that this very figure relies upon repressed concepts of difference. Derrida's *différance* therefore reverses positive science understandings of difference, since rather than an outcome or an exclusion from a norm, the norm cannot exist without *différance*. Moreover, in locating the linguistic operations of difference Derrida's understanding also questions the idea that difference is a foundational property or characteristic of humans.

There are a variety of ways in which these deconstructive notions of *différance* have been put to work within contemporary social theory. Writers such as Stuart Hall have made use of such a strategy to rethink the idea of **identity**, particularly in regard to questions of race. Hall has shown that rather than unitary, uniform or stable formations, identities always rely upon *différance*. Identities, Hall argues, must be read against the grain, 'not as that which fixes the play of difference in a point of origin, but as that which is constructed in and through *différance*' (1996: 5). In rethinking identity in this way Hall has contributed towards a move away from foundational understandings and opened up important avenues for rethinking the relations between identity and difference. Indeed, deconstructionist social theory and, in particular, the notion of *différance* form a backdrop to many recent important interventions in the social theory field, including the work of Judith **Butler** on gender and sexuality, and the work of Anne Game (1991) on deconstructive sociology.

References and further reading

Derrida, J. (1982) *Margins of Philosophy*. Hemel Hempstead: Harvester Wheatsheaf.
Game, A. (1991) *Undoing the Social: Towards a Deconstructive Sociology*. Toronto: University of Toronto Press.
Grossberg, L. (1996) 'Identity and Cultural Studies: Is That All There Is?' in S. Hall and P. du Gay (eds) *Questions of Cultural Identity*. London: Sage.
Hall, S. (1996) 'Who Needs Identity?' in S. Hall and P. du Gay (eds) *Questions of Cultural Identity*. London: Sage.
Hall, S. (ed.) (1997) *Representation: Cultural Representations and Signifying Practices*. London: Sage.

LISA ADKINS

DIFFERENTIATION

Social differentiation is an important attribute of **society**. Differentiation means both a process and a **structure**. In structural terms, it refers to the fact that a unit of analysis, such as a society, consists of a number of distinct parts. These parts may be of the same kind, such as families as the basic components of tribal societies. Or the parts may be different, such as the sub-systems – the economy, the state or the public sphere – making up a modern society. As a process, social differentiation denotes the dynamics which bring about and change a given structure. Sociologists have been especially interested in the dynamics that produce and reproduce the functional differentiation of modern society.

The concept of differentiation spread within sociology after Herbert **Spencer**'s evolutionary theory of societal development 'from incoherent homogeneity to coherent heterogeneity'. Later, Emile **Durkheim**, Georg **Simmel**, Talcott **Parsons**, and Niklas **Luhmann** became important proponents of the concept, while other thinkers such as Karl **Marx** and Max **Weber** who did not explicitly use the term also contributed to our understanding of the kinds of social structures and dynamics it designates. In contemporary sociology, empirical debates on social differentiation are prominent among American 'neo-functionalists' (see **Alexander** and Colomy 1990) and among German sociologists influenced by the work of Luhmann.

Two principal views on the functional differentiation of modern society can be distinguished. For Durkheim and Parsons, as the most important representatives of the first view, functional differentiation is a process of decomposition of a functionally diffuse unit, such as a role or an institution, into at least two functionally more specific units. This idea is modelled on the division of labour in work organizations. In Parsons's highly abstract analytical framework, society is composed of four principal sub-systems (the economy, the polity, the societal community and the fiduciary system), each of which fulfils one of the four fundamental functional prerequisites of societal reproduction. Social differentiation is here seen as tending towards a successive decomposition of each of these sub-systems into second-level sub-systems.

In contrast to the Durkheim–Parsons perspective, Weber portrayed the birth and composition of modern society in terms of the emergence of a number of autonomous 'value-spheres'. One after the other, science, law, art, politics, economics, sexuality, and other spheres free themselves from their former domination by religious ideas. Luhmann radicalizes this second view when he conceives of Weber's 'value-spheres' as operationally closed sub-systems constituted by self-referential chains of **communication**. Luhmann here does not deny manifold mutual dependencies among sub-systems, but he insists that it makes no sense to understand the ensemble of societal sub-systems as a division of labour in which the sub-systems as parts are teleologically oriented towards the performance and maintenance of the whole society. Instead, both Weber and Luhmann emphasize that social differentiation consists of a simultaneous birth and liberation of the parts. These parts emerge and become autonomous in relation each other and to the whole. Moreover, the whole itself does not exist; nothing more than the often tension-ridden and antagonistic interrelationship of the parts exists.

The consequences of functional differentiation for society at large as well as for each individual component of the society are seen by both views as neither totally positive nor totally negative but as a 'mixed blessing'. Parsons drew a largely optimistic picture that stressed the advantages of ongoing functional differentiation, involving technological and economic progress and inclusion of more and more individuals in the 'societal community', as well as value generalization as a basis for a **civil religion** fostering mutual tolerance and **solidarity**. Similarly, Durkheim was obsessed with the question of which mechanisms could produce for 'organic **solidarity**' needed a functionally differentiated society.

More recently, however, uncontrolled evolution of functional differentiation has often been seen as a fundamental danger to the **integration** of modern society, building on Durkheim's theme of **anomie**. On the one hand, enormous increases in the number of options in every societal sphere in modern society allow each person to become an individual in the proper sense of the word: a person who creates autonomously a unique biography for him or herself. On the other, however, this **individualism** is seen as being accompanied by an erosion of traditional meaningful attachments that tie a person to particular cultural worlds, social groups, or **communities**. As a consequence, anomie, **alienation**, and other experiences of meaninglessness are implications of functional differentiation (see **individualism and individualization**). Nevertheless, functional differentiation appears to be a highly effective mode of **social change**. Today world-wide, there seems to be no normative alternative to the adoption of processes of functional differentiation. From the point of view of functionalist analysis, even fundamentalist opposition in some regions of the world may be regarded as something intermittent and recurrent but not sustainable or enduring.

References and further reading

Alexander, J. and Colomy, P. (eds) (1990) *Differentiation Theory and Social Change*. New York: Columbia University Press.

Durkheim, E. ([1893] 1964) *The Division of Labor in Society*. New York: Free Press.

Luhmann, N. (1977a) 'Differentiation of Society', *Canadian Journal of Sociology*, 2: 29–53.

Luhmann, N. (1997b) *Die Gesellschaft der Gesellschaft*. Frankfurt am Main: Suhrkamp.

Parsons, T. (1971) *The System of Modern Societies*. Englewood Cliffs, NJ: Prentice Hall.

Schimank, U. (1996) *Theorien gesellschaftlicher Differenzierung*. Opladen: Leske + Budrich.

Schwinn, T. (2001) *Differenzierung ohne Gesellschaft*. Weilerswist: Velbrück.

UWE SCHIMANK

DILTHEY, WILHELM (1833–1911)
German philosopher

Dilthey sought to provide a solid foundation for the human sciences or *Geisteswissenschaften*. The latter term could equally be translated as sciences of 'mind' or 'spirit'. In this sense Dilthey sought to reveal the unique qualities of the human world in contrast to those of **nature**. There were two key elements in this conception: 'life' and 'history'. The truth of the human world is found in 'life' itself, not in the mechanical abstractions of the natural sciences. The complex amalgam of thought and feeling which constitutes the inner mental life of individuals is the central concern of the human sciences. As the experience of life blends past, present and future, so the human world must be understood as intrinsically historical. In his *Introduction to the Human Sciences* ([1923] 1929), Dilthey created an epistemology for historical study, emphasizing the importance of empathically re-living the experience of actors and its expression in historical artifacts.

Dilthey's influence on **hermeneutics** has been considerable. **Gadamer** accepts the centrality of historical tradition, but rejects as 'psychologism' the attempt to re-live the experience of others as the route to objectivity. **Ricoeur** argues that Dilthey's emphasis on understanding (**Verstehen**) occurs at the expense of **explanation** but can be overcome by incorporating aspects of **structuralism** into interpretation. Dilthey's main influence on sociology has been via **Weber** and the importance attached to **meaning** in interpretative sociology.

Major work

([1923] 1989) *Introduction to the Human Sciences*. Princeton: Princeton University Press.

Further reading

Gadamer, H.-G. (1989) *Truth and Method*. London: Sheed & Ward.

Harrington, A. (2001) 'Dilthey, Empathy and Verstehen: A Contemporary Reassessment', *European Journal of Social Theory* 4(3): 329–47.

Ricoeur, P. (1981) *Hermeneutics and the Human Sciences*. Cambridge: Cambridge University Press.

ALAN HOW

DISABILITY

Disability is a form of social exclusion gaining increasing attention within sociological theorizing (see also **social inclusion and social exclusion**). The term 'disability' is, however, fiercely contested, and is commonly used in two conflicting ways: according to an 'individual model', and according to a 'social model'.

Where many traditional views of disability were once informed by **religion**, the rise of scientific medicine in industrialized countries since the eighteenth century has led to disability being largely conceived in terms of **health and illness** and viewed as a problem of individuals (see **medicalization**). The individual model of disability, typically elaborated by non-disabled professionals, focuses on disability as functional limitation. A three-fold definition is commonly adopted. *Impairment* is seen as denoting any 'loss or abnormality of psychological, physiological or anatomical structure or function'. *Disability* is seen as referring to any 'restriction or lack (resulting from an impairment) of ability to perform an activity in the manner or within the range considered normal for a human being'. *Handicap* is used to describe the 'disadvantage for a given individual, resulting from an impairment or disability, that limits or prevents the fulfilment of a **role** (depending on **age**, sex and social and cultural factors) for that individual' (Wood 1980: 27–9). Thus, according to the individual model, people are disabled by their impairments, and it is the role of medicine and psychology to restore them to 'normality' (see **normal and pathological**). The problem of disability is located within the impaired individual.

In many countries, the latter part of the twentieth century saw the emergence of the disabled people's movement, which redefined disability as a form of oppression on a par with racism and sexism. The *social model of disability* emerged from disabled people's own critiques of the individual model, including its view of **causality**, its assumptions about the existence and nature of 'normality', and its failure to recognize disabled people as the experts on their own situation. A two-fold definition of impairment and disability analogous to the **sex/gender distinction**, was elaborated in Britain by the Union of the Physically Impaired against Segregation (UPIAS), a collective of disabled people. Here, impairment is defined as 'lacking part of or all of a limb, or having a defective limb, organ or mechanism of the body', while disability denotes 'the disadvantage or restriction of activity caused by a contemporary social **organization** which takes no or little account of people who have...impairments and thus excludes them from participation in the mainstream of social activities' (UPIAS 1976: 3–4). No causal link is assumed between impairment and disadvantage; rather, disability is viewed purely as a *social construction* (see **social constructionism**).

The social model is not without its critics, and has been characterized as over-socialized and reductionist by advocates of the individual model. Other critiques have arisen from within the disabled community. These frequently focus on the model's tendency to treat disabled people as an homogenous group and on its failure to adequately theorize impairment. It is argued that failure to theorize impairment adequately may also create disadvantage for those individuals so affected and may itself be seen as socially produced (Thomas 1999) (see **embodiment**). There are further tensions between those assuming materialist and idealist interpretations of the social model. While there is substantial evidence that for centuries people with impairments have suffered discrimination in a range of societies, materialist writers understand disability in its current form to be a logical outcome of the capitalist **mode of production**. The growth of the commodity labour market, and the consequent exclusion and segregation of non-standard workers are identified as key factors in the process of disablement. Hence it is argued that disability will only be eliminated through 'a *radical transformation*, rather than a reform of capitalism' (Gleeson

1997: 196). In contrast, while generally acknowledging the realities of this materialist interpretation, idealist writers understand disability in terms of **liminality** (Shakespeare 1994). On this latter view, equal opportunities within the existing system are advocated to challenge these deep-rooted beliefs and prejudices (see **equality**). However, the failure of reformist measures suggests that for effective change to occur, disability cannot be 'dematerialized' and cannot be explained solely in terms of discriminatory beliefs.

Despite these internal critiques and tensions, the insights of the social model of disability have been vitally important for disabled people, both personally and politically. They have fostered the development of disability studies as an academic discipline and have helped ensure a long-overdue place for disability on the sociological and political agenda.

References and further reading

Barnes, C. *et al.* (1999) *Exploring Disability: A Sociological Introduction.* Cambridge: Polity in association with Blackwell Publishers.

Gleeson, B. J. (1997) 'Disability Studies: A Historical Materialist View', *Disability and Society*, 12(2): 179–202.

Oliver, M. (1996) *Understanding Disability: From Theory to Practice.* Basingstoke: Macmillan.

Shakespeare, T. (1994) 'Cultural Representation of Disabled People: Dustbins for Disavowal?', *Disability and Society*, 9(3): 283–99.

Swain, J. *et al.* (eds) (2004) *Disabling Barriers: Enabling Environments*, 2nd edn. London: Sage.

Thomas, C. (1999) *Female Forms: Experiencing and Understanding Disability.* Buckingham: Open University Press.

UPIAS (1976) *Fundamental Principles of Disability.* London: Union of the Physically Impaired Against Segregation.

Wood, P. (1980) *International Classification of Impairments, Disabilities and Handicaps.* Geneva: WHO.

ALISON SHELDON

DISCIPLINE

See: social control

DISCOURSE

The concept of discourse and the methods of discourse analysis are established components of contemporary social science. This is immediately evident in the number of empirical studies that employ discourse theory, and the various schools of discourse analysis that have emerged – Critical Discourse Analysis (Fairclough 1989), Argumentative Discourse Analysis (Hajer 1995), and Discourse Theory (Laclau and Mouffe 1985; Laclau 1990). Bound up with the rise of the concept of discourse has been the **linguistic turn** in the 1960s and 1970s which stimulated the emergence of new approaches such as **semiotics**, **hermeneutics**, **critical theory** and **post-structuralism**, as well as the resurgence of Marxist theory and the wider dissemination of psychoanalytic ideas in the social sciences. Equally important have been developments within linguistics itself (e.g. Fowler *et al.* 1979).

The *Oxford English Dictionary* defines discourse as 'talk, conversation; dissertation, treatise, sermon', or in its verb form to 'talk, converse; speak or write at length on a subject'. Hayden White's more detailed etymology of the concept stresses 'the connotations of circularity, of movement back and forth, which the Indo-European root of this term (*kers-*) and its Latinate form (*dis–*, "in different directions", + *currere*, "to run") suggest' (White 1979: 82). In the social sciences, the term has acquired greater technical sophistication, while accruing additional meanings and connotations. It has also engendered debate among those who use the concept as to its precise **meaning**, scope and application, while encountering fierce criticisms from those who oppose the culturalist and linguistic turns in social science (Geras 1990) (see **cultural turn**).

Theories of discourse might be classified in three ways. First, traditional discourse analysis is concerned with the investigation of 'language in use' or 'talk or text in context' (van Dijk 1997). For example, speech-act theory focuses on the fact that by saying something, we are also doing something (Austin 1975). When someone utters a statement such as 'I promise' or 'I name this ship the Queen Mary', and meets the requisite 'felicity conditions' – i.e. intends to keep the promise or is authorized to name ships – the person is also performing an act. In a related vein, conversation analysts drawing largely on **Garfinkel**'s (1967) sociological method of **ethnomethodology** endeavour to deduce from observation what speakers are doing and how they are doing it (Trask 1999: 57). For instance, conversation analysts such as Schegloff and Sacks (1973) examine the organization and logic of 'turn-taking' in conversations to show that a key principle that structures conversations is the avoidance of 'holes' and 'intersections' between speakers.

A second approach to discourse analysis, which emerged alongside the development of **structuralism**, post-structuralism, hermeneutics and **Marxism** in the 1960s and 1970s, is evident in the writings of Michel **Foucault** and his followers. Foucault's (1970, 1973) earlier 'archaeological' writings examine the way discursive practices form the objects and subjects of discursive formations. Discourses are thus 'practices that systematically form the objects of which we speak', and consist of historically specific 'rules of formation' that determine the difference between grammatically well-formed statements and 'what is actually said' at particular times and places (Foucault 1972: 49; Foucault 1991: 63). In his later 'genealogical' writings, Foucault (1987) modifies his quasi-structuralist approach, and focuses on the way in which discourses are shaped by social practices, and the way discursive practices in turn shape social relationships and institutions (see **praxis and practices**). In his later writings, the 'archaeological' and genealogical strategies are combined in a method of 'problematization'. In this reconfiguration, archaeology provides the means to delimit research objects by describing the rules in a given period that condition the elements of a particular discourse – its objects, subjects, concepts and strategies. Examples of this for Foucault are 'madness' or 'illness' in the nineteenth century. Genealogy, on the other hand, analyzes the constitution of the elements of a discourse by recounting the historical practices from which they were constructed. The latter enables research to show the contingency of identities and practices, and foregrounds possibilities foreclosed by the dominant logics.

A third type of discourse analysis, which develops partly out of Foucault's contributions, and partly from Derridean, Marxist and post-Marxist insights, expands the scope of discourse analysis to include non-linguistic practices and elements. Fairclough's 'critical discourse analysis' includes the analysis of political texts and speeches, as well as the contexts in which they are produced, although discourses are still understood in terms of the semiotic dimension of social practice, thus remaining at a distinct level of the social system. By contrast, Laclau and Mouffe's post-Marxist discourse theory enlarges the scope of discourse analysis to include all social practices, so that discourses and discursive practices are synonymous with structurally incomplete systems of **social relations**.

This latter type of approach arguably offers the most comprehensive and systematic attempt to employ discourse analysis in the social sciences. It synthesizes developments within post-structuralism, psychoanalysis, Marxism, and post-analytical philosophy in an endeavour to account for the political structuring of social orders and the constitution of subjective **identities**. The core of this research programme centres on the idea that all objects and practices are meaningful, and that social meanings are contextual, relational and contingent. In addition, its advocates assert that all systems of meaningful practice rely upon discursive exteriors that partially constitute such orders, while potentially subverting them.

A little less abstractly, social relations exhibit four properties: **contingency**, historicity, **power**, and the primacy of politics (Laclau 1990: 31–6). The identities of social agents are constituted within structures of articulatory practice, and political subjects arise when agents identify anew under conditions of dislocation. Such assumptions represent the formal ontological presuppositions of post-Marxist discourse theory. A fuller expression would suggest the introduction of further concepts and logics pertaining to the constitution and dissolution of political identities, the processes of hegemonic construction, and the structuring of social spaces (see Howarth 2000; Torfing 1999).

References and further reading

Austin, J. L. (1975) *How to Do Things with Words*. Oxford: Oxford University Press.

Butler, J., Laclau, E. and Žižek, S. (2000) *Contingency, Hegemony, Universality*. London: Verso.

Fairclough, N. (1989) *Language and Power*. London: Longman.

Foucault, M. (1970) *The Order of Things: An Archaeology of the Human Sciences*. London: Tavistock.

Foucault, M. (1972) *The Archaeology of Knowledge*. London: Tavistock.

Foucault, M. (1973) *The Birth of the Clinic: An Archaeology of Medical Perception*. London: Tavistock.

Foucault, M. (1987) 'Nietzsche, Genealogy, History', in P. Rabinow (ed.) *The Foucault Reader*. Harmondsworth: Penguin Books.

Foucault, M. (1991) 'Politics and the Study of Discourse', in G. Burchell, C. Gordon and P. H. Miller (eds) *The Foucault Effect: Studies in Governmentality*. London: Harvester Wheatsheaf.

Fowler, R., Hodge, B., Kress, G. and Trew, T. (1979) *Language and Control*. London: Routledge & Kegan Paul.

Garfinkel, H. (1967) *Studies in Ethnomethodology*. Englewood Cliffs, NJ: Prentice Hall.

Geras, N. (1990) *Discourses of Extremity: Radical Ethics and Post-Marxist Extravagances*. London: Verso.

Glynos, J. (2001) 'The Grip of Ideology: A Lacanian Approach to the Theory of Ideology', *Journal of Political Ideologies*, 6(2): 191–214.

Hajer, M. (1995) *The Politics of Environmental Discourse: Ecological Modernization and the Policy Process*. Oxford: Clarendon Press.

Howarth, D. (2000) *Discourse*. Buckingham, Open University Press.

Laclau, E. (1990) *New Reflections on the Revolution of Our Time*. London: Verso.

Laclau, E. and Mouffe, C. (1985) *Hegemony and Socialist Strategy*. London: Verso.

Schegloff, E. and Sacks, H. (1973) 'Opening up Closings', *Semiotica*, 8: 289–327.

Searl, J. (1969) *Speech Acts*. Cambridge: Cambridge University Press.

Torfing, J. (1999) *New Theories of Discourse: Laclau, Mouffe and Žižek*. Oxford: Blackwell.

Trask, R. L. (1999) *Key Concepts in Language and Linguistics*. London: Routledge.

van Dijk, T. (1997) *Discourse as Social Interaction*. London: Sage.

White, H. (1979) 'Michel Foucault', in J. Sturrock (ed.) *Structuralism and Since*, Oxford: Oxford University Press, p. 82.

DAVID HOWARTH

DIVISION OF LABOUR

See: differentiation.

DOMINATION

Domination refers to a structural relationship of unequal **power** resources in which the more powerful routinely gain the compliance of the less powerful. A 'one-off' exercise of power, however exploitative, which does not reflect structural relationships, does not constitute domination in the sociological sense of the term. For instance, the capitalist system constitutes a set of **structures** that are central to a specific form of domination. Hence, the power which factory owners routinely exercise over their workers constitutes domination. However, if particular workers manage to exercise power over their employers through once-off strategic action, this does not constitute domination. Only if workers organize themselves into a movement (through trade unions or political parties) and alter the surrounding social structures in order to exercise power, can we speak of domination.

Max **Weber** describes domination in terms of the probability that a command will be obeyed in a structural relationship and explains that the cause of compliance can arise from several sources. He distinguishes between forms of domination which are based upon legitimacy and domination that is coercive. The former involves **authority** (see **legitimacy** and **legitimation**). The latter is at its most obvious when based upon the threat of **violence** but can equally derive from control over other resources – a bank which exploits a restricted **market** can be in a position of domination.

Michael **Mann** (1986) has argued that there are four sources of power, which are central to the reproduction of relations of domination. Military power entails coercion by physical force; political power corresponds to authority; economic power involves the control of physical resources; and ideological power entails control over ideas. While in some systems of domination, one source of power appears more prominent than the rest (for instance, the economy in **capitalism**), it is almost invariably the case that any system of domination is based upon a complex interdependence of all four sources. Capitalism did not simply evolve out of economic advances but was a consequence of developments at the military, ideological and political levels. Militarily, the feudal knight was made superfluous by the invention of cheap weaponry – the rifle. Capitalist production presupposes the existence of a workforce that is disciplined through **state** monopoly of **education** – a combination of ideological and political power.

Each system of domination has an internal logic that entails particular relations of empowerment and disempowerment. Social actors change relations of domination by 'organizationally outflanking' (Mann 1986; Clegg 1989) existing relations of domination. Conversely those who wish to maintain existing relations of domination (the status quo) do so through 'organizationally outflanking' any of the would-be challengers to the system. Organizational outflanking generally takes place through innovation in any of the sources of power but in some instances, organizational out-flanking can also be influenced by chance (Clegg 1989). One of the factors which contributed to the 'organizational outflanking' of the **aristocracy** by the **bourgeoisie** was not only innovation but also the bubonic plague – a contingent event.

While the term 'domination' suggests relations of radical **inequality**, in practice, relations are rarely entirely one-sided. Dom-ination usually entails relations of mutual dependence (**Giddens** 1984). First, there is usually no useful purpose to be gained from dominating the entirely powerless. To be worth dominating, dominated actors need to have some power resources at their dis-posal. These resources usually give the dominated some **autonomy** and, because the dominating party wish to acquire control of these resources, the latter are, to an extent, dependent upon the dominated. Second, since domination is not once-off, it is in the interests of the dominating party that the dominated gain some advantage from the relationship; otherwise they cannot be relied upon routinely to reproduce the structures in question. While feudal serfs are dominated by having to render all sorts of services and a percentage of production to the feudal lord, in turn, they gain pro-tection and the right to hold land (see **feudalism**). Similarly, while workers are not entirely 'free' to sell their labour power (as some libertarians would like to suggest), it is the case that they gain some empow-erment from these relations of domination.

While much of modern **critical theory** aims at overcoming domination, many **postmodern** thinkers, including **Foucault** (1980) and Laclau and Mouffe (1985), would argue that domination is both ubi-quitous and without a well-defined source or centre (see also **centre and periphery**). However, they do not conclude from this that domination should be accepted uncritically;

instead, relations of domination should be resisted through the micro-practices of **everyday** life. One way of accomplishing this is through an awareness of the con-tingent nature of any relations of domina-tion. **Contingency** implies 'could have been otherwise', which in turn suggests 'can be otherwise'. Such awareness will not lead to **utopia** but it does have the potential to empower agents to be more than simply the effect of **social relations** of domination which define 'what' and 'who' they are.

References and further reading

Clegg, S. (1989) *Frameworks of Power*. London: Sage.
Foucault, M. (1980) *Power Knowledge*. Brighton: Harvester Press.
Giddens, A. (1984) *The Constitution of Society*. Cambridge: Polity.
Laclau, E. and Mouffe, C. (1985) *Hegemony and Socialist Strategy*. London: Verso.
Mann, M. (1986) *The Sources of Social Power*, vols 1, 2. Cambridge: Cambridge University Press.
Scott, L. (2001) *Power*. Cambridge: Polity.
Weber, M. (1978) *Economy and Society*, vols 1, 2. Berkeley, CA: University of California Press.

MARK HAUGAARD

DOUGLAS, MARY (1921–)
British anthropologist

Douglas was employed during the Second World War in a section of the British gov-ernment responsible for colonial affairs, an experience that stimulated her to write a doctorate in anthropology under Evans-Pritchard, based on fieldwork among the Lele in the African Congo. Her two best-known works are *Purity and Danger* (1966) and *Natural Symbols* (1973).

Purity and Danger is a powerful reassess-ment of the identities and differences between 'primitives' and 'moderns'. In oppo-sition to the evolutionary series of magic – **religion** – **science**, Douglas emphasizes the need in any society for differentiation, hierarchy and borderlines, against the danger of contagious disorder, while recognizing both that there is a need for the occasional creative breaking of the rules, and that corruption, as part of life, also belongs to the **sacred**.

Natural Symbols introduces the conceptual pair 'grid versus **group**', denoting the symbolic system of **classification** and the pressure to conform. The combination of high or low **values** on these two axes differentiates hierarchy from **individualism**, but also contrasts **church** and **sect**. The book presents a defence of **ritual** for social life, including unreformed Catholicism, and a condemnation of both free market individualism and what she perceives as the millennial sectarianism of oppositional movements.

Major works

([1966] 1996) *Purity and Danger: An Analysis of the Concepts of Pollution and Taboo.* London: Routledge.

([1973] 1996). *Natural Symbols: Explorations in Cosmology*, revised edn. London: Routledge.

([1978] 1996) (with B. Isherwood) *The World of Goods.* London: Routledge.

(1982) (with A. Wildavsky) *Risk and Culture: Essays on the Selection of Environmental Dangers.* Berkeley, CA: University of California Press.

Further reading

Fardon, R. (1999) *Mary Douglas: An Intellectual Biography.* London: Routledge.

ARPAD SZAKOLCZAI

DRAMATURGICAL SCHOOL

The stage has been a fruitful source of inspiration for the study of the social. In numerous passages Shakespeare employed metaphors of the theatre to depict social life. The use of such metaphors by sociologists has sometimes led to overly determinist pictures of the social, where people are portrayed as performing **roles** and following scripts. Erving **Goffman**, however, compared social life with the stage without succumbing to a view that neglected human **agency**. In Goffman's depiction, people are portrayed as active, using various props to influence their surroundings. Although the dramaturgical approach is mainly associated with Goffman, other authors have also contributed (e.g. Cochran and Claspell 1987; Hare and Blumberg 1988)

Goffman initially studied to become a film director before entering graduate school in sociology at the University of Chicago (see **Chicago School**). His earlier training and interest in film and theatre remained visible in his sociological work. Partly because of his studies in Chicago, commentators tend to associate him with the school of **symbolic interactionism**. Like other interactionists, his concerns are the micro-settings of face-to-face interaction, attending to pay attention to how individuals share **meaning** and how they are able to anticipate what their gestures mean to other individuals. Individuals are able to monitor their conduct and manipulate their environment, picking up on clues and aching accordingly. In his *Presentation of the Self in Everyday Life* (Goffman 1959), Goffman explained how individuals use various devices to impose a particular definition of themselves and of the situation on others. It is important for individuals to show themselves in a good light, to emphasize certain aspects and hide others. Goffman called this 'impression management', which individuals use various props or devices to accomplish.

Impression management takes place at the 'front stage' before the 'audience'. The front consists of the 'setting' and the 'personal front'. The setting is the scene where the performance takes place. For instance, lawyers meet clients in their office. A neat, well-organized office may induce confidence in their abilities. The personal front refers to the identifiable items, which the performer carries or is expected to carry. The personal front consists of 'appearance' and 'manner'. Appearance gives clues to the status of the performer. The outfit of a judge provides an idea of his or her importance, and the judge may appear authoritative and confident. People use the backstage to prepare for the preparation or as an emotional outlet. For instance, the restaurant kitchen allows waiters to let off steam.

Goffman insisted that members of the audience help performers in various ways. As in the theatre, people tend to suspend disbelief, ignoring mistakes in the performance. They also help the performer by not entering the backstage. In addition, Goffman recognized that how someone is perceived is often affected by the performances of others. In this context, Goffman talked about political parties as 'teams'. The activities and misdoings of one of its members may affect how the wider public perceives the party, leading possibly to expulsion or sanctions. Goffman studied diverse aspects of role distancing and stigmatizing (Goffman 1961, 1963), as well as 'total institutions' such as asylums (Goffman 1962).

Goffman never tried to develop a coherent theoretical framework and has sometimes been criticized for being his journalistic style. Some social theorists, however, have tried to incorporate the dramaturgical approach within a more systematic theoretical framework. One example is **Giddens**, whose structuration theory partly draws on Goffman's insights. Social order is seen here as an ongoing accomplishment of knowledgeable individuals who display tacit, practical knowledge in **everyday** life (Giddens 1984).

References and further reading

Cochran, L. and Claspell, E. (1987) *The Meaning of Grief: A Dramaturgical Approach to Understanding Emotion.* New York: Greenwood.

Dahrendorf, R. (1973) *Homo Sociologicus.* London: Routledge & Kegan Paul.

Giddens, A. (1984) *The Constitution of Society: Outline of the Theory of Structuration.* Cambridge: Polity.

Goffman, E. (1959) *Presentation of the Self in Everyday Life.* Garden City, NY: Anchor.

Goffman, E. (1961) *Encounters: Two Studies in the Sociology of Interaction.* Indianapolis, IN: Bobbs Merrill.

Goffman, E. (1962) *Asylums: Essays on the Social Situation of Mental Patients and other Inmates.* Chicago: Aldine.

Goffman, E. (1963) *Stigma: Notes on the Management of Spoiled Identity.* Englewood Cliffs, NJ: Prentice Hall.

Hare, A. and Blumberg, H. (1988) *Dramaturgical Analysis of Social Interaction.* London: Praeger.

Manning, P. (1991) *Erving Goffman and Modern Sociology.* Cambridge: Polity.

PATRICK BAERT

DU BOIS, WILLIAM EDWARD BURGHARDT (1868–1963)
US theorist

Du Bois was the first African-American to receive a PhD from Harvard University, and was founder of the National Association for the Advancement of Colored People. Du Bois's central concern was the significance of 'race' in social life (see **'race' and racism**). He wrote extensively on the social construction of 'race', being one of the first social scientists, along with Franz Boas, to deconstruct essentialized, biological notions of racial differentiation (see **essentialism**). He analyzed the causes and consequences of racism and the intersection of racial constructs with **class**, **gender**, **crime**, **religion**, and **education**. His micro-level, social-psychological assessment of racialized **identity** is exemplified in his famous discussion of 'double-consciousness', and his macro-level analysis of international racial division is developed in his many pioneering studies of global **capitalism** and **colonialism** and their relationship to the ever-salient 'color line' (see **post-colonial theory**). Similar to **Durkheim**, Du Bois emphasized the social, communal bonds that come with religious involvement. Similar to **Weber** – with whom he maintained a strong personal and professional relationship – Du Bois infused his sociological writings with extensive historical analysis. Du Bois relied heavily on

Marx in his many critiques of **imperialism** and unfettered **capitalism**, but chastised Marxist theory for ignoring the independent importance of racial divisions in social and historical **conflict**. Urban sociology, rural sociology, criminology, sociology of religion, sociology of education, and the sociology of race are all indebted to Du Bois's under-recognized but unparalleled pioneering scholarship.

Major works

([1898] 1903) *The Souls of Black Folk*. New York: Bantam Books.

([1899] 1998) *The Philadelphia Negro: A Social Study*. Philadelphia, PA: University of Pennsylvania Press.

([1915] 2001) *The Negro*. Philadelphia, PA: University of Pennsylvania Press.

([1920] 1999) *Darkwater: Voices From Within the Veil*. New York: Dover Publications.

(1940) *Dusk of Dawn: An Essay Toward an Autobiography of a Race Concept*. New York: Harcourt, Brace.

(1945) *Color and Democracy: Colonies and Peace*. New York: Harcourt, Brace.

Further reading

Lewis, D. L. (1993) *W. E. B. Du Bois: Biography of a Race*. New York: Henry Holt.

Zuckerman, P. (2004) *The Social Theory of W. E. B. Du Bois*. Thousand Oaks, CA: Pine Forge Press.

PHIL ZUCKERMAN

DURKHEIM, EMILE (1858–1916)

French theorist, Professor of Education and Sociology at the Sorbonne. Considered the founder of theoretically grounded empirical sociology in France, Durkheim argued that the mode of association of human individuals creates 'a specific reality,' which is different from 'the sum of its parts'. This *sui generis* reality is the source of 'social facts', the object of a critical sociological knowledge.

Durkheim identifies two different kinds of society based on the type of **solidarity** which integrates them – *mechanical solidarity*, based on similarity, or, the more modern, *organic solidarity*, based on differentiation and interdependence. True organic solidarity could be realized only after appropriating and redistributing inherited wealth to abolish the 'forced division of labour', for this blocks people's ability to achieve social positions commensurate with their merit.

Considered a major influence on the development of **functionalism** and **structuralism**, Durkheim's work is a crucial resource for non-humanist critical realist work in **epistemology** and **ontology**, for general sociological concepts including **solidarity** and the **sacred**, and in the areas of **deviance**, **law** and **religion**. His innovative theory of the democratic socialist state is a major influence on theories of 'associative democracy' (see also **association**).

Major works

([1893] 1984) *The Division of Labour in Society*. London: Macmillan.

([1895] 1982) *The Rules of Sociological Method*. London: Macmillan.

([1897] 1951) *Suicide: A Study in Sociology*. New York: Free Press.

([1912] 1995) *Elementary Forms of the Religious Life*. New York: Free Press.

([1950] 1957) *Professional Ethics and Civic Morals*. London: Routledge & Kegan Paul.

([1955] 1983) *Pragmatism and Sociology*. Cambridge: Cambridge University Press.

Further reading

Lukes, S. (1973) *Emile Durkheim: His Life and Work*. Harmondsworth: Penguin Books

Pearce, F. (2001) *The Radical Durkheim*, 2nd edn. Toronto: Canadian Scholars Press.

Stedman-Jones, S. (2001) *Durkheim Reconsidered*. Cambridge: Polity Press.

FRANK PEARCE

E

ECOLOGY AND ENVIRONMENTALISM

Beginning with the German biologist Ernst Haeckel, who introduced the term 'ecology' in 1866, ecological **science** has traditionally stressed connections and interrelationships above individual entities. A pivotal characteristic of ecology until the middle of the twentieth century was that it represented a kind of borderland between the geographical, biological, and the social sciences. From the social science perspective, undisturbed **nature** was often assumed to achieve a balance or a stability without humans, since people were seen as active agents who determined the physical configurations of the geographical environment. This concept also encouraged public ecological thought and the rise of modern environmentalism as a new **social movement** (see **socialist movements**). This movement had many precursors, but its most recent version can be traced to the publication of the biologist Rachel Carson's book *The Silent Spring* (1962). In the period after the book's publication, the term ecology came to connote philosophical, moral, and political viewpoints as well as a specialized field of scientific inquiry. In the 1970s members of the environmental movement began to regard themselves as 'ecologically aware' or even as ecologists. Explanations for this surge in new environmental movements prominently include an increase in 'post-material' values and the observation of a general **social change** in **post-industrial society**, where radical political groups are more concerned with cultural rather than economic transformation. The **globalization** of environmentalism is evident in the decentralized and spontaneous growth of grass-roots environmental groups in less-developed countries. At the global level, environmental concern is not limited to post-material elites.

Different ideas and ideological positions adopted by many environmental groups and organizations have led to the view that there is no monolithic unit called the environmental movement. In its simplistic form, environmentalism since the 1970s can be divided into the camp of those who favour conservation and preservation of nature for nature's sake and those who wish to maintain the environment as a necessary habitat for humankind. Along with what Mary **Douglas** (1992) has termed 'myths of nature', one can categorize four core streams of environmental thought based on the assumed character of nature: (1) traditional expansionism; (2) mainstream environmentalism; (3) deep ecological egalitarianism; and (4) fatalism. The idea of a benign nature is the underlying ideal of expansionism, the **myth** that nature is robust. Whatever adverse effects **industrialization** has on nature, human technology and reasoning will always see to it that all disturbances in the very end will work out for the good. This myth is based on the idea of a global equilibrium. According to the mainstream environmentalist myth, the ecosystem is perceived as vulnerable, hence human intervention must be controlled and regulated by scientific findings in order not to destroy the natural equilibrium. In this notion strict standards for resource usage are needed, but this does not mean that industrial production has to come to an end. In many deep and radical ecological streams instead, one can detect a plea for a radical hands-off policy. According to this view, whatever humans do can mean a catastrophic collapse of the ecological equilibrium. The ideal is to live in small-scale communities on an egalitarian basis (see **egalitarianism**). Practically every human intervention in nature is regarded as bad. Other radical streams of the environmental movement, such as eco-feminism, have made the point that ecological degradation is based on **patriarchy** and thus the **domination** of women parallels the domination of nature. The fourth myth of nature, the fatalist way of thinking about ecosystems, regards the management of nature as useless, because nature cannot be managed at all. Here there is no point in theorizing about or intervening in nature since it is impossible to know how nature works.

It is important to understand that in all four categories there are two underlying ideas about the natural world that inform most environmentalist thinking: (1) the idea of a balance, an equilibrium, or a strict order of nature which is disturbed by humans only; and (2) the tendency to see nature as essentially separate and different from human **society**. The ideal of a balance of nature is still especially relevant for contemporary environmental thinking and often serves as a normative category, as a test against which to judge human activities. It was the prerequisite for how environmental problems were to be defined, and how their solution should be envisaged. The idea of a balance in nature was seen not as human desire, but as a necessity imposed by nature. Thus, environmentalism in the 1970s seemed to be a radical movement, but the ideas on which it was based represented a resurgence of early twentieth-century

ecology blended with Romantic myths about nature (see **Romanticism**). Consequently, some late twentieth-century ecologists claim that the findings of recent ecological currents which indicate a general change of understanding from the idea of a natural ecosystem balance to something that is naturally in constant flux, have led to many of the failures of environmentalism, since public debates on 'ecology' and 'sustainability' have little to do with scientific ecology (Botkin 1990).

In a similar fashion, social theory has mostly excluded the idea of natural action in accounting for social development. For Emile **Durkheim**, for instance, it was always the idea of a steady state of nature as a basis for his theoretical ideas. He wrote: 'As for the physical world, since the beginning of history it has remained sensibly the same, at least if one does not take account of novelties which are of social origin' ([1893] 1933: 348). Thinking in this tradition sociologists have rarely cared about the character of society's natural environment. Nature was implicitly treated as static whereas society was the dynamic factor. However, if sociologists, like most twenty-first-century ecologists, no longer believe in any balance of nature, social theory has also lost its steady foundation for society to take place. As long as social theorists could believe that nature undisturbed was constant, they were provided with a simple standard against which to judge societal **development**. In more recent streams of the environmental movement since the 1990s, as in ecological restoration (Jordan 2003), an understanding of the ecological world that accommodates ecosystems' dynamism and unpredictability, and especially its understanding of humans as a mature part of nature, is being taken seriously. If one takes the view that nature is in constant flux and natural activities are influencing societal processes, then the question arises whether sociology should explain social facts with other social facts or whether the debates in ecology and related fields should also affect social theory.

From a different angle, but closely related to the above problem, in some streams of sociology the claim has been made that new environmental movements, citizen initiatives and other forms of non-formal politics are a force to rethink traditional sociological categories. Authors like Ulrich **Beck** (1999) take the world-wide public perception of ecological risks (see **risk**) and the engagement in non-formal ecological organizations as an indication that informal types of political activity, what Beck called 'subpolitics', have taken on a greater significance in modern societies and need to be faced as a challenge to traditional forms of theorizing the human place in nature, as well as how ecological thinking emerges and connects with environmental politics. Furthermore, if this discourse goes hand in hand with an understanding of humans as part of a dynamic nature, social theory might be well advised to rethink some of its traditional approaches to a fixed differentiating between a dynamic society and a nature in balance. Some observers already claim that in the twenty-first century the entwinement between the natural and the human realm has become so powerful (see **actor-network theory**; **cyborgs**) that focusing solely on the social side will not do justice to theorize and understand contemporary societies.

References and further reading

Baldwin, D., de Luce, J., and Pletsch, C. (eds) (1994) *Beyond Preservation: Restoring and Inventing Landscapes*. Minneapolis, MN: University of Minnesota Press.

Beck, U. (1999) *World Risk Society*. Oxford: Polity.

Botkin, D. B. (1990) *Discordant Harmonies: A New Ecology for the Twenty-First Century*. New York: Oxford University Press.

Carson, R. (1962) *The Silent Spring*. Boston: Houghton Mifflin.

Douglas, M. (1992) *Risk and Blame: Essays in Cultural Theory*. London: Routledge.

Durkheim, E. ([1893] 1933) *The Division of Labor in Society*. Glencoe, IL: Free Press.

Gross, M. (2003) *Inventing Nature: Ecological Restoration by Public Experiments*. Lanham, MD: Lexington Books.

Humphrey, C. G., Lewis, T. L. and Buttel, F. H. (2002) *Environment, Energy, and Society: A New Synthesis*. Belmont, CA: Wadsworth.

Jordan, W. R. (2003) *The Sunflower Forest: Ecological Restoration and the New Communion with Nature*. Berkeley, CA: University of California Press.

Mitman, G. (1992) *The State of Nature: Ecology, Community, and American Social Thought, 1900–1950*. Chicago: University of Chicago Press.

Mol, A. P. J. and Sonnenfeld, D. A. (eds) (2000) *Ecological Modernisation around the World: Perspectives and Critical Debates*. London: Cass.

MATTHIAS GROSS

ECONOMY

See: political economy

EDUCATION

It is important to note that people who write on the topic of education are themselves invariably highly educated. They are equipped with the **knowledge**, experiences, **language**, and communicative abilities that testify to major features of education success. Education empowers and emboldens, whether it be in ways supportive or opposed to the status quo.

Primary socialization takes place within the **family**. Of **institutions** providing secondary **socialization** education is regarded as among the most important. Education is a nurturer of **values**, beliefs and **morality**, a transmitter of skills and competencies, and is the major provider of approved credentials in contemporary society which contributes to social mobility.

Emile **Durkheim** placed emphasis on education's ability to instil communal values in the young. For Durkheim, this sense of belonging, fostered through the teaching of a nation's history, and through the encouragement of allegiance to its government, was a crucial counter-weight to tendencies towards increased individualism in modern societies. Durkheim's functionalist approach has exercised a major influence in the study of education, from both ends of the political spectrum. While the Left sometimes see education as inculcating passivity in the lower orders, the Right may regard it as an essential way of preserving order. In reality, however, education has rarely been entirely successful in either of these regards. In a post-modern epoch, characterized by differences and volatility, it is hard to see education simply or solely as inculcating communal values.

Researchers tend to distinguish between the external relations bearing on education (**government**, industry, and employment) and the internal features of educational systems (such as classroom behaviour or curriculum design). Ivan Illich's concept of the 'hidden curriculum' has been influential in drawing attention to the unstated and underestimated aspects of education such as dress codes, the peer **group**, and implicit **role** models presented in schools.

There is evidently a close relationship between industrial growth and educational expansion, though it is imprecise and contestable. While it is true that all industrialized **societies** invest heavily in education, there is considerable difference between nations such as the United States and France, and it is not the case that investment in education leads straightforwardly to industrial success. Talcott **Parsons** (1959) presented an influential version of **functionalism** to argue that education taught the value of achievement through the young's participation in universal standards of examination and assessment. Achievement was essential for industrial success and not something that could be developed in family situations where children are treated in a *particularistic* manner, as distinct from a *universal* manner.

Parsons's analysis fits with the argument that education is a sifter of societal talent, as well as the means by which people are positioned in its hierarchies through the ethos of meritocracy. Meritocracy is the doctrine that ability plus effort ought to be the determinant of educational (and other) success (see Young 1958). It is axial to the doctrine of **equality** of opportunity that is favoured in advanced societies. Parsons's view is that there can be universal standards of examination in which the young seek to achieve individually. Achievement is recognized by the awarding of credentials (certificates, degrees, etc.) to candidates who succeed. Through this meritocratic system the most able and dedicated compete in an equal race and are duly rewarded. On these terms, a major feature of education has been its transformation from an endeavour to tame the masses by teaching them their place to one of socializing the individual to accept responsibility for his or her appropriate position in the class system. In this way, education becomes a central legitimator of **inequality**. So long as there is equality of opportunity in education, inequality of attainment is acceptable.

This doctrine was the basis of the post-war system of education in the UK (and of equivalent systems in other Western countries), where ostensibly objective IQ (intelligence quotient) tests distinguished those who would attend academic institutions (grammar schools) from those (the majority) who would attend less academic and more technically oriented schools. The introduction of non-selective 'comprehensive schools' in the UK from the 1950s onwards was an expression of dissatisfaction with the unfairness of the grammar school system and the limitations of IQ tests administered at age 11. The continued attendance of 7 per cent of the age-group at fee-paying independent schools in the UK remains an important instance of inequality of opportunity since it relies upon parents having the resources to pay for it. Because it offends the core value of equality of opportunity, private education gets a disproportionate amount of attention at the expense of other barriers to equality.

It is not surprising that much attention has been paid to the relationship between education and social mobility, given that education is the major filtering mechanism for entry into occupations. It is demonstrably the case that educational performance is socially skewed. There may be formal equality of opportunity, but outcomes are highly dependent on origins. British researchers in the 1970s and 1980s, notably A. H. Halsey *et al* (1980) and John Goldthorpe (1980), showed in large-scale surveys that educational attainment is not explicable in terms of meritocracy theory. Children whose parents work in manual occupations perform much worse than those from non-manual backgrounds, even when of equal intelligence. While there has been considerable social mobility throughout the twentieth century, Halsey and Goldthorpe account for this in terms of changes in the occupational structure. Large increases in white-collar positions have meant an absolute increase in upward mobility among talented working-class children, but the relative chances of these working-class children, compared to middle-class children, have changed little over the twentieth century.

Some accounts of educational inequality focus on material deprivation where middle-class parents can pay for private schools, or buy property in the catchment areas of desirable schools. Other accounts, such as that of Basil Bernstein (1975), focus on socio-linguistic codes, suggesting that the restricted code of working-class children disadvantages them in school, while the ability of the middle class to adopt an elaborate code aids their progress. Still other accounts in the cultural vein suggest that aspirations of parents, children and schools are important in achievement. The most influential explanation for educational disadvantage this framework is explained by the French sociologist, Pierre **Bourdieu**. His account suggests that the education system requires mastery of speech, comportment and other social accoutrements that together advantage those with high **cultural capital**. Bourdieu goes so far as to argue that education reproduces social

inequality. This pessimistic conclusion is resonant of earlier functionalist approaches to education, though it is at odds with the optimistic belief in meritocracy.

It is indeed hard to imagine how the meritocracy thesis could be accepted by those who fail in the school system. Paul Willis (1977), in his small-scale study of comprehensive school failures in Britain in the 1970s, described a **subculture** of adolescent males who rejected education in favour of an aggressive masculinity associated with working-class jobs. There is particular apprehension today that those at the lower levels of the school system, especially white working-class males, continue to fail in and reject schooling, though there are decreasing numbers of unskilled and semi-skilled occupations for them to occupy on leaving school as educational failures.

There has long been concern that education is inadequately associated with the requirements of **work** and the economy. Some British social historians attribute the relative industrial decline of the UK to its education system propounding values antithetical to competition, industry and market success, values associated with the learned 'gentleman' in preference to the engineer or accountant (Wiener 1981; Barnett 1986). However, since the 1980s a 'new vocationalism' can be discerned in education policy in many countries, where measures have been taken to gear schools and colleges more closely to technical requirements. This has continued, notably in Britain in the tertiary education sector, which has expanded to participation rates of 40 per cent of the age group, where an emphasis on transferable skills, flexibility, and self-directed lifelong learning is thought to fit well with the employment demands of the Information Age (Reich 1991).

References and further reading

Barnett, C. (1986) *The Audit of War*. London: Macmillan.
Bernstein, B. (1975) *Class, Codes and Control*, 3 vols. London: Routledge & Kegan Paul.

Bourdieu, P. and Passeron, J.-C. (1977) *Reproduction in Education, Society and Culture*. London: Sage.

Bowles, S. and Gintis, H. (1976) *Schooling in Capitalist America*. New York: Basic Books.

Goldthorpe, J. (1980) *Social Mobility and Class Structure*. Oxford: Clarendon Press.

Halsey, A. H., Heath, A. and Ridge, J. (1980) *Origins and Destinations*. Oxford: Clarendon Press.

Parsons, T. (1959) 'The School Class as a Social System: Some of its Functions in American Society', in T. Parsons (1964), *Social Structure and Personality*. New York: Free Press.

Reich, R. (1991) *The Work of Nations*. New York: Vintage.

Shavit, Y. and Müller, W. (eds) (1998) *From School to Work: A Comparative Study of Educational Qualifications and Occupational Destinations*. Oxford: Oxford University Press.

Wiener, Martin J. (1981) *English Culture and the Decline of the Industrial Spirit, 1850–1980*. Cambridge: Cambridge University Press.

Willis, P. (1977) *Learning to Labour*. Farnborough: Saxon House.

Young, M. (1958) *The Rise of the Meritocracy*. London: Thames and Hudson.

FRANK WEBSTER

EGALITARIANISM

Egalitarianism refers to a family of social and political ideas that involve philosophical explanations of the value of **equality** and justifications for specific practices thus intended. Since human beings differ considerably in endowments and capabilities, equality rarely means treating everyone exactly alike or making people's conditions the same in any respect. To speak of egalitarianism without historical, social, or philosophical qualification, is to speak elliptically. An egalitarian usually finds some existing social arrangement indefensible – an **inequality** based on allegedly inappropriate grounds for differential treatment – and calls for replacing that system of distinctions. Historically, the focus of egalitarian ideals has shifted continuously to attack the differential treatment of barbarian and Greek, freeman and slave, noble and commoner, black and white, male and female.

In Western European and Anglo-American contexts, modern egalitarian ideas have a long and diverse history. In the English Civil War of the 1640s, the Levellers claimed that the legitimate **authority** of superiors to command inferiors derives from the voluntary agreement of natural equals (see also **voluntarism**). Taking for granted man's rough equality of strength and guile, Hobbes proposed that an absolute sovereign is necessary to ensure lasting **peace**. Locke – whose ideas came to be regarded more as a rejection of egalitarianism than a version of it – nonetheless held that men are by nature equally free, subject only to natural **law**, and possessed the same natural **rights**. In the eighteenth century, Rousseau argued that social **inequalities** were artificial, arising from the pressures of a demand to display a sophisticated way of life to one's peers. Thus, the key problem, answered for Rousseau by the idea of the **sovereignty** of the 'general will', was to reconcile man's natural equality and **autonomy** with political **authority** and social conditions. Similarly, **Kant**'s statement of persons as morally self-governing agents declared all to be equal legislating members of the kingdom of ends, and that they all ought to treat themselves as ends in themselves, and not merely as means. At the end of the century egalitarian ideas found voice in the great revolutionary movements in Europe and America and were made explicit in the declaration of **rights**. In addition to revolutionary movements for political **power**, mid-nineteenth-century Europe saw the evolution of socialist and communist thinking, which targeted economic inequalities as well. In the USA, in the nineteenth century, egalitarian claims were asserted in the struggle to end **slavery**, later fueling the civil rights movement, the **women's movement**, and support for universal human rights.

In modern democratic societies with **market** economies, egalitarianism usually refers to a position that favors a greater degree of equality of income and **wealth** across persons than already exists. The focus on equality is that of **results**, according to which people should be made more nearly equal in actual circumstances. This contrasts with equality of **opportunity** or equality before the law – ideas more commonly associated with modern libertarianism and classical **liberalism** – where the **freedom** and rights of the individual are paramount and of utmost concern in matters of political affairs. Many egalitarians have been suspicious of equal formal rights, pointing to the substantive inequalities they may disguise or exacerbate. The insistence on redistribution toward equalities of income, wealth, capabilities, or life chances shares common ground with **socialism**. Critics have maintained, however, that egalitarianism necessarily reduces aspects of freedom in unacceptable ways. For instance, libertarian arguments claim that redistributive measures to equalize **property** involve a constant and extensive infringement of some individuals' Lockean rights, constraining their liberty to enjoy the fruits of their own labor, and to gain more property than others by trade, inheritance, or assiduousness (see **property and property rights**). Egalitarian rejoinders take goods such as **money** to give one the positive freedom to engage in a wide variety of activities and experiences. Thus, according to egalitarians, little justification can be made for why people should not be able to enjoy this effective freedom to the same extent. Moreover, the injustice lies not in economic inequality alone but in an unequal distribution of economic goods that also forms the source of unequal **power**, **status**, and **prestige**.

Considerable debate surrounds what is required for egalitarian ideas that aim to be sensitive to arguments about markets, individual freedom, fair treatment, and just distribution. Disagreement characterizes attempts to identify inequalities which are arbitrary from a moral point of view. Controversies also hinder attempts to specify the class of people to whom egalitarian norms apply. Some might count an unborn fetus or a very severely demented human as a person,

while others would not. Furthermore, one should not take for granted that the adjustment sought by egalitarianism is strictly for persons or individualized agents. A minority linguistic **community** in a particular society might also seek **government** action, on egalitarian grounds, to promote its flourishing or survival alongside the dominant **group**. Egalitarian claims have been raised against difference of privilege thought to be inappropriately grounded and against qualifications for assuming a role considered unduly restrictive to some. The focus and scope of egalitarian ideals, therefore, have changed and will continue to change in different social and political contexts.

References and further reading

Kymlicka, W. (1990) *Contemporary Political Philosophy*. Oxford: Clarendon Press.

Nielsen, K. (1985) *Equality and Liberty*. Totowa, NJ: Rowman & Allanheld.

Nozick, R. (1974) *Anarchy, State and Utopia*. New York: Basic Books.

Rawls, J. (1971) *A Theory of Justice*. Cambridge, MA: The Belknap Press of Harvard University Press.

Van Parijs, P. (1995) *Real Freedom for All*. Oxford: Clarendon Press.

Young, I. M. (1991) *Justice and the Politics of Difference*. Princeton, NJ: Princeton University Press.

NAOMI CHOI

EISENSTADT, SHMUEL NOAH (1923–)

Israeli sociologist

Eisenstadt is recognized for several macroscopic studies in comparative **historical sociology**, combining a Weberian conception of cultural analysis with a structural functionalist framework of society (see **functionalism**). Eisenstadt began his career with a comprehensive comparative study of the shaping of the political sphere among different historical **civilizations** in his book *The Political Systems of Empires* (1963). He then extended this approach to the emergence of intellectuals as a significant social group in *Tradition, Change and Modernity* (1973), to the prerequisites and results of social **revolutions** in *Revolution and the Transformation of Societies* (1978), and to cultural and religious **world-views** in *The Origins and Diversity of Axial Age Civilizations* (1986). All these works aim to account for the cultural origins and constituent components of **modernity**, a question Eisenstadt takes up directly from the writings on the sociology of religion and capitalism of **Weber** and Sombart. He discerns a crucial event in the process of **modernization**, observable in almost all civilizations, which he defines as the rise of intellectual or clerical **elites** holding a transcendental vision of an ideal world that challenges the traditional normative and political orders (see **modernity and modernization**). Since these developments seem generally to have appeared around the first millennium BCE, Eisenstadt adopts the term 'axial age' from the German philosopher Karl Jaspers to emphasize the centrality of these processes. Since the 1980s, Eisenstadt's comparative historical inquiries have continued to expand systematically on differences between modernization processes displayed by distinct civilizations. The theme of Eisenstadt's project of civilizational cultural comparison is captured in the catchword of 'multiple modernities'.

Major works

(1963) *The Political Systems of Empires.* New York: Free Press.
(1973) *Tradition, Change and Modernity.* New York: John Wiley.
(1978) *Revolution and the Transformation of Societies.* New York: Free Press.
(1986) *The Origins and Diversity of Axial Age Civilisations.* Albany: SUNY Press.
(2002) *Multiple Modernities.* New Brunswick, NJ: Transaction Publishers.

Further reading

Riedel, J. and Sachsenmaier, D. (eds) (2002) *Reflections on Multiple Modernities.* Leiden: Brill.

BERNHARD GIESEN
DANIEL ŠUBER

ELIADE, MIRCEA (1907–1986)
Romanian theorist

Before 1945 his career had obscure political twists: arrested for right-wing activities in 1938, he subsequently occupied diplomatic posts in London and Lisbon. After the Second World War, helped by Georges Dumézil, he lectured in Paris, and joined the University of Chicago in 1957.

Eliade redefines the distinction between the sacred and the profane. Only the **sacred** possesses true reality, manifesting itself in the world through hierophanies. **Symbols** are human responses to the presence of sacred; of particular importance is the symbolism of the centre (*omphalos*). The imitation of primordial acts and heavenly archetypes produces reality. Archaic thought revolts against time, denying history and subordinating change to the logic of eternal recurrence. Religious, mystic and primitive minds live in a permanent present. Initiation rites and ascetic techniques, of which shamanism and yoga are archetypal models, are ways to overcome everyday normality and gain access to sacred truth.

Eliade edited and contributed extensively to a voluminous encyclopedia of religious life. He also published many novels, most famously *The Forbidden Forest* and *The Old Man and the Bureaucrats*. His influential work is controversial due to his youthful involvement in the extreme right and to his refusal to take impartial distance from religious phenomena.

Major works

([1949a] 1958) *Patterns in Comparative Religion.* New York: Sheed & Ward.
([1949b] 1991) *The Myth of the Eternal Return.* Princeton, NJ: Princeton University Press.
([1951] 1972) *Shamanism: Archaic Techniques of Ecstasy.* Princeton, NJ: Princeton University Press.
([1952] 1958) *Yoga: Immortality and Freedom.* Princeton, NJ: Princeton University Press.
(1959) *The Sacred and the Profane.* New York: Harcourt.

([1976–83] 1981–88) *A History of Religious Ideas*, 3 vols. Chicago: Chicago University Press.

(1987) (ed.) *Encyclopaedia of Religion*, 16 vols. New York: Macmillan.

ARPAD SZAKOLCZAI

ELIAS, NORBERT (1897–1990)
German-born sociologist

Elias's aim was to establish a radically processual, relational and trans-disciplinary sociology attuned to the link between 'social' and 'psychological' development. In his magnum opus, *The Civilizing Process* (1939), Elias traced changing standards of socially acceptable behaviour among the secular upper classes of Western societies from the Middle Ages to the present day (see **civilization**) Elias proposed that such societies have been characterized by a 'civilizing process': a multi-faceted process involving, on the one hand, increasing social differentiation, growing structural complexity, and the formation of nation–states, and, on the other, long-term shift in the structure of human emotions and personality. Elias's work constitutes a synthesis of key ideas from theorists such as **Comte**, **Marx**, **Weber**, **Simmel**, **Mannheim** and **Freud**. It presents a means of re-interpreting classical dilemmas within the social sciences such as problems of **structure** and **agency**, the individual/society dualism, and the **culture/nature** split. Central to his work was the concept of **figuration**. However, it was only towards the end of his life that Elias began to gain broader recognition and influence, particularly in relation to the sociology of **violence**, the **body**, and **sport**.

Major works

([1939] 1978–82) *The Civilizing Process*, 2 vols. Oxford: Blackwell.

(1965) (with J. Scotson) *The Established and the Outsiders*. London: Frank Cass.

(1969) *The Court Society*. Oxford: Blackwell.

([1970] 1978) *What is Sociology?* London: Hutchinson.

(1986) (with E. Dunning) *Quest for Excitement*. Oxford: Blackwell.

(1987a) *Involvement and Detachment*. Oxford: Blackwell.

([1987b] 1991) *The Society of Individuals*. Oxford: Blackwell.

Further reading

Mennell, S. (1998) *Norbert Elias: An Introduction*. Dublin: University College Dublin Press.

van Krieken, R. (1998) *Norbert Elias: Key Sociologist*. London: Routledge.

JASON HUGHES

ELITES

The term 'elite', familiar since the eighteenth century, is relatively new but the basic idea underlying it is of ancient vintage. Elites denote small minorities of individuals designated to act for a collectivity – a **society**, an **institution**, an occupation – at the apex of which they stand. Societies look to elites for the realization of major social goals and the maintenance of key social **values**.

The existence of elites is constant in human societies but their shape and form vary from chiefships in preliterate societies to **aristocracies**, first estates, ruling **classes**, power elites, and strategic elites, each connected to a different historic era and a different social order. Elites mirror the societies they crown.

Societies vary by the degree of elite closure from a tightly interwoven comprehensive structure to one looser and more dispersed. Tightly interwoven structures tend to feature a hereditary assignment of elite **status**, whereas in the looser structures, individual achievement plays a greater role. The contrast is evident in an ongoing debate as to whether contemporary elites comprise a ruling class of **wealth** and **property** (**Marx** 1956) or a set of differentiated elites whose number is still under review though typically included are political, economic, military, religious, and cultural elites (see **stratification**).

The proliferation and specialization of elites complicate societal leadership in many ways. When the core elites splinter, the potential for unity and cohesion weakens and the historic umbrella for societal leadership is rent asunder.

Plato focused on the necessity for wise and virtuous 'guardians' selected by birth. Aware of how readily elites become self-serving and exploitative, Plato sought ways to dissociate the **family** from the guardian stratum. This led him into tortuous byways of biological selection deplored by later critics but his reasons for such an extreme step were powerful: to prevent the generational rigidity to which entrenched ruling **groups** are prone. Aristotle, who disagreed with Plato on several critical issues, likewise echoed the need for an effective moral leadership for the ancient *polis* whose threatened decline anguished both thinkers.

Although discussions over the whys and wherefores of elites did not fade in the ensuing centuries, a more recent epoch of concentrated debate, in the aftermath of the French **Revolution**, delineated the modern discussion of elites. Saint Simon (1839), at the start of the century, grasped the emerging significance of technocratic elites, while **Pareto** (1935) followed by Mosca (1939) engaged in a bitter polemic with Marxists in the later decades. Their debate fueled much of the ferment on the nature of elites as these two Italian theorists explicitly challenged the Marxist claim about the supremacy of an economic ruling class.

Karl **Mannheim** (1946) took a different turn when he noted that elites proliferated rather than declined as industrialism advanced. Mannheim proposed a typology of elites that contrasted *integrative* elites of political, economic, and organizational leaders with *sublimative* elites made up of moral, religious, aesthetic, and intellectual leaders who helped direct psychic energies into reflective and creative channels. Some of these ideas appear in the work of C. W. **Mills** (1956) and Keller (1963) in the twentieth century.

Mills analyzed the 'power elite' which combines ruling class and elite theory whereas Keller analyzed 'strategic elites' and the impact of specialized, at times competing, and increasingly achievement-based, elites on the society unfolding.

The questions generated by these works are also treated in important empirical studies of business, political, religious, military, and cultural elites across contemporary societies. Many more theoretically grounded, systematic, and increasingly cross-national studies are needed but there is a base on which to build.

Such studies will need to incorporate the growing complexity of elites as to specialized functions, modes of recruitment, effectiveness and rewards. Some elites continue to stress ancestry, while others stress the highest educational attainments. The corporate elite may stay at the top for decades whereas the political elite is revamped after only a few years. Some elites are rewarded with extraordinary **wealth** while others exercise immense **power** and still others command great respect (see also **prestige**). As for access to the top, the political elite rests on election, the corporate elite on co-optation, the celebrity elite on popular favor.

Ancient questions still abide in these connections. How to keep society's leadership vital, moral, and focused on the public good is as relevant today as it was millennia ago. The ancient question, 'Who will guard the guardians?' takes on ever greater urgency in a world in flux in which an electronically mediated **world-view** must find accommodation with a world-view based on faith and **tradition**. In an era of profound technical, moral, and social dislocation, we need more and better information on the nature, power, and effectiveness of the elites that are entrusted with our fate. This also brings to the fore the matter of the coexistence between democratic forces and powerful elites. Democratic theory grounds **sovereignty** in the will of the people. How can this be reconciled with the persistence of elites?

This is a fundamental dilemma, given the enormous influence of elites as key decision-makers, powerful social actors, and models of style, conduct, and taste. Still, the greater openness of contemporary elites to individual talent and more opportunities for critical public appraisals of elite performance temper the propensity to elite excess and exploitation. Reductions in the autonomy of elites suggest that power has become more circumscribed and the abuse of power more transparent. Saint-Simon's dream of a society governed not by force but by ability, mutual respect, compassion, and trust lives on.

References and further reading

Aristotle (1941) 'Politics', in R. McKeon (ed.) *The Basic Works of Aristotle*. New York: Random House.

Keller, S. (1963) *Beyond the Ruling Class*. New York: Random House.

Keller, S. (1986) 'Celebrities and Politics: A New Alliance', *Research in Political Sociology*, 2: 145–69.

Mannheim, K. (1946) *Man and Society in an Age of Reconstruction*. London: Kegan Paul.

Marx, K. (1956) *Selected Writings in Sociology and Philosophy*. New York: McGraw Hill Book Company.

Mills, C. W. (1956) *The Power Elite*. New York: Oxford.

Mosca, G. (1939) *The Ruling Class*. New York: McGraw-Hill.

Pareto, V. (1935) *The Mind and Society: A Treatise on General Sociology*, 4 vols. New York: Harcourt Brace.

Saint-Simon, H. de (1839) *Œuvres Choisis*, vol. 1. Brussels: Fr. Van Meened et Cie.

SUZANNE KELLER

EMANCIPATION

Originating as a legal term in Roman law referring to **liberation** of children from fathers, the concept of emancipation was later extended to diverse forms of bondage, servitude or limitations on rights, e.g., servants, **slaves**, the **bourgeoisie**, the **working class**, women, and **ethnic** or **religious** groups. It emerged in the late eighteenth century as a political concept associated with **freedom**, **autonomy**, and the **public sphere**. The deeper implications of democratic emancipation were elaborated within the bourgeois **family** as part of the freeing of an inner personal realm that revealed a universal humanity. Though **Kant**'s discussion of **Enlightenment** implicitly referred to this problematic, the term itself did not become widely employed until the 1830s and was radicalized by **Marx** and the Left Hegelians. In the early Marx the 'whole of human servitude' is identified with the alienated labour of workers whose liberation embodied the possibility of 'universal human emancipation'. In the Marxist tradition, such total emancipation became identified with the concept of a collective working-class subject.

Though emancipation was a concern of both **liberalism** and **socialism**, liberalism identified liberation with **rights** of political **citizenship**. For nineteenth-century abolitionists, emancipation was a legal **status** that could be granted from above, as in Lincoln's role as 'the Great Emancipator' of American slaves or the tsarist liberation of serfs (see **slavery**). In Western **Marxism**, however, emancipation became linked to discussions of the social and depth-psychological preconditions of **autonomy**. The distinctive use of emancipation in contemporary social theory as overcoming internalized forms of **domination** stems primarily from the **critical theory** of the **Frankfurt School**, especially the second-generation writings of **Habermas** (1971). In his early writings Habermas referred to a critical-emancipatory **interest** in knowledge that became widely influential in fields that sought to develop forms of critical or emancipatory social science. Similarly, Bhaskar (1986) elaborated a formal analysis of human emancipation as part of his critical **realism**. Nevertheless, Habermas later largely abandoned the concept because of its association with the liberation of collective subjects, a notion that is rejected by the paradigm shift developed in his theory of **communicative rationality**.

Since the 1970s references to emancipatory strategies, projects and possibilities have proliferated in virtually all the human sciences and regions of the world. Though initially often associated with specific reference to Habermas's notion of 'emancipatory sciences', later discussions often appear to be unaware of these specific origins and many draw eclectically on **critical theory**, **post-structuralism**, and **postmodernist** tendencies without worrying about potential inconsistencies. The concept is thus widely used with reference to resistance and empowerment against forms of domination associated with **class**, colonialism, **race**, **gender** and **sexuality**, especially as a part of emancipatory **social movements**. In Latin American discussions the use of emancipation as an alternative to the notion of liberation reflects the belated reception of German critical social theory (Gogol 2002). Though initially having a stronger foothold in **education** (e.g., critical pedagogy and Brazilian educator Paulo Freire's (1970) related notion of *conscientization*), concern with emancipatory strategies can now be found in practice-oriented professional fields such as health, nursing, disability studies, social work and theology. References to emancipatory possibilities also appear in less obvious fields such as urban, organizational and management studies and research on new information technologies.

There have also been a number of more recent, systematic efforts to revitalize the concept of emancipation theoretically, especially in response to postmodernist critiques of political metanarratives that essentialize collective subjects. The critiques of **universalism** that defined **postmodernism** were initially taken by many to have called into question the 'modernist' idea of emancipation as class-reductionist, masculinist, Eurocentric, potentially totalitarian, and complicit with the domination of nature.

Various discussions, however, have attempted to revise the concept rather than abandon it, by speaking of 'emancipations' or even 'postmodern' emancipations to stress the plurality of possibilities that are locally situated and not reducible to any single form or outcome of domination. Similarly, critical theorists have linked Habermas and Freire in the name of an 'emancipatory post-foundationalism' (Morrow and Torres 2002) and theorized emancipatory movements in terms of the tensions between mutual **recognition** and redistribution (Fraser and Honneth 2003).

References and further reading

Alway, J. (1995) *Critical Theory and Political Possibilities*. Westport, CT: Greenwood Press.

Bhaskar, R. (1986) *Scientific Realism and Human Emancipation*. London: Verso.

Fraser, N. and Honneth, A. (2003) *Redistribution or Recognition? A Political-Philosophical Exchange*. London: Verso.

Freire, P. (1970) *Pedagogy of the Oppressed*. New York: Seabury.

Gogol, E. W. (2002) *The Concept of Other in Latin American Liberation*. Lanham, MD: Lexington Books.

Habermas, J. (1971) *Knowledge and Human Interests*. Boston: Beacon.

Koselleck, R. (1972) 'Emanzipation', in O. Brunner, W. Conze and R. Koselleck (eds) *Geschichtliche Grundbegriffe*. Stuttgart: E. Klett.

Koselleck, R. (2002) 'The Limits of Emancipation: A Conceptual-Historical Sketch', in R. Koselleck and T. S. Presner (eds) *The Practice of Conceptual History*. Stanford, CA: Stanford University Press.

Laclau, E. (1996) *Emancipation(s)*. London: Verso.

Morrow, R. A. and Torres, C. A. (2002) *Reading Freire and Habermas*. New York: Teacher's College Press, Columbia University.

Nederveen Pietersen, J. P. (ed.) (1992) *Emanicipations, Modern and Postmodern*. London: Sage.

Ray, L. J. (1993) *Rethinking Critical Theory: Emancipation in the Age of Global Social Movements*. London: Sage.

Santos, B. d. S. (1995) *Toward a New Common Sense*. New York: Routledge.

RAYMOND A. MORROW

EMBEDDING AND DISEMBEDDING

The Hungarian economic historian, Karl Polanyi, developed an institutional approach to the **economy** which emphasized that economic action has always to be interpreted as embedded within social relationships ([1944] 1957). Embeddedness is related to the fact that an economic actor is a social being, with a mixture of motives. Economic action is always part of an instituted process of interaction between actors and their environment and is therefore embedded within relationships of reciprocity and redistribution.

This link between economic and sociological approaches of economic behavior is also the heart of Mark Granovetter's (1985) critical response to the New Institutional Economics and especially the transaction cost approach of R. Coase and O. Williamson (see **institutions and neo-institutionalism**). Granovetter pointed out that this theoretical framework does not explain concretely how social mechanisms or social norms like **trust** or opportunism, through which institutions shape individual behaviour, affect economic outcomes. For many commentators on **globalization**, such as **Giddens** (1990) among others, the disembedding of social relations and **social systems** from local contexts marks a main characteristic of high **modernity**. The main mechanisms in this process are the creation of symbolic tokens, especially **money**, and the establishment of expert systems.

References and further reading

Giddens, A. (1990) *The Consequences of Modernity*. Stanford, CA: Stanford University Press.

Granovetter, M. (1985) 'Economic Action and Social Structure: The Problem of Embeddedness', *American Journal of Sociology*, 91(3): 481–510.

Polanyi, K. ([1944] 1957) *The Great Transformation*. New York: Rinehart.

Polanyi, K., Arensberg, C. M. and Pearson, H. W. (eds) (1957) *Trade and Market in the Early Empires: Economies in History and Theory*. London: Routledge & Kegan Paul.

STEFFEN SIGMUND

EMBODIMENT

The term embodiment refers to the cultural meanings attributed to the **body**, the ways in which these are inscribed on and through individual bodies, as well as the perceptions and experiences of those living in particular bodies. It is a term that indicates the importance of *both* **nature** *and* **culture** (biology and **society**) in understandings and personal experiences of the body.

The body as a 'universal biological entity' has long been the object of study in medicine and the natural sciences. However, it is only recently that a focus on the body and on modes of embodiment has been deemed important within the social sciences and humanities. The prior marginalization of the body by disciplines such as sociology, psychology and philosophy may be explained in terms of the influence of Western Cartesian dualism: that is, the division of mind and body into opposing values, following the work of René Descartes. According to this dichotomous **framing** of the human individual, 'the mind' has been associated with supposedly superior qualities of reason, objectivity, and culture, while 'the body' has been more negatively affiliated with irrationality, animality, and nature (and viewed as the house of the all-important 'self'). The hierarchical division between mind and body has also been mapped onto notions of **gender**, masculinity being aligned with intellect and the public domain of **production**, and femininity with the material body and the private sphere of reproduction (Williams and Bendelow 1998).

The current impetus to study the body and embodied experience in the social sciences is attributed to several contemporary social factors (Nettleton and Watson 1998). For example, political movements of the late twentieth century have been influential in challenging medical constructions of the body, and, in particular, the assumption that the white male body is the norm against which all other bodies are measured.

Along with **postmodern** and **postcolonial theories** on embodiment, **feminist theory** has provided an overt political analysis of how the gendering (and racing) of bodies perpetuate and 'naturalize' **power** differences between men and women, create particular gendered **identities** and experiences, and enable exploitation of certain bodies by others. Demographic issues have also precipitated renewed interest in the body (e.g. the greying of the population, and changes in the nature of disease such as the higher incidence of chronic illnesses). Another factor is the impact of consumer culture (see **consumption**), and the popularity of products and services targeting the rectification, enhancement or modification of the body. In addition, the advent of new technologies has created interest in the innovative ways in which bodies might be reconceived and experienced.

Elizabeth Grosz (1994) categorizes social theories on the body and embodiment as following either an 'inside out' or 'outside in' approach. The 'inside out' perspective views the psychical interior, or mind, as constituted in accordance with the social, cultural and historical meanings attributed to the body (see **psychoanalysis**). 'Outside in' theories of embodiment stress the ways in which the body is a surface to be marked or inscribed by **discourse** and culture (proponents of this perspective include **Nietzsche, Foucault,** and **Deleuze**).

Historian and philosopher, Michel Foucault ([1975] 1979) effectively turned attention away from the privileging of the mind (and the self-conscious subject) towards the constitution of the body and self within discourse, focusing on how bodies become the sites for the operation of power in modern societies. According to Foucault, there can be no access to a 'natural' body – to a fundamentally stable and essential biological being – that exists prior to or apart from cultural and social **practices**. **Subjects** are governed through the deployment of the body within various discourses that constitute the 'nature' of the body. For example, discourses such as medicine and the law produce particular types of bodies through processes of discipline (see also **social control**) and normalization. **Power** may be exercised over populations of bodies through specific **institutions** (such as hospitals, prisons, schools and factories), but the most insidious type of power affecting individuals does not involve overt **authority** directed from above to those at the bottom. Foucault argued that along with the era of so-called political liberation there grew a form of '*disciplinary power*' against the body, which, with its associated anonymous and dispersed micro-powers, operates in a more subtle and productive way through the mundane processes of **everyday** life. The operation of disciplinary power results in individuals becoming self-policing subjects or 'docile bodies'. Foucault's theory can readily be applied to the behaviour of men and women in consumer culture, for example, ageing persons may monitor signs of old **age** and attempt to rectify these through the use of cosmetics and clinical products to combat hair loss, grey hair, skin wrinkles and weight gain. Although Foucault has been criticized for failing adequately to address issues of gender in his analyses of bio-power, his ideas have nevertheless played an important role in contemporary feminist and queer scholarship on the body.

The corporeal **phenomenology** of Maurice **Merleau-Ponty** ([1945] 1962) represents another major theoretical take on embodiment. Emphasizing the inter-relatedness – rather than separation – between mind and body, Merleau-Ponty contends the body is not merely a housing for consciousness and the self, but a necessary locus from which one orientates and experiences the world. He analyzes the ways in which the body is both an object for others and a subject of its own reality, and concentrates on the experiences of the *lived body*, that is, the ways in which embodiment arises from this oscillation between the mind and body.

165

Via its interrogation of the ways in which women have been represented through the body, biology and reproductive sexuality – and of how power is exercised over bodies deemed 'other' – feminist theory has remained at the forefront of academic analysis on embodiment, and has provided an important critique of the works of key male theorists in the area. For example, Luce Irigaray ([1977] 1985) has demonstrated how the masculinist portrayal in psycho-analysis of the female body as deficient or abnormal has restricted women's own bodily understandings, expressions, and desires. She encourages women to experiment with a self-determined female subjectivity, one that is radically alternative to prevalent understandings of femininity that are linked to reproduction and maternity. In the past couple of decades, cultural assumptions about male bodies and modes of masculine embodiment have also been scrutinized in the burgeoning field of masculinity studies. **Queer theory** has also contributed to the **deconstruction** of our ideas about bodies, through its disruption of dichotomous constructions of sex and gender, and its celebration of ambiguous bodies. Judith **Butler** (1990) has been particularly influential in challenging the demarcation between biological bodies and culturally constructed notions of sex difference and gender.

Postmodern theorists of the body disturb dualisms (see also **binary** and **classification**) such as mind/body, culture/nature and masculine/feminine through alternative models of the body and explanations of lived experience. For example, Jean-François **Lyotard** ([1974] 1993) employs the model of a Möbius strip (an inverted three-dimensional figure of eight) to indicate the ways in which cultural meanings and desires are inscribed on and through the flesh to produce certain corporeal experiences. He advocates the proliferation of new desires and experiences by subverting the process through which bodies and their sensations are given particular meanings and classifications in discourse. The **cyborg** theory of Donna **Haraway** (1991) turns attention to the impact of new technologies on modes of embodiment. Haraway's cyborg body comprises a **hybrid** of human and machine (thus combining the 'natural' and the 'unnatural'). She claims the non-dualistic properties of the cyborg have potentially emancipatory implications for humankind, and particularly for women who have historically been relegated to restrictive representations of 'the body'. Importantly, the emergence of innovative technological-human fusions, such as the cyborg, creates new modes of understanding and experiencing embodiment. For example, 'cyber-bodies' provide opportunities to displace the material body from the confines of its immediate geography and capabilities (Featherstone and Burrows 1995).

References and further reading

Butler, J. (1990) *Gender Trouble: Feminism and the Subversion of Identity*. New York: Routledge.

Featherstone, M. and Burrows, R. (eds) (1995) *Cyberspace, Cyberbodies, Cyberpunk: Cultures of Technological Embodiment*. London: Sage.

Featherstone, M., Hepworth, M. and Turner, B. (eds) (1991) *The Body: Social Process and Cultural Theory*. London: Sage.

Foucault, M. ([1975] 1979) *Discipline and Punish: The Birth of the Prison*. London: Penguin.

Grosz, E. (1994) *Volatile Bodies: Toward a Corporeal Feminism*. St Leonards, NSW: Allen & Unwin.

Haraway, D. (1991) *Simians, Cyborgs and Women: The Reinvention of Nature*. New York: Routledge.

Irigaray, L. ([1977] 1985) *This Sex Which is Not One*. Ithaca, NY: Cornell University Press.

Lyotard, J. -F. ([1974] 1993) *Libidinal Economy*. Bloomington, IN: Indiana University Press.

Merleau-Ponty, M. ([1945] 1962) *The Phenomenology of Perception*. London: Routledge & Kegan Paul.

Nettleton, S. and Watson, J. (eds) (1998) *The Body in Everyday Life*. London: Routledge.

Turner, B. S. (1996) *The Body and Society*. London: Sage.

Williams, S. J. and Bendelow, G. (1998) *The Lived Body: Sociology Themes, Embodied Issues*. London: Routledge.

ANNIE POTTS

EMOTION

Emotion has always been important to social theory. In classical times it is found in the philosophy of Aristotle, in the seventeenth century in the thought of Hobbes, Spinoza and Descartes, in the eighteenth century in the writings of Adam Smith, Adam Ferguson and David Hume, and in the nineteenth and twentieth centuries in the work of **Pareto**, **Durkheim**, **Simmel** and other founders of modern sociology. In recent years there has been a renewed and growing interest in emotion in social science and social theory, paralleling similar developments in all the human sciences from the study of literature to neurology.

Emotion is widely understood in terms of feelings and bodily sensations, which relate to the necessary physical basis of emotion. But of particular relevance for social theory is the role of emotion in underscoring **values**, **interests** and **meanings** in social life. Turner (2000: 43–66), for instance, demonstrates that emotions underlie the attunement of interpersonal responses, social sanctioning, moral coding, valuing and exchanging resources, and even rational decision-making. The importance of emotion in these and associated processes dispels common misunderstandings about emotion. For instance, it is important to appreciate that emotions are implicated in rational as well as non-rational and irrational **action** and outlooks, for even the most technical activities require facilitating emotions such as calmness and confidence in order to be successfully executed. In addition, the idea that emotions are necessarily of short duration ignores the importance of enduring emotions required for social commitment and **institutionalization** (Frank 1988). This relates to another misunderstanding, which sees experience of emotion as necessarily leading to its discharge and dissipation. In reality, expression of emotion may often serve to reiterate experience of it, as when expression of political anger maintains political dis-

content, for example. Another common misunderstanding is the assumption that experience of emotion entails consciousness of it. Yet many emotions necessary for social processes are experienced below the threshold of awareness, as Scheff (1988) has shown.

The different approaches to emotion are parallel to methodological and theoretical differences in social theory overall. An approach emphasizing the **cultural** aspects of emotion focuses on the social manipulation, transformation and restraint of emotion. Hochschild (1983), for instance, shows that emotional expression tends to be managed so that it is appropriate to circumstance. Emotion management is achieved through performance of emotional labour, which includes activities designed to induce or suppress feelings productive of emotional expression that would elicit particular states of mind in others. Culturally defined feeling rules, governing the exercise of emotional labour, prescribe the content of emotional expression and its appropriate social context. Another approach, drawing on the work of Emile **Durkheim** and Erving **Goffman**, and most fully developed by Randall Collins (1981) in terms of 'interaction' **rituals**, points to the generation of social **symbols** and emotional energy through social **interaction**. Chains of interaction rituals generate emotional tones and **solidarity**, as well as energy for subsequent interaction chains or sequences and their directions. In this way the micro-sphere of face-to-face interactions is generative of the macro-sphere of institutions through the production of emotional energy.

A structural approach to emotions offers a further characterization of the formation of emotions. Kemper (1978), for instance, argues that all social interactions can be situated on one of two formal dimensions of social relations, namely **power** and **status**, or involuntary and voluntary compliance. The agent of power or status may be the **self** or it may be the **other**. Second, Kemper shows that power and status experiences stimulate broadly different sets of physiological processes. Finally, it can be shown that different emotions are physiologically specific. The point for sociological theory is that the particular emotions experienced arise out of the structure of the relations of power and status in which they are placed. In this way emotion is a necessary link between **social structure** and social actor: experience of insufficient power leads to fear, excess power to guilt; excess status to shame; insufficient status to depression, and so on.

Focus on emotion has played a positive role in the development of a number of areas of social theory. **Feminist theory**, for instance, has shown the ways in which emotional styles tend to be gender-specific, and the differential evaluation of emotional experience by **gender** is associated with manifold social outcomes, including health status, occupational location, consumption patterns, and senses of ontological security. Social theories of the body (see **embodiment**) and of **health and illness** present other areas in which a focus on emotion has taken research in hitherto neglected directions. Cultural theories, from the consideration of **civilizations**, in the manner of Norbert **Elias**, to practices, in the manner of Pierre **Bourdieu**, to writing on rhetoric and **discourse**, have all felt the need to incorporate consideration of emotion in enhancing their epistemic competence.

References and further reading

Barbalet, J. (1998) *Emotion, Social Theory, and Social Structure: A Macrosociological Approach.* Cambridge: Cambridge University Press.

Collins, R. (1981) 'On the Microfoundations of Macrosociology', *American Journal of Sociology*, 86(5): 984–1014.

Frank, R. H. (1988) *Passions within Reason: The Strategic Role of the Emotions.* New York: W. W. Norton.

Hochschild, A. R. (1983) *The Managed Heart: Commercialization of Human Feeling.* Berkeley, CA: University of California Press.

Kemper, T. D. (1978) *A Social Interactional Theory of Emotions.* New York: Wiley.

Lupton, D. (1998) *The Emotional Self.* London: Sage.

Moldoveanu, M. C. and Nohria, N. (2002) *Master Passions: Emotion, Narrative, and the Development of Culture.* Cambridge, MA: MIT Press.

Scheff, T. J. (1988) 'Shame and Conformity: The Deference-Emotion System', *American Sociological Review*, 53: 395–406.

Turner, J. (2000) *On the Origins of Human Emotions.* Stanford, CA: Stanford University Press.

Williams, S. (2001) *Emotion and Social Theory.* London: Sage.

JACK BARBALET

EMPIRICISM

Empiricism is the name given to the general philosophical and scientific attitude that all **knowledge** of the world derives from experience gained through immediate acquaintance or direct observation. In the social sciences it means the acceptance of any of the following propositions: that direct acquaintance with reality defines the limits of knowledge; that concepts and theories are based on directly given data; and that the only reliable **methods** are ones involving experimentation or induction (generalization from observed facts). Empiricism was first formulated by the ancient Greek philosophers, but it is in the context of the early modern scientific movement that it found authoritative articulation.

In opposition to Plato's emphasis on ideas, Epicurus in the fourth and third centuries BCE advanced an anti-**metaphysical** argument in favour of observation as the only source of knowledge. True beliefs were to be inductively derived from sensory experience. In medieval Scholasticism, this early statement was taken up in the doctrine of nominalism which regarded general concepts as at best names given to specific features of things making up reality. Empiricism made its reappearance in the seventeenth century. Francis Bacon stressed the need for all knowledge to be based on experimental and inductive science. Thomas Hobbes and John Locke followed, the latter being the first to articulate the epistemological elements of empiricism in a systematic manner. During the **Enlightenment**, empiricism became one of the strands entering into the emergence of **positivism**, initiated (though not yet named as such) by David Hume and carried forward by the Encyclopedists. In Hume, it appeared as 'impressions' gained through observation, while the Encyclopedists stressed empirical knowledge based on facts established by observation, on 'sensations'. In the nineteenth century, Auguste **Comte** incorporated this current in his proposal for positive science or 'positivism', which John Stuart **Mill** also expounded and which Emile **Durkheim** later presented with explicit reference to sociology in *The Rules of Sociological Method* of 1895 (1966). Durkheim's insistence that sociology should 'consider social facts as things' and that 'all preconceptions must be eradicated', reiterated Bacon's attack on 'idols of the mind' blocking the development of knowledge.

In the older positivism from Hume to Durkheim, induction was central and empiricism was given one of three forms: sensualism, phenomenalism or physicalism. These depended on whether the experiential basis of knowledge was ascribed to sensations, to immediate experience of mental entities representing observables or sense data, or finally to physical entities in commonsense experience. Historically, Durkheim's physicalism proved influential in the social sciences. The emergence in the early twentieth century of neo-positivism, also known as logical empiricism or logical positivism, involved an assault on induction in favour of deduction (reasoning from the general to the particular). Karl **Popper** (1959) famously presented the case against inductivism, while Willard v. O. Quine (1951) launched a devastating attack against the 'dogmas of empiricism'. This immanent critique shifted the principle of empiricism

from verification to falsification, culminating in the thesis of the theory-ladenness of observation, also associated with holism or **paradigm** theory. According to this thesis, only a whole theoretical system can be corroborated or refuted, not discrete individual propositions.

The twentieth-century critiques of positivism by **hermeneutics**, **phenomenology** and **critical theory** all included a frontal attack on empiricism with the argument that the foundational empiricist concept of sensory experience is too narrow to capture the depth of 'communicative experience' (**Habermas** 1988). On this basis, different varieties of qualitative social science have gained currency since the 1960s.

References and further reading

Delanty, G. and Strydom, P. (2003) *Philosophies of Social Science*. Maidenhead: Open University Press; Philadelphia, PA: McGraw-Hill.

Durkheim, E. ([1895] 1966) *The Rules of Sociological Method*. New York: Free Press.

Habermas, J. ([1967] 1988) *On the Logic of the Social Sciences*. Cambridge: Polity.

Popper, K. R. ([1934] 1959) *The Logic of Scientific Discovery*. London: Hutchinson.

Quine, W. v. O. (1951) 'Two Dogmas of Empiricism', *Philosophical Review*, 60: 20–43.

PIET STRYDOM

ENLIGHTENMENT

In contemporary social theory two related notions of Enlightenment are current. On the one hand, Enlightenment designates a social, political and intellectual ideal. On the other hand, as a period in history, the concept of Enlightenment usually designates the mid-eighteenth-century flowering of secular social and philosophical thought in Europe, especially around the French *philosophes* (Hampson 1968). Foremost among these was Voltaire, noted for his advocacy of religious **freedom**, tolerance and freedom of expression.

When the values of the Enlightenment thus conceived are generalized as an ideal, we have what social theorists, after Jürgen **Habermas**, call the 'Enlightenment project', one closely associated with the project of modernity itself (Habermas 1985; cf. **Lyotard** 1984 and McLennan 1996). The ideals of the Enlightenment in this sense refer to such values as **secularization**, **freedom**, **progress**, **equality** and **social justice**. Fidelity to the Enlightenment as a project entails fidelity to the continuing relevance of such specific values, even in a putatively post-modern age. Not all social theorists, however, agree with Habermas on this issue of the continuing relevance of the Enlightenment. Some social theorists, such as John Gray and Zygmunt **Bauman**, believe that these Enlightenment ideals are now finished: indeed, that the Enlightenment itself, with its utopian, rationalizing tendencies, was at the root of the problems, even the disasters, of European secular modernity (Gray 1995; Bauman 1986; Bauman 1987). This attitude towards the ideals of the Enlightenment and their contradictory character has a distinguished genealogy in social theory. One classic expression still remains **Adorno** and Horkheimer's seminal text, *Dialectic of Enlightenment* (1986).

Some social theorists have attempted to redeem the notion of 'enlightenment' as a generic term while still remaining sceptical of the historical legacy of the Enlightenment. Following especially Michel **Foucault**, social theorists invoke a notion of enlightenment in terms less of a particular ideal or a period in history so much as an ethos (Osborne 1998). Here it is not the particular substantive beliefs or values of the Enlightenment which are decisive but rather a critical questioning attitude. Foucault's classic late essay 'What is Enlightenment?' is integral to this perspective (Foucault 1984). In this text, Foucault argued that the legacy of the Enlightenment is far from being best served by a dogmatic adherence to the actual letter of Enlightenment

thought involving specific of substantive principles. Such an adherence represents an un-liberated slavishness towards a very particular **tradition** and remains blind to the real negative effects of some aspects of Enlightenment thought itself. Foucault documented some of these effects in his studies of the modern asylum and the prison (Foucault 1971; 1979). Rather, for Foucault, if the concept of enlightenment is to be redeemed, it is best seen negatively as the on-going and probably endless search for a 'way out'. Foucault draws this sense of enlightenment from **Kant** ([1784] 1970), for whom enlightenment is regarded as an ethical process that releases us from the state of 'immaturity'. Here, immaturity designates any sense of being dogmatically beholden to **authority**. The aim of enlightenment, in this conception, should not be specific or substantive; it should be an ethos or a form: to help us to free ourselves from our continuingly beholden state towards authority, in whatever form such authority disguises itself – even from dogmatic adherence to the authority of the Enlightenment itself.

References and further reading

Adorno, T. M. and Horkheimer, M. (1986) *Dialectic of Enlightenment*. London: Verso.

Bauman, Z. (1986) *Modernity and the Holocaust*. Oxford: Blackwell.

Bauman, Z. (1987) *Legislators and Interpreters*. Cambridge: Polity.

Foucault, M. (1971) *Madness and Civilization*. London: Tavistock.

Foucault, M. (1979) *Discipline and Punish*. Harmondsworth: Penguin.

Foucault, M. (1984) 'What is Enlightenment?', in *The Foucault Reader*. Harmondsworth: Penguin.

Gray, J. (1995) *Enlightenment's Wake*. London: Routledge.

Habermas, J. (1985) 'Modernity – An Incomplete Project', in H. Foster (ed.) *Postmodern Culture*. London: Pluto.

Hampson, N. (1968) *The Enlightenment*. Harmondsworth: Penguin.

Kant, I. ([1784] 1970) 'An Answer to the Question: What is Enlightenment?', in H. Reiss (ed.) *Political Writings*. Cambridge: Cambridge University Press.

Lyotard, J.-F. (1984) *The Postmodern Condition*. Manchester: Manchester University Press.

McLennan, G. (1996) 'The Enlightenment Project Revisited', in S. Hall, D. Held, D. Hubert and K. Thompson (eds) *Modernity: An Introduction to Modern Societies*. Oxford: Blackwell.

Osborne, T. S. D. (1998) *Aspects of Enlightenment: Social Theory and the Ethics of Truth*. London: University College London.

THOMAS OSBORNE

EPISTEMOLOGY

Epistemology is the term used by philosophers since the mid-nineteenth century for the study of the theoretical foundations of **knowledge**. James Ferrier coined the English word 'epistemology' in 1854 to refer to what we now call 'cognitive science', i.e. the scientific study of the mind. However, in the twentieth century, two other senses of 'epistemology' acquired prominence in English, one originating in Germany and the other in Austria.

The German sense harks back to Kant's idea that reality cannot be known in itself but only in terms of our various 'cognitive interests'. In the hands of the German idealists, epistemology in this sense became the philosophy of the university, with the unity of knowledge as its goal and the liberal arts curriculum as its realization. However, for the neo-Kantian philosophers who by 1900 had become the bulwark of German academia, epistemology rationalized the existence of increasingly divergent disciplinary **world-views** (see **Kantianism and neo-Kantianism**). **Weber**'s lifelong attempt to reconcile 'interpretivist' and 'positivist' methodological imperatives in the newly recognized social sciences reflects this epistemological perspective. The early work of **Habermas** ([1968] 1971) is perhaps the last major expression of this project. In this tradition, epistemology is synonymous with the philosophical foundations of the sciences.

The Austrian sense of epistemology, traceable to the late nineteenth-century philosophical psychologist Franz Brentano, began as a theologically inspired backlash against Kant. Brentano returned to Aristotle for a sense of consciousness as indicative of our being in the world. Whereas Kant saw restless quest for knowledge as implying a radical separation from the world, Brentano was more impressed by our fundamental rootedness in the world. This sensibility inspired the later phenomenological tradition, especially the work of Martin **Heidegger**, who came to see epistemology itself as symptomatic of existential alienation that was played out in the proliferation of mutually incommensurable academic disciplines.

These two different senses of epistemology are easily obscured in English, which uses the same words – 'know' and 'knowledge' – for the processes and the products of knowing. In French and German philosophical discourse, the difference is more clearly marked: on the one hand, *connaissance* and *Erkenntnis* and, on the other, *savoir* and *Wissenschaft*. We might translate the former pair of terms as 'cognition' and the latter as 'discipline'. For example, the Baconian motto 'knowledge is power' appears in **Comte** as '*savoir est pouvoir*'.

One consequence of the expressive awkwardness of English in epistemological matters is that Anglophone philosophers have tended to regard socially sanctioned knowledge as simply an aggregation of what is known by individuals. Thus, they obscure the facticity of knowledge as a product of collective action and a normative standard that may contradict what individuals believe. In contrast, just this facticity is taken for granted by French and German theorists of knowledge such as **Foucault** and Habermas. This difference in starting points remains a major source of misunderstanding between contemporary analytic and continental philosophers, which in recent years has led to a call for 'social epistemology' (Fuller 1988).

Within sociology proper, epistemology has had a chequered career, though the character of the controversy surrounding it has shifted over the years. For Comte, sociology was basically applied epistemology, a view he inherited from the **Enlightenment** assumption that societies are defined by their legitimating ideas. Under the influence of **Marx**, legitimatory forms of knowledge came to be seen as ideologies ripe for demystification by the sociology of knowledge. Nevertheless, **Mannheim** (1936) stopped short of demystifying the epistemology of science, not least because sociology itself claimed to rest on it.

By the 1970s, this concern for the reflexive implications of sociological critiques of **science** created a schism within sociology that continues to this day. On the one hand, sociologists of science openly demystify the epistemology of science, while, on the other, more mainstream sociologists reject epistemology in favour of **ontology** as the preferred philosophical foundation for social knowledge. A good sense of the stakes may be gleaned by contrasting Bloor (1976) and **Giddens** (1976). In particular, Giddens is concerned with crediting social agents as 'always already' social theorists whose access to the social world is as valid as that of the social scientists studying them. This view, explicitly indebted to Alfred **Schutz**, is also consonant with that of **Rorty** (1979), who defends a philosophical critique of epistemology that has been influential among postmodernists. Typical of the postmodernist outlook in this sense is the idea that we inhabit different worlds equally, rather than have differential access to the same world.

References and further reading

Bloor, D. (1976) *Knowledge and Social Imagery*. London: Routledge.
Collins, R. (1998) *The Sociology of Philosophies*. Cambridge, MA: Harvard University Press.
Fuller, S. (1988) *Social Epistemology*. Bloomington, IN: Indiana University Press.
Giddens, A. (1976) *New Rules of the Sociological Method*. London. Hutchinson.
Habermas, J. ([1968] 1971) *Knowledge and Human Interests*. Boston: Beacon.
Mannheim, K. ([1929] 1936) *Ideology and Utopia*. New York: Harcourt Brace & World.
Rorty, R. (1979) *Philosophy and the Mirror of Nature*. Princeton, NJ: Princeton University Press.

STEVE FULLER

EQUALITY

The concept of equality is an internally complex idea. It may be preferable to speak instead of conceptions of equality, since many of the varied strands that come into this category bear family resemblances to one another but sit together uncomfortably or conflict with one another. This is because equality is an intrinsically comparative idea. The proposition that two things are equal may be descriptive or it may be normative. Such a proposition is incomplete without further specification of the respects in which the objects compared are thought to be equal. Since no two objects outside the realm of pure mathematics or logic can be equal in all respects – only in all relevant respects – the question of which respects are relevant in social theory yields a spectrum of debates.

The assertion of the equal standing of persons has made equality a central but controversial ideal in social and political theory. The declaration that 'all men are created equal' is not rebutted by pointing to the obvious fact that some are smarter or stronger or better looking than others. The ideal of equality is a prescriptive claim about **social justice**. It says there is some respect in which no difference should be made in the consideration of persons, whatever their actual **differences**. Greater equality in principle leaves open the question of what exactly should be equalized. Should this be opportunities, resources, welfare, capabilities, or another aspect of human life? There are sound arguments for taking any one of these as the basis of public policy; ranging from extreme egalitarian approaches, in which virtually nothing should be exempt from equal treatment, to elitist ones, in which many things should be exempt. Four related but distinguishable forms of equality can be discerned: moral, social, legal, and political.

Moral equality is the idea that people should be regarded as being equal in value or worth, at least insofar as they are the **subjects** of moral reasoning. The equal worth of persons (see **persons and personality**) entitles them to equal consideration in the treatment of their **interests** in a scheme of moral decision-making, as in the utilitarian concern that each one counts as one in aggregation procedures (see **utilitarianism**). *Social equality* demands that all members of **society** enjoy equal access to basic goods that enable them to lead good lives, such as income, **wealth**, **education**, and medical care. *Legal equality*, or equality before the **law**, holds that all those to whom the laws of a particular political **association** apply should be subject to a standard impartial body of laws. No one should enjoy privileges that are not extended to all, nor should anyone in particular be exempt from legal sanctions. *Political equality* demands that all members of a **polity** have an equal say with all others in the selection of leaders and the making of laws. This idea is most obviously violated when some members are disenfranchised.

Provided the relative levels of equality across persons can be measured, the question of *opportunities* versus *outcomes* yields further debates within each of these concepts. For instance, some advocate equalizing opportunities for high incomes even if it leads to exceedingly unequal incomes in the end. On this view, as long as competition for advantages is open to all, the ideal of social equality does not require that everyone ends up with equal or similar advantages. By contrast, those who promote equality of outcomes view equal opportunity as irrelevant or secondary at best if some people end up rich and others poor. Similarly, there are debates over whether and how much political equality concerns eligibility or actual participation. Equal suffrage, for instance, will not offset or correct an imbalance in the political voices on offer, and will only contingently lead to legislative outcomes that conform to some standard of equality.

Tensions also exist between each of the general conceptions of equality. Legal equality and social equality are widely believed to stand in an uneasy relation to one another. Legal equality, as it is usually understood, requires that the law be blind to a great range of differences between those who are subject to it. To apply the law impartially means to apply it without regard to those differences. Yet to promote social equality, it may be necessary to apply the law in ways that are sensitive to **disability**, differences of **gender**, **class**, **race**, **ethnicity** or effects of past discrimination, as some proponents of affirmative action have argued. Even if multiple equalities could be adequately balanced, doing so may impinge on other **values** deemed socially important, such as merit or desert, individual **freedom**, **pluralism**, or communal ties. Radically egalitarian measures can infringe upon some for the sake of others, lead to an unraveling of other aspects of social life for all, or undermine too many of the economic and cultural conditions for stable society.

No social or political theory aims at equality categorically, only at specific conceptions deemed socially important when they are embedded within a broader theory of politics and society. Thus the concept evoked by the term 'equality' actually consists of a range of 'equalities', each of which answers whether and what kinds of equalities of social situations are desirable.

References and further reading

Dworkin, R. (2000) *Sovereign Virtue*. Cambridge, MA: Harvard University Press.

Johnston, D. (ed.) (2000) *Equality*. Indianapolis, IN: Hackett.

Pojman, L. and Westmoreland, R. (eds) (1997) *Equality*. Oxford: Oxford University Press.

Sen, A. (1992) *Inequality Reexamined*. Cambridge, MA: Harvard University Press.

NAOMI CHOI

EROTICISM

The term eroticism refers to the investment of an object, person or event with a sexual charge or desire. The erotic has long held a fascination for artists and poets. Theoretical analysis of the ways in which humans attribute erotic qualities to others (animate or inanimate), and the means by which our experiences are deemed erotic or sexual in nature, has proliferated since the nineteenth century and the emergence of **psychoanalysis** (see **Freud**). Approaches to examining erotic desire and behaviour can be broadly grouped into two camps: those more or less in agreement with psychoanalytic theory, and those who oppose its key tenets, specifically the way in which desire is understood to operate. Freud viewed eroticism as a struggle between two antagonistic drives: life (Eros, generation) and **death** (Thanatos, degeneration). He speculated these two competing forces amalgamated in the strongest sense through orgasm during heterosexual coitus, as this provided the possibility of procreation (life) at the same time as it produced a sense of losing one's **self** (death). In psychoanalysis, desire is conceptualized in negative terms as a response to a **need** or lack (a desire for that which is missing or lost). In contrast, contemporary postmodern theorists such as Jean-François **Lyotard** and Gilles **Deleuze** define erotic desire in distinctly *anti*-psychoanalytic terms: as a primarily positive and productive energy (or 'intensity') that has no specific objective or goal. Their alternative erotologies transgress notions of normative **sexuality**, and disrupt assumptions about what constitute 'bodies' and 'objects' of desire.

References and further reading

Bataille, G. ([1957] 1962) *Eroticism*. London: Calder and Boyars.

Deleuze, G. and Guattari, F. ([1980] 1987) *Anti-Oedipus: Capitalism and Schizophrenia*. Minneapolis, MN: University of Minnesota Press.

Freud, S. (1986) *The Essentials of Psychoanalysis*. Ed. A. Freud. London: Penguin.

Lyotard, J.-F. ([1974] 1993) *Libidinal Economy*. Bloomington, IN: Indiana University Press.

ANNIE POTTS

ESSENTIALISM

The *Compact Oxford English Dictionary* defines essentialism as 'the belief in real essences of things, especially the view that the task of science and philosophy is to discover these and express them in definitions' (1989: 532). One of the important aspects of essentialism is the idea that the properties of things exist prior to the individuals that live with or in some way utilize or embody them. In the social sciences, the concept of essentialism is utilized extensively. Philosophy is concerned to explore whether or not certain concepts are imbued with essence. For instance, what is the constitution of human being? Are there essential properties or qualities to being human (**rationality**, **emotion**, **ethics**, **language**, **tradition**, symbolism)? Sociology tends to be more concerned with essentialism as it applies to social processes. The search for underlying properties that define the essence of a particular entity is best described methodologically by **positivism**, which primarily seeks to understand things through experimental investigation and observation.

A number of sociologists have investigated the extent to which 'sex' and 'race' may be viewed as embodying certain essential qualities. Discussions of essentialism and race have largely been abandoned since they are most often associated with eugenics, prejudice and discrimination. Interestingly, there remains a persistent, if implicit, assumption that sex refers to a set of essential differences between women and men that are grounded in biology. This assumption emerged in contemporary social studies in the form of the **sex/gender distinction**. **Post-structuralism** has most recently argued against any essential qualities of individuals, arguing instead that **subjectivity** is produced through social processes. Interestingly, since these social processes are understood to exist prior to the individual, it could be argued that the social processes themselves are essential qualities of subjectivity, or in other words, that social constructionism (see **constructionism**) is dependent upon essentialism.

References and further reading

The Compact Oxford English Dictionary (1989) 2nd edn. Oxford: Clarendon Press.
Spelman, E. (1988) *Inessential Woman*. London: The Women's Press.
Sydie, R. A. (1987) *Natural Women, Cultured Men*. Milton Keynes: Open University Press.

MYRA HIRD

ETHICS

See: morality

ETHNICITY

From its inception, the term 'ethnicity' has been fluid and elusive, designating attributes and identities (see **identity**) linked indiscriminately to **religion**, **language**, **culture**, physical traits and/or ancestry. It is also a contested term. For some authors, ethnicity is a social category as important for analyzing the twentieth century as **class** was for the nineteenth (Glazer and Moynihan 1975). But it has also been spurned in sociological traditions. **Post-colonial** theorists contend that ethnicity remains a potentially essentializing concept that must be handled with extreme care (see **post-colonial theory**). Scholars have thus been led to differentiate between old and new ethnicities, between

inheritance and social mobilization, and to emphasize the social construction of boundaries and identities (see also **classification**).

According to Warner and Lunt's *Yankee City* (1941) ethnicity is an attribute that characterizes individuals born outside or inside the country, who consider themselves, or are considered to be, members of a **group** with a foreign culture and who participate in the life of the group. However, Warner and Lunt sometimes use the term 'ethnic' to designate all inhabitants of 'Yankee City'. This double sense is associated with the ambiguity of the adjective 'ethnic' from which it derives. In the Greek version of the Bible, *ethnikos* translates the Hebrew *goyim*; that is, Gentiles or heathens (Sollors 1986). In classical Greek, the noun *ethnos* likewise referred to the 'others', while in modern Greek it applies to the Greeks themselves. In English usage from the fifteenth to the mid-nineteenth century, ethnic, sometimes spelled *hethnic*, continues to designate, often negatively, non-Christians and non-Jews. Since the twentieth century, 'ethnic group' has applied mainly to a collectivity within a larger collectivity, differentiated from the rest of the community by ancestry, cultural background and history (Schermerhorn 1970). This restrictive usage of ethnic as 'other' and 'non-standard' has dominated until very recently, in everyday discourses as well as in scholarly ones, despite the position advocated by Hughes and Hughes (1952). These two authors argued that we are all ethnic and that reserving the term exclusively for others constituted a form of **ethnocentrism**.

The term ethnicity resurfaced in the early 1970s in the wake of world-wide ethnic and national movements, which were accompanied by a critique of assimilationism and cultural **domination**. It burst on the American scene in 1972 with a conference of the American Academy of the Arts and the creation of the Committee for the Comparative Study of Ethnicity and Nationality and the journal *Ethnicity* launched in 1974.

When Glazer and Moynihan revived the term in 1975, they meant to describe a new phenomenon, no longer construed as a historical residue.

Theories of ethnicity

Glazer and Moynihan (1975) define ethnicity as a character or quality of an ethnic group. Hence both terms remain intertwined creating a tautological problem observed by Isajiw (1974). Most definitions recorded in Isajiw's study treat ethnicity as a category inseparable from actual concrete groups. Common national or geographic origin or common ancestors, culture and customs, religion, race or physical characteristics, language, consciousness of kind and we-feeling are among the attributes most frequently singled out. Also noteworthy is the overlap between ethnic group and '**race**', which reaches back to the studies of the **Chicago School** on the Race Relation cycle. Today, 'race' is apprehended as a product of an **ideology**, racism, which construes groups as biologically founded, while ethnicity implies reference to acquired cultural differences. That is not to say that all cultural groups are ethnic. Most authors now concur with **Weber**'s incisive definition (Juteau 1999; Jenkins, 1997) which refers to a subjective belief in common descent, real or putative, as a constitutive component of ethnic groups.

New approaches to ethnicity have often been contrasted with former ones. Today constructivism (and **social constructionism**) is presented as a rupture or an **epistemological** break from primordialism, **essentialism** and substantialism. However, understanding theories of ethnicity requires a more nuanced approach, one that tries to overcome this simple dichotomy.

From the very beginning, an **interactionist** approach has characterized the field of ethnic relations, at least as it developed in sociology. Influenced by **Simmel**, the pioneering work of the Chicago School – Park and Burgess

(1921) and Thomas and Znaniecki (1918–20) – on the **migration** of Europeans and Black Americans to the urban centers of the North explored the changing relations between these groups and the host society. Their work is concerned with the transformation of group boundaries, from contact through **conflict**, accommodation, and assimilation, the last stage of the Race Relations cycle, 'race' being used here interchangeably with 'ethnic'. In the 1940s and 1950s, their colleagues Frazier and Hughes questioned assimilation as a necessary or desirable outcome, and focused on unequal relations, be they economic or political. In the 1960s, research examined the cultural and structural processes of assimilation, the changing social organization of ethnic groups, and their institutional parameters and systems of interaction.

Thus, most studies prior to the constructivist turn of the late 1960s cannot be labelled primordialist, although the tendency sometimes was to perceive ethnic groups in an overly substantialist and objectivist way.

While many early anthropological studies often viewed ethnic groups as static and evolving in a vacuum, Barth's (1969) watershed contribution shifted the analysis from the group to the construction of its boundaries. By analysing how individuals are assigned to ethnic categories through processes of auto- and/or hetero-attribution of cultural traits, he traced the construction of boundaries separating insiders from outsiders. Ethnic groups in his picture become vessels of social **organization**, and their boundaries are not to be equated with the cultural stuff they comprise. That is why ethnic boundaries and identities persist even though their cultural content changes.

Barth's constructivist approach, also called 'situational', has often been opposed to the primordialism of **Geertz** (1963), Devereux, Isaac and Shils. Primordialism, it is argued, conceives of ethnic affinities as unaccountable and unchangeable, as ties existing by and of themselves. The primordial character of ethnicity is transmitted within the group, independently of interactions with others. Primordialism must be differentiated from another non-constructivist approach, namely **sociobiology**, which postulates that ethnicity represents a process of kin selection based on the biology of nepotism.

Constructivism – a broad term often used to designate anti-primordialist approaches – has come in different theoretical guises, identified among others by Poutignat and Streiff-Fénart (1995). This paradigm traverses disciplines, producing a shift from the description of ethnic groups to processes of categorization, mobilization and identity formation. Such is the case in Glazer and Moynihan's instrumentalist approach. Ethnicity represents a focus of social and political mobilization, associated with the expanded functions of the state and the need to increase access to resources. Ethnic forms of identification and alliances are used to ensure group organization and **solidarity** for political and economic competition. Theirs is also an optionalist perspective, in the sense that ethnicity involves a form of **voluntarism** that varies according to groups.

When applied to the individual level, instrumentalism corresponds to **rational choice** theory, which contends that social actions aim at maximizing self-interests. Similarly, theories of internal colonialism interpret ethnic and national movements as struggles against an unequal, and culturally assigned, division of labour. According to these theories, ethnicity represents a form of solidarity against discrimination that takes effect through concealed economic **interests**. **Marxism** views ethnicity in relation to **class**, capitalist exploitation and the segmentation of labour markets. For some Marxists, ethnicity is a fiction, a false consciousness masking and conflicting with the real economic antagonisms of class. Others see ethnic differences as real but subordinated to class antagonisms. Some politically focused approaches also look upon ethnicity as an external construction, mainly by a state that categorizes and pigeonholes individuals and groups through census classifications and governmental policies. One position along this line was taken by **Sartre** who argued that anti-Semitism creates the Jew. Neo-Weberian approaches (Rex 1970) emphasize **status** and class and the way in which their interaction fosters monopolistic closure and reproduces social inequalities. Finally, neoculturalist approaches treat ethnicity as a dynamic cultural system that entails the delineation of distinctiveness and its signification.

It should be emphasized that this opposition between 'constructivism' and 'primordialism' is somewhat simplistic, however. The same must also be said of other terminologies such as 'perennial and ubiquitous' versus 'contingent and situated'; or 'primary and expressive' versus 'situational and instrumental'; or 'subjective' and 'objective'; or 'voluntary' and 'imposed' (Jenkins 1997). Geertz, for example, regards primordial attachments as central, but also as putative and stimulated in specific situations. The task, then, is to view ethnicities as embedded in broader contexts, locating social interactions within macro-sociological and state-dominated structures.

Ethnicity in macro-perspective

In his pioneering and comparative work, Schermerhorn (1970) argues that sequences of interaction such as colonialism, annexation and **migration**, from forced **slavery** to formal 'freedom', impact on overall ethnic dynamics. For example, the history of slavery in the USA informs contemporary racialized dynamics, as does colonialism in the case of North Africans in France. These ethnic social relations cut across societies as a whole, traversing their economic, political, cultural and ideological spheres. They can be treated as analytically distinct from gender and social class, which prevents us from reducing one set of social relations to another, and from superimposing, in a deterministic fashion, 'race' and ethnic relations on class. Since these relations intersect at the empirical level, the construction of ethnicity and ethnic boundaries cannot be dissociated from gender and class relations.

At the empirical level, ethnically defined social relations can be examined as 'ethnic-making' situations. Fenton (1999) links differentiated contexts to types of modern ethnicity, thus identifying five distinct situations. Urban minorities comprise migrant workers, including trader minorities. When the descendants of populations who have migrated as coerced, semi-voluntary or voluntary workers come to form distinctive minorities, they constitute ethnic groups. These are to be distinguished from post-slavery minorities, since here groups are racialized, and the descendants of former slaves in the new world are construed as black. Ethnic groups, like the Chinese in Malaysia, can make a claim for a distinct ethno–national status but form a relatively enduring distinct segment of a nations–state system. Some ethnic groups, usually those that have been colonized, define themselves as nations and make a claim to self-government (see **nationalism**). Finally, indigenous minorities dispossessed by colonial settlement voice demands that range from **recognition** to self-government. The status of ethnic groups and their claims thus vary across time and space.

Linking individual and collective interactions and identities to their broader context, and understanding how ethnic social relations are specifically constituted, helps overcome one-sided explanations. Positioning can be understood as relating to ways in which subjective dimensions of ethnicity connect to objective dimensions. An understanding of context reveals that these relations are unequal, and that the capacity to choose and negotiate ethnic identities varies from total choice to complete constraint. Ethnicity is not a given, but nor is it an illusion or simply arbitrary.

Primordialism in the sense of 'perennial' can be reunited with situationism by examining ethnicities in terms of two analytically distinct facets (Juteau 1999). One facet involves unequal social relations underlying the construction of ethnicities and the choice of markers that define ethnic categories. However, to reduce ethnicities to domination is problematic, for dominant groups, be they the **bourgeoisie** or state **elites**, do not construct ethnic boundaries and identities by themselves or from nothing. A second facet therefore refers to the agency of ethnicized minorities who constantly create and recreate their identities in connection to their past and present history, and to their future projects, all of which include manifold social relations.

Of importance here is that unequal relations between groups also express themselves at the discursive level. Dominant groups label subordinate ones as different and ethnic, while defining themselves as universal and as incarnating the norm. In addition, there is a tendency to explain ethnic and national movements in terms of pre-modern ties and essentialized qualities rather than as triggered by domination. When focusing on the internal side of ethnic boundaries, both dominant and subordinate groups are viewed as ethnic since they are both historically specific and situated. Current research on ethnics (Smith, 1987), and on dominant ethnicity (Kaufmann 2004) clearly points to this fact.

Ethnicities should thus be viewed as modern and as centrally located in the world-system (see **world system theory**). They can be dominant or subordinate, and they can form a unified system constituted through unequal social relations, and they can involve ideal and material interests. Their objective and subjective dimensions are typically connected, as are the internal and external facets of their boundaries, and they are typically constantly moving, intersecting with other processes and identities (see **hybridity**). Political campaigns over ethnic relations and ethnicities' struggles and objectives challenge assimilationist ideologies (see **multiculturalism**) and strive to eradicate social **inequality**.

References and further reading

Barth, F. (1969) 'Introduction', in F. Barth (ed.) *Ethnic Groups and Boundaries: The Social Organization of Culture Difference*. Boston: Little Brown and Co.

Fenton, S. (1999) *Ethnicity: Racism, Class and Culture*. Lanham, MD: Rowman & Littlefield.

Geertz, C. (1963) 'The Integrative Revolution', in C. Geertz *Old Societies and New States*. New York: Free Press.

Glazer, N. and Moynihan, D. (eds) (1975) *Ethnicity: Theory and Experience*. Cambridge, MA: Harvard University Press.

Hall, S. (1992) 'New Ethnicities', in J. Donald and A. Rattansi (eds) *Race, Culture and Difference*. London: Sage and Open University.

Hughes, E. and Hughes, H. (1952) *Where Peoples Meet*. Westport, CT: Greenwood Publishers.

Isajiw, W. W. (1974) 'Definitions of Ethnicity', *Ethnicity*, 1(1): 111–24.

Jenkins, R. (1997) *Rethinking Ethnicity: Arguments and Explorations*. London: Sage.

Juteau, D. (1999) *L'ethnicité et ses frontières*. Montréal: Presses de l'Université de Montréal.

Kaufmann, E. (2004) *Rethinking Ethnicity*. London: Routledge.

Poutignat, P. and Streiff-Fénart, J. (1995) *Théories de l'ethnicité*. Paris: Presses Universitaires de France.

Rex, J. (1970) *Race Relations in Sociological Theory*. London: Weidenfeld & Nicolson.

Smith, A. D. (1987) *The Ethnic Origins of Nations*. Oxford: Blackwell.

Sollors, W. (1986) *Beyond Ethnicity: Consent and Descent in American Culture*. New York: Oxford University Press.

Schermerhorn, R. A. (1970) *Comparative Ethnic Relations: A Framework for Theory and Research*. New York: Random.

Warner, W. and Lunt, P. S. (1941) *The Social Life of a Modern Community*. New Haven, CT: Yale University Press.

DANIELLE JUTEAU

ETHNOCENTRISM

The term 'ethnocentrism' is used to refer to habits of thought that misunderstand the distinctness of other peoples who differ in their basic cultural values, beliefs and ideas from the people who make statements about them. Ethnocentrism refers to failed or inadequate understanding of another people on account of prejudice or pre-conceptions. The judging speaker or **group** is said to be too 'centred' in the world of its own **culture**, too guilty of projecting its own 'centre' on to the other, or too lazy in the ethical task of meeting with the other in an attitude of mutual **recognition** and dialogue. Just as the first task of the historian is to overcome ethnocentrism. Typically, however, the act of self-projection on to the other involves a curious fascination with the 'otherness of the other' in which the subject paradoxically forgets its own relation of commonality to the other. European images of the 'noble savage' that entertain an idealized notion of darker-skinned 'races' as less morally corrupted by **civilization** or more in harmony with **nature** are, in this sense, no less ethnocentric than the more blatant attitudes known by the name of **racism**. Essentializing attitudes to other peoples that fetishize cultural difference as something mysterious – typically through ideas of an exotic 'Orient' (see **Orientalism**) – forget that the other cannot be an 'other' except in a *relation* to the subject. As many **post-colonialist** critics demonstrate in response to forms of Western **universalism** (see also **Occident**), the obverse of ethnocentrism is not wholesale self-dissolution in the other's world but critical **reflexivity** on the part of the subject with respect to its relationship to the other.

References and further reading

Geertz, C. (1973) *The Interpretation of Cultures*. New York: Basic Books.

Keesing, R. and Strathern, A. (1998) *Cultural Anthropology: A Contemporary Perspective*. New York: Harcourt Brace.

Price, S. (1989) *Primitive Art in Civilized Places*. Chicago: University of Chicago Press.

Said, E. (1978) *Orientalism*. New York: Pantheon.

Winch, P. (1977) 'Understanding a Primitive Society', in F. Dallmayr and T. McCarthy (eds) *Understanding and Social Inquiry*. Notre Dame, IN: University of Notre Dame Press.

AUSTIN HARRINGTON

ETHNOMETHODOLOGY

Ethnomethodology is a school founded by Harold **Garfinkel**, devoted to the study of micro-dimensions of social life, especially face-to-face **interaction**. Ethnomethodology is the study of the set of common-sense **knowledge** and procedures by which people make sense of their surroundings and act accordingly. It became popular in the 1960s, in reaction to the dominant orthodoxy, which combined **structural functionalism** and positivist **epistemology**. This orthodoxy focused on the meso- and macro-aspects of society, regarded insights from social psychology as irrelevant to sociological questions, and was sceptical of the usefulness of qualitative data. Ethnomethodology provided a welcome alternative to this entrenched position in at least four respects.

First, it showed how detailed accounts of individual interaction provided answers to broader questions about social order. Order is not simply achieved through equilibrium between different parts of the societal system, nor is it achieved through the internalization of central **values** in the personality system. Rather, social order is accomplished through people's continuous employment of tacit knowledge and practical skills in **everyday** life. Second, the sociological orthodoxy in the 1950s tended to consider people as passive recipients of external forces. This ignored the fact that people think, evaluate, consider and anticipate. Ethnomethodologists argued that it was impossible to provide a satisfactory account of social life without paying close attention to people's own accounts and interpretations. Third, ethnomethodologists argued against **Durkheim** that 'social facts' are not external to people, nor do they absolutely pre-determine people's actions.

Rather, social facts are accomplishments by knowledgeable individuals. Fourth, sociological theory in favour of a focus on people's sense-making practices, treating sociology as just one among many possible accounts.

Ethnomethodology draws on a number of philosophical traditions. Alfred **Schutz**'s social **phenomenology** plays an important role, especially his distinction between scientific and everyday **rationality**. Equally important is Ludwig **Wittgenstein**'s conception of rule-following as a social and practical achievement.

Garfinkel's breaching experiments were designed to disrupt the common-sense assumptions that make up people's daily activities. The individuals in question were very upset by these disruptions. In one of these experiments, for instance, high school students were asked to go home and act as if they were boarders. They addressed their parents in a polite and formal fashion, which led to the family's anger and frustration. Like other breaching experiments, this encounter showed the intricate link between the following of rules and feelings of ontological security Some experiments are known under the heading 'documentary method of interpretation'. The documentary method of interpretation shows that people draw on interpretative procedures to make sense of their surroundings so that the procedures remain intact, even when the surroundings potentially question the procedures involved. In one experiment, students were asked to go and see a counselor. They did not know that he was a bogus counselor who gave random advice. Afterwards, students were asked what they thought of the session. Most reported that they learned a lot about themselves and that they valued the experience. They had entered the session with certain expectations and they interpreted the session in such a way that their expectations were met. Thus the interpretative procedures remained intact.

Ethnomethodologists are also interested in accounting practices; that is, how people make sense of their actions or surroundings. They investigate how individuals accept or reject accounts of others. Researchers ought to exhibit 'ethnomethodological indifference': they should not try to evaluate the validity of the accounts. They should simply study how the accounts are employed in practice. Accounts are always reflexive in as much as they help constitute what they describe. In this interest in accounts, ethnomethodologists are typically interested in conversation analysis (e.g. Sacks 1992). They study not only assertions made in conversations, but also other devices such as silences, hesitations, laughter or gestures that people employ to communicate.

References and further reading

Button, G. (ed.) (1991) *Ethnomethodology and the Human Sciences*. Cambridge: Cambridge University Press.

Garfinkel, H. (1967) *Studies in Ethnomethodology*. Englewood Cliffs, NJ: Prentice Hall.

Garfinkel, H. (ed.) (1984) *Ethnomethodological Studies of Work*. London: Routledge & Kegan Paul.

Garfinkel, H. (2002) *Ethnomethodology's Program: Working Out Durkheim's Aphorism*. Ed. A. Rawls. Lanham, MD: Rowman & Littlefield.

Giddens, A. (1984) *The Constitution of Society: Outline of the Theory of Structuration*. Cambridge: Polity.

Heritage, J. (1984) *Garfinkel and Ethnomethodology*. Cambridge: Polity.

Hilbert, R. A. (1992) *The Classical Roots of Ethnomethodology; Durkheim, Weber and Garfinkel*. Chapel Hill, NC: University of North Carolina Press.

Sacks, H. (1992) *Lectures on Conversation*. Ed. G. Jefferson, 2 vols. Oxford: Blackwell.

Schutz, A. (1967) *The Phenomenology of the Social World*. Evanston, IL: Northwestern University Press.

PATRICK BAERT

EUROPE

Europe is often considered to be the birthplace of modern social theory. However, this apparently plausible assertion begs a number of questions. First, which is the 'spatio-temporal envelope', in Bruno **Latour**'s phrase to which the name 'Europe' refers? Second, in which sense is Europe related to **modernity**? Third, how does such a claim for origins relate to the current constellation of European social theory? And, finally, what is the specificity of the social theory that Europe has brought forth?

As a geographical term, the name Europe came into currency after the split of the Roman Empire to denote the area of the empire's Western part, then closely associated with Catholicism. The scope of the meaning was extended over time northeastwards, and the religiously defined boundary with Orthodox **Christianity** and with **Islam** has remained a matter of dispute ever since. During the Middle Ages, Europe – also known as the **Occident** – was considered a religious-politico-territorial unit, however loosely understood. Despite violent strife, the division into two major Western Christian religious denominations – Protestant and Catholic – and into sovereign states at the onset of what is often referred to as early modern times, had relatively little impact on the similarity of intellectual orientations, from the Renaissance to the **Enlightenment**. Instead, the religious conflicts led to a consciousness of common problems in different regions of Europe, problems which came to be identified in political theory from Thomas Hobbes to John Locke and Jean-Jacques Rousseau. It was only with the consolidation of **nation–states** from the late eighteenth century onwards that stronger politico-cultural divisions in Europe came to abound, divisions that only began to decrease after the Second World War.

From the eighteenth century onwards – curiously during an era of deep internal divisions – the view emerged that Europe had a specific role and position in world history. This view found expression in eighteenth-century Enlightenment **universalism**

181

and then in nineteenth-century evolutionary thinking, both movements evoking the idea of Europe as the spearhead of historical **progress**. Historico-sociological research connected with what is now known as 'classical social theory' aimed at investigating and substantiating this view. One of the most influential and ideologically impartial of such analyses was Max **Weber**'s exploration of the specificity of Western rationalism (see **rationality and rationalization**). With varying emphasis, an accumulation of historical events was seen as the background to the specificity of Europe, starting with the rise of the universities, the extension of trade relations, and the increasing autonomy of commercial cities in the late Middle Ages. The series of revolutions reaching from the Reformation to the scientific-philosophical, the market-industrial and the liberal-democratic **revolutions** was later interpreted in terms of steps on a basically linear trajectory of modernization culminating in full-fledged modern society. In the work of **Parsons**, this conception of modernization is theorized in terms of a principle of functional **differentiation**, seen as leading to a higher rationality of societal arrangements (see **modernity and modernization**).

While few historical sociologists and social theorists today would want to discard the relevance of the question of Europe's specificity in world history, few would want to accept the idea of a single course of historical development led by Europe. On the one hand, the European trajectory has been re-interpreted as a more torn, divided one; on the other, the insight has gained ground that Europe can only with difficulty be seen as the avant-garde of history, regardless of which criterion is applied.

The observation that the existence of an identifiable Europe dates back to the Western Roman Empire needs to be disconnected from anything like a normative idea of an 'origin' that gives rise to an **identity** in the form of stably shared **values**

and beliefs. Rather, the Western Roman heritage needs to be seen as resting on divided orientations, or more precisely: being secondary to something else, in two major respects. In terms of **religion**, the Christian orientation is secondary to the Jewish one; and in terms of political philosophy, the Roman republican tradition is secondary to the Greek invention of **democracy** in the form of the *polis*. This 'secondarity' leads to what has been called an 'eccentric identity' that may be a more plausible way of understanding what could be described as a specifically European 'restlessness' – rather than 'rationality' (Brague 1992).

From the early twentieth century onwards, and in particular after the first great intra-European war of that century, the rise of the United States to an economic and military superpower provoked a **crisis** in European consciousness. What led to the feeling of a crisis was less the threat itself to Europe's perceived superiority than the difficulty in making sense of this threat – a threat which was given its most philosophical expression by authors such as Paul Valéry, Edmund Husserl and Martin **Heidegger** (see Patočka 1996). 'America' appeared clearly as more modern than Europe, but also as modern in a more problematic way than the earlier European self-consciousness of being modern. The identification of a particular American incarnation of modernity, emphasizing **individualism** and instrumentalism, inaugurated the debate on what later became an explicit theme of social theory under the heading of 'multiple modernities' (Wagner 1999). Social theory has thus found ways of distancing itself from the condition of modernity from which it itself emerged. In continuing this debate, the European quest has made visible the variety of interpretations of modernity – Western as well as non-Western – and has aimed to situate its own self-understanding within such a plural context.

References and further reading

Brague, R. (1992) *Europe, la voie romaine*. Paris: Gallimard.

Delanty, G. (1996) *Inventing Europe*. London: Macmillan.

Joas, H. and Wiegandt, K. (eds) (2004) *Die Kulturellen Werte Europas*.

Patočka, J. (1996) *Heretical Essays in the Philosophy of History*. Chicago: Open Court.

Therborn, G. (1995) *European Modernity and Beyond: The Trajectory of European Societies, 1945–2000*. London: Sage.

Wagner, P. (1999) 'The Resistance that Modernity Constantly Provokes: Europe, America and Social Theory', *Thesis Eleven*, 58: 35–58.

PETER WAGNER

EVERYDAY

While sociology has predominantly concerned itself with collective entities such as **class**, a counter-tendency with its focus on the 'everyday' persists to the present. In 1937, **Blumer**, drawing on **Mead**'s ideas, coined the term **symbolic interactionism** for his focus on the actively constructive role of the human **subject** as he or she negotiates life in symbolically organized situations. Though this approach originally sought to flesh out the 'everyday' as a complement to the systemic forces which **Parsons** identified as shaping experience, it has become a countervailing view. The emergence of **ethnomethodology** in the 1960s similarly drew attention away from structured concerns, making a topic of the very process by which everyday situations are defined by actors. While these approaches ostensibly eschew wider concerns, they also underpin Dorothy Smith's enterprise in feminist standpoint epistemology in *The Everyday World as Problematic* (1998), revealing the oppressive nature of 'everyday' **gender** relations.

Drawing on phenomenological thoughts, Henri **Lefebvre** championed the importance of the 'everyday' as the real 'meeting place' where the 'sum total of relations' coincide (Lefebvre 1991: 97). Related conceptions of the **lifeworld**, 'being-in-the-world', 'ordinary language' and 'common sense' are also developed in the phenomenological, existentialist and linguistic philosophies of Edmund Husserl, **Heidegger**, **Merleau-Ponty**, **Sartre**, **Schutz** and **Wittgenstein**. According to Western Marxist thought, the everyday can be the site of both **alienation** and potential 'disalienation', the latter idea influencing the Situationists in the 1960s, particularly Debord in *The Society of the Spectacle* (1976). The Situationists sought to undermine the stifling nature of everyday life by sudden intervention with improvised plays (see also **play and game**) and the like. In this they nevertheless parted company with Lefebvre's **Marxist** hope for change led by the **proletariat**. Extending this line of thought, de Certeau in *The Practice of Everyday Life* (1984) analyzes the way people appropriate the 'everyday' to reclaim some **autonomy** from the forces of commerce. **Habermas** also argues that such forces can and ought to be checked to avert the colonization of the **lifeworld** by system imperatives.

References and further reading

Debord, G. ([1976] 1994) *The Society of the Spectacle*. New York: Zone Books.

De Certeau, M. (1984) *The Practice of Everyday Life*. Berkeley, CA: University of California Press.

Lefebvre, H. ([1947] 1991) *Critique of Everyday Life*. London: Verso.

Smith, D. (1988) *The Everyday World as Problematic: A Feminist Sociology*. Milton Keynes: Open University Press.

ALAN HOW

EVOLUTIONARY THEORY

Evolutionary theory generally refers to three types of developmental mechanism: variation, selection, and retention. Obviating concepts of intended production and planning, evolution is seen as operating without origin and direction and instead by recursive iteration, starting from, and leading back to, states of internal and external adaptation.

Both biological and sociological theories deploy evolutionary thinking in a neo-Darwinian mode. Nineteenth-century notions of the 'survival of the fittest' have been reframed both in the Mendelian conception of the 'recombination of genotypes' and in Ashby's conception of 'self-organization' (see **cybernetics**). These terms are translated into the mechanisms of variation, selection, and retention, replacing the older conception of catastrophes in Cuvier, of learning and inheritance in Lamarck, of historical reason in Hegel and 'stages' in **Comte**. Evolution in these respects means more than '**development**' insofar as it combines the idea of circular **causality** with the idea of **differentiation** through systems.

Evolutionary theory began with the observation that cultivated species of plants and animals exhibit greater variability than natural ones. Darwin considered this variability to be the result of the accumulative action of selection by man of successive variations given in **nature**. Generalizing from this observation, Darwin defined the principle of natural selection as consisting in 'the preservation of favourable variations and the rejection of injurious variations' (Darwin 1859: 81), which led him search for 'laws of variation'. These laws he discovered to be complex and obscure. Variations to some extent come from the conditions of life, as effects of use and disuse, as Lamarck might have had it. But most important of all, variations appeared to be consequences of the 'correlation of growth': 'the whole organization is so tied together during its growth and **development**, that when slight variations in any one part occur, and are accumulated through natural selection, other parts become modified' (Darwin 1859: 143). Later biological theory introduced Mendelian genetics, molecular biology, genetic algorithms, and the concept of systems and self-organization in order to account for the role of accident and drift,

on the one hand, and selection and design, on the other (Kauffman 1993).

Contemporary social theory has generally been slow in developing evolutionary conceptions. Evolutionary economics and **organizational** evolution have taken the lead (Nelson and Winter 1982; Hodgson 1993; Aldrich 1999). In sociological theory today, two basic ideas and one vast research programme are predominant.

The first idea is the proposition of the existence of evolutionary societal universals such as **markets**, **money**, **democracy** and institutional offices of **authority**, as theorized by Talcott **Parsons** (1964). Evolutionary universals in this sense refer to states of development which, once reached, do not often disappear. They prove able to cope with contingencies and uncertainties stemming from unstable relations between systems and environments, and in this respect become difficult to replace. This idea of adaptation may be generalized to refer to path-dependence and step-functions, without necessarily implying improvement or **complexity**.

The second basic idea is the proposition of variation and selective retention in sociocultural evolution (Campbell 1969). Here the neo-Darwinian synthesis becomes explicit in social theory. Once again, the goal has been to separate problematic ideas of transformation, development or **progress** from purely descriptive theories of evolutionary mechanisms. These mechanisms have been seen as involving blind (but not random) variation, selection, and retention, transforming a low probability of emergence into a high probability of maintenance, without assuming planning or teleological reason.

The research programme of evolutionary social theory, as developed by **Luhmann**, affirms the idea of evolutionary universals and builds on the distinction between the three evolutionary mechanisms of variation, selection and retention. Differentiation between the three mechanisms is itself seen as a result of evolution, which does not necessarily exclude the possibility of re-integration or short-circuiting between the three. Elaborations of this research programme have involved attempts to examine the three mechanisms more fully, as well as attempts to reintegrate evolutionary theory with other social theories such as **systems theory**, **network** theory, and **media** theory. The decisive step has been to identify **social structures** that act as evolutionary mechanisms. Different theories must come to the assistance of evolutionary thinking in such a way that social theory is itself brought into a state of evolution. How, for instance, do we identify variations? Luhmann (1997) proposes identifying social variation with negation. This means that there is no social evolution without a distinction between 'Yes' and 'No' responses and without an aspect of tolerance and encouragement given to resistance, contradiction, and conflict. Variation requires deviation from a rule. Structures like writing, printing, hierarchy, or politics may be understood as increasing the probability of 'No' responses appearing on a widespread daily basis and being received, maintained, enforced, justified and amplified. Some social systems may take the evolutionary lead in developing means of differentiated negation; others may delay for lack of the skills necessary for internalizing and handling conflict. According to Luhmann, differentiated negation is the key since social evolution does not operate simply by a series of No-reactions but rather by more dialogical reactions such as 'Yes, but' or 'No, but nevertheless', opening up the space for differentiated answering.

To distinguish mechanisms in evolutionary theory implies that there is no evolution without variations being selected, and no evolution without selections being retained. The next step in the research programme therefore consists in trying to identify social structures capable of selecting variations both positively and negatively. Selection is only possible if there are structures that identify deviations as variations rather

than as contradictions. Considerable time must have elapsed before this can become a possibility in socio-cultural evolution. Luhmann (1997) considers the distinction between social members who are present to one another and social members who are both present to and absent from one another. He sees this distinction as the primary mechanism of social selection insofar as it allows for constant and widespread variation among interactions, with some interactions being admitted and others left out. A further mechanism of social selection evolves as the media of **communication** become differentiated in such a way that scientific or monetary communication do not have to be accommodated with, for instance, religious or political communication.

The concluding step for Luhmann is the identification of a mechanism of social *retention*. Since that step consists of describing how the positive or negative selection of a variation is to be made compatible with structures already existing, it is tempting to point to the role of systems or networks accounting for incompatibilities or reducing or compensating for them. Social systems and networks may evolve by relying on instability, choosing retention criteria such as profit, passion, 'reason of state', style, or 'truth' in order to switch between structures when retaining selected variations. Negative selection is theorized in this framework as the refusal of a variation being assigned to the memory of the system.

These ideas are only the starting point for a research programme in evolutionary social theory. Empirically, mechanisms need to be identified for different types of social systems and networks, calling for considerable research in different contexts of social structure.

References and further reading

Aldrich, H. E. (1999) *Organizations Evolving*. London: Sage.

Ashby, W. R. (1956) *Introduction to Cybernetics*. London: Wiley.

Boyd, R. and Richerson, P. J. (1985) *Culture and the Evolutionary Process*. Chicago: University of Chicago Press.

Campbell, D. T. (1969) 'Variation and Selective Retention in Socio–Cultural Evolution', *General Systems*, 14: 69–85.

Darwin, C. ([1859] 1964) *On the Origin of Species By Means of Natural Selection*. Cambridge, MA: Harvard University Press.

Hodgson, G. M. (1993) *Economics and Evolution*. Cambridge: Polity.

Kauffman, S. A. (1993) *The Origins of Order*. Oxford: Oxford University Press.

Luhmann, N. (1997) *Die Gesellschaft der Gesellschaft*. Frankfurt am Main: Suhrkamp.

Nelson, R. R. and Winter, S. N. (1982) *An Evolutionary Theory of Economic Change*. Cambridge, MA: Harvard University Press.

Parsons, T. (1964) 'Evolutionary Universals in Society', *American Sociological Review*, 29: 339–57.

DIRK BAECKER

EXCHANGE THEORY

In exchange theory social **interaction** is viewed as the exchange of more or less rewarding behaviors that lead to relations of mutual dependence over time. This theoretical perspective derives from the early work in sociology by George **Homans** (1958, [1961] 1974), Peter Blau (1964) and Richard M. Emerson (1962, 1972) and in psychology by Thibaut and Kelley (1959). Various anthropologists have also made classic contributions, most famously Marcel **Mauss** in relation to the exchange of gifts and Bronislaw Malinowski (1922) in relation to the exchange of *kula* among the Trobriand Islanders of the Western Pacific. Homans introduced the behavioral version of exchange theory into sociological inquiry. Emerson's work on social exchange relations (1972a) developed further the behavioral analysis of social exchange relations and subsequently social **networks**.

Blau's book, *Exchange and Power in Social Life* (1964), presented a more economic version of exchange theory using concepts like marginal utility and indifference curves. These concepts were employed to explain the relationship between value and behavior in social exchange relations which Blau characterized as reciprocal and involving greater uncertainty than relations of strictly economic exchange. Recent developments in exchange theory build on these primary sources, with the exception of network exchange theory (Willer 1999) which is based on similar concepts derived from 'elementary theory'.

Relations of social exchange are characterized by several distinctive factors: two actors are said to be involved in a social exchange relation to the extent that they value what the other actor has to offer (a resource or behavior that is valued) and form relations of mutual dependence over time (Molm and Cook 1995). A simple direct exchange relation is one in which two actors, A and B, exchange resources of value. But the A – B exchange relation can be embedded in a network of relations connected in various ways, creating structures that differ in terms of size, range, density, degree of connectedness, and in other characteristics. Some of these factors have implications not only for exchange in the dyadic relations in the network, but also for the distribution of **power** and resources in the network at large. Much of the research on exchange networks has focused on these features of connected exchange relations and their implications for the distribution of power in the network. Power in exchange theory is defined in relational terms building on Emerson's original work on power-dependence relations (1962). In this framework power is determined by the dependence of one actor on another for resources of value. This dependence is enhanced when the more dependent party has less access to alternative sources of the resources she or he values. For Emerson, the power of A over B in the A – B exchange relation is a function of the dependence of B on A.

In addition to network determinants of exchange power, recent research in the exchange tradition, especially by Molm (Molm *et al.* 2000), investigates the empirical differences between various forms of exchange, comparing negotiated versus reciprocal exchanges in particular. The key difference between these two forms is the degree of uncertainty involved in the exchange process. In negotiated exchange the terms of trade are worked out through negotiation in a joint decision process that determines the exchange ratio, and transactions are typically binding. In reciprocal exchange there is no negotiation over the terms of trade. Exchange occurs as actors initiate and respond to offers of valued resources over time. Actor A may offer to drive your kids to school one morning in the hope of receiving a reciprocal benefit later. Perhaps you will return the favor and take her kids to the soccer game the next week. In many such events the terms of the actual exchange are unspecified in any given moment and usually are not negotiated in advance, resulting in some degree of uncertainty and **risk**. However, maintenance of the exchange relation depends upon reciprocal acts of giving and receiving. In negotiated exchange the terms are specified in advance of the actual exchange of valued resources or services. Fulfilling the terms of the negotiation is critical to the maintenance of relations of negotiated exchange.

Molm's work specifies some of the dimensions along which these two primary forms of exchange differ, such as in the degree of power exercise, the role of uncertainty and risk, the concomitant **emotions** and affective responses to exchange outcomes, as well as the probability of **trust** emerging. For example, her work suggests that the greater uncertainty involved in reciprocal exchange results in the potential for greater positive affect and trust with successful exchange. Negotiated exchange involves much less uncertainty and, as a result, has less impact on affective feelings of the exchange partners, unless exchange partners fail to fulfill their negotiated obligations. In addition, reciprocal exchange tends to produce lower rates and levels of power use than negotiated exchange and the exchange outcomes tend to be more equal under reciprocal exchange regimes. Greater **equality** transfers into stronger feelings of fairness and higher levels of satisfaction. In negotiated exchange, the greater **inequality** in outcomes may result in feelings of distributive injustice under some circumstances.

It should be acknowledged that important aspects of contemporary American exchange theory build on the foundations of the concepts of interaction and reciprocity developed earlier in the twentieth century by **Simmel** and Mauss and by members of the **Chicago School** of sociology. Mauss notably defined gift-giving as an act of power by which the giver obligates the receiver to render in return, thus establishing a binding circle of reciprocity.

References and further reading

Blau, P. M. (1964) *Exchange and Power in Social Life*. New York: Wiley.

Cook, K. S. and Emerson, R. M. (1978) 'Power, Equity and Commitment in Exchange Networks', *American Sociological Review*, 43: 721–39.

Cook, K. S. and Rice, E. (2001) 'Exchange and Power: Issues of Structure and Agency', in J. Turner (ed.) *Handbook of Sociological Theory*. New York: Kluwer Academic/Plenum Publishers, pp. 699–720.

Emerson, R. (1962) 'Power-Dependence Relations', *American Sociological Review*, 27: 31–41.

Emerson, R. (1972a) 'Exchange Theory', in J. Berger, M. Zelditch, Jr. and B. Anderson (eds) *Sociological Theories in Progress*. Boston: Houghton Mifflin, pp. 38–57.

Homans, G. C. (1958) 'Social Behavior as Exchange', *American Journal of Sociology*, 63: 597–606.

Homans, G. C. ([1961] 1974) *Social Behavior and Its Elementary Forms*. New York: Harcourt, Brace and World.

Malinowski, B. (1922) *Argonauts of the Western Pacific*. New York: E. P. Dutton.

Mauss, M. ([1950] 1990) *The Gift: The Form and Reason for Exchange in Archaic Societies*. New York: W. W. Norton.

Molm, L. D. (2003) 'Theoretical Comparisons of Forms of Exchange', *Sociological Theory*, 21: 1–17.

Molm, L. and Cook, K. (1995) 'Social Exchange and Exchange Networks', in K. Cook, G. Fine and J. House (eds) *Sociological Perspectives on Social Psychology*. Boston: Allyn and Bacon, pp. 209–35.

Thibaut, J. and Kelley, H. (1959) *The Social Psychology of Groups*. New York: Wiley.

Willer, D. (1999) *Network Exchange Theory*. Westport, CT: Praeger.

KAREN S. COOK

EXPLANATION

An explanation is an answer to a 'why' question. The classic forms of explanation are causal, purposive, structural or material, and design, corresponding to the four types of *aetia* or 'reasons for' distinguished by Aristotle. Explanation is often distinguished from 'explication', which concerns the meaning of terms and sentences, and from 'understanding' (see **Verstehen**), which involves intentions, but the lines between these are not clear, and in some accounts the three are mutually interdependent. Many important forms of explanation, such as **rational choice** explanation, do not fit comfortably into this four-fold scheme.

Issues about explanation have played a large role in social theory because many important concepts in social theory have problematic explanatory properties. The notion of function, for example, was developed to replace the terms of classical teleological or purposive explanation (see **functionalism**). In large part, this was because teleological explanations, important in ancient physics, were discredited by the scientific revolutions of the early modern period, which accounted for physical phenomena in terms of causal laws, making appeals to inner forces superfluous. The causes of human **actions**, however, seem to be already described in terms of ends: when we give a motive for an action, it typically describes the purpose of the action – an outcome rather than an input.

Social phenomena have a number of unusual explanatory features. One is over-determination: the same fact typically has multiple causes that would ensure that the same thing would occur even if one of the causes was removed. Also, actions and social phenomena can be described in different ways, each of which requires a different explanation. Often particular descriptions contain within themselves an explanatory account (for example, a 'rational action'). Thus disputes often take the form of disputes over favored description – something that cannot be tested against the facts – rather than over the explanation itself.

References and further reading

Martin, M. and McIntyre, L. C. (eds) (1994) *Readings in the Philosophy of Social Science*. Cambridge, MA: MIT Press.

Nagel, E. (1961) *The Structure of Science: Problems in the Logic of Scientific Explanation*. New York: Harcourt.

Salmon, W. (1990) *Four Decades of Scientific Explanation*. Minneapolis, MN: University of Minnesota.

STEPHEN P. TURNER

F

FAMILY AND HOUSEHOLD

There exists a little confusion over the terms 'family' and 'household', and there is a tendency among both the general public and social scientists to conflate the two. 'Household' is the more clear-cut term relating to the person or persons living under the same roof, whereas the concept 'family' refers to a group of people who share kin ties (see **kinship**) and thus has a more subjective status (see also **intimacy**).

A household can consist of a variety of living arrangements: a single individual, a heterosexual or homosexual couple, a couple with children, an extended family of several generations, one parent with children or unrelated individuals. In many countries of the developed world, there has been a rise in the number of one-person households, with a corresponding decrease in the number of 'family' households consisting of a couple, a couple with children or one parent with children. Because the term 'household' is more easily definable, it tends to be preferred in quantitative survey research such as the British Household Panel Survey (see Scott 1997).

While studies that employ the concept 'household' focus on issues that are relatively easy to measure, such as income, **consumption** and **labour**, studies using the concept of 'family' are more frequently associated with issues such as affect, relationships and parenting. Although the members of a family do not necessarily live together, in common parlance 'family' is understood to consist of family members living in the same household, more specifically the nuclear family consisting of parents and their dependent children. Just as the balance between different household types has undergone many historical shifts, family life keeps changing over time. What it means to be a father, mother, husband, wife, daughter, son, and so on undergoes constant change. For example, since the sixteenth century, the involvement of wider kin in the daily life of the conjugal family has decreased, while the balance of **power** between spouses has shifted from a patriarchal system (see **patriarchy**) to the 'companionate marriage', which was especially promoted in the first half of the twentieth century (see **marriage and divorce**). At the same time, birth rates have decreased in many Western countries, leading to a reduction in the size of the average conjugal family with children. Changes have also occurred in how children are conceptualized within families, with children having become a separate group needing special treatment and adult protection.

The sociological representation of 'family' has also changed over time, reflecting its social and historical context. Mainstream **functionalism**, represented by the work of Talcott **Parsons** (Parsons and Bales 1955), ruled family sociology in the 1950s and 1960s. According to the functionalist view, the modern nuclear family had a positive function in industrialized societies in socializing children and stabilizing adult personalities, where each family member had a distinct **role** to play (see **socialization**). While men and fathers carried out instrumental tasks, such as breadwinning, women and mothers had an expressive role, caring for other family members, physically and emotionally. Parsons's work contributed to the common notion that the nuclear family with a male breadwinner was the 'natural' family model for industrialized societies and that this was the dominant family form.

Mainstream functionalist family sociology, although still influential, has lost much of its significance since the 1970s. The main challenge came from feminist and Marxist (see **Marxism**) sociologists, who highlighted the context-bound, **class**-and **gender**-blind character of Parsons's theories (see **feminist theory**). Their work focused on the diversity of families in different class and ethnic (see **ethnicity**) groups (Collins 1985) and the oppression of women in 'traditional' heterosexual male-breadwinner families (Barrett and McIntosh 1982). Other feminist work focused on family and particularly on motherhood as a locus for resistance to oppression. Whereas much of the earlier focus was on conjugal heterosexual relationships, family sociology has diversified to study other family relationships and actors, such as children as active participants (see **agency**) in family life as well as grandparents.

It would appear that the ideal of the nuclear family has always been stronger than the reality. Nevertheless, the concept of 'family' remains ideologically charged. Debates over whether or not 'the family' is under threat because of a perceived shift in **values and norms** or an increase in family diversity recur at regular intervals. Ideals of 'the family' can be highly normative and employed in an oppressive way, one example being public anxiety about the existence of 'lone mothers' in the USA in the 1990s, when there was talk of the formation of an **underclass** living outside the bounds of 'normal' **society** and supposedly distinguishable by its high proportion of one-parent families and unemployed individuals. In these instances, debates about 'the family' are often a complex mix of issues, concerning gender, class and race (see **'race' and racism**). Popular debates on 'problematic' one-parent families often centre on an ethnic minority (such as African Americans or Afro-Caribbean people in Britain) or on the **working class**.

Family studies have increasingly reflected the diversity of existing family forms, such as nuclear families, one-parent families, step-families, and gay and lesbian families. However, despite an increasing acceptance of a variety of family forms, the modern nuclear family remains the ideal in both popular and scientific discourse and 'family' tends to be delineated as married or cohabiting couples with children. Individuals living in other family forms still risk stigma and social disadvantage.

Another consequence of the diversification of family sociology since the 1970s has been that the concept 'family' has become a highly contested one, leading to an at times heated debate over the correct way to define the term. Some have argued that sociologists should cease using the term altogether as an analytical concept (Bernardes 1986), whereas others have proposed that it would be more appropriate to use the term 'families' (Gittins 1993), as this better reflects the diversity of family forms. Stacey (1992) has maintained that it is justifiable to use the term 'the postmodern family' as this does not indicates a specific family form but rather emphasize the contested and ambivalent character of contemporary kin relations.

Dispute over the correct way to define 'family' has abated somewhat since the early 1990s as the analytical focus has increasingly shifted towards ideas of social construction (see **social constructionism**). The starting point of many studies has been the stories people tell about family life and **everyday** actors' own definitions of 'family'. The term 'family' is no longer understood as a noun, but rather as an adjective or even a verb, with families viewed not as a concrete entity, but as something that people do (Gubrium and Holstein 1990; Morgan 1996). Families are understood to be constructed in everyday practices through which individuals negotiate their family relationships. Whereas the term 'the family' might imply a firm and unchanging reality, the so-called 'new' family studies construct families not as static entities defined by family structure but as ever-changing **networks** of relationships. The focus of such studies is on process and on the dynamic nature of family relationships (Smart and Neale 1999). Researchers have increasingly paid attention to the complexity of family relationships in post-**divorce** families and step-families.

This focus on individual actors has been coupled with theories of late **modernity** and **individualism and individualization**, according to which the norms and traditions that governed family life in the past no longer apply. As the rules have become less strict, the meaning of family has become increasingly fluid and open to negotiation (**Beck** and Beck-Gernsheim 1995). This has not only meant a loss of security, but has also left space for individuals to cobble together their own biographies, rather than following the family patterns laid out for them by dominant cultural patterns (Beck-Gernsheim 2002).

References and further reading

Barrett, M. and McIntosh, M. (1982) *The Anti-Social Family*. London: Verso.
Beck, U. and Beck-Gernsheim, E. (1995) *The Normal Chaos of Love*. Cambridge: Polity.
Beck-Gernsheim, E. (2002) *Reinventing the Family: In Search of New Lifestyles*. Cambridge: Polity.
Bernardes, J. (1986) 'Multidimensional Developmental Pathways: A Proposal to Facilitate the Conceptualisation of "Family"', *Sociological Review*, 34: 590–610.
Collins, R. (1985) *Sociology of Marriage and the Family*. Chicago: Nelson-Hall.
Gittins, D. (1993) *The Family in Question*, 2nd edn. London: Macmillan.
Gubrium, J. F. and Holstein, J. A. (1990) *What is Family?* Mountain View, CA: Mayfield.
Morgan, D. H. J. (1996) *Family Connections: An Introduction to Family Studies*. London: Polity.
Parsons, T. and Bales, R. F. with Olds, J. (eds) (1955) *Family, Socialization and Interaction Process*. Glencoe, IL: Free Press.
Scott, J. (1997) 'Changing Households in Britain: Do Families Still Matter?', *Sociological Review*, 45: 591–620.
Smart, C. and Neale, B. (1999) *Family Fragments?* Cambridge: Polity.
Stacey, J. (1992) 'Backward toward the Postmodern Family: Reflections on Gender, Kinship, and Class in the Silicon Valley', in B. Thorne with M. Yalom (eds) *Rethinking the Family: Some Feminist Questions*, rev. edn. Boston: Northeastern University Press.

VANESSA MAY

FANON, FRANTZ (1925–1961)

French speaking theorist born in Martinique in the French Caribbean. Fanon studied with the poet Aimé Césaire at high school and later fought with the Free French during the Second World War. After graduating from Lyon Medical School, he became chief of psychiatric services at Blida-Joinville Psychiatric Hospital, Algiers (1953), where he joined the Algerian National Liberation Front (1955). Fanon's first book, *Black Skin, White Masks* (1952), addressed the issue of the 'inferiority complex' among the black educated **elite** in France. In a quest for 'disalienation' from black people's internalization of anti-black racism (see **race and racism**), he insisted that his was a 'sociodiagnostic' treatment not only psychoanalytic, taking social and economic realities into account. Engaging key European thinkers – notably **Freud**, Jung, Adler, **Hegel**, **Merleau-Ponty**, and **Sartre** – as well as popular culture and literature, he found that no theory could fully comprehend 'the lived experience of the Black'. Because of its **epistemological** critique,

Black Skin is considered one of the founding texts of postcolonial studies (see **postcolonial theory**). *The Wretched of the Earth*, completed on his deathbed in 1961, is considered a canonical anti-imperialist text (see imperialism). This work and the essay 'The Pitfalls of National Consciousness' map out the internal contradictions of independent Africa. Yet the first chapter of *Wretched of the Earth*, 'Concerning Violence', was controversial in the late 1960s when it was celebrated by Black Power movements in the USA and denigrated by Hannah **Arendt**, among others, as a paean of **violence**. A more rounded Fanon influenced Steve Biko in South Africa. *A Dying Colonialism* (1959) makes clear Fanon's contribution as a revolutionary humanist.

Major works

(1952) *Black Skin White Masks*. New York: Grove.
(1959) *A Dying Colonialism*. New York: Monthly Review.
(1961) *The Wretched of the Earth*. New York: Grove.
(1961) *Toward the African Revolution*. New York: Grove.

Further reading

Gibson, N. F. (2003) *The Postcolonial Imagination*. Oxford: Polity.
Sekyi-Otu, A. (1996) *Fanon's Dialectic of Experience*. Cambridge, MA: Harvard University Press.

NIGEL GIBSON

FASCISM

Fascism as a generic term refers to a generalized historical type of authoritarian political regime (see **authority**). Historically, fascist regimes developed in the inter-war period first after the seizure of power by the Italian Fascist Party and its leader, Benito Mussolini, in Italy (1922–43) and later with the take-over by Adolf Hitler, the charismatic leader of the National Socialist Party and Chancellor of the German Reich (1933–45). Since the 1920s the term fascism has been used as a generalized concept of political theory and political sociology (Wippermann 1997). In particular, it refers to a cluster of common structural features: one-party dictatorship, plebiscitarian **legitimacy**, political repression, a strong state impact on **civil society** and, among the ideological orientation, an extreme **nationalism**, racism (see **'race' and racism**) and the glorification of **violence** and virility.

Studying fascism has been mainly the realm of contemporary history. Nevertheless, since its first manifestation the fascist phenomenon has stimulated social-theoretical reflections too, based on **comparative** analysis and linked to sociological theory and **paradigms**. The most influential social-theoretical frameworks were developed by scholars in the traditions of **Marxism**, **critical theory**, **modernization** theory, and Weberian sociology (see **Weber**).

Marxist analysis attempted to explain the emergence and the structure of fascist regimes referring primarily to its social roots in terms of **political economy** and **class** theory. According to orthodox Marxist social theory, the political sphere and in particular the **state** are generally considered dependent on the constellation of economic forces, social classes, and organized **interests**. In modern **capitalist** society, the state represents and therefore embodies the political interests of the economically dominant classes, principally the capitalist entrepreneurs or the **bourgeoisie**. In this view, fascism and capitalism are closely linked. A more sophisticated conceptualization of fascism by Leftist scholars, however, relates to Marx's theory of Bonapartism. Nineteenth-century Bonapartism has been used to describe a government that forms when the balance of power does not allow a secure class rule and when the military, the police, and the state **bureaucracy** intervene to establish order. In this perspective, the emergence of a fascist dictatorship has been interpreted as a form of a bourgeois state based on the relative independence of the executive power supported by the state bureaucracy and police control of the masses.

The cultural and socio-psychological foundations of fascism were investigated by critical theory, which combined Marxist social theory with **psychoanalysis**. A group of scholars, headed by T. W. **Adorno** and M. **Horkheimer**, identified excessive conformity and submissiveness to **authority** as the main bases of the disposition to anti-Semitism, extreme **conservatism** and anti-democratic violence. These traits of fascist character especially surface within the lower middle class where the oppression of **sexuality** leads to forms of neurosis.

Whereas Marxist interpretations of fascism largely assumed that fascist regimes progressed typically under conditions of **modernity**, characterized by advanced **division of labour** and capitalist economy, another influential group of scholars emphasized exactly the contrary, namely the drive to societal modernization under fascist dictatorship, whether intended by the political leadership or not. In an original and sophisticated manner, Barrington **Moore** (1969) undertook an extensive analysis of the different historical paths to modernity, comparing the European, American and Asian **civilizations**. Moore's study linked the emergence of twentieth-century fascism to the different historical traditions of **feudalism**, in particular to the relationship between landowners and peasants.

Since the 1980s Max Weber's model of charismatic leadership has proved to be a particularly useful analytical tool in explaining the take-over of power by influential leaders like Mussolini and Hitler (see **charisma**). However, in this perspective the focus of analysis does not lie primarily in the personalities of the leaders as such, but refers to the foundations of legitimacy of the political system. On this model, the traditional forms of government were undermined by a shift from monarchic and parliamentarian legitimacy to charismatic legitimacy leading to an erosion of norms, administrative standards and collective conventions. This specific 'revolutionary' strength of charismatic leadership eventually paved the way for the fragmentation of state power, the expansion of arbitrariness, the establishment of 'polycratic' **domination** and the undermining of bureaucratic rationality. This holds true in particular for Nazi Germany, where the destruction of the constitutional and administrative order of the state has been identified as a prerequisite of the **Holocaust**.

References and further reading

Adorno, T. W. and Horkheimer, M. (1950) *The Authoritarian Personality: Studies in Prejudice*. New York: Herper.

Bach, M. (1990) *Die charismatischen Führerdiktaturen: Drittes Reich und italienischer Faschismus im Vergleich ihrer Herrschaftsstrukturen*. Baden-Baden: Nomos.

Fraenkel, E. ([1941] 1969) *The Dual State: A Contribution to the Theory of Dictatorship*. New York: Octagon.

Lepsius, M. R. (1986) 'Charismatic Leadership: Max Weber's Model and its Applicability to the Rule of Hitler', in L. F. Grauman and S. Moscovici (eds) *Changing Conceptions of Leadership*. New York: Springer, pp. 53–66.

Mann, M. (2004) *Fascists*. Cambridge: Cambridge University Press.

Moore, B., Jr. (1969) *Social Origins of Dictatorship and Democracy: Lord and Peasant in the Making of the Modern World*. Harmondsworth: Penguin.

Neumann, F. L. (1942) *Behemoth: The Structure and Practice of National Socialism*. Toronto: Oxford University Press.

Wippermann, W. (1997) *Faschismustheorien: Die Entwicklung von den Anfängen bis heute*. Darmstadt: Wissenschaftliche Buchgesellschaft.

MAURIZIO BACH

FEMINISM

See: women's movement

FEMINIST THEORY

Feminist theory is particularly difficult to characterize since it is not a single unified theory. What makes theory feminist is that it explicitly deals with women and/or **gender**, motivated by a critique of both the position of women within society and the androcentrism of mainstream (or 'malestream') sociological thought. Feminist theory is very diverse and there are feminist variants of most forms of sociological theorizing. It is also difficult to classify into sub-categories: while these can be helpful in creating a conceptual map of the field, they can also be misleading.

The **women's movements** of the late 1960s and early 1970s gave the impetus to the emergence of distinctly feminist forms of theorizing. At first, most feminist theory was addressed to a single, basic question: how can we account for women's subordination? Answers were generally sought in terms of the structure of modern Western society, whether conceived of as capitalist or patriarchal (see **capitalism**; **patriarchy**), reflecting the influence of social structural analysis, especially **Marxism**. During the 1980s, however, the focus moved away from structural inequalities in what has been characterized a '**cultural turn**' in feminist theory (Barrett 1992), paralleling wider trends within social theory as a whole. In the 1990s materialist feminists, those concerned with the actualities of material inequalities, were reasserting themselves and by the turn of the millennium there was more concern with the relationship between the cultural and material.

Theorizing male dominance

In the 1970s and early 1980s Marxism provided a starting point for many of those seeking explanations for male dominance. Since Marxism was developed to explain class relations rather than gender relations, it did not remain unmodified, but gave rise

to a series of debates on the relationship between capitalism and male **domination**. These theoretical differences are often represented in terms of opposition between Marxist and radical feminists, but it is more accurate to conceptualize them in terms of a continuum between those who saw women's subordination as primarily a consequence of capitalism and those who saw it as primarily patriarchal. Theorists at both ends of the spectrum drew upon Marxism, but in rather different ways: the most orthodox sought to fit feminist analysis into existing Marxist conceptual frameworks while others experimented with more radical modifications of Marxism. Among these, many sought to explore potential interrelationships between capitalism and patriarchy.

Patriarchy itself was a highly contentious concept: some worried that it was ahistorical or only applicable to past societies based literally on the rule of fathers. Others, however, defined patriarchy more broadly as a system of male domination and sought to historicize it (Walby 1990). Another set of differences, cutting across the capitalism – patriarchy continuum, concerned where the causes of women's subordination should be located – in economic, productive relations, in reproductive relations, in specifically sexual relations or in the effects of **ideology**. Thus a diverse range of feminisms emerged (see Jackson 1996). For example, among those who concentrated on productive relations, there were those who saw women's disadvantaged position in the **labour** market in terms of their role as a cheap and flexible 'reserve army of labour' for capitalism while others saw gendered labour markets and workplaces as another instance of male control over women's labour; many analyzed housework in terms of the contribution it made to capitalism while a few saw it as the patriarchal appropriation of women's labour (Delphy 1984). Some conceptualized women's domestic work as reproducing capitalist relations through servicing the existing labour force and rearing the next generation of workers while others saw men's control of biological reproduction, as the main issue. Some focused more specifically on **sexuality**, on the sexual exploitation of women or on heterosexuality as a relationship founded upon both sexual and labour relations (see Jackson 2001).

Not all feminists involved in these debates reduced women's subordination to a single cause (see Delphy 1984). Some later attempted to synthesize prior feminist work to produce a multi-dimensional perspective, in which many aspects of patriarchal domination existed in intersection with capitalism, changing over time (e.g. Walby 1990). Particularly significant developments took place in the sphere of ideology and **culture** which shaped the direction of key debates in the 1980s and 1990s.

The cultural and the material

Debates on ideology were ultimately to produce a shift away from materialist analysis on the part of many erstwhile Marxist feminists in favour of a focus on language, discourse and representation. This turn to culture became increasingly evident in the 1980s, spearheaded by the journal *m/f*. The starting point was a form of structural Marxism deriving from **Althusser**. In particular, his conceptualization of ideology as relatively autonomous from economic relations created a space to theorize women's subordination without having to relate it to the capitalist **mode of production**. Althusser's work also contributed to the rehabilitation of **psychoanalysis**, which many feminists had previously rejected, as a means of explaining how ideology is reproduced in our psyche. The work of the French psychoanalyst Jacques **Lacan** was seen as offering a symbolic rather than a biological reading of **Freud**, more in keeping with feminism's insistence on the social origins of women's subordination. In general, there was a growing interest in the structuralist

tradition of French theory (see **structuralism**) and in particular the idea that ideology works through the capacity of language to shape our thoughts and desires. Once the ideas of Michel **Foucault** were added to this mixture, the emphasis shifted from ideology, which was assumed to conceal social truths, to discourse – where 'truth' is an *effect* of discourse. At this point, the link which had moored these new analyses of the symbolic to the material world was severed. Gradually these new forms of feminist theory evolved and merged into poststructuralist and postmodern feminisms.

These new ideas initially had most impact among Marxist feminists. In part, this was a response to the perceived failure of Marxism to deal with such issues as subjectivity and sexuality. Moreover, poststructuralism and postmodernism offered perspectives that were radically anti-essentialist, challenging the idea that 'men' and 'women' were given, natural, essential categories (see **essentialism**). While there were more sociological forms of **social constructionism** available that could have served the same purposes, they were bypassed by a theoretical trajectory leading from structural Marxism to **post-structuralism**.

Some aspects of postmodernism were not particularly new to feminists. Feminists are generally sceptical about claims to 'objectivity' and 'truth', since these so often turn out to be very particular truths, are aware that language is not a transparent medium of communication, that it constructs rather than reflects meaning and often recognize that the idea of a unitary, fixed, rational self does not match the complexities and contradictions of lived experience. However, one aspect of this theorizing that proved problematic was the deconstruction of 'women' – the subject of feminism – which was central to the project of *m/f* and later evident in some of the most celebrated works of postmodern feminism (e.g. Butler 1990).

In this context the immediate concern was to counter the idea of 'women' as a fixed, natural category, to emphasize its historical, cultural and contextual specificity. There was, however, another, and compelling, reason for bringing 'women' into question – the problem of differences among women. Analyses of women's oppression had been framed almost entirely from a white Western perspective and by the end of the 1970s, Black women, Third World women and women of colour were vigorously contesting this ethnocentrism. It became increasingly clear that 'women' was not, and could not be, a unitary category given the complexities of women's lives in a post-colonial era with its global economy, its history of colonial diasporas and its current labour migrations and population displacements (Brah 1996).

All of this was taken by some feminists as a further mandate for postmodern theorizing, seen as a means of avoiding the exclusions of an assumed universal womanhood and the simplifications of causal models of oppression. Not only had the intersections between gender, **racism** and colonialism been under-theorized, but ethnic, religious, national and cultural differences were proving to be complex and context-specific (ibid.). However, while feminist post-colonial theorists who spoke from the position of the previously marginalized 'other' played a major part in re-orienting theory, critics noted that many postmodern writings perpetuated the same exclusions as other theories: presuming to speak for the excluded and professing concern for diversity while refusing directly to confront inequality (Modleski 1991).

Some theorists began to warn of the dangers of turning our backs on structural inequality in the name of scepticism about universalistic truth claims. The most significant of the 'differences' preoccupying postmodernists are, after all, founded upon real, material inequalities such as those deriving from institutionalized racism and local and global divisions of labour. To ignore these is to risk valorizing differences that are products of oppression and inequality. Meera Nanda (1997), for example, argues that the emphasis on cultural difference as a site of resistance to global capitalism, an emphasis that ignores local patriarchal relations, serves to glorify women's status as underdogs. In a global context characterized by extremely stark and worsening material inequalities, it is often women who are most disadvantaged by the intersections between global and local exploitation (Mohanty 1997). In the wealthy Western nations, too, gender, class and racist inequalities are still with us.

As these arguments indicate, a strong counter-critique was being launched by feminists still working with more materialist perspectives. Sylvia Walby (1992), for example, challenged the idea that postmodernism had a monopoly on theorizing diversity and complexity. She argues that postmodernists go too far in fragmenting the categories of 'women', 'race' and 'class', failing to recognize systematic oppressions, cross-cultural regularities and historical continuities in gender relations. Rather than abandoning attempts to explain inequality, she suggests, we should be developing theories of gender, class, and **ethnicity** which recognize the intersections between them and which place them in the context of the international division of labour.

Work of this kind is now being undertaken, for example, Floya Anthias (2001) elaborates a perspective on intersections between class, ethnicity and gender, combining analysis of the material – the production and allocation of resources, and the symbolic – the valuational aspects of inequality. She draws upon earlier forms of Marxist feminist thinking about production and reproduction as well as **Bourdieu**'s analysis of cultural and symbolic capital. In so doing she develops a complex analysis of the ways in which the cultural and symbolic cut across all dimensions of inequality.

In a similar vein Nancy Fraser (1997) has analyzed the cultural and material in terms of the distinction between 'the politics of redistribution' and 'the politics of recognition': claims for equitable distribution of resources and claims for the valuing of differences. She suggests the need to find ways of establishing both the distinctiveness of material and symbolic forms of oppression and the interconnections between them. She places class at the material end of the spectrum and 'despised sexualities' at the cultural end, albeit acknowledging that in reality no form of inequality is *only* material or cultural. This differentiates her position from more Marxist forms of materialism, such as Hennessy's (2000) exploration of the material shaping of sexuality.

Theorizing intersections between the cultural and material has made fields like sexuality, once thought of as primarily cultural, amenable to more materialist analysis. Conversely, issues once approached primarily in material or structural terms have been opened to more cultural analysis – notably class. Feminists drawing on aspects of post-structuralist thought, as well as the work of Bourdieu, were addressing not only the intersections between class and gender but also classed subjectivity. Thus they were bringing the sociology of emotions to bear on a sphere of life traditionally thought of in terms of economic rationality or, in Fraser's terms, bringing issues of recognition, into a field thought of in terms of redistribution (see e.g. Skeggs 2004).

Feminist and sociological theorizing

The history of the interplay between material and cultural analysis, however, is not the whole story. Since the 1970s feminists have undertaken theoretical work outside the major debates and have engaged with a broad spectrum of sociological perspectives. Over time the diversity of feminist theory has become more marked as it continued to develop through continued dialogue among feminists and interventions in wider sociological debates. As a result, feminist theory has played a major role in opening up new avenues of theoretical inquiry, such as sexuality and the body (see **embodiment**). Here they have also ensured that sociological perspectives made due contribution to interdisciplinary feminist debates.

Feminists have therefore made major contributions to sociology, although this has not always been fully recognized, even by those working in fields where feminists have been pioneers. While feminists have consistently engaged with male mainstream theorists, the compliment is only rarely returned.

References and further reading

Anthias, F. (2001) 'The Material and the Symbolic in Theorizing Social Stratification: Issues of Gender, Ethnicity and Class', *British Journal of Sociology*, 52(3): 267–90.

Barrett, M. (1992) 'Words and Things: Materialism and Method in Contemporary Feminist Analysis', in M. Barrett and A. Phillips (eds) *Destabilizing Theory*. Oxford: Polity.

Brah, A. (1996) *Cartographies of Diaspora*. London: Routledge.

Butler, J. (1990) *Gender Trouble*. New York: Routledge.

Delphy, C. (1984) *Close to Home*. London: Hutchinson.

Fraser, N. (1997) *Justice Interruptus*. New York: Routledge.

Hennessy, R. (2000) *Profit and Pleasure*. New York: Routledge.

Jackson, S. (1996) 'Feminist Social Theory', in S. Jackson and J. Jones (eds) *Contemporary Feminist Theories*. Edinburgh: Edinburgh University Press.

Jackson, S. (2001) 'Why a Materialist Feminism Is Still Possible (and Necessary)', *Women's Studies International Forum*, 24(2–3): 283–93.

Modleski, T. (1991) *Feminism without Women*. New York: Routledge.

Mohanty, C. T. (1997) 'Women Workers and Capitalist Scripts: Ideologies of Domination, Common Interests and the Politics of Solidarity', in M. J. Alexander and C. T. Mohanty (eds) *Feminist Genealogies, Colonial Legacies, Democratic Futures*. New York: Routledge.

Nanda, M. (1997) '"History Is What Hurts": A Materialist Feminist Perspective on the

Green Revolution and its Ecofeminist Critics', in R. Hennessy and C. Ingraham (eds) *Materialist Feminism*. New York: Routledge.

Skeggs, B. (2004) *Class, Self, Culture*. London: Routledge.

Walby, S. (1990) *Theorizing Patriarchy*. Oxford: Blackwell.

Walby, S. (1992) 'Post-Post-Modernism? Theorizing Social Complexity', in M. Barrett and A. Phillips (eds) *Destabilizing Theory*. Oxford: Polity.

STEVI JACKSON

FEUDALISM

Feudalism means primarily a stage in the developmental process of European societies in which administrative functions are executed by large land-owners in a barter-economy who obtain fiefs in return for their services. These include military duties which in turn guarantee to their performers a substantial amount of political **power** and lead to the creation of a relatively closed warrior-caste. **Occidental** feudalism thus denotes a process beginning with the collapse of West Roman **authority**, fusing Romanic, Celtic and Germanic **institutions**, and gaining its specific shape under the successors of Charlemagne (Weber 1978: 255). In its narrower sense, feudalism as a dominant formation ends with the consolidation of central power in the late Middle Ages. In its broader sense, feudal remnants can also be found in early twentieth-century **Europe**, and, by analogy, feudal structures can be detected in many parts of the world over various periods. Feudalism's relevance for social theory can be seen under three aspects: (1) *political*, since the modern system of **bureaucratic** and **democratic nation–states** cannot be understood without its feudal precursors and their contrasting properties; (2) *socio-economic*, because modern **capitalism** as a '**mode of production**' can be partly delineated from, and partly contrasted to, feudalism as an economic system; and (3) *cultural*, in so far as feudalism combines a warrior-code of honour ('chivalry')

with physical courage and male **violence** which has deeply shaped European culture up to the present.

Politically, feudalism means a **network** of personal relationships of **domination** and submission between lords and personally free vassals who promise each other loyalty in **exchange** for protection and obedience. Marc **Bloch**'s (1939) classical description paints a vivid picture of **rituals** that include exclusive oaths of fealty and specific gestures (for instance, kisses on the mouth). A whole pyramid of ranks is formed by a system of sub-infeudation.

Against static notions of feudalism, it is better to speak of an extended process of 'feudalization'. In this sense, **Elias** (2000) distinguishes between 'centrifugal' and 'centripetal' **development**. A centrifugal development occurs when the power balance between 'king' or 'overlord' and 'vassal' shifts toward the latter who is able to retain the fief, make it hereditary and thus weakens the power basis of the former. 'Centrifugal' development occurs with commercialization and monetarization where the king rewards his vassals through **money** gained by taxation on towns and merchants and no longer relies exclusively on the military strength of knights.

The classical image of feudalism as largely personal rule contrasts with the bureaucratic, rational character of modern states (see **state and nation-state**). Max **Weber** (1978) saw feudalism, with several Non-Western variations, among them the Japanese Samurai, as a central stage on the path from patriarchalism through patrimonialism to rational bureaucratic rule and democratic **legitimacy**. After Weber, key questions for sociologist have been how to explain the different fates that lead states either to dictatorship or to parliamentary democracy such as in the works of Barrington **Moore** (1973). Equally important have been the role of land-based feudalism (what Weber calls *Standestaat*) versus town-based democracy as the guiding principle of modern parliamentarianism, as well as the role of 'coercion' (**Tilly** 1990) in agrarian territorial states (e.g. Russia) versus 'capital' in sea-faring trading states (e.g. Venice).

Feudalism is also a type of political order that differs radically from the ethnic–national and territorial character of modern nation–states, although it precedes them and leads to a system of competing dynastic states and from there to the often bellicose competition of the European state-system until the Second World War.

Economically, the feudal 'mode of production' has been extensively discussed, especially its aspect of 'serfdom' that deviates most strongly from the asymmetric exchange of commodities between 'free' wage-workers and **capitalists** (see **commodity and commodification**). Marxists writers analyzed the extent to which the feudal system either transformed itself into a **market** economy pushed by an inner contradictory logic of development, or whether it instead received incentives from the outside, from the urban merchant capital of medieval towns, (see Sweezy *et al.* 1976). Karl Polanyi (1944) stressed the closed, static, reciprocal and redistributional character of a traditional economy against the self-destructive tendencies of the market. Historical research has determined varieties of forms and degrees of institutional change in Western feudalism by reconstructing the range of conditions from the serf-like status of manorial farm-hands, based on temporary and hereditary holding, through to those kinds of coercion which stem from feudal monopolies of jurisdiction and manufacturing. In this respect, modern capitalist societies can be seen as resulting from a differentiation of functions into semi-autonomous spheres that once were united under a feudal ruler.

Culturally, European feudalism can be seen as an effective mint that coins lasting models of upper-class behaviour. Elias's (2000) idea of a 'civilizing process' deals with changes in the structure and experience of secular European upper classes from the ferocity of the medieval warrior to the politeness of the tamed courtier (see **civilization**). Elias describes the passage from medieval *courtoisie* to early modern *civilité* and eighteenth-century *civilizations* as a prehistory of modern affect-control. Feudalism thus claims a place in the European history of manners and helps explain properties that can seem alien to us today: a warrior-mentality, the gentlemanly spirit and a preoccupation with honour, all of which have been influential in historians' fascination with the European upper classes, at least until the First World War.

References and further reading

Bloch, M. ([1939] 1961) *Feudal Society*. London: Routledge.
Duby, G. (1984) *L' Europe au Moyen Âge*. Paris: Ernest Flammarion.
Elias, N. ([1939] 2000) *The Civilizing Process*. Oxford: Blackwell.
Moore, B. (1973) *Social Origins of Dictatorship and Democracy*. Harmondsworth: Penguin.
Polanyi, K. (1944) *The Great Transformation*. Boston: Beacon Hill.
Sweezy, P. *et al.* (eds) (1976) *The Transition from Feudalism to Capitalism*. London: NLB.
Tilly, C. (1990) *Coercion, Capital and European States, AD 990–1990*. Oxford: Blackwell.
Weber, M. ([1922] 1978) *Economy and Society*. Berkeley, CA: University of California Press.

HELMUT KUZMICS

FIGURATION

The concept of 'figuration' was developed by Norbert **Elias** as an alternative to, but by no means as the equivalent of, terms such as **structure**, **society** and **system**. Throughout his life, Elias consistently argued that human beings can only be properly understood as pluralities, not as isolated individual actors who variously interact with other individuals or social institutions. Elias called the latter prevailing image of humans *Homo clausus* (the closed person). He aimed to demonstrate how the latter image tended to emerge from the processes of **civilization** whereby human beings come to experience an invisible 'wall of affects' which seemingly separates the 'real me in here' from the 'external world out there'. Elias's aim was to counter this **reification**, as well as the related notions of 'social agencies', '**institutions**', and 'society' as entities existing separately from the people comprising them. He stressed the fundamental interdependence of human beings, first in their biology, and then through their socially developed reciprocal needs (Elias 2000: 482). Such human interdependencies comprise the nexuses of figurations: shifting networks of mutually oriented human beings with fluctuating, asymmetrical **power** balances. Sociologically, the concept directs our attention towards patterns, regularities, directions of change, tendencies and counter-tendencies, in webs of human relationships developing over time.

To explain the concept of figuration, Elias employs the analogy of dance. Viewing dancers on a dance-floor as a mobile figuration of interdependent people helps us to envisage **nation–states**, **cities**, **families**, and even **feudal**, **capitalist** and **communist** societies as figurations. We can talk of recognizable patterns emerging from such shifting figurations, just as we might discern the 'tango', or the 'waltz', or simply 'dance in general'. However, Elias argues that, it is problematic to conceive of 'dance' as a structure somehow 'outside' 'the individual' (ibid.: 482). While different people can dance the same dance figuration, there is no dance as such without dancers. Dance figurations, like any social figuration, are partly independent of the specific individuals forming them at any particular time, but are not independent of individuals as such. Nor are dances mere abstract mental constructions produced from the observation of individuals considered in isolation from one another. While figurations can persist even after the individuals who comprised them at one time have died and been replaced, they only exist through the ongoing participation of constituent members (van Krieken 1998: 58).

The analogy of dance might lead us to conclude that all figurations follow a planned or rational course like dancers following the pre-defined steps of a tango. However, Elias is keen to demonstrate that more complex figurations often follow a 'blind' course. In *What is Sociology?* (1970) he presents a range of game scenarios to serve as models for understanding structural characteristics of figurations (see also **play** and **game**). After first discussing contests without rules, he introduces the model of a two-person game, such as chess, where player A is stronger than player B. In this case, A can force B to play certain moves, but A must also take account of B's response, despite the difference in ability. Thus while A can steer the course of the game, B is not totally powerless. If B had absolutely no strength, there could be no game; the players are, he suggests, always interdependent. However, even in a model where just two players are involved, when their relative strengths become more equal, neither player can easily control the moves of the other. Predicting the game even a few moves ahead becomes difficult, and its overall course follows a path that neither player had intended. In such a case, both players have become increasingly dependent on the game's figuration – its shifting flow – in determining their moves (compare this approach with **game theory**).

Elias further introduces a number of more complex game scenarios – with larger numbers of players, with a range of different respective strengths, involving coalitions and internal conflicts. Such multi-tier game models can be viewed as analogies for complex and extensive social figurations that have no sporting equivalent, such as modern nation–states (see also **sport** and **leisure**). As the number of players in such games increases, so the game's changing course becomes more and more opaque to the participating players so that it appears to them to have a 'life of its own'. Thus it becomes hard to resist the temptation to conceive of such figurations as 'society' or 'social structure', as having their own existence, and as operating 'behind the backs' of human beings. For Elias, 'society', 'system', 'structure' are all better understood figurationally as a 'basic tissue resulting from many single plans and actions of people [which] can give rise to changes and patterns that no individual person has planned or created. . .an order more compelling and stronger than the will of the individual people composing it' (Elias 2000: 366).

While not without its critics – see, for example, Layder (1986) – Elias's concept of figuration has had enormous significance for sociological theory, particularly in relation to contemporary debates concerning the relationship of structure and **agency** (see also **structuration school**).

References and further reading

Elias, N. ([1939] 2000) *The Civilizing Process*, revised edn. Oxford: Blackwell.
Elias, N. ([1970] 1978) *What is Sociology?* London: Hutchinson.
Layder, D. (1986) 'Social Reality as Figuration', *Sociology*, 20: 367–86.
Mennell, S. (1998) *Norbert Elias: An Introduction*. Dublin: University College Dublin Press.
van Krieken, R. (1998) *Norbert Elias*. London: Routledge.

JASON HUGHES

FORM AND FORMS

Form and forms result from a distinction in regard to objects between the substances they consist of and the shape, structure, or configuration these substances attain. For social theory, the main topics are: (1) conceptual forms as epistemological prerequisites for social science; (2) social and cultural forms; and (3) forms in the aesthetic sense and their relationship to society. Historically, the concept of form attained a key status in social theory within neo-Kantianism in the early twentieth century (see **Kantianism and Neo-Kantianism**). A reformulated version is central for recent developments in social **systems theory**.

Form and forms are fundamental categories throughout the history of ideas. Ancient Greek philosophy attributed an independent explanatory status (*causa formalis*) to form. The modern use of the concept dates back to Kant. In Kant's terms, 'forms of intuition' of intuition such as **time** and **space**, and concepts and categories, understood as forms, are conditions of experience and knowledge. **Nature** in Kantian philosophy is consequently conceived as a result of the forming of sensual data by *a priori* categories.

It was this Kantian idea which Georg **Simmel** sought to elaborate in his distinction between 'form' and 'content' as a basis for all humanities disciplines, and for his paradigmatic foundation of sociology in particular. Simmel saw the question 'How is society possible?' ([1905] 1971) as being answered by *a priori* forms of human minds enabling individuals to perceive one another as social beings. This ability synthesizes individuals in societies as members of supra-individual units. Societies are '**interactions**' (Simmel's expression, *Wechselwirkungen*, means literally 'mutual effects'). There is an infinite diversity of motives for establishing interactions, ranging from **work**, **love**, hunger, to religiosity or artistic experience. All these motives are what Simmel refers to as the material or content of association. The realization of such motives depends on specific '*forms* of interactions'. Just as geometry explores the spacial form of objects independent of their empirically given matter, pure or formal sociology describes and analyzes forms of interactions as such. Independent of economic, religious or sexual contents, social forms such as competition, domination and subordination, **division of labour**, **conflict** and imitation display a logic of their own. While many social and cultural forms may have their origin in practical necessities, they attain autonomy once they are established. Thus, science, art and **law** follow an inherent logic in their further development.

According to Simmel, the social forms of games (see **play** and **game**), which involve demonstrations of physical and intellectual prowess, have their origins in capacities for survival, but with time they come to be pursued for their own sake. In this sense, Simmel calls sociability the play-form of sociation. Sociable chatting or flirting is a playful form of conversation or **sexuality**. Chatting and flirting have a social **meaning** beyond the rationalistic dichotomy between purposefulness and irrational purposelessness. In his late phase oriented to *Lebensphilosophie*, Simmel regarded a defining quality of life as being the production of transcendent forms attaining an independent objectified status *vis-à-vis* their creators. His concept of the 'tragedy of **culture**' refers to contradictions between new developments of individual and social life and the persistence of forms once produced by life.

In direct reference to Simmel, and in the broader stream of Neo-Kantianism, the concept of form held a prominent status in several works of leading twentieth-century theorists. Ernst Cassirer's study of German intellectual history is guided by the distinction between a 'principle of form' and a 'principle of freedom'. Cassirer's most important work, *Philosophy of Symbolic Forms* ([1923] 1953), deals with epistemological, mythic and linguistic forms. It had a strong impact on modern **symbol** theory such as Susanne Langer's *Feeling and Form* (1953). In the collection of essays included in *Soul and Form* ([1911] 1974) and other studies in literary theory, Georg **Lukács** explores the connection between aesthetic forms and the social and cultural condition of the time (see **art and aesthetics**). 'Transcendental homelessness' was Lukács's conception of the breakdown of a holistic form of life or the fragmentation of the experience of **totality**, and he saw this reflected in literary forms.

The breakdown of organic forms under **capitalism** is also the core element in Siegfried **Kracauer**'s metaphor *The Mass Ornament* ([1963] 1995). The symmetries of a dance group symbolize 'the fundamental substance of the epoch' in the sense that they are not an organic unity but are merely held together by a rationalistic exterior choreography similar to the 'unity' of a '**group**' of workers on an assembly line. In his earlier epistemological studies, Kracauer distinguished between material sociology and a formal sociology, speaking of a phenomenological 'geometry of experiences'.

In his autopoietic systems theory, Niklas **Luhmann** replaces the traditional form/matter dichotomy with the distinction of form and medium. This reformulation refers to George Spencer-Brown's *Laws of Form* (1969). Observation is based on a distinction. Its unity is a form which requires a medium on which it can be 'inscribed'. According to Luhmann, decisive for social systems are media of communication such as **language** or symbolically generalized media such as **power**, **money**, truth, or love. The general medium of social systems is meaning.

References and further reading

Cassirer, E. ([1923] 1953) *Philosophy of Symbolic Forms*. New Haven, CT: Yale University Press.

Frisby, D. (1985) *Fragments of Modernity: Theories of Modernity in the Work of Simmel, Kracauer and Benjamin*. Cambridge: Polity.

Kracauer, S. ([1963] 1995) *The Mass Ornament*. Cambridge, MA: Harvard University Press.

Langer, S. K. (1953) *Feeling and Form*. New York: Scribner.

Luhmann, N. ([1995] 2000) 'Medium and Form', in *Art as a Social System*. Stanford, CA: Stanford University Press.

Lukács, G. ([1911] 1974). *Soul and Form*. Cambridge, MA: MIT Press.

Simmel, G. ([1905] 1971) *On Individuality and Social Forms*. Chicago: University of Chicago Press.

Spencer-Brown, G. (1969) *Laws of Form*. London: George Allen and Unwin.

HELMUT STAUBMANN

FOUCAULT, MICHEL (1926–1984)
French theorist

Foucault's work had three main stages. In his early work of the 1960s, influenced by Bachelard and Canguilhem, he presented *archaeological* analyses of madness, medicine and the human sciences that focused on delineating *epistemes*, charting the epistemological breaks in ways of reflecting on these topics (see also **health and illness** and **medicalization**). Following a period of methodological reflection, and the events of May 1968, in the 1970s Foucault turned to the **Nietzschean** project of *genealogy* as a critical reflection on the politics of truth and developed the idea of **power–knowledge** relations as a way of addressing the disciplinary constitution of forms of **subjectivity** (see **Nietzscheanism and Neo-Nietzscheanism**). His genealogies of **punishment** and **sexuality** led him to the thesis that modern societies are characterized by bio-power (see **power** and **social control**). Foucault's final period of work concentrated on the issues of **ethics**, enlightenment and governmentality. Through analyses of Greek and Roman practices of self-formation, he developed an approach to **ethics** as a practice of **freedom**. This led him to consider **Enlightenment** as a critical ethos oriented to engaging in the free activity of questioning what appear to us as natural, necessary or obligatory limits on our agency. It is this ethos of Enlightenment that Foucault took his own work to exhibit and which he linked to critical reflection on the ways in which we are governed.

Major works

(1965) *Madness and Civilisation*. New York: Random House.
(1971) *The Order of Things*. New York: Pantheon.
(1972) *The Archaeology of Knowledge*. London: Tavistock.
(1977) *Discipline and Punish*. New York: Pantheon.
(1978) *The History of Sexuality*, vol. 1. New York: Random House.
(1985) *The Use of Pleasure*. New York: Random House.

Further reading

Dreyfus, H and Rabinow, P. (1982) *Michel Foucault: Beyond Structuralism and Hermeneutics*. London: Harvester Wheatsheaf.
Gutting, G. (ed.) (1994) *The Cambridge Companion to Foucault*. Cambridge: Cambridge University Press.

DAVID OWEN

FRAMING

Framing is a concept referring to processes by which reality is classified and ordered by the activation of patterns of expectation, experience, perception and interpretation. In the social sciences, it denotes the cognitive process through which agents structure social reality by drawing on culturally, socially and individually available **knowledge** so as to be able to experience, perceive, interpret and evaluate a situation and whatever appears in it, whether other people, objects or events, and on that basis act in an appropriate manner. The concept of framing derives from **Kantianism** and was carried forward by the psychologist Jean **Piaget** in the twentieth century. It entered sociology when Erving **Goffman** (1974) proposed to deal with the organization of experience, or cognitive structures and processes, by means of the concepts of 'frame', 'framing' and 'frame analysis'. Since the late 1980s, it has attracted increasing attention from sociologists in both North **America** and **Europe**.

The concepts of 'frame' and, 'framing' are related to what Kant termed 'schematization' and to what Piaget termed 'structuration' – the latter being a concept more familiar to sociologists through the work of Anthony **Giddens**. The concept of structuration, however, is also encapsulated in Pierre **Bourdieu**'s (1984) concept of **'habitus'** consisting of a system of internalized, embodied cognitive structures operating as a structuring structure.

The employment of the more specific concept of framing in sociology since the late 1980s exhibits a range of different interpretations. Goffman, who drew on Alfred **Schutz**'s work on 'multiple realities' and on the relevance of particular schemata or typifications (see **type and typification**), focused expressly on the organization of the experience of the individual in social situations. Drawing on Goffman, Giddens (1984) circumscribed framing generally in terms of the ordering of activities and **meanings** through a cluster of rules enabling the participants to make sense of what is going on. David Snow (Snow *et al.* 1986) broadened framing beyond Goffman's individualist stress to refer to the conscious strategic efforts by **social movements** to create a joint understanding of the situation which could motivate and legitimate collective action. Gamson (1988) went still further by including mass media **discourse** and the manner in which particular framings activate or 'resonate' certain cultural themes and counterthemes. The role he ascribed to **culture** as a factor in framing is comparable to both American repertoire theory and the idea of cultural 'tool-kits' and to French pragmatic sociology focusing on cultural **convention** in different social domains. These competing interpretations have fuelled debates about the levels of framing and the precise nature of the structuring occurring in the process.

Criticizing the tendency for the concept to lose its specificity and to be equated with all cultural dimensions, Doug McAdam *et al.* (1996) pleaded for a return to Snow's original confinement of framing to **social movements**. Against McAdam, however, it can be argued that if the relations between a social movement and its adversaries involve intense framing contests producing an outcome shaped by the filter effect of the **media and mass media**, analysis clearly must go beyond the frame of the movement. It must consider the broader framing process taking place through public communication in the given structured situation, as Klaus Eder (1996) has argued. The **framing** of a particular issue requires, first, that the different competing collective actors or agents each use micro-level framing devices drawn from culture to construct its own meso-level actor, **identity** or organizational frame. Second, it requires that these competing meso-level frames be interrelated, played out against one another and selected in public communication, thus discursively producing an emergent joint macro-frame that defines in a collectively valid way the problem situation, the issue at stake in it, an accepted decision about it, and possible courses of action (see **micro-, meso- and macro-levels**).

Clarity about the precise structure of framing remains a desideratum. Two considerations are important. Against the widespread reduction to symbolism (see **symbol**), the first is that the cognitive and symbolic dimensions must be distinguished, so that it is possible to support and internally articulate symbolic analysis by the investigation of cognitive structures and frames. A fruitful theoretical approach to the cognitive side of analysis, second, is suggested by the threefold cognitive concept of culture, embracing a cognitive (in the narrow sense), normative and aesthetic or conative dimension, which is to be found in the writings of **Weber**, Schutz, **Parsons**, **Habermas** and Bourdieu, among others. Such an approach would enable a researcher to focus on the combination of different elements in a dynamic framing process producing an emergent outcome in a non-linear manner.

References and further reading

Bourdieu, P. ([1979] 1984) *Distinction.* London: Routledge & Kegan Paul.

Eder, K. ([1988] 1996) *The Social Construction of Nature.* London: Sage.

Gamson, W. A. (1988) 'A Constructionist Approach to Mass Media and Public Opinion', *Symbolic Interaction*, 11(2): 161–74.

Giddens, A. (1984) *The Constitution of Society.* Cambridge: Polity.

Goffman, E. (1974) *Frame Analysis.* New York: Harper & Row.

McAdam, D., McCarthy, J. D. and Zald, M. N. (eds) (1996) *Comparative Perspectives on Social*

Movements. New York: Cambridge University Press.

Snow, D. A., Rochford, E. B., Worden, S. K. and Benford, R. D. (1986) 'Frame Alignment Processes, Micromobilization and Movement Participation', *American Sociological Review*, 51: 464–81.

Strydom, P. (2000) *Discourse and Knowledge*. Liverpool: Liverpool University Press.

PIET STRYDOM

FRANKFURT SCHOOL

Reference to the 'Frankfurt School' came into use in the 1950s, designating a group of émigré social scientists and philosophers returning to Germany after their flight from that country before the Second World War. The Institute for Social Research, originally founded at Frankfurt University in 1923, was dissolved by the Nazis in 1933, then re-opened in 1945 with American assistance. After emigrating, the members of the circle published the journal they had first founded in 1932 in a range of locations until 1941, first in Geneva, then Paris, then New York. The inner members of the circle were Max **Horkheimer**, Director of the Institute after 1930, together with Theodor W. **Adorno** and Herbert **Marcuse**, as well as Erich Fromm, Walter **Benjamin**, Friedrich Pollock and Leo Löwenthal. In addition, Franz Neumann and Otto Kirchheimer belonged to the circle during its early years in the 1920s and 1930s.

Horkheimer's and Adorno's project involved a unique combination of orthodox and radically revisionist interpretations of **Marx**'s social teachings. On the orthodox side was their adherence to Marx's theory of value in *Capital*, although their interests focused less on the economic intricacies of the theory and increasingly more on its cultural implications. On the revisionist side was their method of subjecting Marxism to the structural fallibility of empirical social research. By the end of the 1920s not only capitalism but also Marxism seemed in to be in a state of severe crisis. **Fascism** now

appeared to have triumphed over **socialism** in **Europe**. Even though many arguments still spoke for Marx's economic theories and for his critique of **capitalism**, great expectations of a radical transformation of experiences of crisis into **revolutionary** consciousness had been disappointed. From this point onward the aims of the Institute were to explain why this was so, through empirical studies drawing on the full spectrum of philosophy and the social sciences. Among the best known of these was their study *The Authoritarian Personality* (1950) (see **authority**).

This falsification of the expectation of revolution was the principal subject of the work undertaken by Adorno and Horkheimer in the USA. In **America** Horkheimer now spoke of **critical theory** without explicit reference to Marx. The fruit of these years was their tragic text, *The Dialectic of Enlightenment*, combining grand philosophical narrative with empirical analysis. The following two decades were dominated by Adorno's philosophy of negative **dialectic**, until Jürgen **Habermas** gave the School a further revisionist but still neo-Marxist turn, orienting the project of critical theory around the concept of **communication**.

References and further reading

Arato, A. and Gebhardt, E. (eds) (1982) *The Essential Frankfurt School Reader*. New York: Continuum.

Benhabib, S. (1986) *Critique, Norm and Utopia: A Study of the Foundations of Critical Theory*. New York: Columbia University Press.

Held, D. (1980) *Introduction to Critical Theory: Horkheimer to Habermas*. London: Hutchinson.

Jay, M. (1973) *The Dialectical Imagination: A History of the Frankfurt School and the Institute of Social Research, 1923–1950*. London: Heinemann.

Wiggershaus, R. (1994) *The Frankfurt School: Its History, Theories, and Political Significance*. Cambridge, MA: MIT Press.

HAUKE BRUNKHORST

FREEDOM

Since Isaiah Berlin's seminal essay 'Two Concepts of Liberty' (1958), discussion of the nature of freedom in social and political philosophy has revolved around two competing concepts – negative and positive liberty (Berlin 1969). Negative liberty denotes the absence of interference or coercion, stating that mere lack of opportunity is not in itself a condition of unfreedom, while the deliberate restriction of our opportunities by others is. Thus I am not unfree because I cannot fly like a bird, since this is merely a brute fact about the human condition. For somebody to prevent me from attempting to fly, on the other hand, would be to have my freedom restricted, however well meaning the person's intentions in this instance.

Positive liberty, on the other hand, suggests that the negative concept is an impoverished account of freedom due to its failure to include the opportunity to be free within its definition of liberty. To say that a penniless person is free to dine at the Ritz Hotel, for example, appears perverse, since this is clearly not a liberty that any penniless person is in a position to act upon. Moreover, as Charles **Taylor** argues (1979), the question arises as to how we can comprehend why some infringements on our freedom offend us more than others unless we have some background notion of what freedom is actually useful *for*. This then brings us back to positive liberty, with its emphasis on freedom as an end-point – the positive realization of a state or goal – whether this is **autonomy**, self-mastery, or some other value-laden account of what it means to be free.

This value-laden aspect of positive liberty is precisely the problem for defenders of negative liberty, however. For, apart from opening itself up to the seemingly intractable debate about what human freedom consists of, there is a danger that those who believe they have discovered the answer might force the rest of us to be free, as Jean-Jacques Rousseau notoriously suggested in his model of government by the 'general will'. Yet counter-intuitive as the idea of being 'forced to be free' appears, we cannot so easily dismiss it, since part of what restricts our freedom is internal – ignorance or prejudice, for example. Under these circumstances, such as when we require children to attend school against their will, it is possible to understand, if not endorse, the argument that our longer-term freedom might occasionally require compulsion.

In a social context, it is also clear that there are times when individual liberty has to be curtailed in the interests of liberty for all. 'Freedom for the pike is death for the minnows', wrote Isaiah Berlin (1969: 124); absolute freedom for all degenerates into the rule of the strong over the weak. J. S. **Mill**'s harm principle, as set out in *On Liberty* ([1859] 1989), is the clearest attempt to address this problem, stating that government is entitled to restrict the exercise of individual freedom only to the extent that this causes harm to others. What exactly constitutes harm, however, is not easy to determine, as in the case of pornography, for example.

Returning to the paradoxical notion of being 'forced to be free', negative libertarians are able to argue that their definition avoids this problem altogether, being open to many different versions of the good life. For non-interference provides the space within which individuals can pursue their own plans and purposes in life. This negative account of liberty is also able to avoid another form of questioning that threatens positive liberty with the possibility of infinite regress, namely: exactly what opportunities do I require in order to be free? Negative freedom is simpler here – no resources are required for me to be free from interference; freedom is deliverable. While we must no doubt address the problem of varying levels of opportunity in society, for negative libertarians this is separate from questions of individual freedom. In Berlin's words: 'Everything is what it is: liberty is liberty, not equality or fairness or justice. . .' (1969: 125).

To see liberty as under discussion only in the terms of negative and positive freedom preferred by **liberalism** would be a mistake, however. Indeed, for Quentin Skinner, who has highlighted a republican (or neo-Roman) notion of freedom, liberty existed before liberalism (1998). Republican liberty, in Skinner's reconstruction of it, emphasizes the political context of freedom, stating that individual freedoms are only realizable in a free **polity**. In other words, to ask 'What does political freedom consist of?' is at once to ask 'What does a free polity require?' For republicans, the answer to this latter question revolves around an account of virtuous citizens who pay due care and attention to the state of freedom in the polity, to threats to that freedom arising from within and without (see **republic**). Republican liberty thus appears better able than liberalism's negative liberty to identify where the unfreedom lies in a benign dictatorship. Such a dictatorship might well respect non-interference in the lives of its citizens – thus ensuring negative liberty – but this is always contingent on the will of the dictator, and republicans are able to condemn this contingency as inimical to freedom properly understood.

References and further reading

Berlin, I. (1969) *Four Essays on Liberty*. Oxford: Oxford University Press.

Mill, J. S. ([1859] 1989) *On Liberty*. Cambridge: Cambridge University Press.

Skinner, Q. (1998) *Liberty before Liberalism*. Cambridge: Cambridge University Press.

Taylor, C. (1979) 'What's Wrong with Negative Liberty', in A. Ryan (ed.) *The Idea of Freedom: Essays in Honour of Isaiah Berlin*. Oxford: Oxford University Press.

GIDEON BAKER

FREUD, SIGMUND (1856–1939)

Austrian psychiatrist and founder of **psychoanalysis**. Freud lived and worked as an analyst and theorist in Vienna until he was forced to emigrate to London in 1938. Freud's psychoanalysis has been interpreted as a product of Viennese modernity and was influenced by Austro-**Marxism** and **Judaism** as well as atheism. Although the appreciation of psychoanalysis in Europe was restricted through the anti-Semitism of his time, Freud's theories became profoundly influential for the humanities and social sciences in the twentieth century. Centrally concerned with the nature of the **unconscious**, **emotion**, **sexuality**, aggressive drives, and the three structures, the id, the ego and the superego, Freud was equally interested in cognition and philosophy. In his meta-psychological writings he sought to give psychoanalysis a purely theoretical dimension, with which he explained the psychic life in its 'dynamic, topic and economic relations' (Freud 1915). He defined a theory of human relationships that was to become a dominant modern psychoanalytical perspective named **object relations theory**. Freud also applied psychoanalysis to cultural issues. His own writings on **religion**, **culture** and **civilization** – *Totem and Taboo* (1913), *Group Psychology and the Analysis of the Ego* (1921), *The Future of an Illusion* (1927), *Civilisation and its Discontents* (1930), *Moses and Monotheism* (1939) – provide models for a social application of psychoanalysis that has been extended by figures such as **Lacan**, **Parsons**, **Elias**, **Marcuse**, Winnicott, Melanie Klein, Nancy Chodorow, Julia Kristeva, and many others.

Major works

(1935–74) *The Standard Edition of the Complete Psychological Works of Sigmund Freud*. London: Hogarth.

Further reading

Gay, P. (1988) *Freud: A Life of Our Time*. London: Dent.

Jones, E. (1953–57) *The Life and Work of Sigmund Freud*, 3 vols. London: Basic Books.

Weber, S. (2000) *The Legend of Freud*, rev. edn. Stanford, CA: Stanford University Press.

MICHAELA WÜNSCH

FRIENDSHIP

Friendship is an interpersonal relationship between two or more human beings over time, based variously on mutual benevolence, personal voluntary choice, **intimacy**, unselfish motives, sincerity, **trust**, discretion, respect, tact and openness of the **self**. It is distinct from passionate sexual or kinship **love** and not determined by social position (see **kinship**). In Parsons's terms, friendship is achieved rather than ascribed. It involves no formal duties, obligations, or legal requirements. In sociological terms friendship may be characterized as a non–institutionalized **institution**.

A universal notion of friendship exists, but in practice it is not culturally invariant. In archaic societies it can have the form of reciprocal obligations and duties. Expressions of friendship can include all kinds of affection, from close erotic and familial ties to political loyalties, sympathies and business partnerships.

In contrast to ancient and medieval authors, modern thinkers suggest that the bond between friends relates to their respective individual or personal qualities. Friends perceive and respond to each other in a unique, genuine, and individual way. The modern definition of friendship underlines the need for openness and self–disclosure among friends as a token of intimacy and trust.

The concept of friendship considered most influential today was defined by Aristotle (1985). He differentiated between: (1) friendship from pleasure; (2) useful friendship; and (3) friendship based on personal character. For Aristotle, true friendship required that friends wish the best for their friends and that their actions are undertaken in their friends' best interests, features characteristic of non–instrumental relationships founded on genuine love and self-love.

The Christian conception of 'perfect love' (*agape* or charity), which defined friendship as a universal and unconditional relationship, did not follow Aristotle. Modern sociological and ethical conceptions discuss friendship as a complex phenomenon involving different types and degrees of companionship, intimacy, attraction by affection, and mutual assistance.

References and further reading

Aristotle (1985) *The Nicomachean Ethics*. Indianapolis, IN: Hackett.

Blum, L. (1980) *Friendship, Altruism, and Morality*. London: Routledge & Kegan Paul.

Derrida, J. (1997) *The Politics of Friendship*. London: Verso.

Hays, R. B. (1988) *Friendship*. New York: Duck Edition.

KLAUS-DIETER EICHLER

FUNCTIONALISM

Drawing on analogies with biological systems, functionalists argue that society should be understood as a system of parts that are both organized and interdependent (see **social system**). Organized interdependence constitutes a functional system, and systems operate as relatively bounded entities in interaction with an environment. Functionalists are interested both in the **organization** of the system and in the organization of its relations with its environment. Emphasis is upon self-regulation and the processing of information and learning via feedback mechanisms.

Functionalism can be traced to Émile **Durkheim** and Herbert **Spencer**. The anthropologists Bronislaw Malinowski and Alfred Radcliffe-Browne drew on Durkheim to develop a distinctive form of functionalist anthropology in the early twentieth century. Functionalism came to prominence as a school of sociology in the United States in the 1950s when it was strongly associated with Talcott **Parsons** and Robert **Merton**, although they differed in approach. While Parsons regarded functionalism as part of a unified general theory, Merton saw it as an adjunct to the development of empirically grounded theories of the 'middle range'. Functionalism was also strongly influenced by fields in **systems theory** such as **cybernetics**, engineering and biology. A 'general systems theory' was proposed by the biologist Ludwig von Bertalanffy as the basis of a unified science, avoiding the older mechanistic view of physical science under which it had proved difficult to include the human sciences. The leading functionalist systems theorist is Niklas **Luhmann**.

Since the 1960s, functionalism has been the subject of major criticism, and few sociologists identified with it again until the 1980s when Jeffrey **Alexander** articulated a neo-functionalist paradigm, arguing for a convergence with functionalism by erstwhile critics such as Jürgen **Habermas** and Anthony **Giddens**.

Functionalism departs from most traditional forms of causal argument where a cause precedes its consequences. Functionalists reverse this by assigning causal powers to effects. When an anthropologist asks, 'Why do the Hopi dance for rain?', a functionalist considers the consequence of the dance and notes that it maintains group **solidarity**. The functionalist concludes that if the rain dance did not have this positive function, it would not be reproduced. Functionalists are aware of illegitimate teleology, arguing that the explanation of the origins of a practice should be distinguished from that of its reproduction. Radcliffe-Browne (1952) distinguished sharply between *diachronic* and *synchronic* analysis, between the analysis of change of a system and the analysis of the interaction among parts of a system at a moment in time. The latter, in Radcliffe-Browne's view, was the proper domain of functional analysis.

Merton (1968) criticized anthropological functionalism, identifying three unsatisfactory postulates: (1) the *functional unity* (or integration) of a society; (2) *universal functionalism*; and (3) *indispensability*. According to Merton,

it may be that some non-literate societies show a high degree of **integration**, but it is wrong to assume this would pertain to all societies. It is also possible that what is functional for society, considered as a whole, does not prove functional for individuals or for some groups within the society and vice versa. This suggests that alongside the concept of function, it is necessary to have a concept of *dysfunction*; that is, where the consequences of an item are negative for some individuals or groups. For Merton, persisting forms have a net balance of functional consequences, either for society considered as a whole or for subgroups. Finally, it is necessary to distinguish between functional prerequisites – preconditions functionally necessary for a society – and the social forms that fulfil those prerequisites. While the former are indispensable, it is not required that particular forms meet those functions. There are always alternative ways of meeting any particular function.

Each of Merton's qualifications was designed to transform the postulates into *variables*. Furthermore, by suggesting that practices can have different consequences for individuals and groups, depending on how they are placed within a social structure, he explicitly made **power** and **conflict** central issues for research within his functionalist paradigm. Where others defined functions in terms of a generalized collectivity, Merton asked, 'Functional for whom?' In this way, Merton anticipated some of the criticisms that conflict theorists were to direct at general functionalism.

Parsons's (1937, 1951) view was that such arguments are *ad hoc*, believing that functions must be theoretically specified in a general framework. For Parsons, there are four different interconnected systems bearing upon human action: the human *organism*, the individual *personality*, the *social system*, and the *cultural system*. The behavioural organism is concerned with the human body as the primary vehicle for engaging the physical environment; that of personality corresponds to the individual actor viewed as a system. It includes conscious and unconscious motivations (or *need dispositions*). Actors respond not only to positive rewards, but also to internalized feelings of guilt, anxiety and the need for approval. The culture system refers to the symbols and meanings that are drawn upon by actors in the pursuit of their personal projects; that of the social system is a system of positions and roles organized by normed expectations and maintained by sanctions.

Parsons's theory of structural **differentiation** is focused on the social system. He proposes four functional imperatives necessary to its constitution and operation (the A–G–I–L scheme). *Adaptation* is concerned with relationships to external environments and the utilization of resources in the pursuit of goals. *Goal attainment* is concerned with the direction of systems toward collective goals. *Integration* refers to the maintenance of coordinated relationships among the parts of the system. *Latency*, or pattern-maintenance, is concerned with the symbolic order as mutually reinforcing meanings and typifications.

The A–G–I–L scheme also allows the classification of societies in terms of their level of structural differentiation or institutional specialization around functions – for example, the extent to which political institutions are separate from economic institutions, or economic institutions separated from the household. The idea of the 'superiority' of higher over lower stages of developmental complexity carries the implication of evolutionary change, where better-adapted forms are realized out of the deficiencies of 'lesser' forms. According to Parsons, **modernity** – or, more specifically, North American society, which Parsons called the new 'lead' society – is the culminating stage of development. This seemed to critics to be an extreme form of teleology, one that revealed an ideological bias inherent in a general conceptual framework that Parsons had presented as being beyond reproach.

For conflict theorists, such as Ralf **Dahrendorf** (1958) and John Rex (1961), functionalism was too one-sided. It gave greater emphasis to **values and norms** than to power and social conflict; its **consensus** model of society needed to be supplemented by a separate conflict model. These criticisms struck a chord, but the opposition was unstable for a number of reasons. In reality, Parsons had sought to account for *both* power *and* consensus in his model. Therefore, it was difficult to argue that the two models could be kept entirely apart and used separately for different purposes, as Dahrendorf and Rex had argued, while expressing a preference for the conflict model. As Parsons saw, the issues of conflict and cooperation, and power and legitimation, are intertwined.

Parsons analyzed social systems in terms of an analytical postulate of perfect **integration**, arguing that this is to be distinguished from concrete social systems, which are to be analyzed in terms of their *tendencies* toward integration, and not in terms of integration as a fully realized state. This has been restated by Jeffery Alexander (1985: 9) as the basis of a neo-functionalist paradigm of **social systems**, where 'equilibrium is taken as a reference point for functionalist systems analysis, though not for participants in actual social systems as such'.

Nonetheless, critics argued that this analytic emphasis on integration ignores conflict, and over-emphasizes equilibrium theoretically, if not concretely. For some systems theorists, the problem is the over-generalized nature of Parsons's theory. According to Walter Buckley (1967), systems theory could be applied directly to concrete systems without any assumption of the priority of equilibrium over 'chaotic complexity', or of **consensus** over **conflict**, and without the artificial constraint of precisely four functions with which to account for differentiation.

Parsons (1937) developed his theory of the social system from the starting-point of the 'action frame of reference'; his aim was to integrate the analysis of systems of action with that of the **agency** of individuals. Critics today, such as Anthony Giddens and Jürgen Habermas, argue that he came to ignore **action** and over-emphasized systems. Nonetheless, each of these critics offers a very similar account of social systems to that of Parsons in their own work. Giddens's theory of structuration (1981) sets out a level of social interaction whose internal differentiation is organized by four structural principles, those of 'allocation', 'authorization', 'legitimation' and 'signification' (see **structuration school**). Habermas (1987) sets out a level of society and a division between the 'system' and 'lifeworld', where each operates in terms of two functions (see **lifeworld**).

The Chilean biologists, Humberto Maturana and his student Francisco Varela, coined the term *autopoiesis* in the 1970s to describe the self-regulation of living systems. This concept has been developed by the German sociologist and student of Parsons, Niklas Luhmann (1995) to develop a constructivist, or self-referential, account of systems. Unlike Habermas, with whom he was engaged in debate, Luhmann argued that the structure/agency and system/lifeworld divisions are false ones. The divisions can be appropriately conflated within a functionalist systems theory based on the communicative *coupling* of actors and systems. According to Luhmann, **communication**, not action, should be the core concept of sociology; modern societies, or social systems, are too complex to be reducible to actors' reasons for acting, which can be multifarious. According to Luhmann's **constructivist** view, autopoietic social systems construct themselves self-referentially as social relationships made up of differentiated sub-systems. These sub-systems interact, but have their own relatively autonomous logics, and are not limited by a pre-given set of functions.

Differentiation increases communication and the scale and **complexity** of society. Luhmann argues that this form of functionalist

systems theory avoids the priority given to integration in Parsons's scheme. His theory is not about the re-establishment of equilibrium in the face of contingent disturbances from the environment, but about the renewal of system elements; all elements must pass away in time and reproduction is a matter of 'dynamic stability'. Disintegration and reproduction are intertwined: 'systems with temporalized complexity depend on constant disintegration. Continuous disintegration creates, as it were, a place and a need for succeeding elements; it is a necessary, contributing cause of reproduction' (Luhmann 1995: 48).

References and further reading

Alexander, J. C. (1985) 'Introduction', in *Neo-Functionalism*. London: Sage.

Buckley, W. (1967) *Sociology and Modern Systems Theory*. Englewood Cliffs, NJ: Prentice Hall.

Dahrendorf, R. (1958) 'Out of Utopia: Toward a Re-Orientation of Sociological Theory', *American Journal of Sociology*, LXIV: 115–27.

Giddens, A. (1981) *A Contemporary Critique of Historical Materialism*. London: Macmillan.

Habermas, J. (1987) *The Theory of Communicative Action*, vol. II. Cambridge: Polity.

Holmwood, J. (2004) 'Functionalism and its Critics', in A. Harrington (ed.) *Modern Social Theory*. Oxford: Oxford University Press.

Luhmann, N. ([1984] 1995) *Social Systems*. Stanford, CA: Stanford University Press.

Merton, R. K. ([1949] 1968) 'Manifest and Latent Functions', in *Social Theory and Social Structure*. New York: Free Press.

Parsons, T. (1937) *The Structure of Social Action*. New York: Free Press.

Parsons, T. (1951) *The Social System*. London: Routledge.

Radcliffe-Browne, A. R. (1952) *Structure and Function in Primitive Societies*. London: Cohen and West.

Rex, J. (1961) *Key Problems of Sociological Theory*. London: Routledge.

JOHN HOLMWOOD

FUNDAMENTALISM

The concept of fundamentalism refers to religious movements, which attempt to overcome the perceived moral crisis of modernity through a return to supposed sacred principles of an ancient past (see religion). Such principles tend to emphasize patriarchal **authority** and **morality**. Even though fundamentalism has secular relatives and at times is fused with **ethnic** and nationalist agendas, it is foremost a religious phenomenon, since religious structures of meaning widely shape its leadership, **ideology**, ethos, goals, and relationship to other social groups.

Originally, the term 'fundamentalism' emerged in early twentieth-century American Protestantism to designate an alliance of orthodox groups opposing biblical criticism and the teaching of evolutionism (Marsden 1980). However, since the 1980s 'fundamentalism' has also been used to refer to religious revival movements outside of Protestantism and **Christianity**, such as in **Islam**, **Judaism**, Buddhism, Hinduism, Sikhism, and even Confucianism (Marty and Appleby 1991, 1993a, 1993b).

A number of authors have rejected the term 'fundamentalism' for different reasons. Some have rightly observed that fundamentalism has become a political catchword used to label and delegitimize religious groups and movements (Juergensmeyer 1995). Others have argued that it should be limited to the Abrahamic tradition of Judaism, Christianity, and Islam, based on sacred scriptures (Lawrence 1989). Others again claim that any extension of the term beyond Protestantism would distort the cultural specificity of other traditions. All fundamentalist movements certainly express features particular to the religious **tradition** from which they have emerged. But from a sociological perspective it seems more relevant that they also share similarities in their ideologies, constituencies, and sources of mobilization.

Fundamentalism is a religious revival movement that can be characterized by its view of history, its ethics, and its anthropology, especially its **gender** ideology. Fundamentalism rejects the **Enlightenment** historical narrative of progress and reform through human reason and effort, and counters it with a narrative of apostasy and decline; human beings cannot save themselves but depend on a return to salvation history. In terms of ethics, fundamentalists tend to adhere to a strict ethic of **law**. The law, as they define it, is timeless and unchanging; since it is of divine origin, it has to be obeyed and enforced literally. In terms of their anthropological assumptions, fundamentalists reject modern gender-neutral **individualism and individualization** and counter it with the doctrine of **gender** dualism according to which men and women are created or naturally designed in relation to each other (Riesebrodt and Chong 1999). A preoccupation with the female body and sexuality seems characteristic for most fundamentalist groups.

Fundamentalists are often regarded as being anti modern, but they are only selectively so. In many respects, they are actually innovative. They have made creative use of modern mass media and have at times borrowed arguments from competing ideologies, such as **nationalism**, **liberalism**, or **Marxism**. Socially, fundamentalism has formed novel kinds of associations and movements that integrate people from diverse social backgrounds and different **class** segments.

In their self-understanding, fundamentalist movements are not class movements but cultural movements, held together by a social moral critique of contemporary society and a vision of an ideal social order based on religious principles. This might explain why their ideology has remained relatively stable, although the centre of the social composition of fundamentalism has shifted from the old middle class to the new middle class and the universities.

Fundamentalisms come in different organizational forms: as communes, subcultures, religious movements, social protest movements, secret societies, or political parties. In the political mobilization of fundamentalist movements, social groups once widely excluded from political participation have entered the political process, often with a new kind of leadership which articulates their specific grievances and demands. Being represented by this new class of preachers and clergy, fundamentalism often undermines traditional religious authority.

Fundamentalism is not predominantly about political mobilization and influence but rather about the mobilization of religious masses for religious goals. It often stresses pious life conduct and the cultivation of a specifically religious ethos and includes people from lower classes and women in these efforts. Since such practices also profoundly influence principles of socialization, their actual cultural and social significance will become more visible in future generations. Because of such consequences, the fundamentalist mobilization and activation of lay people may turn out to represent a cultural revolution of great importance.

References and further reading

Bendroth, M. (1993) *Fundamentalism and Gender, 1875 to the Present*. London: Yale University Press.

Göle, N. (1996) *The Forbidden Modern: Civilization and Veiling*. Ann Arbor, MI: University of Michigan Press.

Juergensmeyer, M. (1995) 'Antifundamentalism', in M. E. Marty and R. S. Appleby (eds) *Fundamentalisms Comprehended*. Chicago: University of Chicago Press.

Kepel, G. (1985) *Muslim Extremism in Egypt: The Prophet and Pharaoh*. Berkeley, CA: University of California Press.

Lawrence, B. (1989) *Defenders of God: The Fundamentalist Revolt against the Modern Age*. San Francisco: Harper & Row.

Marsden, G. (1980) *Fundamentalism and American Culture: The Shaping of Twentieth Century Evangelicalism, 1870–1925*. New York: Oxford University Press.

Marty, M. E. and Appleby, R. S. (eds) (1991) *Fundamentalisms Observed*. Chicago: University of Chicago Press.

Marty, M. E. and Appleby, R. S. (eds) (1993a) *Fundamentalisms and Society*. Chicago: University of Chicago Press.

Marty, M. E. and Appleby, R. S. (eds) (1993b) *Fundamentalisms and the State*. Chicago: University of Chicago Press.

Mitchell, R. P. (1969) *The Society of the Muslim Brothers*. London: Oxford University Press.

Riesebrodt, M. (1993), *Pious Passion: The Emergence of Fundamentalism in the United States and Iran*. Berkeley, CA: University of California Press.

Riesebrodt, M. and Chong, K. (1999) 'Fundamentalisms and Patriarchal Gender Politics', *Journal of Women's History*, 10(4): 55–77.

MARTIN RIESEBRODT

G

GADAMER, HANS-GEORG (1900–2002)
German philosopher

Gadamer is the major proponent of the tradition of **hermeneutics** in twentieth century philosophy, a tradition which includes **Dilthey** and **Ricoeur**. His masterpiece, *Truth and Method* ([1960] 1989) was not widely known in social science until it became the subject of a critical debate with **Habermas** ([1967] 1988).

Gadamer draws on **Heidegger** to show how the human self is a fundamentally situated, self interpreting being (*Dasein*). For this reason the **Enlightenment** ideal of gaining objective, knowledge without forming presuppositions is an illusion. Because the 'prejudgement' of **tradition** constitutes our being-in-the-world, we bring a horizon of tacit expectations to the understanding of things. In understanding the truth of an historical cultural world, we preserve its foreignness while rendering its significance intelligible to our own linguistic tradition. Gadamer calls this process a 'fusion of horizons', describing it as having the character of a 'dialogue'.

Habermas accepted much of Gadamer's critique of objectivism. Indeed, Habermas's account of communicative rationality echoes the significance of dialogue for Gadamer, but he challenges the **authority** Gadamer attributes to a tradition. Habermas argues that there are factors, such as power, which work 'behind the backs of actors' shaping tradition

from the outside. A critical sociology must develop **epistemologies** that accommodate both 'subjective meaning' and tradition's 'externalities'. Habermas recommends a 'hermeneutically informed critical theory' (see **critical theory**). In response to Habermas's challenge, Gadamer explicitly denied emphasizing 'subjective' elements, making it clear that the 'self-awareness of the individual is only a flickering in the closed circuits of historical life' (1989: 276). In Gadamer's view, so-called 'externalities', such as power, happen *within* our language tradition, which continues beyond what we deliberately choose.

Major works

Gadamer, H.-G. ([1960] 1989) *Truth and Method*. London: Sheed & Ward.

Further reading

Habermas, J. ([1967] 1988) *On the Logic of the Social Sciences*. Oxford: Polity.
How, A. (1995) *The Habermas – Gadamer Debate*. Aldershot: Ashgate.
Weinsheimer, J. (1985) *Gadamer's Hermeneutics*. New Haven, CT: Yale University Press.

ALAN HOW

GAME THEORY

Game theory is a set of tools (concepts, assumptions, theorems) for modelling and analyzing rational behaviour in interdependent situations (see also **rational** choice). In such situations, the outcomes of actor A's behaviour also depend on the behaviour of actors B, C,...and vice versa. A typical description of a game situation specifies: (1) the actors involved; (2) the sequence in which they have to make decisions; (3) each actor's information about previous decisions that have been taken and the actor's alternatives when the actor has to make a decision; and (4) a representation of the preferences of each actor over the possible outcomes in terms of a utility function (see also **utilitarianism**). This description is known as the 'extensive form' of a game (see Rasmusen 1994).

A 'strategy' is a plan of action that specifies an actor's behaviour for all possible contingencies the actor may face during the game. Specifying the 'solution' of a game, i.e., the strategies chosen by rational actors, is problematic since actors have to anticipate the decisions of other actors whose behaviour depends on similar anticipations. An important concept for approaching this problem is the Nash (1951) equilibrium. This involves a combination of strategies (one for each actor) so that each actor's equilibrium strategy maximizes the actor's expected utility, given the equilibrium strategies of all others. Thus, in equilibrium, no actor has an incentive to deviate unilaterally from his or her equilibrium strategy. If (1) a unique solution exists; and (2) actors behave as if they anticipate that solution; and (3) actors are rational, it follows that the solution has to be a Nash equilibrium. For many games, an equilibrium exists (at least in so-called 'mixed strategies' that involve elements of randomization in actors' behaviour). However, in general, a game has more than one equilibrium and possibly many. In this case, the problem of equilibrium selection arises. This problem led to various refinements of the equilibrium concept. One modification was Selten's 'subgame perfect equilibrium' which focuses on the credibility of threats and promises implicit in the equilibrium strategies.

Game theory provides flexible tools to account for complex features of inter-dependent situations. The complexity of game situations is indicated by external random events as well as by incomplete information where actors lack information on the preferences or behavioural alternatives of others. In addition, game theory does not focus only on non-cooperative games, i.e. on games without possibilities for binding commitments. It also analyzes cooperative games where they are able to incur binding commitments and to form coalitions, even if these are not explicitly modelled but are externally enforced (see **cooperation**).

Neumann and Morgenstern (1944) established game theory as a scientific discipline. Myerson (1999) provides a concise historical account with a focus on the seminal influence of Nash. Developments since the 1990s include modelling bounded rationality in interdependent situations. One strand has considered whether and in what sense learning processes and evolutionary forces lead to game-theoretic equilibria (Gintis 1999). Behavioural game theory (Camerer 2003) is strongly driven by empirical observation and tries to account for behaviour in standard experimental games (for example, the Prisoner's Dilemma, the Trust and Investment Game, the Dictator Game, the Ultimatum Game and various bargaining games) Here the same theory is used to analyze various utility functions, such as the fairness concerns of actors, or the strategic reasoning of actors. Applications of game theory that aim at generating testable hypotheses from game-theoretic analyses and testing such hypotheses have flourished in economics, in political science, and to a certain extent also in sociology (an early influential account is Schelling 1960; see also Swedberg 2001). Sociological applications include problems of cooperation and **trust** (the problem of social order), in relation to norms, collective **action**, **network** exchange, **power**, and household interaction (Raub and Weesie 1990). Prospects and problems of empirical applications of game theory in the social sciences are discussed in Kreps (1990) and Green and Shapiro (1994). Systematic use of game theory in sociology has certain classical foundations. In **Weber**'s famous definition, sociology is a science that seeks to understand and explain social action, that is, action that 'takes account of the behaviour of others and is thereby oriented in its course'. Social action in this sense is central to the field of game theory.

References and further reading

Camerer, C. (2003) *Behavioral Game Theory*. New York: Russell Sage.

Gintis, H. (1999) *Game Theory Evolving*. Princeton, NJ: Princeton University Press.

Green, D. and Shapiro, I. (1994) *Pathologies of Rational Choice*. New Haven, CT: Yale University Press.

Kreps, D. (1990) *Game Theory and Economic Modelling*. Oxford: Oxford University Press.

Myerson, R. (1999) 'Nash Equilibrium and the History of Economic Theory', *Journal of Economic Literature*, 37: 1067–82.

Nash, J. (1951) 'Non-Cooperative Games', *Annals of Mathematics*, 54: 286–95.

Neumann, J. von and Morgenstern, O. (1944) *Theory of Games and Economic Behavior*. Princeton, NJ: Princeton University Press.

Rasmusen, E. (1994) *Games and Information*, 2nd edn. Oxford: Blackwell.

Raub, W. and Weesie, J. (1990) 'Reputation and Efficiency in Social Interactions', *American Journal of Sociology*, 96: 626–54.

Schelling, T. (1960) *The Strategy of Conflict*. London: Oxford University Press.

Swedberg, R. (2001) 'Sociology and Game Theory', *Theory and Society*, 30: 301–35.

WERNER RAUB

GARFINKEL, HAROLD (1917–)

US sociologist

In the 1960s Garfinkel developed an innovative research agenda for sociology, which he calls **ethnomethodology**. Like **Parsons**, under whose supervision he studied, Garfinkel is preoccupied with how **social order** is brought about, but he addresses this question by turning to the work of **Schutz** and **Wittgenstein**. Garfinkel rejects any theory that portrays people as 'cultural dopes': he is sceptical of the view that the central values of society are simply internalized by individuals. Garfinkel emphasizes that people are skilful individuals who continually employ practical knowledge and interpretative procedures about their surroundings. In so doing they unintentionally contribute to the production of social order. Within this framework, Garfinkel's and his collaborators' experiments on social **trust** demonstrate that the disruption of people's routines can be very upsetting for them. Other research shows the power of the 'documentary method of interpretation': people stick to their interpretative procedures even when confronted with evidence to the contrary. **Giddens**'s '**structuration theory**' draws heavily on Garfinkel's work: people avoid questioning the procedures of everyday life because doing so would erode their feeling of 'ontological security'.

Major works

(1967) *Studies in Ethnomethodology*. Englewood Cliffs, NJ: Prentice Hall.

(2002) *Ethnomethodology's Program: Working Out Durkheim's Aphorism*. Ed. A. Rawls. Lanham, MD: Rowman & Littlefield.

Further reading

Benson, D. and Hughes, J. A. (1983) *The Perspective of Ethnomethodology*. London: Longman.

Coulon, A. (1995) *Ethnomethodology*. London: Sage.

Garfinkel, H. (ed.) (1986) *Ethnomethodological Studies of Work*. London: Routledge & Kegan Paul.

Handel, W. (1982) *Ethnomethodology: How People Make Sense*. Englewood Cliffs, NJ: Prentice Hall.

Heritage, J. (1984) *Garfinkel and Ethnomethodology*. Cambridge: Polity.

Hilbert, R. A. (1992) *The Classical Roots of Ethnomethodology: Durkheim, Weber and Garfinkel*. Chapel Hill, NC: University of North Carolina Press.

Leiter, K. (1980) *Primer on Ethnomethodology*. Oxford: Oxford University Press.

Levingstone, E. (1987) *Making Sense of Ethnomethodology*. London: Routledge & Kegan Paul.

PATRICK BAERT

GEERTZ, CLIFFORD (1926–)

US anthropologist

Since the 1960s, Geertz has been one of the leading figures in the transformation of anthropology into an interpretative discipline contributing to the general **cultural turn** in social theory. Based on field research in Morocco and Indonesia, his influential articles in *The Interpretation of Cultures* (1973) and *Local Knowledge* (1983) combine substantive analysis with methodological reflections. Instead of a systematic 'theory', Geertz develops a series of tools for cultural analysis, above all, those of 'thick description' and of '**culture** as a text'. For Geertz, anthropology is 'not an experimental science in search of law but an interpretive one in search of meaning' (1973: 5). In opposition to **Lévi-Strauss's structuralism** and leaning on theorists such as Gilbert Ryle and Paul **Ricoeur**, these **meanings** are not to be sought in abstract symbolic systems, but in the 'ongoing patterns of life' (ibid.: 17), in perceivable **practices**, **rituals**, and **interactions**. These **actions** are not mere behaviour but 'action which ... signifies' (ibid.: 10), which carries public **symbolic** content for the participants themselves and for the interpreter who reconstructs their meanings through 'thick description'. In this sense, culture is 'read' as a 'text'. In *Works and Lives* (1988), Geertz examines the narrative strategies which anthropologists apply to create the effect of realism, strategies which turn out to be analogous to 'realist' fiction. The 'writing culture' debate of the 1980s was a sign of Geertz's impact on the human sciences as well as of attempts to move critically beyond his approach (see Clifford 1988; Clifford and Marcus 1986).

Major works

(1973) *The Interpretation of Cultures*. New York: Basic Books.

(1983) *Local Knowledge*. New York: Basic Books.

(1988) *Works and Lives: The Anthropologist as Author*. Stanford, CA: Stanford University Press.

Further reading

Clifford, J. (1988) *The Predicament of Culture*. Cambridge, MA: Harvard University Press.

Clifford, J. and Marcus, G. (eds) (1986) *Writing Culture*. Berkeley, CA: University of California Press.

Inglis, F. (2000) *Clifford Geertz*. Cambridge: Polity.

ANDREAS RECKWITZ

GEHLEN, ARNOLD (1904–1976)

German theorist

After Max Scheler and Helmut Plessner, Gehlen is one of the main representatives of German philosophical anthropology. In his principal work, *Man: His Nature and Place in the World* (1940) Gehlen dealt with the question of man's perceived 'special position' in relation to animals. Man as an 'imperfect being' (Herder) and 'undetermined animal' (Nietzsche) is a 'natural cultural being' who does not live bound by instinct within a fixed environment but is 'world-open' and must actively produce its world. Man's use of language is decisive for the way of living of this 'active being'. '**Action**' is a key word for overcoming every kind of dualism of mind and body. Together with Alfred **Schutz**, Gehlen was one of the first German-speaking thinkers to adapt G. H. **Mead**'s theory of the social constitution of ego identity through social **interaction**. Gehlen held that as a creature at the mercy of impulse, man needs the relieving and stabilizing function of social **institutions**. Institutions are 'stabilized tensions' out of which arise objectified impulses and lasting motivations. In *Man in the Age of Technology* (1957), Gehlen developed

217

an interpretation of the modern age with its intellectualism, psychologization and its tendencies toward primitive regression. Concerning painting, this criticism of contemporary issues was clearly defined in his *Zeit-Bilder* (1960), in combination with an acknowledgement of classical modern arts as a *peinture conceptuelle* which reminds us of **Adorno**. However, Gehlen was sceptical of the capacity of modern societies for real innovation and in some respects his conservative thinking anticipates motifs of **postmodernism**. His influence also stands behind the work of **Berger and Luckmann** in their book *The Social Construction of Reality* of 1966.

Major works

([1940] 1988) *Man: His Nature and Place in the World*. New York: Columbia University Press.

([1957] 1980) *Man in the Age of Technology*. New York: Columbia University Press.

(1978–2004) *Gesamtausgabe*, Ed. K.-S. Rehberg, 10 vols. Frankfurt am Main: Klostermann.

Further reading

Klages, H. and Quaritsch, H. (eds) (1994) *Zur geisteswissenschaftlichen Bedeutung Arnold Gehlens*. Berlin: Duncker & Humblot.

KARL-SIEGBERT REHBERG

GELLNER, ERNEST (1925–1995)

Czech-born theorist, resident in Britain. Gellner made important contributions in a number of fields, including the **philosophy of social science** and the theory of **nationalism**. Gellner defended the scientific status of the social sciences against the seductions of **relativism**, arguing that they should aim to meet certain criteria of validity and openness to refutation by evidence. His main influences in this regard were **Popper** and **Weber**. Like Popper, he connected the open spirit of enquiry with a tolerant society. Like Weber, however, he was aware of the 'disenchanting' consequences of the growth of knowledge, though he argued these should not be exaggerated. One of Gellner's main contributions was to identify the social bases of **rationality and rationalisation** in history. He defended an objective account of social change, even if our knowledge of human history is far from complete. In his work dealing with the philosophy of history, Gellner (1988) charted the changing relationship between the three sources of power in society – coercion, cognition and **production**. The distinctive characteristic of cognition in modern society, he argued, is that it becomes separate from the other two realms, and the realm of cognition itself splits into **knowledge** and **culture**.

His best-known work relates to nationalism, and in several books he proposed that nationalism is a product of the transition to **modernity**, putting him at odds with the 'perennialist' school which argues that nationalism exists throughout recorded history. Gellner argued that nationalism results from the fact that **elites** and people in modern society need to share the same culture under the condition of industrial production.

Major works

(1975) *Legitimation of Belief*. Cambridge: Cambridge University Press.

(1983) *Nations and Nationalism*. Oxford: Blackwell.

(1988) *Plough, Sword and Book*. London: Collins Harvill.

(1992) *Reason and Culture: The Historic Role of Rationality and Rationalism*. Oxford: Blackwell.

Further reading

Hall, J. (1998) *The State of the Nation: Ernest Gellner and the Theory of Nationalism*. Cambridge: Cambridge University Press.

Hall, J. and Jarvie, I. (eds) (1996) *The Social Philosophy of Ernest Gellner*. Amsterdam: Rodopi.

Lessnoff, M. (2002) *Ernest Gellner and Modernity*. Cardiff: University of Wales Press.

RALPH SCHROEDER

GEMEINSCHAFT AND GESELLSCHAFT

Ferdinand **Tönnies** saw *Gemeinschaft* (**community**) and *Gesellschaft* (**society**) as the two basic categories of sociology. With these terms, the emergence of **capitalism** from the social forms of the Middle Ages was to be made 'thinkable and describable'. *Gesellschaft* means the rationally constructed social forms that follow the **paradigm** of the social **contract** and the principles of utilitarianism in the economy. *Gemeinschaft* means the traditional forms of communal life, which are 'inherited' and 'transmitted' through the passing on of customs and obligations.

These two concepts have informed a range of sociological work. In his sociology of action, Max **Weber** differentiated between the 'purest types' of '*Vergemeinschaftung*' and '*Vergesellschaftung*', or the processes establishing community and society. **Parsons** claimed to solve the problem of the definition of *Gemeinschaft* and *Gesellschaft* by understanding them as two special cases, determined by 'pattern variables'.

More recently, the relation between rationally constructed social forms and traditional ones has gained systematic importance in **communitarianism**. According to Etzioni (1988), it is 'social collectives', as the manifestation of **values and norms**, which 'form' individual decisions and constitute the basis of all action. Bellah *et al.* (1985) advocate the renewal of commitment by revitalizing the 'habits of the heart' or the traditional patterns of loyalty and obligation that keep the community alive.

References and further reading

Bellah, R. N., Madsen, R., Sullivan, W. M., Swidler, A. and Tipton, S. M. (1985) *Habits of the Heart*. Berkeley, CA: University of California Press.

Etzioni, A. (1988) *The Moral Dimension*. New York: Free Press.

Merz-Benz, P.-U. (1995) *Tiefsinn und Scharfsinn*. Frankfurt am Main: Suhrkamp.

Parsons, T. (1937) 'Note on Gemeinschaft and Gesellschaft', in *The Structure of Social Action*. New York: Free Press.

Parsons, T. (1951) *The Social System*. London: Routledge & Kegan Paul.

Tönnies, F. (1979) *Gemeinschaft und Gesellschaft*. Darmstadt: Wissenschaftliche Buchgesellschaft.

Weber, M. (1972) *Wirtschaft und Gesellschaft*. Tübingen: J. C. B. Mohr (Paul Siebeck).

PETER-ULRICH MERZ-BENZ

GENDER

The term 'gender' is commonly used to describe the social and cultural elaboration of sexual **difference** – that is, masculinity and femininity. The language of gender, as differentiated from biological sex, was especially taken up by Anglophone feminists in the 1970s as a means of understanding the observable social differences and inequalities between men and women as socially constructed (see **social constructionism**). In doing so, they developed the earlier observation of Simone de **Beauvoir** (1949) that 'one is not born, but made a woman'. Gender is seen as historically and culturally variable, and subject to reconstruction through conscious social and political action. Because gender is seen as a key mechanism of social **power**, as an analytic construct, it remains important in linking **feminist theory** to the politics of feminism as a social movement (see **women's movement**).

Understanding the construction and operation of gender grounds an important theoretical problematic in its own right. However, the concept of gender has also been important in critiquing overly universalistic concepts in mainstream social theory. This is why, in addition to the work of bringing women's lives and experiences into the purview of the social, and documenting gender inequality and gendered social processes, feminists have insisted that *all* theories and methodologies need to take gender into account in more than a peripheral way. Thus, in addition to theories of gender, the gendering of theory needs to be considered.

Theorizing gender

Theories about differences between men and women and about the acquisition of appropriate sex-linked identities and behaviours long pre-date the language of 'gender'. Theories in psychology and **psychoanalysis**, for example, posited a masculine or feminine self-identity congruent with the anatomy of one's body as one of the outcomes of successful personality development. While it is difficult to pinpoint the first usage of the term 'gender' in the social sciences, the distinction between 'sex' and 'gender' was most clearly elaborated in mid-twentieth-century clinical psychology as therapists grappled with cases of 'gender identity disorder' – characterized by a *lack* of congruity between one's physical sex and one's subjective gender identity.

Some theorizations of gender focus on the acquisition of gender **identity** and gender **roles**. In these approaches, gender is understood as primarily a characteristic of individuals, although one rooted in social relations. Nancy Chodorow's *The Reproduction of Mothering* (1978), for example, used **object relations theory** to argue that the gendered **division of labour** in parenting, which assigns most childcare responsibilities to women, creates different developmental paths for boys and girls – one which tends to reproduce that gendered division of labour by creating a greater propensity to nurture in girls. Suzanne Kessler and Wendy McKenna's (1978) ethnomethodological treatment (see **ethnomethodology**) emphasized the manner in which gender as a dichotomy produces typifications that individuals use in negotiating everyday life, and in classifying themselves and others accordingly. In doing so, they anticipated later critiques of the **sex/gender distinction** as a natural/cultural one, as well as subsequent work on the symbolic dimensions of gender.

Other theorists focus on gender as less a characteristic of individuals than of social **structure** and social **inequality**. In an extremely influential article, which drew

on anthropological work on kinship, psychoanalytic theory and **political economy**, Gayle Rubin (1975) posited a 'sex-gender system' in which compulsory heterosexuality, the exchange of women in marriage, and a gendered division of labour produce the social and psychic structures in which masculine gender dominance is rooted. Rubin's work was one of a number of attempts to develop socialist-feminist analyses of gender and sexuality in relation to social and economic power structures. Some of these were known as 'dual-systems theories', as they drew on analyses of both **capitalism** and **patriarchy** as interlocking **social systems** to explain the convergence of economic and gender hierarchies.

As feminism has become more internationalized, so too has its thinking about gender, and considerations about how gender is related to national and ethnic processes have been central to its development as an analytic category. Flora Anthias and Nira Yuval-Davies (1992), for example, have elaborated a multi-dimensional theory for understanding the interrelationships of gender, **ethnicity** and **nationalism** which involves complex processes of bodily and reproductive practices, cultural reproduction, labour and political struggles.

Australian theorist R. W. Connell (2002) has proposed a sophisticated theorization of gender as a way of structuring social practice in relation to bodies, arguing that gender relations form one of the central structures of all known societies. He locates the practice of gender at all levels of analysis, including the individual, cultural, economic, and institutional. He argues that gender should be analyzed as structured around four constellations of social relations: relations of power, relations of **production**, relations of **emotion**, and symbolic relations.

Destabilizing gender: feminist debates

Seyla Benhabib (1989) has suggested that gender is to feminist theory what class or production is to Marxist theory, or the unconscious to psychoanalytic theory – that it defines a 'problem horizon'. However, against this horizon, numerous debates have emerged within feminist theory regarding the various theoretical and tactical uses to which the concept of gender has been put.

The very distinction between sex and gender has been criticized as reproducing a nature/culture **binary** and reinforcing assumptions of sexual dimorphism. It has been argued that theorizing gender as social has implicitly or explicitly left sex untheorized as a biological category. Studies of inter-sexuality, transexuality/transgendering and third genders, for example, challenge the dichotomies of both sex and gender and their relationship as categories.

Other critiques contend that the very concept of 'gender' is too universalizing and too over-determining, implicating it as shot through with racism, classism and heterosexism (see **race**, **class**, and **sexuality**). For example, generalizations about gender based on a division of labour in which women stay home and raise children ignore the fact that this is a situation that historically has never been practiced by, nor possible for, large proportions of the population. To invoke gender, it is argued, is to necessarily invoke some sort of **essentialism**, constructing overly homogenous categories called 'women' and 'men'. While in earlier feminist approaches, attention to 'gender difference' meant the mapping out of differences between the categories of 'men' and 'women', more recent work has turned the question of difference inward, to see gender categories themselves as infinitely differentiated. Black feminist theorists such as Patricia Hill Collins (1990) have eloquently demonstrated the inadequacy of conceptions of gender that erase differences of race. Collins argues that instead of starting with gender, and then adding on other characteristics of interest, gender, race and class must be seen as interlocking and interdependent systems of oppression from the start. The import of

such critiques has been to make clear that 'gender' does not just signify ready-made difference, but is productive of difference – difference that is always mobilized in and through other modalities of difference.

Certainly postmodern and post-structuralist theories have been significant in the destabilization of gender, calling into question the both the unity and the stability implied by some conceptions of gender (see **postmodernism and postmodernity**; **post-structuralism**). Particularly influential has been the work of Judith **Butler** (1990). Butler advocates a radically discontinuous relationship between sex and gender, asserting that gender is **performative**, and that it has no originary, ontological status apart from those acts which continually constitute it (see **ontology**). Butler argues that the very idea of a core gender identity is a fiction, an illusion that is produced by its repetitive performance. This illusion can be subverted through parody, and here she takes such practices as drag and cross-dressing as paradigmatic. Through such parodic practices, Butler argues that not only is the fiction of gender identity and its relationship to any particular sorts of sexed bodies revealed, but the possibility of a multiplicity of 'genders' is opened up.

A related line of critique focuses on the extent to which heterosexuality is inscribed as normative in the social construction of both sex and gender categories as 'opposite' and related. Instead, heterosexuality might be seen as a social matrix that links sex and gender categories in a particular and rather arbitrary way. An emphasis on incoherency and instability in configurations of sex, gender, and sexual desire, and the chain of significations that link them, is the hallmark of contemporary **queer theory**.

The postmodern shift in emphasis to seeing gender as unstable and fluid has, for some, signalled a shift that cedes too much to **discourse** and **culture** at the expense of a more materially grounded analysis (see **materialism**). Here, it is argued that the persistence of macro-social and material gender inequalities demand analytic tools that admit some form of material and/or structural analysis of gender. Sylvia Walby (1997), for example, argues that an analytic focus on the macro-level is necessary to adequately grasp the manner in which gender, ethnicity and class continue to structure important and intersecting social divisions.

Some feminists have also argued that the language of gender has meant a depoliticizing turn away from 'women', arguing that an explicit focus on 'women' as a category whose members share some something – some 'otherness' (see **other**) – has provided a crucial political link to the politics of women's movements. Related arguments, which sometimes object to the increasing space that a focus on masculinity has taken up in the remit of 'gender studies', charge the conceptual shift to gender with positing an unwarranted symmetry between the categories 'men' and 'women', ignoring the continuing effects of patriarchy in the production of, not just difference, but inequality.

The concept of gender also seems to have little currency in non-Anglophone feminist scholarship, with French and continental traditions preferring to speak of sex and 'sexual difference'. One important exception is French feminist theorist Christine Delphy (1993), who uses the distinction between sex and gender to argue that gender actually precedes sex. Conceptualizing both gender and sex as social, not natural, distinctions, she argues that hierarchy is a constitutive element of gender, and sex acts mainly as a signifier of this hierarchy.

Despite these varied critiques, some notion of gender remains important in contesting the naturalness of sexual difference, and it remains a key 'problem horizon' for feminist theory.

Gendering theory

One of the most important insights of the various ways in which gender has been theorized, all of which move away from seeing gender as merely a consequence of pre-existing sexual difference, is that gender suffuses thinking about things which may not necessarily present themselves as immediately gendered. Social theory is no exception here, and numerous feminist contributions have demonstrated the extent to which social theory has been – and continues to be – shot through with unarticulated gender assumptions. The need to expose the gendered subtext of mainstream social theory was influentially articulated by Canadian social theorist Dorothy E. Smith (1990). In her feminist sociology of **knowledge**, she has argued that social scientific theories, methods, concepts and practices are all rooted in a 'male social universe' that has masqueraded as a universalistic standpoint. To take a different standpoint – for Smith, an explicitly gendered one – constitutes a radical critique, one that unmasks the presumptions of masculinity that underpin taken-for-granted conceptions of **objectivity** (see **standpoint epistemology**).

Thus, feminists argue that gender was not absent from the discourse of **modernity** that shaped the development of social theory, but that its masculinist form has remained largely unarticulated. For example, feminist re-examinations of classical social and political theory have demonstrated the extent to which some of its pivotal concepts are rendered both literally and metaphorically in the masculine. They are literally masculine where men are explicitly identified as the empirical basis on which the theory is built, and they are metaphorically masculine where qualities derived from the latter are rendered as more generally 'social'. For example, in **Durkheim**'s *Elementary Forms of Religious Life*, religious rituals to which only men are admitted are taken as the empirical basis of a theory regarding the development of human capacities to think conceptually. As Nancy Jay (1981) points out, by his own gendered logic, Durkheim renders women unable to think!

The success of feminist attempts to revise the core assumptions and categories of social theory has been uneven. Despite the fact that gender is quite firmly established as a key concept in social analysis, mainstream theory has not yet been revolutionized. When gender is taken up in theoretical discussions, it is almost always in relation to women, signalling their presence in the text. This often takes the form of special qualifying clauses or footnotes to explain that women do not always experience the social processes under discussion in the same way as men. Men, however, are more likely to enter the text unmarked, as generic social actors. Even in contemporary social theory, specifically masculine forms of **embodiment**, **individualization** and **agency** continue to be presumed as normative. However, it is not necessarily the case that the familiar, privileged masculine subject is simply being *reinstated* in contemporary social theory. Rather, as Lisa Adkins (2002) argues, the exclusions and erasures that operate in relation to the reflexive subject of much contemporary theory may serve to re-gender in new ways the concept of the social, even as the dissolution of gender is claimed. Therefore, continued interrogation of the gendering of social theory remains necessary (Marshall and Witz 2004).

References and further reading

Adkins, L. (2002) *Revisions: Towards a Sociology of Gender and Sexuality in Late Modernity*. Buckingham: Open University Press.

Anthias, F. and Yuval-Davies, N. (1992) *Racialized Boundaries*. London: Routledge.

Beauvoir, S. de ([1949] 1974) *The Second Sex*. Trans. H. M. Parshley. New York: Vintage Books.

Benhabib, S. (1989) 'On Contemporary Feminist Theory', *Dissent*, 36: 366–70.

Butler, J. (1990) *Gender Trouble: Feminism and the Subversion of Identity*. London: Routledge.

Chodorow, N. (1978) *The Reproduction of Mothering: Psychoanalysis and the Sociology of Gender*. Berkeley, CA: University of California Press.

Collins, P. H. (1990) *Black Feminist Thought: Knowledge, Consciousness and the Politics of Empowerment*. Boston: Unwin Hyman.

Connell, R. W. (2002) *Gender*. Cambridge: Polity Press.

Delphy, C. (1993) 'Rethinking Sex and Gender', *Women's Studies International Forum*, 16(1): 1–9.

Jay, N. (1981) 'Gender and Dichotomy', *Feminist Studies*, 7(1): 38–56.

Kessler, S. and McKenna, W. (1978) *Gender: An Ethnomethodological Approach*. New York: Wiley.

Marshall, B. and Witz, A. (eds) (2004) *Engendering the Social: Feminist Encounters with Sociological Theory*. Buckingham: Open University Press.

Rubin, G. (1975) 'The Traffic in Women: Notes on the "Political Economy" of Sex', in R. R. Reiter (ed.) *Toward an Anthropology of Women*. New York: Monthly Review Press.

Smith, D. E. (1990) *The Conceptual Practices of Power: A Feminist Sociology of Knowledge*. Toronto: University of Toronto Press.

Walby, S. (1997) *Gender Transformations*. London: Routledge.

BARBARA L. MARSHALL

GENERATION

In sociological literature, five meanings of the concept of generation can be distinguished: (1) generation in the sense of age-unspecific contemporaries; (2) genealogical generation both as kinship descent and as familial generation; (3) historical generations and/or political generations as age-independent communities sharing the same experiences and interpretations of a contemporary historical event; (4) different ages, age-groups and age-stratifications; and (5) cohort (birth cohort) as a statistical aggregate of people born within the same time interval. In empirical contexts, the aspects denoted by these terms often overlap (see also **age**).

The concept of genealogical generation corresponds to a cyclical understanding of history which links successive kinship descent generations to their origins (see also **kinship**). The son replaces the father to reproduce the way of life handed down by the father.

This identity of simultaneously reproducing both social life-styles and generations is broken down by the experience of **social change** in the course of modernity. The genealogical understanding of history is replaced by the future-oriented concept of **progress**. Against this background, the classic question among generation sociologists arose as to the relationship between the natural succession of generations and social change. The first responses in the nineteenth and early twentieth centuries – formulated by John Stuart **Mill**, Auguste **Comte**, and José Ortega y Gasset – still maintained a close connection between social progress and the natural succession of generations whose average duration was assumed to be about 30 years. Two questions, however, remain unanswered: (1) When does a new generational interval commence?; and (2) How is the continuous succession of generations linked to the discontinuous process of social change?

Since the late 1980s, the topic of generation has attracted renewed attention. This has occurred against the backdrop of the profound demographic development towards ageing societies in the advanced industrialized countries (see **demography**), as well as in the context of the historical upheavals in Eastern bloc countries. In this frame, many studies have referred to the cultural and socio-political dimensions of Karl **Mannheim**'s approach to generation research and have underlined its relevance for a globalized world (Fietze 1997; Edmunds and Turner 2002).

In the 1920s, Mannheim elaborated the social inter-connectedness of nature and culture and is therefore seen as the actual founder of the sociology of generations. Mannheim linked processes of social change and the natural succession of generations, the exit and new entry of cultural agents, by means of age-independent perceptions and interpretations of social processes of change. Historical generations do not emerge with natural regularity, but only under specific social circumstances. Mannheim only speaks of a historical generation once a generation nexus has been constituted among contemporaries by a decisive collective event, such as a war or revolution. By 'generation nexus' Mannheim meant an age-dependent perception of the situation and a resulting age-dependent consciousness and identity.

Although open to criticism, the Mannheimian concept has been taken up by numerous writers, particularly by political sociologists, who use the term 'political generation' with regard to **social movements** and political **elites** (Heberle 1951; Fogt 1982). Within the context of world-wide youth movements in the 1960s, the topic of generations was once again widely debated from a socio-political angle, linking it to aspects of youth and the family (Bengtson and Laufer 1974) (see also **family and household**).

The concept of cohort, adopted by the sociology of generations from demography, has somewhat greater scientific clarity. It connects with Mannheim's concept of 'generation location', but excludes cultural dimensions. The cohort analysis does not assume that the succession of generations (demographic metabolism) causes social change, but rather that it renders it possible (Ryder 1965). Social transformation can be studied by analysing aggregate collective biographies with the help of intra- and inter-cohort analyses. Many studies have borne out the time-specific influence on members of one birth cohort throughout their life-courses. Because cohort affiliation, age and life-cycle overlap (Elder 1974), it is necessary to distinguish, methodologically, the effects of generation, period and age.

From a structural-functionalist point of view, age as an aspect of social structuring has gained relevance (**Eisenstadt** 1956). Integrating different age-groups, particularly the youth groups, into the social order is not only a significant organizational principle in so-called 'primitive' societies. In developed societies, too, age serves as a criterion for accessing positions of **status**.

Thus the issue of generation conflict between age-groups is of particular interest.

References and further reading

Bengtson, V. L. and Laufer, R. S. (eds) (1974) 'Youth, Generations, and Social Change', *Journal of Social Issues*, 30(2–3).

Edmunds, J. and Turner, B. S. (2002) *Generations, Culture and Society*. Milton Keynes: Open University Press.

Eisenstadt, S. N. (1956) *From Generation to Generation*. Glencoe, IL: Free Press.

Elder, G. H., Jr. (1974) *Children of the Great Depression*. Chicago: University of Chicago Press.

Fietze, B. (1997) '1968 als Symbol der ersten globalen Generation', *Berliner Journal für Soziologie*, 7(3): 365–86.

Fogt, H. (1982) *Politische Generationen*. Opladen: Westdeutscher Verlag.

Heberle, R. (1951) *Social Movements*. New York: Appelton Century-Crofts.

Mannheim, K. ([1928] 1952) 'The Problem of Generations', in P. Kecskemeti (ed.) *Essays on the Sociology of Knowledge*. New York: Oxford University Press, pp. 276–320.

Ryder, N. B. (1965) 'The Cohort as a Concept in the Study of Social Change', *American Sociological Review*, 30(6): 843–61.

BEATE FIETZE

GENETICS

Genetics refers to a branch of biology which studies the ways genes operate within an organism and are transmitted from parents to offspring in a similar, yet varying fashion. This field of **science** emerged in 1900 following the independent 'rediscovery' of Gregor Mendel's laws of inheritance. William Bateson coined the term genetics in 1906, and Wilhelm Johannsen introduced the term 'gene' in 1909 to refer to the 'unit factors' or traits that are inherited during reproduction. Following the elucidation of the self-replicating structure of deoxyribonucleic acid (DNA) in 1953 by James Watson and Francis Crick, DNA became identified as the material basis of genes. From the 1970s onwards, it became possible to manipulate DNA at the molecular level and redesign it to suit human needs, giving rise to a field known as genetic engineering or biotechnology. Throughout the 1990s, a major international effort, known as the Human Genome Project, was undertaken to develop a map of human DNA. The Human Genome Project introduced a range of tools for characterizing and manipulating DNA which can be used to produce information about an individual's genetic make-up in diverse areas such as forensic investigations, paternity disputes, or in the prenatal and presymptomatic identification of illness.

Genetics is particularly relevant to a number of theoretical debates and concerns within the social sciences. One point of convergence focuses on the relationship that figures between **science** and **society** (see **social studies of science**). Refuting the claim that science is value-free and independent of social context, a number of scholars have drawn attention to how in the early twentieth-century eugenics movement, genetics was seen as a solution to many social problems, and used to explain and justify differences in terms of gender, race, and intellectual capacity (Kevles 1985; Paul 1998). In many liberal democracies, genetic explanations throughout this period were used to justify the exercise of control (see **social control**) over the reproduction of those considered to pose a threat to the quality of the race or nation through their sterilization, segregation, and ultimately, extermination in Nazi Germany. The pervasiveness of genetics in late twentieth-century popular culture (Nelkin and Lindee 1995) has given rise to concerns over how genetics is reshaping conceptions of personhood, **health and illness**, individual and group identities, and personal and familial responsibilities (see **self**; **subject and subjectivity**).

The forms of reductionism and **essentialism** present in the fields of biology and genetics has formed a topic of concern within **feminist theory**. Molecular genetics is understood as being essentialist by many feminists since it posits biological causes as the root of who we are, therefore ignoring the role of socio-cultural factors in shaping **gender** or **sexuality**. Molecular genetics is also reductionist by its exclusive concentration on the role of DNA in directing the development of an organism, thus neglecting the role of other factors such as the environment (Hubbard and Ward 1999). Given these concerns, feminists, alongside disability scholars, have been attentive to the social implications of genetics, especially its reliance upon abortion to prevent the occurrence of genetic disease. They have argued that genetics reinforces medical-genetic definitions of disability, makes judgements about the social worth of disabled persons, and ultimately involves decisions about what kinds of persons ought to be born (Kerr and Shakespeare 2002).

Biotechnology brings into question the relationship between technology, political economy, and nature. As genetic engineering enables intervention upon living organisms and the exploitation of their capacities for the purposes of extracting surplus value, biotechnology contributes to the commercialization of academic research (Thackray 1998). A related concern raised by the development of the biotechnology industry is the commodification of life itself through the patenting of human DNA sequences and genetically modified plants or animals. Biotechnology has a number of implications for developing countries through the patenting of natural and agricultural products by transnational corporations, in many cases without compensating local people for their knowledge of the properties of these organisms, often referred to as biopiracy (Shiva 1997). As biotechnology involves the creation of novel plants and organisms, environmentalists and social scientists have conceptualized the processes by which experts construct, assess and communicate the risk presented by genetically modified organisms to ecosystems and human health.

Conceptualizing the social and political implications of genetics poses major challenges for critical social thought in the twenty-first century. As more aspects of human biology become open to understanding and technological mediation, there are continuing consequences for the establishment of difference along the lines of gender, **race** and ability.

References and further reading

Hubbard, R. and Ward, E. (1999) *Exploding the Gene Myth*. New York: Beacon.
Kay, L. E. (2000) *Who Wrote the Book of Life?: A History of the Genetic Code*. Stanford, CA: Stanford University Press.
Keller, E. F. (2000) *The Century of the Gene*. Cambridge, MA: Harvard University Press.
Kerr, A. and Shakespeare, T. (2002) *Genetic Politics: From Eugenics to Genome*. Cheltenham: New Clarion Press.
Kevles, D. J. (1985) *In the Name of Eugenics: Genetics and the Uses of Human Heredity*. Berkeley, CA: University of California Press.
Nelkin, D. and Lindee, M. S. (1995) *The DNA Mystique: The Gene as a Cultural Icon*. New York: W. H. Freeman and Co.
Paul, D. B. (1998) *Controlling Human Heredity: 1865 to the Present*. New York: Humanity Books.
Shiva, V. (1997) *Biopiracy: The Plunder of Nature and Knowledge*. Toronto: Between the Lines.
Thackray, A. (1998) *Private Science: Biotechnology and the Rise of the Molecular Sciences*. Philadelphia, PA: University of Pennsylvania Press.

CARLOS NOVAS

GIDDENS, ANTHONY (1938–)
British sociologist

In *New Rules of Sociological Method* (1976) and *Central Problems of Sociological Theory* culminating in *The Constitution of Society* (1984), the core of Giddens's social theory is his account of 'social structuration' (see **structuration school**). Here the key concept is the 'duality of structure' in which '**structure**' is presented as the medium and outcome of the conduct or **agency** that it recursively organizes. Structure in this sense is both 'enabling' and 'constraining'. Drawing on a range of social theories including **functionalism**, **ethnomethodology** and **structuralism**, Giddens's work involves a comprehensive refurbishing of central sociological concepts. In *A Contemporary Critique of Historical Materialism* (1990a) and *The Nation State and Violence*, he presents social change as 'contingent', involving a stretching of social relations across **time** and **space** that undermines the validity of any closed conception of **society**. Rather than being simply Westernization, Giddens portrays **globalization** in *The Consequences of Modernity* as involving a dialectic of the local and global. Although appearing to us as a 'runaway world', globalization in Giddens's view is potentially controllable. Taking issue with **postmodernism**, he argues that changes presented as 'postmodernity' are aspects of radicalized **modernity and modernization**. In *Modernity and Self-Identity* (1991) and *The Transformation of Intimacy* (1992), Giddens explores the implications of the centrality of **reflexivity** in modern society, including changes in 'ontological security', 'self-identity', **trust** and **risk**. In the 1990s Giddens recast himself as a public intellectual influencing the thinking underlying the politics of 'the Third Way' and Tony Blair's New Labour Party.

Major works

(1976) *New Rules of Sociological Method*. London: Hutchinson.
(1984) *The Constitution of Society*. Cambridge: Polity.
(1990a) *A Contemporary Critique of Historical Materialism*. London: Macmillan.
(1990b) *The Consequences of Modernity*. Cambridge: Polity.
(1991) *Modernity and Self-Identity*. Cambridge: Polity.

Further reading

Bryant, C. and Jary, D. (eds) (2001) *The Contemporary Giddens*. London: Palgrave.

DAVID JARY

GIFT EXCHANGE

See: exchange theory

GLOBALIZATION

Globalization seems to mean all things to all people. For some, globalization is the welcome erosion of nation–state boundaries and barriers to free trade; for others it is a monolithic tidal wave sweeping over the helpless local; or it is the way in which technology facilitates the diffusion of **networks** and enables dialogue between societies. Globalization for some is something to be championed; for others, it is to be opposed. For some, it is occurring apace, for others not at all. Globalization for some is a transformation within the logic of **modernity**; or it is a historical process predating modernity; or even a process which brings to an end the modern age altogether.

Popular though it may be with journalists, politicians and activists, the usefulness of the concept of globalization for social theorists is not self-evident, and disagreement abounds over the concept's reference. As with earlier debates over the nature and extent of **industrialization** or modernization, globalization can be presented as one way of describing what might be happening in the world today; and if this is the case, its relationship with alternative models of contemporary global **social change** needs to be carefully and analytically researched. If we follow this logic, 'balkanization' is used to describe a world increasingly divided along **cultural** or **ethnic** lines, 'Americanization' to a world increasingly dominated and reshaped politically, militarily and culturally by the last remaining superpower, 'McDonaldization' to an increasingly standardized and homogeneous world, and 'globalization' to a world in which nation–state borders are losing their significance, as organizations, individuals, events and ideas treat the world itself as a single stage on which to perform. If the term itself is to have any value here, it is necessary to avoid the careless essentialism which often accompanies its use and interrogate instead the extent to which globalization might be an appropriate description for specific different fields of the social world. In all likelihood,we should expect to find that as a process, globalization is more advanced and thus more appropriate a term to be used in some areas than in others.

Some of the most typical and influential contributions to the debate over what globalization 'is' and how it came about have come from Held and McGrew (2003), Robertson (1992), **Giddens** (1990), Harvey (1990), Sklair (2002), and Hall (1991) among many others. For Robertson, globalization refers to the increasing consciousness of the world as a single place, a process originating in **Europe** in the fifteenth century which speeds up dramatically during the twentieth century. For Giddens, by contrast, it is a continuation of **modernity and modernization**, the intensification of modernity's logic to drive forward, which is facilitated by new technologies and characterized by time–space distantiation, the experience of compression of **time** and **space and place**. Harvey and Sklair both agree with Giddens that globalization is a process beginning in the late twentieth century, but they locate its origins in significant transformations within the logic of **capitalism**, rooted for Harvey in a crisis of over-accumulation and a need to seek out new markets, and for Sklair in the declining significance of the nation–state in the regulation of capitalism (see **state and nation-state**). Hall links globalization instead to post-colonialism and the resultant blurring of cultures and ethnic identities (see **post-colonial theory**). Subsequent theorists have sought to present a dialectic of globalization, positing a systemic or capitalist-driven 'globalization from above' with an emancipatory or socialist 'globalization from below' (Brecher *et al.* 1993; Sklair 2002; O'Byrne 2003).

Economic globalization

According to its champions and its critics, economic globalization represents a distinct and significant shift in the dynamics of capitalism. Effectively the last quarter of the twentieth century has seen an uncoupling of the capitalist **market** from the political nation–state, thus ending (or at least eroding) a marriage of convenience which had defined **political economy** for the preceding centuries. Unrestricted by the burden of nation–state regulation, capitalism operates globally irrespective of borders, thus uniting the world in a single global marketplace (Ohmae 1990).

According to Sklair (2002), there are three main characteristics of this new global capitalism. First is the presence, and power, of transnational corporations (TNCs). Annually, the world's richest corporations benefit from gross sales figures which exceed the gross domestic product of relatively stable and advanced nation–state economies. These TNCs own a significant percentage of the world's assets and exert considerable influence on the policies of major economies, raising concerns about accountability. The international **division of labour** empowers these TNCs to operate beyond the regulative scope of any single nation–state, disembedding and re-embedding their operations so as to best maximize their profits (see **embedding and disembedding**).

Disembedding and re-embedding are among the major transnational practices which comprise the second characteristic of global capitalism. The shift in production practices from Fordism to **post-Fordism** necessarily benefits from globalized conditions and an international division of labour. Not only are corporations enabled to operate at the level of production in dispersed spaces across the globe, but they are able to exploit global **media and mass media** and the culture of consumerism to market themselves as global brands. Coca-Cola's famous 'teach the world to sing' advertising campaign of the 1970s is a fine example of this exhibition of corporate globality, in directly addressing not an American market, nor even just a Western one, but instead identifying and presenting itself as an actor on a global stage with a global audience.

The third characteristic is the emergence of a transnational capitalist **class**. Although doubts remain as to whether this collection of wealthy and powerful individuals constitutes a class (in the orthodox **Marxian** sense) or is better defined as a global **elite**, the major corporate tycoons, financiers and entrepreneurs who are responsible for the running of the TNCs, whose budgets are greater than many national economies, and who able to exchange citizenships with relative ease, possess considerable political and economic influence.

According to Sklair, these new dynamics of capitalism require us to move beyond earlier theoretical frameworks, including orthodox Marxian approaches, which continue to over-emphasize the significance of the nation – state in the world economy, a charge Sklair also makes against the **world-systems theory** of **Wallerstein** and others. Although world systems analysis moves beyond orthodox Marxism in identifying capitalism as a system extending beyond nation–states, its insistence on still treating nation–states as the primary units of analysis, this wider economic system, either as oppressor or oppressed, renders it insensitive to the dynamics of a globalized capitalism in which the principal actors operate across and regardless of nation–state borders.

Any suggestion that these characteristics represent a new stage in capitalist development should be treated carefully, however. Already in the eighteenth century, Adam **Smith** based his economic theories on the assumption that an unregulated market would necessarily extend beyond the nation–state, and **Marx** himself recognized the need for capitalism to seek out new markets. Contemporary critics continue to

assert the importance of the nation–state in economic practices, and identify consistencies between the international capitalism of the nineteenth century and today's economy (Hirst and Thompson 1996).

Political globalization

At first glance it would seem premature to suggest that 'globalization' is as evident in the political sphere as it is in the economic. While there are indeed significant challenges to state **sovereignty** – transnational regulatory bodies such as the United Nations and the European Union, economic institutions such as the World Bank, international legal conventions recognized by nation–states (Held 1991: 211–12) – the political significance of the nation–state appears to have been far less compromised than its economic significance. The political and military power of the United States and the prevalence of inter-state conflict in the twenty-first century are testament to this.

Nonetheless, the presence of these transnational regulatory bodies and conventions suggests a small but significant step along the process of political globalization which should not be underestimated. Despite its deficiencies, the United Nations, although international in composition, is at least global in scope, and a fully functioning International Criminal Court would represent a major challenge to state autonomy and provide much-needed empowerment to such otherwise abstract legal concepts as 'crimes against humanity'. The culmination of this particular process of political globalization would involve the formation of a world state under a single world government – but this is not a likely prospect at this point in history.

However, political globalization need not be synonymous with this incremental unification of the world, viewed in terms of globalization of political **institutions**. At least two other forms of political globalization are identifiable. The first involves the globalization of political practices. In its classical formation, commentators from the liberal right and the Marxian left agreed that despite superficial ideological differences, the strategies and operations of states in the late twentieth century were becoming or had become increasingly similar. A more contemporary version of this position is presented by John Meyer, who suggests that a single institutional culture, prioritizing the establishment of a democratic framework, is fast becoming the standardized norm for nation–states (Meyer *et al.* 1997). This form of political globalization does not require the erosion of nation–state boundaries.

A third form of political globalization which is equally independent of the unification of political institutions is the globalization of political values. Accordingly, the shift in values from nation–state concerns to global ones such as human **rights**, **ecology and environmentalism**, and **world peace** reflects what Giddens (1990) identifies as the move from class politics to life politics. Traditional forms of political expression, such as participation in established political parties, are inadequate for directly addressing these wider global concerns. Thus, participation in global **social movements** (coupled with declining involvement in nation–state political institutions) is indicative of a new, globalized form of politics.

Cultural and social globalization

As with politics, in the field of culture at least three alternative models are identifiable, which can for the sake of convenience be labelled 'Americanization', 'McDonaldization', and 'creolization'. The Americanization model begins with the Marxian assumption that culture and ideology serve to reproduce power relations and protect the interests of the dominant group. Cultural globalization is thus defined in terms of the global reach of media images, brands, advertising, television and cinema. Those who control the media and communications industries wield vast amounts of power and influence, and they tend to be Western, primarily American. Particular cultural products – Hollywood blockbusters, fashionable clothing, television programmes such as *Dallas*, *Baywatch* and *Friends* – permeate local cultures and duly promote the consumerist **ideology** which sustains capitalism and Western interests. Cultural globalization is thus synonymous with cultural **imperialism**. Ritzer's (1993) McDonaldization thesis, which amounts to the globalization of cultural practices, suggests a similar 'top-down' view of cultural globalization, but in fact takes its lead from the Weberian tradition which emphasizes **rationalization** and standardization.

The creolization argument takes issue with the simplistic, one-directional view forwarded by advocates of both the Americanization and McDonaldization theses. While champions of this position readily accept that for the most part cultural flows go from the core to the periphery, they are more sensitive towards the reception and consumption of these products, and do not see these flows as 'one way traffic'. That is to say, the process of cultural globalization is not 'merely a matter of constant pressure from the center toward the periphery, but a more active interplay' (Hannerz 1996: 68). Rather than being swept under from the pressure of the Western tidal wave, local cultures appropriate these imported objects, invest in them new and specific meanings, blend them with local cultural products to produce new hybridized ones (see **hybridity**). The result is that even products such as Coca-Cola are 'attributed with meanings and uses within particular cultures that are different from those imagined by the manufacturers' (Howes 1996: 6). Global culture is thus a hybrid culture, a culture of **difference** rather than sameness, within which emerge new identity formations intersect national boundaries and are dislocated from any traditional sense of place (Hall 1992: 310).

That these globalizing processes enable the flow of people around the world is uncontested. That they impact upon lifestyles, behaviour patterns, and self-identities, seems equally obvious. Clearly the 'presentation of self' – in the form of **body** images, modes and manners of communication and **interaction** – is susceptible to the influence of a globalized media, and thus represents a possible form of social globalization. Equally, the spread of social networks and relationships around the world, and the ways in which communication technology sustains the depth of these relationships regardless of time and space, is a clear example of this. If one's '**society**' is composed of people and the institutions those people create in order to best facilitate their activities, clearly 'society' can no longer be bound up within nation–state borders. It is curious, then, that sociologists and social theorists have largely overlooked this social dimension in any depth. One exception is Niklas **Luhmann** (1990) who suggests that, largely because of technological developments, a 'world society' is now visible and meaningful, as a society of increasingly interlinked and interdependent societies.

While journalists and politicians continue to use the term synonymously with global capitalism, most social theorists now recognize that globalization is a multifaceted process with no obvious single direction. If one road leads to a single unregulated market which further polarizes the rich North and the poor South, another leads to inter-cultural dialogue and awareness, to new identities and citizenships unconstrained by the 'assimilationist' frame of old, and to respect for universal human rights. If one road threatens to wash away local differences and remake the world in a single image, another allows for those voices of difference to be heard.

References and further reading

Appelbaum, R. and Robinson, W. (eds) (2005) *Critical Globalization Studies*. New York: Routledge.

Brecher, J. *et al.* (eds) (1993) *Global Visions*. Boston: South End Press.

Giddens, A. (1990) *The Consequences of Modernity*. Cambridge: Polity.

Hall, S. (1991) 'The Local and the Global: Globalization and Ethnicity', in A. King (ed.) *Culture, Globalization and the World-System*. Basingstoke: Macmillan.

Hall, S. (1992) 'The Question of Cultural Identity', in S. Hall, D. Held and A. McGrew (eds) *Modernity and Its Futures*. Cambridge: Polity.

Hannerz, U. (1996) *Transnational Connections*. London: Routledge.

Harvey, D. (1990) *The Condition of Postmodernity*. Oxford: Blackwell.

Held, D. *et al* (1999) *Global Transformations: Politics, Economics and Culture*. Cambridge: Polity Press.

Held, D. and McGrew, A. (eds) (2003) *The Global Transformations Reader*. Cambridge: Polity Press.

Hirst, P. and Thompson, G. (1996) *Globalization in Question*. Cambridge: Polity.

Howes, D. (ed.) (1996) *Cross-Cultural Consumption: Global Markets, Local Realities*. London: Routledge.

Luhmann, N. (1990) 'The World Society as a Social System', in N. Luhmann (1990) *Essays on Self-Reference*. New York: Columbia University Press.

Meyer, J. W., Boli, J., Thomas, G. and Ramirez, F. (1997) 'World Society and the Nation–State', *American Journal of Sociology*, 103(1): 144–81.

O'Byrne, D. (2003) *The Dimensions of Global Citizenship*. London: Frank Cass.

Ohmae, K. (1990) *The Borderless World*. London: Collins.

Ritzer, G. (1993) *The McDonaldization of Society*. Newbury Park, CA: Pine Forge.

Robertson, R. (1992) *Globalization*. London: Sage.

Sklair, L. (2002) *Globalization: Capitalism and Its Alternatives*. Oxford: Oxford University Press.

DARREN J. O'BYRNE

GOFFMAN, ERVING (1922–1982)
Canadian-born sociologist

Goffman made substantial and distinctive contributions to the sociology of **everyday** life, influenced by **Simmel** and **Durkheim**. Like Simmel, Goffman studied interactions in urban settings, and also felt no compulsion to develop a systematic theoretical framework. Many commentators locate him primarily within the tradition of **symbolic interactionism**: like **Mead** and **Blumer**, Goffman is sensitive to the way in which individuals can anticipate the meanings others might attribute to their actions. Because individuals can anticipate meanings, they are able to influence their surroundings. This is not to say that Goffman depicts people as cynical manipulators. He insists that they operate in a moral universe: they exhibit tact, adhere to systems of secrecy and try not to lose face. Initially Goffman described his research strategy as the 'dramaturgical approach' (see **dramaturgical school**), referring to his use of metaphors from the theatre to understand people's interactions. The societal relevance of Goffman's approach became more apparent in his later work on labelling processes, 'total institutions', advertising and gender. Even today, Goffman remains an engaging and provocative author, not least because of his anecdotal, journalistic writing style.

Major works

(1959) *Presentation of Self in Everyday Life*. Harmondsworth: Penguin.
(1961a) *Asylums*. Harmondsworth: Penguin.
(1961b) *Encounters: Two Studies in the Sociology of Interaction*. Indianapolis, IN: Bobbs-Merrill.
(1964) *Stigma*. Englewood Cliffs, NJ: Prentice Hall.
(1967) *Interaction Ritual: Essays on Face-to-Face Behavior*. New York: Anchor.
(1970) *Strategic Interaction*. Oxford: Blackwell.
(1971) *Relations in Public: Microstudies of the Public Order*. New York: Basic Books.
(1974) *Frame Analysis: An Essay on the Organization of Experience*. New York: Harper & Row.
(1979) *Gender Advertisements*. London: Macmillan.
(1981) *Forms of Talk*. Oxford: Blackwell.

Further reading

Drew, P. and Wootton, A. (eds) (1998) *Erving Goffman: Exploring the Interaction Order*. Cambridge: Polity.

Manning, P. (1992) *Erving Goffman and Modern Sociology*. Cambridge: Polity.

PATRICK BAERT

GOVERNANCE AND GOVERNMENTALITY

'Governance' was introduced in the political sciences and organizational theory as an academic term in the 1980s, while today it is used in a general sense to refer to any strategy, process, procedure or programme for controlling, regulating or managing problems on a global, national, local or organizational level. Thus texts proliferate on global corporate and environmental governance. While in political and social science, 'government' is traditionally associated with the activities of political authorities and state agencies (see **state and nation–state**), the literature on governance stresses that there are important mechanisms of social regulation besides the state, such as the **community** and the **market**. In this perspective, governance includes informal arrangements and decision-making processes below state institutions and it goes beyond the competence of political authorities and questions of legality and law: 'Governance is the sum of the diverse ways individuals and institutions, public and private, manage their common affairs' (CGG 1995: 2).

The literature on governance is characterized by two main aspects. The first is descriptive. Governance accounts for growing interdependencies between political authorities and social and economic actors. It tries to capture the policy networks and public–private partnerships that emerge from the interactions between a variety of bureaucracies, organizations and associations. Governance refers to the appearance of new actors on the scene of government that indicate a fundamental transformation in statehood and a new relation between state and **civil society**. This encompasses, on the one hand, the displacement of practices formerly defined in terms of the **nation–state** to supranational levels (e.g. the European Union or the United Nations), and, on the other, the development of forms of sub-politics 'beneath' politics in its traditional meaning (e.g. **social movements** or humanitarian organizations).

The descriptive dimension of governance is often linked to a second, normative sense. Governance tends to be judged 'good' when political strategies seek to minimize the role of the state in the management of societal affairs. The 'reinvention of government' (Osborne and Gaebler 1992) calls for the privatization of state corporations and the downsizing of the political apparatus. The proponents of the 'good governance' discourse (including organizations such as the World Bank) claim that decentralization, deregulation and liberalization provide solutions to key social and political problems since they replace sovereign authority and hierarchic bureaucracies by spontaneous interactions between equal and autonomous actors.

A more comprehensive and critical account of this political transformation is presented by the French philosopher Michel **Foucault** in his lectures of 1978 and 1979 at the Collège de France. Foucault introduces the notion of 'governmentality' (*gouvernementalité*) as a guiding principle in his 'genealogy of the modern state'. The semantic linking of governing (*gouverner*) and modes of thought (*mentalité*) indicates that it is impossible to study the technologies of power without an analysis of the political rationality underpinning them. In addition, Foucault uses the notion of government in a sense geared strongly to the older meaning of the term, as well as adumbrating a close link between forms of power and processes of subjectification (see **subject and subjectivity**). He demonstrates that in addition to management by the state administration, 'government' in the past also signified problems of self-control, guidance for the family, management of the household or direction of the soul. For this reason, Foucault defines government as 'the conduct of conduct', thus giving the term a meaning ranging from 'governing the self' to 'governing others'(Foucault 1982: 220–1).

Following this line of inquiry, Foucault concentrates on the question of **power** more explicitly than the governance discourse. For Foucault, power relations are not restricted to the government of the state; they also include all forms of directing and guiding individuals and collectives in civil society and in the economic sphere. In this perspective, the differences between state and society, politics and economy, the private and the public sphere do not function as universal foundations or essential borderlines, but as elements and effects of technologies of government (Foucault 1991: 103). In light of this approach, the 'retreat of the state' can itself be read as a governmental technology and a political programme.

References and further reading

Burchell, G., Gordon, C. and Miller, P. (eds) (1991) *The Foucault Effect: Studies in Governmentality*. Hemel Hempstead: Harvester Wheatsheaf.

CGG (Commission on Global Governance) (1995) *Our Global Neighbourhood*. Oxford: Oxford University Press.

Foucault, M. (1982) 'The Subject and the Power', in H. Dreyfus and P. Rabinow (eds) *Michel Foucault: Beyond Structuralism and Hermeneutics*. Brighton: Harvester.

Foucault, M. (1991) 'Governmentality', in G. Burchell, C. Gordon, and P. Miller (eds) *The Foucault Effect: Studies in Governmentality*. Hemel Hempstead: Harvester Wheatsheaf.

Lemke, T. (1997) *Eine Kritik der politischen Vernunft: Foucaults Analyse der modernen Gouvernementalität*. Berlin: Argument.

Osborne, D. and Gaebler, T. (1992) *Reinventing Government: How the Entrepreneurial Spirit is Transforming the Public Sector*. Reading, MA: Addison-Wesley.

Rose, N. and Miller, P. (1992) 'Political Power beyond the State: Problematics of Government', *British Journal of Sociology*, 43(2): 173–205.

Senellart, M. (1995) *Les arts de gouverner: Du régimen médiéval au concept de gouvernement.* Paris: Seuil.

THOMAS LEMKE

GRAMSCI, ANTONIO (1891–1937)
Italian theorist

Gramsci was inspired by Labriola and Croce's anti-determinist interpretation of Marxism. He studied at the University of Turin where he became a leader of the socialist factory council movement. He was co-founder of the Italian Communist Party (PCI) in 1921 and served as its Comintern representative until 1924 when he became the leader of PCI. He was imprisoned by Mussolini in 1926 and died shortly after release from prison.

In his *Prison Notebooks*, first published in Italy in 1948, Gramsci rejected the economic determinism of Marxism that reduced politics to a superstructural level whose form and function are determined by the economic laws of **capitalism**. Instead, he inverted the classical Marxist hierarchy of economy and state with his claim that the highest moment in the struggle for **hegemony** by a social **class** is not seizure of economic power, but establishment of a political and moral–intellectual leadership. In this way, a social class manages 'to become a state'. Gramsci here conceives of the state as the articulation of political society with **civil society**. His concept of the 'historical bloc' describes a complex, contradictory and only relatively unified ensemble of state, economy and civil society, whose articulation is the result of hegemonic struggles.

Gramsci also attacked the class reductionism of classical Marxism. The formation of collective wills is not a result of the imposition of the **ideology** of the dominant class, but rather a product of 'intellectual and moral reform' that rearticulate social meanings and **identities**. The goal of intellectual and moral reform is not the advancement of a narrow class interests, but the formation of a collective will with a 'national-popular' character.

Major works

(1971) *Selections from the Prison Notebooks.* London: Lawrence and Wishart.
(1977) *Selections from Political Writings 1910–1920.* London: Lawrence and Wishart.
(1978) *Selections from Political Writings 1921–1926.* London: Lawrence and Wishart.
(1985) *Selections from Cultural Writings.* London: Lawrence and Wishart.

Further reading

Laclau, E. and Mouffe, C. (1985) *Hegemony and Socialist Strategy.* London: Verso.
Sassoon, A. S. (1982) *Approaches to Gramsci.* London: Writers and Readers.
Simon, R. (1982) *Gramsci's Political Thought.* London: Lawrence and Wishart.
Torfing, J. (1999) *New Theories of Discourse.* Oxford: Blackwell.

JACOB TORFING

GROUNDED THEORY

Grounded theory is a methodology for generating theory inductively from systematically gathered and analyzed data. Grounded theory emerged during the 1960s to counter the dominance of hypothetico-deductive theory in social science research. In particular, the 'great men' theories of **Parsons**, **Weber**, **Durkheim**, and others preoccupied a generation of scholars whose work focused on testing them. In *The Discovery of Grounded Theory* (1967), Glaser and Strauss maintained that the prevailing tendency within the discipline to undervalue new theory stymied the advance of sociological theory and practice. Another criticism concerned the quality of the connection the 'great men' theory established – or failed to establish – between theory and data obtained from the field. Often initially conceived from *a priori* assumptions separate from data, 'great men' theory did not always fit the social phenomena researchers were trying to explain (ibid.: 3). This was especially true for new areas of study emerging in the discipline during this period. This misfit between theory and field, together with the overemphasis on theory testing, was the impetus for the creation of grounded theory (ibid.: 220; Glaser 1978: 2–3).

As a research method, grounded theory is appropriate for use in qualitative studies of either qualitative or quantitative data (see **methods and methodology**). Although grounded theory originated within sociology, this general research methodology is appropriate for use in any social science discipline. Grounded theory turns the logic of verification methodology on its head. Whereas the logic of verification methodologies is primarily deductive, the dominant logic of grounded theory is inductive. In contrast to verification methodologies that use data to validate preconceived theory, grounded theory uses data to generate theory. Often called the *constant comparative method*, grounded theory compares every piece of data, concept, category, and relationship to every other to formulate an explanatory theory.

In contrast to verification methodologies, which begin with a preconceived research problem deduced from a given theory, grounded theory methodology begins with a broad area of interest (e.g. becoming a professional nurse). Inductive analysis and coding of data eventually yield the research problem. Because the problem is allowed to emerge from the data, the grounded theorist really does not know what the study is about at the outset. Indeed, the focus of the study may change several times as more data is collected and analyzed. Emergence and relevance are core principles counselling the researcher to be patient, and to continue constant comparison until the data reveal the research problem from the perspective of study participants, and not from preconceived theory. Two general research questions guide the research process: 'What is the chief concern or problem of the people in the substantive area, and what accounts for most of the variation in processing the problem? What category or what property of what category does this incident indicate?' (Glaser and Strauss 1967: 210).

Once the research problem emerges, theory generation continues using a combination of coding and theoretical sampling. Beginning with narrative data (e.g. transcribed interviews, field notes, writings, documents), researchers use the above questions to identify patterns in the data. From the narrative data, researchers induce concepts and code the data by writing the concept in the blank margins. This is called *open coding*. Typically incidents yield concepts, and comparative analysis of concepts and incidents yield new concepts or more general categories. New data are selectively gathered to elaborate and refine the emergent theory. Through a process called memoing, the researcher continuously records relationships, possible bias, and potential explanatory hypotheses as they occur to her or him throughout the research process. Eventually the data yield no further concepts or categories. When this occurs, the data are saturated, and theoretical coding begins. *Theoretical coding* refers to the process of relating categories to create hypothetical relationships and explanations for the research problem. Thus the products of grounded theory are probabilities, hypothetical statements about a substantive area of inquiry such as dying or nursing. Unlike formal theory, substantive theories are not predictive. To become formal theory, Glaser and Strauss proposed treating a collection of substantive theories as data and subjecting them to the same coding and theoretical sampling procedures of grounded theory.

The theory has been used in sociology, anthropology, political science, and professional fields such as nursing, medicine, and education (Strauss and Corbin 1997). Their ground-breaking study, *Awareness of Dying* (Glaser and Strauss 1965), is the prototype for grounded theory researchers who continue to refine and clarify the original formulation in *Discovery* (Glaser 1967). Ironically, Glaser and Strauss ended their collaboration in 1987 over differences related to the infusion of verification methods into grounded theory, the very issue that had spawned their collaboration (Glaser 1992).

References and further reading

Conrad, C. (1990) *A Grounded Theory of Academic Change*. Needham Heights, MA: Ginn.

Glaser, B. (1978) *Theoretical Sensitivity*. Mill Valley, CA: Sociology.

Glaser, B. (1992) *Basics of Grounded Theory Analysis*. Mill Valley, CA: Sociology.

Glaser, B. and Strauss, A. (1965) *Awareness of Dying*. Chicago: Aldine.

Glaser, B. and Strauss, A. (1967) *The Discovery of Grounded Theory*. Chicago: Aldine.

Kinach, B. (1995) 'Grounded Theory as Scientific Method: Haig-Inspired Reflections on Educational Research Methodology', in A. Neiman (ed.) *Philosophy of Education 1995*. Urbana, IL: University of Illinois at Urbana Champaign.

Schreiber, R. and Stern, P. (eds) (2001) *Using Grounded Theory in Nursing*. New York: Springer.

Strauss, A. (1987) *Qualitative Analysis for Social Scientists*. New York: Cambridge University Press.

Strauss, A. and Corbin, J. (1997) *Grounded Theory in Practice*. Thousand Oaks, CA: Sage.

BARBARA M. KINACH

GROUP

The term 'group' designates a set of persons tied to each other through repeated **interaction** and a collective **identity**. Groups are amorphous social phenomena without a formalized **structure**. They are located on the meso-level of sociological enquiry (see **micro-, meso- and macro-levels**). Examples are **families**, **sects**, peers, gangs, and ethnic groups. **Associations** and **social movements** often build on group segments. Groups differ from interaction systems in their endurance and from **organizations** in their informal character. Until the 1960s, the group was one of the most important concepts of sociology. Today, the group concept is only of secondary importance in sociology, but features prominently in social psychology.

The theory of social groups was first propounded by Georg **Simmel** (1908) and Leopold von Wiese. Simmel and von Wiese saw the dyadic social relation between two persons as the basic building block of sociology. Coupling of these dyads makes for larger groupings of three or more persons (for example, in the family). The larger these social groups, the more independent they become of single persons. According to Simmel, the persistence of social groups depends on the existence of favourable **emotions** such as **love** and **friendship**, among its members. Simmel regarded the individual as the product of cross-cutting social groups.

A second important strand in group sociology is to be found in the writings of **symbolic interactionism**. Charles Horton Cooley highlighted the importance of primary groups such as the family and the peer group for the formation of beliefs and the sense of **self** (1909). According to Cooley, these primary groups are characterized by intimate social relations, mutual identification, and a 'we-feeling'. Cooley's work was only a first step in the many works on groups by members of the **Chicago School**. Herbert **Blumer** pointed out that **meaning** arises out of interaction in human groups (1969). In this vein, sociologists studied the culture of ethnic groups, of gangs, of religious and ideological groups, of baseball teams and many other groups. An important part of this work focussed on the mechanisms that made for the evolution and persistence of cultural differences between a group and its environment. Howard Becker's *Outsiders* (1963) argued that sub-cultural forms evolve in the interaction within a group (see **subculture**). Equally important was the labelling of the group as deviant by the surrounding society, and vice versa, leading to the construction of symbolic boundaries. Similar work was undertaken by Norbert **Elias** and John Scotson in the context of figurational sociology (see **figuration**) and by Fredrik Barth (1969) in his cultural anthropology of ethnic groups.

Until the 1960s, diverse theorists ranging from Becker and Elias to Robert Bales and George C. **Homans**) worked with the group concept. In general, all of these writers agreed of the following broad propositions. Social relations and group membership mutually enforce each other. In repeated interaction, groups exert compelling **social control** on their members. Individuals are shaped by groups such as the family and peer groups in childhood and adolescence, while adults are influenced by work colleagues, neighbours, and friends. The values and norms of a group **culture** depend on **symbols**, an argot, a group identity and the drawing of a group boundary. Often the group identity is tied to a common goal or activity. Stereotypes are also often constructed in groups, with a positive light thrown on members and a negative evaluation made of non-members or members of rivalling groups. The group identity often implies a negative reference to a rival group, imagined or real. The construction of these 'outgroups' (William Graham Sumner) or 'negative reference groups' (Robert K. **Merton**) is part of the group culture. The conflict with outgroups makes for a strong integration in the in-group (Simmel 1908). Groups with a strong emphasis on **difference** and conflict depend on **recognition** of this difference by the public or other groups. Some groups use personal traits such as **age**, **gender**, **ethnicity** or **religion** as markers of distinction, markers which need to be perceived as natural. The choice of these traits, though, is always arbitrary and contingent. Without formal regulations of inclusion and decision-making processes, groups usually show an informal hierarchy with leadership based on **charisma** and commitment to the group. Thus members are assigned **roles** within the group. At the core of the role structure are those exerting leadership and **power** over the group with a high level of commitment to the group identity and group activities. At the edge, influences from various groups cross-cut and make for a lower level of engagement. Through the drawing of a boundary, every group defines criteria for inclusion and exclusion, establishing a basic measure of **inequality**. In general, the larger a group, the more dependent it becomes on the construction of a common identity.

After the 1960s, interest in the concept of groups faded with the influence of **functionalism** on the macro-level of societal subsystems and with **exchange theory** and **rational choice** theories at the micro-level of individual decisions. Social psychology, in contrast, still works with the group as one of its core concepts, most prominently in the Bristol School around Henri Tajfel (1981; Hogg and Abrams 1988). The Bristol scholars have focused on the rootedness of stereotypes in group cultures and on the social dynamics of inter-group conflict. Their methods include the experimental creation of groups in artificial settings. Tajfel and his colleagues found that division of groups by aesthetic taste or even by coin flips sufficed to create strong in-group favouritism.

In more recent years, a further problem has contributed to the decline of 'the group' as a conceptual tool. The concept implies a boundedness, connectedness, and homogeneity seldom found on the empirical level. As a consequence, first in social anthropology, later in sociology, the **network** concept increasingly displaced the group concept.

References and further reading

Barth, F. (ed.) (1969) *Ethnic Groups and Boundaries: The Social Organization of Cultural Difference*. Bergen: Universitetsforlaget.

Becker, H. (1963) *Outsiders: Studies in the Sociology of Deviance.* New York: Free Press.

Blumer, H. (1969) *Symbolic Interactionism.* Englewood Cliffs, NJ: Prentice Hall.

Brown, R. (1988) *Group Processes: Dynamics within and between Groups.* Oxford: Blackwell.

Cooley, C. H. (1909) *Social Organization: A Study of the Larger Mind.* New York: Scribner.

Elias, N. and Scotson, J. (1965) *The Established and the Outsiders.* London: Cass.

Hogg, M. and Abrams, D. (1988) *Social Identifications: A Social Psychology of Intergroup Relations and Group Processes.* London: Routledge.

Homans, G. C. (1950) *The Human Group.* New York: Harcourt Brace.

Mills, T. M. (1967) *The Sociology of Small Groups.* Englewood Cliffs, NJ: Prentice Hall.

Shibutani, T. (1962) 'Reference Groups and Social Control', in A. Rose (ed.) *Human Behavior and Social Processes.* Boston: Houghton Mifflin.

Simmel, G. (1908) *Soziologie.* Leipzig: Duncker & Humblot.

Tajfel, H. (1981) *Human Groups and Social Categories.* Cambridge: Cambridge University Press.

JAN FUHSE

H

HABERMAS, JÜRGEN (1929–)
German theorist

Habermas's life-project may be summed up as an attempt to elaborate a theory of society oriented to democratic norms of social transformation by means of what Habermas defines as 'communicative rationality'. Habermas's early work from the 1960s reflects the outlook of the **Frankfurt School** and the particular conception of **Marxist** social theory known as **critical theory**. In several major treatises Habermas has restated the emancipatory ambitions of the Marxist critique of **instrumental reason** in the form of a theory of rational communication oriented to democratic consensus formation. Drawing on classical theorists from **Durkheim**, **Weber** and **Mead** to **Parsons** as well as analytical philosophy of language, Habermas argues that over the course of processes of **modernization**, society is divided into different spheres of rational competence. Scientific-technical spheres governing the economy and systemic social organization come to 'colonize' what Habermas defines as the **lifeworld** of ordinary social interaction mediated by normative linguistic agreements between individuals. However, Habermas argues that these tendencies toward 'colonization of the lifeworld' can be checked and, in principle, overcome by forms of collective action that strive after critical **reflexivity** in public affairs. Habermas defines this possibility as the 'unfinished project of modernity'. Habermas's work has had a major impact on debates about **postmodernism, modernity and modernization** and the **public sphere**.

Major works

([1962] 1989) *Structural Transformation of the Public Sphere*. Cambridge: Polity.
([1967] 1988) *Logic of the Social Sciences*. Cambridge, MA: MIT Press.
([1968] 1971) *Knowledge and Human Interests*. London: Heinemann.
([1981] 1984–87) *The Theory of Communicative Action*, 2 vols. Cambridge: Polity.
([1985] 1987) *The Philosophical Discourse of Modernity*. Cambridge: Polity.
([1992] 1995) *Between Facts and Norms*. Cambridge, MA: MIT Press.

Further reading

McCarthy, T. (1978) *The Critical Theory of Jürgen Habermas*. Cambridge, MA: MIT Press.
Outhwaite, W. (1995) *Habermas*. Cambridge: Polity.

AUSTIN HARRINGTON

HABITUS

Habitus is a key concept developed by Pierre **Bourdieu**. It was intended as an instrument to assist analysis rather than as itself a representation of reality. Many of the comments on its imprecision ignore this fundamental aspect of Bourdieu's **philosophy of social scientific** explanation. Following the Neo-Kantian (see **Kant and**

Neo-Kantianism) thinking of Ernst Cassirer, Bourdieu opposed positivist (see **positivism**) assumptions and believed that concepts are relational or 'functional' rather than 'substantive', using the term 'habitus' as a way of dealing with the problems of **agency** and **structure**. The behaviour of humans is not determined by prior social conditions ('mechanism'), nor by being part of a process leading inevitably towards some future end ('finalism'). Bourdieu opposed **Marxist** determinism and advanced instead a 'soft' determinism which recognizes that humans have some freedom to make social choices within the parameters of opportunity which they inherit. The habitus of agents defines their capacity to modify constraints embodied in social structures. The concept therefore underpins Bourdieu's notion of the process of gradual **social change** effected by the inter generational modification of structures. It is particularly useful in describing the process of parental and student choice in the sociology of **education**. It offers an alternative to **rational choice** theory because it insists that the ability to think rationally is the consequence of socially acquired prior dispositions. Bourdieu was influenced by **Merleau-Ponty** in arguing that the habitus does not simply apply to attitudes but to physical comportment and body language. Earlier uses of the term with a different, but not unrelated, sense were made by Max **Weber** and Norbert **Elias**.

References and further reading

Bourdieu, P. (1985) 'The Genesis of the Concepts of Habitus and Field', *Sociocriticism*, II(2): 11–24.
Bourdieu, P. ([1997] 2000) *Pascalian Meditations*. Cambridge: Polity.
Ostrow, J. M. (2000) 'Culture as a Fundamental Dimension of Experience: A Discussion of Pierre Bourdieu's Theory of Human Habitus', in D. M. Robbins (ed.) *Pierre Bourdieu*, vol. I. London: Sage.

DEREK ROBBINS

HARAWAY, DONNA JEANNE (1944–)

American biologist, philosopher and feminist theorist of science, Professor of History of Consciousness, University of California at Santa Cruz. Haraway is best known for her 1985 essay which used the metaphor of the **cyborg** to argue that we are all technoscientifically produced amalgams of organism and machine, 'reality' and 'fiction' – a metaphor which suggested both a heterogenous and fluid **ontology** and a politics which rejects universalizing theory. This was a key intervention into debates within **feminist theory** and **social studies of science**, the insights of which she has continued to develop. Her studies on primatology demonstrate how, as a science, it rests upon and reproduces a series of cultural binaries – including **nature/culture** and male/female. More recently she has turned her attention to the construction of such scientific objects as 'genes', 'fetuses' and 'race'. As she has consistently argued, such scientific objects are 'boundary projects' which only materialize through the interaction of human and non-human actors in specific historical and geo-political contexts.

Haraway rejects conceptions of science as an objective, representational enterprise. She contributed the concept of 'situated objectivity' to feminist post-positivist **epistemology** in the 1980s. In her later work, the term 'modest witness' is used to stake out this epistemological position – one that acknowledges both its location and its responsibility.

Major works

(1985) 'A Manifesto for Cyborgs: Science, Technology and Socialist Feminism in the 1980s', *Socialist Review*, 80: 65–108.
(1989) *Primate Visions: Gender, Race and Nature in the World of Modern Science*. London: Routledge.
(1991) *Simians, Cyborgs and Women: The Reinvention of Nature*. London: Routledge.
(1997) *Modest_Witness @Second_Millennium. FemaleMan★ Meets OncoMouse: Feminism and Technoscience*. London: Routledge.

(2000) *How Like a Leaf* (interview with Thyrze Nichols Goodeve). London: Routledge.
(2004) *The Haraway Reader*. London: Routledge.

BARBARA L. MARSHALL

HEALTH AND ILLNESS

Lay notions of health and illness long predate medical understandings, the two terms constituting a binary opposition: health referring to states of well-being, or less positively, simply to the absence of illness; illness to some disorder of the body, or more broadly to a state of not being or feeling well. Key indicators of illness are pain and suffering, some form of incapacity – not being able to perform one's usual tasks – and an increased chance of death. The potential breadth of the notions of health and illness is reflected in the World Health Organization's frequently cited definition of health as 'a state of complete physical, social and mental well-being'. As these definitions indicate, health and illness are evaluative concepts: to talk of health is to make a positive judgement of the state in question, if only that a person is not ill; to talk of illness is to make a negative judgement that something is wrong. The evaluative character of the concepts helps to explain certain social features of health and illness. First, the common expectation that some form of intervention to assist the sick individual is appropriate – one of the expectations that **Parsons** formulated as governing the sick role that individuals occupy once sickness is identified. Second, it helps to explain the fact that the boundaries of health and illness change over time as understandings and values change. For instance, as populations live longer and as standards and expectations of health are raised, the boundaries of illness tend to widen (see **medicalization**). Finally, it also helps to explain the variation in people's ideas about health and illness. Sociologists have emphasized the way in which demographic, social, economic and cultural factors shape concepts and understandings of

health and illness, as well as their importance in structuring the ways in which individuals respond to illness – their 'illness behaviour'. Since the 1980s they have also paid particular attention to lay concepts and understandings of health and illness, particularly exploring them through 'illness narratives' – that is, accounts of the experience of illness provided by sick individuals (Kleinman 1988).

The ideas and practices of professionals, particularly members of the medical profession who have established extensive legal powers over the diagnosis and treatment of illness, are a key force shaping lay understandings of illness (see **professions and professionalization**). Modern medical thinking and practice are grounded in the natural sciences, which provide an important foundation for the profession's claims to expertise, though medical work is commonly defined as a mixture of both art and **science**. Medicine's earlier focus on anatomy and physiology was replaced by a greater attention to the inner workings of the body, first at the level of the organs, and then at the level of chemical processes, with biochemistry, neurology and **genetics** now playing the dominant role in scientific understandings of illness. Medicine's reliance on the natural sciences extends to, and is especially visible in, the treatments it uses. Surgery and pharmacology are the major weapons in medicine's therapeutic armoury, with twentieth-century developments in treatment transforming medical practice.

An important feature of medical thinking about illness that provides the foundation for diagnosis is the idea of distinct disease entities, with sociologists often distinguishing between the social category of illness as the experience of being unwell, and the medical category of disease as an objectively identifiable bodily malfunction. Current ideas about disease entities have been heavily influenced by nineteenth-century developments in the understanding of infectious diseases, and the identification of distinctive infectious micro-organisms, such as the tubercle bacillus, whose presence in the body is a necessary condition for the occurrence of a particular illness. As a result, aetiological specificity became a key basis for differentiating diseases, though for diagnostic purposes the symptom cluster, onset, course and outcome are also important. In practice, however, medical classifications are hybrid in character since many disorders lack the aetiological specificity of infectious illnesses, and diseases are often grouped either in terms of similarity of biological process, as with cancers, or by the organs of the body affected, as with respiratory conditions and heart diseases. The range of conditions that may be identified as illnesses extends from the very severe, often fatal, to the milder, less severe illnesses, which though inconvenient and sometimes painful, are frequently self-limiting. Another common distinction is that between acute and chronic illnesses, with heart attacks and many infectious illnesses such as pneumonia or measles falling into the acute category and others such as rheumatism or arthritis with a much longer trajectory falling into the chronic category, though the acute – chronic contrast can also be applied to the stage of an illness.

Although medicine has given increasing attention to the inner workings of the body in its understandings of illness and its treatments, illness has broader social and psychological causes. The importance of social factors is highlighted by the marked variations in health over time in human populations and between social groups, variations that have been clearly established in a wide range of epidemiological work. Historically, improvements in health, as measured by increases in life expectancy, have usually been associated with economic **development** and the attendant improvements in standards of living, including nutrition and sanitation. In many countries life expectancies increased rapidly in line with economic growth over the nineteenth and twentieth centuries – from average life expectancies of around forty or fifty years

to life expectancies of around eighty years. These increases were associated with marked changes in patterns of health and illness. In poorer countries, infectious illnesses, such as malaria and tuberculosis, to which infants and children are especially vulnerable, are a common cause of **death**. Consequently, levels of infant mortality are high and a far smaller proportion of people survive to older ages. And if, as is common, this pattern is associated with high levels of fertility, the result is a demographic profile in which the young, notwithstanding their high death rates, are far more numerous than the elderly. In richer countries, improved nutrition and sanitation reduce the exposure to, and vulnerability to, infectious illnesses, infant and child mortality are far lower, and diseases associated with the deterioration and ageing of the body, such as cancers, heart diseases and respiratory problems, become the usual causes of death. Since lower mortality rates tend to be associated with lower fertility rates, this produces a demographic profile with far higher proportions of elderly people. What is also striking, however, is that, as noted, as life expectancies rise, so expectations of health increase and people in richer countries, who have better access to medical services, frequently set the boundaries of illness more widely and identify more ill-health.

Health also varies between groups within a society at a given moment in time. In most advanced industrial societies, where women typically have fewer children and the attendant toll on their health is considerably less, women live longer than men, often as much as six or seven years longer. However, the size of the **gender** difference varies considerably and is linked to differences in health-related behaviours, such as smoking and diet, and to differences in employment (men have typically had less healthy and more dangerous work), as well as to patterns of childbearing. There are also marked inequalities in health by social **class** and **ethnicity**. Whereas it is usually accepted that in poorer countries much of the difference in life expectancy is due to the lack of material resources of those lower down the social and income scale, there is considerable debate as to whether the differences in life expectancy within richer countries are due to material factors or to psychosocial processes. There is evidence, for instance, that a lack of social **status** and control over one's life, which tend to be more common among lower-income groups, can lead to stress and to a greater likelihood of illness (Marmot 2004) – a view that suggests that social **inequality** is itself bad for health (Wilkinson 1996).

The improvements in health experienced by individuals in richer countries measured by life expectancy present an optimistic picture of what can be achieved for human health. However, there are also major threats to human health. First, the low life expectancy in many poorer countries is unacceptable and makes a strong case for the need for support for economic improvement in these countries. Second, populations, rich as well as poor, have long been vulnerable to major epidemics and increasing **globalization** is likely to mean that infectious diseases will spread more rapidly than in the past. Third, major social changes in richer societies are having negative consequences for health. Affluence, transformed via over-eating and lack of exercise into obesity, could well reduce life expectancies in the future. There are no grounds for complacency.

References and further reading

Freidson, E. (1970) *The Medical Profession*. New York: Little Brown.

Kleinman, A. (1988) *The Illness Narratives*. New York: Basic Books.

Marmot, M. (2004) *Status Syndrome*. London: Bloomsbury.

Parsons, T. (1951) *The Social System*. London: Routledge & Kegan Paul.

Wilkinson, R. (1996) *Unhealthy Societies*. London: Routledge.

JOAN BUSFIELD

HEGELIANISM AND NEO-HEGELIANISM

Hegelianism is the name for the variety of philosophical positions inspired in different and sometimes opposed ways by Hegel's philosophy. These positions vary considerably in terms of how close they remain to Hegel's original doctrines and to the extent which they either appropriate or critically revise Hegel's ideas. The term neo-Hegelianism is generally given to philosophical positions of the twentieth and twenty-first centuries which combine various Hegelian insights with philosophical issues that Hegel himself could not have anticipated. It is clear that neither Hegelianism nor neo-Hegelianism can be taken as conventional philosophical labels which stand for particular principles. And philosophers identified as 'Hegelians' might think they had little in common with others so labelled. However, it can be seen that any position which belongs to the stream of Western philosophy known as Hegelianism holds that philosophical analysis involves an holistic rather than atomistic approach to phenomena.

The early appropriations of Hegel, following his death in 1831, were attracted to Hegel's idealist claim that reality, a finite set of conceptual relations, is ultimately transparent to reason (see **idealism**). Hegel himself employed this principle to discover the inner rationality of **metaphysics**, **science**, **art**, history, **religion** and the modern state, as did his orthodox followers. Important innovations in Hegelianism emerged with the so-called 'Young Hegelians' – some of whom had studied under Hegel – who maintained that Hegel was correct to hold that reality as it manifests itself is the product of concepts, but that Hegel had been too conservative in failing to realize that these concepts were in all cases human and historical, a criticism which laid the foundations for the subsequent 'materialization' of Hegel's metaphysics. Hegelianism in this form came to be associated with an essentially demythologizing activity (exemplified in the works of

D. F. Strauss and Ludwig Feuerbach). In a similar vein, radical critiques of Hegel's validation of religion and his account of political reality emerged with the Left Hegelians, most famously Karl **Marx**, who held that Hegel had correctly identified that history has a structure, that its momentum is achieved by the overcoming of **conflicts**, but that in no sense could current society be regarded as rational, containing, as it seemed, nothing but antagonistic **social relations**. On these grounds Hegel's dictum that 'the real is the rational, and the rational is the real' was rejected as the axiom of **conservativism** and of so-called Right Hegelianism. Soon after, the politically neutral 'historicist' (see **historicism**) school in Germany, inspired by Hegel's notion of **cultures** as historically specific and held together by certain operative ideas (their 'form of consciousness'), developed **hermeneutic** methodologies as means of deciphering the 'spirit' of a culture (outstandingly, Wilhelm **Dilthey**).

The vast riches of the *Science of Logic* – Hegel's **ontology**, in effect – was bound to be exploited. In Britain and the USA, between approximately 1860 and 1920 it inspired philosophers who, taken with Hegel's view that reality is a holistic set of relations, not atomic facts, were keen to devise anti-empiricist forms of analysis of issues in metaphysics (F. H. Bradley and T. H. Green, in England, for example, and in the USA a wide circle of thinkers who contributed to the *Journal of Speculative Philosophy*, edited at the University of St Louis). In this period, prior to the foundation of analytic philosophy, Hegelianism was the orthodox philosophy at Oxford and Cambridge, and virtually the only possibility in the USA until the development of **pragmatism** (by philosophers who, like their British analytic counterparts, had been educated by Hegelians).

Neo-Hegelianism differs in character from Hegelianism as a consequence of the application of Hegelian ideas to a radically changed context. Neo-Hegelianism is generally the selective development of certain Hegelian themes, combined with non-Hegelian questions. For instance, there are the neo-Hegelians of the **Frankfurt School** of **critical theory**, who developed one of Marx's Hegelian theses that consciousness determines the form of reality that we can accept and that material forces determine consciousness, a thesis they combine with an anti-Hegelian suspicion of the notion of **totality**. Ideas of '**dialectic**' and 'consciousness' have played significant roles in continental philosophy in general, but the principle of systematicity – greatly emphasized by Hegel – is specifically rejected in many cases, often thanks to the Nietzschean dimensions of continental philosophy (see **Nietzscheanism and neo-Nietzscheanism**).

A similar pattern might be found in Neo-Hegelian aspects of contemporary American philosophy. Wilfrid Sellars referred to his epochal **Wittgensteinian** polemic against the 'myth of the given' as Hegelian. The recent Quinean conceptualist and inferentialist philosophies of John McDowell and Robert Brandom, which draw on Hegel's concept of mediation, have given rise to the term 'Pittsburgh Hegelianism' (both philosophers being professional academics there). However, these philosophers, unlike Hegel, are primarily philosophers of the era of the **linguistic turn**. It might also be noted that the recent interest in **communitarianism** (especially, Michael Sandel) is a kind of neo-Hegelianism which appropriates Hegel's critique, in the *Philosophy of Right,* of Kantian **liberalism**, but employs it in a context of institutional and democratic **norms** which would have been unknown to Hegel.

References and further reading

Brandom, R. (1999) 'Some Pragmatist Themes in Hegel's Idealism', *European Journal of Philosophy*, 7: 164–89.

Dearmey, M. (ed.) (2002) *The St. Louis Hegelians*. Bristol: Thoemmes.

Mackintosh, R. (1990) *Hegel and Hegelianism*. Bristol: Thoemmes.

Robbins, P. (1982) *The British Hegelians: 1875–1925*. New York: Garland.

Schacht, R. (1975) *Hegel and After*. Pittsburgh, PA: University of Pittsburgh Press.

Toews, J. (1980) *Hegelianism*. Cambridge: Cambridge University Press.

BRIAN O'CONNOR

HEGEMONY

Hegemony refers to a type of political and ideological leadership that is obtained mainly, but not exclusively, by articulating a generally accepted **value** system or **worldview**. In International Relations theory, hegemony is used descriptively to designate the leadership, **authority** and influence of one state in a group of states. Hence, it is common to speak about the hegemony of the USA within the Western world in the post-war period. In the Marxist tradition, and within certain strands of **post-structuralist** discourse theory, hegemony is used as an analytical category for analysing the predominance of an alliance of social classes or a particular set of ideas, meanings or **identity** constructions. As Laclau and Mouffe (1985) argue, hegemony introduces and expands a supplementary *logic of contingency* that tends to undermine and replace the *logic of necessity* that dominated orthodox **Marxism**. For example, Karl Kautsky's dogmatic reassertion of economic determinism in the wake of the consolidation of **capitalism** at the end of the nineteenth century threatened to eliminate reference to contingent forms of political intervention. By contrast, the role of politics is gradually enhanced in Eduard Bernstein's revisionism and Rosa Luxemburg's and George Sorel's revolutionary syndicalism. However, it was in the revolutionary struggles in Russia that the contingent logic of politics acquired its name. Axelrod and Plekhanov introduced the term hegemony in order to account for the extraordinary historical situation in which one **class** – the **proletariat** – should carry out the task of another class, that is, the destruction of the feudal order in a **bourgeois revolution**. After the successful revolution in 1905, Lenin believed that the 'uneven and combined development' in Russia made it possible for the proletariat to advance a socialist revolution by forging a broad class alliance of workers, peasants and soldiers (see **socialism**). Lenin saw the political leadership of the working class as a political intervention that was prompted by the exceptional circumstances in Russia capitalism. Trotsky, on the other hand, argued that the uneven and combined development was a general condition of the age. This radically expanded the validity of the logic of hegemony, although it was still conceived in terms of an alliance of separate identities held together by the tactical leadership of the communist vanguard party. If Trotsky generalized the call for the struggle for hegemony, Antonio **Gramsci** reformulated the conception of hegemony which he defined as a political as well as moral–intellectual leadership aiming to articulate a collective will with a national-popular **identity** (Gramsci 1971). Hegemony was now no longer defined as an alliance of pre-constituted identities, but rather as a new collective identity that was constructed and unified by **ideology**, **symbols** and **myth**. Gramsci insisted that only the fundamental classes (i.e. the bourgeoisie and the proletariat), who are firmly anchored in the capitalist economy, can become hegemonic. However, by insisting on the ultimately political character of the economy, Gramsci removed this last residue of **essentialism** and **reductionism**. This made it possible for post-structuralist discourse theorists, like Laclau and Mouffe, to see hegemony as a general concept for the political practices that articulate social meanings and identities within contingent forms of discourse (see **discourse**).

245

References and further reading

Bocock, R. (1986) *Hegemony*. London: Tavistock.
Gramsci, A. (1971) *Selections from the Prison Notebooks*. London: Lawrence and Wishart.
Laclau, E. and Mouffe, C. (1985) *Hegemony and Socialist Strategy*. London: Verso.
Torfing, J. (1999) *New Theories of Discourse*. Oxford: Blackwell.

JACOB TORFING

HEIDEGGER, MARTIN (1889–1976)

German philosopher

A highly influential figure in European philosophy and social theory, Heidegger's thought influenced the early development of **phenomenology**, and then of existentialism, of **hermeneutics**, **post-structuralism** and **deconstruction** (see **Merleau-Ponty**, **Sartre**, **Gadamer**, **Ricoeur** and **Derrida**). His influence via Merleau-Ponty has been felt in the sociology of the **body**; via Sartre on de **Beauvoir** and **feminism**; via Gadamer on **Habermas** and **critical theory**; via Derrida on **Spivak** and **post-colonial theory**. It can be also discerned in **Schutz**'s phenomenological sociology. Much debate has also focused on Heidegger's brief notorious support of Nazism in the 1930s.

In his major work *Being and Time* ([1927] 1962), Heidegger distinguishes between a secondary 'ontic' level of existence and the **ontological** (the level of Being). He argues that man's immersion in empirical 'things' such as technology has meant that we have lost our closeness to the nature of Being, and are no longer 'at home in the world'. He seeks to uncover Being through an analysis of human being (*Dasein*), as it alone has a tacit awareness of its own nature. Heidegger illuminates the temporal nature human being as happening in **time**. *Dasein* has a projective quality that anticipates the implications of things. For example in Van Gogh's painting of peasants' shoes we do not just see shoes, for the picture speaks of *Dasein*'s connection to toil, weariness and ripening grain (1978: 163). In his later work, Heidegger emphasizes the open-ended nature of **language** as both disclosing the Being of the world and concealing it or putting it under erasure. Heidegger distinguishes between a secondary 'ontic' level of existence represented by science and a more primordial 'ontological' level of understanding of Being.

Major works

([1927] 1962) *Being and Time*. Oxford: Blackwell.
([1929] 1997) *Kant and the Problem of Metaphysics*. Bloomington, IN: Indiana.
([1936–68] 2000) *Elucidations of Hölderlin's Poetry*. New York: Humanity Books.
([1950–59] 1971) *On the Way to Language*. New York: Harper & Row.
([1951–52] 1968) *What Is Called Thinking?* New York: Harper & Row.
([1955–57] 1969) *Identity and Difference*. New York: Harper & Row.
([1962–64] 1972) *On Time and Being*. New York: Harper & Row.
(1978) *Basic Writings*. London: Routledge.

Further reading

Adam, B. (1990) *Time and Social Theory*. Cambridge: Polity.

ALAN HOW

HERMENEUTICS

Hermeneutics is the name given to theories of interpretation in the social sciences and humanities. The term derives from the Greek verb 'to interpret', *hermeneuein*. In social theory, hermeneutics denotes a school of thinking that emphasizes that **actions**, events and social processes must be understood and interpreted from the standpoint of their subjective meaning for the actors under consideration and from the standpoint of their specific historical and cultural context. Hermeneutics is opposed to the view that actions, events and social processes can be adequately explained by reference to invariant laws of cause and effect or statistical regularities, as with positivist, behaviourist and **functionalist** thinking. The school is associated with theorists and philosophers such as Wilhelm **Dilthey**, Max **Weber**, Alfred **Schutz**, Martin **Heidegger**, Hans-Georg **Gadamer**, Paul **Ricoeur**, Peter Winch and Charles **Taylor**.

Hermeneutics has its origins in biblical criticism. Among German Protestant writers of the seventeenth and eighteenth centuries, the term came to refer to the study of the art of interpreting passages of scripture in the light of linguistic analysis and historical evidence. After Martin Luther established the principle of the **autonomy** of the written word of scripture, in opposition to the institutional **authority** of the Catholic Church, questions arose as to how fragmentary, obscure and allegorical parts of the text of the Bible were to be correctly interpreted. These kinds of questions were also thought to apply to the interpretation of statutes of law. Since linguistic meanings change over time, ancient texts of law and scripture could not be read literally; they had to be interpreted and reconstructed in the light of historical changes in the structures of society. In the early nineteenth century, the German theologian F. D. E. Schleiermacher argued that all interpretation – whether religious, legal, poetic or philosophical – had to proceed from an understanding of the total context of social relations from which the text originates. Schleiermacher argued that the act of understanding a problematic text revolved around a 'hermeneutic circle' in which the parts of a text could be interpreted only in terms of the whole and the whole only in terms of the parts, where the text was itself a part in the wider whole of lived social understandings in historically specific worlds or contexts.

In modern social thought, the first thinker to develop a distinctively hermeneutic conception of the methods of the social sciences is Wilhelm Dilthey. Writing in the 1880s, Dilthey (1976) distinguished between two domains of scientific inquiry: on the one hand, the natural sciences; on the other, the human sciences. Dilthey defined the human sciences as sciences of the works of the human mind, or *Geisteswissenschaften*. Dilthey argued that whereas the natural sciences proceed by explaining phenomena according to laws of regular correspondence between cause and effect, the human sciences proceed by understanding phenomena in terms of their meaning: in terms of the reasons or intentions with which actors carry out particular actions and in terms of collectively shared symbolic structures. Dilthey held that to interpret a particular historical event or social process in terms of its context of meaningfully lived experience was itself to account adequately for the occurrence of the event or process and did not require the support of law-like naturalistic explanations in order to gain scientific validity.

Dilthey's distinction between **explanation** and 'understanding', or *Erklären* and *Verstehen*, was influential for German Neo-Kantian philosophers of the early twentieth century, who likewise distinguished between the 'nomothetic', law-like and generalizing methods of the natural sciences and the 'idiographic', interpretive and particularizing methods of the sciences of **culture** (see **Kantianism and Neo-Kantianism**.

For Max Weber, Dilthey's ideas underlined the importance of the orientation of sociology toward 'empathic understanding' of 'subjectively intended meanings' and the fallacy of any attempt to model the study of social action on a search for physical or psychological laws of behaviour, as with the positivist programmes of nineteenth-century writers from Auguste **Comte** to J. S. **Mill** and Herbert **Spencer**.

A second key source for hermeneutic social thought in the twentieth century is phenomenological and linguistic philosophy (see **phenomenology**). In the 1920s and the 1930s the philosophers Edmund Husserl and Martin Heidegger argued that before all methodical and scientific forms of thought, human beings possess a more primordial ontological understanding of the world which they expressively enact and communicate to one another in daily life (see **everyday**). These ideas became important for writers such as Max Scheler, Maurice **Merleau-Ponty** and, notably, Alfred Schutz who sought to restate Weber's programme of interpretive sociology in the form of a phenomenology of the social world, based on the concepts of **intersubjectivity** and the **lifeworld**. Similarly, drawing on Ludwig **Wittgenstein**'s philosophy of language, Peter Winch (1958) argued that social science involves analysis of the ways in which social relations and practices are performatively constructed in everyday norms and rules of linguistic communication.

In a major synthesis of classical philological scholarship and modern phenomenological philosophy from 1960, Hans-Georg Gadamer (1975) argued that hermeneutics is the self-interpretation of human consciousness in the medium of a universal linguistic dialogue with other cultures and civilizations across time and history. Hermeneutics for Gadamer is not the methodical study of past cultural productions in historical contexts; it is the self-interpretation of the present in the light of what Gadamer calls 'tradition'. All understanding is structured by what Gadamer describes as certain deep-seated 'pre-judgements'. He argues that while these pre-judgements cannot be eliminated, they can be brought into a state of reflective awareness by means of an orientation towards what he calls a 'fusion of horizons' between the standpoint of the interpreter and the standpoint of the other culture.

Gadamer's conception of hermeneutics was criticized by Jürgen **Habermas** on grounds of failure to address issues of **power**, **ideology** and material conflict in social life. In texts from the 1960s and the 1970s, Habermas (1988) argues that hermeneutics raises a false claim to universality when it overlooks aspects of the imbrication of linguistic **communication** with unequal relations of power and domination and concealed material interests. Habermas therefore argues that Gadamer's and all other hermeneutic philosophies need to be amended to incorporate critical assessment of the rationality of social practices in ways that avoid simple cultural **relativism**. Habermas demonstrates this by means of a comparison between **Marxian** critique of **ideology** and Freudian **psychoanalysis**. In the same way that Marx showed how historical analysis requires exposure of the ways in which dominant ideologies can be disguised and internalized in the collective consciousness of society, so **Freud** shows how interpretive dialogue with the patient is guided toward enlightenment and **emancipation** from irrational repressions.

One criticism is that Habermas's view of hermeneutics is problematic insofar as it ignores the sense in which both ideology-critique and Freudian psychoanalysis are themselves situated in a specifically Western post-**Enlightenment** context of thought and are therefore not free from interpretive pre-judgements, as Gadamer himself maintained in his reply to Habermas. However, in general, it can be argued that Habermas's criticisms point to some important limits around the scope of the applicability of hermeneutics in social theory. Recent critics such as Bhaskar (1979), **Giddens** (1993) and **Bourdieu** (1977) argue that hermeneutics is informative for social theory only when it does not collapse material, economic and systemic factors and forces in social life into purely 'mental' or 'subjective' elements in the consciousness of actors. Hermeneutic thinking brings to light the fallacies of positivist and objectivist approaches to social research, but it should not be seen as refuting or obviating the requirements of a realist **epistemology** in social science (see **realism**). Hermeneutics demonstrates that all conceptions of social reality are dependent on some form of interpretation, but it does not show that all social reality is reducible to interpretation, or that all relations of cause and effect in social life are solely functions of meaning and symbolization.

References and further reading

Bauman, Z. (1981) *Hermeneutics and Social Science*. London: Hutchinson.

Bhaskar, R. (1979) *The Possibility of Naturalism*. Brighton: Harvester.

Bleicher, J. (1980) *Contemporary Hermeneutics*. London: Routledge.

Bourdieu, P. (1977) *Outline of a Theory of Practice*. Cambridge: Cambridge University Press.

Dilthey, W. (1976) *Dilthey: Selected Writings*. Ed. H. P. Rickman. Cambridge: Cambridge University Press.

Gadamer, H.-G. (1975) *Truth and Method*. London: Sheed & Ward.

Giddens, A. (1993) *New Rules of Sociological Method*. Cambridge: Polity.

Habermas, J. (1988) *On the Logic of the Social Sciences*. Cambridge, MA: MIT Press.

Harrington, A. (2001) *Hermeneutic Dialogue and Social Science: A Critique of Gadamer and Habermas*. London: Routledge.

Ricoeur, P. (1991) *From Text to Action*. London: Athlone.

Taylor, C. (1985) 'Interpretation and the Sciences of Man', in *Philosophical Papers*, I. Cambridge: Cambridge University Press.

Winch, P. (1958) *The Idea of a Social Science and its Relation to Philosophy*. London: Routledge.

AUSTIN HARRINGTON

HISTORICAL SOCIOLOGY

Historical sociology can be approached in two different ways. It might be considered as one subfield applying the tools of sociological research to the vast field of history. Given the central interest of sociology in contemporary issues, this does not look very promising. It can, however, also be defined as dealing with questions of vital interest for the present: what rendered possible the rise of the modern world? What is the source of its dynamism, and where does it lead us? Approached in this way, historical sociology shifts to the centre of interest for social theory, and for sociological understanding in general.

This claim can be supported by the prominent role of historical questions in classical sociology (Delanty and Isin 2003). The nineteenth-century pioneers produced grandiose schemes to explain the modern social order, using functionalist and evolutionary schemes. Saint-Simon and **Comte** combined **Enlightenment** philosophy, especially the ideas of Adam **Smith** and Adam Ferguson with French medical theory, while Herbert **Spencer** was influenced by Darwin's biological theory of evolution, which itself drew on Malthus's economics (see **evolutionary theory**). All these approaches were imbued with nineteenth-century liberal ideas of **progress**, with the emphasis placed on individual freedom and rationality.

The two most influential thinkers of the later nineteenth century, Karl **Marx** and Friedrich **Nietzsche**, radically broke with this framework. For Marx, the founder of 'historical **materialism**', the driving force of history was **class** struggle, and the capitalist system emerged out of the 'original accumulation' of capital based on the land enclosures of the sixteenth century. Nietzsche similarly questioned the optimism of Enlightenment **liberalism**, defining his time as nihilistic in its ethos. But instead of Marx's materialist theories, Nietzsche emphasized the self-elimination of Christian morality and the crisis in European cultural self-understanding.

The classical sociologists of the decades of 1890–1920 produced a critical synthesis of some of these positions. **Durkheim** attempted to correct the teleology of Comte or Spencer by paying closer attention to social and national problems, and later turned to anthropology for further comparative analysis of cultural forms and religious life. **Simmel** drew on both Marx and Nietzsche extensively, but he did not systematically develop a historical approach. The most important work was completed by Max **Weber**.

Paying only lip service to evolutionary or functionalist accounts, Weber drew inspiration from Marx and Nietzsche, guided by Simmel, while avoiding the excesses of both (Szakolczai 1998). Following Marx, he posed as his central concern the rise of modern **capitalism**, this 'most fateful force in our modern life' (Weber 1976), but in approaching the problem through Nietzsche, Weber emphasized the role of science and methodical conduct of life.

After completing his classic study of the **Protestant ethic** Weber realized that the substantiation of his argument required a comparative historical approach. This led to the essays on the 'Economic Ethic of World Religions' and the planned five-volume 'Collected Essays on the Sociology of Religions', of which only one was published in his lifetime. These contained Weber's three major summaries, known as the *Vorbemerkung*, the *Einleitung* and the *Zwischenbetrachtung*. They also contained the essays on the Protestant ethic and the Protestant sects, and on China, India and ancient Israel. The central question of this project was not the justification but the problem of universality in modern Western culture (see **Occident**).

As a consequence of the world wars and the ideologically divided world, and the absence of a developed Weberian 'school', the spirit of the Weberian synthesis was not maintained. Instead, the academic scene in social theory and historical sociology after 1945 was split. On the one hand, it became dominated by the path-breaking but in some respects misguided work of Talcott **Parsons** who read Weber only in a functionalist and evolutionary key (see **functionalism**), laying the foundations of 'modernization' theory'. On the other hand, Marxism was given renewed historical credibility through the work of the **Frankfurt School**. In both cases, interest in comparative study was abandoned in favour of grandiose schemes – evolutionary functionalism in one case, Hegelian Marxism in another.

New impetus for historical sociology came from the 1970s onward. The arguably less innovative part of these developments was the attempt to create a synthesis between academic philosophy and **critical theory**. This led to various forms of 'neo-Weberian neo-Marxism'. Notable contributors have been Reinhard **Bendix**, Anthony **Giddens**, Michael **Mann**, Immanuel **Wallerstein**, Barrington **Moore**, Theda **Skocpol** and Charles **Tilly**.

Further developments have come from two different but interlocking sources. One is the liberation of Weber's work from the spell of **structural functionalism** and modernization theory represented by the work of Wilhelm Hennis, Friedrich Tenbruck, Wolfgang Schluchter, and others. The second is based on the recognition that history and the history of thought cannot and should not be separated (Koselleck 1985; Sewell 1996; Smith 1991; Somers 1995; Szakolczai 2000). Here there has been a break away from claims to deal with 'facts' of the past, in order to 'test' contemporary theoretical models.

Also influential has been the pioneering work of Norbert **Elias** (1983, 2000) on the 'civilizing process' (see **civilization**). In opposition to Weber's interest in religious factors, Elias emphasized the impact of the 'court society', through the centralization of taxation and the monopolization of violence, but especially by spreading new models of self-control. While the high-spending consumers of the court are radically opposed to Weber's thrifty Protestant ascetics, the two are connected through the systematic and individualized regularization of everyday conduct of life.

Another important thread in contemporary historical sociology is provided by the genealogical and archaeological studies of Michel **Foucault** (1975, 1979, 1986). Foucault drew inspiration from Nietzsche, but eventually recognized the parallels with Weber's undertaking. Starting with the formative impact of scientific knowledge on modernity, focusing on the sciences of life, Foucault in his last period shifted the emphasis onto the distant sources of the identity of the modern subject, especially in Greek and Roman thought (see **subject and subjectivity**).

Weber's 'inner-worldly asceticism' and methodical everyday life-conduct, Elias's 'civilizing process' as progress towards increasing self-control, and Foucault's 'disciplinary society' and 'care of the self' are complementary approaches to the joint shaping of modern society and the modern **self**. In Elias's terminology, 'sociogenesis' and 'psychogenesis' are inseparable, while in Foucault's language, the 'totalizing' and individualizing tendencies of the modern condition belong together (see **individualism and individualization**).

While Elias and Foucault started from the 'micro' level, other thinkers continued the Weberian project through a long-term comparative study of civilizations. Interest in this area was kept alive by Benjamin Nelson, and recently received a further boost in 'civilizational analysis'. A central role is played here by the concept of 'axis time' or 'axial age', proposed by Karl Jaspers, an important disciple of Weber, and this was later taken up by Eric **Voegelin** (1974), Shmuel **Eisenstadt** (1986) and Johann Arnason.

The emphasis of most of these approaches on the links between history and the history of thought implies that the present has been produced neither by 'historical laws' nor through 'class struggles', but rather through human efforts to resolve the existential problems of experience, and through a search for a meaningful and dignified life. In this sense the task of theoretically oriented historical sociology is to move beyond ideas of historical necessity, objective interests, or general rules of rationality. Instead its task is to identify the formative impact of transitional or 'liminal' periods of crisis: moments in which previously taken for granted certainties are dissolved and the dividing lines between thought and reality become porous.

References and further reading

Delanty, G. and Isin, E. (2003) *Handbook of Historical Sociology*. London: Sage.

Eisenstadt, S. N. (ed.) (1986) *The Origins and Diversity of Axial Age Civilisations*. New York: SUNY Press.

Elias, N. ([1938–39] 2000) *The Civilizing Process*. Oxford: Blackwell.

Elias, N. ([1969] 1983) *The Court Society*. Oxford: Blackwell.

Foucault, M. ([1963] 1975) *The Birth of the Clinic*. New York: Vintage.

Foucault, M. ([1975] 1979) *Discipline and Punish*. New York: Vintage.

Foucault, M. ([1984] 1986) *The Use of Pleasure*. New York: Vintage.

Horvath, A. (1998) 'Tricking into the Position of the Outcast', *Political Psychology*, 19: 331–47.

Koselleck, R. (1985) *Futures Past: On the Semantics of Historical Time*. Cambridge, MA: MIT Press.

Sewell, W. (1996) 'Historical Events as Transformations of Structures: Inventing Revolution at the Bastille', *Theory and Society*, 25(6): 841–81.

Smith, D. (1991) *The Rise of Historical Sociology*. Cambridge: Polity.

Somers, M. (1995) 'What's Political or Cultural about Political Culture or the Public Sphere? Toward an Historical Sociology of Concept Formation', *Sociological Theory*, 13(2): 115–43.

Szakolczai, A. (1998) *Max Weber and Michel Foucault: Parallel Life-Works*. London: Routledge.

Szakolczai, A. (2000) *Reflexive Historical Sociology*. London: Routledge.

Voegelin, E. (1974) *Order and History*, vol. 4: *The Ecumenic Age*. Baton Rouge, LA: Louisiana State University Press.

ARPAD SZAKOLCZAI

HISTORICISM

Historicism is a controversial and contested term. Articles were written against its very use and important books published with altered titles (Antoni 1962), while Karl **Popper** devoted to it one of his sharpest polemics (Popper 1957). It has recently been stated that '[t]he term has been much used and misused, and it is probably too late to correct misunderstandings' (Kelley 1998: 267). The problem is largely due to the fact that 'historicism', apart from an important predecessor

(Vico) and some late affiliates (Croce and Collingwood), is a nineteenth-century German concern, and is linked to some troublesome aspects of German history.

Historicism in the classical sense has two main branches: cultural and political. Cultural historicism starts with Herder's interest in **language**. Herder argued that Kant never asked the fundamental question of how human understanding arose and developed through history (Kelley 1998: 259). This was because **Kant**, starting with concepts, misconceived the central characteristic of language. Words were first expressions of all human reactions, and only later acquired conceptual meaning as names. Herder also returned to Renaissance ideas of microcosm and macrocosm, arguing that man is a mid-point of the universe, between the heavens and the Earth. Historicism in this sense developed in close alliance with the ideals of *Bildingsbürgertum*, implying the full development of the human personality (Goldman 1988), and its main propagator, Wilhelm von Humboldt (see **humanism**). On the more problematic side, Herder proposed unifying concepts such as the *Volkgeist* (the unique spirit of a people) with the *Zeitgeist* (the spirit of the time).

Political historicism originates with Ranke, the founder of modern historiography (Iggers 1997). Its main concern is diplomatic history and great powers, *Realpolitik* and the doctrine of 'reason of state' (Meinecke 1957), ignoring economic and social history. Ranke's legacy was carried on by the 'Prussian school,' underlining the ethical values embodied in the state and shifting the emphasis from culture to the nation–state.

Common to both branches of historicism is the contrast between history as the realm of the unique and nature as dominated by laws. The central value of historicism, according to Troeltsch and Meinecke, its late representatives and historians, was that it managed to break with the idea of 'natural law'. In the flux of history, permanence is assured by great individual personalities and lasting institutions.

The fight against time, and against **relativism**, requires will-power rather than reason. Historicists opposed the idea of **progress**, and were often charged with irrationalism.

Historicism can also be read in a slightly different light: defined as a concern with restoring texts and material documents to life, involving a sensitivity, even a certain degree of 'empathy', to ways and forms of life of the past. In particular, historicism may be seen as involving not only understanding of the past on its own terms, but also grasping how the present itself has come to be formed. In this sense historicism is close to the **hermeneutical** philosophies of Schleiermacher, **Dilthey**, **Heidegger** and **Gadamer**, the cultural history of Burckhardt (and **Nietzsche**), the interpretive sociology of **Weber**, or the 'new historicism' (Veeser 1989).

Central to historicism in this sense is the work of Wilhelm Dilthey. Dilthey returned to the objections of Herder and Schleiermacher against Kant's neglect of history, and set up the task of preparing the missing fourth '**Critique**', of historical reason. He aimed at restoring life to history and creativity in opposition to the 'conceptual fixing' characteristic of idealist philosophy (Makkreel 1975: 279), by liberating the humanities from the explanative and constructionist ideals of the natural sciences, relying especially on history and anthropology. Instead of capturing the 'essences' of phenomena, by setting up dichotomies and their **dialectic** in overarching conceptual frameworks, characteristic of both the Kantian and **Hegelian** versions of **idealism**, Dilthey proposed to start in the middle, focusing on what is transitory in time and lying in-between in **space**. Thus, he explained the characteristics of German thought by its in-between character.

Central to Dilthey's thought is the idea of 'experience' – followed by 'expression', followed by 'understanding' (Makkreel 1975: 293). Experience (*Erlebnis*) is what happens to somebody undergoing an event; it is the in-the-middle, matter-of-fact starting point

(Antoni 1962: 11). Such experiences are immediately expressed, through plain language or artistic means. The third element, understanding, is a reflexive attempt to make sense of the way events are experienced and expressed (see **Verstehen**). Instead of starting from statements as propositions, the aim is to go into the composition of the work, by linking the movement of experience with the movement of understanding.

Dilthey had a huge (and not fully acknowledged) impact on Max Weber, while in his last writings Victor Turner recognized in him a forerunner of '**liminality**' (Turner 1985). The influence of his thought was impaired by the unfinished character of his writings, earning the reputation of a 'man of first volumes' (Makkreel 1975: 51), and by the unfair attacks of Neo-**Kantians** like Heinrich Rickert.

Some of the controversy about historicism can be attributed to the one-sidedness of its opponents, especially the neo-Kantians, who shared some of the worst legacies of German **idealism** (**reification** of concepts, the attempt to capture 'essences', and a hubristic exaggeration of theory) as well as to the Prussian state which at that time was responsible for the compartmentalization of scientific **knowledge** and a ruthless use of academic politics.

References and further reading

Antoni, C. ([1949] 1962) *From History to Sociology*. London: Merlin.

Goldman, H. (1988) *Max Weber and Thomas Mann: Calling and the Shaping of the Self*. Berkeley, CA: University of California Press.

Iggers, G. ([1968] 1997) *The German Conception of History*. Vienna: Böhlau.

Kelley, D. (1998) *Faces of History*. New Haven, CT: Yale University Press.

Makkreel, R. (1975) *Dilthey, Philosopher of the Human Sciences*. Princeton, NJ: Princeton University Press.

Meinecke, F. ([1924] 1957) *Machiavellism: The Doctrine of Raison d'État and its Place in Modern History*. Oxford: Oxford University Press.

Popper, K. (1957) *The Poverty of Historicism*. London: Routledge.

Turner, V. (1985) 'Experience and Performance: Towards a New Processual Anthropology', and 'The Anthropology of Experience', in *On the Edge of the Bush*. Tucson, AZ: University of Arizona Press.

Veeser, A. (1989) *The New Historicism*. London: Routledge.

ARPAD SZAKOLCZAI

HOLOCAUST

'The Holocaust' was coined as a name in the early 1960s, probably by Eli Wiesel, to refer to the Nazi genocide of the Jews. The term means 'burnt offering' and was drawn from Jewish theology. Another term commonly used is 'Shoah' which translates as 'catastrophe'. The term the Nazis used to refer to this same event was the 'Final Solution'.

The Holocaust was the series of actions taken by the Nazi regime against Jews between the years 1933 and 1945. These included: the deprivation of political and civil rights for all Jews; forced deportation of Jews; forced concentration of Jews into 'ghettoes'; systematic starvation and demoralization of Jews in ghettoes; rounding up and shooting of Jews behind the German lines; deportation of Jews by cattle train to concentration and death camps; forced labour and starvation of Jews in the camps; mass gassing and burning of Jews in the camps. The mass killing of Jews took place between 1941 and 1945.

Special duty troops of the Nazi Security Service and Security Police, the *Einsatzgruppen*, were assigned to each of the German armies invading the Soviet Union and were given the task of rounding up Jews and killing them through crude and primitive methods of shooting. It is estimated that some two million Jews were murdered in this way. To murder the rest of European Jewry the Nazis built six installations with large-scale gassing and sometimes crematorium facilities: these were Auschwitz, Belzec, Chelmo, Majdanek, Sobibor and Treblinka. The technology used here was barely more sophisticated than the brute violence of the

Einsatzgruppen and it was only when death camps were combined with labour camps (as was the case at Auschwitz and Majdanek) that the architectural relics of 'industrial killing' were left behind. All in all, about 3.5 million Jews were murdered in this way. A further half a million Jews were killed through hunger, disease and exhaustion in the ghettoes and as victims of random terror and reprisal. The Holocaust was not only the mass murder of Jews and the attempt to eliminate Jews from the face of the earth; it was also the attempt to exercise total **domination** over Jews and instil total terror prior their extermination.

The use of the name 'Holocaust' in social theory raises a number of thorny questions. First, the Nazis terrorized and then murdered many other people in addition to the Jews, including Roma, Communists, Polish nationals, homosexuals and the disabled. Sometimes all these different categories were sent to the same camps. Thus the question arises: does the word 'Holocaust' embrace these other victims of Nazi terror? Second, the name 'Holocaust' refers originally to one particular event or series of events in history. It is only by extension that the term can be used to cover other events like, say, the genocide in Rwanda of 1994. Here the question arises: is the Holocaust unique or is it comparable with other forms of genocide and totalitarian terror, such as occurred in Russia under Stalin? Third, the name 'Holocaust' is drawn from theology. This expresses a feeling that it is beyond all human understanding: a mystery, ineffable, and incapable of representation. This raises the further question: is the Holocaust nonetheless understandable in terms of the categories employed by the social sciences, that is, through the normal conventions of historical, political and sociological investigation? A major debate occurred among German historians in the 1980s, known as the Historians' Dispute, about whether the Nazi terror could be compared to that of the Soviet Union and other

totalitarian and fascist regimes (the view taken by Ernst Nolte), or whether the German route to the Holocaust must be seen as unique and specific, as a *Sonderweg* or 'special path' (the view taken by **Habermas**).

References and further reading

Arendt, H. (1979) *The Origins of Totalitarianism.* New York: Harcourt Brace.
Bauman, Z. (1989) *Modernity and the Holocaust.* Cambridge: Polity Press
Browning, C. R. (c2004) *The Origins of the Final Solution: The Evolution of Nazi Jewish Policy, September 1939 – March 1942.* Lincoln, NE: University of Nebraska Press.
Fine, R. (2001) 'Understanding Evil: Arendt and the Final Solution', in M. P. Lara (ed.) *Rethinking Evil: Contemporary Perspectives.* Berkeley, CA: University of California Press.
Gigliotti, S. (2005) *The Holocaust: A Reader.* Oxford: Blackwell.
Gilbert, M. (2004) *The Routledge Atlas of the Holocaust.* London: Routledge.
Horkheimer, M. and Adorno, T. W. and ([1947] 1972) *Dialectic of Enlightenment.* New York: Herder and Herder.
Langerbein, H. (2004) *Hitler's Death Squads: The Logic of Mass Murder.* College Station, TX: Texas A&M University Press.
Stoke, D. (2004) *The Historiography of the Holocaust.* Basingstoke: Palgrave Macmillan.

ROBERT FINE

HOMANS, GEORGE C. (1910–1989)
US theorist

Homans was the founder of behavioral sociology. His treatment of social behavior as **exchange** emerged in reaction to the growing dominance of **functionalism** in American sociology in the 1950s. Homans argued that theory should focus on the sub-institutional level of analysis, specifying the determinants of 'elementary' social behavior that formed the bedrock of **groups** and **organizations**. For Homans this meant a primary emphasis on the **actions** of individuals in direct interaction, and a rejection of the focus of **Parsons** on **institutions** and institutional behavior driven by social prescriptions or normative elements in society.

Homans's most sustained work on social exchange appears in his book, *Social Behavior and Its Elementary Forms* (1961). Here he lays out various propositions of elementary social behavior, based to a large extent on the work of the behavioral psychologist, B. F. Skinner (see **behaviourism**). Influenced by deductive theorizing and **logical positivism**, Homans believed that many important aspects of social behavior could be derived from a small number of simple propositions. He embraced **reductionism**, arguing that the behavior of collectivities could be reduced to principles of elementary behavior.

Homans focused on the social behavior that emerged as a result of mutual reinforcement of two parties involved in a dyadic exchange. His theoretical consideration of distributive justice, balance, **power**, **status**, **authority**, leadership and **solidarity** are all based on an analysis of direct or indirect exchange.

Major works

(1950) *The Human Group*. New York: Harcourt Brace.

(1961) *Social Behavior and Its Elementary Forms*. New York: Harcourt, Brace and World.

(1964) 'Bringing Men Back In', *American Sociological Review*, 19: 809–18.

(1984) *Coming to My Senses: The Autobiography of a Sociologist*. New Brunswick, NJ: Transaction Books.

Further reading

Turner, J. H. (2003) 'Behavioristic Exchange Theory: George C. Homans', in *The Structure of Sociological Theory*. Belmont, CA: Wadsworth Thomson Learning.

KAREN S. COOK
and ALEXANDRA GERBASI

HORKHEIMER, MAX (1895–1973)

German theorist

Director of the Institute for Social Research at Frankfurt after 1930 (see **Frankfurt School**) and close friend of **Adorno**, Horkheimer's conception of **critical theory** began in a sharply **empiricist** mode opposed to *a priori* philosophizing and committed to the post-**metaphysical** project of a materialist rationalism. In some respects in a similar fashion to American **pragmatism**, Horkheimer's original aims were to open up the philosophy of society to the empirical social sciences. In the 1920s he maintained a close intellectual relationship with Otto Neurath, the Viennese positivist philosopher and close associate of Rudolph Carnap of the Vienna Circle. However, in the mid-1930s, after emigration from Nazi Germany to Geneva, Paris, and then the USA, Horkheimer not only substituted the concept of 'critical theory' for **materialism** – fearful of any association with **Marxism** in the American anti-**communist** climate of the 1940s – but also sought to rehabilitate the claims of philosophy against **empiricism**. However, the impetus of his thinking remained anti-metaphysical when he joined with Adorno in Californian exile in composing *The Dialectic of Enlightenment* of 1944/1947, a work that prefigured by Horkheimer's own *The Eclipse of Reason* of 1947. After the war, Horkheimer's thinking turned in the direction of negative theology, expressed in short aphoristic observations of the time aimed at the restorative spirit of Adenauer's Germany.

Major works

(1947) *The Eclipse of Reason*. Oxford: Oxford University Press.

(1972a) *Critical Theory: Selected Essays*. New York: Herder and Herder.

(1972b) with T. W. Adorno, *Dialectic of Enlightenment*. New York: Herder and Herder.

Further reading

Jay, M. (1973) *The Dialectical Imagination: A History of the Frankfurt School and the Institute of Social Research, 1923–1950*. London: Heinemann.

HAUKE BRUNKHORST

HUMANISM

Humanist ideas and beliefs thematize the existence or agency or dignity of human beings as self-interpreting social beings. Roughly speaking, at least five distinct kinds of humanism can be distinguished with a relevance to modern social theory: (1) Renaissance humanism; (2) post-**Enlightenment** liberal humanism; (3) atheistic and anti-clerical humanism; (4) **Marxist** or socialist humanism; and (5) existentialist humanism.

Renaissance humanism describes the world-view of the intellectual elites of the early modern European nations, especially Italy and the Low Countries, founded in idealizing imitation of the manners and mores of the classical Greek and Roman philosophers and statesmen. Sixteenth-century Renaissance humanism enshrines the principle of independent free inquiry and learning by the **individual**, defining man or the human mind as mediator between God and the lower creatures of the earth within a 'great chain of being' (Burckhardt 1995; Lovejoy 1936).

The second wave of humanistic thought and belief that emerged in the later eighteenth century, especially in Germany, celebrated values of individual self-cultivation or **education** or *Bildung*, based on the Greek idea of *paideia* (Jaeger 1945). It is associated with poets such as Goethe and Schiller, and especially with Schiller's conception of the 'many-sided personality' in the *Letters on the Aesthetic Education of Man*. These ideas exerted a wide-ranging influence on later nineteenth-century social thinkers, including **Marx**, **Weber** and **Simmel** and twentieth century philosophers such as Ernst Cassirer. They mark the beginning of the movement of **historicism** as the informing ethos of the 'human sciences', thematizing **cosmopolitan** understanding of other cultures and past ages. In a more sociological sense, nineteenth-century humanism can be seen as a certain kind of **ideology** held by the members of the educated middle classes (then known in Germany as the *Bildungsbürgertum*), as holders of property with interests in the maintenance of a pluralistic **civil society**. In its close association with political **liberalism**, humanism is also linked to the cause of the **emancipation** of the Jews in nineteenth-century society, and more generally with the establishment of civil rights and universal human **rights**.

Atheistic and anti-clerical humanism arises out of the more militantly anti-authoritarian aspects of the eighteenth-century Enlightenment, especially in France. It explicitly repudiates religious faith in favour of a secular vision of human beings as autonomous rational agents capable of defining moral norms without need for appeal to a deity. Humanism, in this sense, considers both religious belief and the institutional power of the **church** to be remnants of a primitive or backward stage in the evolution of the human species, which has definitively been superseded by the authority of positive science, especially as exemplified by the Darwinian account of the descent of man from apes. It can be associated with Auguste **Comte**'s **positivism** and with English **utilitarian** thought from Bentham to J. S. **Mill** and Herbert **Spencer**. In early twentieth-century sociological thought, its clearest advocate is **Durkheim**, involving a call for secular education founded in **civil religion** or **civic education**.

Marxist or socialist humanism grows out of Ludwig Feuerbach's thesis of the 'species-being' of humanity which learns to recognize itself as the creator of God, not as the creature of God. Marx's materialist transformation of this idea from German idealist philosophy – especially from **Hegel**'s philosophy – is expressed in his vision of work as the medium of the self-**production** of human beings through **praxis and practices**, which is at once the cause of human **alienation** and the precondition for its overcoming. Many twentieth-century intellectuals combine this vision with ideas drawn from **phenomenological** and existentialist philosophy, and from American **pragmatist** thought, from **Freudian psychoanalysis** and from **Nietzsche**'s diagnosis of religion as a 'necessary illusion' that comes to be troubled by the 'death of God'. Representatives of this synthesis of Marxist and existentialist humanism include Georg **Lukács**, Alexandre Kojève, and famously Jean-Paul **Sartre** (1948).

Critiques of humanist thought and belief have several distinct yet interconnecting strands. Neo-religious critiques question the presumption of making man 'the measure of all things' or of making a god out of man. These can be associated with the anti-secularist polemics of figures such as Kierkegaard, Tolstoy and Dostoyevsky and neo-orthodox modernist theologians such as Karl Barth. Such critiques also find their way into some of the more sophisticated versions of existentialist humanism, notably that of Martin **Heidegger**, which thematize an idea of the radical finitude, transience or 'throwness' of man in the face of death, without accepting the postulate of a deity. Some forms of contemporary environmentalist philosophy import elements of this thinking into the critique of technological civilization and exploitative attitudes to **nature** (Jonas 1984) (see **ecology and environmentalism**). Anti-Eurocentric critiques of liberal humanism are prominent in debates in the arts and humanities about ethical and aesthetic value, especially in relation to forms of European intellectual universalism, accused of ignoring its own **ethnocentrism** in relation to other cultures. Closely allied to this have been feminist critiques of the androcentric linguistic bias of the words 'man' and 'human' (even when some languages, such as German, distinguish between *Mann* and *Mensch*) (Irigaray 1985). **Postmodernist** critiques draw on the '**deconstructive**' and '**poststructuralist**' arguments of Jacques **Derrida** and Michel **Foucault** about the illusions of expressive, unitary, meaning-giving

human **agency**. In the 1960s Foucault spoke explicitly of the 'end of man' and of the 'anthropological slumber' of modern philosophy. Some of this thinking is paralleled today in a questioning of **ontological binary** differences between 'man and machine' in the field of neurological science. It also appears in a more speculative vein in the conception of '**cyborgs**' or techno-human hybrids, defined by the feminist theorist Donna **Haraway** (1991).

References and further reading

Burckhardt, J. ([1860] 1995) *The Civilization of the Renaissance in Italy*. London: Phaidon.

Foucault, M. (1970) *The Order of Things*. London: Tavistock.

Haraway, D. (1991) *Simians, Cyborgs and Women*. London: Free Association Books.

Irigaray, L. (1985) *This Sex Which Is Not One*. Ithaca, NY: Cornell University Press.

Jaeger, W. (1945) *Paideia: The Ideals of Greek Culture*. Oxford: Oxford University Press.

Janicaud, D. (2005) *On the Human Condition*. London: Routledge.

Jonas, H. (1984) *The Imperative of Responsibility*. Chicago: University of Chicago Press.

Lovejoy, A. (1936) *The Great Chain of Being*. Cambridge, MA: Harvard University Press.

Sartre, J.-P. (1948) *Existentialism and Humanism*. London: Methuen.

AUSTIN HARRINGTON

HYBRIDITY

Hybridity has become a key concept in contemporary cultural criticism. It has been deeply inscribed in colonial ideologies maintaining white supremacy and prominently used in scientific debates on **race and racism** in the nineteenth century (Young 1995). However, the use of the term hybridity has undergone a transformation particularly in the ongoing debates of **post-colonial theory** in the late twentieth century. The term is currently characterized by its subversive capacity to put into question essentializing (see **essentialism**) assumptions of cultural categories such as the notions of **gender**, race, **class** or conceptions of **identity** and **representation**. The contours of a theory of hybridity are strongly influenced by the works of Homi K. Bhabha (1994), Edward W. **Said** (1979), Stuart Hall (1996) and Gayatri C. **Spivak**.

The rejection of a stable cultural identity, signified by essential distinctions such as the binary opposition between 'us' and 'them', is considered to be one of the crucial features of conceptual debates on hybridity. In contrast, hybrid identities are thought to emerge within an unstable and precarious process of **identity** formation in the unmarked space between these distinctions. They are regarded as the result of a cross-cultural encounter, the merging of different **traditions**, **discourses** and **technologies** and of techniques such as **bricolage**, i.e. the fusing and mixing of cultural objects. In challenging the taken-for-granteds of homogenous cultural formations the concept can further be understood as a fundamental epistemological critique of the notion of pure and bounded national identities (see **nationalism**).

The concept of hybridity has also been applied to other theoretical frames, notably **actor-network theory** (**Latour** 1993) with its denial of a clear-cut distinction between 'natural' and 'social', or the merging of human and nonhuman entities in feminist theoretical accounts (see **Haraway**). Therefore, along with post-colonial theoretical approaches, debates on hybridity open up space for the recovery of a critical and multi-disciplinary cultural self-reflexivity.

References and further reading

Bhabha, H. (1994) *The Location of Culture*. London: Routledge.

Hall, S. (1996) 'When Was the Postcolonial? Thinking at the Limit', in I. Chambers and L. Curti (eds) *The Postcolonial Question: Common Skies, Divided Horizons*. London: Routledge.

Haraway, D. (1991) *Simians, Cyborgs and Women*. London: Free Association Books.

Latour, B. (1993) *We Have Never Been Modern*. London: Harvester Wheatsheaf.

Papastergiadis, N. (2000) *The Turbulence of Migration: Globalization, Deterritorialization and Hybridity*. Cambridge: Polity.

Said, E. W. (1979) *Orientalism*. New York: Vintage.

Werbner, P. and Modood, T. (eds) (1997) *Debating Cultural Hybridity: Multi-Cultural Identities and the Politics of Anti-Racism*. London: Zed Books.

Young, R. J. C. (1995) *Colonial Desire: Hybridity in Theory, Culture and Race*. London: Routledge.

IL-TSCHUNG LIM

I

IDEAL TYPE

The concept of the 'ideal type' was originally introduced by Max **Weber** in the early twentieth century (Weber [1904] 2003). In his program of social-science explanation, analytical concepts were to emulate typified, 'pure' (idealized) schemes which in turn serve to explain empirical social phenomena. In this endeavour, he stressed the researcher's **knowledge** interest as all-important since it led to the focus on an 'historical individual', on a paradigmatic case that epitomized the subject matter of inquiry. Weber illustrated this in his *The Protestant Ethic and the Spirit of Capitalism* where the 'spirit of **capitalism**' was exemplified through commentary on passages from Benjamin Franklin (see **Protestant ethic**). Weber referred both to the 'historical individual' and equally to ideal types to find sociological explanations that accounted for historical social facts. He recommended ideal types as methodological devices. Through the construction of ideal types as conceptual schemes, frames of reference were to be formed. They, in turn, helped structure the analysis of the social world. Indeed, frames of reference composed of one or more ideal types were what made social inquiry scientific. If sociological knowledge was to be 'objective', Weber argued, sociologists must never think that their approach could grasp reality in the same manner in which natural scientists treat their subject matter. In his chapters on the sociology of **religion, law**,

and **domination** in *Economy and Society*, Weber juxtaposed two or more ideal types in his historical reconstructions, showing how empirical explanations could convincingly constitute substantive theory (see also **type and typification**).

In the decades that followed Weber's untimely death in 1920, ideal-type **methodology** was recognized in three different settings. In all three, however, ideal types were not used in a strictly Weberian way. The three uses most prominent between the 1920s and 1940s were those of Alfred **Schutz**, Talcott **Parsons** and Theodore Abel. Schutz (1967) extended Weber's idea from methodology to the social world, as he made ideal types the centre-piece of his explanatory construction of **meaning** in **everyday** life, though separate from the taken-for-granted world when it also used ideal types, but also of social theory. Parsons (1937) partly abandoned Weber's idea of ideal type, replacing it with the methodological principle of Alfred Whitehead that empirical knowledge avoids the 'fallacy of misplaced concreteness' – a principle which in fact was fully compatible with Weberian concept formation and also allowed Parsons to introduce a two-pronged 'action frame of reference'. On the one hand, Parsons considered that an analytical level of sociological thought must be separated from an empirical level of society, and, on the other, that the action systems structure comprised both **anomie** and **integration**. This juxtaposition in fact owed more to Weber's ideal-type conception of sociology than Parsons seems to have realized. Theodore Abel (1948) disavowed the tradition of Weberian thought altogether insofar as he claimed that **Verstehen** – whether or not based on ideal types – was no different from any other sociological explanation. This view came to prevail throughout the 1950s. As survey research became the main genre of sociological investigation, social theory tended to rely on explanation using elementary conceptual models taken for replica of social systems. Misconceptions regarding Weber's methodology were not challenged until the 1960s.

On the occasion of a conference in Germany devoted to the centenary of Weber's birth, in 1964, Weber's conception of 'objectivity' in its relation to evaluation became a hot topic (Parsons 1965). In the following decade, the Weberian accomplishments eventually were rediscovered (Bendix and Roth 1971). In the 1990s, Weber's idea of ideal types made yet another comeback, this time as a method for empirical research. Ideal-type methodology became an approach in qualitative analysis, due to the fact that it could handle interview data on a systematic case-comparison basis (Gerhardt 1994).

In recent years it has become clear that Weberian ideal-type methodology has a philosophical background of its own, dating back beyond the origin of its apparent rival, so-called quantitative methodology. Here it is evident that ideal-type thinking relates to the beginnings of anti-**positivist** thought in modern sociology – a beginning that Weber was fully aware of and a line of thought which he took into account as he established ideal-type methodology (Gerhardt 2001). It was against this background that the relationships between the cultural sciences in the late nineteenth century, particularly Wilhelm **Dilthey**'s philosophy of the cultural sciences, and the early sociology of Georg **Simmel** became a noteworthy theme.

References and further reading

Abel, T. (1948) 'The Operation called Verstehen', *American Journal of Sociology*, 54: 211–18.

Bendix, R. and Roth, G. (1971) *Scholarship and Partisanship: Essays on Max Weber*. Berkeley, CA: University of California Press.

Bruun, H. H. (2005) *Science, Values and Politics in Max Weber's Methodology*, 2nd edn. Copenhagen: Munskgaard.

Gerhardt, U. (1994) 'The Use of Weberian Ideal-Type Methodology in Qualitative Data Interpretation: An Outline for Ideal-Type Analysis', BMS *Bulletin de Méthodologie Sociologique* (ISA Research Committee 33), 45: 74–126.

Gerhardt, U. (2001) *Idealtypus: Zur methodologischen Begründung der modernen Soziologie*. Frankfurt am Main: Suhrkamp.

Parsons, T. (1937) *The Structure of Social Action*. New York: McGraw Hill.

Parsons, T. (1965) 'Evaluation and Objectivity in Social Science: An Interpretation of Max Weber's Contribution', *International Social Science Journal*, 17: 46–63.

Schutz, A. ([1932] 1967) *The Phenomenology of the Social World*. Evanston, IL: Northwestern University Press.

Weber, M. ([1904] 2003) 'The "Objectivity" of Knowledge in Social Science and Social Policy', in S. Whimster (ed.) *The Essential Weber*. London: Routledge

UTA GERHARDT

IDEALISM

Although the history of philosophy has generated an equivocal concept of idealism – referring both to Plato's notion of **metaphysical** subsistent forms and to the modern philosophy of consciousness – all connotations share a rejection of **materialism**, the thesis that meaning is a product of **nature**.

The term first emerges in Plato's philosophy, in which his contention that there are non-relative truths – absolute justice, absolute goodness – is supported by a theory of 'forms' or 'ideas'. Plato's dialogues attempt to demonstrate the necessity of these 'ideas' to our most basic assertions about the world, arguing that the very concept of relations implies a fixed standard (e.g. A is more beautiful than B makes sense only against an assumed standard of beauty), and that each general concept implies a perfection not actually to be experienced in the material world (e.g. no triangle is perfect). (Aristotle criticized Plato for thereby proliferating the range of 'ideas', thus leading to a virtual mirror world of perfect exemplars.) In Plato's application of this thesis to the question of society – in the book, *The Republic* – a theory of justice that transcends convention is proposed, namely the 'idea' of 'the Good'. It is no doubt from Plato's position that the everyday sense of idealism – as implying an unrealistic concern for perfection – is derived. Plato's **metaphysical** idealism exerted an enormous influence on early medieval philosophy, in which Christian theology united with the theory of forms to provide a theory of being in which the material world is understood as an 'emanation' from a divine perfect idea.

However, in the modern period, beginning with Descartes, idealism acquired a quite different, and almost entirely opposite meaning. The essence of modern idealism is that, since 'ideas' are the necessary mediating point between mind and independent world, we can assert that our experience of the world is fundamentally 'ideal', i.e. composed of ideas. This claim was produced as a reaction against materialist epistemology which seemed to be subject to the unsustainable claim that independent material objects are directly known to us as non-material ideas. Why should we believe in any direct correlation between the two? Immanuel Kant and his immediate followers emphasized the closely related idea that experience was ultimately representational (see **Kantianism and Neo-Kantianism**).

The concept of idealism gained significance for social theory during the period of German idealism. The pertinent claim is that since experience is a matter for consciousness, it follows that the world as we experience it is not a given; that is, it is constituted in accordance with consciousness. G. W. F.

Hegel explains the notion of consciousness as 'the attitude of thought towards objectivity'. For Hegel, consciousness provides the criterion of objectivity. That is, what we take as objectivity – what we judge things to be – is determined by our criterion of **objectivity**. (For this reason it is possible to speak of different consciousnesses which determine in different ways what the world is, either for that person or for a **culture** with which a person identifies.) Now if it can be shown that consciousness is itself malleable – that it can be transformed – then reality can be transformed by changes of consciousness. Idealism in this form was therefore directly in opposition to the naturalistic theories of society which claimed that some preferred concept of society or other was the inevitable manifestation of certain features of unalterable human nature: society in that preferred form was therefore allegedly natural. It is significant that the philosophers of this period – Fichte, Schelling, Schiller, Hegel – commonly understood the task of political liberation as an adjustment of the consciousness through which social relations are construed (see **emancipation**). Hence the notions of idealism and modernism – the rise of individual consciousness, the rejection of **naturalism** – are closely connected. An additional element of German idealism is the Spinoza-inspired holistic dimension, which holds that meaning is intelligible only within systems of belief (which sometimes appear to transcend individual agency) (see **Hegelianism and neo-Hegelianism**).

The metaphysical dimensions of German idealism, problematical for the more positivist climate of the nineteenth and twentieth centuries, led to widespread rejection of the very notion of idealism. However, what remains obscured are the residual idealist elements even in social theories which, like that of **Marx**, defined themselves as overcoming idealism through historical **materialism**. For instance, the notion of false consciousness or **ideology** – in so far as it is committed to the idea that reality is in some way correlative with the ways in which consciousness apprehends it – is an idealist thesis. In contemporary **epistemology** the term 'idealism' continues largely to be avoided – no doubt because of its traditional associations with metaphysics and scepticism – yet 'conceptualism', which might be traced back to Kantian and Hegelian forms of philosophy is a respected position, as too are the theses of linguistic **pragmatism** that meaning arises through human **practices** and that **language** is constitutive of the possibilities of our experience.

References and further reading

Boucher, D. (ed.) (1997) *The British Idealists*. Cambridge: Cambridge University Press.

Grube, G. M. A. (1935) *Plato's Thought*. London: Methuen.

Hegel, G. W. F. ([1807] 1975) *Phenomenology of Spirit*. Oxford: Oxford University Press.

McDowell, J. (1996) *Mind and World*. Cambridge, MA: Harvard University Press.

Rescher, N. (1973) *Conceptual Idealism*. Oxford: Blackwell.

Schelling, F. W. J. ([1800] 1978) *System of Transcedental Idealism*. Charlottesville: University of Virginia Press.

Taylor, C. (1975) *Hegel*. Cambridge: Cambridge University Press.

Vesey, G. (ed.) (1982) *Idealism, Past and Present*. Cambridge: Cambridge University Press.

BRIAN O'CONNOR

IDENTITY

'Identity' is one of the most fundamental of all social theoretical concepts. In its most general meaning, it refers to the marking by humans of similarities and differences between things of all kinds and their use to classify, and impart meaning to, the world. Within social theory, the notion of identity is shorthand for humans believing they know who they themselves are, and who others are, in a manner that because it is encoded in **language** and a range of non-verbal symbolic registers is infinitely more elaborate than the affiliational and oppositional repertoires of other higher primates. Without this complex capacity to know and name self and others, the human world, as we know it, would be an impossible creation.

Identity is also consequential. There is no highway or byway of the human world that is not organized, to a greater or lesser extent, in terms of identification and **classification**. In any situation, how people identify themselves and others, and how others identify them, create a vista of advantages and disadvantages, permissions and denials, opportunities and costs, and rewards and penalties. While it may not *determine* what human individuals do, identification is a major dimension of the interplay between habit, **emotion** and **rationality** that characterize human **practice**.

Philosophers have discussed the ins and outs of identity for millennia. Social theoretical discourse about aspects of identity is as old as social theory itself: **Marx** talked about humans making themselves and **class** formation, **Freud** groped towards an understanding of the foundations of personal identity in early childhood, **Durkheim** problematized the **division of labour**, **Weber** theorized class and **status** and laid the foundations of the study of **ethnicity**, while **Simmel** thought that the relationship between similarity and difference was the key to understanding human cultural history. These were not, however, explicit theorizations of identity in general. For that we have to wait for George Herbert **Mead**. Coming out of American **pragmatism**, with an intellectual genealogy including C. S. Peirce, William James and Charles Horton Cooley, the papers that Mead published during his lifetime, and the lectures that appeared posthumously as *Mind, Self and Society* (1934), laid the foundations for **symbolic interactionism**. More specifically, they outlined a social theory of identity and identification that arguably remains the bedrock of most contemporary understandings of the topic.

The key to this perspective is that although Mead is clear that the predisposition to identification is part of human nature, identity is not a stand-alone individual property. Rather, identity emerges out of the interaction between **self** and others, both actual individual others and a 'generalized other' that is the internalized voice of collective **knowledge** and values learned during **socialization**. Rooted in a sociology of mind that insists that we cannot know ourselves without knowing others – and without first knowing others – Mead distinguishes the 'I', the ongoing unreflective agency of individual human beings, from the 'me', the sense of personal identity that is the individual's reflexive response to others. Combined, the 'I', the 'me' and the 'generalized other' add up to selfhood: embodied individual identification, framed and constructed within the symbolic riches of language and only possible within an **intersubjective** human world.

Scepticism about Mead's tripartite 'committee' model of self-identification is necessary. The basic scheme remains robust, however. Identity emerges out of the, effectively simultaneous, interactions between how we see ourselves, how we see others, and how they see us. Identity is not fixed or 'given'. Identity is definitively an ongoing process of identification (which is arguably a better generic theoretical term). Identification, mind and selfhood are all embodied. Finally, identification is rooted in symbolization, particularly in language.

Loud echoes of Marx and Freud can be heard in Mead. His own work has echoed influentially down the subsequent decades: in the sociological interactionism of Erving **Goffman** (1959), in the transactional social anthropology of Fredrik Barth (1969), and, although it is rarely acknowledged, in the social psychology of identity inspired by Henri Tajfel (Robinson 1996).

The most systematic recent development of the basic interactionist model conceives of identification as a **dialectic** between internal self-identification and the external categorization done by others (Jenkins 2004). Embodiment and early socialization are emphasized: although the negotiated, open character of identification is recognized, identities such as **gender**, entered into early in life or defined with reference to the **body**, are likely to be robust and resistant to change. Nor is the interactional playing field level: whose identification of self and others will count and the consequences of identification are emergent products of **power** and **authority** relations. In its most radical departure, this version of the interactionist model proposes that one basic theoretical scheme – the internal-external dialectic of identification – can be used to understand both individual and collective identification.

From the 1980s onwards, another discourse about identity began to appear in the public social theory domain. Eschewing the interactionist interest in generic human process at the micro level, this approach drew on an enormous diversity of theory, from **post-structuralism** to **psychoanalysis** to **feminist theory** to subaltern studies to **social constructionism**. From this coalesced a comprehensive vision of identity and its role in human affairs under the sign of **postmodernity**. With roots in the despair of the Left, it was an attempt to theorize a radical new understanding of a human world in which the old certainties of **class** no longer seemed to hold and new possibilities for progressive 'identity politics' based on diversity of lifestyle, individual as well as collective, needed to be nurtured. Acknowledging that doing so homogenizes a wide range of opinion within a loose coalition of minimally shared positions, this approach can be summarized as the 'cultural model of identity' (Hall and du Gay 1996; Lash and Friedman 1992). It is characterized by several core themes. First, modernity seguing into postmodernity – or 'high modernity' or 'late modernity' – is distinguished from earlier eras as the great age of multiple identities, an open terrain of diversity and flux. People are no longer doomed to the identities into which they are born, and there is a wide array of identity choices, or at least options, available to them (Giddens 1991). This is emancipatory, at least in principle, although **conflict** over identity claims is likely. At its most extreme, generic human attributes such as consciously reflexive self-identification are claimed as definitively of the era (**Giddens** 1991). Second, the assumption that existence is fundamentally the realization, assertion and cultivation of identities has created an overarching theoretical framework within which all human life – from selfhood to shopping to sex to intergroup conflict to cyberspace – can be interpreted. Third, **globalization** has increasingly provided the historicist meta-narrative within which this cultural model of (post)modern identification is anchored. Once again at its most extreme, commentators write about the decline of the state and the opening up of a world 'beyond societies', in which everything is mobile (Urry 2000).

The cultural model can be criticized on several grounds. Apart from a strong tendency to overstatement and to inadequate grounding in evidence generated by more systematic inquiry, it has in large part merely re-invented the wheel, generally without acknowledging the source. To recognize that identification is, in principle, flexible, negotiable and open is to do little more than restate one of the fundamentals of the interactionist model. The concerns of the interactionist and cultural models of identity may be converging in recent critical discussions of the consequences of identity. Contemporary research needs to focus on the questions of when identity matters, how, to what extent, and why (Brubaker and Cooper 2000). Although these are essentially empirical issues, they require a theoretical framework within which to be addressed.

References and further reading

Barth, F. (ed.) (1969) *Ethnic Groups and Boundaries*. Oslo: Universitetsforlaget.
Brubaker, R. and Cooper, F. (2000) 'Beyond Identity', *Theory and Society*, 29: 1–47.
Giddens, A. (1991) *Modernity and Self-Identity*. Cambridge: Polity.
Goffman, E. (1959) *The Presentation of Self in Everyday Life*. New York: Anchor.
Hall, S. and du Gay, P. (eds) (1996) *Questions of Cultural Identity*. London: Sage.
Jenkins, R. (2004) *Social Identity*, 2nd edn. London: Routledge.
Lash, S. and Friedman, J. (eds) (1992) *Modernity and Identity*. Oxford: Blackwell.
Mead, G. H. (1934) *Mind, Self and Society from the Standpoint of a Social Behaviorist*. Chicago: University of Chicago Press.
Robinson, W. P. (ed.) (1996) *Social Groups and Identities*. Oxford: Butterworth-Heinemann.
Urry, J. (2000) *Sociology Beyond Societies*. London: Routledge.

RICHARD JENKINS

IDEOLOGY

The notion of 'ideology' questions the complex relations between ideas and (social) reality. The forms in which these relations are articulated range from mere epistemological problems of true and false representations of reality to sociological questions about the connections of forms of thought and political power. All hitherto history of 'ideology' is the history of struggles for its definition, a struggle of various theoretical inscriptions trying to substitute one another.

Although the notion of ideology is usually associated with **Marx** and the Marxist tradition, its actual origin lies in the thought of the French philosopher and economist Destutt de Tracy, who introduced it for the first time in a lecture in 1796 at the *Institut Nationale* in Paris. De Tracy, who became the leading theorist of the school of *Idéologistes*, used the term 'ideology' according to the Greek etymology of the word as a science of (Greek-*ologie*) human ideas (Greek *idea/eidos*), their genesis, impartation, combination and their socio-political relevance. De Tracy's fundamental idea was that all human ideas and every abstract notion of the world have their origin in elementary sensual perceptions which he comprehended as true sources of all further intellectual activity. De Tracy aimed to orientate his conception of ideology towards a mathematical model of methodical rigor and exactitude. Thus, ideology was founded as rationalist project targeting the tradition of what de Tracy called 'métaphysique nébuleuse' which he criticized as an ensemble of abstract speculation on man and the world. Ideology started its career as an affirmative concept and can even be considered as the climax of French **Enlightenment**. Only later did it receive its negative, even pejorative connotation. The inversion is connected with the name of Napoleon who criticized the *Idéologistes* out of a genuinely political interest. Napoleon's critique originated out of the fact that the *Idéologistes* did not limit their enquiries to epistemological problems but expanded their rationalist project by questioning all theological mystifications and metaphysical irrationality in the constitution of social and political life. Therein, Napoleon perceived a threat to every form of statist **authority** and **power**, above all to his own as emperor of France. All of a sudden the *Idéologistes* were now themselves accused of being blind metaphysicians and political idealists who failed to take into account that every society is based on a necessary theological and non-rationalist **imaginary** core. Against their 'diffuse metaphysics', Napoleon appealed to the 'knowledge of the human heart and the lessons of history', claiming to speak as a political pragmatist.

When Marx and Engels wrote about ideology for the first time comprehensively in their co-authored work *The German Ideology* (1845/6), they perpetuated the negative usage of the term, albeit it was situated in a modified context and served a different purpose. Their declared adversaries were no longer the French *Idéologistes* but

German speculative philosophy, especially the idealism of the Young **Hegelians**. Their idealistic outlook was based on the presupposition that the structure of human society and history is determined by abstract ideas. Every change in the structure of a given society is explained by a change of ideas. According to idealistic philosophy, it is consciousness that structures and dominates being, including the material relationships between individuals and social **classes**. In the view of Marx and Engels, this idealistic outlook of history is grounded on a complete inversion of the real relationship between being and consciousness, material activity and thinking (to describe this inversion Marx and Engels evoked the metaphor of a *camera obscura*). Ideology is the name for this inversion. For Marx and Engels, the only way to escape the ideological representation of real material history consists in revealing the real conditions which regulate human society: material production of the means of subsistence through living individuals conditioned by historical circumstances, i.e. the **division of labour** which gives rise to social contradictions between different – dominant and dominated – classes. Thus, conscious ideas on the material world are theorized, on the one hand, as mere echoes and reflections but, on the other, also as serving a specific function in social conditions which are structured by an antagonism between social classes. 'The ideas of the ruling class are in every epoch the ruling ideas, i.e. the class which is the ruling material force of society, is at the same time its ruling intellectual force' (Marx and Engels 1845–46: 59). By transposing the particular **interests** of a **dominant** social **class** onto the level of general validity for society as a whole, by creating it as an imaginary reconciled **totality**, the ideological 'ruling intellectual force' reproduces the given power structures.

The German Ideology marked the first attempt to elaborate a materialist concept of ideology: it was an attempt not without

265

ambiguities, which is followed by further enquiries that are not always consistent with its initial formulations. Moreover, Marx's succeeding analyses were themselves elliptic and far from unequivocal. A good example of this ambiguity is the *Preface to A Contribution to the Critique of Political Economy* ([1859] 1987). Here Marx tried to clarify the concept of ideology by inscribing it into the relation of two new terms: *base* and *superstructure*. The 'base' refers to the economic structure of society, constituted by the totality of relations of **production** which corresponds to a specific stage of development of material productive forces. On this real foundation arises a political and legal 'superstructure' and corresponding definite social forms of consciousness. Every time the productive forces come into conflict with the relations of production, an epoch of social revolution arises. Whereas radical change can be stated scientifically, in the legal, political, religious, artistic or philosophical, in short, ideological forms, 'men become conscious of this conflict and fight it out' (Marx 1857/58: 263).

How exactly to conceive the relations between base, superstructure and ideology has always been a controversial question within the succeeding Marxist discourses. Answers vary from the economically determinist in which the ideological spheres are understood as mere reflections of the economic base to Engels's remarks about 'interaction' between these spheres. Particularly prominent has been **Gramsci**'s conception of organic ideologies which produce the social cohesion of every social formation, as well as Lenin's conception of ideology as political expression of different class interests arising from economic conflicts.

Another strand has focused strongly on Marx's mature analyses of capitalist society in *Capital*, especially on the notion of *commodity fetishism*. In capitalist society, people as private producers fabricate things and exchange them on the market. The exchange value of things is grounded in the social character of human labour. **Commodity**

exchange is therefore a product of definite social relations between people. But 'since the producers do not come into social contact with each other until they exchange their products, the specific social character of each producer's **labour** does not show itself except in the act of exchange' (Marx [1867] 1996: 81–93). In the act of exchange it appears as if the commodities have a life of their own and that all social relations between people seem to be material relations, social relations between things (see **reification**).

Georg **Lukács** clung to this argument in his *History and Class Consciousness* (1923). According to Lukács, capitalist society appears to the bourgeoisie as a natural phenomenon governed by 'eternal' laws of nature accepted as unchangeable (later the **Frankfurt School** will conceive the misrecognition of relations between people as natural, reified relations of things as *the* ideological mechanism *par excellence*, which is at work in all forms of positivist thought). Ideology is here understood as 'false consciousness', i.e. the inability of the bourgeoisie to grasp capitalist society in its **totality**, as a historical product of human **praxis** that can again be transformed through practical-revolutionary activity. For Lukács, only the **proletariat**, the subject-object of history, is able to gain insight – via historical **materialism** – into the totality of social relations and processes, which also means that only the proletariat is enabled to become the agent of revolutionary transformation of capitalist society as a whole.

Lukács's work can be regarded as the climax of a Marxist tradition considering ideology as a question of (false) consciousness. Against this tradition another important Marxist attempt to reconsider ideology in the twentieth century is to be found in the work of Louis **Althusser**, who insisted that ideology is not a problem of consciousness but rather of unconsciousness. Ideology is understood as a process of subjecting individuals to a given social structure by allocating them a fixed position in that structure. Althusser's conception crystallizes around three moments: (1) ideology has no history. It is a transhistorical invariant detectable in every social formation; (2) ideology represents the imaginary relations of individuals to their real conditions of existence and has itself a material existence (in ideological state apparatuses such as schools, **family**, etc.); and (3) ideology 'interpellates' individuals as 'subjects'. After Althusser, the imaginary dimension of ideology was further developed in the work of Ernest Laclau and Slavoj **Žižek**, who related it to the psychoanalytic discourse of Jacques **Lacan**. According to this position, ideology attempts to present society as a stable reality sustained by the phantasm of its imaginary fullness. What ideology therefore forecloses is the Real of the non-symbolizable antagonism of classes which prevents the closure of every social formation, making it non-whole.

Besides these Marxist discourses on ideology, a non-Marxist line of theorizing ideology also emerged in the first half of the twentieth century (A. Seidel, M. Scheler, K. **Mannheim**). One of its main objectives consisted in the depoliticization and deradicalization of the concept of ideology by reformulating it in terms of a neutral, value-free typology of different world outlooks. Mannheim spoke of a 'total conception' of ideology according to which all social knowledge is determined by the social structure. Every class or group has, in accordance with its place in the social structure, a specific perspective on the (social) world. Because he feared that the term ideology could not be evacuated of denunciatory connotations, Mannheim argued that the study of general social perspectivism finds its very first scientific realization in his own 'sociology of knowledge' (Mannheim 1929) (see **knowledge and knowledge society**).

References and further reading

Althusser, L. ([1969–70] 2001) 'Ideology and Ideological State Apparatuses', in *Lenin and Philosophy and Other Essays*. New York: Monthly Review Press.
Balibar, E. (1995) *The Philosophy of Marx*. London: Verso, pp. 42–79.
Eagleton, T. (ed.) (1994) *Ideology*. London: Longman.
Larrain, J. (1979) *The Concept of Ideology*. London: Hutchinson.
Lukács, G. ([1923] 1971) *History and Class Consciousness*, Cambridge, MA: MIT Press.
Mannheim, K. ([1929] 1952) *Ideology and Utopia*. New York: Routledge & Kegan Paul.
Marx, K. and Engels, F. ([1845–46] 1976) *The German Ideology* (*Collected Works*, vol. 5). New York: International Publishers.
Marx, K. and Engels, F. ([1859] 1987) *Preface to A Contribution to the Critique of Political Economy* (*Collected Works*, vol. 29). New York: International Publishers, pp. 261–6.
Marx, K. and Engels, F. ([1867] 1996) *Capital*, vol. 1 (*Collected Works*, vol. 35). New York: International Publishers.
Žižek, S. (ed.)(1994) *Mapping Ideology*. London: Verso.

LARS BULLMANN
and FRANK RUDA

IMAGINARY

The term 'imaginary' in social theory has its origins mainly in the work of Jacques **Lacan** and Cornelius **Castoriadis**. In a famous essay originally published in 1949, 'The Mirror Stage as Formative of the I', Lacan argued that the subject is shaped by an 'imago', an image, which is a product of **language**. As a result, **subjectivity** is constructed by language: words uttered by the subject have the same reality as the image in the mirror. The 'imago' allows a subject to be formed. The basic form of this process occurs when a child is confronted with a mirror image, which it mistakes for real. Language, Lacan, argues, has a similar function to the mirror, namely one of 'misrecognition'. The imaginary is the psychological mechanism that converts symbolic images into linguistic realities. Lacan's notion of the imaginary can be contrasted with **Althusser**'s Marxist use of the term. For Althusser, the imaginary stands in contrast to real relations and is sustained only as an ideological distortion.

Castoriadis's use of the term is closer to that of the 'imagination'. Where Lacan was concerned with language and the formation of the subject, Castoriadis's focus is on how societies symbolically constitute themselves. Further, the issue for Castoriadis is not misrecognition but creativity. According to him, all societies possess an imaginary dimension, since they must answer certain symbolic questions as to their basic **identity**, their goals and limits. **Modernity** has come to rest on two kinds of imaginary significations, the imaginary of rational and technical control and the radical imaginary of **autonomy**.

A related, but quite different and more sociological sense of the term imagination/imaginary is Benedict Anderson's (1983) notion of 'imagined communities'. Anderson's use of the term refers more specifically to the way social **institutions** and collective identities are invented (as **tradition**).

References and further reading

Althusser, L. (1984) 'Ideology and Ideological State Apparatuses', *Essays on Ideology*. London: Verso.

Anderson, B. (1983) *Imaginary Communities: Reflections on the Origin and Spread of Nationalism*. London: Verso.

Castoriadis, C. ([1970] 1987) *The Imaginary Institution of Society*. Cambridge: Polity.

Lacan, J. ([1949] 1977) 'The Mirror Stage as Formative of the I', in *Écrits: A Selection*. London: Tavistock.

GERARD DELANTY

IMPERIALISM

The concept of imperialism means the rule and administration of an empire which is considerably larger than a regular **nation–state**. A type of foreign politics is also called imperialistic when it is carried out in an aggressive manner, taking advantage of a strong position in terms of military (see **war and militarism**), economic and financial resources and even a more subtle form of oppression by cultural dominance.

Any kind of dominance, whether based on political, military, economical or even **cultural** grounds, can be called imperialism if it is seen as oppression by those who are subject to it, at least in a polemical sense. A narrower and more historically scientific meaning of imperialism denotes the period between 1880 and 1918 and the contest of the European powers in establishing colonies and settlements in order to secure trade and flow of resources. J.A. Hobson's (1938) theory of imperialism initiated the widespread use of the term that is related to that period, together with Lenin's theory. The practice of imperial foreign policy was continued in the twentieth century by the USA and the USSR over their more or less formally connected satellite states.

Today there are attempts within social and political sciences to establish imperialism as a term for analysing two connected aspects: an interior aspect, concerning how imperial policy affects the internal life of a state practising it and an exterior aspect, concerning the effect of imperial policy on the international system.

On an international scale, imperialism can mean any form of unilateral political **action** which is aimed at the establishment of spheres of dominance. Used polemically by any opponent to dominance, it denounces the foreign policy of the dominator as imperialistic. Hans Morgenthau (1978) sought to leave this polemical aspect of imperialism behind and to establish a *realist* concept. Morgenthau concentrated purely on the struggle of the two superpowers to extend their spheres of influence over the world in order to prevent the other from doing so. He defined imperialism as a strategy to increase political influence by means of coercion, distinguishing three aims (creating a world-wide empire, continental hegemony, and local domination) and three methods (military, economic, and cultural).

The theory of 'dependencia' emphasizes the economic method in order to analyse the political superiority of one state over another without touching its formal **sovereignty**. Even the cultural method can involve coercion of the will of another nation by convincing it of the superiority of the imperialist's culture. Before Morgenthau, Max **Weber** had discussed psychological factors which could establish a dynamic imperial foreign policy. He made a link between imperialism and **prestige**. The subjective image of one's power may differ from any objective estimate, but can nevertheless be decisive. Thus a government may feel compelled to demonstrate political **power** to prevent an image of weakness that may encourage other states to free themselves from the dominating state.

Approaches focusing on the internalist aspect of imperialism examine the impact of a state's imperial foreign policy on its own political system, especially in democracies. Hobson, who is famous for his economic explanation of imperial policy, discussed the rise of militarism and its impact on democracy in the domestic arena. It was Hannah **Arendt** who regarded imperialism in foreign policy as the first step to establishing a polity based on the relation between ruling masters and ruled subjects without **rights**. The experience of Europeans in underdeveloped countries gave them the impression of a personal superiority in ruling over so many people. Arendt thought it a remarkable achievement of the British Empire to transform itself into a Commonwealth. In other countries like Germany the connection of the imperial form of total **bureaucracy** with an ideology of racism underlay the Nazi version of the **totalitarian paradigm**. Hence Arendt paid much attention to the ideological aspects of imperialism, especially its 'missionary' character, examining how the basic normative claims of missionary imperialism undermine the rule of **law** in the constituted **democracy**.

Debates about cultural imperialism typically follow the older 'dependencia' theory concerning asymmetrical development in the first and third worlds. On this reading,

globalization processes serve the imperial intentions of the industrialized countries of the West by levelling borders that might otherwise have permitted more autonomous trajectories of development among Third World countries. It is argued that the enforcement of the social institutions of **modernity**, **capitalism**, bureaucracy, urban industrialism and Western cultural practices (Tomlinson 1991: 162) replaces older techniques of oppression with new canons of cultural **domination** based particularly on commerce. On this view, a globalized system of 'informational capitalism' increases the influence of imperialist nation–states over under-developed countries in a more subtle way than military strength alone (Golding and Harris 1997).

References and further reading

Arendt, H. (1951) *Origins of Totalitarianism*. New York: Harcourt and Brace.

Golding, P. and Harris, P. (eds) (1997) *Beyond Cultural Imperialism: Globalization, Communication and the New International Order*. London: Sage.

Hobson, J. A. (1938) *Imperialism: A Study*, 3rd edn. London: Allen and Unwin.

Koebner, R. and Schmidt, H. D. (1964) *Imperialism: The Story and Significance of a Word 1840–1960*. Cambridge: Cambridge University Press.

Morgenthau, H. J. (1978) *Politics among Nations: The Struggle for Power and Peace*, 5th revised edn. New York: Knopf.

Semmel, B. (1993) *The Liberal Ideal and the Demons of Empire: Theories of Imperialism from Adam Smith to Lenin*. Baltimore, MD: Johns Hopkins University Press.

Tomlinson, J. (2002) *Cultural Imperialism: A Critical Introduction*. Baltimore, MD: Johns Hopkins University Press.

Weber, M. (1970) *Essays in Sociology*, 7th edn. London: Routledge.

MARCUS LLANQUE

INCEST

Incest is defined as illicit sexual relations between close **family** members. Most

269

known societies classify parent–child and brother–sister sexual relations as incestuous and therefore **taboo** (exceptions are aristocratic relations in stratified societies such as Ancient Egypt).

Freud argued that incest was a natural inclination that social prohibitions repressed. An opposite popular belief holds that humans avoid incest because it runs against natural inclinations. The dominant biological theory builds on natural selection principles, since outbreeding has reproductive advantages over inbreeding. However, this does not explain why cousin relations are considered incestuous in some societies, while favoured in others. Moreover, why do individuals still reject incest when unaware of possible genetic effects? Anthropological theories refer back to the British evolutionist Edward Tylor's argument that 'savage tribes had the alternative between "marrying out or being killed out"'. Equally stressing the *social* advantages from outbreeding, Claude **Lévi-Strauss** saw the incest prohibition in terms of a qualitative leap from **nature** to **culture**: co-operating social units developed alongside the need to exchange marriage partners. However, incestuous relations may co-exist with out-marrying. In addition, the nature – culture jump is also incongruent with the fact that other primate species prefer outbreeding.

Sociologists emphasize how the incest prohibition functions to reduce competition between nuclear family members. It has also been suggested that avoidance of sexual partners is determined by co-residence rather than 'blood'. 'Familiarity breeds contempt' theories draw on research in settings such as adoptive families and kibbutzim where biologically unrelated children still tend to avoid sexual relations: sexual (non)drives are co-produced by social arrangements. From an applied perspective, incestuous urges may still be treated as distorted sexuality. In the case of child-abuse by parents or other close kin, psychological approaches still prevail.

References and further reading

Arens, W. (1983) *The Original Sin: Incest and its Meaning*. New York: Oxford University Press.
Sherper, J. (1983) *Incest: A Biosocial View*. New York: Academic Press.

BJØRN THOMASSEN

INDIVIDUALISM AND INDIVIDUALIZATION

One can hardly think of words more loaded with misunderstandings than 'individualism' and 'individualization'. It is therefore necessary to establish and keep in mind the distinction between 'individualism' as the **neo-liberal** idea of the free-market individual and the concept of 'individualization' in the sense of institutionalized individualism. 'Individuation' is a psychological concept used by depth-psychologists to describe the process of becoming an autonomous individual.

Neo-liberal economics rests upon an image of the autonomous human self. It assumes that individuals alone can master their entire lives, that they derive and renew their capacity for action from within themselves, 'self-entrepreneur', for instance. Yet this **ideology** openly conflicts with everyday experience in (and sociological studies of) the worlds of **work**, **family** and the local **community**, which show that the individual is not a monad and fully self-insufficient but increasingly tied to others on a level of world-wide **networks** and **institutions**. The ideological notion of the self-sufficient individual ultimately implies the disappearance of a sense of mutual obligation – which is why neo-liberalism threatens the existence of the welfare state.

The *social-scientific* sense of 'individualization' should be distinguished from the political neo-liberal sense. A history of sociology could be written in terms of how its principal theorists – from **Marx** through **Weber**, **Durkheim** and **Simmel** to **Parsons**, **Foucault**, **Elias**, **Luhmann**, **Habermas** and **Giddens** – have varied the basic idea that individualization is a product of complex, contingent and thus high-level **socialization**. For although they tell quite different – some optimistically, many pessimistically tinged – narratives of individualization, and although some see it as a danger to society and/or individuality itself, the thread running through them all is that individualization is (1) a structural characteristic of highly differentiated societies, and (2) does not necessarily endanger their integration but actually makes it possible. The individual creativity which it releases is seen as opening space for the renewal of society under conditions of radical change. In developed **modernity**, human mutuality and community no longer rest on solidly established **traditions**, but, rather, on a paradoxical collectivity of reciprocal individualization.

'Individualization' in this sociological sense means institutionalized individualism. Central institutions of modern society – basic civil, political and social rights, but also paid employment and the training and mobility necessary for it – are geared to the individual and not to the group. Insofar as basic rights are internalized and everyone wants to or must be economically active to earn a livelihood, the spiral of individualization destroys the given foundations of social coexistence. So – to give a simple definition – 'individualization' means *disembedding without re-embedding*.

But what, then, is specific about individualization and second modernity? In the society of second modernity, the separation between subjective and objective analysis, consciousness and class, *Überbau* and *Unterbau*, is losing its significance. Individualization can no longer be understood as a merely subjective reality which has to be relativized by and confronted with objective class analysis. Because individualization not only affects the *Überbau* – 'ideology', 'false consciousness' – but also the economic *Unterbau* of 'real **classes**', the individual is becoming the basic unit of social reproduction for the first time in history.

To put it in a nutshell, individualization is becoming the social structure of the society of second modernity itself. Institutionalized individualism is no longer Talcott **Parsons**'s idea of linear self-reproducing systems; it means the paradox of an 'individualizing structure' as a non-linear, open-ended, highly ambivalent, ongoing process. It relates to a decline of narratives of given sociability. A 'micro foundation of macro sociology' (in Randall Collins's sense) may not be possible. But sociology as an institutionalized rejection of individualism is no longer possible either.

So what does individualization beyond the **collectivist** biases of the social sciences mean? It means an institutionalized imbalance between the disembedded individual and global problems in a **risk** society. The Western type of individualized society tells us to seek biographical solutions to systematic contradictions. For example, the tension in family life today is the fact that equality of men and women cannot be created in an institutional family structure which presupposes and enforces their inequality.

But does this not mean that all individuals just revolve around themselves, forgetting how much they rely on others for the assertion of their own 'push-and-shove' freedom? Certainly the stereotype in people's heads is that individualization breeds a me-first society, but this is a one-sided picture of what in fact happens in family, **gender** relationships, **love** and **sexuality**, youth and old **age**. There are also signs that point towards an ethic of 'altruistic individualism'. Anyone who wants to live a life of his or her own must be socially sensitive to a very high degree.

To adapt Habermas's concept of the 'ideal speech situation', we might speak here of an 'ideal intimacy situation'. If the former refers to general norms, the latter establishes specific rules for the intimate interactions involved in relationships, **marriage**, parenthood, **friendship** and the family – a normative horizon of expectations of reciprocal individuation which, having emerged under conditions of cultural **democratization**, must be counterfactually assumed and sustained. The result is that 'natural' living conditions and inequalities become political. For example, the division of **labour** in the family or workplace can no longer claim to be a 'natural' matter of course; like much else besides, it must be negotiated and justified. But part of the same phenomenon is the right to a life of one's own (**space**, **time** and **money** of one's own) within relationships and the family. The issues of fairness and recognition of the **other**'s identity thus become highly charged as they get caught up in the partner's distribution of daily tasks and career chances, and as the 'family' more and more becomes the rubbish bin for all the social problems around the world that cannot be solved in any other way.

Here the concept of 'individuation' as distinct from 'individualization' is pertinent. It involves an awakening of, or a fight for, co-operative individualism, which presupposes that each has a right to a life of his or her own and that the terms of living together have to be renegotiated in each case. The twofold search for individuation, which is often unsuccessful, might be termed the *freedom culture*. This daily culture of **freedom** also has political implications, for it stands in blatant contradiction with the global victory of neo-liberalism. The smouldering conflict is called 'capitalism or freedom' (in an inverted allusion to the old conservative election motto: 'Freedom or Socialism!'). The freedom culture is in danger of being destroyed by capitalism.

What does the dimension of power, the relationship between power and individuation (individualization) add to the argument? **Hegel**'s philosophy bequeathed the idea that people at the top of society also develop a richer **subjectivity**. In modern management, this conception takes the at once intensified and degraded form that anyone climbing the career ladder not only

knows better what they want, but forgets that they depend on those they have left behind, entertaining the illusion that they can do the job of anyone else working for them. Today, the new '**capitalism**' intensifies social inequalities throughout the world and changes their historical characteristics. When Marx talked about the proletariat, he had in mind the need of capital for cheap labour **power**. But today this seems to be less and less the case: global capital, in bidding farewell to unskilled labour, dismisses more and more people to a state beyond society in which their services are no longer needed by the labour market.

This suggests the following objection: the farewell to class conceptualization by individualization theory may have been applicable yesterday, but it is no longer applicable today and will be invalid tomorrow. The concept of class, so often pronounced dead, has been undergoing a renaissance in the new global context. For the new inequalities growing world-wide are also a collective experience. Yet this is precisely the question. Paradoxically, it is the individualization and fragmentation of growing inequalities into separate biographies which offer a collective experience. The concept of class actually plays down the situation of growing inequalities without collective ties. Class, social stratum, or gender presuppose a collective moulding of individual behaviour: the old idea that by knowing that someone was a Siemens apprentice, one also knew the things he would say, the way he would dress and enjoy himself, what he would read and how he would vote. This kind of syllogistic reasoning has now become questionable. Under conditions of individualization, it is necessary to work out if and when new collective forms of action take shape, and which forms they are. The key question is how the bubbling, contradictory process of individualization and denationalization can be cast into new democratic forms of organization.

However, it would be a big mistake to equate the crisis of the concept of class with a denial of increasing inequalities. To invoke individualization theory is, on the contrary, to consider that social inequality is on the rise precisely *because* of the spread of individualization. Instead of suppressing the question of how collectivity can be generated in global modernity, or shifting it to the premises of a sociology based upon uncertain class collectives, the non-class character of individualized inequalities poses it in a more radical way.

No doubt the question of the frontiers of individualization is becoming ever more pressing. Many think that objective limits of collectivity are set in advance, rather as there are natural limits to growth, and this suggests that the limits of individualization should be sought in the individualization process itself – or, to put it mechanically, the more people are individualized, the more they produce de-individualizing consequences for others. Take the case of a woman who files for divorce and whose husband finds himself facing a void. In the tussle over the children, each one tries to impose on the other the dictates of his or her life. Not only is there a positive sum game of co-individualization; probably more often there is also a negative sum game of contra-individualization. It would seem reasonable to suppose that the irritation caused by the other's resistance strengthens the urge for a new, and perhaps seemingly 'democratic', **authoritarianism**.

References and further reading

Beck, U. and Beck-Gernsheim, E. (1995) *The Normal Chaos of Love*. Cambridge: Polity.
Beck, U. and Beck-Gernsheim, E. (2001) *Individualization*. London: Sage.
Giddens, A. (1992) *The Transformation of Intimacy*. Cambridge: Polity.
Leisering, L. and Leibfried, S. (1999) *Time and Poverty in Western Welfare States*. Cambridge: Polity.
Schroer, M. (2001) *Die Individuen der Gesellschaft*. Frankfurt am Main: Suhrkamp.

ULRICH BECK

INDUSTRIALIZATION

'Industrialization' is a transition process whereby economies based mainly on agriculture or trading ventures adopt machine **technologies** and **rational** systems of work directed to the manufacture of goods. Where capital and **labour** are plentiful, the diffusion of these systems rapidly eclipses other forms of economic activity and eventually transforms entire **social structures**. This 'great transformation', as Karl Polanyi (1944) called it, engenders consistent annual output growth; is usually associated with an increasing dependence on an international **division of labour**; and therefore with the import and export of foodstuffs, raw materials, semi-finished and finished goods. Britain's 'industrial revolution' of the early nineteenth century was the first instance of such a transition; later that century **America** and Germany had emerged as the leading industrial economies which were, in their different ways, to dominate the world for much of the twentieth century. By the late twentieth century the newly industrialized countries, among them Korea, Japan, Mexico and Brazil, had adopted a similar path to economic growth.

By the last third of the nineteenth century Britain was the most urbanized of modern economies (see **urbanism and urbanization**). Employment and economic activity in agriculture declined sharply with Britain's adoption of free trade. On the eve of the Great War some 35 per cent of the French population lived in towns and cities with more than 3000 inhabitants; in Britain 78 per cent of the population did so. Likewise, in 1913, 42 per cent of French workers were rural workers, as against 8 per cent of British workers. As late as the mid-1950s some 25 per cent of the German and French workforce remained in agricultural employment. The Common Agricultural Policy of the EEC sought to transfer this pool of rural labour to urban factories. At the end of the twentieth century the distribution of Polish employment between agriculture, manufacture and services was similar to that of Western European economies fifty years earlier. However, as with Portugal and Spain in the 1980s, the decline of **European** manufacturing employment now directs labour out of agriculture into service sector occupations (see **post-industrial society**).

'Industry' was originally understood to mean purposeful human activity directed to any end, not a sector of the economy linked specifically to the **production** of goods by enterprises that combined human labour with machine production. Adam **Smith** (1776) saw **wealth** as the outcome of human industry, applied both in town and in country. The idea that the rise of manufacturing had the **power** to transform economies was first formulated in by Adolphe Blanqui, who wrote of an 'industrial revolution' that had transformed Britain in much the same way as the French Revolution had swept away Europe's *ancien régime*. Karl **Marx**'s *Capital* of 1867, taking British industrialization as his model, identified irreversible changes that would, he argued, sweep the world. Here the sheer abundance of which industrial production was capable served as a model for the future of mankind. But it was not until the 1880s that 'modern society' began to be routinely thought of as 'industrial society'. Arnold Toynbee lectured to Oxford students on the 'industrial revolution of the eighteenth century in England' (1884) and the first textbook of English economic history was entitled *The Growth of English Industry and Commerce* (Cunningham 1882).

The idea that industrialization could serve as a model for economic development was first adopted in Soviet Russia. The mechanization of agricultural production and the electrification of the countryside were part of a process of rural industrialization intended to modernize rural Russia. This vision of a modern society integrated around industrial production proved difficult to realize. Shortfalls in grain collection, leading to **collectivization** as an instrument of **social control**, led to a catastrophic famine in the early 1930s. In response, forced industrialization as a series of five-year plans was adopted. Imposed upon Eastern Europe in the late 1940s, later the forced industrialization of China's Great Leap Forward had similar disastrous results for entire populations.

Soviet industrialization did, however, seem to produce impressive results. During the 1950s the Soviet bloc boasted that its planning mechanisms would enable it to catch up and overtake the West. Competition between the world powers became economic, and newly-independent states increasingly looked to the Soviet model. Western states responded with development programmes which sought to place the recipient countries on the kind of growth path typical of the industrial economies.

As the industrial economies matured, manufacturing output and employment declined proportionally. During the recessions of the 1970s and 1980s commentators talked of 'de-industrialization': sectors such as retailing and finance eclipsed traditional branches of manufacturing. The occupational changes associated with the consequent decline in skilled manual work hitherto dominated by men contributed to the argument that Western societies were becoming 'post-industrial'.

References and further reading

Blanqui, A. (1837) *Histoire de l'économie politique en Europe*. Paris: Guillamain.

Cunningham, W. (1882) *The Growth of English Industry and Commerce*. London: Cambridge University Press.

Hilger, D. and Hölscher, L. (1982) 'Industrie, Gewerbe', in O. Brunner, W. Conze and R.

Koselleck (eds) *Geschichtliche Grundbegriffe*, Bd. 3. Stuttgart: Klett-Cotta.

Lewin, M. (1985) *The Making of the Soviet Economic System*. New York: Pantheon Books.

Polanyi, K. (1944) *The Great Transformation: The Political and Economic Origins of Our Time*. New York: Rinehart and Co.

Smith, A. ([1776] 1976) *An Inquiry into the Nature and Causes of the Wealth of Nations*. Oxford: Oxford University Press.

Toynbee, A. (1884) *Lectures on the Industrial Revolution of the Eighteenth Century in England*. London: Longmans, Green & Co.

Tribe, K. (1981) '"Industrialisation" as a Historical Category', in K. Tribe *Genealogies of Capitalism*. London: Macmillan.

KEITH TRIBE

INEQUALITY

The analysis of inequality in the social sciences is based on three different approaches (see also **equality**). First, inequality is conceptualized as the differential distribution of valued resources, attributes or items (let goods be the generic term) among units. These units can be individuals, households (**families**), **groups**, **regions** or **nations**. They are seemingly unequal to the extent that they possess those goods in different amounts. This approach is typical for economics. Its main advantage is that the distribution of goods can be analyzed in quantitative terms. From a sociological point of view, however, it suffers from conceptualizing social **structure** in terms of persons who possess goods (that is, things distributed among persons), not in terms of **social relations**.

The second approach, preferred in sociology, sees inequality centred in unequal access to different spheres of society. Social relations can be characterized by different degrees of openness or closure. The archetype of an open social relationship is the competitive **market** for goods and services. Access is limited whenever private **associations** are successful in establishing the monopolistic closure of a social sphere (cf. **Weber** 1922). In this approach, a precondition of inequality

is that some members of a society are deliberately excluded from participating in an activity, thus limiting competition in this activity. Consequently, inequality is studied in terms of **social inclusion and social exclusion**. A case in point is the differential access to the **labour** market in **capitalist** societies, although the same differential access may also dominate the political and educational spheres. However, exclusion does not necessarily translate into inequality. It is true that the more open a social relation is, the less it is prone to inequality; but a conditional access to a social sphere is not automatically an unequal one. For instance, if jobs are distributed according to qualifications, access to them is restricted but not necessarily unequal.

The first two mentioned approaches are macro approaches. A third approach is micro in character. Here inequality is typical for a social relation between two or more **actors**. It is not the access to it that is unequal, but the relation itself. An example is **friendship** or **love**. Though everybody is free to have friends or to fall in love, access to a specific friendship is limited to a very few, but this does not constitute inequality. However, within the relationship itself, it can happen that relations of precedence or subordination are established. Then the relation may be shaped by differences either of **power** or of reciprocal **recognition** and esteem.

Though it is useful to separate these approaches analytically, they are interrelated. For instance, participation in elections is, as a rule, restricted to the citizens of a nation–state. The possession of the resource (nationality or **citizenship**) governs access to a social sphere. Conversely, access to a social sphere such as the system of higher **education** may provide its graduates with highly valued resources for a professional career. Not surprisingly, there is a micro–macro link. Differential possession of goods may shape **interactions**. Relationships affected by inequality, if repeated in a large number, may turn into a

275

quality of the social system characterized by unequal access or unequal possession of goods.

The goods that can be distributed unevenly differ according to the social sphere for which they are typical. How many types of goods exist depends on how many types of social spheres or subsystems can be distinguished. According to a venerable tradition established by Talcott **Parsons**, a modern society consists of four subsystems: the economy, the **polity**, the (societal) **community** and the socio-cultural system. The goods distributed in these different systems are income and **money**, political **power**, **prestige** (including **rights**, for Parsons, and for some other authors) and finally **knowledge** mediated by formal education. Recently it has become common to speak of different types of 'capital': economic capital (money or physical capital), human capital (education and skills), **social capital** (networks of social relationships), political capital (the ability to make decisions binding for a group) and **cultural capital**.

Goods whose differential distribution constitutes dimensions of inequality can be classified along various lines. They are either monadic (definable without reference to another unit) or relational. Examples of the first class are talent or health; examples of the second are prestige and power (Wright 1994). Or they are separable from its owner (e.g. **wealth**) or inseparable (e.g. ability). Only separable resources can be redistributed. Since people are not equal in terms of their capabilities, the question arises as to whether **social justice** requires compensating them for natural disadvantages. Egalitarians answer this in the affirmative (see **egalitarianism**), whereas liberals answer it in the negative (see **liberalism**). Finally, goods are either acquired (e.g. skills) or inherited (e.g. wealth and genetic traits).

A naïve conception of inequality assumes it exists whenever resources are differentially distributed among units, be they individuals, households or nations. Following this idea, income equality, for instance, is not reached

before every unit earns exactly the same amount of money. This conception draws no distinction between equality of *outcome* and equality of *opportunity*. Equality of outcome implies that an absolute value should be equal; equality of opportunity only that the expected value of the variable in question be equal (Barr 1998: 144). According to this idea of equality, the purpose of an equal-opportunity policy is to 'level the playing field' (Roemer 1998: 5). However, there is a more restricted version of this concept, which amounts to establishing an anti-discrimination principle. Chances should not vary with irrelevant attributes like **sex** or **race**, although it is admissible that they may vary with relevant attributes such as skills. Chances are here regarded not as equal for everybody but only for the bearers of the relevant attributes. According to this anti-discrimination variant of the equal opportunity principle, individual traits may affect the distribution of resources without causing inequality; among these traits may belong both natural attributes such as age and behavioural attributes such as individual choices (cf. Barr 1998: 144).

It is hard to find an aspect of inequality that has not been taken up by an ever growing inequality research. As large and diverse as it is, however, the literature is driven by three basic questions: (1) is inequality inevitable?; (2) does it increase or decrease in the course of history?; and (3) what are its ultimate causes?

The view that inequality is *inevitable* is ascribed to functionalist sociology (see **functionalism**). In a classic paper, Davis and **Moore** (1945) argued that unequal remunerations are necessary to allocate labour efficiently to different tasks. To this extent, **stratification** is an 'unconsciously evolved device by which societies ensure that the important positions are conscientiously filled by the most qualified persons' (ibid.: 243). We must doubt whether this is a cogent argument for demonstrating that all human societies independent of the stage of development are necessarily stratified in terms of unequal rewards. The argument presupposes that there exists a system of occupations which differ primarily according to the qualifications needed to fulfil them, and it also presupposes mobility. 'Primitive' societies lack the first trait, while a feudal society lacks the second (see **feudalism**). That is, feudal society limits mobility to such an extent that the mechanism described by Davis and Moore is unlikely to operate. However, whether a society without equal rewards is at all conceivable – let alone, whether such a society is, as **Marx** assumed, the destination of history under capitalism – is entirely another matter. Unequal rewards in Davis and Moore's sense are compatible with the antidiscrimination version of the principle of equal opportunity. To this extent, a society that realizes this principle without hurting the mechanism necessary to allocate labour efficiently is both conceivable and feasible.

The view that the 'gradual and progressive development of social equality is at once the past and the future of . . . history' was first formulated by de **Tocqueville** ([1834] 2000: 7). De Tocqueville conceived of social equality as equivalent to abolishing the barriers of rank, leading to a society with equal civil and political rights for all. In this sense, equality is indeed the culmination of a long-lasting historical development. However, the question remains as to whether the same applies for economic equality, i.e. as to whether a historical tendency towards income equality can be observed. Here it is helpful to split the issue into two parts: inequality *within* countries and inequality *between* countries. Kuznets (1955) assumed that inequality within countries would at best be depicted by an inverted U: in the course of history it first increases, then, after reaching a climax, it decreases. The empirical evidence for this hypothesis is mixed. As a cross-sectional comparison shows, inequality in developing countries is much higher than in developed

countries. However, the Kuznets hypothesis is not a cross-sectional but an intertemporal one. Inequality in industrial countries undoubtedly decreased over the course of the twentieth century; but it has increased again since the 1980s (Gottschalk and Smeeding 2000).

As for inequality between countries, this inequality has increased substantially since the first modern country, England, entered the 'epoch of modern economic growth' (Kuznets 1973). According to a calculation by Pritchett (1997) the gap in income per head of the poorest and the (second) richest country (the USA) has increased since 1870 from approximately a factor of nine to a factor of over 45 in 1990. Yet the picture of a rapidly increasing inter-national inequality changes if the average incomes of nations are weighted by population size. From this frame of analysis, income inequality across nations peaked sometime around 1970 and has been declining since (Firebaugh 2003: 19). Nevertheless, inequality *within* nations has increased. This is the essence of what Firebaugh calls the 'new geography of global income inequality'. Inter-national inequality must be distinguished from *global inequality*, where the latter term denotes global personal income distribution involving a weighted sum of inequality both within and between countries.

Concerning the *causes* of inequality, here it is again helpful to distinguish between *within*-and *between*-countries inequalities. In the former case, empirically incomes are shaped by practically all the forces that in regression analyses are used to explain the mean of many other dependent variables: sex, race, age, working hours, qualification, region, industry, etc. Theoretically, in a market economy, because income is the product of productive services multiplied by their price, income differences can only occur either (1) because the endowment of individuals with productive resources differs or (2) individuals' services are paid differently. In a competitive market system the latter ought to be impossible (Berger 2003). There are mainly two sources causing prices to deviate from their competitive level, thereby entailing inequality: (1) economic rents, i.e. payments above the level necessary to keep a resource in its present use; and (2) discrimination.

Concerning income differences between countries, a distinction should be made between immediate and ultimate causes of growth. Discussion of the immediate causes concentrates on technology versus factor accumulation. Either **technological** progress or investment in human and physical capital is held to account for growth differentials. In discussions of the ultimate causes, most researchers agree that secure property rights are the key to economic success (Rodrik 2003).

References and further reading

Barr, N. (1998) *The Economics of the Welfare State*, 3rd edn. Oxford: Oxford University Press.

Berger, J. (2003) 'Sind Märkte gerecht?' *Zeitschrift für Soziologie*, 32: 462–73.

Davis, K. and Moore, W. E. (1945) 'Some Principles of Stratification', *American Sociological Review*, 45: 242–9.

Firebaugh, G. (2003) *The New Geography of Global Income Inequality*. Cambridge, MA: Harvard University Press.

Gottschalk, P. and Smeeding, T. M. (2000) 'Empirical Evidence on Income Inequality in Industrial Countries', in A. B. Atkinson and François Bourguignon (eds) *Handbook of Income Distribution*, vol. I. Amsterdam: Elsevier.

Kuznets, S. (1955) 'Economic Growth and Income Inequality', *American Economic Review*, 45: 1–28.

Kuznets, S. (1973) 'Modern Economic Growth: Findings and Reflections', *American Economic Review*, 63: 247–58.

Pritchett, L. (1997) 'Divergence, Big Time', *Journal of Economic Perspectives*, 11: 3–17.

Rodrik, D. (ed.) (2003) *In Search of Prosperity: Analytical Narratives on Economic Growth*. Princeton, NJ: Princeton University Press.

Roemer, J. E. (1998) *Equality of Opportunity*. Cambridge, MA: Harvard University Press.

Tocqueville, A. de ([1834] 2000) *Democracy in America*. New York: Bantam.

Weber, M. (1922) *Wirtschaft und Gesellschaft*. Tübingen: J. C. B. Mohr.

Wright, E. O. (1994) 'Inequality', in *Interrogating Inequality*. London: Verso.

JOHANNES BERGER

INFORMATION

Information refers to a record or communication of something, such as a person, an event or a place. This neutral meaning of the word supersedes the notion that information involves the formation of mind or character, as in the novice being instructed for entry into the clergy, **law** or teaching. The latter sense of the word connotes a superior condition, as in someone being an informed person.

The primary meaning of information is normally positioned on an ascending scale, above 'data', but below '**knowledge**' and 'wisdom'. Information is more than data but less than knowledge or wisdom. Although precise distinctions between data, information, knowledge and wisdom are impossible to make, an implied hierarchy is always evident. Where knowledge is more generalizable than information, wisdom signifies a high level of learning combined with rich experience and a capacity to make sound judgements. It is not difficult to appreciate these distinctions, but their application is fraught with ambiguity. While the terms are distinguishable in terms of a continuum which runs from the specific towards the general and abstract, they may only be accurately perceived in context.

Information is generally conceived semantically – i.e. as having meaning, since it is 'about' something or someone. Shannon and Weaver (1964), however, defined information in a different way. According to their Information Theory, information is a quantity that is measured in 'bits' and defined in terms of the probabilities of occurrence of **symbols**. This explicitly ignores information as a semantic phenomenon. Their notion has been enormously influential in mathematics, engineering and computer science, but it is a specialist definition at odds with more everyday conceptions.

Information is associated with a reduction in uncertainty insofar as it enhances control. The uncertainty-reducing features of information are central to economic analyses of decision-making, just as they are to the identification of errors in transmission of signals in engineering. However, a countervailing tendency, particularly prominent in postmodern thought, associates information with an *increase* in uncertainty. The argument here is that so much information is now available and unceasingly generated that scarcely anything may be held any longer with surety. Previously firm beliefs are routinely challenged by alternative information in such quantities that people easily come to abandon convictions, whether moral or **religious** convictions or everyday beliefs about occurrences and regularities in the world. A result is uncertainty, insecurity and anxiety (**Bauman** 1997).

Information has become a popular prefix to a range of concepts that claim to identify features of a new sort of society. The Information Age, the Information Economy, and especially the Information Society have become common descriptors (Webster 2002) (see **knowledge and knowledge society**). The concepts appear to capture similar phenomena, yet on inspection centre often on different things. For example, their concern ranged from a general increase in symbols and signs that accelerated since the 1960s (the 'information explosion'), on the development of information and communications technologies, especially the Internet (the 'information superhighway'), on the increased prominence of information in employment ('information scientists', 'information labour', 'information professions'), on the growing significance of tradable information (the 'information economy'), and on new forms of **inequality** (the 'information divide', the 'information rich/poor').

There is a **consensus** that the expansion and ubiquity of information are distinguishing features of contemporary societies. For instance, one can think of the growth of media **technologies** (video, cable, satellite), in advertising (campaigns, posters, placements), in news and entertainment services (from DVD movies to computer games), in fashion, image and style, in information-intensive occupations (teaching, accountancy, design), and in the development of **education** systems around the world. A problem is that the term 'information' may here be over-extended, purporting to unite too many different areas under a common theme. It is questionable whether such different activities can be legitimately seen in these homogeneous ways. The extraordinary range and differences among things so encompassed may not fit the single category.

Conceptions of an 'information society' typically embrace evolutionary themes, the term suggesting a higher stage of development than hitherto. In this way, the information society retains something of the suggestion of a higher order state evident in the implication of an informed populace. When most commentators speak of an information society, the implication is that this is a desirable condition. Where observers recognise problems of inequality in the 'information age', claims may be made not against a misdistribution of material resources (money, food, housing, etc.), but rather against unequal informational access (e.g. to education, libraries, Internet facilities). The proposed solutions tend to offer not redistribution of **wealth** but improved access to information.

References and further reading

Bauman, Z. (1997) *Postmodernity and Its Discontents*. Cambridge: Polity.
Castells, M. (1996) *The Information Society, I: The Rise of the Network Society*. Oxford: Blackwell.
Lash, S. (2002). *Critique of Information*. London: Sage.

Shannon, C. and Weaver, W. ([1949] 1964) *The Mathematical Theory of Communication.* Urbana, IL: University of Illinois Press.

Webster, F. (2002) *Theories of the Information Society*, 2nd edn. London: Routledge.

FRANK WEBSTER

INSTITUTIONS AND NEO-INSTITUTIONALISM

In Latin, *institutiones* originally meant principles of law – such as those published in the Emperor Justinian's *Corpus juris civilis* of 533 AD – bearing on civil matters such as norms of **property** and **marriage**. At the time of the Protestant Reformation the term referred to the debate about whether institutional **authority** could be based only on Christ or also indirectly on the **Church**.

Widespread as an **everyday** term, institutions are said by sociologists to mediate between social **structures** on the macro- and micro-level, on the one hand, and **actors**, on the other. They are said to constitute regulations of **action** that are relatively long-lasting and make rules of behaviour binding on the basis of **values and norms**, and **sanctions**. They are seen as forming the **habitus** of particular groups and as symbolically expressing a certain order.

Herbert **Spencer** spoke of domestic, political, industrial, ecclesiastical, ceremonial, and professional 'basic institutions' in an evolutionary manner, in a sense analogous to 'basic **needs**'. point of view. William G. Sumner, viewed as a 'fanatical social Darwinist', considered institutions to be evolutionary adaptation performances, distinguishing between 'crescive institutions' (in early societies) and 'enacted institutions' (in advanced civilizations). Institutions on this view always consist of a 'concept (idea, notion, doctrine, interest) and a structure', and are based on needs and the folk customs that shape their satisfaction. The anthropologist Bronislaw Malinowski (2002) shifted the emphasis from 'biological heritage' to the cultural **development** of

multi-functional and dynamic institutions whose performances (and limitations) each produce resultant needs which in turn are worked over by institutions. However, **Durkheim** (1982), who defined sociology as 'the science of institutions, of their development and mode of action' has been seen as the real father of the theory of institutions, notably by Fauconet and **Mauss**. In Durkheim's work institutional dimensions are salient in the transition from early, segmentary **communities** to differentiated industrial societies, in the operation of 'social facts' and in the historical effects of ancient institutions reaching back to totemistic **religion**. Mary **Douglas** (1986) understands institutions neither in a **metaphysical-collectivistic** way nor as a mere field of action for individual calculations. As an anthropologist, she investigates how binding **conventions** are established mostly by institutional **classification** systems, following Durkheim, Mauss, and **Lévi-Strauss**.

In distinction to the idea of institutions as collective entities, action-oriented approaches emphasize that institutions arise from interaction between individual human agents. Max **Weber** (1979) used the idea of institution only in passing, but in section 5 of the opening chapter of *Economy and Society* he concisely connects the foundations of institutional validity to the idea of the existence of a 'legitimate order'. Weber saw the process of the 'routinization of **charisma**' as involving the institutionalization and legitimation of a leader who originally appears to break with received institutions (see **legitimacy and legitimation**).

From the social-psychological point of view, Floyd H. Allport (1933) emphasized that institutions consist solely of actions. Thus, a university was nothing other than 'teaching, learning, and cooperating in academic relationships generally'. Concerning the theory of interactions, **Mead** considered institutionalizing to be connected to the **intersubjectivity** of individual action. Significant **symbols** and processes of taking a **role** foster both the development of a personal **identity** and the 'common reaction to a certain situation by all members of the community'. In **Blumer**'s **symbolic interactionism** and in **Goffman**'s idea of '**frames**' and 'total institutions', face-to-face interaction is key. This is also dealt with in the analyses of **Schutz**, for whom sociality is based on common relevance systems and stocks of knowledge. From the **phenomenological** point of view, **Berger and Luckmann** (1979) combined anthropological and interactionist approaches in describing the institutional worlds of **meaning** in terms of objectified human action whose validity claims are to be analysed in terms of the sociology of **knowledge**.

Beginning from the 'unit act', **Parsons** (1991) defined the concept of institution in the 1950s as a complex of institutionalized role elements or '**status** relationships'. For him and the **structural functionalist** school, institutions rest on the connection between roles and status and on processes of socialization and internalization of 'cultural patterns'. In this case, 'institutionalizing' means communication between personal, social, and cultural systems based on norms and symbols. **Merton**, who also emphasized the functional relevance of social deviance, further developed this into analyses of relationships of power and mutual interdependences.

Stimulated by Weber's comparative **historical sociology**, **Eisenstadt** extended the theme to comparative studies, combining evolutionary perspectives and correlation analyses, looking at various kinds of institutions such as **kinship**, ecological patterns and modes of subsistence on the one hand and kinds of political organization, on the other hand. Examples are his studies on axial age civilizations or on 'multiple modernities'.

Luhmann determined institutions in terms of the 'reduction of complexity' through the coordination of individual actions and sub-systems. After his 'autopoietic turn' he replaced the term 'institution', which he had assigned to the **tradition**-based world of 'stratified societies', by more explicitly system-theoretic terms. Much of Luhmann's work on social systems can be seen as describing the autonomizing of institutional forms, particularly in the **law**, economy and the fine arts.

Lévi-Strauss defined the regulation of social **groups** in structuralist terms by systems of kinship, **myths**, and formal principles of organization, although he did not explicitly use the term 'institution'. **Foucault** similarly developed his reconstruction of orders of knowledge and practises of **social control** and disciplining while referring to the power of including and excluding **discourses**. Starting out from **Sartre**'s theory of the group and the radical spirit of the 1960s, Foucault, Jaques **Lacan**, Lévi-Strauss, and **Althusser** investigated the 'act of instituting' as a meaning which comes from the hidden and the **unconscious** and combines with the objectivations of society. From this, **Castoriadis** (1987) developed an emphasis on the imaginary and creative power involved in the forming of institutions, showing how social institutions necessarily pressuppose a dimension of the symbolic (see **imaginary**). According to Castoriadis, institutions are creative and determining at one and the same time. From the revolutionary destruction of existing institutions necessarily arises the instituting of new orders. This view found prominence most clearly in the radical criticism of institutions led by the anti-psychiatry movement of the 1970s.

Within the frame of philosophical anthropology, Arnold **Gehlen** (1988) determined institutions as the most important 'compensating relief' for man as a creature overburdened by impulses and instincts in need of control. Following Durkheim, institutions for Gehlen are born from group actions, including totemistic rituals in archaic societies. Their task is the stabilization of tensions and the binding standardization of motives for action by an institutionalized 'end in itself'. Thus, what Maurice Hauriou called 'idées directrices' appear and at the same time come to function as differences based on power. In modern times, however, Gehlen suspected an increasing decline of institutions. In critically discussing this conservative institutionalism, the analysis of institutional mechanisms considers institutions to be 'symbolic orders', involving validity claims and mechanisms of institutional stabilization based on particular orders of space and time (Rehberg 1994). In postmodern discourses and in concepts of a second, 'reflexive' modernity (**Beck** and **Giddens**), long-lasting institutional structures are dynamized by processes of individualization and of globalization (see **reflexivity** and **individualism and individualisation**). In contrast to this, **Dahrendorf** while deviating from his earlier dualism of personal freedom versus social constraint, recently emphasized the significance of 'ligatures', i.e. institutional standardization.

Against the predominance of neo-classical economic model theory with its search for extensive 'laws' with the aid of mathematizeable models, there has been an inclusion of institutional frames of economic action since Thorstein Veblen's 'evolutionary economy'. Other main representatives are Wesley C. Mitchells, John R. Commons, and Clarence E. Ayers (in the wider field also Joseph A. **Schumpeter** and Karl Polanyi). The German Historical School (e.g. Gustav Schmoller), the social-critical American 'meliorism' and the reforming pragmatism of Peirce, James and Dewey have also been influential. In opposition to philosophies of *laissez-faire*, attention came to be focused on the formation of trusts and monopolies in the last third of the nineteenth century and on increasing social divisions. J. R. Commons looked to the tradition of German *Socialpolitik*, searching for possibilities of political intervention by pointing out the exogenous institutional factors of economic cycles. He showed

how wars, domestic political influences, harvests and diseases, as well as regional and sectoral specialities, militate against any idea of law-based periodicity. This stimulated C. E. Ayre's criticism of capitalism and **Keynes**'s anti-cyclic economic policy.

After the 1970s there developed a 'New Institutionalism' in economic theory. Although this movement appears to build on the older institutionalists, it in fact involves an extension of **neo-liberal** theory, expanded to include '**property rights**', 'public choice', and 'transaction-cost' theories. Institutional performances on the macro-level have been investigated among others by Meyer and Rowan (1977) and DiMaggio and Powell (1983) and on the micro-institutionalistic level by Zucker (1977). These have examined innovation, habitualizing, objectivation, and sedimentation as phases of a process and levels of intensifying institutionalizing.

In sociology, the renaissance of the subject of institution is based on a cultural-sociological approach on the one hand, and on **rational choice** theory on the other hand. Writers such as James **Coleman** and Hartmut Esser have also sought to combine these approaches in their analyses of action situations.

References and further reading

Allport, F. H. (1933) *Institutional Behavior*. Chapel Hill: University of North Carolina Press.
Berger, P. L. and Luckmann, T. (1979) *The Social Construction of Reality*. Harmondsworth: Penguin.
Castoriadis, C. (1987) *The Imaginary Institution of Society*. Cambridge: Polity.
DiMaggio, P. J. and Powell, W. W. (1983) 'The Iron Cage Revisited', *American Sociological Revue*, 48: 147–60.
Douglas, M. (1986) *How Institutions Think*. Syracuse, NY: Syracuse University Press.
Durkheim, E. (1982) *The Rules of Sociological Method*. London: Macmillan.
Gehlen, A. (1988) *Man: His Nature and Place in the World*. New York: Columbia University Press.
Malinowski, B. (2002) *A Scientific Theory of Culture and Other Essays*. London: Routledge.

Meyer, J. W. and Rowan, B. (1977) 'Institutional Organisations', *American Journal of Sociology*, 83: 340–63.

Parsons, T. (1991) *The Social System*. London: Routledge.

Rehberg, K.-S. (1994) 'Institutionen als symbolische Ordnungen', in G. Göhler (ed.) *Die Eigenart der Institutionen*. Baden-Baden: Nomos.

Weber, M. (1979) *Economy and Society*. London: University of California Press.

Zucker, L. G. (1977) 'The Role of Institutionalization in Cultural Persistence', *American Sociological Revue*, 42: 726–43.

KARL-SIEGBERT REHBERG

INSTRUMENTAL REASON

Max **Horkheimer**'s phrase 'instrumental reason', appearing in the German title of this book, *Die Kritik der instrumentellen Vernunft* (1967) (translated from the English original, *The Eclipse of Reason*, 1947), refers at once to Kant's subjectivist reconstruction of the ancient Greek idea of logos and to **Weber**'s 'purposive rationality' or means–end rationality (*Zweckrationalität*). With Weber, Horkheimer understood historical processes of rationalization in terms of 'disenchantment' (see **rationality and rationalization**), and with **Marx** in terms of processes of **reification** of consciousness. Horkheimer analyzed the history of Western thought in terms of the twin poles of objective and subjective reason (see also **Occident**). Where the objective reason of classical antiquity and the monotheistic world religions was able to evoke an encompassing sense of the meaning of life and of the nature of goodness and freedom, this capacity is lost in modern times with the transition to subjective reason undertaken by Francis Bacon and Descartes. What is gained instead is a more effective technical **knowledge** of control that brings about unprecedented possibilities of domination over inner and outer nature and a definite increase in the freedom of the subject of such domination. The problem, however, is not only, as classical Marxism held, that some become subjects of this instru-

mental power while the dominated classes remain objects of it. Now the instrumental power that was originally thought to make possible the **freedom** of all subjects becomes an **autonomous** and anonymous machine, gathering ever greater speed long after the driver has lost control. At this point a return to objective reason is impossible because the good life that is guaranteed by it is only available for the freedom of a few on condition of the **slavery** of the rest. Objective reason in this context is **ideology**. Subjective reason instrumentalizes itself in the process of its scientistic self-criticism; and the product of this instrumentalization consequently ossifies into an 'iron cage', in Weber's phrase. In this situation, repressed nature takes revenge in the form of a regressive **fascist** exodus from all reason *tout court*.

Habermas in the 1960s and the 1970s critically adapted and transformed this earlier legacy of the **Frankfurt School**, speaking neither of subjective nor of objective reason but instead of '**intersubjective**' or '**communicative**' reason, targeted at the systemic entrenchment of **functionalist** reasoning in the maintenance of societal domination or 'colonization of the **lifeworld** by the **system**'.

References and further reading

Adorno, T. W. and Horkheimer, M. (1972) *The Dialectic of Enlightenment*. New York: Herder and Herder.

Horkheimer, M. (1947) *The Eclipse of Reason*. Oxford: Oxford University Press.

HAUKE BRUNKHORST

INTEGRATION

One of the central assumptions of social theory is that some degree of integration or order is necessary for social life. 'That all human societies must have *some* degree of integration is a matter of definition', writes Robert **Merton**, 'and begs the question.' How much integration is necessary and how it is to be conceptualized have proved highly controversial. Social theorists in the Western tradition have been divided. For some, society can overcome a disorder intrinsic to the 'state of **nature**', whether by the force of a central authority (Hobbes), by an 'invisible hand' governing the operation of selfish interests (Adam **Smith**), or by unifying collective sentiments (**Durkheim**). For others, society itself is the source of the 'war of all against all' and can only moderate a tendency toward disintegration intrinsic to it (Montesquieu; Rousseau), while collective values can express conflict as much as they unify (**Weber**).

In sociology, the problem of integration was famously summed up by Talcott **Parsons** as the 'Hobbesian problem of order', which he set about solving. For Parsons, the very idea of a society means that there is a tendency toward integration among its parts. Since the different parts of a society are maintained in human **action**, this was also interpreted to mean the integration of the subjective **meanings** and motives of actors. Parsons argued that actors operated within a common **culture** that provided both the definition of **role** expectations and provided them with internalized need dispositions that served to define wants. Actors respond not only to positive rewards, but also to internalized feelings of guilt, anxiety and the need for approval; a functioning social system is also a *normative* order. At the same time, a normative order is reinforced not only by internalized dispositions, but also by external **sanctions**, coercive **power** and material rewards or interests. Processes of systems and of action are mutually reinforcing (see **functionalism** and **social system**).

Although Parsons had sought to provide an all-encompassing theory, it seemed to others that it was too one-sided. For conflict theorists, such as Ralf **Dahrendorf** and John Rex, for example, it gave greater emphasis to **values and norms**, than to power and **conflict**. For Dennis Wrong, it placed too much emphasis on the internalization of norms and thus proposed an 'over-socia-lized conception' of the human actor, neglecting pre-social drives. Rather than a **consensus** model of society, these theorists argued that a conflict model would be both more preferable and more realistic.

These criticisms had force, but the alternative conflict model was unstable for a number of reasons. Parsons had in fact sought to account for *both* power *and* consensus in his model. It was difficult to argue that the two models could be kept entirely apart and used separately for different purposes, as Dahrendorf and Rex argued, while expressing a preference for the conflict model. The issues of conflict and cooperation, and power and **legitimation** cannot be easily separated. Nonetheless, it seemed that the fault of Parsons's analysis was that these elements were conceptualized both as intertwined *and* as serving integration. This was evident in his overarching analytical concept of *perfect integration* and his tendency to see disintegration in terms of the contingent deviance of individual actors, rather than as something systematic.

Drawing on **Marx**'s analysis of **capitalism**, David Lockwood suggested that what was missing was a concept of *system contradiction*. Simply put, functionalism had no place for the idea that the parts of a social system may contain tendencies toward disintegration or contradiction (the exception was Robert **Merton**'s idea of 'dysfunction'). According to Lockwood, those tendencies may eventually come to the surface in the form of oppositional interests and conflicts among actors. These conflicts may or may not be contained by the normative order (for Lockwood, this is an empirical question).

Rather than proposing two separate models, Lockwood argued that it is necessary to consider the question of **cooperation**, conflict and **social change** in terms of two distinct, but inter-related, sets of processes. One is concerned with normative processes of *social integration*, the other with material processes of *system integration*. The problem with functionalism was that it conflated the two and emphasized the mutually consistent operation of both sets of processes. Lockwood's ideas have been taken further in Jürgen **Habermas**'s development of the concepts of social system and **lifeworld**.

More recently it has seemed that the problem of making an equal acknowledgement of the sources of order and disorder in social life has derived from the central place given to the actor in much social theory. According to **Luhmann**, and other theorists influenced by the rise of chaos theory or complexity theory in the natural sciences, social systems are too complex to be reducible to actors' reasons for acting. Since the latter can in principle be multifarious, this gives rise to the analysis of social systems in terms of how they manage the coordination of the motivations of actors and this must give precedence to order over disorder. For Luhmann, continuous disintegration is integral to the dynamic of social systems.

References and further reading

Alexander, J. (1985) *Neo-Functionalism*. London: Sage.
Giddens, A. (1984) *The Constitution of Society*. Cambridge: Polity Press.
Habermas, J. (1987) *The Theory of Communicative Action*, vol. 2. Cambridge: Polity Press.
Lockwood, D. (1964) 'System Integration and Social Integration', in G. Zollschan and W. Hirsch (eds), *Explorations in Social Change*. London: Routledge.
Luhmann, N. (1997) *Die Gesellschaft der Gesellschaft*. Frankfurt am Main: Suhrkamp.

JOHN HOLMWOOD

INTELLECTUALS

Intellectuals neither perform primarily physical work nor hold command over coercive means, but rather act conceptually, in the form of talking and writing, teaching, planning, suggesting, and thinking. The implications of this basic characteristic are complex enough, encompassing the social division of mental and manual labour and pointing to the fact that intellectual **elites** are typically 'not among the primary holders of political power or controllers of economic resources' (Parsons 1969: 21). But intellectuals are also seen as taking on tasks of addressing issues of public interest. The natural scientist or the professor of Greek philosophy is not an intellectual *per se*; but if the scientist refuses research that contributes to the development of the atom bomb, or if the professor writes pamphlets propagating a restitution of Aristotelian virtues, both figures are deemed to be intellectuals. This deviation from normal role expectations also implies a third quality, whereby intellectuals tend to escape fixed social topologies and become 'socially unattached' or 'free-floating' (*freischwebend*) in Karl **Mannheim**'s key phrase (Mannheim [1929] 1936: 137). It was in this sense that Mannheim and Georg **Lukács** spoke grandiosely of the homelessness of the modern intellectual.

If intellectuals as a specific category or social **group** are to be distinguished from general knowledge workers or cultural guardians such as engineers or magicians, the time and place of their historical emergence varies widely. Often the Greek sophists with their universal teaching and questioning program are described as the first intellectuals. The French historian Jacques Le Goff (1956) traces them to the formation of an independent intellectual life in the late-medieval city. Mannheim, on the other hand, wavers between placing their emergence in the period of Renaissance humanism 'and the period of bourgeois ascendancy' in the seventeenth and eighteenth centuries onwards (Mannheim 1936: 139). However, the concept of intellectuals in its modern received sense developed only in the course of the nineteenth century, and only gained relevance at the end of this century. When the false accusation and condemnation of the French Jewish army officer, Dreyfus, led to an outcry among French artists and scientists in the

1890s, famously including Èmile Zola, as well as Èmile Durkheim, his supporters soon came to be called *les intellectuels*. Yet the term at first carried a strongly negative connotation which was first systematized by the right-wing French writer Maurice Barrès, defining the intellectual 'as an artist or scientist who lacks political power but nevertheless forms a social ideal' (cited in Bering: 1978: 45). Barrès's statements fuelled a continuous wave of anti-intellectual resentment that lasted throughout the early twentieth century in Europe, reinforced by anti-Semitism and culminating in the rise of fascism. Intellectuals tended to be perceived as decadent, Jewish, practically incompetent and lacking in instinct and patriotism (see **Judaism**).

Two factors have been seen as crucial in explaining the role of intellectuals in society: on the one hand, intellectuals' difficult and diminished relationship to the sources of formal political power, and on the other hand the role of intellectuals class backgrounds. Antonio **Gramsci**'s conception of the 'organic intellectual' and Mannheim s conception of the 'free-floating intelligentsia' from the 1920s and 1930s are exemplary in these respects. Where for Gramsci the intellectual function of forming a **worldview** and shaping a social **consensus** is intimately linked to the struggle of social classes for political **hegemony**, Mannheim held that the discourses of the educated strata are the only place in which social particularity can be overcome. But Mannheim also emphasized that intellectual activity was conditioned by affiliations with antagonistic classes, while Gramsci conceded a relatively de-particularized space of intellectual activity, writing that 'the relationship between the intellectuals and the world of production is... mediated by the whole fabric of society and by the complex of superstructures, of which the intellectuals are, precisely, the "functionaries"' (Gramsci 1971: 12). Later, Jean-Paul **Sartre** ([1965] 1974) drew together these different perspectives, arguing that

while intellectuals occupy particular functions within the hierarchies and power relations of the of the state and the economy, they also seek to think and act on behalf of the 'universal' – so that they either strive to transcend their particular function or else live a life of resignation. Since Sartre's time, however, this language of the 'universal intellectual' has been subject to serious scepticism. For **Foucault** and **Bourdieu**, the way historically specific intellectuals gain their social reputation, form their will to opposition, and realize their chances to resist, is more important than the manifest content of their messages.

References and further reading

Bauman, Z. (1987) *Legislators and Interpreters: On Modernity, Post-Modernity, and Intellectuals*. Ithaca, NY: Cornell University Press.
Benda, J. ([1927] 1955) *The Betrayal of the Intellectuals*. Boston: Beacon Press.
Bering, D. (1978) *Die Intellektuellen. Geschichte eines Schimpfwortes*. Stuttgart: Klett-Cotta.
Gramsci, A. (1971) *Selections from the Prison Notebooks*. New York: International Publishers.
Le Goff, Jacques (1956) *Les Intellectuels au Moyen Age*. Paris: Le Seuil.
Mannheim, K. (1936) *Ideology and Utopia*. London: Routledge.
Parsons, T. (1969) "The Intellectual': A Social Role Category', in P. Rieff (ed.) *On Intellectuals: Theoretical Studies, Case Studies*. Garden City, NY: Anchor/Doubleday.
Rieff, P. (ed.) (1969) *On Intellectuals: Theoretical Studies, Case Studies*. Garden City, NY: Anchor/Doubleday.
Sartre, J.-P. ([1965] 1974) 'A Plea for Intellectuals', in *Between Existentialism and Marxism*. London: New Left Books.

TILMAN REITZ

INTERACTION

There have been numerous attempts to develop systems to describe social interaction throughout the history of the social sciences. The topic of interaction is salient for social thought since the reciprocally attentive and mutually effective relationship between two or more individuals can be seen as the essence of social existence, as in Max **Weber**'s near-canonical definition of 'social action' as individuals whose conduct is rooted in, and oriented by, their awareness of each other. In contemporary sociology since the Second World War, the significance of social interaction has been the subject of two contested questions: (1) is the presence of interaction extensively, if not entirely, excluded from mainstream schemes of sociological theory?; and (2) is society reducible to interactions between individuals?

A key figure in the contribution of a distinct possibility for sociology was Georg **Simmel** who cultivated the idea of a 'formal sociology', one that would examine social relationships in terms of their '**form**' rather than their content; that is, in terms of the kind of relationship that individuals are involved in, without regard for the nature of whatever practical matters their relationship might be sub-serving. Thus, one could examine relationships in terms of the effects that the number of people involved in it might have, no matter whether the people are playing games, arguing, eating lunch, or trying out the fitting of a tailored suit. The possibilities of relationship available to two people are different from those available to three people: the latter relationship allows that there may be 'ganging up' whereas the former does not.

The most significant inheritor of Simmel's idea was Erving **Goffman** who complained of what he called a 'neglected situation', namely, that of face-to-face interaction or more accurately, that of 'co-presence' situations. These are situations in which people are physically present to each other in the same locality, though not necessarily in face-to-face engagement with each other (as when people sit in parallel disregard on a shared bus seat). Goffman viewed such situations as an autonomous domain of social life in the sense of displaying a system of distinctive properties that could be

understood in their own terms: there were always ways in which **social relationships** could be specifically affected by being carried on under conditions of co-presence.

Goffman conceived co-presence as an informational transaction, shaped by the access to information about each other that parties to the transaction have, and as centrally connected with the capacity of individuals to claim and sustain an **identity**. The availability of segregation between **public and private** occasions was a key consideration in respect of the 'presentation of **self**', as Goffman termed it. In contrast to strongly methodological-individualist theories such as **rational choice** theory or **utilitarianism**, Goffman affirmed that: (1) purportedly individual qualities and properties such as identity are to be understood as held through joint **action** and **cooperation**; and (2) that institutional givens determine the possibility of segregation between 'public' and 'private' domains. Thus in his *Presentation of Self in Everyday Life* (1959) Goffman developed a concept of 'establishments', including organizations such as hotels, restaurants, and theatres in which team-like interactions generate and sustain the identity claims of particular individuals. *Asylums* (1961) expounds the concept of 'total institution' to categorize establishments such as prisons, concentration camps, mental hospitals. In these establishments all segregation of public and private **spaces** is denied to the parties (often inmates), with the routine consequence that claims to personal identities are routinely undermined. The concept of 'total institutions' forcefully embodies Goffman's formal approach. His comparison of heterogeneous organizational kinds such as prisons, military schools and monasteries enables him to highlight their common formal attributes, despite considerable variation in their practical purpose and **moral** ethos, and it also allows him to impute these common features to the administrative consequences of co-presence rather than to the purpose of the organization or to the character of the persons contained within them. Thus, a key argument of *Asylums* was that purportedly therapeutic practices are better understood as manifestations of disciplinary necessities orientated to managing the daily co-presence of inmates.

Goffman was sceptical about the major theoretical enterprises within sociology, but by no means opposed to the idea that interactions are **embedded** in large environing complexes of social **organization**.

Harvey Sacks, a student of both Goffman and **Garfinkel**, sought to develop a more systematic form of analysis of interaction than Goffman had attempted. Before the early 1960s, when Sacks began to set out his ideas, it had often been argued that it was the non-verbal aspects of **communication** that were decisive in interpersonal communication. Sacks noted that this conviction was not based on any extensive or thoughtful analysis of the verbal component of face-to-face interaction. Thus taking advantage of the availability of tape-recorders and accessible phone-lines to mechanically capture the details of speech exchanges, he began to examine social interaction in terms of talk.

His aim was to develop a systematic way of using 'conversational data as a way of doing sociology', as he put it. This project of studying talk-in-interaction under the title of 'conversation analysis' was realized through concentration on the composition and distribution of turns-at-talk between parties to conversation. Viewing contributions to conversation as actions, and the alternation of turns at talk as constituting cases of social interaction, conversation analysis has come to develop ways of identifying generic organizing properties of action and interaction sequences. These are analyzed predominantly in terms of (1) the manner in which actions (exemplified in utterances) manifest a specific orderliness which is designed by the participants on the basis of sensitivity to the properties of prior

utterances and the immediate situations in which those utterances are produced; and (2) the way in which parties to the talk jointly endow the alternation of their single turns with features that place them in an overall conversational sequence that they jointly build.

Where Goffman's work has been seen as involving a personalized style that is hard to convert into a systematically applicable method, conversation analysis provides a generally accessible method giving rise to a large and vigorous industry in sociology and cognate disciplines such as linguistics and pragmatics. Often these related disciplines use the terminology of turn-taking as a baseline for the exploration of **language** exchange in workplaces and other social settings.

Sometimes the work of Goffman and Sacks and other conversation analysts is seen as implying a view that social life consists in nothing but face-to-face interactions and as thus denying any reality to large-scale **social structures**. Certainly, even among those concerned with the analysis of interaction, conversation analysis is criticized for its concentration on patterns of speech at the expense of (for example) the 'multimodal' character of interaction. However, there is no reason to suppose that these approaches necessarily preclude concern with the phenomena that other sociological schemes elect to address, such as systems, structures and organization. Some commentators argue that Goffman and conversation analysis can be treated as identifying a distinct 'level' of social reality that can be incorporated into a more general theoretical scheme that postulates and integrates a variety of such levels, often by way of combining complementary elements from different theoretical **traditions** into new synthesis. One exponent of this synthetic approach is Anthony **Giddens**, who has sought to treat social interaction as the observable site of social organization.

References and further reading

Goffman, E. (1959) *Presentation of Self in Every-day Life*. New York: Doubleday.
Goffman, E. (1961) *Asylums*. New York: Double-day.
Sacks, H. (1992) *Lectures on Conversation*, 2 vols. Oxford: Blackwell.

WES SHARROCK

INTERESTS

The term 'interests' is a central concept aimed at explaining the behaviour of actors, whether individuals or collective actors. Interest-motivated action is a specific manner of conduct oriented by purposive rationality (see also **preferences** and **needs**). Interest-driven action is characterised by four elements: (1) individual or collective actors motivated by goals, needs and desires; (2) rational calculation, involving estimation of costs, benefits, and alternative means; (3) competition from opponents, often in conflictual relations to one another; and (4) opportunity structures, which both constrain and articulate the realization of interests. Objects of interests may include money, power, prestige, or security.

In seventeenth and eighteenth century social and political thought, the effects of interest-driven action were seen as consisting both in emancipation from traditionalistic moral ideas of virtue and restraint of the 'passions'. In eighteenth-century political thought, especially on the writing of Montesquieu on 'the softening' effect of commerce ('*doux commerce*'), one particular type of passion was thought capable of taming or pacifying the other passions. This was seen as the passion for money: love of lucre was seen as opposing and bridling other passions insofar as it promised relatively predictable and constant behaviour of men and thus a peaceful and stable society. According to Albert Hirschman's classic study, passions were thereby thought to give way to *interests* (Hirschman 1977).

However, this reasoning soon met with criticism. Many social thinkers of the mid-nineteenth century onwards demonstrate the ways in which interests alone do not fully explain the character of social action. With differing theoretical nuances, many thinkers from J. S. **Mill** and Vilfredo Pareto to **Tönnies**, **Durkheim** and **Weber** articulate the ways in which action can also be driven by non-self-regarding motivations, notably by **values and norms**, and can aim at non-self-regarding goals. They make clear the questionableness of the assumption that competition or conflict of interest entails the common good as some kind of happy by-product. A **republic** or 'commonwealth' cannot legitimately rest purely on self-interest and conflict. In politics, interests are served and become effective by intermediation through collective action. In addition, there is the further problem that the very propensity to struggle collectively and voluntarily in pursuit of common goals presupposes a starting-point of unequal distribution of resources. Not every interest will therefore have an equal chance to find articulation, organization and realization.

In political sociology, **institutions** play a key part in the opportunity structures that affect the emergence and design of interests. From this perspective, three typical accounts of the institutional origins and context of interests can be identified. According to **Marx**, objective interests derive from an actor's position in the process of production and the social division of labour. Individuals affected by the same objective social circumstances are said to possess common interests. These interests are the 'necessary condition' for the emergence of **class** conflict and for the driving of basic social change. However, the 'sufficient condition' is that individuals must become *subjectively aware* of these interests in class struggle, through class organisation and through a common epistemic act (Lukes 1974). For Theodor Geiger (1949), on the other hand, interests rest only on the privation or non-satisfaction of something, and can only be subjective in nature, dependent on individual valuation and interpretation: there is no objectively 'true interest' of labour and the working class. Lastly, a third typical position is represented by Ralf **Dahrendorf** (1959), who reformulates the distinction between objective and subjective interests by pointing out that both the social situation as an external world and the inner psychological preferences of the individual actor must feature in the content of the same individual actor's interests. Dahrendorf thus reformulates Marx's 'objective interests' as 'latent interests', stemming from the actor's social position and role. To the extent that an actor becomes conscious of such interests, they are the actor's 'manifest interests'. In this sense, 'objective' or 'latent' interests describe a purely hypothetical assumption about possible individual orientations. This debate highlights the way in which durable coincident interests can only emerge from social differentiation in the form of mediated conflicts between citizens and states, between socio-economic groups or classes, between producers and consumers, and between states and private corporations.

References and further reading

Dahrendorf, R. (1959) *Class and Class Conflict in an Industrial Society*. London: Routledge & Kegan Paul.

Geiger, T. (1949) *Die Klassengesellschaft im Schmelztiegel*. Cologne: Kiepenheuer.

Hirschman, A. O. (1977) *The Passions and the Interests: Political Arguments for Capitalism before its Triumph*. Princeton, NJ: Princeton University Press.

Lukes, S. (1974) *Power: A Radical View*. London: Macmillan.

Mansbridge, J. J. (ed.) (1990) *Beyond Self-Interest*. Chicago: University of Chicago Press.

Neuendorff, H. (1973) *Der Begriff des Interesses: Eine Studie zu den Gesellschaftstheorien von Hobbes, Smith und Marx*. Frankfurt am Main: Suhrkamp.

Olson, M. (1965) *The Logic of Collective Action: Public Goods and the Theory of Groups*. Cambridge, MA: Harvard University Press.

Schmitter, P. and Streeck, W. (1999) *The Organization of Business Interests: Studying the Associative Action of Business in Advanced Industrial Societies* (Discussion Paper 99/1). Cologne: Max Planck Institute for the Study of Societies.

CHRISTIAN BRÜTT

INTERSEXUALITY

See: sex/gender distinction

INTERSUBJECTIVITY

'Intersubjectivity' denotes the connection and interpenetration of individual human subjectivities. Some writers approach this issue from the perspective of the individual, asking how it is that one solitary ego is able to know, recognize, connect and/or communicate with other solitary egos. The question of 'other minds' in Anglo-American philosophy is one example of this, so too is Edmund Husserl's famous phenomenological theory of intersubjectivity, outlined in his *Cartesian Meditations* (1973) (see **phenomenology**). The subjective life of others is given to us in our everyday life, Husserl argues, both in the respect that we can experience ourselves as experienced by them (e.g. when we feel others looking at us, their eyes burning into our back) and in the respect that we experience the world as one experienced by others (e.g. when we point things out to others and/or feel surprised when they claim not to see what we see). This sense is extremely important, he argues, as it grounds our sense of **rationality** and **objectivity**, not to mention **ethics**. Rationality, in the final instance, entails that we can make ourselves understandable to others, which of course presupposes that they have a subjective life. Likewise, objectivity presupposes that 'the world' is more than my mere subjective apprehension of it: that it exists for others as it exists for me. Ethics is founded upon my recognition of others as subjects like me, deserving of the same consideration. The mystery, for Husserl, is how all of this is possible for an individual consciousness. How does subjectivity transcend itself and achieve intersubjectivity? The answer, for Husserl, resides in a transference of subjective states from ego to alter, which is, in turn, based on perceived similarities between ego and alter.

Other writers, such as G. H. **Mead** and Alfred **Schutz**, approach the issue from the other way round. On their view, human agents are always already involved in interactions and relations with others. Moreover, any concept of '**self**' presupposes an 'other' who is not self. One cannot have self without other. From this standpoint, our senses of both 'self' and 'other' arise simultaneously out of interactions which precede them. In contrast to Husserl, 'primary' forms of intersubjectivity are said to precede the development of individual subjectivity. Moreover, developing a **Hegelian** thread that this approach is based upon, it is argued that individual egos seek **recognition** from one another and need this recognition for their full subjective development. Subjective interdependency is thus deemed fundamental to the human condition.

References and further reading

Crossley, N. (1996) *Intersubjectivity: The Fabric of Social Becoming*. London: Sage.
Haney, K. M. (1994) *Intersubjectivity Revisited: Phenomenology and the Other*. Athens, OH: Ohio University Press.
Husserl, E. (1973) *Cartesian Meditations: An Introduction to Phenomenology*. The Hague: Nijhoff; Dordrecht: Kluwer.
Theunissen, M. (1984) *The Other: Studies in the Social Ontology of Husserl, Heidegger, Sartre, and Buber*. Cambridge, MA: MIT Press.

NICK CROSSLEY

INTIMACY

The term lacks a precise definition in both **popular culture** and much social theory.

Moreover, its meaning has changed over time. 'Intimacy' is often defined by **practices** thought to generate affective and binding qualities of relationship although the precise **nature** and consequence of these practices are contested. The term is occasionally used more narrowly to refer to sexual familiarity with another. In everyday current usage, intimacy is often presumed to involve practices of close association, familiarity and privileged **knowledge**, strong positive emotional attachments, such as **love**, and a very particular form of 'closeness' and being 'special' to another person, associated with high levels of **trust**. Whether loyalty and **moral** responsibility are typical features of intimacy in the present is more contested. More recent discussions of intimacy emphasize one particular practice of generating 'closeness' above all others: self-disclosure. Intimacy of the inner **self**, 'disclosing intimacy' or 'self-expressing intimacy' has become celebrated in popular culture as the key to a 'good relationship' although some academic work has suggested that this type of intimacy may be more of an ideological construct than an everyday lived reality. Debate also focuses on **gender** differences in 'doing intimacy'.

Classical theorists' accounts of the development of '**modernity**' provide a starting point for understanding the significance of intimacy. Necessary precursors to intimacy are: a degree of **individualization**, including the conceptualization of individuals as having unique inner selves and the separation, whether ideological or 'real', of 'public' and 'private' domains, creating the opportunity for intimacy to be associated with private personal relationships (see also **public and private**, **subject and subjectivity**). Of the classical theorists, Georg **Simmel** offers the most detailed account of intimacy. Simmel notes that the intimate dyad is a relationship which, by definition, only lasts as long as both parties participate. In its pure form, voluntary, mutual and exclusive participation, what each shows or gives *only to the other*, sustains the relationship. Private, exclusive, exchange generates trust and affect. There is no externally imposed institutionalization of the relationship. Although Simmel emphasized that people put their whole person into intimate relationships, tact and discretion remained aspects of relationships.

Subsequent theorists echo many of these themes with rather different emphasis. For example, Erving **Goffman** discusses intimate relationships in terms of people who not only go 'back stage' into the private domain but with whom tact and discretion, which he associates with role performance, are significantly less important. Much of Simmel's account of intimacy in dyadic relationships is echoed by the contemporary British theorist, Anthony **Giddens** in his discussion of 'the pure relationship' but Giddens places more emphasis on a dialogue of mutual disclosure and argues that a distinctive shift in intimacy occurred in the late twentieth century. In a climate in which people became more self-conscious of change, risk and being the makers of their own 'narrative-of-the-self', self-disclosing intimacy became a means of anchoring the self in one or more particularly intense personal relationships. Relationships became both more fragile, lasting only as long as they provide mutual satisfaction, and are more satisfactory, **equal** and **democratic**.

Whereas Giddens suggested that the cultural emphasis on 'disclosing intimacy' is indicative of positive **social change**, there are a number of **postmodern** theorists who offer more pessimistic accounts. Unrestrained **market** forces and mass consumer cultures are accused of promoting a self-obsessive, self-isolating or competitive individualism which renders people incapable of sustaining meaningful intimate relationships. The work of Zygmunt **Bauman** (2003) is typical, but there are elements of this critique in many other works including that of Richard Sennett and the feminist

work of Arlie Hochschild. Barbara Misztal controversially sums up the practical consequences of disclosing intimacy in terms of the replacement of a concern to be sincere and responsible to each other in relationships with worry about authenticity, and being true to the self. These debates overlap with discussion of **social capital** and concern that private intimacy supplants or undermines sociability, **community** and **civil society**.

There has been continued discussion of whether and why women's relationships appear to involve more 'self-disclosing intimacy' than men's. Some **feminist theory** draws on **psychoanalysis** to claim that a greater capacity for intimacy among women is a psychological consequence of the conventional divisions of labor in parenting and the distinctiveness of mother – daughter and mother – son relationships. Feminist theorists also offer accounts that give greater explanatory weight to material factors such as inequalities in social, economic and political opportunities constraining women to specialize in caring work and intimacy. Feminists have also analyzed gendered cultural discourses about men's and women's differential emotional and romantic needs that are folded into their conceptions of the self. Some feminist theorizing suggests that Giddens underestimated the underpinnings of gender inequality and the ideological strength of a conventional heterosexual culture.

References and further reading

Bauman, Z. (2003) *Liquid Love*. Cambridge: Polity.

Berlant, L. (ed.) (2000) *Intimacy*. Chicago: University of Chicago Press.

Duncombe, J. and Marsden, D. (1995). '"Workaholics" and "Whingeing Women": Theorising Intimacy and Emotion Work', *Sociological Review*, 43: 150–69.

Giddens, A. (1992) *The Transformation of Intimacy*. Cambridge: Polity.

Hochschild, A. (2003) *The Commercialization of Intimate Life*. Berkeley, CA: University of California Press.

Holland, J., Weeks, J. and Gillies, V. (2003) 'Families, Intimacy and Social Capital', *Social Policy and Society*, 2: 339–48.

Jamieson, L. (1998) *Intimacy: Personal Relationships in Modern Societies*. Cambridge: Polity.

Misztal, B. (2000). *Informality: Social Theory and Contemporary Practice*. London: Routledge.

Sennett, R. (1998) *The Corrosion of Character: The Personal Consequences of Work in the New Capitalism*. London: W. W. Norton.

LYNN JAMIESON

ISLAM

Islam begins with a series of revelations received by Muhammad (570–632) during the 610s CE. The nature of these revelations has a family resemblance to many tropes found within the cultural milieu of the Nile to Oxus region, which can also be found at work in Jewish and Christian **sacred** stories (see **Judaism** and **Christianity**) . Islam orders these narratives of Abrahamic monotheism, placing itself as the culmination of a series of revelations associated with a diverse group of prophets including Abraham, Moses and Jesus. Despite the degree of overlap between these Abrahamic revelations, Islam is not usefully considered to be either a Jewish or Christian heresy. It inaugurated a new semantic universe, which succeeded in radically transforming the Nile to Oxus region so that themes that continued beyond the arrival of Islam could only do so through a cultural lexicon dominated by the venture of Islam.

Encouraged by his wife Khadijah, the Prophet Mohammed gradually began to gather around him a small group of followers who formed the *Umma*, the **community** of the faithful. The decade following these revelations was a taxing one in which the Prophet and other members of the Umma found themselves increasingly harassed and ostracized from Meccan society. In 622 they moved to Medina after the Prophet was invited as an arbiter by conflicting Medinese factions. In his role as arbiter, he was able to establish the first Islamic state in Medina, prior to its incorporation of Mecca (630), and eventually the rest of the Arabian peninsula (630–32). As such, the Islamic state pioneered the political unification of Arabia, amalgamating both its settled and nomadic communities.

From 630 to 715 the Islamic state mounted a number of spectacular military campaigns, which brought areas ranging from Spain to Sind under its control. The Muslim armies' success did not result from **technological** or numerical superiority over their foes; rather, it was a function of the **discipline** and cohesion inculcated by the discourse of Islam as well as the capacity of the Islamicate state to direct military operations on a continental scale. (The adjective 'Islamicate' is used to refer to institutions informed by Islam but not directly a part of Islam defined in the strict sense of a set of sacred discourses.) The expansion of Islam included two related but distinct processes: it entailed the expansion of an Islamicate public order in which states ruled by Muslim elites brought under their domain regions in which Muslims were either marginal or absent; and it also involved the process whereby individuals and communities transformed themselves by embracing Islam and thus becoming members of the Umma. With the fragmentation of the unified Islamic state, the jihad also became fragmented and the expansion of Islam began to take the form of missionary activities performed by merchants and preachers and small-scale campaigns of conquest. The corpus of texts that constitute Islam as a system of beliefs and values were consolidated for the most part by the tenth century CE. After this period, the survival of a complex and huge social formation as constituted by Islam is a testimony to its capacity to adapt to a variety of spatial and temporal contexts.

The configurations of the Islamicate world are normally narrated in a series of

dynasties that ruled the increasingly fragmented Umma. In these narratives the
pristine unity and simplicity of the early
Islamicate order gave way to decadence and
a fissiparous 'Oriental despotism'. Such a
sequence reflects the scheme used by classical
Muslim scholars, which has been too often
uncritically appropriated by **Orientalism**,
and as such tends to smooth over the contingent and deeply contested context of
these transformations and re-configur-
ations. Rather than narrating a cycle of
dynasties, it is more useful to focus on four
major themes contributing to the shaping
of Muslim history.

The first theme refers to the oscillation
between the boundaries of the Umma and
the boundaries of an Islamicate political
order. In various periods the Umma has
exceeded the Islamicate state(s); in other
periods the boundaries of the Islamicate
government(s) have gone beyond the confines of the Umma. Membership of the
Umma and the Islamicate state remained
synonymous until Al-Andulas broke away
from the unified Islamicate state (the Caliphate) in 757. Despite the severance of its
political links with the Caliphate, the Muslims of Al-Andulas continued to see themselves and were seen by other Muslims as
members of the community of the faithful.
This de-linking between being members of
a faith community and being members of a
political community has continued to the
present, in which the idea of being Muslims
living under non-Muslim rule has become
not only accepted but common.

The second theme refers to processes of
de-centralization and re-centralization of
the Islamicate political order, and specifically to the number of units it has been
divided into, ranging from the single unitary state to the metaphor of the '72
nations'. The development of the Shia and
what later became the Sunni political
movements and their over-determination as
sectarian divisions were one of the major
forces undermining the single universal

Caliphate. It was not, however, until the
conflict between the Fatimids and the
Abassids from 909 until 1071 that the order
saw a proliferation of (anti-)Caliphates
initially centred in Andulus, Egypt and
Iraq. The Islamicate state was replaced by a
Muslim 'commonwealth' of powerful
regional Muslim polities: Ottoman, Safvid
and Timurid (Mughal) empires and a host
of smaller local states in Africa and the
Malay archipelago. These centrifugal tendencies were often countered by various projects to restore a centralized order, which
sometimes took the form of eschatological
movements such as those of the Mahdi in
Sudan (1884), and at other times took the
form of state expansion, where a single
Muslim regime sought the mantle of the
leadership of the Muslim world, as with the
pan-Islamism of the late Ottomans at the
end of the ninteenth century.

The third theme is concerned with tensions
between processes of Islamization (i.e deepening of the 'Islamic' element in Islamicate) societies and de-Islamization.
Islamization often occurred in the wake of
the establishment of an Islamicate public
order, as those subject to Muslim rule become
Muslims. The notion of subjugated populations choosing Islam on pain of death, however, owes more to anti-Muslim polemics
than to available historical records. De-Islamization involved the coercive elimination
of Muslim **identity**. This was the experience of enslaved West Africans (perhaps as
many as a third of Africans shipped to the
Western hemisphere may been Muslims) (see
slavery), as well as of the Muslims of Iberian
peninsula, and the Muslims of most of the
'**Communist**' world, and Muslims subject to
colonial rule. De-Islamization also occurred as a result of projects of **secularization**
initiated either by colonial or post-Inde-
pendence 'Kemalist' regimes.

The final theme refers to the relationship
between the Islamicate entities and the rest
of the world, in particular the degree of centrality or marginality of Islamicate formations.

The marginalization of Islam is largely a product of the two most serious challenges to the existence of Islam. The Mongol invasions, culminating in the sack of Baghdad in 1258, threatened the Islamicate public order with extinction. The Mongol invasions took place in the context of the weakening of the central leadership of the 'universal' Caliphate. The Muslim victory at Ayn Jalut (1260) inflicted the first major defeat on the Mongol armies and signalled the process by which Muslims were able to turn the tide, with the eventual Islamization of the Mongol empire's successor elites. It left in its wake an Islamicate world divided into a Muslim commonwealth of regional and often contending political entities that faced the second major challenge to the Ummah: that of European colonization of large parts of Afro-Eurasia, often resulting in clashes between Islamicate ruling elites and European colonial forces. The success of European colonization was such that by 1920 the bulk of the Muslim population of the world was living under European rule. The challenge posed by the European colonization was initially political and military. However, by the late nineteenth century it took on **economic**, **intellectual** and **cultural** aspects, so much so that in 1924 the Turkish leader, Mustafa Kemal, unilaterally abolished the Caliphate. Kemal's intervention ruptured the link with an autonomous Muslim presence and its past, ushering in a strident project of westernization, which was also pursued in less stringent forms in other parts of the Islamicate world.

Much of the current unrest in Muslim communities can be seen as an attempt to recover from the effects of European colonization. The Muslim recovery or 'Awakening' takes the form of a re-politicization of Islam. This project of re-politicization (Islamism) takes place in the context of a world marked by the logic of post-colonialism (see **post-colonial theory**), in which the cultural underpinnings of Western **dominance** find it difficult to translate Western economic and political **power** into global **hegemony**. Furthermore, the process of **globalization** allows the articulation of a universal Islam increasingly unencumbered by particularistic local accretions. Thus the formation of a Muslim commonwealth and an increasing integration of the Umma indicate that the assertion of Islam is not a nativist reaction to globalization but an alternative form of globalization. Islamism is a project that draws much of its strength from a conviction that there is no need for a detour through the labyrinths of Western history before one can arrive at a vision of the good life and a just order: universal **values** can be generated from Islam. The possibility of articulating such visions inspired by divergent readings of Islam's canonical texts is, however, complicated by the way the Muslim Umma finds itself without geopolitical representation, while many of the world's major powers (the United States, the Russian Federation, China, the European Union and India) confront restive Muslim populations. In the absence of an Islamicate great power, some Muslim activists have resorted to insurrectionary warfare in large parts of the world inhabited by the Umma. Other Muslims hope that 'intellectual and **moral** reform' will free the Umma to make its own history.

References and further reading

Berkey, J. P. (2003) *The Formation of Islam*. Cambridge: Cambridge University Press.

Blinkshap, K. Y. (1994) *The End of the Jihad State*. Albany, NY: SUNY Press.

Hodgson, M. G. (1977) *The Venture of Islam*. Chicago: University of Chicago Press.

McGraw, F. D. (1981) *The Early Muslim Conquests*. Princeton, NJ: Princeton University Press.

Sayyid, B. S. (2003) *A Fundamental Fear: Eurocentrism and the Emergence of Islamism*. London: Zed Press.

BOBBY S. SAYYID

J

JAMESON, FREDRIC (1932–)

US theorist

One of Jameson's central theoretical aims is to connect aesthetics with political and economic theories. As a Marxist theorist, he critically incorporates into his framework different currents of contemporary social thought, including **structuralism**, **post-structuralism**, **psychoanalysis**, and **critical theory**. In his attempt to link **Freud**, **Marx**, **Lacan** and **Althusser**, Jameson proposes a theory of the 'political unconscious' by, which he understands history as the history of **class** struggle. The latter resembles the Freudian **unconscious** or the Lacanian Real in so far as it cannot be analyzed directly: class struggle can only be analyzed through the narratives in which it has become sedimented. Jameson carries out many such analyses on cultural sources ranging from literature to architecture, video and film, arguing that the cultural form of **postmodernism** corresponds to today's stage of multinational capital or **post-industrial society**, while in earlier stages modernism corresponded to monopoly **capitalism**, and realism to market capitalism. Although critical of what **Lukács** called **reification**, Jameson always seeks to excavate the hidden utopian moments in even the most commodified cultural texts (see **utopia**). Jameson has contributed decisively to what has come to be called the **cultural turn**.

Major works

(1971) *Marxism and Form*. Princeton, NJ: Princeton University Press.
(1972) *The Prison House of Language*. Princeton, NJ: Princeton University Press.
(1981) *The Political Unconscious*. London: Routledge.
(1988) *The Ideologies of Theory*, 2 vols. Minneapolis, MN: University of Minnesota Press.
(1991) *Postmodernism, or, The Cultural Logic of Late Capitalism*. London: Verso.
(1998) *The Cultural Turn*. London: Verso.

Further reading

Burnham, C. (1995) *The Jamesonian Unconscious*. Durham, NC: Duke University Press.
Homer, S. (1998) *Fredric Jameson: Marxism, Hermeneutics, Postmodernism*. Cambridge: Polity Press.

OLIVER MARCHART

JUDAISM

The determination of the character of modern Jewish social thought must focus on elucidating what is distinctively Jewish in it (see also **Christianity** and **Islam**). Once this is done, one can proceed to examine some ways in which Jewish themes influence modern social thought in general. Three problems, however, make this undertaking especially difficult.

First, the temptation of a certain kind of sociology of **knowledge** that asserts a significant relation between circumstances of one's birth and **intellectual** accomplishment should be resisted. It is indeed the case that perhaps even before the destruction of the First Temple in Jerusalem by the Babylonians in 586 BCE and certainly afterwards, the **religion** of the Jews became 'textual' (Schniedewind 2004). Given this ancient textual environment of Judaism as a religion of a people exhibiting significant **literacy**, continual disputation and commentary were not only engendered but became the norm, resulting in the Mishnah, Talmud and Rabbinic Responsa, involving institutional **differentiation** and heterodoxy. The bearers of this textual preoccupation were the clerics, as **intellectuals**. Initially they included the Pharisees, and subsequently the rabbis. With the development of the *Haskalah* (enlightenment) in the eighteenth century and the emancipation of the Jews in Europe, the hitherto mostly unquestioned supremacy of rabbinic-*halakhic* (legal) orthodoxy was challenged (Nemoy 1952; Scholem 1971). The walls of the ghetto tumbled down before the more generalized *lex terrae* of the national state, with its principle of religious toleration. One can say here, borrowing from Max **Weber**'s (1967) contested category, that the Jews were no longer a 'pariah people' (see Momigliano 1994; Eisenstadt 1981): they became, both in the United States and **Europe**, citizens of what had now become their respective states (see **citizenship**). As a consequence, the intellectualism of the Jewish textual **tradition** was now turned outward, as exemplified by the reception of the thought of Baruch Spinoza, Heinrich Heine and Moses Mendelssohn.

In general it seems that the large number of Jewish-born modern intellectuals bears witness to this textual tradition of Judaism. Indeed it may be that the messianic potential within Judaism, conveyed specifically by the prophetic writings and the Talmud, had an influence on those radical socialists who were either born Jews, such as Leon Trotsky, or born in families that had converted to Christianity, such as Karl **Marx**.

However, whatever the degree of that influence, it had been refracted through both an 1800-year-long Christian tradition and a briefer but increasingly important tradition of scientific **rationalism** that qualitatively transformed Jewish messianism in a consistently cosmopolitan direction (see **cosmopolitanism**). It may also be that the centuries-long history of the Jews as 'outsiders' in the diaspora may have had a bearing on other intellectual developments such as Georg **Simmel**'s essay 'The Stranger'. Nonetheless, Simmel's father had converted to Roman Catholicism; and his mother had been baptized as a Protestant, as was the younger Simmel. Whatever Jewish influence there might have been on the work of a Marx or a Simmel, it is indirect; for it is hard to identify anything openly Jewish in their writings. The same can largely be said of the work of other Jewish-born intellectuals such as Emile **Durkheim** and Edmund Husserl. Still, the Jewish textual tradition and the status of the Jew as outsider were surely factors in the emergence of a large number of Jewish intellectuals preoccupied with themes of marginality and exclusion, exile and alienation, duty, repression and the law – such as Freud and Kafka, to name only two of the most famous names.

A second problem, however, involves the very idea of 'modern Jewish social thought'. While the changing circumstances of the nineteenth and twentieth centuries – full citizenship for Jews, the persistence of anti-Semitism, the **Holocaust**, Zionism and the existence of the state of Israel – required different and often new responses, modern Jewish thought remains inconceivable without reference to the *TANAKH* (the Hebrew Bible) and the rabbinic tradition. The common observation that Zionism is a modern nationalist movement is only a half-truth, as the concluding line of the Passover seder alone makes clear, 'next year in Jerusalem'. It is certainly the case that the toleration of gentiles by the 'enlightened Jew' of the *Aufklärung*, for example, Moses Mendelssohn and, later, the neo-**Kantian** Hermann Cohen, rested upon the assertion of the rationality of Judaism which is difficult to justify either biblically or from the rabbinic tradition. Yet even this assertion that found its culmination in the **universalism** of the **ethical** monotheism of Reform Judaism was justified by a tendentious translation of the biblical *ger* as 'stranger' instead of 'resident alien', as in the phrase 'you shall love the stranger, for you were strangers in the land of Egypt' (Deuteronomy 10:19); reference to the Noahide covenant in Genesis 9 (understood as the natural law); and Maimonides understanding of Christians as 'righteous', hence, worthy of salvation because of their acceptance of that covenant (see Katz 1961). Lastly, a third and obvious problem is that there has never been a single Judaism. There has always been a wide-ranging variety of Judaisms; for example, during the period of the Second Temple, Sadducees, Pharisees, Essenes, and today, Orthodox, Conservative, Reform and secular Jews. The significant conceptual differences between today's currents pose difficulties in ascertaining what is distinctively Jewish about modern Jewish social thought.

Despite these problems, the distinctiveness of Jewish thought can be ascertained as a paradoxical, simultaneously held recognition of two heterogeneous orientations: both the *nation* as conceptually legitimate (the putative lineage of Abraham, Isaac and Jacob) and a *universal monotheism*. The variety of Judaisms in modern times has sought in correspondingly different ways to ameliorate this tension-filled heterogeneity. For example, Reform Judaism has emphasized the universalism of an ethical monotheism – hence social activism 'to repair the world' – while Zionism has emphasized the nation. However, given these heterogeneous poles, the attempts within Judaism to eliminate the problem of the relation between the two orientations – the primordial and the universal – can not succeed.

Because of the asserted **legitimacy** of the particularism or distinctiveness of 'Israel', the universalism of monotheism, although accorded primacy, is always qualified. As such, it never attains, insofar as it remains Jewish, a consistent cosmopolitanism. Thus, even though Jews have achieved full **citizenship** in the modern **state**, there will always be, from the perspective of a rationalistic theory of the state, as Marx formulated it, 'the Jewish problem'. The distinctive contribution of Jewish social thought to modern social thought are the different ways in which this paradoxical orientation has been expressed and addressed.

When in the sixteenth and seventeenth centuries predominantly Christian societies such as England and Holland asserted their national distinctiveness from Spain, the 'Israel' of the Old Testament and Judaism was appealed to in order to justify the nation within a monotheistic **civilization**. A similar appeal justified the separation of Protestant countries from Roman Catholicism; and this combination of nationality and universal mission is also to be found in the political tradition of the United States. This appeal represents a significant influence of Judaism on the political developments of the **Occident**. The combination of these two heterogeneous orientations, exploited by the 'Christian Hebraism' of the sixteenth and seventeenth centuries in its adaptation of the biblical concept of the 'national covenant' (for example among the Dutch Calvinists and the English Puritans) indicated that the God of Judaism was 'national-universal' (see Orlinsky 1974; Dubnow 1958). This contrasted with the internationalist God of Christianity which recognized a universalism among individuals and not, as in the Jewish tradition, among nations. It is thus perhaps no coincidence that numerous scholars of nationality have been Jewish; for example, Hans Kohn, Elie Kedourie, Ernest **Gellner**, Eric Hobsbawm, Anthony Smith and Liah Greenfeld.

It is likely that one consequence of Jewish thought explicitly maintaining both of these orientations is a greater sensitivity to the place of the finite and primordial within otherwise universal aspirations, as in the work of Franz Rosenzweig ([1921] 1971), or in Martin Buber's (1937) analysis of the encounter between the I and the You, or in Edward Shils's (1975) discussion of the relation between primordial, personal, sacred and civil ties (see **sacred**). Certainly this influence is to be observed in Emmanuel Levinas's (1994) observation that a historical religious tradition is the condition of access to what is not conditioned. This **phenomenological** formulation of the relation between distinctiveness and the universal is a reformulation of the problem that history poses to universal monotheism: the problem of the Old Testament prophets and, later, of Judah ha-Levi's *The Kuzari*. The modern Jewish preoccupation with the relation of the historically particular to the universal aspirations of humanity finds expression in modern social thought in the relation between the unique and the universal (Talmon 1965), the encounter of one civilization with another (Momigliano 1971, 1987) and the analysis of the 'axial age' (Eisenstadt 1986).

References and further reading

Buber, M. (1937) *I and Thou*. Edinburgh: T. & T. Clark.

Dubnow, S. (1958) 'Letters on Old and New Judaism', in K. Pinson (ed.) *Nationality and History*. Philadelphia, PA: Jewish Publication Society.

Eisenstadt, S. N. (1981) 'Max Webers antikes Judentum und der Charakter der jüdischen Zivilisation', in W. Schluchter (ed.) *Max Webers Studie über das antike Judentum*. Franfurt am Main: Suhrkamp.

Eisenstadt, S. N. (1986) *The Origins and Diversity of Axial Age Civilizations*. Albany, NY: State University of New York.

Katz, J. (1961) *Exclusiveness and Tolerance*. Oxford: Oxford University Press.

Levinas, E. (1994) *Nine Talmudic Readings*. Bloomington, IN: Indiana University Press.

Momigliano, A. (1971) *Alien Wisdom*. Cambridge: Cambridge University Press.

Momigliano, A. ([1980] 1994) 'A Note on Max Weber's Definition of Judaism as a Pariah Religion', in *Essays on Ancient and Modern Judaism*. Chicago: University of Chicago Press.

Momigliano, A. (1987) *On Pagans, Jews and Christians*. Middletown, CT: Wesleyan University Press.

Nemoy, L. (1952) *Karaite Anthology*. New Haven, CT: Yale University Press.

Orlinsky, H. (1974) 'Nationalism-Universalism and Internationalism in Ancient Israel', in *Essays in Biblical Culture and Bible Translation*. New York: KTAV.

Rosenzweig, F. ([1921] 1971) *The Star of Redemption*. New York: Holt, Rinehart & Winston.

Schniedewind, W. (2004) *How the Bible Became a Book*. Cambridge: Cambridge University Press.

Scholem, G. (1971) *The Messianic Idea in Judaism*. New York: Schocken.

Shils, E. ([1957] 1975) 'Primordial, Personal, Sacred, and Civil Ties', in *Center and Periphery*. Chicago: University of Chicago Press.

Talmon, J. (1965) *The Unique and the Universal*. London: Secker & Warburg.

Weber, M. ([1921] 1967) *Ancient Judaism*. New York: Free Press.

STEVEN GROSBY

K

KANTIANISM AND NEO-KANTIANISM

Immanuel Kant (1724–1804) is celebrated in the history of philosophy as the progenitor of a systematic theory of **knowledge**, **morality** and aesthetics, based on '**transcendental** deduction' of the necessary structures of experience Although Kant's writings on history, politics and **society** were relatively limited, his influence in the history of social thought has been immense.

Kant's immediate followers, notably Fichte, Schelling, and **Hegel** believed they were 'completing' Kant by constructing speculative systems. Their philosophies, however, soon came to be challenged in the nineteenth century by forms of **positivism** and **materialism**. F. A. Lange's *Geschichte des Materialismus* (1866) was not so much a history of materialism as a history of materialism's mistakes and helped pave the way for a return to **idealism**. It was the work of Kuno Fischer and Hermann Lotze in the mid-nineteenth century that began the Neo-Kantian movement that sought to apply Kant's insights into the conditions of the possibility of knowledge. Whereas Kant had sought to justify Newtonian physics, the Neo-Kantians sought to establish the conditions for the sciences of history, psychology, and sociology: the new human sciences. The Neo-Kantians sought to avoid both the positivists' emphasis on the senses and the Hegelians' extravagant claims of reason.

Although he is not technically regarded as a Neo-Kantian, Wilhelm **Dilthey** worked in this spirit by creating a critique of historical reason and a 'philosophy of life' (*Lebensphilosophie*), notably laid out in his *Einleitung in die Geisteswissenschaft* (1883). Wilhelm Windelband influentially distinguished between 'nomothetic' and 'idiographic' knowledge, where the first seeks universal causal **laws** and is operative in the **natural** sciences, while the second focuses on non-repeatable individual events and is operative in the human sciences. The 'Southwest German School' of Neo-Kantianism, represented by Windelband and by Heinrich Rickert, concerned itself with problems of **value** and **culture**. They strove to develop the 'cultural sciences' – *Kulturwissenschaften* – based upon the study of the positing of values by individuals. In *Die Grenzen der naturwissenschaftlichen Begriffsbildung* (1902) Rickert sought to show historical research implies concepts of historical uniqueness that are crucial for a philosophy of culture. He stressed the importance of **methods and methodology** in the analysis of value relations in different social contexts. These ideas were further developed by Max **Weber** in his methodological writings. Weber's contributions included the distinction between 'facts and values' and the concept of the **ideal type**. Georg **Simmel** also contributed significantly to the project of a philosophy of history and culture based on Neo-Kantian premises. His Kantian background was particularly evident in his opposition between '**form**' and 'content'.

At the Marburg School of Neo-Kantianism, Hermann Cohen developed the idea of **objectivity** in Kant's theory of knowledge and experience, while Paul Natorp defended on anti-psychologistic understanding of Plato's philosophy, claiming that Plato was a 'Kantian before Kant'.

The year 1911 in Germany saw the foundation of *Logos* (1911–33), an international journal for the philosophy of culture with contributions by Rickert, Weber, Simmel, Troeltsch and the Marburg neo-Kantians, as well as by Nicolai Hartmann and Ernst Cassirer. It also published Edmund Husserl's key text *Philosophie als strenge Wissenschaft*. All these contributions dealt with a wide range of issues covering philosophy, **art**, **religion** and social reform.

References and further reading

Adair-Toteff, C. (2003) 'Neo-Kantianism', in T. Baldwin (ed.) *The Cambridge History of Philosophy 1870 – 1945*. Cambridge: Cambridge University Press.

Dilthey, W. ([1883] 1990) *Einleitung in die Geisteswissenschaft*. Stuttgart: Teubner.

Husserl, E. (1911) 'Philosophie als strenge Wissenschaft', *Logos*, 1: 289–341.

Lange, F. A. ([1866] 2003) *Geschichte des Materialismus und Kritik seiner Bedeutung in der Gegenwart*. Waltrop: Manuscriptum.

Ollig, H. (1979) *Der Neukantianismus*. Stuttgart: Metzler.

Rickert, H. ([1902] 2004) *Die Grenzen der naturwissenschaftlichen Begriffsbildung*. Stuttgart: Frommann, Friedrich, Verlag Günther Holzboog.

Willey, T. (1976) *Back to Kant*. Detroit, MI: Wayne State University Press.

CHRISTOPHER ADAIR-TOTEFF

KEYNES, JOHN MAYNARD (1883–1946)
British economist

Keynes served in the British government at the Treasury and as a member of the Versailles Treaty delegation, and was an influential political advisor at the Bretton Woods Treaty. His major work, the *General Theory of Employment, Interest and Money* (1936) revolutionized economic thought and policy. Keynes founded his claim to a general theory on the demonstration that traditional economic theory was limited to dealing with the special case of full employment equilibrium (see **political economy**). In his macroeconomic theory of aggregate output and employment, Keynes explained the causes of unemployment by refuting conventional economic theories of the social advantages of thrift, of the role of the rate of interest in adjusting savings and investments. He conclusively demonstrated the fallacies of the quantity theory of **money** and *laissez-faire* economics. Keynes's theory was adapted to neoclassical economic thought by J. R. Hicks (1937), but it fell into disrepute after the failure of Keynesian policies in the 1970s. For social theory, Keynes's economic theory implies the recognition that the normal state of **society** is one of dynamic disequilibrium rather than one of order or a tendency to equilibrium. In other respects, Keynes's social thought is characterized by a concern with economic efficiency, **social justice** and individual **liberty**. His theory had an exceptional impact on the policies of twentieth-century Western nation–states, supporting greater government intervention, not only to achieve full employment but also to redistribute income.

Major works

([1919] 1971) *The Economic Consequences of the Peace*. London: Macmillan.

([1921] 1963) *A Treatise on Probability*. London: Macmillan.

([1930] 1971) *A Treatise on Money*. London: Macmillan.

([1931] 1972) *Essays in Persuasion*. London: Macmillan.

([1933] 1972) *Essays in Biography*. London: Macmillan.

([1936] 1991) *General Theory of Employment, Interest and Money*. San Diego, CA: Harcourt Brace Jovanovich.

Further reading

Hicks, J. R. (1937) 'Mr. Keynes and the "Classics": A Suggested Interpretation', *Econometrica*, 5(2): 147–59.
Skidelsky, R. (1983, 1992, 2000) *John Maynard Keynes*, 3 vols. London: Macmillan.

HEINER GANßMANN

KINSHIP

Kinship refers to relations between humans built on descent and in-marriage. Types of descent and **marriage** differ widely between **cultures**, while what a **family** is and means is equally open to cultural elaboration. Describing and explaining these variations and the way in which societies organize around kinship have been central concerns of anthropology.

Most societies distinguish between 'real' family and 'in-laws', the former related through descent, the latter through marriage. In Euro-American societies, the distinction is conceptualized as 'blood-related' or 'consanguineal' relatives versus in-laws who do not 'share blood'. Other societies use different metaphors, but the idea of a common substance or spirit uniting descent groups is very common.

Descent is either bilateral (from the two parents) or unilineal (from one of the parents). However, no descent principle is pure. While inheritance may be passed on along a bilateral principle, surnames and other real or symbolic items may not. Unilineal descent is either patri- or matrilineal. Descent systems are not always indicators of power: societies with matrilineal descent are not necessarily matriarchal. Descent groups are, in theory, biological facts, but the actual means for acquiring membership of a kin group vary: virtually no societies use biological criteria plus in-marriage alone, and ideas about conception and procreation are themselves culture-relative. In some cases, simply the importance of a social relationship suffices to make it thought of as kinship.

Two main types of marriage exist: monogamy and polygamy. Monogamy is frequent in complex societies but can also be found in small-scale societies. Polygamy (found in many African and Asian societies) normally takes the form of polygyny (marriage between one man and more than one woman) but it is usually limited to a minority of men possessing **wealth** and **prestige**. In a few societies, mainly in the Himalayan area, polyandry (marriage between one woman and more than one man) is practised. There are many subtypes of these basic marriage forms. Early anthropological theory sought, with very partial success, to organize these types on an evolutionary ladder.

Marriage and descent are related to locality and the arrangement of households, although in no **law**-like manner. Monogamy typically combines with nuclear families (a married couple and their offspring living together), while polygamy is combinable with multiple households or extended families (domestic groups consisting of two or more nuclear families or multigenerational households). The most common forms of post-marital residence (important since kinship groups often have a territorial basis) include patrilocality, matrilocality and neolocality. Marriage caught the attention of anthropologists because it seems to be one of those rare universals that allows for comparison. G. P. Murdock (1949) wrote that marriage exists 'when the economic and sexual functions are united into one'. Anthropologists have struggled to establish a more covering definition for marriage, as indeed for the concepts of 'family' and kinship; but each attempt has been challenged by ethnographic exceptions (for example, some societies arrange marriages involving a dead member of a descent group). The **universalism** versus cultural particularism debate has loomed large in the study of kinship.

In anthropology, two larger schools developed in the study of kinship systems: descent theory and alliance theory. Both were reactions to evolutionist theory, and directed attention away from hypothetical origins towards social function and **structure**. The main proponents of descent theory included Meyer Fortes, A. R. Radcliffe-Brown, and E. E. Evans-Pritchard. They suggested that kinship systems function to ensure that lineage groups persist over time as political entities. According to Evans-Pritchard's study of segmentary organization among the Nuer (1951), segmentary systems are made of descent groups (lineages) organized around a principle of opposition to one another. If conflict breaks out between members of closely related lineages, only members of those two lineages will be involved in solving it. If conflict breaks out between lineages that stand farther away from each other (distance being measured by closeness to a common ancestor), larger descent groups will be involved. If threatened from the outside, the whole Nuer **tribe** will be activated as a political unit. Similar systems of fission and fusion have been found elsewhere. According to descent theorists, kinship systems may also serve to allocate rights and duties in societies.

Alliance theory focused on marriage and the rules surrounding it: **kinship** systems exist primarily to create possible marriages. Claude **Lévi-Strauss** (1969) distinguished between 'complex' and 'elementary' kinship systems. In complex systems, marriage rules are negative as definitions are provided only for those one cannot marry (normally defined by the **taboo** on **incest**). Individual choice in this case is important. In 'elementary' kinship, on the other hand, a spouse is selected according to much more sharply defined social rules, which are positive, singling out the group of persons one *should* marry. Cross-cousin marriage (marrying a cousin related through an opposite-sex sibling link) is one of the most favoured types of marriage, and formed part of Levi-Strauss's theory of elementary structures. It is the norm among Dravidian groups in Southern India, which prescribe bilateral cross-cousin marriage, and similar

systems have been found among Australian Aborigines and South American natives. Analyzing kinship structures among these 'elementary' societies, Lévi-Strauss believed he found a universal 'atom of kinship', consisting of the relations husband/wife and brother/sister, and father/son and mother's brother/sister's son. The last addition is crucial because Lévi-Strauss claims that kinship is primarily a means of creating alliances and reciprocity *between* descent groups: hence the role of mother's brother who has exchanged his sister for another woman.

Alliance and descent theorists argued along different paths, as they often represented (British) **functionalist** approaches versus (French) structuralist approaches. It can also be suggested that the two schools developed different theories to explain different societies: descent theorists drew mostly on African data, alliance theorists on Asian/American data. Yet it is not clear why descent and marriage should be regarded as separate realities, and many anthropologists have sought to overcome the dualism between the two directions.

Both approaches have also been criticized by more actor-oriented scholars. In *Outline of a Theory of Practice,* Pierre **Bourdieu** (1977) develops a theory of practice drawing on his fieldwork in Kabylia (Algeria), with a special focus on marriage strategies. In his critique of structuralism, Bourdieu uses the concept of **habitus** to show how individuals always seek to manipulate social rules in order to seek advantage within a dynamic system. One must distinguish between formal kinship rules and social interaction. Kinship **ideology** may justify behaviour, but it cannot explain it. Since the 1980s, kinship studies have occupied a less central role in anthropology, and have been partly replaced by a new interest in **ethnicity**.

Bourdieu's study of Kabyle kinship introduced the important concepts of 'symbolic power' and 'symbolic capital' to social theory. Here it is worth thinking about how important the role of kinship is to social theory and to sociologists. Anthropologists tend to focus on 'kinship-based societies' where social arrangements in general evolve around kinship ties. Sociologists, by contrast, analyze modern **industrialized** societies where political organization, economic exchange, **education** and other primary social institutions are in theory reproduced outside the world of kinship. Sociologists tend to restrict their analysis the family and household. Here the tendency has been to see family as part of the private domain: family is functional to society mostly as 'primary **socialization**'. Talcott **Parsons** saw the isolated nuclear family as the ideal family form for the workforce of industrial society, and claimed that family had become 'on the "macroscopic" levels, almost completely functionless' (Parsons 1955: 16). Family has been related to issues of **gender**, **personality** and **role**, but less systematically to social **structure**. Consequently, the study of family and kinship has remained somewhat peripheral to mainstream social theory, geared towards social transformations on the more 'macroscopic' level in Western societies.

Moreover, social theorists since **Durkheim** have continuously emphasized the erosion of the family in industrialized societies. Such views have typically been based on claims about growing **individualization**. From the 1960s, arguments for a near collapse of the family were also adopted by feminist and **Marxist** critical traditions that saw the (**patriarchal**) family as oppressive; here the demise of family became part of a political program. From the 1990s such arguments were given further impetus by the new reproduction technologies.

Yet these views may be challenged. First of all, the by now old idea of a breakdown of 'traditional' family overlooks how family forms have always adapted to changing conditions, frequently surviving the most radical socio–economic transformations. The empirical indicators for such a breakdown

are also debatable. Rising divorce figures, for example, do not necessarily mean that people care less about marriage; empirically, they are accompanied by widespread serial monogamy. It is also noteworthy that one of the main political demands of homosexual couples is to be recognized as family. This may represent a challenge to one type of family, but is hardly the end of it. Living in families is still the normative reference point. Descent groups are also functional within the economic realm, as a high percentage of modern private companies are family businesses. In (post)industrial societies, extended kin networks are also activated in the organization of the workforce, in money exchanges, and in international migration. Clientelism and informal networking, often kin-based, continue to exert influence on modern politics.

Furthermore, the ties between **public and private**, micro and macro, may be more intricate than assumed by functionalist approaches. Euro-American societies today practise bilateral descent and monogamy (the mismatch between theory and practice being part of the system), and late marriage followed (or preceded) by neolocality. When, how and why did this system come into being? This is still a matter of dispute, but the developments of kinship practices must be related to wider social arrangements. The Marxist-evolutionist theory proposed by Engels (1972) that the nuclear family was a consequence of private property has not stood the empirical test. Other authors have since examined the **dialectic** between family forms and key social, political, and economic developments in European history, including **Christianity**, **feudalism**, and the industrial revolution. In his comparative, long-term analysis of the European family, Jack Goody (1983) argues that the nuclear family was established well before the industrial revolution (see also Macfarlane 1978). Far from functioning as superstructure to the **economy**, the developments of **love**, inheritance and marriage can be seen as causing socio-economic change. If this is so from a historical and anthropological perspective, there is little reason to assume that things are so radically different in modern societies today. The question of the interrelation between family forms and the development of modern institutions remains open to further research.

References and further reading

Bourdieu, P. (1977) *Outline of a Theory of Practice*. Cambridge: Cambridge University Press.

Engels, F. ([1902] 1972) *The Origin of the Family, Private Property and the State*. London: Lawrence & Wishart.

Evans-Pritchard, E. E. (1951) *Kinship and Marriage among the Nuer*. Oxford: Clarendon Press.

Goody, J. (1983) *The Development of the Family and Marriage in Europe*. Cambridge: Cambridge University Press.

Lévi-Strauss, C. ([1949] 1969) *The Elementary Structures of Kinship*. London: Eyre & Spottiswoode.

MacFarlane, A. (1978) *The Origins of English Individualism: The Family, Property and Social Transition*. Oxford: Blackwell.

Parsons, T. (1955) 'The American Family: Its Relations to Personality and Social Structure', in T. Parsons and R. F. Bales *Family, Socialization and Interaction Process*. New York: Free Press.

BJØRN THOMASSEN

KNOWLEDGE AND KNOWLEDGE SOCIETY

Knowledge may be defined broadly as a *capacity for action*. This use of the term is derived from Francis Bacon's observation that knowledge is **power**. The definition of knowledge as capacity for action indicates that implementation of knowledge is open, that it is dependent on or embedded within the context of specific social, **economic** and **intellectual** conditions.

On this definition too, knowledge is a peculiar entity with properties unlike those of commodities or of secrets, for example. Knowledge exists in objectified and embodied forms. If sold, it enters other domains – and yet it remains within the domain of its producer. Unlike **money**, property rights and **symbolic** attributes such as titles, knowledge cannot be transmitted instantaneously. Its acquisition takes time and often is based on intermediary cognitive capacities and skills. Despite its reputation, knowledge is virtually never uncontested. *Scientific and technical knowledge* is uniquely important because it produces *incremental* capacities for social and economic action that may be 'privately appropriated' (see **property rights**), at least temporarily.

Knowledge has of course always had a major function in social life. That human action is knowledge-based might even be regarded as an anthropological constant. Social **groups**, social situations, social **interaction** and social **roles** all depend on, and are mediated by, knowledge. Power too has frequently been based on knowledge advantages, not merely on physical strength.

The foundations for the transformation of modern societies into knowledge societies continues to be based, as was the case for industrial society, on changes in the structure of the economies of advanced societies. Economic capital – or, more precisely, the source of economic growth and value-adding activities – increasingly relies on knowledge. The transformation of the structures of the modern economy by knowledge as a productive force constitutes the 'material' basis and justification for designating advanced modern society as a *knowledge society*. The significance of knowledge grows in all spheres of life and in all social institutions of modern society.

The historical emergence of knowledge societies does not occur suddenly; it does not represent a revolutionary development, but rather a gradual process during which the defining characteristics of society change and new traits emerge.

Until recently, modern society was conceived primarily in terms of property and labor. On the basis of these attributes, individuals and groups were able or constrained to define their membership in society. While the traditional attributes of labor and property certainly have not disappeared entirely, a new principle, 'knowledge', has been added which, to an extent, challenges as well as transforms property and labor as the constitutive mechanisms of society.

The emergence of knowledge societies signals first and foremost a radical transformation in the structure of the economy. Productive processes in industrial society are governed by factors that have greatly changed in significance as preconditions for economic growth: the dynamics of the supply and demand for primary products or raw materials; the dependence of employment on production; the importance of the manufacturing sector that processes primary products; the role of manual **labor** and the social organization of **work**; the role of international trade in manufactured goods and services; and the function of time and place in **production**. The common denominator of the changing economic structure is a shift away from an economy driven and governed by material inputs into the productive process and its organization, toward an economy in which the transformations of productive and distributive processes are increasingly determined by symbolic or knowledge-based inputs.

One of the remarkable consequences of this transformation is the extent to which modern societies become *fragile*. Modern societies tend to be fragile from the viewpoint of those large and once dominant social institutions that find it increasingly difficult to impose their will on all of society. However, from the perspective of small groups and **social movements** that are more uncoupled from the influence of the **traditional** large-scale social institutions, modern societies are not more fragile, at least in the first instance. For such groups and social movements, the social transformations underway mean a gain in their relative influence and participation, even if typically mainly in their ability to resist, delay and alter the objectives of the larger institutions.

Knowledge societies are, to adopt a phrase from Adam Ferguson, the results of human action, but often not of deliberate human design. They emerge as adaptations to persistent but evolving needs and changing circumstances of human conduct. Among the most significant transformations in circumstances is the continuous 'enlargement' of human action, including an extension of its 'limits to growth'.

The enlargement in capacities to act occurs at an uneven pace and to an uneven degree. The outcome is a hitherto unknown contradiction: an increasingly larger proportion of the public acquires and exercises political skills, choosing for example non-institutionalized participation, while the ability of the state and its **agencies** to exercise **sovereignty** is arrested, and even decreases. It is in this sense that the growth and broader dissemination of knowledge produces greater uncertainty and **contingency** rather than the foundations for a resolution of disagreements or the basis for a more effective **domination** by central societal institutions.

Modern societies are also increasingly *vulnerable* entities. More specifically, the economy, the **communication** or traffic systems are vulnerable to malfunctions of self-imposed practices typically designed to avoid breakdowns. Modern infrastructures and technological regimes are subject to accidents including large-scale disasters as the result of fortuitous, unanticipated human action, to non-marginal or extreme natural events that may dramatically undermine the taken-for-granted routines of everyday life in modern societies or to deliberate sabotage.

Present-day social systems may be seen to be fragile and vulnerable entities in yet another sense. Such fragility results from conduct as well as the deployment of artifacts designed to stabilize routine and delimit social action. This refers specifically to the so-called 'computer trap' or, more generally, the unintended outcomes of intentional social action. In the process of even more deeply **embedding** computers into the social fabric of society, that is, re-designing and reengineering large-scale social and socio-technical systems in order to manage the complexities of modern **society**, novel **risks** and vulnerabilities are created.

Hence, a basic fragility is inscribed into **social systems** via the deployment of technical regimes designed to achieve the opposite, namely to stabilize, constrain, routinize and even control conduct. Such an outcome of computerization might be particularly unexpected, cataclysmic and far-reaching but does not differ in principle from the unintended and unanticipated consequences of the widespread deployment of other technical devices in the past.

Contemporary societies are also fragile because individuals are capable, within certain established rules, of asserting their own interests by opposing or resisting the – not too long ago – almost unassailable monopoly of truth of major societal institutions. That is to say, **legitimate** cultural practices based on the enlargement and diffusion of knowledge enable a much larger segment of society to effectively oppose power configurations that turned out or are apprehended to be tenuous and brittle.

Among the major but widely invisible social innovations in modern society is the immense growth of the '**civil society**' sector. This sector provides an organized basis through which **citizens** can exercise individual initiative in the **private** pursuit of **public** purposes.

References and further reading

Baldi, P. (2001) *The Shattered Self: The End of Natural Evolution.* Cambridge, MA: MIT Press.

Bell, D. (1976) *The Coming of Post-Industrial Society,* second edition. New York: Basic Books

Drucker, P. F. (1969) *The Age of Discontinuity: Guidelines to our Changing Society.* New York: Harper & Row.

Gouldner, A. W. (1976) *The Dialectic of Ideology and Technology: The Origins, Grammar and Future of Ideology.* New York: Seabury.

Hardin, R. (2003) 'If It Rained Knowledge', *Philosophy of the Social Sciences,* 33(1): 3–24.

Luhmann, N. ([1992] 1998) *Observations on Modernity.* Stanford, CA: Stanford University Press.

Lyotard, J.-F. ([1979] 1984) *The Postmodern Condition: A Report on Knowledge.* Minneapolis, MN: University of Minnesota Press.

Mannheim, K. ([1929] 1936) *Ideology and Utopia: An Introduction to the Sociology of Knowledge.* London: Routledge & Kegan Paul.

Scheler, M. ([1924] 1990) 'The Sociology of Knowledge: Formal and Material Problems', in V. Meja and N. Stehr (eds) *Knowledge and Politics: The Sociology of Knowledge Dispute.* London: Routledge.

Stehr, N. (2001) *The Fragility of Modern Societies: Knowledge and Risk in the Information Age.* London: Sage.

Stehr, N. (2002) *Knowledge and Economic Conduct: The Social Foundations of the Modern Economy.* Toronto: University of Toronto Press.

Stehr, N. (2004) *Knowledge Politics: Governing the Consequences of Science and Technology.* Boulder, CO: Paradigm.

NICO STEHR

KRACAUER, SIEGFRIED (1889–1966)
German theorist

Kracauer is best known for his post-war studies in film theory. A trained architect, Kracauer devoted himself to philosophical and sociological inquiry after the First World War, becoming a journalist and editor for the *Frankfurter Zeitung* in the 1920s. His early studies included *On Suffering under Knowledge and the Desire for the Deed* (1917), *Sociology as Science* (1920–22), *On Expressionism* (1918), *Georg Simmel* (1919) and *The Detective Novel* (1922–25). These works stressed the 'spiritual homelessness' of the **rationalized** modern condition – a theme also underpinning his ethnographic study of Berlin's burgeoning white-collar workforce, *The Salaried Masses* (1929). A prolific 'feuilletonist' and perceptive film reviewer, Kracauer deciphered modern metropolitan culture as 'organized distraction', prefiguring the **Frankfurt School**'s thesis of the 'culture industry'. Written in exile in Paris (1933–

41), his 'societal biography', *Jacques Offenbach and the Paris of His Time* ([1937] 2002) explores the cultural habits of the Parisian **bourgeoisie** under the Second Empire through the life and work of its leading composer. Escaping to New York in 1941, Kracauer began work on *From Caligari to Hitler* (1949), a study tracing the development of **authoritarian** tendencies in Weimar Germany as manifested in popular cinema. *Theory of Film* (1960) examines the fundamental properties of the cinematic medium, arguing that the camera's inherent ability to penetrate physical reality promises to redeem qualities lost through the disenchantment of the world.

Major works

([1929] 1998) *The Salaried Masses: Duty and Distraction in Weimar Germany*. London: Verso.

([1937] 2002) *Jacques Offenbach and the Paris of His Time*. New York: Zone.

(1947) *From Caligari to Hitler: A Psychological History of the German Film*. Princeton, NJ: Princeton University Press.

(1960) *Theory of Film*. Oxford: Oxford University Press.

([1969] 1995) *History: The Last Things before the Last*. New York: Oxford University Press.

(1995) *The Mass Ornament: Weimar Essays*. Cambridge, MA: Harvard University Press.

Further reading

Barnouw, D. (1994) *Critical Realism*. Baltimore, MD: Johns Hopkins University Press.

Frisby, D. (1986) *Fragments of Modernity*. Cambridge: Polity.

Koch, G. (2000) *Siegfried Kracauer*. Princeton, NJ: Princeton University Press.

GRAEME GILLOCH

L

LABOUR

See: work

LACAN, JACQUES (1901–1981)

French psychoanalyst

Lacan's linguistic and philosophical reworking of **psychoanalysis** has strongly influenced **cultural**, literary and **gender** theories. The most important aspect of Lacan's theory is the concept of a decentred or divided **subject** as an effect of **language** that structures the **unconscious**. Alongside **Freud**, Lacan was influenced by **Hegel**, **Lévi-Strauss** and structuralist linguists (see **structuralism**). Lacan's fundamental classification system is built around the terms of the **imaginary**, the *real* and the *symbolic*, each of which describe different aspects of psychoanalytical experience (see **symbol**).

The concept of desire, particularly of unconscious desire, is also at the centre of Lacan's thought. This socially constituted desire as 'desire of the **Other**' (Lacan 1977) does not tend toward an object, but is a relation to a *lack* that is described by Lacan as a lack of a signifier or as *lack of being*, a term used by Lacan as synonymous with *castration*. Although Lacan's definition of castration and the phallus is not determined by biological thoughts like Freud's, his concepts have been critized as phallocentric by feminist theorists (Grosz 1990) and by **Derrida** (1975) (see **phallocentrism**).

Major works

(1977) *Ecrits: A Selection*. London: Tavistock.

Further reading

Bowie, M. (1991) *Lacan*. London: HarperCollins.

Derrida, J. (1975) *The Post Card: From Socrates to Freud and Beyond*. Chicago: University of Chicago Press.

Felman, S. (1987) *Jacques Lacan and the Adventure of Insight: Psychoanalysis in Contemporary Culture*. London: Cambridge University Press.

Gallop, J. (1985) *Reading Lacan*. Ithaca, NY: Cornell University Press.

Grosz, E. (1990) *Jacques Lacan: A Feminist Introduction*. London: Routledge.

Ragland-Sullivan, E. (1986) *Jacques Lacan and the Philosophy of Psychoanalysis*. Urbana, IL: University of Illinois.

Roudinesco, E. ([1993] 1999) *Jacques Lacan*. New York: Columbia University Press.

MICHAELA WÜNSCH

LANGUAGE

Language is a system of conventional signs, both auditory (speech) and visual (writing), used by people for a huge variety of cognitive, practical and social tasks. A distinction should be made between *langue*, the system of signs considered abstractly, and *parole*, the system in use by people in everyday life (Saussure 1974).

Language uses include drawing attention to something, 'Voilà!'; controlling other people, 'Get the bread!'; expressing personal experiences and states of mind, 'That hurts'; describing situations and objects, 'The car was black'; creating **institutions** by discussing and agreeing a **constitution**, and many others, including giving verdicts, speculating, apologizing, and so on. The study of language has traditionally been divided into semantics, the study of **meaning**, syntax, the study of grammar, and pragmatics, the study of linguistic **practices**. The distinctness of these categories has been brought into question in various ways.

Meaning has been variously defined as the object or state of affairs signified by a word or sentence, as a mental image associated with the word or sentence, and as the use to which people routinely put a linguistic sign. Objections to the idea of meaning as object signified include the problem of words which do not seem to refer to anything, for example, the numerals. Objections to the idea of meaning as mental association point out that in order to make use of an association to grasp the meaning of a word one must already know the meaning of the accompanying image.

Saussure (1974) argued that a sound or mark can serve as a sign if it has a place in a **network** of relations with other similar entities (see **semiotics**). On the syntagmatic dimension, a sign has a place in an open sequence of sign-structures; for example, a word in a sequence of sentences. On the paradigmatic dimension, the appearance of a certain sound or mark is a sign if it is understood to exclude other signs. For example, hearing 'horse' excludes hearing 'donkey' or 'car'. A sound or mark that has a place in a sign system can acquire specific meanings in various ways (see also **symbol**).

Language is not only a system adapted to **communication** between one person and others. It is also the main medium of cognition. A great deal of thinking, remembering, forecasting, planning, classifying, and so on, is realized in linguistic forms (see **classification**). This raises the question of whether differences between languages are reflected in differ-

ences between cognitive processes in diverse cultures (see **culture**). For example, how, if at all, do differences in colour vocabularies affect discriminations of colours? According to Whorf (1956), there is a strong link between linguistic resources and **cognition**, perception, **emotion** and other psychological aspects of human life. Anthropologists have pointed to significant differences in emotion vocabularies that seem to be related to differences in the repertoires of emotions expressible in diverse cultures (Lutz 1988).

A similar issue has been raised with respect to the possibility of a link between **social relations** and linguistic resources. Pronouns differ greatly between languages, and there is some evidence that the expression of social relations is both inhibited and facilitated there by. The differences in second person between English and other European languages illustrate this phenomenon (Brown and Gillman 1960). The impoverishment of the English second person vocabulary can be associated with changes in the structure of English society in the seventeenth century.

Language use is bound by unstable and ephemeral but locally demanding standards of correctness. The concept of 'rule' seems handy for expressing linguistic norms. Traditionally, 'grammar' consisted of the rules for the locally correct construction of sentences, with respect to the standard pattern of word classes, thus, in French that the adjective usually follows the noun, 'Le ballon rouge'. **Wittgenstein** extended the use of the word 'grammar' to cover all kinds of normativity in language, including conventions of meaning. Along with that, he made a wider use of the concept of a rule, including not only rule as explicit instruction, but rule as a metaphor for any kind of normative constraint, whatever its psychological status, blurring the sharp distinction between syntax and semantics (see also **discourse**).

Pragmatics has also been assimilated to the rule-following model. The study of **performative** uses of language, initiated by J. L.

Austin (1959), showed a parallel between the truth conditions for correct descriptive uses of a sentence, and the felicity conditions for an effective performative use. These included such conditions as the right of a **person** using the sentence to perform that particular social act. Only a judge can sentence someone to a term in gaol. Austin distinguished between the illocutionary force of an utterance, the special act thereby performed, and the perlocutionary effect, whatever is brought about by the performance of that social act. The words of the wedding ceremony bring about a marriage, which has all sorts of long and short consequences. Austin's analysis of the uses of language to perform social acts has been influential in discursive psychology, an approach which is based on the idea that the social world is largely a symbolic construction in which language plays a fundamental part (see **social constructionism**).

Instead of three distinct sub-disciplines constitutive of the science of language, we have three aspects of the one approach, based on diversity of uses and adherence to **norms**. The question of whether there are common elements in all languages has been debated with respect to **Chomsky**'s (1986) thesis of a universal grammar, and Wierzbicka's (1992) claim to have identified several semantic universals. The idea of a universal syntax is tied in with the distinction between surface and deep grammar, the former derived from the latter by rules of transformation. For example, noun phrase/verb phrase (NP/VP) is a universal which can be transformed into a sentence by applying such rules as 'Noun phrase to noun plus adjective'.

If there are universal grammatical features of all human languages, what is their origin? Chomsky's claim is based on the idea that human beings are equipped from birth with a LAD, a language acquisition device, which extracts linguistic forms from the infant's environment. The LAD is inherited. Underlying this claim is the belief that language is too complex for it to be learned from the speech of others by generalizing from particular cases. Alternative proposals include Bruner's thesis of a common **culture**, especially mother–infant games, in the course of which an infant acquires the basic principles of its language (see **play and game**).

Wierzbicka points to a number of semantic features common to all lexicons, such as words for the first person, for reference to objects in the environment, for negation and so on. These features provide an analytical scheme for extracting the root meanings of any vocabulary. However, they pick out features at a high level of abstraction, while individual languages differ in how these features are realized.

Natural languages display many instances of words with a variety of uses. Are there linguistic essences, underlying common meanings which account for the use of the same word with apparently different meanings? Wittgenstein identified the assumption that there are linguistic essences as a prime source of philosophical errors. He introduced the idea of family resemblances, patterns of similarities and differences in the use of a word, which, once revealed, dispel the error. The word 'rule' is an important case, since it is a mistake to think that all uses of the word imply a process of following an instruction.

The phenomenon of indexicality raises doubts about the stability of meanings even in the short run. An indexical is a word, like 'now', the meaning of which depends on the current situation of its use. It has been argued that all uses of words are to some degree indexical, the meaning depending on the actual situation of use. This leads to the question of how languages grow. One way is through the displacement of concepts; the use of words established in one context in a new environment, and in general 'metaphor'.

A metaphorical use of a word is not a comparison, that is, it is not a condensed simile. In an example such as 'My pen is my sword' the meanings of both 'pen' and 'sword' are transformed in a mutual interaction.

Continual use of the metaphor can permanently enlarge the meaning of words. The sciences are rich in examples of metaphors which have given rise to new terminology, suited to the expression of novel ideas; for example, Darwin's metaphor of 'natural selection' for the process of **evolution**. The vocabulary that has grown up to describe the use and characteristics of computers has a rich metaphorical base, 'saving', 'crashing', 'hacking', 'virus', and so on. Languages can also be enlarged by explicit formal definitions of new terms.

References and further reading

Austin, J. L. (1959) *How to Do Things with Words*. Oxford: Clarendon Press.

Brown, G. and Gillman, A. (1960) 'Pronouns of Power and Solidarity', in T. Sebiok (ed.), *Style in Language*. Cambridge, MA: MIT Press.

Chomsky, N. (1986) *Knowledge of Language: Its Nature, Origin and Use*. New York: Praeger.

Lutz, C. (1988) *Unnatural Emotions*. Chicago: University of Chicago Press.

Ortony, A. (1993) *Metaphor and Thought*. Cambridge: Cambridge University Press.

Saussure, F. de (1974) *A Course in General Linguistics*. London: Collins.

Whorf, B. L. (1956) *Language, Thought and Reality*. Cambridge, MA: MIT Press.

Wierzbicka, A. (1992) *Semantics, Culture and Cognition*. Oxford: Oxford University Press.

Wittgenstein, L. (1953) *Philosophical Investigations*. Trans. G. E. M. Ancombe. Oxford: Blackwell.

ROM HARRÉ

LATOUR, BRUNO (1947–)

French theorist

The work of Bruno Latour is most closely associated with **social studies of science** and **actor-network theory**. However, since the early 1990s his concerns have increasingly turned towards the study of politics, and the relations between science and politics, an interest that emerged explicitly in *We Have Never Been Modern* (1993) and is developed further in *The Politics of Nature* (2003).

Latour's work first became widely known following the publication (with Steve Woolgar) of *Laboratory Life: The Social Construction of Scientific Facts* (1986), a pioneering ethnographic study of a scientific laboratory (see **social constructionism**). The title of the book is, however, misleading, and indeed was corrected in the second edition. For the idea of social construction implied the existence of a '**society**' that was distinct from '**nature**'. On the contrary, for Latour, what needed to be explained was how the separation of the realm of nature from society was locally achieved through scientific practice, not given. In Latour's account, scientific facts are neither mere fictions, nor do they exist independently of the laboratories and technical apparatuses that sustain and circulate them. As he made clear in *Pandora's Hope* (1999), his argument is a metaphysical one. In his account, there is no essential distinction between social and natural, or between human and non-human entities. Instead, all entities are entangled in relations with others, an idea signified through terms such as **actor-network**, **association** and **collective**. In his writings on politics Latour interrogates what he terms the modern **constitution** that restricts politics to the realm of society, and at the same time points towards an analysis of the construction of both political and scientific forms of **representation**.

Major works

(1986) (with S. Woolgar) *Laboratory Life: The Construction of Scientific Facts*, 2nd edn. Princeton, NJ: Princeton University Press.

(1987) *Science in Action*. Milton Keynes: Open University Press.

(1988) *The Pasteurization of France*. Cambridge, MA: Harvard University Press.

(1993) *We Have Never Been Modern*. Hemel Hempstead: Harvester Wheatsheaf.

(1996) *Aramis, or the Love of Technology*. Cambridge, MA: Harvard University Press.

(1999) *Pandora's Hope: Essays on the Reality of Science Studies*. Cambridge, MA: Harvard University Press.

(2003) *The Politics of Nature.* Cambridge, MA: Harvard University Press.

ANDREW BARRY

LAW AND LEGALITY

Social theory of law is concerned with the theoretical analysis of law in society. In a broad sense, it forms part of the law-and-society movement and of socio-legal studies. However, it constitutes something of a conundrum: it is a **hybrid** insofar as it is neither legal philosophy nor sociological theory, although borrowing major insights from both disciplines.

Social theory of law differs from strict normativist and empiricist approaches. It comprises both interdisciplinary theorizing and attempts to form a separate discipline. Within social theory of law we can distinguish middle-range theories, such as dispute processing, from grand theory discussing foundations of law in society, such as legal **positivism**, legal pluralism and legal autopoiesis.

The beginnings of social theory of law can be traced back to the sociological classics and early sociologists of law. Most of these approaches were influenced by the concerns of Neo-Kantian philosophers and were aimed at an understanding of the conditions that enable social and economic processes to occur (see **Kantianism and Neo-Kantianism**). This is particularly true for the sociology of law of Max **Weber** (1967). His social theory of law emphasizes three aspects of modern law: (1) its coercive character; (2) its formal logical **rationality**; and (3) its function as the main source of legitimation of **power** (see **legitimacy and legitimation**. In section 6 of his 'Basic Sociological Terms' in the opening chapter of *Economy and Society,* Weber introduces the following definition of law: 'An order will be called…"law" if it is externally guaranteed by the probability that physical or psychological coercion will be applied by a *staff* of people in order to bring about compliance or avenge violation' (1967: 5).

In the section of *Economy and Society* entitled 'Sociology of Law', Weber distinguishes four modes of legal thinking based on distinct forms of legal rationality: (1) substantive irrationality; (2) formal irrationality; (3) substantive rationality; and (4) logically formal rationality. In his political sociology, law plays a crucial role in relation to **domination** and power for which it serves as the predominant form of legitimation in modern society, largely replacing **tradition** and **charisma**.

Neo-Kantianism also provides the philosophical background for Eugen Ehrlich (2002), Weber's contemporary, who wrote the first textbook on the sociology of law. Ehrlich's concept of 'living law' was a frontal attack on legal positivism and lawyer's law that is exclusively concerned with official statutory norms. Ehrlich insisted on the importance of customary law for legal and in particular judicial practice. In his view, **society**, and not the **state**, is the ultimate source of norm production. His practical jurisprudence emphasizes the dependency of law enforcement and legal sanctions on the existence of social sanctions.

Ehrlich's living law concept was influential in American debates on legal realism and in legal anthropology where it figured prominently in debates about *legal pluralism* (see also **pluralism**). The theory of legal pluralism was originally developed as a critical assessment of the relationship of colonial and indigenous law, thereby arguing for a horizontal rather than vertical arrangement of these legal orders. In a second wave, legal pluralism was applied in studies of contemporary modern law in which a multitude of legal orders operating next to each other were discovered in Western law (Griffiths, Galanter, Benda-Beckmann). More recently, in a third wave, the concept of legal pluralism has been used to analyze the multiplicity of sources from which the new global law derives (Teubner) (see **globalization**).

313

Social theory of law is influenced in many ways by its opposite which is widely regarded to be the theory of *legal positivism*. Legal positivism has been the dominant theory of law among legal practitioners for most of the past two centuries. Its main characteristic is the rejection of natural law and any other theory postulating that law has a basis outside of law. Most versions of legal positivism share the assumption of a strict separation of **moral** and legal questions. Whereas the English tradition of legal positivism (Austin, Bentham, Hart, Raz) emphasizes the sovereignty of parliament and the rule of law as key elements of the legal order (Dicey 1981), the continental European school of legal positivism (Kelsen 1967) is mainly concerned with the logical character of a system of legal norms. For Kelsen, the only relevant question of a 'pure theory of law' pertains to the validity of law. In his view, the modern legal system is capable of justifying itself because the validity of any legal **norm** can be established by reference to a higher ranking norm. At the apex of the hierarchy of norms rests the basic norm which is a logical presumption rather than a really existing norm. In Kelsen's theory, legality and the rule of law are internal affairs of the legal order.

Legal positivism has been criticized from different directions. A prominent critic of Kelsen was Carl **Schmitt** (2004) who emphasized the limits of parliamentary norm production. For Schmitt, legal positivism robs the concept of law of every substantive relationship to reason and **justice** and overlooks the interplay of legality and (political) legitimacy. It renders law defenceless against abuse by dictators. (This criticism was, however, ironic, as Schmitt was later to compromise himself by support for Hitler's dictatorship, and has been regarded by many critics as an apologist for fascist politics.)

Contemporary social theory of law has to some extent taken up issues discussed between Kelsen and Schmitt in the debate about the **autonomy** of law. A radical approach to redefine the concept of modern law as completely autonomous is proposed by social systems theory. For Niklas **Luhmann**, legal positivism is successful as a theory of reflection in the legal system because it understands the need for self-justification of the system and its closure to its environment (Luhmann 1985, 2004). Luhmann developed his **systems theory** of law in three stages. First, law is conceptualized in relation to expectations generated in society whereby law's function consists in congruent generalization of structures of expectations along meaning dimensions. Second, law is defined as a system of **communication** that is capable of reproducing itself on the basis of self-reference of specific legal communications (legal 'autopoiesis'). And third, law is analyzed as part of the world society in which a genuine world law emerges.

Günther Teubner (1993) has, by applying abstract systems theory to specific discussions in law, developed a social theory of law called 'reflexive law'. Prominent topics in Teubner's reflexive law are a system-specific legal **epistemology**, processes of juridification of social spheres and the reformulation of the history of law in terms of **evolutionary theory**. Teubner is especially known for his insights on legal regulation, self-regulation and regulatory failure. Further, he has analyzed new legal constructs that combine notions of **contract** and **organization** in establishing **networks**. These so-called legal hybrids include joint ventures, corporate **groups** and franchises, which he discusses both from a jurisprudential and a doctrinal perspective.

A quite distinct path is followed by normative social theories of law. Most prominent is John **Rawls**'s (1971) *A Theory of Justice*. Rawls's theory combines Kantian concepts with traditions of **utilitarianism**, **liberalism**, and social contract theory. Justice for Rawls constitutes the main aspect for the justification of modern law and social order (see **social justice**). Central to

Rawls's theory of justice is recourse to an idea of social contract which is translated into the concept of an original position in which, behind a veil of ignorance, two main principles of justice are adopted, centring on redistribution offset by the 'priority of liberty'.

Another example of a normative social theory of law is Jürgen **Habermas**'s (1996) discourse theory of law. His thinking about law aims at the normative and ethical foundation of modern law. Central is the concern with legitimation and why modern law is dependent on the possibility of a **discourse** to resolve claims that challenge its validity. Habermas's theory of law originally formed part of a general theory of communicative action that distinguishes between law as a medium and law as an **institution**. In *Between Facts and Norms* (1996), he advanced his theory of law to include analyses of the modern constitutional and **welfare state**, the rule of law, and **democracy** in **civil society**. In particular, the distinction between facticity and normativity is now seen as constitutive of the inherent tension in modern law.

References and further reading

Banakar, R. and Travers, M. (eds) (2002) *An Introduction to Law and Social Theory*. Oxford: Hart.

Berman, H. J. (1983) *Law and Revolution: The Formation of the Western Legal Tradition*. Cambridge, MA: Harvard University Press.

Cotterell, R. (2006) *Law, Culture and Society: Legal Ideas in the Perspective of Social Theory*. Aldershot: Ashgate.

Dicey, A. V. (1981) *Lectures on the Relation between Law and Public Opinion in England during the Nineteenth Century*. New Brunswick, NJ: Transaction.

Ehrlich, E. (2002) *Fundamental Principles of the Sociology of Law* (reprint of 1936 English edn; German edn 1913). New Brunswick, NJ: Transaction.

Friedman, L. and Macaulay, S. (eds) (1977) *Law and the Behavioral Sciences*. Indianapolis, IN: Bobbs-Merrill.

Habermas, J. (1996) *Between Facts and Norms* (German edn 1992). Cambridge: Polity.

Kelsen, H. (1967) *Pure Theory of Law* (German edn 1960). Berkeley, CA: University of California Press.

Luhmann, N. (1985) *A Sociological Theory of Law* (German edn 1972). London: Routledge & Kegan Paul.

Luhmann, N. (2004) *Law as a Social System* (German edn 1993). Oxford: Oxford University Press.

Penner, J., Schiff, D. and Nobles, R. (eds) (2002) *An Introduction to Jurisprudence and Legal Theory*. London: Butterworths.

Rawls, J. (1971) *A Theory of Justice*. Oxford: Oxford University Press.

Roach Anleu, S. L. (2000) *Law and Social Change*. London: Sage.

Schmitt, C. (2004) *Legality and Legitimacy* (German edn 1932). Durham, NC: Duke University Press.

Teubner, G. (1993) *Law as an Autopoietic System* (German edn 1989). Oxford: Blackwell.

Weber, M. (1967) *Law in Economy and Society*. Ed. M. Rheinstein. New York: Simon & Schuster.

RALF ROGOWSKI

LEFEBVRE, HENRI (1901–1991)
French theorist

Underpinning all Lefebvre's work is a detailed engagement with the writings of **Marx**, and the relation of his work to other philosophers, notably **Hegel**, **Nietzsche** and **Heidegger**. Lefebvre held that Marx (both his early and late work) was in need of supplementation with ideas drawn from other sources. But these other elements demanded immanent critique, aimed at stripping away their mystifying or reactionary tendencies. In this sense, Lefebvre's readings were close to the way Marx himself read Hegel. Lefebvre was particularly interested in the concept of **alienation** which he read in Hegel and Marx's writings and compared to Heidegger's idea of the **everyday** (see also **phenomenology**). Lefebvre saw alienation under **capitalism** as no longer confined to the economic sphere but found in social and cultural life in the widest sense. This theme ran throughout his work, notably in the three volumes of

315

the *Critique of Everyday Life* (1991, 2002, 2003). Rural and urban life in France was a long-term concern, leading to his most cited work, *The Production of Space* (1991), which analyzes the philosophy, politics and **political economy** of space (see **space and place**). This was partnered by an ongoing rethinking of the categories of **time** and history. Lefebvre wrote extensively on a wide range of topics, and English language work has yet to fully take the measure of this output.

Major works

(1976–78) *De l'État*, 4 vols. Paris: UGE.
(1991) *The Production of Space*. Trans. D. Nicolson-Smith. Oxford: Blackwell.
(1991, 2002, 2003) *Critique of Everyday Life*, 3 vols. Trans. J. Moore, London: Verso.
(1996) *Writings on Cities*. Trans. E. Kofman and E. Lebas. Oxford: Blackwell.
(2003) *Key Writings*. Ed. S. Elden, E. Lebas and E. Kofman. London: Continuum.

Further reading

Elden, S. (2004) *Understanding Henri Lefebvre: Theory and the Possible*. London: Continuum.
Hess, R. (1988) *Henri Lefebvre et l'aventure du siècle*. Paris: A.M. Métailié.
Shields, R. (1999) *Lefebvre, Love and Struggle: Spatial Dialectics*. London: Routledge.

STUART ELDEN

LEGITIMACY AND LEGITIMATION

When and why do people comply and cooperate with **authority**? When and why do human beings obey? For Max **Weber** (1978), obedience is determined by highly robust motives of fear and hope – fear of the vengeance of the power-holder and hope for reward (see **power**). Voluntary compliance may arise from simple habituation or the most purely rational calculation of advantage. Yet, as Weber claims, for authority to achieve a sufficiently reliable and permanent basis, more than custom, personal advantage, and purely affectual or ideal motives, are needed. Voluntary compliance

is complemented by an acceptance by the ruled of the validity of the claims put forward by the ruler (and his or her staff). These claims depend on acceptance that there are inner justifications for the exercise of their rule and for their expectation to find obedience for their commands. Obedience to authority may therefore be based on the belief in the legitimacy of **domination**. Ideal-typically, the ultimate grounds of the validity of domination may be the authority of the 'eternal yesterday', as in 'traditional' domination (see **tradition**); the authority of the extraordinary and personal **charisma** of an individual, as in 'charismatic' domination; and, finally, the authority of rationally created legal rules on the basis of constitutionally correct procedures (see **law and legality**). Yet how beliefs in legitimacy are generated, Weber does not discuss in any detail. Randall Collins (1986) has, controversially, argued that legitimacy for Weber was tied to the power position of the state in the international arena (see **state and nation–state**). Domestic legitimacy is the good sought by political leaders when they engage in external military competition with other states. Military success and 'Great Power' status generate feelings of legitimacy, while defeat leads to a crisis of legitimacy.

Even if this did indeed identify a key reason proffered by Weber for a psychological disposition to accept claims of legitimacy, however, it does not address the question of the conditions under which normative validity claims (*innere Rechtfertigungsgründe*) may be successfully redeemed. **Habermas**'s theory of '**discourse** ethics', in general, and the theory of deliberative **democracy**, in particular, have focused on this question. According to Cohen and Arato (1992: 347–8), drawing on Habermas, the principle of discourse ethics postulates that 'a norm of action has validity only if all those possibly affected by it (and by the side-effects of its application) would, as participants in a practical discourse, arrive at a (rationally motivated) agreement that such a norm should come into or remain in force'. This principle contains a theory of legitimation as it proposes to consider as legitimate only those norms and institutions that would be validated by individuals who engage in a practical discourse. But for such a discourse to produce a rational **consensus** on the validity of a norm and its **institutionalization**, procedures must be in place that give all those affected an equal chance to partake in the public deliberations and to initiate and continue **communication** unconstrained by economic or political force on the basis of a mutual and reciprocal **recognition** of each by all as autonomous, rational **subjects** whose claims will be acknowledged if supported by valid arguments. There is no assumption – such as is made by David Beetham (1991) – that the norms that ground legitimacy claims can only be justified by reference to beliefs shared by both dominant and subordinate. On the contrary, not only is there no reference to shared beliefs, but there is also no closure with regard to either the question as to which items may be put on the agenda of conversation or the **identity** of the participants to the conversation. Indeed, the **community** of communicants is open to each person or **group** that can justifiably show that they are relevantly affected by the proposed norm under question (see **values and norms**).

Beetham is right, however, to identify two concerns which, in particular, need normative justification. First, who or what is the rightful source of authority (if not 'the people', for example, then who?). Second, what are the proper ends and standards of government? Legitimacy claims are the concern not only of discourse ethics and the analyst but, above all, of political contestation and the citizen. Legitimacy depends not only on words but also on deeds. For authority to be legitimate, it needs confirmation by express consent or affirmation of appropriate subordinates.

When consent or **recognition** is publicly withdrawn or withheld, authority is delegitimized. What counts as consent? The **conventions** prevailing in a particular society are a starting point for addressing this question; but they, in turn, must also meet the legitimacy requirement to be relevant in the context of the assessment of the legitimacy of a particular system of domination.

References and further reading

Barker, R. (1990) *Political Legitimacy and the State*. Oxford: Clarendon Press.
Beetham, D. (1991) *The Legitimation of Power*. Houndsmills: Macmillan.
Benhabib, S. (1994) 'Deliberative Rationality and Models of Democratic Legitimacy', *Constellations*, 1(1): 26–52.
Cohen, J. and Arato, A. (1992) *Civil Society and Political Theory*. Cambridge, MA: MIT Press.
Collins, R. (1986) *Weberian Sociological Theory*. Cambridge: Cambridge University Press.
Habermas, J. (1976) *Legitimation Crisis*. London: Heinemann.
Habermas, J. (1996) *Between Facts and Norms: Contributions to a Discourse Theory of Law and Democracy*. Cambridge, MA: MIT Press.
Manin, B. (1987) 'On Legitimacy and Political Deliberation', *Political Theory*, 15(3): 338–68.
Weber, M. (1978) *Economy and Society: An Outline of Interpretive Sociology*. Berkeley, CA: University of California Press.

ROLAND AXTMANN

LEISURE

There are two distinct but not unrelated etymological sources of modern understandings of leisure. There is the French word *loisir*, from the Latin root *licere*. *Licere* is interesting because it reveals ambivalence: on the one hand, leisure implies freedom; on the other hand it implies permission or licence. The other **etymological** source is the Greek term *skholé* which at its most basic level means to be free from obligation. Like *licere*, however, *skholé* has a more complex meaning and was considered by the Greeks to be an ideal state guided by the appreciation of moderation. In this sense, *skholé* was an elitist theorization that considered leisure to be a serious business – both a privileged and studious occupation – which was suggestive of a restrictive economy of pleasure. What this contained was the tacit acknowledgment of an affiliation between leisure and **work**.

In modern social thought the significance of work for understanding leisure has also loomed large. In *The Theory of the Leisure Class* (1899), Thorstein Veblen established the notion of leisure as a means of conspicuous **consumption** for those who had no need to work and who used it as means of acquiring reputability and **status**. In their neo-**Marxist** account of leisure in industrializing Britain, Clarke and Critcher (1985: 53) suggest that for the majority of **working class** people at this time leisure did not exist in the modern sense and 'work and leisure intermingled'. The public house was the well-spring of most popular working-class pastimes which were often accompanied with overt **violence** and brutality as well as drinking. But by the early to mid–1800s the kinds of leisure forms that **popular culture** had traditionally promoted were increasingly seen through the eyes of establishment figures as problematic, signifying a social **class** struggle over leisure. In explaining this change in outlook, scholars have identified two major factors: on the one hand, the emergence of a civilizing trend (**Elias** 1994) in relations between **state** formation and changes in individual conduct, including new forms of **morality** and controlled, ordered and self-improving leisure forms (Cunningham 1980) (see **civilization**), and on the other, the suppression of the threat posed by extant forms of popular culture to the emergence of clock-time paid work.

What could not have been anticipated at this time was what would in the 1900s become a mass consumer **market** for leisure and with it the idea of leisure as cultural competition for 'distinction' between different status groups across the social spectrum

(**Bourdieu** 1984). Yet despite these massive changes in the ways people were now experiencing leisure, a number of scholars continued to theorize the concept as little more than a domesticated modern understanding of *skholé* (Parker 1983; Stebbins 1999).

In response to these **functionalist** accounts, other scholars have suggested that leisure activities are not necessarily structurally prescribed and expected by individuals to reflect their own individual choices and tastes. Csikszentmihalyi (1974) argued that the definitive illustration of leisure of this kind is that characterized by flow, or the existential experience of total involvement in leisure activities freely chosen, which are self-rewarding and contain an uncertainty of outcome that allows for individual creativity.

Most contemporary leisure scholars have avoided elitist and **individualist** understandings of leisure and have developed some innovative analyses to uncover the inequalities of class, **gender**, **ethnicity**, **age** and **disability** which tend to establish and limit opportunities for leisure. This has spawned a range of empirical studies, but some of the best theoretical work on leisure in Britain has come from Chris Rojek. His *Capitalism and Leisure Theory* (1985) helped to establish leisure studies as a serious area of academic study, while his *Decentring Leisure* (1995) provides a radical **critique** suggestive of a **postmodern** theory of leisure which recognizes that if today human lives are marked by their **freedom** from the **hegemony** of any one specific meaning it is concepts such as **risk**, **contingency**, fragmentation, speed, change and de–differentiation which best reveal the **complexity** of leisure in those lives. This decentring of leisure is also related to another key aspect of Rojek's critique, which argues that if leisure cannot be separated from other aspects of people's lives, then the study of leisure should better proceed as cultural studies.

References and further reading

Bourdieu, P. (1984) *Distinction: A Social Critique of the Judgement of Taste*. London: Routledge & Kegan Paul.

Clarke, J. and Critcher, C. (1985) *The Devil Makes Work: Leisure in Capitalist Britain*. London: Macmillan.

Csikszentmihalyi, M. (1974) *Flow: Studies of Enjoyment*. Chicago: University of Chicago Press.

Cunningham, H. (1980) *Leisure in the Industrial Revolution*. London: Croom Helm.

Elias, N. (1994) *The Civilizing Process: The History of Manners and State-Formation and Civilization*, integrated edn. Oxford: Blackwell.

Parker, S. (1983) *Leisure and Work*. London: George Allen and Unwin.

Rojek, C. (1985) *Capitalism and Leisure Theory*. London: Tavistock.

Rojek, C. (1995) *Decentring Leisure: Rethinking Leisure Theory*. London: Sage.

Stebbins, R. (1999) 'Serious Leisure', in T. L. Burton and E. L. Jackson (eds) *Leisure Studies: Prospects for the Twenty-First Century*. State College, PA: Venture Publishing.

Veblen, T. ([1899] 1970) *The Theory of the Leisure Class*. New York: Macmillan; London: Unwin.

TONY BLACKSHAW

LÉVI-STRAUSS, CLAUDE GUSTAVE (1908–)

Belgian-born anthropologist

An exponent of **structuralist** anthropology, Lévi-Strauss rejected **evolutionary**, **empiricist**, **historicist** or **humanist** approaches to cultural inquiry, instead treating social order, **subjectivity** and symbolic **culture** as products or effects of basic structural relations. He proposed that **myths**, **ritual**, **kinship** and **exchange** involve systems of **classification** in which **binary** categories are combined or transformed according to specific rules, producing a range of culturally-specific outcomes. Such categories condition mythical thought but escape its comprehension. The task of science is to make them evident in a way that myth itself cannot. Lévi-Strauss suggested that comparative studies of the **semiotic** organization of myth could demonstrate cognitive universals of human thought. In making this claim, he challenged **essentialist** distinctions between **science** and myth, 'primitive' and 'modern', echoing **Durkheim**'s positing of structural affinities between science and religion (though Lévi-Strauss located these in psychology rather than in the social). His theoretical insights were taken up by **Althusser**, **Lacan**, and **Barthes**, and provoked a critical response from **Derrida** concerning Lévi-Strauss's ambiguous treatment of certain binaries (e.g., **nature/culture**) as both topics of and resources for scientific inquiry; an ambiguity implicated in his reflections on the status of science itself. There is a danger in reducing Lévi-Strauss to a marker in debates over structuralism and **post-structuralism**: he was an elegant and catholic writer on many topics, including music, and his work resists easy categorization. His superb anthropological memoir, *Tristes Tropiques* ([1955] 1974), combines recollections of his Brazilian fieldwork with compelling philosophical insight.

Major works

([1949] 1971) *The Elementary Structures of Kinship*. Boston: Beacon.

([1955] 1974) *Tristes Tropiques*. New York: Atheneum.

([1958] 1967) *Structural Anthropology*. New York: Doubleday.

([1962] 1966) *The Savage Mind*. Chicago: University of Chicago Press.

([1964] 1983) *The Raw and the Cooked*. Chicago: University of Chicago Press.

Further reading

Badcock, C. R. (1975) *Lévi-Strauss: Structuralism and Social Theory*. London: Hutchinson.

Henaff, M. (1998) *Claude Lévi-Strauss and the Making of Structural Anthropology*. Minneapolis, MN: University of Minnesota Press.

Leach, E. (1989) *Claude Lévi-Strauss*. Chicago: University of Chicago Press.

Segal, R. A. (1996) *Structuralism in Myth: Lévi-Strauss, Barthes, Dumezil and Propp*. New York: Garland Publishers.

WILLIAM RAMP

319

LIBERALISM

Liberalism has a long pedigree, preceding the other major ideologies of **modernity** – **conservatism**, **socialism** and **fascism** – which to a great extent have defined themselves in opposition to various of liberalism's tenets. The liberal emphasis on individual liberties, initially from the **church**, then from the **state**, arose out of the sixteenth and seventeenth centuries in Europe shaped by the Protestant Reformation – especially the notion of the priesthood of all believers, which defined individuals as relating directly to God without the mediation of priests or pope. In the eighteenth century **Enlightenment**, the liberal call for the **freedom** of the individual found its voice in opposition to the monarchical state built upon the divine right of kings. Thus, the two great political **revolutions** of this era – the American (1776) and the French (1789) – were carried out in the name of the **rights** of man: 'We hold these truths to be self-evident, that all men are created equal, that they are endowed by their Creator with certain inalienable Rights, that among these are Life, Liberty, and the pursuit of Happiness. That to secure these Rights, Governments are instituted among Men, deriving their just powers from the consent of the governed' (American Declaration of Independence, 1776).

Anticipated here are some of the key principles of contemporary liberalism and **democracy and democratization**. Human nature is defined as fundamentally unencumbered, rather than socially constituted; individuals are seen as innately free and rational. For John Locke, who expounded a theory of natural rights, humans beings are born 'in a state of perfect freedom, to order their **actions** and dispose of their possessions, and persons, as they see fit' ([1690] 1988). To put Locke's point another way: their predisposition to rationality and freedom means that individuals are capable of running their own lives in opposition to paternalism, involving guardians – whether of the church or the state – who claim to define how to live the good life. As Tom Paine, whose *Rights of Man* ([1791] 2000) was a key early statement of the liberal rejection of **traditional authority**, put it: 'my own mind is my own church'. Since the pursuit of happiness is a matter for individuals, liberal **government** is understood as necessary, not in upholding the good life but as instrumental to individual freedom. Government therefore requires the consent of the people and should also be limited in scope, with individuals protected from over-extensive, oppressive, government by sets of rights, such as to freedom of **religion**, speech and association.

The place of limited government within liberalism has, however, been the source of its major schism in the past hundred years. Nineteenth-century forms of liberalism – following Adam **Smith**'s *Wealth of Nations* (1776) arguing that the free **market** constitutes a 'system of natural liberty' – celebrated the capacity of the market economy, free from government interference, to provide equal opportunity for all. The free market was here seen in contrast to feudal society, where social station, and with it economic opportunity, were determined at birth. So strong was this Victorian attachment to limited government intervention in the market economy, or *laissez-faire*, that for John Stuart **Mill** 'every departure from it, unless required by some great good, is a certain evil'. As the nineteenth century wore on, however, the market-capitalist society was seen to have created its own, extreme, **inequalities**, apparently falsifying the notion that the negative freedom (freedom as non-interference) offered by the market provided equal opportunities for all. Subsequently, the so-called new liberalism of the late nineteenth and early twentieth centuries, which in turn influenced the development of **welfare state** liberalism in the inter- and post-war period, argued that freedom from **poverty** (or positive freedom) was indispensable to genuine **equality** of opportunity, and that only the state could achieve this through redistributive interventions in markets as a means to providing goods such as **education** and universal **health** care.

By the 1970s, however, a new move in liberal philosophy – 'neo-liberalism' – argued that liberalism must abandon this statist path and 'return' to a minimal state philosophy prioritizing negative over positive freedoms. Neo-liberalism was heavily influenced by the philosophy of market libertarians such as Robert Nozick, who argued that the welfare state, in taxing its citizens, transgressed fundamental rights of self-ownership in the pursuit of social goods. According to Nozick (2001) there are no social goods, only individual goods. Taxation is therefore a form of economic **slavery**, forcibly appropriating what has been legitimately acquired by individuals through free exchange in the market. It was on the basis of this individualistic view of society, and subsequent hostility to the collectivist politics of redistribution, that neo-liberal politicians such as Britain's Margaret Thatcher argued for 'rolling back' the state from the market in the form of policies such as the privatization of state-owned industries.

A central debate within contemporary liberalism concerns applying liberal principles to **multiculturalism**. This revolves around the extent to which liberalism is neutral between visions of the good life. For philosophers such as John **Rawls**, liberalism is capable of providing an 'overlapping consensus' between otherwise very different forms of life and **community**. It is uniquely a political doctrine, rather than a substantive view of the good (Rawls 1993). For some multiculturalists, however, the liberal emphasis on individual rights as the framework for compromise in pluralist societies prioritizes secular **individualism** over other models of the good life that instead privilege community in various ways (see **pluralism** and **communitarianism**). Liberalism, retreating from its universalistic assertions, must therefore recognize the particular claims of communities in the form of **group rights** (see Kymlicka 1995).

Traditional, individualistic liberalism has also been criticized recently, particularly by **feminist theory**, for its 'difference blindness'. This approach to managing diversity, it is argued, far from preventing **discrimination**, actually reinforces the exclusion of disempowered groups who may have different needs that require acknowledgment – for example, through positive discrimination legislation (see Young 1990). For opponents of this view, such as Brian Barry (2001), liberalism is either a doctrine of individual freedom – positing equal rights and opportunities – or it is not liberalism at all. Citizens of liberal societies must be able to voluntarily choose or reject community, and this requires that they be seen as individuals first, with certain rights attached, and members of a community second.

References and further reading

Barry, B. (2001) *Culture and Equality: An Egalitarian Critique of Multiculturalism*. Cambridge: Polity.

Kymlicka, W. (1995) *Multicultural Citizenship: A Liberal Theory of Minority Rights*. Oxford: Clarendon.

Locke, J. ([1690] 1988) *Two Treatises of Government*. Cambridge: Cambridge University Press.

Mill, J. S. (1978) *Three Essays: On Liberty, Representative Government, The Subjection of Women*. Oxford: Oxford University Press.

Nozick, R. (2001) *Anarchy, State, and Utopia*. Oxford: Blackwell.

Paine, T. ([1791] 2000) *Rights of Man*. New York: Dover.

Rawls, J. (1993) *Political Liberalism*. New York: Columbia University Press.

Smith, A. ([1776] 1998) *Wealth of Nations*. Oxford: Oxford Paperbacks.

Young, I. M. (1990) *Justice and the Politics of Difference*. Princeton, NJ: Princeton University Press.

GIDEON BAKER

LIBERATION

See: emancipation

LIBERTY

See: freedom

LIFEWORLD

The concept of the lifeworld originates in the phenomenological philosophy of Edmund Husserl (see **phenomenology**). It denotes the world as lived; the lifeworld is the lived world. As such, it can be contrasted to the world as construed by science. Where science construes **space** in abstract geometrical terms, space, as we live, it is arranged around us; near and far, high and low, left and right. Likewise, where **science** construes the human **body** narrowly, in terms of physiological mechanisms, in the life world, bodies are moral, aesthetic and expressive beings. The contrast between science and the lifeworld, and particularly the tendency of science to bracket out or deny aspects of it, are a source of **critique**, both philosophical and social, for Husserl.

The lifeworld is socially 'constructed'. The world as we live it is a world which we perceive, think about and where we act in habitual and typified ways. Alfred **Schutz**, in particular, developed this aspect of the concept. An exploration of the lifeworld, for Schutz, is an exploration of the '**typifications**', assumptions, 'recipe **knowledge**' and habitual orientations that inform an agent's experiences and actions (see **type and typification**). Such exploration is an essential component of any action–theoretic, interpretative social science (see **action**).

Jürgen **Habermas** (1987) develops this notion in his work, fusing it with **Parsons**'s concept of the 'societal **community**'. The lifeworld, for Habermas, is the world of everyday life, the 'space' in which **identities**, **norms**, **culture** and **knowledge** are reproduced. He revives the critical element of the concept, moreover, by suggesting that

this **everyday** world is now under threat from colonization by the **structures** of the **economy** and the **state** or the **social system**.

References and further reading

Crossley, N. (1996) *Intersubjectivity: The Fabric of Social Becoming*. London: Sage.

Habermas, J. (1987) *The Theory of Communicative Action*, vol. 2: *Lifeworld and System: A Critique of Functionalist Reason*. Cambridge: Polity.

Luckmann, T. (1983) *Life-World and Social Realities*. London: Heinemann Educational.

Outhwaite, W. (1994) *Habermas: A Critical Introduction*. Cambridge: Polity.

Schutz, A. and Luckmann, T. (1973) *The Structures of the Life-World*. Evanston, IL: Northwestern University Press.

Wagner, H. R. (1983) *Phenomenology of Consciousness and Sociology of the Life-World: An Introductory Study*. Edmonton: University of Alberta Press.

NICK CROSSLEY

LIMINALITY

The technical meaning of liminality derives from anthropological studies of **ritual** passages in small-scale societies. Ritual passages (such as the transition from boyhood to manhood) were conceptualized by Arnold van Gennep ([1909] 1960) as made up of three steps: (1) separation; (2) liminality; and (3) reintegration. During liminality, the initiands live outside their normal environment and are brought to question their **self** and the existing social order through a series of rituals that often involve acts of pain: the initiands come to feel nameless, spatio-temporally dislocated and socially unstructured. Liminal periods are both destructive and constructive, as the formative experiences during liminality will prepare the initiand (and his/her cohort) to occupy a new social **role** or **status**, made public during the reintegration rituals.

In a more extended **meaning**, liminality can refer to any 'betwixt and between' situation or object (Turner 1969). The wider importance of liminal experiences in large-scale societies has been suggested by Turner (1974) and **Eisenstadt** (1995), and developed by Arpád Szakolczai (2000) to include both personal and collective liminality, temporal as well as spatial. The idea is that historical moments or whole epochs can be understood as liminal. During such periods, characterized by a wholesale collapse of order and a loss of background, **agency** is pushed to the forefront and reorientations in modes of conduct and thought are produced within larger populations. Thus the concept of liminality may add a temporal and spatial dimension to the structure/agency debate. In this vein, political or social **revolutions**, or other **crisis** periods, may be thought of as liminal, which has consequences for theorizing **social change**.

References and further reading

Eisenstadt, S. N. (1995) 'The Order-Maintaining and Order-Transforming Dimensions of Culture', in S. N. Eisenstadt *Power, Trust, and Meaning, Essays in Sociological Theory and Analysis*. Chicago: University of Chicago Press.

Szakolczai, A. (2000) *Reflexive Historical Sociology*. London: Routledge.

Turner, V. (1969) *The Ritual Process*. Harmondsworth: Penguin.

Turner, V. (1974) *Dramas, Fields, and Metaphors*. Ithaca, NY: Cornell University Press.

van Gennep, A. ([1909] 1960) *The Rites of Passage*. Chicago: University of Chicago Press.

BJØRN THOMASSEN

LINGUISTIC TURN

The term 'linguistic turn' denotes a fundamental change in the methods of philosophy, based on the idea that mistakes about **language** emerge as bad philosophy. Largely drawing on the work of Ludwig **Wittgenstein**, philosophers in Britain and the USA in the 1950s and the 1960s sought to show that persisting philosophical puzzles are due to enticing errors in the understanding and use of the relevant aspects of language (Wittgenstein 1953).

They argued that the assumption that every substantive must have a referent had led philosophers to populate the universe with all sorts of bogus objects, from Plato's forms to Meinongs's inexistence. Already in 1915 Bertrand Russell developed a technique for 'trimming Plato's beard with Ockham's Razor', arguing that close attention to the logical form of descriptive statements can dispel the illusions that lead to the postulation of an inflated universe.

Moral philosophy also followed this pattern. G. E. Moore (1903) argued that studies of the meaning of words like 'good' and 'right' should displace discussions of how to rank actions as good and bad. Some philosophers went so far as to argue that **moral** talk was not descriptive, but advisory (Hare 1952).

Later in the century, realizing that the prime medium of thought and **action** was language or language-like symbolic systems, a new school of cognitive and social psychologists turned their attention to studies of the relevant linguistic forms. They were influenced by Lev Vygotsky's (1962) studies of the way **cognitive** skills were acquired by **embedment** in the **family** conversation, and by the identification of **performatives** by J. L. Austin (1959), that is, words used to accomplish social acts. One of the most recent and influential exponents of a linguistic turn in philosophy has been the American pragmatist philosopher Richard **Rorty** (1979) (see **pragmatism**).

References and further reading

Austin, J. L. (1959) *How to Do Things with Words*. Oxford: Oxford University Press.

Hare, R. M. (1952) *The Language of Morals*. Oxford: Clarendon Press.

Moore, G. E. (1903) *Principia Ethica*. Cambridge: Cambridge University Press.

Rorty, R. (1979) *Philosophy and the Mirror of Nature*. Princeton, NJ: Princeton University Press.

Russell, B. A. W. (1915) *Introduction to Mathematical Philosophy*. London: Allen and Unwin.

Vygotsky, L. S. (1962) *Thought and Language*. Cambridge, MA: MIT Press.

Wittgenstein, L. (1953) *Philosophical Investigations*. Oxford: Basil Blackwell.

ROM HARRÉ

LIPSET, SEYMOUR MARTIN (1922–)
US theorist

Lipset is one of the most influential American social scientists the later twentieth century. Working in the tradition of social research as established by Paul Lazarsfeld at Columbia University, Lipset's predominant concerns are with the conditions of individual political participation and the concept of social cleavages. A major representative of political sociology, Lipset's cooperation with Rokkan earned him the reputation of an eminent scholar in European studies. However, his main focus has been **America**. *American Exceptionalism* (1995) and *The First New Nation* (1973) analyze – following **Tocqueville** – the qualities of US **democracy**. In *Agrarian Socialism* ([1950] 1972), Lipset gives a picture of a specific North American (Canadian) concept of socialism, and his *Union Democracy* (1956) is a classic study of the workings of **trade unions**, reflecting the influence of Robert Michels. His most quoted book is *Political Man* (1981), an exemplary outline of the liberal understanding of politics and democracy (see also **democracy and democratization**).

Major works

([1950] 1972) *Agrarian Socialism: The Cooperative Commonwealth Federation in Saskatchewan*, revised edn. Berkeley, CA: University of California Press.

(1956) (with Martin Trow and James Coleman) *Union Democracy: The Internal Politics of the International Typographical Union*. New York: Free Press.

(1973) *The First New Nation: The United States in Historical and Comparative Perspective*. New York: Basic Books.

(1981) *Political Man: The Social Bases of Politics*, expanded and updated edn. Baltimore, MD: Johns Hopkins University Press.

(1995) *American Exceptionalism: The Double-Edged Sword*. New York: W. W. Norton.

Further reading

Horowitz, I. L. (ed.) (2004) *Civil Societty and Class Politics: Essays on the Political Sociology of Seymour Martin Lipset*. New Brunswick: Transaction.

ANTON PELINKA

LITERACY

The term literacy signifies that a major part of societal **communication** is based on or carried out in writing. While **language** is a correlate of **society** as such, literacy and printing are evolutionary achievements of societal communication. The main focus of classical social theory was on the structural consequences of literacy for societal organization. Literate scholarship, literate **intellectualism** and **bureaucracy** play a constitutive role in the rise of advanced **civilization** and **modernity**, according to Max **Weber**. For Talcott **Parsons** (1964), well-institutionalized literacy is a prerequisite to more advanced 'evolutionary universals'. Modern **law**, **science**, the emergence of **states**, religious heterodoxy, and the formation of a **public sphere** are tied to literacy. In what manner, however, is disputed.

Since the late 1960s a field of intensive research has emerged which, from a sociological and philological-linguistic perspective, has shed new light on the problem of literacy. These interdisciplinary explorations share common grounds insofar as they: (1) focus on the medium itself and its operative application; (2) analyze literacy not only with regard to its recording and memory functions but also as a communication medium; and (3) dispense with linear developmental models and instead adopt the assumption of diachronic and synchronic differences in literacy. This new interest in literacy thus inevitably entails a study of orality. Each can only be defined and determined in contrast to the other. New insights into orality follow from anthropological studies of the consequences of literacy. The theory of the 'homeostatic' organization of oral cultures (Goody and Watt 1963) which allows a dynamic stabilization through reconstructing the past in accordance with the present situation is one example of such work.

Although Marshal **McLuhan** in the 1960s postulated the decline of book culture and the emergence of a new 'orality' in the age of the **media and mass media**, the notion that media never serve purely as substitutes for other media has recently gained more and more ground. Rather, by only seeming to replace earlier media, new media tend to modify them. Hence, linguistic studies distinguish between 'conceptional literacy' and 'conceptional orality' (Raible 1994). Once a society has both forms available, each can be found in either medium. Text forms emerge in the medium of speech that would be neither conceivable nor utterable without literacy. In addition, the practice of juridical, economic and scientific communication is characterized by a continuum of orality, literacy and imagery.

Derrida (1967) adopts a global historical perspective on the problem of literacy and sees book culture on the verge of its demise. What will follow, according to Derrida, however, is a new 'writing situation'. He proposes a modified, generalized concept of writing, encompassing everything that can be a matter of inscription: cinematography, choreography, but also the 'writing' of an image, of music, of a sculpture. Speech is not preliminary to this primary writing, but rather already a part of it. Hence Derrida's critique of phonocentrism leads him to a concept of writing encompassing those signs that depict speech as well as those that do not.

A thorough analysis of the writing systems of the world challenges the notion of the superiority of the alphabet over forms of literacy based on pictograms and hieroglyphs, which, according to authors from Humboldt to Havelock, is responsible for the Greek **revolution** of literacy and its cultural consequences. Today, the constraints and limitations of the Greco-centric perspective on writing systems have been made clear (Coulmas 1989). Admittedly, the alphabet lends itself more easily to learning, thus facilitating its public use. However, cross-cultural analyses prove the assumption of a causal relationship between literacy and societal transformation is implausible, showing that the effects of literacy and printing are dependent on cultural and institutional circumstances and thus vary historically and locally. In particular, the invention of the printing press was far more consequential in **Europe** than it was in China and Korea, owing to the decentralized, marketed distribution of printed works as opposed to the centralized, governed distribution in the eastern countries.

Sociological analyses increasingly focus on operative changes in communication that become possible through the introduction of literacy and printing into societal communication. Such changes themselves can again trigger structural and semantic adaptations. Written communication differs from speech in that it can be carried out without co-presence: absentees can also be addressed communicatively. However, the effects of literacy are not limited to an increase in possible addressees or, with regard to printing, to the consequence of addressee anonymity. Rather, the dissolution of simultaneity and spatial proximity of communication leads to a reordering of time and **culture**. With written communication it is possible to dissect communicative **meaning** into its factual, temporal and social dimension. Written communication escapes interactional control and thus increases the risk of rejection. According to Luhmann, communication media such as **money**, truth, and **power**, are outcomes of socio-cultural **evolution** reacting to this problem (Luhmann 1997). While speech has an inherent inclination towards **consensus**, written communication promotes the possibility of disagreement.

An institutionalization of critical faculties follows from the many characteristics of written communication: spatial and temporal distance, the possibility of comparison, the pressure of consistency, and the combination of mass literacy and book printing generating a surplus of uncontrollable information. As one of the long-term effects, literacy potentializes communicative reactions: written communication is released from the burden of immediate response and thus can defer acceptance and rejection; it can also refer to something already rejected. Further, it leads to a *modalizing* of reality: fiction becomes possible. Finally, reality can be observed in terms of its prospective possibilities and conceived as a contingent realization of mere possibility. Consequently, literacy does not introduce permanence and stability into societal communication, but instead promotes an awareness of **contingency**. As one of the fundamental semantic effects of literacy, the notion of sociality itself changes (Bohn 1999, Calhoun 1998). Communication is no longer merely a reciprocal, face-to-face process as suggested by the model of speech. Rather, literacy with all its contingencies becomes a form of sociality itself.

References and further reading

Bohn, C. (1999) *Schriftlichkeit und Gesellschaft.* Opladen: Westdeutscher Verlag.
Calhoun, C. (1998) 'Community without Propinquity Revisited: Communication Technology and the Transformation of the Urban Public Sphere', *Social Inquiry*, 68(3): 373–97.
Coulmas, F. (1989) *The Writing Systems of the World.* Oxford: Blackwell.
Derrida, J. (1967) *De la Grammatologie.* Paris: Les Editions Minuit.
Eisenstein, E. L. ([1979] 1993) *The Printing Press as an Agent of Change: Communications and Cultural Transformations in Early-Modern Europe,* vols I, II. Cambridge: Cambridge University Press.
Goody, J. and Watt, I. (1963) 'The Consequences of Literacy', *Comparative Studies in Society and History*, 5: 304–45.
Havelock, E. (1982) *The Literate Revolution in Greece and its Cultural Consequences.* Princeton, NJ: Princeton University Press.
Luhmann, N. (1997) *Die Gesellschaft der Gesellschaft*, 2 Bde. Frankfurt am Main: Suhrkamp.
Parsons, T. (1964) 'Evolutionary Universals in Society', *American Sociological Review*, 29: 339–57.
Raible, W. (1994) 'Orality and Literacy', in H. Günther and O. Ludwig (eds) *Writing and Its Use.* Berlin: Walter de Gruyter.
Thomas, R. (1992) *Literacy and Orality in Ancient Greece.* Cambridge: Cambridge University Press.

CORNELIA BOHN

LOGICAL POSITIVISM

See: positivism

LOGOS AND LOGOCENTRISM

The noun *logos*, from the Greek verb *legein*, has a number of meanings, including account, reason, speech, and rational **discourse**. It was a key term in ancient philosophy, beginning with Heraclitus and especially with Plato. In a variety of ways, logos has figured as that which accounts for the unity of thinking and world. The term 'logocentrism' implies criticism of man's dependence upon a certain idea of logos. The term first appeared in the work of Ludwig Klages ([1929–32] 1981), where it was opposed to 'biocentrism'. In Klages's account, logocentrism has determined Western culture since Socrates, implying dominance of the mind (*Geist*) and disruption of the primordial unity of **body** and soul. More commonly, however, the term is associated with the work of Jacques **Derrida** and his program of **deconstruction** (1967, 1972a, 1972b). Logocentrism is

Derrida's name for the dominant formation of Western metaphysics from Plato to Hegel and beyond. In Derrida's thesis, logocentric metaphysics is organized around the ideal of a discourse that is absolutely present and proximate to itself, forming a closed, homogeneous and pure sphere of **meaning**. Logocentrism is criticized by Derrida for its reduction of **difference**, alterity, and exteriority. From within the tradition of metaphysics, how Derrida seeks to show how logos is in fact constituted by an excluded 'other' and is only an idealized effect of a differential, impure and exterior force which Derrida terms '*différance*'. In **feminist theory**, logocentrism is closely linked with the term **phallocentrism**.

References and further reading

Derrida, J. ([1967] 1974) *Of Grammatology*. Baltimore, MD: Johns Hopkins University Press.
Derrida, J. ([1972a] 1981) *Dissemination*. Chicago: University of Chicago Press.
Derrida, J. ([1972b] 1981) *Positions*. Chicago: University of Chicago Press.
Klages, L. ([1929–32] 1981) *Der Geist als Widersacher der Seele*. Bonn: Bouvier.

THOMAS KHURANA

LOVE

'Love' is considered to have three sociologically relevant aspects. First, it designates an affection that arises out of or generates social relations or ties of different kinds (parental love, attraction based on sexual desire, affection based on admiration, benevolence, or common interests). Second, love is addressed as a historically and culturally variable code of conceiving, organizing and enacting such relationships (e.g. 'companionate love', 'passionate love', 'romantic love'). Third, 'love' is variously considered as a means of either social **integration** or individuation, or as mediating both of these processes.

Historically, social theory has mainly considered 'love' as referring to heterosexual relations (to an extent that it is often used as a synonym for heterosexual '**sexuality**' and '**eroticism**' or is collapsed with 'marriage'). Other conceptions of love, such as 'human kindness' or 'fraternal love' receive less attention. 'Love' is thus understood as constituting, mediating, and/or organizing relations between men and women, and conceptualizations of love go hand in hand with theories of sexual **difference**, femininity and masculinity. Theorizations of love have, especially in classical theories, also served to prescribe women's place and function in society.

Conceptualizations of love can be found in various strands of social theory, although it is often introduced as an ephemeral topic while fulfilling a systematic function in the theoretical argument. This is the case in various classical theories where love is identified as the affective correlate of functional integration in modern society. In the context of arguments on disintegration as an effect of excessive differentiation, love is credited with the compensatory function of constituting a bulwark against the loss of social bond. This function is, very commonly, attributed to women (see e.g. Auguste **Comte**, Ferdinand **Tönnies**). This understanding of love as the indispensable '**other**' of what constitutes modern **society** is continued in classical texts around 1900. Here, love is accredited with a redemptive function *vis-à-vis* **alienation** and excessive rationalization. For Max **Weber** (1920), erotic love is a means of innerworldly salvation, constituting a re-enchanted sphere of experience beyond the ordinary and the rationalized (see **rationality and rationalization**). Georg **Simmel** (1907) understands (modern) love as a feeling that grounds and generates distinctive personalities and creates a social reality that is, in analogy to **art** and **religion**, not imbued with instrumentality. As both Weber and Simmel ascribe instrumentality to masculinity and non-instrumentality to femininity, their conceptions of love are genuinely gendered. Elements of these arguments were continued in Talcott **Parsons**'s (Parsons and Bales 1955) theory of the benefits to the nuclear family of women's specializing in expressive action and men's specializing in instrumental action. However, in contrast to Simmel and Weber, Parsons considers heterosexual love exclusively with respect to the institutional arrangement of the nuclear **family**, tying it to **marriage**, biological reproduction and parenthood.

Feminists have criticized this assumption of women's specialization in love for its underlying **ontology** of sexual difference and its resulting normative prescriptions for women. It has been criticized as an **ideology** camouflaging female subjection and patriarchal power (see e.g. Simone de **Beauvoir**). **Psychoanalytic** feminists approach the 'femininity' of love as explained not in ontological terms but as an outcome of early gender-specific socialization (see **object relations theory**). This approach has been criticized for reifying the distinction between feminine expressiveness and masculine instrumentality. Various feminist engagements with love since the nineteenth century imply a rehabilitation of love as a means of female **emancipation** when understood as constituting reciprocal **recognition** of two individual and equal personalities.

A focus on the connection between love and individuality or individuation (see **individualism and individualization**) has been continued in different theoretical contexts. Niklas **Luhmann** ([1982] 1986) conceives of love as a symbolically generalized **media** of **communication** which makes relatively improbable personalized communication possible. Within the transition from a primarily stratified form of differentiation of the **social system** to one which is primarily functional, love takes over the function of addressing one's whole personality. In approaches that synthesize theories of

intersubjectivity, psychoanalysis, and **critical theory**, love is conceptualized as a relation of reciprocal recognition that takes the form of a symbiotic relation cross-cut by individuation that is propelled by this very relation (see e.g. Benjamin 1986). Since the late 1980s, there has been an intensified theoretical interest in the topic of love, nourished by the observation of changing codes, institutional arrangements, normative models and practices of couple and familial relationships (**Giddens** 1992; **Beck** and Beck-Gernsheim [1990] 1995) as well as by a growing sociological interest in **emotion** and **intimacy**.

References and further reading

Beck, U. and Beck-Gernsheim, E. ([1990] 1995) *The Normal Chaos of Love*. Cambridge: Polity.

Benjamin, J. (1986) *The Bonds of Love: Psychoanalysis, Feminism, and the Problem of Domination*. New York: Pantheon.

Bertilsson, M. (1986) 'Love's Labour Lost? A Sociological View', *Theory, Culture & Society*, 3(2): 19–35.

Giddens, A. (1992) *The Transformation of Intimacy: Sexuality, Love and Eroticism in Modern Society*. Cambridge: Polity.

Illouz, E. (1997) *Consuming the Romantic Utopia*. Berkeley, CA: University of California Press.

Luhmann, N. ([1982] 1986) *Love as Passion: The Codification of Intimacy*. Cambridge: Polity.

Parsons, T. and Bales, R. F. (1955) *Family, Socialization and Interaction Process*. New York: Free Press.

Simmel, G. ([1907] 1984) 'On Love (A Fragment)', in *On Women, Sexuality and Love*. New Haven, CT: Yale University Press.

Weber, M. ([1920] 1993) *The Sociology of Religion*. Boston: Beacon.

CAROLINE ARNI

LUHMANN, NIKLAS (1927–1998)
German theorist

Luhmann's social theory began in the late 1960s in the form of a **critique** of the work of Talcott **Parsons**. Modifying Parsons's understanding of the relationship between **structure** and function (see **functionalism**), Luhmann developed a more dynamic and process-oriented type of **systems theory**. In his second period Luhmann defined **social systems** as consisting of autopoietic communication networks, rather than of individuals or **actions**. Referring both to analogies with the biological concept of 'autopoiesis' and to Edmund Husserl's **phenomenology**, Luhmann defined a social system as a system composed of communicative events, which emerge over time with the effect of enabling the system to manage **contingencies** in its environment (see **communication**).

Modern **society** for Luhmann has to be described as functionally differentiated, consisting of systems for politics, **economy**, **law**, **science**, **religion**, **art**, **education**, and the mass **media**. All these functional systems are conceptualized as 'autopoietic' systems, or functionally self-generating systems. Modern society in this regard reproduces itself without a single organizing centre. Luhmann emphasizes a theory of society which eschews societal self-descriptions of normative integration, collective goals, or self-sufficiency.

Major works

([1984] 1995) *Social Systems*. Stanford, CA: Stanford University Press.
(1986) 'The Autopoiesis of Social Systems', in R. F. Geyer and J. van der Zouwen (eds) *Sociocybernetic Paradoxes: Observation, Control and Evolution of Self-Steering Systems*. London: Sage.
(1990) *Essays on Self-Reference*. New York: Columbia University Press.
([1992] 1998) *Observations on Modernity*. Stanford, CA: Stanford University Press.

Further reading

Rasch, W. (2000) *Niklas Luhmann's Modernity: The Paradoxes of Differentiation*. Stanford: Stanford University Press.

ARMIN NASSEHI

LUKÁCS, GEORG (1885–1971)
Hungarian theorist

A major exponent of Western **Marxism** and influence on **critical theory**, Lukács

held political positions in the governments of Béla Kun 1919, as Commissar for Education and of Imre Nagy 1956, as Minister of Culture, in Hungary. Lukács's early work on literature and **art and aesthetics** was influenced by neo-**Kantian** philosophy and by the work of **Dilthey**, **Simmel**, and **Weber**. During the First World War, he became engaged in studies of **Marx** and **Hegelianism and neo-Hegelianism**. An outcome of these 'years of apprenticeship in Marxism', as he later wrote, was *History and Class Consciousness* ([1923] 1991). This collection of studies in Marxist **dialectic** became Lukács's most influential book. With reference to Marx's analysis of the fetish character of capitalist **commodity** production, he developed the concept of **reification**. With his numerous essays as a literary theorist he is acknowledged as the founder of the sociology of literature. The theme of reconstructing the prehistory of ideologies of the twentieth century out of the history of literature and literary forms is taken up in *Destruction of Reason* ([1954] 1980) with respect to philosophy and sociology (see **form and forms**). Included in this portrayal of the development of irrationalism are his early teachers Simmel and Weber.

Major works

([1920] 1971) *Theory of the Novel*. London: Merlin.
([1923] 1991) *History and Class Consciousness*. London: Merlin.
([1948] 1980) *Essays on Realism*. Cambridge, MA: MIT Press.
([1954] 1980) *Destruction of Reason*. London: Merlin.
(1962 –) *Georg Lukács Werke* [Works], 17 vols. Neuwied: Luchterhand.
(1995) *The Lukács Reader*. Cambridge, MA: Blackwell.

Further reading

Kadarkay, A. (1991) *Georg Lukács: Life, Thought, and Politics*. Cambridge, MA: Blackwell.

HELMUT STAUBMANN

LYOTARD, JEAN-FRANÇOIS (1924–1998)
French theorist

Lyotard is best known as the author of *The Postmodern Condition* (1979), which introduced the term **postmodernism and postmodernity** to philosophical **discourse** and provoked widespread discussion. Contrary to some misunderstandings of the term, Lyotard did not intend to proclaim an age 'after' modernity, but rather to encourage a 'rewriting' or 'working through' of modernity that takes into account the '**crisis** of foundations' of the modern world after the end of 'grand narratives' (see **modernity and modernization**). For Lyotard, this crisis of foundations is connected to a basic problem of **justice** that he explores in his major work *The Differend* (1983). Following **Kant** and **Wittgenstein**, Lyotard here translates the social bond in the philosophy of **language**, understanding **society** as a struggle of different 'genres of discourse' that get entangled in a dispute or 'differend'. Since a universal rule of judgment that could decide this 'differend' is generally lacking, Lyotard draws attention to a forgotten 'rest' in every act of **communication**. This 'rest' has different names: the 'unpresentable', the 'sublime', 'the Jews'. It is often thematized in the context of aesthetic questions, both in relation to perception, in general, and to **art**, in particular. In *The Postmodern Condition*, Lyotard focuses particularly on problems of **legitimacy and legitimation** in **science**, **knowledge**, **education** and **social control**. He writes of a condition in which expert knowledge cannot justify its authority other than by recourse to norms of performance and **technocratic** efficiency. Part of this work can be related to debates on **trust**, **risk**, **reflexivity** and the **information** society.

Major works

([1974] 1993) *Libidinal Economy*. Indianapolis, IN: Indiana University Press.

([1979] 1984) *The Postmodern Condition*. Manchester: Manchester University Press.

([1983] 1988) *The Differend*. Minnesota, MN: University of Minnesota Press.

([1988] 1990) *Heidegger and 'the Jews'*. Minnesota, MN: University of Minnesota Press.

([1988] 1992) *The Inhuman*. Stanford, CA: Stanford University Press.

([1991] 1994) *Lessons on the Analytic of the Sublime*. Stanford, CA: Stanford University Press.

Further reading

Malpas, S. (2003) *Jean-François Lyotard*. London: Routledge.

CHRISTINE PRIES

M

MADNESS

See: mental illness

MANN, MICHAEL (1942–)
British sociologist

Initiator of a major study of the history of
power, Mann is a leading figure in **historical sociology**. The first volume of Mann's
The Sources of Social Power, subtitled *A History of Power from the Beginning to A.D. 1760*
(1986) covers the period from the earliest
civilizational formations of Mesopotamia up
to the emergence of European nation–states
in the eighteenth century (see **state and
nation–state**). The second volume, subtitled
*The Rise of Classes and Nation-States, 1760–
1914* (1993), explores the stages of **industrialization** traversed by Western European
societies in the high modern period. Opposing both **Marxist** and excessively culturalist
and idealist vantage points, Mann focuses
particularly on technological, political and
military aspects of social relations. He avoids
a conventional concept of **society** by replacing it with a more open-ended notion of
'**networks** of power'. Mann distinguishes four
primary sources of power: ideological power,
economic power, political power, and military power.

Mann dates the emergence of modern
European **civilization** further in the past than
many traditional accounts. He particularly
attributes the **dominance** of the West to
achievements in the early Middle Ages based
on military and technical inventions inherited
from civilizations of the Middle East. Also
important in his account of the rise of the
Occident is the role of local informal **communication** networks that eventually prepare
the way for the emergence of key social and
political institutions, including the **capitalist
market** economy, the nation–state and laws of
private **property and property rights**.

Major works

(1986) *The Sources of Social Power*, vol. 1: *A History of Power from the Beginning to A.D. 1760*.
Cambridge: Cambridge University Press.

(1988) *States, War and Capitalism: Studies in
Political Sociology*. Oxford: Blackwell.

(1990) (ed.) *The Rise and Decline of the Nation
State*. Oxford: Blackwell.

(1993) *The Sources of Social Power*, vol. 2: *The
Rise of Classes and Nation-States, 1760–1914*.
Cambridge: Cambridge University Press.

(2003) *Incoherent Empire*. London: Verso.

(2004a) *The Dark Side of Democracy: Explaining
Ethnic Cleansing*. New York: Cambridge
University Press.

(2004b) *Fascists*. Cambridge: Cambridge University
Press.

Further reading

Anderson, P. (1992) 'Mann's Sociology of Power',
in P. Anderson (ed.) *A Zone of Engagement*.
London: Verso.

Skocpol, T, Evans, P. and Rueschemeyer, D.
(eds) (1985) *Bringing the State Back In*. Cambridge: Cambridge University Press.

BERNHARD GIESEN
DANIEL ŠUBER

MANNHEIM, KARL (1893–1947)

Hungarian theorist, resident in Germany until 1933 when he emigrated to Britain. Mannheim's intellectual biography falls into three main phases: (1) a Hungarian phase until 1919; (2) a German phase until 1933; and (3) a British phase until 1947. Important intellectual influences were Georg **Lukács**, Georg **Simmel**, Edmund Husserl, Karl **Marx**, Max **Weber**, Max Scheler and Wilhelm **Dilthey**. Through these figures, Mannheim's work was shaped by the movements of German **historicism**, **Marxism**, **phenomenology**, and American **pragmatism**. In his German phase, Mannheim turned from philosophy to sociology, inquiring into the roots of **culture**. His essays on the sociology of knowledge have become classic texts of this discipline (see **knowledge and knowledge society**). In his British phase, Mannheim undertook a comprehensive analysis of the structure of modern **society**, underlining the normative importance of democratic social planning and **education**.

Ideologie und Utopie (1929) was the most widely debated book by a living sociologist in Germany during the Weimar Republic. His other main work, *Conservatism* ([1925] 1986), was a study of conservative political **discourse** in the nineteenth century and its relation to dominant **social structures** (see **conservatism**). Mannheim's conception of the social relations and determinants of knowledge represents a critical adaptation and qualification of the Marxist theory of **ideology**. He described all knowledge as standing in definite relations to social facts in historical contexts and places. However, he did not subscribe to a position of **relativism** in which all knowledge, or all claims to knowledge, are treated as possessing equal validity.

Major works

([1922–24] 1980) *Structures of Thinking*. London: Routledge & Kegan Paul.
([1925] 1986) *Conservatism: A Contribution to the Sociology of Knowledge*. London: Routledge & Kegan Paul.

([1929] 1936) *Ideology and Utopia*. London: Routledge.
(1940) *Man and Society in an Age of Reconstruction*. London: Routledge.

Further reading

Kettler, D. and Meja, V. (1995) *Karl Mannheim and the Crisis of Liberalism*. New Brunswick, NJ: Transaction.
Meja, V. and Stehr, N. (eds) (1990) *Knowledge and Politics: The Sociology of Knowledge Dispute*. London: Routledge & Kegan Paul.
Wolff, K. H. (ed.) (1993) *From Karl Mannheim*. New Brunswick, NJ: Transaction.

VOLKER MEJA
NICO STEHR

MARCUSE, HERBERT (1878–1971)

German theorist, resident in the USA. A major figure in the **Frankfurt School**, Marcuse was also the School's most politically outspoken member. Born into a Jewish bourgeois family, Marcuse fled Nazi Germany for the USA, where he joined the Office of Strategic Studies of the US State Department during the Second World War. Shaped by his experience of the political upheavals in Germany in 1918, Marcuse's lifelong thinking revolved around the question of how collective **emancipation** was to be conceived in times that appeared to have bid farewell to the idea of **revolution**. Influenced in his early work by the **phenomenological** ideas of Husserl and **Heidegger**, Marcuse addressed the issue of how a world marked by total **reification** was to be overcome through an existentially motivated total social revolution. This project came to a conclusion in the 1970s with his ironically entitled book *Counter-Revolution and Revolt* (1972) which defended the student revolt of 1968 but also recognized the overwhelming **power** of counter-revolutionary forces, ending with what **Habermas** called a certain 'defensive message of the beautiful', drawn from J. C. F. Schiller's utopian philosophy of 'aesthetic education' (see **utopia**). In his study of Hegel, *Reason and Revolution* (1941) and his best-known work, *One-Dimensional Man* (1964), Marcuse arrived at his most mature account of the destruction of the qualities of human existence under the effects of capitalist rationality. This project was extended in his study of **Freud**, *Eros and Civilization* (1955), which fused the Marxian critique of **ideology** with an examination of the libidinal structures of social repression (see **psychoanalysis**).

Major works

(1941) *Reason and Revolution: Hegel and the Rise of Social Theory.* New York: Oxford University Press.
(1955) *Eros and Civilization: A Philosophical Inquiry into Freud.* Boston: Beacon Press.
(1958) *Soviet Marxism: A Critical Analysis.* New York: Columbia University Press.
(1964) *One Dimensional Man: Studies in Ideology of Advanced Society.* Boston: Beacon Press.
(1972) *Counter-Revolution and Revolt.* Boston: Beacon Press.
(1978 –) *Schriften.* Frankfurt am Main: Suhrkamp.

Further reading

Bokina, J. and Lukes, T. L. (eds) (1994) *Marcuse: From the New Left to the Next Left.* Lawrence, KS: University Press of Kansas.
Brunkhorst, H. and Koch, G. (1987) *Herbert Marcuse zur Einführung.* Hamburg: Junius Verlag.
Kellner, D. (1984) *Herbert Marcuse and the Crisis of Marxism.* Berkeley, CA: University of California Press.

HAUKE BRUNKHORST

MARKET

Markets are the outcome of producers and consumers competing for revenue and **status**. Markets are considered essentially economic phenomena, but are common in other spheres, including the spheres of politics, **science**, **religion**, **art**, **education**, **law**, and **organizations**, as well as **labour** and **professions**. Markets emerge as soon as signals are reproduced and interpreted with respect to qualities and volumes of products or services, **actions** or events supplied and demanded.

Markets are second-order phenomena. They emerge as **structures** relating **roles** and rules, games and **institutions**. This is one reason why Max **Weber** ([1918] 1978) understood the market as a rational means of **socialization**. Markets make producers compete with each other for chances of **exchange** while dealing with a third party, the purchaser, and without necessarily involving personal links of any kind. The second reason is that most markets use **money** or some other form of currency as a medium of exchange that refers to potential action by indeterminate others. Georg **Simmel** ([1908] 1950), in his **conflict** theory of competition, emphasized the same structure of relations between two parties who observe each other while taking a third instance into account. Options and chances are calculated with respect to both **risks** and better chances. Markets transform comparison and comparability into basic features of the search for opportunities of action and their reproduction.

Classical social theory was well aware of the importance of markets. Talcott **Parsons** and Neil J. **Smelser** (1956) describe the structure of markets in terms of the institutionalization of contractual relationships, i.e. of relationships that are deliberate, involve bargaining over the settlement of terms, and are subject to rules of sanctioning (see **contract**). Markets combine competition and **regulation** so that symmetry of types of **interest** is possible.

Yet it has proved difficult to theorize about markets. How are decoupling and self-regulation to be combined with overall social structure? How exactly are **trust** and **power** institutionalized in this potentially dubious theatre of interaction? What are these markets that in economic theory must somehow act as substitutes for individual rationality?

Social theory has only recently begun to deal with these and other questions. Markets arise from self-reproducing social structures based on producers' roles that consist in observing others' behaviour (White 1981). They consist of feedback structures based on self-selections of producers who read and interpret the signals of prices and infer volume signals sent by other producers. Any one volume shipped for a price means that there is a market that can be explored and exploited by means of different qualities shipped for different prices leading to a different volume. Finding one's own role as a producer *vis-à-vis* the roles of other producers is what constitutes the market and what defines the possibility of competition. White proposes a $W(y)$ model, deducing the worth W of a shipment of a volume y, to describe the mechanism of markets.

Other theories have followed suit, most of them accepting the metaphor presented by White of the market as a 'mirror'. Producers observe each other when searching for signals that tell them what actions the market sustains. They do not try to observe the other side of the market, for instance, by searching for the 'needs' of consumers.

Niklas **Luhmann** (1988) extends this model to describe both sides of the market, both of them looking at a mirror, the producer observing producers, the purchaser observing purchasers. This approach defines markets as the boundaries of the economic system. They are not social systems in their own right but interfaces of the economic system, turning the indeterminate **complexity** outside the economic system into determinate complexity inside it. Firms and households are necessary to test, and to maintain, these markets. Overflowing and **framing**, as Callon (1998) argues, are not exclusive but inclusive of each other: producers overflow, and purchasers overshoot, in order to settle for the frames that prove sustainable. Yet these framings are not institutional givens but **networks** which are always in the process of testing for, and

being tested for, deviant action; that is to say, entrepreneurial action.

Architectures of markets can be modelled that describe incentives versus risks and expectations versus **information** as a topology of market orientations which both decouple and embed possible action within and beyond the frames of the market (Baecker 1988). Accounting for possible moral hazard and adverse selection defines how opportunities and needs are pursued. Elaborations are proposed that describe how **status** based on the quality of both the product and the producer helps to signal the quality, to reduce transactions costs and finance costs of finance, and to discourage comparisons with qualities of lesser status (Podolny 1993). Competition in markets looks for non-redundant contacts that may provide opportunity (Burt 1992). Markets are understood as 'fields' that combine stability and complexity, and fluidity and efficiency on the basis of social roles. These define how the dynamism of technology and competition is received, encouraged, and enacted by firms and households (Fligstein 2001).

White (2002) argues that older exchange markets are replaced by production markets that work by pumping product flows downstream. These newer production markets replace the **institutionalized** frame of more or less chance meetings between buyers and sellers. **Production** markets account for the fact that most of business is done with other business, not with consumers. Social theory in this context must take account of networks which focus on simultaneous (i.e., oscillating) decoupling and **embedding** by presenting actors' opportunities to deal with their commitments and fears. Producers and purchasers can only adapt if they know where to look and how to explore variance. Markets offer a choice between looking upstream or looking downstream. One direction is accepted as it is; the other direction becomes the target for deal testing. The $W(y)$ model is fleshed out in White (2002) in great detail, defining a market profile mechanism, which consists of a rule for producers to maximize the worth of a shipment minus its costs while looking for a position in a pecking order of qualities that allows purchasers to compare qualities with respect to substitutability. Markets emerge when firms succeed in nesting their cost schedules in the same order used by purchasers to nest their satisfaction schedules. This means that markets may unravel when firms 'freeload' their volumes with too low a quality to sustain a footing.

Markets become embedded within business cultures and allow for framing and networking, for entrepreneurship and strategies contingent on **discourses**, including discourses of religious **legitimacy**, which describe and picture what can be done and what can be talked about (cf. Swedberg 1998). A social theory of markets begins where firms and markets are seen to interact in networks that define how identities shape, and are shaped by, control. Markets show how operation and context, commitment and indeterminacy, are equally present in the domain of social action (see also **embedding and disembedding**).

References and further reading

Baecker, D. (1988) *Information und Risiko in der Marktwirtschaft*. Frankfurt am Main: Suhrkamp.

Burt, R. S. (1992) *Structural Holes: The Social Structure of Competition*. Cambridge, MA: Harvard University Press.

Callon, M. (ed.) (1998) *The Laws of the Markets*. Oxford: Blackwell.

Fligstein, N. (2001) *The Architecture of Markets*. Princeton, NJ: Princeton University Press.

Luhmann, N. (1988) *Die Wirtschaft der Gesellschaft*. Frankfurt am Main: Suhrkamp.

Parsons, T. and Smelser, N. J. (1956) *Economy and Society*. London: Routledge & Kegan Paul.

Podolny, J. (1993) 'A Status-Based Model of Market Competition', *American Journal of Sociology*, 98: 829–72.

Simmel, G. ([1908] 1950) *The Sociology of Georg Simmel*. Glencoe, IL: Free Press.

Swedberg, R. (1998) *Max Weber and the Idea of Economic Sociology*. Princeton, NJ: Princeton University Press.

Weber, M. ([1918] 1978) *Economy and Society*. Berkeley, CA: University of California Press.

White, H. C. (1981) 'Where Do Markets Come From?', *American Journal of Sociology*, 87: 517–47.

White, H. C. (2002) *Markets from Networks*. Princeton, NJ: Princeton University Press.

DIRK BAECKER

MARRIAGE AND DIVORCE

The term 'marriage' is strongly associated with concepts of the 'family', involving heterosexual relationships and reproduction (see **family and household**). However, the **values and norms** that govern marriage never remain static but keep changing with the times, and at any given time, individuals from different **classes** and ethnic backgrounds consider marriage differently. For example, in fifteenth-century England, marriages among the upper classes often had the strategic purpose of preserving and increasing **property** or political and social **power**, while many in the poorer strata of **society** could not afford to wed formally. Romantic **love** as the basis for marriage has since gained increasing importance, as has the notion of the couple independently choosing their spouse. Some historians argue, however, that also in previous eras, marriages served **emotional** as well as practical purposes (Bailey 2003: 201) (see also **intimacy** and **eroticism**).

Over the past half century in many Western countries, the average **age** at first marriage has risen while marriage rates have declined. These changes can partly be attributed to the growing popularity of cohabitation and to women's increased participation in higher **education**. There has also been a shift from religious to secular marriages (see **secularization**). In the early twenty-first century, two-fifths of all marriages in Britain were of couples of whom at least one had been married before.

335

Marriage today is a legal **contract**, offering married couples many forms of legal and financial protection. As legislation and norms governing marriage have changed, the power balance between husbands and wives has shifted. Since the later twentieth century, a strict **division of labour** and friendship **networks** between husbands and wives has given way to the ideal of the companionate marriage based on mutuality and **equality**. In Britain, a degree of equality within marriage was not gained until the 1970s, in relation to ownership of **property** and the upbringing of children. However, these improvements in formal equality have not necessarily translated into practice and it is debatable to what extent the ideal of the companionate marriage has been realized. There remain power imbalances and a division of labour between men and women in marriage.

Still, attitudes within and towards marriages have changed and continue to change (Lewis 2001). **Giddens** (1992) has argued that as the power of prescription has faded, contemporary marriages are based on choice rather than obligation. The connection between marriage and parenthood has also changed in character. Norms governing illegitimacy have become less strict, while married couples are no longer to the same degree expected to have children. Further, children are no longer seen as a major hindrance to divorce. Since the late 1990s, the focus of debate in many Western countries has increasingly been on gay marriage as several Western countries have implemented laws on gay marriage or partnerships. This debate has highlighted how ideologically charged the concept is.

Marriage continues to be based on the ideal of 'till death us do part', but in reality, not all marital relationships survive that long. Prior to the second half of the twentieth century, divorce was rare. Although many marriages did break down, only a small minority of couples could afford to divorce. There was also a strong stigma attached to

divorce, and divorced couples, especially women, were often shamed and ostracized by their **communities**. As the norms and legislation concerning divorce became more **liberal** during the twentieth century, divorce became more accessible. The number of divorces rose steadily in many Western countries in the decades after the Second World War although there has been a decreasing trend since the 1990s in several countries. In contemporary Western societies, divorce can be viewed as a form of liberation and is connected with modern ideas about **individualism and individualization** (Giddens 1992). Still, although the stigma of divorce has decreased, rising divorce rates have been the cause of **moral** panics and widespread concern.

In the 1990s, researchers began increasingly to regard divorce not as a discrete event but as a process. Smart and Neale (1999) and **Beck** and Beck-Gernsheim (1995) have argued that divorced couples rarely cut all ties, but go on living in a 'post-marital marriage' based on continuing material support, parenting and a shared biography. Whereas in the past, it was not unusual for the divorced father to absent himself, contemporary fathers are expected to continue bearing their parenting and financial responsibilities towards their children also after divorce, as reflected in legislation such as the Child Support Act in Britain in 1991 and equivalent legislation elsewhere.

References and further reading

Bailey, J. (2003) *Unquiet Lives: Marriage and Marriage Breakdown in England, 1660–1800.* Cambridge: Cambridge University Press.

Beck, U. and Beck-Gernsheim, E. (1995) *The Normal Chaos of Love.* Cambridge: Polity.

Davidoff, L., Doolittle, M., Fink, J. and Holden, K. (1999) *The Family Story: Blood, Contract and Intimacy, 1830–1960.* London: Longman.

Giddens, A. (1992) *The Transformation of Intimacy: Sexuality, Love and Eroticism in Modern Societies.* Cambridge: Polity.

Lewis, J. (2001) *The End of Marriage? Individualism and Intimate Relationships.* Cheltenham: Edward Elgar.

Simpson, B. (1998) *Changing Families: An Ethnographic Approach to Divorce and Separation.* Oxford: Berg.

Smart, C. (1984) *The Ties That Bind: Law, Marriage and the Reproduction of Patriarchal Relations.* London: Routledge, Kegan & Paul.

Smart, C. and Neale, B. (1999) *Family Fragments?* Cambridge: Polity.

Stone, L. (1977) *The Family, Sex and Marriage in England, 1500–1800.* London: Weidenfeld & Nicolson.

VANESSA MAY

MARSHALL, THOMAS HUMPHREY (1893–1982)

British theorist

Marshall was influenced by **Durkheim**, **Weber** and **Mannheim**. His essay *Citizenship and Social Class* (1950) is his most important contribution to sociology. His analysis of the simultaneous development of social **class** and **citizenship** in Britain from the eighteenth to the twentieth century is the founding text of contemporary studies of citizenship. It is Marshall's central argument that the **institution** of citizenship bestows a **status** of formal **equality** on all members of **society**, which permits the acceptance of social **inequalities** as legitimate. However, these inequalities are mitigated over time with the extension of **rights**, beginning with legal and political rights in the eighteenth and nineteenth centuries, moving to **social rights** in the twentieth century with the foundation of the **welfare state**.

Marshall's analysis of the effects of social **rights** on the inequalities generated by the capitalist class system has become influential in many fields of sociology concerned with **stratification**, **social change**, social **integration**, and **social justice**.

Major works

(1950) *Citizenship and Social Class and Other Essays.* Cambridge: Cambridge University Press.

(1965) *Social Policy in the Twentieth Century.* London: Hutchinson.

(1981) *The Right to Welfare and Other Essays.* London: Heinemann Educational Books.

Further reading

Dahrendorf, R. (1988) *The Modern Social Conflict: An Essay on the Politics of Liberty.* New York: Weidenfeld & Nicolson.

Turner, B. S. (ed.) (1993) *Citizenship and Social Theory.* London: Sage.

JÜRGEN MACKERT

MARTINEAU, HARRIET (1802–1876)

First woman sociologist to produce writings which posed genuine sociological questions and sparked empirical research. Asking how different societies could be analyzed and understood, she developed an original method and set up methodological principles to govern research into social reality. Some 60 years before **Durkheim**'s *Rules of Sociological Method*, Martineau worked out the basics of a quantitative and qualitative concept for social research. She did not stop at simply reflecting on research strategies, but applied these empirically, looking for the relationship between theory and **practice** in particular societies. In comparing societies, she always combined **micro-** and **macro**-sociological perspectives. Martineau recognized the ubiquity of unequal social relationships which for her resulted systematically and simultaneously from categories of **class**, **sex** and **race**. Social antinomies were grounded in the 'circumstances' or social relationships of individuals, not in their psycho-physical or biologically-determined dispositions. In 1851 she began a translation of Auguste **Comte**'s *Cours de philosophie positive* with the aim of promoting Comte's ideas. To achieve a broader acceptance of the work, she decided to condense the original into two volumes. This interpretive achievement was such a success that Comte preferred the English edition to his own French version, and used it as the basis for a revised edition.

337

Major works

(1837) *Society in America*, 2 vols. Paris: Baudry's European Library.

([1838] 1989) *How to Observe Morals and Manners*. New Brunswick, NJ: Transaction.

(1848) *Eastern Life, Present and Past*, 3 vols. London: Edward Moxon.

(1853) *The Positive Philosophy of Auguste Comte.* Trans. and condensed by Harriet Martineau, 2 vols. New York: Appleton, Chapman.

Further reading

Hill, Michael R. *et al.* (2002) *Harriet Martineau: Theoretical and Methodological Perspectives*. London: Routledge.

CHARLOTTE MÜLLER

MARX, KARL (1818–1883)
German theorist

Assisted by Engels, Marx reformulated Hegelian ideas of history and **labour** into sociological concepts (see **Hegelianism and Neo-Hegelianism**). Marx's and Engels's **materialism** portrayed ruling-**class** expropriation of direct producers' surplus product and consequent class struggles as history's secret motor. The political catechism for **communism**, their *Communist Manifesto* ([1848] 1976), exhorted workers to revolt, establish a classless **society**. Marx ([1851] 1979) also addressed France's second Napoleonic dictatorship, which foreshadowed communist and **fascist authoritarianism**. Marx's unfinished magnum opus, *Capital* ([1867–94] 1996–98) theorized that ever more rationalized capitalist expropriation of workers' unpaid portion of **labour** time produces **poverty** alongside **wealth** and technical **progress**, generating eventually concentration, centralization, boom–bust cycles, permanent underemployment, and systemic **crisis**.

Countering Adam **Smith** and other representatives of classical **political economy**, Marx held that society precedes individuals and that 'modern industry's' complex **cooperation**, interdependence, and 'socialized' **pro**-duction create bases for comprehensive public planning, collectivized productive property, and **communism**. The late twentieth-century erosion and collapse of oppressive, actually existing communism led many theorists to dismiss Marx. But US-led **globalization** has produced a global **working class**, expanded the **underclass**, and heightened political instability, renewing the relevance of Marx's materialist analytical tools.

Major works

Marx and Engels references are from: *Karl Marx, Frederick Engels, Collected Works*, 50 vols. New York. International Publishers.

Marx, K. (1979) *The Eighteenth Brumaire of Lewis Bonaparte*, vol. 11.

Marx, K. (1996–98) *Capital, I – III*, vols 35–7.

Marx, K. and Engels, F. (1976) *Manifesto of the Communist Party*, vol. 6.

Further reading

Seigel, J. (1993) *Marx's Fate*. University Park, PA: Pennsylvania State University Press.

ROBERT J. ANTONIO

MARXISM

Being identified with some of the twentieth-century's major **emancipatory** struggles and worst repressions, no modern social theorist has generated more intense feelings among more widely dispersed audiences than Karl **Marx**. As **capitalism** moved from its original centres in Europe and North America, Marx's ideas spread worldwide, were revised, blended with local **traditions**, and applied diversely. Marxism's contributions to **communism**, **labour movements**, and diverse Left criticism, resistance, and insurgency have opened it to intense debate.

Breaking with **transcendental** philosophy, **Hegel** aimed to derive 'what should be' from 'what is coming to be' and to execute an 'immanent critique' of **modernity**, stressing humanity's self-creation through labour.

Assisted by Engels, Marx revised Hegelian **historicism**, dropping Hegel's stress on 'spirit' and transforming his ideas of history and labour into sociological concepts. Marx anchored his normative critique in a materialist analysis of society as a whole (see **materialism**). Founding the **critical theory** tradition, he theorized an emancipatory path by analyzing history's actual features and tendencies (see **emancipation**). He criticized capitalism's **class**-based social order from the perspective of its emergent, contradictory structural characteristics, its **ideology** of **freedom**, **equality**, and plenty, and its nascent **social movements**. Marx saw ruling class appropriation of direct producers' surplus product and consequent 'class struggles' to be history's 'secret' formative force (see **class**). Marx argued that the **bourgeoisie**'s ever more rationalized expropriation of workers' unpaid portion of labour time produces **poverty** along with **wealth** and technical **progress**, eventually generating concentration, centralization, boom–bust cycles, permanent underemployment, and systemic **crisis**. He held that the capitalist **mode of production**'s contradictory facets lead ultimately to **proletarian** class struggle and communism.

Marxist theory has been variously employed. It has been an ideology for communist movements. Later nineteenth- and early twentieth-century social democrats debated materialist theory along with politics. Karl Kautsky proposed a **deterministic** materialism that supposedly would reveal to Party intelligentsia the proletariat's 'real interests' and the proper moment for worker revolt. He argued that Party leaders should institute reforms by parliamentary means until material conditions are ripe for **revolution**. Interpreting materialism differently, Rosa Luxemburg opposed reformism and stressed **working-class** consciousness and spontaneous revolutionary action. The 'revisionist' Eduard Bernstein abandoned materialism and revolution, fusing **socialism** with **liberalism**. After World War I's **nationalist**

mobilization and the Russian Revolution, Lenin's ideas of the 'vanguard party' and the 'dictatorship of the proletariat' supplanted democratic socialist visions. His materialist 'reflection theory' of **knowledge** consecrated Party officialdom, as the infallible revolutionary guide. Codifying mechanical materialism, Bukharin stressed deterministic natural laws. Stalin made 'Marxism–Leninism' or 'dialectical materialism' ('diamat') the Soviet **state**'s meta-ideology and scientific warrant. Invalidating competing systems of thought, diamat neutralized intellectual and political debate, justifying Soviet destruction of **civil society**. In the post-war era and after, Mao and Third World Marxists reshaped diamat to fit **peasant** revolution and new communist regimes.

The borders between Marxist ideology and Marxist social theory are fluid, and mixed forms predominate. In the 1920s, **Lukács**, **Gramsci**, and Korsch founded 'Western Marxism', breaking with diamat and stressing **culture** and consciousness. Gramsci's concept of cultural **hegemony** has been employed centrally in later twentieth-century 'cultural Marxism' and 'cultural studies'. Lukács's *History and Class Consciousness* also had a wide impact on Marxist theory. Employing concepts of **reification**, rooted in Marx's argument about 'commodity fetishism', and **rationalization**, originating from **Weber**, Lukács held that false consciousness and cultural domination block revolutionary agency.

Influenced by Lukács and founded in the 1920s, the Frankfurt 'Institute for Social Research' severed connections with the Communist Party. The **Frankfurt School** theorists abandoned claims that Marxism was integral to social theory, engaging plural traditions, eliminating warrants about historical 'inevitability', overthrowing the Party's **epistemological** privilege, and embracing contingent, multi-causal historicism. Their work on **fascism**, authoritarianism, anti-Semitism, and the 'culture industry' focused on the absence of a revolutionary

proletariat. **Horkheimer** and **Adorno** employed Nietzsche, Weber, and other non-Marxists widely in their analyses of 'total administration,' **instrumental reason**, and the 'dialectic of **enlightenment**'. Shifting the focus from **capitalism** to Western rationality, they held that social critique had been neutralized by the **media and mass media** and the unparalleled capacity for terror, propaganda, and regimentation. Although remaining Marxist, **Marcuse** held that legitimacy, in post-war capitalism, was based on **consumption** rather than ideology. In the late twentieth century, **Habermas** tried to revive Marxism's 'Enlightenment Project' and restore critical theory's emancipatory thrust, substituting a 'quasi-transcendental' method for Hegel-Marxism's historical immanent critique. His '**discourse ethics**' manifested a broader **linguistic turn** in social theory.

In post-World War II France, **Sartre**, and others fashioned heterodox Marxisms. In 1956, Soviet repression of the Hungarian revolt and Khrushchev's revelations about Stalinism split the French Communist Party. Joining the *gauchistes*' left alliance, which broke with the Party and Marxism, Henri **Lefebvre** declared that philosophy is autonomous from politics and that mass consumption and new forms of fragmentation, **alienation**, and administration required fresh non-Marxist analyses. Borders between Marxist, Marxist-influenced, and post-Marxist theory became blurred. For example, neither Garaudy's **humanism**, drawing on the early Marx's ideas on alienation, nor **Althusser**'s **structuralism**, stressing the later Marx, resembled orthodox materialism. During the 1970s, Althusser attacked economic determinism, and stressed the **autonomy** of theory. His 'decentred' idea of totality suggested heterogeneous sources of change and that ideology or politics as well as economics can be dominant structural principles. He connected theory to Eurocommunism's alliance politics and parliamentary socialism. The New Left suggested a plural revolutionary subject composed of Third World peoples and First World students, minorities and the poor. Even in Eastern Europe, heterodox Marxists spoke more critically about materialism and communism.

By 1980, Eurocommunist Parties had failed, the New Left had fizzled out, and the USSR and Third World communism had declined. Marxism was exhausted as an ideology of the state and of insurgency. In the 1980s, Perry Anderson, Martin Jay, Ernesto Laclau and Chantal Mouffe, Ellen Meiksins Wood and other leftists addressed Western Marxism's lost vitality. 'New Social Movements' theorists shifted from labour-centred, class politics to 'cultural politics' and from **solidarity** to plural alliance. Convergent 'postmodernists' rejected 'grand narratives', embracing discourse, **difference**, and 'local politics' (see **postmodernism and postmodernity**). In the wake of the 1989 communist collapse, the neo-conservative Francis Fukuyama declared Marx dead and free-market liberalism's global triumph over socialism and social democracy. Diverse theorists announced an 'end of left and right' and the 'end of alternatives'.

However, Marxist-influenced sociological analysis has continued to thrive in the social sciences and humanities. New fusions have appeared. 'Regulationists' and 'structures of accumulation' theorists have blended Marxism with institutional economics, analytical Marxists have borrowed from neo-classical economics, and socialist feminists have mixed Marxian materialism with new gender critiques. Since the turn of the millennium, neo-liberal **globalization**'s international division of labour has expanded working classes, increased economic inequality, deregulated global markets, eroded welfare states, and generated the kind of economic and political instability Marx foresaw.

References and further reading

Anderson, P. (1983) *In the Tracks of Historical Materialism*. London: Verso.

Grossberg, L. and Nelson, C. (eds) (1988). *Marxism and the Interpretation of Culture.* Urbana, IL: University of Illinois Press.

Habermas, J. ([1981] 1984–87) *The Theory of Communicative Action*, 2 vols. Cambridge, MA: MIT Press.

Harvey, D. (1989) *The Condition of Post-modernity.* Oxford: Blackwell.

Jay, M. (1984) *Marxism and Totality.* Berkeley, CA: University of California Press.

Kolakowski, L. (1978) *Main Currents of Marxism*, 3 vols. Oxford: Oxford University Press.

Lukács, G. ([1923] 1968) *History and Class Consciousness.* Cambridge, MA: MIT Press.

Mandel, E. ([1972] 1978) *Late Capitalism.* London: Verso.

Przeworski, A. (1985) *Capitalism and Social Democracy.* Cambridge: Cambridge University Press.

Sassoon, D. (1996) *One Hundred Years of Socialism.* New York: New Press.

Wiggershaus, R. ([1986] 1994) *The Frankfurt School.* Cambridge, MA: MIT Press.

ROBERT J. ANTONIO

MASS CULTURE AND MASS SOCIETY

The terms 'mass society' and 'mass culture' are no longer in fashion in the twenty-first century. Before societies and cultures were called 'mass', the term 'masses' was used for political reasons. It had both reactionary and radical inflections. For conservatives, it was another word for 'mob', designating the unruly populace who occasionally rioted, thereby causing civil disturbance that needed to be put down. For revolutionaries in the **Marxist**-Leninist tradition, 'the masses' was another word for the **proletariat**, the 'universal' **class**. In their book, *Empire* (2000), Michael Hardt and Antonio Negri use the term 'multitude' to refer to the dispossessed and, potentially, revolutionary masses. It was the revolutionary connotation that prompted Theodor **Adorno** and Max **Horkheimer**, in their book of 1944, *Dialectic of Enlightenment*, to dispense with the term they themselves had coined in the late 1930s, namely 'mass **culture**'. Instead, they favoured the term 'culture industry'.

By the 1950s, however, both 'mass society' and 'mass culture' were established concepts of sociology, supposedly providing neutral descriptions of contemporary conditions, not necessarily with the pejorative connotations of cultural criticism.

In social theory, 'mass society' and 'mass culture' are predicated on a tacitly assumed model of societal hierarchy, that of **elite** and mass. From this point of view, **industrialization**, **urbanization** and **democratization** place most people in a uniform situation, that of a homogeneous mass. Waged **labour**, modern cities, universal suffrage and 'mass media' of **communication** bring about what is viewed as a standardized way of life. The masses are viewed as subject to manipulation by propaganda – as in **communist** and **fascist** movements of the 1930s.

After the Second World War, especially in the USA, there emerged the much discussed phenomenon of mass conformity, 'organizational men' in the sphere of **production** and 'suburban housewives' in the sphere of **consumption**, and the much vaunted 'American way of life'. Automobiles, televisions, washing machines and other labour-saving devices were now available to the social majority. Minority privileges were apparently no longer confined to the social elite: mass consumption of standardized **commodities** in an affluent **society** was becoming the norm. 'Levelling down' was occurring.

Some of this thinking reflected elitist views about the regrettable losses brought about by greater **democracy** and equal opportunities. This was particularly enunciated with regard to an alleged decline of the finer values and standards of educated culture in an increasingly egalitarian consumer society. There remained a perception of mass culture as inferior in worth. From the 1930s, the literary critic F. R. Leavis complained about the threat of mass entertainment and publicity to genuine

Culture with a capital C. The tasteful and embattled elite were not, according to Leavis, so much aristocrats or a *haute bourgeoisie* but, rather, an educated minority, a discriminating elect. The modernist avant garde and Marxist critics took a not dissimilar view, including **Adorno** and **Horkheimer**'s **Frankfurt School**.

However, as Raymond Williams persistently argued, the masses are always other people, never us. And, it is especially unfortunate, he believed, to understand modern-day communications as homogeneous mass culture and degrading mass media. In contemporary social and cultural theory there is much more emphasis on difference and heterogeneity than on sameness and homogeneity. This is particularly associated with **identity politics**. Identities today are understood to be complexly composed and hybrid. Such understanding challenges the very idea of standardized mass culture and conformist mass society. The shift from Fordism to **post-Fordism** – 'keeping up with the Joneses' to 'being different from the Joneses' – has complicated processes of production and consumption, apparently creating greater choice of commodities and, by extension, self-construction through consuming **practices**. However, it should be warned that this argument for de-massification is easily open to exaggeration. At a minimum, the sheer scale and reach of contemporary mediated communications justify the nomination 'mass', at least in reference to magnitude and concentration.

MASTER–SLAVE DIALECTIC

Hegel's **dialectic** of master and slave appears in his *Phenomenology of Spirit* ([1807] 1977) as a kind of a philosophical parable or fable in that master and slave stand for particular kinds of social **actors** working through the forms of **society** prior to modern civic society. It is a dialectic in that each actor grows by stages through experience towards a deepened ('completed') self-consciousness, in which one understands oneself as an individual among others, through mutual and equal **recognition** of each other's individuality, within a rationally achieved social order.

The dialectic proceeds broadly as follows: (1) the emergence of the first awareness of oneself through awareness of an other, experienced as a threat to one's original absoluteness; (2) a life or **death** struggle between the two; (3) the experience that the destruction of the other leaves the self at a loss of that which first brought it to awareness of itself; (4) enslavement, rather than destruction, of the other; (5) the instability of the master and slave relationship. Neither party relates satisfactorily to nature (the master through the slave, the slave through coercion), and the conditions for mutuality of recognition are still absent (the master is affirmed by the inferior slave who in turn is recognized simply as an inferior). Here the story ends, and only in the further exposition of the **Phenomenology** does it become clear how the full conditions behind the emergence of completed self-consciousness are possible.

References and further reading

Adorno, T. and Horkheimer, M. ([1944] 1972) *Dialectic of Enlightenment*. New York: Herder and Herder.

Giner, S. (1976) *Mass Society*. London: Martin Robertson.

Hardt, M. and Negri, A. (2000) *Empire*. Cambridge, MA: Harvard University Press.

Hoggart, R. (2004) *Mass Media in a Mass Society*. London: Continuum.

JIM MCGUIGAN

References and further reading

Hegel, G. W. F. ([1807] 1977) *Phenomenology of Spirit*. Oxford: Oxford University Press.

Hegel, G. W. F. (1991) *Elements of the Philosophy of Right*. Cambridge: Cambridge University Press.

Hyppolite, J. (1974). *Genesis and Structure of Hegel's Phenomenology of Spirit*. Evanston, IL: Northwestern University Press.

Norman, R. (1976) *Hegel's Phenomenology*. London: Sussex University Press.

BRIAN O'CONNOR

MATERIALISM

Materialism posits the primacy of matter over ideas, mind, values, spirit, and other incorporeal phenomena. Modern materialism is rooted in the ancient Greek view that physical things are composed of indivisible, ultimate objects of the same material in perpetual motion in **space**. Galileo and Newton revised this perspective into modern physics, Hobbes and Locke brought materialism into modern philosophy; **Enlightenment** philosophies employed it in theories of social **progress**; and Darwin made it the basis of biological science.

At **Marx**'s grave, Engels ([1883] 1989: 467) declared 'Just as Darwin discovered the law of development of organic nature, so Marx discovered the law of **development** of human history...' Explaining materialism's core tenet, Marx ([1894] 1998: 777–8) argued: the 'direct relationship' between ruling **classes** and producing classes is the 'hidden basis of the entire social structure' and the 'specific economic form, in which unpaid surplus labour is pumped out of direct producers, determines the relationship of rulers and ruled, as it grows directly out of **production** itself and in turn, reacts upon it as a determining element'. Marx saw 'social formations' to be shaped by their **'mode of production'**. He held that this *base* is composed of 'productive forces' (which contribute directly to production of necessary and surplus product; i.e., natural resources, tools, **labour** power, **technology/science**, modes of **cooperation**) and of **'property** relations' (by which ruling classes exert effective control over production and product and set the terms of direct producers' labour). Marx also stressed *superstructure*, or non-productive 'modes of intercourse' and '**ideology**', which reproduce the base. He saw the **state**'s military, **police**, legal, and administrative arms to be the primary means of **social reproduction**. However, he also stressed 'ruling ideas,' or leading public justifications of the mode of production, and other organizations, **associations**, **groups**, and cultural factors that, indirectly, help control, socialize, indoctrinate, or otherwise fit people to the base. Marx did not reduce all non-economic social and cultural relations to superstructure. He held that all parts of a social formation bear the mode of production's imprint, but that they have variable connections to reproduction and often have considerable **autonomy** (e.g., he understood that anti-hegemonic groups and forms of literature, art, and science sometimes have enormous social impact; see **hegemony**). Marx's materialism is social as well as natural, stressing socially-mediated material needs, productive **organization**, and 'class struggles' over productive property, focusing more on social relations oriented to material interest than on material factors *per se*.

Theorizing materialist historical stages, Marx argued that epochal shifts (e.g., from **feudalism** to **capitalism**) fundamentally transform socio-cultural life in similar ways over wide expanses. However, he also held that each social formation manifests particular circumstances and consequent variations demand empirical study. Marx held that relations of 'correspondence' facilitate reproduction and that relations of 'contradiction' undermine it. For example, feudal regulations forbidding unrestricted sale of land and free movement of **peasants** perpetuated the manor's productive forces and class structure. By contrast, emerging capitalist labour organization and technology contradicted these feudal regulations, becoming a focus of class struggles between the **bourgeoisie** and feudal **aristocrats**. Victorious capitalists created new political, legal, and socio-cultural forms corresponding to and nurturing emergent capitalism. Stressing the primacy of material factors, Marx held that all epochal transformations are rooted in basic productive force shifts and consequent superstructural changes and that most other large-scale **social changes** have similar material causes. However, Marx's claims about material primacy varied in strength, and have been an enduring topic of Marxist debate

343

and anti-Marxist criticism. He acknowledged that **causality** is manifold and contingent, but his assertions about 'inevitable' or historically 'necessary' social changes implied that socio-cultural conditions are 'reflections' or 'epiphenomena' of economic forces. 'Mechanical' Marxists have expressed such **determinism** in ideological warrants for political ends, while 'critical' Marxists usually have stressed the relative autonomy and contingency of politics, culture, and society.

Overall, Marx suggested a complex, historically-contingent materialism, rather than narrow 'technological determinism' or 'reflection theory'. After Marx's death, Engels criticized the crude materialism of younger Marxists. Although admitting that Marx and he sometimes overstated their position, Engels ([1890] (2001) argued that they meant simply: 'the determining factor is, *in the final analysis*, the production and reproduction of actual life.' Suggesting a historically-contingent materialist sociology, he contended that history is shaped by 'innumerable conflicting forces' and cannot be grasped *a priori*. As Engels implied, materialism is employed best as a heuristic principle pointing to likely sources of **structure**, **conflict**, and change and to distinctive types of questions about variable historical processes. Still, Engels understated his and Marx's deterministic moments. Many Marxists have since exhibited similar determinist tendencies, while anti-Marxists and post-Marxists, opposing **reductionism**, often have attributed sweeping or total autonomy to culture and rejected materialism and Marx *in toto*.

References and further reading

Marx and Engels references are from: *Karl Marx, Frederick Engels, Collected Works*, 50 vols. New York. International Publishers.
Cohen, G. A. (1978) *Karl Marx's Theory of History: A Defence*. Princeton, NJ: Princeton Press.
Engels, F. (1989) 'Karl Marx's Funeral', vol. 24.
Engels, F. (2001) 'Letter to Joseph Bloch', vol. 49.
Marx, K. ([1859] 1987) 'Preface' of *A Contribution to the Critique of Political Economy*, vol. 29.
Marx, K (1998) *Capital, III*, vol. 37.

Marx, K. and Engels, F. ([1845–46] 1976) *The German Ideology*. New York: International Publishers.
McMurtry, J. (1978) *The Structure of Marx's World-View*. Princeton, NJ: Princeton University Press.

ROBERT J. ANTONIO

MAUSS, MARCEL (1872–1950)

French social anthropologist, nephew and collaborator of Emile **Durkheim**. Mauss helped edit the *Année Sociologique*, which disseminated ideas central to the development of social anthropology and comparative mythology. With Durkheim, he wrote *Primitive Classification* ([1903] 1967), a comparative study of forms of **classification** evident in **myth** and **ritual**, arguing for the origins of **modern** logic in these domains. In *The Gift* ([1925] 1963), Mauss proposed that ceremonial and obligatory forms of gift **exchange** were important elements in social **solidarity**, illuminating non-utilitarian features of modern economic life. A key feature of obligatory reciprocity is **recognition** of the social status of the other. Mauss also wrote on prayer, ritual assemblies and collective effervescence, the category of the **person**, sacrifice and magic. He emphasized the importance of 'total social facts', social phenomena with economic, political and spiritual dimensions characteristic of an entire social **type**. With Durkheim, he promoted the comparative ethnographic study of archaic or 'elementary' social **forms**. Much of his work took the form of essays and reviews, and is suggestive rather than systematic. He was an important influence on **Lévi-Strauss**.

Major works

([1903] 1967) (with Emile Durkheim) *Primitive Classification*. Chicago: University of Chicago Press.
([1904] 2001) *A General Theory of Magic*. London: Routledge.

([1909] 2003) *On Prayer*. New York: Berghahn; Oxford: Durkheim Press.

([1925] 2000) *The Gift: The Form and Reason for Exchange in Primitive Societies*. New York: W. W. Norton.

(1968) *Marcel Mauss: Œuvres*. Ed. V. Karady, 3 vols. Paris: Minuit.

Further reading

Allen, N. J. and James, W. (eds) (1998) *Marcel Mauss: A Centenary Tribute*. New York: Berghahn.

Fournier, M. (1994) *Marcel Mauss*. Paris: Fayard.

Karsenti, B. *L'Homme total: Sociologie, anthropologie et philosophie chez Marcel Mauss*. Paris: Presses Universitaires de France.

Lévi-Strauss, C. (2001) *Introduction to the Work of Marcel Mauss*. London: Routledge.

WILLIAM RAMP

McLUHAN, MARSHALL (1911–1980)

Canadian theorist of media and communications. McLuhan's early work developed a **mass culture** critique of modern society that is similar to the early **Frankfurt School**. However, he later reversed these reflections by abandoning the view that modern **technology** is essentially alienating. For McLuhan, technology is best viewed as an outgrowth of the human body. By this he means that the radio is an extension of the ear and the book the development of the eye. Influenced by fellow Canadian theorist, Harold Innis, McLuhan's most important contribution was in recognizing the effects of technological **media** on the organization of **time** and **space**. His key insight is summed up in the idea that 'the medium is the message'. The media's **power** is to be found not in its message, but in its ability to impact upon human perception. For example, print culture permitted the spread of national forms of identification allowing the spread of national **languages**, dictionaries and readerships. In McLuhan's terms, print culture is a 'hot media' to the extent that readers are rendered passive in shaping the cultural content and its high level of informational

content. However, the transition to electric culture has both shifted our shared perceptions of time and space and allowed the development of 'cool media'. The mass development of the telephone and the television in the 1960s fostered high levels of participation by the audience. Further, the mediated development of the 'global village' means that time and space have become irrelevant in determining the content of contemporary **culture**. Electronic media have shattered national forms of identification, replacing them with a global mosaic.

Major works

(1967) (with Q. Fiore) *The Medium is the Massage*. Harmondsworth: Penguin.

(1968) (with Q. Fiore) *War and Peace in the Global Village*. New York: Gingko Press.

(1989) (with B. R. Powers) *The Global Village*. Oxford: Oxford University Press.

(1994) *Understanding Media: The Extensions of Man*. London: Routledge.

Further reading

Meyrowitz, J. (1985) *No Sense of Place: The Impact of Electronic Media on Social Behavior*. New York: Oxford University Press.

Stevenson, N. (2002) *Understanding Media Cultures*. London: Sage.

NICK STEVENSON

MEAD, GEORGE HERBERT (1863–1931)
American psychologist

Mead was a **pragmatist** philosopher in the sense that he regarded the standard assumption that knowledge depends on contemplation as misleading and as better thought of as being created through activity.

Mead saw sociology and psychology as continuous. The mind evolves only within society and plays a formative role in the further development of society. Mead's 'social psychology' saw the development of mind

345

and society as a stage in biological evolution. The critical question for him was the acquisition of **language**, since it is the possession of language that enables reflective intelligence. Human beings do not simply react by stimulus and response to circumstances (see **hegemony**). They reason about their situation, their effects.

Thought, for Mead, is an 'inner conversation', and such a conversation must go on in some medium – in language. Thought may consist in an inner process, but it is not separate from conduct but continuous with it. Thinking is part of the problem-solving activity of human beings. The mind is not privately secreted.

In Mead's analysis, self-conscious thought involves adopting an attitude towards oneself as an object. For other people, the ego is an object, and to understand through communication how others respond to the ego is to understand how the ego is an object to others. I incorporate how I am thought of by others into how I think of myself, 'taking over' or 'internalizing' the attitudes of others as the 'generalized **other**'. The individual 'self' is formed in and through sociality and **socialization**.

Mead's greatest impact has been through his influence on **symbolic interactionism**, as formulated by Herbert **Blumer**, in close association with the work of the **Chicago School**.

Major works

(1932) *The Philosophy of the Present*. Ed. Arthur E. Murphy. Chicago: Open Court.

([1934] 1972) *Mind, Self, and Society*. Ed. Charles W. Morris. Chicago: University of Chicago Press.

(1936) *Movements of Thought in the Nineteenth Century*. Ed. Merritt H. Moore. Chicago: University of Chicago Press.

([1938] 1972) *The Philosophy of the Act: Mead's Carus Lectures of 1930*. Ed. Charles W. Morris. Chicago: University of Chicago Press.

Further reading

Hamilton, P. (ed.) (1992) *George Herbert Mead: Critical Assessments*. London: Routledge.

Joas, H. (1985) *G. H. Mead: A Contemporary Re-examination of His Thought*. Cambridge: Polity.

WES SHARROCK

MEANING

The concept of meaning is of special relevance in the sociological, philosophical and linguistic analysis of **action**, **communication** and **language**. Meaning can be attributed to verbal or non-verbal behaviour and its products such as gestures, words and sentences, texts or works of **art**, thus giving them the status of interpretable signs. Beside artificial or non-natural signs of this kind, there is a class of natural signs which, for an experienced observer, are interpretable as symptoms (see **semiotics**), e.g. red spots on the skin mean (i.e. indicate) measles (Grice 1957).

Concerning non-natural meaning, four closely interrelated aspects are of special relevance: (1) the *meaning-intention* of an actor or speaker who produces a certain kind of behaviour or meaningful object; (2) *conventionalized rules* for the attribution of meaning; (3) the *context* of a behaviour or meaningful object; and (4) the meaning as it is ascribed not by the actor or speaker, but by *other interpreters*. Theories of meaning differ concerning the aspect they view as *primarily* relevant for the ascription of meaning:

Concerning meaning–intention: suppose A and B have an appointment to meet at a place, but A must leave before B has arrived. Given these circumstances, leaving a note with his name and telephone number would be a possible way for A to tell B that A was there but couldn't wait for B's arrival and wants B to call him, though there is no conventional rule of language determining that a name and a number on a piece of paper have that meaning. Relying on this kind of evidence, Grice (1957) argues that *intentional* meaning is more basic than *conventional* meaning so that the reconstruction of the evolution of conventions would have to start with meaning intentions.

Concerning conventionalized rules: advocates of the conventionalist view, such as Searle and **Habermas**, claim that the production of intersubjectively shared meanings under standard conditions requires acting in conformity with the rules of language (see **intersubjectivity**). According to Searle (1969), to perform speech acts (e.g. assertions, promises or requests) is equivalent to the selection of a behaviour conforming to *constitutive rules* defining the meaning of the behaviour, similar to the way that the rules of chess determine the meaning of the moves in the game. Without constitutive rules it would be impossible to promise to checkmate the king. Therefore, the autonomy of a speaker's intention to ascribe a certain meaning to his behaviour seems to be restricted by the realm of possible meanings defined by the rules of language and social action. Even more than conventionalist speech act theory, **structuralism** from de Saussure to **Lévi-Strauss** reduces the relevance of speaker's intention to a marginal factor compared with structural meaning, following from the objective interrelations of signs within a sign system.

Concerning context: performance of speech acts in accordance with constitutive rules presupposes the fulfilment of contextual conditions which the speaker is not able to completely control or explicate. Starting with this assumption and summarizing **Derrida**'s (1977) objections to speech act theory, Culler (1982) notes that the meaning of an utterance is fully determinable neither by a speaker's intention nor by conventionalized rules, but depends on the conditions of *context* an interpreter supposes to be the case. So, if the context supposed as background of an utterance changes, its meaning

changes too. Moreover, as **Garfinkel** insists, the application of a rule under given circumstances demands interpretation and a judgement as to whether these circumstances are part of the class of situations the rule is applicable to.

Concerning other interpreters: placing the main accent on the relevance of context, the point of emphasis in the ascription of meaning shifts to the position of *interpreter(s)*. To reach intersubjectively shared meanings, a common definition of context and joint background knowledge have to be presupposed which allow the congruent interpretation and application of conventional rules we make tacit use of to understand an utterance (see **Verstehen**). Fish (1980), therefore, from a deconstructionist view, stresses the role of 'interpretive communities' in the creation of shared meanings.

Emphasizing the recipient's interpretation as a primary source of the construction of meaning in communication is not restricted to **deconstruction**. Paradigmatically illustrated by the use of religious and juridical texts, it is one of the main assertions of **Gadamer** against traditional intentionalist positions within the realm of **hermeneutics** that the meaning of a text is constituted by its application to a problem situation, defined from the perspective of the interpreter. According to **Mead**, the meaning of an utterance in communication is given or stated in terms of response, presupposing a specific interpretation of the preceding utterance. Similarly, **Luhmann**'s systems theory (1984) and conversational analysis point out that meaning in communication is constituted through understanding, displayed in consecutive utterances. Referring to face-to-face communication, conversation analysis, here again in convergence with Mead and **systems theory** (Schneider 2000), has shown that each congruence or incongruence between the speaker's ascription of meaning and the evident interpretation of the hearer is registered (Heritage 1984: 254–64), thus making possible the sequentially organized co-construction of *intersubjectively ratified* meanings.

References and further reading

Culler, J. (1982) *On Deconstruction*. Ithaca, NY: Cornell University Press.

Derrida, J. (1977) *Limited Inc.* Baltimore, MD: Johns Hopkins University Press.

Fish, S. (1980) *Is There a Text in this Class?* Cambridge, MA: Harvard University Press.

Gadamer, H.-J. ([1960] 1993) *Truth and Method*. New York: Continuum International.

Grice, P. (1957) 'Meaning', *The Philosophical Review*, 66: 377–88.

Heritage, J. (1984) *Garfinkel and Ethnomethodology*. Cambridge: Polity.

Luhmann, N. ([1984] 1995) *Social Systems*. Stanford, CA: Stanford University Press.

Schneider, W. L. (2000) 'The Sequential Production of Acts in Conversation', *Human Studies*, 23(2): 123–44.

Searle, J. (1969) *Speech Acts*. Cambridge: Cambridge University Press.

WOLFGANG LUDWIG SCHNEIDER

MEASUREMENT

Both in the natural sciences, and in ordinary usage, measurement is usually identified with estimating quantities relative to a defined standard unit. However, in discussions of **methods and methodology** among social scientists, a broader use of the term predominates. Here measurement is taken to encompass a wide range of procedures, from qualitative **classification** to scoring on complex indices (such as GNP) that combine multiple quantitative indicators. In this perspective, measurement has a variety of forms, the common feature of which is the assignment, in accordance with specified rules, of **symbols** or numbers to represent specified properties of objects. First developed in the field of psychometrics by S. S. Stevens (1946), this perspective has been the starting point for most methodological discussions of measurement in social science since the early 1950s. While there are proponents of an alternative perspective

(Michell 1999) that would, if adopted, imply that most social science procedures discussed as measurement should not be so conceived, this contention has made little headway in altering the entrenched usage.

In social science, measurement is distinguished from other ways of assigning symbols or numbers by its specification of the properties represented, and of the rules to be followed, in the process of assignment. Scholars who make assignments on the basis of intuitive, holistic judgments are not engaged in measurement. For an assignment process to constitute measurement, the content of that process has to be explicated. First, there must be a conceptual specification of the property to be represented. Usually the property is broken down into component attributes, each of which is explicitly defined. Second, for each such attribute, empirical indicators need to be identified, on which the assignment of symbols or numbers will be based. Finally, if there is more than one such indicator, it must be specified how those symbols or numbers will be combined in a summary representation of the property. Max **Weber**'s application of his **ideal type** of **bureaucracy** is not an example of measurement because, while attributes are indeed specified, he does not explicate indicators for these attributes or how they are combined in summary representations.

The specification that is the prerequisite of social science measurement supports two standards – reliability and validity – used in the evaluation of measurement procedures. Reliability assessment focuses on the rules of assignment. It estimates the extent to which scholars with the appropriate training would, if they repeated those rules for the same case, consistently assign the same symbol or number. Validity assessment takes as its starting point the conceptual specification of the property to be measured. It queries how well the representations produced by following the rules of assignment succeed in capturing that conceptual content.

In addition to discussions of the above topics, there is a further line of conversation usually called 'measurement theory'. Here the assignment processes at the heart of measurement are conceptualized as mapping empirical properties onto abstract systems with formal properties spelled out in axiomatic form. On this basis, measurement theory has developed an extensive, formal analysis of multiple issues regarding measurement. The one aspect of this literature to receive broader attention among social science methodologists is its classification of scales of measurement, such as nominal, ordinal, interval, and ratio scales. Identification of a measurement procedure with a particular scale of measurement allows for a formal analysis of which mathematical and statistical tools can and cannot be meaningfully applied to the data produced by that procedure. The limitations implied by such an analysis are, however, frequently hedged, challenged, or ignored by social science practitioners.

Methodological discussions often simply assume that social scientists should devote the substantial time and energy that it takes to develop and apply measurement procedures with some degree of reliability and validity. The presuppositions and implications of this stance are only rarely explicated or defended. It is, however, far from philosophically self-evident that measurement, with its stress on explicating concepts and rules, should be preferred over the intuitive, holistic judgment of individual scholars well versed in their subject matter. This preference is usually premised on a belief that measurement is more objective, but this belief is itself dependent on a contestable construction regarding what objectivity consists in and how it is best approximated in practice (see **object and objectivity**). Along another line, it can also be argued, as **Habermas** ([1967] 1988) illustrates, that measurement in social science needs to take into account the conceptually preconstituted character of its object domain, and that doing so implies that **phenomenological** and/or linguistic analysis is a necessary precursor to measurement endeavors.

References and further reading

Blalock, H. (1982) *Conceptualization and Measurement in the Social Sciences*. Beverly Hills, CA: Sage.

Campbell, D. T. and Russo, M. J. (2000) *Social Measurement*. Thousand Oaks, CA: Sage.

Coombs, C. H. (1953) 'Theory and Methods of Social Measurement', in L. Festinger and D. Katz (eds) *Research Methods in the Behavioral Sciences*. New York: Dryden.

Duncan, O. D. (1984) *Notes on Social Measurement: Historical and Critical*. New York: Russell Sage Foundation.

Habermas, J. [1967] (1988) *On the Logic of the Social Sciences*. Cambridge, MA: MIT Press.

Krantz, D., Luce D., Suppes, P. and Tversky, A. (1971) *Foundations of Measurement*, vol. 1. New York: Academic. (See also Suppes *et al.*, vol. 2, 1989, and Luce *et al.*, vol. 3, 1990).

Lazarsfeld, P. F. and Barton, A. H. (1951) 'Qualitative Measurement in the Social Sciences: Classification, Typologies, and Indices', in D. Lerner and H. D. Lasswell (eds) *The Policy Sciences: Recent Developments in Scope and Methods*. Stanford, CA: Stanford University Press.

Michell, J. (1999) *Measurement in Psychology: A Critical History of a Methodological Concept*. Cambridge: Cambridge University Press.

Stevens, S. S. (1946) 'On the Theory of Scales of Measurement', *Science*, 103: 677–80.

ROBERT ADCOCK

MEDIA AND MASS MEDIA

Media is the plural of 'medium' – the means by which messages can be sent from senders to receivers. By mass media we mean those industries or organizations that are engaged in the distribution of media messages or texts to usually large numbers of people in a wide range of social settings. Mass media may be further understood by examining ownership structures, technologies employed (see **technology and technocracy**), media genres, and **information** theory.

Sociological significance of the mass media

Given the media saturation that characterizes modern and post-modern societies, the sociological significance of the mass media cannot be understated. The mass media are agents of **social change** and transformation. As transnational corporations, they have played – and continue to play – a central role in the **globalization** of everyday life. They are key agents of **socialization** and the texts or messages they distribute, and play a crucial role in the construction of social reality for **society**'s members. Media messages or texts are powerful sources of social **meaning**. They are commodities (see **commodity and commodification**) as well as being products that have cultural and political purchase (Devereux 2003). Because of their centrality in **everyday** life, mass media continue to have a fascination for social theorists. Mass media are also the subject of theoretical work in the fields of social psychology, communications, cultural studies and social informatics, for example.

Power and the media

Within the three main strands of social theory concerned with media and mass media, **power** is the unifying theme. Theorists have examined the determining power of the media message or text; the excessive power of (global or transnational) **capitalist** media organizations in the erosion of the **public sphere** and the power of audience members to exercise **agency** in the face of hegemonic (and other forms of) media **discourse** (see **hegemony**). Although media technologies and genres develop and change, a core set of questions concerning **structure** and agency remain central to how social theorists understand the role of the mass media. Significant theoretical differences exist between structuralists (see **structuralism**) post-structuralists and postmodernists over the relative power possessed by media audiences, media organizations and media texts or messages (see **postmodernism and postmodernity**).

The power of the media message

Over time, a range of theories have concentrated on the power of the media message or text to shape or determine public beliefs. The effects paradigm, best exemplified in the writings of the **Frankfurt School** (and **Adorno** and **Marcuse** in particular), saw the power of the media message in essentially negative terms. They witnessed how mass media messages were used to disseminate propaganda in Nazi Germany. They also believed that the mass media were responsible for the spread and perpetuation of capitalist **ideology** through the creation of false consciousness. Marcuse (1964: 12) famously asserted that the media manufacture products that 'indoctrinate and manipulate; they promote a false consciousness which is immune against its falsehood'. In the earliest version of the effects **paradigm**, audience members were constructed as being passive and easily duped by media content – a theme developed further by Postman in his seminal (1986) text, *Amusing Ourselves to Death*.

Marxist theories in either classical or neo-Marxist guises (see **Marxism**) also hold that media messages have a power over media audiences. Media content is responsible for the perpetuation of unequal or asymmetrical relationships of power between social and especially **class groups**. This is achieved through the transmission of ideology across a wide range of media genres. There has, however, been a degree of slippage within the Marxist perspective over the existence or not of agency on the part of audience members *vis-à-vis* media content that contains hegemonic or counter-hegemonic ideology (see **Gramsci**). In an attempt to rescue the concept of ideology from a growing number of opponents, Thompson's (1990) *Ideology and Modern Culture* asserts that in order to investigate how the mass media assist in the perpetuation of unequal or asymmetrical relationships of power, we need to examine the production, construction and reception of media messages (Corner 2001). Marxist interpretations of media messages, whether operating from a 'relaxed' or a 'restricted' understanding of ideology, recognize the potency of the media message in the spread of ideologies in everyday life.

This is something that is also acknowledged within **feminist** representation in particular (Dyer 2001). Mainstream media content is seen as a key source of patriarchal (see **patriarchy**) and heterosexist ideology and discourse. Theorists have commented upon, for example, the invisibility of gays, lesbians and bisexuals in mainstream media discourse. They have also repeatedly stressed the ways in which women are 'symbolically annihilated' in a mass media setting through misrepresentation, under-representation and objectification.

Semiotic theory (see **semiotics**) and discourse theory (focusing on both text and talk) have also emphasized the power of media content in examining how media messages or texts 'work' at a symbolic (see **symbol**) and discursive (see **Foucault**) level in the creation of meaning for audiences. Van Dijk's (1991, 1998) path-breaking work on **'race'/ethnicity** and ideology demonstrates how media discourse can impact upon public beliefs and social (in)action. Other theories such as **framing** theory and agenda-setting theory have been applied to analyses of media content in order to explain how hegemonic ideologies – often masquerading as 'commonsensical' explanations of the social world – come to occupy a position of dominance in media and public discourse. Theories that privilege the media message or text stress the determining power of media content and allow for either little or no agency on the part of audience members.

Power and media organizations

Another body of social theory focuses on power and media organizations with particular reference to their ownership, management and control. **Political economy** theory, **critical theory**, **feminist theory** and liberal-pluralist (see **liberalism**, **pluralism**) theory have all been applied to investigations of the internal workings of media organizations. Liberal-pluralists would cast doubt on the domination of media organizations by elite individuals and groups, preferring to stress the degree to which diverse **world-views** are evident within media content. **Globalization** theory and more recent versions of political economy theory have stressed the significance of the growing levels of ownership concentration and conglomeration within the media industries. Such changes not only have an economic significance but also a political and cultural importance in terms of the apparent shrinkage in the range of voices heard in a media setting (Mosco 1996).

Political economy theory seeks to explain how the capitalist class manage to secure and maintain their dominant position in society. In this view, any understanding of media content (and especially its ideological importance) has to begin with an appreciation of the ownership structure of the media industries. According to McQuail (2002), the restructuring of the media industries in an age of media globalization has, from a political economy perspective, meant

> [a] reduction in independent media sources, concentration on the largest markets, avoidance of risks, and reduced investment in less profitable media tasks (such as investigative reporting and documentary film-making). We also find neglect of smaller and poorer sections of the potential audience and often a politically unbalanced range of news.
>
> (ibid.: 82)

The likelihood therefore of the mass media operating as a public sphere (see **Habermas**) has been even further curtailed (Verstraeten 1996). The ideal of the mass media as a public sphere – if it ever actually existed – seems even more remote in an age of media globalization (McChesney 1999) in spite of

351

the utopian possibilities suggested by some social theorists, such as **McLuhan**.

Globalization theory recognizes the pivotal role played by mass media organizations in the overall globalization process. As agents of globalization, mass media organizations possess considerable power. The globalization of the mass media has resulted from technological developments, most notably in the form of information and communications technologies (ICTs), and from the re-structuring of media ownership in the shape of global media conglomerates. The globalization of the mass media has resurrected older theoretical concerns (most notably about new forms of cultural imperialism – first developed extensively by the late Herbert Schiller) as well as new concerns about cultural sameness or homogenization and hybridization (see **hybridity**). Media globalization is also held to have resulted in the intensification of local identities as well as the creation of new hybrid identities in the shape of 'glocalization'. Other anxieties about the globalization of the mass media concern the extent to which the much-heralded 'global village' is accessible to all through the use of new media technologies or ICTs. Worries about its implications for **democracy** are seen in the apparent rise of 'infotainment' – the merging of information and entertainment especially within factual media genres such as news and current affairs – which has come to replace more critical media coverage of social issues. **Bourdieu**, for example, commenting on the postmodern mediascape, noted the degree to which media content is now swamped by what he terms 'cultural fast-food'. This is in evidence in, for example, re-runs, copycat and 'reality' television programming.

Power and media audiences

Although still evident within some public discourse about the supposed negative effects of media genres such as 'video nasties',

virtual reality games or soap operas, the effects paradigm was replaced in the last quarter of the twentieth century by a range of theoretical perspectives that recognized the **agency** or creativity of audience members. However, theorists who have focused on audience agency differ in the degree to which they accept whether ideology or discourses exist independently of the media text. The very notion of the existence of the 'mass' media audience has also been thrown into doubt by postmodern theory. However, some of this speculation is based upon very little or no empirical observation.

Dating from the 1940s, uses and gratifications theory marked the initial break with the effects model, stressing, as it did, the ways in which audiences used a variety of media genres to gratify their needs for entertainment or information. Reception analysis, however, put the question of audience agency centre stage. In reality, reception analysis draws upon a number of distinct theoretical models. These are the Marxist encoding/decoding model, the feminist/ethnographic model and the postmodern constructionist/discursive model.

In examining the circulation by the mass media of dominant and other forms of ideology, Stuart Hall's encoding/decoding paradigm argued that we need to examine the initial encoding of media texts or messages by media professionals with reference to the dominant and professional codes employed. Audience interpretations of the message or text are best understood in terms of whether audience members accept the dominant encoding or whether they use a negotiated or oppositional code in their interpretative activities.

The feminist-inspired ethnographic model witnessed theorists and empirical researchers entering the domestic spaces and places of real people's (and especially women's) lives (see **women's movement**). Theorists wanted to understand more about how female audience members make sense of certain forms (usually fictional) of media discourse. This work has focused on **gender** discourses in a media setting. It has also been used to understand more about the adoption and control of new media technologies in the domestic sphere.

The constructionist or discursive approach sees its task as reaching a deeper understanding of the complexities inherent in the post-modern mediascape (see **social constructionism**). The focus is on the broader discursive context of media in everyday life. Audiences are reflexive, capable of considerable agency, and have been characterized by some theorists as being 'guerrilla readers' who live their media lives in a polysemic democracy. Theorists such as **Baudrillard** argue that structuralist concerns with the relationship between 'reality' and 'media representation' are outdated. In the postmodern context media 'reality' serves as a 'hyper-reality' for members of society.

New media and old questions

Media globalization and developments in media technologies in particular have radically altered the contemporary mediascape. New possibilities have been created for media organizations and (some) audience members. Social theorists have responded to these developments by adopting either a utopian stance as exemplified by the global society and global culture approaches, or a more critical perspective as exemplified by **world systems** and global capitalism theories. Both world systems and global capitalism theories are heavily critical of the inequalities associated with (media) globalization. The domination of the world's media by the profit-driven transnational capitalist class and the well-documented digital divide between the 'information rich' and the 'information poor' suggest that some of the key concerns of traditional social theory – namely those of power and **inequality** – are manifest in new ways in the information age. There is an obvious

danger in theorists focusing on either the 'ecstasy of communication' (Baudrillard) or the delights of new media technologies without much recourse to the sociological realities of new forms of mass media.

References and further reading

Devereux, E. (2003) *Understanding the Media*. London: Sage.

Dyer, R. (2001) *Culture of Queers*. London: Routledge.

Gitlin, T. (1983) *Inside Prime Time*. New York: Pantheon.

Inglis, F. (1990) *Media Theory: An Introduction*. Oxford: Blackwell.

Luhmann, N. (2000) *The Reality of the Mass Media*. Cambridge: Polity Press.

McChesney, R. W. (1999) *Rich Media, Poor Democracy: Communication Politics in Dubious Times*. Champaign, IL: University of Illinois Press.

McLuhan, M. (1964) *Understanding Media*. New York: McGraw-Hill.

McQuail, D. (2002) *McQuail's Mass Communication Theory*. London: Sage.

Meyrowitz, J. (1985) *No Sense of Place: The Impact of Electronic Media on Social Behaviour*. Oxford: Oxford University Press.

Mosco, V. (1996) *The Political Economy of Communication*. London: Sage.

Postman, N. (1986) *Amusing Ourselves to Death*. London: Viking Penguin.

Schudson, M. (1995) *The Power of News*. Cambridge, MA: Harvard University Press.

Silverstone, R. (1999) *Why Study the Media?* London: Sage.

Thompson, J. B. (1990) *Ideology and Modern Culture*. Cambridge: Polity Press.

Thompson, J. B. (1995) *The Media and Modernity: A Social Theory of The Media*. Cambridge: Polity Press.

van Dijk, T. A. (1991) *Racism and the Press*. London: Routledge.

Verstraeten, H. (1996) 'The Media and the Transformation of the Public Sphere: A Contribution for a Critical Political Economy of the Public Sphere', *European Journal of Communication*, 11(3): 347–70.

EOIN DEVEREUX

MEDICALIZATION

Medicalization is a concept used to describe, often critically, the processes in which medicine takes over a particular domain of life and treats it as part of the proper province of medicine. It has been used, in particular, to describe the increased medical involvement in areas of **everyday** life over which doctors formerly had no claims to special knowledge or expertise, such as old **age**, sexual behaviour and human unhappiness, changes that extend the boundaries of illness (see **health and illness** and **sexuality**). The term was first used in the 1970s by writers such as Zola (1972), who emphasized medicine's role as an institution of **social control**, and Illich (1976), who was highly critical of the extended role of medicine which he claimed undermined people's autonomy. It was also widely used in feminist discussions of the expanding role of medicine in relation to childbirth, manifest in the shift in the location of childbirth from home to hospital and the growing resort to medical interventions such as episiotomies, inductions, foetal monitoring and caesareans. While the concept has frequently been used simply descriptively, albeit critically, without making any claims about the factors that underpin the greater range of medical activity in contemporary life, on occasions it has been used to suggest an active medical **imperialism** – an account that connotes both conscious **agency** and medical **power**. However, the forces shaping the range of medical activity are numerous. Although members of the medical profession have often been keen to protect their interests, including securing new areas of **work**, the profession is not monolithic and others have entered new areas with reluctance, under the pressure of external factors (see **professions and professionalization**). Moreover, there are areas where the range of medical activity has decreased and the profession's power has been reduced.

References and further reading

Illich, I. (1976) *The Limits to Medicine*. Harmondsworth: Penguin.
Zola, I. K. (1972) 'Medicine as an Institution of Social Control', *Sociological Review*, 20: 487–504.

JOAN BUSFIELD

MENTAL ILLNESS

A term modelled on that of physical illness (see **health and illness**), in which a judgement is made that there is a disorder of mental functioning. Whether there is necessarily a concomitant disorder of physical functioning underpinning the mental disorder is a matter of debate. Psychiatrists assume that, as with physical illness, there is a set of discrete disorders of mental functioning that can be distinguished from one another and have different symptom clusters, onset, course and outcome. The mental illnesses so distinguished range from the very severe and highly incapacitating, but much less common conditions, to the milder, far more common conditions. At the more severe end of the spectrum are schizophrenia and manic-depression. Such disorders involve a disturbance of reason (see **Foucault** 1967) or thought, sometimes reflected in symptoms such as delusions and hallucinations that are the archetypical signs of madness and suggest a 'loss of contact with reality' – that the person no longer inhabits, at least for a while, the everyday world as it is known and accepted by others. Psychiatrists have commonly focused on the physical causes of these disorders, with heredity identified as a key contributory factor, though the evidence indicates that environmental factors are also important in causation. The various forms of senile dementia, such as Alzheimer's disease, also belong to the severe end of the spectrum. Symptoms typically involve a loss of memory and intellectual ability and far less frequently psychotic thinking produced by structural changes in the brain. At the less severe end of the spectrum are anxiety states, phobias and milder forms of depression. These used to be termed, following **Freud**, the psychoneuroses – that is, disorders with a psychological origin. However, official classifications now usually avoid this term because of its aetiological connotations. In addition, there are various types of mental illness where the symptoms focus on behavioural problems. The behavioural or personality disorders include various forms of substance abuse such as alcoholism and drug dependence, as well as psychopathic behaviour. The official psychiatric classifications that list the different mental disorders have changed considerably over time, though there have been strong moves towards international standardization. The two dominant international **classifications** are the section on mental disorders in the World Health Organization's *International Classification of Diseases* and the American Psychiatric Association's *Diagnostic and Statistical Manual of Mental Disorders*, first produced in 1952 and currently in its fourth edition. A comparison of the various editions shows two related features: first, growth in the number of disorders listed, and, second, an expansion in the boundaries of mental illness.

The concept of mental illness and the psychiatric classifications that give formal meaning to the term, as well as issues of causation, have been hotly contested. In 1961 the psychiatrist, Thomas Szasz, asserted that mental illness was a myth, arguing that the concept was simply a metaphor and that in reality there were only either organic brain diseases that affected mental functioning, as in the case of the various senile dementias, or else there were 'problems in living'. From a sociological perspective Thomas Scheff (1966) contended that mental illness was best viewed as 'residual' **deviance**. However, Alan Horwitz (2002), drawing on the work of other writers, argues that there are some valid mental illnesses: those conditions involving some

psychological dysfunction (the universal component) that is defined as inappropriate in a particular social context (the culturally specific component). Responses to stressful conditions are not mental disorders; nor are many of the behavioural deviations currently listed as mental disorders – these are better viewed, as many have argued, as forms of social deviance rather than as mental disorders.

Certain mental disorders have attracted especial controversy and debate. These include schizophrenia because of its central status as the archetypical mental disorder. On rather different political foundations, a campaign was launched in the 1960s on the status of homosexuality, which had been included in psychiatric classifications as a mental illness in its own right from the late nineteenth century. The campaign was fuelled by the growth of civil **rights** movements and the political activism of gay and lesbian groups, and led to homosexuality's removal from the list of mental disorders, though it may still be regarded as a symptom of some other sexual dysfunction. Similarly, there has been major controversy over the inclusion of premenstrual tension as a mental illness, with **feminists** arguing that the disorder transforms into a psychiatric problem what should be viewed as a normal bodily process, albeit that some may experience considerable physical pain and discomfort.

In the nineteenth century and first half of the twentieth century severe mental illness usually led in industrial societies to confinement in an asylum or mental hospital. However, since the 1950s there has been an expansion of **community** care – that is, of efforts to maintain psychiatric patients, especially those with long-term problems, outside hospital. In Western countries the standard treatment of psychiatric patients across the spectrum of mental illness is some form of psychotropic medication. New chemically synthesized drugs for the treatment of mental illnesses began to be developed and marketed in the 1950s and their use is now widespread, including for individuals who never come into contact with specialist mental health services.

References and further reading

Foucault, M. (1967) *Madness and Civilisation*. London: Tavistock.

Horwitz, A. V. (2002) *Creating Mental Illness*. Chicago: University of Chicago Press.

Scheff, T. J. (1966) *Being Mentally Ill*. London: Weidenfeld & Nicholson.

Szasz, T. (1961) *The Myth of Mental Illness*. New York: Hoeber-Harper.

JOAN BUSFIELD

MENTALITIES

Mentalities are **individual** and **collective** forms of consciousness, interpretation and **action**. As a technical term mentality goes beyond collective interests in order to explain the emergence of common interests within heterogeneous social groups. Mentalities are not only rational ideas, but rather encompass the **emotional** and irrational dimension of human consciousness. The concept of mentality analyzes collective actions through mental dispositions and world-views that underlie the particular contents of individual consciousness. Mentalities mediate between the individual and the collective, especially as they concern collective attitudes towards life, **death**, childhood, **sexuality**, **love**, **family**, **health and illness** and other aspects of **everyday** life.

The French sociologist Emile **Durkheim** was the first to bridge the gap between the individual and the collective level through the concepts of the *conscience collective* and the *representations collectives*. His approach was taken up by the French *Annales* school around Lucien Febvre and Marc Bloch in the 1920s. They applied the concept of mentalities to the history of medieval and early modern society. A second generation of *Annales* historians after 1945, led by

Fernand Braudel, overcame the high culture bias of the first generation by using quantitative and statistical **methods** to describe the historical cycles of economic and social mentalities. It was the third generation after 1970 (represented by Georges Duby, Jacques LeGoff, Le Roy Ladurie), that reoriented the *Annales* school theoretically around the concept of mentality by combining history with anthropology, sociology and psychology.

But there have been other traditions as well. Norbert **Elias** explained modern **civilizations** through the taming and disciplining function of collective mentalities. German and Anglo-American historians and social scientists have focused more on social and cultural **representations**. Recent debates have criticized the descriptive approach of the *Annales* school and reoriented mentalities towards the original question of why and how collective action is possible and how collective mentalities develop. In current historiography mentalities are often understood as 'collective representations' and the history of mentalities has become an established part of cultural history and social anthropology.

References and further reading

Braudel, F. (1995) *A History of Civilization*. New York: Penguin Books.

Chartier, R. (1989) 'Le Monde comme représentation', *Annales*, 44: 1505–20.

Durkheim, E. (1893) *De la Division du travail social*. Paris: Alcan.

Durkheim, E. (1924) *Sociologie et Philosophie*. Paris: Alcan.

Elias, N. (1992) *Über den Prozess der Zivilisation*. Frankfurt am Main: Suhrkamp.

Halbwachs, M. (1985) *Das kollektive Gedächtnis*. Frankfurt am Main: Fischer.

Hutton, P. H. (1981) 'The History of Mentalities: The New Map of Cultural History', *History and Theory*, 20: 237–59.

SIEGFRIED WEICHLEIN

MERLEAU-PONTY, MAURICE (1908–1961)

French philosopher

Merleau-Ponty was one of the key proponents of existential **phenomenology** in France in the 1940s and 1950s, alongside Jean-Paul **Sartre** and Simone de **Beauvoir**. Like Sartre and de Beauvoir, he drew strongly upon the thought of **Hegel**, **Husserl** and **Heidegger** in his own version of existential philosophy. However, he criticized the residual aspects of Cartesianism that he found in Sartre, and also Sartre's extreme and uncompromising attitude towards **freedom** and **transcendence**. His interest in social and historical structures led in his early work to an attempt to construct an existential form of **Marxism**. However, he soon became critical of Marxism and was beginning to move away from it at about the time Sartre was starting to embrace it.

Merleau-Ponty's critique of Marxism, *Adventures of the Dialectic* (1973), is his best-known political work. However, he is more generally known for *The Phenomenology of Perception* (1962), a study which seeks to explain the nature of human being-in-the-world from the starting point of embodied sensory perception (see **embodiment**). This study explores issues of freedom, thought, temporality, **language** use, the cogito and, most famously, the *embodied* nature of human **subjectivity**. In a critique of Cartesianism and related strands of thought, Merleau-Ponty sought to root human subjectivity in the practical activities of the human **body**, and to question many dominant philosophical assumptions about the nature of the body.

Other aspects of Merleau-Ponty's work include a sympathetic but critical engagement with **psychoanalysis**, which is revisited at points throughout his *œuvre*, and a critique of the **structuralism** of de Saussure and the early **Lévi-Strauss** which anticipates both **post-structuralist** critiques and certain aspects of **structuration** theory.

Major works

(1962) *The Phenomenology of Perception*. London: Routledge.
(1973) *Adventures of the Dialectic*. Evanston, IL: Northwestern University Press.

Further reading

Carman, T. and Hansen, M. B. N. (eds) (2005) *The Cambridge Companion to Merleau-Ponty*. Cambridge: Cambridge University Press.

NICK CROSSLEY

MERTON, ROBERT K. (1910–2003)

US sociologist.

Merton was Professor at Columbia University until 1976 and collaborated with Paul F. Lazarsfeld for more than 35 years as head of the Bureau of Applied Social Research. Mainly influenced by **Durkheim**, Malinowski, W.E. Thomas and F. Znaniecki, Merton was a student of Talcott **Parsons** and Pitirim Sorokin. Merton codified functional analysis by rejecting some common assumptions of **functionalism** as it had developed in British anthropology. He introduced the concept of unintended consequences of purposive action and distinguished between functions and dysfunctions, as well as between manifest and latent functions.

In opposition to Parsons's efforts to develop a 'grand theory', Merton outlined his conception of 'middle-range' theories. This approach seeks to detect key social mechanisms in order to explain social processes, arguing in favour of the interplay between theoretical assumptions and empirical work. Merton's general contribution to social theory includes his approach to structural analysis, where the term 'opportunity structure' refers to the idea of an analysis of socially patterned choices of individuals and their consequences for the institutional order. Merton's contributions to sociological analysis, social theory, concept formation and empirical investigation can hardly be over-estimated. Many of his concepts, such as the 'self-fulfilling prophecy' or the 'Matthew principle', are important tools in sociology and well known to the wider public.

Major works

(1965) *On the Shoulders of Giants*. Chicago: University of Chicago Press.
(1968) *Social Theory and Social Structure*, enlarged edn. New York: Free Press.

Further reading

Coser, L. A. (ed.) (1975) *The Idea of Social Structure: Papers in Honour of Robert K. Merton*. New York: Harcourt Brace Jovanovich, Inc.
Crothers, C. (1987) *Robert K. Merton*. London: Tavistock.
Mongardini, C. and Tabboni, S. (eds) (1998) *Robert K Merton and Contemporary Sociology*. New Brunswick, NJ: Transaction Publishers.
Sztompka, P. (1986) *Robert K. Merton*. New York: St Martin's Press.

JÜRGEN MACKERT

METAPHYSICAL

Metaphysics is the traditional philosophical discipline that investigates the nature of reality. It might be thought that the sciences have replaced such philosophical questions with empirical ones internal to their enterprise. However, even apart from the more general questions of reality as such, it is still possible to ask what sort of things must exist for a theory to be true, and thus about its presupposed **ontology**. In this sense, Martin Hollis (1977) among others shows that social scientific theories entail 'models of man', or deeper and interconnected sets of metaphysical and normative assumptions. Such assumptions have been discussed under a variety of rubrics, from individualism to holism, the intentional and the causal order, aggregation and emergence, parts and wholes, among others, that together make up some of the issues of social ontology:

what the world must be like given the nature of social facts, or what must be true if various explanations and theories are correct.

Two sorts of **reductionism** are at issue in current debates about social ontology. In the first, Elster (1989) and other methodological individualists argue that social phenomena can be explained solely in terms of the property of individuals and their **interactions** (1989), while Gilbert and other holists hold that explanation is to be found at the level of collective intentionality or **institutions** (1992). Metaphysical commitments to positions such as **individualism** are often tied to methodological strictures. The second dispute about reductionism is between naturalists, who see norms in terms of causal regularities, and anti-naturalists, for whom normativity is the irreducible mark of the social.

References and further reading

Elster, J. (1989) *Nuts and Bolts in the Social Sciences*. Cambridge: Cambridge University Press.
Gilbert, M. (1992) *On Social Facts*. London: Routledge.
Habermas, J. (1992) *Postmetaphysical Thinking*. Cambridge, MA: MIT Press.
Hillel-Ruben, D. (1985) *The Metaphysics of the Social World*. London: Routledge.
Hollis, Martin (1977) *Models of Man*. Cambridge: Cambridge University Press.

JAMES BOHMAN

METHODS AND METHODOLOGY

While not all social theory is intended to be empirically testable and not all social theory is developed from research, there is an important relationship between theory and method or methodology. Social research nearly always has the role of developing or testing theory. Consequently, methods and methodology are the bridge between social theory and the everyday social world. The term 'methodology' is sometimes incorrectly used synonymously with 'methods'. While the two concepts are interrelated, they are distinct.

Research methods are the means by which concepts from one or other theoretical level are represented through empirical investigation. Thus the postulates of, say, a theory of social class are tested for their representative validity through research instruments such as social surveys or experiments. In this sense, method is a technical procedure, particularly so when the representations take the form of numerical quantities. Social **class**, for example, may be represented in forms of **classification** such as those used in government surveys (Williams 2003: 43). Individuals will be allocated to a class (e.g. I Professional through to VI Manual Unskilled) and this allocation will be achieved through questions about occupation and the like in the survey. Class operationalized in this way comes to stand in for class as a theoretical concept. Other variables within the survey – for instance, **education**, income, housing tenure or attitudes – can then be analyzed for statistical associations or, in some circumstances, causal processes (see **statistics**). At the level of method, the efficacy with which a survey or experiment is designed, conducted or analyzed is judged on the basis of its validity, reliability and the appropriateness and significance of the statistical procedures employed in the analyses.

Qualitative methods (variously described as ethnographic, interpretive or **hermeneutic**) can be also viewed as technical procedures within social scientific method, but many of their practitioners would eschew such an approach, or at least insist that technical control or quantification plays a minimal role (Seale 1999). Nevertheless, at an empirical level the relationship between theory and ethnography as method is also one of **representation**. Ethnographic approaches, which include observational field research, in-depth interviewing or documentary analysis may be located within a particular theoretical approach (e.g. **symbolic interactionism** or **realism**), but will usually develop theory through interpretations of agents' **actions** or **meanings** within particular contexts.

In each of these general approaches to method there are field level decisions about how one can maximize the efficacy of representation. For example, in survey research we may ask whether a researcher should use a cross-sectional or longitudinal design. In ethnography should one conduct an observational study or in-depth interviews? If the former, how much of an observer or participant should the researcher be?

Methodology itself has two aspects. It is: (1) the translatory bridge between theory and method; and (2) the (often critical) study of choices of method and the relationship between theories and method.

In the first sense, to describe something as a 'methodological strategy' is to do more than, say, choose a cross-sectional survey. Rather, it is the intellectual justification for the choice of this method to represent one's research question and theoretical position. A methodological strategy moves beyond purely technical issues and is an explication of how the methods used provide valid representations of the theory to be tested, or how the methods used are the best way to develop theory. In survey method, for example, a key issue is how one operationalizes a concept (Williams 2003: 39–43). For example, how would a battery of questions about relationships to workplace superiors or subordinates represent or help build a theory of **authority**? What do we mean by 'authority'? These kinds of issues connect methodology with **epistemology**.

In the second sense, debates in methodology can be specific about how one might 'operationalize' a theory into specific methods, or they may be more abstract and general. They may be about how to decide between the relative advantages and disadvantages of quantitative methods over qualitative methods.

Though the claim has been challenged by some writers (e.g. Bryman 1988) most methodologists hold that higher-level epistemological issues also run through methodology and impact upon choice of method. Perhaps the most fundamental of these has been the subject of dispute between those who favour a nomothetic (scientific) approach and those who believe an ideographic humanistic approach to representation to be more efficacious. In the first case, it is held that social theory can be translated into measurable concepts (such as class or **alienation**) and the relative quantities of these and their relationship to other concepts can be known (see **measurement**). There is an affinity between nomothetic approaches to methodology and method and certain theoretical positions, such as **functionalism**, **structuralism**, and **rational choice** theory – though this is not universally the case, and the theoretical approaches may themselves be logically mutually exclusive. Similarly, ideographic approaches have theoretical cognates such as **hermeneutics** or **poststructuralism**. Those who take an ideographic approach often argue that there is a divide between the cultural world – produced by autonomous, self-reflecting human agents – and the physical world. The latter may be known objectively by human observers, but the social world must be studied subjectively through a strategy of interpretation. Broadly speaking, the naturalistic approach to social theory maps onto a nomothetic approach to methodology and in turn translates into quantitative methods (see **naturalism**). Conversely, the humanistic approach to theory implies an ideographic approach to methodology and qualitative methods (see **humanism**). In a general sense, this divide was characterized and played out in the last third of the twentieth century as a dispute between **positivism** and 'interpretivism' (Bryman 1988).

The latter dispute continues to be recapitulated and misunderstood in some methods textbooks, but, generally speaking, debates have moved on today, at both the level of method and methodology. Increasingly there is an awareness that the social sciences (and to an extent the natural sciences) have both a nomothetic *and* an ideographic character and that to successfully represent or develop theoretical concepts there is a requirement for both methods of measurement and interpretation. This approach is often known as 'methodological pluralism' (Dow 2001). It has two interrelated aspects. First, it is the view that some research problems require quantitative methods and others qualitative and that the full toolkit of methods should be available to researchers. Second, it is the view that more than one method should be used where necessary. For example, while survey methods can demonstrate the existence or extent of a phenomenon or its statistical relationship to other phenomena, their ability to access the subjective meanings of agents has certain limits. Access to subjective meaning is the strength of interpretivist approaches, but the limits of interpretivist approaches turn on their ability to generalize from one context to another.

Social scientists face two polar difficulties in their understanding of the relationship between methods, methodology and theory. The first concerns how to translate theories into testable propositions and, second, how to build theory from empirical research. If the first is to be achieved, the terms of the theory need to be spelt out clearly and logically. This is difficult with 'grand theory' which is often general and abstract, but there have been a number of attempts to phrase social theory in such a way that it can be developed methodologically. The best known of these was Robert **Merton**'s 'middle-range theories'. He advocated, for example, theories of 'reference groups, social mobility, of role-conflict and of the formation of social norms' (1968:

40). He saw these as involving theoretical abstractions, but as being close enough to the data to be turned into testable propositions. More recently, the methodology/theory link has been further developed in this way by Layder (1993) and among others Pawson (2000).

The converse problem in the development of theory is most often tackled through ethnographic approaches which allow flexibility in the exploration of agents' actions and meanings. One of the best-known approaches to this is **grounded theory** (Strauss and Corbin 1997). This relies on concept construction through interpretive methods. The constructs are then clarified and further developed through further interpretations. This process does not imply the complete absence of theory. Theories already exist at least at the level of the experiential or **everyday**. Indeed, most research combines elements of each, and a key role for methodology is to clarify the relationship between testing and building theory.

References and further reading

Bryman, A. (1988) *Quantity and Quality in Social Research*. London: Routledge.

Dow, S. (2001) 'Methodology in a Pluralist Environment', *Journal of Economic Methodology*, 8(1): 33–40.

Layder, D. (1993) *New Strategies in Social Research: An Introduction and Guide*. Oxford: Polity.

Merton, R. (1968) *Social Theory and Social Structure*. New York: The Free Press.

Pawson, R. (2000) 'Middle Range Realism', *European Journal of Sociology*, XLI(2): 283–325.

Seale, C. (1999) *The Quality of Qualitative Research*. London: Sage.

Strauss, A. and Corbin, J. (eds) (1997) *Grounded Theory in Practice*. Thousand Oaks, CA: Sage.

Williams, M. (2003) *Making Sense of Social Research*. London: Sage.

MALCOLM WILLIAMS

MICRO-, MESO- AND MACRO-LEVELS

Sociological theory and methodology distinguish between different levels of analysis.

Microsocial units, such as **actions**, sequences of face-to-face **interaction** or the interrelations of members of small **groups**, contrast with meso- and macro-social units, such as **organizations**, **social systems** and **structures** of social **stratification**.

The micro-macro distinction can be interpreted as an analytical instrument whose application and contents vary with the explanatory ends of the social scientist. In the analysis of short sequences of interaction, recurrent structural patterns characteristic of intra-organizational **cooperation** might be classified as macro-structures. But the same patterns of cooperation might alternatively be addressed as micro-structures, if evolutionary changes concerning the composition of a population of organizations in a segment of an economic **market** are investigated. In multi-level analysis, adjacent levels of **complexity** or aggregation can be treated as micro-*and* macro-level in relation to each other, iterating the micro-macro distinction as often as necessary so that there may be no need to specify a certain level as 'meso'.

Micro- and macro-levels have also been interpreted in an *ontological* mode (see **ontology**). In this sense they refer to different levels of society as a result of an evolutionary process of social **differentiation**. On these premises, the real existence of a separate meso-level may be observed as a product of a long-term historical process. Thus **Luhmann**'s (1987) **systems theory** assumes that modern world **society** has developed through evolutionary differentiation between the macro-level of society as a population of functional systems (see **functionalism**) and the micro-level of face-to-face interaction. Luhmann analyzes the development of organizations as a meso-level type of social systems that makes differentiation between the other two levels possible. Social **networks**, too, are often discussed by sociologists as meso-level phenomena.

Several answers have been given to the question of the causal relation between micro- and macro-levels (see also **causality**). Proponents defending macro-determination of micro-relations are attacked by those who argue for the relative **autonomy** of micro-processes against macro-structures. Others opt for a complementarity thesis, asserting that different mechanisms operate on each level and hence that different kinds of theories are necessary to reconstruct them.

Durkheim is one of the classical proponents of a macro-deterministic position. According to his approach, sociology analyzes social facts exterior to the consciousness of individuals. Collectively shared categories and norms functioning as a primary device of social integration are explained as a result of the structure of **social relations**, depending on the degree of the **division of labour** in a society. Compared with Durkheim, who localized the determining macro-variables on the level of social structure, **Parsons**'s conception of social **integration**, assumed a double process of institutionalization and individual internalization of **values and norms** which generate motivational dispositions and lead actors to act in conformity with rules of social order. This is often described as a more culturalistic version of macro-determinism.

In contrast to macro-determistic approaches, **symbolic interactionism** and **ethnomethodology** maintain the relative autonomy of the micro-level, specified as the level of interaction. Criticizing functionalism's macro-cultural **determinism**, **Garfinkel** (1967: 69ff.) accused Parsons of portraying members of society as 'cultural dopes', ignoring the interpretive and judgemental work of actors in relation to rules and norms. Similarly, conversation analysts defend the relative autonomy of interaction with respect to macro-structural variables such as differences of **status** and **power** between actors (Schegloff 1987). In their view, it is the micro-level of interaction that decides which macro-level elements are called up as structural premises, guiding

the sequential production of social acts *in situ*.

A more radical approach is advocated by Collins (1981, 1987), reducing the macro-level to a pure aggregate of micro events i.e. to a collection of interactional episodes, distributed in space and time. Synthesizing the theses of the autonomy of interaction in a macro-theoretical framework, authors such as **Giddens** and Luhmann maintain a circular relation between action or **communication** and structure, where macro-structures function as rules and resources for actors in micro-processes who in turn make selective use of or modify macro-structures, thereby reproducing or transforming them.

In his assertion of the micro-unit of the individual actor and his or her actions as the basic level of **explanation** in sociology, **Weber** is one of the classical proponents of methodological **individualism**. For **Popper** (1958, vol. 2: Chapter IV), only explanations of this type are acceptable in social sciences, whereas 'collectivistic' explanations of a macro-analytical type are to be rejected (see **collectivism**).

Based on the premise that actors choose from sets of possible actions those that maximize their subjective expected utility, **rational choice** theorists such as **Coleman** advocate an individualistic approach that views the relation on the micro-level between actor's definition of the situation and his or her selection of an action as the central element in sociological explanation. Coleman (1987) proposes a standard model of explanation connecting micro- and macro-levels. On this model, macro-structural variables such as the social distribution of resources or cultural values and institutionalized norms are relevant determinants for the micro-level selection of actions by individual actors in so far as they become elements of each actor's subjective definition of the situation. To return from the micro- to the macro-level, it has to be shown how the individual decisions of many actors are transformed into macro-level effects by institutionalized rules (determining, for example, the distribution of seats in parliament according to the number of votes in political elections) or by social mechanisms (for example, mechanisms of price fixing in economic markets).

In contrast to approaches assigning primary explanatory relevance to micro- or macro levels, Peter Blau (1987) argues that micro- and macro-levels are both relatively independent from and complementary to each other, and therefore have to be investigated from different perspectives with different kinds of theories. On the micro-level, interaction must be analyzed in terms of a theory of **social exchange**. Macro-parameters, concerning the distribution of persons over social positions defined in terms of ethnic group membership, categories of status, or power, must be analyzed as restrictions and opportunities, making it more or less probable that relations of social exchange between actors in specified social positions will occur.

References and further reading

Alexander, J. C., Giesen, B., Münch, R., Smelser, N. J. (eds) (1987) *The Micro-Macro Link*. Berkeley, CA: University of California Press.

Garfinkel, H. (1967) *Studies in Ethnomethodology*. Cambridge: Polity.

Knorr, K. and Cicourel, A. V. (eds) (1981) *Advances in Social Theory and Methodology: Toward an Integration of Micro- and Macro-Sociologies*. Boston: Routledge.

Popper, K. (1958) *The Open Society and its Enemies*, 2 vols. London: Routledge.

Smelser, N. J. (1997) *Problematics of Sociology*. Berkeley: University of California Press.

WOLFGANG LUDWIG SCHNEIDER

MIDDLE CLASS

The middle class has been the subject of considerable debate in sociology, not least about its definition. This has been further complicated by different understandings of the term in **Europe** and North **America**. In Britain and Europe the term has generally been used to describe those social groups who are neither members of the **working class** nor the upper class, or in **Marxist** parlance the **proletariat** or the **bourgeoisie**. In North America, middle class has been used to refer to the employed middle mass of both blue- and white-collar workers. However, there is a stronger consensus over what the middle class is *not* and over the nature of its boundaries with proximate social **groups**. Successive generations of sociologists have tried to resolve these definitional and conceptual problems by renaming the middle class. In recent years debates have revolved around the terms 'service class' and 'new class'.

During the 1980s in Britain the term 'service class' was the favoured term (Goldthorpe 1982; Abercrombie and Urry 1983). This term derived from the work of Karl Renner who saw the main role of the class in servicing the functions of the state. Compared to the working class, its relations to the employing class were based on **trust**, for which it was compensated by a salary, as distinct from a paid wage. The term 'salariat' is sometimes still used to describe this group. Goldthorpe argued that its members acted rationally to maximize their advantages and maintain them intergenerationally. While he noted differences between those in managerial and professional occupations, he treated the service class as a single relatively propertyless class that is dependent on the 'trust relationship'.

Urry and his fellow authors saw the main functions of the service class as 'servicing' the needs of capital through the administration, control and the regulation of social reproduction. It is the possession of credentials and lack of capital assets that mark the boundaries between the classes above and below them. For Urry and his co-authors, some members of the service class could be radical in social and political orientation. Particularly those involved in the regulation of the reproduction and organization of welfare could define their interests as being in conflict with more dominant members.

Crompton (1998) has criticized both these approaches to the service class for over-identifying issues of occupation and for under-identifying sectoral and gender differences within the service class. In more recent work, Urry appears to have heeded these criticisms by giving less emphasis to class in what he sees as an emerging order of 'disorganized capitalism'.

The concept of the 'new class' was developed in North America to account for the growth of a new group of managerial and professional workers in the late 1970s in the context of the decline of industrial production and the growth of quaternary services (Gouldner 1979). This group was distinguished from both traditional **professionals** and the middle class of blue- and white-collar employees. It was seen as an essentially urban, insecure and 'new economy'-based class (Ehrenreich 1989; Ley 1996).

In Britain, work on the middle classes in recent years has become the focus for a renaissance in class analysis (Savage, Barlow *et al.* 1992; Butler and Savage 1995; Savage 2000). Savage's approach, deriving from the work of Erik Olin Wright and particularly Pierre **Bourdieu**, stresses the role of assets. Bourdieu originally identified a tri-partite division within the middle class between those reliant on property assets (a petty bourgeoisie), organizational assets (managers) and educational credentials (professionals). Bourdieu has developed this into a more rounded approach that sees the middle classes operating across a number of 'fields' and drawing strategically on their assets and resources in relation to different forms of capital: cultural, economic, social and symbolic, ensuring not only their own comparative advantage but also those of their children (see **cultural capital**).

For many decades the middle class was *de facto* defined as not being the working class.

These accounts of class were based almost exclusively on accounts of occupation and production and class culture was read off from this. The current renaissance in class analysis is largely based on accounts of the middle class and its fields of **consumption**. Work on gentrification indicates that **space and place** are now an important element in processes of class formation in the middle class (Butler and Robson 2003).

References and further reading

Abercrombie, N. and Urry, J. (1983) *Capitalism, Labour and the Middle Classes*. London: Allen & Unwin.

Butler, T. and Robson, G. (2003) *London Calling: The Middle Classes and the Remaking of Inner London*. Oxford: Berg.

Butler, T. and Savage, M. (eds) (1995) *Social Change and the Middle Classes*. London: University College London Press.

Crompton, R. (1998) *Class and Stratification: An Introduction to Current Debates*. Cambridge: Polity.

Ehrenreich, B. (1989) *Fear of Falling: The Inner Life of the Middle Class*. New York: Pantheon.

Goldthorpe, J. (1982) 'On the Service Class, Its Formation and Future', in A. Giddens and G. Mackenzie *Social Class and the Division of Labour*. Cambridge: Cambridge University Press.

Gouldner, A. (1979) *The Future of Intellectuals and the Rise of the New Class: A Frame of Reference, Theses, Conjectures, Argumentation and an Historical Perspective*. London: Macmillan.

Ley, D. (1996) *The New Middle Class and the Remaking of the Central City*. Oxford: Oxford University Press.

Savage, M. (2000) *Class Analysis and Social Transformation*. Milton Keynes: Open University Press.

Savage, M., Barlow, J. *et al.* (1992) *Property, Bureaucracy and Culture: Middle Class Formation in Contemporary Britain*. London: Routledge.

TIM BUTLER

MIGRATION

Human migration is the process by which individuals or **groups** of people change their usual place of residence, crossing administrative boundaries. The administrative unit they leave is the place of origin and they arrive at the place of destination. This concept implies the existence of a place of residence, so nomads are usually excluded from the counts of migration in many countries. Similarly, commuting is not seen as migration, even if distances can be substantial and the impact on an **economy** and **society** might be important and deserve study. While the notion of administrative boundaries is difficult to apply in historical perspective this element is important in defining and understanding modern migration movements. The sheer variety of migration types also makes it difficult to establish exact quantitative accounts of the extent of migration.

One approach to categorizing migration is to distinguish between *internal* and *international* migration. Internal migration occurs if place of origin and place of destination remain in the same sovereign country. International migrants cross a national border in their move. There are various types of internal migrations. Today in many developing countries, rural-urban migration is predominant, as it was in the past in European countries. In developed countries in the twentieth century, suburbanization brought a migration of families from the cities to suburbia, where land was cheaper and the conditions for raising families were considered to be more favourable than in densely populated cities (see **urbanism and urbanization**).

Another characteristic distinguishing types of migration relates to the length of stay. Permanent migrants make a definitive decision to stay. However, in many regions of the world temporary migrants are common. They return after some time to the place of origin (return migration) or move to another destination. The duration of stay can range from a few months to many years. Seasonal movements are often not considered migration in the strict sense, although they are sometimes referred to as seasonal migration. In most cases it is labour migration related to harvests. This occurs during certain periods of the year and the duration is usually shorter than three months.

Although there are many reasons to migrate, one distinction in migration motives is fundamental and identifies two types of migration: voluntary and forced. The reasons for voluntary migration are manifold and are discussed below. In the case of forced migration, migrants are either compelled by public authorities to leave their place of residence (displaced persons) or they must escape in order to safeguard their lives from persecution, natural disasters or war (refugees). Refugees usually migrate of their own accord, although they are generally under strong pressure or in danger while making this decision.

International migrants cross borders and stay in the country of destination either as documented ('legal') migrants or as undocumented ('illegal') migrants. The legal status of immigrants is defined differently in various countries. Undocumented immigrants often find it difficult to integrate in the country of destination and are subject to **discrimination**.

Migration research divides the reasons for migration into *push factors*, resulting from the country of origin, and in *pull factors*, attracting migrants to the area of destination. Push factors might be unfavourable changes in climatic and environmental conditions, food shortages, population pressure on land or water, **poverty**, high **unemployment** and/or underemployment, ethnic and religious discrimination or expulsion, war or civil war. Pull factors might include political and economic stability and transparency, religious tolerance and respect, real or perceived opportunities to seek work and income and find access to health services and education, often for children. Religious motives have been important for a substantial share of migration in the past. The distinction between push and pull factors has been questioned, since it is typically the differential between conditions in the country of origin and the country of destination that makes people migrate. Focusing on the differential also helps us understand the direction of migration movements to certain countries of destination.

For most countries of destination there are only vague and often conflicting estimates of undocumented immigration (the 'flow') and of the number of undocumented immigrants (the 'stock'). But even the size of documented immigration from abroad is often not precisely known. Usually immigrants should register at their new place of residence; temporary migrants should register if they leave the country of destination again. The contribution of international migration to overall population dynamics depends on a difference between gross immigration (arrivals) in a period of time and emigration (departures) in the same period. In many countries of destination there have been periods of net-immigration and periods of net-emigration is recorded in history.

The total number of international migrants is currently estimated at between 175 to 185 million people world-wide. This amounts to 3 per cent of the world population; the percentage of international migrants has not increased substantially since c. 1965. These estimates include about 30 million people living in the successor states of the former Soviet Union, who had previously been internal migrants but became international migrants with the dissolution of the Union. The annual number of people actually migrating in one year is estimated currently to be about 12 million people world-wide. Between 1.5 and 2 million of them are students; between 7 and 8 million immigrants reach developed countries annually.

Family unification is quantitatively the most important form of international migration today. The second largest group of immigrants are **labour** migrants; the third largest group are asylum-seekers and refugees. The USA is the country with the largest absolute number of immigrants world-wide, estimated at 35 million in 2000. Second in the absolute size of the immigrant population is the Russian Federation, with 13.2 million in 2003; third is Germany with 7.4 million immigrants in the same year. However, a different picture appears if the relative size of the immigrant population is measured. The country with the highest share of immigrants in total population is the United Arab Emirates, which saw more than 70 per cent immigrant population in 2000, followed by Kuwait, Jordan and Israel.

In the case of voluntary migration, migrants can expect both personal losses and gains from the decision to move. Typically they abandon property, friends and relatives, as well as inheritance rights. Educational certificates and qualifications may not be recognized, on account of language and cultural barriers as well as plain discrimination. In a lifetime perspective the net gains for migrants are higher if they are younger. Some migrants consider the gains of a migration for their children. These considerations might be one of the reasons why younger people constitute the majority of international migrants. This effect has been called self-selection of migrants. Usually immigrants are substantially younger than the population in the country of destination and better educated than the majority of the population in the country of origin.

In many countries of origin, unemployment is high and the emigration of young people tends to ease supply pressure on the labour **market**. However, since many emigrants are highly qualified, a brain drain of talent is typically the consequence. In countries of destination, since immigrants

tend to be younger than the native population, employed documented immigrants
contribute more to the pension system and
to health insurance than they draw from
these systems. Most studies of the economic
consequences of immigration to developed
countries agree on its positive impact in the
past decades. However, while immigrants
fitted well into the labour markets, particularly in manufacturing in the 1960s and
the 1970s, demand for this type of labour
has decreased substantially. Some authors
see the integration of immigrants into the
labour markets and societies of West European countries today as more difficult than
in the recent past. Yet, some of these
countries are certain to experience demo-
graphically induced shortages of labour in
the near future making immigration policy
a vital topic of political debate.

Key related terms in debates about
migration in social theory are the concepts
of the **stranger**, **social inclusion and
social exclusion**, **'race' and racism**, **liminality**, and the positions of marginality
often occupied by people of forced or
voluntary transitional mobility, people
crossing boundaries whose life habits, ideas
and cultural values may be stranded
between hegemonic categories in both the
country of origin and the country of destination.

References and further reading

Brettell, C. B. and Hollifield, J. F. (eds) (2000)
Migration Theory Talking Across Disciplines.
New York: Routledge.

Castles, S. and Davidson, A. (2000) *Citizenship
and Migration: Globalization and the Politics of
Belonging.* New York: Routledge.

Castles, S. and Miller, M. J. (2003) *The Age of
Migration: International Population Movements
in the Modern World*, 3rd edn. New York:
Guilford.

Cornelius, W. A., Tsuda, T., Martin P. L. and
Hollifield, J. F. (eds) (2004) *Controlling
Immigration: A Global Perspective*, 2nd edn,
revised and expanded. Stanford, CA: Stanford University Press/CCIS.

Joppke, C. (ed.) (1998) *Challenge to the Nation-
State: Immigration in Western Europe and the
United States.* Oxford: Oxford University
Press.

Massey, D. S., Arango, J., Hugo, G., Kouaouci,
A., Pellegrino, A. and Taylor, J. (1998)
*Worlds in Motion: Understanding International
Migration at the End of the Millennium.* Oxford:
Clarendon.

RALF E. ULRICH

MILL, JOHN STUART (1806–1873)
English philosopher

Mill was educated by his father, the philosopher and political economist, James Mill,
in the expectation that the younger Mill
would implement the utilitarian ideas
espoused by his father and the family friend,
Jeremy Bentham, in order to promote
rational social administration. As a civil
servant for the East India Company in his
youth, Mill's public and private interests
were combined in his despatches and
debates over the relationship between **civilization** and political **liberty**.

Mill sought to reconcile public policy
geared towards promoting the common
good with an implacable defence of the
autonomy of the individual, expressed in
his 'harm principle'. He fused Romantic
themes of individual fulfilment, derived
from Samuel Coleridge and Wilhelm von
Humboldt, with **utilitarianism**, to defend
the liberty-enhancing capacities of representative government (see **freedom**). But
influenced by de **Tocqueville**, he worried
about the relationship between democracy
and social conformity.

Mill's concern to grant both voice and
vote to all was noticeably radical in its time,
as was his account of the subjection of
women, a work influenced by his wife,
Harriet Taylor, which defended women's
rights and the virtues of marriage as an
intellectual partnership. This was a theme
he pursued in Parliament as an MP for
Westminster after 1865, along with
numerous considerations on parliamentary

reform. Mill is the classic theorist of political liberalism. To some extent he has also been interpreted as favouring **socialism**, given his remarks about ownership of production in his economic writings, but he worried about the effects of its excessive socialist **bureaucracy** on human freedom.

Major works

([1859] 1977) 'On Liberty', in *Collected Works of John Stuart Mill*, vol. XIX: *Essays on Politics and Society*. Ed. J. Robson. Toronto: University of Toronto Press.

([1861] 1969) 'Utilitarianism', in *Collected Works of John Stuart Mill*, vol. X: *Essays on Ethics, Religion and Society*. Ed. J. Robson. Toronto: University of Toronto Press.

([1861] 1977) 'Considerations on Representative Government', in *Collected Works of John Stuart Mill*, vol. XIX: *Essays on Politics and Society*. Ed. J. Robson. Toronto: University of Toronto Press.

([1873] 1980) 'Autobiography', in *Collected Works of John Stuart Mill*, vol. I: *Autobiography and Literary Essays*. Ed. J. Robson and J. Stillinger. Toronto: University of Toronto Press.

Further reading

Burns, J. H. (1969) 'J. S. Mill and Democracy, 1829–61', in J. Schneewind (ed.) *Mill: A Collection of Critical Essays*. London: Macmillan.

Capaldi, N. (2004) *John Stuart Mill: A Biography*. Cambridge: Cambridge University Press.

Robson, J. M. (1968) *The Improvement of Mankind*. London: RKP.

Ryan, A. (1978). *J. S. Mill*. London: Routledge.

Urbinati, N. (2002) *Mill on Democracy*. Chicago: Chicago University Press.

DUNCAN KELLY

MILLS, CHARLES WRIGHT (1916–1962)

US theorist

Mills was an intellectual radical who explored, both empirically and theoretically, the dynamics of **power** and **stratification** in **American** society, raising in the process challenging questions about the ethical and moral responsibility of social scientists. Influenced by American **pragma-**

tism and by Thorstein Veblen, Mills's subsequent engagement with European social theorists was facilitated by his collaboration with the German émigré sociologist, Hans Gerth. Mills is best known for his book, *The Sociological Imagination* (1959). In it, Mills debunks trends then current in the discipline, lambasting both 'grand theory' for its pretension, vacuity and lack of empirical referent, and 'abstracted empiricism', or the accumulation of atheoretical empirical studies. Mills argues that the task and promise of sociology lies in the ability to grasp the interrelationship between 'public issues' and 'private troubles'. Sociological imagination grows out of 'intellectual craftmanship', the creative, self-disciplined engagement with research materials rather than the ritualistic application of methodological techniques.

In his work on post-war American society, Mills produced powerful portrayals of organized **labour**, the newly emergent **middle class**, and the intertwining of corporate, political and military **elites**. This work challenged conventional assumptions that emphasized the pluralist and consensual nature of American society. In his later writing, Mills explored world politics, US **hegemony**, especially in relation to Latin America, and the Cold War.

Major works

(1951) *White Collar*. New York: Oxford University Press.

(1956) *The Power Elite*. New York: Oxford University Press.

(1959) *The Sociological Imagination*. New York: Oxford University Press.

(1960) *Listen Yankee: The Revolution in Cuba*. New York: McGraw-Hill.

Further reading

Aronowitz, S. (2004) *C. Wright Mills*. Thousand Oaks, CA: Sage.

Horowitz, I. (1983) *C. Wright Mills: An American Utopian*. New York: Free Press.

RAYMOND LEE

MODE OF PRODUCTION

For **Marx**, a mode of production comprises: 'forces of production' – specific kinds of human **labour**, instruments of production and the materials upon which these elements are applied to produce the means of subsistence and other goods; and 'relations of production' – specific ways in which the forces of production are controlled, combined and their products distributed, thereby reproducing and possibly expanding the forces of production, including the number and well-being of direct producers (and their **kinship** networks).

In **class** societies, a non-productive class, through its control of one or more of the forces of production and their mode of combination, has the ability to enhance its social position by appropriating and determining the use of any surplus produced by the forces of production. Marx identifies primitive **communist**, Asiatic, **slave**, **feudal**, **capitalist**, **socialist** and post-scarcity communist modes of production.

According to more recent Althusserian elaborations of this concept (see **Althusser**), if a mode of production is articulated with compatible political, legal institutional 'superstructures' and if the horizon of thought of most of its members is shaped by accommodative **institutionalized ideologies**, then these together may constitute a reproducible social formation. However, the social logic of class modes of production and social formations, particularly capitalistic ones, consists in the likely development of internal contradictions, possibly generating crises. These crises may be temporarily contained, or may contribute to societal collapse or to the emergence of a new mode of production and social formation.

If suitably applied, the concepts of mode of production and social formation provide a potentially powerful analytic tool for understanding how the overall social organization and development of societies relate to continuities and changes in their socio-economic relations and their conditions of existence.

References and further reading

Althusser, L. and Balibar, E. (1970) *Reading Capital*. London: New Left Books.

Marx, K. (1961, 1962) *Capital, I, II and III*. Moscow: Foreign Languages Publishing House.

Sekine, T. (1997) *An Outline of the Dialectic of Capital*, vols 1 and 2. London: Macmillan.

Wolpe, H. (1980) *The Articulation of Modes of Production*. London: Routledge.

FRANK PEARCE

MODERNITY AND MODERNIZATION

The analysis of contemporary Western societies has long been based on the idea that those societies emerged through some rupture with the past. In this sense, the social sciences have long theorized 'modernity' as the attempt to grasp the specificity of the present, even though the term has been used only rather recently. The dominant strand in the social sciences has aimed at capturing this specificity by *structural-institutional* analysis. Modern institutions are here seen as the embodiments of the modern promise of **freedom** and reason. Against and beyond this dominant strand, different conceptualizations of modernity have been proposed. In parallel to the history of the 'modern social sciences', *critiques of modernity* have provided an alternative institutional analysis, emphasizing the undermining of the promise of **autonomy** in and through the workings of modern institutions.

Both of these views have recently been considered too limited in their approach, committing themselves to an overly specific understanding of modernity. On the one side stand the excessive confidences of 'modernization theory' in functional evolutionary necessity. On the other side stand the potentially self-defeating gestures of **postmodernism**. More interpretative approaches to modernity demonstrate the breadth of possible interpretations of what is commonly understood as the basic self-understanding, or imaginary signification, of modernity. The conception of modernity as an *ethos* and an *experience* underlines the normative and agential features of modernity. Here the emphasis is on the lack of any given foundations and the possibility of pushing the 'project of modernity' ever further, as well as on creativity and openness. The experiential understanding thus complements the interpretative approach by underlining the large, potentially infinite, *variety of forms of modernity*. At the same time, however, it raises the stakes for an analysis of settings of modernity as entire societal configurations.

Modernity as an era and a set of institutions

In the form of the announcement of a possible new era, the term 'modernity' was made prominent in the *quérelle des anciens et des modernes* in the seventeenth and eighteenth centuries. From then onwards, most uses of the term have retained a strong temporal implication, the later concept of 'modern society' being a key example. Drawing such a distinction between eras, however, also demands specification as to how they differ, i.e., a conceptualization of what is modern. Such conceptualization regularly transcends historical time, and thus invites analyses that go beyond the initial preference for the present over the past. In other words, the term inevitably carries a double connotation; it is always both philosophical and empirical, or both *substantive* and *temporal* (Yack 1997), or both *conceptual* and *historical* (Wagner 2001).

Sociologists of 'modern society' often found themselves in the dilemma of reconciling these two concerns, that is, as having, on the one hand, to claim a historical break with '**traditional society**', but having, on the other, difficulties in empirically identifying such clear-cut breaks. Thus, spatio-

temporal reference points were created and employed in various combinations. First of all, the idea of the emergence of 'modern society' has often referred straightforwardly to the 'history of the **West**'. More specifically, it has referred to the history of **Europe**, and from some time onwards also to North **America**. Modern social life then begins at the earliest in the fifteenth century with the Renaissance, the Reformation and the voyages of discovery. At the latest, it starts in the early twentieth century with modernism in the arts and architecture and with the new form of self-inspection provided by **psychoanalysis**. Economic modernity is said to begin with the market revolution and the industrial **revolution**, and political modernity has its take-off with the revolutions in America and France in the late eighteenth century. Scientific and philosophical revolutions towards modernity can be variously dated along this temporal line – from Cartesian **rationalism** and experimental method to the *fin-de-siècle* critique of science and metaphysics and to the theory of relativity (Toulmin 1990).

However one looks at this range of dates, the tension between any historical description of a rupture and conceptual understandings of modernity comes immediately to the fore. The conceptual imagery of a 'modern society', as known in twentieth-century sociology, characterized by a **market**-based **economy**, a **democratic polity** and autonomous knowledge-producing institutions developing empirical-analytical sciences, sits in an uneasy relation to these historical dates. Were one to insist that the full set of those institutions needs to exist before a society can be called modern, social modernity would be limited to a relatively small part of the globe during only a part of the twentieth century.

This tension between conceptuality and historicity was resolved for some theorists by introducing an evolutionary logic in societal development. Based on the assumption of a societally effective voluntarism of human **action**, realms of social life were considered to have gradually separated from one another according to social functions. **Religion**, **politics**, the economy, and the arts all emerged as separate spheres in a series of historical breaks – known as the scientific, industrial and democratic revolutions – following a logic of **differentiation** (**Parsons** 1964). A sequence of otherwise contingent ruptures is thus read as a history of **progress**, and the era of modernity emerges by an unfolding from incomplete beginnings. In conceptual terms, this perspective aimed at combining an emphasis on free human action with the achievement of greater mastery over the natural and social world (**Alexander** 1978). The differentiation of functions and their separate institutionalization was seen as both enhancing human **freedom** and as increasing the range of **action**. Thus, it provided a sociologized version of the **Enlightenment** combination of freedom and reason, or of subjectivity and rationality (Touraine 1992).

The grand critiques of modernity

Starting out from considerable doubt about such facile harmony between freedom and reason, a series of major critical inquiries into the dynamics of modernity set in from the middle of the nineteenth century up until the 1930s. These grand critiques identified basic structural problems in the practices of modernity, without at the same time abandoning a commitment to the idea of modernity as a project. They all problematize, although in very different ways, the tension between the unleashing of the modern dynamics of freedom and rational mastery and its often unintended consequences.

The first of these critiques was the *critique of political economy*, developed mainly by **Marx**. In contrast to some of the conservative critics of **capitalism**, such as the German historical economists who flatly denounced its rationalist individualism,

Marx basically adhered to the Enlightenment tradition of personal autonomy. His ideal was 'the free association of free human beings.' In the workings of the 'free market' in capitalism, however, he discovered a societal effect of human economic interaction that asserted itself 'behind the backs' of the actors.

The second grand critique was the *critique of large-scale organization and bureaucracy*, as analyzed most prominently by Robert Michels and Max **Weber**. With a view to the enhancement of rational mastery of the world, it postulated the tendency for the formation of stratified bodies with hierarchical chains of command and abstract rules of action. In the context of a universal-suffrage polity and a **welfare state**, i.e. in 'large' societies in which all individuals had to be included on a formal, legally equal, basis in all major regulations, such 'iron cages' had emerged as state apparatuses. Alongside this, large industrial enterprises and mass parties would spread further into all realms of social life. While such institutions enhanced the reach of human action generally, they limited it to the application of rules, leading to perceptions of imprisonment within a bureaucratic order and to conditions of 'disenchantment' and 'meaninglessness'.

A third related critique of modernity is the *critique of modern philosophy and science*. Weber, too, was aware of the great loss, the 'disenchantment of the world', entailed by rational **domination**. But still, he understood his own project of social science in rational and **value**-neutral terms, as he thought no other approach could prevail under conditions of modernity. In contrast, radical and explicit critiques of science were put forward by others in very different forms. In idealist *Lebensphilosophie* the elaboration of a non-scientist approach to science was attempted, as well as in a different manner by early twentieth-century 'Western' Marxism, notably by Max **Horkheimer** and the early **Frankfurt School**. In some

371

respects, **pragmatism** in the USA can also be ranged under the critiques of science in its uniting of theoretical and practical understanding in lived experience.

Interpretive approaches to modernity

Although the authors of these grand critiques in some respects anticipated the more recent idea of modernity as a *space of interpretive possibilities*, Marx, Horkheimer and to some extent even Weber had assumed that their critique provided a uniquely superior account. It is only from the 1970s onwards that the openness of modernity towards a variety of interpretations has become an explicit topic of social theory.

Following Cornelius **Castoriadis** (1990), modernity can be considered as a situation in which the reference to autonomy and mastery provides for a double 'imaginary signification' of social life. By this term, Castoriadis refers to what more conventionally would be called a generally held belief or an 'interpretative pattern' (Arnason 1989). More precisely, the two components of this signification are the idea of the autonomy of the human being as the knowing and acting subject, on the one hand, and, on the other, the idea of the basic rationality and intelligibility of the world. In this sense modernity refers to a situation in which human beings do not accept any *external guarantees*. Although the authors of these grand critiques in some respects anticipated the more recent idea of modernity as a *space of interpretive possibilities*. That is, human beings do not accept any guarantees that they *themselves* do not posit, concerning political order, knowledge and the idea of self-hood (see **subject and subjectivity**) (Wagner 2001).

The sociology of modern society – and, by inversion of the topic, the grand critiques as well – claimed to derive a particular institutional structure from this double imaginary signification. One problem with this assumption that a modern set of insti-

tutions can be derived from the imaginary signification of modernity is that it overlooks the way in which the two elements of this signification are ambivalent and in tension with one another. The interpretative approach consequently takes such tensions to indicate the possibility of a variety of institutional forms. The relation between autonomy and mastery institutes an interpretative space that is to be specifically filled in each socio-historical situation through struggles over the situation-grounded appropriate meaning. Theoretically, there is always a plurality and diversity of interpretations of this space.

With its emphasis on openness, the interpretive approach links up to the idea of modernity as an *ethos* and *experience*. A common view of the history of social life in Europe holds that a 'culture of modernity' spread gradually which is individualist in a broad sense and gives an important place to self-exploration (Taylor 1989: 305). Such an emphasis on individuality and individualization is quite alien both to the more formalized 'modern' discourses of the individual, as in **rational choice** theory, or in liberal political philosophy and to the totalizing critiques of modernity. Yet in literature and the arts, the idea of the experience of modernity as a quest for personal autonomy has always been at the centre and, as an experience, it concerned in the first place the singular human being (Berman 1982). Michel **Foucault**'s lecture 'What is Enlightenment?' very succinctly distinguished in this sense between modernity as an ethos of self-examination and modernity as an institutional Leviathan. Modernity as an attitude and experience demands the exploration of one's self and is counterposed to modernity as an epoch and a set of institutions, which demands obedience to agreed-upon rules. At least in some writers, such Jean-François Lyotard, the idea of postmodernity was inspired by a return to what had been a modern self-understanding since at least the Enlightenment, and much less by the idea of a new era 'after' modernity.

Varieties of modernity

In attempts to combine insights from the variety of approaches without abandoning the objective of analyzing spatio-temporally extended configurations, research interest in what may be called the 'cultures of modernity' has recently increased (Friese and Wagner 2000). Such research investigates the variety of socio-historical interpretations of the double imaginary signification of modernity and the resources such interpretations draw on and mobilize. In Western Europe (for example, in France and Germany) or within the more broadly defined 'West' (for example, in Europe and the USA), those resources are much richer and much more varied than earlier research had been able to identify. Both richness and variety increase considerably as soon as one focuses on the so-called non-Western societies. Research on 'multiple modernities' aims at analyzing such wider, present and past, plurality of interpretations of the modern signification (**Eisenstadt** 1998; 2002). Such sociologies of modernity break with any reasoning that associates modernization unequivocally with Westernization. Without disregarding the problem of the 'specificity of the West', interest is accordingly revived in the comparative-historical study of societal configurations.

References and further reading

Alexander, J. C. (1978) 'Formal and Substantive Voluntarism in the Work of Talcott Parsons: A Theoretical and Ideological Reinterpretation', *American Sociological Review*, 43: 177–98.

Arnason, J. P. (1989) 'The Imaginary Constitution of Modernity', in G. Busino *et al. Autonomie et autotransformation de la société: La philosophie militante de Cornelius Castoriadis*. Geneva: Droz.

Berman, M. (1982) *All That Is Solid Melts into Air: The Experience of Modernity*. New York: Simon and Schuster.

Castoriadis, C. (1990) *Le monde morcelé: Les carrefours du labyrinthe III*. Paris: Seuil.

Eisenstadt, S. N. (1998) *Antinomien der Moderne*. Frankfurt am Main: Suhrkamp.

— (ed.) (2002) *Multiple Modernities*. New Brunswick, NJ: Transaction.

Foucault, M. (1984) 'What Is Enlightenment?', in P. Rabinow (ed.) *The Foucault Reader*. London: Penguin.

Friese, H. and Wagner, P. (2000) 'When the Light of the Great Cultural Problems Moves On: On The Possibility of a Cultural Theory of Modernity', *Thesis Eleven*, 61: 25–40.

Lyotard, J.-F. (1979) *La Condition postmoderne*. Paris: Minuit.

Parsons, T. (1964) 'Evolutionary Universals in Society', *American Sociological Review*, 29: 339–357.

Taylor, C. (1989) *Sources of the Self*. Cambridge, MA: Harvard University Press.

Toulmin, S. (1990) *Cosmopolis: The Hidden Agenda of Modernity*. Chicago: University of Chicago Press.

Touraine, A. (1992) *Critique de la modernité*. Paris: Fayard.

Wagner, P. (2001) *Theorizing Modernity: Inescapability and Attainability in Social Theory*. London: Sage.

Yack, B. (1997) *The Fetishism of Modernities*. Notre Dame, IN: University of Notre Dame Press.

PETER WAGNER

MONARCHY

Originating from Greek, the word 'monarchy' denotes the undivided rule of a single person. But contemporary **language** does not permit extension of the terms 'monarch' and 'monarchy' to the rule of dictators, life-time presidents or other 'despots' (indeed a restriction of this kind is already present in the writings of Aristotle). 'Monarchy' is usually reserved for the rule of kings, emperors or important princes, with the implication of **legitimacy**.

It is possible to study the institution of monarchy under three aspects: (1) a historical concept of European origin and variety; (2) a broader anthropological concept traceable to the Neolithic agricultural state; and (3) a story of the decline, limitation or abolition of monarchy through **constitutions**, republics and **democratic nation–states**, as theorized by thinkers from Hobbes to Montesquieu and dramatized in events such as the French **Revolution**.

The Greeks, during the classical era of the republican *polis*, knew 'kingship' only from Homer's writings or from their neighbour Macedonia. While Celtic, Germanic and other ancient European peoples knew 'warlords' (**Weber** 1978: 1141), the most significant early understanding of monarchy developed in the Roman Empire: as an incremental, largely unplanned process generating central imperial structures that emerged from the oligarchy of a *polis*. Historical sociologists such as Michael **Mann** (1986: 259) consider Rome the first 'territorial empire of world history', based on coerced cooperation of the masses, organized by an **elite** with the help of a centralized army and **bureaucracy**. Medieval kingship is closely connected to the rise of a militarized feudal society and to the 'Roman' conception of empire to which these kings were tied by the bonds of fealty since Charlemagne. The origins of this kind of kingship lie in what Max Weber called the 'charismatic heroism' (Weber 1978: 1141) of war-princes, supported by voluntary vassals, engaged in near permanent **war**. These 'conquering' kings initially derived legitimacy from 'magical' **charisma**. The historian Marc Bloch (1924) stressed their **sacred** gift to heal through miracles (*Les rois thaumaturges*). Yet such charisma was soon transmitted into a hereditary and acquired 'depersonalized' **authority**, culminating eventually in a condition of 'traditional authority' with 'patrimonial' elements.

The peak of absolutist royal **power** can be explained in terms of what Norbert **Elias** (2000) called a 'royal mechanism'. According to this framework, the king benefits from a historically singular constellation of an equal power balance between declining aristocratic power on the one hand and the rising bourgeois power of merchants and officials, on the other, tipping the scale in favour of his own domineering position (see **aristocracy** and **bourgeoisie**). Absolutist rule in its purest form only took shape in a few countries. The model example is France under Louis XIV until the eve of the French Revolution. In other countries absolutism remained only a tendency (e.g., England under the Tudors). Perry Anderson (1974) also distinguishes between 'Western' and 'Eastern Absolutism'. In addition to hereditary kingship, ancient **Europe** knew several kingships based on the principle of election: the Holy Roman Empire itself, Poland, as well as Hungary and Bohemia before the Habsburgs.

Outside Europe, kingship is found in many societies with at least a horticultural or agricultural basis. The roots of kingship may lie in the transition from reciprocal to redistributive institutions of **exchange** (Harris and Johnson 1999). They are not restricted to heroism in war but can also be traced to magicians or shamans who may eventually become priestly princes or kings (Weber 1978). Hierocracy, theocracy and what Weber called 'caesaro-papism' tend to derive from origins of these kinds. Thus Mesopotamian and Egyptian kingship had similar **economic** roots (agriculture based on irrigation) and similar **religious** nuclear functions. Steward (1963) sees lineages such as these as significant in the European conquest of the Americas through the spread of empires based on (largely) standing armies and on sacred elements of royal rule. But before this conquest, pastoral nomads, too, had their king-like heads of '**state**'. In the East, it was not before the guns of Ivan IV, the Terrible, developed a destructive capacity against Russia's former Mongolian overlords, that the power-balance shifted in favour of settled peasant empires over mobile, warring and violent nomads.

The decline of the European monarchies began with the rise of limitations on the monarch's monopoly on use of **violence** and access to taxation. This occurred through the agency of aristocratic parliaments (especially in the case of England) and through the rise of the **industrialized** bourgeois nation–state. The European **network** of dynastic elites began to cede power to the **middle classes** and to the **urban** and rural **working classes**. Bonds of loyalty to kings and princes came to be replaced by identification with an abstract 'nation' (**Gellner** 1983). By the turn of the nineteenth century, Europe was still a deeply monarchical continent; yet by 1918 it saw the abolition of three empires (Austria, Russia, Germany) as the legitimacy of dynastic rule was fatally damaged by defeat in war and revolution (Skocpol 1979).

References and further reading

Anderson, P. (1974) *Lineages of the Absolutist State*. London: NLB.

Bloch, M. (1924) *Les Rois thaumaturges*. Strasbourg: Librairie Istra; Oxford: Oxford University Press.

Elias, N. ([1939] 2000) *The Civilizing Process*. Oxford: Blackwell.

Elias, N. ([1969] 1983) *The Court Society*. Oxford: Blackwell.

Gellner, E. (1983) *Nations and Nationalism*. Oxford: Blackwell.

Harris, M. and Johnson, O. (1999) *Cultural Anthropology*. Boston: Allyn and Bacon.

Mann, M. (1986) *The Sources of Social Power*, vol. 1. Cambridge: Cambridge University Press.

Skocpol, T. (1979) *States and Social Revolutions*. Cambridge: Cambridge University Press.

Steward, J. H. (1963) *Theory of Culture Change*. Urbana, IL: University of Illinois Press.

Weber, M. ([1922] 1978) *Economy and Society*. Berkeley, CA: University of California Press.

HELMUT KUZMICS

MONEY

Social theorists have predominantly been interested in the **market** monies used in capitalist economies (see **capitalism**). Neoclassical economists argue that these so-called 'modern' monies facilitated the rise of a more complex, capitalist economic system by replacing barter and making possible economic specialization. Modern money is usually attributed with four functions: a medium of **exchange**; a unit of account; a store of **value**; and a means of payment. For Karl Polanyi (1971) the ability to perform all these functions, to be 'all purpose,' is precisely what differentiates modern money from the 'special' monies of 'primitive' societies such as cowry shells or yap stones. But this functionalist approach to modern money hardly captures the dynamic social relations that produce and reproduce monetary exchange.

Money and modernity

In the late nineteenth and early twentieth centuries, money held a central place in social theory, becoming a diagnostic device for coming to terms with modernity. Karl **Marx**'s assessment of generalized commodity **production** under capitalism, for example, has at its heart a theory of money (Marx 1977). Money is a kind of *über*-**commodity**: it is a medium of exchange, rooted in a commodity form (gold), but it is also used as a measure of value. By capturing the value of **labour**, money makes possible a particular form of wage economy associated with a capitalist system of production, which in turn facilitates the specialization of labour. Yet modern money, according to Marx, also acts as a universal equivalent: it becomes the value against which all other values are commensurable. Hence money, argues Marx, functions as a 'radical leveller,' whereby quantities are substituted for qualities, and **subjects** are turned into **objects**. In terms of social relations, money empties the personal from exchange, and transforms the relations between people into a material relation between things (see **reification**).

This Marxian concept of homogenization followed by **alienation** in capitalist socitey resurfaces in a different form in the writings of Georg **Simmel** (1991) and Max **Weber** (1978). Both Simmel and Weber argue that the abstraction of social relations brought about by the transition to a money economy leads to rationalization and bureaucratic regulation of daily life, turning the world into an 'arithmetic problem'. Weber's model of bureaucratization (see **bureaucracy**) emphasizes the role of the **state** in this process, particularly with respect to the issuing and valuation of currency. Simmel, by contrast, provides a broader cultural analysis that analyzes money's impact on social interactions. He suggests that money embodies the heartlessness of **modernity** insofar as it encourages the dissolution of community, the shift from *Gemeinschaft* to *Gesellschaft* (see **Gemeinschaft and Gesellschaft** and **Tönnies**). Simmel's outlook, however, is not entirely gloomy. In his view, the erosion of social ties by money can open up possibilities that were previously constrained by social obligations.

Central to these various accounts is an evolutionary model of monetary development, with modern money being represented not simply as an outcome of these events but as a forceful agent of social and economic change. Some **postmodernist** theories have pushed the evolutionary model yet further, aligning the increasing dematerialization of commodities in the late twentieth century with the emergence of a society of **signs** and **simulacra**. Brian Rotman (1987) draws upon Jean **Baudrillard** and Jacques **Derrida** to develop a theory of 'xenomoney', that is a money which is no longer redeemable in specie – in gold or silver – but which, like paper money or the electronic blips of the stock market, can be redeemed only for identical copies of itself (for more paper, more blips). Given that money acts as the universal equivalent, parallel patterns of inconvertibility and deferral are replicated in other systems of representation, from texts to number systems. Similarly, for Jean-Joseph

Goux (1990) the crisis of **representation** associated with postmodernism is but a radicalization of the logic of equivalence in which all things are made commensurate, a logic which structures styles of thought as varied as **semiotics**, **psychoanalysis** and economics.

What these social theories have in common is the centrality they attribute to money in capitalist society and its impact on social relations. Marx's original formulation of **alienation** and homogenization, rooted in the evolution of the commodity form, is reconfigured in the postmodern accounts, but the foundations of his analysis are not disrupted. These accounts provide a seductive critique of capitalist **anomie**, and they challenge the tendency of economic accounts to detach economic and social realms. Geoffrey Ingham (1999) argues, however, that an evolutionary model of money actually provides a limited and distorted account of capitalist production and exchange. In particular, he argues it does not adequately deal with contemporary forms of money such as bank-generated credit-money (e.g. debt) that have become ubiquitous. Moreover, classical social theories of money do little in explaining the social dynamics of money in terms other than its role as a universal equivalent. In Ingham's view, these theories provide little sense either of the social conditions through which money is produced and of the agencies among which money circulates.

Money networks

Since the end of the twentieth century, there has been an attempt to rethink the role of money in terms of the particular social **networks** through which it circulates. Thus Viviana Zelizer (1994) examines the ways in which people store, earmark, and deface money, hence inscribing it with individual values. Her work on money in the United States pays particular attention to the gendering of monetary relations at the turn of the nineteenth century (see **gender**). At that time, women, who were then infrequently in the wage economy, had very little control over money and almost no legal entitlement to a husband's wage. Household expenses, which women were expected to manage, were thus a constant source of tension; funds were often doled out as an allowance, supervised by the husband, but also sought through pleading and/or deception. Looking at the uses of money in this way illustrates that money does not simply hollow out social relations, but can produce them and reproduce them in new ways. This presents a much more dynamic understanding of money, more closely attuned to the individualized dimensions of monetary transactions.

Nigel Dodd (1994) also argues that tackling the meaning of money requires an understanding of it in terms of its social relations. Dodd, however, is less interested in a micro-analysis of the individual uses of money than in setting out a new general theory of money. He argues that money needs to be examined in terms of the five properties vital to monetary networks: accountancy; regulation; spatiality; reflexivity; and sociality. In so doing, attention is shifted away from money's role as a general equivalent, and away from individualized transactions, towards the rational, fiduciary, and political relationships that exist among transactors within monetary exchange. **Information** binds the network together and generates the necessary **trust** in **institutions** or in money forms that enable the more fleeting, extensive and conclusive transactions associated with market economies. Because the information about money is never complete – it is either lacking, imperfect or there is too much of it – all monetary transactions are accompanied by an element of **risk** and are inherently tenuous. Thus, while Dodd presents a general theory of money, it is one that points towards the fragility of monetary networks.

Dodd's analytic framework enables the premises of monetary networks to be questioned rather than taken-for-granted. **Actor-network theories** of money also emphasize the **contingency** and recursivity of monetary networks, but with greater attention to their iterative relationship with the object they put into circulation. Leyshon and Thrift (1997), for example, identify four actor-networks that are largely responsible for the structures of **governance** in the new international financial system: nation–states; the media; the financial services industry; and machine intelligence (see **governance and governmentality**). As with Dodd's thesis, information is crucial to the maintenance of networks, but it is also a question of how information is translated across the network to mediate the relationship between actors and intermediaries. One need think only of the stock exchange, and the ways that information flows, filtered through expert systems or through the mood of the market, impact upon decision-making and in turn on prices and stock values; these re-valuations create new kinds of information, and the dynamic intensifies (see also **exchange theory**).

Network approaches thus present a model of monetary exchange that is clearly embedded in social behaviour. The interactions are iterative and context-dependent. Money impinges upon social relations not only as a measure of value but also in and through its circulation from person to person, from place to place, and through time. Hence the emphasis is much more on the performativity of money, of the significance of actors and objects in interaction (see **performative**). Money is not a totalizing social phenomenon but a changing and often ambivalent social network. Moreover, the model of society that is presented is more complex and messier than the elegant narratives of evolutionary **development**.

Money and power

Another strain of work in the study of money has provided a more considered analysis of the modern money form. Often drawing upon anthropological studies of non-modern monies, this research has questioned whether monies such as coins and paper money are really as empty of signs as has been suggested. Much of this research has focused on the emergence of modern monies in particular places and at particular moments in time. The role of states in this process is central, for the history of modern money is largely a history of state-issued currency. The ascendance of paper currencies, for example, was made possible by the trust invested in the state to secure the circulation and redeemability of currency. The **legitimation and legitimacy** of money was orchestrated through the centralized **power** of the state, and its authenticity regulated by state-controlled **police** who were authorized to prosecute counterfeiting and other forgeries. The result was the territorialization of currencies along national lines. But it was not simply that states made possible the proliferation of paper currencies, but that these territorialized currencies in turn reinforced and legitimated the authority of the state (Gilbert and Helleiner 1999).

Social theorists have also examined how one of the outcomes of this territorialization has been the formation of national identities (see **identity**). Subject-positions are created as people identify themselves and each other through monetary transactions, through the implicit rules and regulations which authorize certain kinds of transactions. The iconography on money has often been used to naturalize newer forms of money, particularly that which is no longer valuable in and of itself (such as gold and silver), by conveying social, cultural and political narratives. At the same time, **nationalist** imageries have also been harnessed to help produce and reproduce what

Benedict Anderson (1983) calls the 'imagined community' of the nation. Hence the images on money that also circulate as part of the transaction help to **frame** the kinds of subject positions that are legitimized via the state (McGinley 1993).

Power relations are crucial in the formation of national currencies, but perhaps nowhere more so than when modern monies are imposed by a colonizing power (see **post-colonial theory**). The Australian government, for example, used various tactics to replace the 'primitive' monies of Papua New Guineans with bank notes. Robert J. Foster (1998) describes how media from advertising to newspaper columns were used to educate and demystify the national currency being introduced. A national identity was constructed based on a model derived from Australia, and infused with a capitalist work ethic that emphasized the links between labour, wealth and social values. Similarly, Wambui Mwangi (2002) reveals how the new currency introduced into Kenya in the late 1950s, as approved by the East African Currency Board, reconfigured the colonial relationship into a narrative of capitalist development. Gone were iconographic representations of **naturalism** and 'noble savages', replaced by agricultural products such as cotton and tea. Questions of **race** were at once muted, while Kenya's place in the global economy was asserted.

Studies of national currencies have been very much concerned with questions of power, relating to the question of who issues money and with what effects on social relations. Context-specific, these studies reveal that modern monies are not empty, impersonal or disembedding but produce and reproduce identities, values and **communities**, particularly (but not only) at the national scale. This tracing of modern money's historical and geographical development also helps to defetishize the modern money form. For the most part, however, these substantive analyses tend not to illuminate our understanding of the more diffuse social networks in which money circulates, except at the level of the state, and they do not offer a general, explanatory theory of money's role in society.

According to Fine and Lapavitsas (2000), what is needed is a new theory of money which both draws on substantive empirical studies and is of general explanatory value. A great challenge for such a theory would be how to reconcile the micro- and macro-dimensions of money under one roof (see **micro-**, **meso-**, **and macro- levels**). The influx of new money forms – including transnational currencies such as the euro, electronic commerce, and local currencies – suggests some of the added difficulties in setting out an overarching theory of money. In addition, in different theories and understandings money itself plays a significant role in how the economy and social relations are theoretically enacted by the theorist. In this sense, money raises a number of paradoxes: it is at once a symbol, a social relation and an object. Always in circulation, on the move, its slipperiness evades a totalizing definition.

References and further reading

Anderson, B. (1983) *Imagined Communities: Reflections on the Origins and Spread of Nationalism*. London: Verso.

Dodd, N. (1994) *The Sociology of Money: Economics, Reason and Contemporary Society*. New York: Continuum.

Fine, B. and Lapavitsas, C. (2000) 'Markets and Money in Social Theory: What Role for Economics?', *Economy and Society*, 29(3): 357–82.

Foster, R. J. (1998) 'Your Money, Our Money, the Government's Money: Finance and Fetishism in Melanesia', in P. Spyer (ed.) *Border Fetishisms: Material Objects in Unstable Spaces*. London: Routledge, pp. 60–90.

Gilbert, E. and Helleiner, E. (eds) (1999) *Nation-States and Money: The Past, Present and Future of National Currencies*. London: Routledge.

Goux, J.-J. ([1973] 1990) *Symbolic Economies: After Marx and Freud*. Ithaca, NY: Cornell University Press.

Ingham, G. (1999) 'Capitalism, Money and Banking: A Critique of Recent Historical Sociology', *British Journal of Sociology*, 50(1): 76–96.

Leyshon, A. and Thrift, N. (1997) *Money/Space: Geographies of Monetary Transformation*. London: Routledge.

Marx, K. ([1867] 1977) *Capital: A Critique of Political Economy*. New York: Random House.

McGinley, C. L. (1993) 'Coining Nationality: Woman as Spectacle on 19th Century Currency', *American Transcendental Quarterly*, 7(3): 247–69.

Mwangi, W. (2002) 'The Lion, the Native and the Coffee Plant: Political Imagery and the Ambiguous Art of Currency Design in Colonial Kenya', *Geopolitics*, 7(1): 31–62.

Polanyi, K. ([1944] 1971) *The Great Transformation*. Boston: Beacon.

Rotman, B. (1987) *Signifying Nothing: The Semiotics of Zero*. Stanford, CA: Stanford University Press.

Simmel, G. ([1907] 1991) *The Philosophy of Money*. Boston: Routledge & Kegan Paul.

Weber, M. ([c1920] 1978) *Economy and Society*. Berkeley, CA: University of California Press.

Zelizer, V. A. (1994) *The Social Meaning of Money: Pin Money, Paychecks, Poor Relief and Other Currencies*. New York: Basic Books.

EMILY GILBERT

MOORE, BARRINGTON (1913–)

American sociologist and political scientist

Having begun his career in the shadow of **Parsons** and **Mills**, Moore inspired a generation of scholars from the 1960s onwards who helped to promote the sub-discipline of macroscopic **historical sociology**. He became renowned in the 1950s for his sociological analyses of the Soviet system. His later works, *Social Origins of Dictatorship and Democracy* (1966), *Reflections on the Causes of Human Misery and on Certain Proposals to Eliminate Them* (1972), and *Injustice: The Social Bases of Obedience and Revolt* (1978), display a clear inter-disciplinary and **comparative** historical approach, challenging prevailing diagnoses of the sources of **social change** and the moral underpinnings of modern society. In his major study *The Social*

Origins of Dictatorship and Democracy, Moore accounted comparatively for developments in various Western and Eastern states during the span from 1300 to the twentieth century. Blending **Marxist** and **Weberian** findings, he claimed that **modernization** could not be portrayed adequately in an evolutionary **structural functionalist** model, nor in a framework centered on economic factors. Instead, he saw it a matter of alternative paths that had to be grasped with historical comprehension. Moore explained the underlying roots of **democratic, communist** and **fascist** political systems with reference to corresponding revolutionary transitions from an agrarian to a modern stage of development. On the basis of these transformations, Moore examined shifts in **class** alliances that conditioned particular societal institutions and political cultures. Moore's works have also inspired many sociological studies, including notably on the historical role and preconditions of **revolutions**.

Major works

(1966) *Social Origins of Dictatorship and Democracy: Lord and Peasant in the Making of the Modern World*. Boston: Beacon.

(1972) *Reflections on the Causes of Human Misery and on Certain Proposals to Eliminate Them*. London: Allen Lane.

(1978) *Injustice: The Social Bases of Obedience and Revolt*. New York: Sharpe.

Further reading

Skocpol, T. (ed.) (1998) *Democracy, Revolution, and History*. Ithaca, NY: Cornell University Press.

Smith, D. (1983) *Barrington Moore, Jr.: A Critical Appraisal*. Armonk, NY: Sharpe.

BERNHARD GIESEN
DANIEL ŠUBER

MORALITY

Morality, at least from one fairly widespread modern perspective, consists in the rightness or wrongness of **action**. An action is moral if it is judged to be right or good, and immoral in so far as it is judged to be wrong. From this schematic definition arise at least two strands of sociological debate and controversy. The first strand can be described as '**epistemological**', the second as '**ontological**'.

The 'epistemological' side of the problem of morality for social theory relates to the common presumption in everyday consciousness that there exist criteria of moral judgment that are independent of action, and which can then be applied to an action in order to determine whether it is moral or immoral. The category of morality here refers to a consciousness of *what ought to be* the case with the world. For centuries this consciousness or sense of the moral or ethical has presented innumerable problems for philosophers and theologians; and for social theorists, too, it is especially difficult to examine and to conceptualize. In a nutshell, the problem of morality for social theory is that social theory is an empirically and not normatively informed discipline. This foundation of sociology is clearly expressed in **Durkheim**'s contention that sociology is the science of 'social facts'. These facts are understood as being external to any given individual insofar as they exist before the individual, and any given individual is only one small part of the totality that the fact represents. For example, a church exists before my entrance into it, and my participation in the rites of that church does not represent everything that constitutes that church. Social facts are to be treated 'objectively' or 'value-neutrally' (Durkheim 1982). This means that from the Durkheimian perspective, morality cannot be understood sociologically if it begins from the standpoint of the normative consciousness of the individual. Rather, morality consists in prevalent 'social facts'.

Similarly, though with different nuances, Max **Weber** also argued that sociology can say nothing about the 'ought' and can only deal with morality in terms of what it entails for the actions of social actors. Weber expressly stated in *The Protestant Ethic and the Spirit of Capitalism* that, 'we are here naturally not so much concerned with what concepts the theological moralists developed in their ethical theories, but, rather, what was the effective morality in the life of believers'. Weber's sociology concentrated on 'how the religious background of economic ethics affected practice' (Weber 1930: 267). These classical formulations of Durkheim and Weber have underpinned a consensus among many academic sociologists that sociology cannot make legitimate comments about 'what ought to be'. Sociology can analyze different social expressions of the 'ought' (compare **Parsons** on **values and norms**), but as a discipline it cannot legitimately make value-statements. It is felt that this is a facet of the epistemology of sociology that is endangered when the discipline is harnessed to a political platform or moral agenda. This view, however, tends to command less adherence from more politically engaged forms of social theory such as **Marxism** – for example, the **critical theory** of the **Frankfurt School** – or **feminist theory**.

From the 'ontological' side of the problem, it must be observed that various sociological analyses of morality are built on different – and often incompatible – *a priori* conceptualizations of the nature of human being. Durkheim took a definite stand on this matter. His stress on social facts implied that human beings *need* external constraint and symbolic and emotional processes of positive integration if any kind of social order is to be possible (see **values and norms**). For Durkheim, morality was a social fact that plays a role in the establishment and maintenance of social order, and this is necessary because, without the power of the social facts of morality, human nature cannot itself be the basis of an orderly life. Morality, then, is a social addition to what it means to be human.

There are traces of the philosophies both **Kant** and Hobbes in this argument, which is represented most clearly in Durkheim's notion of *homo duplex*. This conceptualization of human being suggests that every individual contains an opposition between egoistic and social (moral) impulses. Where the social order is not felt sufficiently powerfully, the individual will be able to follow only egoistic impulses, and an orderly life in common will be prejudiced (see **anomie**).

A variation on the theme of *homo duplex* appears in Norbert **Elias**'s theory of the civilizing process. Elias provides a wealth of historical evidence to support the thesis that '**civilization**' consists of the renunciation of egoistic impulses in favour of the acceptance by individuals of external constraints and restraints (Elias 2000). Elias proposes that it is through 'civilization' that men and women become moral.

The ontological *a priori* that Durkheim and Elias share in different ways is the presumption that men and women become moral, and need to become moral, through acceptance of the external **power** of social norms. In contrast, expressing a humanistic current in social theory, both **Simmel** and Weber identify moral activity more with an attitude of personal autonomous self-creation – an attitude that, in their view, was being increasingly restricted by social constraints (see **autonomy** and **humanism**). This humanist sensibility is encapsulated in Weber's famous declaration about the 'iron cage' of modern capitalist **rationality** (Weber 1930). In more recent times, it is in the work of Zygmunt **Bauman** that it is possible to find the boldest contemporary sociological expression of this humanist *a priori*, as well as one of the most direct critiques of the Durkheimian approach to morality.

For Bauman, Durkheim's approach collapses morality into the problem of social order and, specifically, into the question of social **integration**. Bauman comments that 'the most formidable of Durkheim's influences on social-scientific practice was the conception of society as, essentially, an actively moralizing force' (1989: 172). Bauman criticizes Durkheim on the grounds that the argument that it is '**society**' that makes men and women moral leads inevitably to the conclusion that morality involves merely the *passive* acceptance of social demands; to be moral is to do as one is told and to obey. Bauman develops this criticism in the context of his analysis of the **Holocaust**, contending that the Durkheimian position leads to the conclusion that Nazi officers responsible for the Holocaust behaved morally (because they obeyed orders, rules, norms, imposed by **authority**), while those men and women who came to the assistance of Jews were immoral because they refused to accept the demands of social integration. Bauman rejects this mode of analysis and instead draws on a humanist ontology to propose that the rescuers were moral because they were attending to the pre-social moral demand that is made by the human **Other**, which the social systems tends to manipulate or to efface.

According to Bauman, it is not 'society' that makes us moral. On the contrary, it is 'society' – especially **totalitarian** society – that prevents us from being moral. Bauman's counter to the Durkheimian approach to morality draws on the work of the philosopher Emmanuel Levinas, who identifies an ethics of a pre-social demand to care for the Other. Levinas's position is summed up in a passage from Dostoevsky: 'We are all responsible for all and for all men before all, and I more than all the others' (cited in Bauman 1989: 182). Consequently, in the context of the Holocaust, it was those who disobeyed the law in Nazi Germany, who refused to be integrated into that particular social order, who earn our moral acclaim, and it was those who were well integrated and who upheld social order who were most able to accept persecution of the victims.

However, it is important to note that Bauman does not seek to establish the Levinasian ethic of care for the Other as a sociological 'ought'. Bauman deduces the Levinasian position from a sociological investigation into the Holocaust, and thereafter deploys it as the foundation of a critical sociology. In his view, sociology is to be ethically informed and at the same time respectful of the epistemological foundations of the discipline. We see here that morality lies at the centre of social theory, but the study of morality continuously tests the limits of social theoretical epistemology. For this reason it is a matter of constant debate, and rarely of consensus.

References and further reading

Bauman, Z. (1989) *Modernity and the Holocaust*. Cambridge: Polity.
Bauman, Z. (1993) *Postmodern Ethics*. Cambridge: Polity.
Benhabib, S. and Dallmayr, F. (eds) (1990) *The Communicative Ethics Controversy*. Cambridge, MA: MIT Press.
Durkheim, E. (1974) 'The Dualism of Human Nature and its Social Conditions', in R. N. Bellah (ed.) *Emile Durkheim on Morality and Society*. Chicago: University of Chicago Press.
Durkheim, E. (1957) *Professional Ethics and Civic Morals*. London: Routledge.
Durkheim, E. (1982) *The Rules of Sociological Method*. London: Macmillan.
Elias, N. (2000) *The Civilizing Process*. Oxford: Blackwell.
Levine, D. (1995) *Visions of the Sociological Tradition*. Chicago: University of Chicago Press.
Weber, M. (1930) *The Protestant Ethic and the Spirit of Capitalism*. London: George Allen & Unwin.

KEITH TESTER

MULTICULTURALISM

Multiculturalism regards the coexistence of distinct cultural **groups** in a **society** as a positive **value** that should be supported by public policies. The term was coined in the mid-1960s in Canada, where multiculturalism was also for the first time declared official policy by Prime Minister Trudeau in 1971. The idea can, however, be traced back to

1915 when Horace Kallen (1915) advocated 'cultural pluralism' as an alternative to the **American** melting pot. Multicultural societies are subdivided into groups defined by cultural markers, especially **language**, **religion**, **ethnic** origin or distinct ways of life. Although such boundaries are often fluid and overlapping, multiculturalism regards them as significant for individual **identity** and public policy. In philosophy and political theory debates about multiculturalism raise questions about: (1) moral relativism; (2) the limits of toleration; (3) justice for cultural minorities; and (4) democratic stability and national unity in diverse societies.

For many critics, the problem with multiculturalism is that it generates cultural **relativism**, i.e. the view that all moral values emerge from shared beliefs within particular **communities** and cannot be applied across cultural boundaries. Radical cultural relativism is indeed logically incoherent since the idea that all societies and cultures can only be judged by their internal values postulates a universal value of abstaining from external judgment. The ban on criticizing other cultures because values are relative rather than universal is itself a universalizing statement. This idea is also sociologically incoherent since passing judgments on other groups, their beliefs and ways of life, seems to be a universal feature of human cultures.

Philosophical questions about value **pluralism** become more urgent and more political when they are posed within a culturally divided society whose members share a common **citizenship**. If citizens passionately disagree on fundamental issues concerning the nature of human beings, the good life or religious obligations, the question arises as to how they can agree on **constitutional** principles and accept the authority of **laws** that apply equally to them all. John **Rawls** (1993) suggests that social members may hope for an 'overlapping consensus' on principles of justice even in

deeply divided societies, if these principles are not derived from any particular philosophy, including **liberalism**, but are instead seen as responding to the question of what all free and equal citizens owe to each other in the abstract. Citizens of a multi-religious country may, for example, agree on religious toleration and the separation of **church** and **state**. In a liberal society, this **consensus** is not a mere *modus vivendi* that each side would want to overturn in order to establish its religion.

Other theorists have taken opposite views. For Chandran Kukathas (2003), liberal toleration, **freedom** of conscience and association imply that the state has no **authority** to intervene in cultural communities in order to enforce, for example, equal citizenship rights for women. Others have argued that liberal principles of justice and **equality** take priority over respect for cultural diversity. Susan Moller Okin (1999) believes that women in some repressive minority cultures would be better off if their cultures became extinct, while Brian Barry (2001) accuses multiculturalism of undermining the liberal agenda of difference-blind equality (see **difference**).

Debates about the limits of toleration have generally focused on religious diversity but fail to address conflicts over demands for language protection or territorial autonomy raised by ethno-national minorities. Will Kymlicka (1995) suggests two arguments for why granting such rights is a matter of justice. First, while liberal states may be neutral between religious beliefs, they cannot possibly be neutral towards the use of languages in government institutions and public education. Since all nation-building involves establishing particular languages and cultural traditions at the expense of alternative ones, cultural minorities have a right to 'external protection' against assimilation pressure from a dominant majority. Second, language-based cultures do not constrain individual **autonomy** in the way that some religious doctrines do, but provide instead a 'context of choice' that makes individuals aware of the value of different options for their lives. For Kymlicka these arguments justify self-government and special **representation** rights for national and indigenous minorities, and 'poly-ethnic rights' for immigrant groups, which allow them to negotiate the conditions of their cultural **integration**.

Many authors are more concerned with democratic stability and conflict management than with justice for minorities. From this perspective, too, there is little agreement. Some believe that stable democracies need a shared history and identity and that multiculturalism promotes minority **ethnocentrism** that undermines national unity (Schlesinger 1992). Yet most societies in the global context are much more deeply divided along ethnic and religious lines than Western democracies are. Once coercive assimilation is ruled out as illegitimate, democratic stability can hardly be obtained without accommodating minorities through autonomy and power-sharing arrangements.

Multicultural theories and polices must, however, try to avoid the danger of **essentializing** group identities and entrenching community boundaries. All cultural identities are socially constructed and malleable, and protecting minorities is no excuse for imposing unwanted identities on their members.

References and further reading

Barry, B. (2001) *Culture and Equality*. London: Polity.

Kallen, H. (1915) 'Democracy versus the Melting Pot', *Nation*, 100(2): 18–25.

Kukathas, C. (2003) *The Liberal Archipelago*. Oxford: Oxford University Press.

Kymlicka, W. (1995) *Multicultural Citizenship*. Oxford: Oxford University Press.

Okin, S. M. *et al.* (1999) *Is Multiculturalism Bad for Women?* Princeton, NJ: Princeton University Press.

Parekh, B. (2000) *Rethinking Multiculturalism*. Basingstoke: Macmillan.

Rawls, J. (1993) *Political Liberalism*. New York: Columbia University Press.

Schlesinger, A. (1992) *The Disuniting of America*. New York: W. W. Norton.

Taylor, C. *et al.* (1992) *Multiculturalism and the Politics of Recognition*, Princeton, NJ: Princeton University Press.

RAINER BAUBÖCK

MYTH

According to the *Oxford English Dictionary*, myth may refer to: (1) a traditional story, typically involving supernatural beings or forces, which embodies and provides an explanation, aetiology, or justification for something; (2) a widespread but untrue or erroneous story or belief; a widely held misconception or a misrepresentation of the truth; (3) a person or thing held in awe or generally referred to with near reverential admiration on the basis of popularly repeated stories; or (4) a popular conception of a person or thing which exaggerates or idealizes the truth.

The term, used predominantly in the first of these senses, entered modern social theory through the work of the German Romantics, especially Johann Gottfried von Herder, who viewed myths as products of the spirit (*Geist*) of the people-nation (*Volk*) and as resources through which social life was maintained. Perhaps the first attempt to establish the term on a scientific basis was the work of Haymann Steinthal and Moritz Lazarus on *Völkerpsychologie* (the psychology of peoples/nations or social psychology). These thinkers argued that the common activity of individuals gives rise to **objective** cultural forms that in turn produce the individual psychological **subjects** who engage in common activity. As Lazarus put it in 1865, 'Wherever several people live together, it is a necessary result of their companionship that there develops an objective mental content which then becomes the content, norm and organ of their further subjective activity' (Danziger 1983: 305). **Language**, mythology and custom together form a *Volksgeist* or 'objective spirit' of the

Volk, an 'inner activity common to all individuals' (Lazarus quoted in Danziger 1983). The positions articulated by Steinthal in particular were further elaborated by Franz Boas and by modern social anthropology. *Völkerpsychologie* was developed in the work of Wilhelm Wundt, who argued that the 'seat' of collective cultural phenomena such as myth was the *Volksseele* or popular soul, which was held to be but 'a convenient way of referring on the one hand to general psychological processes that emerge from the reciprocity (*Wechselwirkung*) between individuals and on the other to the mental products resulting from it such as language and myths' (Clarke and Nerlich 1998: 182).

In the work of nineteenth-century theorists such as Herbert **Spencer** and Max Müller, myth was considered an irrational belief of primitive man that arose as a result of the metaphorical deficiencies of language, and persisted in superstition. The dominance of this approach ended with the work of Emile **Durkheim**, who drew on the work of Wundt and the anthropologist William Robertson Smith to recast the German idealists' 'objective spirit' as 'collective representations'. Myths and **ritual** were now viewed as elements of a **religious** system and the means by which **communities** focus their collective attention, thereby re-creating themselves. The content of myths represents certain **values** that are embodied in social life and reflects certain facets of the social **structure**. Myths serve to bind together a given social **group** and to differentiate one group from another, providing, the cultural means for categorizing the world (see **classification**). Myths are thus precursors of philosophical and scientific knowledge, but, unlike scientific truths, 'mythological truths' are accepted without verification, because of collective pressure (Lukes 1973: 492). Durkheim's approach drew upon the **tradition**, which goes back to ancient Greece, of differentiating between *mythos*, the word as a decisive or final pronouncement, and *logos*, the word whose

validity or truth can be argued and demonstrated (Heehs 1994: 3). One of Durkheim's most influential followers, Lucien Lévy-Bruhl, argued that while myth is a 'pre-logical' form of belief characteristic of primitive societies, it should not be regarded as an unambiguously negative phenomenon.

This more nuanced approach subsequently made its way into the idealist philosophy of Ernst Cassirer (1955), for whom reality is a totality of symbolic **forms**. Myth is now seen as a primordial form of symbolic activity from which all other forms evolve. Mythical thought is, however, precritical in that it allows no detachment: the world is perceived intensely as permeated with emotional qualities, a 'solidarity of life' in which the observer has no privileged place. Scientific thought has systematically to liberate the observer from the observed phenomenon, progressively restricting mythical thought to the initial stages of expressive symbolization. The development of critical culture is the systematic emancipation of symbolic forms from the common matrix of myth.

This approach, largely stripped of its idealist assumptions, made its way into Soviet accounts of the cultural legacy of primitive **communism** in the work of the linguist Nikolai Marr, the classicist Ol'ga Freidenberg and the cultural theorist Mikhail **Bakhtin**. In the latter's work, the periodic re-emergence of the semantic forms of primitive communal **solidarity**, what Bakhtin calls 'carnival' throws critical light on social **inequalities** and forms of thinking that are themselves dominated by mythos at the expense of logos. As in the phenomenon described by Durkheim as 'effervescence', myth here is a resource for revitalizing social orderings and thus both the source of dogmatic thought and a resource for its elimination.

In contemporary social theory, myth is often associated with **ideology** in the sense of a belief system that derives from a specific social situation and serves to further or legitimize the interests of a specific social group (see also **legitimacy and legitimation**). The distinction generally drawn between the two terms is that whereas myth is a zone of contact between irrational drives and rational **communication**, ideology is a zone of rational communication and social competition (Halpern 1961: 143). The French syndicalist Georges Sorel, for instance, argued that myth derives from and expresses a personally experienced will to action, while ideology is a rational structure with roots in that myth which carries the force of myth beyond the immediate period and social circle. Ideology may then either communicate the power of personal experience in pursuit of progressive action, or serve as a façade for reactionary forces rooted in dead myths. Karl **Mannheim** adopts a similar position, but arrives at a different evaluation, arguing that myth is an irrational and conservative drive for stasis, while ideology serves myth as a rationalization of the status quo (see **conservatism**).

One of the most influential approaches to myth is that developed by the **Frankfurt School**. In their study *The Dialectic of Enlightenment*, Max **Horkheimer** and Theodor W. **Adorno** combined **Marxism** with Max **Weber**'s work on the 'disenchantment of the world' to argue that *logos* and *mythos* become entwined in modern society so that the prevailing rational perspective becomes an uncritically adopted *doxa*, that is, an assumption rooted in the prevailing social order – a myth. Weber argued that scientific thinking in the modern day remains powerless against other value spheres within social life that have taken on the spectral form of latter-day gods and demons. Even more boldly, Horkheimer and Adorno contend that purposive rationality has itself become a myth, one that imposes itself on other modes of thought through **violence**.

In recent years, the notion of the entanglement of *logos* and *mythos* has been combined with **structuralist** principles derived from the work of the French anthropologist Claude **Lévi-Strauss**, for whom myth serves as a structure for posing and mediating experienced contradictions. According to Lévi-Strauss and his many followers, the mind works through **binary discriminations**, but in myths the mind seizes whatever material is at hand and builds a structure in which categories are related systematically. This makes myth the precursor of science. Myths express the basic structural characteristics of the mind, demonstrating the hard structure beneath surface transformations. Roland **Barthes** (1972) extended the structuralist approach to myth to include certain cultural forms or texts characteristic of modern **bourgeois** society, such as advertising. In **post-structuralist** thought, however, structure becomes a mobile, shifting phenomenon, with the effect that rationality dissolves into ambiguity. The structures of myths and scientific explanation are reduced to mere narratives as the distinction between realistic and fictional discourses is dissolved and the referent of language 'bracketed out'. In the work of Hayden White, for instance, the characteristic feature of myth is, as in the case of Cassirer, the presumption of discursive adequacy. Myths and ideologies assume the adequacy of narratives to the phenomena they purport to reveal (White 1990).

While many so-called '**postmodern**' thinkers see no escape from the violence of myth, Jürgen **Habermas**, a student of Horkheimer and Adorno, returns to the neo-**Kantian** thinking of Durkheim and Cassirer, to argue that communicative reason holds the key to curtailing the influence of myth (see **communication**). While critique and theory, enlightenment and grounding are intertwined, the adherence of participants in argument to the 'unforced force of the better argument' is crucial for breaking the hold of mythical thinking while preserving the 'light radiating from the semantic potentials also preserved in myth' (Habermas

1987: 130). Pierre **Bourdieu** (2000) has argued that such a type of discourse has identifiable institutional preconditions.

References and further reading

Adorno, T. W. and Horkheimer, M. (1973) *Dialectic of Enlightenment*. London: Allen Lane.

Barthes, R. (1972) *Mythologies*. London: Cape.

Bourdieu, P. (2000) *Pascalian Meditations*. Cambridge: Polity.

Cassirer, E. (1955) *The Philosophy of Symbolic Forms*, vol. 2: *Mythical Thought*. New Haven, CT: Yale University Press.

Clark, D. and Nerlich, B. (1998) 'The Linguistic Repudiation of Wundt', *History of Psychology*, 1(3): 179–204.

Danziger, K. (1983) 'Origins and Basic Principles of Wundt's *Völkerpsychologie*', *British Journal of Social Psychology*, 22: 303–13.

Habermas, J. (1987) *The Philosophical Discourse of Modernity*. Cambridge: Polity.

Halpern, B. (1961) '"Myth" and "Ideology" in Modern Usage', *History and Theory*, 1(2): 129–49.

Heehs, P. (1994) 'Myth, History, and Theory', *History and Theory*, 33(1): 1–19.

Lukes, S. (1973) *Emile Durkheim: His Life and Work*. Harmondsworth: Penguin.

White, H. (1990) *The Content of Form*. Baltimore, MD: Johns Hopkins University Press.

CRAIG BRANDIST

N

NATIONALISM

Nationalism may be understood as a **discourse** that is expressed, on the one hand, as the **identity** project of a national **movement** mobilizing for cultural-political transformation and, on the other, as an institutionalized national identity code shaping political **ideologies** and **everyday mentalities**. Nationalism is conceptually distinguished from **ethnicity** by the explicit aspiration of achieving dominance within a single nation–state (see **state and nation–state**). It is conceptually distinguished from the nation–state in its status as an identity code, defending the **values** and interests associated with nation identification amidst co-existing and often competing identity projects and institutional **cultures**. Nationalist discourse is pre-eminent in specifying criteria of who belongs to the political **community** of the nation, along lines of ethnicity, 'race', **language**, **religion**, and other forms of cultural identification.

The relationship between nationalism and social theory has never been a comfortable one. While in one way or another nationalism was addressed in the classical sociologies of **Marx**, **Weber** and **Durkheim**, it was never prominent. Nor was it prominent in the later theoretical **hegemony** of **functionalism**, though this theoretical movement did inspire a more sustained, specialized literature on the subject. The focus of these two generations of social theory instead lay in the social processes and cultural orders associated with the emergence and consolidation of **modernity** as a **society** of free individuals, with the classical emphasis more on the aspiration, the functionalist more on the assumed accomplishment. Whether in aspiration or in fact, the association drawn between modern **rationalized** forms of **organization**, and universalistic cultural orientations excluded much attention to nationalism, which was perceived as a local, ascriptive and particularistic phenomenon (see **universalism**).

Notwithstanding these problems, theorists of nationalism in the functionalist tradition made a significant contribution to the field. Nationalism was conceived of as one of the critical forces that respond to the need of a differentiated society for an integrated cultural order (see **integration** and **differentiation**). Ernest **Gellner** is the exemplary exponent of this style of thinking (Gellner 1983). For Gellner, using a strong explanatory model, **industrialization** is the key to understanding nationalism. Industrialization requires a complex **division of labour**, which leads to an increase in knowledge work, which in turn requires a high culture. The standardization of culture in an expanded educational systems leads to the creation of this high culture on a nationalist basis, the nationalization of culture (see **education**). The thesis of the nationalization of culture and its complement, the formation of national communication systems, recalls the work of another influential functionalist theorist, Karl Deutsch

(1953). Gellner's second thesis is that the diffusion of nationalism follows in the wake of modernization, associated with the spread of industrialization. Assumptions of the equality of mobilized ethnic cultures come to collide with existing political and material inequalities. The thesis of uneven development combining with nationalist mobilization is also to be found in some Marxist accounts of nationalism, indicating common functional premises, though with different political orientations (Hechter 1975).

One peculiarity of the study of nationalism is the relatively narrow canon of relevant texts. Important works that bridge nationalism and theoretical concerns are often not included in this canon. Works in the differentiation/integration tradition of this kind include Stein Rokkan's magisterial study of the formation of national territories in **Europe**, with its wide-ranging exploration of how multiple **centre–periphery** relations led to the formation of the European system of nation–states and their distinctive identity configurations (Rokkan 1999). It also includes the work of Norbert **Elias**, notably his development and application of the concept of the national **habitus**, a national cultural interpretation system that is responsive not only to the standard nationalist discriminators of language, culture and religion but also to distinctive historical experiences. Elias draws attention to nationalism as an integrative ideology generated within the inter-state context, an emphasis that is poorly developed in the wider literature.

Over against the preceding functionalist and Marxist traditions, the '**cultural turn**' in a variety of existing and newly emerging disciplines since the 1960s emphasized the **autonomy** of culture and the creativity of social **action**. Both dimensions gave fresh impetus to the study of nationalism in the past two decades. The influential approach of Benedict Anderson (1983), marked a shift from Gellner's explanation-oriented emphasis towards interpretive understanding

of the nation **form**. Nations are here conceived as 'imagined communities' between people who mostly are strangers to one another, forged through new technologies and modalities of the diffusion of culture in societies becoming disembedded from traditional communities (see **tradition**, **stranger** and **imaginary**).

A further area of debate in nationalist studies has focused on the longevity and 'origins' of the nation. In this debate, between so-called traditionalists and modernizers, the issue has been twofold. First, it has concerned the question of whether nationalist interpretations of history were based on the real foundations of enduring cultural traditions or were simply invented for political purposes. Second, it has centred on the question of whether nationalism existed only in the past two centuries or whether it has deeper historical roots. It appears reasonable to conclude from this debate so far that nationalist discourses are constructed out of *both* relatively 'authentic' and relatively 'invented' traditions, but only in contexts where a significant historical sense of collective belonging is manifest. The continuity of a sense of collective belonging could in fact owe as much to the medium-term actions of political centres in creating nationalities, or to common historical experiences only later constructed as ethnically relevant.

What appears probable after several decades of **constructionist** analysis in a variety of fields is that nationalist discourses are likely to be highly mutable, depending on a large variety of short- to medium-term factors related to changes in **group** interests, events, patterns of opportunity, cultural models, belief systems, mediation channels and mobilization capacities (see **social constructionism**). Indeed, a constructivist turn is recently becoming evident in studies of nationalism, of which Brubaker's (1996) study is a prominent example. A further notable development in a constructivist direction is the systematic use of linguistic and discursive methods to analyze nationalist discourses, exemplified by the work of Bhabha, Billig (1995) and Wodak (1999).

The re-orientation of social and political theory touched on here affects not only empirical-theoretical frameworks in the study of nationalism but also ongoing contention over its normative evaluation. Normatively inclined theorists have increasingly come to regard forms of ethnic and national identification as expressive of legitimate difference rather than simply as empty fabrication. At the same time, however, theorists have also emphasized that extended reciprocal **recognition** of these forms of collective identity must occur within a politics of participation and inclusion across boundaries (see **multiculturalism**). Hidden in this inter-cultural turn is the acknowledgement that the long-run tendency to ignore nationalism in normative political theory led to a certain immunizing of the hegemonic, latent **ethnocentrism** of the nation–state from **critique**, perpetuating associated practices of **exclusion** and **inequality**, which was **class**-based and **gendered** as well as ethnic and racial. The softening of such ethnocentric tendencies brought on by the politics of **difference** and by more cosmopolitan attitudes points to the need for an attenuation of nationalism as a strong collective identity (see **cosmopolitanism**). In future, if it is possible to remove its latent ethnocentrism, nationalism might continue as a weak collective identity force compatible with argumentatively redeemable political values. In any such incarnation, the dimension of cultural we-feeling would need to be reduced to a collective sentiment that knows appropriate limits.

References and further reading

Anderson, B. (1983) *Imagined Communities: Reflections on the Origins and Spread of Nationalism*. London: Verso.

Billig, M. (1995) *Banal Nationalism: Nationhood*. London: Sage.

Brubaker, R. (1996) *Nationalism Reframed: Nationhood and the National Question in the New Europe*. Cambridge: Cambridge University Press.

Calhoun, C. (1997) *Nationalism*. Buckingham: Open University Press.

Delanty, G. and O'Mahony, P. (2002) *Nationalism and Social Theory*. London: Sage.

Deutsch, K. (1953) *Nationalism and Social Communication*. Cambridge, MA: MIT Press.

Elias, N. (1992) *Studien über die Deutschen*. Frankfurt am Main: Suhrkamp.

Gellner, E. (1983) *Nations and Nationalism*. Oxford: Blackwell.

Hechter, M. (1975) *Internal Colonialism: The Celtic Fringe in British National Development*. Berkeley, CA: University of California Press.

Hutchinson, J. and Smith, A. D. (1994) *Nationalism*. London: Oxford University Press.

Kohn, H. (1962) *The Age of Nationalism: The First Era of Global History*. New York: Harper.

McCrone, D. (1998) *The Sociology of Nationalism*. London: Routledge.

Ozkirimli, U. (2000) *Theories of Nationalism*. London: Macmillan.

Rokkan, S. (1999) *State Formation, Nation-Building, and Mass Politics in Europe: The Theory of Stein Rokkan, Based on His Collected Works*. Oxford: Oxford University Press.

Wodak, R. (1999) *The Discursive Construction of National Identity*. Edinburgh: Edinburgh University Press.

PATRICK O'MAHONY

NATION–STATE

See: state and nation–state

NATURALISM

Ancient doctrines of naturalism maintain that **nature** is the whole of reality, or that what takes place in the world is an immanent necessity of nature. Naturalism has a long lineage stretching from the ancient Greek philosopher Democritus to Francis Bacon and Thomas Hobbes, Jean-Jacques Rousseau, Karl **Marx** (in the sense of 'historical **materialism**') and Emile **Durkheim** (in the sense of the study of 'social facts').

While epistemologically the doctrine varies between **rationalism** and **empiricism**, the dominant naturalistic tradition in the social sciences during the nineteenth and twentieth centuries leaned toward the latter pole, taking the form of **positivism**. Here naturalism meant that society can be studied in essentially the same way as physical phenomena. Following the questioning of positivism, new approaches to naturalism emerged in the late twentieth century. Under the influence of Willard von O. Quine and John Dewey, the idea of a 'naturalization of **epistemology**' (Kornblith 1985) came to take hold. Along these lines, Bhaskar (1979) proposes a new naturalism based on an ontological **realism** focusing on generative mechanisms as the foundation for a naturalistic social science which is in principle the same as the natural sciences yet differs from them in respect of both object and methods. In comparable manner, **Habermas** ([1999] 2003) rejects Quine's strong naturalism in favour of a weak version which ontologically accepts continuity between nature and **culture**, but epistemologically draws a distinction between the natural and social sciences. In distinction to Bhaskar's realism, however, a pragmatic rather than an ontological realism informs Habermas's work (see **pragmatism** and **philosophy of social science**.

References and further reading

Bhaskar, R. (1979) *The Possibility of Naturalism*. London: Harvester.

Delanty, G. and Strydom, P. (eds) (2003) *Philosophies of Social Science*. Maidenhead: Open University Press; Philadelphia, PA: McGraw-Hill.

Habermas, J. ([1999] 2003) *Truth and Justification*. Cambridge: Polity.

Kornblith, H. (ed.) (1985) *Naturalizing Epistemology*. Cambridge, MA: MIT Press.

PIET STRYDOM

NATURE

Sociological questioning pertaining to the role of nature in **society** is as old as the discipline of sociology itself. For many classical authors, society always remained in a dual relation with nature: society is incorporated into nature and yet it stands opposed to it, stands looking at it. In this view, nature is anything that is not part of human intention and activity, opposed to everything which is called human, to what is artificially worked and produced, to everything which is defining of society. The range of connotations of the word nature, with its roots in the Latin *natura*, to give birth, covers meanings distinct and often antithetical to one another in their implications. Nature has also had different meanings through history.

In most nineteenth-century social theory, the impact of nature on society was perceived as determining. Social thinkers of the time were driven by the view that environments shape **culture**; that is, not only that geographical factors determine cultural characteristics, but also that these factors directly act on cultures. This geographical or environmental determinism addressed questions of how cultural features originate, change, adapt, and function. Human activities, in this stream of thought, simply belong to a network of cause and effect in 'the order of nature' (see **functionalism**). This view made it possible to explain all cultural features and accounts for cultural diversity by reference to influences of the geographical environment. Thus, the primary ecological issue here was less the origins of environmental degradation and environmental problems, but how societies are held in check by their natural environment. Yet, the human transformations and influences of the natural environment on human societies (global warming, the smell of mountains of waste, smog, etc.) can very well ricochet back on human societies. The insights of early thought on the influence of the material environment on human societies can be helpful in understanding today's environmental problems and the challenges of how to theorize the natural environment and the reciprocal interaction between nature and society.

In early twentieth-century sociology, the notion of nature carried at least two different core meanings, one referring to 'inner nature' (see **humanism**; **sociobiology**) which often meant an early stage in the development of a person, the other is the 'outer nature,' that is, the all-inclusive complex of the material world outside of human societies, but sometimes also the materiality together with the social side as connected in causal chains. Here nature often referred to all life including people, but not the products people made. In social theory, all these meanings have been used in reference to society. For classical theorist, Georg **Simmel**, for instance, the 'whole history of mankind is a gradual rise of the spirit to mastery over the nature which it finds outside, but in a certain sense also within, itself' (1958: 379). Especially with the rise of new environmental movements (see **ecology and environmentalism**) since the late 1960s, nature in social theory is normally synonymous with the great amorphous mass that surrounds the planet, with ecosystem, or in connection with the degradation of the geographical environment. The focus was on the human influence on the natural environment.

Since the 1970s the sub-discipline of environmental sociology has sought to theorize the reciprocal connection between human societies and the natural environment (Dunlap *et al.* 2002). Today's theorists normally reject one-dimensional environmental determinist descriptions of society. This yielded to the sociological approach that reality, including the natural world, is socially constructed. **Social constructionism** asserts the view that nature can never speak unmediated to humans, since its meaning is constructed inside a society. Without local interpretation it is devoid of meaning (see **relativism**). This, as some environmental sociologists lament, can be misused by 'realist' critics as a form of **idealism** that denies the reality (see **realism**) of environmental problems. Since these two perspectives still employ a disciplinary division between the world of social facts and the world of natural facts, some authors such as Bruno **Latour**

(1993), have criticized both the sociological representation of nature as a social construction as well as an objective given. Latour claims that the modern divide between nature and society was never real, but the most powerful metaphor or 'tool' for modern society to emerge. The nature/society divide is regarded as the great fiction of **modernity**. As soon as the distinction was invented, Latour believes, collectives between nature and society begin to proliferate. For Latour, there is neither nature nor society, but only hybrids. Consequently, in a method called **actor-network theory**, the imposing of analytical categories such as nature and society from the outside is abandoned in favour of tracing developing networks between a multiplicity of entities, including natural 'actors'. Thus, nature continues to be a meeting place for debate in social theory.

References and further reading

Cronon, W. (ed.) (1995) *Uncommon Ground: Rethinking the Human Place in Nature*. New York: W. W. Norton.

Dunlap, R. E., Buttel, F. H., Dickens, P. and Gijswit, A. (eds) (2002) *Sociological Theory and the Environment*. Lanham, MD: Rowman & Littlefield.

Eder, K. (1996) *The Social Construction of Nature*. London: Sage.

Franklin, A. (2002) *Nature and Social Theory*. London: Sage.

Gross, M. (2001) *Die Natur der Gesellschaft: Eine Geschichte der Umweltsoziologie*. Weinheim: Juventa.

Latour, B. ([1991] 1993) *We Have Never Been Modern*. Cambridge, MA: Harvard University Press.

Michael, M. (2000) *Reconnecting Culture, Technology and Nature: From Society to Heterogeneity*. London: Routledge.

Simmel, G. ([1911] 1958) 'The Ruin', *The Hudson Review*, 11(3): 379–85.

MATTHIAS GROSS

NEEDS

Human needs are the necessary conditions and aspirations of full human functioning.

The idea of human need has always been a central component of social and political discourse. However, its association with Soviet **communism**, which lived up to its billing as the 'dictatorship over needs' (Fehér *et al.* 1983), has made it the conceptual equivalent of a *persona non grata*. The result is an artificial exclusion of the concept from the mainstream of theory. This has proved detrimental for an understanding social and political **practices** since most of these are characterized by constant recourse to the idea of need.

Human needs manifest themselves in the three main forms: instrumental, vital and **agency**. In the first form, normally need-claims treat 'need' as a verb and have the logical or analytical form: A needs X in order to Y. This form calls attention to the fact that need statements tend to be triadic. This fact about needs enables us to ask what X is needed for. Y then becomes the crucial variable: the need-claim can be evaluated in the light of Y (Connolly 1983: 62). This emphasizes the instrumental nature of most needs; that they are means to other acts, or states of being or becoming. In the second form, needs are the necessary conditions for minimal human functioning. These include the need for water, shelter, adequate nutrition, mobility, and social entertainment. These have been called 'vital' needs because their satisfaction is a necessary condition for *vita*, or life. This is more obvious with regard to needs such as oxygen and water than it is with others, like adequate shelter, but the lack of satisfaction of any these needs tends to impair healthy human functioning (Hamilton 2003: 23; 27–31). In the third form, needs are the necessary conditions and aspirations for individual and political agency that is characteristic of full human functioning, for example, **autonomy** (or **freedom**), **recognition**, and so on. These have been called '**agency**' needs because they are ongoing aspirations whose development increases an agent's causal **power** to carry out intended **action**, as well as to satisfy and

evaluate needs. Met agency needs provide the feelings of safety, self-esteem and confidence that provide individuals with the ability to function fully, individually and politically (ibid.: 24; 35–47).

These characteristics of needs explain common usage: we use the notion of need, often in contrast to want, to denote a degree of seriousness, priority and **objectivity**. However, there is a tendency among theorists to overstate the case in two different, equally problematic ways. First, some theorists argue that needs are universal, basic, material requirements of continued human existence. In doing so, they focus exclusively on the second form of needs. This is most apparent in the 'basic needs' approach within **development discourses** on **inequality** (Stewart 1985). One important exception to this rule is the work on inequality and capability developed by Amartya **Sen**. Second, more nuanced political theorists shift the emphasis towards the third component of needs, and conceive of needs as universal **ethical** goals whose lack creates objective harm (Doyal and Gough 1991; Braybrooke 1987; cf Wiggins 1998). In both cases, an emphasis on an unchanging list of universal needs enables theorists to draw a clear, strict distinction between needs and wants. This is seemingly reinforced by the fact that, 'wanting something does not entail needing it, and vice versa. [S]omeone may have a need without having a desire *for what he needs* and. . .and he may have a desire without having a need for what he wants' (Frankfurt 1998: 30). For example, someone can have a need for periodic exercise without ever desiring to exercise in any way, and they may have a strong desire to smoke cigarettes. Needs are not simply strong wants. Needs are objective and normative (Thomson 1987), and their state of development and satisfaction have a direct effect on human functioning. In contrast, wants are subjectively felt desires or second-order desires for a specific object or state of being, and normally they depend on actual conditions of the world. However, this popular clear, analytical distinction between needs and wants rests on an over-simplification of the nature of needs that belies a more complicated causal reality. First, particular wants can over time become interpreted as needs. Think how easily the desire for refrigerators and televisions became a legitimate need for these commodities (see **commodity and commodification**). Second, new satisfiers and commodities generate new wants which affect our ability to satisfy our needs. For example, the car produces both the desire for a car and a need for more motorways. Subsequent political decisions that shift investment from the upkeep of an efficient public transport to the construction of more motorways ensures that in order for me to be able to satisfy my need for mobility I need a car. The three forms of need highlight the fact that human needs are not simply normative and objective, but also historical, social and political. Their objectivity is not universal: they are affected by wants and **institutions** and change as human nature changes. Understanding these effects and changes requires a contextual, historical analysis of existing institutions and how they determine the formation, interpretation, articulation and satisfaction of needs.

References and further reading

Braybrooke, D. (1987) *Meeting Needs*. Princeton, NJ: Princeton University Press.

Connolly, W. E. (1983) *The Terms of Political Discourse*. Oxford: Martin Robertson.

Doyal, L. and Gough, I. (1991) *A Theory of Human Need*. London: Macmillan.

Fehér, F. *et al.* (1983) *The Dictatorship Over Needs*. Oxford: Blackwell.

Frankfurt, H. (1998) 'Necessity and Desire', in Brock, G. (ed.) *Necessary Goods*. Lanham, MD: Rowman & Littlefield.

Hamilton, L. (2003) *The Political Philosophy of Needs*. Cambridge: Cambridge University Press.

Stewart, F. (1985) *Basic Needs in Developing Countries*. Baltimore, MD: Johns Hopkins University Press.

Wiggins, D. (1998) *Needs, Values, Truth*. Oxford: Clarendon.

LAWRENCE HAMILTON

NEO-KANTIANISM

See: Kantianism and Neo-Kantianism

NEO-LIBERALISM

See: liberalism

NETWORKS

Focusing on structural elements in social life, the concept of networks describes and explains how actors, roles, and positions interlock in such a way that action is reproduced and fresh action is generated. Networks refer to ties whose maintenance and variation generate and control identity. Networks combine heterogeneous elements such as **institutions**, **roles**, talk, **ideologies**, and **individuals** into self-reproducing practices that globally define a structure without any one actor locally having to know about it or understand it. The basic feature of a network is self-similarity; that is, the same basic **structure** is recursively reproduced independently of scale, scope, and size.

Like the concepts of complementary roles, **media** of **exchange** and **communication**, and **social systems**, networks belong among the major theoretical innovations of twentieth-century sociology. Invented as a means to model aggregates without recourse to categories such as '**class**' or 'stratum' and substantive agencies such as '**religion**', 'political party', 'income' or '**education**', networks account for the way social action comes about, is shaped, and is reproduced. Thus, the concept of networks combines social theory, empirical research, and modelling. They are strictly relational (Fuchs 2001), are opposed to normative modernist discourse (**Latour** 1993), and are suitable for mathematical presentation (White 2000).

The concept of 'block models' interprets networks in terms of closed systems of roles (Boorman and White 1976) involving a structural equivalence of ties between actors (White *et al.* 1976). Block models are concerned with partitions of a population of actors that go beyond sets in describing games that combine known and unknown, or determinate and indeterminate, elements. A block model is a hypothesis about which sections of a population cluster into a system of roles and which do not. A block model, in this sense, is a structure in search of actors and **action**, and is identified by actors in their attempts to control their range of opportunities. Structural equivalence means that actors are disposed to serve in the system of roles. Individual actors are not seen as possessing prior intentions or motives; rather, these elements are seen as the correlates of structure (White 1995a).

Harrison C. White (1992) takes **identity** and control to be the mechanism that produces action via networks. Networks define identities by joining roles, disciplines, institutions and ideologies with individuals, all of whom gain an idea of who they are from their part in a network. But participation in the network involves control both of one's contribution and of the contribution of others. Identity and control involve pleading, seducing, bargaining, commitment, and fixing. Identity and control consist in a system of roles shaped by complementary expectations that define any one role and position by relating it to other roles and positions. Stories are told, and listened to, which count for how specific roles and positions solve problems of double **contingency**, interrelate, and decouple from other roles and positions (Parsons and Shils 1951; Luhmann 1984). Disciplines of pecking orders emerge to order action and actors according to criteria of quality, purity, or **prestige** (White 1992: 16), all of them defining identity in terms of control, or conversely control in terms of identity.

As sections and not just sets, networks are composed of ties as well as of failed ties, and switches of ties. They combine the actual and the potential, consisting of strong ties that can be relied upon and weak ties that are held in reserve. They allow for ambiguity and ambivalence, for interpretation and evasion, incorporating uncertainty and at the same time keeping it at bay. Networks feature their own boundaries, which, however, do not always provide shelter but often repeat the vagaries and vicissitudes from which they derive. Boundaries, therefore, are subtle and complex products of action (ibid.: 127). They do not always run where actors expect them to run; and they cannot always be changed or manipulated as actors believe they can.

White gives abundant examples of these states of affairs. One is the urban dinner party: 'A sit-down urban dinner party among professional couples is an arena discipline.' That is, it deals with questions of purity, ranging from friendly to hostile. 'It is concerned with establishing some sort of identity of the evening' (ibid.: 30). The elements of the network are couples, individuals, professions, the **city**, and dining. A discipline emerges that counts topics of conversation and contributors to conversation according to an attempt to establish **equality** among them, which allows comparisons between, for instance, performances and claims. The idea of 'purity', in distinction from other valuation principles such as 'quality' or 'prestige' contributes to the ordering of performances and claims by means of control over possible dangers and threats. All actors and all actions must ensure that the evening is attributed an identity, which distinguishes 'friendly' issues from 'problem' issues in the context of urban married professional life. Stories are told, and ties are both strengthened and weakened, making the evening remembered as revealing a way of life either to be wished or to be avoided. The identities of the individuals and the couples present are addressed only insofar as they either contribute or do not contribute to the identity of the evening.

Similarly *publics* are networks that consist in constraints on the possibility of switches in membership (White 1995b). The heterogeneous elements are people, social spaces, entry and exit points, imaginary possibilities and boundaries with other publics. A closed system of roles emerges that needs no more than **Goffman**'s (1959) basic distinction between performance and audience to generate rules of tact, encounter, and tactlessness. The tram, the line at the cinema box, and the reading of a newspaper all make use of the network features presented by publics.

A further example is **organization**. Organizations may be considered networks as soon as **integration**, i.e. loss of degrees of freedom, works across formal boundaries (Nohria and Eccles 1992). Networks here cluster together types of **social relations** (of professional membership or **friendship**) around **markets** or around **status** or strategy. Switches of roles, positions, and attention are both possible and restricted. Identities are sought, and generated, among products, profits, or resources of legitimation. Measures such as efficiency, entitlement, or **charisma** are invented to account for variations in these identities. Ecological settings and environments are established that provide the organization with factors of production that it controls by externalizing.

Common to all these examples of networks is the feature not only of 'self-similarity' – of recursively reappearing structures – but also the feature that **interactions** in networks involves three, not just two, layers of actors. Networks break with the common-sense visualization of the social as consisting of more or less complicated dyads and refer instead to the importance of the third. Hierarchy, marriage, or the making and consumption of art are all impossible without reference to a third who watches and judges the identities that are brought forward, risked or confirmed or changed. Networks consist in control over identities

through the presence of absent thirds, which both fix them and keep them fluid. Networks are considered by Manuel Castells (1996) to be the cardinal feature of contemporary global socio-economic processes, movements and relations (see **globalization**).

References and further reading

Boorman, S. A. and White, H. C. (1976) 'Social Structure from Multiple Networks: Part II. Role Interlock', *American Journal of Sociology*, 81: 1384–446.

Castells, M. (1996) *The Information Age: Economy, Society and Culture*, vol. I: *The Rise of the Network Society*. Oxford: Blackwell.

Fuchs, S. (2001) *Against Essentialism*. Cambridge, MA: Harvard University Press.

Goffman, E. (1959) *The Presentation of Self in Everyday Life*. New York: Anchor.

Latour, B. ([1993] 1994) *We Have Never Been Modern*. Cambridge, MA: Harvard University Press.

Luhmann, N. ([1984] 1995) *Social Systems*. Stanford, CA: Stanford University Press.

Nohria, N. and Eccles, R. G. (eds) (1992) *Networks and Organizations*. Boston: Harvard Business School.

Parsons, T. and Shils, E. A. (eds) (1951) *Toward a General Theory of Action*. Cambridge, MA: Harvard University Press.

White, H. C. (1992) *Identity and Control*. Princeton, NJ: Princeton University Press.

White, H. C. (1995a) 'Social Networks Can Resolve Actor Paradoxes in Economics and in Psychology', *Journal of Institutional and Theoretical Economics*, 151: 58–74.

White, H. C. (1995b) 'Network Switchings and Bayesian Forks: Reconstructing the Social and Behavioral Sciences', *Social Research*, 62: 1035–63.

White, H. C. (2000) 'PARAMETERIZE! Notes on Mathematical Modeling for Sociology', *Sociological Theory*, 18: 505–9.

White, H. C., Boorman, S. A. and Breiger, R. L. (1976) 'Social Structure from Multiple Networks, Part I: Blockmodels of Roles and Positions', *American Journal of Sociology*, 81: 730–80.

DIRK BAECKER

NEW SOCIAL MOVEMENTS

See: social movements

NIETZSCHEANISM AND NEO-NIETZSCHEANISM

The emergence of philosophical approaches indebted to the work of Nietzsche has been significant at least since the publication of **Deleuze**'s *Nietzsche et la philosophie* ([1962] 1983). Three main strands of Nietzscheanism can be identified in contemporary French philosophy. The first, associated with Deleuze, develops Nietzsche's emphasis on becoming as a purely immanent process and the articulation of a naturalistic metaphysics of **difference**. The second, developed by De Man, **Derrida** and Kofman, takes up Nietzsche's (early) reflections on **language** and truth as offering a deconstruction of **metaphysics**. The third, adopted by **Foucault**, extends Nietzsche's project of a genealogy of morals. To this may be added two important strands in Anglo-American philosophy. The first, developed by Bernard Williams, focuses on Nietzsche's critique of **morality** and on genealogy as a non-reductive naturalistic approach to **ethics**. The second, associated with William Connolly and James Tully, takes up Nietzsche's emphasis on the agonic character of **freedom**. Critical reactions to the emergence of Nietzscheanism in its various forms have been advanced by Alasdair MacIntyre, Jürgen **Habermas** and Charles **Taylor** as well as through the polemical collection edited by Luc Ferry and Alain Renault, *Why We Are Not Nietzscheans* (1997).

These disparate strands of Nietzscheanism are characterized by certain family resemblances in which the following themes are prominent:

1. The naturalization of ethics. Whether developed through Deleuze's stress on desire, Foucault's conception of the subject of **power** or Williams's appeal to the notion of a minimalist moral psychology, these authors see Nietzsche's project of translating man back into **nature** as a central task for contemporary philosophy (see also **subject and subjectivity**). In each case, these thinkers are concerned with how to accomplish such a naturalization of ethics without succumbing to the essentially reductive strategy exhibited by evolutionary psychology. To this end, they all stress the ethnological point that human beings are naturally cultural beings.

2. The critique of morality in its dominant **Kantian** and utilitarian forms. This theme links Foucault's criticisms of Habermas's reinterpretation of Kantian ethics with Williams's criticisms of the peculiar institution of morality as involving an incoherent notion of the voluntary. More generally, all of the strands of Nietzscheanism reject attempts to provide foundations for morality and stress the importance of ethics as an ethos (or mode of self-formation) that is not reducible to a set of moral principles or rules.

3. The critique of metaphysical realism and the commitment to the perspectival character of knowledge. This theme is stressed by Derrida in terms of a **deconstruction** of the terms of Western metaphysics but is equally (if differently) developed by Foucault's view of genealogy as a perspectival form of critical reflection designed to free us from the grip of a given perspective. Whereas Derrida's project seems to echo Nietzsche's early stress on the fictive and limiting character of concepts, Foucault's work takes up Nietzsche's mature recognition that the perspectival character of knowledge is precisely not a limitation on knowing but a condition of its possibility.

4. An agonistic concept of freedom that rejects the opposition of freedom and constraint in favour of a view of situated subjects who act freely in transforming, to varying degrees, the conditions of their **agency** by, for example, extending and re-interpreting the norms

397

immanent to the practices in which they are engaged. This point is particularly stressed by Foucault and by Deleuze and has been developed by Connolly and Tully.

More generally, the common concern of Nietzschean and neo-Nietzschean philosophy has been to explore the implications of what Max **Weber** called the 'disenchantment of the world' for our common ways of thinking about the world.

References and further reading

Connolly, W. (1995) *The Ethos of Pluralization*. Minneapolis, MN: University of Minnesota.

Deleuze, G. ([1962] 1983) *Nietzsche and Philosophy*. London: Athlone.

De Man, P. (1979) *Allegories of Reading*. New Haven, CT: Yale University Press.

Derrida, J. (1979) *Spurs: Nietzsche's Styles*. Chicago: University of Chicago Press.

Ferry, L. and Renault, A. (eds) (1997) *Why We Are Not Nietzscheans*. Chicago: University of Chicago Press.

Foucault, M. (1984) *The Foucault Reader*. Harmondsworth: Penguin.

Kofman, S. (1993) *Nietzsche and Metaphor*. London: Athlone.

MacIntyre, A. (1981) *After Virtue*. London: Duckworth.

Williams, B. (2002) *Truth and Truthfulness*. Princeton, NJ: Princeton University Press.

DAVID OWEN

NORMAL AND PATHOLOGICAL

'Normal' and 'pathological' are terms proposed by **Durkheim** for a scientific **classification** of social phenomena and a basis for sociologically informed statecraft. Just as physicians identify pathologies in the human organism and recommend appropriate treatment, so the future 'statesman' would formulate policy correctives for properly diagnosed social pathologies, free from **idealism** or **moralism**. 'Normal' social phenomena are found in the average of a given social type or 'species' at a given level of **development**, and thus may be determined statistically (e.g., generality of distribution; level and consistency of occurrence). However, the difficulty of determining the actual 'level of development' of a given social 'type' (or of defining full development), led Durkheim to propose a second way of determining the normal: its occurrence could be linked to conditions of existence of 'collective life' in a given social type. Conversely, exceptionally occurring phenomena which detracted from such type-specific conditions of existence could be designated as pathological. Durkheim defined pathology as an extension or mutation of normally occurring processes, and thus subject to scientific examination; an examination which must treat questions of cause and function separately.

Durkheim's most famous examples of normalcy and pathology are from his discussions of **crime** and **suicide**. Crime is 'normal' in that acts which could be called criminal (which break explicit social rules) are found in all societies, and occur at relatively steady rates. Further, crime (more accurately, its exposure, representation and punishment) serves a social function, making rules and consequences manifest in exemplary spectacles. Like crime, suicide itself is less a pathology than a condition of social life; however, elevated or depressed *rates* of suicide, like variations in crime rates, can indicate a social pathology. **Anomie** (an attenuation of the force of social norms, allowing a pathological exercise of will), egoism (weakened connections between individuals and the larger society), excessive altruism (over-identification with the collective) or fatalism (a response to an inescapable and burdensome normative order) can be pathological in their consequences. However, both pathology and consequences will vary with the social type and its level of development, and with the specific circumstances in which the pathology occurs. Durkheim's discussion of economic anomie hints at a social pathology of modern

capitalism, though he cautioned that the question of what constituted a developed 'type' of modern industrial society was complex. Durkheim argued that pathological phenomena could indicate an evolutionary development: what is pathological at one period might appear later as prophetic, and what was once normal could become pathological (e.g., the institution of family inheritance which, Durkheim argued, reinforced a forced division of labour).

Durkheim's use of the term 'normal' reflects a nineteenth-century interest in **statistical** studies of human populations and statistical norms (e.g., Quetelet and Galton), and theoretical developments in internal medicine (e.g., Claude Bernard's assertion that pathology is an extension of 'normal' physiological processes, is scientifically explainable, and can be expressed quantitatively). The normal/pathological distinction also exhibits Durkheim's **structuralist** affinity for **binary** conceptual pairs.

Normalcy and pathology did not become central sociological concepts; nor did they link theory to practice as Durkheim had intended. Along with the organic analogy, they came to be seen as unworkable in sociological circles because of the difficulty of defining social types (without which an average could not be determined) and of ascertaining functional 'conditions of collective life'. The normal/pathological distinction was more commonly found in medical, psychological or criminological contexts, in the symptomatic surveillance of deviant actions, individuals, and populations (see **deviance** and **social control**). Such usage contradicted Durkheim's emphasis on a strictly social level of analysis, inasmuch as pathology or 'dysfunction' became less an indication of a social condition than a label attached to individuals and groups.

The normal/pathological distinction was subsequently resurrected as a topic in the history of science by Georges Canguilhem (1991), who explored how its development in nineteenth-century medicine was linked to specific social, technological, political or economic priorities. Canguilhem rejected statistical definitions of normalcy, or definitions implying some pre-existing harmony, but his own usage still had, at least in form, some affinity with those of Durkheim and Bernard. Canguilhem's work was an inspiration for **Foucault**'s detailed history of practices of separation and incarceration through which ideas of madness were transmuted into modern concepts of psychopathology (see **mental illness** and **medicalization**). Foucault displaced the idea of scientific or conceptual **progress**, examining instead specific shifts, transformations and ruptures in the ways in which madness was talked about, examined and treated. Similarly, Ian Hacking (1986) has explored the reciprocal interplay of actions, practices and statements in the formation of psychological categories and of the kinds of persons they were applied to. Nikolas Rose (1996) has examined the formation of **subjects** as **agents** in relation to 'public' powers and forms of authority in modern 'psy' **discourses** (see **subject and subjectivity**). Like the later Foucault, Rose stresses the 'productive' **power** of psychological categories, including normalcy and pathology, and more recently function and dysfunction, in the formation of a modern biopolitics. These are not simply 'imposed', but are also actively appropriated, modified, internalized and applied by subjects in ways that shape their self-definition as agents and **citizens**.

References and further reading

Canguilhem, G. ([1943] 1991) *The Normal and the Pathological*. New York: Zone Books

Durkheim, E. ([1893] 1984) *The Division of Labour in Society*. New York: Free Press.

Durkheim, E. ([1894] 1982) *The Rules of Sociological Method*. New York: Free Press.

Economy and Society 27, 2–3. 'The Normal and the Pathological': special double issue in honour of Georges Canguilhem.

Foucault, M. (1976) *Histoire de la folie à l'âge classique*. Paris: Gallimard.

Gane, M. (1988) *On Durkheim's Rules of Sociological Method*. London: Routledge.

Hacking, I. (1986) 'Making Up People', in T. Heller *et al.* (eds) *Reconstructing Individualism*. Stanford, CA: Stanford University Press.

Katz, S. and B. Marshall (2004) 'Is the Functional "Normal"? Aging, Sexuality and the Bio-Marketing of Successful Living', *History of the Human Sciences*, 17(3): 53–75.

Rose, N. (1996) *Inventing Our Selves: Psychology, Power and Personhood*. New York: Cambridge University Press.

WILLIAM RAMP

O

OBJECT AND OBJECTIVITY

Questions about the nature or existence of objects in the social world, and about whether we can know the social world objectively, have been fundamental throughout the history of the social sciences. The issue of the existence or nature of objects is an **ontological** matter, while whether we can know the social world objectively is an **epistemological** one. This entry will consider the meaning and issues concerning the use of objectivism, objectification and objectivity, but will begin by considering the issue of objects in the social world.

If there are objects in the social world, they possess different properties to physical objects, and cannot be defined by mass and trajectory alone. Some theorists deny that there can be social objects, on the grounds that social life is constituted of shared meanings which are constructions relative to time and place and are hence the antithesis of the solid or enduring properties normally associated with (physical) objects. 'Anti-object' views range from a moderate position where it is allowed that people act toward the social world 'as if' it had an objective existence – **Giddens**, for example, accords social structures a 'virtual existence' (Craib 1992: Chapter 7) – to more militant relativist positions, such as those held by **postmodernists**.

Those who maintain that there are objects in the social world hold equally disparate views, but they can be broadly categorized

as 'realists' (see **realism**). An early assertion of one of these views was **Durkheim**'s insistence that social facts are equivalent to those in the physical world. More nuanced contemporary versions accord different ontological statuses to social objects. For example, many realists define objects as something with 'causal powers', that is, identified properties, which, if actuated, can 'cause' something to happen (see **causality**). Thus, TNT has the 'causal power' of explosion, or 'people have the causal powers of being able to work (labour power), speak, reason, walk, reproduce etc.' (Sayer 1992: 105).

A further and pejorative conception of social objects is that of 'objectification'. This term originally came into use in connection with **Marxist** concepts of **reification**, but it has also been developed by feminist theorists such as Catharine MacKinnon and Andrea Dworkin, referring to the androcentric tendency to depict women as sexual things, objects or commodities and consequently to dehumanize them (see **feminist theory**). While there would be agreement that such dehumanization is the case in many social spheres, including sexual and **ethnic** relations, it raises questions about what is meant by treating another human as an 'object' (Nussbaum 1995). It seems unavoidable to attribute characteristics to individuals and groups as markers of differentiation. Whether these are pejorative for those so described would seem to be the product of both individual intent and the

401

symbolic structures of the particular social milieu in which the objectification is said to occur.

In the nineteenth and early twentieth centuries the social and the natural sciences were dominated by the epistemological view that, in R. J. Bernstein's words, there could be 'a permanent, ahistorical matrix or framework to which we can ultimately appeal in determining the nature of **rationality**, **knowledge**, truth, reality, goodness or rightness' (Bernstein 1983). Thomas Kuhn in *The Structure of Scientific Revolutions* ([1962] 1970) challenged this orthodoxy in natural **science** (and by extension in social science), claiming that **progress** in science is not linear. Instead there are '**paradigms**' of thought and practice that represent scientific truth at particular times. These are subject to occasional and dramatic revolution which can be accounted for more readily by social and psychological factors than by objective facts about the world.

Arguably, Kuhn's work had more influence on the social sciences than the natural sciences and was the motivation for a number of anti-objectivist positions including **subjectivism** and **relativism**. Subjectivists take a philosophically idealist position that denies the existence of an objective reality outside of agents' perceptions or constructions of it. Relativists go one step further by denying that knowledge and/or morality can be judged from a perspective that is not embedded in subjective positions. According to relativism, it follows from this that there can be no privileging of any one truth or moral position over another.

Objectivism has long been out of fashion. In the form described by Bernstein, it today has very few adherents. Likewise, extreme forms of subjectivism or relativism are not widely held, mainly because they imply ultimately that investigative social science is impossible.

The concept of objectivity is closely related to objectivism, but is not reducible to it. Objectivism can be seen as an exaggerated form of objectivity usually associated with claims to 'value freedom'. Indeed, objectivity and value freedom are often falsely conflated. While value freedom implies a radical form of objectivity, the obverse is by no means the case. Those who advocate or oppose value freedom usually take the term to mean that investigations can be conducted from a position of moral or political value neutrality. In the social sciences, where the subject matter itself or the choice of subject focus invariably possesses moral or political content, this view has long been discredited.

There is, beginning with Max **Weber** (1974), a long tradition of recognizing that any social science investigation inevitably starts from a value-laden perspective. In Weber's view, once this had been recognized, it is possible to bracket off value judgements and conduct an impartial investigation. In empirical social research this is possible to some extent and more sophisticated variants of this position have their supporters (Hammersley 2000). However, in the past three decades since the 'Kuhnian revolution', philosophers of natural and social science have questioned the role of values in each, and there have been a number of attempts to provide alternative programmes for objectivity in the social sciences. Often these focus on the self-examination of individual values. However, one philosopher, Helen Longino, has developed a version of objectivity applicable to the natural and social sciences which treats values as inevitably social.

Longino (1990) maintains that all science has both constitutive values and contextual values. The former are the internal values of science, such as accuracy and explanation, while the latter are individual or moral/political values. This much was implicit in Weber, but Longino goes further by claiming that contextual values influence constitutive ones and, moreover, that this is to be welcomed. In social science the early history of statistics illustrates the concatenation of contextual and constitutive values. For example, the concept of the normal distribution, 'discovered' by Quételet in the early nineteenth century, nevertheless required a notion and definition of what counts as 'normal' in order to know how other values are distributed in relation to it. Indeed, upon examination, virtually all constitutive values can be traced to a contextual origin.

Longino's redefined concept of objectivity begins from values, but as values are social, she maintains it is possible to examine those values communally in a 'transformative interrogation'. This might be likened to **Habermas**'s 'ideal speech situation' insofar as it aims to be an inclusive activity taking place within an enlightened discursive **community**. She maintains that this would produce scientific theories which are 'better not as measured against some independently accessible reality but better as measured against the **cognitive** needs of a genuinely democratic community' (1990: 214).

Longino's position is a sophisticated advance on that of Weber. By making the transformative interrogation the arbiter of objectivity, 'truth' is re-interpreted as a matter of intersubjective agreement (see **intersubjectivity**). However, one problematic implication of this conception is that views deviant to the consensus must be rejected. Consequently, Longino's conception of social objectivity has the effect of deferring truth about social or physical 'objects' to the existence of a **consensus**. While Longino is right that objectivity is a social value, the question still arises as to whether it is necessary to think of objects as states of the world that exist in a particular way, independently of how the scientific community happens to believe they exist. If so, we may ask: what is their ontological status (Williams 2000)?

The question of objects and objectivity in social science is a vexed one, but a social science without an orientation to objectivity has no means of adjudicating between the subjectively held theories of social scientists.

References and further reading

Bernstein, R. J. (1983) *Beyond Objectivism and Relativism: Science, Hermeneutics and Praxis.* Oxford: Blackwell.

Craib, I. (1992) *Anthony Giddens.* London: Routledge.

Hammersley, M. (2000) *Taking Sides in Social Research: Essays in Partisanship and Bias.* London: Routledge.

Harrington, A. (2001) *Hermeneutic Dialogue and Social Science: A Critique of Gadamer and Habermas.* London: Routledge.

Kuhn, T. ([1962] 1970) *The Structure of Scientific Revolutions*, 2nd edn. Chicago: University of Chicago Press.

Longino, H. (1990) *Science as Social Knowledge: Values and Objectivity in Scientific Enquiry.* Princeton, NJ: Princeton University Press.

Nussbaum, M. (1995) 'Objectification', *Philosophy and Public Affairs*, 24(4): 249–91.

Sayer, A. (1992) *Method in Social Science*, 2nd edn. London: Routledge.

Weber, M. (1974) '"Objectivity" in Social Science and Social Policy', in G. Riley (ed.) *Values, Objectivity and the Social Sciences.* Reading, MA: Addison-Wesley.

Williams, M. (2000) *Science and Social Science: An Introduction.* London: Routledge.

MALCOLM WILLIAMS

OBJECT RELATIONS THEORY

Since **Freud**, **psychoanalysis** has undergone a shift, from looking at the intrapsychic world of the **self** to interpersonal relations between self and **others**. Rather than focusing on pleasure-seeking or its denial – the need to reduce drive energy – the school of object relations sees the self as object-seeking and gratified by connections with others. The internal structure of the psyche is the product of early relations with others, in particular, those of mother. Good enough relations to [m]other provide the recognition and attachment that are preconditions for rich relations to others. In their absence, lack of **trust** and **security** makes it difficult for the child to successfully separate from mother and form meaningful relations. The focus on pre-oedipal relations between mother and infant acted as a corrective to the Freudian focus on the significance to relations to father. Central figures of the British school are W. R. D. Fairbairn, Melanie Klein, D. W. Winnicott, and John Bowlby. They were particularly significant in the 1950s, though their significance endures, with Anthony **Giddens** a contemporary proponent. In contrast to **post-structuralist** psychoanalysts (Jacques **Lacan**, Slavoj **Žižek**) who focus on the creativity of the unconscious, the illusory nature of self and a split self; object relations theorists strive to integrate **unconscious** aspects into the self to make its effects less destructive. In the 1960s, British **feminists** were critical of the assumption that mothers were responsible for their children's mental health. Feminist psychoanalysts Nancy Chodorow (*The Reproduction of Mothering*) (1978) and Jessica Benjamin (*The Bonds of Love*) (1988) have been influenced by this theory of self-formation, but historicize the role of mother. They believe that **traditional gender** identities for boys and girls are effects of the gendered **division of labour** where women are assigned nurturing roles, and as this changes, they believe so will traditional gendered **identities**.

References and further reading

Benjamin, J. (1988) *The Bonds of Love*. New York: Pantheon.
Chodorow, N. (1978) *The Reproduction of Mothering*. Berkeley, CA: University of California Press.

ELAINE STAVRO

OCCIDENT

The Occident, or the West, is an 'essentially contested concept', to borrow W. B. Gallie's much cited phrase. 'The West' is not west viewed from the Pacific Ocean; and even when it is viewed from the more terrestrial hemisphere, it includes many regions and states spatially to the east of the Mediterranean (Japan, Australasia, Israel). If the West refers to the more prosperous regions of the world (the 'developed world', the 'First World'), it is only marginally better understood as a 'North' in distinction to a 'global South'. For a great number of reasons implied in the term **globalization**, the West is an almost geographically meaningless referent today. Yet as a normative signifier with an immense legacy of history behind it, the West remains an important and urgent matter of debate.

Debates about the West in social theory thematize at least four different issues: (1) the issue of the '**identity**' or cultural particularity of the West; (2) the issue of the association of the West with **modernity**, and the reasons for this association; (3) the issue of when, why and how the West achieved economic, political and cultural **dominance** over the rest of the world; and (4) the issue of **intellectual** and **ideological** opposition to the West, including Western claims over the definition of reason and modernity and the West's construction of its **Other** as 'the East' (see **Orientalism**).

Hegel declared in *The Philosophy of History* that as the sun rises in the East and sets in the West, so the history of humanity finds its infancy in Asia, its childhood in Greece, its adolescence in Rome, and its maturity in Germany and Western **Europe**. **America**, which was not part of world history, **Hegel** consigned to the 'future of humanity'; while Africa went without mention except as a land of bestial '**nature**'. Hegel's lapidary words redound throughout the eighteenth and nineteenth centuries in close and sinister association with European ideas about the direction and goal of world history, **progress**, **civilization** and the universal validity of Western values – especially as expressed by the men of the **Enlightenment** – and the evolution of the 'races' (see '**race**' and racism). Oswald Spengler's best-selling adventure in historical obscurantism and **romanticism** *The Decline of the West*, of 1918, only disguised these notions through a narrative trope of the collective European 'tragedy'.

No essay in explaining the rise of the West in genuinely non-chauvinist terms appears in the history of social thought until Max **Weber**'s analysis of 'occidental rationalism' in the early years of the twentieth century. In his Preface to the collection of essays in the sociology of religion he published shortly before his death in 1920, Weber declared:

> A product of modern European civilization studying the problem of universal history is bound to ask himself, and rightly so, to what combination of circumstances the fact should be attributed that in Western civilization, and in Western civilization only, cultural phenomena have appeared which (as we like to think) lie on a line of development having *universal* significance and validity.
>
> (Weber 1930: 13)

Weber acknowledged in this and other passages that Western social scientists can never expect to put aside fully the influence on their research of their own historical world with its particular cultural value-orientations. Nevertheless, Weber's aim was to proceed as far as possible in value-neutral terms: not to suggest that the Western experience of **rationalization** was inevitable or bound to take a single unbroken line of development. He did so by pointing to a unique combination of factors: *economic* factors (**capitalism**, fostered by laws of private **property**, laws against arbitrary taxation, international trading ports, merchant adventurers, double-entry book-keeping, banks); *political* factors (the rise of the **state**, **bureaucracy** and legal-rational forms of domination through the rule of **law**, untrammelled in their operations by the teachings of the **church** and other traditional sources of **authority**); *cultural* dimensions (positive **science** harnessed to technical invention, dissociated from **myth** and philosophical metaphysics); and especially *religious* factors capable of conferring spiritual legitimacy on all of these named activities.

Unique to the West in Weber's analysis was the phenomenon of 'inner-worldly asceticism', exemplified in the **Protestant ethic** and its contribution to the moulding of a 'capitalist spirit' through attitudes of 'methodical conduct of life'.

Since the late twentieth century, at least two basic *topoi* have dominated discussion about the status of the West. One is the dating and historical causation of the rise of the West. Some historical sociologists dispute Weber's early focus on the sixteenth and seventeenth centuries, instead setting the decisive watershed as late as the eighteenth and early nineteenth centuries in connection with European **industrialization** (McNeil 1963; **Mann** 1986–93; Hall 1986). Others, such as **Wallerstein**, writing in a more **Marxian** vein, emphasize the rise of a **world-system** marked by shifting relations of economic dominance in world trade between **centre and periphery**. The other, more normative and theoretical focus is the link between Western historical experiences and ideas of '**modernity**'. Writing in the 1950s, Talcott **Parsons** interpreted Weber's thesis as suggesting a general process of convergence in world history around a paradigmatic type of 'modern society'. In Parsons's thesis, this was exemplified by the rise to prominence of North America as the world's 'lead society' oriented to liberal **democracy** and industrial capitalism.

One response to this Parsonian thesis is to dissent from the privileged normative status it accords to Western experiences as *cultural* models, but nevertheless to accept its identification of certain structural *societal* components as essential to any strict definition of modernity. These components might include the development of a capitalist economy, separation of religious institutions from the state, codification in positive law, differentiation between the **public and private** spheres. It is argued that from the fact that Western countries were the first to acquire these structures, it by no means follows that other counties that subsequently acquire them become modern merely by dint of imitation of the West or by having Western institutions foisted upon them as the result of cultural imperialism. This reading roughly describes the position taken by **Habermas**, among others (see also Schluchter 1981).

Another response, which is more sympathetic to ideas of **difference**, **cosmopolitanism**, **multiculturalism** and **post-colonial theory**, argues that Western experiences imply no universalizable model, either in the sense of the West's cultural values or in the sense of Parsons's or Habermas's 'modern societal structures'. In preference to any single unitary concept of modernity, this position advocates 'multiple modernities'. The phrase 'multiple modernities' allows for different civlizationally inflected trajectories of modernization, based on no strict dichotomy between the aspect of the modern, on the one hand, and the aspect of **tradition**, on the other (**Eisenstadt** 2002).

References and further reading

Baechler, J., Hall, J. A. and Mann, M. (eds) (1988) *Europe and the Rise of Capitalism*. Oxford: Blackwell.

Buruma, I. and Margalit, A. (2004) *Occidentalism: The West in the Eyes of Its Enemies*. New York: Penguin Press.

Eisenstadt, S. N. (ed.) (2002) *Multiple Modernities*. New Brunswick, NJ: Transaction.

Hall, J. A. (1986) *Powers and Liberties: The Causes and Consequences of the Rise of the West*. Berkeley, CA: University of California Press.

Harrington, A. (2006) *Concepts of Europe in Classical Sociology*. London: Routledge.

Mann, M. (1986–93) *The Sources of Social Power*, 2 vols. Cambridge: Cambridge University Press.

McNeil, W. (1963) *The Rise of the West: A History of the Human Community*. Chicago: University of Chicago Press.

Schluchter, W. (1981) *The Rise of Western Rationalism*. Berkeley, CA: University of California Press.

Venn, C. (2000) *Occidentalism: Modernity and Subjectivity*. London: Sage.

Weber, M. (1930) 'Author's Introduction', in *The Protestant Ethic and the Spirit of Capitalism*. London: Routledge.

AUSTIN HARRINGTON

ONTOLOGY

An ontology is a catalogue of the most fundamental beings, the existence of which is presupposed by the meaningfulness of a **discourse** and/or the viability of a practice. It is also the study of existential presuppositions. Ontologies are rarely formulated explicitly as one or more existential hypotheses. The logic of existential hypotheses is different from that of descriptive statements. A general statement such as 'Carrots improve night vision' is confirmed, to some extent, by favourable evidence, but falsified by counter-examples. Existential statements, however, are fully confirmed by the discovery of an instance of the kind in question. 'This is a carrot' confirms 'There are carrots' absolutely. Failure to find an instance does not falsify the hypothesis. 'This is not a carrot' has no immediate bearing on the belief-worthiness of the general claim.

In the 1950s the question of the relation between existential presuppositions and descriptive statements led to the important idea of non-truth functional relations between propositions. If its existential presuppositions were true, a statement could be assessed for 'truth or falsity', but the statement was void if that presupposition was false. Bertrand Russell had tried to maintain the principle of bivalence, that every meaningful statement can be assessed for truth and falsity. But it also held that ontological presuppositions did not behave like ordinary descriptive statements, nor were their relations to ordinary descriptive statements truth-functional (see **linguistic turn**).

Existential hypotheses, expressing ontological presuppositions, proved awkward for Karl **Popper**'s (1959) conception of meaningfulness as falsifiability, since they were unfalsifiable but strongly confirmable. It could hardly be denied that they were empirically meaningful.

Ontology is linked closely to grammar, in the most general sense. The favoured sentence form in Indo-European **languages** is subject-predicate. The subject term refers to an individual or substance while the predicate expresses one of its attributes. It seems that substance/attribute grammar fixes the form of ontology in advance of any philosophical analyses. Whatever constitutes an ontology must be a catalogue of substances or instances of substances. Material things, the criteria of **identity** of which are related to location in space and time, are prime candidates for the basic ontology of our world. The rise of the physical sciences had a profound effect on the properties that the basic material beings of our world were defined by. The success of mechanics in the seventeenth century led to a distinction between primary qualities of things, the properties handled by mechanics, and secondary qualities, the ideas of which did not resemble their material causes. Not only did Newtonian mechanics favour basic material things, but because of the dominance of mechanics, only the primary qualities of 'bulk, figure, texture and motion' of the simple material entities were real. Colour, taste, and so on were attributes of human sensibility only (Locke 1690).

Throughout the rise of modern science, the mechanistic account of **nature** was challenged by an alternative ontology. Newton's atoms were passive and interacted only when in contact. According to Descartes, the evolution of the material universe was just the redistribution of the original divine impetus by collisions among the basic beings. The alternative ontology consisted of active beings, with unobservable causal powers that were manifested in the behavioural dispositions of material beings. The monads of Leibniz's (1714) ontology were realizations of primitive active and passive forces, in the balance of which the material world was maintained. The current dominant ontology of physics, charges and fields, is a linear descendant of the activity ontology.

What of human beings? Are they to be likened to Newtonian atoms or Leibnizean monads? Despite appearances, are they really only passive responders to stimuli? Or must we treat them, as the basic particulars

of the social world (Strawson 1962), acting like the charges of the physicist's world?

Psychology, whether under the influence of **behaviourism** or in the **Freudian** mould, has tended to deny people the status of ontologically basic particulars. Instead, for behaviourists, they are reduced to the sites of stimulus–response relations, or for Freudians, to beings driven by unobservable cognitive 'machinery'. August **Comte** (1832), the father of modern **positivism**, rejected the idea of an ontology of powerful particulars as a kind of hangover from animism. In the positive stage of social science, he believed, only observable regularities would count scientifically. Thus, positivism presupposes an ontology not unlike that of behaviourism.

In recent years, a new ontological debate has sprung up between those who hold that the social world is a discursive construction, a **network** of meaningful exchanges between people, and those who hold that there is a transcendental structure over and above the patterns of mutual **interaction** among actual human beings, within which human beings live out their lives (Bhaskar 1979). This ontological debate echoes the debate between those who argue for a psychology of active beings against the advocates of ontological passivity. The constructionists argue that the only source of activity in the social world is people, while the transcendentalists argue for causally efficacious social structures exercising their powers on individuals (Nightingale and Cromby 1999).

References and further reading

Bhaskar, R. (1979) *The Possibility of Naturalism.* Brighton: Harvester.

Comte, A. (1853) *The Positive Philosophy of Auguste Comte.* London: Chapman.

Leibniz, G. ([1714] 1930) *The Monadology.* London: The Favil Press.

Locke, J. ([1690] 1974) *An Essay Concerning Human Understanding.* London: Dent.

Nightingale, D. J. and Cromby, J. (1999) *Social Constructionist Psychology.* Buckingham: Open University Press.

Popper, K. R. (1959) *The Logic of Scientific Discovery*. London: Hutchinson.

Strawson, P. F. (1962) *Individuals*. London: Methuen.

ROM HARRÉ

OPEN SOCIETY

The 'open society' is a concept articulated and championed by Karl **Popper** (1945) who sought to denote a society characterized both by open, rational debate and by its evolution along an unpredictable trajectory. Popper argued that the growth of **knowledge** is inherently unpredictable, though the character of a society depends on the knowledge the society has acquired. Thus a society with a predictable pattern of evolution must be one that is intellectually stagnated. '**Tribal**' societies approach this condition. Within societies marked by rational debate, **intellectual progress**, and therefore unpredictable **social change**, some may desire a return to stasis. Such are (perhaps unwitting) enemies of the open society. Their tendency of mind represents 'tribalism' according to Popper. One signature of tribalism is **collectivism**, the doctrine that each individual's essence or good is defined by the social collective as a whole. Like the (related) conception that society is an organism, collectivism is suitable only for 'tribal' societies, not for an open society. Popper asserted that notably collectivist thinkers such as Plato and **Marx** hold that an ideal society would not be subject to change. Their ambitions for social reform are impossibly 'utopian' (see **utopia**). To embrace, by contrast, the ideal that society should be open is incompatible with utopianism. In an open society, the appropriate way forward is 'piecemeal engineering'. The goal, with regard to J. S. **Mill**'s doctrine of **utilitarianism**, is not to maximize happiness, so much as to ameliorate, by trial and error and by limited reforms, the conditions that all rational people agree to be harmful. This 'negative utilitarianism'

represents a middle path between moral dogmatism and moral scepticism or nihilism. It avoids any pretense that there are truly general laws of society or of history, for there are none.

References and further reading

O'Hear, A. (2004) 'The Open Society Revisited', in P. Catton and G. Macdonald (eds) *Karl Popper: Critical Appraisals*. London: Routledge.

Popper, K. (1945) *The Open Society and Its Enemies*, 2 vols. London: Routledge.

PHILIP CATTON

ORGANIZATION

'Organization' derives from the Latin verb *organisare*, implying both 'to furnish with organs' and 'to endow with a coordinated structure' (Starbuck 2003). Today the term is generally applied as an adjective to refer to a collection of people, in conjunction with other material and non-material resources, whose activities are coordinated through a series of explicit procedures towards the pursuit of specified objectives or outcomes. Organizations are thus a key object of systematic analysis, particularly in the business and administration oriented social sciences.

While organization encompasses a range of forms and functions – from **nation–states** through to corporate multinational companies or local voluntary **groups** or **kinship** arrangements – the primary focus in the burgeoning social scientific field of **organization studies** has tended to be that of the **work** organization, or formal organizations, as they predominate in the regulative framework of the modern **capitalist economy**. The dominance of such organizational forms is a relatively contemporary phenomenon, the emergence of which can be traced back to earlier phases of capitalist development in Europe during the eighteenth and late nineteenth centuries and the requirements for ever more extensive and complex modes of administration and coordination.

Yet despite this shared framework, disagreement has prevailed over the ontological character of organizations. Much of this disagreement has been conducted within the dualities of **structure** versus **agency** and **realism** versus nominalism. Throughout the twentieth century a largely structuralist orthodoxy pervaded the academic understanding of organization with its roots in the work of **Marx**, **Durkheim** and Max **Weber** and his **ideal type** representation of the bureaucratic form of organization. Weber's (1978) analysis of **bureaucracy** addressed not only the pervasive organizational features of formal work and administrative bodies but also the increasingly rational organization of society itself, leading to a range of studies which have sought to evaluate levels of structural congruity with Weber's ideal typology (**Merton** 1949; Blau 1955).

In general, these systemic understandings of organizational bodies are premised on the view that by virtue of their capacity to cause effects in the **market** place or on the behaviour of their members, organization can be ascribed a supra-individual ontological status. Often such **structuralism** is integrated with a functionalist understanding of organized activity, in that organizational structures are conceived of as a functional response to environmental contingencies, particularly **technological** and market changes (Lawrence and Lorsch 1967) (see **functionalism**). Yet despite the adaptive possibilities that such **contingency** understandings of organization produced, such work continued to envisage the optimum organization as characterized by high levels of functional **differentiation** and hierarchical controls adopted from Weber's analysis.

From the 1960s onwards, this largely structural understanding of organization and the realist **ontology** which underpinned it came under critical scrutiny from a range of sociological and other sources. In addition to historical and comparative work that demonstrated that organizational forms clearly differ between societies and historical and institutional locations, social psychologists and social interactionists, such as Karl Weick (1969) in the USA and David Silverman (1970) in the UK, challenged the very notion that organizations exist as objective entities in themselves. Instead, they posited the idea, heavily influenced by advocates of **social constructionism** such as **Berger and Luckman** (1967), that they must first and foremost be understood as processes and outcomes of meaningful social interaction. Organization thus increasingly came to be seen as a *process* rather than a static entity, as something emerging through the ongoing, subjective mobilization of differing symbolic and cultural resources within the context of dominant economic and political regimes of accumulation and **governance**.

With the advent of **postmodernism** in organization studies, this latter understanding established even greater prominence with a shift from what Cooper and Law (1995) have referred to as a proximal to a distal conception of organization. A distal conception understands the organization as a relatively stable entity that has bounded parameters and an enduring character. Alternatively, a proximal conception recognizes the ontological instability of the organizational domain, identifying its form and composition as essentially unstable, as composed of disparate and often uncoordinated acts and processes, open-ended in their nature and bounded only by temporary and unstable conjunctions.

As a consequence of the general inability to grasp the nature of organization in anything approaching a definitive sense, the application of *metaphor* has attained prominence among a number of contemporary commentators. Metaphor has been seen as describing the variety of forms and contours of organization more comprehensively and reflexively than attempts to apply a purely representationalist definition. Particularly prominent has been Gareth Morgan's (1997) *Images of Organisation* which proposes employing multiple metaphors to achieve a richer understanding of the complexities of organization and the institutional forms it takes, as well as recognizing the constitutive role played by pre-conceptualizations of organization. Examples of the metaphors offered by Morgan include the machine and the 'psychic prison'. The former thematizes independent but regulated functions contributing to the pursuit of an overarching goal or imperative. This is the organization of mass industrial production associated with Henry Ford and scientific management where the defining principles of the organization are rationality, efficiency and centralized control (see **Post-Fordism**). The latter understands organizations as reified outcomes of human agency which serve to constrain human creativity and freedom of action (Weber's 'iron cage'). Organizations are here conceptualized as highly normalizing outcomes of social relations which are able to reproduce themselves through the concomitant reproduction of the psychological characteristics of their members.

Contemporary thought has increasingly focused on the idea that organizations are evolving into diffuse **networks** of practitioners, often only temporarily united via loose cellular structures. Such networks are, by their very nature, characterized by a proximal logic of organization, taking many contrasting forms and adopting an array of levels of formality and goal orientation. This has been increasingly facilitated by the growth and spread of **information** technology which has dramatically reconfigured the spatial and temporal parameters of forms of organizing, exemplified in, among other things, the growth of remote home working. The idea of virtual organizations is also becoming increasingly prominent. In this picture no central organizational hub is said to exist in physical space; instead, activities and interactions are undertaken via a web of communication technologies such as e-mail.

Often the primary function of such organizational forms is the generation and transference of **knowledge** among internal members and beyond. An organization's longevity is then seen as dependent not upon the coordination of physical tasks but rather on the unimpeded generation and flow of knowledge both as a resource for, and as an outcome of, its activities (Newell *et al.* 2002). For some commentators, organization is thus increasingly coming to inhabit a permeable world of flows and processes in which rigid, modern conceptions of organization as bounded by time and place are increasingly pushed toward the global and economic periphery.

References and further reading

Berger, P. L. and Luckman, T. (1967) *The Social Construction of Reality*. Harmondsworth: Penguin.

Blau, P. M. (1955) *The Dynamics of Bureaucracy*. Chicago: University of Chicago Press.

Burrell, G. (1997) *Pandemonium: Towards a Retro-Organization Theory*. London: Sage.

Cooper, R. and Law, J. (1995) 'Organization: Distal and Proximal Views', *Research in the Sociology of Organizations*, 13. Greenwich, CT: JAI Press.

Lawrence, P. R. and Lorsch, J. W. (1967) *Organization and Environment*. Boston: Harvard University Press.

Merton, R. (1949) *Social Theory and Social Structure*. New York: Free Press.

Morgan, G. (1997) *Images of Organization*. Thousand Oaks, CA: Sage.

Newell, S. *et al.* (2002) *Managing Knowledge Work*. Basingstoke: Palgrave.

Perrow, C. (1972) *Complex Organizations: A Critical Essay*. Glenview, ILL: Scott Foresman.

Perrow, C. (2002) *Organizing America: Wealth, Power, and the Origins of Corporate Capitalism*. Princeton: Princeton University Press.

Reed, M. (1993) 'Organizations and Modernity: Continuity and Discontinuity in Organization Theory', in J. Hassard and M. Parker (eds) *Postmodernism and Organizations*. London: Sage, pp. 163–82.

Silverman, D. (1970) *The Theory of Organizations*. London: Heinemann.

Starbuck, W. H. (2003) 'The Origins of Organization Theory', in H. Tsoukas and C. Knudsen (eds) *The Oxford Handbook of Organization Theory*. Oxford: Oxford University Press.
Weber, M. ([1922] 1978) *Economy and Society*. Berkeley, CA: University of California Press.
Weick, K. (1969) *The Social Psychology of Organizing*. Reading, MA: Addison-Wesley.

PHILIP HANCOCK

ORGANIZATION STUDIES

Organization studies is a multi-disciplinary field in the social sciences, concerned with the operational, **cultural** and **political** activities of complex *work-organizations* and their members. Often deployed as a synonym for a range of complementary fields such as organizational analysis and theory, organization studies is characterized by its disciplinary inclusiveness and a holistic approach to **organization** as a socio-cultural as well as an economic and political phenomenon.

The origins of contemporary organization studies lie in the **economic** and **intellectual** developments of the eighteenth and nineteenth centuries in Europe. It has been noted, for example, how it was Saint-Simon who called for the rational organization of society as an antidote to the unfettered individualism and looming **anomie** unleashed by the political, intellectual and cultural **revolutions** of **Europe** (Wolin 1960).

The earliest systematic approach to the study of the increasingly complex organizational forms of contemporary capitalism appears in the work of Max **Weber** (1978). For Weber, there was an inevitable tendency for contemporary organizations to structurally converge in the form of a **bureaucracy**. Much research has since been conducted on the continuing prevalence and relevance of bureaucratic forms of organization in an increasingly flexible global economy.

Equally influential on the field's evolution throughout the first half of the twentieth century was the emergence of a body of management theory associated with the prescriptions of Frederick Winslow Taylor in the USA and Henri Fayol in Europe. Taylor is closely associated with the emergence of what came to be known as scientific management revolving around the systematic evaluation of working practices and the imposition of managerially conceived practices and procedures designed as the 'one best way' to minimize wasted effort and maximize individual, and thus organizational, productivity. Fayol, while more concerned with **authority** than efficiency, shared many of Taylor's ideas, particularly in relation to the implementation of uniform procedures and a functional **division of labour**.

By the 1930s, the rational actor model of the organizational member presupposed by these accounts came under increasing critical scrutiny largely as a result of a series of studies carried out by Roethlisberger and his associates at the *Hawthorne Works of the Western Electric Company* in the USA. Rather than witnessing efficiency gains through the implementation of techniques associated with scientific management, what they found was that productivity was best achieved through nurturing relations of spontaneous cooperation among employees, including supervisors and management. This focus on the social relations of organizational life was central to the formation of the human relations movement in modern organizational and management thinking.

At present, the field remains largely dominated by various offshoots of what is known as general **systems theory**. Such approaches have tended to combine the empirical-analytical tenets of the natural sciences and the normative assumptions of functionalist sociology, analyzing organizational performance with a view to prescribing technocratic solutions to problems of under-performance in the marketplace. The most prominent variation of this has been **contingency** theory which, while rejecting the proposition that there is one best way to structure any given organization, argues that the key to understanding and promoting successful organizational performance is to ensure that design is congruent with a range of internal and external contingencies, including, for example, organizational size and the **market** environment.

Yet while contingency theory continues to maintain its prominence in the USA, organization studies in the international context has become an increasingly pluralistic and paradigmatically diverse field (see Burrell and Morgan 1979). In particular, a number of less managerial and more **hermeneutically** sensitive approaches have embedded themselves within the field, opening up a range of methodological possibilities and novel objects of analysis. While some of these have their origins in well-established traditions, such as in industrial sociology, others have embraced the influence of **post-structuralism**. This in turn has led to the emergence of new sub-fields of study such as those of **gender**, **emotion** and aesthetics within organizations.

Today, while there are those who continue to demand managerial relevance and methodological coherence from organization studies (Donaldson 2001), there are also those who reject such strictures in the name of experimentation and heterodoxy, arguing that the field must look beyond its traditional focus on the work organization and into the realms of informal and even pre-industrial types of organization (Burrell 1997).

References and further reading

Burrell, G. (1997) *Pandemonium*. London: Sage.
Burrell, G. and Morgan, G. (1979) *Sociological Paradigms and Organisational Analysis*. London: Heinemann.
Clegg, S. R., Hardy, C. and Nord, W. R. (eds) (1996) *Handbook of Organization Studies*. London: Sage.
Donaldson, L. (2001) *The Contingency Theory of Organizations*. London: Sage.
Tsoukas, H. and Knudsen, C. (eds) (2003) *The Oxford Handbook of Organization Theory*. Oxford: Oxford University Press.

Weber, M. ([1922] 1978) *Economy and Society*. Berkeley, CA: University of California Press.
Wolin, S. (1960) *Politics and Vision*. London: Allen and Unwin.

PHILIP HANCOCK

ORIENTALISM

Orientalism emerged as the study of non-Western societies by Europeans in the wake of the European voyages of discovery of the fifteenth and sixteenth centuries. Armed with scientific knowledge and new ways of seeing how human beings control and shape their physical surroundings, explorers, travelers, scholars and writers ventured into other parts of the world and collected information about distant places and cultures. The term Orientalist became widely used in the nineteenth century to describe scholars who studied 'Oriental cultures'. However, it was Edward **Said** who completely redefined the term in his seminal book, *Orientalism* (1978).

In *Orientalism*, Said argues that the Orient, far from being a physical entity, was an invention – a **discourse** – constructed by travelers, writers and scholars. The main assumption of Orientalist discourse was the existence of an ontological difference between the Orient and the **Occident**. This **ontological** difference, which is created by Orientalist knowledge, was not a neutral one but embedded in power relationships that helped to define the Occident against the Orient. If the Orient was the site of the exotic, the irrational, the effeminate and the weak, then the Occident became the site of reason and all that was familiar, masculine and strong. **Knowledge** produced by scholars, stories told by travelers and writers, and statements made by colonial bureaucrats all contributed to the creation of Orientalism and its particular **representation** of peoples and cultures in remote places. What is absent in Orientalist representations is the voice of the people who have been the subject of representation.

Orientalism, according to Said, enabled the West to classify other societies, evaluate them, and reduce complex social **structures** to simple generalizations. As a result, Said argues, Orientalism presented a distorted image of non-Western peoples and cultures, thereby feeding misunderstanding between different cultures. According to Said, Orientalism involved a certain way of 'dealing with' the Orient by 'making statements about it, settling it, ruling over it' (Said 1978: 3).

Influenced by **Foucault**'s concept of **power**, Said illustrated that producing knowledge about other peoples and **cultures** was not an innocent act but resulted in a set of representations which constituted the Orient on the Occident's terms. As a result, the **hegemony** of the Occident over the Orient was maintained first and foremost by turning remote cultures and peoples into objects of knowledge and then by using this knowledge to control and rule them. Said's discussion of Orientalism turned the **Marxist** theories of **imperialism** and colonization upside down. Classical Marxist theories of colonization and imperialism considered **capitalism**'s desire to expand into new markets as the main impetus behind the conquest of remote places and cultures. Said argued, however, that in order for conquest to happen, there was a need for ideological justification. By inventing the Orient, producing knowledge about it, and authorizing statements about its nature, Orientalism provided the necessary background and justification for **colonization**. By emphasizing the role of Orientalism in creating a hegemonic relationship between the Orient and the Occident, Said pointed out the role of culture in colonialism and imperialism.

The debate about Orientalism gave an impetus to the development of **post-colonial theory** and had a profound impact on the way other cultures are studied. However, some post-colonial writers criticized Said for reproducing the logic of Orientalism by creating the same sharp distinction between the Orient and the Occident. Homi Bhabha

argued that in Said's account the Orient appears to be a monolithic bloc devoid of agency and initiative (Bhabha 1984). This inevitably reproduces the logic of Orientalism and ignores the complexity and heterogeneity of cultures defined under the rubric of the Orient. In addition, Bhabha pointed out that the subjects of the Orient are not powerless agents. So too, the encounter with the colonized is always a destabilizing experience for the colonizer as it brings out the insecurity of the identity of the colonizer. In his *Culture and Imperialism*, Said addressed this criticism by arguing that the relationship between Orient and Occident is mutually constitutive and can only be understood by reading divergent experiences simultaneously — or what Said described as 'contrapuntally'. Said's 'contrapuntal reading' requires a juxtaposition of the nonsynchronized and discrepant moments that exist within a discourse. Such an exercise not only restores the multiplicity of voices within the Orient but also reveals the constituted nature of the Occident. Since the initial publication of *Orientalism*, Orientalist scholarship has undergone significant transformation with greater sensitivity now paid to the relationship between power and knowledge in the study of other cultures.

References and further reading

Bhabha, H. (1984) 'Of Mimicry and Man: The Ambivalence of Colonial Discourse', *October*, 28: 125–33.

Dossa, S. (1987) 'Political Philosophy and Orientalism: The Classical Origins of a Discourse', *Alternatives*, 4: 343–57.

Mani, L. and Frankenberg, R. (1985) 'The Challenge of Orientalism', *Economy and Society*, 14: 174–92.

O'Hanlon, R. and Washbrook, D. (1992) 'After Orientalism: Culture, Criticism and Politics in the Third World', *Comparative Study of Society and History*, 34: 41–167.

Said, E. (1978) *Orientalism*. New York: Pantheon Books.

Said, E. (1993) *Culture and Imperialism*. New York: Alfred Knopf.

Young, R. (1990) *White Mythologies: Writing History and the West*. London: Routledge.

FEYZI BABAN

OTHER

Otherness or alterity, from the Latin *alter*, describes a condition of being different. As something can only be different with respect to something else, the term other (or otherness) is employed as an antonym of **self**, ego, **subject**, or **identity**. The way the relation between the other and its antonyms is envisaged, however, varies. In the twentieth century, the **Hegelian master-slave dialectic** was taken up by Kojève (1969) who claimed that the subject's desire for **recognition** is based on his/her *desire of an other desire* and, thus, of the desire of the other. In **psychoanalysis**, Jacques **Lacan** adopted this formula but capitalized the term by now referring to 'the Other' as the **symbolic** order of **language** and as the subject's **unconscious**. Conversely, for Emmanuel Levinas (1969), the other (*autrui*) is radicalized into an inassimilable calling to which one must respond with infinite responsibility. In social thought, the Hegelian dialectic of recognition was critically employed in **Fanon**'s discussion of the colonizer/colonized relationship (1967). **Post-colonial theory** and studies of **Orientalism** and subalternity have pointed out ways in which the other is 'made other' through construction or projection (Said 1978). While **racism** is premised upon the wish to exclude the other and to establish a homogenous identity without alterity, these studies underline the impossibility of ever sustaining a clear-cut separation between identity and alterity (see **hybridity** and '**race**' and racism).

References and further reading

Fanon, F. (1967) *Black Skin, White Masks*. New York: Grove Press.

Kojève, A. (1969) *Introduction to the Reading of Hegel*. New York: Basic Books.

Levinas, E. (1969) *Totality and Infinity*. Pittsburgh, PA: Duquesne University Press.

Said, E. (1978) *Orientalism*. New York: Pantheon Books.

Todorov, T. (1984) *The Conquest of America*. New York: Harper & Row.

OLIVER MARCHART

P

PARADIGM

This widely used and abused concept was first introduced by Thomas Kuhn (1970) to capture the historical role that singular achievements have played in providing a blueprint for the conduct of scientific research. Indeed the possession of a paradigm is the defining feature of **science** for Kuhn. The concept is loosely based on a 'paradigm' in grammar, such as the conjugation of *amare* as the model for a class of Latin verbs. Kuhn believed that the worked-out problems in physics textbooks functioned much the same way, and that the entire discipline of physics could be seen as the elaboration of such textbook problem-solving. This core meaning of 'paradigm' remains current in **social studies of science**.

Kuhn's one clear example of a paradigm is Newton's *Principia Mathematica*. The virtual consensus surrounding Newton's theory and method for two centuries (roughly 1700–1900) enabled physicists to have a clear sense of the progress made and still to go. The Einsteinian revolution occurred only once the Newtonian paradigm failed to solve its own problems, rendering future progress problematic.

Kuhn specifically said that the social sciences – along with most of the biological sciences – lack paradigms because their research **communities** have lacked an overall sense of direction at any given time. Unlike Newton or Einstein in physics, social science's would-be paradigmatic figures – say, **Marx** or **Freud** – have been subject to intense controversy about the amount of progress made under their influence. Kuhn would thus find the idea of a 'multiple paradigm science' (George Ritzer's description of sociology) an oxymoron.

References and further reading

Barnes, B. (1982) *T. S. Kuhn and Social Science*. London: Macmillan.

Fuller, S. (2000) *Thomas Kuhn: A Philosophical History for Our Times*. Chicago: University of Chicago Press.

Kuhn, T. ([1962] 1970) *The Structure of Scientific Revolutions*. Chicago: University of Chicago Press.

STEVE FULLER

PARETO, VILFREDO (1848–1923)
Italian economist and sociologist

Influenced by theoretical physics, **positivism**, and marginalist theory of economics, Pareto developed a unique social-theoretical system based on **action** theory. According to Pareto, the central issue of sociological theorizing is the non-rational conduct of human action, based on pre-rational constellations of consciousness, which he called 'residues', and normative orientations, reasonings and illusions, which he called 'derivations'. Non-rational actions, such as magic **ritual**, **religion** or collective **solidarity**, are defined as the cornerstones of social **integration**.

Consequently, it is not **rationality** in the ordinary sense of logical conduct and **rational choice** that defines the object and scope of sociology. Instead the cement of society, is seen by Pareto as rooted in the sphere of non-rational discourses, notably in religious superstitions, prejudices and defective reasonings, as well as in the mobilization of mass **emotion**, **ideology** and political rhetoric.

The perception of Pareto as a classic in contemporary sociology is mainly based on his original and widely recognized contribution to the theory of **elites**. According to this theory, societies, and especially the political sphere, are generally subdivided into a privileged and ruling class, on the one hand, and an underprivileged majority as the object of **domination**, on the other. In **democracies**, the **power** and autonomy of the governing elite depend mainly on their capacity to make use of the residues, of mass emotions, in order to gain **consensus** by political rhetoric.

Major work

(1935) *Mind and Society: A Treatise on General Sociology*. New York: Dover.

Further reading

Bach, M. (2004) *Jenseits des rationalen Handelns. V. Paretos soziologische Handlungstheorie.* Wiesbaden: VS Verlag.
Parsons, T. ([1937] 1968) *The Structure of Social Action*. New York: Free Press.

MAURIZIO BACH

PARSONS, TALCOTT (1902–1979)
US theorist

Trained in economic theory, Parsons was the leading exponent of the **functionalist paradigm** in sociology, teaching sociology at Harvard University from 1927 until his death. In his first major work, *The Structure of Social Action* ([1937] 1968), Parsons synthesized the works of four European thinkers (Alfred Marshall, Vilfredo **Pareto**, Emile **Durkheim**, and Max **Weber**) in a solution of Hobbes's problem of how to secure a social order over against an impending chaos – on the eve of World War II. Parsons demonstrated the convergence of these thinkers around the morally obliging role of a common system of **value** attitudes as the basis of social order. Parsons singled out values as the central category of social order since they were at once a guarantee for free choice and for personal effort as basic characteristics of the **voluntarism** of action.

Parsons conceded that the second version of his theory, known as 'structural functionalism', was unable to provide an adequate account of both structure and *process* in **social systems** and therefore could only provide 'a second best type of theory' (Parsons [1951] 1959: 20). Nevertheless, in the 1950s his work became the dominant functionalist paradigm of **American** sociology. In the 1960s the dominance of functionalism waned under the onslaught of competing theoretical currents. In this period Parsons developed *systemic functionalism*, which had at its core the notion of inter-systemic **communication** based on generalized **media**, chiefly involving **money** and **power** (Parsons 1963).

Major works

([1937] 1968) *The Structure of Social Action*. New York: Free Press.
([1951] 1959) *The Social System*. Glencoe, IL: Free Press.
(1963) 'On the Concept of Political Power', *Proceedings of the American Philosophical Society*, 107: 232–62.

Further reading

Alexander, J. (1984) *Theoretical Logic in Sociology: Talcott Parsons*. Berkeley: University of California Press.
Gerhardt, U. (2003) *Talcott Parson*. Cambridge: Cambridge University Press.
Smelser, N. and Trevino, A. J. (eds) (2001) *Talcott Parsons Today*. Lanham: Rowman and Littlefield.

HARALD WENZEL

PARTY

The term 'party' derives from the Latin *pars* (part) and very generally means an **organization** of citizens to articulate their political interests in public decision-making by holding public offices and positions. The defining feature of a party (distinguishing it from other organizations) is – at least in **democracies** – its participation in elections. Modern party research conceptualizes parties as vote, office, and/or policy seekers. Thus it is assumed that a central aim of parties is competition for votes. By maximizing these votes, they can fill offices in the political system, enabling them to transform programmatic goals into policies.

While **rational choice** theory (Downs *et al.* 1957) considers parties mainly as vote and office seekers, whose exclusive rational interest is the maximization of votes, other schools (Budge and Keman 1990; Laver and Schofield 1990) emphasize the formulation and implementation of policies as the central goal of parties. Political parties in Western democracies linked both functions in the second half of the twentieth century. On the one hand, modern parties want to maximize votes in the political contest to occupy the state's offices of authoritative decision-making; on the other, it cannot be denied that vote maximization happens only within the limits of values and programs and that the carrying out of specific policies remains the central interest of parties.

Historically, modern political parties emerged with the introduction of the general franchise and the establishment of parliaments, mobilizing along social and cultural cleavages. The more heterogeneous the societal interest structure, the more plural the party system is generally (Sartori 1976). According to the cleavage theory of **Lipset** and Rokkan (1967), cleavages in Western democracies have largely persisted since the 1920s. Social groups and parties formed coalitions along these 'frozen cleavage structures', which have by and large endured in 'frozen party systems' (ibid.). Only the disintegration of **traditional** milieus, the emergence of new social movements, and citizens' fading party identification in the last third of the twentieth century provide the conditions for the formation of new parties (above all, green-ecological or right-wing populist parties). In most (Western) societies, liberal, conservative, labor, agrarian, regional, Christian, communist, fascist, right-wing populist and ecological parties can be classified as 'ideological party families' (Beyme 1985).

Parties can be conceptualized in various ways: into notable, cadre, mass and cartel parties, according to organization **structure**; into **interest**, **class** and **national** parties, according to the structure of their members and voters; into **labor**, agrarian and entrepreneurial parties, according to the voters' social and professional background; into **communist**, **socialist**, **liberal**, **conservative** or **fascist** parties, according to programmatic values; into national and regional parties, according to geographic region; into system and anti-system parties, according to their position in the political system; into established and non-established parties, according to the degree of their institutionalization; and into democratic, authoritarian, **totalitarian** or unified state parties, according to their claim to power. Complex party typologies underline the various dimensions in the development of parties and party systems (cf. Beyme 1985).

If one looks at such multi-dimensional types, four phases of party development can be differentiated according to Katz and Mair (1995), at least in **Europe**: The first elite parties emerged in the nineteenth century due to property-owning and working classes. After 1880 (approximately until 1960) the first mass parties, initially in the labor movement, were founded on the basis of fierce class conflicts. People's parties of a new type (catch-all parties) only emerged with the gradual dissolution of these old class conflicts after 1945. Catch-all parties, according to Kirchheimer (1965), are characterized by a decline in **ideology**, partial **autonomy** of the party's leadership from its members, expansion of the party's clientele to practically every citizen, and opening of the party to various interest groups. Anthony Downs (1957) developed a theoretical model of this concept of 'catch-all party' within the theoretical framework of rational choice. Here, the de-ideologization of the party, stated by Kirchheimer, finds its equivalent in the rational strategy of vote maximization, which is no longer primarily oriented towards ideology but the median voter. Indicators of such a development were tendencies in professionalizing party organization (see **professions and professionalization**), a stronger intra-party democracy, an increase in the ability to form coalitions, and related to these a de-ideologization of party goals for election-campaign purposes (vote seeking, catch-all). The transformation of the people's parties of the 1960s and 1970s into 'cartel parties' (Katz and Mair 1995) or 'professionalized vote-seeking parties' marks the final step of this development, which is explained particularly by the aspect of professionalization and the formation of new electoral milieus and the new volatile opinion voters (Panebianco 1988).

For modern democracies parties fulfill mainly six functions: they (1) articulate societal and political aims and write them down in programs; (2) articulate and aggregate interests; and (3) mobilize citizens during elections and recruit political elites. Further, (4) parties form governments and control them in parliaments; (5) influence government policy and activity; and, ideally, (6) provide for the communication between the elite and citizens.

According to **systems theory**, parties function as organizers of citizens' loyalty by ensuring, through their role as transmitters, the specific and diffuse support for the political system (Easton 1965). It is parties, above all, which channel demands to the political system and translate them into political programs.

Critical reviews of parties and party systems point to the fact that parties want to push through particular interests at the expense of public interest. Robert Michels ([1911] 1966) first formulated the 'iron law of oligarchy', which postulates for organizations the inexorable separation of the leadership from the rest of the organization. Applied to parties, this means that, with a growing number of party members, the tendency increases for the leadership to become oligarchic. The consequence is a decline in intra-party democracy. The assertion of an 'inexorable' trend towards party oligarchy has considerably weakened. Legal regulations on intra-party democracy and direct participation in particular have at least contained tendencies towards oligarchic forms in most Western democracy parties.

Nevertheless, there are tendencies towards a 'party state' and 'state parties', because parties acquire more and more state resources. The point can be made at least that modern parties have tapped considerable state resources through the financing of parties by the state as well as through their access to publicly owned **media**. However, in view of the **pluralist** character of Western societies, this omen seems to be inordinate. In addition, the criticism ignores the fact that parties perform necessary functions in democracies, which up to now have not been carried out by any other organization. Political parties as intermediaries between citizens and the state thus appear to be indispensable.

Nonetheless, party researchers continue to discuss hypotheses on party decline. They base their hypotheses on changes in the social **stratification** of the electorate, declining party identification, changes in voters' normative orientations, decreasing electoral participation and increasing volatility. According to the so-called Michigan School (Campbell *et al.* 1966), which has prevailed in party research for a long time, a voter's decision can be traced back to mainly three factors: party identification, issue orientation, and candidate assessment. In particular, party identification has been seen as the central explanatory variable for a long time. The underlying assumption is that individuals adopt central **values and norms** of a party for their individual system of values and beliefs in the course of their political socialization and, thus, establish a durable psychological identification with this party. Such identification is considered to be stable over a long time. However, nowadays, the increasing number of volatile voters casts doubts on the persistent validity of party-identification theory. Since the 1980s, empirical research has observed a clear decline in party identification (dealignment) (Dalton 1996). Situative factors, such as issue and candidate orientations, need to be added to explain electoral behavior. Thus, it can be assumed that the rational voter is knowledgeable about alternative policy offers and makes his or her decision for a party according to rational individual preferences. Moreover, the category 'candidate orientation' also includes the consideration that voters assign performance-oriented (competence, strong leadership quality, etc.) and personality-oriented (reliability, sympathy) characteristics to the candidates running for election, and allow them to influence their electoral decisions. Campbell *et al.* (1966) arranged these three components into a 'funnel of causality' for the explanation of electoral behavior. Thus, parties are confronted with the problem that they can no longer rely on their loyal electorate, but need to approach the ever increasing number of volatile voters with programmatic offers.

How do parties deal with these challenges? Parties' reactions range from mere non-reaction to changes in party organization (professionalization) and selection of candidates (geared towards the media), strategic reactions to the electorate (acquisition of new target **groups**) and political competitors (electoral alliances) to new programmatic, ideological or policy orientations. Although these transformation processes can be very slow-moving, one cannot speak of a crisis of political parties. Only in very rare cases, when the political system as a whole enters a crisis

(such as Italy in 1994), will the party systems collapse. Otherwise, parties have proven to be able to change and adapt to new conditions in the medium term, and party systems have turned out to be relatively stable.

References and further reading

Beyme, K. (1985) *Political Parties in Western Democracies*. New York: Palgrave Macmillan.

Budge, I. and Keman, H. (1990) *Parties and Democracy: Coalition Formation and Government Function in Twenty Democracies*. Oxford: Oxford University Press.

Campbell, A. *et al.* (1966) *Elections and the Political Order*. New York: John Wiley and Sons.

Dalton, R. J. (1996) *Citizen Politics in Western Democracies*. Chatham, NJ: Chatham House.

Downs, A. (1957) *An Economic Theory of Democracy*. New York: Addison-Wesley.

Duverger, M. (1954) *Political Parties: Their Organisation and Activity in the Modern State*. New York: John Wiley and Sons.

Easton, D. (1965) *A Systems Analysis of Political Life*. New York: John Wiley and Sons.

Katz, R. S. and Mair, P. (1995) 'Changing Models of Party Organization and Party Democracy: The Emergence of the Cartel Party', *Party Politics*, 1: 5–28.

Kirchheimer, O. (1965) 'The Transformation of West European Party Systems', in J. Lapalombara and M. Weiner (eds) *Political Parties and Political Development*. Princeton, NJ: Princeton University Press.

Laver, M. and Schofield, N. (1990) *Multiparty Government: The Politics of Coalition in Europe*. Oxford: Oxford University Press.

Lawson, K. and Merkl, P. H. (eds) (1988) *When Parties Fail: Emerging Alternative Organizations*. Princeton, NJ: Princeton University Press.

Lipset, S. M. and Rokkan, S. (eds) (1967) *Party Systems and Voter Alignments*. New York: Free Press.

Michels, R. ([1911] 1966) *Political Parties*. New York: Free Press.

Panebianco, A. (1988) *Political Parties: Organization and Power*. Cambridge: Cambridge University Press.

Sartori, G. (1976) *Parties and Party Systems*. Cambridge: Cambridge University Press.

Ware, A. (1996) *Political Parties and Party Systems*. Oxford: Oxford University Press.

Webb, P., Farrell, D. M. and Holliday, I. (eds) (2002) *Political Parties in Advanced Industrial*

Democracies. Oxford: Oxford University Press.

SASCHA KNEIP
WOLFGANG MERKEL

PATRIARCHY

Patriarchy is generally understood to be a system of social relations and institutions that give men control and advantages that are withheld from women. Like all social systems, patriarchy consists of economic, legal, political relations and of ideas, **values**, beliefs and norms. Patriarchal societies grant privileges to men and permit or encourage their **domination** over females. They allow men as a group to accrue more social resources at the expense of women as a group. While in its narrowest definition patriarchy means 'rule by the father' within the family and the consequent subordination of both his wife and children, a broader concept of patriarchy characterizes a society dominated by men, both within the family and outside it. Patriarchy has assumed various forms throughout history and has existed in most though not all **societies**.

Many patriarchal formations have been and still are fundamentally rooted in **kinship** alliances ruled by fathers (Lerner 1987). Some historians have argued that eighteenth-century Western society saw the transition from father-based patriarchy to regimes in which fraternal rather than patriarchal relations dominate. Such an understanding of patriarchy attempts to take into account changing formations of patriarchy and to rethink how patriarchal **power** works in a **post-industrial society** (McCannell 1991). In **industrialized** countries, family-based patriarchy has been unevenly and gradually displaced by bourgeois and postmodern forms of patriarchy. In **bourgeois** patriarchy, kinship alliances are subordinate to a social organization split between a wage **economy** and unpaid domestic production, both of which are regulated by ideologies of race, gender, and sexuality. In advanced **capitalist** countries, **postmodern** patriarchy has recently emerged as the prevailing form, characterized by the hyper-**development** of consumption and the joint wage earner family, the relative transfer of power from husbands to professional men and women, the rise of the single mother and other 'alternative' households, and sexualized **consumption** patterns.

Patriarchal formations are unevenly developed. One form of patriarchy may dominate in a particular society, but it often co-exists with other contesting or residual forms. Patriarchal relations are also differential. This means that women as a group are positioned the same in relation to men, but they are positioned differently in relation to each other and at times in relation to some men. For example, some women have access to resources – they may be in the owning class or in the **middle class** sector of the **working class**; they may own a home and a car, have a cleaning lady and are able to purchase a lot of **commodities** – all of which are only possible because of the labor of other women and men. Because patriarchy functions in concert with a system of white supremacy, disproportionate numbers of people of color have occupied the most exploited, under-resourced social positions. That more women than men fill the ranks of the hyper-exploited speaks loudly to the ways patriarchal structures shore up **class** relations. However, white women and women of color are differently positioned in relation to each other; white women can claim power over black women and men of color by virtue of their **race**. But even women who benefit from their class positions are disadvantaged in some areas of their lives in a society that systematically accords men power over women. The persistence of rape and domestic violence against women across class sectors are two examples. Rather than invoke a homogeneous 'patriarchy,' recent feminist research attempts to address these differential relations.

In positing male and female as distinct and opposite sexes that are naturally attracted to each other, heterosexuality is integral to patri-archy. Women's position as subordinate other, as sexual property, and as exploited laborer depends on this heterosexual matrix. As a pervasive institution within other institu-tions (**state**, **education**, **church**, the **media**), heterosexuality helps guarantee patriarchal regulation of women's bodies, labor, and desires (Wittig 1992).

While many feminists still find patriarchy a useful term for conceptualizing a system of male dominance over resources and ideas, there has been much debate over the con-cept's limitations and uses. Some have cri-tiqued the concept of patriarchy for the ways it over-generalizes the historically variable hierarchically structured relations between men and women. Some **feminists** have substituted the concept of **phallocentrism** for patriarchy in order to highlight the lin-guistic dimensions of a male dominant social order (Irigaray 1974). Phallocentrism refers to a symbolic discursive system, the meanings through which power circulates. Another set of debates involves the relationship of patriarchy to other social systems. Some socialist feminists have argued that there are two interlocking and mutually dependent systems of oppression – patriarchy and **capitalism** – and have called for a theory that would adequately address their intersec-tion. Critics of this dual systems approach contend that domestic labor is not really so separate from capitalist **production** but rather a necessary though invisible component of it. Women's labor of caring for children, elders, husbands, the labor of preparing food and other basic necessities is not wage work, but it is socially necessary for capitalist production in the sense that it enables those who are working for wages to return to work the next day. From this vantage point, any explanation of women's place in capitalist class relations needs to begin not with the presumption that there are two systems of oppression but rather with the ways capitalism uses patriarchal structures that preceded and developed alongside it (German 1989).

In certain parts of the developing world, patriarchy is still primarily rooted in kinship relations. The trajectories of patriarchy and capitalist development have not been linear, but have had different impacts on various groups and social sectors. In spite of the improvements in the social and economic position of women that capitalist 'develop-ment' has brought, the persistence of patri-archal structures has been a major influence on the possibilities for women's full parti-cipation in the modernizing process. Some of the questions raised in research on patri-archy and 'development' have addressed the integrated relations between patriarchal for-mations in the colonies and the metropolitan areas of empire (Mies 1986), have considered whether the patriarchal structures of colo-nized societies reproduce existing **inequalities** and result in further deterioration in the social position of women, and evaluated whether the social struggles and the insti-tutional changes in the achievement of national independence moderate, exacerbate, or eliminate certain traditional characteristics of the societies influencing **gender** relations (Moghadam 1996).

References and further reading

Bartky, S. L. (1991) *Femininity and Domination: Studies in the Phenomenology of Oppression.* New York: Routledge.

Carby, H. (1987) *Reconstructing Womanhood: The Emergence of the African American Woman Novelist.* New York: Oxford University Press.

Ferguson, A. (1989) *Blood at the Root: Motherhood, Sexuality, and Male Dominance.* London: Pan-dora.

German, L. (1989) *Sex, Class and Socialism.* London: Bookmarks.

Hennessy, R. and Ingraham, C. (1997) *Materi-alist Feminism: Class, Difference and Women's Lives.* London: Routledge.

Irigaray, L. (1974) *This Sex Which is Not One.* Trans. C. Porter with C. Burke. Ithaca, NY: Cornell University Press.

Lerner, G. (1987) *The Creation of Patriarchy.* London: Oxford University Press.

McCannell, J. F. (1991) *The Regime of the Brother after the Patriarchy.* New York: Routledge.

Mies, M. (1986) *Patriarchy and Accumulation on a World Scale: Women and the International Division of Labor*. London: Zed.

Moghadam, V. (1996) *Patriarchy and Economic Development: Women's Positions at the End of the Twentieth Century*. Oxford: Clarendon.

Walby, S. (1990) *Theorizing Patriarchy*. London: Oxford.

Wittig, M. (1992) *The Straight Mind and Other Essays*. Boston: Beacon.

ROSEMARY HENNESSY

PEACE

The nineteenth-century English lawyer Sir Henry Maine wrote, '**War** appears to be as old as mankind, but peace is a modern invention.' Peace as a concept may not be a modern invention but what we mean by peace now is vastly changed from what it might have meant a hundred or so years ago. In general usage, peace is understood to mean a state of tranquillity. Linked to the notion is the idea of obtaining peace of mind, denoting a degree of mental calm or serenity. To be at peace with oneself and with the world is not only to refrain from violent action, but to cast off all semblance of anger or anxiety. According to Spinoza: 'Peace is not the absence of war; it is a virtue, a state of mind, a disposition for benevolence, confidence, and justice.'

In modern international relations theory, the first and probably least contentious interpretation of the concept refers to the absence of war or **violence**: 'Peace is an armistice in a war that is continuously going on', wrote Thucydides. This is often referred to as *negative peace*, a term coined by the Norwegian scholar, Johan Galtung. It can be expanded to mean not only the cessation of hostilities, but also a period when war is neither imminent nor actually being fought. Peace in this negative sense may be regarded as a 'construct'. According to Michael Howard (2001), war starts in the minds of men, but so does peace. At the other end of the scale is the notion of 'positive peace' – a state of harmonious relations between peoples. The attainment of this kind of positive peace requires the attainment of certain normative goals, such as the existence of peaceful social and cultural beliefs and norms, a commitment to non-violence, the presence of justice at all levels (economic, social, and political), and a democratic political system.

The last requirement is particularly contentious and implies the imposition of **democracy** as an element in *peace-building*. It is linked to the notion of a democratic peace – the theory that democratic states or republics are more peaceful in their external relations and are less inclined to go to war with one another. Modern democratic peace theory is often associated with Immanuel **Kant**'s conception of 'perpetual peace', wherein a league of republican states would find no cause for war since their interests and societies closely resembled one another. Yet Kant acknowledged the difficulty of establishing such a peace: 'With men, the state of nature is not a state of peace, but war.'

Twentieth-century proponents of democratic peace theory include Karl Deutsch, writing in the 1950s, who put forward the idea of 'security communities' – groups of states (such as Western **Europe**) in which there is little likelihood that states will resort to violence and a concrete commitment to settle disputes by negotiation. the idea was revived in the mid-1980s by the **American** political scientist, Michael Doyle, and became a major theme of academic and public debate on the nature of the post-Cold War international order. One of the most notorious proponents was the former US government official Francis Fukuyama, who proclaimed in the summer of 1989 that world society had reached the 'End of History'. Fukuyama's thesis was that the end of the Cold War division marked a huge victory for both capitalism and democracy, heralding the beginning of a new phase in which **liberal** economic values would prevail. However, critics have questioned the reliability of the statistical evidence for democratic peace, especially in the pre-1945 period and point to alternative explanations for regional clusters of peaceful states, or security communities, in Europe and the Americas. In addition, evidence suggests that while established democracies may be peaceful, democratizing states, especially in unstable regions, may be more prone to conflict than **authoritarian** regimes.

Support for the idea of positive peace entails that cessation of hostilities can only be the first step towards peace. Aristotle wrote, 'It is more difficult to organize a peace than to win a war; but the fruits of victory will be lost if the peace is not organized.' What happens in the aftermath of conflict is key to determining whether it results in merely a temporary cessation of hostilities or a lasting – positive – peace. According to Vasquez, 'certain types of peace have been fairly successful in avoiding a repeat of the war, while others have actually promoted a war's recurrence.' More recently, scholars have focused on the 'critical juncture' in the transition between war and peace when the foundations for lasting peace might be laid (Colson 2000). As well as the emphasis on democracy, much has been made of the importance of justice in this process, and the developments that have led to the establishment of international tribunals or courts and a permanent international criminal court are directly linked to the recognition of the synthesis between peace and justice.

One ancient view has been that in order to enjoy positive peace, it may be necessary to sacrifice negative peace. On this view, war may be necessary in order to create a society in which positive peace is established (Wazer 2000). Standing in opposition to this thinking is pacifism, which rests on the belief that war and violence are morally unjustified and that all disputes should be settled by peaceful means. Closely linked is the notion of passive or non-violent resistance pioneered by Mahatma Gandhi in his campaign against the British government in India in the 1930s and 1940s. The power of passive resistance rests on its moral force. It was unsuccessful in Czechoslovakia in 1968, but enjoyed greater success in the American civil rights movement of the late 1950s and early 1960s, culminating in the Civil Rights Act of 1964.

References and further reading

Ceadel, M. (1987) *Thinking about Peace and War*. Oxford: Oxford University Press.

Colson, A. J. (2000) 'The Logic of Peace and the Logic of Justice', *International Relations*, 15(1): 51–62.

Gallie, W. B. (1987) *Philosophers of Peace and War*. Cambridge: Cambridge University Press.

Howard, M. (2001) *The Invention of Peace and the Reinvention of War*. London: Profile Books.

Nardin, T. (ed.) (1996) *The Ethics of War and Peace*. Princeton, NJ: Princeton University Press.

Walzer, M. (2000) *Just and Unjust Wars*, 3rd edn. London: Penguin.

RACHEL KERR

PEASANTRY

In historical accounts, peasantry is used to refer to the majority population residing in villages and mostly working in agriculture in pre-industrial **Europe**, but also in China, India and other continents. Today the term is often similarly used to refer to the majority population in developing countries, in Africa, Asia and Latin America. The latter use carries an implicit connotation that the rural majority in the contemporary world is a counterpart to the majority in the pre-industrial **civilization**. This connotation is problematic since it implies a misleading **modernization** or evolutionary perspective. It is important to note that the words 'peasantry' and 'peasant' carry condescending connotations. This notwithstanding, social theorists such as A. V. Chayanov, E. R. Wolf and T. Shanin have made important contributions in defining peasantry as a theoretical term.

423

The Russian agricultural economist A. V. Chayanov (1986) played an important role in the debate about the agrarian question in Russia both before and after the revolution (see **feudalism**). Throughout this period he engaged in a more or less outspoken polemic with Lenin and his theories about the development of **capitalism** in agriculture ([1899] 1960). Since then, the debate about rural and agricultural development in rural sociology, history, anthropology and other fields and disciplines, has largely been in dialogue with Chayanov.

Lenin's views on the peasantry were a typical product of late nineteenth-century **evolutionary theory**. Lenin leaned heavily on **Marx**, and the latter shared the evolutionism of his contemporaries, which implied that the peasantry was a relic of earlier social forms, bound to disappear or to transform itself in the course of capitalist **development**. Similarly, from a **Weberian** and **Durkheimian** perspective, peasants were part of traditional societies and village communities.

With neo-evolutionism in anthropology, peasantry studies received an important impetus from E. R. Wolf (1966). Wolf's work defined peasants as surplus producers in a broadly Marxist sense, viewing the peasantry as subordinated to lords, living from the surplus. Wolf postulated an evolutionary line from peasants to farmers, seen as motivated by profit and oriented towards the **market** rather than towards subsistence and towards the village **community**.

Chayanov's contribution has been reformulated by several writers, some of them influenced by Marxist theory and some by the early neo-classical tradition in economics. Shanin (1988), in his definition of a 'peasant society', stressed both the Weberian element of **tradition** and the Marxian focus on surplus appropriation by lords. Djurfeldt (1996) has suggested that Chayanov's insight is fruitfully formulated in terms of the conditions of reproduction of peasant households. Due to their reliance on family **labour**, the conditions of reproduction of peasant farms are different from those of capitalist firms, mainly because labour costs are not accounted for as a cost (see **family and household**). This again accounts for the resilience of peasant reproduction and more generally for family labour farms. A reproduction perspective implies not the disappearance of a historical relic but the resilience of family-based economic **organization**, in competition with economic organizations based on hired labour.

The concept of peasantry seems to be losing its centrality in contemporary development studies, although it remains important in historical enquiry. In line with the Chayanovian tradition, the focus on family labour remains in the sociological study of agriculture (see Gasson and Errington 1993; Goodman and Redclift 1991). While in development studies, concepts such as smallholders and small farmers seem to be gaining currency over peasants, Chayanov continues to influence authors such as Netting (1993) in his focus on small family labour farms, in the context of American populism, and can also be found in the work of Schultz (1983) and in other current studies of agricultural and rural **development**.

At the same time, the modernist theme of the disappearing peasantry has retained its resonance in the work of Bryceson, who uses the terms *de-agrarianization* and de-peasantization to describe what appears to be a global trend in the subsistence strategies of poor people in developing countries (Bryceson and Jamal 1997). Similarly, in the West, the modernist theme of a disappearing family farm sector continues to be central to social research. Many contemporary family farms in developed countries are best understood as forms of business organizations (see e.g. Barlett 1993).

References and further reading

Barlett, P. F. (1993) *American Dreams: Rural Realities*. Chapel Hill, NC: University of North Carolina Press.

Bryceson, D. F. and Jamal, V. (eds) (1997) *Farewell to Farms*. Aldershot: Ashgate.

Chayanov, A. V. ([1966] 1986) *On the Theory of Peasant Economy*. Madison, WI: University of Wisconsin Press.

Djurfeldt, G. (1996) 'Defining and Operationalising Family Farming from a Sociological Perspective', *Sociologia Ruralis*, 36 (3): 340–51.

Gasson, R. and Errington, A. (1993) *The Farm Family Business*. London: CABI.

Goodman, M. and Redclift, M. (1991) *Refashioning Nature*. London: Routledge.

Lenin, V. I. ([1899] 1964) *The Development of Capitalism in Russia*. Moscow: Progress Publishers.

Netting, R. M. (1993) *Smallholders, Householders*. Stanford, CA: Stanford University Press.

Schultz, T. W. ([1964] 1983) *Transforming Traditional Agriculture*. Chicago: University of Chicago Press.

Shanin, T. (1988) 'Introduction: Peasantry as a Concept', in T. Shanin (ed.) *Peasants and Peasant Societies*. Oxford: Blackwell.

Wolf, E. R. (1966) *Peasants*. Englewood Cliffs, NJ: Prentice Hall.

GÖRAN DJURFELDT

PERFORMATIVE

In *Gender Trouble* (1990), Judith **Butler** sees **gender** as a performance. Gender is not a social fact but an accomplishment – it is not what you are, but what you do. She calls for women to resist stable and pre-given gender identities and to invent new ones, thereby challenging **essentialism**. Following **Foucault**, she theoretically disturbs the presumed links between sex, gender and desire – separating gender and **sexuality** from women's reproductive capacities, seeing gender and desire as free floating rather than determined by women's social roles. She prefers the term performativity to performance, for the latter assumes a stable, rational humanist **self**. She is critical of second-wave feminism for normalizing gender binaries (male/female) and installing heterosexuality as compulsory. To subvert restrictive **binary** identities, she calls for queer performance – ways of troubling the normal and freeing us from the dominant heterosexual norms. In this move she became one of the forerunners of **queer theory**. Wary of the charge of **voluntarism** (that you choose your gender or sex as you choose your clothes), Butler revisited the category of sexed body and the problem of materiality in *Bodies that Matter* (1993). One is not radically free to re-invent oneself, rather, one must take up the processes that have been materialized on the body. In *Excitable Speech* (1997) (a Derridean re-writing of Austin), she explores the racist practices in **America** – how speech acts construct 'identity' and bring into being that which is being named – how speech can be injurious. Performance has been taken up as a transgressive strategy in critical **race**, queer and gender politics.

References and further reading

Butler, J. (1990) *Gender Trouble: Feminism and the Subversion of Identity*. London: Routledge.

Butler, J. (1993) *Bodies that Matter: On the Discursive Limits of 'Sex'*. London: Routledge.

Butler, J. (1997) *Excitable Speech: A Politics of the Performative*. London: Routledge.

ELAINE STAVRO

PERSON AND PERSONALITY

'Persons' are organic embodied individuals, centres of consciousness, morally responsible for their **actions** and protected against the actions of others. 'Personality' refers to the totality of social and psychological characteristics of a person.

For more than three centuries, the dualism of Descartes ([1641] 1984) dominated discussions of personhood. His argument depended on two moves: first, the division of personal attributes into two groups, the bodily attributes having their roots in the material property of extension, the mental having no material attributes. The second move was to argue that each group required an appropriate substance in which to inhere. The **body** was a divisible material substance, and the mind an indivisible immaterial substance, identical with the soul of traditional **Christian** belief. Resistance to the Cartesian account of persons came from **materialists**, such as La Mettrie ([1749] 1960), who held that the mental aspects of persons were caused by their material attributes. Resistance also came from **idealists**, who held that the universe was essentially mental in character, denying the independent existence of matter. In recent years, there has been a vigorous attempt to materialize the mind as an emergent property of the brain, the most complex thing we know of (Searle 2002). Reductionists have tried to show that the language of neuroscience can systematically replace the language of mentality; 'brain state' replaces 'belief' (Churchland, 1984).

John Locke's ([1690] 1974) treatment of the problem of personal identity remains the starting point for contemporary discussions of the issue. He distinguished between the criteria for being the same man or woman, and criteria for being the same **self**. The former were rooted in bodily **identity**, and the latter in the reach of conscious awareness. However, if this self is a unity, how is it revealed to the person? Hume ([1739] 1975) pointed out that the self was never given as something of which a person could be aware, since the being that was aware was that very self. **Kant** ([1787] 1996), using his powerful conception of the transcendental condition for something to be possible, argued that the unity of self was a condition for the nature of our experience (see **subject and subjectivity**). The person, he thought, had a place in the realm of causes, and a place in the realm of reasons. There was a noumenal self, free to choose, though every aspect of our lives of which we could be aware displayed causality. In this way persons were free agents and subject to the demands of **morality**.

There are three main forms in which the natures of individuals are displayed in public interactions: (1) personality, one's social attributes; (2) character, one's moral attributes; and (3) temperament, involving attributes that seem to have a biological basis. Traditionally four personality types were recognized, the choleric, the phlegmatic, the melancholic, and the sanguine (Allport 1961).

Attempts were made in the twentieth century to substitute a more 'scientifically' based catalogue of personality types for the traditional four. This began with the idea of a personality trait or disposition to behave in certain ways in well-defined situations. (Eysenck 1952). Did individuals have stable and consistent traits? Were there stable and persistent traits that characterized every human being in different degrees? Both questions have been disputed. Idiographic studies of individuals tend to show wide variations in responses to situations, with some stabilities. Efforts to answer the second question have been hampered by unsatisfactory methodology, using factor analysis of answers to questionnaires to identify 'source traits', which seem to have little psychological plausibility (Cattell 1965). The method emphasizes what people say about personality rather than how they behave. Despite the criticisms to which this approach has been subjected, it continues to be practised, offering a five-fold set of source traits. Some of the terminology of trait theory has entered everyday speech. Many people talk about 'extroverts' and 'introverts'.

An alternative approach, based on extensive observations of people in real settings, is to see personality displays in terms of a repertoire of ways of behaving with others, based on a dramaturgical metaphor (Goffman 1959). This opens up the possibility of people deliberately managing their self-presentations, as well as being trained to present personalities that are more acceptable (see **Goffman** and **dramaturgical school**).

The relation between temperament and personality is unsettled, though there has been a tendency to ascribe temperamental differences to genetic endowment (Wilson 1978). Ties between neuro-physiological structures and personality traits have also been suggested, though the research has been inconclusive.

References and further reading

Allport, G. W. (1961) *Pattern and Growth in Personality*. New York: Holt, Rinehart and Winston.

Cattell, R. B. (1965) *The Scientific Analysis of Personality*. Harmondsworth: Penguin.

Churchland, P. M. (1984) *Matter and Consciousness*. Cambridge, MA: MIT Press.

Descartes, R. ([1641] 1984) 'Meditations on the First Philosophy', in *The Philosophical Writings of Descartes*, vol. 2. Cambridge: Cambridge University Press.

Eysenck, H. (1952) *The Scientific Study of Personality*. London: Routledge & Kegan Paul.

Goffman, E. (1959) *The Presentation of Self in Everyday Life*. Garden City, NY: Anchor.

Hume, D. ([1739] 1975) *A Treatise of Human Nature*. London: Collins.

Kant, I. ([1787] 1996) *Critique of Pure Reason*. Indianapolis, IN: Hackett.

La Mettrie, J. O. ([1749] 1960) *L'Homme machine*. Princeton, NJ: Princeton University Press.

Locke, J. ([1690] 1974) *An Essay Concerning Human Understanding*. London: Dent.

Searle, J. R. (2002) *Consciousness and Language*. Cambridge: Cambridge University Press.

Wilson, E. O. (1978) *On Human Nature*. Cambridge, MA: Harvard University Press.

ROM HARRÉ

PETTY BOURGEOISIE

See: bourgeoisie, middle class

PHALLOCENTRISM

Phallocentrism refers to the privileged position in western culture of the **symbol** of the phallus. Psychoanalyst Jacques **Lacan** ([1966] 1977) argued that the phallus is the signifier that transcends all others and therefore provides the basis around which all cultural **meanings** are **valued**. Men, by virtue of their anatomical possession of a penis, are considered closer to phallic power; women are regarded as 'castrated' because they lack the organ that stands in for the phallus. However, while possessing a penis may grant men certain advantages in a phallocentric world, it cannot guarantee their absolute appropriation of the power of the phallus. Thus, normative masculine subjectivity requires various rivalries between men (enacted through, for example, competitive sport) in order to acquire the closest approximation to phallic power (Buchbinder 1998).

Feminist theory has played a crucial role in contesting phallocentric culture and those social theories that prioritize the phallus. In particular, it has challenged the notion that power and authority are determined according to one's position with respect to the phallus. Some of the most rigorous critique has come from the French feminists, through their interrogation of **psychoanalytic** assumptions pertaining to the influence of the phallus in language and modes of desire (Cixous 1976; Irigaray [1977] 1985; Kristeva [1977] 1980). Feminist theory has also produced alternative symbolism to oppose the negative portrayals of women's bodies and female sexuality prevalent in phallocentric **discourse**.

References and further reading

Buchbinder, D. (1998) *Performance Anxieties*. St Leonards, NSW: Allen & Unwin.

Cixous, H. (1976) 'The Laugh of the Medusa', *Signs*, 1(4): 875–93.

Irigaray, L. ([1977] 1985) *This Sex Which is Not One*. Ithaca, NY: Cornell University Press.

Kristeva, J. ([1977] 1980) *Desire in Language*. New York: Columbia University Press.

Lacan, J. ([1966] 1977) *Écrits*. London: Routledge.

ANNIE POTTS

PHENOMENOLOGY

Phenomenology is a current of philosophical thought stemming from the work of

427

Edmund Husserl (1859–1938). Like many philosophical founders, Husserl formulated and reformulated his project at various points in his life, drawing out different applications and implications. From the point of view of social theory, it is his later formulations, where he began to consider questions of history, **embodiment**, habit, intersubjectivity and what he called 'the **lifeworld**', that are most significant. This later work is regarded by many to have heralded a shift towards a more social or existential form of phenomenology. Certainly it is the later portion of Husserl's *œuvre* which most inspired the existentialist phenomenologists, the best known of whom include Martin **Heidegger**, Jean-Paul **Sartre** and Maurice **Merleau-Ponty**. And it is this portion of Husserl's work which inspired the more sociological applications of Alfred **Schutz**.

In its Husserlian form, phenomenology takes as its point of departure the evidence of consciousness. Whatever else philosophy might throw into doubt, it cannot lead the ego to doubt its own existence as a conscious being. 'I think, therefore I am', as Descartes famously put it. Consciousness in this sense provides an indubitable ground from which philosophical activity can proceed. For some philosophers, notably Descartes, the task of philosophy is to build upon this certainty of consciousness to establish the certain existence of a world beyond consciousness. Husserl disagrees, however. According to Husserl, one can only be conscious of the contents of consciousness. It is logically impossible to be conscious of what lies beyond consciousness. The task of philosophy is therefore not to go beyond consciousness, to the 'external world', but rather to explore consciousness itself. This, however, is not to say that Husserl's philosophy doubts the existence of the external world. For Husserl, it would only make sense to doubt the existence of a world external to consciousness if there was some way in which we could determine

the matter one way or another. But we cannot. Thus, Husserl concludes that phenomenology should bracket out questions of the existence (or not) of the external world, focusing instead upon consciousness of the world and of **objects** within the world. This bracketing is referred to as 'phenomenological reduction' or *epokhé*.

According to Husserl, consciousness is always consciousness *of* something. Husserl refers to this directedness of consciousness as 'intentionality'. Consciousness has an intentional **structure**. It 'intends' objects in the respect that it is conscious-of them. Phenomenology is an exploration of the different ways in which objects are intended in consciousness. Yet the relationship between the object and the **subject** of consciousness is not one of simple **representation** of objects. In a similar fashion to **Kant**, Husserl shows how consciousness of objects involves active synthetic activity on the part of the ego, such that the object can be said to be 'constituted' in consciousness. When we listen to music, for example, we hear a sequence of notes as a sequence. Each note modifies the **meaning** or effect of all of the others. This temporal structure cannot derive solely from the sensory data themselves. Rather, it is imposed, or a temporal synthesis is effected, by consciousness. We do not normally notice this constitutive activity. In our 'natural attitude' we experience the world constituted by us as a world wholly independent of us; a world with a 'pre-given' structure. Phenomenology unpicks the natural attitude and explores this constitutive activity.

Husserl is at pains to argue that this type of analysis is not psychology but philosophy. His reasoning turns on the claim that phenomenology is not interested in empirical facts about the mind, as psychology is, but rather seeks to explore the grounds upon which we come to know and distinguish facts and an empirical world in the first place. Moreover, in place of the empirical mind, about which testable and probabilistic claims to truth can be made, phenomenology deduces backwards from the certain truths of consciousness to what must be the necessary foundation of these certain truths. It thus deals with the 'transcendental' rather than the 'empirical' ego.

Much of Husserl's early work has a disembodied and ahistorical feel to it. In his later work, however, he began to reflect on the embodied and socially situated nature of consciousness. These themes were taken up by Heidegger, Sartre and Merleau-Ponty, among others. For these writers, the latter two of whom seek a realignment with psychology and the social sciences, the concept of intentionality is considerably broadened and the purpose of the *epokhé* redefined. According to Merleau-Ponty, the purpose of these phenomenological operations is to allow us to explore the nature of our multiple connections to and inherence within the world, our being-in-the-world, in Heidegger's phrase. Moreover, this connectedness is not simply a matter of what we know consciously and reflectively, but of what we imagine, feel and 'grasp' practically through pre-reflective bodily habits and skills.

This theme of habit (or **habitus**) is also evident in Husserl's later work. Here he argues that useful ways of perceiving and acting in the world take root within and structure the ego. This theme is taken up by both Merleau-Ponty and Schutz, the latter of whom popularized it under the rubric of the '**typifications**' and 'recipe knowledge' which structure **action**, combining this idea with Max **Weber**'s theory of social action (see **type and typification**). Weber recognizes that the world is meaningful for social agents, Schutz argues, but fails to investigate the constitutive acts of consciousness through which that meaning is bestowed. Moreover, he takes the 'facticity' of the world for granted, remaining in the 'natural attitude'. Phenomenology for Schutz allows us to take Weber's project to its proper conclusion, exploring the acts of

consciousness which constitute the world as we experience it. And it thereby enables us to investigate rather than rely upon the natural attitude.

Throughout his work Husserl also focused upon the nature of **language** and its role. This concern found later expression both in **hermeneutics** (largely via Heidegger) and in **Derrida**'s **deconstruction**.

References and further reading

Heidegger, M. ([1927–75] 1982) *The Basic Problems of Phenomenology*. Bloomington, IN: Indiana University Press.
Husserl, E. ([1900–1] 2001) *Logical Investigations*, vols 1, 2. London: Routledge.
Husserl, E. ([1912] 1980) *Ideas Pertaining to a Pure Phenomenology and to a Phenomenological Philosophy*. The Hague: Nijhoff.
Merleau-Ponty, M. ([1945] 1996) *Phenomenology of Perception*. London: Routledge.
Moran, D. (2000) *Introduction to Phenomenology*. London: Routledge.
Smith, B. and Smith, D. W. (eds) (1995) *The Cambridge Companion to Husserl*. Cambridge: Cambridge University Press.
Sokolowski, R. (2000) *Introduction to Phenomenology*. Cambridge: Cambridge University Press.
Spiegelberg, H. (1960) *The Phenomenological Movement*. The Hague: Nijhoff.

NICK CROSSLEY

PHILOSOPHY OF SOCIAL SCIENCE

The philosophy of social science attempts to unify and validate the diverse enterprises and activities that come under the name 'social science'. While philosophers since Aristotle have talked about the nature of social arrangements and its norms and conventions, for there to be philosophy of social science, there must first be social sciences, and these are a relatively recent modern invention. For some, this means that it is a subdiscipline of the philosophy of **science**; for others, the social sciences have their own distinctive problems, standards and **epistemology**. While empiricists and positivists have emphasized prediction and control and other goals continuous with the natural sciences, others see them as human sciences with moral and political ends. The diversity of answers to such philosophical questions reflects the great methodological, theoretical and disciplinary diversity within the social sciences themselves.

The philosophy of social sciences can be thought of as having several distinctive stages that may be distinguished not only historically but also by the distinct questions that predominated within them. Beginning in the mid to late nineteenth century, its first phase was marked by debates about the scientific status of the social sciences and their methodology. Here the main lines of debate formed around the **neo-Kantian** distinction between the object domains of two types of science: between the *Geistes-* and the *Naturwissenschaften*, each with their distinctive methodologies of explanation and understanding. This phase culminates in a synthetic approach offered by Max **Weber**, who held that the social sciences combine both in a still distinctive form of 'explanatory understanding', typical of **historical sociology** (Weber 1949). At the same time, Weber also saw that the social sciences were internally diverse, with distinctive methodological problems and approaches and practical 'vocations' (see **explanation** and **Verstehen**).

The re-emergence of **positivism** in the twentieth century marked the next phase of the debate. While the Vienna Circle positivists actually had a fundamentally practical understanding of the social sciences (as articulated by Neurath), the next phase of the debate engaged their immediate successors and centered on the highly formal 'covering law' model of explanation proposed by Carl Hempel in the 1930s. While the **'laws'** that he offered sparked much debate and alternatives such as **Popper**'s falsification criterion, a strong countermovement began with *The Idea of a Social Science* (1958), in which Peter Winch denied both the very

idea of causal laws and the assumption of an invariant conception of **rationality**. Winch's arguments sparked a long debate about rationality and **relativism** (Winch 1970), in which interpretive ethnography became the primary point of reference. At the same time, similar debates began in continental philosophy between hermeneutical approaches and **critical theory**, in which **Habermas** in particular argued that unavoidable interpretive access to the social domain does not undermine the possibility of normative criticism (see **hermeneutics**). Similar to Weber, Habermas argued for a methodological pluralism, in which the intertwining of pluralist methods and perspectives gave the social scientist critical purchase on social and historical reality (Habermas 1988).

The final and most recent phase marks a return to fundamental issues of **ontology** and takes up issues spurred at the end of the rationality and relativism controversy: issues related to normativity, in general, and the normativity of reasons, in particular. This phase is engendered by the increasing predominance of two fundamentally naturalistic approaches to the social sciences: the potential universal applicability of **rational choice** and **game theory**, on the one hand, and Darwinian **evolutionary theory**, on the other. In the first case, rationality loses its normative character and becomes simply a ubiquitous assumption in light of which social scientists can explicate any social **action** as rational. Even if some phenomena can be explained in this way, the critics of such a **methodology** argue that its conception of rationality is too thin to understand social norms. Similarly, many argue that the explanatory reduction of social life to natural selection cannot easily explain norms and rules. The social sciences now have become the focus of debates about whether or not norms, including scientific norms, can be naturalized; if not, then the alternative is that norms must be taken to be primitives. Or, as Brandom (1994) puts it, in the social world it is 'norms all the way down', so that the requisite **knowledge** is practical, available from the point of view of the competent participant in practices.

While this possible periodization tracks shifts in the focus of debate, underlying themes remain in each. The first phase sought to distinguish various sorts of sciences by ontological domains and methodologies, only to see that actual social science often cuts across them; the second phase sought to unify science in causal explanations, only to see such a program shatter into explanatory **pluralism**; and spurred by discussions of assumptions about rationality in intentional explanation, the third phase considers the status of social norms in the face of various unifying naturalistic theories. Nonetheless, questions of explanation, rationality, and normativity can be found throughout, transforming the distinction of the human and natural sciences into issues of methodological, explanatory and theoretical unification and pluralism.

When confronted with the **tradition** of methodological dualism inherited from the nineteenth century, one response was to seek a general methodology based on an account of explanation that could unify diverse sciences. When the reconstructions of Hempel's deductive–nomological model only produced trivial laws, philosophers turned against such formal models and began to reconstruct the actual explanations used in the social sciences. Debates about explanation then splintered into various fields, from sociology to economics, leading to the broad *de facto* acceptance of what might be called 'explanatory pluralism'. Instead of laws, Jon Elster (1989) and others sought particular 'mechanisms', or social processes sufficient to bring about some event or state of affairs, such as the presence or absence of social **cooperation**, whether that be individualist or functionalist in form. If explanation is a retail and not wholesale affair, then we cannot expect one type or another to cover the whole social domain.

One advantage of the formal covering law model was that it was agnostic about the fundamental terms, so that laws could refer to intentional terms by making rationality the explanation of an action or event. Winch challenged all causal strategies of this sort (including Weber's) by showing that terms involved in **agency** or rationality could only be understood in terms of the rules of practices that are constitutive of specific 'forms of life'. The way around this objection is to show that some rules are indeed universal, and this gave rise to debates focused on anthropological examples of odd and seemingly irrational practices such as Azande witchcraft that must be instead seen from the agents' point of view. At least in philosophical circles, these debates about relativism lost their momentum after David Davidson's transcendental argument that we can understand others only if they have the same largely true and trivial beliefs as the interpreter (Davidson 1980). At a more general level, Habermas turned relativism on its head by arguing that interpretation necessarily involves evaluation, the assessment of the reasons that others offer as reasons from the interpreters' point of view in order to yield understanding.

Along with rational choice theory, explanation of social phenomena such as cooperation in evolutionary biological or rational choice terms marks the reemergence of a new and comprehensive form of naturalism. Against such reductive forms of **naturalism**, defenders of normativity no longer appeal with Winch to explicit rules, but rather to necessary but implicit practical knowledge possessed by competent participants in social practices. Far from being the source of relativism, such norms make it possible that discursive practices produce both objectivity and shared conceptual contents. A middle ground might be found in the explanatory pluralism of Weber and critical theory that permits a return to what **Marx** calls an 'active naturalism', with its emphasis on human creative powers and capacities. Practical social science could be thought of as promoting practical knowledge, the capacity of knowledgeable actors to shape institutions and practices. In joining social facts and norms non-reductively, such a critical social science once again may take up the **Enlightenment** task of realizing ideals and norms within the factual constraints of large-scale, modern societies.

References and further reading

Bohman, J. (1991) *New Philosophy of Social Science*. Cambridge, MA: MIT Press.

Brandom, R. (1994) *Making It Explicit*. Cambridge, MA: Harvard University Press.

Davidson, D. (1980) *Essays on Action and Events*. Oxford: Oxford University Press.

Elster, J. (1989) *Nuts and Bolts for the Social Sciences*. Cambridge: Cambridge University Press.

Habermas, J. (1988) *Logic of the Social Sciences*. Cambridge, MA: MIT Press.

Hempel, C. (1965) *Aspects of Scientific Explanation*. New York: Free Press.

Hollis, M. and Lukes, S. (eds) (1982) *Rationality and Relativism*. London: Blackwell.

Pettit, P. (1993) *The Common Mind*. Oxford: Oxford University Press.

Turner, S. and Roth, P. (eds) (2003) *The Blackwell Guide to the Philosophy of the Social Sciences*. London: Blackwell.

Weber, M. (1949) *The Methodology of the Social Sciences*. New York: Free Press.

Winch, P. (1958) *The Idea of a Social Science*. London: Routledge.

— (1970) 'Understanding a Primitive Society', in B. O. Wilson (ed.), *Rationality*. Oxford: Blackwell.

JAMES BOHMAN

PIAGET, JEAN (1886–1980)
Swiss psychologist

From his beginnings as a naturalist, biologist and philosopher of science until his late works, Piaget always considered the scientific and psychological study of human development as part of a wider philosophical and anthropological project. Central to this project was Piaget's '**genetic epistemology**', an empirically based theory of children's cog-

nitive development systematized over the course of about fifty books. He sought not only to redefine the child as an active, intelligent, and creative subject of his or her own development, but also to resolve many traditional problems of both philosophical **empiricism** and **rationalism**. Drawing on models from **evolutionary theory**, **structuralism**, logic, **Kantian** epistemology and moral philosophy, and influenced by Protestant individualism and the anti-authoritarian Rousseauian spirit of his native *Suisse Romande*, Piaget intended his work to create both a new developmental psychology of the logico-mathematical mind, and a **constructivist** experimental philosophy of cognitive development and **education** that revolved around the idea of individual **agency**. Although he did not entirely ignore social issues, many socioculturally oriented psychologists following among others Vygotsky – have criticized his egocentric perspective of the child as a solo learner who develops exclusively according to universal biological and cognitive laws and principles in a world without **language**, **emotion**, and any other cultural and historical constraints, such as **politics**, **economy**, **race**, and **gender**.

Major works

([1936] 1952) *The Origins of Intelligence in Children*. New York: International Universities.

([1950] 1954) *The Child's Construction of Reality*. London: Routledge.

([1965] 1972) *Insights and Illusions of Philosophy*. London: Routledge.

([1967] 1971) *Biology and Knowledge*. Chicago: University of Chicago Press.

([1974] 1976) *The Grasp of Consciousness*. Cambridge, MA: Harvard University Press.

(1977) *The Essential Piaget*. New York: Basic Books.

Further reading

Silverman, H. (1997) *Piaget, Philosophy and the Human Sciences*. Evanston: Northwestern University Press.

JENS BROCKMEIER

PLANNING

See: governance and governmentality

PLAY AND GAME

When contemporary social science attends to the idea of play, it is typically in the form popularized by the game theory that can be traced back to the work of von Neumann in the 1940s and its manifestations in **rational choice** theory, 'decision theory' and 'strategic gaming' today. There is, however, a much richer tradition of thought devoted to role of play in the human sciences. Reflection on the nature of play and gaming has its origins in Romantic responses to **Enlightenment** philosophy. The seminal encounter here is between the cognitive rationalism of **Kant**'s theory of the mind and Friedrich Schiller's rejection of Kant's views in favour of a vision of the human condition based on aesthetics and creative play (see **art and aesthetics**). Schiller links the spirit of play to the very idea of **education** (*Erziehung*) and cultural development (*Bildung*). In his famous *Letters on the Aesthetic Education of Mankind*, Schiller rejected Kantian formalism and formulated the first clear definition of the human condition that sees aesthetic play as the singular feature of human being-in-the-world. Play – exemplified by the *beaux arts* – is the supreme form of human **action** as an end in itself. Play in other words is autotelic praxis (see **praxis and practices**). Through the intermediary of **Hegel**'s philosophy of Spirit, this conception of human activity as play enters modern thought in Marx's *Economic and Philosophical Manuscripts* (1844) as part of the creative powers of the 'species being' of humanity articulated in the humanizing work of culture – in symbolic expression, **language**, and art.

For classical sociology the centrality of play is defended in Georg **Simmel**'s theory of 'sociation'. Simmel distinguishes social forms from what he calls their 'play-forms' (for example, the serious social relationships of human **sexuality** are replicated in the play forms of flirtation and coquetry; the malign conflicts of **war** are represented in the benign polemics of debate and controversy). For later sociology and social theory, the rediscovery of play as a category of social inquiry begins with the work of the Dutch scholar, Johan Huizinga in his work *Homo Ludens* (1950). Huizinga historicizes gaming by investigating the changing social forms through which individuals and groups have defined their **identity** through play. The next major elaboration of this type of comparative **historical sociology** occurs in the work of Norbert **Elias**. In his magisterial history of the 'civilizing process' the rituals of play and competitive gaming occupy a prominent position. Essentially Elias relates the development of **civil society** to the 'civilizing' functions of play in medieval courtly life.

Explicit accounts of play enter mainstream sociology by way of three philosophical perspectives: **pragmatism**, interactionism (particularly the tradition known as **symbolic interactionism**), and **phenomenology**.

Four major perspectives can be distinguished: first, the **interactionist** approach to 'mind, self, and society' is associated with the writings of George Herbert **Mead**. Mead's innovation was to see the emergence of thought (or 'mind') as a product of symbolic learning, and particularly of the reciprocal role-taking process involved in childhood games and play activities (see **role**). In Mead's theory, human beings acquire consciousness and self-consciousness through the social rules of gaming. Second, after Mead, the theatrical or 'dramaturgical' model of role playing and symbolic participation through the activities of the 'generalized other' becomes the axiom of 'symbolic interactionism' (codified by Mead's student Herbert Blumer) (see **dramaturgical school**). From here it enters mainstream thinking about the reciprocal relationships between individual and society in work of Erving **Goffman** and others. Third, it emerges in the phenomenological

433

tradition, with the work of Alfred **Schutz** and his studies of the social **lifeworld**. In particular, Schutz emphasizes the role of symbolism and play as a 'finite province of meaning' through which reality is both constructed and transcended. For Schutz, as for Mead, sociation is symbolic **communication** acquired through participation in play and games. Schutz's work has been extended and augmented in the approach known as 'the social construction of reality' (associated with **Berger and Luckmann**). Finally, mention must be made of the later work of Ludwig **Wittgenstein** and his view of language as an open totality of 'language games' (*Sprachspiele*).

In addition to these 'modernist' conceptions of play in social action, today we find a wide spectrum of approaches that are broadly defined as '**postmodernist**' perspectives, making play central to all forms of signifying practices. Thus, Jacques **Derrida** speaks of the 'play' of *différance*, the interminable operations of intertextuality in language and culture, Jean-François **Lyotard** adapted the theory of *Sprachspiele* in his diagnosis of postmodern culture as the 'end of grand narratives'; while Jean **Baudrillard** sees the 'end of the social' as a consequence of the implosion of culture and the expansionary play of simulacra in consumer society.

References and further reading

Callois, R. (1961) *Man, Play and Games*. New York: Free Press.
Elias, N. (2000) *The Civilizing Process*, reprint edn. Oxford: Blackwell.
Goffman, E. (1959) *The Presentation of Self in Everyday Life*. Garden City, NY: Doubleday.
Huizinga, J. (1950) *Homo Ludens: A Study of the Play Element in Culture*. New York: Roy.
Levy, J. (1978) *Play Behaviour*. New York: John Wiley.
Mead, G. H. (1934) *Mind, Self and Society*. Chicago: University of Chicago Press.
Schutz, A. (1967) *The Phenomenology of the Social World*. Evanston, IL: Northwestern University Press.
von Neumann, J. and Morgenstern, O. ([1944] 1953) *Theory of Games and Economic Behaviour*. Princeton, NJ: Princeton University Press.

BARRY SANDYWELL

PLURALISM

Pluralism is a widely used yet contested concept in the social sciences. 'Cultural' pluralism, broadly speaking, signifies a diversity of overlapping and conflicting cognitive ideas and normative frames. 'Structural' pluralism indicates a diversity of overlapping and conflicting social **groups**, **associations**, **organizations**, and **institutions**. Practices of cultural and structural pluralism are linked to each other in complex ways, and have influenced competing pluralist theories.

Modern, differentiated and stratified societies tend to display extensive pluralism. Societies with liberal-democratic constitutions are often called 'pluralist' as opposed to '**totalitarian**' societies. If guarantees exist for **freedom** of political communication, social groups may organize, mobilize and conflict with one another as interest groups seeking to influence public opinion, **parties**, and different branches of **state**. Theories of political pluralism such as that of the early Robert Dahl (1970), informed by the American political system, claim that such **conflict** does not threaten the stability of 'liberal democracies'. It is claimed that the 'private' **power** of cross-cutting cleavages and overlapping membership does not systematically spill over into 'political' power. As a normative theory, this political pluralism seeks to keep 'private' associations and organizations outside of state policies, holding that they should receive no public subsidies and no official role in the political process.

Many political pluralists acknowledge the criticism, emphasized by particularly Marxist writers, that, as Schattschneider (1975: 34) puts it, 'The flaw in the pluralist heaven is that the heavenly chorus sings with a strong upper-class accent'. Democratic 'institutional' pluralism here takes account of this criticism by going further than purely political pluralism in two regards. First, it demands that the existing plurality of groups, organizations and political units must not only be formally recognized but must also be integrated into the political process of problem-definition, deliberation, decision-making, and implementation. Second, it demands that such **recognition** and **integration** be combined with significant decentralization and institutional **autonomy**. All institutionally pluralist arrangements can thus be characterized as 'power-sharing' systems. Power (of states, of private property, and of administration) must be divided, delegated and limited. This implies a decisive break with ideas of absolute undivided sovereignty and with ideas of monistic, unitarian or majoritarian government.

Theories of institutional pluralism begin with Althusius, are well developed in French legal institutionalism (Duguit, Durkheim), in the German historical school (von Gierke), in English nineteenth and twentieth century authors from Sir Henry Maine and Maitland to Figgis and Laski, and in American writers such as Follett and Dewey. Practices and theories of institutional pluralism fall into three basic types (Bader 2003). First, there is the pluralism of power-sharing systems in territorially bounded units or polities. Here power-sharing may occur even in polities claiming to realize supreme **sovereignty** and **law**. Systems of these kinds are central to comparative **democracy** research (Lijphart 1984), to theories of legal pluralism (Griffith, Teubner), and to multi-level polity research such as EU policy studies (Scharpf, Benz). These accounts of institutional pluralism tend to be critical of 'Westminster' types of 'consensus democracy'. Second, there is the social-functional pluralism associated of **classes**, **professions**, **elites**, categories of producers, and consumers as clients in the political process. This is characteristic of feudal, guild, and Catholic

corporatism as well as of modern neo-corporatism (Schmitter, Lehmbruch, Streeck), of 'negotiated governance' (Mayntz), and democratic corporate governance (Scott). In normative theory it finds its sources in classical social democracy and recently in 'associative democracy' (Hirst 1994, Schmitter 2000). Third, there is the minority pluralism of ethnic, national, and religious groups, as well as women, lesbians and gays, and disabled people, and their involvement the political process. Here research focuses typically on the consequences of colonial and post-colonial racism (Schermerhorn 1970) and on the implications of ethno-cultural and religious institutional pluralism (Sisk 1996). Institutional pluralism of this 'consociational' and 'associative' kind is theorized among others by Hirst and Bader (2001) and by theorists of group rights (Kymlicka 1995), of 'multiculturalism' (Phillips 1995), and of **rights** and **representation** for women, and for disabled people (Minow 1990).

Cultural pluralism in the sense of a diversity of practices, habits, and ways of life is constitutive for modern state societies whether it may increase due to immigration and **individualization**, or decrease due to perceived global 'McDonaldization' processes. While nationalists may see it as a threat to a minimally needed social coherence, value-pluralism or 'reasonable pluralism of the good' (Rawls 1993) seems inescapable in modern societies.

References and further reading

Bader, V. (2001) 'Problems and Prospects of Associative Democracy', in P. Hirst and V. Bader (eds) *Associative Democracy: The Real Third Way*. London: Frank Cass, pp. 31–70.

Bader, V. (2003) 'Democratic Institutional Pluralism', in D. Juteau *et al.* (eds) *The Social Construction of Diversity*. New York: Berghahn, 131–67.

Dahl, R. (1970) *After the Revolution*. New Haven, CT: Yale University Press.

Galston, W. (2002) *Liberal Pluralism*. Cambridge: Cambridge University Press.

Hirst, P. (1989) *The Pluralist Theory of the State*. London: Routledge.

Hirst, P. (1994) *Associative Democracy*. Cambridge: Polity.

Kymlicka, W. (1995) *Multicultural Citizenship*. Oxford: Oxford University Press.

Lijphart, A. (1984) *Democracies*. New Haven, CT: Yale University Press.

Minow, M. (1990) *Making All the Difference*. Ithaca, NY: Cornell University Press.

Phillips, A. (1995) *The Politics of Presence*. Oxford: Clarendon.

Rawls, J. (1993) *Political Liberalism*. New York: Columbia University Press.

Schattschneider, E. (1975) *The Semi-Sovereign People*. New York: Holt, Rinehart and Winston.

Schermerhorn, R. (1970) *Comparative Ethnic Relations*. New York: Random House.

Schmitter, P. (2000) *How to Democratize the European Union*. Oxford: Rowman & Littlefield.

Sisk, T. (1996) *Power Sharing and International Mediation in Ethnic Conflicts*. Washington, DC: US Institute of Peace.

VEIT BADER

POLICE

Police in the modern sense is one of the core **state** agencies, in essence, a distinct and professional body of people patrolling public spaces with a large mandate for 'maintaining daily order'. We must keep in mind here that this definition of 'police' is a distinctly modern one. From the beginning of state formation around the fifteenth century, the 'police' (defined as 'science of the police' or in German '*Policewissenschaft*') covered all duties of what would be called today the **welfare state** (see also **state and nation–state**). According to the ancient meaning of the Greek concept of *polis*, police was the activity intended to achieve stability of the social order and the happiness of its individual members (**Foucault** 1981; Paoli 2003). In the history of European nation–states it was only with the creation of the centralized 'Lieutenance générale de police' in Paris (1667) and the English municipal counterpart 'London Metropolitan Police force' of Sir Robert Peel (1829)

that the concept and social form of the police came to acquire its distinctly modern face, confined to the safeguarding of daily order and to the enforcement of **law and legality**. But even these institutionalized and specialized forces were an exception, since in France, Britain and for a much longer time in the United States, police tasks in the eighteenth and nineteenth centuries were mostly executed by non-professional citizen 'volunteers'.

The concept of police can be seen both as an *institution* and as a *function*. The police are an institution embodying the core of the state's monopolization of legitimate force over its territory (see **legitimacy and legitimation**). As such, the police are the strong arm of the state or of the law. However, considering the wide scope of the tasks of modern police forces in maintaining '**public** order', an individual police officer must exercise considerable discretion in choosing actual targets and tasks. As such, the mandate of the police considered in the light of the actual practices of its members consists more in 'peace keeping' than in 'enforcing the law'. In their daily **social control** function, beat or patrol police officers are expected to respond potentially to all kinds of public concerns. In consequence, the narrower legal definition of 'police' in fact has very little to do with the wider social facts of 'policing'. In a sociological sense, the police are the institution in charge of every situation in which 'something that is happening ought not to be happening and ought to be dealt with by someone now' (Bittner 1980). Defined in this sociological sense of real **actions**, the police in fact uses force to a relatively small extent. It can be argued that far from exercising force as its core function, the police is the only occupation which consists in 'doing everything' (Brodeur *et al.* 2001). A similar approach focusing on the growth of **information** flows in **postmodern** societies is to consider the police as '**knowledge** workers' (Ericson and Haggerty 1997).

This structural sociological conception of policing in some respects concurs with common police perceptions of their own activities, defined as the 'thin blue line' perception: the police see themselves constantly confronted with **deviance**, disorder, **crime** and deprived people, and as at the same time disregarded by society. A shared 'cop culture' (Skolnick 1966) helps strengthen the ranks of an institution which brings under the same seal people and occupations that do not have much in common: rank-and-file constables, managers, and plain-clothes detectives.

On another level, the increasing need for professional workers to confront new or increased threats (such as narcotics trade, organized **crime**, or **terrorism**) tends to give an ever more diverse role to the police as 'state-like actors' in defining international or domestic legal provisions. In view of growing internal cleavages of tasks within police forces, the difficulty of defining the police as an *institution* is becoming increasingly problematic. But equally, the difficulty of defining the police as a *function* is also increasing in view of diminishing differentiation between police officers and other kinds of actors in society.

References and further reading

Banton, M. (1964) *The Policeman in the Community*. London: Tavistock.

Bittner, E. (1980) *The Functions of the Police in Modern Society*. Cambridge: Oelgeschlager, Gunn and Hain Publishers.

Bittner, E., Brodeur, J.-P. and Jobard, F. (2001) 'Comprendre l'habilation à l'usage de la force policière', *Déviance et Société*, 3: 325.

Brodeur, J.-P., Gill, P. and Töllborg, D. (eds) (2003) *Democracy, Law and Security: Internal Security Services in Contemporary Europe*. Aldershot: Ashgate.

Ericson, R. and Haggerty, K. (1997) *Policing the Risk Society*. Oxford: Clarendon.

Foucault, M. (1981) '*Omnes et singulatim*: Towards a Criticism of Political Reason', in S. McMurrin (ed.) *The Tanner Lectures on Human Values*, 2. Salt Lake City, UT: University of Utah, pp. 223–54.

Newburn, T. (2003) *Handbook of Policing*. Devon: Willan.

Skolnick, J. (1966) *Justice without Trial*. New York: Wiley.

Westley, W. (1970) *Violence and the Police: A Sociological Study of Law, Custom, and Morality*. Cambridge, MA: MIT Press.

FABIEN JOBARD

POLITICAL ECONOMY

Oeconomia refers to *oikos*, the house, and thus to the traditional organization of **production** and reproduction in the **family and household**. The adjective 'political' signified the goal of explaining the **economy** of the *polis*, the commonwealth, and giving advice to policy-makers. The expression emerged in the early seventeenth century in France (Groenewegen 1987), signaling a new concern with economic matters beyond the question of how **feudal** rulers could maximize their income. As the young **Marx** indicated when he translated political economy as 'the rule of **society** over **wealth**', the subject matter of political economy was seen to involve tensions. Not only should society – rather than the monarch – rule over wealth, but if individuals were left free to pursue their own enrichment, as the emerging **bourgeoisie** demanded, how would it be possible to harness economic forces to serve common social goals? How would it be possible to prevent the translation of economic into political **power**?

Political economy developed in three stages: classical, **Keynesian** and neo-classical. **Marx** used the term 'classical' political economy to refer to a period of thought ranging roughly from the French Physiocrats to John Stuart **Mill**. These early radical thinkers unabashedly expressed the interests of the rising bourgeoisie against feudal fetters, but were at the same time attentive to the new social problems of the capitalist mode of economic organization. While Adam **Smith** celebrated the social advantages of the **division of labor** and the ensuing increases in productivity driven by self-interest, he never hesitated to note soberly the degrading nature of **work** under modern conditions, as well as conflicts between the interests of particular social **classes** and the general interest. David Ricardo emphasized the stark opposition of class interests in relation to income distribution, arguing that investment in machinery could result in **unemployment**, and seeking to demonstrate specifically that the 'interest of the landlords is always opposed to the interest of every other class in the **community**.' (Ricardo 1815: 21).

The main characteristics of classical political economy are the concern with **capitalism** as a self-reproducing system, presented in a macro-perspective as an interplay of classes of economic agents in the typical roles of landowners, capitalists and workers. These three classes are distinguished according to the typical kinds of endowments which they are able to feed into the production process (work, capital, land) and according to the type of revenue they receive in return (wages, profits, interest and rent). Classes are not *a priori* held to be collective agents (in the sense of being organized to pursue collectively defined goals), but are conceived as aggregates formed by classifying individuals according to their typical economic activities, in standard situations, using their typical means. The generalized assumption of self-interested behaviour then allows for the imputation of class **interests**, most prominently those which result in **conflict** over the distribution of the surplus produced. Surplus refers to the part of output exceeding the replacement of means of production. Despite conflicting interests, classes have to cooperate if **production** – the core of all economic activity – is to take place. Cooperation is achieved through **exchanges**. Landlords allow the use of their land (or other appropriated natural resources) in exchange for rent; workers concede the command over their ability to work to the capitalist in return for wages; capitalists use their capital to buy means of production,

hire workers and rent the land, all in order to organize production in such a way that the resulting products can be sold with a profit. As Quesnay and – in a more developed form, Marx – showed, the system is self-reproductive in so far as means of production are replaced and the surplus generated is sufficient to pay incomes that will induce a sufficient number of the members of each of the three classes to continuously reappear on the market as sellers of their factors of production. Apart from the requirement to produce as outputs the inputs for the next round of production, the exchanges leading to reproduction have to be based on prices which, on the one hand, give agents and their households sufficient purchasing power to reproduce themselves, and which, on the other hand, offer them sufficient incentives to continue participation in the capitalist process.

This line of analysis was resumed by Sraffa (1960), who demonstrated that prices including evaluations of capital are dependent on the distribution of the surplus. Classical political economists emphasized the uniquely dynamic development of the **capitalist** economy by focusing on capital accumulation and on productivity increases induced by the growing division of labor. The system puts a premium in the form of extra-profits on cost-reducing and product innovations and it rewards the reinvestment of profits, leading to historically unprecedented economic growth. The costs of this dynamic growth were found to be recurring cyclical crisis (Ricardo) accompanied by mass poverty (Malthus), and – in the case of Marx – in the ultimate self-destruction of the system due to the twin forces of a falling rate of profit and **revolution** led by the exploited working class.

Political economists after Smith relied mostly on a simple notion of **agency** that was a forerunner of **utilitarianism**. Individuals were seen as pursuing their self-interest in the institutional framework of the division of labor and private **property and property rights** while rationality was forced upon them by competition. Partly due to this rather crude theory of **action** and partly due to problems inherent in the labor theory of **value**, and partly due also to the desire for a more harmonistic view of the capitalism, classical political economy was pushed aside in the late nineteenth century by the marginalist school, which defended a notion of economic value based on scarcity and individual subjective **preferences**. Marginalism implied a switch to a microeconomic perspective, although in general equilibrium theory as first conceived by Walras this was elaborated to present the working of a total economic system.

Apart from continuous strands of Marxist economic thought, a return to the macroperspective of circular flows and reproduction occurred only in the 1930s under the impact of the deep world economic crisis. Against the background of widespread mass unemployment, **Keynes** (1936) rejected neo-classical microeconomics as implicitly dealing with the special case of a full employment economy, demonstrating the need for political intervention to reach the level of effective demand required for full employment. However, as in previous variants of political economy, the state was here the addressee, rather than the subject matter, of theoretical argument. This changed once Kalecki (1943) discussed the issue of political obstacles to full employment, given that Keynes had demonstrated its economic feasibility.

The renewed emphasis on the role of the state in the economy provided a transition to the third stage of political economy. A theory of **market** failures, in which it was taken to be self-evident that the state, acting in the public interest, would assume the role of correcting market failures, developed within the neoclassical framework. However, this implicitly functionalist view of the state was demolished by conservative economists who – drawing on **Schumpeter**'s economic theory of democracy – questioned the notion of the benevolent state implicit

in earlier political economy. Politicians and bureaucrats were seen as pursuing their own interests (Stigler 1975), raising the question of how they could be brought to follow the will of the majority in a democratic system. Solutions to the question have been seen to turn on the role of institutions that combine both market and **state** allocations of resources and distributions of income in ways that allow the exercise of democratic control to improve the results of an economy bugged by inefficiencies if left to self-regulation (Przeworski 2003).

References and further reading

Groenewegen, P. (1987) 'Political Economy' and 'Economics', in J. Eatwell *et al.* (eds) *The New Palgrave Dictionary of Economics*, vol. IV. London: Macmillan.

Kalecki, M. ([1943] 1972) 'Political Aspects of Full Employment', reprinted in E. K. Hunt and J. G. Schwartz, *A Critique of Economic Theory*. Harmondsworth: Penguin, pp. 420–30.

Keynes, J. M. (1936) *The General Theory of Employment, Interest, and Money*. London: Macmillan.

Marx, K. ([1867] 1954) *Capital*, vol. 1. Moscow: Progress Publishers.

Przeworski, A. (1990) *The State and the Economy under Capitalism*. New York: Harwood.

Przeworski, A. (2003) *States and Markets: A Primer in Political Economy*. Cambridge: Cambridge University Press.

Ricardo, D. ([1815] 1951) *Principles of Political Economy and Taxation*. Reprinted as vol. 1 of *The Works and Correspondence of David Ricardo*, ed. P. Sraffa. Cambridge: Cambridge University Press.

Schumpeter, J. A. (1943) *Capitalism, Socialism and Democracy*. London: Harper.

Smith, A. ([1776] 1976) *An Inquiry into the Nature and Causes of the Wealth of Nations*. Reprinted as vol.2 of *The Glasgow Edition of the Works and Correspondence of Adam Smith*, ed. R. H. Campbell *et al.* Oxford: Oxford University Press.

Sraffa, P. (1960) *Production of Commodities by Means of Commodities: Prelude to a Critique of Economic Theory*. Cambridge: Cambridge University Press.

Stigler, G. (1975) *The Citizen and the State: Essays on Regulation*. Chicago: University of Chicago Press.

Walsh, V. C. and Gram, H. (1980) *Classical and Neoclassical Theories of General Equilibrium: Historical Origins and Mathematical Structure.* New York: Oxford University Press.

HEINER GANßMANN

POLITY

Aristotle called the *politeia* the **power** of the people exercised according to the rule of **law**. Today the term 'polity' is used to refer to a certain key aspect of political systems that is not fully captured by the words 'politics' or 'policy'.

In the Aristotelian tradition *politeia* means broadly the **constitution**, covering both the institutional framework of a given political system and its basic moral norms. 'Polity' or **republic** is the common English translation of Aristotle's preferred type of government within his sixfold scheme of constitutions (Aristotle, *The Politics*, Book. 3, Chapter 7). There Aristotle differentiates constitutions by the number of people participating in power (one, many, or all) and by the broader aim of government (the **interest** of the rulers or the common interest). Hence he compares tyranny with **monarchy**, oligarchy with **aristocracy** and **democracy** with the republic or polity. In this scheme, polity stands for the rule of all **citizens** seeking the common interest and upholding the political will through laws.

Recently this tradition was revived by Hannah **Arendt** and her pupils. In opposition to the **behaviourist** approach which dominated the 1950s, Arendt tried to revitalize what she called the ancient view of the political, based on the significance of **praxis**, **action** and experience. In her view, modern social science had replaced the moral significance of action by functional labour and production and thus was guilty of failing the essence of the political. Polity covered the normative aims of political action in order to establish a system enabling men to be free and equal citizens (Arendt 1958).

In most contemporary political science, 'polity' describes macropolitical aspects of the political system. Unlike German and French, the English language provides political science with a richer terminology with regard to political phenomena and their analysis. In French and German only one word is used: *politique* or *Politik*. However, in English we find 'policy' as well as 'politics' and 'polity' describing different aspects of the political realm (Heidenheimer 1963). Interdisciplinary polity analysis refers to juridical, philosophical and historical research that explores the **institutional** and normative roots of a political system. Here polity may indicate the religious background of a social practice (Höpfl 1982; Elazar 1995) or a certain political philosophy concerning the concept of the political. Whereas 'politics' (as process) and 'policy' (as topic) operate usually against the background of the historically given political system, 'polity' inquires into the constitutive factors of that system with a view to discussing possible alternatives (Rohe 1994: 61–7). Thus polity is logically prior to politics and policy insofar as it marks the frame in which politics and policy are set to work.

The macropolitical dimensions of the concept of polity allow scholars to move beyond the state-centred framework of conventional political research. Conceptions of a 'world polity', for example, seek to focus on a global political system that is constituted by non-governmental organizations. Here the **nation-state** no longer constitutes the sole political **paradigm**. Non-governmental actors initiate a new political culture operating on the global scale. Although closely connected with the state system, non-governmental organizations establish a new political culture of **universalism** and world **citizenship** through the increasing density of their **networks** (Boli and Thomas 2000).

As a reaction to the scientific turn of political science, the concept of polity typically indicates a more normative approach.

Often used loosely regarding Aristotelian thinking, the term 'the good polity' focuses on the problem of the common good as the aim of all politics. This approach criticises standards of efficiency and functionality as too narrow. A question remains here as to the standards by which a good polity can be measured. The answer mainly given by political philosophers today is *justice*. In the meaning claimed by Hamlin and Pettit, the good polity is the link between the methodological basis of **rational choice** theory and aspects of **legitimacy** beyond efficiency (Hamlin and Pettit 1989).

References and further reading

Arendt, H. (1958) *The Human Condition*. Chicago: University of Chicago Press.

Aristotle (1984) *Politics*. Chicago: University of Chicago Press.

Boli, J. and Thomas, G. (eds) (2000) *World Polity Formation since 1875: World Culture and International Non-Governmental Organizations*. Stanford, CA: Stanford University Press.

Elazar, D. J. (1995) *Covenant and Polity in Biblical Israel: Biblical Foundations and Jewish Expressions*, vol. 1: *Covenant Tradition in Politics*. New Brunswick, NJ: Transaction.

Hamlin, A. and Pettit, P. (eds) (1989) *The Good Polity: Normative Analysis of the State*. Oxford: Blackwell.

Heidenheimer, A. J. (1963) 'Politics, Policy, and Polity as Concepts in English and Continental Languages', *Review of Politics*, 48(1): 3–30.

Höpfl, H. (1982) *The Christian Polity of John Calvin*. Cambridge: Cambridge University Press.

Miller, F. D. (1995) *Nature, Justice, and Rights in Aristotle's Politics*. Oxford: Clarendon.

Rohe, K. (1994) *Politik: Begriffe und Wirklichkeiten*. Stuttgart: Kohlhammer.

MARCUS LLANQUE

POPPER, KARL RAIMUND (1902–1994)

Austrian-born philosopher, resident in Britain. An early critic of the **positivism** of the Vienna Circle, Popper championed a modified **Kantianism** that he termed 'critical rationalism' maintaining a middle path between dogmatism and scepticism within the separate spheres of **science** and **morals**. Against the positivists, Popper held that moral and other metaphysical views are meaningful and thus are serious issues for critical debate. Opposed to naïve **empiricism**, Popper nonetheless compared much social and psychological theory invidiously with the theories of empirically testable physical science. With a single word, 'unfalsifiable', he launched probably the most damaging, if tendentious, attack on the integrity of social thinkers from **Marx** to **Freud**, maintaining that each was a mere pseudo-scientist, Freud for having advanced 'logically unfalsifiable' conceptions, Marx for having advanced conceptions rendered 'methodologically unfalsifiable'. Popper challenged the **historicism** of Hegel's contention that human history unfolds according to historical laws. He criticized social **collectivism** as a return to unreasoned 'tribalism' and defended 'piecemeal engineering' over against 'utopian' socialism. Against the **utilitarianism** of J. S. **Mill**, he championed his own distinct 'negative **utilitarianism**'.

Major works

([1939] 1959) *The Logic of Scientific Discovery* (translation of *Logik der Forschung*). London: Hutchinson.

(1945) *The Open Society and Its Enemies*, 2 vols. London: Routledge.

(1961) *The Poverty of Historicism*, 2nd edn. London: Routledge.

(1963) *Conjectures and Refutations: The Growth of Scientific Knowledge*. London: Routledge.

(1994) *The Myth of the Framework: In Defence of Science and Rationality*. London: Routledge.

Further reading

Catton, P. and Macdonald, G. (eds) (2004) *Karl Popper: Critical Appraisals*. London: Routledge.

PHILIP CATTON

POPULAR CULTURE

The term 'popular' has historically meant 'of the people'. The popular was at the heart of the creation of a national sense of belonging in the construction of modern **nationalism**. In the late-eighteenth century, Johan Gottfried Herder spoke of *Kultur des Volkes*, which rapidly translated into English as 'folk **culture**'. In the German territories of the nineteenth century, the fusion of the people with the nation laid the foundations for a Germanic **nation–state**, not necessarily to justify German superiority, as in Nazism, but to bring a disparate people into an '**imagined** community' (Anderson 1983). The modern nation had to be imagined because its members are only personally familiar with a tiny proportion of the membership unlike in a traditional agrarian **community**, typically a village. Today, modern media of **communication**, particularly broadcasting, are crucial for producing imagined communities and for fostering identification with such abstractions as the nation. In this sense **media and mass media** have succeeded the church in the construction of popular belonging.

The popular is available for differential articulation. On the one hand, it may inhere in resistance from below to arbitrary **authority** and alien **power**. On the other hand, it may enact a national-popular **ideology** aimed at excluding others from the chosen people. To a great extent, successful articulation of the people is the key to politics. Yet popular culture is not always explicitly thought of in this political sense.

How the popular and culture interrelate may be conceptualized in different ways. Residually, folk culture is the obscure source of the populist conception that sets popular culture against an educated high culture. However, popular culture has also been distinguished from 'mass culture' (see **mass culture and mass society**), viewed as inauthentic culture foisted upon the people from above. Popular culture as the authentic culture of the people, in one formulation or another, is the residuum of self-made culture. That distinction has greater relevance now in poorer parts of the world where popular **traditions** of music and ritual are maintained to a sig-

nificant extent in spite of the onslaught of mass-commercial culture from above and elsewhere, especially through the channels of the global media. It has less relevance in more affluent countries where considerably less remains of traditional folk culture.

Until quite recently, social scientists tended to assume that folk culture was actively produced by the people themselves whereas mass culture was passively consumed. That assumption was overturned in cultural studies by the theory of active **consumption**. From this perspective, television viewers, for instance, should no longer be thought of invariably as the passive recipients of information and entertainment transmitted to them by corporate power. Rather, they are to be seen as active in choosing programmes to watch and in interpreting televised meanings according to their own predilections. Television messages do not have simple effects on viewers; instead, there is a complex process by which audiences actively seek use and gratification from television viewing. People are not the passive dopes of mass culture. Such thinking was generalized by John Fiske (2002, 2004), among others, to suggest that cultural consumption is always active and, therefore, productive through appropriation and re-inflection across the board. In effect, consumer activity turns mass culture into popular culture. The old **binary** opposition between 'mass' and 'popular' is thus eliminated.

However, it can be argued that this elimination has occurred at the cost of a more *critical* analysis of mass-popular culture. It has been argued that the active consumer of populist cultural studies meets up with the sovereign consumer of **neo-liberal** economics, the dominant ideology and prevailing conventional wisdom. Critics of cultural populism claim that it succumbs to free-market ideology. Some argue that it has become so relativistic that critical judgements as to quality and value are rendered impossible. A danger is that populism misunderstands real structures and processes of power in the cultural field and awards inordinate power to consumers, thereby repeating the nostrums of marketing and, more generally, a pervasive consumerist ideology.

Cultural populism is an extreme reaction to an equally extreme and unsatisfactory position that saw popular culture as having been superseded by an entirely manipulative mass culture. In many ways, the populist reaction is reasonable; it has certainly rectified faults in earlier social-scientific approaches to popular culture. There is no doubt that popular culture is a worthy and important object of study. Its dismissal by academic conservatives in the past and still, to an extent, today has been arrogant and deeply mistaken. Yet it is perplexing that in reaction to cultural elitism, some researchers have gone very far in the other direction. Popular culture matters, especially in its mass-distributed forms and post-modern collapsing of hierarchies and blurring of boundaries, if we want to understand social life in the late-modern world. A certain detachment, however, is advisable that is supported by a cautious willingness to make criticisms. The powers of the capitalist culture industry and the activities of people regarding what is on offer are two sides of a complex, multi-dimensional object.

References and further reading

Anderson, B. (1983) *Imagined Communities: Reflections on the Origin and Spread of Nationalism*. London: Verso.

Fiske, J. (2002) *Reading the Popular*. London: Routledge.

Fiske, J. (2004) *Understanding Popular Culture*. London: Routledge.

Gans, H. (1975) *Popular Culture and High Culture*. New York: Basic Books.

McGuigan, J. (1992) *Cultural Populism*. London: Routledge.

—— (1996) *Culture and the Public Sphere*. London: Routledge.

JIM MCGUIGAN

POSITIVISM

Positivism refers – often pejoratively – to any **philosophy of social science** that claims that the social sciences should directly emulate the **objectivism** and **reductionism** of 'the scientific method' of the natural sciences. Positivism is also identified with the post-Enlightenment **world-view** of **modernity** that has been criticized as 'scientism'. Key themes of positivism have included a naively realistic **ontology** suggesting that concepts correspond directly to reality; an empiricist **epistemology** based on the unity of scientific methods understood in terms of verification of theories by facts; and a search for causal **explanation** with an ideal hypothetico-deductive logical structure. Also salient in positivist programmes is a strong emphasis on the value-neutrality of the researcher. Defenders of the scientific aspirations social science complain that the term has been used indiscriminately and does not take into account the more sophisticated justifications of **naturalism** in social science. For example, **functionalism** and **systems theory** draw upon biological models quite distinct from classical positivism.

Positivism can be traced to **Comte**'s early nineteenth-century formulation of a 'positive philosophy' as an alternative to the negativism of **Enlightenment** criticism. Positivist philosophies were characterized by an anti-**metaphysical** stance based on a faith in science as the basis of progress. Scientific methods were understood in empiricist terms as validation of knowledge by facts and applying equally to the natural and social sciences. Forerunners can be found in British **empiricism** and later representatives included **Spencer**, **Mill** and **Durkheim**. In the nineteenth century positivism was often associated with reformist causes that included both liberals and socialists. In Latin America in the nineteenth century, Comtean positivism had a more specific **ideological** function as part of the legitimation of a form of liberalism that promised to link 'order and progress'. The philosophers of the Vienna Circle attempted in the 1920s to use formal logic to construct a rigorous logical positivism based on a strict verification principle and the unity of science.

Positivism remained dominant into the 1960s, resulting in the primacy of quantitative methods and functionalist theory in sociology. Nevertheless, as long ago as the late nineteenth century, positivism has been challenged by **neo-Kantianism**, and especially by **hermeneutics**, in terms of a distinction between the natural sciences, based on nomothetic or universal generalizations, and the cultural sciences, oriented toward the idiographic interpretation of unique cases. Many influential contemporary social theorists have challenged this polarization, following the lead of **Weber**, **Mannheim** and the early **Frankfurt School**, in suggesting that social research should be grounded in a mediating perspective that links **agency** with the causal effects of structure.

The most influential critique of positivism emerged from historians and philosophers who criticized it for not providing an adequate account of the natural sciences. The critical **rationalism** of **Popper** challenged the preoccupation with verification rather than falsification, but the residual scientism of his position was challenged by **Adorno** (1976) in the 'positivism dispute' in Germany in the 1960s. Most decisively, historians of science, especially as exemplified in Kuhn's account of scientific **paradigms**, drew upon hermeneutic arguments to demonstrate how the theory-laden character of facts undermined positivist views of **science**.

The term *post-positivism* (or post-empiricism) is now widely used in inconsistent ways to designate a turning point. Discussions of post-positivism typically begin by referring to Kuhn and science studies and other accounts of the construction of knowledge, e.g., hermeneutics (**Gadamer**), the **linguistic turn** in philosophy (**Wittgenstein**), the French post-structuralist stress on the arbitrariness of language and representation (**Derrida**), or the effects of ideology (**Frankfurt School**) and power (**Foucault**). Responses to the post-positivist turn, however, have

split along two lines that can be characterized as a radical and more moderate **social constructionism** (Phillips and Burbules 2000). Though some authors speak of a 'post-positivist paradigm', they proceed to discuss variations that cannot easily be subsumed in a single perspective, e.g., **feminist theory**, constructivism, **critical theory**, and post-positivist empirical research. At one extreme, post-positivism has been identified with **relativism**, or with strongly anti-realist, sceptical, anti-universalistic and politicized views of research that are associated with **postmodernism**. Alternatively, post-positivism has been associated with more moderate forms of **constructivism** that defend the autonomy of inquiry and the rational basis of critique, thus rejecting scepticism, strong anti-realism, and the depreciation of empirical methodologies. In research methodology, post-positivism has been used as a label for justifying multivariate analysis within a more pluralist understanding of methodology where quantitative and qualitative methods have equal status. Social theorists as varied as **Alexander**, Bhaskar (critical **realism**), **Bourdieu**, **Giddens**, and **Habermas** have defended post-positivist conceptions of a critical social science. Such moderate constructionists argue in different ways that contextualism and the universality of interpretation do not undermine the pragmatic significance of the capacity of theories to represent social reality or that evidence may adequately – if provisionally – justify valid interpretations.

References and further reading

Adorno, T. W. *et al.* (eds) (1976) *The Positivist Dispute in German Sociology*. London: Heinemann.

Bryant, C. G. A. (1985) *Positivism in Social Theory and Research*. London: Macmillan.

Gartrell, C. D. and Gartrell, J. W. (2002) 'Positivism in Sociological Research: USA and UK (1966–1990)', *British Journal of Sociology*, 53(4): 639–57.

Halfpenny, P. (2001) 'Positivism in the Twentieth Century', in G. Ritzer and B. Smart (eds) *Handbook of Social Theory*. London: Sage.

Phillips, D. C. and Burbules, N. C. (2000) *Post-positivism and Educational Research*. Lanham, MD: Rowman & Littlefield.

RAYMOND A. MORROW

POST-COLONIAL THEORY

Emerging in the late 1970s and the early 1980s, and influenced by **post-structuralism** and **postmodernism**, postcolonialism (now mainly without a hyphen) has less of a chronological meaning than an epistemic one with a focus on a study of the **discourses**, **institutions** and **identity** constructions of modern (especially eighteenth and nineteenth centuries) European (especially British and French) colonialism. Expressed first in terms of the colonial discourse analysis that developed after the **cultural** and **linguistic turn** in the academy, postcolonial studies was first situated in literature departments with a cultural, rather than a historical and sociological, focus. Yet, even at its most **aesthetic**, postcolonialism has been connected to debates about economics, politics and history.

With its roots in other critical discourses (such as **psychoanalysis** and **Marxism**) postcolonialism rejects linear ideas of **development**, and from its beginnings has been critical of its 'own' positioning as a historical phase coming *after* colonialism, i.e., 'post' colonial as linearly and developmentally following 'pre-colonial' and colonial periods. Influenced by anti-colonial thinkers and 'Third World' Marxists, postcolonialism attempts to produce another vantage point, to 'speak back' to the colonial **representation**. In other words, postcolonialism's agenda has been to open up the privileged site (and sight) of the colonial power and to challenge the dominance of the colonial standpoint and the **binary** of **master and slave**, colonizer and colonized. In other words, as a **standpoint epistemology**, postcolonial theory looks critically not only at the master

narratives of European **Enlightenment** and European **imperialism** but, drawing on psychoanalysis, **gender** and **race** theory, also challenges and subverts established notions of **self** and **identity** that are produced by the colonial gaze. A postcolonial standpoint is then concerned with shifting the geography of reason, 'mov[ing] the centre' (Ngugi) and emphasizing a discourse of **space** over **time**, opening up the idea of multiple time.

However, despite its rejection of temporal linearity, postcolonialism does come 'after' colonialism, not only as a reflexive **critical theory** but also in the creative and critical works of writers and artists living in the postcolonial world. Thus, it is argued that the 'post' in postcolonial is not the same as the 'post' in postmodernism (Appiah). In the early 1980s, already established university courses in 'Commonwealth', 'Third World' and 'World Literature' soon became clustered as postcolonial, though often changing their titles rather than their contents. The tension is now not so much between theory and **art**, but between the life of the multitude in the postcolony, often represented by literary works and the theoretical practices of postcolonialist theorists in the metropole. While the importance of ideas of **hybridity**, **migration** and diaspora to postcolonial studies is underlined by the experiences of the postcolonial theorists who have migrated from the postcolony, their **cosmopolitanism** is often an **elite** one and their experiences are quite different from the majority of people in the postcolonial world. Thus, postcolonial theorists, especially migrants from the postcolonies, were among the first to problematize their own subject position as well as the first to be criticized for re-representing 'the people'.

The notion of 'speaking back' creates new problems of representation. With its epistemological critique, postcolonialism refuses to fall into **essentialism** when discussing postcolonial subjectivity. The more politically engaged, who are often also critics of the institutionalization of postcolonialism, have attempted to bracket off the debilitating bind of representation through a 'strategic essentialism' (**Spivak**). Other critics have insisting on holding onto such terms as colonizer and colonized, oppressor and oppressed, to emphasize the different realities of colonial domination and movements that respond to it (Parry). While some tend to dismiss the discourses of nation and **nationalism** as colonial derivatives, others often following **Fanon** and other anticolonial intellectuals and activists, argue that there is a need to engage the difference between 'bourgeois' nationalism and a more radical, if often contradictory, popular national consciousness (Lazarus). By engaging all these tensions productively, postcolonial theory keeps challenging and deconstructing the very concepts that itself brings forward. Thus, one issue for postcolonial studies is whether the study of the very concepts its wishes to undermine valorizes those concepts.

As postcolonial studies have become accepted in the academy, they have encouraged a sensibility to cultural, and especially **media**, representation of '**others**'. Postcolonialism has become particularly important for critically rethinking issues such as identity, hybridity, border-crossings, as well as the nature of the politics of (multi) culturalism. Postcolonial questionings have begun to influence and borrow from such fields as anthropology, economics and politics, problematizing such issues as ethnography, **development**, **modernization** and nation building. Postcolonial theory has also made headway into international relations, as 'area studies' lost part of its *raison d'être* after the collapse of **communism**, and such old dominant forms that were used to think about the world no longer apply. As the field developed, texts by **intellectuals** from the anti-colonial period, such as those by Fanon, Césaire, and C. L. R. James became part of an emerging canon. Finding its roots in the theoretical

practice of anti-colonial **freedom** struggles, a politics of postcolonial critique, often integrated with global studies, has emphasized the increasing inequalities between 'the North' and 'the South' and has turned its attention to anti-systemic movements.

As a term, post-colonial (with a hyphen) was first employed by historians and political scientists, particularly those who were interested in the nature of the 'post-colonial state' that arose in Asia and Africa after the post-war decolonizations. Like the under-development and Marxist critics of modernization theory who employed the term 'neo-colonial', those interested in 'the post-colonial state' contextualized its development in an economic and structural continuity with colonial **domination**. This contextualization, based on an understanding of the spatial ordering of the world system in terms of **centre and periphery**, has carried over into postcolonial studies.

The emergence of contemporary postcolonial studies is usually associated with Edward W. **Said**'s *Orientalism* (1978) as a founding text, as well as with works by Gayatri C. Spivak and Homi Bhabha. By the 1990s Said, Spivak and Bhabha were considered a 'Holy Trinity' (Young 1991), the principal representatives of postcolonial theory, each employing high French theory to disrupt the master concepts and dominant epistemologies of colonial discourse. Said's *Orientalism* was one of the first applications of Foucauldian theory to a discourse analysis of the connections of Western **culture** and imperialism, of Western **power**, **knowledge** and representations and creations of 'the Other', 'the Oriental', 'the African', and so on. Homi Bhabha used Lacanian **psychoanalysis**, especially in his **Lacanian** reading of Frantz Fanon's *Black Skin White Masks*, to disrupt the binaries of colonial and colonized, white and black, and **self** and other, focusing on the 'in-betweenness' and 'ambiguity' of the colonial encounter which introduce into resistance what Bhabha called the 'third space of enunciation', the ambivalences, slippages and fluidity located in colonial 'mimicry'. Spivak's often misunderstood essay, 'Can the Subaltern Speak?' which was criticized as elitist, employed Derridean deconstruction to argue that the subaltern could not make a 'speech act' and thus was always already represented by a **discourse**. Disrupting the master concepts and dominant **ideology** of colonial discourse, Spivak, and to a lesser extent, Said and Bhabha, maintain that there is no such thing as an 'essential' 'subaltern' identity or voice of the marginalized. Each is already represented in **language**. Because there is no way that postcolonial discourse can escape this dilemma it must embrace it critically and be sensitive to issues of language.

Whether one traces postcolonialism through Marxism, through post-structuralism, through **Freudian** and Lacanian psychoanalysis (or a hybrid of all three), the common focus is on shifting the geography of reason. Thus the postcolonial critic also demands the end of postcoloniality, that is to say, the day when the object of study of colonial discourses, 'the native', 'the colonized', 'the subaltern', refuses to be an object of study.

References and further reading

Appiah, A. K. (1993) *In My Father's House: Africa in the Philosophy of Culture*. Oxford: Oxford University Press.

Bhabha, H. (1994) *Location of Culture*. London: Routledge.

Fanon, F. (1967) *Black Skin White Masks*. New York: Grove Press.

James, C. L. R. (1989) *Black Jacobins: Toussaint L'Ouverture and the San Domingo Revolution*. New York: Random House.

Lazarus, Neil (1999) *Nationalism and Cultural Practice in the Postcolonial World*. Cambridge: Cambridge University Press.

Mbembe, J.-A. (2001) *On the Postcolony*. Berkeley, CA: University of California Press.

Ngugi Wa Th'iongo (1993) *Moving the Centre: The Struggle for Cultural Freedom*. London: Heinemann.

Parry, B. (2004) *Postcolonial Studies: A Materialist Critique*. New York: Routledge.

Said, E. W. (1978) *Orientalism*. New York: Vintage Books.

Said, E. W. (1993) *Culture and Imperialism*. New York: Random House.

Spivak, G. C. (1999) *Critique of Postcolonial Reason: Toward a History of the Vanishing Present*. New York: Routledge.

Young, R. J. C. (1991) *White Mythologies: Writing History and the West*. New York: Routledge.

NIGEL GIBSON

POST-FORDISM

Post-Fordism is a key term in **regulation** theory, and describes a specific historical stage of **capitalist society** which emerged out of the political, economic, and cultural **crisis** of the mid-1970s. It is characterized in ideal-typical terms (see **ideal type**) as a contrast to the previous phase of Fordism and stresses the ongoing change in the methods of **production** and regulation as a result of 'search' strategies attempting to institutionalize a new project of economic growth.

The neo–Marxist concept of post-Fordism relies on the insight that there is no single form of **capitalism**, but rather spatially and temporally distinct formations of society which, however, on an abstract level share the essential structural principles of the capitalist **mode of production**. Each formation is a 'historical bloc' (see **Gramsci**) in which a certain 'accumulation regime' and a 'mode of regulation' (see **regulation**) are articulated in a way which enables phases of relatively stable growth. Fordism, the archetypal example of such a formation, developed from the 1930s to the 1950s in the wake of the world economic crisis and the Second World War. It rested essentially on the Taylorist reorganization of the **labour** process, based on the assembly-line principle and the unique combination of mass production and mass **consumption**, economic growth, and full employment (it is therefore named after the successful strategy of the American automobile industrialist Henry Ford). It was based on a social **consensus** between capital, **trade unions**, and the **state**, and was associated with corporatism, Keynesianism (see **Keynes**), a bureaucratized **welfare state**, and a disciplined **subjectivity**.

The crisis of Fordism led to the world-wide collapse of this formation and the transition to a new phase, called post-Fordism. The prefix 'post' is used to highlight the (dis)-continuities between Fordism and its successor. The new pattern of post-Fordist capitalism is said to be characterized by a **knowledge**-based economy and flexible production to ensure a diversity of products, rather than the diminishing costs of standardized **commodities** and mass production typical of Fordism. The post-Fordist labour process requires a flexible workforce: outsourced jobs, self-employed or subcontracted skilled labour, and teamwork are the emerging features of this process, together with very insecure working and social conditions. These combine to produce an 'entrepreneurial self'. In terms of political formation, there is said to be a shift from the national **security** state to a national competition state as an answer to **globalization** (Bonefeld and Holloway 1991). Whereas the former was responsible for social *and* repressive security, the latter is – whether on the local, the national, or the supra-national level – mainly engaged in the management of internationalization, the mobilization of knowledge, and the subordination of extra-economic spheres to the discursively construed needs of competitiveness (Jessop 2002); this is accompanied by **authoritarian** statism. Scholars differ on the question of whether a new formation already exists or if we are still witnessing the crisis of Fordism (Alnasseri *et al.* 2001).

This periodization has been challenged, however. It has been accused of formalism and teleologism, and it has been argued that there is a danger of imposing reified normative general models on a complex reality (Bonefeld 1991). Furthermore, it has come under attack for neglecting the relevance of collective social **agency** and ideas, and therefore perpetuating the structuralist and functionalist proclivities which the approach was originally intended to overcome as a move away from the structural Marxism of **Althusser** (Holloway 1991; Jenson 1991). The regulationists reply by insisting that actors and struggles, and not solely economic '**laws**', play an important role in post-Fordism (Esser 1998). Hence there are different types of post-Fordism, and the transition is not seen as inevitable (Jessop 2002). It is also argued that this abstract concept should not be fetishized as a way of identifying historical specificity (Lipietz 1993).

Finally, from a feminist point of view, it seems obvious that **gender** relations are neglected, as the process of regulation is described as a conflict only between **classes** and **production** as a gender-neutral process. In fact, Fordism has to be analyzed as the result of a masculinist class compromise, while post-Fordism is characterized by a pluralization of gender practices and simultaneously a doubling of the demands on the growing number of women in employment (Kohlmorgen 2004).

References and further reading

Alnasseri, S., Brand, U., Sablowski, T. and Winter, J. (2001) 'Space, Regulation and the Periodisation of Capitalism', in R. Albritton, M. Itoh, R. Westra and A. Zuege (eds) *Phases of Capitalist Development: Booms, Crises and Globalization*. London: Palgrave.

Amin, A. (ed.) (1994) 'Post-Fordism: Models, Fantasies and Phantoms of Transition', in *Post-Fordism: A Reader*. Oxford: Blackwell.

Bonefeld, W. and Holloway, J. (eds) (1991) *Post-Fordism and Social Form: A Marxist Debate on the Post-Fordist State*. Basingstoke: Macmillan.

Esser, J. (1998) 'Fordismus/Postfordismus', in D. Nohlen, O. Schlutze and S. Schüttemeyer (eds) *Lexikon der Politik: 7, Politische Begriffe*. Munich: Beck.

Hirsch, J. and Roth, R. (1986) *Das neue Gesicht des Kapitalismus: Vom Fordismus zum Post-Fordismus*. Hamburg: VSA.

Jenson, J. (1991) 'Thinking (a Feminist) History: The Regulation Approach as Theatre', *Cahiers de Recherche Sociologique*, 17: 185–98.

Jessop, B. (2002) *The Future of the Capitalist State*. Cambridge: Polity.

Kohlmorgen, L. (2004) *Regulation, Klasse, Geschlecht: Die Konstituierung der Sozialstruktur im Fordismus und Postfordismus*. Münster: Westfälisches Dampfboot.

Lipietz, A. (1993) 'Fordism and Post-Fordism', in W. Outhwaite and T. Bottomore (eds) *The Blackwell Dictionary of Twentieth-Century Social Thought*. Oxford: Blackwell.

SONJA BUCKEL

POST-INDUSTRIAL SOCIETY

The concept of post-industrial society aims at an understanding of the broad structural changes experienced by Western advanced industrial societies in the latter half of the twentieth century. These include most notably the decline of employment in manufacturing and a rise in the service sectors, the spread of tertiary **education** and growth in the field of professional, technical and administrative occupations, and the central role of **science** and **technology**.

Post-industrial society is seen as a new stage in socio-economic evolution. Much like many classical conceptions, societal evolution is thought to involve three stages, moving from traditional to industrial to post-industrial society. The theoretical underpinning for this was paradigmatically expounded by Daniel **Bell** (1976). In his view, society could be viewed as differentiated into three relatively autonomous spheres: politics, **culture** and **social structure**, the latter encompassing economic activities, technology and the occupational structure. Following **Marx**, Bell further differentiates the social structure into relations of production and productive forces. However, against Marx, he argues that these do not need to coincide, and should be viewed as independent axes. Thus, social change can proceed along either axis, and in the case of post-industrial society, it is the axis of the productive forces which is dominant.

The concept of post-industrial society grew out of discussions on the future course of socio-economic development in advanced industrial societies starting roughly in the 1940s. Besides the growth of science and technology and the question of a rising technocracy (Ellul 1954; Richta *et al.* 1969), a central theme was the sectoral dynamic, elaborated, among others, by Clark (1940). According to this theorem, economic activity could be split into extraction (agriculture, mining), manufacture and services. The dynamic of industrial development could then be traced to the different average rate of productivity increase in these sectors, which is highest in agriculture and lowest in services, thus leading to a shift of employment first from agriculture to manufacturing and services, then from manufacturing to services. The emergent society in this perspective need not be a 'service society' (Fourastié); it could as well be more of a 'leisure society' (Riesman), or possibly even a 'do-it-yourself-society' (Gershuny).

With the concept of post-industrial society a more concise and coherent understanding of these and associated changes was sought, most prominently by Bell (1976) and Alan **Touraine** (1969). Touraine's concept of a 'programmed society' gives a general account of the structural changes leading to the emergence of post-industrial society. He focused on the shifts in power relations between social **classes** and the rise of a new social class of technocrats. In his view, economic struggles have been losing significance. In particular, with the institutionalization of industrial conflict, the working class no longer attains the role of an active force in societal change. In this situation, new **social movements** arise as a counterforce to technocracy. Here Touraine hoped to find the outlines of a new historical subject that could be the bearer of societal **emancipation**.

Bell explains the concept of post-industrial society through five dimensions: a shift from manufacturing to services in the economy; the predominance of technical, professional and administrative occupations in the social structure, higher education being the common denominator; the centrality and codification of theoretical **knowledge** as the axial principle, being the basis for technical development, economic growth and policy-making; a certain future orientation as to the projection and planning of technological progress, but also concerning a range of externalities, such as environment and health; and an **intellectual** technology based on algorithms and models and powered by computers.

Due to its speculative nature, Bell hesitated to develop the concept of the post-industrial society in a linear fashion. Rather, he sought to synthesize the various strands of his analysis by schematically contrasting post-industrial with industrial and traditional societies. While traditional society can be understood as a game played against nature, industrial society seems to resemble more of a game played against fabricated **nature**, with the factory as the quintessential place of **work** and the capitalist as the central figure. Post-industrial society, on the other hand, seems to resemble a game between people, epitomized by interaction in an office or practice and by the notion of career, and by the scientist as the central figure. Conflict would not predominantly be rooted in economic class, but in site-specific functional strata (**power**) and in claims on behalf of **status** or other **groups** (distribution). According to Bell, post-industrial society can be viewed from different perspectives. In terms of change in the character of work and change in consumption from quantity of goods towards quality of life, it is a service society. In terms of the axial principle of the codification and centrality of theoretical knowledge, it is a 'knowledge society'. In terms of a more conscious future orientation, combined with knowledge-based tools of modelling and planning and a value orientation towards quality of life and the possible subordination of the corporation, it is a communal society.

Among the core issues discussed are the changing class structure and the role of the 'new class' of professional, administrative and technical occupations; the changing character of work implied in the move from goods to services and the attenuation of education and skills; issues of power and technocracy; and the role of knowledge and science. With particular regard to the move to services, matters of interest have been the future of **trade unions**, with typically low participation rates, and the implications for **gender** relations, with typically high rates of female employment. Also of concern has been the overall economic relation between manufacturing and services, especially problems of economic growth in light of the low rate of productivity increase in the service sectors.

Critique of the concept of post-industrial society has focused on the questions of change in occupational structure and the centrality of theoretical knowledge. Generally, it is held that the view of a sequence from agriculture to manufacturing to a 'march through the sectors' (Gershuny) disregards the complexity of the processes involved, and does not account adequately for differences between countries. Aside from the fact that, at least until the 1980s, employment in manufacturing was rather stable, some of the rise in services is due to rising **labour** participation, some of the decline in manufacturing due to the **globalization** of **production**, and some of the shift between these categories a statistical artefact of what is really the outsourcing of activities such as accounting, PR or transportation to foreign countries. Thus, if the interpretation of the move from manufacturing to services as a radical break seems overstated, the same can be said of the role of theoretical knowledge. In this vein, critics have questioned the disjunction of industrial society and post-industrial society, arguing that most tendencies claimed for the thesis of post-industrial society are strongly related to the very formation of industrial society.

Critique has also focused on the pertinent issue of an implicit, sometimes even explicit, logic of convergence, which is probably exhibited by most society concepts, particularly if they are derived from the analysis of a single country, as in Bell's case, the USA. Here there is the issue of a technological or techno-economic bias if analyses aimed at the axis of the productive forces and the social structure entail changes for culture and politics, thus subsuming the latter under the former, and also leading to an image of convergence.

While the notion of post-industrial society is still being used as a tagline, debates today have shifted considerably toward the concepts of knowledge and information society.

References and further reading

Bell, D. (1976) *The Coming of Post-Industrial Society: A Venture in Social Forecasting,* 2nd edn, with new foreword. New York: Basic Books.

Clark, C. (1940) *The Conditions of Economic Progress.* London: Macmillan.

Ellul, J. (1954) *La technique ou l'enjeu du siècle.* Paris: Armand Colin.

Kumar, K. (1995) *From Post-Industrial to Post-Modern Society.* Oxford: Blackwell.

Richta, R. *et al.* (1969) *Civilization at the Crossroads: Social and Human Implications of the Scientific and Technological Revolution.* White Plains, NY: International Arts and Sciences Press.

Steinbicker, J. (2001) *Zur Theorie der Informationsgesellschaft.* Opladen: Leske Budrich.

Touraine, A. (1969) *La Société post-industrielle.* Paris: Denoël.

Webster, F. (1995) *Theories of the Information Society.* London: Routledge.

JOCHEN STEINBICKER

POSTMODERNISM AND POSTMODERNITY

The concept of postmodernity appeared at a specific moment in the debate over modernity and cannot be separated from that debate. Towards the end of the twentieth century the conditions that had for some time been known as 'modern' seemed to have altered so strikingly that several new concepts burst forth. Among them, 'postmodern' stuck most strongly, and it remains a complex and contested concept within social theory.

The concept of postmodernism, on the other hand, appeared within literary, architectural, philosophical and cultural theory, designating some supposed shifts within modern*ism*. In this case some significant canons of modern culture were in question, such as the stability of texts and the foundations of science. As far as social theory is concerned, this was heralded by some as an important '**cultural turn**' that would even permit sociology to acknowledge 'the end of the social' or to go 'beyond society'.

Initial discussions of the 'postmodern condition' opened up new vistas for social theory. While some complained that 'postmodernity' raised few, if any, distinctively new questions for sociology, many others could foresee hopeful possibilities for this discipline and others beyond the constraints of sclerotic concepts and rigid 'methodologies'. Moreover, the condition of postmodernity seemed to speak to actually existing conditions, such as globalizing tendencies, **new social movements** and the rise of digital technologies, which seemed peripheral to more mainstream sociologies. To many, this seemed like an exciting new opportunity for social theory.

In both cases, postmodernism and postmodernity, the debate was a deep one, referring both to the historical periodization of 'modernity' and to the philosophical currents, emanating from the **Enlightenment**, that accompanied its development. 'Modernity' normally encapsulates those features of the world that are often taken-for-granted today: science and technology as a means to '**progress**', liberal democratic polity, and varieties of capitalist economy. These are associated in turn with the growth of **cities** and a dependence on inanimate power sources for **production**, which gave much of twentieth-century sociology its core focus, 'urban–industrial society' (see **modernity and modernization**).

However, mainstream social theory had always insisted on the active role of cultural influences – religious, literary, philosophical – in the genesis and maintenance of modern social formations. Max **Weber**'s exploration of the role of the **Protestant ethic** in the emergence of capitalism is only the most celebrated (and controversial) of these. True, some social theory had been pursued on the assumption that such cultural influences have become less central (seen in the mid-twentieth century penchant for a strong **secularization** theory, for instance) many others were dubious about the prospects for social theory evacuated of cultural elements.

The debate over the postmodern has several starting points and thus seems to lead in several different directions. The strongest suggests that a new era has dawned, beyond modernity, to which there can be no return. Others hint at the exhaustion of modernity rather than at the clearly visible contours of a new phase of human history. Yet others, such as Anthony **Giddens**, are dubious about the supposed end of modernity but acknowledge that some major changes have occurred since the mid-twentieth century. These they dub 'late' modernity. This position is congruent with that of another group, who argue that while 'modernity' still exists is the designation of the new phase, the conditions of modernity still have to be reckoned with.

For Giddens, the globalizing impact of media contributes to the '**reflexivity** of modernity' and to the ways in which remote localities are now linked. Older, modern social relations are disembedded, or 'lifted out' of local contexts to be reorganized across large time–space distances (see **embedding and disembedding**). **Risk** and uncertainty characterize life more and more. Giddens says that these conditions do

not yet add up to 'postmodern society'. Zygmunt **Bauman** offers another interpretation, speaking of the advent of 'liquid society', where consumer orientations signal the shift to the postmodern, in a world that is the site of constant mobility and change, but without a clear direction of **development**.

So the debate over postmodernity, sociologically speaking, has to do with the subtle interplay of social and cultural conditions that were present, but only in embryonic form, in modernity. Today, aspects of modernity, above all consumerism and new **communications** technologies (or 'new **media**'), have expanded so much that they constitute the contours of what to some appeared as 'new' social terrain. That which was present in a minor way has now inflated so much that the original shape of modernity is almost unrecognizable.

Another aspect of this social transformation is that it contains forces and features that tend to destabilize the more settled sense of reality that many sought in modernity (despite Marx's sense that in modern times 'all that is solid melts into air'). That is to say, many features of postmodernism may be properly understood as relating to tectonic movements deep within the subterranean levels of the social. Of course they resonate with cultural concerns over risk and uncertainty, seen particularly sharply in the radicalizing of modern skepticism in postmodernist **discourse**. And this skepticism is understandable. If Providence was secularized into the shallow optimism of Progress, what would happen when Progress was unmasked as mythical?

At the same time, it is clear that no one – including social theorists – can live with the sheer nihilism or relativism which some postmodernists are sometimes charged with fostering. So it is hardly surprising that attention turns to older sociological questions, now in fresh forms, of normativity or 'how we should live'. Indeed, if the debate over the postmodern has achieved anything it is a revitalizing of the connections between sociology, **ethics** and politics.

Appropriately enough, such concerns refer both to the largest and smallest scale of social activity, from the **body** to the globe, along with a range of intermediary issues. This is turn has helped catalyze theoretical reflection on '**other**ness' in a world where cultural contacts proliferate between people of very different backgrounds, or on the boundaries of human bodies, given the possibilities not only for consumer-oriented medical modification but for seeing bodies as an outcome of competing discourses. This both connects with pressing political questions, to do with the regulation of mobility or of bodies, and pushes the ethical envelope to ask whether there are, after all, some shared priorities for life on earth without which that life may not only be 'not worth living' but practically unsustainable.

Other 'body and globe' questions are prompted not just by long-term processes but also by dramatic events such as '**terrorist**' attack and **war**. After all, it is precisely the sharp and shocking culture contact engendered by 9/11 that raises numerous questions about inter-cultural relationships in a globalizing world. The destruction of the World Trade Center was a blow struck precisely at those postmodern **symbols** of consumerism and new media, but it also forefronted questions ignored by some modern social theorists regarding the role of religion as a basic factor of social life. It remains to be seen whether the 'othering' of strangers or the embrace of the 'other' will become the dominant mode, or how far religion will indeed be taken seriously as a feature of postmodernizing social life.

In the end, however, basic questions about 'the social' still have to be confronted in today's world of accelerating social and cultural change. They are bound up with issues of digital media and with new cosmopolitan and local identities but simultaneously call to mind the kinds of analysis that Emile **Durkheim** (the radical realist,

not the supposed 'father of **functionalism**') espoused. This in turn calls for choices to be made, not only about areas of analysis or about their political consequences, but also about how far the 'human' condition is basically 'social'.

While postmodern*ist* analyses may reject the view that the social *really* exists, sociologists will likely continue to work within some kind of realist frame that sees the social as **ontologically** given (and even, ethically, that our responsibility to and for the other has priority) (see **realism**). For the debate over the postmodern, with its '**hermeneutic** of suspicion', not only discloses some underlying assumptions of all social theory, it also obliges us to lay bare our own commitments. And this is by no means a bad thing.

References and further reading

Bauman, Z. (1992) *Intimations of Postmodernity*. London: Routledge.

Giddens, A. (1991) *The Consequences of Modernity*. Stanford, CA: Stanford University Press.

Lyon, D. (1999) *Postmodernity*. Milton Keynes: Open University Press.

Lyotard, J.-F. ([1979] 1984) *The Postmodern Condition: A Report on Knowledge*. Minneapolis, MN: University of Minnesota Press.

Rosenau, P. M. (1992) *Postmodernism and the Social Sciences*. Princeton, NJ: Princeton University Press.

Sassen, S. (2001) *The Global City*. Princeton, NJ: Princeton University Press.

DAVID LYON

POST-STRUCTURALISM

Post-structuralist thinking encompasses a broad range of concepts and theories that are critically related to French **structuralism** (Ferdinand de Saussure, Claude **Lévi-Strauss**). It shares with structuralism the interest in the generation and the constitution of **meaning**, but also emphasizes the necessary failure of any process of meaning.

Post-structuralism is not simply a theoretical movement after structuralism, but a 'working-through' of structuralism, which started in the late 1960s and which has been taken up by social theorists in the English-speaking world since the early 1980s. Crucial representatives of post-structuralist thought include Jacques **Derrida**, Michel **Foucault**, Jean-François **Lyotard**, Jacques **Lacan**, Ernesto Laclau, Judith **Butler** and Homi Bhabha. In contrast to some theories of **postmodernism**, post-structuralism does not claim that a new era or epoch has started, but rather it tries to establish a new mode of philosophical and social theorizing, starting from the concept of **difference**.

Linguistic structuralism assumes that meaning is generated within a system of differences, thus abandoning the idea of atomistic elements that are meaningful by themselves. It is always difference from other elements which produces meaning. This originally linguistic conception has been transferred to a wide range of social and cultural spheres leading to ideas of society as basically constituted by structures of meanings. These can be seen, for example, in the analysis of **myth** and fairytales, in kinship systems and in fashion systems (see also **Barthes**).

Post-structuralism radicalizes the role of difference and in the process undermines certain assumptions of structuralism. First, post-structuralism is *anti-foundational*, since the foundation of a system (be it God, **rationality**, or a material essence) loses its pre-given position. Derrida (1978) calls these foundations 'transcendental signifiers' because they open up the horizon of a system of meaning. The strategy of post-structuralist thinking is to show how the idea of a pure foundation or origin is itself part of the play of differences. Thus, the effect of anti-foundationalism is a radical decentring of any structure of meaning. Second, such a decentring is accompanied by a critique of the *sign*. Although poststructuralist accounts assume that social structures are discursive structures, they do not accept structuralist and hermeneutic models of meaning (see

hermeneutics). This critique takes different paths. Derrida deconstructs the distinction between 'signifier' and 'signified', since the privileged position of the signified participates in the metaphysical illusion of a pure origin. Instead, the 'sliding of the signifier' manifests a necessary deferral of any fixed signified. Foucault (1972) suggests a mode of **discourse** analysis, which is no longer interested in intentions and hidden layers of meaning, but in the regularity of utterances. Third, hierarchical distinctions (such as speech/writing or culture/nature) are seen as essentially contested and unstable since there is neither a prior foundation, nor is it pos1-structuralism introduces a de-constructivist epistemology, which questions the very distinction between **representation** and the represented, and between reality and fiction.

This **deconstruction** of structuralism was first mainly discussed in literary criticism, although later these ideas proved to be fruitful for social and political theory. Post-structuralist thinkers emphasize that the process of the fixation of meaning within essentially unstable systems becomes the terrain for struggles of **power**. The very diverse post-structuralist social theories share the idea that the **subject** is not pre-given, but created within and through processes of power and knowledge. Subjectivation is understood as subjection/domination *and* as the making of a subject. This idea has been taken up in the analysis of social and cultural **identities** based on **class**, **gender**, **sexuality** and **ethnicity**. A post-structuralist analysis of identities shows the constitutive **exclusions**, which are necessary to produce an **identity** and how the 'constitutive outside' subverts any claim to a fully achieved identity. Typically, a post-structuralist social analysis traces the failures of maintaining stable identities. A post-structuralist understanding also has crucial consequences for any totalizing concept of society. Laclau and Mouffe's (1984) theory of **hegemony** claims that society becomes impossible, because it will never be able to achieve its full identity. This impossibility, however, does not mean that there is no society, but rather that there are always competing attempts at totalizing society.

Post-structuralism has been heavily criticized for its deconstruction of key categories of social thought and its alleged **epistemological relativism**. The interest in the generation and failure of meaning has been accused of textualism, which neglects analysis of material **social structure**. Critiques also worry about the political implications of the deconstruction of the subject and the challenge to the ideas of **rationality** One of the most vocal critics in this regard has been **Habermas** (1988).

References and further reading

Butler, J. (1997) *The Psychic Life of Power*. Stanford, CA: Stanford University Press.

Derrida, J. (1978) *Writing and Difference*. London: Routledge.

Foucault, M. (1972) *The Archaeology of Knowledge*. London: Tavistock.

Game, A. (1991) *Undoing the Social: Towards a Deconstructive Sociology*. Milton Keynes: Open University Press.

Habermas, J. (1988) *The Philosophical Discourse of Modernity*. Cambridge: Polity.

Laclau, E. and Mouffe, C. (1984) *Hegemony and Socialist Strategy*. London: Verso.

Lemert, C. (1997) *Postmodernism Is Not What You Think*. Oxford: Blackwell.

Stäheli, U. (2000) *Poststrukturalistische Soziologien*. Bielefeld: Transcript.

URS STÄHELI

POVERTY

When some people live below a level which **society** defines as a reasonable minimum, they are in poverty, but there is no agreement on how to define it more precisely. Poverty is often associated with the causes or deleterious consequences of a lack of resources, but **meanings** and usages change over time. Debate often focuses on people in poverty ('the poor') or disparate **measure-** **ment** methods rather than the concept of poverty itself. Many incompatible **discourses** are separately but simultaneously used to discuss its forms, dimensions, causes and cures, and to address different audiences in industrialized societies and in developing nations, with little attempt to integrate the approaches (see **industrialization**).

Until the twentieth century, 'poverty' was used to describe the conditions in which much of the urban and rural working population ('the poor') lived. Poverty was an accepted aspect of stratified class societies, where resources were unequally distributed without respect to human **needs** (see **stratification**). Georg **Simmel**, like Edmund Burke before him, distinguished between normal **working class** mass poverty, and the problematic individual poverty **status** of dependence on charity or the Poor Law. Personal social status was critical: the 'respectable' poor 'deserving' to be helped were distinguished from the 'rough' or 'undeserving', to be deterred or punished. For the non-poor, the social problem was poverty's extreme and visible manifestations: squalid living conditions, disreputable and criminal behaviour, precarious social and economic marginality, and threats to social order from an '**underclass**'.

From 1901, Seebohm Rowntree's systematic attempts to analyze the nature and extent of the causes of poverty led to a focus on measuring the resources, chiefly disposable incomes, needed to escape poverty in **market economies**. To avoid argument about culpability for squalor, Rowntree devised his heuristic 'primary poverty' household expenditure budget sufficient only for physical but not social life, to show what proportion of the poor had incontrovertibly inadequate incomes. But its popularity among social investigators wanting a quantitative measure to count the poor, obscured his emphasis on the social relativity of poverty. Throughout **Europe** and North **America**, the idea of poverty became synonymous with incomes insufficient for physical subsistence, also called 'absolute' poverty, not least because this was the period of the **development** of **welfare state** income maintenance systems which needed minimum standards against which to rationalize cash benefits. The social problem became a political problem of dependence on the state, within which the high **risk** causes of low incomes (large families, **unemployment**, sickness and **disability**, old **age**) became paradoxically seen as identifiers of the condition, even though found across the income distribution.

This **paradigm** of poverty as insufficient income for levels of living prescribed by experts and politicians was overturned in the 1960s by Peter Townsend. He criticized the normative sources of the evaluative standards of adequacy used, especially 'absolute' notions, as merely **ideological** constructs and instead emphasized the **relativity** of all possible conceptions of poverty. While accepting that poverty is a socially defined concept, subsequent theoreticians have argued over the authenticity of expressed needs, and how to derive criteria **empirically** from society as a whole instead of normatively from **elites**. Derivations of this relativistic approach are now generally used in social analysis. Poverty measures used include socially defined indicators of **deprivation** as direct criteria of unmet needs; inadequate incomes as their proxies; and qualitative accounts of the experience of poverty. However, references to 'absolute' poverty persist in debate about deprivation and need on a global basis, and many governments still use elitist stipulative definitions of poverty in their policy-making.

Focus on the adequacy of incomes and other disposable resources to achieve minimally acceptable levels of living also makes comparisons difficult between societies which vary in the kinds of resource flows and stocks relevant to overcoming their poverties. Amartya **Sen** suggested that instead of the commodities and their char-acteristics which are analyzed as needed to overcome poverty within any society, a more fruitful approach would be to study the capabilities which people in any society should have to meet their needs, poverty being the condition in which they are prevented from doing so. This perspective shifts the focus from static comparisons of commodities to the dynamics of **power** relations in which people can act or are prevented from acting. Social theorists have become increasingly aware that stipulative formulations of acceptable standards treat people in poverty and its related social and economic exclusions as lacking **agency**, contradicting the essential human value that all members of society should be ascribed equal **rights**. Qualitative social research with and by people in poverty (Narayan *et al.* 2000) has shown the inadequacy of elitist formulations. It has demonstrated that, for this right to be implemented, the experience of living in poverty must be acknowledged as an indispensable perspective on both poverty conceptualization and policy formation. The lack of social and economic integration and the sufferings of socially excluded people, traditionally seen as symptoms of morbidity, become expressed as reflections of powerlessness against unjust shares of resources essential to integration and participation. Nevertheless, research into **deprivation and relative deprivation** (Runciman 1966) has shown that many of those who are objectively poor may not want to identify themselves as such, while dynamic studies reveal that many more are poor over time than at one time.

By the late twentieth century, the concept of poverty accumulated many meanings. Paul Spicker (Gordon and Spicker 1999) identified eleven clusters, three of which referred to material conditions (inadequate level of living, unmet need, multiple deprivation), three to economic position (lack of resources, **inequality** of resources, **class**) and four to social position (lack of entitlements, lack of security, dependency and exclusion). All can be found, though not all congruently, in the seven discourses identified by John Veit-Wilson (1998) in use among government policy-makers in ten countries. Each discourse packaged the poverty concept with its manifestations and appropriate measures in a paradigmatic analysis and vocabulary effecting closure on other competing discourses. Three were asocially abstracted, expressing poverty in terms of a legal status, a theoretical economic model, or a **statistical** position on an income distribution. Four discourses were **humanistic**, referring to persons and behaviours. Of these, one was structural: the consequence of an unequal distribution of power over resources through time created the need to ensure that no one's level of living should fall below the standards acceptable to society in general. The other three covered poverty as a set of deviant behaviours, as life-experiences too divergent from the acceptable average, and as social exclusion. Each of these meanings and the discourses in which they are expressed generates its apposite definitions and related measures. However, confusions abound, so that, for instance, what is measurable often becomes described as 'poverty' without acknowledgement of the limitations of the measure, or causal proxies (such as low income levels) become identified as the substantive unacceptable level of living. The European Union's institutions express poverty as social exclusion (see **social inclusion and social exclusion**), measuring poverty in terms of arbitrary points in national income distributions with no empirical relationship to income levels needed to combat social exclusions and to enable dignified lives. Social exclusion is given meanings far wider than the usual idea of market exclusion as poverty. Further misunderstandings arise from the failure to address questions about the variety of standards of need or adequacy used – needed or adequate for what, for how long, for whom, and from whose perspective – each of which elicits different answers from different, often unvoiced, premises.

A synthesis of current widely accepted definitions of poverty in the early twenty-first century would express it as a condition of levels of living and life experiences unacceptable according to relative and unstratified social standards, caused by a lack of power over tangible and intangible resources needed over time to take part in society and achieve those expected levels of living and experiences without which people are effectively excluded both from participation and from full dignified status. But because of the lack of agreement and the looseness of the many definitions used in social theory, social policy and politics, constructive social analysis is vitiated and argument continues on what policy measures are socially and politically feasible to overcome the poverties revealed by different discourses and methodologies.

References and further reading

Gordon, D. and Spicker, P. (eds) (1999) *The International Glossary on Poverty*. London: Zed Books.

Lister, R. (2004) *Poverty*. Cambridge: Polity.

Narayan, D. *et al.* (2000) *Voices of the Poor*. New York: Oxford University Press for World Bank.

Runciman, W. G. (1966) *Relative Deprivation and Social Justice*. London: Routledge.

Townsend, P. (1993) *The International Analysis of Poverty*. London: Harvester Wheatsheaf.

Veit-Wilson, J. (1998) *Setting Adequacy Standards: How Governments Define Minimum Incomes*. Bristol: Policy Press.

JOHN VEIT-WILSON

POWER

At a most general level the study of power is the analysis of the capacity of individuals both to act in concert and to make others do things which they would not otherwise have done. The first sense can be thought of as 'power *to*' (power to achieve something)

The second sense can be thought of as 'power *over*' (power over someone)

In the literature, there is no agreed definition of the concept because power is what the philosopher **Wittgenstein** termed a '**family** resemblance' concept. In the same way that members of a family resemble each other without there being one single characteristic which they all have in common, a family resemblance concept is a word which has an overlapping set of meanings without the existence of a single core essence to link all uses. There are many characteristics shared by phrases such as 'A exercises power over B', 'the power of **authority**', 'the power of delusion', yet there is no single essence which links them together.

At the broadest level, social theorists are divided between two perspectives. There are those who primarily view power as 'power over'. This is a conflictual perspective that goes back to Thomas Hobbes and receives its first explicit sociological articulation in **Weber**'s definition of power as 'the probability that one actor within a social relationship will be in a position to carry out his will despite resistance' (Weber 1978: 58). This view also informs the analysis of **Mills** (1956), Dahl (1968), Bachrach and Baratz (1962), Lukes (1974), **Mann** (1986) and Poggi (2001). In contrast, some social theorists prefer to interpret power as a capacity for action, which entails a focus on 'power to'. They include **Arendt**, **Parsons** (1963) and Barnes (1988). This contrast should not be considered an absolute distinction but as a scalar one. Arendt, Parsons and Barnes would claim to provide conceptual space for 'power over', but only as a subset of 'power to'. **Giddens** (1984), **Foucault** (1979, 1981), Clegg (1989) and Haugaard (2003) put the two perspectives into a balance.

The power debate began in the 1950s with Mills's (1956) argument to the effect that in the USA power was distributed among an **elite** of approximately 400, who controlled the **economy**, military and political spheres. Because the needs of the three arenas are interdependent, and due to shared **socialization** among the 400, this power elite constituted a united group that set the political agenda.

In response, Dahl argued that Mills had an unsophisticated view of power. In particular, Mills confused power with power *resources*. For Dahl, power is synonymous with the exercise of power: one actor makes another actor do something which he or she would not otherwise have done. Resources are only forms of potential power. **Wealth** may be used to purchase art or to lobby politicians, but only the act of such purchasing or lobbying constitutes power. Hence, Mills had shown only that there existed an inequality in power resources – in potential, not in actual power. Dahl argued that, in order to verify the claim that there exists a power **elite**, key decisions have to be examined to demonstrate that a unified **group** initiates and vetoes decisions. Dahl undertook such a study of decision-making in New Haven. Three key issue areas were examined and those responsible for decisional outcomes were identified. He found that there were elites who dominated specific issues but no single 'power elite'. Furthermore, these elites were in competition with each other, creating a pluralistic balance of power (see **pluralism**).

While Bachrach and Baratz (1962) accepted that power was not equivalent to power resources, they argued that Dahl's exclusive emphasis upon decision-making made him blind to an important aspect of relations of **domination**: the existence of **institutional** bias. Any **organization** has a bias whereby certain issues are placed inside the political process, while others are removed from it. By focusing upon decision-making, Dahl had excluded the possibility that non-decision-making could be taking place. Elites can exercise power by making sure that certain issues are left off the agenda. Consistent with **behaviourism**, Bachrach and Baratz insisted that this 'second face' of power was a form of decision-making in which specific actors should be identifiable.

Lukes (1974) joined the debate by arguing that Bachrach and Baratz did not go far enough in their critique of Dahl. Structural bias is not simply attributable to identifiable decision and non-decision-makers, but is the consequence of the general structural conditions in which social interaction takes place. Furthermore, the ultimate and most effective exercise of power takes place when the powerless do not know what their 'real' **interests** are. What Lukes calls this 'third dimension' of power is a theoretical development of the Marxist concept of 'false consciousness' and **ideology**, where it is used to explain the non-engagement of the **working class** in revolutionary activity. It is held that the members of the working class do not know what their 'real interests' are. In this connection, Lukes calls for a redefinition of power in terms of interest whereby 'A exercises power over B when A affects B in a manner contrary to B's interests' (1974: 27).

While Lukes is undoubtedly correct to point out that power relations can be sustained by the social consciousness of the relatively powerless, the concepts of 'real interests' and 'false consciousness' are inherently problematic because they entail an unacceptable privileging of a particular perspective. For instance, from the vantage-point of Western **feminists**, the **patriarchal** relations of domination that are internalized by women in some non-Western traditional societies may well constitute a form of Lukes' third dimension of power. However, the description of this social knowledge as 'false consciousness' may also be guilty of **ethnocentrism**.

Like Dahl, Parsons developed his theory of power in response to Mills, but he argued that Mills's exclusive emphasis on 'power over' was inherently superficial. In Parson's view, any such analysis had to incorporate 'power to'. Membership of societies gives actors a capacity for social **action** which

they would not otherwise have. Power is created by **social systems** and is not zero-sum – there is not a fixed quantity of power. Consequently, a system in which there is an unequal distribution of power may be more efficient at creating power than a more egalitarian one. Hence an unequal distribution of power may be to the benefit of the worst off.

Arguing from the standpoint of **functionalism**, Parsons maintained that within the polity of social systems, power exists as a circulating medium which is functionally equivalent to **money** in the economy. Essentially he argued that 'power to' is created by the institutionalization of authority through **legitimacy**. This view has found several critics. Among others, Giddens criticized the theory on the grounds that it failed to provide conceptual space for 'power over'. However, Parsons's theory retains importance as one of the first perspectives to observe the significance of 'power to' and to distinguish power from coercion.

Barnes (1988) theorizes 'power to' through the development of a theory of social order based on a combination of the work of Thomas Kuhn and **rational choice** theory. Barnes argues that social order is a massive self-fulfilling prophecy, derived from a shared, paradigmatic, perception of the social world. He explains this through an analogy between a spherical object and a mountain summit. If you wish to check if the former is indeed spherical, you examine its entire surface. In contrast, if you wish to ascertain if a large rock is the summit of a mountain, you examine all the surrounding peaks of rock to decide which is the highest. The surrounding rocks constitute a 'ring of reference' which establishes a rock as the summit. Social **objects** are analogous to mountain summits, except that their ring of reference is the perceptions of social actors. For instance, what makes a particular dot a 'target' is the fact that a group of actors believe it to be a target – they throw missiles at it. This shared perception of the 'order of things' is a self-fulfilling prophesy which gives actors a capacity for action and is also the basis of leadership. If we all believe that John is a leader – and hence behave appropriately towards him – John's leadership becomes a social fact. Barnes provides conceptual space for illegitimate power through rational choice theory. This includes, for instance, 'fear of being first': the first actor to rebel against an illegitimate leadership is confronted by the, as yet, undiminished power of the leader. Hence, everyone will wish to be second with the consequence that the illegitimate leader remains in power.

Giddens develops his analysis of power from the perspective of **structuration** theory. Central to this perspective is the idea that social structures exist only in the moment of reproduction – they are not external to social action. Outside the moment of reproduction, structures exist as 'practical consciousness' or tacit **knowledge**, or **habitus**, which enables actors to 'go on'. The specific goals which agents pursue are largely expressed in discursive consciousness, in knowledge they can put into words. For instance, at this moment I am discursively conscious of the fact that I wish to explain Giddens's theory of power; but what enables me to accomplish this task is my practical consciousness of the structures of the English language. The latter gives me capacity for action – 'power to'. Every utterance contributes to the reproduction of linguistic structures, to what Giddens calls structuration. In so far as these structures are reproduced repeatedly, they are experienced as constraining, and this latter experience of constraint is integral to our capacity for action. If I were to 'invent' new words or grammatical constructions as I went along (i.e. to engage constantly in novel acts of structuration), I would be unable to communicate. Consequently, the constraining aspect of social structures is a prerequisite for them being enabling. In this sense, structures are both enabling and constraining.

Giddens argues that 'power over' is a subset of 'power to'. In particular, he argues that both are premised on structural constraint and that neither form of power exists to the exclusion of the other. For instance, if an employer exercises 'power over' an employee, this gives the former 'power to' produce commodities; but it also, gives the latter 'power to' in the form of a wage. Hence, relations of domination entail mutual dependence.

Foucault similarly argues that 'power to' and 'power over' cannot be conceptually separated. Foucault practised social critique by writing 'histories of the present' learning the past to understand our present condition. Essentially, Foucault views social agents as interpretative beings whose reality is defined by a specific, historically contingent, interpretative horizon which he terms *episteme* or **discourse**. Foucault argues that over the last five hundred years there have been three dominant discourses (corresponding to the Renaissance period, the Classical period and the Modern period). Each of these is discontinuous with the other and defines the reality of actors in an epoch differently. So, for instance, in the Renaissance period, a relation of 'resemblance' was part of the interpretative horizon of society. In this episteme, individuals perceived the human face as resembling the sky: seven orifices in the face reflected seven planets in the heavens. This shared system of thought gave agents 'power to' act in concert, while simultaneously defining the 'rules of the game' concerning any conflict ('power over'). The Modern period is unique for its discovery of the human subject as the object of knowledge, expressed in the idea of 'Man'. In Foucault's thesis this entails the division of social subjects into **normal and pathological** ways of being, which in turn necessitate control of the **socialization** process. Foucault argues that Bentham's Panopticon – a circular building in which prisoners were constantly visible – became paradigmatic of a disciplinary regime of normalization. The Panopticon is a socialization machine in which social subjects have power exercised over them through the internalization of micro practices. But, furthermore, once such a process has successfully taken place, this also constitutes the basis of social agency – 'power to'. The objects of socialization resist, but compliance is sought through an appeal to truth and to normal behaviour. Social subjects are informed that their resistance is scientifically established 'pathology' – hence inherently unreasonable. If **violence** has to be used against the subject, this represents failure in the use of truth, and a failure of power. Foucault's social critique works in this sense by exposing the contingent manufactured nature of modern moral discourse.

From a post-modern perspective, Clegg (1989) argues that there are three circuits of power. The first is the dispositional circuit in which A exercises power over B. However, within the context of complex **social relations**, this occurrence presupposes a set of dispositions which constitute the background social conditions of possibility. This 'dispositional' circuit of power defines the 'rules of the game', and these are reified through 'obligatory passage points'. In turn, dispositional power only makes sense within an overall system of domination. The former does not exist in isolation; it has to be fought for by social agents through organizational outflanking.

Drawing on Giddens, Haugaard (2003) argues that Lukes's third dimension of power is better theorized in terms of a distinction between 'practical consciousness' and 'discursive consciousness'. Because the majority of structures exist as practical consciousness, many actors reproduce social structures which render them relatively powerless without being discursively aware of this. Consequently, social critique does not entail dispelling 'false consciousness'; it entails consciousness-raising. In this sense, feminist or socialist critique attempts to bring actors to a more discursive awareness of how their

practically conscious acts of structural reproduction contribute to relations of domination. In the tradition of **historical sociology**, Michael **Mann** (1986) examines the sources of social power from 3000 BC to the present. Mann argues that societies are not unitary entities but constituted through a complex interweaving of the economic, ideological, political and military sources of power. Within this interweaving the state cannot be associated with one source; rather its evolution shows a complex exploitation of networks of power sources. Criticizing Mann, and defending Weber's definition of the state as possessing a monopoly of violence, Poggi (2001) argues that political power should not be distinguished from military power. Instead, Poggi espouses a more cynical, Machiavellian model of 'power over'.

References and further reading

Bachrach, P. and Baratz, M. ([1962] 2002) 'The Two Faces of Power', *American Political Science Review*, 56. Reprinted in M. Haugaard, *Power: A Reader*. Manchester: Manchester University Press.

Barnes, B. (1988) *The Nature of Power*. Cambridge: Polity.

Clegg, S. (1989) *Frameworks of Power*. London: Sage.

Dahl, R. ([1968] 2002) 'Power', in *International Encyclopedia of the Social Sciences*, vol. 12. New York: Macmillan. Reprinted in M. Haugaard, *Power: A Reader*. Manchester: Manchester University Press.

Foucault, M. (1979) *Discipline and Punish*. Harmondsworth: Penguin.

Foucault, M. (1981) *The History of Sexuality*. Harmondsworth: Cambridge.

Giddens, A. (1984) *The Constitution of Society*. Cambridge: Polity.

Haugaard, M. (2002) *Power: A Reader*. Manchester: Manchester University Press.

Haugaard, M. (2003) 'Reflections on Seven Ways of Creating Power', *European Journal of Social Theory*, 6: 1.

Lukes, S. (1974) *Power: A Radical View*. London: Macmillan.

Mann, M. (1986) *The Sources of Social Power*, vol. 1. Cambridge: Cambridge University Press.

Mills, C. W. (1956) *The Power Elite*. Oxford: Oxford University Press.

Parsons, T. ([1963] 2002) 'On the Concept of Political Power', in M. Haugaard, *Power: A Reader*. Manchester: Manchester University Press.

Poggi, G. (2001) *Forms of Power*. Cambridge: Polity.

Popitz, H. (1992) *Phänomene der Macht*. Tübingen: Mohr Siebeck.

Weber, M. (1978) *Economy and Society*. Berkeley, CA: University of California Press.

MARK HAUGAARD

PRAGMATISM

Pragmatism is a philosophical doctrine that originated in the United States, though some European thinkers developed similar ideas (e.g. Friedrich **Nietzsche**) or borrowed from American pragmatism (e.g. Jürgen **Habermas**). There are two stages in the history of American pragmatism. The first refers to the period 1890–1930 when pragmatism was the dominant philosophical tradition in the United States, with C. S. Peirce, William James, G. H. **Mead** and John Dewey as central figures. The second stage refers to the more recent revival of pragmatism since 1900, Richard J. Bernstein and Richard **Rorty** being particularly relevant for social theory.

Pragmatism can be subdivided into different camps. There is the juxtaposition between Peirce's attention to the **intersubjectivity** of a community of inquirers and James's focus on individuals' thought processes. There is also the contrast between pragmatists, like Sidney Hook, who wish to impose scientific **rationality** onto other aspects of **culture**, and the likes of Rorty who do not wish to attribute more rationality to **science** than to **art**, politics and **religion**. There are nevertheless a number of key ideas that most pragmatists have in common.

First, most pragmatic philosophers reject what John Dewey called the 'spectator theory of **knowledge**' (Dewey 1930: 233ff.). The spectator theory of knowledge sees knowledge as predominantly a way of representing the inner **nature** of an outer world as accurately as possible. Pragmatism wishes to break with this metaphor of vision (Rorty 1980). Inspired by Darwinian **evolutionary theory**, it expounds an 'anti-representationalist' view, in which knowledge acquisition is seen as active and as a way of coping with life's demands. It would, in the light of biological evolution, be an extraordinary coincidence if people's cognitive functions were so radically transformed as to allow for adequate representation. For rationalists, reality is ready-made, complete and waiting to be discovered; for pragmatists, it is always in the making.

Second, most pragmatist writings argue against a **transcendental** form of inquiry that supposedly grounds aesthetic, ethical or cognitive claims. For a long time philosophers thought their discipline consisted of doing precisely that. While non-philosophers were able to articulate the historically and culturally specific, philosophers assumed they were able somehow to provide atemporal foundations. Pragmatists, on the other hand, argue that the validity of this project has been compromised because none of the attempts so far to find foundations have proved to be successful. Pragmatists therefore talk about the 'agent's point of view', referring to the fact that people cannot escape using a conceptual system. But recognizing the situated nature of human inquiry need not imply that people's knowledge is merely subjective (if by subjective, we mean that this knowledge fails to correspond to the inner nature of reality).

Third, pragmatists try to settle theoretical disputes by gauging what effects they have. They are particularly dismayed by the extent to which philosophers and scientists get involved in pointless debates. These discussions often concern the 'inner' nature of things, alleged 'necessities' or 'first principles'. Pragmatists like James argued that many disputes of this kind are merely 'specious' or 'verbal' (James 1907). To know whether a debate is worth having, so their argument goes, we should simply ascertain whether it makes any difference to take up one position or another, and we should abandon the debate if there are no observable consequences by taking one position or another. In science, pragmatists tend to argue that *empirical* effects matter; in social sciences other effects (such as repercussions in terms of social policy) may be considered.

Fourth, for centuries philosophers have been preoccupied with providing a theory of truth. Philosophers have also often treated scientific **progress** as a gradual progression towards truth. By contrast, contemporary pragmatists are sceptical of any philosophical search for the meaning of 'truth'. To ascertain whether an idea or a theory is true is a pointless exercise if by 'true' is meant something unconditional or a correspondence to an absolute reality. Pragmatists might say that truth is simply a name attributed to that which all true statements share. For pragmatists, what is more important is whether the idea of theory is successful: that is, whether it accomplishes what we want to achieve. So they might be willing to retain the notion of truth in so far as it is defined in terms of successful consequences.

Pragmatism has influenced social theory in a number of ways. G. H. Mead's work inspired Herbert Blumer's (1969) **symbolic interactionism**. It studies how people adopt someone else's perspective, reflect on themselves from this outside perspective and act accordingly. C. S. Peirce's work influenced **Habermas**'s and Karl-Otto Apel's theories of 'communicative rationality' and 'universal pragmatics'. Habermas (1978) studies the relationship between knowledge and cognitive interests. Recently, neo-pragmatism has inspired the emergence of a non-foundationalist **philosophy of social science** (Baert 2005).

References and further reading

Baert, P. (2005) *Philosophy of the Social Sciences: Towards Pragmatism*. Cambridge: Polity.
Bernstein, R. J. (1986) *Philosophical Profiles: Essays in a Pragmatic Mode*. Cambridge: Polity.
Blumer, H. (1969) *Symbolic Interactionism: Perspective and Method*. Englewood Cliffs, NJ: Prentice Hall.
Dewey, J. (1930) *The Quest for Certainty: A Study of the Relation of Knowledge and Action*. New York: Minton, Balch.
Habermas, J. (1978) *Knowledge and Human Interests*. London: Heinemann.
James, W. (1907) *Pragmatism: A New Name for Some Old Ways of Thinking*. New York: Longmans, Green and Co.
Joas, H. (1993) *Pragmatism and Social Theory*. Chicago: University of Chicago Press.
Mead, G. H. (1934) *Mind, Self, and Society: From the Standpoint of a Behaviorist*. Chicago: University of Chicago Press.
Rorty, R. (1980) *Philosophy and the Mirror of Nature*. Oxford: Blackwell.
Rorty, R. (1982) *Consequences of Pragmatism*. New York: University of Minnesota Press.

PATRICK BAERT

PRAXIS AND PRACTICES

The concept of practice operates in pairs or contrasts, particularly with theories or rules. Praxis denotes the realm of **knowledge** and **action** that cannot be fully accounted for by theory, particularly the theory of revolutionary political action. It is sometimes suggested, as it was by Georg **Lukács**, that there must be a dialectical relationship between the two, in which theory can learn from practice as well as direct and inform it.

In contemporary social theory, practice plays a different role, which can best be understood through the contrast between the concept of practice and the concept of social norm (or models of society in terms of rules). The contrast is well expressed by Pierre **Bourdieu** in his classic study, *Outline of a Theory of Practice* (1972). The 'rules' or 'norms' model of **society** is a misleading abstraction; practice is a concept that better captures the fact that living in society is a matter not simply of following rules, but of practical mastery of the cues and expectations of others, of the use of **symbols**, and of a process of continuous mutual adjustment.

The differences are sometimes subtle, but they have meant that the concepts have played quite different roles: rule-like concepts, such as **culture** and **ideology**, can be thought of as super-structural, concepts explained and determined by some other kind of fact, such as fundamental economic relations. Practice, however, is a fundamental concept. It is not explained in any simple way by a different **structure**, but it is itself a basic (and hidden) structure that produces visible or overt structure, according to the internal logic of the strategies it permits, and that lead to its continuation.

The family of concepts of practices includes two large sub-families of concepts. One includes notions like **frames**, **worldviews**, and **paradigms**, and the other includes **habitus**, embodied knowledge, skills, and *mores*, among other things. All of these concepts are theoretical in the sense that we must infer their existence and their powers from their observable effects. We cannot observe a 'culture' or a 'paradigm' directly. We see only manifestations, consequences, and effects. So there is an open question about what these entities really are. Are they supra-individual 'external' realities, like Emile Durkheim's 'social facts'? Or are they no more than convenient descriptions of enduring patterns that are composed, like the strands of a rope, not of anything continuous but of short elements, such as individual skills, beliefs, actions, habits, and expectations?

The issue here may be seen most simply through an example. If one were to claim, for example, that there is a 'European skiing culture', and point to the evidence of certain typical behaviours of skiers in Europe that are less common elsewhere, is one describing an outcome of the various individual skills, habits, beliefs, and actions of skiers in Europe, or describing the outcome of a collective process that guarantees the pattern, holds the skiers to it, and also in some fashion assures its own continuation? This is a very deep and basic question about the nature of social reality and 'the social' itself: whether a practice or world-view is understood to be located in some sort of supra-individual place, such as 'the social', or is no more than what exists within individual brains and bodies. Thomas Kuhn's concept of a 'paradigm', presumably, is social *and* cognitive; 'social' because it is 'shared' rather than individual.

Like Kuhn's concept of paradigm, the most common and familiar usages in both branches of the practice family are social rather than individual. It is essential to the argument of Bourdieu, for example, that individual properties, such as dispositions, are constituted or produced by *collective* processes. The habitus of the participant includes dispositions, which produce actions, which produce responses in persons similarly programmed, which assure the continuation of the activity, which in turn 'programs' dispositions that make the activity possible. The basic point is this: practices have both a causal primacy and a kind of **autonomy** in relation to the individual, what Durkheim called 'externality' ([1895] 1982) – though it is often unclear what is meant by this.

There are, however, those who seem to reject this kind of objectification of collective notions who nevertheless also seek to employ notions like **tradition** and skill, and who also accord the 'tacit' a large and significant role, such as Michael Oakeshott (1962) or Michael Polanyi ([1946] 1964). For these thinkers, the content is carried in the (different) skills of the *individuals*, whose common actions constitute the 'tradition'. The patterns, however, are descriptive facts. These thinkers do not assume that practices are the sorts of things that can assure their own continuation. For them, that which is 'external' or 'social' is simply the actions and sayings of others, and 'continuation' is a result of the ongoing activities of individuals, and not of collective forces.

References and further reading

Bourdieu, P. ([1972] 1977) *Outline of a Theory of Practice*. Cambridge: Cambridge University Press.

Durkheim, E. ([1895] 1982) *The Rules of Sociological Method*. New York: Macmillan.

Kuhn, T. ([1964] 1996) *The Structure of Scientific Revolutions*, 3rd edn. Chicago: University of Chicago Press.

Oakeshott, M. (1962) *Rationalism in Politics*. London: Methuen.

Polanyi, M. ([1946] 1964) *Science, Faith, and Society*. Chicago: University of Chicago Press.

Turner, S. P. (1994) *Social Theory of Practices*. Chicago: University of Chicago Press.

STEPHEN P. TURNER

PREFERENCES

Preferring one state of affairs to another amounts to desiring it more strongly or favouring it. Philosophers of mind debate how to characterize such attitudes. Some hold that by a preference we mean a possible cause of action; on this view, a person's preference (say, for health over illness) should be defined as the attitude that would cause her to do certain things (say, to exercise) in certain circumstances. It has also been suggested that a preference is merely a disposition to act: a person's tendency to perform certain actions under certain conditions. Or that it is a disposition to feel – for instance, a person's tendency to feel better imagining one scenario rather than another, or to feel better receiving the news that one rather than the other has come true. Two further views are that the concept of a preference is respectable but unanalyzable; or that it is hopeless and should be boycotted.

Preferences pervade social theory because they pervade both the **explanation** and the evaluation of **action**. Consider again a person's preference for health. This preference might help us explain her exercising, but it might also confer various kinds of normative status on this and other actions. For one thing, it might make exercising the prudent, reasonable course of action for that person, thus building a bridge from explaining to understanding or rationalizing

her behaviour. Preferences loom large, therefore, in the quest for *Verstehen* that informs **hermeneutics** and in **rational choice** theory as conceived by **game theory** and methodological **individualism**. Then there is the moral part of the normative. A person's preference for health might be the feature of the world that would make it good and right for others to promote her health, and wrong for them to interfere with her health. Her preferences might be the source of other people's obligations to her. Such proposals to centre **morality** and all **values and norms** around preference satisfaction are typically rooted in **utilitarianism**. The moral good is seen as an aggregate of all the individuals' good, and an individual's good as the satisfaction of her preferences or desires.

However, putting preferences centre-stage has its problems. Preference-based explanations of behaviour threaten to become vacuous if the very concept of a preference is behavioural - for how could my tendency to do something explain my doing it? If we steer clear of this vacuity by employing a less behavioural concept of preference, large portions of real-life behaviour may fail to match preferences and, *a fortiori*, to be explained by them. Another challenge comes from the hard sciences, for they aspire to provide physical explanations of everything, human action included. Can talk of attitudes like preferences be made to fit in with talk of atoms or neurons? The normative domain, too, is controversial. In assessing actions as rational or right, it has been objected, we should not give a say simply to *any* preference - not, for example, to preferences that are sadistic or caused by brain-washing or by false information. If this objection holds, and if thus preferences themselves have to meet normative constraints in order for an individual action or social policy prompted by them to qualify as wise or good, the reduction of reason and value to subjective preference is incoherent.

465

References and further reading

Dennett, D. (1987) *The Intentional Stance*. Cambridge, MA: MIT Press.

Elster, J. (1983) *Sour Grapes*. Cambridge: Cambridge University Press.

Elster, J. and Hylland, A. (eds) (1986) *Foundations of Social Choice Theory*. Cambridge: Cambridge University Press.

Fehige, C. and Wessels, U. (eds) (1998) *Preferences*. Berlin: de Gruyter.

Millgram, E. (ed.) (2001) *Varieties of Practical Reasoning*. Cambridge, MA: MIT Press.

von Wright, G. H. (1971) *Explanation and Understanding*. London: Routledge.

CHRISTOPH FEHIGE

PRESTIGE

Prestige researchers deal not with one but with two concepts of prestige: with prestige as a hierarchy of positions and prestige as an attribute of socially closed **groups**. By and large, **stratification** theories that emphasize order in society (e.g. **functionalist** theories) conceive prestige as an attribute of individuals or of individual social positions that form a hierarchy. Stratification theories that emphasize **conflict** (e.g. the work of **Weber**) think of prestige as designating social aggregates, or individuals within social aggregates, influenced by social closure processes.

Other researchers find it necessary to distinguish between prestige as a subjective evaluation and prestige as objective reality. If, however, it is conceived as purely subjective, prestige would be of little relevance; it would constitute nothing more than a psychological response. It must, therefore, reflect at least some aspect of the objective social world. On the other hand, if prestige is conceived as a straightforward measure of that reality, sociologists would not gain from introducing the concept either. Clearly, prestige must be subjective as well as objective. However, to construe prestige as being both confronts us with a problem of **action** and order, as is always the case when sociologists focus on the individual

Table 1. Types of prestige theories

Sources of stratification	Orientations of social action	
	Normative	Rational
order (hierarchy)	charisma (Shils 1968)	achievement (Davis and Moore 1945)
conflict (social closure)	honour (Weber 1972)	esteem (Blau 1964)

actor as an active **agency** whose choice of ends is a random factor. If sociologists deny the objectionable implication of the randomness of ends, the independence of the actor disappears and is assimilated to the conditions of the situation. The solution suggested by Talcott **Parsons**, is to distinguish between two different types of orientations of social actions: the rational and the normative. Drawing on this idea, we can then cross-tabulate two types of stratification theories: order and **conflict** theories, with the two types of orientations of social action which these theories primarily consider. We then have (1) rational-order theories of prestige, (2) rational-conflict theories, (3) normative-conflict theories, and (4) normative-order theories (Wegener 1992). Table 1 lists these theories, their basic defenders, and the four different foundations of prestige the theories imply: achievement, esteem, honour, and **charisma**.

In this scheme, the property from which prestige flows is *achievement* if occupational success is considered central to society (Davis and Moore 1945). It is *esteem* if *power* relations are deemed important (Blau 1964). It is *honour* if it is a quality shared by members of one and the same status group or *Stand* (Weber 1972). Finally, it is *charisma* if based on deference entitlement conferred to occupational roles that harmonize with central collective **values** (Shils 1968) (see also **status** and **charisma**).

In empirical research, a dominant view has been to think of prestige as a hierarchy of positions that individuals may possess.

This research follows 'Edward's paradigm' (Edwards 1938) in so far as it assumes that social positions are visible to everyone and that they are ordered along a single value dimension. North and Hatt (1947) were among the first to ask respondents of popular surveys to rate occupational titles according to their 'social standing'. The resulting NORC occupational prestige scale is updated regularly, serving as a model for all national and international inquiries into the prestige of occupations. Based on these standard scales, socio-economic indexes (SEI) have also been constructed by regressing mean **education** and income levels on prestige, thereby also generating scores for those occupations (or census codes) for which no direct prestige measures have been determined.

In spite of its apparent success in terms of providing occupational prestige scales, this dominant view has been challenged on a number of accounts. Evidence has accumulated that judgments of prestige differ depending on the social positions of the observers themselves. In particular, there is less consensus in the attribution of prestige in the lower than in the upper strata of society. This finding has been attributed to the fact that members of lower status groups tend to lack expert knowledge. In addition, however, social perception research indicates that high status observers tend to polarize the prestige continuum, increasing inter-rater correlations, whereas low status observers level the continuum generating lower correlations. Evaluators of prestige also typically distinguish between positions and incumbents of positions, especially with regard to gender. The difference in the judgement of male and female incumbents depends on the **gender** composition of the occupations. In particular, women receive higher prestige ratings than men in traditionally female occupations; and men are judged higher than women if they are in occupations typically held by men. It is likely, therefore, that gender-typed prestige perceptions prevent men as well as women from entering gender-atypical occupations.

References and further reading

Blau, P. M. (1964) *Exchange and Power in Social Life*. New York: Wiley.

Davis, K. and Moore, W. E. (1945) 'Some Principles of Stratification', *American Sociological Review*, 10: 242–9.

Edwards, A. M. (1938) *A Social-Economic Grouping of Gainful Workers of the United States*. Washington, DC: US Department of Labor.

Goode, W. J. (1978) *The Celebration of Heroes: Prestige as a Control System*. Berkeley, CA: University of California Press.

North, C. C. and Hatt, P. K. (1947) 'Jobs and Occupations', *Opinion News*, 9: 3–13.

Shils, E. A. (1968) 'Deference', in J. A. Jackson (ed.) *Social Stratification*. Cambridge, MA: Harvard University Press, pp. 104–32.

Weber, M. (1972) *Wirtschaft und Gesellschaft*, 5th edn. Tübingen: Mohr-Siebeck.

Wegener, B. (1992) 'Concepts and Measurement of Prestige', *Annual Review of Sociology*, 18: 253–80.

BERND WEGENER

PRODUCTION

Most uses of the concept of 'production' in sociology and social theory refer to production of material goods or **commodities** in economic contexts. There are, however, additional uses of the concept involving accounts of the ways in which cultural elements can be said to be conditioned or in some sense produced by material factors. In a more abstract sense, some theorists speak of the 'production of society' by individuals acting within structural constraints that are themselves said to be products of **action** and **agency**. For some theorists of **postmodernism** and **post-industrial society**, social theory and research since the 1970s–80s is said to have made a turn away from what has been called a 'production **paradigm**' of analysis towards a focus on the salience of **consumption**.

The classic account of the significance of economic production in social theory is **Marx**'s historical **materialism**, drawing on the classical liberal economic theories of the eighteenth- and early nineteenth-century British and French **political economists**. Marx's concept of the **mode of production** describes the conjunction of the 'forces and relations of production' that make up the economic systems of socially organized **labour** that condition and 'determine in the last instance' the distinct political and cultural institutions of historical ages. Marx explained **social change** by postulating moments of historical **crisis** when the productive 'forces' eventually become 'fettered' by the existing productive 'relations', precipitating a **revolution** which extends the development of the productive forces (Cohen 1978). After the transition from **feudalism** to **capitalism**, the future communistic mode of production is one in which the power of the **proletariat** to produce goods that satisfy human **needs** ceases to be a commodified product of the production process. According to Marx's materialist reading of **Hegelian** philosophy, non-alienated labour presupposes the ability of workers to recognize in the products of their own **work** an externalization of their own inner essence or creative agency. According to classical Marxism, the capitalist economy attempts to solve its constant crises of overproduction through expediencies such as dumping of excess goods on colonial markets (as in Lenin's and J. A. Hobson's theory of **imperialism**) or intervention and **regulation** by the **state**.

Before Marx, Hegel in *The Philosophy of Right* had already spoken of a contradiction in **civil society** between the production of ever greater quantities of goods and an ever growing mass of producers unable to appropriate these goods. Hegel's conception of the need for an ethically integrating state later influenced the movements for social reform, social democracy and **socialism** in the early twentieth century. The idea of ethically

meaningful production within the framework of nationalized or state-owned industry was essential to the social philosophies of the European **welfare states** after 1945.

Contemporary **neo-liberal** economic policies aimed at coercing the unemployed into any available occupation without significant regard to previously acquired skills or to job **security** manipulate the originally socialist idea of work as the paramount medium of human self-realization. By construing production in instrumental terms as the *end* for which welfare payments are the *means* (as in 'welfare-to-work'), such policies tend to remove the productive performance of labour from the wider social context of collective **solidarity** that alone lends it ethical meaning. An emasculated idea of production then becomes the foil against which qualitatively different, less utilitarian, kinds of labour can be stigmatized as forms of idleness, parasitism or wastefulness. Use of the term 'productivity' by economists appears to denote some recognition of the frailties of this **discourse**, as in the observation that some relatively labour-friendlier European economies display relatively higher rates of output per number of hours worked. But this term, too, is vulnerable to reification. 'Productivity' can at most describe the outcome of a labouring activity that is meaningful or satisfying for the worker; it cannot itself describe the worker's conscious ends.

Henry Ford's management of the eponymous automobile company in the 1920s encouraged its labour-force to behave as avid consumers of the high quantities of goods it was exhorted to produce (see **Fordism** and **post-Fordism**). Frederick Taylor codified this thinking in a series of pamphlets advocating 'scientific management' of the production process. During the Cold War, the figure of Stakhanov in the Soviet Union as Stalin's near-mythic champion worker formed an ironic homology to these doctrines on the other side of the ideological divide. Fordism, Taylorism and 'Stakhanovite' attitudes are today household names for production management philosophies operating by the dual **sanction** effect of coercion, on the one hand, and consumer inducement, on the other – otherwise known in colloquia English as 'the carrot and the stick'.

Neither these doctrines nor any of their neo-liberal avatars gain normative foundation from ideas in Hegelian Marxism and phenomenological and existentialist philosophy about the self-realization of the subject in the object through labour and *praxis* (see **praxis and practices**). Marx's early Hegelian thinking echoed ancient Greek teaching in Aristotle about the intertwinement of *praxis* and *poiesis*, where 'practice' stood to 'production' as the enfolding medium of an ongoing expressive process whose productive outcomes could never be contrived in advance. Numerous twentieth-century intellectuals adapted these ideas to the critique of **technological** civilization founded on domination by **instrumental reason**. Drawing partly on J. C. F. Schiller's conception of *play* in the moral and aesthetic education of the self (see **play and game**), **Gramsci**, **Marcuse** and **Sartre** spoke of the travails of the human self to produce its own reality and to 'make history'. **Lukács** combined Marx's theory of the declining power of wages to purchase the products of the wage-earner's labour with **Simmel**'s thesis of the diminishing ability of humanity spiritually to re-appropriate the products of its own producing process – Simmel's 'tragedy of culture'. Henri **Lefebvre** spoke of the availability of a **space and place** for work, dwelling, leisure and politics not as given but as *produced* through conflict and struggle, especially in the modern **city**. Today the Canadian '**communitarian**' philosopher Charles **Taylor** (1989) refers to all these accounts of the sources of the modern self with the label of the 'expressivist model of the subject' (see also **humanism**).

In a less openly normative vein, phenomenological and anthropological concepts of production feed into the theories of **institutions** developed by Arnold **Gehlen** and later by **Berger and Luckmann**, partly under the influence of **Schutz**'s conception of the meaningful production of the social world by acting subjects. Related uses of a concept of production occur in the areas of the sociology of **culture** and **knowledge**, from the work of Karl **Mannheim** to the exponents of British cultural studies in the 1970s (Hall 1980 *et al.*) and contemporary American cultural sociology organized around the theme of the 'production of culture' (Peterson 1976).

Some theorists of postmodernism and post-industrial society have, however, spoken of the declining validity of a 'production paradigm' in social theory. Authors such as **Jameson** (1991), Harvey (1990) and other commentators on the 'new' or 'late' capitalism and its more dispersed, de-centralized or 'disorganized' forms (Lash and Urry 1987) point to the effect of images of consumer lifestyle choices in concealing general social consciousness of the class bases of capitalist production. In the 1970s Daniel **Bell** wrote of a climate in which the ability of productive labour in a vocation to sustain the cement of capitalist society would have to be taken up by a new myth of consumer freedom playing proxy for Weber's moribund **Protestant ethic** (see also Campbell 1987). Not without a dose of overstatement, Jean **Baudrillard** claims that where the Marxian concept of production might once have made sense of predominantly manufacturing-based industrial economies, the only theoretical framework adequate to contemporary realities is one that thematizes the 'implosion' of relations of production into mediated consumer signs and **simulacra** and is radically sceptical of notions of an inner human essence seeking redemption for itself through work.

References and further reading

Bell, D. (1973) *The Coming of Post-Industrial Society*. New York: Basic Books.
Bell, D. (1979) *The Cultural Contradictions of Capitalism*. London: Heinemann.

Campbell, C. (1987) *The Romantic Ethic and the Spirit of Modern Consumerism*. Oxford: Blackwell.

Cohen, G. A. (1978) *Karl Marx's Theory of History: A Defense*. Oxford: Oxford University Press.

Hall, S. *et al.* (eds) (1980) *Culture, Media, Language*. London: Hutchinson.

Harvey, D. (1990) *The Condition of Postmodernity*. Oxford: Blackwell.

Jameson, F. (1991) *Postmodernism, or, the Cultural Logic of Late Capitalism*. London: Verso.

Lash, S. and Urry, J. (1987) *The End of Organized Capitalism*. London: Sage.

Peterson, R. A. (ed.) (1976) *The Production of Culture*. Beverly Hills: Sage.

Taylor, C. (1989) *Sources of the Self*. Cambridge: Cambridge University Press.

AUSTIN HARRINGTON

PROFESSIONS AND PROFESSIONALIZATION

Professions are occupational categories whose members have degrees of statutory **power** and **autonomy**, because they successfully claim to solve better than others relevant problems of their clients or of society in general. The expertise of their members is validated by advanced university degrees, theoretical **knowledge** and technical skills. Medicine and law are archetypal examples. Profession is both a **status** category (see **stratification**) and a category for a certain type of occupation. *Professionalization* is the historical process by which a single occupation gains the status of a profession (i.e. by establishing a monopoly for a specific activity); it also refers to the general upgrading of qualification level in society, by which more and more occupations make academic or specialist training a prerequisite of their practice. *Professionalism* is the idea guiding the **culture** (**values**, **ethics**, **ideology**) of the profession and the **habitus** of its members. In nineteenth century USA, professionalism arose as part of the culture of the new **middle class**, exposing elements like self-control, self-reli-

ance, self-esteem and shaping an **individualism** based on social responsibility (Bledstein 1976). The rise of the professions occurred mainly in the nineteenth century. The historical roots, however, are deeper. The medieval academic groups, originally called learned professions (clergy or divinity, medicine, and **law**), were the first occupational groups to be called professions. Thus, besides medicine and law, teaching is a privileged case as a model for professional **action**.

We find the main roots of the theory of the professions in classical European sociology. For Max **Weber**, professionalization is part of the **rationalization** process of Western **modernity**. Professional action is not simply a technical task or instrumental activity, but a **vocation** or calling (*Berufung*), a value-oriented practice. For Emile **Durkheim** the cohesion and integration of society were mainly guaranteed by professional or corporate **associations**. Since the 1930s, some attempts have been made to define the distinguishing characteristics of modern professions. This approach (sometimes called 'trait' or 'check-list' approach) has been frequently criticized as being only descriptive and arbitrary.

With Talcott **Parsons**'s early essay ([1939] 1954), a more theoretical approach began to emerge. Parsons made a sharp distinction between the logic of action of economic occupations (entrepreneur) and of the professions, or profit orientation vs. client orientation. Later, the therapeutic relation between doctor (especially the psychotherapist) and patient became the model for Parsons's theory of professional action (*clinical focus*). The patient is dependent on the doctor, and therefore the institutional setting of the professional relationship must secure the protection of the patient, mainly by professional **ethics** which encourages the patient to develop **trust**. Since this institutional setting must be protected from influences of pressure groups and from economic interests, a certain independence of the professional is necessary. There are structural similarities between the therapeutic and the socializing pattern. In later years, Parsons saw the academic profession as a model for the profession as such, where the logic of action – the relationship between professional and client – differs systematically from three other models, namely, **bureaucracy**, **market economy**, and **democracy**. The academic profession is a trustee of *cognitive rationality*, and helps to maintain the fiduciary function of the university system for cultural values. Even more emphasis on the *clinical focus* of the teaching profession can be found in the work of German sociologist Ulrich Oevermann who stressed the primacy of professionals' orientation towards clients' value problems instead of the application of scientific knowledge.

Since the 1960s, a critical approach has gained prominence (Johnson 1972; Freidson 1970, 1986; Larson 1977). It emphasizes **power** and **autonomy** of the profession as an organized occupational group (association), protected by the state, and legitimized by professional ethics serving as an ideology to maintain power and privileges. For these critics, autonomy – understood as the power of the professional organization to define and to control their own work and thus avoiding external **control** – is the distinctive trait of the profession. Larson hardly sees a difference between professional and market orientation. In the tradition of the **Chicago School**, Andrew Abbott (1988) developed professions theory further by considering the professions as a system of interdependent occupational groups with conflicting interrelations. His key term is *jurisdiction*, meaning the social and legal acceptance of a profession's claim for exclusive problem solving. In **systems theory** and the theory of functional **differentiation** (see **Luhmann**) there is some doubt about whether professions are still necessary in a functionally differentiated modern society.

References and further reading

Abbott, A. (1988) *The System of Professions: An Essay on the Division of Expert Labor*. Chicago: University of Chicago Press.

Bledstein, B. J. (1976) *The Culture of Professionalism*. New York: W. W. Norton.

Freidson, E. (1970) *Profession of Medicine*. New York: Dodd & Mead.

Freidson, E. (1986) *Professional Powers: A Study of the Institutionalization of Formal Knowledge*. Chicago: University of Chicago Press.

Johnson, T. J. (1972) *Professions and Power*. London: Macmillan.

Larson, M. S. (1977) *The Rise of Professionalism*. Berkeley, CA: University of California Press.

Parsons, T. ([1939] 1954) 'The Professions and Social Structure', in T. Parsons, *Essays in Sociological Theory*. Glencoe, IL: Free Press.

Parsons, T. and Platt, G. (1973) *The American University*. Cambridge, MA: Harvard University Press.

Witz, A. (1992) *Professions and Patriarchy*. London: Routledge.

GÜNTER BURKART

PROGRESS

Progress is one of the main concepts to capture **social change**. Unlike **development** and **evolutionary theory**, progress is confined to the social and psychological realm due to the idea's central proposition: humanity is not only gifted with the ability for **rationality** (animal rationable) but can transform itself to become rational (animal rationale) (**Kant** 1798: 321). The idea of perfectibility then becomes the driving force of social change. Thus, **knowledge** of the past obtained in the present can transform the future along a normatively defined direction towards improving human welfare (Condorcet 1955). The idea of progress has two origins: the Judaeo-Christian **tradition** leading to linear time and a positive evaluation of the future and the project of **Enlightenment** which emancipates humanity from tradition and allows for self-determination.

In the nineteenth century, progress was the central idea in the social sciences culminating

471

in **Marx**'s *Communist Manifesto* (Marx and Engels 1998). However, the twentieth century witnessed the fall of the idea of progress. **Metaphysical** constructions of history became outdated and the perspective shifted towards unintended consequences of action and ambivalent outcomes of modernity. At the end of the twentieth century **postmodernism** put a final end to the naïve idea of progress (see also **modernity and modernization**). Recently, progress has been reinterpreted as reflexive and has been replaced by the idea of sustainable development, taking into account the effect of today's **action** on the ability of future generations to meet their needs (WCED 1987: 5).

References and further reading

Alexander, J. C. and Sztompka, P. (eds) (1990) *Rethinking Progress*. Boston: Unwin Hyman.

Condorcet, A.-N. ([1794] 1955) *Sketch for a Historical Picture of the Progress of the Human Mind*. London: Weidenfeld & Nicolson.

Kant, I. ([1798] 1968) 'Anthropologie in pragmatischer Hinsicht', in *Kants Werke: Akademie-Ausgabe*, vol. 8. Berlin: de Gruyter.

Marx, K. and Engels, F. ([1948] 1998) *Manifesto of the Communist Party*. London: Verso.

Nisbet, R. (1980) *History of the Idea of Progress*. New York: Basic Books.

WCED (1987) *Our Common Future: Report of the World Commission on Environment and Development*. Oxford: Oxford University Press.

CHRISTIAN SCHMIDT-WELLENBURG

PROLETARIAT

The term proletariat, denoting the poorest **class**, became widely used in the industrial **revolution** and **Marxism**. In academic theories, it became synonymous with the **working class**.

Popularized Marxism expected **capitalism** to downgrade the middle classes into the factory proletariat, being deskilled, exploited, and demoralized. United by factory discipline, it would overthrow capitalism, instructed by **communist** theory and **parties**.

Historians like Thompson found that, in the **underclass** (mainly Irish immigrants) 'immiseration' instead produced fatalism. Data disproved general wage decreases. Class formed from the skilled popular classes and their traditions of dissent, opposing not machinery, but political repression and the changed way of life under *laissez-faire* capitalism. Conflicts became antagonistic only as a 'special' historic case. After 1848, movements turned to institutionalized struggles for civil and economic rights curbing capitalism.

In Russia, these rights being denied, Lenin revived the revolutionary model: workers could only develop **trade union** consciousness, needing leadership from party **intellectuals**. Instead, as Rosa Luxemburg ([1906] 1971) argued, skilled workers, participating in power conflicts, could develop autonomous political competences. The Russian Revolution followed Lenin, and the vision of proletarian abolition of **domination** became the legitimating **ideology** for domination *over* the working class.

After 1960, **Marcuse** modified the model for rebellious intellectuals. As workers were 'integrated', fundamental opposition could only come from marginalized groups or the Third World.

References and further reading

Engels, F. ([1845] 1958) *The Condition of the Working Class in England in 1844*. Oxford: Blackwell.

Lenin, V. I. ([1902] 1978) *What Is To Be Done?* Moscow: Progress Publishers.

Luxemburg, R. ([1906] 1971) *The Mass Strike, the Political Party and the Trade Unions*. New York: Harper & Row.

Marcuse, H. (1964) *One-Dimensional Man*. London: Routledge.

Marx, K. and Engels, F. ([1848] 1964) 'The Communist Manifesto', in *Selected Works*, vol. 1. Moscow: Progress Publishers.

Thompson, E. P. ([1963] 1968) *The Making of the English Working Class*. Harmondsworth: Penguin.

MICHAEL VESTER

PROPERTY AND PROPERTY RIGHTS

Property is a relationship between a person and an **object** or a trait. Its Latin origin *proprius* denotes something owned by or specific to a person (or **group** of persons). Property rights are rights to acquire, use, and transfer something (see also **rights**). They imply exclusivity – the property of a person in some thing has to be respected by everyone else. Therefore, property as a social **institution** is the complex of relationships among persons, concerning things. Three themes will be discussed below: first, property as an institution; second, property and the concept of efficiency; third, property in its relationship to **rationality**, justice and **power**.

Property exists in every **society**, but since property rights regulate relationships among persons, their form depends on the character of these relations. **Differences** between societies concerning property can be found with respect to:

* who the *bearers* of property rights can be – only natural persons or also juridical persons, **families**, clans, **communities**, the society at large;
* the *kind and scope* of property rights – they may be restricted and shaped in one of many ways;
* the *objects* in which property rights may be held (some or all kinds of tangible objects, intangibles like stocks, patents, copyrights or entitlements to receive social-insurance payments). In some legal systems, property in other persons can be held, but this is impossible where a person is seen as an entity endowed with unalienable rights. In the latter case, a person cannot even be his/her own property – one cannot trade away the rights which define oneself as a person. Related and normatively contested questions include whether a person may alienate parts of his/her body or something which cannot be physically separated from oneself, such as one's working capacity.

A theoretically prominent special case is unrestricted private property. Here the rights of acquisition, use, and alienation of an object, concentrated in one owner, are confined only by the general legal order, but not by the property relationship: one may not use one's knife to stab one's neighbour, not because one's specific right in the knife is restricted, but because a certain type of **action** is generally prohibited. In most legal systems the **nature** of an object and of the relevant social relationships determines the shape of property rights: unrestricted private property rights are common with respect to standard **consumption** goods, whereas other forms of property rights are often restricted. For example, rights in land are often restricted by zoning ordinances or distributed over different people (e.g. by easements). Rights to means of production occasionally are restricted by codetermination requirements, and some rights, such as social security entitlements, are often not freely transferable. Property in patents is limited in time everywhere and rules of succession often restrict transfer options.

Modern attempts to explain the shape and development of property institutions focus mainly on efficiency aspects. If property rights are not well delineated – that is, if everyone has an unlimited right to use a resource (a common pooled resource) – then everyone has an incentive to over-use that resource, since the costs of one person's overuse fall partly on other people and the benefits of self-restriction would be partly reaped by other users. This is known as the 'Tragedy of the Commons' (Hardin 1968). Put in more abstract terms, if the social rate of return of some activity differs from its private rate of return, inefficiency results. This is true not only for the use of physical resources; it is also true for activities which produce intangibles, like **knowledge**. If property rights in (the use of) knowledge

473

are nonexistent then often it will not be provided at all. Nearly as important for efficiency as the clear delineation of ownership rights is the absence of restrictions on their use. If people can freely command resources and are free to exchange them, then resources will flow towards their most productive uses.

Efficiency considerations can be used in normative arguments, but are relevant for positive theory as well. The argument is an evolutionary one: societies which have (for whatever reasons) comparatively more 'efficient' property rights will gain an edge over societies with less efficient property rights; this induces competitive pressure to adopt the most advanced institutions everywhere, although it is a tendency mitigated by analyzable path dependences (Demsetz 1967; Posner 1977; North 1990).

Efficiency as a central explanatory variable is not disputed. It is also not disputed that well defined property rights are a vital prerequisite of efficiency. However, this is not, as suggested frequently, a question of private versus common property. The 'tragedy' is not a tragedy of the 'commons', but rather the tragedy of a resource which is 'up for grabs'. The argument only shows that some **governance** of the resource is needed, but it does not demonstrate that one specific governance type – private property – is the most efficient governance type under all circumstances.

What about the idea of commons taken seriously – as joint governance? The piece of reasoning quoted most frequently in this context is the Coase theorem (1960). In principle, private property can be efficient under all circumstances. When external effects of individual behaviour are absent, this is obvious; where externalities exist, still joint governance is not immediately necessary, since those affected by an externality have incentives to negotiate with the actor/ owner whose behaviour is harmful or beneficial to them. If everybody is well informed and if transaction costs are negligible, private property is efficient: there is no need to

bother about more cumbersome forms of governance. This, however, is a special case. Generally, it depends on the properties of the matter and on the available instruments of governance what institution can be considered as most efficient – sometimes it is private property, sometimes it is the state, sometimes forms of governance in between are best (Ostrom 1990).

Efficiency is, of course, a normative criterion, but not a seriously contested one. If nothing else was at stake, intense discussions about the shape of property rights would not be plausible. Since, however, the shape of property rights affects not only efficiency, but is also consequential with respect to rationality, power, and justice, we find persistent normative conflict.

Rationality problems are connected to the different dynamics of a private property system versus joint governance. In the first case, the state and path of a society evolve from autonomous individual decisions, in the second it is the result of explicit design. Evolution, as opposed to design can be seen as a strength of the institutional arrangement, since it best fits our limited information processing capacities (von Hayek 1960: 54ff.). However, it can also be seen as a weakness, making society go along blindly, driven by 'natural' forces – the Marxian critique.

Justice problems with respect to property are problems of access and of distribution. Many advocates of private property accept the idea of equal access to property (Waldron 1988), beginning with Locke's proviso that everyone has a right to appropriate 'at least where there is enough, and as good left in common for others' (Locke [1689] 1960: para. 26; cf. MacPherson 1962). Adherents of a system of private property have consistently opposed the idea of **social justice**, since this idea belongs to a system of joint governance. So if justice with respect to property is understood as requiring more than just equal access to property or some minimal endowment, then one will tend to argue for joint governance instead of private property.

Finally, **power** relationships are shaped by the way property is governed. Given joint governance, power is basically political power – the possibility of the prevention of some coalition's or person's will prevailing over other members of the group. Given private property, power is basically bargaining power, generated by the shape of the property distribution. No one can literally force his/her will on someone else, but someone who can do so without cooperation has power if his/her prospective partner needs the cooperation. Theories of exploitation, most prominently that of **Marx**, focus on these kinds of asymmetries endemic in a private property system, in particular where the means of production are concentrated in the hands of a minority. The preference for private property or for joint governance then depends on what kind of power – political or economic – one considers as being more dangerous.

References and further reading

Coase, R. H. (1960) 'The Problem of Social Cost', *Journal of Law and Economics*, 3: 1–44.

Demsetz, H. (1967) 'Towards a Theory of Property Rights', *American Economic Review*, 57: 347–59.

Hardin, G. (1968) 'The Tragedy of the Commons', *Science*, 162: 1243–8.

Locke, J. ([1689] 1960) *Two Treatises of Civil Government*. Cambridge: Cambridge University Press.

MacPherson, C. B. (1962) *The Political Theory of Possessive Individualism*. Oxford: Clarendon.

North, D. C. (1990) *Institutions, Institutional Change and Economic Performance*. Cambridge: Cambridge University Press.

Ostrom, E. (1990) *Governing the Commons: The Evolution of Institutions for Collective Action*. Cambridge: Cambridge University Press.

Posner, R. A. (1977) *Economic Analysis of Law*. Boston: Little, Brown.

Waldron, J. (1988) *The Right to Private Property*. Oxford: Oxford University Press.

von Hayek, F. A. (1960) *The Constitution of Liberty*. Chicago: University of Chicago Press.

REINHARD ZINTL

PROTEST

Protest is defined as collective **action** directed against others considered to be responsible for some injustice. Charles **Tilly** (1986) provided the first systematic account of protest as a generic form of collective action and at the same time a comparative historical analysis of protest events. Protest accompanies the formation of the modern **state** and continues to produce events within the modern **nation–state** (Franzosi 1995).

The object of protest is highly variable. It is, first of all, protest against injustice. The forms of such injustice range widely – from the high price of bread to the working conditions of the industrial proletariat, to discrimination against **women** or minorities – and related protest may take on a range of spontaneous or organized forms (see also **social movements**). Another class of protest has to do with forms of non-**recognition**, i.e. with identity issues. Protest based on **identity** claims reacts to the experience of **cultural difference** and the **power** relations that shape these differences. Protest can finally be based on claims for securing common goods against their destruction by those following individual self-interests. Protest in this last sense is directed against those who produce 'the tragedy of the commons', and against the institutional structures that do not prevent the self-destructive use of collective goods. In each of these senses, the object of protest refers to three kinds of objective: justice, recognition and **environment**.

Protest events provide the data source for analyzing and explaining the causes and course of mobilization of collective action (Rucht and Neidhardt 1998). But what count as protest events? Protest in the traditional sense implies some kind of action such as a demonstration or the destruction of **symbols** of power – substantive action linked to some observable phenomenon in space and time. Protest is in this way a mode of communicating a claim for more justice or for recognition or for a better environment, supported by publicly visible **action**.

Theories that explain protest work on different levels. A micro-explanation is offered in the theory of **deprivation and relative deprivation**. A typical macro-explanation is the assumption of structural strains, of structural contradictions such as market effects or of power effects such as the relation of domination between peasants and landlords (**Moore** 1966) (see **micro-, meso- and macro-levels**). In this way **capitalism** or the modern state as such have become explanatory variables. Both these models, however, turn out to be too simplistic. Social-psychological models have been extended by **framing** theories which state that any complaint needs to be socially *constructed* as a complaint to become a collective claim. This frame of a complaint is a social process that interferes with the individual experience of a deprivation. Thus relations among people are used to explain the way people frame their mode of experiencing the world. Macro-structural explanations have turned out to be too general to survive the test of comparative evidence. Situational contexts are much more complicated and time-space-specific, and such constellations need to be specified before we are in a position adequately to analyze and explain protest.

Protest is also linked to a specific action *repertoire*. This includes demonstrations, blockades, strikes, anything that interrupts the normality of public life. Traditional views of the protest action repertoire, however, are no longer sufficient. Protest has changed its form and function in modern societies. The more complex these societies become, the more direct action is complemented by 'verbal action', especially involving claims made through the channels of the **media and mass media**. This double structure of protest action becomes visible when moving onto the level of global protest. Here there is direct action (such as anti-**globalization** demonstrations) as

well as conferences where discursive claims are made, typically through NGOs. Today, collective claims-making appears to be more prevalent than ever, even though traditional social protest in the sense of its heyday in the nineteenth and twentieth centuries appears to be on the decline.

The strict traditionalists among those doing research on protest events base their definition of protest on the occurrence of some observable collective behaviour. Yet in a society in which politics is mediated by mass media, protest becomes more and more contingent on new kinds and methods of claims making. As soon as we accept that verbal action, as collective claims-making, is part of the action repertoire of protest, we start to see that there is a lot of collective action going on, not only in national contexts, but also in the transnationalizing world.

A concept that attempts to target the diversity of forms of protest is 'contentious politics' (Imig and Tarrow 2001). Contention is a concept used by Tilly to make sense of protest in Europe since the eighteenth century. Apart from extending the definition of a repertoire of action to include verbal action ('collective speech acts'), the concept of contentious politics allows for a differentiated view of the relationship between protest and **institutions**. The adversarial mode is no longer the exclusive characteristic of this relationship. Protest does not necessarily need to attack institutions. Institutions and movements often even act jointly when they moralize on political issues and campaign for the same issues. (One can see this, for instance, in the resemblance between the anti-racist campaigns organized by the European Commission and those organized by anti-racist activist groups.) Institutions can therefore protest too, in ways that become visible when they use the action repertoire of social movements, and conversely when social movements use the action repertoire of institutions.

476

References and further reading

Franzosi, R. (1995) *The Puzzle of Strikes: Class and State Strategies in Postwar Italy*. Cambridge: Cambridge University Press.

Imig, D. and Tarrow, S. (eds) (2001) *Contentious Europeans: Protest and Politics in an Emerging Polity*. Lanham, MD: Rowman & Littlefield.

Moore, B. (1966) *Social Origins of Dictatorship and Democracy: Lord and Peasant in the Making of the Modern World*. Boston: Beacon Press.

Rucht, D. and Neidhardt, F. (1998) 'Methodological Issues in Collecting Protest Event Data: Units of Analysis, Sources and Sampling, Coding Problems', in D. Rucht, R. Koopmans and F. Neidhardt (eds) *Acts of Dissent: New Developments in the Study of Protest*. Berlin: Sigma, pp. 65–89.

Tilly, C. (1986) 'European Violence and Collective Action Since 1700', *Social Research*, 53: 158–84.

KLAUS EDER

THE PROTESTANT ETHIC

Max **Weber** claimed that a 'Protestant ethic' played a significant part in calling forth the modern version of **capitalism** that appeared in the West or **Occident** in the eighteenth and nineteenth centuries. In his classic study, *The Protestant Ethic and the Spirit of Capitalism*, Weber (2002a) argued that a causal analysis of capitalism's rise and expansion that referred to technological advances, population increases, human greed, and the interests of 'economic supermen' (Carnegie, Rockefeller) must be viewed as incomplete. Further, structural changes and the **power** of an increasingly cohesive **bourgeoisie** only partially explain the advent of this new 'economic form'. In Weber's view, Adam **Smith**'s focus upon a 'natural propensity to truck, barter, and exchange', also proved inadequate.

Rather, **cultural** forces specific to the West must be acknowledged. A specific 'frame of mind' (*Gesinnung*), an eighteenth-century 'spirit of capitalism' assumed an important causal **role**, according to 'the Protestant **ethic** thesis'. This secular spirit located its roots, Weber held, in the realm of **religion**, in the social dynamics (1985, 2002b) and rigorous doctrines of the ascetic Protestant **sects** and **churches**, particularly the pastoral exhortations of sixteenth- and seventeenth-century English Puritans (2002a: 103–25).

John Calvin (1509–1564), the Swiss theologian, enunciated the pivotal Predestination doctrine, according to which a few were saved, most were condemned, and no earthly good works could change one's 'salvation status'. This bleak decree introduced among the devout an unbearable anxiety and fatalism. However, interpretations by theologians and pastors in England assisted the faithful to believe they belonged among the saved and simultaneously gave birth to a systematic work ethic and a positive evaluation of **wealth**, material success, a search for profit, and entrepreneurial activity generally. In this connection Weber argued that a leap back in history was necessary into the subjective meanings dominant in a *religious cosmos* in which a single question ruled: 'Am I among the saved'?

The Puritans, who defined their purpose on earth as the creation of God's kingdom, believed that an earthly realm of abundance would best praise His majesty. **Work** comprised an appropriate means to fulfill this goal. Moreover, God explicitly commanded that all should **labor** in a continuous manner, for 'work in a calling' (*Beruf*) would diminish egocentric wishes and provide constancy to life. In turn, wants and desires, which distracted the devout from a focus upon their Deity and His commandments, would be tamed. Doubt and anxiety regarding one's salvation status would be simultaneously dispelled. In short, God 'willed' methodical labour. The faithful also knew that their intense devotion, capacity for righteous conduct, and energy to work hard derived from God who is omnipotent and omniscient. Yet this awesome God would not 'operate within' and assist just anyone. If the devout sought to labor in a systematic manner and discovered a capacity to do so, it could be concluded that a *sign* of the Deity's favor had been given. They were, or so they could convince themselves, among the predestined elect. Powerful religious **values** now directly penetrated routine work, which acquired thereby a 'providential' character.

Furthermore, owing to God's desire for an earthly kingdom of abundance to praise His glory, believers concluded that their Deity willed the faithful to create wealth. Indeed, its actual production constituted a positive sign from God. Because the devout knew that an all-knowing and all-powerful Deity exclusively bestowed personal riches (which thus belonged to Him and must be used for His purposes), wealth itself became important *evidence* to the faithful of a favorable salvation status. With Puritanism, riches now lost entirely their immoral stigma, as conveyed emphatically by the Catholic Church, and became sanctified, that is, their possession signified salvation. The search for profit became viewed in a parallel manner: opportunities to increase one's wealth were perceived as given to certain entrepreneurs by God and hence indicated His favor. The increase of one's wealth and its successful reinvestment, rather than its hoarding or squandering on worldly pleasures (which only distracted the faithful from their appropriate orientation to their Deity), proved a further effective means to create God's kingdom of abundance and to convince the faithful of their elect status. Anxiety and worry declined as activity *in* the world (but not *of* the world) oriented to material success intensified.

For Weber, this new 'economic ethic' implied a significant alteration: the *entire* life of the believer became *organized* methodically around work in a calling. A monumental shift away from a 'traditional' economic ethic and toward an 'inner-worldly asceticism' and 'rational' economic

ethic took place, involving a new frame of mind, or **habitus**.

Weber's identification of a religion-based root of modern capitalism never sought simply to substitute an **idealist** for a **materialist** approach. His modest goal instead aimed to unveil a neglected cause of modern capitalism's rise and expansion (2002a: 125). Modern capitalism was given a push by a certain entrepreneurial 'spirit' involving a 'utilitarian ethos' that descended directly from the Protestant ethic as a **secularized** legacy. It was this ethos that became cultivated, for example, by Benjamin Franklin (2002a: 13–16). However, once 'in the saddle' the **market economy** no longer required a constellation of values and operated instead simply on the basis of manifold instrumental constraints. Neither a religious sanctification nor a secular spirit fuels its viable functioning today. Modern capitalism's internal driving forces have been replaced by an external and mechanistic 'steel-hard casing', or 'iron age', which follows its own **pragmatic laws** (2002b: 18, 123–4).

Vehement debate has accompanied the 'Weber thesis' since its original formulation. Many commentators have incorrectly understood the argument as offering an explanation for the unfolding of a far more complex phenomenon – modern capitalism – rather than for the rise of a *spirit* of capitalism. (Weber leaves the exact influence of the latter upon the former open and a subject for nation-by-nation investigation.) Others view values and beliefs, and even the economic ethics of great religions, as outgrowths alone of prior economic, political, and technological forces. Yet the Protestant ethic's **autonomy** and influence have been repeatedly defended (Marshall 1980). Weber's study offers a forceful demonstration of the way in which cultural forces may significantly, and in the long term, influence economic change, place work at the center of life, and comprehensively organize and direct conduct.

References and further reading

Chalcraft, D. J. and Harrington, A. (eds) (2001) *The Protestant Ethic Debate: Max Weber's Replies to his Critics, 1907–1910*. Liverpool: Liverpool University Press.

Kalberg, S. (1996) 'On the Neglect of Weber's *Protestant Ethic* as a Theoretical Treatise: Demarcating the Parameters of Postwar American Sociological Theory', *Sociological Theory*, 14(1): 49–70.

Lehmann, H. and Roth, G. (eds) (1993) *Weber's Protestant Ethic*. New York: Cambridge University Press.

Marshall, G. (1980) *Presbyteries and Profits*. Oxford: Clarendon.

Weber, M. ([1904–5, 1920] 2002a) *The Protestant Ethic and the Spirit of Capitalism*. Oxford: Blackwell.

Weber, M. ([1906] 1985) '"Churches" and "Sects" in North America', *Sociological Theory*, 3(1): 7–13.

Weber, M. ([1920] 2002b) 'The Protestant Sects and the Spirit of Capitalism', in *The Protestant Ethic and the Spirit of Capitalism*. Oxford: Blackwell.

STEPHEN KALBERG

PSYCHOANALYSIS

Psychoanalysis refers to the theory of subjectivity and psychological method of therapy developed by Sigmund **Freud** and his followers at the end of the nineteenth century and elaborated in different ways by later theorists. Although Freud did not discover the **unconscious** originally, his assumption of the **self** as radically divided, split between consciousness and a repressed unconscious, influenced **modern** and **postmodern** theories of the **subject and subjectivity**.

Freud's starting point, influenced by Charcot's experiments with hysterical female patients at the Salpêtrière hospital, was his *Study on Hysteria*, published in 1893, with the Viennese physician Josef Breuer. They discovered that the hysterical symptoms could be traced to traumatic experiences in the patient's past that had become located in the unconscious. Freud abandoned his early efforts to recover repressed material by means of hypnosis, thanks to Breuer's famous Patient Anna O. (Berta Pappenheim) and Freud's patient Elisabeth von R., who discovered the *talking cure* and *free association*. Freud replaced hypnosis with this technique which remains, alongside transference in the analytical relationship, an essential aspect of psychoanalytical method.

The most controversial part of Freud's theory in his time was the determinate role he gave to human **sexuality**. Although his sexual theory stood alongside the theories of other sexual scientists such as Richard von Krafft-Ebing, Havelock Ellis or Magnus Hirschfeld, most physicians and psychologists disputed Freud's view of the importance of sexuality, including his young follower, Carl Gustav Jung, who saw the *libido* as a more general energy. Jung succeeded in founding a school of psychoanalysis that is independent of Freud. Beside the division between Jung and Freud, there was a dispute with Alfred Adler, who had a biologically based interpretation of human behavior in terms of responses to feelings of organic inferiority. The ideas of other early figures in the psychoanalytical movement, such as Sandor Ferenczi, Otto Rank, Karl Abraham, Sabrina Spielrein, Lou Andreas-Salomé and Marie Bonaparte were incorporated into Freudian theory.

In the 1920s and the 1930s some female psychoanalysts criticized Freud's concepts of femininity in terms of penis envy resulting from a perception of castration and biological lack. Melanie Klein, Joan Rivière and Helene Deutsch developed an alternative perspective on the female psyche and Karen Horney, in particular, focused on the relation between the individual and society.

Melanie Klein established her own psychoanalytical school, referred to also as the British school of **object relations**, which is based on the hypothesis that relations to external objects are mediated by representations of objects in fantasy. On that basis

Klein developed a model of the mind as incorporating a fantasized inner world composed of internal figures and exhibiting certain key structures and patterns of activity determining crucial aspects of the subject's relation to objects in reality. Klein's work has been extended in the post-Kleinian work of Donald Winnicott and Hannah Segal.

One of the most important aspects of Freudian psychoanalysis is the relation between **unconscious** mental phenomena and conscious **knowledge** in mental life. The model of the mind as a 'place' with unconscious, preconscious, and conscious systems built Freud's *topographic theory*. This model was later replaced with the 'structural theory', the concept of three interacting psychic structures, the ego, the superego and the id (Freud 1961).

The id is the mental structure that contains the functions according to the primary process and the representatives of the drives, that is, the motivations that Freud described in his dual drive theory of Eros and Thanatos or the sexual or **love** drive and the death drive (Freud 1955). The ego is the seat of the consciousness as well as of unconscious defence mechanisms that, in the psychoanalytical treatment, appear as resistance to free association. Freud located the functions of censoring or judging the ego in the superego or ego ideal. Freud arrived at the idea of excessive mourning or melancholia as reflecting the unconscious internalization of the representation of an ambivalently loved and hated object (Freud 1957). In unconsciously identifying the self with that object interjected into the ego, the individual now attacks its own self in place of the previous unconscious hatred of the object; the result of this internalization is the superego's unconscious **morality**.

Freud traced the origins of the superego or 'ego ideal' to the overcoming of the double Oedipus complex, the positive and the negative, via unconscious identification with the parents. Freud assumed that every child has an initial bisexual disposition and *identifies* with one parental object, while *desiring* the other parent. When he or she has to give up the parent as a sexual object, the child can identify with this lost love object or strengthen identification with the parent of the other gender.

Post-structuralist gender theorists like Judith **Butler** have shown how central these identifications are to the formation of **gender** and sexual identity, an assumption which is inherent in Freud's theory. However, Butler criticizes Freud for articulating the role of the prohibition on **incest** in these identification processes, but not the cultural prohibition on homosexuality. Since the 1980s there has been a broader debate on the usability of psychoanalytical assumptions on homo- and heterosexuality and gender in parts of **Queer theory**.

The writings of more linguistic and Lacanian-oriented authors such as Julia Kristeva, Luce Irigaray, Jacqueline Rose and Joan Copjec have significantly influenced contemporary sociological perspectives. Other gender theorists, appealing more to the work of Michel **Foucault**, have questioned the so-called *repression hypothesis* as a psychoanalytically-based **discourse**, which asserts the repression of sexuality while producing sexual norms.

In the 1970s psychoanalytical terms were discussed by feminists like Juliet Mitchell, who defended and connected Freudian psychoanalytical ideas with feminist, **Marxist** sociological theory in her book *Psychoanalysis and Feminism* (1974). In addition, Nancy Chodorow (1978) worked with psychoanalysis to develop an understanding of female and male **socialization** processes.

Alongside the role of sexuality and gender relations in society, Freud's ideas on the relations between self and society as well as the mix of reason and irrationality in politics and society have been appropriated in social analysis and sociological theory. The sociological theory developed by the **Frankfurt School** of critical theory (namely,

Theodor **Adorno**, Erich Fromm, Max **Horkheimer**, Herbert **Marcuse**) unified psychoanalysis and Marxism to explain **capitalism** and features of **modernity** such as **mass culture** and **fascism**.

From the late 1960s onwards, French theory, particularly structuralism and **post-structuralism**, became increasingly influential in terms of theorizing the general dimensions of psychoanalysis for issues of subjectivity, society and politics. Jacques **Lacan** stressed the importance of the discourse of the **Other** and the role of **inter-subjectivity** for the subject as well as the centrality of **language**, which 'structures the unconscious', as he famously argues. His interpretation of Freud brings psychoanalysis to the level of a philosophical discourse, an approach which has been endorsed by many French philosophers and literary theorists who have made use of Lacanian ideas. Lacan's essay *The Mirror Stage as Formative of the Function of the I* (1949) and his concept of the subject constituted lack has been his most influential contribution to sociological theory. Lacan's reworking of Freud's core concepts in the light of modern linguistics and Hegelianism influenced post-Marxist political philosophers like Louis **Althusser**, Étienne Balibar, Chantal Mouffe, Ernesto Laclau and Slavoj **Žižek**. Jean Laplanche and Jean-Baptiste Pontalis's *The Language of Psychoanalysis* ([1967] 1973) was the first conceptual dictionary of psychoanalysis, rooted in the French tradition of the **epistomology** of the sciences.

Postmodern social theory has also been shaped by psychoanalysis to analyze anew the self and self-identity. The writings of Jean-François **Lyotard** and Jacques **Derrida**, which have also had a strong influence on sociological theory, discussed the fate of the individual or 'death of the subject' in postmodernist culture. Film and other cultural theorists use psychoanalysis as a method for culture-decoding. **Post-colonial theory** questions the Western (European and North American) perspective of psychoanalysis, but

evolved, like Frantz **Fanon**, also a psychoanalytical theory of racial relations.

References and further reading

Althusser, L. (1984) *Ideology and Ideological State Apparatuses*. London: Verso.

Chodorow, N. (1978) *The Reproduction of Mothering: Psychoanalysis and the Sociology of Gender*. Berkeley, CA: University of California Press.

Copjec, J. (1994) *Read My Desire: Lacan against the Historicists*. Cambridge, MA: MIT Press.

Dean, T. and Lane, C. (2001) *Homosexuality and Psychoanalysis*. Chicago: University of Chicago Press.

Elliot, A. (1992) *Social Theory and Psychoanalysis in Transition: Self and Society from Freud to Kristeva*. Oxford: Blackwell.

Evans, D. (1996) *An Introductory Dictionary of Lacanian Psychoanalysis*. Chicago: University of Chicago Press.

Freud, S. (1935–74) *The Standard Edition of the Complete Psychological Works of Sigmund Freud*. London: Hogarth.

Lacan, J. (1977) *Écrits: A Selection*. London: Tavistock.

Laplanche, J. and Pontalis, J.-B. ([1967] 1973) *The Language of Psychoanalysis*. London: Methuen.

Mitchell, J. (1974) *Psychoanalysis and Feminism*. Harmondsworth: Penguin.

Rose, J. (1986) *Sexuality in the Field of Vision*. London: Verso.

MICHAELA WÜNSCH

PUBLIC AND PRIVATE

The general meaning of public denotes the whole of a **society** as this is articulated in the idea of a shared **interest** or good (thus, the public interest and public good). To this meaning is added the political connotation of 'public', the idea that the construction of this shared interest is a political affair that should include all those who belong to the society concerned either directly by way of their participation in government (electing those who govern or participating in the business of government) or indirectly by way of making those who are engaged in decisions that affect the whole accountable to the wider public for their **action** (the norm of publicity). Private is not public in either of these senses. Thus, private denotes, first, the idea of something that concerns people in their distinct rather than shared interests, and second, this being so, their private affairs are subject to their discretion, and do not need to be **communicated** except as these private actors choose.

Social theory deploys these **meanings** of public and private in its account of modern social **differentiation**. The idea of the state is associated with 'a public authority' (Locke's term) that supplies the institutional framework for the constitution of a society as a public body of citizens. The state is responsible also for the articulation of the shared interest or good of these citizens in both law and policy (see **state and nation–state**). The idea of **civil society** refers to the sphere of voluntary association between people in their private capacity; this sphere includes the market economy. Actors who engage with each other in a private capacity have a shared and thus 'public' interest in these engagements being lawful and equitable, and the state is charged with securing **law** and equity in these privately oriented relationships. The idea of **family** and personal life refers to the sphere of intimate **association** between people who are oriented to loving and caring for each other as unique individuals. In order to engage in **intimacy**, people need privacy for the development and exploration of such attachments, which are understood as based in the privately oriented decisions of people regarding with whom they want to share intimacy and whether they want to parent or not. Society has an interest in such attachments as fostering the well-being and integrity of those who are involved in them, especially children who are vulnerable to parental abuse of **power**. The state articulates this societal interest in the integrity of personal and parental relationships in its regulation of **marriage** and child welfare.

In this perspective, public and private are not antagonistic but interdependent values. They denote distinct aspects of what it is to be a person in modern social life. The person can be oriented publicly to the good of the whole society of persons, or the person can be oriented privately to his or own good or well being which s/he may choose to share with his/her domestic or personal intimates. Both orientations are predicated on an account of the **subject** as a social being, and both are relational. While the public orientation trumps the private orientation, the public orientation readily degenerates into a despotic abuse of state authority if it is not held accountable to a respect for persons in their two private capacities (the relationships of civil society and the individualized attachments of family and personal life). The standing of civil society is ambiguous: it is both public when it is the site of a public sphere of communicative **interaction** and **critique**, and private when it is the site of the pursuit of private interest.

The social differentiation of public and private is first theorized by **Hegel**, and it is built on by sociological theorists like **Durkheim** and theoretical social democrats like Raymond Plant. It overcomes the difficulties of the alternate account of the public and the private, one that sees the private as beyond or outside the public. Vulgar **liberalism** (not the liberalism of political thinkers like Locke) argues that private action should be free from 'state interference' and cannot provide a coherent account of how the integrity of private action depends on 'state interference'. There is also the neoclassicist argument of Hannah **Arendt** that the private sphere of the household (the *oikos*), being subject to the necessity of the biological maintenance and reproduction of the human species, should not be allowed to deflect the public sphere from its supremely political task of articulating the **freedom** of human beings as actors who engage in self-disclosure through speech, and self-

knowledge through shared reasoning about the significance of such speech.

When private action is thought of as outside and antagonistic to public action, sociologists point out that this kind of **binary** construction makes no sense: both private and public action are subject to social patterning. 'The social' becomes that which contains both the public and the private, an approach that for theorists like Nancy Fraser underlies their conception of the welfare state.

Sociologists (especially **feminists**) also focus their attention on how what C. Wright **Mills** called 'personal issues' become politicized and turned into 'public issues'. These sociological interventions which demonstrate the social character of private life, and thus its connection with public life, make sense as far as they go. When they call into question the differentiation of public and private life itself, they forego insight into the internal differentiation of a modern society.

References and further reading

Arendt, H. (1958) *The Human Condition*. Chicago: University of Chicago Press.
Calhoun, C. (1992) *Habermas and the Public Sphere*. Cambridge, MA: MIT Press.
Durkheim, E. (1992) *Professional Ethics and Civic Morals*. London: Routledge.
Fraser, N. (1989) 'Women, Welfare and the Politics of Needs Interpretation', in *Unruly Practices*. Cambridge: Polity Press.
Hegel, G. W. F. (1991) *Elements of the Philosophy of Right*. Cambridge: Cambridge University Press.
Locke, J. (1970) *Two Treatises of Government*. Cambridge: Cambridge University Press.
Mills, C. W. (1967) 'The Promise', in *The Sociological Imagination*. Oxford: Oxford University Press.
Pitkin, H. (1981) 'Justice: On Relating Private and Public', *Political Theory*, 9(3): 327–52.
Plant, R. (1996) 'Social Democracy', in D. Marquand and A. Seldon (eds) *The Ideas that Shaped Post-War Britain*. London: Collins.

ANNA YEATMAN

PUBLIC SPHERE

The making of modern society is shaped by a double process: the formation of an **economic** sphere and the formation of a public sphere as spheres distinct from the household. This double process constituted **civil society** as a world separate from, and even opposed to, the world of political **power**.

Within this civil society, two different logics of action are set free: rational 'self-interested' action as the basis of the **market** and 'communicative' **action** as the action basis of a public sphere (see **communication**). Both logics – that of the public sphere and that of the market – are constitutive for civil society. The term 'public sphere' describes the 'communicative' side of civil society. It represents the context of debate in which a new semantics for making sense of the emerging modern society is formed: the semantics of an unbound economic sphere (thematized by **Smith** and **Marx**) and the semantics of an unbound public sphere (thematized by **Kant** and J. S. **Mill**). These two semantics still shape debates in political and social theory today.

The semantics of an unbound public sphere has received a sociological reinterpretation in the work of **Habermas** ([1962] 1989). Habermas combines a historical reconstruction of theories of the public sphere with a systematic sociological analysis of the social evolution of a public sphere in the course of Western modernization. This allows him to contrast the reconstruction of the ideal of a public sphere with its real working. His ideal model of the public sphere is based on three particular assumptions: the model of the association of **free** and **equal** people capable of entering a discursive relationship. This model is read off from the structure of the social order that replaced the traditional order in **Europe**: the model of the free and equal association of **citizens**, constituted by public debate. This model of an egalitarian and discursive order replaces the **sacred** order of the past by an order in which the rules are self-constituted as a positive legal order (see **law and legality**). The public sphere is the space wherein the rational force of collective arguing is triggered by free communication.

Habermas identifies these structural features in his historical account of the formation of a sphere of public debate that accompanied the making of a **bourgeois** class in the eighteenth century. The places of this emerging public sphere were found in coffee-houses and literary salons, political clubs and **intellectual** circles in European cities. Such modes of public togetherness were popularized as **associations** discussing all number of subjects, from the **moral** quality of the **lower** classes to the protection of birds. However, these manifestations of equal and free communication did not necessarily live up to the requirements of the model. In some cases they perverted the model, as Habermas himself argues in relation to the marketization of mass communication. Social inequality remained in public communication, in terms of both access and influence. Many were excluded, and those included could accumulate 'mass media power'. Nevertheless, in Habermas's (1996) thesis, the normative model of the public sphere cannot be done away with: it retains its critical task of challenging those in power. Habermas's perspective paves the way for approaches combining normative accounts of the public sphere with empirical sociological research on public communication (see also the range of historical responses to Habermas's thesis in Calhoun 1992).

Theoretically informed empirical research on the public sphere follows two different lines. The first relates to the people as 'the public' or audience of public communication. It develops into 'public opinion research' – one of the main branches of survey research. The second line follows the **tradition** of news making research. It relates to what and how news is communicated 'in public'. It analyzes the discourses that represent – in a more or less distorted fashion – reality. The combination of European cultural criticism and American empirical social research in recent years has made this type of analysis a dynamic field in which notions of **ideology** and **power** have again played a prominent role.

Yet these two lines of research have tended to presuppose a traditional communicator to the receiver model that assumes a causal link from the communicators via what they communicate to the receiver. This model has proved to be rather misleading. Both sides of the issue – public **discourse** as the communicator side and public opinion as the receiver side – have been increasingly decoupled. The idea of a public sphere which mediates those speaking and those listening into a dynamic interrelationship here tends to get lost.

In some accounts, the *receiver* side dominates research and theory, especially in its version of public opinion research. The public is seen as having an 'opinion' that reacts to ongoing political communication (Bennett 1980). Public opinion in this research is an environment for public discourse. It is defined as the distribution of attitudes among a random sample of people which can be identified through a sample survey with pre-coded response categories. It is thus an emergent effect of the sum of individual opinions. Converse (1964) has criticized this claim, arguing that stability on the level of mass publics goes together with instability on the individual level. This makes public opinion an unstable empirical phenomenon. In defending the notion of public opinion as an emergent property of the sum of individual opinions, Inglehart (1985) explains the apparent instability of survey responses over time as the result of manifest attitudes and stability as the result of latent attitudes. Public opinion as the collective effect of public communication on individual attitudes has proved to be a theoretical idea with consequences for the practice of public communication – as is shown by the daily communication of public opinion in political communication, especially through the mass media.

The *speaker* side of public communication concentrates on the fabrication of public discourse through the **media and mass-media**. This 'public discourse analysis' dissects the process by which agenda setting is initiated by **elites**, interest groups, **social movements** and finds media coverage. Its particular theoretical focus is the representation of reality in public discourse. Whereas some denounce public discourse as a distortion of reality, an alternative theoretical perspective understands distortion as the normal *process of constructing* social reality. This direction is taken in the 'power-balance' model which explains what is communicated in public by the strategic interaction of actors active on the public stage. In this model there is **agency** – most of it strategic – and there are organizational resources and institutional opportunities. What is communicated is the result of a negotiation process going on between, and within, media institutions (media actors such as journalists are the most important element) which have to take into account their social environments as their (paying) audiences.

Recent contributions combine public discourse and public opinion research by giving it a constructivist twist (see **constructivism**). The construction of issues among people, in the media and among elites, contribute to conflictive political interaction as the mechanism which shapes a public sphere (Gamson 1992). Not only the speakers on the public stage talk, but also people, the audience.

A radicalized view of such constructionism is found in **Luhmann** (2000) who conceives public opinion as a mirror that society uses to look at itself. What we perceive as society we see through the mirror of what is said publicly about it and from the position we have taken while looking into this mirror. **Differences** in perception are effects of differences in the social position of the observer looking into the mirror. Whether the social position of observers leads them to a critical or an affirmative stand toward society

depends on where the observers stand. The idea of a public sphere as a sphere of opposition to power is thus no longer an inherent *property* of a public sphere but rather an *opportunity* offered by a public sphere.

If there *is* such a capacity of observation of power by diverse publics, the link between the reasoning public and those observed here returns as a central theoretical issue. The model resulting from this perspective can be described as a two-step observation: people observe their representatives, who again observe those who act in the name of the state. This is what is called '**democratic** control', the idea of people observing their representatives.

This pattern of the observation model found a relatively stable institutional form in the **nation–state**. But to the extent that supranational institutions have been growing in recent times, the form of the issue again becomes complex: who observes whom and how do they do it? Is democracy – defined as the observation of those in power by a public – possible beyond the nation–state? This raises the theoretically challenging question of a transnational public sphere, and possibly of a global public sphere.

References and further reading

Bennett, W. L. (1980) 'The Paradox of Public Discourse: A Framework for the Analysis of Political Accounts', *Journal of Politics*, 42: 792–817.

Calhoun, C. (ed.) (1992) *Habermas and the Public Sphere*. Cambridge, MA: MIT Press.

Converse, P. E. (1964) 'The Nature of Belief Systems in Mass Publics', in D. E. Apter (ed.) *Ideology and Discontent*. New York: Free Press, pp. 207–61.

Gamson, W. A. (1992) *Talking Politics*. Cambridge: Cambridge University Press.

Habermas, J. ([1962] 1989) *The Structural Transformation of the Public Sphere: An Inquiry into a Category of Bourgeois Society*. Cambridge, MA: MIT Press.

Habermas, J. (1992) 'Further Reflections on the Public Sphere', in C. Calhoun (ed.) *Habermas and the Public Sphere*. Cambridge, MA: MIT Press, pp. 421–61.

Habermas, J. (1996) *Between Facts and Norms: Contributions to a Discourse Theory of Law and Democracy*. Oxford: Polity Press.

Inglehart, R. (1985) 'Aggregate Stability and Individual-Level Flux in Mass Belief Systems: The Level of Analysis Paradox', *American Political Science Review*, 79: 97–116.

Luhmann, N. (2000) *The Reality of the Mass Media*. Cambridge: Cambridge University Press.

KLAUS EDER

PUNISHMENT

See: social control

Q

QUEER THEORY

While Queer theory is a relatively loose term for an approach to cultural studies which emerged in the late 1980s, it can be broadly understood as an extension of lesbian and gay scholarship that illuminated issues of **power** and ambiguity in cultural productions of **gender** and **sexuality**. While **post-structuralist** in orientation, Queer theory's preoccupation with questions of **culture**, power and structures of gender has led to ongoing engagement with sociology, particularly **feminist** and lesbian and gay sociological work. Queer theorists have extended **Foucault**'s theoretical framework of power/resistance to explore the possibilities of resistance through the transgression and subversion of dominant **discourses**. The target of this resistance is any form of essentialized or naturalized **identity**, often leading to theoretical elaborations on how **ontology** is socially produced and maintained through disciplinary operations of **knowledge**. However, while many dimensions of 'natural' identities have been subject to Queer analysis, the overwhelming substantive engagement has been around issues of gender and sexuality.

The heritage of Queer theory can be traced to Foucault's studies on sexuality and his thesis on the ubiquitous operation of power through discourses; constituting objects of knowledge, social identities, **subjectivity** and hierarchies of social relationships. This provided the theoretical framework for the post-emancipation politics of gay and lesbian activism which is characterized as Queer politics and which emerged in the late 1980s and early 1990s in the USA and the UK, through groups such as Aids Coalition to Unleash Power (ACT-UP), Queer Nation, Lesbian Avengers and OutRage! This connection between political identity and political goals is central to an understanding of the development and preoccupations of Queer theory. Differences of perspective and experience in terms of **race**, gender and **class** emerged within the increasingly commercialized lesbian and gay communities of the 1970s, and this dissent converged with radical critiques of homogenous feminist, lesbian and gay identity politics, which were based on 'minority' models and assimilationist strategies. Furthermore, the impact of AIDS in the early 1980s reminded many gays and lesbians that minority politics based on a semi-**ethnic** identity had its limits in a heterosexually-ordered world.

Queer theory developed out of this political and intellectual context, combining post-structuralist theories of identity and post-**Marxist** analyses of political struggle in order to forge a new perspective on both sexual identities and political engagement. In this sense, Queer theory has always been explicitly political in that social identities are regarded as manifestations of power. Since essentialist sexual identities emerged from the operation of power as knowledge through certain dominant discourses (legal, medical, psychiatric, **educational**) a politics of effective 'liberation' must be concerned with resisting power and its associated discursive effects, including the idea of an essential 'gay' or 'lesbian' identity. Resistance is possible because power is open to appropriation since if it multiplies itself through the creation of sexual identities, it is constitutive rather than simply restrictive: 'discourse transmits and produces power; it reinforces it, but also undermines and exposes it, rendering it fragile and makes it possible to thwart it' (Foucault 1980: 101). Resistance to the discursive **practices** and **meanings** of homophobia is what Halperin (1995) regards as the proper function of Queer *politics*: this entails countering the effects of power as it is manifested within **essentialist** categories and through **binary** divisions of gender/sexuality. Halperin (1995) describes the strategies of Queer as threefold in terms of identities, practices and discourses: creative appropriation and resignification; appropriation and theatricalization to undermine dominant forms and exposure and demystification of the same. The reappropriation of the once stigmatizing term 'queer' is, of course, the most obvious example of Queer resistance. The increasingly abstract academic Queer theory still resonates with Queer politics in its consistent focus on the transgression of norms of behaviour and exclusion, and the illumination of heteronormativity as the key structure to identity, knowledge, power and politics.

While Queer theory resonates with feminist, lesbian and gay politics, Queer strategies have proved controversial precisely because these are based on a radical theoretical rejection of categories of identity, despite the fact that these categories structure social existence and experience. The two works most often cited as canonical in Queer theory are **Butler**'s *Gender Trouble* (1990) and Sedgwick's *Epistemology of the Closet* (1990). While the authors of other articles and books provided the critical mass

necessary for this development of lesbian and gay studies to be characterized specifically as Queer theory, both Butler and Sedgwick provide the most detailed theoretical elaborations of identity and epistemology and have remained key influences in current work. Butler's work has been particularly influential in contesting the foundational ontological basis of sex/gender categories, arguing that it is the heterosexual matrix which serves to instate these categories as exclusive, natural and dependent. Butler analyzes 'drag' to argue that all genders are constructed through repeated performance. This is the central example through which she develops the notion of performativity, the disruption of which holds the potential for subversion and resistance (see **performative**).

This rejection of the authenticity of identity categories has provoked sociologists to challenge Queer theory to account for the evident social structures in gender and sexuality, and the fact that these also provide a structure to experience, identity and action. This vigorous and on-going debate is a manifestation of the impact of – and resistance to – the **'cultural turn'** within social theory, but it is also a critique of the **voluntarism** implied in the concept of performativity and the potential implosion of authenticity implied by the radical destabilization of identity. Materialist feminists in particular have provided consistent critiques of the dangers of a Queer analytics which is divorced from understandings of **patriarchy** and **capitalism** as social systems which anchor discursive regimes and contextualize experience and agency (Hennessy 2000; Jackson 2001).

However, feminist and lesbian and gay sociologists have also recognized the positive impact of Queer theory, framed largely around its **epistemological** challenge to 'universalizing' or 'minoritizing' ways of thinking about sexuality and gender. Indeed, Sedgwick's work on the relations between men lays the foundation for her claim that the epistemological binarism of 'natural' gendered and sexual identity has profoundly structured all Western knowledge on identity. Specifically, she argues that 'many of the major nodes of thought and knowledge in Western culture as a whole are structured – indeed, fractured – by a chronic, now endemic crisis of homo/heterosexual definition' (1990: 1) which, she suggests, indicates that any analysis of culture must depart from an awareness of this epistemological **paradigm**. The elaboration of ideas which propose that subjecthood is an unstable and arbitrary construction, forged out of multiple and historically contingent ways of thinking about self-identity, significantly extends the sociological gaze to 'naturalized' ontologies of human character (Seidman 1996). Queer analysis has sensitized sociology to the ubiquitous and ambiguous operations of power as a disciplinary force in the construction of identities, centring attention on the dynamic of inclusion/exclusion necessary to arrive at identity and, most influentially, in moving studies of sexuality on from an implicit focus on 'deviant' sexualities to a consistent focus on heteronormativity as the disciplinary matrix of gender and sexuality (Epstein 1996; Stein and Plummer 1996).

While the confrontational and transgressive direct actions of Queer politics is in decline and 'queer' has become synonymous with 'lesbian and gay' in some activists' perceptions and within the younger lesbian and/or gay **communities**, Queer theory has become institutionalized in the academy within a relatively short space of time, particularly in North America and the UK. There is a range of work which is self-described as Queer which often uses fairly simplistic versions of concepts of performativity or

simply aims to illuminate the inscription of essentialism. However, there is also further conceptual development of Queer theory, often in the engagement with sociologists on issues such as the conditions for effective **agency**, the materiality of existence and **embodiment**, and the structural formations of discursive regimes (Butler 1993; Hennessy 2000).

References and further reading

Abelove, H., Barale, M. A. and Halperin, D. (eds) (1993) *The Lesbian and Gay Studies Reader*. New York: Routledge.

Butler, J. (1990) *Gender Trouble*. New York: Routledge.

Butler, J. (1993) *Bodies That Matter*. New York: Routledge.

Epstein, S. (1996) 'A Queer Encounter: Sociology and the Study of Sexuality', in S. Seidman (ed.) *Queer Theory/Sociology*. Oxford: Blackwell, pp. 145–67.

Foucault, M (1980) *The History of Sexuality*, vol. 1. New York: Vintage.

Halperin, D. (1995) *Saint Foucault: Towards a Gay Hagiography*. New York: Oxford University Press.

Hennessy, R. (2000) *Profit and Pleasure*. New York: Routledge.

Jackson, S. (2001) 'Why a Materialist Feminism Is (Still) Possible', *Women's Studies International Quarterly*, 24(3): 283–93.

Phelan, S. (ed.) (1997) *Playing with Fire: Queer Politics, Queer Theories*. New York: Routledge.

Sedgwick, E. K. (1990) *Epistemology of the Closet*. Berkeley, CA: University of California Press.

Seidman, S. (1996) 'Introduction', in S. Seidman (ed.) *Queer Theory/Sociology*. Oxford: Blackwell, pp. 1–30.

Stein, A. and Plummer, K. (1996) '"I Can't Even Think Straight": "Queer" Theory and the Missing Sexual Revolution in Sociology', in S. Seidman (ed.) *Queer Theory/Sociology*. Oxford: Blackwell, pp. 129–44.

MOMIN RAHMAN

R

'RACE' AND RACISM

'Race' denotes the belief that humans can be grouped according to visible characteristics such as skin colour or hair type, personality, cultural traits, or all of these. This belief is the basis of 'racism' and 'racialism', two terms that we may usefully, if somewhat artificially, distinguish. 'Racialism' is a view that human beings are fundamentally grouped into races. 'Racism' starts from the belief that human beings are grouped into races and then adds the belief that these races are of differential intrinsic worth. Racialism does not necessarily imply ranking racial **groups**, but it always asserts that they exist in some stable fashion. This ideal-typical distinction would allow us to separate race-based world-views that are pluralist, from those which are invidious because they advocate unequal treatment on racial grounds. Students of 'race' and racism differ on whether both are integral vices of modern Western thought, or whether they are degenerate departures from an **Enlightenment** project that still promises the transcendence of racism through its aspiration to moral **universalism**.

Neither biology nor **genetics** offers support for the idea of human beings being divided into distinct racial groups. Only a small fraction of our genetic make-up accounts for the visible differences that are seen to mark 'race'. Furthermore, any two randomly selected individuals from one 'race' will have greater genetic variation between themselves than that between any two randomly selected individuals of two different races. So, although visible difference is the means whereby 'race' is usually understood, genetics offers no reliable support for differentiating people on the basis of phenotype. The fact that people remain attached to the idea of racial groups suggests that we might usefully turn to history and the social sciences for explanations of what is evidently a social and cultural, rather than a 'natural', phenomenon.

Racial thinking peaked in Western thought in the nineteenth century, when attempts were made to set it on scientific ground. This scientific racism was founded in the belief that 'race' is rooted in biological **difference** and that racial characteristics were therefore inherited. Further, scientific racists sought to infer essential, inner characteristics from external, phenotypical differences. Though scientific racism as theory was dealt fatal blows by the defeat of Nazism and by subsequent developments in genetics, 'race' is still often discussed as if it were a fixed biological category akin to species. Much racial thinking is based on an implicit notion of a natural group. An important question is therefore: how and why can 'race' be seen as constituting a natural group? Guillaumin (1990) makes a distinction between a natural group as understood biologically (say a species) and a social group regarded as natural. For Guillaumin, the conventional mark (length of hair or cut of clothing) preceded natur-alization of a system of marking (where some biological attribute such as skin col-our is taken as a permanent and 'thus' natural mark); systems of **slavery** (at least as old as civilization) preceded taxonomies of living things, which themselves preceded racist theories. Racial consciousness and practice were the result of the coming together in the modern era of the social construction of natural groups *and* the system of marking of social groups, the latter having had a history which pre-dated the modern.

Although the historical processes by which 'race' came to be constituted as a fundamental characteristic of persons have been seen as modern developments, how racial thinking relates to modern thought is a point of contention. On the one hand, some writers argue that racism is deeply interwoven within Enlightenment thought (Gilroy 1993; Goldberg 1993); while, on the other, oth-ers see racism as a degenerate by-product of post-Enlightenment thinking (Malik 1996; Miles 1993).

Those who see racialist and racist ideas as integral to modern Western thought point to the many instances of racist representations to be found in the work of key Enlight-enment thinkers such as **Kant**, Hume and Locke. They also draw our attention to the systematic oppression of non-Europeans under Atlantic slavery during the unfolding of European **modernity**. The coexistence of universalistic ideals of the Enlightenment and the reality of racial oppression is thus seen to demonstrate that racism and Enlight-enment thought were not incompatible and indeed, that a racialist world-view was refined into racist ideas and practices over three centuries of European modernization and colonial expansion. Critics taking this per-spective have also pointed to the conjunction of 'high **culture**' and extreme racism under Nazism. The opposite perspective sees racial thinking and racism as a degeneration of Enlightenment universalistic ideals. From this standpoint, the ideas of inclusive

democratic citizenship without regard to 'race' (or **class** or **gender**) are still in the process of being struggled over. Over-coming racist thinking and practice, then, would entail striving to bring these ideals ever closer to full realization.

Many social and cultural anthropologists early in the twentieth century insisted that 'race' was a social and not a natural cate-gory (Montagu [1964] 1998). Some sug-gested that '**ethnicity**' or 'culture' might be a better marker for large-scale differences between human groups (Banks 1996). The move away from biologically based notions of difference between human populations to one grounded in a concept of culture was pioneered by Franz Boas (Boas 1948). For Boas, what mattered in differentiating human groups was not what they looked like, not some notion of 'race' understood through phenotype, but 'culture': a deter-mining **symbolic**, belief, communication and reasoning system which shaped the individual. Human groups were different because culture manifested itself in different ways. Committed to human equality in general terms, Boas was the sponsor of mod-ern cultural **relativism**, from which some strands of anti-racism have evolved.

The study of 'race' and racism has grown into a major area in sociology, political science, social policy and social/cultural anthropology since the 1960s, principally in the USA, the UK and France. The field may be divided into several theoretical approaches: race relations; **Marxist** and neo-Marxist approaches; **social construction-ism**; and approaches influenced by feminist thought. The race relations perspective is the longest established of these, especially in the English-speaking world, where it emerged in the 1950s. It understands racial conflict as resulting from a clash between groups with different cultures and histories (under-stood as 'races'). This perspective takes the category of 'race' as a tool of analysis and not just an object of analysis. In race relations policy, racism is to be combated by a policy of eliminating discrimination in the **public sphere** and by fostering good relations between the races through public **education**. The race relations approach rests on the liberal assumption of tolerance on the part of a supposed racial majority toward various minorities; it is rooted in US and UK experience mainly. The main criticism of race relations theory and practice is that it does not have a sufficiently critical and theoretically sophisticated understanding of 'race'.

The second and third approaches emerged as critiques of the race relations approach. Marxist and neo-Marxist perspectives on 'race' and racism begin with a structural analysis of political economy and the history of racial **domination** under European colonialism. Their proponents see 'race' and class as closely interlinked. Social constructionist perspectives have been informed by class analysis as well as feminism, but their principal influences have been those of participant fieldwork and ethnography, and more recently, **structuralism** and **post-structuralism**. In this perspective, 'race' and racism are examined in terms of subjectivity, identity and representation, 'race' and racism are seen as made and re-made in practice: in communication, and in disciplines and representations of the **body**. Since the 1970s a vibrant body of work has grown up out of a critique by Black feminists of the gender blindness of much early work on 'race', as well as the 'race' blindness of much pioneering **feminist theory** and politics (Collins 1990). There are close affinities between much recent constructionist and feminist work on 'race', in that both see racial discourse and racist practice as constantly being constructed and reconstructed on an everyday basis in contexts shaped by gender.

Ideas of ethnicity are increasingly employed to gloss over the continued fuzziness of racial classification. This development is theoretically inadequate in that it uncritically replaces, rather than questions, the underlying assumption that 'race' is a valid and

reliable way of grouping human beings. Critical observation, the life sciences, and even simple logic deny the existence of 'races' as clearly defined groups of people. Yet, the idea that 'race' is somehow natural and even immutable retains much currency. This remains a key area for social research.

References and further reading

Banks, M. (1996) *Ethnicity: Anthropological Constructions*. London: Routledge.

Boas, F. (1948) *Race, Language and Culture*. New York: Free Press.

Collins, P. H. (1990) *Black Feminist Thought: Knowledge, Consciousness and the Politics of Empowerment*. London: Unwin.

Gilroy, P. (1993) *The Black Atlantic: Modernity and Double Consciousness*. Cambridge, MA: Harvard University Press.

Goldberg, D. (1993) *Racist Culture: Philosophy and the Politics of Meaning*. Oxford: Blackwell.

Guillaumin, C. (1995) *Racism, Sexism, Power and Ideology*. London: Routledge.

Malik, K. (1996) *The Meaning of Race: Race, History and Culture in Western Society*. London: Macmillan.

Montagu, A. ([1964] 1998) *Man's Most Dangerous Myth. Fallacy of Race*. Walnut Creek, CA. Altamira.

Miles, R. (1993) *Racism after Race Relations*. London: Routledge.

BRIAN ALLEYNE

RATIONAL CHOICE

Rational choice is a multi-disciplinary research program in the social sciences that is based on the assumption of rational behaviour. Rational choice assumes that an agent chooses among alternatives in accordance with certain rationality postulates. These postulates can be expressed as normative statements. They tell us what ought to be done if an agent accepts certain criteria of rationality in a particular situation. In the social sciences, however, the rationality assumption is usually interpreted as a **law-like**, empirical regularity of individual behaviour. Consequently, the approach aims to generate testable hypotheses. These empirical propositions refer to the micro- and to the macro-levels (see **micro-, meso-, and macro-levels**). The applicability of action principles to macro-phenomena follows from methodological **individualism** which is accepted by most rational choice theorists. Methodological individualism and rational choice are dominant perspectives in contemporary neo-classical economics and are also influential in political theory. In addition, there are many legal theorists and moral philosophers who work in this tradition. In sociology, the approach is associated with the names of James S. **Coleman**, Raymond Boudon, Hartmut Esser, Michael Hechter, Douglas Heckathorn, Siegwart Lindenberg, Karl-Dieter Opp, Werner Raub and Viktor Vanberg, among others. In a looser sense, Max **Weber** can also be seen as a forerunner of rational choice analysis.

The basic model of **action** used by rational choice theorists is akin to that of neo-classical economic theory: actors choose among a set of alternatives in accordance with their **preferences**. The set of available actions (opportunities) depends on restrictions and resources, namely **time**, income, budget, **market** prices of goods, and so on. These are determined by social-structural variables such as **class** position and by institutional constraints (such as formal and informal norms with associated sanctions). Rational choice implies choice of the outcome that is valued highest in the light of the actor's preferences. If the preferences are consistent (and fulfil some formal rationality postulates), they may be represented by a utility function. Rational choice then implies maximizing utility under certain constraints or restrictions (see **utilitarianism**). A more complex theory is necessary if **agents** cannot merely choose among definite outcomes (whereby every action leads with certainty to a particular outcome) but must consider **risk** or uncertainty. In this case, rationality requires additional rationality postulates. These imply that agents act as if they choose the action with the highest expected utility. Utility functions which represent preferences among risky alternatives were derived axiomatically by von Neumann and Morgenstern in the 1940s. These ideas are contained in the core of modern *decision theory*. Another variant of rational choice is used to analyze game situations of interacting rational agents. Social interactions imply strategic interdependencies among rational decision-makers: agent A's outcomes not only depend on A's choices (and, possibly, on risk or uncertainty) but also on the choices of other rational actors B, C,. . .(and vice versa). **Game theory** refers to formal tools used to form predictions for outcomes in these strategic interactions. There has been an explosion of research on game situations since the 1970s which has led to a reorientation of much of rational choice thinking in the social sciences.

The term 'rational choice' has been in use since the 1960s. However, there are important antecedents in the much earlier eighteenth century social theories of the Scottish **moralists**. Adam **Smith** demonstrated individual purposive action may generate unintended consequences, and that individuals who pursue self-interests under certain social conditions create a 'spontaneous order' (F. Hayek) of market equilibria. A similar mechanism appears in David Hume's explanation of the evolution of informal social norms ('artificial virtues') that contribute to social order in a market society. The principle of methodological individualism was explicitly introduced by members of the Austrian School of economics, including Joseph **Schumpeter**. In sociology, Max Weber's methodological writings assert that sociology aims to explain causally the macro-level results of individual purposive action. Understanding and explaining individual action through the concept of *Zweckrationalität* (means–ends rationality) for Weber is a useful first approximation. But in contrast to most contemporary rational choice analysis, Weber argued that *other* kinds of motives are important in explaining choices between alternatives, namely **tradition**, affect and **value**-rationality. Weber introduces *Wertrationalität* (value rationality) as a second type of rationality that involves a categorical commitment to certain values. Many contemporary rational choice theorists disagree with Weber's typological approach for methodological reasons. According to Harsanyi: 'If we make our motivational assumptions complicated enough, we can "explain" any kind of behavior – which of course means that we are explaining absolutely nothing' (Harsanyi 1976: 122).

In contemporary sociology, rational choice theory evolved in the 1960s in the context of social **exchange theory**. Peter M. Blau, George C. **Homans** and others argued that social **interaction** and small group processes can be explained by principles adopted from elementary microeconomic theory. Similarly, Coleman, beginning in the 1960s, explicitly modelled social behaviour in systems of social exchange and collective decision-making as rational action. Coleman's models are closely related to work in the fields of new **political economy**, 'public choice' and the 'new institutional economics' (see **institutions and neo-institutionalism**). Authors such as Kenneth J. Arrow, James M. Buchanan, Anthony Downs, John C. Harsanyi, Douglass C. North, Mancur Olson, Amartya **Sen** and Oliver Williamson have pioneered the application of rational choice principles to political phenomena and to the **economic** institutions of capitalism as well as moral institutions.

Another seminal contribution is Gary S. Becker's economic approach to sociology that comprises testable predictions about a variety of sociological explananda. These include: investment decisions with regard to human capital (in particular, **education**) and its consequences for social **inequality**; the forming and dissolution of **marriages**; the number and quality of children within the **family**; the creation and consequences of **social capital** and the emergence of habits, addictions and traditions. Becker's approach deeply transformed hypothesis-building and empirical research in the sociology of the family and **demography**. And there have been many other related fields of application in sociology (see Voss and Abraham 2000).

In a general sense, rational choice analysis addresses the problem of social order. Many classical theorists such as **Durkheim** and **Parsons** denied the possibility of a narrowly rationalistic explanation of social order. Parsons alluded to the Hobbesian 'state of nature', the condition of a 'war of all against all', to argue that it is impossible to construct a social order of mutually respected rules of cooperation purely on the basis of self-interest. Modern discussions point out similarities of the state of nature and the Prisoner's Dilemma or public goods production problem. The possibility of cooperation among egoists (without a central authority) can be demonstrated by using game theoretic principles. Cooperation is possible if the game is not a one-shot but is repeated indefinitely (Michael Taylor, Robert Axelrod, Ken Binmore). It is argued that using game theory, a rational reconstruction of Hume's explanation of informal **norms** via repeated interactions and 'reciprocity' (conditional cooperation) will become available (Binmore 1998). This approach may also explain the emergence of informal social norms (Ellickson 1991).

However, some critics of rational choice (such as Green and Shapiro 1994) have reviewed empirical anomalies where real human beings do cooperate in various experimental and real-life settings and contribute to public goods – even in cases of non-repeated games. Some proponents of rational choice consequently argue for redirections of the program to deal with these anomalies. Though an assumption of 'egoism' is by no means implied in rational choice, work on *interdependent* 'social preferences' is quite rare (see Becker and Murphy 2000, for an exception). Formal models of social preferences are useful for the elaboration of motivational assumptions informed by the ideas of fairness, altruism and reciprocity (Gintis 2000). Given these types of preferences, rational agents may cooperate in cases of one-shot games. Other arguments favour behavioural principles of boundedly rational choice and evolutionary explanations that may yield more realistic empirical predictions about the conditions of **cooperation** and other outcomes.

References and further reading

Becker, G. S. (1976) *The Economic Approach to Human Behavior*. Chicago: University of Chicago Press.

Becker, G. S. and Murphy, K. M. (2000) *Social Economics: Market Behavior in a Social Environment*. Cambridge, MA: Harvard University Press.

Binmore, K. (1998) *Game Theory and the Social Contract*, vol. II: *Just Playing*. Cambridge, MA: MIT Press.

Coleman, J. S. (1990) *Foundations of Social Theory*. Cambridge, MA: Harvard University Press.

Ellickson, R. C. (1991) *Order without Law*. Cambridge, MA: Harvard University Press.

Gintis, H. (2000) *Game Theory Evolving*. Princeton, NJ: Princeton University Press.

Goldthorpe, J. H. (2000) *On Sociology*. Oxford: Oxford University Press.

Green, D. P. and Shapiro, I. (1994) *Pathologies of Rational Choice: A Critique of Applications in Political Science*. New Haven, CT: Yale University Press.

Harsanyi, J. C. (1976) *Essays on Ethics, Social Behavior and Scientific Explanation*. Dordrecht: Reidel.

Hedström, P. and Swedberg, R. (eds) (1998) *Social Mechanisms: An Analytical Approach to Social Theory*. Cambridge: Cambridge University Press.

Voss, T. and Abraham, M. (2000) 'Rational Choice Theory in Sociology: A Survey', in S. Quah and A. Sales (eds) *The International Handbook of Sociology*. London: Sage.

THOMAS VOSS

RATIONALITY AND RATIONALIZATION

The cluster of terms around rationality appears in a variety of social science contexts. Rationality is discussed as part of the categorization of different types of social **action**, but also in the context of criteria for truth. Rationalism can be regarded as a current in the history of ideas, but also as a key feature of **industrialized** societies. Rationalization is sometimes used simply to mean increasing efficiency, but it is most famously associated in sociology with Max **Weber**'s thesis of the rationalization of **modern** society, by which he meant the increasing pervasiveness of instrumental rational action and **institutions**. Difficulties often stem from the links – or the slippage – between these various contexts.

It is best to begin with the most complex issue, rationality as a criterion for truth, which flared up in an important debate in the 1970s and 1980s (Wilson 1970; Hollis and Lukes 1982). The debate took place in the wake of the so-called **positivism** dispute of the late 1960s (**Adorno** 1976), which pitted the adherents of the view that social scientific **knowledge** should advance by means of scientific methods, most notably linked with **Popper** against those arguing that rationality should be a philosophical or critical standard with which to evaluate social learning processes – a position associated with **Habermas**.

The positivism dispute could be regarded as having been mainly located in the **philosophy of social science**, but in the rationality debate of the 1970s and the 1980s the issue was broadened to being about the rationality of – and in – different societies. Anthropologists joined the fray with (longer-standing) questions such as whether the beliefs relating to certain practices – 'healing', for example – if believed to be effective within the context in which they are practised, could be regarded as 'untrue' or irrational or ineffective from a 'Western' or scientific standpoint. Sociologists of science entered the debate from the other side: they argued that up close, the truth seeking practices of scientists were determined by many local social circumstances, and that the validity of this knowledge was also inextricably tied to this local context.

Rationality thus became a question about society as much as about knowledge and belief. This point was lucidly elaborated, by Ernest Gellner (1992). Gellner argued that it was not individual actions that could be described as rational or irrational from within a particular context, but that knowledge and belief must be regarded as part and parcel of different societies. From this vantage point of comparative history, he insisted, it is clear that modern societies are pervaded by a specific form of knowledge with consequences that were different from that in other, pre-modern societies. This specific form of knowledge is **science**. In Gellner's view, science has imposed on the modern world a form of knowledge which is singularly effective, causing unprecedented economic growth and making secular knowledge – based on testable evidence – ever more pervasive at the expense of other beliefs.

Gellner regarded the rise of science as part of a broader **world-view**, that made the modern world unique. Other commentators either take a more expansive view of rationalism, seeing it as part of a longer-term Western or Euro-centric tradition of knowledge going back to the ancient Judaeo-Christian or classical worlds, or more narrowly they see it as a particular strand of thought associated with certain thinkers in intellectual history since the European Enlightenment (Cottingham 1988). Interestingly, Gellner was closer to an anthropological position than this historical (or history of ideas) viewpoint. He pointed out that rationalism or rational science was also a form of belief, one option of belief among other options. Yet unlike these for whom this way of thinking led to **relativism** Gellner thought, again, that this

option, rationalism, with its distinctive criteria of validity, also entailed the inevitable consequence of a rapid growth of knowledge. Randall Collins (1994) speaks here of 'high-consensus rapid-discovery science', which, in turn, had other social consequences.

Gellner is also one of many thinkers who has taken seriously and elaborated on Weber's *rationalization thesis* (Schroeder 1995). Weber's comparative-historical project of analyzing cultural change (mainly through the role of the major world-**religions**) led him to conclude that modern capitalist society was uniquely pervaded by **instrumental rationality** (Schroeder 1992). This was part of his **Protestant ethic** thesis, which argued that Protestant religiosity ultimately led to a restless striving to improve oneself, translating into instrumental rational economic activity. Weber also attributed the increasing dominance of instrumental rationality to the growth of rational rule-bound **bureaucracy** and ever more effective and impersonal and scientific knowledge (Brubaker 1984). Ultimately, for Weber, the modern world therefore becomes, in his famous words, an 'iron cage' in which our lives are ever more bound by instrumental rational institutions. Rationalization leads, to use his other, equally famous formulation, to the 'disenchantment of the world', a world in which non-instrumental (or, another of Weber's concepts, 'value rational') forms of action and belief are increasingly displaced by more rule-bound, instrumentally efficient forms of action and belief (for Weber's various concepts, see Swedberg 2005).

Weber's rationalization thesis has a pessimistic tone; he thought that this direction of social development was ever more powerful and inescapable. The debate in **historical sociology** has not greatly progressed since. The notion of rationalism, outside of the history of ideas, is no longer much invoked in arguments about the transition to modernity, or about whether certain societies are dominated by a distinctive type of knowledge which can be separated from belief or culture. Instead, arguments focus more on the nature of scientific knowledge – how unique is it? How central was its role in the transition to modernity? Rationalization has remained associated with Weber, but the question of the extent to which modern social institutions are pervaded by instrumental rationality is discussed less often today as an overall theory of modern society than in the context of particular institutions in modern society (see DiMaggio and Powell 1983).

These debates will only be resolved when we have a thoroughly sociological account of the role of science (and its twin, **technology**) and of the distinctive features of modern, industrial and **post-industrial society**. A thoroughly sociological account would be able to strip rationality, rationalism and rationalization of their immediate positive and negative connotations and replace value judgements with an account based on the evidence about the actual **embeddedness** of these three phenomena in social institutions.

References and further reading

Adorno, T. *et al.* (1976) *The Positivism Dispute in German Sociology.* London: Heinemann.

Brubaker, R. (1984) *The Limits of Rationality: An Essay on the Social and Moral Thought of Max Weber.* London: Allen and Unwin.

Collins, R. (1994) 'Why the Social Sciences Won't Become High-Consensus, Rapid-Discovery Science', *Sociological Forum*, 9(2): 155–77.

Cottingham, J. (1988) *The Rationalists.* Oxford: Oxford University Press.

DiMaggio, P. J. and Powell, W. W. (1983) 'The Iron Cage Revisited: Institutional Isomorphism and Collective Rationality in Organizational Fields', *American Sociological Review*, 48: 147–60.

Gellner, E. (1992) *Reason and Culture: The Historic Role of Rationality and Rationalism.* Oxford: Blackwell.

Hollis, M. and Lukes, S. (eds) (1982) *Rationality and Relativism.* Oxford: Blackwell.

Schroeder, R. (1992) *Max Weber and the Sociology of Culture.* London: Sage.

Schroeder, R. (1995) 'Disenchantment and its Discontents: Weberian Perspectives on Science and Technology', *Sociological Review*, 43(2): 227–50.

Swedberg, R. (2005) *The Max Weber Dictionary: Key Words and Central Concepts.* Stanford, CA: Stanford University Press.

Wilson, B. (ed.) (1970) *Rationality.* Oxford: Blackwell.

RALPH SCHROEDER

RAWLS, JOHN (1921–2002)
US political philosopher

In his main work, *A Theory of Justice* ([1971] 1999), he defends a strongly egalitarian form of **liberalism**. Rawls's leading idea is that of justice as fairness. A just society maximizes for the least advantaged the value of the basic liberties shared by all (see also **equality and egalitarianism**). Rawls employs his method of 'reflective equilibrium': coherence in our moral views is to be achieved through mutual adjustment between particular moral judgements, general principles, sociological and psychological background theories, and the heuristic device of the hypothetical social contract which models the idea of **morality**. We are to imagine ourselves in an 'original position' of **equality**, in which – behind a 'veil of ignorance' – we do not know the socially significant facts about ourselves and are free to choose rationally what principles are to govern the basic structures – political, economic and social – which determine people's chances in life. In his later work, *Political Liberalism* (1993), Rawls develops a political conception of the just and stable liberal **society** that can be endorsed from within a variety of reasonable comprehensive moral views. His last writings explore the principles that should govern the relations among 'decent well-ordered' (liberal and non-liberal) societies and their relations to societies that are not well ordered.

Major works

([1971] 1999) *A Theory of Justice*, 2nd revised edn. Cambridge, MA: Harvard University Press.

(1993) *Political Liberalism*. New York: Columbia University Press.

(1999a) *Collected Papers*. Ed. S. Freeman. Cambridge, MA: Harvard University Press.

(1999b) *The Law of Peoples; with, The Idea of Public Reason Revisited*. Cambridge, MA: Harvard University Press.

(2000) *Lectures on the History of Moral Philosophy*. Ed. B. Herman. Cambridge, MA: Harvard University Press.

(2001) *Justice as Fairness: A Restatement*. Ed. E. Kelly. Cambridge, MA: Harvard University Press.

Further reading

Freeman, S. (ed.) (2002) *The Cambridge Companion to Rawls*. Cambridge: Cambridge University Press.

LUKAS H. MEYER

REALISM

Realism is the doctrine that the world exists independently of human existence, and that it can be known in part. Realism has a vernacular use to describe a point of view uninfluenced by sentiment or wishful thinking. In **philosophy**, there are four main uses, each emphasizing a different contrast. There is realism in contrast to **idealism**, realism in contrast to **phenomenalism** or sensationalism, realism in contrast to **positivism**, and realism in contrast to intuitionism.

Idealism is characterized by advocacy of the coherence theory of truth, that a proposition is true when it fits without contradiction into the existing body of human **knowledge** (Blanshard 1939). Realism is characterized by advocacy of the correspondence theory of truth, that the truth or falsity of propositions is determined by states of the world, that exist independently of **language** and thought

Based on the principle that all that one can ever know are one's own experiences, phenomenalists denied that human beings could have access to the source of those experiences in an independent world. Patterns among the kinds of sensations that succeeded one another in the consciousness of a person were the only source of knowledge (Mach 1914). Even this was restricted by scepticism as to how far present experience could be generalized to the future. Realism, in this context, involves the claim that in perception at least some aspects of a world independent of human experience are revealed.

Scientific realism concerns the meaning of theories. Even a cursory examination of the vocabulary of the natural sciences reveals an apparent distinction between words, the meaning of which is determined by observable states of the world (for example, 'track in cloud chamber') and words which purport to refer to entities, properties and relations that are not or even could not be observed by a human scientist (for example, 'electron'). Positivists hold that theoretical terms serve merely to build a logical structure from which predictions of further observables and explanatory retrodictions can be drawn. 'Operational definitions' require that the meaning of an expression in a scientific discourse be fixed by the operations required to assign a numerical value to the property it denotes (Bridgman 1936).

The presumption according to which theoretical terms do refer to unobservables has been the basis of innumerable research programs, and has inspired the construction of sense-extending instruments to test the relevant existential propositions; for example the proposition, that bacteria exist, supports 'policy' realism. Analysis of the process of theory construction shows that theories are based on models or analogues of the unobservable processes to which theories refer (Harré 1986). For example, Darwin was quite explicit in setting out the analogy between breeding plants and animals in gardens and farms and the processes of natural selection. 'Natural selection' thereby acquired a meaning in biology independent of Darwin's observations. The fact that all claims to knowledge are revisable implies indefinite refinements of our theories.

Logical positivism, as the Vienna Circle developed it (Ayer 1946), involved generalizations of the main themes of phenomenalism and the denial of scientific realism. The verification theory of **meaning**, the trademark doctrine of the Vienna Circle, asserted that the meaning of a proposition was its method of verification, a generalization of the concept of the operational definition. The rejection of unobservables was intended to rid science of unwarranted speculations, but had the unfortunate consequence of ridding it of its capacity to use theory to reach beyond the limits of current experience.

'Anti-realism', as defended by Dummett (1978), derives from the intuitionist philosophy of mathematics. Originally a matter of proofs of unprovability of certain theorems in mathematics, it has been extended to questioning the appropriateness of the true/false distinction in general. This distinction should be replaced by something like 'well attested'. This form of anti-realism is consistent with scientific realism. The meaningfulness of theoretical terms, as fixed by models, is compatible with the perpetual revisability of scientific theories. The degree of verisimilitude of models to what they represent allows for an epistemology that falls short of a strong concept of truth (Aronson *et al.* 1994).

Recently, **social constructionism** has posed another threat to realism. Generalizing from the plausible thesis that social reality is a human construction (**Berger and Luckmann** 1967), the claim has been forcibly made that the reality, which the natural sciences purport to describe and explain, is also a social construction (**Latour** 1987). The criteria for the acceptability for scientific theories turn out, it is argued, to be social, for instance, the consensus among a group of scientists influenced by the views of their leader. Some feminist theorists and other theorists have developed a version of **post-structuralism**, rejecting all binary oppositions, to arrive at the claim that there are no definitive criteria for choosing among **discourses**, other than their role in the politicizing of society (Cixous 1986).

References and further reading

Aronson, J. L., Harré, R. and Way, E. C. (1994) *Realism Rescued*. London: Duckworth.

Ayer, A. J. (1946) *Language, Truth and Logic*. London: Gollancz.

Berger, P. L. and Luckmann, T. (1967) *The Social Construction of Reality*. London: Penguin.

Blanshard, B. (1939) *The Nature of Thought*. London: Allen and Unwin.

Bridgman, P. W. (1936) *The Nature of Physical Theory*. Princeton: Princeton University Press.

Cixous, H. (1986) *The Newly Born Woman*. Manchester: Manchester University Press.

Collier, A. (1994) *Critical Realism: An Introduction to Roy Bhaskar's Philosophy*. London: Verso.

Dummett, M. A. E. (1978) *Truth and Other Enigmas*. London: Duckworth.

Harré, R. (1986) *Varieties of Realism*. Oxford: Blackwell.

Latour, B. (1987) *Science in Action*. Milton Keynes: Open University Press.

Mach, E. (1914) *The Analysis of Sensations*. Trans C. Williams. Chicago: Open Court.

ROM HARRÉ

RECOGNITION

Recognition can be defined as the identification of something, as the attribution of a **status**, or as the positive evaluation of the **identity** or specific features of an individual or a **group**. The idea of a struggle for recognition as a structural feature of **intersubjectivity** was first elaborated by Hegel. **Hegelianism**, and especially the **master–slave dialectic** from *The Phenomenology of Spirit* (1807), had a strong influence on twentieth-century French philosophy from **Sartre** to **Althusser**. In social theory, the importance of recognition and misrecognition for the **legitimation** and reproduction of social **inequality** is emphasized among others by

Bourdieu. A systematic theory of recognition has been elaborated by Honneth (1992). Distinguishing various spheres of recognition (**love**, legal and moral respect, social esteem and **solidarity**), he claims that: (1) recognition by others is a condition of being a **person** and of leading a good life (anthropology and **ethics**); (2) reciprocal recognition of the equal value of each person is what we owe to each other (moral philosophy); (3) socio-economic conditions which make this kind of relationship impossible are pathological (**critical theory** of **society**); and (4) the quest for recognition has been at the centre of many recent **social movements** (political analysis). The negative experience of systematic misrecognition is seen as fuelling struggles for recognition that are leading to more reciprocal **social relations**. As Charles **Taylor** has argued, claims for recognition become particularly relevant in the current debates about **multiculturalism**, minority **rights** and the politics of identity and **difference** (Gutmann 1994). The relation between the theory and politics of recognition to issues of **social justice** and redistribution is, however, still very much debated (Fraser and Honneth 2003).

References and further reading

Fraser, N. and Honneth, A. (2003) *Redistribution or Recognition?* London: Verso.

Gutmann, A. (ed.) (1994) *Multiculturalism: Examining the Politics of Recognition*. Princeton, NJ: Princeton University Press.

Hegel, G. W. F. ([1807] 1977) *Phenomenology of Spirit*. Oxford: Oxford University Press.

Honneth, A. ([1992] 1995) *The Struggle for Recognition*. Cambridge: Polity.

Lash, S. and Featherstone, M. (eds) (2002) *Recognition and Difference*. London: Sage.

Markell, P. (2003) *Bound by Recognition*. Princeton, NJ: Princeton University Press.

Ricoeur, P. (2004) *Parcours de la reconnaissance*. Paris: Stock.

Taylor, C. (1992) *Multiculturalism and 'The Politics of Recognition'*. Princeton: Princeton University Press.

ROBIN CELIKATES

REDUCTIONISM

Reductionism is typically used pejoratively to refer to what are held to be the logical fallacies of **explanations** whose **determinism** commits the **epistemological** error of focusing on one level of analysis to the exclusion of others. According to Mouzelis (1991), upward reductionism denies the explanatory significance of higher levels in the hierarchy of **social relations**, whereas 'downward' reductionism suggests lower levels can be explained by higher ones. For example, positivist explanatory accounts entail upward reductionism when **meanings** are nothing but the causal effect of **structures**. By focusing on a lower causal level, higher level emergent properties are considered epiphenomenal, hence without further explanatory importance. More holistic approaches, however, do not necessarily deny the value of lower level explanations, but argue that emergence must be taken into account. Whereas upward reductionism was the explanatory ideal of **positivism** (e.g. **behaviourism**, **rational choice** theory, biologism), extreme anti-reductionism is associated with anti-scientific stances that reject the very idea of social **causality**. **Marxism** has been associated with **class** and **economic** reductionism. Variants of downward reductionism can be found in **post-structuralism** and **discourse** theories. The concept of supervenience is now widely used by philosophers to analyze how higher level phenomena are correlated with more basic ones, but cannot be reduced to them (Le Boutillier 2001). Such a perspective is congenial for those who seek naturalistic and materialist analyses that avoid reductionism.

References and further reading

Le Boutillier, S. (2001) 'Theorising Social Constraint: The Concept of Supervenience', *Sociology*, 35(1): 159–75.

Mouzelis, N. (1991) *Back to Sociological Theory*. London: Macmillan.

Mouzelis, N. (1995) *Sociological Theory: What Went Wrong?* London: Routledge.

Sawyer, R. K. (2001) 'Emergence in Sociology: Contemporary Philosophy of Mind and Some Implications for Sociological Theory', *American Journal of Sociology*, 107(3): 551–85.

RAYMOND A. MORROW

REFLEXIVITY

Reflexivity refers to the human ability to reflect upon our attitudes and behaviours, and in the light of new experiences, change the ways we think and act in the world. In sociological theory this concept has featured heavily in debates over the potential for individuals and social **institutions** to engage in a conscious and deliberate process of social transformation. Theoretical accounts of reflexivity have often taken place in the context of a more wide-ranging debate over the relationship between **agency** and **structure** in modern societies. Debates on reflexivity tend to feature in efforts to account for the relative amounts of social **power** and cultural resources available to those seeking to initiate a critical challenge to the prevailing status quo. On this understanding, reflexive thinking and reflexive practice take place in contexts where individual and institutional agency is constrained by structures of the **economy**, **polity**, **culture** and **society**.

It may be helpful to think about reflexivity in relation to two broad terrains of sociological interest. The first of these concerns the **intellectual** attitudes with which sociologists approach the study of society. Here reflexivity is championed as a form of methodology. For social theorists such as Alvin Gouldner (1970) and Pierre **Bourdieu** (1994), reflexivity refers to an approach in which researchers aim to reflect upon, and make clear to their readers, their personal standpoint in relation to the subjects and objects of their research. A reflexive sociology aims for a 'deepening of the sociologist's own awareness of who and what he is, in a specific society at any given time, and of how both his social role and his personal praxis affect his work as a

sociologist' (Gouldner 1970: 494). Such an approach is understood to lead sociologists to be more sensitive towards the influence of particular value positions upon the ways **knowledge** of society is produced. It is also presented as a means to guard sociologists against the conceit of presenting themselves as somehow 'above' or 'removed' from the worlds they seek to explain. A reflexive sociology aims to liberate the terms of sociological inquiry from cold-calculating science so as to enable a process of critical reflection upon the ways in which research takes place as sets of human relationships in distinctly moral and political circumstances. Considerable debate surrounds the impact of such an approach on the academic **authority** of social science. Moreover, there appears to be no overall agreement as to the means by which sociologists are made self-consciously and self-critically alert to the values and assumptions that shape their work. Certainly, there is no sociological consensus as to the limits of reflexivity, or whether we can ever be reflexive enough. On the negative side, reflexivity can be viewed as the cause of a great deal of ethical anxiety and **epistemological** uncertainty. On the positive side, it may be approached as critical activity that aims to bring the values of humanity to bear upon the conduct of social science for the sake of building more humane forms of society.

The second area of debate in which matters of reflexivity feature as an interest for sociological theory concerns the cultural character and institutional formation of contemporary processes of modernization (see **modernity** and **modernization**). Indeed, some would go so far as to identify processes of 'reflexive modernization' as among the most distinctive features of advanced industrial societies (Beck *et al.* 1994). Here sociologists are preoccupied by the suggestion that individuals and institutions are becoming increasingly reflexive in their approach to day-to-day life. For example, Anthony **Giddens** maintains that, insofar as terms of employment and conditions of **family** life have become increasingly varied and subject to change, populations are displaying signs of an enhanced capacity for reflexivity. He argues that insofar as we forced to live in social environments which are constantly made to change, we increasingly find ourselves in the position of having 'no choice but to choose how to be and how to act' (Giddens 1994: 75). On this understanding, such a state of affairs is bound to make people more anxiously preoccupied with matters of personal **risk** as they struggle to maintain control over the overall direction and **meaning** of their lives. For theorists such Zygmunt **Bauman** (1993) and Ulrich **Beck** (1992), such circumstances have an emancipatory and tranformative potential; for they argue that these everyday anxieties may awaken populations to more critical thinking about the economic conditions and political decisions that produce such a world. Accordingly, debates over the character of reflexivity are intimately related to long-standing sociological concerns for populations to acquire forms of political consciousness in support of world-changing initiatives that radically reform the principles and practices of Western modernization.

References and further reading

Bauman, Z. (1993) *Postmodern Ethics*. Oxford: Blackwell.

Beck, U. (1992) *Risk Society: Towards a New Modernity*. London: Sage.

Beck, U., Giddens, A and Lash, S. (1994) *Reflexive Modernization: Politics, Tradition and Aesthetics in the Modern Social Order*. London: Sage.

Bourdieu, P. (1994) *In Other Words*. Cambridge: Polity.

Giddens, A. (1994) 'Living in a Post-Traditional Society', in U. Beck, A. Giddens and S. Lash (eds) *Reflexive Modernization: Politics, Tradition and Aesthetics in the Modern Social Order*. London: Sage.

Gouldner, A. (1970) *The Coming Crisis of Western Sociology*. London: Heinemann.

IAIN WILKINSON

REGION AND REGIONALISM

Since the later twentieth century there has been a dramatic increase in regionalist movements pointing to particular regions as strategic territories and places of identification. Causes of these developments are predominantly seen in the variety of **globalization** processes, which on the one hand fuel motives for economic co-operations aimed at improving regional competitiveness in the global market place and, on the other hand, encourage attachments to local regional peculiarities as resistance to processes of global cultural homogenization. There are different theories to explain why regionalism has been of growing importance. Hurrell (1995) distinguishes three main types. First, neo-mercantilist or realist theories focus on motives of stabilising political and/or economic **power**. These theories mostly concentrate on top down regionalist processes administered by formal organizations. Second, constructivist theories focus on bottom-up movements, emphasising regional identification, **solidarity** and mutual **trust**. Third, there are theories that point to globalization processes as increasing functions of structural interdependence between regions.

Regional units may be established either (1) as sub-national federal states (e.g. the states of the USA or the German *Bundesländer*), or (2) as cross-national regions (e.g. the Euro-Regions) or (3) as inter-governmental co-operations (e.g. the EU, NATO or NAFTA). Bottom-up regionalist movements may be driven either politically, aiming at **autonomy** with regard to the central state, or economically, aiming at competitiveness (often in regard to tourism), or as the expression of a cultural or ethnic or linguistic **identity** movement.

In the case of the three intergovernmental cooperations represented by the EU, NAFTA and ASEAN, regionalization is believed to enhance competition, expressed by export surplus and foreign investment. The three continental regions, however, are based on very different understandings of regionalism concerning the status of autonomy of the **nation-states** (Coleman and Underhill 1998). In the EU-context, particularly in the rhetoric among exponents of federalism, regionalism is said to support regional uniqueness. Furthermore, it is said to reduce the democratic deficit on the European leven since regionalism is associated with an efficient and 'close to the citizens' policy. Under the headline of 'Europe of the Regions' an efficient and decentralised regional administration with a high level of competence is demanded, based on a logic of subsidiarity (Ruge 2003). Simultaneous developments are the formation of strategic network coalitions on the regional level by businesses. This type of strategic networking was at first implemented in regions whose economy was lagging behind, but increasingly it has proceeded in larger and more economically sound agglomerations (Camagni 1995; Lange 2005). In this context new forms of public private-partnerships between the increasingly entrepreneurial political subdivisions and the companies or their stakeholders and lobbyists are established.

Bottom-up-processes of regionalization tend to be driven by a fear that globalization leads not only to intensified economic subordination of the peripheral regions but also to cultural infiltration. Thus strong claims to regional cultural identity arise, appealing to indigenous language, preservation of traditional handicraft skills, cultivation of unique regional architecture, and the like (Lindner 1994). This is also true of cities (see **urbanism and urbanization**) demanding greater local autonomies and rights. One indicator of this in the European context is networks such as the Assembly of European Regions (AER) or the Eurocities, together with intensified regional lobbying activities.

References and further reading

Camagni, R. (1995) 'The Concept of Innovative Milieu and its Relevance for Public Policies in European Lagging Regions', *Regional Science*, 4: 317–40.

Coleman, W. and Underhill, G. (eds) (1998) *Regionalism and Global Economic Integration: Europe, Asia and the Americas*. London: Routledge.

Döring, D. (2001) *Regionalismus in der Europäischen Union*. Berlin: Verlag für Wissenschaft und Forschung.

Hurrell, A. (1995) 'Regionalism in Theoretical Perspective', in L. Fawcett and A. Hurrell (eds) *Regionalism in World Politics: Regional Organization and International Order*. Oxford: Oxford University Press.

Lange, S. (forthcoming) 'Landscapes of Scenes: Socio-Spatial Strategies of Culturepreneurs in Berlin', in A.-M. d'Hauteserre and T. S. Terkenli (eds) *Landscapes of a New Cultural Economy of Space*. Deventer: Kluwer Academic Publishers.

Lindner, R. (1994) *Die Wiederkehr des Regionalen: Über Formen kultureller Identität*. Frankfurt am Main: Campus.

Rosamond, B. (2000) *Theories of European Integration*. New York: St Martin's Press.

Ruge, U. (2003) *Die Erfindung des 'Europa der Regionen': Kritische Ideengeschichte eines konservativen Konzepts*. Frankfurt am Main: Campus.

JENS DANGSCHAT

REGULATION

The concept of *régulation* was first developed by French political economists in the 1970s (Aglietta 1979; Benassy *et al.* 1977; Lipietz 1979) and refers to the mode by which **social relations** are reproduced in spite of, and because of, their conflictual and contradictory character (Lipietz 1988). Regulation in its broad sense goes beyond political regulation by the **state** and implies the whole social fabric of regularities, norms and **institutions** relevant to **social reproduction**. With its emphasis on social conflicts and contradictions, the concept of regulation as used by the 'regulation school' (Boyer 1990; Boyer and Saillard 2002) has little in common with the meaning of the same term used in **cybernetics** and **systems theory**, where regulation is conceived of in an entirely **functionalist** way. The inspiration of the 'regulation school' is **Marxist**. Society is seen as a complex structured whole determined by its **mode of production**. The contradictory nature of the **capitalist** mode of production implies that social reproduction is a **crisis**-ridden process which can be stabilized only temporarily. Regulation does not secure social reproduction *a priori*. Only an *ex post* analysis can reveal that forms of regulation are functional for reproduction. However, a 'mode of regulation' is the outcome of social struggles and compromises between antagonistic forces, a 'happy coincidence' from the standpoint of capitalist reproduction.

Regulation theory is opposed not only to mainstream neo-classical economics and its harmonious view of the **market**, but also to deterministic and functionalist variants of Marxism which reduce social development to an expression of a 'logic of capital'. Influenced by **Althusser**, but superseding his **structuralism**, regulation theory is critical of **Hegelianism** and assumptions of linear **causality** (Lipietz 1993). This general orientation is not confined to the 'Parisian regulation school' in the narrow sense. Bob Jessop (1990) distinguishes seven regulationist schools which share more or less basic methodological and substantive concerns of the regulationist research programme.

To account for the historical and spatial variety of capitalist development, regulation theory develops a series of concepts which mediate between **Marx**'s relatively abstract level of analysis in his 'critique of political economy' and the analysis of concrete and complex societies. The starting point of the analysis is the process of capital accumulation which can be typified in several ways. Accumulation can be predominantly *extensive* (through an extension of wage labour and labour time, the construction of new industries, privatization, **commodification**) or *intensive* (by raising **labour** productivity, transforming wage earners' conditions of life); it can be more or less introverted or extroverted (directed toward the domestic **market** or the world market); and it can be dominated by industrial capital or by financial capital. The concrete nexus between the allocation of capital, the transformation of the conditions of production, the distribution of the social product and the transformation of the conditions of **consumption** defines the regime of accumulation. It is crucial that a regime of accumulation which allows for a more or less regular growth process cannot come about and exist by itself. It relies on a configuration of institutional forms regulating basic social relations, such as **money**, the wage relation, competition, the **state**, the international arena).

The forms of regulation in different parts of society need to be compatible with each other and with the accumulation process in order to enable regular social reproduction. This implies that there are a number of crisis tendencies which need to be differentiated. First, even a 'successful' mode of **development** which comprises a specific regime of accumulation and a predominant mode of regulation is never free from crises. Business cycles and 'small' crises define the normal mode of operation of any regime of accumulation. Second, each mode of development is characterized by specific structural crisis tendencies which sooner or later lead to the transformation of the mode of development. Contradictions can develop between the regime of accumulation and its mode of regulation, as well as between forms of regulation in different spheres of society. Although typical structural crisis tendencies of a mode of development can be analyzed and determined, the outcome of a structural crisis cannot be predicted. History remains open and indeterminate.

References and further reading

Aglietta, M. ([1976] 1979) *A Theory of Capitalist Regulation*. London: Verso.

Benassy, J. P., Boyer, R., Gelpi, R. M., Lipietz, A., Mistral, J., Munoz, J. and Ominami, C. (1977) *Approche de l'inflation: L'exemple français*. Paris: Centre d'études prospectives d'économie mathématique appliquées à la planification (CEPREMAP).

Boyer, R. ([1986] 1990) *The Regulation School: A Critical Introduction.* New York: Columbia University Press.

Boyer, R. and Saillard, Y. (eds) ([1995] 2002) *Regulation Theory: The State of the Art.* London: Routledge.

Jessop, B. (1990) 'Regulation Theories in Retrospect and Prospect', *Economy and Society*, 19(2): 153–216.

Jessop, B. (ed.) (2001) *Regulation Theory and the Crisis of Capitalism.* Cheltenham: Edward Elgar.

Lipietz, A. (1979) *Crise et inflation, pourquoi?* Paris: Maspero.

Lipietz, A. (1988) 'Accumulation, Crisis, and Ways Out: Some Methodological Reflections on the Concept of "Regulation"', in F. Moseley (ed.) *Limits of Regulation: International Journal of Political Economy*, 18(2).

Lipietz, A. (1993) 'From Althusserianism to "Regulation Theory"', in E. A. Kaplan and M. Sprinker (eds) *The Althusserian Legacy.* London: Verso.

THOMAS SABLOWSKI

REIFICATION

Reification means the transfer of human agency to **objects** creating objectified social relations so that the latter come to exercise a coercive force over human beings. The concept is a key element in **Marxist** theory and is especially associated with the philosopher and literary theorist Georg **Lukács**. The term has pre-Marxist roots in **Hegel** and his followers and critics. For Feuerbach, religion is the projection of an ideal human existence onto God, and thus as an expression of man's **alienation**. **Marx** integrated such ideas into his analysis of **money** in the *Grundrisse* and into his theory of **commodity** fetishism in *Capital*. To the extent that commodities become 'personified' – i.e. acquire agency – humans become 'objectified'. The social and historical conditions of **capitalist production** are thus obscured behind their apparent objectivity and universality. Lukács treated reification as a quality of **bourgeois class** consciousness; as an 'uncritical attitude to the fact that its own standpoint is conditioned' (1971: 150) (see

standpoint epistemology). The extreme antinomies of reified consciousness can only be overcome by a truly universal, and thus totalizing, **world-view**: that of the **proletariat**. Whereas Marxists treat reification as: (1) specific to capitalism; and (2) a coercive force, for Georg **Simmel** all human communities deposit their 'life' in external 'forms'. Such 'objective culture', which becomes more pronounced in **modernity**, both enables and constrains. For example, money both constricts individuals' options and extends their agency spatially and temporally. Although the term 'reification' is now less frequently used, the problematic lives on, for example, in the ascription of agency to objects in **actor-network theory**.

References and further reading

Kolakowski, L. (1978) *Main Currents of Marxism*, vol. 3. Oxford: Oxford University Press.

Löwith, K. ([1932] 1982) *Max Weber and Karl Marx.* London: Allen & Unwin.

Lukács, G. ([1923] 1971) 'Reification and the Consciousness of the Proletariat', in *History and Class Consciousness: Studies in Marxist Dialectics.* London: Merlin.

Marx, K. ([1857–58] 1973) *Grundrisse.* London: Penguin.

Marx, K. ([1867] 1976) *Capital: A Critique of Political Economy*, vol. 1. London: Penguin.

Simmel, G. ([1900] 1990) *The Philosophy of Money.* London: Routledge.

ALAN SCOTT

RELATIVISM

Though relativism can be traced back to sceptical sophism in classical Greece, the modern problematic arises from post-**Enlightenment** attempts to confront cultural diversity and the thesis that **knowledge** and **values** are historically and socially constructed. A theory or truth claim is said to be relative because it is self-referential and cannot provide criteria of validity outside of itself; hence its truth value is only 'relative to' its context of origin and not universal. Relativism first became widely discussed as cultural relativism in early anthropology and nihilism in philosophy. Given the contradictory and shifting uses of the term, however, it has become a rather confusing concept.

The meanings of relativism depend primarily on the specific contrasting positions at stake, that is, on the kind of absolutist or objectivist claims that are opposed. Historically, targets of relativist criticism have included Platonism, Christian metaphysics, scientific **positivism**, and **humanism**. Discussions of relativism in social theory, however, are generally plagued by a failure to clearly differentiate the different contexts of relativist attributions, e.g., **ontological**, epistemological and value relativism. Popular and postmodern forms of relativism have flourished under the assumption that truth is absolute or it is nothing, hence that there is a simple choice between relativism and totalizing claims about absolute foundations that imply a universal or **transcendental** standpoint outside of history. Though relativism has been widely embraced under the heading of **postmodernism** in the humanities, social theorists with backgrounds in social science have more often attempted to develop a historical, **pluralistic** and **pragmatic** understanding of the diversity of forms of reason and valid knowledge without embracing radical relativism.

Despite the post-Enlightenment dominance of positivism, various relativist arguments were elaborated in the late nineteenth and early twentieth centuries, e.g., the perspectivalism of **Nietzsche** and the German crisis of **historicism**. Such themes were most clearly articulated by **Mannheim**'s sociology of knowledge which exempted natural science from social determination. More recently, **standpoint epistemologies** have been used to justify perspectival group claims to knowledge (especially in **feminist theory**), but suggest only a partial relativism with contested epistemological implications.

With the rise of post-empiricist philosophies of science (e.g., Kuhn's theory of **paradigms**) in the 1960s, a new cycle of epistemological relativism emerged with reference to the natural sciences, e.g. the 'strong programme' of the sociology of knowledge, the **linguistic turn**, **actor-network theory** in science studies, and the revival of pragmatism and **hermeneutics**. Such tendencies were reinforced by **post-structuralism's** account of the arbitrariness of the sign and related relativistic claims made on behalf of postmodernism. It is now common in many fields to refer to these developments as having eclipsed positivism, a transition identified with the ambiguous notion of post-positivism's recognition of the 'constructed' character of all knowledge.

The crucial issue in social theory has not been so much the principle of **social constructionism**, as the specific kind of relativistic epistemological and normative implications. The current of strong relativism associated with postmodernism – especially in the humanities – not only stresses (and embraces) both cognitive and normative relativity, but also suggests, ostensibly following **Foucault**'s notion of subjugated knowledges, that scientific claims have inherent **authoritarian** and **violent** effects resulting from **power–knowledge** relations. In its more radical forms, some anti-colonial and eco-feminist defenders of indigenous and local knowledge, such as Sandra Harding (1998), have challenged the universalism of Western science as Eurocentric and **phallocentric**. Sociological critics such as Raymond Boudon (1998) have claimed that postmodernist relativism makes hyperbolic and logically questionable use of social constructionism, a strategy whose success can be explained by the sociology of knowledge. Anti-relativists are often lumped together as defending **rationalism** – though this obscures the diversity of post-positivist, yet anti-relativist positions and their concessions to partial relativity (Hollis and Lukes 1982).

Debates relating to relativism have taken place under the heading of oppositions such as rationalism and anti-rationalism, positivism and anti-positivism, **objectivism** and subjectivism, **universalism** and particularism, **realism** and anti-realism, and foundationalism and anti-foundationalism. Discussions of universalism versus relativism with respect to **rights** have recently become an important topic in the context of **globalization** and **post-colonial theory**. In all such discussions imputations of relativism (and rationalism) must be treated with caution. Whereas one widely recognized relativist has proclaimed that he is not a relativist (Richard **Rorty**), another often cited as an anti-relativist (Jürgen **Habermas**) proclaims himself to be post-foundationalist and post-metaphysical.

Post-positivist alternatives to strong relativism in social theory have taken many different forms, e.g., transcendental, critical realism (Bhaskar), the **structuration school** (**Giddens**), reflexive sociology (**Bourdieu**), a 'project of universalism' (**Alexander** 1995), and a post-foundational, pragmatist critical theory (Habermas) that claims to move 'beyond objectivism and relativism' (Bernstein 1983).

References and further reading

Alexander, J. C. (1995) *Fin de Siècle Social Theory: Relativism, Reduction, and the Problem of Reason*. London: Verso.

Bernstein, R. J. (1983) *Beyond Objectivism and Relativism: Science, Hermeneutics, and Praxis*. Philadelphia, PA: University of Pennsylvania Press.

Boudon, R. (1998) 'The Social Sciences and the Two Types of Relativism', *Comparative Sociology*, 2(3): 424–40.

Harding, S. (1998) *Is Science Multicultual? Postcolonialism, Feminisms, and Epistemologies*. Bloomington, IN: Indiana University Press.

Harré, R. and Krausz, M. (1996) *Varieties of Relativism*. Cambridge, MA: Blackwell.

Hollis, M. and Lukes, S. (1982) *Rationality and Relativism*. Oxford: Blackwell.

Kirk, R. (1999) *Relativism and Reality: A Contemporary Introduction*. New York: Routledge.

Norris, C. (1996) *Reclaiming Truth: Contribution to a Critique of Cultural Relativism*. Durham, NC: Duke University Press.

RAYMOND A. MORROW

RELIGION

Definitions of religion abound, with most tracing their origins back to the nineteenth century. In the social sciences, two types of definitions prevail: substantive ones based on structures of **meaning**, and functional ones based on the alleged effects of the '**sacred**'. Most substantive definitions characterize religion as a system of **practices** predicated on references to personal or impersonal superhuman powers. Most functional definitions identify religion with the sacralization of **cognitive** and **moral** principles that give unity and coherence to **community**, **society** or the **self**. Substantive definitions are often combined with functional explanations.

The term 'religion' has been primarily, although not exclusively, conceptualized and systematized sociologically in the modern West. Not surprisingly, debates about religion have routinely given rise to fundamental reflections on the nature of Western **modernity**. For some, religion represents an indispensable element in the construction of the social, an *a priori* faculty of the human mind, or the foundation of morality and ethics. Yet others interpret it as a survival from a pre-scientific era, an **ideology** serving worldly interests, a symptom of **alienation**, an infantile illusion, or romantic escapism. Religion can be defined so generally that everyone is 'somehow' religious, or so specifically that no one is 'really' religious. Depending on one's understanding, religion is believed to be a phenomenon waning in the process of **secularization** or one that cannot disappear although it may change its form or function.

Religion and Enlightenment rationalism

These different understandings of religion can be interpreted as various responses to the **Enlightenment** critique of reason and the institutional differentiation of Western societies through which traditional religions have lost their metaphysical and moral centrality. Many of the debates on religion, therefore, implicitly or explicitly address questions of **rationality**. Although some **Enlightenment** authors, especially in France, rejected religion altogether as a priestly swindle, most of them actually attempted to reconcile religion and reason by rationalizing religion. Deism, the dominant religion of Enlightenment intellectuals, often informed rationalistic reinterpretations of **Christianity** and also stimulated biblical criticism. Deism undermined the authority of tradition and revelation by making science the new form of revelation. God could best be known through the scientific study of the laws that He had written into nature and the human mind.

This reconciliation of reason and religion, however, met with different kinds of criticism. Sceptics, like David Hume, rejected this intellectualist view of religion and claimed that religion is based on affect rather than reason. **Romantics** attempted to protect religion from Enlightenment rationalism by linking religion to aesthetics rather than to **metaphysics** or **morality**. For them, religion referred to an experience based on an inborn sensibility of the human mind comparable to poetry or music.

Debates in the social sciences are grounded in and continue these diverse understandings of religion. Most social scientists have assumed that religion changes its form in relation to processes of social transformation. With regard to Western **modernization**, some view religion as a fundamentally irrational phenomenon, while others regard it as an anachronistic but basically rational mode of thought or assume that religion is compatible with modernity when it becomes rationalized into ethics. Some expect the ongoing secularization of religion; others, the replacement of conventional religions by national ideologies, and others again, the privatization of religion.

Auguste **Comte** set the tone for much of nineteenth-century interpretations of religion. In his early writings he formulated his famous 'law of three stages' claiming that human thought had progressed from the theological via the metaphysical to the scientific. This cognitive approach to religion has dominated **evolutionist** theories in sociology and anthropology, especially in the British anthropological tradition. Comte's later writings, however, emphasized religion's significance in its capacity to integrate individuals into society intellectually, morally, and emotionally, thereby foreshadowing **Durkheim**'s theory of religion as a requisite of social order.

Projection theories

A rather different understanding emerged in the German critique of religion. The left-Hegelians, Ludwig Feuerbach and Karl **Marx**, and later Sigmund **Freud**, offered three different kinds of theories of projection, which agree in their diagnosis of religion as an irrational force. For Feuerbach, religion expressed human **alienation**. By attributing all of human perfection to a **transcendental** God who in turn overawes His creators, humans alienate themselves from their full humanity. For Freud, religion represented an infantile projection of unfulfilled wishes into an illusory realm. Religion was thus an expression of the human failure to face reality. Marx's socioeconomic explanation of religion, building on Feuerbach's critique and to a certain degree anticipating Freud's, was perhaps the most elaborate and influential of these projection theories.

According to Marx, religion represented a false consciousness, a misrecognition of the structures of social relations as they emerged in the transformation of nature into culture through human **labour**. In early socioeconomic stages, religion expressed the mysteriousness of natural forces. With increasing understanding of and control over nature, religion would disappear. However, in modern **capitalism**, increasing **class** differentiation between manual and intellectual labour, on the one hand, and the owners of the means of production and wage labourers, on the other, religion would make 'society' increasingly unfathomable. Hence social relations would not usually be comprehended as they actually are, but rather would be misunderstood, misrepresented, and mysticized. The reasons for this mystification were manifold, but all were based on the alienating structures of modern socioeconomic relations. Moreover, this misrecognition lay in the very nature of **commodity** production itself, since the interaction between social actors appeared in the form of an exchange relation between products. Religion expressed the irrationalities and contradictions of social relations. It served the ruling classes as an ideology of **legitimation** and provided the lower classes with an illusory happiness. Religion would disappear, once the alienating social conditions were overcome.

Durkheim

Durkheim's approach was both similar to and different from Marx's. Marx and Durkheim were not far apart in their assumption that religions legitimate and symbolize the structures of **social relations**. But what Marx formulated as a social critique, Durkheim affirmed as a social necessity based on arguments borrowed from the evolutionism of his time. For Durkheim, religion was rational in terms of the functions it serves for society and its survival. By simultaneously sacralizing cognitive and moral categories, as well as collective representations and conscience, and providing **emotional** attachment through **ritualization** and **symbolization**, religion guarantees both the socialization of egoistic individuals into moral ones and the coordination of individual actors into participants in the social **division of labour** and societal reproduction.

Durkheim's view of religion represented a major break with conventional under-

standings of religion and had far-reaching consequences. Religion for Durkheim, as earlier for Hobbes, was social and public. However, the concept of religion did not refer primarily or exclusively to religious communities and traditions but to sociopolitical units. Durkheim made tribal religion the prototype, or the 'elementary form,' of religion. In his analysis he swiftly moved from **tribe** to nation, ignoring important periods in history when any such close relationship between religion and political **community** was either tenuous or absent. His analysis also implied that traditional religions had outlived their functionality for society at large and that the modern age was in need of a new religion, a secular humanistic religion.

Weber

Max **Weber**, Durkheim's contemporary, had a rather different approach to the study of religion. Although Weber recognized what he called 'communal cults' as a typical early formation of religion, he did not link the concept of religion to societies as a whole. While religion always had communal as well as individual dimensions, Weber was most interested in religion as an independent principle of **association** and community formation. Although Weber abstained from an **essentializing** definition, he implicitly employed a substantive definition of religion. In his analyses he focused primarily on the study of 'salvation religions', because, in contrast to earlier religious formations, salvation religions distinguish between worldly and other-worldly interests. The interest in salvation represents a relatively autonomous religious interest that could come into conflict with worldly interests.

Linking religion to institutionalized interests in salvation rather than to the systemic needs of society generated questions different from Durkheim's. Weber mainly explored how salvation **interests** impacted the life conduct both of *virtuosi* and lay people, and what kinds of tensions these interests created *vis-à-vis* other interests, such as political, economic, **aesthetic**, erotic, or scientific ones. Such tensions, or the lack thereof, shape cultures and personalities in specific ways. Because Weber regarded all ultimate values on which cultures are based as irrational, the difference between Western and non-Western cultures represented not a difference between rational and irrational cultures, but between cultures whose rationalization had taken different directions based on their ultimate attitudes towards the world. Weber linked such developments not only to an inner logic of world views, but also to dominant social classes, forms of religious organizations, theodicies, and plausibility structures in conjunction with broader economic or political trends.

Social psychology

In reaction to Durkheim's supposed sociological determinism, on the one hand, and the individualistic cognitive psychology of Tylor and Frazer, on the other, other classical explanations of religion began from social psychology. Authors like the psychologists William McDougall and William James and the anthropologists Robert R. Marett and Bronislaw Malinowski linked religion to affect rather than reason. For them, the religious experience begins as an experience of awe and powerlessness, but it does not end there. Religions also help humans to overcome situations of **crisis** through public rituals that empower and reintegrate communities and selves. These approaches should be clearly distinguished from earlier Romantic and later phenomenological ones, like those of Rudolf Otto or Mircea **Eliade**, that model their understanding of religion on the concept of revelation. Social psychological approaches locate religion not in a specifically religious experience but in the interpretation of experiences as religious.

Postclassical trends

The classical **paradigms** have widely dominated the paths along which religion has been conceptualized and theorized during the twentieth century. Later authors have mostly elaborated, reformulated, or revised them. The Marxists focused either on religion as a response to the socio-economic irrationalities of **colonialism** and **capitalism** or, via **Gramsci**, on religion as a resource for resistance. The Durkheimians have analyzed religion as collective representations and public **rituals**. And the Weberians have been mostly interested in the impact of religion on attitudes towards the world and on life conduct. The approaches of Durkheim and Weber have often been combined with little attention to their profound differences.

The Durkheimian legacy of linking religion to societal and national integration has been prominent in the writings of Talcott **Parsons** and the authors he influenced, such as Robert Bellah and Clifford **Geertz**. Parsons argued that modern industrial societies, especially the USA, have not relegated Christianity to a subordinate position, but, on the contrary, have been permeated by the Christian values of **voluntarism** and **individualism**. Bellah further argued that Rousseau's notion of a **civil religion** has become a reality in America. American civil religion has its own ritual calendar and sacred language that is regularly invoked at solemn occasions, or in presidential addresses.

Peter **Berger** (1967) and Thomas **Luckmann** (1967) have combined Durkheimian and Weberian perspectives with Alfred **Schutz**'s phenomenological approach. Both are concerned with the social construction of reality and its reproduction through processes of externalization, **objectification**, and internalization, although they disagree on the definition of religion and the question of secularization. Berger, employing a substantive definition of religion, argues that the pluralization of religions in modern societies undermines their truth claims, leading to a lack of plausibility and ultimately to secularization. Luckmann, in turn, favouring a formal definition and linking it to the formation of a self, makes religion a universal necessity of human identity formation. For him, institutional differentiation and pluralization do not lead to secularization but to the privatization of religion.

Each of these theoretical approaches has generated timely criticism. In the 1960s Melford Spiro debunked **functionalism** for conflating the definition and explanation of religion and for being fundamentally disinterested in religion itself. David Martin, comparatively studying institutional dynamics that generate different secularization outcomes, questioned the secularization thesis in its undifferentiated form. Later Karel Dobbelaere further refined Martin's conceptualization and analysis of secularization.

The decades since the 1970s have produced a plethora of studies that suggest a conceptual ambiguity regarding what constitutes the object of the study of religion. Durkheim's concept of 'effervescence' has often been appropriated to legitimize studies of various kinds of group enthusiasm, from football games to barbecues, as religious phenomena. Moreover, the privatization and subjectivization of religion have contributed to a fuzziness regarding the boundaries of religious phenomena. The term 'spirituality' is too often introduced to give unity to all the manners of personal idiosyncrasy. The concept of 'implicit religion' looks for 'quasi'-religious phenomena in a secular world, offering another example of such vagueness.

However, the resurgence of religious movements and their increased public and political visibility, often associated with **fundamentalism**, and the new religious vitality triggered by processes of **globalization**, **urbanization** and **migration** have also revitalized and refocused the study of religion. Economic approaches based on variations of **rational choice** theories have contributed to the analysis of religious markets and the success and failure of religious organizations. Pierre **Bourdieu** elaborated Weber's model of religious competition and explored the uses of religious capital in the general social struggle over **power** and **prestige**. Niklas **Luhmann** has developed his own functional approach to religion based on the distinction between the familiar and the unfamiliar, the immanent and the transcendent.

In general, postclassical approaches have paid much more attention to competition between religious organizations and actors. Instead of religious monopolies, **pluralism** has become the privileged model. The secularization thesis, while still contested, is now mainly understood in relation to processes of institutional differentiation. Yet, as Luhmann has pointed out, these processes require more precise analysis. Nevertheless, the last few decades have corrected the perception that scholars of religion are studying a vanishing phenomenon.

References and further reading

Banton, M. (ed.) (1966) *Anthropological Approaches to the Study of Religion*. London: Tavistock.

Bellah, R. (1970) *Beyond Belief*. New York: Harper & Row.

Berger, P. (1967) *The Sacred Canopy: Elements of a Sociological Theory of Religion*. Garden City, NY: Doubleday.

Bourdieu, P. (1992) 'Genesis and Structure of the Religious Field', in C. Calhoun (ed.) *Religious Institutions*. Greenwich, CT: JAI Press.

Durkheim, E. ([1912] 1995) *The Elementary Forms of the Religious Life*. New York: Free Press.

Luckmann, T. (1967) *The Invisible Religion*. New York: Macmillan.

Malinowski, B. (1948) *Magic, Science, and Religion*. Boston: Beacon Press.

Martin, D. (1978) *A General Theory of Secularisation*. Oxford: Blackwell.

Parsons, T. (1963) 'Christianity and Modern Industrial Society', in E. Tiryakian (ed.) *Sociological Theory, Values, and Sociocultural Change*. New York: Free Press.

Preus, J. S. (1987) *Explaining Religion*. New Haven, CT: Yale University Press.

Smart, N. *et al.* (eds) (1985) *Nineteenth Century Religious Thought in the West*, 3 vols. Cambridge: Cambridge University Press.

Taylor, M. (ed.) (1998) *Critical Terms For Religious Studies*. Chicago: University of Chicago Press.

Weber, M. ([1922] 1993) *The Sociology of Religion*. Boston: Beacon Press.

Young, L. (ed.) (1998) *Rational Choice Theory and Religion: Summary and Assessment*. New York: Routledge.

MARTIN RIESEBRODT

REPRESENTATION

Use of the term 'representation' in the social sciences should ideally be confined to contexts in which representation is *intended* by social *actors*. Two primary senses of the term can be distinguished. On the one hand, if social actors, by virtue of their personality, specific characteristics, actions, occupation or membership of distinct **groups**, adhere to certain representations of the world – in the sense of religious beliefs, political ideologies, philosophies, prejudices, **world-views**, or any other kinds of 'collective representation' in **Durkheim**'s sense – we may speak generally of *symbolic representation*. If, on the other hand, social actors 'stand in' for other, real or possible, even perhaps fictive actors – as in a lawyer who represents a client, a member of parliament who represents a constituency, or an actor on the theatrical stage who represents a character – we may speak, in a rather narrower sense, of *social representation*. In this second case, it is most often human individuals who are the media of representation, the agents of the act of representing, the 'representatives'; and, decisively, what or whom these representatives 'stand in' for can only be individuals, or groups of individuals, people, or communities, such as religious or political communities or economic enterprises or 'nations'. Such collective actors or corporate actors, particularly in modern societies, frequently have the status of 'legal personalities' (cf. Coleman 1990).

Social representation presupposes that those who are represented have the power to act. Entities which lack, or have been denied, the power to act – that is, the ability or right to act on their own behalf – cannot be represented, at least not in the *social* sense; at most, they can be represented in the *symbolic* sense. Representation is a social fact to the extent that a corresponding relationship is taken for granted by both sides and a social environment is taken as given. Socio-cultural interpretations and definitions decide who can be represented by whom and in what respect.

The most general formula to describe social representation is: A (the representative) represents B (the represented) before C (the addressee of the representation) with respect to matter X. Here 'represent' means not only 'act or speak in place of' or 'in the interests of', but also 'in the name of', in such a way that the person(s) represented must assume at least the consequences of this representation as the consequences of his or her *own* action. This is described most accurately in the formula from Roman law, *alieno nomine agere*.

The social tasks for which representation occurs vary to an extraordinary degree both historically and culturally. But in all cases limits are imposed on actors, which they are not able or not permitted to transgress in their own name, but whose transgression is of great importance for them. These limits can be of a factual or physical or spatio-temporal nature, or based on a lack of competence, or be generated from social-moral or religious prescriptions as to what is permissible and not permissible for certain actors.

There is a very wide-ranging literature in the social sciences on political representation, with particular reference to the principles, functional preconditions and functional problems of modern parliamentary, i.e. representative, democracies (cf. de Grazia 1968; Mill 1958). Abbé Sieyés, before the French Revolution, pointed out that 'everything is representation in the social state' (*tout est représentation dans l'état social*), and indeed in many other sub-systems representation is of constitutive significance and is always disputed. The spectrum of facts to be examined here ranges from the religious or quasi-religious idea and institution of representative suffering or dying to representation within the legal system and, predominantly legally regulated, economic conditions via the more or less formalized representation arrangements provided by the professions. Also salient is the claim to representation with respect to classes, nations or the whole of humanity, maintained and disputed by **intellectuals** (cf. Weiss 1992). Finally there is the currently vital question of an 'advocatory decision' about the life and death of the unborn or severely ill person.

References and further reading

Coleman, J. S. (1990) *Foundations of Social Theory*. Cambridge, MA: Harvard University Press.

De Grazia, A. (1968) 'Representation (I): Theory', in D. L. Sills (ed.) *International Encyclopedia of the Social Sciences*, vol. 13. Glencoe, IL: Macmillan/Free Press, pp. 461–5.

Mill, J. S. ([1861] 1958) *Considerations on Representative Government*. New York: Arts Press.

Pennock, J. and Chapman, J. W. (eds) (1968) *Representation: Yearbook of the American Society for Political and Legal Philosophy*. New York: Atherton Press.

Pitkin, H. F. (1967) *The Concept of Representation*. Berkeley, CA: University of California Press.

Weiss, J. (1992) 'From Representative Culture to Cultural Representation', in R. Münch and N. J. Smelser (eds) *Theory and Culture*. Berkeley, CA: University of California Press, pp. 121–44.

Weiss, J. (1998) *Handeln und handeln lassen: Über Stellvertretung* [To Act and to Let Act: On Representation]. Wiesbaden: Westdeutscher Verlag.

Williams, R. (1976) 'Representative', in *Keywords: A Vocabulary of Culture and Society*. London: Croom Helm, pp. 222–5.

JOHANNES WEISS

REPUBLIC

The republic is as old a political concept as **democracy** and like democracy, its exact meaning is mutable. 'Republic' is best considered as both a specific form of **organization** and an ideal state or harmonious **community**. In republics, order is not imposed by absolutist rulers such as monarchs or a priesthood; nor is it spontaneously generated through the deliberation of the people as in an ideal democracy (or **anarchy**). Rather, order is actively legislated through **laws** and customs. What varies, both in theory and practice, are the means by which good laws are derived and the composition of the **citizen** body from which they emerge.

Plato's fourth-century BC philosophical *Republic* (1974) sought to derive the nature of justice and good political conduct. The results formed a repudiation of Athenian democracy, which Plato likened to a ship on which 'the sailors are quarrelling about the navigation. Each man thinks that he ought to navigate, though up to that time he has never studied the art' (*Republic*: para. 488). Ships – and republics – needed a navigator with **authority** and experience. Therefore, instead of handing responsibility for lawmaking over to a capricious mass, the Platonic ideal was rule by 'philosopher-kings' (*Republic*: Book VI): men whose long study of good conduct and justice qualified them to craft legislation under which citizens would live harmoniously. Plato acknowledged that one could not take for granted the benevolence of philosopher-kings. What protections existed against their corruption? But he said that it was when rulers courted the masses that corruption occurred. A multitude cannot but have conflicting interpretations of the good life, so 'a multitude cannot be philosophical' (*Republic*: para. 494). Good laws were therefore to be found not in democracy but in **objective**, **philosophical** enquiry into the nature of truth. Plato admitted good philosopher-kings were very rare, but that was why they should be actively courted as rulers.

513

The Roman historian Livy disagreed with Plato's dismissal of the citizenry. A healthy republic:

> could be linked directly to respect for authority, religious and secular, and to the 'modesty, fairness and nobility of mind' which belonged to the whole people. Such a frame of mind could be sustained when civic virtue triumphed over factionalism; that is, when the common business of citizens...prevailed over the tendency to corrupt political practices – the pursuit of private interests in public affairs.
>
> (quoted in Held 1996: 44)

This idea of civic virtue – broadly, citizens' glorification of their republic and desire for its betterment – was developed by the first significant Renaissance republican, Machiavelli (1519). In his *Discourses on Livy*, Machiavelli agreed that without reviving the Athenian idea of active citizenship, a republic would decay. While admitting that the political masses were imperfect, he noted that all their faults were amplified in **aristocracies** or princes. At the same time, he was a realist and recognized the need to accommodate the powerful ruling classes of Renaissance Italian **city–states**. The people and the **aristocracy** therefore balanced each other. An unchecked aristocracy would decay into a tyranny; but an unchecked democracy would also decay into a state where 'each individual lived according to his own wishes, so that every day a thousand wrongs were done' ([1519] 1979: Chapter II). Machiavelli therefore wrote that 'those who were prudent in establishing laws recognized this fact...[that] where there is in the same city-state a principality, an aristocracy, and a democracy, one form keeps watch over the other' (ibid.). In his ideal republic, order would therefore arise through a balance of **powers**, fortified by the citizens' civic virtue.

Held (1996: 44–5) terms Machiavelli a 'protective' republican. That is, political participation is valuable, but only because these make republics strong and enable them to protect citizens' rights, objectives and interests. Held contrasts this with a more 'developmental' republicanism, in which participation has a more inherent value, being important for the happiness and **moral development** of citizens. The epitome of the developmental republican was Rousseau, particularly in *The Social Contract* ([1762] 1968). Here the republic returned to an idealist democratic state in which citizens deliberated on the 'general will' and enacted this without the control of a prince or aristocracy. But Rousseau's book was also a warning that as society continued to develop and **nation–states** grew vastly larger than the small city-states of his (or Machiavelli's, or Plato's) time, the conditions under which a general will could be democratically formed would be lost.

Modern republics are not small city-states but typically large nations, in which **autonomy** is delegated to representatives. The 'balance of power' does not necessarily include the citizens themselves. Active citizenship is seen as a challenge by many governments, rather than as a supporting pillar. An ideal republican **community**, however, is accountable only to *all* members of the community itself, both rulers and citizens. Therefore, like many political concepts, republics are both ideals and fallible, real-world attempts to emulate those ideals.

References and further reading

Held, D. (1996) *Models of Democracy* 2nd edn. Cambridge: Polity.

Livy (1951) *History of Rome.* Cambridge, MA: Harvard University Press.

Machiavelli, N. ([1519] 1979) 'The Discourses', in P. Bondanella and M. Musa (eds) *The Portable Machiavelli.* Harmondsworth: Penguin.

Plato (1974) *The Republic.* Harmondsworth: Penguin.

Pocock, J. (1975) *The Machiavellian Moment.* Princeton, NJ: Princeton University Press.

Rahe, P. (1994) *Republics Ancient and Modern.* Chapel Hill, NC: University of North Carolina Press.

Rousseau, J.-J. ([1762] 1968) *The Social Contract.* Harmondsworth: Penguin.

ANDREW WHITWORTH

REVOLUTION

The modern sense of the term 'revolution' refers to a process of political and **social change** based on use of violent force that aims to overthrow existing forms of government. The modern concept of revolution was profoundly shaped by the French Revolution of 1789 and by successive **intellectual** movements marking the beginning of the concept's career in social scientific **discourse**. **Marx**'s adaptation of revolution in a **materialist** historical framework has been the main point of reference for an abundance of social and political theories in the twentieth century. Since the 1960s sociologists have been repeatedly concerned with the causes, social preconditions and consequences of revolutionary movements and uprisings.

The **modern** notion of revolution must be distinguished from its ancient meaning. From classical antiquity to the Renaissance, 'revolution' stood for a cyclical movement, based on the image of the movement of planets. As Koselleck (1969) demonstrates, it was the French Revolution that coined the modern sense of the term, introducing the element of singularity and completeness of transformation. Marx, in this sense, emphasized the thrust of modern revolutions to overcome the past for the sake of an open and unstructured future. With Engels, Marx provided a long-term account of societal change of Western **civilization**, referring to dominant **modes of production** leading necessarily to class antagonisms which can be overcome only by the revolutionary **agency** of the exploited. In this scheme, the revolutionary process marks the end of an old era and the beginning of a new one,

from **feudalism** to **capitalism**, and from capitalism to **communism**. Revolution is conceived of as a motor of social change in the service of human progress, and all negative perceptions of the phenomenon are thrown aside. Despite its teleological implications, the Marxian conception of revolution had a major impact on subsequent theories of revolution. It drew social-scientific attention towards the significance of revolutions for the transitional passage from traditional to modern stages of society, setting a sweeping agenda for research and political mobilization in the twentieth century.

O'Kane (2000) summarizes the varieties of approaches towards the explanation of revolutions, distinguishing between two basic types of definition prevalent in the early twentieth century. One type conceives of revolution as a sub-category of collective **violence**, focusing on a universal psychological disposition of the masses (Le Bon, **Durkheim**), and in this way tending to neglect historical contexts and peculiarities. The other type aims at the 'world-historical meaning' of revolutions, in the spirit of Marx.

In the first third of twentieth century, remarkable attempts to delineate common patterns and uniformities of varied revolutionary transformations were made by scholars such as Edwards, Brinton, and Pettee, making up the 'natural history' school. Their main interest lay more in extrapolation of the dynamics of processes incited by uprisings than an examination of their driving forces. But in focusing solely on the classic cases of 'successful' revolutions – the British, American, French, and Russian – they have been criticized for a truncated outlook that fails to adequately account for differences among developments.

A more explicit inductive method was pioneered by Barrington **Moore** in his influential study *Social Origins of Dictatorship and Democracy* (1966), blazing the trail for a younger generation of scholars such as Charles **Tilly**, Theda **Skocpol**, and others.

Reconstructing concepts from Marx, Moore avoided the quandary engendered by too close an adherence to theoretical or ideological claims and instead remained sensitive to empirical variation. He conducted a large-scale comparative historical analysis of **modernization** developments in various civilizational regions from 1300 until the twentieth century, tracing the roots of **democratic**, communist, and **fascist** regimes in relation to models of transition from agrarian to capitalist stages of development. He thus avoided the biases of previously dominant modernization theories that had tended to impose Western categories on dissimilar contexts.

Moore's methodological recommendations have been taken up and fleshed out by Tilly (1978, 1993) and Skocpol (1979). Tilly's analysis of revolutionary energy and collective discontent focuses on the organizational capacity of groups eager for power. Refining **comparative methods**, Tilly seeks to account for the vast diversity of contingencies that precede the outcome of revolutionary outbreaks in various European regions. Revolutionary upheaval in his picture appears to be more the result of happy coincidence than of planned action. In the same vein, Skocpol draws attention to events that render states incapable of functioning in their basic provisions due to fiscal collapse or military threats from neighbouring states. She brings to bear a wide range of aspects that shaped the outcome of revolutions in France, Russia, and China, accounting principally for the international context of states and the pressures put on them.

The comparative historical approach of Moore, Tilly and Skocpol has prompted some critical responses from other writers. **Eisenstadt** (1978) and Sewell (1985) take issue with their neglect of cultural dimensions of social change and their restriction purely to institutional and social-structural aspects. In his comparative analysis of diverse civilizations, Eisenstadt discerns forms of institutional change beyond the

implications of labor division related to cultural symbolic orientations such as **centre** and **periphery** relations, hierarchical structuring of social relations and basic rules of interaction. In a similar manner, Sewell argues, mainly against Skocpol, that 'ideology plays a crucial role in revolutions, both as cause and as outcome' (1985: 86).

Another rival paradigm has been established by **rational choice** theorists. Focusing on social settings in which it may appear reasonable for individuals to engage in revolutionary activity, authors such as Tullock, Popkin, and Silver draw their conclusions from observations about types of **group** membership, especially **peasant** groups. In their analysis, individuals are likely to pursue revolutionary action primarily on grounds of **private** payoffs and with indifference towards **public** matters. Since the late 1980s, however, these hard-nosed accounts have been criticized by scholars who demonstrate that public goods can indeed serve as incentives for individual revolutionary action and who challenges the individualist assumptions of **rational choice** theory, emphasizing the agency of social groups as key actors in revolutions.

Although scholars do not agree either on any conclusive definition of revolutions or on any royal road to their methodical analysis, the transformations in Eastern Europe and many other parts of the world since the early 1990s continue to place the phenomenon of revolution at the top of the social-scientific agenda.

References and further reading

Aya, R. (1990) *Rethinking Revolutions and Collective Violence: Studies on Concept, Theory, and Method*. Amsterdam: Het Spinhuis.

Eisenstadt, S. N. (1978) *Revolutions and the Transformations of Society: A Comparative Study of Civilizations*. New York: Free Press.

Foran, J. (ed.) (1997) *Theorizing Revolution*. London: Routledge.

Koselleck, R. (1969) 'Der neuzeitliche Revolutionsbegriff als geschichtliche Kategorie', *Studium Generale*, 22: 825–38.

Moore, B., Jr. (1966) *Social Origins of Dictatorship and Democracy: Lord and Peasant in the Making of the Modern World*. Boston: Beacon.

O'Kane, R. H. T. (2000) 'Revolution and Social Science: Movements in Method, Theory and Practice', in R. H. T. O'Kane (ed.) *Revolution: Critical Concepts in Political Science*, vol. 1. London: Routledge.

O'Kane, R. H. T. (ed.) (2000) *Revolution: Critical Concepts in Political Science*, 4 vols. London: Routledge.

Sewell, W. H., Jr. ([1985] 2000) 'Ideologies and Social Revolutions: Reflections on the French Case', in R. H. T. O'Kane (ed.) *Revolution: Critical Concepts in Political Science*, vol. 1. London: Routledge.

Skocpol, T. (1979). *States and Social Revolutions: A Comparative Analysis of France, Russia and China*. Cambridge: Cambridge University Press.

Taylor, S. (1984) *Social Science and Revolutions*. London: Macmillan.

Tilly, C. (1978) *From Mobilization to Revolution*. Reading, MA: Addison-Wesley.

Tilly, C. (1993) *European Revolutions, 1492–1992*. Oxford: Blackwell.

BERNHARD GIESEN
DANIEL ŠUBER

RICOEUR, PAUL (1913–2005)

French philosopher

One of the leading protagonists of the project of philosophical **hermeneutics**, Ricoeur dedicated himself to the exploration of human understanding and, in particular, imagination, as a process of *interpretation*. Four aspects may be seen as central in Ricoeur's life-long studies of philosophical, poetic, historic, and theological understanding, and **action**. All interpretation is: (1) linguistic or a **language**-like process; (2) socially, **culturally**, and historically contextualized; (3) creative and originating new meaning ('meaning surplus'), rather than just realizing given meaning; and (4) open-ended and indeterminate. After dealing in his early work with Husserl's **phenomenology** and existentialism, he published studies on **psychoanalysis**, *Freud and Philosophy* ([1965] 1970) and **structuralism**. In *Hermeneutics and the*

Human Sciences (1981), he suggested a systematic theory of interpretation based on the model of the text, a view that was extended in *From Text to Action* ([1986] 1991) to non-textual forms of action. In *The Rule of Metaphor* ([1975] 1977) and *Time and Narrative* ([1983–85] 1984–88), Ricoeur sought to explicate the crucial role of figurative language and narrative **discourse** in **meaning** construction, particularly focusing on the narrative fabric of our notions of **time** and temporality. Only the narrative configuration of time, he argues, gives shape to the temporal dimension of human existence. In *Oneself as Another* ([1990] 1992), Ricoeur formulated the consequences of his social–existential hermeneutics for the dialectic of **self** and **other**, and, in *La mémoire, l'histoire, l'oubli* (2000), for human self-understanding in memory and history.

Major works

([1965] 1970) *Freud and Philosophy*. New Haven: Yale University Press.

([1975] 1977) *The Rule of Metaphor*. Chicago: University of Chicago Press.

(1981) *Hermeneutics and the Human Sciences*. Cambridge: Cambridge University Press.

([1986] 1991) *From Text to Action*. Evanston: Northwestern University Press.

([1983–85] 1984–88) *Time and Narrative*. Chicago: University of Chicago Press.

([1990] 1992) *Oneself as Another*. Chicago: University of Chicago Press.

(2000) *La mémoire, l'histoire, l'oubli*. Paris: Seuil.

Further reading

Wood, D. (ed.) (1991) *On Paul Ricœur: Narrative and Interpretation*. London: Routledge.

JENS BROCKMEIER

RIESMAN, DAVID (1909–2002)

US sociologist

In his best-selling book *The Lonely Crowd* (1950), Riesman developed a social psychology concerned with **mass culture and** mass society and popular culture in an era that seemed to be experiencing a new era of economic abundance. Influenced by Erich Fromm's neo-Freudian psychoanalysis as well as by Thorstein Veblen's sociology of the 'leisure class', Riesman argues that in every society a 'mode of conformity' secures the relation between individual and society through the construction of social character types. Corresponding to the shift from an age of production to an age of consumption, the work-driven character type that he calls 'inner-directed' becomes increasingly supplanted by a consumption-driven character type that he calls 'other-directed'. During the same process, a shift occurs in the field of decision-making from dominance by a ruling class to power dispersal among a plurality of competing 'veto groups'. This places Riesman within the pluralist school of social thought. Given his focus on culture, leisure and mass media (see media and mass media), Riesman's work continues to exert an influence in American studies and cultural studies.

Major works

(1950) (with R. Denney and N. Glazer) *The Lonely Crowd: A Study of the Changing American Character.* New Haven, CT: Yale University Press.

(1952) (with N. Glazer) *Faces in the Crowd: Individual Studies in Character and Politics.* New Haven, CT: Yale University Press.

(1953) *Thorstein Veblen: A Critical Interpretation.* New York: Scribner.

(1954) *Individualism Reconsidered and Other Essays.* Glencoe, IL: Free Press.

(1964) *Abundance for What? and Other Essays.* Garden City, NY: Doubleday.

Further reading

Gans, H. J., Glazer, N., Gusfield, J. R. and Jencks, C. (eds) (1979) *On the Making of Americans: Essays in Honor of David Riesman.* Philadelphia, PA: University of Pennsylvania Press.

OLIVER MARCHART

RIGHTS

Although used freely in political debate, what constitutes a right is the subject of intense controversy. Following W. N. Hohfeld's (1923) classic modern analysis, most scholars have interpreted rights in a fourfold fashion: first, as *privileges*, where a person owes no duty to another to do or not to do something; second, as *claim-rights*, where individual rights entail duties to uphold these rights on the part of others; third, as *powers*, where rights are thought of as permitting a change in the legal relationships between peoples; and fourth, as *immunities*, where rights are a security against a change in legal status. Today, human rights are often thought of as entailing an assortment of these conditions, in order to provide some sort of constitutional guarantee of a universal right to life, liberty and security. Most political and social theorists discuss rights in terms of the claims or duties that they make upon others. They are usually broadly understood as either negative (implying that a right to something is an absence of constraint in making good one's claim to it), or positive, which implies that some sort of action is required to enforce one's right in the first place. Most writers retain Hohfeld's assumption that rights constitute some form of advantage.

However, Jeremy Bentham ([1791] 1973) famously attacked the idea of the natural 'rights of man', claiming that if all persons had universal rights, there was no way of distinguishing between who had a right to something or not, and hence the question of justification and enforcement was overly muddied (see utilitarianism). Bentham's analysis was updated in a seminal modern essay by H. L. A. Hart ([1955] 1984), who argued that if one suggests that rights claims are moral claims, then justifying political interference or intervention with persons on the basis of such moral claims presupposes in the first place that all persons have a natural and equal interest in and right to freedom. From a more radical perspective, Karl **Marx** asserted that a focus on rights obfuscated real problems of **inequality** within a particular society, and were **liberal** illusions.

These discussions consider whether individual rights are universal or whether positive law must be used to enforce particular rights claims. Prior to this, early-modern discussions often tried to reconcile the idea of a natural right to do everything possible to uphold the natural law of self-preservation. Thus the notion of rights was bound up with questions of individual liberty and **property** in a different sense. Indeed, in one of the most famous of discussions, John Locke claimed that all human beings had a natural and God-given right to life, liberty and property, but that the right to property in particular could only be maintained if it was used by persons in a very particularly **Christian** way, by mixing their **labour** with it. This was then underpinned by a distinctly **religious** account of the proper use of property. In the absence of such proper use by the American Indians, for example, Locke thought (along with numerous other theorists from Grotius to Hobbes) that the effectively **colonial** acquisition of land and the conduct of **war** were justifiable. However, writers such as these also effectively bridged traditional discussions of natural **law** with their focus on subjective individual rights that were defended and recognized as such only when the civil law under a Commonwealth had been established. This notion of political rights would be amended and later codified in such documents as the American Declaration of Independence, and the French *Déclaration*, initiating a special relationship between rights and **democracy**.

Modern discussions have, as Jeremy Waldron (1984) suggests, attempted both to render more explicit precisely what a right is in relation to positive law (see **law and legality**), while at the same time excavating the foundations of rights and in particular their relationship to the notion of duty,

something which he suggests Hohfeld's analysis left under-theorized. Broadly, we can say that the relationship between rights and duties is often theorized in terms of the power that a bearer of rights has over the person who has a duty to uphold the right, and the choice that they are able to make in order to relieve someone of that duty. Or it has been considered in terms of the interest or benefit that someone has in having his or her rights claim enforced. One of the central problems faced by those who claim a clear relationship between rights and duties on the one hand, alongside the assessment which suggests that individual rights form the basis of discussions of political **morality** and **value**, on the other, is that they may neglect to consider the other, non-individualistic bases of political morality.

Since the recent work of Ronald Dworkin (1979) in particular, rights are often perceived within liberal thought as 'trumps' that instantiate certain claims over and above a basic social structure that is broadly held together by a particular political philosophy (here, a version of **utilitarianism**). Hence, rights and political morality are related within a discussion that seeks to maximize liberty through the promotion of **equality**, but in which specific rights claims can have priority over the general interest. This has led to questions of which rights are to be justified, and how considerations of the general good are to be established, whether by virtue of utility or by virtue of other, non-welfarist considerations. Joseph Raz (1988) has developed powerful criticisms of such positions. He argues that other goods and values, in particular respect for persons and notions of self-respect, are elements of prime importance to conceptions of political life that go beyond a focus on the rights of the individual.

Alongside this focus on the boundaries of rights, debate has increasingly been divided on the issue of **conflict** between rights themselves, in particular in terms of whether special status should be accorded to the rights claims of particular **groups** on the basis of such issues as **race**, **gender** and **culture**, or whether the rights of groups should simply be seen as derivative of the universal rights of individuals. The most obvious case here again is that of human rights. However, if one is sceptical about the religious basis of individual rights as well as the capacity for finding practical means for their universal enforcement, one might try to avoid the problem of cultural and moral **relativism** by suggesting that a sceptical and secular humanism, alongside a focus on moral reciprocity, is quite simply the best that we can achieve if we take the view that all violations of human rights should be subject to similar penalties. That one cannot and should not pick and choose, for example, which abuses to challenge on this basis, and that in fact all human rights claims should be defended and supported equally, is a theme that one can find in various recent liberal analyses.

Others, such as A. J. Simmons (2001), take a position termed philosophical **anarchism**, to suggest that political obligation (a variation on the duties owed to those with specific rights claims) is an almost entirely voluntary undertaking, which cannot be justified in terms of the fact that we all share in the life of a political association (see also **voluntarism**). Similarly, other neo-Lockean positions have developed to defend the right to private property and various forms of libertarianism. Liberals such as Waldron (1984) defend the idea that under a properly representative democracy, by guaranteeing the right of participation in the selection of political actors, individual **citizens** are given a basic right to have rights. In effect, this can appear as another variation on the idea that rights are in some senses 'trumps' over other political claims and which can justify the maintenance and procedural neutrality of a liberal regime. But such an account could also be used to justify redistributive taxation and the promotion of positive rights as well, as

various liberals have done, and debates on this issue are likely to continue for the foreseeable future.

References and further reading

Bentham, J. ([1791] 1973) 'A Critical Examination of the Declaration of Rights', in B. Parekh (ed.) *Bentham's Political Thought*. New York: Barnes and Noble, pp. 257–90.

Dworkin, R. (1979) *Taking Rights Seriously*. London: Duckworth.

Hart, H. L. A. ([1955] 1984) 'Are There Any Natural Rights?', in J. Waldron (ed.) *Theories of Rights*. Oxford: Oxford University Press, pp. 77–90.

Hohfeld, W. J. (1923) *Fundamental Legal Conceptions*. New Haven, CT: Yale University Press.

Ignatieff, M. (2001) *Human Rights as Politics and Idolatry*. Cambridge, MA: Harvard University Press.

Jones, P. (1994) *Rights*. Basingstoke: Macmillan.

Locke, J. ([1690] 1988) *Two Treatises on Government*. Ed. P. Laslett. Cambridge: Cambridge University Press.

Rawls, J. (2001) *The Law of Peoples*. Cambridge, MA: Harvard University Press.

Raz, J. (1988) *The Morality of Freedom*. Oxford: Oxford University Press.

Simmons, A. J. (2001) *Justification and Legitimacy*. Cambridge: Cambridge University Press.

Steiner, H. (1994) *An Essay on Rights*. Oxford: Blackwell.

Tuck, R. (1979) *Natural Rights: Their Origins and Development*. Cambridge: Cambridge University Press.

Waldron, J. (ed.) (1984) *Theories of Rights*. Oxford: Oxford University Press.

DUNCAN KELLY

RISK

The concept of risk has a long history, and provides sociologists with a vantage point from which to study the ways in which people place confidence in their relative powers of control over possible future dangers. The precise origins of the word 'risk' are uncertain, but it may be derived from the Arabic word *risq*, meaning 'riches' or 'good fortune'. It is also possible to trace its origins to the Greek word *rhiza*, meaning 'cliff', and the Latin *resegare* meaning 'to cut off short', so that it appears to have first featured as part of a maritime vocabulary to evoke the danger of sailing too closely to inshore rocks. Where the concept 'risk' has featured in modern times as a principle of insurance, both of these possible derivations colour the ways in which this is put to use. It was during the Commercial Revolution (*c.* 1275–1375) that Italian shipping merchants first used modern-style insurance contracts as a means to manage their business affairs (de Roover 1945). Here, the concept of risk was used with reference to a process of calculation that has taken place in order to assess the likelihood of commercial success in a world of hazardous contingencies. For insurers to place confidence in their calculations of risk, they must be willing to **trust** that their **knowledge** and experience of past events are a reliable guide for predicting what is most likely to take place in the future. Where merchants are prepared to approach risk as an acquisitive opportunity, this implies that a society has successfully established a range of legal **institutions**, administrative practices and technological innovations that place a measure of guarantee upon the predicted outcomes of their investment decisions For this reason, sociologists contend that historical developments in the meaning and application of risk mirror the social and technological processes by which nature and **society** have been made subject to the law of calculable rules. The history of risk is a vital part of the history of modern processes of rationalization (see **rationality, rationalism and rationalization**) (Ewald 1991).

In contemporary social theory, the concept of risk is often associated with the works of Ulrich **Beck** (1992, 1999), Mary **Douglas** (1986, 1992) and **Foucauldian** theorists of 'governmentality' (Dean 1999a, 1999b; O'Malley 1996) (see **governance and governmentality**). While writing from different traditions of sociological analysis, they all share the understanding that, where

the **language** of risk has risen to prominence in contemporary public debate, it signals a profound transformation in the cultural experience of modern societies. For Beck and Douglas, this concerns the ways in which we relate to the hazards of modern technologies (see **technology and technocracy**) and construct the political **meaning** of disaster. Both observe that, at the level of popular discourse, the concept of risk is losing its positive **associations** with acquisitive opportunity, and is used exclusively to evoke the threat of danger. For Beck, this is connected with the extent to which societies are alert to the hazardous 'side-effects' of industrial **modernity and modernization**), especially the threat of ecological catastrophe (see **ecology and environmentalism**). By contrast, Mary Douglas emphasizes the extent to which, under the force of **globalization**, changes in people's experiences of social **solidarity** lead them to experience heightened states of anxiety and to become increasingly hostile towards the knowledge claims of expert authorities. Where Beck claims that 'risk consciousness' grows in proportion to our knowledge of the threat posed by new forms of technological hazards (i.e. industrial pollution), Douglas maintains that it is not so much that we are faced with increasing amounts of danger, but that we are now socially disposed to feel more afraid (Wilkinson 2001). Theorists of 'governmentality' are not so much interested in advancing a critical point of view on the reality of possible dangers as they are with the ways in which the conduct of individuals and institutions is now disciplined in relation to the language of risk. For Foucauldian theorists such as Mitchell Dean, the sociological importance of risk lies predominantly in the ways in which the concept is used in managerial practices and governmental techniques designed to shape human conduct for specific ends. For example, they may be interested to understand how the labelling of certain social behaviours as 'risky' (e.g.

521

smoking, drinking, driving) leads people to adopt a more precautionary attitude towards life. Here, the language of risk is used as a means to persuade individuals to take more personal responsibility for their **health** and safety. Such analysis is often related to a more broad-ranging discussion of the impacts of neo-liberal market reforms on the **welfare state** and health services.

In the domain of sociological theory, there is now a '**hermeneutics** of risk' for devising cultural narratives of modernity. Debates on the social meaning of the concept of risk are approached as an opportunity to analyze contemporary attitudes and responses to modern processes of rationalization. Differences in the ways sociologists theorize risk tend to be closely related to their favoured accounts of the 'trustworthiness' of expert knowledge and the 'reality' of possible dangers (see **trust**). The risk debate in social science is approached as an opportunity to advance political points of view on the 'hazards' of modernization and the forms of institutional and individual behaviours that are best suited to respond to these. It also presents social researchers with opportunities to map the various ways in which risk discourse serves as a means to regulate organizational and individual behaviour according to the values of 'self-management', 'self-interest' and 'voluntary risk avoidance'.

References and further reading

Beck, U. (1992) *Risk Society: Towards a New Modernity*. London: Sage.
Beck, U. (1999) *World Risk Society*. Cambridge: Polity.
Dean, M. (1999a) *Governmentality: Power and Rule in Modern Societies*. London: Sage.
Dean, M. (1999b) 'Risk, Calculable and Incalculable', in D. Lupton (ed.) *Risk and Sociocultural Theory: New Directions and Perspectives*. Cambridge: Cambridge University Press.
de Roover, F. E. (1945) 'Early Examples of Marine Insurance', *Journal of Economic History*, 5: 172–200.
Douglas, M. (1985) *Risk Acceptability According to the Social Sciences*. London: Routledge & Kegan Paul.
Douglas, M. (1992) *Risk and Blame: Essays in Cultural Theory*. London: Routledge.
O'Malley, P. (1996) 'Risk and Responsibility', in A. Barry, T. Osborne and N. Rose (eds) *Foucault and Political Reason: Liberalism, Neo-Liberalism and Rationalities of Government*. London: University College London Press.
Perrow, C. (1984) *Normal Accidents: Living with High-Risk Technologies*. New York: Basic Books.
Wilkinson, I. (2001) *Anxiety in a Risk Society*. London: Routledge.

IAIN WILKINSON

RITUAL

Rituals can be defined as formally regulated, repetitive, collective acts of behaviour, standing apart from normal social life. The extraordinary character of the ritual event is established through the use of **symbols**, transforming functions and **meanings** of **actions** and objects by connecting them to 'tradition' or to the **sacred** in society. Examples of rituals are weddings, funerals, **church** ceremonies, coronation ceremonies, carnivals, **family** reunions. Ritual passages are those rituals that signal a passage from one state to the other (the passage from life to **death** in a funeral ritual, for example). Since they involve collective participation, rituals are related to the creation of human collectivities, although the precise nature of this relationship remains a matter of dispute.

The meaning of ritual can also be interpreted as 'routine behaviour', as everyday acts performed without special attention for example, 'my morning-coffee ritual'). In his dramaturgical approach, Erving **Goffman** (1967) wrote about '**interaction** rituals', meaning those largely unconscious codes of ritualized behaviour through which we acknowledge a shared reality, upholding a mutual sense of **self**.

In **Durkheim**'s *The Elementary Forms of Religious Life* (1961), rituals are seen as the life-giver to **society**. Through his study of Australian totemism, Durkheim argued that in religious rituals an individual is 'lifted out of himself', and made part of the social **group**. It is in ritual that the 'individual soul is regenerated, by being dipped again in the sources from which its life comes'. For Durkheim, these sources were society itself, where 'society' represents a sociological equivalent of the **Kantian** moral *a priori*. While rituals thus belong to the sacred realm, they are in reality a society's mode of self-worship. Durkheim tied this theory to the concept of social **solidarity**, arguing that in modern forms of organic solidarity, rituals lose their integrative function. Durkheim worried that with the decline of ritual dipping, **individualism, and individualization** in modern society threatened to run amok, creating **anomie**.

Social theorists since Durkheim have all recognized that rituals, although formalized and stereotypical in form, are not solely acts of **leisure** or ornament. However, Durkheim placed little emphasis on the relationship between ritual and **power** hierarchies. Durkheim only saw ritual as the moment when a society's basic **values and norms** were established through a collective 'effervescence'. More critical approaches, Marxist as well as non-Marxist, have argued that rituals relate to power in either of two ways: either by supporting social **structure** or by concealing power. Rituals do so by evoking the power of the transcendental over the normal, a 'celestialization' of social life (investing hierarchies with 'givenness', as in royal rituals). Further, in ritual forms, discussion and criticism are narrowed down to a minimum, **roles** and conclusions being pre-established (as in role reversals during carnivals that ultimately reinforce the status quo). Rituals in this approach lead to submission, forcing people to accept social hierarchy, and sometimes even to celebrate it against their self-interest. Rituals are here seen as conservative and mystifying (Bloch 1989).

Functionalist approaches have been criticized on a series of accounts: for neglecting **agency** of the participants, for assuming a shared interpretation of symbols, and for obscuring the transformative potential of rituals. These points of criticism are related: the variability in individuals' perception of rituals is one reason why change is inbuilt. In anthropology, the assumption that rituals always support social structure was challenged by Victor Turner (1969). Focusing on ritual passages and on playful behaviour in **liminality**, Turner claimed that ritual periods represented a kind of 'anti-structure', or lay outside social structure altogether. He also showed how in ritual passages human subjectivity (see **subject and subjectivity**) is really transformed. If so, rituals must be crucial to role theory. Turner (1974) also used his studies of African **tribal** society as a springboard for the analysis of ritual and **play and game** in complex societies, claiming that the 'subjunctive mood' found in ritual had here been replaced by art and leisure. Turner's student, Richard Schechner (1993), has extended these insights into the seriousness of play by relating them to drama and performance theory.

Other approaches have tried to demonstrate how rituals may in fact serve to challenge power. If ritual is 'play' or 'social theatre', it may function as a form of **protest** movement, as not all rituals are controlled from above (Cohen 1993). Examples could be the Ghost Dance movement in North America or political protest movements. These tend to develop ritual forms that serve to question the givenness of existing powers. In short, depending on specific contexts, rituals can be studied as constitutive moments of individuals and social groups that may serve either to legitimize and solidify or to question and alter both personhood and social structure.

References and further reading

Bloch, M. (1989) *Ritual, History and Power: Selected Papers in Social Anthropology*. London: Athlone Press.

Cohen, A. (1993) *Masquerade Politics: Exploration in the Structure of Urban Cultural Movements*. Oxford: Berg.

Durkheim, E. ([1912] 1961) *The Elementary Forms of Religious Life*. New York: Collier Books.

Goffman, E. (1967) *Interaction Ritual: Essays on Face-to-Face Behaviour*. Chicago: Aldine.

Schechner, R. (1993) *The Future of Ritual: Writings on Culture and Performance*. London: Routledge.

Turner, V. (1969) *The Ritual Process*. Harmondsworth: Penguin.

Turner, V. (1974) *Dramas, Fields, and Metaphors*. Ithaca, NY: Cornell University Press.

Van Gennep, A. ([1909] 1960) *The Rites of Passage*. Chicago: University of Chicago Press.

BJØRN THOMASSEN

ROLE

Social theorists and sociologists sometimes use analogies with the stage in order to account for social life. This has led to an interest in roles, role-playing and related concepts. Social theorists were not the first to conceive of the social in this way. Over the centuries, many novelists and playwrights have depicted individuals as enacting roles. The difference is that social theorists have tried to systematize these metaphors and analogies into a coherent theory.

The concept of role came to prominence in sociology in the 1950s and 1960s. The concept was often used in conjunction with other notions, such as 'social position', '**status**', and 'expectations'. A role was defined as a set of expectations **society** has of individuals in a given social position or status. It is possible to talk about a 'role theory', applicable not only to sociology, but also to social psychology and social anthropology. Sociologists who used this framework were trying to indicate the extent to which people's **agency** is curtailed by the positions or status they occupy. To occupy a position means that one possesses specific roles, and this implies that others have expectations about how one should act. These expectations are likely to affect

what one does: failing to comply with them leads to **sanctions**, whereas complying is rewarded. Positions and roles also ensure continuity, even if new people occupy the positions in question. This partly accounts for a level of predictability in social life: independent of who occupies a specific position, it entails certain roles, expectations and behaviour. Roles thus make for continuity, but this does not come without a cost. Hence, social research has focused on the tensions caused by role-playing for the individual: for instance, 'role strain' or 'role overload' (due to the various expectations related to a role) and 'role conflict' (due to incompatible expectations related to a role).

Role theory was compatible with some of **Durkheim**'s central guidelines for sociological method. Durkheim (1982) argued that sociology studied social facts, which are general, external and constraining, and have predictive **power**. Role theory operates in a similar fashion. Roles are also general, applying to everybody in a certain position. Roles are external to individuals, imposed onto them, and they are constraining in that they entail guidelines regarding what is permissible and desirable for certain positions. Roles also have a predictive power. The role of pupil, for example, implies a set of assumptions and expectations, applicable to every teacher. Pupils do not choose the guidelines; they exist prior to their arrival. There are clear guidelines and expectations about what pupils can and cannot do. Some of these rules are strict and have legal repercussions; other rules are less formal, but not necessarily less binding: pupils are supposed to do their homework, be attentive, cooperative and well behaved. Once we know these rules and expectations, the conduct of pupils becomes more predictable.

This traditional role theory was once so dominant that it was regarded as characteristic of any sociological perspective. For instance, Ralf **Dahrendorf**'s (1973) *Homo Sociologicus* saw the notion of role as central to the sociological view of people, as opposed to *homo oeconomicus*. Whereas other disciplinary perspectives take a more atomistic view, sociology is sensitive to the binding nature of social life, and 'role' is the key concept for accomplishing this. Structural-**functionalism** was the dominant framework in the 1980s and its proponents regarded role theory as compatible with it. In their view, roles persist because they fulfil vital functions for the larger **social systems** in which they are embedded (**Merton** 1957). In the course of the 1960s and the 1970s, however, social theorists became increasingly uneasy with the neglect of **agency** in functionalism and related theories. Dennis Wrong's (1961) article 'The Over-socialised Conception of Man' pointed out that many sociological accounts overstate the constraining influence of society on human conduct. Role theory was then seen as particularly suspect and in need of adjustment. This re-assessment took place in various ways, through a rediscovery of George Herbert **Mead** and through the work of Erving **Goffman**.

Influenced by German **idealist** philosophy and American **pragmatism**, Mead developed his 'social **behaviourism**' in the beginning of the twentieth century. He became particularly well known for his posthumously published *Mind, Self and Society* (1934), in which he argued that we, as human beings, put ourselves in other people's perspectives to look upon ourselves. This enables us to choose between alternatives lines of conduct and to steer our behaviour. **Symbolic interactionists** wrote about 'taking the perspective, attitude or role of the other', and they emphasized that the notion of role is now no longer associated with a deterministic picture. Individuals take on the role of other individuals in ways that enable them to control their own conduct (**Blumer** 1969). Unsurprisingly, symbolic interactionists tend to couple the concept of role to a notion of agency. Ralph Turner (1979, 1998) examined how individuals' gestures

and actions assert a particular role, how each individual infers from other people's gestures what role they play, and how he or she verifies those inferences. Jonathan Turner developed this perspective further by arguing that people's stock of knowledge includes fine-tuned, shared role-conceptions, which provide generative potential for role taking, imputation and verification (Turner 1988). He integrated these insights into a broader theory of **interaction**.

This dynamic view is consistent with Erving Goffman's writings. Goffman operated within the tradition of symbolic interactionism, but he takes a distinct angle. Influenced by Emile Durkheim and Georg **Simmel**, Goffman's (1959) *Presentation of Self in Everyday Life* employs analogies with the theatre to depict social life. This approach has been described as exemplary for the **dramaturgical school**. Unlike traditional role theory, however, people are not depicted as passive recipients of external social forces. For Goffman, individuals are constantly involved in 'performances': they impose a definition of who they are onto others, and they are able do so with the help of various props and devices. People act out roles that they themselves at least partly design. Not all performances are individual, however. Often people depend on the collaboration of others to consolidate the roles they play. There are sanctions for those members of the team who discredit its image. Even when an individual is not a member of a team, the successful accomplishment of his or her performance will depend on the collaboration of the audience.

While the significance of role theory has decreased in the past couple of decades, the role-concept has played a significant role in contributions to the sociology of **gender** (see, for instance, Lipman–Blumen 1984; Lindsey 1994). Gender roles are here seen to refer to the behavioural expectations associated with being male or female, the durability of these expectations, the power relations involved, and the positive and negative sanctions associated with them.

References and further reading

Banton, M. (1965) *Roles: An Introduction to the Study of Social Relations*. New York: Basic Books.

Biddle, B. J. (1979) *Role Theory*. London: Academic Press.

Blumer, H. (1969) *Symbolic Interactionism: Perspective and Method*. Englewood Cliffs, NJ: Prentice Hall.

Dahrendorf, R. (1973) *Homo Sociologicus*. London: Routledge & Kegan Paul.

Durkheim, E. (1982) *The Rules of Sociological Method; and Selected Texts and its Methods*. London: Macmillan.

Goffman, E. (1959) *Presentation of Self in Everyday Life*. Harmondsworth: Penguin.

Lindsey, L. L. (1994) *Gender Roles: A Sociological Perspective*. Englewood Cliffs, NJ: Prentice Hall.

Lipman-Blumen, J. (1984) *Gender Roles and Power*. Englewood Cliffs, NJ: Prentice Hall.

Merton, R. K. (1957a) *Social Theory and Social Structure*. New York: Free Press.

Merton, R. K. (1957b) 'The Role-Set: Problems in Sociological Theory', *British Journal of Sociology*, 8: 106–20.

Turner, J. H. (1988) *A Theory of Social Interaction*. Cambridge: Polity Press.

Turner, R. H. (1979) 'Strategy for Developing an Integrated Role Theory', *Humboldt Journal of Social Relations*, 7: 114–22.

Turner, R. H. (1998) 'Role Taking: Process versus Conformity', in A. Rose (ed.) *Human Behaviour and Social Processes: An Interactionist Approach*. London: Routledge, pp. 20–40.

Walker, S. G. (ed.) (1987) *Role Theory and Foreign Policy Analysis*. Durham, NC: Duke University Press.

Wilson, E. K. (1971) *Sociology: Rules, Roles, and Relationships*. Homewood, IL: Dorsey Press.

Wrong, D. (1961) 'The Oversocialized Conception of Man', *American Sociological Review*, 26(2): 183–93.

Znaniecki, F. (1965) *Social Relations and Social Roles: The Unfinished Systematic Sociology*. San Francisco: Chandler.

PATRICK BAERT

ROMANTICISM

Romanticism as an historical period is commonly viewed as lasting from approximately 1780 (represented, for example, by Goethe's *Sorrows of Young Werther* to 1834, the year of the death of Samuel Coleridge in England. For social theory, Romanticism is often understood in terms of a 'German ideology' carrying a particular dialectical relationship to the **Enlightenment**. Its main discourses and practices were first defined by German thinkers in the late eighteenth century and largely in reaction to the French Revolution. The perennial re-appropriation of its preoccupations with mythic origins, redemptive politics, organic societies and folk cultures, mythic heroes and aesthetic gods, heroes and geniuses, have had lasting effects on modern Europe, not least in the killing fields of **imperialism**, **fascism** and **communism**. Romanticism has found numerous critics and adherents in **hermeneutics**, **critical theory**, anthropology, **art and aesthetics**, and cultural studies. While it remains a contested and ambiguous term denoting a chameleon phenomenon, it can be typified as having three main abiding concerns: **culture**, subjectivity (see **subject and subjectivity**), and **nature**, that are explored via hermeneutical, historicist, and aesthetic modes of critical inquiry and practice. Romanticism is a persistent trope in contemporary social theory because it is a perennially renewed form of modernism (see **modernity and modernization**), at once in dialogue with and in conflict with our idea of rationality, radicalism and rationalization (see **rationality and rationalization**).

References and further reading

Blechman, M. (ed.) (1999) *Revolutionary Romanticism*. San Francisco: City Lights.

Bowie, A. (1997) *From Romanticism to Critical Theory*. London: Routledge.

Dumont, L. (1994) *The German Ideology*. Chicago: University of Chicago Press.

Löwy, M. and Sayre, R. (2001) *Romanticism against the Tide of Modernity*. Durham, NC: Duke University Press.

Roberts, D. and Murphy, P. (2004) *Dialectic of Romanticism: A Critique of Modernism*. London: Continuum.

TREVOR HOGAN

RORTY, RICHARD (1931–)

US philosopher

Having started his career as a promising young philosopher in the analytic tradition, Rorty soon became one of the most influential critics of the idea of knowledge as representation and Cartesian dualism in **epistemology** and the philosophy of mind. As an initiator of the **linguistic turn** his whole work is marked by a struggle against **metaphysical** residues in contemporary thinking, especially the idealist belief in the Subject, the True and the Good. Rorty's own philosophy is an original blend of **hermeneutics** (**Heidegger**, **Gadamer**), American **pragmatism** (Dewey), **post-structuralism** (**Derrida**), **Wittgenstein** and analytic philosophers such as Quine, Davidson and Putnam. Rorty argues for a sociological account of truth and justification: **solidarity** and not **objectivity** is the aim of intersubjective **discourse**, both in morality **and** science. His belief that all practices (see **praxis and practices**) and vocabularies are marked by historicity and **contingency** has often provoked the reproach of **relativism**. Rorty, however, is himself a liberal ironist, someone who believes that values cannot be ultimately grounded but is nevertheless committed to the cause of freedom and justice. In addition to the impact of his work on various debates in philosophy, social and cultural theory and literary studies Rorty is one of the most influential liberal public intellectuals in the USA today.

Major works

(1979) *Philosophy and the Mirror of Nature*. Princeton, NJ: Princeton University Press.
(1989) *Contingency, Irony, and Solidarity*. Cambridge: Cambridge University Press.
(1991–98) *Philosophical Papers I – III*. Cambridge: Cambridge University Press.
(1998) *Achieving Our Country*. Cambridge: Cambridge University Press.
(1999) *Philosophy and Social Hope*. London: Penguin.

Further reading

Brandom, R. (ed.) (2000) *Rorty and His Critics*. Oxford: Blackwell.
Festenstein, M. and Thompson, S. (eds) (2001) *Richard Rorty*. Cambridge: Polity.
Guignon, C. and Hiley, D. (eds) (2003) *Richard Rorty*. Cambridge: Cambridge University Press.
Malachowski, A. (2002) *Richard Rorty*. Princeton, NJ: Princeton University Press.

ROBIN CELIKATES

S

SACRED

Emile **Durkheim** in *The Elementary Forms of Religious Life* (1995) critically interrogated the nature of religious phenomena to demonstrate the importance of the categories of the sacred (and the profane). When people experience their lives as subject to forces more powerful than themselves, they often see this as proof of God's existence, Durkheim argues that while they are right to identify the existence of transcendental forces, they are wrong about its source which is the *sui generis* reality of society: God is a metaphor. Although many people see monotheistic **religions** as somehow nearer to the essence of true religiosity, this view is further subverted through his analytical clarification of the meaning of the term, **Church**, i.e. 'a unified system of beliefs and practices relative to sacred things, that is to say, things set apart and forbidden-beliefs and practices which unite into one single moral community...all those who adhere to it.' Monotheism is not essential for religiosity, for it is only found in some societies and this is true also of anthropomorphic conceptions of gods. Further, the idea of spirits is absent in religions like Buddhism and there are sacral dimensions to phenomena that are not normally thought to be religious, e.g. **progress**, the flag, and such historical events as the French Revolution. Nevertheless, there remains one element common to all religious phenomena and that is that believers experience the cosmos as being made up of the sacred and the profane, which are 'always and everywhere conceived by the human intellect as separate genera, as two worlds with nothing in common'.

Religious phenomena, Durkheim (1975) argues, are premised upon faith, i.e. 'any belief experienced or accepted without argument,' and are enforced by 'a collective discipline', thus regulating consciousness and conduct and these latter are always associated with **rituals**, rendered equally obligatory by their imbrication in myth and dogma. This experience of a compulsion to think and act in particular ways is produced from social forces by sacred things 'whose representation society itself has fashioned'. The sacred is a particular way of conceiving of, and relating to, a realm of things (objects, places, beings, rituals, images, words, and times) replete with high and potentially creative and/or destructive energy. Not surprisingly, human beings feel the need to treat these with deference and/or caution and to take steps to ensure that the sacred does not come in contact with its other, the profane. The profane refers to phenomena, like eating, which are merely satisfying basically **utilitarian** and physical needs. Although he seems to assume that when alone the human individual's cognitive and **emotional** attributes are extra-social, untransformed and unmediated by the experience of a social life, he also argues that the more **emancipated** we are from our individual sensations, and the more able to think conceptually, the more we become persons and, moreover, that 'sacred ideals' retain their **power** after collective religious rituals have finished because 'they penetrate the individual consciousness where they are organized in a lasting fashion' (Durkheim 1960). In other words, once we have truly become members of society – for example, through the acquisition of **language** and through transformative initiation rites – we always remain members and hence 'nothing but their heterogeneity is left to define the relation between the sacred and the profane' (Durkheim 1995).

Ultimately, this sacred is generated by collective effervescences found in particularly intense collective rituals such as the Australian Intichiuma rites, designed to assure, under uncertain conditions, the fecundity of the animal or vegetable species which serves a clan as a totem or god. These rites are in reality sacrificial: first, in that they involve 'an offering', a 'gift', 'an act of renunciation' by which clan members hope to aid their god by giving to it some of the forces at their disposal; and, second, and for Durkheim this seems much more important, this offering is part, but only part, of how members of the collectivity intensely commune with each other and with their god.

George **Bataille** agrees with Durkheim that the sacred is generated by sacrifice and that this process involves the subsumption of individuals within totalizing **group** processes but he believes that this is at its most powerful when group members are participating in the killing of those who fearlessly confront **death** and are willing to be sacrificed. When the victim dies, 'the witnesses participate in an element which his death reveals… The sacred is precisely the continuity of being revealed to those who fix their attention, in a solemn rite, on the death of a discontinuous being' (Bataille 1988). He recognizes that in practice such a willingness to die is doubtful and that various forms of surrogacy are routine but his

argument that severe 'acts of renunciation' are an essential element in the genesis of the sacred is powerful. René Girard (1977) provides a somewhat different account of sacralization when he argues that in more primitive **communities** a situation of escalating interpersonal **violence** is often produced by mimetic rivalry exacerbated by excessive egalitarianism and may only be ended by the scapegoating and collective murder of a marginal group member, a process which is subsequently misrepresented in **myths** and sacrificial rituals where the victim is often sanctified and may be represented as a saviour. These processes are less likely in societies with developed legal systems which impersonally regulate and contain interpersonal relations and in Christian societies where the development of an understanding of the scapegoat mechanism means that it can be avoided. However, it may well be that whole populations are scapegoated through the legal system and also those who create 'scandal' by understanding **Christianity** but refusing it may become victims of yet another sacrificial mechanism.

References and further reading

Bataille, G. (1985) *Visions of Excess: Selected Writings 1927–1939*. Trans. A. Stoekl. Minneapolis, MN: University of Minnesota Press.

Bataille, G. (1988) *Inner Experience*. Trans. L. A. Boldt. Albany, NY: State University of New York Press.

Caillois, R. (1950) *L'homme et le Sacré*. Paris: Gallimard.

Durkheim, E. ([1960] 1977) 'The Dualism of Human Nature and its Social Conditions', in R. Girard, *Violence and the Sacred*. Baltimore, MD: Johns Hopkins University Press.

Durkheim, E. (1975) 'Concerning the Definition of Religious Phenomena', in W. G. Pickering (ed.) *Durkheim on Religion*. London: Routledge & Kegan Paul.

Durkheim, E. (1995) *The Elementary Forms of Religious Life*. Trans. K. E. Fields. New York: Free Press.

Eliade, M. (1965) *Le Sacré et le Profane*. Paris: Gallimond.

Girard, R. (1977) *Literature and the Sacred.* Baltimore: John Hopkins University Press.

Otto, R. ([1917] 1987) *Das Heilige.* Munich: Beck.

Wolff, K. H. (ed.) *Essays on Sociology and Philosophy by Emile Durkheim et al.* New York: Free Press.

FRANK PEARCE

SAID, EDWARD W. (1935–2003)
Palestinian-born, US theorist

Although Said was a leading theorist of comparative literature, his major contribution was to **post-colonial theory** with his book *Orientalism*, first published in 1978. Said here discusses the ways in which the 'Orient' is constructed as a **discourse** by scholars, travelers, colonial bureaucrats and artists. Influenced by **Foucault**'s concept of power, Said highlights the role of **knowledge** in defining the relationship between the Orient and the Occident as a form of **domination**. In *Culture and Imperialism*, Said argues that in order to understand **imperialism**, one needs to read simultaneously or 'contrapuntally' the contradictory and competing narratives of the colonized and colonizer. Said's work has been influential in introducing concepts such as **hybridity**, the **Other** and exile into cultural studies and postcolonial theory. A public **intellectual**, Said believed that intellectuals have a responsibility to go outside the confines of academic circles, initiating public debate to influence change. He regularly published on literature, art, music, cinema and American and Middle East politics. In addition to prolific writing, Said was a political activist dedicated to the Palestinian cause. He was a strong advocate of a **democratic** secular Palestine in which Arabs and Jews were equal citizens.

Major works

(1975) *Beginnings: Intention and Method.* New York: Basic Books.

(1978) *Orientalism.* New York: Pantheon Books.

(1981) *Covering Islam: How the Media and the Experts Determine How We See the Rest of the World.* New York: Pantheon.

(1983) *The World, the Text, and the Critic.* Cambridge, MA: Harvard University Press.

Further reading

Bayoumi, M. and Rubin, A. (eds) (2000) *The Edward Said Reader.* New York: Vintage Books.

Gauri, W. (2002) *Power, Politics and Culture: Interviews with Edward Said.* New York: Vintage Books.

FEYZI BABAN

SANCTION

See: social control

SARTRE, JEAN-PAUL (1905–1980)
French philosopher

Unlike the philosophy of **Heidegger**, Sartre's existentialism is expressed in a decisively social and political form. Sartre's leading idea was to define what he called 'atheist existentialism' as a form of **humanism** aimed at engaged social **praxis and practices**. The human being who is 'condemned to unconditional **freedom**' creates his or her own essence, and in this permanent process takes up responsibility for his or her own existence. According to Sartre, this activity at the same time encompasses responsibility for all people and defines the context of unending social praxis in which discovery of truth first becomes possible. Sartre saw this philosophy of action as involving the requirement for a permanent **revolution** of the **proletariat**, a requirement that does not exclude the possibility of justification for **violence** but which at the same time must make possible a 'philosophy of freedom'. Sartre's **voluntaristic** philosophy appears in his chief political *œuvre*, *The Critique of Dialectical Reason* (1960), a work that seeks to avoid the more dogmatic tendencies of Marx's **dialectical materialism** in order to open up its true humanistic potentialities.

Through his works for the theatre and political essays as well as his early involvement in the French resistance against **fascism**, Sartre established a lasting place for himself in French political life, together with Simone de **Beauvoir** as a morally engaged public **intellectual**. Although he persisted for a long while in a rather uncritical attitude toward Soviet **communism**, inviting criticism from a number of writers, including notably Raymond **Aron**, Sartre distanced himself from any apology for Stalinism after 1968 and made clear his support for **anarchist** and anti-authoritarian causes.

Major works

([1946] 1973) *Existentialism and Humanism*. London: Methuen.

([1949] 1957) *Being and Nothingness*. London: Methuen.

([1960] 1991, 2004) *The Critique of Dialectical Reason*, 2 vols. London: Verso.

Further reading

Hayim, G. J. (1996) *Existentialism and Sociology*. New Brunswick, NJ: Transaction.

Lévy, B.-H. (2003) *Sartre*. Cambridge: Polity.

KARSTEN FISCHER

SCHMITT, CARL (1888–1985)
German legal and political theorist

Schmitt's early thought fused themes drawn from Catholicism, **romanticism**, Max **Weber**, and the history of political thought (in particular Thomas Hobbes), to criticize contemporary **liberal** parliamentary **democracy**. Schmitt argued that such a political form avoided real politics through procedural neutrality, and was a halfway house between the two major principles of political forms he perceived – identity (homogeneity) and representation. By contrast, he argues, a properly political body, typically the state, can distinguish between political friends (see **friendship**) and enemies, thereby maintaining **legitimacy** as well as legality (see **law and legality**). His polemics with contemporary legal and political scholars during the Weimar Republic show his concern with the problem of maintaining and sustaining political order, and highlight the apparent disregard within liberal legal scholarship of the 'moment' in which political decisions are made. His decisionism has been the subject of numerous critiques, especially by Jürgen **Habermas**, and his accommodation with the Nazis has been rightly attacked. Schmitt's thought had a profound influence on postwar German academia and his later writings focus on international law. They maintain an interest in Hobbes, worry about the rise of modern **technology and technocracy**, and consider how sovereign communities are founded through land appropriation.

Major works

([1919–25] 1986) (ed.) *Political Romanticism*. Cambridge, MA: MIT Press.

([1923–26] 1985) (ed.) *The Crisis of Parliamentary Democracy*. Cambridge, MA: MIT Press.

([1927–32] 1996) (ed.) *The Concept of the Political*. Chicago: University of Chicago Press.

([1928] 1993) *Verfassungslehre*. Berlin: Duncker & Humblot.

([1950] 1997) *Der Nomos der Erde*. Berlin: Duncker & Humblot.

Further reading

Bendersky, J. (1983) *Carl Schmitt: Theorist for the Reich*. Princeton, NJ: Princeton University Press.

Kelly, D. (2003) *The State of the Political: Conceptions of Politics and the State in the Thought of Max Weber, Carl Schmitt, and Franz Neumann*. Oxford: Oxford University Press.

McCormick, J. (1997) *Carl Schmitt's Critique of Liberalism*. Cambridge: Cambridge University Press.

Müller, J. W. (2003) *A Dangerous Mind*. New Haven, CT: Yale University Press.

DUNCAN KELLY

SCHUMPETER, JOSEPH ALOIS
(1883–1950)
Austrian economist

From 1919 to 1920 Schumpeter served as Finance Minister in the Austrian Republic. In 1932 he left for the United States, where he worked at Harvard University until his death in 1950. He is primarily known for his ideas on entrepreneurship and his theory of **democracy**, as formulated in *Capitalism, Socialism and Democracy* (1942). He is also the author of two hefty works on business cycles and the history of economic analysis.

Schumpeter's most important early work is *The Theory of Economic Development* ([1911] trans. 1934), which contains his famous theory of entrepreneurship. In Schumpeter's formulation, entrepreneurship consists of 'putting together a new combination of already existing elements'. An important obstacle for the entrepreneur is the difficulty of letting go of the past. Innovations include such things as a new type of product and the creation of a new **market**. It is not so much **money** that drives the entrepreneur as the satisfaction of being creative, being better than others and creating one own's empire.

Capitalism, Socialism and Democracy contains a well-known analysis of monopolies and 'creative destruction'. Its main claim to fame, however, is connected to its critique of the existing theory of democracy and Schumpeter's attempt to create an alternative. According to the old theory, democracy is about realizing the will of the people, in the manner expressed by Rousseau. The new theory, in contrast, views democracy as a competition among leaders for the votes of the masses. Despite its elitist overtones, Schumpeter's alternative theory of democracy is considered considerably more realistic than the old theory.

Major works

([1911] 1934) *The Theory of Economic Development.* Cambridge, MA: Harvard University Press.
([1942] 1994) *Capitalism, Socialism and Democracy.* London: Routledge.

Further reading

Swedberg, R. (1991) *Schumpeter: A Biography.* London: Polity.

RICHARD SWEDBERG

SCHUTZ, ALFRED (1899–1959)
Austrian theorist

The work of Alfred Schutz was devoted to the construction of a specifically **phenomenological** sociology. Schutz's initial sociological orientation was rooted in the **Weberian** tradition. When he encountered the phenomenological philosophy of Edmund Husserl, however, he came to question some aspects of the Weberian framework, seeking to deepen and extend the Weberian theory of **action**. In his major work *The Phenomenology of the Social World* he examined the '**typifications**' and 'recipe **knowledge**' that social agents use to constitute the meanings of social situations. He explored the conditions which allow those situations to be understood through communication and **intersubjectively**; that is, which allow agents to form working agreements over the meaning of their shared situations and thereby enable them to collectively accomplish whatever is required by those situations.

In his later work, Schutz brought the phenomenological perspective into engagement with other key sociological theorists, including **Parsons** and **Mead**. The essays of his later period focus on topics such as temporality, 'multiple realities' (different 'worlds' of dreams, drama, and **games**), and most centrally 'the **lifeworld**' – the world of everyday life as it is lived by its inhabitants. Alongside his theory of action, Schutz's theorization of the lifeworld is perhaps his most influential legacy in the sociological literature.

Major works

([1932] 1972) *The Phenomenology of the Social World.* London: Heinemann.

(1964–66) *Collected Papers* (3 vols.), ed. M. Natanson. The Hague: Nijhoff.

Further reading

Srubar, I. (1988) *Kosmian: Die Genese der pragmatischen Lebenswelttheorie von Alfred Schütz*. Frankfurt am Main: Suhrkamp.

NICK CROSSLEY

SCIENCE

Science is the term for the most highly valued form of social **knowledge**, in terms of which all belief and action are ultimately held accountable. Science is distinguished primarily by its comprehensive and systematic character, which is associated with virtues such as '**rationality**', 'objectivity' (see **object, objectification, objectivism and objectivity**) and 'validity'. The exemplars of science have shifted markedly throughout Western history. In the ancient world it was geometry, in the Middle Ages theology, in the nineteenth century it was history, and in the twentieth century physics (Fuller 1997). The vast differences in the structure and content of these exemplars suggest that what counts as science is defined mainly in terms of its relationship to other forms of social knowledge.

A hallmark of the eighteenth-century **Enlightenment** was the belief that science could be the motor of social **progress**, mainly through mass **education** and the **technological** transformation of the environment. This belief, which fuelled the positivist movement in the nineteenth and early twentieth centuries, came under severe challenge after the two world wars, in which science was instrumental in raising the overall level of devastation to unprecedented heights. **Adorno** and **Horkheimer**'s work ([1943] 1972) remains the template for these concerns. However, whereas Adorno and Horkheimer spoke in terms of science having betrayed its own rational potential, more recent critiques have tended to stress alternative forms of knowledge that 'Western' science (now specifically named as such) has suppressed in its complicity with **power**, especially in imperial settings (Harding 1991).

The sociological character of science is manifested in five types of account:

1. A style of reasoning that pervades just about everything in the modern era. It is epitomized in Max **Weber**'s process of 'rationalization', the inexorable replacement of local folkways and traditions with formal administration. While this conception correctly stresses science's historical tendency towards global **colonization** it obscures the uneven and reversible ways in which scientific styles of reasoning have become implicated in social processes.

2. Common sense rendered self-conscious, which, over the course of evolution, has enabled humans to flourish in an ever wider variety of environments. This view is associated with the American **pragmatists**, especially John Dewey. While correctly stressing science's aim at controlling – and, indeed, remaking – the natural environment, it overestimates the naturalness of this way of being in the world (to the point of rendering it 'biological') and hence obscures the historical contingency of our world happening to become (and remain) a scientific one. From this perspective, positivistic vigilance in policing the precincts of science begins to make sense, regardless of the acceptability of specific positivist strategies for demarcating science from non-science.

3. The content of scientific beliefs, which today spread faster than any other kind, often enjoying the authority previously reserved for **religious** beliefs. This point is most vividly illustrated today in the colonization of one's health by medical science, such that people now need

to consult physicians in order to learn 'how they feel' (see **medicalization**). Yet, while correctly stressing how science can be an **ideology** held by scientists and non-scientists alike, this account downplays science's distinctiveness, which lies in its procedures and methods, not the content of its beliefs. Indeed, scientific beliefs are popular often because they are already rooted in political, religious, and other traditionally non-scientific forms of thought. What matters, then, is whether those beliefs are subject to 'scientific' scrutiny.

4. The ethos of practising scientists, in terms of which they routinely justify their work. Robert K. **Merton** (1977) identifies the entire 'normative structure of science' with such professions of faith, which he encapsulates in four principles: **universalism**, communalism, disinterestedness, and organized scepticism. While this conception captures the self-understanding of many scientists and often constitutes the public rhetoric that scientists use to legitimate their activities (typically the only exposure that the public has to science at all), it presupposes a simplistic notion of normativity that fails to allow for how the same public rhetoric can legitimate widely divergent practices.

5. A set of principles for organizing imperfect reasoners to enable them to make the world bend to their collective will so as to allow them to do more of the same in the future. Science, in this sense, is both 'rhetorical' and 'experimental': it aims to alter the behaviour of reasoners under specifiable and changeable conditions. This is the sense in which science can be regarded as a highly disciplined social movement, akin to a religious order in its dedication to, in Weber's memorable phrase, a '**vocation**'.

Although the overriding significance of science for modern societies had been recognized from the dawn of social science, it was only in the 1970s that the sociology of science started to be studied as something other than the institutional correlate of normative epistemology. Merton (1977) was a frequent target of the so-called new sociology of science, the main schools of which included the strong programme in the sociology of scientific knowledge and a**ctor-network theory**, the latter probably the dominant school of what is now called 'Science and Technology Studies' (Pickering 1992).

The history of recent sociology of science can be read as three successive solutions to the 'problem of scientific rationality': (1) *relativize* it; (2) *bracket* it; and (3) *eliminate* it:

1. Ludwig Fleck (1979) in the 1930s pioneered the relativistic approach, which foreshadows the 'anthropologization' of science associated with **Latour** and Woolgar's (1979) ethnography of the laboratory. Fleck, a practising medical scientist, explained the discovery of the syphilis vaccine in terms of 'thought collectives' that many believe anticipated Kuhn's (1970) influential concept of '**paradigms**' and, in any case, showed that science could be understood as if the natives were a tribe whose activities acquire meaning solely from things happening in their environment rather than in terms of some socially transcendent sense of reality.

2. Scientific rationality is next 'bracketed' in the sense that apparent differences in the rationality of a scientific practice or the truth of a scientific theory depend on whether the analyst has chosen an evaluative framework internal or external to the practice in question. Otherwise, there is no empirical reason for treating one set of practices as more

rational than another set. This move has significant implications for the historical study of science. It means that a proper appreciation of the agents' rationality requires that the historian see them as confronting a future open to several different directions, and not simply the one that eventually prevailed. The classic work in this vein is Shapin and Schaffer's *Leviathan and the Air-Pump* (1985), which recounts a debate between Thomas Hobbes and Robert Boyle that resulted in the triumph of experiment over philosophy in the establishment of claims to scientific knowledge.

3. The third and most recent stage would have scientific rationality 'eliminated' altogether. This radical proposal is associated with the tendency to erase any strong distinction between science and the larger society. This undifferentiated entity, called 'technoscience', is nowadays identified as the proper object of Science and Technology Studies. Accordingly, scientific rationality does not exist as a uniquely truth-oriented or objective mode of operation, but simply as a special case of political rationality. According to one influential formulation, those who maintain the longest technoscientific networks for the longest time simply come to be defined as both the most knowledgeable *and* most powerful, with the former predicate used to explain the latter by obscuring the local struggles faced along the way (Latour 1987).

By the time we reach stage (3), it is legitimate to ask whether what is described is still a sociology of knowledge (Fuller 2000). However we answer this question, the phenomenon is itself worthy of study as an episode in the sociology of knowledge. The technoscientific turn may be radical from the standpoint of the intellectual history of Science and Technology Studies, but it also provides an explication, perhaps even legitimation, for associated social tendencies that have accompanied the decline of the **welfare state** and the rise of neoliberalism. These are associated with the claims that we live in 'knowledge societies' in need of 'knowledge management' (see **knowledge society**).

References and further reading

Adorno, T. and Horkheimer, M. ([1943] 1972) *The Dialectic of Enlightenment*. New York: Continuum.

Fleck, L. ([1935] 1979) *The Genesis and Development of a Scientific Fact*. Chicago: University of Chicago Press.

Fuller, S. (1997) *Science*. Milton Keynes: Open University Press.

Fuller, S. (2000) *The Governance of Science*. Milton Keynes: Open University Press.

Harding, S. (1991) *Whose Science? Whose Knowledge?* Ithaca, NY: Cornell University Press.

Kuhn, T. S. ([1962] 1970) *The Structure of Scientific Revolutions*. Chicago: University of Chicago Press.

Latour, B. (1987) *Science in Action*. Milton Keynes: Open University Press.

Latour, B. and Woolgar, S. (1979) *Laboratory Life*. London: Sage.

Merton, R. (1977) *The Sociology of Science*. Chicago: University of Chicago Press.

Pickering, A. (ed.) (1992) *Science as Practice and Culture*. Chicago: University of Chicago Press.

Shapin, S. and Schaffer, S. (1985) *Leviathan and the Air-Pump: Hobbes, Boyle and the Experimental Life*. Princeton, NJ: Princeton University Press.

STEVE FULLER

SECT

The term sect refers to a specific form of religious association. In principle, definitions of sect focus either on the inner structure of the **group** or its relation to the external social environment. But many definitions and applications of the term have actually combined both dimensions.

Weber, focusing on inner structure, defines sect as a voluntary **association** of the religiously qualified with a strict code of conduct enforced by a regime of social control. He contrasts sect with '**church**' as an organization lacking comparable strictness into which one is born. For Weber, sects represent the most complete form of congregational **religion** and are, therefore, capable under certain circumstances of contributing to the ethical **rationalization** of the laity.

Johnson (1963) and authors following him, like Stark (1985), have defined sect by its tensions with the external social environment. Whereas churches tend to embrace dominant social **roles**, **values**, and **norms**, sects repudiate them.

These two definitions express different perspectives and interests. While Weber is interested in the impact a specific organizational form has on the life conduct of its members, Johnson and Stark focus on social **integration** and **deviance** as well as organizational dynamics over time that transform sects into churches or that lead to sect formations through church schisms.

References and further reading

Gerth, H. and Mills, C. W. (eds) (1956) *From Max Weber: Essays in Sociology*. New York: Oxford University Press.

Johnson, B. (1963) 'On Church and Sect', *American Sociological Review*, 28(4): 539–49.

Riesebrodt, M. (2001) 'Religiöse Vergemeinschaftungen', in H. Kippenberg and M. Riesebrodt (eds) *Max Webers Religionssystematik*. Tübingen: Mohr Siebeck.

Stark, R. (1985) 'Church and Sect', in P. Hammond (ed.) *The Sacred in a Secular Age*. Berkeley, CA: University of California Press.

Wilson, B. (1973) *Magic and the Millennium*. New York: Harper & Row.

Weber, M. ([1922] 1968) *Economy and Society*. Berkeley: University of California Press.

MARTIN RIESEBRODT

SECULARIZATION

Approached most broadly, secularization is the process by which religious structures, values, and behaviours are seen to diminish in importance as societies develop greater complexity, employ increasing rationality, and achieve a measure of modernity. In most standard definitions, secularization refers to 'decline in the scope of control exercised by religious authority' (Chaves 1994: 757) or more widely to 'the process whereby religious thinking, practice and institutions lose social significance' (Wilson 1966: xiv). In the transition from simple communities to highly differentiated social systems, groups encounter a greater variety of populations, greater diversity in ideologies, a refinement of role definitions, increased complexity in thought and expression, and a reliance on scientific evidence and impersonal administration to accomplish collective aims. These developments are said to wear down the solidity of old patterns and institutions. The result is an erosion of religious customs and beliefs, or a 'loss of the presidency which religion once exercised over practically all of man's doing' (Wilson 1982: 41).

Debate about secularization is as old as modern sociology itself, for the concept is 'nested in an even broader theory of modernization' whose naïve attachment to an image of societal evolution functioned as '*the* master model of sociological inquiry' (Hadden 1987: 588). Auguste **Comte** predicted that traditional religion, with its orientation to the supernatural, would yield its place to scientific reasoning, and that positive science would then be joined by a new 'Religion of Humanity'. Few who have followed Comte have resorted to formulations so doctrinaire and forecasts so far-fetched. Today it is only the rare theorist today who adheres to the view that secularization is the inevitable fate for religions everywhere: the end-point in a linear, unidirectional, and irreversible sequence of decline. But many, beginning with Max **Weber**, have advanced a claim that the widening influence of rationality, along with differentiation and specialization of parts in society, undermines the existence and normative claims of religion. In this sense the secularization debate is at least partly about basic visions and philosophies of history. The key conceptual question remains as what kinds of social facts can be held to indicate secularization. Can it be said to be observable in reports of personal piety, within the practices of congregations and denominations themselves, or in structures across the whole of society? In this respect the debate is about 'dimensions of secularization' and about levels of analysis that are pertinent to these dimensions and locations (Riis 1993). Some commentators go so far as to hold that the topic is incapable of rigorous study because it is more the foothold of an anti-religious tendency in social thought than a foundation for empirical knowledge. One of the few certainties is that researchers disagree ardently about the definition of the term, about how to detect it, about where it is most likely to be found, and about the implications of these findings for general theories of religion. In addition, there are differences in how to interpret current events such as the global growth of new religious movements and the power of fundamentalist factions within several world religious traditions. Are these signs of a revivified role for faith under modernity, or are their long-term portents ephemeral?

It has been argued that the European experience of secularization since the early modern period can no longer be held up as paradigmatic for social engagements with religion in a global context. In the Eurocentric context of classical sociology it was thought for a long while that the puzzling contradiction presented by the continuing prominent presence of religious movements, institutions and organizations in US society against the background of a strict constitutional norm of separation of church and state was another aspect of 'American exceptionalism'. Today commentators are more inclined to consider whether it is

Europe, rather than America, that presents the exception. Compared with other world continents, including South America, Africa and large parts of Asia from the Indian sub-continent to the Middle East, Western Europe's experience of secularization appears to be considerably more of the exception in comparative global terms than the phenomenon of continuing religious mobilization in the USA (see Casanova 1994; Joas 2004). It in this framework that Peter Berger (1999) even speaks of a process 'de-secularization'.

References and further reading

Beckford, J. A. (2003) *Social Theory and Religion*. Cambridge: Cambridge University Press.

Berger, P. (ed.) (1999) *The Desecularization of the World: Resurgent Religion and World Politics*. Washington: W. B. Eerdmans.

Bruce, S. (1996) *Religion in the Modern World: From Cathedrals to Cults*. Oxford: Oxford University Press.

Bruce, S. (2002) *God Is Dead: Secularization in the West*. Malden, MA: Blackwell.

Casanova, J. (1994) *Public Religions in the Modern World*. Chicago: University of Chicago Press.

Chaves, M. (1994) 'Secularization as Declining Religious Authority', *Social Forces*, 72(3): 749–74.

Dobbelaere, K. (1981) *Secularization: A Multi-Dimensional Concept*. London: Sage.

Gorski, P. S. (2000) 'Historicizing the Secularization Debate: Church, State, and Society in Late Medieval and Early Modern Europe, ca. 1300 to 1700', *American Sociological Review*, 65(1): 138–67.

Hadden, J. K. (1987) 'Toward Desacralizing Secularization Theory', *Social Forces*, 65(3): 587–611.

Joas, H. (2004) *Braucht der Mensch Religion?* Freiburg: Herder.

Lechner, F. J. (1991) 'The Case against Secularization: A Rebuttal', *Social Forces*, 69(4): 1103–19.

Lyon, D. (1985) 'Rethinking Secularization: Retrospect and Prospect', *Review of Religious Research*, 26(3): 228–43.

Martin, D. A. (1978) *A General Theory of Secularization*. New York: Harper & Row.

Martin, D. A. (2005) *On Secularization: Towards a Revised General Theory*. Burlington, VT: Ashgate.

537

Riis, O. (1993) 'Recent Developments in the Study of Religion in Modern Society', *Acta Sociologica*, 36(4): 371–83.

Smith, C. (ed.) (2003) *The Secular Revolution: Power, Interests, and Conflict in the Secularization of American Public Life.* Berkeley, CA: University of California Press.

Swatos, W. H., Jr. and Olson, D. V. A. (eds) (2000) *The Secularization Debate.* Lanham, MD: Rowman & Littlefield.

Wilson, B. R. (1966) *Religion in Secular Society: A Sociological Comment.* London: C. A. Watts.

Wilson, B. R. (1982) *Religion in Sociological Perspective.* Oxford: Oxford University Press.

KEVIN J. CHRISTIANO

SECURITY

Security is a classical collective good. Protection of the life, liberty and **freedom** of the people, viewed as defense of the political **community** against internal and external threats, has been seen as the highest duty of the state and its institutions. The history of modern statehood could be described as the history of structures and institutions to guarantee security against internal and external enemies, which may include powerful **economic** and societal forces.

Yet security is a contested topic of controversial political value. As a topic of reflection, it has mostly been left to writers in international relations and criminologists. There is, however, in social research, much talk about **risk** and insecurity (**Beck** 1992; Earle and Cvetkovich 1995; **Luhmann** 1979; Ewald 1986). Security refers to a broader and much more complicated phenomenon than simply **crime**, or the internal security of a given state or 'national security', or the threat of **terrorist** attacks. Even though crime and crime prevention are at the core of public unease, other aspects are of importance in relation to the 'security question': **technological** risks, economic uncertainties, social welfare and social security, threats to internal security by political extremists and militant political groups, the so-called 'enemy from within'.

Security is a societal concept based on the absence of threats in an objective sense, and in a subjective sense on the assumption that a situation is safe and could be described as lasting, reliable and without danger or risk. The concept of security combines a certain physical condition with a state of mind. It also refers to the prevention and upholding of a certain social **status**, standard of living or living conditions of individuals and social **groups**. In addition, security has been understood in terms of the assurance of **rights** ('social rights') and the provision of procedures to uphold these rights against violation, whether by other individuals or by societal forces or state-institutions. This is enshrined in the principle of the rule of **law**.

Lawrence Freedman (1992: 732) defines security 'as the extent of a state's confidence in its capacity to withstand another's **power**'. This definition refers to the traditional distinction of internal and external security. 'External' security is mainly aimed at risk through the threat of military intervention from another state. This scenario refers to the two-level interplay of armed offensive and defensive capabilities of states, and states' perceptions of each other's intentions. 'Internal' security appears to refer to social and political stability. Statehood in the modern world has been the primary source for political stability as a precondition for security in a context of crime, subversion and the activities of disaffected groups rejecting the **authority** of a given order. States are also the main pillars of international order and stability. However, a growing number of states are too weak to conduct their responsibilities to their citizens in full and have resorted to foreign support, which often comes close to military intervention. These states and their system of government lack the institutional stability to protect their citizens and to provide for basic services in the community often leading to a lack of **legitimacy** and to further instability.

However, this distinction between 'internal' and 'external' security has become considerably blurred in the present day. Organized crime and international terrorism are only the most obvious examples of the link between external and internal threats to and a new vulnerability of modern societies.

The term 'societal security' refers to a framework needed to withstand these challenges to the sustainability of a given society. A social and political order cannot be defended or changed in the face of the **alienation** of the people but only in accordance with the will of the people and **democratic** procedures of decision-making.

Security in a narrow sense would mean providing for the rules, regulations and **institutions** 'to establish justice, insure domestic tranquillity, protect against external threats, promote the general welfare, and secure the blessings of liberty to ourselves and our posterity', as the American Constitution puts it in its preamble. Yet the modern state's obligation to provide security reaches far beyond these duties. It also includes the welfare of the political community and its members (Walzer 1983: 68), which necessarily touches on the economic and social sphere, and includes the basic **values and norms** of a society. This makes security an overarching concept, which cannot be limited to one segment of a society and political order. It constitutes basic duties and goals of the state as the institutional form of a political community.

However, in modern societies today, security cannot be guaranteed, and the state can no longer pretend to fully secure life, liberty, property and the well-being of its citizens. The quest for absolute security would mean absolute power of the state, without any guarantee that this goal could be achieved. If there is any chance for security, it is only by minimizing insecurity, uncertainty and risks. In modern societies the security and freedom of human collectives and a political community are jeopardized by different factors (Buzan 1991: 19). Likewise, economic security can no longer be maintained. **Globalization** has become the driving force of economic developments, and **Keynesian** visions of economic policy have largely vanished. States, supranational institutions and international regimes today have limited influence on the economy. Instead of providing 'security' by state-intervention and anti-cyclic activities to stimulate the slowdown of the economy, **nation–states** and supranational institutions such as the EU tend to retreat to a politics of order, setting legal standards, **regulations** and/or restrictions for economic actors and potential competitors. The same holds true for social security. Contemporary political actors often concentrate on not alienating key public constituencies or on not disadvantaging key clienteles, while comprehensive social security, as was known in European states in the post-1945 period, is no longer maintained – in part, as a consequence of **demographic** factors. Finally, there is also a perception that political security is threatened by international crime, terrorism, and the consequences of cross-border economic migration. A modern state's ability to provide security in all these spheres is thus increasingly heavily restricted. Authoritarian regimes and dictatorships might resort to repression in order deal with these problems, while democracies might be tempted to trade security for liberty only to find that this is an illusion.

References and further reading

Beck, U. (1992) *Risk Society: Towards a New Modernity*. London: Sage.

Buzan, B. (1991) *People, States and Fear: An Agenda for International Security Studies in the Post-Cold War Era*. Hemel Hempstead: Harvester Wheatsheaf.

Earle, T. C. and Cvetkovich, G. T. (1995) *Social Trust: Toward a Cosmopolitan Society*. Westport, CT: Praeger.

Ewald, F. (1986) *L'État providence*. Paris: Bernard Grasset.

Freedman, L. (1992) 'The Concept of Security', in M. Hawkesworth and M. Kogan (eds) *Encyclopedia of Government and Politics*. London: Routledge.

Glaeßner, G.-J. (2003) *Sicherheit in Freiheit: Die Schutzfunktion des demokratischen Staates und die Freiheit der Bürger*. Opladen: Leske+Budrich.

Jones, T. and Newburn, T. (1998) *Private Security and Public Policing*. Oxford: Clarendon.

Luhmann, N. (1979) *Trust and Power: Two Works by Niklas Luhmann*. Chichester: Wiley.

Scheingold, S. (1984) *The Politics of Law and Order: Street Crime and Public Policy*. London: Longman.

Townsend, C. (1993) *Making the Peace: Public Order and Public Security in Modern Britain*. Oxford: Oxford University Press.

Walzer, M. (1983) *Spheres of Justice: A Defense of Pluralism and Equality*. Oxford: Blackwell.

GERT-JOACHIM GLAESSNER

SELF

In social theory the concept of the self is heavily contested. From interactionist and interpretative perspectives, the self is something that emerges as meaningful in the context of symbolically mediated **action**, **communication** and **interaction**. For George Herbert **Mead** (1972) for example, the self or the 'me' emerges as an entity separate from the 'I' or the ego in the process of interaction. Moreover, the self is continuously reshaped and reframed in interaction. Given that we often occupy a variety of (sometimes conflicting) social positions (for instance, as employee, manager, brother, sister, friend, partner or parent), it is likely that any given individual may have several overlapping, and possibly contradictory, selves. While Mead's as well as other interactionist accounts of the formation of the self (such as **Goffman**'s (1969)) have been influential, informing some ground-breaking sociological studies, in recent years, certain core assumptions of interactionist understandings of the self have come under scrutiny. For example, the tendency within such accounts to assume that a more 'authentic' or 'real' self (denoted by terms such as the 'I') exists alongside a more social or collective self has come under question. This tendency is evident in the dramaturgical metaphors of 'frontstage' and 'backstage' used by Goffman to describe the social **framing** of the self. The problem with the use of such metaphors is that they imply that the social self is a self-conscious, strategically managed and performed artifice. As Lois McNay (1999) has recently observed (in a critique of Anthony **Giddens**'s (1991) arguments regarding the increasingly self-conscious shaping and management of the self), such a formulation tends to underplay the significance of unconscious or pre-reflexive practices in the process of self and **identity** formation, including those unconscious **practices**, perceptions and habits captured by Pierre **Bourdieu** (1977) in his concept of the habitus.

One author who has radically disrupted the idea that people are in possession of a 'true' or 'real' self is Michel **Foucault** (1987, 1990). In his work on the operation of modern forms of **power**, Foucault discusses what he terms 'technologies of the self' and their significance for the articulation and elaboration of the self. Technologies of the self are sets of (often institutionalized) practices which allow historically specific modes of the self to be constructed (and other to be disallowed). Such practices include the confession (think, for example, of the confessional style of many television chat shows such as *Oprah Winfrey*) and the techniques of writing, especially genres of writing which allow stories of the self to be told such as autobiography (Steedman 2000). In this view then the 'self' (including the experiences and sensations we may have of 'having' a self or an interior, and of being a 'unique' individual) must be understood as an historical invention, associated with the emergence of specific technologies. Foucault's insights have been extended by many theorists to argue that technologies of the self are also central to the operations of **class** and **gender** in **modernity**.

While Foucault's understanding of the self clearly problematizes ideas of a real or true self, recent work on **media** and new communications technologies is suggestive of some important ways in which contemporary techniques of the self are shifting, and working to produce new experiences of the self. While Foucault showed that technologies of the self worked to produce a sense of interiority, or the sensation of an inner life, media and communications technologies are stripping this away. For example, in her work on photography Celia Lury (1998) argues that experimentation is now a central technology of the self which is working to undo previous conceptions of human selfhood (especially the properties of consciousness, memory and embodiment). Lury's argument is that photography as a way of seeing is a technology which, via its capacities to freeze, frame and fix its objects, is contributing to a culture which encourages experimentation – a process in which people can increasingly lay claim to features of context or environment as if they were 'the outcome of the testing of his or her personal capacities' (ibid.: 3). The self here is not defined with reference to the internal properties of consciousness and self-knowledge but is externalized and achieved via experimentation with (non-human) objects. Lury's thesis is suggestive of a radical restructuring of the self in contemporary societies. In particular, it suggests that in contemporary media-mediated cultures it is not face-to-face human interaction which is productive of the self, but rather engagements with non-human media objects, engagements which are fundamentally redrawing the boundaries of 'human' selfhood in ways which pose radical challenges for social theory.

References and further reading

Bourdieu, P. (1977) *Outline of a Theory of Practice*. Cambridge: Polity Press.

Foucault, M. (1987) *The History of Sexuality*, vol. 2: *The Use of Pleasure*. Trans. R. Hurley. London: Penguin.

Foucault, M. (1990) *The History of Sexuality*, vol. 3: *The Care of the Self*. Trans R. Hurley. London: Penguin.

Giddens, A. (1991) *Modernity and Self-Identity*. Cambridge: Polity.

Goffman, E. (1969) *The Presentation of Self in Everyday Life*. London: Allen Lane.

Lury, C. (1998) *Prosthetic Culture*. London: Routledge.

McNay, L. (1999) 'Gender, Habitus and the Field: Pierre Bourdieu and the Limits of Reflexivity', *Theory, Culture & Society*, 16(1): 95–117.

Mead, G. H. (1972) *Mind, Self and Society*. Chicago: University of Chicago Press.

Steedman, C. (2000) 'Enforced Narratives: Stories of Another Self', in T. Cosslett, C. Lury and P. Summerfield (eds) *Feminism and Autobiography*. London: Routledge.

LISA ADKINS

SEMIOTICS

The term 'semiotics' derives from the Greek *semeiotikos* – 'interpreter of signs' – and is also referred to as 'semiology'. Broadly definable as the 'science of signs', semiotics deals with a range of issues and concepts, involving **meaning**, cognition, **culture** and behaviour and is therefore not a homogeneous discipline. It intersects with many well-established disciplines, including logic, philosophy of **language**, linguistics, anthropology and psychology. In particular, it seeks to specify the place of language among other sign systems. Although semiotics emerged as an independent activity only in the mid-twentieth century, reflection on signs and the functioning of sign systems has a long tradition in Western thought. Aristotle posited the distinction between natural and conventional signs, which became the crux of the debate between the Stoics and the Epicureans. St Augustine, whose influence extends to William of Ockham (*c.*1285–1349) and John Locke, identifies in the word, on the one hand, a relationship between the sign and the thing and, on the other hand, a relationship between the speaker and the listener; this constitutes the first attempt to combine an elaborated account of language and signification with a psychological theory of **communication**.

Major contributions to the establishment of semiotics were made in twentieth-century **philosophy**. Notably where the work of Ernst Cassirer on symbolic forms emphasized the role of language in articulating reality and the unique capacity of language to refer to itself and to other symbolic systems. In logic, Charles Morris distinguished between the semantic, the syntactic and the pragmatic aspects of the sign. The founding fathers of semiotics, however, are generally considered to be the Swiss linguist Ferdinand de Saussure and the American logician Charles Sanders Peirce. Saussure conceived of the sign as constituted by a dyadic relationship between a signifier (or 'sound-image', i.e. the psychological representation of a sound) and a signified (or mental concept); the sign in turn refers to a referent, or the object in the real world. Saussure further proposed that the connection between signifier and the signified is arbitrary, and a product of social convention. His posthumously published *Course in General Linguistics* represents a breakthrough in its conception of language as, on one hand, an abstract system, or *langue*, posited as synchronic, and on the other hand *parole*, or language in actual use. Peirce's model of the sign is triadic: it involves what he called a 'representamen' (the sign) or 'First'; its object or 'Second'; and an 'interpretant' or 'Third' (located in the sign system itself). He further defines a number of sign types, among them the icon, the index and the symbol. His theory of the sign is dynamic in that the interpretant can become the sign in a succeeding triad, thus opening up the possibility of 'unlimited semiosis'. These two approaches conceive of their object either as constructed (Saussurean semiology) or as observable (Peircean semiotics). The First Congress of the International Association for Semiotic Studies in 1969 opted for 'semiotics'.

The Danish linguist Louis Hjelmslev introduced the distinction between *denotation*, the relationship between signifier and signified, and *connotation*, the relationship between signs, which would be crucial to Roland **Barthes**'s work on 'mythologies', notably on petty bourgeois ideology pervading popular culture and on fashion and eating habits as systems of signs. Following Hjelmslev, Claude **Lévi-Strauss**, Barthes and Algirdas Julien Greimas developed 'structural semiotics' extending the linguistic model to the study of social and cultural forms from **myths** to **kinship** systems and narrative. A number of theorists, notably Julia Kristeva and Umberto Eco, also engaged in a radical questioning of the structural principles of semiosis and of the sign to develop a theory of the reader as active participant in the generation of the text. Roman Jakobson elaborated a model of communication (inspired by Karl Bühler and his 'organon model'). In this model, six functions of language combine into a hierarchy within which any one function may be dominant. Another representative of Czech structuralist thought, Jan Mukarovsky, focused on the aesthetic as socially constituted, emphasizing the presence of a communicative function in aesthetic objects. Soviet semiotics, more specifically Jurij Lotman and the Tartu School, developed a semiotics of culture, based on the notion of 'secondary modelling systems', which draws upon information theory and prefigures **cybernetics**. In North America, Thomas Sebeok advanced the idea of 'meaning-plan', which brings together the environment (a notion derived from Jakob von Uexküll's *Umwelt*) and the organism in an interrelation of semiosis, thus pursuing the Peircean tradition of study of both verbal and non-verbal signs.

References and further reading

Barthes, R. (1993) *Mythologies*. Trans. A. Lavers. London: Vintage.

Deely, J. (1982) *Introducing Semiotics: Its History and Doctrine*. Bloomington, IN: Indiana University Press.

Eco, U. (1976) *A Theory of Semiotics*. Bloomington: Indiana University Press.

Peirce, C. S. (1982 –) *The Writings of Charles S. Peirce: A Chronological Edition*. Ed. M. H. Fisch, 30 vols. Bloomington, IN: Indiana University Press.

Saussure, F. de (1959) *Course in General Linguistics*. Trans. W. Baskin. New York: McGraw-Hill.

Sebeok, T. (1994) *Signs: An Introduction to Semiotics*. Toronto: University of Toronto Press.

Todorov, T. (1982) *Theories of the Symbol*. Trans. C. Porter. Ithaca, NY: Cornell University Press.

KARINE ZBINDEN

SEN, AMARTYA K. (1933–)

Indian economist and philosopher, Nobel Prize Winner in Economics 1998. Sen's principal concerns are the nature and distribution of welfare. He starts out from the classical theory of social choice that puts individual **preferences** centre-stage. Preferences, Sen argues, may fail to be transitive, reflexive, and complete, but they come in different intensities. Any attempt to do justice to this fact will face the problem of interpersonal comparability. Sen shares and expands on the view that the problem can be solved by extended sympathy. However, a fundamental doubt remains: if individual preferences themselves can be shaped by unfair conditions (for instance, by a culture of oppression), how can they serve as our guides to what is fair and right? Sen therefore submits an alternative proposal, focusing on capabilities to achieve valuable functionings. Functionings are beings and doings, such as avoiding premature **death** or taking part in communal life; capabilities are the **freedom** to choose among various functionings.

While both functionings and capabilities constitute individual welfare, only capabilities determine social welfare: a good **society** is a society of freedom. Using social choice theory and, in his later writings, welding it to the capability approach, Sen also discusses a variety of more applied questions: how to address economic **inequality**, **deprivation and relative deprivation**, **poverty** (including famines), **class** and **gender** disparities, and the violation of basic **rights**.

Major works

(1970) *Collective Choice and Social Welfare*. Amsterdam: North-Holland.

(1973) *On Economic Inequality*. Oxford: Clarendon.

(1981) *Poverty and Famines*. Oxford: Clarendon.

(1982) *Choice, Welfare and Measurement*. Cambridge, MA: Harvard University Press.

(1987) *On Ethics and Economics*. Oxford: Blackwell.

(1992) *Inequality Reexamined*. Cambridge, MA: Harvard University Press.

Further reading

Basu, K. (ed.) (1995) *Choice, Welfare and Development*. Oxford: Clarendon.

ULLA WESSELS

SEX/GENDER DISTINCTION

Since the 1950s, the sex/gender distinction (also referred to as the sex/gender **binary**) has circulated throughout the social sciences: in **Giddens**'s latest edition of *Sociology* (1992); in psychology's *Psychology of Sex Differences* (Maccoby and Jacklin, 1975); in medical accounts such as Money's (1965) *Sex Research*; and in feminist theory such as Oakley's (1972) *Sex, Gender and Society*. Within **feminist theory**, the distinction provided a powerful foundation for a **material** account of women's oppression. 'Sex' referred to the biological differences between women and men, while '**gender**' signified the practices of femininity or masculinity within social relations. This bifurcation served a number of functions, the most immediate of which was to provide a convenient, tangible means to constitute **identity** and proceed with the immediate concern of challenging the hierarchical relationships which subordinate women to men.

Over the past two decades, the distinction between sex and gender has undergone vigorous challenge. The major criticism of this distinction is that it appears to substantiate the assumption that while gender differences may be socially constructed, 'sex' remains an immutable essential difference between women and men (see **essentialism**). On this basis, feminists have recently argued that inequalities between women and men are legitimized as natural and therefore unchangeable, and that the 'immutability' of sex places severe limitations on any **critiques** of gender. The critique of the sex/gender distinction has utilized two complementary types of argument. Combining **post-structuralism** and **social studies of science**, some feminists concentrate on the **social construction** of scientific knowledge. These studies begin their analyses from the perspective that scientific 'facts' are socially mediated and can only be understood within their particular social and cultural milieu. For instance, Christine Delphy argues that rather than seeing sex as the baseline from which gender emerges through sociality, 'gender...create[s] anatomical sex' (1984: 144). By conflating the biological with the natural, 'sex' becomes the natural that initiates the social. Feminist studies of science examine what are often viewed as the 'essence' of sex differences: gonads, hormones, chromosomes and genes. For instance, Emily Martin (1991) analyzes how the inscription of cultural notions of sex differences on to the physical processes of egg and sperm activity provides the basis for an analysis of human gonads as another site deployed in the social construction of sexual difference. As Anne Fausto-Sterling suggests, behind debates about sexual reproduction

'lurk some heavy-duty social questions about sex, gender, power, and the social structure of European culture...In the work of the established evolutionary biologists, past and present, talking about eggs and sperm gives us permission to prescribe appropriate gender behaviors' (1997: 54, 57).

A second challenge to the sex/gender distinction concentrates more on explorations of matter (sex) itself. For example, John Hood-Williams (1996) focuses on three inter-related assumptions which underlie this (often) taken-for-granted distinction. First, the biological distinction between women and men assumes that a distinction can be made between biology (sex), on the one hand, and culture (gender), on the other; second, while gender is changeable, sex is immutable. Third, the distinction depends upon the idea that biology itself consistently distinguishes between females and males. A number of feminist scholars now argue that the concept of sex differences should be replaced by a notion of sex diversity, to reflect the diversity of sex found in human and non-human animal species.

Both challenges to the sex/gender distinction recognize that within our current discursive field, to exist at all means being a woman or a man, or in Judith **Butler**'s terms, 'sex is the norm by which the "one" becomes viable at all' (1993: 2). Thus, feminist theory continues to labor definitional concerns based on the 'sex'/'gender' template.

References and further reading

Butler, J. (1993) *Bodies that Matter*. London: Routledge.

Delphy, C. (1984) *Close to Home*. London: Hutchinson.

Fausto-Sterling, A. (1997) 'Feminism and Behavioral Evolution: A Taxonomy', in P. Gowaty, *Feminism and Evolutionary Biology: Boundaries, Intersections, and Frontiers*. New York: Chapman and Hall, pp. 42–60.

Giddens, A. (1992) *Sociology*. Oxford: Polity Press.

Hird, M. J. (2000) 'Gender's Nature: Inter-sexuals, Transsexuals and the "Sex"/"Gender" Binary', *Feminist Theory*, 1(3): 347–64.

Hood-Williams, J. (1996) 'Goodbye to Sex and Gender', *Sociological Review*, 44(1): 1–16.

Maccoby, E. and Jacklin, C. (1975) *The Psychology of Sex Differences*. London: Tavistock.

Martin, E. (1991) 'The Egg and the Sperm: How Science Has Constructed a Romance Based on Stereotypical Male-Female Roles', *Signs: Journal of Women in Culture and Society*, 16(3): 485–501.

Money, J. (1965) *Sex Research: New Developments*. New York: Holt, Rinehart and Winston.

Oakley, A. (1972) *Sex, Gender and Society*. London: Maurice Temple Smith.

MYRA HIRD

SEXUALITY

As a concept, sexuality has a relatively recent origin, its first usage in scientific literature occurring in the early nineteenth century to describe types of **persons** and their sexual **preferences** (such as homosexual, heterosexual and bisexual) (Bristow 1997). Today sexuality is a broad term that encompasses sexual **identity**, sexual preferences, sexual **practices**, and sexual **meanings**. The history of sexuality has been a battlefield of diverse and competing theoretical perspectives, which can be grouped into two key opposing schools of thought: **essentialism** and anti-essentialism. The essentialist model, which is affiliated with biological science, orthodox sexology, socio-biology, psychiatry, and medicine in general, claims that sexuality is a natural biological instinct associated with the evolutionary need to reproduce. According to this model, sexuality is essentially ahistorical, transcultural and unchanging. The anti-essentialist approach, which is associated with alternative scholarship in the fields of sociology, **philosophy**, psychology, **feminist** and **gender** studies, argues that sexuality is not biologically determined, but rather that sexual meanings, identities and practices are produced in **culture** and through **language**, and have particular political and discursive implications. Some of the ways that sexuality has been understood within these two main schools of thought can be traced through a historical overview of key theorists in the field.

During the late nineteenth century, and first half of the twentieth century, sexology (defined as the 'scientific study' of human sexuality) and **psychoanalysis** vied for authority over the classifications and meanings of sexuality. Early orthodox sexologists, such as Richard von Krafft-Ebing and Havelock Ellis, aimed to determine via scientific method the various forms sexuality took, categorize these according to notions of 'natural' and 'unnatural' ('normal' and 'abnormal'), and develop interventions for those deemed 'unnatural' or 'perverse'. Maintaining a close affiliation with medicine, orthodox sexology primarily employed biological and evolutionary understandings of sexuality, maintaining that heterosexuality (and penis – vagina sex) was the most normal mode of sexuality due to its reproductive purpose. Sexologists in the second half of the twentieth century, such as Alfred Kinsey, William Masters and Virginia Johnson, shifted the scene from a focus on 'sexual perversion' to a more medically-influenced notion of 'sexual pathology'. The current classification system of sexual difficulties utilized by sexologists, medical practitioners and sex therapists is based on Masters and Johnson's (1966) 'human sexual response cycle', a model depicting physiological response during sexual stimulation which comprises several distinct phases: desire, arousal, and orgasm. According to the biomedical model of sexuality, the human sexual response cycle operates in men and women regardless of historical factors, gender and cultural difference, or sexual orientation (although most sexologists and clinicians would acknowledge these various factors influence the cycle). Deviations from the human sexual response cycle are deemed pathological and constitute 'sexual dysfunctions'.

545

Since its inception in the late nineteenth century, psychoanalysis has challenged the sexological and medical model through its refusal to view sexuality as a strictly instinctual imperative. While maintaining some affinity with the scientific approach, **Freud** ([1925] 1986) disputed the prioritization of biology, theorizing that sexuality was a 'drive' affected by the 'psyche' and by 'unconscious desires'. Freud postulated the existence of the 'libido', defined as the psyche's capacity for sexual energy. Unlike the biological model in which genital sexuality becomes most important as a result of maturation and puberty, Freud claimed that sexuality originates in infancy and progresses during human **development** through distinct stages at which attention is fixated at particular erogenous zones: oral, anal, and genital. Early experiences associated with each of these stages influence one's sexual preferences and experiences throughout adult life. Freud disputed the assumed link between the sexual and the genital, as well as the 'naturalness' of heterosexual (and coital) sex espoused in the traditional biological model of sexuality. He argued that desire does not always manifest in ways that facilitate genital reproductive sex (examples of non-reproductive desires including kissing). Freud also claimed that desires that were **taboo** within culture were repressed into the **unconscious**. Traditional psychoanalysis has perhaps had most impact on theories of 'sexual identity'.

In the late twentieth century the predominance of scientific sexology and traditional psychoanalysis over sexual matters was effectively contested by alternative theory arising from the radical movements of the 1970s such as feminism, and gay and lesbian activism. **Post-structuralism** also had a profound impact on theory on sexuality. These various perspectives emphasized the historical, cultural and political construction of sexual 'truths' within language. In his landmark text, *The History of Sexuality*, French philosopher and historian Michel **Foucault** ([1976] 1978) argued that sexual meanings and forms, as well as sexual identities, are products of language, **discourse**, and **power**. Discourses in this context are ways of understanding the world and our experiences that involve a relationship between a certain form of **knowledge** and power. How we make sense of sexuality is contingent on the various discourses regarding sexual matters – termed 'technologies of sex' – that are circulating in a given culture at a given time. Dominant (or normative) discourses are those with most **authority** within a society – such as biological and evolutionary understandings of sexuality in contemporary Western culture – and they therefore tend to be the most prevalent ways by means of which individual men and women will also make sense of their own sexual identities and experiences. While one discourse may be considered more authoritative, there are always multiple alternative discourses in existence (for example, feminist, queer and postmodern perspectives on sexuality) that disrupt and resist the privilege of the normative discourse.

Foucault challenged what has been termed 'the repressive hypothesis' of sexuality: that is, the idea that sexuality had been restricted during the nineteenth century and subsequently liberated in the twentieth. Instead he claimed that power, rather than denying the forms of expression that sexuality might take, *produces* and *proliferates* types of sexualities and modes of desire. Power in this sense is not interpreted as a unitary and over-bearing force, but rather as an unstable and diverse phenomenon that operates through the very *constitution* and *regulation* of sexual identities, desires, and practices. The so-called 'sexual **revolution**', which Foucault views as a form of social control exercised through the sexual domain, brought about a 'confessional mode' of governing the sexual **subject**, as sexuality became aligned with expressions of one's true identity and self-awareness: we have come to think of *ourselves* as being *our sex*. Foucault contends that, through the operation of 'disciplinary power', discourses of the sexual play a key role in controlling populations.

Queer theory has also influenced contemporary understandings of sexuality. Where once the term 'queer' was employed as derogatory slang for homosexual, it is now used to connote a marginal sexual self-identification or to refer to a nascent theoretical perspective derived from gay and lesbian studies (Jagose 1996). Queer theory disrupts dualistic notions of sex (such as male/female), gender (masculinity/femininity) and sexuality (heterosexual/homosexual), and blurs cultural assumptions about 'natural' sex and sexual identity. In analytic terms, queer theory is most closely associated with **deconstruction** and psychoanalytic theory, although neither wholly determines queer theory as it seeks to remain distinctly political, marginalized and resistant to definition.

Judith **Butler**'s (1990) provocative book *Gender Trouble* is often credited with being the most widely cited Queer theory text. Expanding on Foucauldian theory, Butler questioned the ways in which marginalized identities (e.g., woman, feminist, queer) are inevitably complicit with those systems or discourses they are trying to dispute. She challenged the idea that one's sense of gender identity (as masculine or feminine) followed from one's anatomical sex (as male or female), instead asking whether it was not the case that gender *preceded* sex. This contention rocked previous thinking on sex and gender, which had assumed sex was a natural given and gender was an outcome of environment, culture or social learning. In contrast to the traditional nature = sex/nurture = gender division in medicine (and in mainstream social science), Butler argued that anatomical sex itself was not necessarily grounded in nature, positioning *both* sex *and* gender as cultural constructions. She

contended that the current categorization of bodies as male or female is the condition for the naturalization of heterosexuality (termed 'the heterosexual matrix' in *Gender Trouble*), and the marginalization of ambiguously sexed bodies, alternative sexualities and genders. However, Butler went further to insist that *all* sexualities need to be 'denaturalized'; this position conflicts with the tenets of early gay and lesbian liberation and radical feminism (see **women's movement**). She theorized gender as a **performative** act, the result of imitative acts and gestures repeated on the surface of the body.

References and further reading

Bristow, J. (1997) *Sexuality*. London: Routledge.

Butler, J. (1990) *Gender Trouble: Feminism and the Subversion of Identity*. London: Routledge.

Foucault, M. ([1976] 1978) *The History of Sexuality*, vol. 1. New York: Pantheon.

Freud, S. ([1925] 1986) *The Essentials of Psychoanalysis: The Definitive Collection of Sigmund Freud's Writing*. Ed. A. Freud. London: Penguin.

Jagose, A. (1996) *Queer Theory*. Dunedin: University of Otago Press.

Masters, W. and Johnson, V. (1966) *Human Sexual Response*. Boston: Little, Brown.

Potts, A. (2002) *The Science/Fiction of Sex: Feminist Deconstruction and the Vocabularies of Heterosex*. London: Routledge.

Weeks, J. (2003) *Sexuality*, 2nd edn. London: Routledge.

ANNIE POTTS

SIGNS

See: semiotics

SIMMEL, GEORG (1858–1918)

German theorist

Influenced by **Kantianism and Neo-Kantianism**. Simmel's early **philosophy** of history is a rendering of Kant's conception of 'nature' as a forming of sensual material by means of categories of the mind. *A priori* categories of the scientific mind shape lived experiences into 'history.' This same **form**–content distinction is the basis for the definition of sociology as a discipline dealing with the forms of social processes. **Society** is an emergent unity of **interactions**, in the broad sense of mutual influences between individuals. The most diverse motives and interests such as **love**, **work**, or **religiosity** which are not social in themselves are the content or material of countless social forms. **Domination** and subordination, **conflict**, **exchange**, and sociability are famous examples of Simmel's 'pure' or 'formal' sociology. His most celebrated work, *The Philosophy of Money* ([1900] 1990), deals with analytic questions of monetary values and the implications of a **money economy** for individual **freedom**, **culture** and style of life. Influenced by **Nietzsche** and Bergson, in the course of his studies of Goethe and Rembrandt, Simmel's late work is based upon elements of *Lebensphilosophie*. There he developed a concept of culture as a form created by, but transcending, life. Life realizes itself in culture, but inherent in this process is also a 'tragedy': as a fixed **objec**tification, culture constrains life's flow.

Major works

([1900] 1990) *The Philosophy of Money*. New York: Routledge.

([1916] 2004) *Rembrandt*. New York: Routledge.

(1950) *The Sociology of Georg Simmel*. New York: Free Press.

(1971) *On Individuality and Social Forms*. Chicago: University of Chicago Press.

(1989) *Georg Simmel Gesamtausgabe* [Collected Works], 24 vols. Frankfurt am Main: Suhrkamp.

(1997) *On Culture*. London: Sage.

Further reading

Dahme, H. -J. (1981) *Soziologie als exalte Wissenschaft*, 2 vols. Stuttgart.

Köhke, K. (1996) *Der junge Simmel in Theoriebeziehungen und Sozialen Bewegungen*. Frankfurt am Main: Suhrkamp.

—(1981) *Sociological Impressionism: A Reassessment of Georg Simmel's Social Theory*. London: Heinemann.

HELMUT STAUBMANN

SIMULACRUM

In everyday usage 'simulacrum' refers to an imitation or copy of an original. In social theory, it is associated with **Baudrillard**'s theory of contemporary society which holds that the 'real' has been displaced by 'hyperreal' orders of **signs** and simulated experiences. The theory of simulacra is explored in Baudrillard's *Symbolic Exchange and Death* and *Simulacra and Simulations*. With the combined expansion of mass-mediated sign processes, the 'implosion' of signs into **society**, and the dominance of coded realities, we face what Baudrillard calls the 'end of **representation**' and the beginning of hyperreality (see **media and mass media**). We have moved beyond the 'society of the spectacle' of advanced consumer **capitalism** into an information **civilization** dominated by image spectacles in which every sphere of life has been displaced by models and simulacra of reality. Hyperreality is 'the generation by models of a real without origin or reality: a hyperreal. The territory no longer precedes the map, nor survives it. . . it is the map that engenders the territory' (1983a). Baudrillard speculates that we now live in a world in which all representation is simulacral. There are no longer 'original' objects to be represented, no independent referents but simply practices and strategies of hyperreality. We witness the 'end of the social': 'Whereas representation tries to absorb simulation by interpreting it as false representation, simulation envelops the whole edifice of representation as itself a simulacrum' (1983a). Speculation about simulacra is a central theme in contemporary debates about **postmodernism**, the **media and the mass media**, and cultures of **consumption**.

References and further reading

Baudrillard, J. (1975) *The Mirror of Production.* St Louis, MO: Telos Press.

Baudrillard, J. (1983a) *Simulations.* New York: Semiotext(e).

Baudrillard, J. (1983b) *In the Shadow of the Silent Majorities; Or, the End of the Social and Other Essays.* New York: Semiotext(e).

Baudrillard, J. (1988) *Selected Writings.* Ed. M. Poster. Stanford, CA: Stanford University Press; Cambridge: Polity Press.

Kellner, D. (ed.) (1994) *Baudrillard: A Critical Reader.* Oxford: Blackwell.

Sandywell, B. (1995) 'Forget Baudrillard', *Theory, Culture & Society,* 12: 125–52.

BARRY SANDYWELL

SKOCPOL, THEDA (1947–)

American sociologist and political scientist

Influenced by Barrington **Moore**, Skocpol has been an important figure in **historical sociology** recognized for ground-breaking studies of large-scale **social change**, including **revolution** and **state** politics. In her edited volumes *Vision and Method in Historical Sociology* (1985a) and *Bringing the State Back In* (1985b), Skocpol discusses forms of methodological and conceptual reorientation capable of accounting for the state as an independent social. Countering both structural **functionalist** and neo-**Marxist** conceptions, Skocpol argues that states should be viewed as 'configurations of **organization** and **action** that influence the **meanings** and methods of politics' (1985b: 28). Rectifying the shortcomings of Moore's description of modernization processes in European states, Skocpol examines the problem faced by pre-revolutionary regimes in keeping abreast of international competition, notably focusing on the French Revolution, the Russian Revolution and the Chinese Revolution. In *States and Social Revolutions* (1979) and *Social Revolutions in the Modern World* (1994), she argues that it was this component rather than **ideologies** that prompted

revolutionary outbreaks and set the path to **modernity**. She combines a structural with an institutional framework for the cases of France, Russia, China, and Iran, emphasizing rigorous comparative empirical method shorn of ideological slogans.

Major works

(1979) *States and Social Revolutions.* Cambridge: Cambridge University Press.

(1985a) (ed.) *Vision and Method in Historical Sociology.* Cambridge: Cambridge University Press.

(1985b) *Bringing the State Back In.* Cambridge: Cambridge University Press.

(1994) *Social Revolutions in the Modern World.* Cambridge: Cambridge University Press.

Further reading

Chirot, D. (1997) 'Social Revolutions in the Modern World', *Social Forces,* 75: 1121–6.

Dunn, J. (1982) 'States and Social Revolutions', *Ethics,* 92: 299–315.

BERNHARD GIESEN
DANIEL ŠUBER

SLAVERY

Slavery is a system that legally and socially designates 'slaves' as being entirely under the control of those termed 'masters'. While slavery had existed in various forms from the earliest days of human **civilization**, the institution was transformed from the late fifteenth century AD onwards into one of the most important phenomena of modern history. The **European** exploration of Africa brought them into contact with people who were willing to trade slaves in return for European goods and the opening up of new lands in the **Americas** from 1492 gave a fresh economic impetus to the slave trade. Europeans first coerced Native Americans into **labour** in the Americas, but the devastating impact of Old World diseases on New World populations forced the Spanish and Portuguese to look elsewhere for a labour force. Since African princes were willing to sell slaves, there was an alternative source of labour, but in order to meet European demand, African rulers were forced to increase their supplies of slaves by seizing members of neighbouring **ethnic groups**. The slave trade started by the Portuguese and Spanish eventually grew to include all European imperial nations with territories in the Americas. Roughly ten million Africans were forcibly transported to America. No European colony in the Americas existed without slavery, and the staples produced by slave labour contributed vastly to the wealth of Britain, France, Spain, Portugal and the Netherlands.

Slavery in the Americas had several distinct features. While the impetus for the introduction of slaves in the Americas was primarily **economic**, slavery quickly became a racialized institution. Early modern Europeans did not see **race** as an individual's most significant characteristic since **language**, dress, and **religion** also defined status. However, by the eighteenth century the words 'slave' and 'Negro' had become almost synonymous. As Europeans increasingly classified the world's flora and fauna, they also classified humanity, with Africans being generally regarded as inferior subhumans, incapable of rational thought or self-improvement. As a form of **property**, slaves were effectively de-humanized. Slave-owners treated slaves much as they treated their livestock, meting out brutal punishments for resistance. This is not to claim that slaves lacked **agency** in their dealings with masters, however, since the day-to-day operation of plantations inevitably involved a degree of negotiation and accommodation. Slaves could disrupt the rhythm of plantation life in a variety of ways and prudent masters realized that they obtained more from their labour force by granting small privileges and overlooking minor infractions (see **master–slave dialectic**).

By the late eighteenth century, **Enlightenment** ideas of universal human **rights** suggested that slavery was incompatible with civilized societies and gradually agitation for the abolition of slavery grew. In the 1830s Britain formally **emancipated** its slaves in its West Indies. However, the United States wrestled with the issue of abolition for far longer because there the pro-slavery voice was considerably more politically powerful. The rise of abolitionists such as William Lloyd Garrison in the 1830s, who made a vocal **moral** and religious case for ending slavery, encouraged a determined pro-slavery defence by southern intellectuals. Slavery, it was claimed, was not only a 'necessary evil' for economic reasons, it was also a 'positive good' – the most suitable existence for bondspeople. Slave owners claimed to provide a paternalistic cradle-to-grave welfare system (unlike Northern employers) with moral guidance for their slaves, arguing that emancipation would lead to widespread suffering by people unaccustomed to fending for themselves.

By 1865, slavery in the Americas had ended in all but the Spanish Caribbean islands and in Brazil, but this did not mean equal rights for emancipated slaves. In the Caribbean the British used an apprenticeship system for a transitional period, while in the USA share-cropping became one of the few employments open to freedmen. Yet both these systems might be described as slavery in all but name. Inter-racial **violence** grew with whites using lynching and intimidation to maintain racial hierarchies once the legal distinctions between slave and free had been swept away. For more than a century the oppression of racial **minorities** by ruling classes was the norm in Western society. The achievements of civil rights activists in the second half of the twentieth century went some way towards ending racial discrimination in the West, though slavery and other forms of coerced labour still persist in many parts of the world and are globally diffused by increasingly entrenched forms of transnational criminal networks, including prostitution rings.

References and further reading

Blackburn, R. (1988) *The Overthrow of Colonial Slavery*. London: Verso.
— (1997) *The Making of New World Slavery*. London: Verso.
Genovese, E. (1976) *Roll Jordan Roll*. New York: Random House.
Heuman, G. and Walvin, J. (eds) (2003) *The Slavery Reader*. London: Routledge.
Jordan, W. (1968) *White over Black*. Chapel Hill, NC: University of North Carolina Press.
Patterson, O. (1969) *The Sociology of Slavery*. Rutherford, NJ: Fairleigh Dickinson University Press.
— (1982) *Slavery and Social Death*. Cambridge, MA: Harvard University Press.
Stinchcombe, A. (1995) *Sugar Island Slavery in the Age of Enlightenment*. Princeton: Princeton University Press.
Wood, B. (1997) *Origins of American Slavery*. New York: Hill & Wang.

TIM LOCKLEY

SMELSER, NEIL J. (1930–)
US sociologist

Started as an adherent of structural **functionalism** and published *Economy and Society* in 1956 with Talcott **Parsons**. Aware of the major shortcomings of this school, he stressed **social change** rather than social order, **social movements** rather than institutionalized actors. His *Social Change in the Industrial Revolution* (1959) and his *Theory of Collective Behavior* (1962) became landmarks in the research on collective action and mobilization. A second trait of his work is methodology. His study of **comparative methods** as well as his reflections upon the problematics of sociology revolve around two of the most pressing problems in the social sciences: comparative reasoning and the epistemological levels of sociological analysis, sometimes referred to as the 'micro-macro-link' (see **micro-, meso- and macro- levels**). A third line in his work concerns economic sociology. In the tradition of Adam **Smith**, Max **Weber** and Joseph **Schumpeter**, Smelser discusses the relationship of economy and society and

demonstrates the strengths of a sociological approach to the **economy**. Economic matters are much too important to be left to neo-classic economists. In this sense, Smelser is a pioneer of the revival of neo-**institutionalism**.

Major works

(1956) (with T. Parsons) *Economy and Society*. London: Routledge.
(1959) *Social Change in the Industrial Revolution*. Chicago: University of Chicago Press.
(1962) *Theory of Collective Behavior*. New York: Free Press.
(1976) *Comparative Methods in the Social Sciences*. Englewood Cliffs, NJ: Prentice Hall.
(1991) *Social Paralysis and Social Change*. Berkeley, CA: University of California Press.
(1994) (ed., with R. Swedberg) *The Handbook of Economic Sociology*. Princeton, NJ: Princeton University Press.
(1997) *Problematics of Sociology: The Georg Simmel Lectures, 1995*. Berkeley, CA: University of California Press.

Further reading

Alexander, J., Giesen, B., Münch, R. and Smelser, N. J. (eds) (1987) *The Micro-Macro Link*. Berkeley, CA: University of California Press.

HANS-PETER MÜLLER

SMITH, ADAM (1723–1790)
Scottish philosopher

Smith's (1776) *Wealth of Nations* is one of the founding texts of economic theory, mostly admired for the idea of the self-regulating **market**, governed as if by an 'invisible hand'. In modern 'civilized society' individuals pursue their **self**-interest in a 'system of natural **liberty**' built on property and the division of **labour**, and made possible by the uniquely human 'propensity to truck, barter and exchange'. Because Smith argued strongly against absolutist state intervention, he is often claimed to be an advocate of *laissez-faire* economic policies, although he argued for a quite extensive role of the state in defense, in the rule of law, **education** and the provision of public goods. In considering the emerging **capitalist** economy as a process of reproduction activated by individuals assuming the typical roles of landlord, capitalist and worker, Smith drew a picture of society as composed of social **classes** with opposing interests.

A relatively neglected but important aspect of Smith's work is his theory of the emergence of moral values in *The Theory of Moral Sentiments* (1759). He analyzed social **interaction** in terms of sympathy, mutual observation and reflection to arrive at the construction of the 'impartial spectator'. On this theory, each individual observes her or his actions with the eyes of an internalized impartial spectator – a figure similar to G. H. **Mead**'s 'generalized other' – to monitor the 'propriety' of actions. This non-**utilitarian** theory of normative action has sometimes been found to be inconsistent with the idea of self-interested actors on markets. However, Smith had a sufficiently complex view of society to see that distinct **action** orientations dominate in different social realms.

Major works

([1759] 1976–87) 'The Theory of Moral Sentiments', in A. S. Skinner *et al.* (eds) *The Glasgow Edition of the Works and Correspondence of Adam Smith*, 7 vols. Oxford: Clarendon.
([1766] 1976–87) 'Lectures on Jurisprudence', in A. S. Skinner *et al.* (eds) *The Glasgow Edition of the Works and Correspondence of Adam Smith*, 7 vols. Oxford: Clarendon.
([1776] 1976–87) 'An Inquiry into the Nature and Causes of the Wealth of Nations', in A. S. Skinner *et al.* (eds) *The Glasgow Edition of the Works and Correspondence of Adam Smith*, 7 vols. Oxford: Clarendon.

Further reading

Skinner, A. S. *et al.* (eds) (1976–87) 'Introduction', in *The Glasgow Edition of the Works and Correspondence of Adam Smith*, 7 vols. Oxford: Clarendon.

HEINER GANßMANN

SOCIAL CAPITAL

The concept of social capital captures the relation between social norms and **networks** and the quality of economic and political performance in a society. It is also employed to measure the quality of a **civil society**. Two major theorists of the term are Robert D. Putnam and James S. **Coleman**. A more critical use of the term can be found in the work of Pierre **Bourdieu** who speaks of the power of social networks and connections which actors and classes are able to mobilize in the pursuit of their own interests.

According to Putnam (1993, 2000) and Coleman (1990), **trust**, norms and networks among **citizens** reduce transaction costs and allow for a more efficient functioning of the **economy** and political institutions. The term was originally introduced by Loury (1977) to explain variations in the individual accumulation of human capital as a consequence of social **status**. Insights into the structural promotion of collective action in the economy and in international relations through regimes and contracts also added to the concept (see Granovetter 1985; Keohane 1984). Since the mid-1990s, social capital has increasingly been used as a value in itself to evaluate the civil and moral capacities of a **society**.

References and further reading

Alexander, J. C. (1992) 'Shaky Foundations: The Presuppositions and Internal Contradictions of James Coleman's Foundations of Social Theory', *Theory and Society*, 21(2): 203–18.
Coleman, J. S. (1990) *Foundations of Social Theory*. Cambridge, MA: harvard University Press.
Granovetter, M. S. (1985) 'Economic Action and Social Structure: The Problem of Embeddedness', *American Journal of Sociology*, 91(November): 481–510.
Keohane, R. O. (1984) *After Hegemony: Cooperation and Discord in the World Political Economy*. Princeton, NJ: Princeton University Press.
Loury, G. C. (1977) 'A Dynamic Theory of Racial Income Differences', in P. A. Wallace

and A. M. LaMond (eds) *Women, Minorities, and Employment Discrimination*. Lexington, MA: Lexington Books.

Portes, A. and Landolt, P. (1996) 'Unsolved Mysteries: The Tocqueville Files II: The Downside of Social Capital', *The American Prospect*, 7(26): 18–21.

Putnam, R. D. (1993) *Making Democracy Work*. Princeton, NJ: Princeton University Press.

Putnam, R. D. (2000) *Bowling Alone: The Collapse and Revival of American Community*. New York: Simon & Schuster.

Putnam, R. D. (ed.) (2002) *Democracies in Flux: The Evolution of Social Capital in Contemporary Society*. Oxford: Oxford University Press.

SUSANNE FUCHS

SOCIAL CHANGE

In contrast to the continuous and static properties of all social systems it refers to the discontinuities and dynamics of social phenomena: e.g. **demographic** change, change in social structures and cultural patterns of **societies**, **organizations**, **institutions** and **groups**. Theories of social change have two main tasks: they provide descriptions and explanations of processes of change. Descriptions of the regular patterns of the process have to denote its quantity (increasing – decreasing), its quality (cyclical – linear) and its speed (accelerating – decelerating). In order to achieve an explanation of these processes, all theories of social change face the same three constituting problems when constructing models: they have to specify the relation between **structure** and elements, designate a mover of the process and indicate a source of innovation. Theories of social change vary according to the solutions offered for description and explanation, leading to different types of sociological analysis. Historically, the emphasis in social theory has shifted from description of patterns to explanation by means of refined models, which abandon simple analogies between the growth of society and that of an organism. In addition, teleological ideas of **progress** have been replaced by the idea of multi-linear directions

of change, referring to the **reflexivity** of human **action** and the indeterminacy of its outcomes. At the beginning of the twenty-first century, change is now seen as the effect of an underlying, continuous process, fuelled by innovations deriving not only from immanent potentials but also from contextual conditions.

Nineteenth-century social theory looked to the natural **sciences** in developing the project of explaining world history by the use of universal historical **laws**. These theories are often called **evolutionary theory** due to their conceptualization of the process of social change as a unilinear path consisting of necessary stages of **development** towards a known final state. **Comte** captures this process in idealistic terms in his 'law of the three stages', asserting that the mind progresses in its development from a theological through a **metaphysical** into a **positivist** state. The way the mind thinks leads to different theoretical systems, which in turn shape the political and social systems. The process of change is fuelled by the human thirst for knowledge and drives towards a consistent **world-view**.

From a **materialist** point of view, **Marx** argues that social change stems from systemic contradictions necessarily leading to social **conflict**. Societies can be characterized according to their **mode of production** deriving from the antagonistic relationship between the productive forces and the relations of production. Continuous **technological** and organizational innovation leads to a mismatch between forces and relations of production. In a revolutionary process, the latter are abolished and new, adequate relations of production introduced, resulting in a transition from one stage of Marx's descriptive model to another.

In addition to Comte and Marx, **Spencer** focused on the increase in complexity of societies as they progress, analyzing social change as **differentiation**, understood as change from an incoherent homogeneity to a coherent heterogeneity.

553

At the beginning of the twentieth century the emphasis shifted towards actor-centred models taking into account the cultural diversities and historical differences of the societies in question. While **Pareto**, and following him Sorokin (1937) developed cyclical models of change, it was **Weber**'s linear idea of rationalization (see **rationality and rationalization**) that had the by far greatest and lasting impact. Rationalization is a universal property of all societies and cultural circles, understood as the systematization of thought and the increasing importance of **instrumental reason**. Human beings are perceived as cultural beings with the ability to generate innovative ideas and creative thoughts based on their material and idealistic context. The possible impact of new ideas and process of their routinization then depend on the societal constellation of **institutions** and **interests**, held by the carriers of the idea as well as other members of society. Since rationalization receives its specific and unique meaning from the cultural context in question, Weber uses not only a multilinear model of change, but also opts for an **empirical** and historical-comparative approach.

Drawing on this idea and the earlier tradition of evolutionary thought **Parsons** attempted a great synthesis in the mid-twentieth century known as neo-evolutionism. Societies are conceived of as stable **social systems** in dynamic environments. Change is understood as a reaction to endogenous or exogenous sources of disturbance that cannot be controlled by the integrative and adaptive mechanisms of the system, and hence leads to a state of disequilibrium. Following Spencer, Parsons models the movement towards a new equilibrium as differentiation: disturbance, differentiation, **integration** and inclusion, value generalization and specialization. The effect is a more generalized adaptive capacity and controllability of a more complex society that has reached more **autonomy** in relation to its environment. By means of this adaptive upgrading, it might also have gained an advantage over adjacent societies, escaping the fate of extinction or retreat into a niche. In this evolutionary process Parsons singles out structural inventions which are necessary but not sufficient for higher levels of a generalized adaptive capacity, which he labels as evolutionary universals (see **universalism**). The logic of general societal progress can then be spelled out along these evolutionary universals leading to a general idea of evolution in addition to the specific evolution of certain societies.

At the end of the twentieth century social theory faces a new schism with respect to conceptualizing social change: On the one hand, neo-Darwinian approaches, on the other structuration theories (see **structuration school**). Neo-Darwinian theories adapt the central model of explanation used in biological evolutionary theory, resting on the premises that not only reproduction but also mutation of elements takes place continuously on the micro-level according to a mechanism of variation. A second mechanism of selection specifies the circumstances under which a mutation **conveys** an advantage on its carrier in a given context that increases the chance of its reproduction, change being the effect. These two mechanisms are interconnected by chance: variation is random and cannot be aligned with the process of selection. W. G. Runciman (1983–97) uses both mechanisms in his actor, role and conflict centred approach. On the micro-level, practices enacting **roles** guarantee reproduction. Variations result from actors striving for **power**, thereby producing and altering social practices. The reproduction of recombined or new practices depends on the amount of power they lend **roles**. If new or altered practices are selected in the second mechanism, role-relations and thus the overall distribution of power in society is changed on the macro-level.

Luhmann (1997) also uses the Darwinian concatenation of mechanisms in a system- and communication-theoretical framework. The elements are communications, selected according to their ability to reduce complexity in a given context and their compatibility with the existing structures. Neo-Darwinian approaches refrain from detailed descriptive models due to the open-ended character of the self-organized process of the two interlinking mechanisms. The direction of change can only be given in abstract terms of the criterion of selection: an overall increase in complexity or power resources. Concrete paths of change have to be reconstructed retrospectively in an empirical and comparative-historical analysis.

Theories of structuration are interested in overcoming four dualisms which have plagued social theory: static/dynamic, synchronicity/diachronicity, action/structure and subject/object. These dualisms can be dissolved by the idea of structuration – that is, the interplay of structure and actor in action conceived of as societal **praxis**. Actors are seen as practical conscious human beings equipped with bounded rationality, producing actions in a given opportunity structure, thus reproducing the structural context. Since rationality is bounded, any action is accompanied by unintended consequences. Different models capture these insights. **Giddens**'s (1984) theory of structuration uses the concept of the duality of structure interlinked with the idea of the ongoing de-routinization of the natural character of everyday interaction to explain social change. In addition, Archer (1988) presents a cultural theory of structuration. Her concept of morphogenesis concentrates on the interface between the cultural system and socio-cultural interaction of actors in specific situations and locates processes leading towards change or stability in their interplay. The process is understood as a self-transforming cycle consisting of three temporal sequences: cultural conditioning, cultural interaction

and cultural elaboration. Finally, **Bourdieu**'s (1998) theory of praxis is an attempt to interlock a structural and cultural approach by use of a triad: structure, **habitus** and praxis. The resources available to individuals or groups, located in practical fields, coin their habitus, defined as a set of dispositions that generate actions in a strategic praxis leading to the reproduction of the structural distribution of resources. Change is initiated by the temporal disparity of field and habitus, bringing forth a praxis in which the structure is not reproduced but altered.

References and further reading

Archer, M. (1988) *Culture and Agency.* Cambridge: Cambridge University Press.

Bourdieu, P. ([1980] 1998) *Practical Reason.* Cambridge: Polity Press.

Boudon, R. ([1984] 1986) *Theories of Social Change.* Oxford: Polity Press.

Giddens, A. (1984) *The Constitution of Society.* Cambridge: Polity Press.

Luhmann, N. (1997) *Die Gesellschaft der Gesellschaft.* Frankfurt am Main: Suhrkamp.

Runciman, W. G. (1983–97) *A Treatise on Social Theory*, 3 vols. Cambridge: Cambridge University Press.

Sorokin, P. A. (1937) *Social and Cultural Dynamics*, 4 vols. New York: American Book Company.

Sztompka, P. (1993) *The Sociology of Social Change.* Oxford: Blackwell.

CHRISTIAN SCHMIDT-WELLENBURG

SOCIAL CONSTRUCTIONISM

Social constructionism is not a single perspective, but rather a range of perspectives that are usually taken to stand in opposition to **essentialism**. Against biological essentialism, it is maintained that human attributes, practices and institutions – such as **gender**, sexual relations or **marriage** – are social in origin rather than ordained by nature. Social constructionism, however, has a second, broader, meaning where no object in our social landscape – whether the economy or homosexuality – can be con-sidered to have essential, given properties prior to the social **practices** that constitute it. It was in this second sense, which now often encompasses the first, that the term first entered the sociological lexicon. In the 1960s and 1970s, the ideas associated with social constructionism were widespread within **symbolic interactionism** and **phenomenology**, perspectives that share an understanding of the social world as con-stituted by its participants through their everyday activity and making of meaning Later forms of social constructionism, those deriving from **post-structuralism** and **postmodernism**, took up some similar themes, but were also subtly different. Social constructionism has its opponents, in particular critical realists (see **realism**), who are generally most sceptical about its post-modern variants and in particular the idea that all social reality is a product of language and discourse, although they are sometimes willing to accept that gender and **sexuality** might legitimately be thought of as socially constructed (see Sayer 2000).

The first full theoretical explication of the process of social construction was **Berger and Luckman**'s *The Social Construction of Reality* (1967), which drew upon **Schutz**'s phenomenology as well as inter-actionist ideas such as W. I. Thomas's dic-tum that if a situation is defined as real, it is real in its consequences and G. H Mead's conceptualization of a reflexively constructed social **self** (see **Mead, reflexivity**). Their starting point is the tension in sociological thought between society as the product of human action and as possessing objective facticity. They tend, however, to place the emphasis on the former. Where **Durkheim** had insisted that social facts should be trea-ted as 'things' external to individual actors, Berger and Luckman argued that these things were produced by social action. The common-sense world is created through intersubjectively constituted meanings and everyday practical activities which, once they become habitual, become 'objecti-vated' as our taken-for granted reality: they are real because we define them as such and can and can, though habit and history become **institutionalized**. They do not, therefore, maintain that there is no objec-tive reality, rather that reality is *realized* through human activity, through sedimented past activity and a double realization in our daily lives – we realize, apprehend, that a social reality exists and we continuously produce this reality through recognizing and acting upon this realization. This same social reality also produces our subjectivity (see **subject and subjectivity**): in a dialectic relationship 'man [*sic*] produces reality and thereby produces himself ' (ibid.: 204).

One problem this perspective creates is an attenuated conceptualization of power as the ability to impose a definition of the sit-uation on others. Nonetheless, social con-structionist assumptions within **interactionist** and **phenomenological** sociology in the 1960s and early 1970s, did make possible certain forms of social critique. For exam-ple, there were challenges to the 'objecti-vist' view of **knowledge** as 'truth' external to its social production (Young 1971) and to the idea of deviance as an attribute of criminal or 'sick' mind rather than a product of socially constructed rules and their application to particular acts and individuals (Becker 1963).

Where social constructionism has had a lasting critical impact is in its ability to challenge biological determinism, especially in relation to gender and sexuality, where it was taken further. It produced critiques of the concept of repression in the interac-tionist work of Gagnon and Simon (1974), for whom nothing was sexual unless defined as such, and in **Foucault**'s (1978) conceptualization of sexuality as a dis-cursive apparatus. This radical anti-essenti-alism has persisted in post-structuralist and postmodernist analyses. For example, in Judith **Butler**'s (1993) analysis of the mate-rialization of sexed bodies through citational practices there are echoes of Berger and Luckman's earlier notion of realization.

Here, though, there is a different emphasis, from the embedding of language and meaning in everyday activity to the effects of **language** and especially **discourse** per se. While Berger and Luckman ask how it is 'possible that human activity should create a world of things', Foucault seeks to substitute for "things" anterior to discourse, the regular formation of objects that emerge only in discourse' (1972: 47). With the growing influence of post-modern ideas of social construction, everyday social practices have given way to the circulation of discourses external to the individual, which constitute the individual as subject. Social constructionism has thus moved from a critique of the idea of social facts and social structures external to individual to the proposition that discourses are external to and constitutive of individual subjectivity and agency.

References and further reading

Becker, H. (1963) *Outsiders*. New York: Free Press.
Berger, P. L. and Luckman, T. (1967) *The Social Construction of Reality*. London: Allen Lane.
Butler, J. (1993) *Bodies That Matter*. New York: Routledge.
Foucault, M. (1972) *The Archaeology of Knowledge*. London: Tavistock.
Foucault, M. (1978) *The History of Sexuality*, vol. 1. New York: Random House.
Gagnon, J. and Simon, W. (1974) *Sexual Conduct*. London: Hutchinson.
Sayer, A. (2000) *Realism and Social Science*. London: Sage.
Schutz, A. (1972) *The Phenomenology of the Social World*. London: Heinemann.
Young, M. (ed.) (1971) *Knowledge and Control*. London: Collier-Macmillan.

STEVI JACKSON

SOCIAL CONTROL

The view of social control generally accepted in the earlier twentieth century held that it denotes the patterned and systematic ways in which **society**, on the one hand, enforces or encourages conformity and, on the other, deals with any form of **deviance** that violates its accepted **values and norms**. The major assumption was the idea that human behaviour is: tacitly and routinely socially controlled. Sociologists tended to conceptualize a category which yoked **socialization** and social control together as one and the same. This view was that social order is maintained not only by the state – judiciary, legal systems, **police** forces and prisons – but also by public opinion, **culture**, **religion**, popular beliefs, **family**, **education**, and so on. To this extent it was assumed that social control converged around all efforts that induce the populace to behave willingly and voluntarily in ways that the 'value **consensus**' of society considers proper and appropriate.

Talcott **Parsons** (1951) made this functionalist perspective more analytically complex when he suggested that social control mechanisms are both necessary and inevitable 'secondary defences' to combat the deviance that is inevitable in all societies (see **functionalism**). Foremost among these is the utilization of sanctions which are filtered through individuals and institutions. Positive **sanctions** are used to reward desirable social behaviour, while negative sanctions in the form of punishments are aimed at deterring unwelcome social behaviour. Formal sanctions tend to be institutionally rooted, while informal sanctions are in most cases exercised through the immediate 'off the record' responses of significant others. But, according to functionalism, the backbone of any system of sanctions is 'the basic and irreducible' function of social institutions, such as the family, imbued with its sexual, reproductive, **economic** and educational functions, and the occupational structure, driven by the pervasive authority of the work ethic.

In the 1960s there emerged a more radical way of interpreting social control which was more explicitly concerned with the role of **power**. In a much used citation, Edwin Lemert (1967) turned Parsons's thinking on its head when he suggested that it is not deviance that precedes social control, but that, on the contrary, it is social control that invariably leads to deviance. Following Lemert's lead, the problem of social control in sociology now changed from how to deal with recalcitrant individuals and **groups**, to asking questions about how and why 'society' deems it necessary to socially control the behaviours of particular individuals and social groups more, and in different ways, than others. This alternative **epistemology** offered by Lemert earmarked a new challenge to the hegemony of functionalism. It was now the task of the emerging sub-discipline of the sociology of deviance, through its more complex and multi-perspectival understanding of social control, to give sociology a perspective on **conflict** that it previously lacked, resisting in the process functionalism's remorseless abstraction of human experience.

If not entirely shaking off the pervasive influence of functionalism, Lemert's (1967) own work on 'primary' and 'secondary' deviance and Becker's (1963) influential study of the socio-historical context of marijuana usage neatly encapsulated the growing influence of *labelling theory*. This offered the view that if society creates deviance, in the sense that the application of deviant labels may produce more deviance than it prevents, it follows that one cannot understand deviance without understanding social control in the form of the response of society to rule breaking behaviour. Labelling theorists suggested that it should be the role of micro social analysis to examine the social audience and its reaction to deviance since labels are not automatically imposed on all rule-breakers and some people escape labelling altogether. From this perspective, social control was seen to be coercive and repressive, its main aim being to bring under control those perceived to be troublesome.

The upshot was that a 'new' sociology of deviance came more and more to focus on the actions of powerful groups, characterized by a willingness to 'side with the underdog'. One example in Britain was Paul Willis's (1977) study of cultural reproduction and subcultural resistance in education was a case in point. Drawing on a theoretical blend which encompassed different aspects of structural and cultural **Marxism** and **symbolic interactionism**, Willis offered an understanding of the ambivalence of an education system which ostensibly prepares **working-class** boys for their subordinate and inferior adult roles in society, but in its crystallization does not appear to be particularly effective as an agency of social control.

If Willis had added class conflict to the understanding of social control, in *Policing the Crisis*, Hall *et al.* (1978) theorized the issues of '**race**' and **ethnicity** to deal with the racial motivations behind what they called the moral panic generated around the category of 'mugging' in Britain in 1972. Drawing on a Marxist theoretical amalgam inspired by **Althusser** and **Gramsci** and augmented through an adaptation of Cohen's (1972) theorization of *Folk Devils and Moral Panics*, Hall *et al.* turned their attention to the role of establishment authority figures and institutional arrangements in the assignment of social control to young unemployed black populations. In a nutshell, they argued that if the involvement in street **crime** by young black men could to some extent be attributed to their social, economic and political marginalization, their criminality was more a result of institutional social control intensified through a mass media–inspired moral panic about 'mugging'. Regardless of its originality *Policing the Crisis* was subject to widespread criticism, not only because of its dubious empirical consistency but also for being silent on the matter of the social control of women. And it was left to **feminist** critics to put the issue of **gender** and social control on the political agenda.

While in the 1970s a good deal of feminist scholarship exposed the tendency of 'malestream' sociology to overlook the institutional features of the social control of women, particularly in relation to criminality and **health** and welfare, others began to focus their attention on how the structural and everyday features of patriarchal capitalist societies combine to prevent women having the same **freedoms** as men and how this results in their lives being for the most part circumscribed by their gender (see **patriarchy**). The central organizing theme of feminist scholarship in **leisure** studies, for example, revealed both the contingency and the multi-levelled ways in which women's leisure is constrained, not only directly due to the narrow range of activity options open to them, but also because of the temporal, spatial, economic, ideological, socio-psychological factors involved, as well as the influence in this process of the categories of social **class**, 'race', ethnicity, familial and gender roles.

In the 1980s more and more materialist and structuralist thinkers were diverting their theoretical interests into **post-structuralism** and in particular the work of Foucault. If classical Marxism had emphasized a reductive economy of power related to the means of production, it was Foucault who exposed in a **dialectical** fashion the imbrication of social control in a 'microphysics of power' with the normalizing judgements that persisted through this collusion. Foucault offered an alternative view which understood power as having no substantive content and in an innovative twist he suggested it would be more profitable to analyse it as a **technology** of **knowledge**, rather than being something possessed or centralized in the state or some other institution.

In *Discipline and Punish* (1977), Foucault used a startling juxtaposition to chart the unfolding of the machinery of a new disciplinary society. And in so doing he suggested that in modern societies there has been a historical movement from brutal, overt repression and social control to rational, scientific and **bureaucratic** control of 'deviant' populations through surveillance. Foucault evoked the image of Jeremy Bentham's Panopticon in order to argue that the all-seeing 'gaze' (*le regard*) comes to serve as a metaphor for surveillance connected with governmentality in the modern state. A significant feature of panopticonism is that like Orwell's *Big Brother* surveillance, it is indiscernible: those under surveillance are always unsure whether or not they are being watched. This model of surveillance keeps those being watched subordinate by means of uncertainty and as a consequence the 'watched' act in accordance with the Panopticon, because they do not know 'when' or 'who' might be watching. Foucault argued that these social controls – the panopticonisms of everyday life found in schools, work, and leisure – micro-manage individuals more efficiently than previous carceral systems because they thwart deviant behaviour through self-actuating prohibitions reinforced by the subject's own certainty in the omnipresence of the all-seeing power of the gaze.

In more recent years, thinking about social control has floated indecisively between applications and critiques of the Panopticon model. The model suffers from severe problems of legitimacy because the power of the state and other large social institutions has diminished in significance, while the ability of individuals to say 'no' has spectacularly increased (Stehr 2001). Consequently, more recent analyses of social control have been concerned with the ways in which public perceptions of crime have become sensitized to danger and how the right to censure as a result of 'dangerization' has come to feature more extensively in crime control. Lianos and Douglas (2000: 110) consider this new way of thinking as a 'tendency to perceive and analyse the world through categories of menace', which invokes the tacit assumption that the world 'out there' is unsafe. The upshot is that social control has become managerial rather than curative. For **Bauman** (1995: 100), cool distance is of the utmost importance here since social control is not merely used to differentiate 'us' from 'them', it also allows 'us' to construct 'them' as 'the objective of aesthetic, not moral evaluation; as a matter of taste, not responsibility'. This process is what Bauman describes as *diaphorization*, which essentially marks the comfortable but anxious majority's disengagement with a commitment and responsibility for those who do not conduct themselves as 'we' do.

Bauman also argues that the configuration of economic arrangements associated with consumer capitalism may be of greater importance in explaining patterns of social control today. To put it another way, social control, like much else in **liberal democracies**, has by and large been commodified and privatized. The comfortable majority no longer live in the shadow of state tyranny; instead they create their own turmoil, or in **Baudrillard's** (1998) terminology, their own paroxysm, driven by market forces that they have no authority over, but at the same time have no final authority over them. In what Bauman (2000) calls 'liquid **modernity**', private **consumption** replaces work as the backbone of the reward system in a society which is under-patterned rather than patterned, disorganized rather than ordered. It is only the poor – the 'flawed consumers' – who are still controlled through the work ethic. In this sense, contemporary modernity redraws the boundaries between social class divisions as a relationship between those who happily consume and those who cannot, despite their want of trying. Instead of being repressively controlled, fragmented society is driven by the 'pleasure principle'. Social control is barely noticeable, except in the behaviour of the flawed consumers, whose subordinate position prevents them from participating freely in what appears to them as a dream world of consumption.

It is the poor too who continue to experience the hard edge of exclusionary and repressive surveillance. In Bauman's critical theory, expert systems play an important role in enforcing and preserving the weapons of *seduction* and *repression*. Contra Foucault, however, Bauman (1998) suggests that the repressive apparatus of the Panopticon has largely been supplemented by the seductive allure of Synopticon watching. And in our present-day society social control is by and large not about the few *who watch the many* (Panopticon), but rather *the many who watch the few* (Synopticon). For the comfortable majority, 'normalization' is thus replaced by precarization, and when the 'normal' lost its authority, the world became committed, as Bauman might say, on people revealing themselves. In this sense, social control for the most part today has become rather more like the world of the TV show *Big Brother* than Orwell's dystopia.

References and further reading

Baudrillard, J. (1998) *Paroxysm: Interviews with Philippe Petit*. London: Verso.

Bauman, Z. (1995) *Life in Fragments: Essays in Postmodern Morality*. Oxford: Blackwell.

Bauman, Z. (1998) *Work, Consumerism and the New Poor*. Buckingham: Open University Press.

Bauman, Z. (2000) *Liquid Modernity*. Cambridge: Polity Press.

Becker, H. (1963) *Outsiders: Studies in the Sociology of Deviance*. London: Free Press.

Cohen, S. (1972) *Folk Devils and Moral Panics: The Creation of the Mods and Rockers*. London: MacGibbon Kee.

Foucault, M. (1977) *Discipline and Punish: The Birth of the Prison*. Harmondsworth: Penguin.

Hall, S., Critcher, C., Jefferson, T., Clarke, J. and Roberts, B. (1978) *Policing the Crisis: Mugging, the State and Law and Order*. London: Macmillan.

Lemert, E. (1967) *Human Deviance, Social Problems and Social Control*. Englewood Cliffs, NJ: Prentice Hall.

Lianos, M. with Douglas, M. (2000) 'Dangerization and the End of Deviance: The Institutional

Environment', in D. Garland and R. Sparks (eds) *Criminology and Social Theory*. Oxford: Oxford University Press.

Parsons, T. (1951) *The Social System*. Glencoe, IL: Free Press.

Stehr, N. (2001) 'Modern Societies as Knowledge Societies', in G. Ritzer and B. Smart (eds) *Handbook of Social Theory*. London: Sage.

Sumner, C. (1997) 'Social Control: The History and Politics of a Central Concept in Anglo-American Sociology', in R. Bergalli and C. Sumner (eds) *Social Control and Political Order*. London: Sage.

Willis, P. (1977) *Learning to Labour: How Working Class Kids Get Working Class Jobs*. London: Saxon House.

TONY BLACKSHAW

SOCIAL INCLUSION AND SOCIAL EXCLUSION

'Social exclusion' has only recently gained currency in social theory. Until the 1980s the word existed on the margins of the discipline (Klanfer 1969) and the concept was mostly expressed through 'marginalization'. 'Exclusion' was understood as akin to '**culture of poverty**' and '**underclass**' (see **poverty and underclass**). Observers of Western culture at that time were shocked to see persistent poverty in the midst of affluence.

There are three occurrences in the 1990s that made the concept of 'exclusion' more popular, two political, one theoretical. First, the fifth EU research programme, 1994–98, had a (small) section of research on 'social exclusion'. Second, the Blair government in the UK installed an inter-ministerial 'Social Exclusion Unit' in 1997 to develop programmes in a new type of welfare policy aimed at 'preventing social exclusion', which replaced the traditional labour idea that effective welfare policy aims at reducing poverty and **inequality**. Third, in 1994, and Niklas **Luhmann** published an article on social exclusion which brought the concept into **systems theory**. All three events helped to popularize the terminology of 'exclusion' in the European political

and research communities and to stabilize its use. Its plausibility is connected to that of a 'horizontal' model of inequality, in which it is decisive to 'belong' at all, no matter in what position, and in which there are qualitatively different subcultures that are not necessarily ranked hierarchically. Such a model was at the same time used in the sociology of **stratification** as 'life-styles' instead of classes or strata. Its plausibility is certainly supported by the experience of **migration** where the first problem is to cross the border and then to stay 'inside'.

'Inclusion', in contrast, had a place already in **Parsons**'s **functionalist** model and is unproblematic in systems theory. 'Inclusion', in this tradition, denotes the fact of 'belonging' to a certain system and the process of becoming a member. 'Inclusion' and 'exclusion' are related in that every regime of inclusion necessarily excludes some characteristics or **persons**, but the two can follow different logics. In 'functionally differentiated' societies, inclusion in one subsystem is independent from that in another, but exclusion can still encompass all subsystems and, accordingly, be 'total'. In approaches that are more alert to relations of **power** and **domination**, 'inclusion' is seen to have aspects of repression (down to the closed 'total institution') and is more likely to be theorized as 'participation' (see **citizenship**). In the same vein, exclusion, even if possibly universal as long as there is differential inclusion, can assume different forms and degrees and is an instrument of domination inside and between social units down to the extremes of 'redundancy', 'cleansing' and genocide. Instead of a differentiation framework, exclusion is seen as a multi-dimensional and dynamic, contested process and not as a stable state, irreversibly self-reinforcing (Steinert and Pilgram 2003).

In the UK, 'social exclusion' acquired a place in research on the **welfare state** that is roughly equivalent to 'social problems'. The New Labour orientation of welfare thinking made homelessness, teenage pregnancy, truancy and neighbourhood deterioration major symptoms or instances of 'social exclusion' (see Hill *et al.* 2002). In this welfare and social work context, 'inclusion' is understood as the simple opposite of 'exclusion' and is prominently applied in work against the **discrimination** of disabilities (as in 'inclusive **education**') (see **disability**). In the USA, this usage is found in the welfare field, otherwise 'exclusion' is not a frequently used concept.

If 'social exclusion' can avoid being turned into a mere 'umbrella concept', not least by theoretical work (e.g. Byrne 1999) that adds precision and scope, it can open up and organize an important field of inquiry: the social and political **institutions** of boundary definition and maintenance, including **war** and other forms of mass destruction, exile, transportation and imprisonment. Since 'exclusion' usually means that persons are treated as exemplars of a broad category, labelling theory and more generally **social constructionism** are relevant. The study of the creation and application of categorical identifications, as developed for the ascriptions of 'criminal', 'mad' and 'handicapped', can be generalized to include nationalist, racist, sexist and classicist categorizing (see **nationalism**, **'race' and racism**, **women's movement**) and the processes, from politically and administratively organized to private, in which such categories are applied and fought against (see **classification**). The most extremely exclusionary categories define a 'sub-human' character ('barbarian', 'savage') to which human **rights** and the rules of civilized conduct do not apply (see **slavery**, **Holocaust**).

At present, a theory of 'exclusion' and the development of the concept's potential for social theory and research is very much a work in progress.

References and further reading

Byrne, D. (1999) *Social Exclusion*. Buckingham: Open University Press.

Hill, J., LeGrand, J. and Piachaud, D. (eds) (2002) *Understanding Social Exclusion*. Oxford: Oxford University Press.

Klanfer, J. (1969) *Die soziale Ausschließung: Armut in reichen Ländern*. Vienna: Europa.

Kronauer, M. (2002) *Exklusion: Die Gefährdung des Sozialen im hoch entwickelten Kapitalismus*. Frankfurt am Main: Campus.

Luhmann, N. (1994) 'Inklusion und Exklusion', in H. Berding (ed.) *Nationales Bewusstsein und kollektive Identität*. Frankfurt am Main: Suhrkamp.

Steinert, H. and Pilgram, A. (eds) (2003) *Welfare Policy from Below: Struggles against Social Exclusion in Europe*. Aldershot: Ashgate.

HEINZ STEINERT

SOCIAL JUSTICE

Social justice refers to the distribution of goods, positions and burdens in a **society**. Social justice entails an evaluative aspect and often involves a moral conception as to what is valuable in social life, as well as to what is fair in terms of social cooperation. Accordingly, just distributions are those that meet certain normative criteria established by a political **community** or by various forms of deliberation. Social justice matters at many different levels of social aggregation and is generally assumed to be crucial for the 'moral fabric' of society. Justice matters because only social systems that are regarded as just can count on social cooperation, **legitimacy** and allegiance. Justice research is divided into two factions, namely normative theories of justice and **empirical** justice approaches. Whereas the first is interested in elaborating universal normative standards which can be used to evaluate social distributions or to establish a just social order, the latter examines justice at an attitudinal, **behavioural** or **institutional** level.

As far as normative justice theories are concerned, there are many, often competing theoretical approaches and claims. Taking a historical perspective, one of the most influential **paradigms** was established by Jeremy Bentham. He formulated the utilitarian principle which approves of an **action** in so far as an action has an overall tendency to promote the greatest amount of happiness. This objective should be achieved by summing up all individual preferences and wants, and finding a means of satisfying the greatest number of them. While **utilitarianism** defends some degree of redistribution and seeks the maximization of the overall **wealth** and well-being in society, the economic libertarian position of Friedrich A. von Hayek (1960) objects to state intervention and sees unlimited *laissez-faire* **capitalism** as morally justified. **Freedom** as the individual right to pursue one's own economic interests and the right to appropriate resources are the normative maxims of this line of thought. Hayek takes the position that goods are not to be distributed but rather left to individual decision-making and the **market**. On the opposite end of the theoretical spectrum are strict egalitarians who propose that everyone should have the equal chance to satisfy needs or to develop basic capabilities (Sen 1985) (see **equality and egalitarianism**).

The milestone for thinking about justice has been John **Rawls**'s (1971) liberal theory of social justice. He supplied the philosophical rationale for a fair society based on substantive principles of justice. In order to establish these basic principles, Rawls proposes a thought experiment: people are invited to imagine themselves as founders of society, being in the 'original position' and behind a 'veil of ignorance' that enables them to take a position of impartiality. Given such a situation, it is asked which principles of allocation would be agreeable to everybody, and therefore just, from a rational point of view. Following from this, Rawls claims that two principles will be agreed upon. The first principle is that each person should have the most extensive equal basic liberties and rights. The second principle, the '**difference** principle' demands that social and economic **inequalities** are to be arranged so that they are (1) to the

greatest benefit of the least advantaged, and (2) attached to offices and positions open to all under conditions of fair equality of opportunity (Rawls 1971: 102). Ronald Dworkin (2000) has put forward a sceptical view for the Rawlsian justice theory, as he sees it as potentially subject to moral hazard. In order to overcome some of the shortcomings of Rawls's theory, he introduces the so-called 'envy-test' as the criterion of a just distribution. The theory attempts to be sensitive to unequal distribution of talents, but disregards those factors that are under the control of individuals.

Challenges to the contractualist theories of justice can be found in Michael **Walzer**'s *Spheres of Justice* (1983) which represents a communitarian account (see **communitarianism**). While Walzer maintains a normative focus, he departs from the search for overarching and universal standards of justice and claims that distributional principles differ across societal spheres. He demonstrates that it makes a difference whether we distribute medical goods, specialized **education** or set up regulations for immigration. His spheres of justice are constituted by common-sense understanding and social **meaning** attached to the social good in question. Another example of making justice more context-specific is Jon Elster's (1992) investigation into the distributional practices of intermediary institutions and organizations. Rather than formulating normative principles of justice, he demonstrates that many distributional problems are of a local nature, conditioned by specific actors, experiences and circumstances.

A large part of the empirical social justice literature deals with judgements of justice and insists that 'justice is in the eye of the beholder' or shaped by the observer's characteristics and social location. Rather than looking for consistent and defendable justice theories, these authors scrutinize the distribution and determinants of justice attitudes. Two different principles operate to produce ideas of justice: the principle of micro-justice relates to the question of 'who should get what?' and the principles of macro-justice relate to patterns of overall distribution. Findings indicate most people do object to other society members falling into **poverty** (Frohlich and Oppenheimer 1992). While there is some support for providing for basic **needs**, generally people are only modestly egalitarian favouring some degree of income inequality reduction but also stating that inequalities should be allowed and that earnings should reflect economic merits.

References and further reading

Barry, B. (1989) *Theories of Justice*. London: Harvester Wheatsheaf.

Dworkin, R. (2000) *Sovereign Virtue*. Cambridge, MA: Harvard University Press.

Elster, J. (1992) *Local Justice*. New York: Russell Sage.

Frohlich, N. and Oppenheimer, J. (1992) *Choosing Justice*. Berkeley, CA: University of California Press.

Hayek, F. von (1960) *The Constitution of Liberty*. London: Routledge & Kegan Paul.

Kymlicka, W. (1990) *Contemporary Political Philosophy*. Oxford: Clarendon.

Miller, D. (1999) *Principles of Social Justice*. Cambridge, MA: Harvard University Press.

Rawls, J. (1971) *A Theory of Justice*. Oxford: Oxford University Press.

Sen, A. (1985) *Commodities and Capabilities*. Amsterdam: North-Holland.

Walzer, M. (1983) *Spheres of Justice*. New York: Basic Books.

STEFFEN MAU

SOCIAL MOVEMENTS

Social movements have been ever present both in traditional societies and in the **modernization** of modern societies since then (**Tilly** 1978; McAdam *et al.* 2001). They continue to be a relevant political phenomenon in the context of **globalization** as anti-globalization mobilizations

have shown since the 1990s (Smith and Johnston 2002).

Apart from **Marx** and his theory of **class** struggle which explained the dynamics of the workers movement, social movements entered social theory with the rise of the 'new social movements' in the 1970s. **Touraine** (1977, 1981) was one of the first to state a particular theory of social movements in terms of a general social theory, arguing that social movements were forms of **collective** action distinct from the collective action of interest groups or parties (see **interests** and **party**). He further claimed that social movements have become the central element of the dynamics of modern societies and, therefore, have become the key to social analysis. The theory of society, he argued, had to be reformulated as a theory of social movements. Claiming that movements are substituted for **class**, that **culture** is replaced by the orientations of collective actors, that identity is created through collective action, and that **institutions** are secondary to social life, Touraine's project represented a paradigmatic shift.

However, these claims could not be upheld. Class still seems to be an important determinant of social movements – as the thesis of **middle-class** radicalism holds. Culture is much more shaped by implicit references to memory than by collective projections orienting social change, and movements more often react to social changes than guide them. **Identity** constructions are still well anchored in traditional images with an eminent political force that also shape the identity constructions of social movements. One example would be the conservative/reactionary identity elements in some green movements. Finally, institutions shape social life more than social movements; the participation of movements in the reorganization of the institutional system in modern societies points to a process in which social movements interact with institutions.

These arguments can be summarized in the thesis that movements are more shaped by social reality than social reality is shaped by social movements.

Despite its faults, however, Touraine's theory has shaped the research agenda of social movements studies since the last quarter of the twentieth century. Central issues of research have been changes in class structure, the emergence of post-**materialist** values, new political identities manifest in the idea of a 'new politics', and the decline of the traditional political institutions, be it political parties or the state as such (Eder 1993) (see **state and nation–state**).

A parallel development has been resource mobilization theory (Zald and McCarthy 1979, 1987). This approach, called the American approach, as opposed to the European approach, marks a divide in social movement theory on both sides of the Atlantic. It simply claimed that social movements are a particular kind of organization, depending on mobilizing resources like any other organization for its reproduction. This approach transformed the analysis of social movements into an analysis of social movement *organizations*. Empirically, it helped to understand the effects of formal **organization** as a characteristic of modern society on social movements.

The American variant won the battle by embedding resource mobilization theory in macro-historical contexts. It is characterized by a **paradigmatic** settlement of social movement analysis as a normal field of social research. It emphasizes the complementarity of the perspectives in empirical research.

From this **consensus** emerged the dominant and quasi-orthodox model of social movement theory today, represented by Tarrow, McAdam and Tilly (Tarrow 1998; McAdam *et al.* 2001). This orthodox version is in movement itself since the term movement has more or less disappeared from the restatement of the orthodox consensus in recent publications (McAdam *et al.* 2001).

This consensus states a three-dimensional model of **explanation** which includes: opportunities given by historical situations, modes of bonding actors in episodes of collective mobilization, and interpretative constructions of the meaning of such collective actions. Thus, we have three 'independent' variables, which interact (not specified by the explanatory model) and produce outcomes: successful or failed protest, widespread or limited, politically effective or ineffective.

The orthodox model works with a first assumption that the movements we have analyzed since the 1970s are 'rational' movements. This means that they have a clear political goal and are guided by rational motives. This assumption implicitly defines social movements as a special type of goal-oriented collective action that raises its voice in public and relies on networks that crosscut traditional links between people which are created in the course of collective action.

Such a concept, however, is to be questioned on two grounds. First, it contains an over-culturalized conception of movements which reduces movements to what they believe they are, and sees movements as the outcome of rational motives of actors. Second, it contains an over-politicized conception which sees movements as mere competitors with other collective actors for political power on the political market.

The alternative is a more sociological conception of social movements which takes seriously the label 'social'. Movements are based on social relations, in links between people. This conception is what **Marx** and **Durkheim** had already proposed in terms of a social analysis: to ground social phenomena in the structure of social relations that generate social reality such as collective action. Such structures can be described as **network** structures (Diani and McAdam 2003). Networks need, in addition, some criteria to define the boundaries of the networks, i.e. some symbolic boundary markers that separate the movement from the non-movement. Such a conception requires network analysis as the basic **methodological** strategy of social movement research.

At the turn of the millennium, the end of the post-war constellation has also affected the dynamics of social movements. A new cycle of mobilizations has begun which is no longer tied to the optimism of this period, to the ideals of justice and sustainability. Questions of **meaning**, of identity, of life issues supersede these old questions. New movements form around such issues and only weakly resemble what we have seen and experienced in the preceding thirty years.

The institutionalization of movement politics is accompanied by the rise of identity politics. Traditionally excluded from social movement research have been issues related to right-wing protest, **nationalisms**, Queer politics, lifestyle politics, music, New Age sentiments. All these now enter the terrain of social movement research, while the previously defined 'new social movements' increasingly follow the logic of symbolic action in an environment of ever increasing public **communication**. All this challenges the 'rationalist' model of new social movement theory, opening the way for a 'post-rationalist' theory of the 'new' new social movements.

The emerging new paradigm seeks regularities that emerge in the course of collective action in terms of processes that produce outcomes. Social movements are conceived as a special type of process which can be explained by regular patterns that shape the processes through which they are constituted over time. Such regular patterns are called 'mechanisms'. Situational mechanisms refer to regularities in situations that foster mobilization processes in the form of social movements. Cognitive mechanisms refer to learning processes which come up regularly in collective mobilization processes. Finally, relational mechanisms refer to those interaction processes that typically help to shape such mobilization (McAdam *et al.* 2001). In this way it becomes possible to ask why some mobilizations produce **revolutions** (which define the end of a movement), why others end up in social movements (at least for a while), and why others produce neither outcome. This emerging **paradigm** goes beyond sweeping generalizations and analytic narratives of single cases towards the explanation of regularities in mobilizations events that lead to social movements.

That social movements are endemic to **social change** still needs theoretical explanation. One option is to represent them as ingredients of a '**civil society**'. The existence of procedures of mediation and dispute settlements, for example, are empirical indicators for such an institutionalist interpretation of social movements. Social movements, on this account, can be seen as mechanisms that force civil society to enter into conflictive interaction with the state. Another option is to conceive of social movements as integral to the **public sphere**. From this perspective they appear as special carriers of political communication that sharpen social cleavages, raise new issues and provide a dynamic environment to political institutions. In any case, social movements are less than a historical collective subject and more than noise. It is the interaction of institutionalized power and self-organizing collective action which is the central mechanism of the accelerating change of modern societies.

References and further reading

Diani, M. and McAdam, D. (eds) (2003) *Social Movements and Networks: Relational Approaches to Collective Action*. Oxford: Oxford University Press.

Eder, K. (1993) *The New Politics of Class: Social Movements and Cultural Dynamics in Advanced Societies*. London: Sage.

McAdam, D., Tarrow, S. and Tilly, C. (2001) *Dynamics of Contention*. New York: Cambridge University Press.

Smelser, N. (1962) *Theory of Collective Behaviour*. New York: Free Press.

Smith, J. and Johnston, H. (eds) (2002) *Globalization and Resistance: Transnational Dimensions of Social Movements*. Lanham, MD: Rowman & Littlefield.

Tilly, C. (1978) *From Mobilization to Revolution*. Reading, MA: Addison-Wesley.

Touraine, A. (1977) *The Self-Production of Society*. Chicago: University of Chicago Press.

Touraine, A. (1981) *The Voice and the Eye*. Cambridge: Cambridge University Press.

Zald, M. N. and McCarthy, J. D. (eds) (1979) *The Dynamics of Social Movements*. Cambridge, MA: Winthrop.

Zald, M. N. and McCarthy, J. D. (eds) (1987) *Social Movements in an Organizational Society*. New Brunswick, NJ: Transaction.

KLAUS EDER

SOCIAL RELATIONS

The term 'social relations' or 'social relationships' stands generally, and somewhat unspecifically, for any relation between actors within a social **space** of some kind. The concept of *soziale Beziehung* was one of the basic sociological terms outlined by Max **Weber** in the first chapter of *Economy and Society* ([1920] 1968). Weber here defines social relationships as 'the behavior of a plurality of actors insofar as, in its meaningful content, the **action** of each takes account of the others and is oriented in these terms' (ibid.: 26). Social relations, for Weber, need in no way be normatively positive, nor need they be symmetrical in character. Thus, **friendship** and **love** are social relationships as much as enmity, hate and **conflict**. Furthermore, Weber does not assert reciprocity in a social relationship. Some relations may involve actors with different **subjective** definitions of the same situation. Weber also emphasizes that social relations can vary from the fleeting to the very strong, from the constant and continuous to the brief and interrupted, and so on.

There is no general theory of social relations in sociology, although there are several theories that bear meaningfully and fruitfully on the term. Two examples are Mark Granovetter's theory of the 'strength of weak ties' (Granovetter 1983), as well as **network** analysis in general (Wassermann and Faust 1994), and James **Coleman**'s theory of action (Coleman 1990). In general, the concept of social relations is especially thematized among theorists who begin from the premises of methodological **individualism**.

References and further reading

Coleman, J. (1990) *Foundations of Social Theory*. Cambridge, MA: Harvard University Press.

Granovetter, M. S. (1983) 'The Strength of Weak Ties: A Network Theory Revisited', *Sociological Theory*, 1: 203–33.

Wasserman, S. and Faust, K. (1994) *Social Network Analysis: Methods and Applications*. Cambridge: Cambridge University Press.

Weber, M. ([1920] 1968) 'Basic Sociological Terms', in *Economy and Society*, vol. 1. Ed. G. Roth and C. Wittich. Berkeley, CA: University of California Press.

ARMIN NASSEHI

SOCIAL REPRODUCTION

Social reproduction is linked to the concepts deployed by **Bourdieu**, notably his concepts of **habitus** and **cultural capital**. Bourdieu first discussed reproduction in a book of that title which was published in 1970 with the sub-title: 'Elements for a theory of the system of **education**' ([1970] 1977). This was an analysis of pedagogic **communication** in which the concept of cultural capital was elaborated. Within the schooling system, **power**, **social control** and **domination** are all concealed or 'misrecognized'. The capacity of institutionalized schooling to exercise power is dependent on its ability to delude participants into the belief that the values and **knowledge** transmitted are of absolute validity, so that parents and pupils acquiesce in accepting the social subordination which is the consequence of failing to perform adequately in authorized assessment situations. So, far from providing equal opportunities, Bourdieu argued that the schooling system was a social mechanism for **legitimizing** the reproduction of the hierarchical status quo. It becomes necessary, therefore, to analyze the extent to which educational institutions transmit 'arbitrary' knowledge and to analyze the ways in which their **status** as institutions is differentially constructed so as to perpetuate social distinctions. A corollary of Bourdieu's conviction that the educational process was one of 'selecting the elect' was that he saw the practice of pedagogy as one of **socialization** in which successful students were initiated into the values of the dominant. The hidden agenda of pedagogy was to secure a homology between students and institutions. The real purpose of the process was to safeguard the reproduction of exclusive and distinct institutions.

In 1970, Bourdieu gave an important paper at the Durham conference of the British Sociological Association which was subsequently published as 'Cultural Reproduction and Social Reproduction' (1973). It was here that it became explicit that social reproduction was not simply concerned with the ways in which the educational system perpetuated social disadvantage. The relationship between social and cultural reproduction is partly a question of the relationship between inherited habitus and acquired cultural capital, and the educational system is only one socially and historically contingent mechanism for transmitting values inter-generationally or between social groups. The recognition that cultural value is not absolute but contingent or subject to movement on the stock exchange or the cultural market meant that Bourdieu was able to move towards the analysis of competing cultural values within any society. His researches were no longer contained within the field of the sociology of education but were able to consider the implications for social reproduction of all

kinds of cultural competition within **multicultural** societies. One outcome of this change was the work which led to the publication of *Distinction* in 1979 ([1979] 1986). There Bourdieu was able to analyze the complex **network** of allegiances and affiliations whereby cultural choices in the widest sense such as between wine or beer drinking and between support for golf, horse-racing, soccer or rugby, and between aesthetic and gastronomic tastes, were all arbitrary practices which consolidated differences and ensured the social reproduction of these differences.

This was not a systemic analysis of static relationships but rather an analysis of the dynamic possibilities which are available to all to transform their habitus by the strategic deployment of cultural capital. Early in the 1970s, Bourdieu developed the notion of 'strategies of reconversion'. We transfer the cultural capital which we acquire in one field in order to invest in securing power in another field. The observation of social reproduction is not the preserve of the sociologist. Rather, an implicit recognition of the mechanisms of reproduction guides the actions which we all take in contriving to become socially mobile. It followed that Bourdieu sought to analyze the processes of reconversion which enabled individuals to achieve authority within academic institutions (*homo academicus*) and in the sphere of politics and **state** administrative **authority** (*state nobility*).

In a wider context, Bourdieu's theory of social reproduction was a way of accounting for the continuing manifestations of **aristocratic class** domination in French society. The dominant were always in a position to change the rules of the game and to ensure that their class-specific values appeared to have absolute validity. Bourdieu pursued this tacit ratification of value in relation to the claims of 'pure **art**' and he opposed attempts to exempt the study of art and artistic values from sociological scrutiny. Similarly, Bourdieu's theory enabled him to analyze the phenomena of colonialism and **post-colonialism**, seeking to expose the extent to which the particular values of occupying powers masquerade as universal values as a mechanism for reproducing social and political control.

References and further reading

Bourdieu, P. with Passeron, J.-C. ([1970] 1977) *Reproduction in Education, Society and Culture*. London: Sage.

Bourdieu, P. (1973) 'Cultural Reproduction and Social Reproduction', in R. Brown (ed.) *Knowledge, Education, and Cultural Change*. London: Tavistock.

Bourdieu, P. ([1979] 1986) *Distinction: A Social Critique of the Judgement of Taste*. London: Routledge & Kegan Paul.

Bourdieu, P. ([1984] 1988) *Homo Academicus*. Cambridge: Polity.

Bourdieu, P. ([1989] 1996) *The State Nobility*. Cambridge: Polity.

Bourdieu, P. (1992) *Les Règles de l'art: Genèse et structure du champ littéraire*. Paris: Seuil.

Jenkins, R. (2000) 'Pierre Bourdieu and the Reproduction of Determinism', in D. M. Robbins (ed.) *Pierre Bourdieu*, vol. 2. London: Sage.

DEREK ROBBINS

SOCIAL STRUCTURE

See: structure

SOCIAL STUDIES OF SCIENCE

It has been common to assume that the social institution of **science** has quite particular characteristics. Science, it has often been assumed, is carried out by clearly distinct **communities** of specialists who, through the use of scientific methods, are able to make claims to objective **knowledge** concerning a particular domain. While there has been much debate among social scientists about whether it is possible to establish a science of **society**, there has generally been comparatively less doubt that the natural sciences yield objective facts about **nature**.

Social studies of science, as they have developed since the 1970s, challenge this received view in different ways. The term 'social studies of science', as distinct from the more general sociology and philosophy of science, is particularly associated with the work of Bruno **Latour** among others. In this approach, first, contributors question the idea that there is any straightforward unity to science. The various sciences are marked by considerable heterogeneity, whether in terms of technical practice, theoretical **language**, institutional forms, or ontology. Second, social studies of science question the idea that there is a scientific method of the kind once imagined by **philosophers**, and instead direct empirical attention towards the material and literary **culture** of scientific laboratories. Sociologists of science here explore the ways in which scientific research itself involves complex forms of technical practice. The technical practice of laboratory science does not simply produce observational data or test scientific theories but produces a whole series of artefacts and effects, which may be difficult to interpret or connect to anything produced in other laboratories or in the field. Third, the idea that a clear distinction can be made between science, conceived as an **objective** body of knowledge, and lay knowledge and understanding, is increasingly questioned. Studies have pointed to the ways in which non-scientists (such as farmers, industrial workers, or patients with particular diseases) may possess forms of knowledge that may both complement and problematize orthodox forms of science.

In the 1980s and 1990s social studies of science developed in a quite distinct direction from the broader discipline of sociology. While some sociologists of science generated very general accounts of the production and function of scientific knowledge in society, dominant approaches to the social study of science took the form of detailed case studies of particular laboratories, controversies or scientific fields. In so far as it was informed by mainstream sociology, research in social studies of science has tended to be more influenced by micro-sociological traditions such as **symbolic interactionism**, **phenomenology** and **ethnomethodology**. At the same time, there is a close relation between debates in the social studies of science and arguments in **post-structuralist** and **feminist theory** concerning, among other issues, the construction of nature and the politics of medical knowledge (see **medicalization**). The work of **Foucault** and Haraway, in particular, established connections between feminist theory and social studies of science.

In recent years research in social studies of science has increasingly come to intersect with a wider range of interests in social theory. First, sociologists of science have begun to apply many of the tools developed in studies of the natural sciences, to the study of fields of expertise such as **economics**, **law** and accountancy. In this way, social studies of science promise to make a significant contribution to rethinking economic sociology and socio-legal studies. Second, particularly following the publication of Ulrich **Beck**'s *World Risk Society* (1999), there has been a broad convergence of interests of sociologists of science and social theorists in the changing status of scientific knowledge, the importance of **risk** and uncertainty, and in the relation between experts and non-experts. For example, recent research has focused on the ways in which both experts and non-experts establish public claims to knowledge concerning, for example, politically controversial matters such as genetic modification or global warming. In this context, theoretical and empirical research in social studies of science is increasingly relevant to the study of **politics** and **government**. Third, the development of new bio and media technologies raises questions about the relation between the biological and the

social sciences and the emergence of new forms of intellectual property and new economies of knowledge production.

References and further reading

Beck, U. (1999) *World Risk Society*. Cambridge: Polity.

Haraway, D. (1992) *Primate Vision: Gender, Race and Nature in the World of Modern Sciences*. London: Verso.

Knorr-Cetina, K. (1999) *Epistemic Cultures: How the Sciences Make Knowledge*. Cambridge, MA: Harvard University Press.

Latour, B. (1987) *Science in Action*. Milton Keynes: Open University Press.

Martin, E. (1994) *Flexible Bodies: The Role of Immunity in American Culture from the Days of Polio to the Age of AIDS*. Boston: Beacon.

Nowotny, H., Scott, P. and Gibbons, M. (2001) *Re-thinking Science: Knowledge and the Public in an Age of Uncertainty*. Cambridge: Polity.

Pickering, A. (1995) *The Mangle of Practice*. Chicago: University of Chicago Press.

Shapin, S. and Schaffer, S. (1985) *Leviathan and the Air-Pump: Hobbes, Boyle and the Experimental Life*. Princeton, NJ: Princeton University Press.

ANDREW BARRY

SOCIAL SYSTEM

Concepts of 'social systems' or of 'the social system', are common in sociology, although no consensus exists over the precise reference of these terms. In common-sense language, a social system evokes the idea of any persistent patterning of social relations across 'time-space' and with stable structures for reproducing practices. Compare here Anthony **Giddens**'s analysis in Giddens (1984). Such common-sense notions can be found also in social theories that are not associated with any definite **systems theory**. For example, James **Coleman**, one of the most stringent advocates of methodological **individualism**, emphasizes his interest not primarily in the explanation of individual behavior but in the 'explanation of the behavior of social systems' (Coleman 1990: 2).

The idea of a social system has at least two general implications. On the one hand, 'system' stands for the *context* in which individual behavior can be observed and to some extent meaningfully predicted. On the other hand, 'system' stands for the emerging *result* of **interactions** between individual **actions** and individual **actors**. The common-sense reference of the notion thus indicates a level of order that cannot be understood purely in terms of individual actions taken as isolated phenomena. The idea of a social system stands generally in use for different meso- or macro-levels (see **micro-, meso-** and **macro-levels**) of analysis – levels which, in Coleman's words, 'may be as small as a dyad or as large as a society or even a world system' (Coleman 1990: 2).

A more specific and technical use of the concept appears in the framework of systems theoretical approaches in sociology. Here the concept of a social system is adapted from general systems theory under the influence of **cybernetics** and biological and mathematical theories of systemic dynamics. The best-known concept of social systems derives from Talcott **Parsons**'s sociology (1977). Here the social system means the integrating sub-system of the general action system, where the social system has the function of coordinating interactions between actors or actions. The social system presupposes the cooperation of four sub-systems in Parsons's AGIL scheme: 'adaptation', 'goal attainment', 'integration' and 'latency', or pattern maintenance. Each of these subsystems fulfils one particular function, conceived as necessary for the maintenance of the structure of the system as a whole. This conception of functions is explicitly conceptualized by Parsons as an analytical scheme, serving to guide the sociologist's empirical observations.

Parsons employs cybernetics and general systems theory in his description of various relationships between different functions. Social systems in this account are units in which the four functions are related by mutual interaction, by interchange processes, and by interchanging parameters that adapt and adjust to dysfunctions in any one of the four sub-systems. The *systemic* aspect of the social system consists in its way of stabilizing itself through internal interactions and control hierarchies. The *social* aspect of the social system consists in its integration of the elements of actions and actors.

Parsons's conception of social systems was once a dominant paradigm in sociology. Since the late 1960s, however, it has come under fire for its over-estimation of structure maintenance and for its inflexible assumptions about 'functional prerequisites'. A more recent approach is that of Niklas **Luhmann**. Like Parsons, Luhmann draws on general systems theory but shifts the emphasis away from conditions of stability towards a focus more on the dynamics of emerging orders. Luhmann also does not regard social systems purely as analytical categories designed to arrange miscellaneous empirical observations in various ways. Instead, Luhmann begins with one basic strong ontological assertion: 'There *are* systems' (Luhmann [1984] 1995: 12). However, this strong **ontological** assumption does not lead him to presuppose a set of pre-operational and pre-requisite functions. Rather, Luhmann conceptualizes social systems as operating units that themselves *produce* the relation between problems and solutions with which a system must cope (ibid.: 53). Whereas older systems theories regarded the frame of references to problems as essentially external, Luhmann emphasizes that social systems produce both problems *and* compatible functional solutions to these problems by drawing on their own resources. Social systems consist of a network of communications, which emerge in time, from one event to another. Social systems in this sense have the attribute of being *autopoietic* or self-generating, and *operationally closed*, or self-referential. Self-reference does not mean that such systems are unable to

571

experience contact with their environments at all, but only that the only mode in which contact with an environment is possible is through their own operation. Thus, in general, unlike earlier theories of social systems, Luhmann here focuses especially on the dynamic and operational aspects of the system's reproduction, rather than on functionally presumed structures.

References and further reading

Coleman, J. (1990) *Foundations of Social Theory*. Cambridge: Belknap.

Giddens, A. (1984) *The Constitution of Society*. Cambridge: Polity.

Luhmann, N. ([1984] 1995) *Social Systems*. Stanford, CA: Stanford University Press.

Parsons, T. (1977) *Social Systems and the Evolution of Action Theory*. New York: Free Press.

ARMIN NASSEHI

SOCIALISM

Socialism developed, in the first half of the nineteenth century, from the double experience of the Industrial Revolution and the French Revolution (Hobsbawm 1962). Given the embattled history of the concept, socialism remains notoriously difficult to define. However, it is possible to distinguish two core dimensions on the basis of its double origin. On the one hand, socialism represented a reaction to new forms of **poverty** and social dislocation resulting from early **industrialization** and the emergence of a growing **working class**. Against the background of this experience, central socialist demands were formulated in the nineteenth century, reaching from the socialization of the means of production to the abolition of wage labour (see **work**) and the establishment of a classless society. These demands were fuelled by the ideal of a **community** in which preference would be given to **cooperation** over competition. On the other

hand, they were very much located within the political horizon of the French democratic **revolution** of 1789–94. If, in the first instance, the French Revolution opened up the democratic horizon of liberty (see **freedom**), **equality** and **solidarity**, socialism can be understood as the subsequent attempt at deepening the social dimension of these categories.

The aim to extend political **emancipation** towards full social emancipation is best represented by François Noël Babeuf in the eighteenth century who violently argued for 'real', social and economic equality. His Jacobin emphasis on the total transformation of society by way of revolutionary insurrection – his own 'conspiracy of the equals' failed and he was executed – became one of the sources of **communism** (see **egalitarianism**). While the Babouvian model of conspirational insurrection lived on in many secret societies of the nineteenth century, a diverse group of early socialists, developed non-revolutionary models of social transformation. Claude-Henri de Saint-Simon welcomed the effects of industrialization, advocating the rule of an enlightened **elite** of scientists and 'industrialists' who would replace rule over men by the administration of things. A rather different vision of socialist life was advocated by Charles Fourier who proposed small and harmoniously run communities, so-called *phalansteries*, based on agriculture and organized in egalitarian fashion. Pierre-Joseph Proudhon, one of the progenitors of **anarchism**, proposed what he called 'mutualism': a system of mutual exchange of goods between individual producers that would sideline the **state** or any other centralized regime. In Britain, Robert Owen advocated cooperative communities but also tried to organize a national union of the working class. The term 'socialism' first appeared in an Owenite journal in 1827, and in the early 1830s circulated on the continent among the followers of Saint-Simon.

These early socialists were subsumed by **Marx** and Engels under the heading of 'utopian socialism', against which Marx and Engels propounded their own version of 'scientific socialism' (see **utopia**). Among other things, they were critical of the early socialists' preference for small-scale communal alternatives to **capitalism**. Marx and Engels, on the other hand, reverted to the revolutionary model as they assumed that the new order could only be established via a complete break with the old one. Here one encounters the main crux of the socialist tradition, for the historical problem was not only how to envisage a future socialist society but also how to conceptualize the passage between the present and the future society. The early socialists firmly believed in the intrinsic persuasiveness of their models whose establishment would not necessarily imply the seizure of political **power**. In their vision, the passage towards socialism could be forged by piecemeal engineering and the exemplary establishment of model communities without any wider engagement in politics. The revolutionary solution, on the other side, saw the movement as requiring some form of political **organization**. This political tendency in **Marxism**, however, ran counter to its 'scientific' tendency. From Marxism's 'scientific' point of view – an amalgamation of classical economics and **Hegelianism** – socialism would be the necessary point of culmination of capitalist **development**. What results is a peculiar tension within Marxist thought. If on the one hand, the passage towards socialism (and eventually communism) is to be forged by political action, on the other, it is determined by economic laws leading inevitably to the simplification of the social structure, pauperization, and eventually **revolution**.

This tension between a conception of socialism as the necessary outcome of capitalist development and of socialism as the contingent outcome of political struggle – that is between an economic and a political

tendency – can be detected in the later history of Marxism. At the time of the Second International (founded in 1889), the tendency to economistic **determinism** had established dominance over Marxist thought. This 'orthodox' position, set up by Karl Kautsky and Giorgi Plekhanov, was characterized by the belief in an imminent breakdown of capitalism resulting from the necessary unfolding of its internal contradictions. What may have had some plausibility against the background of the protracted economic **crisis** in the second half of the nineteenth century, turned out to be rather premature when a new phase of capitalist consolidation set in. 'Orthodoxy' came under attack from Eduard Bernstein and other so-called 'revisionists' who urged the German Social Democrats to abandon economic fatalism and to acknowledge the presuppositions of their own practice, namely, that socialism had to be achieved gradually and by non-revolutionary means. In Britain, where Marxism did not take hold until the twentieth century, the latter view was always dominant. It is encapsulated in the ideas of the Fabian Society, founded in 1884. The Fabians, constituting what today would be called a lobbying group, advocated a form of 'administrative socialism', reminiscent of earlier Saint-Simonian ideas. The naming of Fabianism after the Roman general, Fabius Cunctator, who is famous for his non-confrontational 'delaying' and waiting tactics against Hannibal, makes Fabianism a synonym for gradualism.

At the beginning of the twentieth century, the exact opposite to gradualism emerged with French syndicalism (see **trade unions**). In the Charter of Amiens of 1905, the French trade unions declared the general strike to be the only feasible instrument of revolution. According to Georges Sorel, the goal of the general strike was to bring about total social transformation through a single political action by the united working class. While for proponents of gradualism and reformism, a socialist society would result from a multitude of small political steps and a series of social reforms, for syndicalism, the passage towards socialism would lead through the eye of a needle: the general strike. After the Russian Revolution of 1917 and the end of World War I, the difference between reformist and revolutionary strategies – which would be deconstructed only by **Gramsci** in the 1920s – came to correspond to the split between socialist and communist parties (announced by the earlier split between Mensheviks and Bolsheviks in Russia. After World War II, while in Eastern Europe the regimes of 'actually existing socialism' were established, social democracy in Western Europe embarked on the establishment of the **welfare state**. Leaving behind many tenets of traditional socialism, such as the propagation of state-ownership of the means of production, social democrats ceased thinking of socialism as a goal external to capitalism. The troubling question as to the nature of the passage to socialism lost some of its importance in the West. Simultaneously, however, this question assumed new meaning in other areas of the world as de-**colonization** gathered pace. 'Maoism' became the leading **ideology** of many national liberation movements. The idea of an 'Arab Socialism' was developed by the Egyptian statesman, Gamal Abdel-Nasser. 'African Socialism' was proposed as a concept by the poet and statesman Léopold-Sédar Senghor of Senegal, who sought to articulate socialist ideas with what he considered indigenous community values of pre-colonial Africa.

In Western European countries after World War II, socialism entered a long phase of transformation when in the 1950s and 1960s an independent 'nouvelle gauche' or New Left emerged as a reaction to changing political and social circumstances. If it was to adjust to the new situation, socialism had to take into account the

pluralization of social **identities** and not restrict its scope to questions of **class**. On the political scene, the so-called New Social Movements of the 1970s and the 1980s demonstrated the need for calling into question forms of social subordination not reducible to economic **inequality**, such as questions related to issues of **peace** and **ecology**, or '**race**', **ethnicity**, **gender**, and **sexuality**. On a theoretical level, the new situation was taken into account by theorists such as **Touraine** or Ernesto Laclau and Chantal Mouffe (1985) who proposed a socialist strategy of extending the democratic horizon of freedom and equality in directions other than the 'economic' one. It thus seems that today socialist thought, after having concentrated for a long time on questions related to class, returns to the democratic revolution as one of its early sources.

References and further reading

Bauman, Z. (1976) *Socialism: The Active Utopia*. London: George Allen & Unwin.

Cole, G. D. H. (1953–60) *A History of Socialist Thought*, 5 vols. London: Macmillan.

Crick, B. (1987) *Socialism*. Milton Keynes: Open University Press.

Hobsbawm, E. (1962) *The Age of Revolution*. London: Weidenfeld & Nicolson.

Laclau, E. and Mouffe, C. (1985) *Hegemony and Socialist Strategy: Towards a Radical Democratic Politics*. London: Verso.

Sassoon, D. (1996) *One Hundred Years of Socialism*. London: I. B. Tauris.

Senghor, L.-S. (1959) *African Socialism*. New York: American Society of African Culture.

OLIVER MARCHART

SOCIALIZATION

Socialization can be defined as the transmission of the **culture** of a given society from one generation to the next or as processes through which we learn to be competent members of **society**. It may seem obvious that we each must acquire the **language** and culture of the particular society into which we have been born in order to be able to function within it and, conversely, that any form of social life would be impossible if members of society did not come to share taken-for-granted assumptions about ways of engaging in routine social activity and at least some basic **values**. Yet the concept of socialization has become contested and has, since the 1970s, become less widely used. It fell into disrepute in part because of explicit **critiques** of the way it was conventionally deployed by sociologists and psychologists and also because of the rise of new perspectives, especially those deriving from **post-structuralism**, **postmodernism** and **psychoanalysis** within which it was simply an alien concept.

Until the 1960s socialization was generally conceptualized as the internalization of norms and values through early experiences within families (primary socialization) and later in terms of the wider social and institutional settings in which we live (secondary socialization). One of the most consistently theorized versions of this perspective was that of Talcott **Parsons**, for whom socialization was necessary to maintain social integration (Parsons 1951; Parsons and Bales 1956). Parsons stressed the 'plasticity' of the children: their basic personality structure became established through early socialization within **families**. Children then gradually internalized the 'value orientations' of society in general and those appropriate to specific social statuses and also the social expectations associated with the roles they were destined to play in society (see **status**; **role**). Ascribed roles – roles an individual is born to play, such as **gender** 'sex roles' – were learnt early in life as part of basic personality structure while achieved roles, as the term suggests, were learnt later, even in adulthood in the case of occupational roles.

Socialization theory in general, however, tended to concentrate on children and envisaged them as blank slates on which

society inscribes its norms and values or empty vessels into which norms and values are poured. Social norms thus came to be seen as constituting human behaviour rather than merely regulating it. One of first and most influential critiques of this conventional view was provided by Dennis Wrong (1961). He suggested that socialization might be seen as a mean by which sociologists had answered the 'Hobbesian question' of how social order is possible and the '**Marxist** question' of how, in complex societies, conflict between social groups is regulated and contained. This answer, he maintained, had produced 'an over-socialized view of man [*sic*]... and an over-integrated view of society' (Wrong 1961: 184). He suggested that we should distinguish between socialization as the transmission of a particular society's culture and as the process whereby we become fully human through **interaction** with others. If we confuse the two we arrive at an over-socialized, disembodied, conformist view of human nature. Drawing on **Freud**, Wrong suggests that we may be social creatures but we are never entirely socialized.

Parsons had used Freud to explain mechanisms of socialization but had assumed that these processes, through the creation of a conformist super-ego, tamed anti-social impulses (see **psychoanalysis**). Wrong's interpretation of Freud, however, emphasizes embodied drives and internal conflicts and antagonisms that render us resistant to socialization. Wrong's interpretation is more in keeping with later variants of psychoanalysis, which were, from the 1980s, to provide an influential alternative to socialization theory among some sociologists. These more recent approaches, influenced by the French post-structuralist psychoanalyst Jacques **Lacan**, emphasized the shifting effects of language in shaping our entry into culture and the fractured, precarious character of **subjectivity**, which was always vulnerable to the unsettling effects of the **unconscious**.

575

This is an account of how we become social, how we enter into culture and culture constitutes us but it leaves little room for **agency** except through unpredictable, disruptive eruptions of the unconscious.

Liz Stanley and Sue Wise ([1983] 1993) provide an alternative critique that does account for agency. Drawing upon interactionist and phenomenological approaches they contest 'the socialization model' from a feminist perspective (see **symbolic interactionism**; **phenomenology**). They point out that the socialization model cannot explain those of us who do not conform to 'gender roles'; it does not allow for different ways of being men or women, for agency and reflexivity in the ways gender is lived and continually renegotiated. Importantly they challenge the dualistic and often contradictory opposition between 'the individual' and 'society' whereby socialization presupposes internal psychological mechanisms of internalization but at the same time *what* is internalized is entirely determined by a society existing separately from the individual. Through the work of G. H. **Mead** and Alfred **Schutz** they suggest instead that we become social – able to relate to and co-operate with others – through the acquisition of a social **self** reflexively constructed through everyday action and interaction with others. Rather than being socialized into pre-determined values and conduct, self and social milieu are interdependent, both constructed through interaction. Since this is an ongoing process, it follows that selves are not fixed but subtly evolve and change in different contexts.

Some theorists developing post-structuralist approaches made similar criticisms, particularly of the individual-society dualism and of the deterministic mechanistic processes envisaged by conventional socialization theorists (Henriques *et al.* 1984; Davies 1989). For post-structuralists we are not pre-existing individuals moulded by society, but 'subjects' constituted through and subject to the social (see **subject and subjectivity**). 'Subjectivity' is entirely socially constituted, but understood as a fluid and dynamic product of our locations within shifting discourses or discursive practices rather than a coherent individual personality (see **discourse**). Where agency is admitted, it is generally through an *ad hoc* formulation whereby we are assumed to take up positions or locate ourselves within discourses (Hollway 1984; Davies 1989). With the rise of **postmodernism** subjectivity came to be seen as even more fragmentary and decentred, leaving even less scope for agency. Subjectivity is seen as social but 'socialization' has become irrelevant – there is no unified subject to be socialized and no coherent social order for her to be socialized into. Thus, Wrong's 'Hobbesian question' has been bypassed and the 'Marxist question' is no longer pertinent since pre-given social **groups** and lines of social cleavage can no longer be presupposed in a fluid postmodern social landscape (see **postmodernism and postmodernity**).

Many post-structuralists and postmodernists do not ask how our subjectivity comes to be constituted in the first place, those who do so often employ variants of psychoanalysis, although others treat psychoanalysis with scepticism. There is one problem, however, common to much psychoanalytic, post-structuralist and postmodern theorizing: it effects the disappearance of the everyday social contexts in which we come to be social and in which our social being is enacted. This is not true of all – and particularly not for those who use post-structuralism in empirical research. For example, Bronwyn Davies's study of pre-school children in Australia provides a nuanced and grounded account of the ways in which very young children begin to create a sense of gendered subjectivity. However, in achieving this, she supplements her post-structuralism with interactionist and phenomenological insights.

While the critique of 'over-socialization' is well founded, it still seems necessary to consider how we come to be competent social beings at all. We have long had the conceptual tools to do so, for example through the phenomenological and inter-actionist **traditions** favoured by Stanley and Wise. These posit a fundamentally social account of human self-hood achieved through **everyday** practical activity or interaction entailing constant reflexive dia-logue between self and others. Since the 1990s these accounts have begun to be uti-lized in conjunction with post-structuralism in re-thinking the social self as both narra-tive construction and lived experience (see Holstein and Gubrium 2000). Such approaches may enable us to conceptualize the process of becoming social without conceding either to the socialization para-digm or to a vision of subjectivity so frag-mentary and unstable it is barely socially meaningful at all. Whether the term 'socia-lization' itself can ever be reclaimed from its negative connotations remains to be seen – and, after more than four decades of critique, some twenty-first-century sociol-ogists continue to use it as if it had never been problematized.

References and further reading

Davies, B. (1989) *Frogs and Snails and Feminist Tales*. Sydney: Allen & Unwin.
Henriques, J., Hollway, W., Urwin, C., Venn, C. and Walkerdine, V. (1984) *Changing the Subject*. London: Methuen.
Hollway, W. (1984) 'Gender Difference and the Production of Subjectivity', in J. Henriques *et al.*, *Changing the Subject*. London: Methuen.
Holstein, J. and Gubrium, J. (2000) *The Self We Live By*. Oxford: Oxford University Press.
Parsons, T. (1951) *The Social System*. London: Routledge & Kegan Paul.
Parsons, T. and Bales, R. (1956) *Family: Sociali-zation and Interaction Process*. London: Rou-tledge and Kegan Paul.
Stanley, L. and Wise, S. ([1983] 1993) *Breaking Out/Breaking Out Again*. London: Routledge.
Wrong, D. (1961) 'The Over-Socialized Con-ception of Man in Modern Sociology', *American Sociological Review*, 26(2): 183–93.

STEVI JACKSON

SOCIETY

'Society' is the most basic concept of sociology and social theory, yet its definition is far from self-evident. 'A society' denotes a macrological composite of social order. The term is employed for historical dis-tinctions, as when we speak of 'modern', 'pre-modern', 'traditional' or 'archaic' socie-ties; or we use it for regional or national distinctions, as with 'American society', 'German society', or 'European society'. Or we refer to particular structures or features, as with 'industrial society', 'rural society', '**class** society', or perhaps one singular 'world society'. There are also diagnostic uses of the term, as with '**risk society**', '**knowledge** society', or the '**network** society', and the like.

The idea of society shares a fate common to other basic concepts in the social sciences and humanities, concepts that are frequently used without general agreement as to their meaning. **Education**, for instance, is a basic concept in pedagogy, but is also one of the most unclear words in this discipline. Something similar can be said about '**politics**' or 'the **state**' in political science, or about '**language**' in linguistics, or 'consciousness' in psychology, or 'culture' in cultural studies.

An attempt to define society in the most general terms suggests an idea of the largest conceivable social entity, an idea of the whole or **totality** that is more than the sum of its parts. The idea has a long tradition and is akin to the Aristotelian *koinonía poli-tiké*: the idea of a more general unit under which all parts are subsumed. Today most discourse about society involves some reference to a general level of order.

Society as a historical concept

Although a general word for social order has its roots in Greek philosophy, the idea of a social order that is open to *design* or intentional agency in some way emerges only in the post-medieval and early modern period. Here it poses a new problem: that of reconciling the idea of individual freedom

577

with the necessity of social order. All early modern political philosophers from Hobbes and Spinoza to Locke, Rousseau, Montesquieu and **Kant** sought for ways of mediating between individual aspirations and social limitations on freedom. The idea of a social world as both limiting and resulting from the experience of freedom was itself a product of more differentiated social relations with increasingly self-referential social practices. In the course of the emergence of **modern** forms of social relations, new possibilities of action and new necessities for decision making processes begin to arise. In the gradually differing spheres of politics, economics, **science**, as well as in **arts**, education and legislation, degrees of **freedom** increase in terms of new institutions and decision making processes; and these new spaces of agency in turn operated in new contexts of **contingency** that led to a search for new or particular reasons for decisions in courses of action. The historical experience of a designable world was not an academic idea, but an everyday experience involving new kinds of practical exigency.

The modern idea of living in a society, rather than solely in a world with well-ordered structures, immutable evidences, and routines beyond criticism, has two sources. The first source is the experience of handling individual interests in the horizon of socially negotiable **values and norms**. The second is the experience of different parts or 'spheres' of society *de-coupling* from one another, not in the sense of becoming independent from each other but in the sense of developing their own distinct routines and semantics of practice.

The modern idea of society can be observed in one its most representative forms in G. W. F. Hegel's *Philosophy of Right* (see **Hegelianism and neo-Hegelianism**). Here Hegel speaks of society (*Gesellschaft*) as a basic frame of reference which is able to reconcile subjective aspirations with the objective needs of a reasonable shape of

order. At the centre of his diagnosis is the differentiation or 'diremption' of the family, **civil society** and **state**. What was formerly called *societas civilis* Hegel now divides into two basic spheres: *civil society*, or ('*bürgerliche Gesellschaft*'), on the one hand, comprising economic, cultural, scientific and religious dimensions; and the *state*, on the other hand, comprising the political dimension. In civil society, individuals are private persons with individual interests and the need to live their own lives. But the state as the 'actuality of the ethical idea' (Hegel ([1821] 1967): para. 257) is the point of unification which is able both to command subordination from its citizens and to present this subordination as freedom. With this figure of thought Hegel breaks with Kant's atomism of the individual in favour of the ethical place of the individual within the social 'substance', which becomes conceptualized as the most general and most rational standpoint.

Hegel's *Philosophy of Right* is one of the first philosophies of society in the narrow sense. His philosophy rejects individualistic ideas in favour of a dialectical mediation of particularity and universality. It addresses itself to the problem of the coordination of individual actions and decisions and the problem of the integration of different fields within a single encompassing order. Hegel reflects on a world with basic differences: *temporal* historical differences between past and present; *functional* differences between fields or spheres of action; and *social* differences between individuals willing to subordinate themselves to a ruling power under the free acceptance of the necessity of a larger ethical totality. This is the starting-point for all subsequent sociological thinking about society as a general area of social order. The vision of mediation between 'subjective spirit' (denoting individuals and their separate particularistic interests) and 'objective spirit' (denoting laws, morality and ethical life) became known in later sociology by the name of normative **integration**. The basic Hegelian idea of objective spirit as the determining element of society continues in **Durkheim**'s *conscience collective* and in **Parsons**'s *societal community*, as well as in **Habermas**'s idea of the 'rational identity' of a 'complex society'.

Sociological approaches

As against grand historical philosophies of society such as Hegel's, more specifically sociologically conceptions of society have been associated with ideas of **differentiation**. For Durkheim and **Weber**, the idea of society raises the question of how unity can be reconciled with the observation of decoupling and differentiation. Durkheim's diagnosis of **modernity** addresses the problem of how a society that lacks the premodern security of a shared knowledge about what keeps the world together can achieve stable structures. Durkheim looks for a functional equivalent for archaic *conscience collective*. He finds this in **morality**, which is able to represent values and norms in such a way that radical differentiations in a society with a high degree of division of **labour** can be mediated.

In contrast, Weber rarely willingly speaks of a general concept of 'society', even though the appearance of the word in the title of his posthumously published magnum opus *Economy and Society* appears to have gained his consent. Weber doubted the meaningfulness of a unitary concept of society and was highly sceptical of the possibility of mediation between different 'value-spheres'. A similarly pessimistic interpretation occurs in Ferdinand **Tönnies**'s distinction between **Gemeinschaft and Gesellschaft**.

Yet, as different as all these conceptualizations of society are, they all share a common frame of reference. The concept of society has to do with the experience of the co-presence of different spheres which have to become readjusted and coordi-

nated. All sociological concepts of society seek to offer solutions to this problem of observing both differentiation between zones and an emergent global order that transcends this differentiation. One of the commonest solutions to this problem is the idea of normative integration, first propounded by Talcott Parsons.

Parsons defines a society as a social system with 'the greatest self-sufficiency of any type of social system' (Parsons 1977: 182). The integrative function of the societal community is here regarded as the decisive guarantor of the self-sufficiency of a society. Although Parsons's theory has been subject to extensive criticism on grounds of its over-estimation of stability and under-estimation of **conflict** and **social change**, his conception of the significance of normative integration is generally accepted in contemporary social theory. Today, ideas of 'society' are very frequently associated with ideas of normative integration, collective **solidarity** or social commitment. It would not be an exaggeration to note that this Parsonian heritage is part of the collective unconscious of contemporary sociology.

In many similar respects, uses of the word 'society' in everyday language serve to make collectivities addressable and to simulate a form of self-sufficiency by drawing a line between different societies which become integrated by norms and by culture. Yet in these connections the idea of society is very often linked closely to the idea of the nation–state as the typical shape of social order in the Western hemisphere. Both in classical sociology and in many contexts of public discourse, the concept of a society is frequently thought of by analogy with the concept of a **nation–state**. Nation – state boundaries have been taken as implying boundaries between one society and another society. This assumption is by no means satisfactory today. In the context of what is currently called **globalization**, the boundaries of societies are not as stable as the idea of a self-sufficient system might suggest. Societal structures clearly transcend national and nation–state boundaries. National and nation–state boundaries can at most be regarded as contingent political constructs, constructs that are constantly being cross-cut by 'trans-national' social and economic processes, flows and networks, invading flows of capital, people and **technology** as well as cultural and **intellectual exchanges** and legal developments (Beck 2000; Castells 1996; Urry 2000). 'Methodological nationalism' is no longer an acceptable framework for theorizing the concept of society today.

Social research today suggests a need for a concept of society that gains greater distance from the self-descriptions of collective goals and patterns of collective identities than the heritage of nineteenth-century Hegelian, **positivist**, **evolutionary** or otherwise largely metaphysical conceptions has bequeathed to us. Niklas **Luhmann**'s work suggests clues leading in this direction. Luhmann conceptualizes society as the highest level of social order, but rejects many of the basic assumptions of classical sociology. Luhmann's proposal is to regard society not as a **community** of human beings and their relationships but as the sum of all possible and accessible 'communications'. In his thesis, the idea of society is not bound to similar cultural codes, beliefs or life-forms, but only to the interaction of social processes. This concept of society implies an image of integration processes neither as general functional prerequisites nor as general achievable goals, but only as discrete empirical possibilities. Whereas in the Parsonian tradition the boundaries of society are still identical with the boundaries of nation–states, the Luhmannian conception of the totality of all communications or actions implies another idea. In this view, national boundaries are only patterns of political semantics, regarded as points of criteria for the recognizability of one bundle of **communications**

and **actions** to another bundle of communications and actions. In this sense, there is no reason for the existence of more than one society in the world – not because all life-conditions or cultural commitments are the same but because life-conditions and cultural commitments constantly interact and interpenetrate with one another empirically. This is the background for the concepts of **world system** or 'world society' (Burton 1972; Luhmann 1982).

References and further reading

Beck, U. (2000) *What is Globalization?* Cambridge: Polity Press.

Burton, J. W. (1972) *World Society*. Cambridge: Cambridge University Press.

Castells, M. (1996) *The Rise of the Network Society*. Oxford: Blackwell.

Habermas, J. ([1981] 1984–87) *The Theory of Communicative Action*, 2 vols. Boston: Beacon.

Hegel, G. W. F. ([1821] 1967) *The Philosophy of Right*. Oxford: Clarendon Press.

Lockwood, D. (1964) 'Social Integration and System Integration', in G. K. Zollschan and W. Hirsch (eds) *Social Change*. Boston: Houghton Mifflin.

Luhmann, N. (1982) 'The World Society as a Social System', *International Journal of General Systems*, 8: 131–8.

Nassehi, A. (2004) 'Die Theorie funktionaler Differenzierung im Horizont ihrer Kritik', *Zeitschrift für Soziologie*, 33(2): 98–118.

Parsons, T. (1977) *Social Systems and the Evolution of Action Theory*. New York: Free Press.

Urry, J. (2000) *Sociology beyond Societies: Mobilities for the Twenty-First Century*. London: Routledge.

ARMIN NASSEHI

SOCIOBIOLOGY

Since Darwin devised his radical theory in *The Origin of Species* ([1859] 1998), hundreds of evolutionary scientists have expounded on natural selection and evolution. Edward Wilson coined the term 'sociobiology' to describe a branch of **evolutionary theory** concerned with 'the systematic study of the biological basis of all social behavior' (2000: 4). Although Wilson is the best-known proponent of sociobiology, a number of other researchers, including Richard Dawkins, Robert Trivers and David Buss have written from this theoretical perspective. Popularized during the 1970s, it was preceded in the 1960s by the work of those such as Konrad Lorenz and Desmond Morris: its most contemporary reincarnation is in evolutionary biology.

Drawing data mainly from non-human animal data, but also early human animal cultures, sociobiology presents the 'human condition...as an epiphenomenon of evolution by natural selection based on the "drive" by individual genes to reproduce copies of themselves' (Rose and Rose 2001: 6). The theory focuses on aspects of social behavior such as altruism, **communication**, **dominance**, **roles** and **castes**, social spacing including territories, animal homosexuality, and behavior seen to be related to sex such as parental care, monogamy, homosexuality and sex selection.

Sociobiology has been subjected to major criticism from social scientists, biologists and particularly feminist biologists, who are concerned about a number of its axiomatic assumptions and assertions. First of all, natural and social scientists alike are concerned with sociobiology's attempt to provide an all-embracing grand theory of social behavior across all time and for all individuals. That is, sociobiology tends to be conservative insofar as morphology and behavior of living organisms are confined by law-like parameters dictated by nature. For social scientists in particular, the proclamation of a 'grand theory' eschews **poststructural** criticisms of the **Enlightenment** project (this attempt is evident in the title of the most famous book on sociobiology, Wilson's *New Synthesis*). A second critique is that sociobiology anthropomorphizes animal behaviors. Terms such as 'rape', 'coy', 'cuckoldry', 'adultery', 'harem' 'homosexual', 'marry' and 'divorce' are extensively used in sociobiology studies of animal behavior. Patricia Gowaty strongly objects to the use of these terms on the grounds that they have potentially damaging social repercussions, are more emotionally evocative, and their use is often sensationalized (1982). For instance, the term 'rape' is used by Randy Thornhill in his study of 'Rape in *Panorpa* Scorpionflies and a General Rape Hypothesis' (1980). Thornhill defines rape as the apparent forced insemination or fertilization that enhances male fitness and decreases female fitness (fitness as defined entirely in sexually reproductive terms). Gowaty was asked at a scientific meeting 'is it rape when a virgin is forced to intercourse?' and 'is it rape when a postmenopausal woman is forced to intercourse?' In human terms, both of these instances are clear acts of rape. However, in Thornhill's sociobiology terms, neither is rape because the virgin's fitness may be increased if she becomes pregnant, and the fitness of the male who copulates with the menopausal woman could not increase, nor is the fitness of the menopausal woman decreased.

Another criticism is that sociobiology often appears to provide a biological explanation for culturally conservative practices that reinforce unequal roles in society such as those of **class**, sex and **ethnicity**. For instance, much emphasis is placed on competition and dominance in studies of animals, with inferences from the interpretation of observations of animals made to human society. Wolfgang Wieser (1997) observes that studies focus on competition rather than cooperation because this reflects the Western emphasis on aggression and competition in human social systems. These studies clearly associate dominance with the male sex of most species and passivity with the female sex. However, social phenomena are by no means necessarily the result of 'nature' through evolution. This observation is linked to the strongest criticism of sociobiology, that it reduces what shapes human behavior to evolutionary (and more recently genetic) forces, ignoring 'cultural and historical variability and the significance of individual experiences, social practices and normative institutions in shaping human behavior' (Smith 2001: 136). Steven Rose points out that whereas sociobiology maintains that behaviors are *caused* by physical and chemical processes, they are in fact only *enabled* by these processes. Moreover, sociobiology over-emphasizes evolutionary theory as a set of law-like principles while failing to acknowledge contingency, diversity and variation as key elements of evolution (see Hird 2004).

References and further reading

Darwin, C. ([1859] 1998) *The Origin of Species.* Ware: Wordsworth Editions.

Gowaty, P. A. (1982) 'Sexual Terms in Sociobiology: Emotionally Evocative and Paradoxically, Jargon', *Animal Behavior*, 30: 630–1.

Hird, M. (2004) *Sex, Gender and Science.* Houndsmills: Palgrave.

Rose, H. and Rose, S. (eds) (2001) *Alas Poor Darwin: Arguments against Evolutionary Biology.* London: Vintage.

Smith, B. H. (2001) 'Sewing Up the Mind: The Claims of Evolutionary Psychology', in H. Rose and S. Rose (eds) *Alas Poor Darwin: Arguments against Evolutionary Biology.* London: Vintage, pp. 129–43.

Thornhill, R. (1980) 'Rape in *Panorpa* Scorpionflies and a General Rape Hypothesis', *Animal Behavior*, 28: 52–9.

Wieser, W. (1997) 'A Major Transition in Darwinism', *Trends in Ecology and Evolution*, 12: 367–70.

Wilson, E. O. (1975) *Sociobiology: The New Synthesis.* Cambridge, MA: Harvard University Press.

Wilson, E. O. (2000) *Sociobiology: The New Synthesis*, 25th anniversary edn. Cambridge, MA: Harvard University Press.

MYRA HIRD

SOLIDARITY

A term denoting cohesion or integration in a social body or whole. As a sociological concept, it derives from three sources: (1) the organic 'social physiology' of H. de St. Simon; (2) Fourier's social 'law of attraction' (analogous to the Newtonian law of gravity); and (3) the 'social physics' of **Comte**, who stressed the consensual basis of social order and cohesion. All three sought, in different ways, to extend a broadly Newtonian **world-view** to the study of society. Emile **Durkheim** made a **binary** distinction between two different types of solidarity which he claimed were associated more or less strongly with different social types. 'Mechanical' solidarity was characteristic of 'segmental' societies, typically small-scale with little internal differentiation, and a simple **division of labour** (see **differentiation**). Members of such societies are bound together by likeness and by a strong *conscience collective*, a body of shared and emotionally-freighted beliefs, norms (see **values and norms**) and symbolic **representations** to which they respond in similar ways. Conversely, Durkheim argued that 'organic' solidarity was characteristic of societies with a highly-developed division of labour; in which specialization of tasks encouraged social **differentiation**, individualization (see **individualism and individualization**) and individual **autonomy**. Members of such societies are bound together by interdependence expressed in complex networks of co-operation, reciprocity and economic exchange. Durkheim held that organic solidarity was as yet imperfectly realized in modern industrial societies. He called for the development of occupationally-based **associations** to provide economic life with a stronger integrative fabric and more adequate moral **regulation**, as well as a legal framework appropriate to modern economic organization (especially in the regulation of contracts, the definition of **property** and the adjudication of individual and collective rights and responsibilities). These would be necessary to check the social pathologies (see **normal and pathological**) of egoism and **anomie**.

Durkheim claimed that one index of mechanical solidarity was the relative predominance of 'repressive' **law**, in which a detailed set of collective norms (relating to beliefs, values and **symbols**, often religious in nature), backed by strong social sanctions (see **social control**), were applicable to all members in most aspects of their lives. On the other hand, organic solidarity is characterized by the development of 'restitutive' forms of law which seek to restore a social balance appropriate to specific activities or situations, rather than to impose universal **sanctions**.

However, mechanical and organic solidarity, and their respective legal forms, are not mutually exclusive. Durkheim claimed that both types of solidarity, and of law, are found in both simple and complex social types. In complex societies marked by a strong development of organic solidarity, there is still a normative order (albeit, a restricted one) to which all members may be called to comply; for example, at times of national emergency or war. Further, within a complex social order, smaller social bodies, with which people affiliate on the basis of likeness (e.g., similar interests, purposes or beliefs, or tastes), may impose some degree of moral order backed by sanctions, though these manifestations of mechanical solidarity are often limited and restricted. In addition, the co-operation and exchange characteristic of organic solidarity is itself subject to moral and legal regulation: parties to a contract are, to some extent, moral **subjects**, subject to normative requirements for fair dealing.

Durkheim's later discussion of collective effervescence allows an application of the concept of solidarity to extraordinary occasions in social life or in a society's history, in which individuals are called out of their differentiated everyday existence by a collective force which profoundly marks or transforms their identities. Examples include **ritual** occasions on which solidarity is reinforced, or **revolutionary** moments in which entirely new social bases of solidarity may develop. In this light, Durkheim's sociology of solidarity anticipates both the sociology of **emotions** and the focus on collective **identity** found in new **social movement** theory.

Durkheim's concern for solidarity reflects a context in which *solidarisme* was a focus of political and pedagogical concern in *fin de siècle* France, arising from a republican desire to develop a secular moral basis for a modern social order; however, Durkheim's usage of the term *solidarité* was distinctive and not reducible to this context. Durkheim's discussion of solidarity was subsequently reinterpreted by Parsons in terms of a general theory of action in which the cohesion of social actors, and the existence of social order, are guaranteed by a cultural **value** consensus. Aside from a more restricted usage in the sociology of working-class **communities**, and the anthropology of **kinship**, solidarity subsequently fell out of favour as a sociological concept, but was revived in relation to Bellah's discussion of religion in American **civil society**, **Goffman**'s studies of interactional solidarity, and also mass media (see **media and mass media**) studies. It also retained some power as a reference point for discussion of fundamental dilemmas of **modernity**, and of a nostalgia for absolutes. Traces of a Durkheimian approach can be seen in Bataille's discussion of the oscillation of homogeneity and heterogeneity, and in his analysis of **fascism**, and more recently in discussions by Tiryakian, **Alexander** and others of differentiation and disenchantment as features of modernity.

References and further reading

Bellah, R. (1967) 'Civil Religion in America', *Daedalus*, 96: 1–21.

Durkheim, E. ([1893] 1984) *The Division of Labour in Society*. New York: Free Press.

Durkheim, E. ([1913] 1996) *The Elementary Forms of Religious Life*. New York: Free Press.

Emirbayer, M. (ed.) (2003) *Emile Durkheim: Sociologist of Modernity*. Oxford: Blackwell.

Lukes, S. (1973) *Emile Durkheim: His Life and Work.* London: Allen Lane.

Lukes, S. and Scull, A. (1984) 'Introduction', in S. Lukes and A. Scull (eds) *Durkheim and the Law.* Oxford: Blackwell.

Parsons, T. (1937) *The Structure of Social Action.* New York: Free Press.

Pearce, F. (2001) *The Radical Durkheim*, 2nd edn. Toronto: Canadian Scholars' Press.

Tiryakian, E. A. (1992) 'Dialectics of Modernity: Reenchantment and Dedifferentiation as Counterprocesses', in H. Haferkamp and N. J. Smelser (eds) *Social Change and Modernity.* Berkeley, CA: University of California Press.

WILLIAM RAMP

SOVEREIGNTY

The concept of sovereignty refers to a form of political rule that is intrinsically entwined with the emergence and existence of the modern **state** system states (see **state and nation–state**). In Europe, after the medieval patchwork of overlapping political and religious rule had crumbled, thinkers such as Jean Bodin and Thomas Hobbes saw the state as sovereign, as the ultimate guarantor of authority and order. With centralized states starting to dominate the political landscape, debate ensued about the legitimacy of their authority (see **legitimacy and legitimation**). Since John Locke and Jean-Jacques Rousseau, debate has been particularly concerned with popular sovereignty, defining the people's mandate as the source of the legitimacy of the ruler. Yet first and foremost, any arrangement of rule inside a territorial state, whether a **democracy**, a **monarchy** or a dictatorship, external intervention in order to be sovereign. As 'the idea that there is a final and absolute political authority in the political community', sovereignty entails the condition that 'no final and absolute authority exists elsewhere' (Hinsley 1986: 26). Without recognition by outside forces, a state's sovereignty remains impaired. Altogether, sovereignty is a set of norms (see **values and norms**) that comprises an internal (absolute authority), an external

(autonomy) and an **intersubjective** (recognition) dimension. To the extent that it shapes expectations and behaviour, sovereignty becomes a fundamental political **institution**. One of its main purposes is the peaceful co-existence of states with very different internal systems of rule.

Frequently, the Peace of Westphalia that ended the Thirty Years War in 1648 is said to symbolize the shift towards a modern international system of sovereign states. In reality, sovereignty's breakthrough was a much more gradual process, climaxing after de-colonization in the twentieth century with a globe carved up into some 200 sovereign states. Today, sovereignty's validity both as a concept and as an institution is increasingly disputed. One line of criticism highlights the manifold instances in which sovereignty is being violated or only nominally or partially upheld. Some arguments point to the fact that most major **peace** treaties limit the autonomy of defeated states through external obligations. Also, the emergence of universal human **rights** and humanitarian interventions are seen as developments that run counter to the concept of sovereignty. Further dilemmas relate to states that enjoy external sovereignty and **recognition** by other states, but possess little internal authority, e.g. due to civil wars, for which the term 'quasi-states' has been coined (Jackson 1990). All this can lead to the conclusion that sovereignty is 'organised hypocrisy' (Krasner 1999) – an institution that demands general respect but is constantly being infringed. However, such an evaluation remains problematic as long as it only counts deviations, and many observers claim that sovereignty continues to be the effective basic norm of world politics.

Another line of criticism views **globalization** as threatening sovereignty, because intensifying cross-border interdependencies appear to diminish states' autonomy (Smith *et al.* 1999). Here, it is important to consider the variety of senses of state autonomy – as the right to make rules (authority) and the capacity to enforce them (see **social control**), and states' authority as their 'meta-political authority' to decide what belongs to their realm of authority and what remains under non-state authority (see **public and private**) (Thomson 1995: 223–5). Autonomy then becomes a relative criterion: authority is never all-encompassing nor is control ever full. Tax avoidance, for example, has always endangered states' sovereignty by reducing their control and authority over taxation. **Globalization** makes international tax evasion easier and forces states to find new ways of guarding their tax **autonomy**. Key questions in the debate about globalization and sovereignty are how much loss of control leads to a loss of authority, and whether globalization empowers other actors *vis-à-vis* states, e.g. transnational corporations and **civil society** organizations or supranational institutions. Some argue that states, using their meta-political authority, deliberately decide to give up parts of their sovereignty, via privatization or the transfer of authority to international institutions, in order to achieve goals like economic growth or security. The European Union's system of rule above and between its member states is a prime example of such 'sovereignty bargains' (Mattli 2000). Simultaneously, the EU has grown into a new political entity that defies the very concept of sovereignty, because the supremacy of EU law diminishes the internal and external dimensions of member states' sovereignty.

All in all, the extent of individual states' sovereignty is a matter of degree that varies enormously over time and across countries. Crucial challenges for sovereignty as a form of political rule arise from non-state actors and institutions that acquire independent rule-making authority at the expense of states.

References and further reading

Biersteker, T. J. and Weber, C. (eds) (1996) *State Sovereignty as Social Construct*. Cambridge: Cambridge University Press.

Held, D. (1995) *Democracy and the Global Order*. Cambridge: Polity.

Hinsley, F. H. (1986) *Sovereignty*. Cambridge: Cambridge University Press.

Jackson, R. H. (1990) *Quasi-States: Sovereignty, International Relations, and the Third World*. Cambridge: Cambridge University Press.

Krasner, S. D. (1999) *Sovereignty: Organized Hypocrisy*. Princeton: Princeton University Press.

Mattli, W. (2000) 'Sovereignty Bargains in Regional Integration', *International Studies Review*, 2(2): 149–80.

Smith, D. A., Solinger, D. J. and Topik, S. C. (eds) (1999) *States and Sovereignty in the Global Economy*. London: Routledge.

Spruyt, H. (1994) *The Sovereign State and Its Competitors*. Princeton, NJ: Princeton University Press.

Thomson, J. E. (1995) 'State Sovereignty in International Relations: Bridging the Gap between Theory and Empirical Research', *International Studies Quarterly*, 39: 213–33.

PETER HÄGEL

SPACE AND PLACE

The concepts of space and place play a prominent role within disciplines such as geography, sociology and anthropology, and are also of significance for a range of professional fields such as architecture, landscape design and urban planning. If we explore the evolution of these concepts, we find that they have changed markedly over time in response to wider developments in philosophy and social theory and that the relationship between the two concepts has also oscillated between phases of relative antinomy and reciprocity.

In the 1950s a tension emerged between the concepts of space and place driven by a sense that the study of place had hitherto been excessively descriptive and had produced little in the way of rigorous scientific **knowledge**. This sense of unease was driven in part by the perceived low academic status of disciplines such as anthropology, geography and other fields of knowledge that appeared unable to offer substantive contributions to key **intellectual** debates over the causality of social phenomena. A number of scholars, particularly from within human geography, sought to promote the study of space as a distinctive spatial science capable of generating universal laws comparable with the natural sciences. By the mid-1960s this changing emphasis had become widely known as the 'quantitative revolution' on account of the extensive deployment of mathematical models and the implicit acquiescence in positivist scientific methods. The change of emphasis in the 1960s from description to explanation also marked a rediscovery of attempts to explore the spatial patterns of phenomena such as agricultural zones, urban neighbourhood change and the distribution of settlements developed in earlier decades by figures such as Walter Christaller, August Lösch and Johann Heinrich von Thünen.

In the early 1970s, however, we encounter a growing dissatisfaction with positivist spatial science emerging from two quarters: first, a humanistic emphasis on the subjective meanings of place and space influenced by **hermeneutic** and **phenomenological** philosophical traditions; and second, a perception that spatial science was remote from critical challenges such as environmental pollution, **poverty**, **racism** and the geo-political impact of **imperialism** (see Harvey 1973) (see also **ecology and environmentalism**). The growing sense of political frustration with the putative ethical neutrality of positivist spatial science played a decisive role in bringing **Marxist** analysis to the fore so that spatial phenomena were increasingly interpreted as the outcome of structural economic and political forces, notably in the work of Henri **Lefevbre** (see also Harvey 1974). By the 1980s, however, at the peak of Marxism's influence within geography, there were concerns that the universal models of spatial science had been substituted by a new set of generalizations which left relatively little scope for an engagement with the lived experience of place and space. Various approaches

emerged which sought to explore the specificity of particular places within a more general explanatory framework through, for example, the development of 'structuration theory' by Anthony **Giddens** and the recognition of the significance of 'spatial divisions of labour' in the production of regional disparities (see Gregory 1994; Massey 1984).

During the 1990s the earlier emphasis on so-called Grand Theory, whether positivist or Marxist, was challenged by a new diversity of approaches influenced by developments in **feminist theory**, **psychoanalytic** concepts and **post-structuralist** approaches. Emphasis on place as a space of **identity** and belonging has been supplemented by awareness of the exclusionary dangers of socially or ethnically homogenous conceptions of place (see Young 1990). The omniscience of masculinist forms of knowledge has been challenged by feminist insights into the gendered production of space (Deutsche 1996; Rose 1993), and the relationship between concrete and imaginary spaces has been developed in new directions through the influence of Gilles **Deleuze** and other scholars concerned with non-hierarchical conceptions of spatial difference (see Rajchman 2000).

More recently, it has been claimed that space and place are of declining significance because of the 'dematerialization' of social and economic transactions and the increasing importance of so-called 'virtual spaces'. When taken to extremes, however, the notion of a radical 'deterritorialization' appears to deny any clear role for space or place in social or economic life. Recent research demonstrates that an over-emphasis on the deterritorialization of space and power is misplaced because spatial dispersal within the global economy has paradoxically necessitated the recombination and reconcentration of power in specific places (see Castells 2000; Sassen 2001). Yet this influential body of literature on **networks** and the paradoxical enhancement of spatial propinquity has a tendency to overlook those marginal or 'ordinary' spaces where unequal **power** relations, **violence** and **social exclusion** are most powerfully manifested.

References and further reading

Castells, M. (2000) *The Rise of the Network Society*, 2nd edn. Oxford: Blackwell.

Deutsche, R. (1996) *Evictions: Art and Spatial Politics*. Cambridge, MA: MIT Press.

Gregory, D. (1994) *Geographical Imaginations*. Oxford: Blackwell.

Harvey, D. (1973) *Social Justice and the City*. London: Edward Arnold.

Harvey, D. (1974) 'Population, Resources and the Ideology of Science', *Economic Geography*, 50(3): 256–77.

Massey, D. (1984) *Spatial Divisions of Labour*. London: Macmillan.

Rajchman, J. (2000) *The Deleuze Connections*. Cambridge, MA: MIT Press.

Rose, G. (1993) *Feminism and Geography*. Minneapolis, MN: University of Minnesota Press.

Sassen, S. (2001) *The Global City: London, New York, Tokyo*, 2nd edn. Princeton, NJ: Princeton University Press.

Young, I. M. (1990) *Justice and the Politics of Difference*. Princeton, NJ: Princeton University Press.

MATTHEW GANDY

SPENCER, HERBERT (1820–1903)

Spencer saw himself as a social philosopher, and long before he undertook the study of sociology, he had written major treatises on ethics, psychology, and biology. His larger project was termed 'Synthetic Philosophy' which, Spencer believed, would unify the sciences under a common set of theoretical principles that were loosely derived from the physics of his time.

Spencer's sociological work can be divided into three groups. The sixteen volumes of *Descriptive Sociology*, which sought to classify ethnographic and historical data under a common category system, appeared throughout Spencer's life and even after his death. Spencer's first sociological book *The Study of Sociology* (1873) outlined the

potential sources of bias in sociological inquiry, and represents the most sophisticated **methodological** treatise of the late nineteenth century. The three volumes of *The Principles of Sociology* ([1874–96] 2001), over 2,000 pages long, unfold empirically the theoretical argument that as human populations grow, selection pressures are generated that lead to the differentiation of the population along three axes: (1) operation (production and reproduction); (2) regulation (the consolidation of power to coordinate and control); and (3) distribution (the use of infrastructures and markets to move resources, people, and information). As differentiation proceeds along these three axes, a structural and cultural base is created that allows for further differentiation and population growth. Yet, Spencer emphasized that the selection pressures on a population to differentiate are not always met, leading to dissolution of the population and disintegration of society.

Spencer was primarily a theorist of **power** – despite contemporary sociology's emphasis on his **functionalism** – and he was particularly interested in the internal and external forces that led to the centralization of power. For Spencer, as power is consolidated, inequalities increase and power is used to conquer other populations. As the logistical loads of controlling conquered populations mount, pressures build up and cause the decentralization of power and, if these pressures are sufficiently intense, to the disintegration of a society and its empire. He also studied a range of **institutional** systems to analyse how centralized power and **inequality** influence their internal **structure** and operation. Spencer is the least read of the founders of sociology today, but his work deserves more respect from, and scrutiny by, sociologists.

Major works

(1873) *The Study of Sociology*. London: Routledge.

(1873–1934) *Descriptive Sociology, or Groups of Sociological Facts*, 16 vols. Various publishers.

([1874–96] 2001) *The Principles of Sociology*. New York: Appleton-Century-Crofts, reprinted by Transaction Publishers.

Further reading

Turner, J. (1985) *Herbert Spencer*. Beverley Hills: Sage.

JONATHAN TURNER

SPIVAK, GAYATRI CHAKRAVORTY (1942–)

Indian Marxist, feminist, literary and cultural theorist, Professor of Humanities at Columbia University, New York. Spivak first gained critical attention in social theory for her English translation of and 'Translator's Preface' (1976) to **Derrida**'s *De la grammatologie* which sparked debate on deconstruction among English speaking scholars. Since then, she has advocated the overtly political use of **deconstruction** to disrupt the colonial legacies of western intellectual traditions which continue to produce their subjects through 'epistemic violence'. She has crucially interrogated the manner in which the vocabularies of theory – even those varieties that understand themselves as critical – are unable to know or represent the experiences of the oppressed. For example, she has criticized western **feminism** for its blind spots regarding third world women, just as she has criticized subaltern studies for an inability to allow for a place from which the 'sexed subaltern' can speak (1988). While critical of **essentialist** categories such as 'Third World' and 'woman', she has argued that deploying a 'strategic essentialism' – an explicitly political, and avowedly temporary use of identity categories – may be useful as a means of interrupting the silences in these intellectual traditions. Relentlessly disregarding disciplinary boundaries and traditions, and taking a deconstructive stance towards texts

of all sorts (literary, cultural, economic, political) Spivak's continuing critical interventions make her a key figure in contemporary social theory.

Major works

(1976) Translator's preface to J. Derrida, *Of Grammatology*. Baltimore, MD: Johns Hopkins University Press, pp. ix – lxxxvii.

(1987) *In Other Worlds: Essays in Cultural Politics*. New York: Methuen.

(1988) 'Can the Subaltern Speak?' in C. Nelson and L. Grossberg (eds) *Marxism and the Interpretation of Culture*. London: Macmillan, pp. 271–313.

(1993) *Outside in the Teaching Machine*. London: Routledge.

(1999) *A Critique of Colonial Reason: Toward a History of the Vanishing Present*. Cambridge, MA: Harvard University Press.

Further reading

Harasym, S. (ed.) (1990) *The Post-Colonial Critic: Interviews, Strategies, Dialogues*. London: Routledge.

Landry, D. and MacLean, G. (eds) *The Spivak Reader*. London: Routledge.

Morton, S. (2003) *Gayatri Chakravorty Spivak*. London: Routledge.

BARBARA L. MARSHALL

SPORT

The modern term 'sport' is a shortened version of the word 'disport', which literally means 'to indulge (oneself) in pleasure'. 'Disport' is in turn based on the French word *desporter*, which is derived from the Latin etymological root *disportare*, meaning 'to carry away'. Where some sociologists have tended to reduce the idea of sport to modern recreational pursuits in which the outcome is affected by physical skills and prowess (Loy, McPherson and Kenyon 1978), others have identified what they see as sport's essential features (Haywood *et al.* 1995). Social theorists, in contrast, have found it impossible to set limits on what constitutes a sport, because culturally sport is experienced in myriad ways.

Accordingly, they have explicitly rejected the kind of nut-and-bolts definitions that emphasize the essential structural properties of sport forms, or which focus their attention on elite performance, as these sidestep more interesting and difficult questions suggested by the role of sport in historical and contemporary social formations.

In relation to questions about the historical development of sport, the figurational sociologist Norbert **Elias** (1971) convincingly argued that most modern forms of organized sport have their antecedents in eighteenth-century Britain, where they developed through the 'sportization' of pastimes. This occurred in two main phases which saw the emergence of sports such as cricket, boxing, fox hunting and horse racing, followed by association football, rugby, tennis and track and field games in the mid-nineteenth century. Elias developed the concept of sportization to argue that what came to be known as 'sport' emerged as part of a wider civilizing tendency where the rules governing 'sporting' contests became not only more exacting, but also established a balance between the ability to gain a high degree of 'combat-tension' with what was perceived to be an acceptable use of protection against injury (Elias and Dunning 1986). What Elias was in effect offering was a domesticated modern understanding of the Aristotelian concept of 'mimesis'; involving a processual theory of the 'imitation of men in action', which despite the protestations of his followers was latently **functionalist**.

Functionalist sociologists themselves have considered the ways in which sport meets the 'needs' of the social system by concentrating their attention on the way it not only contributes to individual personal development, but more importantly maintains **value consensus** and social order. Yet functionalism has been heavily criticized not least because it underplays the extent to which sport may actually discourage people from participation because the way in which it is structured in **capitalist** socie-

ties allows for few 'winners'. If this counter-argument acknowledges that some individuals might rationally conclude that their own efforts might not be enough and instead might resort to dishonest ways of improving their chances of winning, it also suggests that sport, whatever its public and moral **hegemony**, offers myriad opportunities for the pursuit of deviance, from ritualized rule-breaking activities, to outright **violence**, as in football hooliganism.

As well as criticizing functionalism for overlooking the multi-faceted ways in which sports manifest themselves in contemporary social formations, social theorists writing from Marxist, feminist and race and ethnicity perspectives have in their own ways viewed the social relationship with sport as one of **domination** and social **inequality** which maintains unequal power relations in support of hegemonic, patriarchal and racist conditions. **Marxist** accounts have also suggested that sport in capitalist societies merely serves as a spectacle (Debord 1967) or opiate (Brohm 1978) which diverts people's attention away from more pressing issues and that sport participation ultimately leads to **alienation**, because the **body** is reduced to an instrumental means to an end – a virtual machine set with the task of maximizing capitalist production.

Interest in the body has become central to current theorizing about sport but more often in relation to **consumption** than **production**. This interest in consumer culture has often been combined with a growing interest in the reciprocal relationship between sport and the **media**. There has also developed an increasing recognition that if people's experiences of sport are better understood through their contingency rather than their fixity, sport also presents myriad possibilities for **identity** constructions.

References and further reading

Brohm, J.-M. (1978) *Sport: A Prison of Measured Time*. London: Ink Links.

Coakley, J. and Dunning, E. (eds) (2000) *Handbook of Sports Studies*. London: Sage.

Debord. G. ([1967] 1995) *The Society of the Spectacle*. New York: Zone Books.

Elias, N. (1971) 'The Genesis of Sport as a Sociological Problem', in E. Dunning (ed.) *The Sociology of Sport*. London: Frank Cass.

Elias, N. and Dunning, E. (eds) (1986) *Quest for Excitement: Sport and Leisure in the Civilizing Process*. Oxford: Blackwell.

Haywood, L., Kew, F., Bramham, P., Spink, J., Capenerhurst, J. and Henry, I. (1995) *Understanding Leisure*, 2nd edn. Cheltenham: Stanley Thornes.

Loy, J. W., McPherson, B. D. and Kenyon, G. (1978) *Sport and the Social System*. Reading, MA: Addison-Wesley.

TONY BLACKSHAW

STANDPOINT EPISTEMOLOGY

Standpoint epistemology is a methodology and a political strategy that addresses the problem of what is true (**epistemology**) in a way that aims to validate the **knowledge** of oppressed **groups**. 'Standpoint' refers to a shared social 'position' that is shaped by divisions of labor (property) and structures of **power**. Standpoint epistemology claims that knowledge arising from the social locations of the exploited and oppressed has an authority that is less partial, more critically powerful, and potentially transformative.

Standpoint theory acknowledges that **values and norms** shape what counts as 'true', including the content and methods of scientific research. Against scientific claims to speak for universal truths, standpoint theory contends that knowledge is shaped by the social location of specific groups. Standpoint theory rests its authority on the premise that the restrictions an oppressed or exploited position impose on individuals give them the capacity to see and know the world from a less partial, more critical perspective. In other words, one's exploited or excluded social location can afford critical insight, especially about a dominant group and its **practices**. Standpoint theory highlights those ways of knowing that might be characterized as 'the outsider within' or the knowledge of the marginalized – the views of women responsible for everyday care, the engaged perspectives of the hyper-exploited factory workers, the small farmers scraping together a subsistence living, or the double consciousness of **colonized** peoples. Standpoint theory claims that the oppressive restrictions imposed on the exploited and oppressed give them an ability to see what is masked to others.

Standpoint theory confronts the dominant knowledge claim to universal truth by making evident the interested values and vision it speaks from and offers instead an alternative perspective situated in the history of social struggle over what is real and true. Standpoint theory embraces a critique that reads social realities (history, **culture** and **identities**, labor and **law**) from locations that can more adequately explain the systemic relations, particularly under capitalism, that organize what we know, including our experiences. Implicit in this perspective is a normative vision of alternative social relations where the needs of all can be met

There is no clear agreement on how to explain the relation between social location and knowledge One of the issues here is how a particular standpoint is different from a marginalized person's 'experience'. At times 'standpoint' is equated with a group identity (e.g. 'women of color') and other times it is synonymous with a way of knowing that is not necessarily the same as a group identity (e.g. a **feminist** or socialist standpoint). Some standpoint theorists turn to theories of **ideology** as a concept that calls attention to the fact that knowledge is a site of class struggle (Hennessy 1993). Much recent work, however, has a more postmodern, pro-democratic socio-cultural emphasis (Harding 2004; Hekman 1997; Sandoval 1991).

Socialist feminists developed the notion of standpoint in the late twentieth century from the insights of **Marx**, Engels and **Lukács** in order to expand the standards of what counts as knowledge and to formulate a more coherent explanation of feminism's **authority**, who it speaks for, and the social relations it contests.

Feminist standpoint theorists posit feminism as a way of conceptualizing from the vantage point of women's lives: their activities, interests, and values. In attending to the complex material forces that structure the relations between social positioning and ways of knowing, feminist standpoint theorists have challenged the assumption that simply to be a woman guarantees a clear understanding of the world. Instead they argue that the feminist standpoint is a socially produced position not necessarily accessible to all women.

Feminist standpoint theorist Dorothy Smith (1974) critiques sociology's claim to objective knowledge of daily life for the ways it substitutes the concerns of administrators for ordinary people and women in particular whose perspectives can discredit sociology's 'objective' claims. Political scientist Nancy Hartsock (1983) addresses the class struggle in feminist knowledge. Hilary Rose (1994) confronts the ways the division of labor is responsible for some of the partial truths and distorted understandings in the medical and health sciences. Other feminist standpoint theorists draw upon postmodern theories of the subject as a way to understand the differential construction of 'woman' across ethnic, racial and sexual locations (Sandoval 1991; Haraway 1991). The relations between women's/feminist standpoints and the locations and knowledges of other oppressed groups are also points of continued debate.

References and further reading

Collins, P. (1986) 'Learning for the Outsider Within: The Sociological Significance of Black Feminist Thought', *Social Problems*, 33(6): S14 – S32.

Haraway, D. (1991) 'Situated Knowledges: The Science Question in Feminism and the Privilege of Partial Perspective', in *Simians, Cyborgs, and Women: The Reinvention of Nature*. New York: Routledge.

Harding, S. (2004) *The Feminist Standpoint Theory Reader*. New York: Routledge.

Hartsock, N. (1983) 'The Feminist Standpoint: Developing the Ground for a Specifically Feminist Historical Materialism', in M. B. Hintikka and S. Harding (eds) *Discovering Reality*. Dordrecht: Reidel, pp. 283–310.

Hekman, S. (1997) 'Truth and Method: Feminist Standpoint Theory Revisited', *Signs: Journal of Women in Culture and Society*, 22(21): 341–65.

Hennessy, R. (1993) 'Feminist Standpoint, Discourse and Authority: From Women's Lives to Ideology Critique', in *Materialist Feminism and the Politics of Discourse*. New York: Routledge.

Jameson, F. (1998) 'History and Class Consciousness as an Unfinished Project', *Rethinking Marxism*, 1(1): 49–72.

Rose, H. (1994) *Love, Power and Knowledge: Towards a Feminist Transformation of the Sciences*. Bloomington, IN: Indiana University Press.

Sandoval, C. (1991) 'U.S. Third World Feminism: The Theory and the Method of Differential Oppositional Consciousness', *Genders*, 10: 1–10.

Smith, D. (1974) 'Women's Perspective as a Radical Critique of Sociology', *Sociological Inquiry*, 44: 1–13.

ROSEMARY HENNESSY

STATE AND NATION–STATE

The term 'state' can be traced back to the Latin *status* (state of affairs, **constitution**, condition, composition) and to the French *état souverain* (sovereign situation, sovereign state). 'State' can be defined as:

1. all political and social **institutions** of a political entity and their interrelations in a defined territory;
2. the political and legal order of a nation, a territory, or a sovereign **authority** to ensure certain purposes;
3. in a narrower sense, the institutions of government (executive, legislature, and jurisdiction).

Max **Weber** defines the core of the state as 'that entity which possesses a monopoly upon the legitimate (and successful) use of force within a defined territory' (Weber 1958). A modern state, according to Weber, is characterized by a legitimate authority of people over people, functioning through a rational constitution and jurisdiction, executed by an administration bound to law.

Systems theory understands the state as a sub-system of the **social system** responsible for authoritative decision-making of society as a whole. While traditional systems theory in political science assigns to the state a superior position (Easton 1953), modern autopoietic systems theory defines the state as the 'self-description' of the political system (**Luhmann** 1989), which can only claim for itself the status of being one of several 'partial social systems'.

The modern state owes its existence to a **legitimacy** and governability crisis in a certain historical period in continental Europe. **Secularization** in **Europe** caused a power vacuum, since rule could not be legitimated by any 'God given order'. The secular order of the modern state replaced religious rule. Therefore, **sovereignty** became a central feature of the state. This sovereignty distinguished the modern state from medieval times when a sovereign political authority not legitimated by God and **religion** would have been inconceivable.

A consequence of becoming a sovereign modern state was the separation of state (monopoly on the use of force) and society (subject to the use of force). Modern understandings of sovereignty, however, do not conceptualize **citizens** as subjects but – since Thomas Hobbes's *Leviathan* (1651) – as the ultimate legitimate instance of a unified and centralized state. The modern state bases itself exclusively on the free consent of each individual. In the normative sense, the state is sovereign only as long as it represents the sovereignty of its citizens.

Two fundamental distinctions should be made concerning political orders. First, states can be differentiated as either **democratic** or autocratic regimes according to their type of rule. Thus, democracies and autocracies can be distinguished by the *legitimacy* of power (popular sovereignty v. tradition), *access* to power (open through universal franchise v. restricted or closed access), the *monopoly* of power (democratically legitimated institutions v. Führer-principle or oligarchies), the *structure* of power (pluralist rule by control of power v. monistic rule), the *claim* to power (closely limited by rule of **law** v. comprehensive or unlimited), and the *execution* of power (based on the rule of law v. repressive).

Second, states can be characterized as either unitarian or federal. Federal states distinguish themselves mainly by attributing the legislative and executive powers both at the central and at federal levels of the state. Unitarian states, on the other hand, ground their authority on legislative and executive bodies that are centralized and hold their prerogatives for the entire national territory. Important goals of federally organized states include: the taming of power by means of the vertical separation of powers between the federation and its federal states, the preservation of the **autonomy** of single states, and the protection of **minorities** in ethnically and culturally heterogeneous countries.

Parsons's (1951) and Easton's (1953) system theories emphasize the functioning of the state and its sub-systems. Here, not only the stability of the state, but also its functional crises, e.g., legitimacy crisis (**Habermas** 1975), were taken into account. As a consequence, the performance of the state and political systems, as well as issues of political control became the focus of analysis. In this process the pessimistic modern system theory (Luhmann 1989) has slowly been replaced by a position that admits the possibility of an indirect context control in complex societies.

Klaus von Beyme (1986) distinguishes four central concepts of the state: the state based on the rule of law (*Rechtsstaat*); the nation–state; the democratic state; and the **welfare state** (the list could be expanded by the concepts of the 'power state', 'the cultural state', 'the constitutional state', or 'the **totalitarian** state'). Historically, states based upon the rule of law and democratic states have rarely developed simultaneously but rather successively, only coming together in the modern democratic constitutional state. Jürgen Habermas (1996) spoke of the *Gleichursprunglichkeit* or simultaneous emergence of the two concepts. Although both concepts developed and became generally accepted one after the other in history, their functional link is grounded on their inevitable mutual dependency: on the one hand, democratic self-rule is only feasible within the framework of a **liberal** constitutional state in which citizens recognize each other as equal and are equipped with equal rights; on the other, these rights have to be specified and granted in a democratic process (Merkel 2004).

Linked to these concepts, the central responsibilities of the state can be distinguished. First, one central responsibility of a state is the guarantee of internal and external security (Hobbes), the granting and ensuring of liberal human and civil rights (Locke), and the right to political participation (**Mill**). Second, the state has the duty to integrate (Smend) its citizens politically (and culturally). Third, the state must provide the infrastructural conditions for the economy, to guarantee free competition, and to supply necessary public goods. However, for the modern state under conditions of **globalization**, this latter task is increasingly difficult to carry out (Held 1995). Fourth, the state as a welfare state has the obligation to institutionalize re-distribution for the benefit of the weak, thereby securing ('positive') freedom for all citizens and creating the prerequisites for equal democratic participation and political

inclusion (Heller). In a modern state, a fifth responsibility may be to take care of and to preserve the natural conditions of life. Thus, the protection of environment as an objective of the state has been part of many democratic constitutions. While the first three responsibilities are recognized by all political **groups** as core functions of the state, welfare and ecological responsibilities on the part of the state, especially with regard to their extent, are disputed.

The more specific concept of the nation–state can generally be defined as the political organization of a nation within a state. Thus, the nation–state combines two principles: the political, territorial principle of the state (a territory within established borders; the monopoly on the legitimate use of force; binding regulations for solving conflicts in society) and the historical, cultural principle of the nation. Max Weber (1958) defined nation–state as the 'worldly organization of authority of the nation' in a cultural and/or political **community**.

Historically, the formation of nation–states can be explained by three factors: nation–states emerged first due to internal revolution (expression of the self-determination of citizens) or, second, due to the formation of a new state by the amalgamation of previously separated parts of a population which defined themselves as a 'nation' (e.g., Germany and Italy) or, third, due to the breakdown of empires (e.g., the Habsburg Empire).

Here, two terms of 'nation' can be distinguished: a constitutional crafting of a nation (France, but also the USA: *jus solis*) and an **ethnic**-cultural orientation (Germany, but also Central and Eastern Europe: *jus sanguinis*). The frequent distinction between a 'community of intent' and a 'community of fate' emphasizes a similar aspect. The French understanding of **citizenship**, which underlines the participation principle as the decisive characteristic of a nation, can be clearly distinguished from the German ethnic, historical, and cultural understanding of the nation as an objective community of fate. Abbé Sièyes ([1798] 2003) had defined the French nation as the 'totality of united individuals who are under one common legislation and represented by one and the same legislative assembly'. The ethnic-cultural nation–state concept, however, understands nation as an 'objective community of fate', which cannot be joined voluntarily by an individual but which has to be accepted as objectively given. This view of the nation–state seems largely out-dated today (see **nationalism**).

Today, the nation–state is facing diverse problems which may go beyond its capacity to solve them: globalized markets spoil its allocation of resources; **terrorism** and **crime** have become international, just like traffic and **communication networks**, **migration**, or environmental pollution. There are four core functions of the state and its legitimacy in particular which are challenged by globalization (cf. Habermas 2001): law and order and effective public administration; sovereignty; collective identity of the political community; and democratic legitimacy.

Because of these challenges, supporters of a 'post-national' or 'cosmopolitan' democracy have already postulated the end of the nation–state (e.g., van Crefeld 1999; Held 1995; Axtmann 2004), but this prognosis is premature (see **cosmopolitanism**). On the one hand, findings about the general inability of the nation–state to solve problems are not clear; on the other, the viability of a post-national democracy must be assessed sceptically. First, it is doubtful whether there can be a democratic legitimacy beyond the nation–state and, second, it has to be asked to what extent states and supra-national actors can change so that they see themselves as members of an international community able to accept their mutual and common interests (Habermas 2001).

The historical success of the nation–state, to which there is (still) no real alternative,

makes the end of the nation–state highly improbable. Wherever a democratic system has been successfully established, this has always occurred within the framework of a nation–state.

References and further reading

Axtmann, R. (2004) 'The State of the State: The Model of the Modern State and its Contemporary Transformation', *International Political Science Review*, 3: 259–79.

Beyme, K. von. (1986) 'The Contemporary Relevance of the Concept of the State', *International Political Science Review*, 2: 115–19.

Easton, D. (1953) *The Political System: An Inquiry into the State of Political Science*. New York: Knopf.

Habermas, J. (1975) *Legitimation Crisis*. Boston: Beacon Press.

Habermas, J. (1996) *Between Facts and Norms: Contributions to a Discourse Theory of Law and Democracy*. Cambridge, MA: MIT Press.

Habermas, J. (2001) *The Post-National Constellation: Political Essays*. Cambridge, MA: MIT Press.

Held, D. (1995) *Democracy and the Global Order*. Cambridge: Blackwell.

Hobbes, T. ([1651] 1962) *Leviathan; Or the Matter, Form and Power of a Commonwealth Ecclesiastical and Civil*. New York: Simon & Schuster.

Luhmann, N. (1989) *Ecological Communication*. Chicago: University of Chicago Press.

Merkel, W. (2004) 'Embedded and Defective Democracies', special issue of *Democratization*, 11(5).

Parsons, T. (1951) *The Social System*. London: Routledge.

Sieyès, E. J. ([1978] 2003) *Political Writings*. Indianapolis, IN: Hackett.

van Creveld, M. (1999) *The Rise and Decline of the State*. Cambridge: Cambridge University Press.

Weber, M. (1958) *Essays in Sociology*. Oxford: Oxford University Press.

SASCHA KNEIP
and WOLFGANG MERKEL

STATISTICS

Statistical tools play a critical part in the development and testing of sociological theory, and hence in the accumulation of reliable **knowledge** about human behavior and the basic socio-behavioral processes.

Two statistical tools are paramount – probability distributions and the descriptive and inferential apparatus for estimation and testing. Probability distributions are used in three kinds of sociological analysis: (1) developing a framework, where they provide the modeling distributions for the fundamental quantities, which then become the building-blocks for theories; (2) theoretical analysis, where they enable derivation of testable predictions; and (3) empirical analysis, where they provide sampling distributions and the models for characterizing underlying distributions and unobservables. The descriptive and inferential tools are used in all types of empirical analysis, from **measurement** of single variables to estimation of relations between them to testing the predictions of deductive theories and the propositions suggested by non-deductive theories.

To illustrate our daily dependence on statistical tools, we can draw on the study of justice, focusing on one ingredient – the *justice evaluation function* (JEF) – and tracing its operation in development and testing of justice theory.

When people assess the fairness or unfairness of the rewards that they and others receive, the ensuing assessment – called the justice evaluation – is thought to vary with the logarithm of the ratio of the *actual reward* to the observer's idea of the *just reward*:

$$justice\ evaluation = \theta \ln \left(\frac{actual\ reward}{just\ reward} \right).$$

The JEF seemed so appealing that it was immediately proposed as a Law of Justice Evaluation (Jasso 1978) and used as the first assumption of a new justice theory (Jasso 1980).

When the JEF was first introduced, its appeal rested on three properties: (1) faithful mapping from combinations of the actual reward (A) and the just reward (C) to the representation of the justice evaluation (J) by the full real-number line; (2) unification of two rival views of the justice process as a ratio and difference (via properties of logarithms); and (3) loss aversion, namely, that deficiency is felt more keenly than comparable excess. These were and remain the most often cited properties (Wagner and Berger 1985). Twelve years later a proof was presented that the log-ratio form of the JEF is the only functional form that satisfies two conditions, scale-invariance and additivity (Jasso 1990). Subsequently, two more properties were identified: symmetry, and the feature that the JEF is the limiting form of the difference between two power functions, simultaneously strengthening both the unification of the rival ratio and difference conceptions and forging a new link between the rival power and logarithmic functions (Jasso 1996). More recently, a remarkable new property has been identified: analysis of the JEF and loss aversion yields a result involving the Golden Number, triggering speculation that the JEF may be more than a beautiful and convenient representation, that it may have deep roots in human nature.

Probability distributions are immediately used to model three kinds of distributions of justice evaluations – the observer-specific distribution for a collectivity, the rewardee-specific distribution, and the reflexive distribution; assembling all the justice evaluations for a collectivity in a matrix, these three distribution are represented, respectively, by the rows, columns, and diagonal of the matrix. Probing further, by assigning probability distributions to the underlying actual reward and just reward, we obtain a large new family of probability distributions which show how the combination of shapes of the A and C distributions and of the relations between A and C determine the form of the distribution of justice evaluations.

595

This simple use of probability distribution immediately yields theoretical results expressing the effects of A and C on the mean an inequality of the J distribution, including the result that as inequality in A increases, the mean of J decreases – putting on a firm footing the relation so often asserted between **inequality** and justice.

But much more is to come. Using the JEF as first postulate and a derivation technique called the macro-model yields numerous testable predictions for a wide array of disparate phenomena, underscoring the long reach of justice: (1) subgroup conflict is an increasing function of economic inequality, but the exact way that conflict depends on the proportions in the two subgroups depends on the shape of the income distribution; and (2) the proportions Selfista, Subgroupista, and Groupista in a society depend on the shape of the income distribution.

Once the true just rewards are estimated, it becomes possible to estimate the observer-specific principles of micro-justice, such as the just returns to school and experience and just **gender** effect, and the principles of macro-justice, such as the just inequality.

Further, the theory-based predictions and propositions are ready to test. These include such predictions as 'The rate of vocations to the **religious** life is an increasing function of economic inequality', 'Parents of two or more children will spend more of their toy budget at an annual gift-giving occasion rather than on the children's birthdays', and 'Blind people are less susceptible to eating disorders' (Jasso 2001).

Finally, development of justice indexes for entire societies enables two new lines of inquiry: (1) estimation of the decomposition of overall injustice into injustice attributable to poverty and injustice attributable to inequality; and (2) assessment and calibration of well-being based on inequality measures and well-being based on justice measures.

In all these activities to understand more deeply and more reliably the operation of the sense of justice, and more generally to develop and test sociological theory, statistical tools are our daily helpers.

References and further reading

Jasso, G. (1978) 'On the Justice of Earnings: A New Specification of the Justice Evaluation Function', *American Journal of Sociology*, 83: 1398–419.

Jasso, G. (1990) 'Methods for the Theoretical and Empirical Analysis of Comparison Processes', *Sociological Methodology*, 20: 369–419.

Jasso, G. (1996) 'Exploring the Reciprocal Relations between Theoretical and Empirical Work: The Case of the Justice Evaluation Function', *Sociological Methods and Research*, 24: 253–303.

Jasso, G. (2001) 'Comparison Theory', in J. H. Turner (ed.) *Handbook of Sociological Theory*. New York: Kluwer Academic/Plenum, pp. 669–98.

Jasso, G. and Liao, T. F. (2003) 'Distribution', in M. Lewis-Beck, A. Bryman and T. F. Liao (eds) *The Sage Encyclopedia of Social Science Research Methods*, vol. 1. Thousand Oaks, CA: Sage, pp. 276–80.

Wagner, D. and Berger, J. (1985) 'Do Sociological Theories Grow?' *American Journal of Sociology*, 90: 697–728.

GUILLERMINA JASSO

STATUS

Status is used as a synonym for social position and to refer to the relative ranking of individuals, **groups**, and **objects**. The Latin root *sta* or 'standing' is used in related words like stature, state, stage, station and estate. Until the nineteenth century, status referred primarily to the rights accorded to different feudal estates and implied both being in a given social position and the ranking of these positions.

Ralph Linton, Robert K. **Merton**, and others used 'status' to refer to a *social position* and linked this with **role** to refer to the set of cultural expectations relevant to a particular position (Clark 1999). *Status-set* designated the array of positions a particular person held. *Status-sequence* referred to a set of linked social positions that a given individual moved through over time, for example, infant, child, adult, or freshman, sophomore, junior. 'Social position' has, however, become the more common usage to designate a condition, office or role, and status more commonly refers to ranking, though both uses are still found in the sociological literature.

Max **Weber**'s (1968) essay '**Class**, Status, and **Party**' played a crucial role in shaping the conceptualization of **inequality** in general and status in particular. He contrasted the *status situation* to the 'purely economically determined' *class situation*, He defined status as a 'positive or negative, social estimation of honour' (ibid.: IX: 932). While status is often associated with class position, it is based on and expressed by conformity to a particular *style of life*. This involves following the appropriate fashions and manners, and restricting social **interaction** with those who are not members of one's particular social circle. A social formation based on status honour is a *status group*, which is often tied to **kinship** and is more of a **community** than classes or political parties. Indian castes, feudal **aristocracies**, and outcast groups, are important examples (see **caste**). **Ethnic** groups are a closely related phenomenon. The concept of 'status group' is on the same analytical level as the notions of 'class' and 'political party.'

Weber's placement of status on a par with economic and political **power** had numerous impacts on sociology. It became the basis of a multidimensional concept of social inequality, which served as critique of what was seen as **Marx**'s over-emphasis on economic power in general and control of the means of production in particular. This multidimensional concept of power became the basis of what was called **stratification** theory, which was sometimes contrasted to Marxian class analysis. Studies by W. L Warner (1960), August Hollings-head and many others placed individuals and **families** on various scales of socio-economic status. Reputation measures used panels of informants to rate people's standing in a local community. Subjective measures ask informants to rank themselves. Objective measures ranked people according to some combination of their education, occupation, income, etc. Extensive debates emerged about the virtues and vices of these various forms of **measurement**.

This multidimensional concept of inequality was a prerequisite to considering whether an individual's various statuses were inconsistent, for example, a high educational level but low occupational status and income, or vice versa. Gerhard Lenski, who conducted the first, careful quantitative study of this matter, used the term *status crystallization* to refer to individuals who have approximately the same levels on various dimensions of status. Lenski hypothesized that those who had crystallized statuses would experience less stress in social interaction and would be more politically conservative. Lenski's notions were intuitively appealing and have led to several hundreds of research articles testing the effects of *status inconsistency* on an array of factors from voting behavior to coronary disease. Extensive theoretical, methodological, and statistical issues emerged about which there is no conclusive agreement. In general, the empirical studies seem flawed in various respects and show little independent effect of such status inconsistency (Smith 1996).

Another important development known as *status attainment* models grew out of attempts to understand the placement of individuals in the stratification system. This had roots in earlier attempts to measure the rates of social mobility using tables that cross-tabulated a son's social strata, class, or occupation with those of his father. (Most studies ignored women.) The concern was to determine whether positions of privilege (or under-privilege) were inherited or achieved. Status attainment models, first developed by Peter Blau and Otis Dudley Duncan (1967), specified some of the social processes – parent's occupation and **education**, child's education, child's first job – that accounted for adults' location in the structure of **inequality**. An important prerequisite for such analyses was the development of *occupational prestige* scales that assigned occupational categories a quantitative score indicating their relative prestige rank within the occupational structure. This made possible the use of regression techniques. Later analyses added a number of different variables including measures of IQ and personality. The *reproduction theory* of Pierre **Bourdieu** also deals with the issue of how social status and other privileges are reproduced across generations, though he focuses on a wide array of different forms of symbolic capital including styles, accent, credentials, and social contacts, and elaborates how these are means of inheriting privileges, even under conditions where direct control of economic capital may be less relevant.

Micro-sociology that focuses on the details of interpersonal **interaction** has also devoted much attention to people's status. This includes the ethnographic work of everyday life by Erving **Goffman**. *Status expectation theory*, developed by Joseph Berger and his colleagues (Wagner and Berger 2002) and based on small group experiments, focuses on how individuals use clues, e.g. **race** or **gender**, to develop expectations of others and how these expectations in turn shape their behavior toward those individuals. Jasso (2001) has suggested a mathematically oriented framework for studying status that distinguishes between the characteristics of individuals and groups and their relationship and links micro- and macro-levels of analysis.

A *theory of status relations*, developed by Milner, explains people's behavior when status is not simply a function of economic or political power. Status is the accumulated expressions of approval and disapproval. The theory has been applied to the Indian **castes**, religious behavior, political **legitimacy**, and American teenagers (Milner 2004). Conformity to a group's norms is a key source of status. **Elites** defend group boundaries and their rank by elaborating and complicating the norms, e.g. the elaborate rules of purity in the Indian caste system and the arcane forms of conformity required by teenage crowds. In traditional societies copying the lifestyle of superiors is forbidden; in modern societies, superiors constantly change what is required to conform, and hence the importance of fashions. Association is the other source of status. Associating with high status people or objects improves one's status and with lower status people or objects degrades it – especially for intimate expressive relationships such as eating and sex. The caste system regulates who one can marry or eat with; teenagers are preoccupied with whom their peers are 'going with' and eat with in the lunchroom. In contrast to economic and political power, status is a relative rank and therefore is inflexible. For some to move up, others must move down, and vice versa. This is the source of the restricted mobility and put-downs common in status-conscious systems.

A considerable anthropological literature focuses on honor and shame (Peristany 1966). Historical work on traditional social structures (e.g. Clark 1995) continues. Notions of honor and respect have been central to analyzing urban gangs (Horowitz 1983). Various movements including prohibition, the 1990s 'culture wars', ethnic and homosexual pride movements, and religious **fundamentalism** have been referred to as status politics and are closely related to issues of respect, honor, and **sacredness**. Increasing evidence indicates that in developed societies **health** and well-being are related as closely to relative status ranking as to absolute levels of wealth

(Marmot 2004). This calls into question whether the 'good society' can be based on opportunity and growth while ignoring inequality *per se*. All these issues are in large part rooted in concerns about social status.

References and further reading

Blau, P. and Duncan, O. D. (1967) *American Occupational Structure*. New York: Wiley.

Clark, J, Modgil, C. and Modgil, S. (1999) *Robert K. Merton: Consensus and Controversy*. Philadelphia, PA: Falmer, chaps 11–13.

Clark, S. (1995) *State and Status*. Montreal: McGill-Queen's University Press.

Horowitz, R. (1983) *Honor and the American Dream*. New Brunswick, NJ: Rutgers University Press.

Jasso, G. (2001) 'Studying Status: An Integrated Framework', *American Sociological Review*, 66(1): 96–124.

Milner, M., Jr. (2004) *Freaks, Geeks, and Cool Kids*. New York: Routledge.

Marmot, M. (2004) *The Status Syndrome*. New York: Henry Holt.

Peristany, J. G. (ed.) (1966) *Honour and Shame*. Chicago: University of Chicago Press.

Smith, R. D. (1996) 'The Career of Status Crystallization: A Sociological Odyssey', *Sociological Research Online*, 1(3) (http://www.socresonline.org.uk/socresonline/1/3/3.html).

Wagner, D. G. and Berger, J. (2002) 'Expectation States Theory...', in J. Berger and M. Zeldich, Jr. (eds) *New Directions in Contemporary Sociological Theory*. Lanham, MD: Rowman & Littlefield.

Warner, W. L. (1960) *Social Class in America*. New York: Harper.

Weber, M. ([1925] 1968) *Economy and Society*. New York: Bedminster Press, IX(6): 926–40.

MURRAY MILNER, JR

STRANGER

The concept of the stranger has to be distinguished from the concept of alterity which formulates the otherness we experience in relation to any other human being (see **Other**). The stranger is a social **role** category we find in the historical semantics of nearly all human **societies**. This near universality of the semantics of the stranger makes it a very interesting **subject** for the comparative study of social **structures** of human **societies**. The semantics of the stranger is in many societies closely related to patterns of hostility and hospitality, as the stranger may function as enemy or as guest and often as both in an oscillatory movement.

Five diverging patterns of dealing with strangers can be distinguished in historical terms. First, there were societies which were incapable of recognizing strangers as strangers. In being confronted with them they easily classified strangers as ancestors or gods or other figures provided for in their **world-view**; but the disturbance in dealing with unexpected foreign persons did not arise in these societies. Second, there are societies which recognize strangers but concentrate all their reactions on eliminating the fact of strangeness. They either kill or expel strangers or integrate them by cleansing rites and adoption to **kinship** which divests them of all outer signs of strangeness. A third pattern was developed by the stratified social systems which determined a greater part of the social history of the past few thousand years. Stratified societies were the first to offer strangers a plurality of possible statuses, corresponding to the diversified social **structures** of the stratified societies themselves. There were now inner and outer strangers; tolerated, privileged and subjugated strangers (Gilissen 1958); occupations and societal enclaves that were reserved for strangers and **prohibited** for locals. Strangers filled status gaps (Rinder 1958) and **communication** gaps which are characteristic of stratified systems. In nineteenth- and twentieth-century **modernity** a fourth and again radically simplified pattern arose together with the genesis of the nation–state. Instead of a plurality of statuses, binary classifications now appeared, aimed at distinguishing local inhabitants who were conceived of as fully-fledged members of the **nation–state** from strangers who had no such claims to membership (see **classification**). But, parallel to the rise of the nation–state, a fifth and most contemporaneous pattern already became visible. In **urban**, **cosmopolitan** settings it was soon perceived that social intercourse mostly involves interacting with people who are strangers. Therefore, we have to do with the universalization of the stranger and this implies that the strangeness of the other comes to be seen as a normal everyday occurrence, whereby it loses its disturbing character. The same condition is sometimes called the disappearance of the stranger or his/her invisibility.

It is a significant fact about the genesis of the discipline of sociology that it was closely intertwined with the last two patterns of the societal relevance of the stranger. The major figures of the classical sociology of the stranger which was formulated between 1890 and 1945 – **Simmel**, Michels, Park and **Schutz** among many others (Stichweh 1992) – were either focused on the nation–state circumstance or on the urban, cosmopolitan variant or on both. After World War II the stranger loses its central place in social theory, only to reappear in much more fragmented variants.

The first major treatment of the sociology of the stranger after World War II – Benjamin Nelson's 'From Tribal Brotherhood to Universal Otherhood' ([1949] 1969) – belongs to a much more macrohistorical variant and may function as a prelude to an adequate study of the stranger in present world society. It makes use of the formula of 'universal otherhood', and in looking at natural rights theories from seventeenth-century Europe it goes one further step in deciphering the paradoxical structures of modern attitudes towards strangers. Alberico Gentili Nelson speaks of 'calculated benevolence' towards other persons – and this may be related to numerous kindred formulations of our universalized attitudes towards other persons:

'civil inattention' (**Goffman**); 'commonplace folk' (Shaler); 'disciplined individuality' (**Elias**); 'detached concern' (Fox). Each of these attitudes towards others as strangers is obviously paradoxical. We are indifferent towards other persons in the world and there is no longer a need to dissolve or institutionalize strangeness as role category. We are used to it. But we have a minimal sympathy and minimal interest towards other persons as members of a common humanity and we treat them as individuals. From this one may derive a paradoxical oscillation between these two poles of generalized attitudes towards other people, and there is always the potential path from indifference to neglect and hostility.

References and further reading

Fox, R. C. (1959) *Experiment Perilous: Physicians and Patients Facing the Unknown*. New York: Free Press.

Gilissen, J. (ed.) (1958) *L'Étranger*, 2 vols.

Goffman, E. (1972) *Relations in Public*. Harmondsworth: Penguin

Michels, R. (1925) 'Materialien zu einer Soziologie des Fremden', *Jahrbuch für Soziologie*, 1: 296–317.

Nelson, B. ([1949] 1969) *The Idea of Usury: From Tribal Brotherhood to Universal Otherhood*, revised edn. Chicago: University of Chicago Press.

Park, R. E. (1964) *Race and Culture*. New York: Free Press.

Rinder, I. D. (1958) 'Strangers in the Land: Social Relations in the Status Gap', *Social Problems*, 6: 253–60.

Schütz, A. (1944) 'The Stranger', *American Journal of Sociology*, 49: 499–507.

Shaler, N. S. (1904) *The Neighbor: The Natural History of Human Contacts*. Boston: Houghton, Mifflin.

Simmel, G. (1908) 'Exkurs über den Fremden', in *Soziologie*. Berlin: Duncker & Humblot.

Stichweh, R. (1992) 'Der Fremde: Zur Evolution der Weltgesellschaft', *Rechtshistorisches Journal*, 11: 295–316.

RUDOLF STICHWEH

STRATIFICATION

Social stratification means that both groups and individuals are regarded as belonging to differentiated strata or classes of people in a society. The term began to be used in the social sciences in the 1940s, replacing older notions such as social **class**. Analytically, social stratification implies three aspects: (1) a distributive aspect, referring to unequal distribution of resources; (2) a relational aspect, referring to the formation of homogenous social groups or sub-collectivities according to common resource status; and (3) a positional aspect, referring to the ranking of these sub-collectivities or groups into a social hierarchy. Stratification not only refers to the horizontal differentiation of a society into different sub-populations but also involves evaluation as to why some strata are viewed as 'better' than others. This evaluation refers to the crucial dimensions of **wealth** or **money**, **power**, **education** and social **prestige**. Although it is a commonplace that wealth typically enables acquisition of power, educational qualifications and social reputation (this is sometimes referred to as the 'Matthew effect', after St Matthew's gospel, 25:29 – 'For unto every one that hath shall be given, and he shall have abundance'), these dimensions do not always coincide. They are interdependent in a social sense but independent in an analytical sense. Thus, it is advisable to speak of either 'status consistency' and 'status crystallization' or 'status inconsistency' (see **status**). For example, a physician may be high-earning, highly qualified, influential and have a good reputation. On the other hand, a pimp may possess considerable financial resources but few formal qualifications and low occupational prestige.

Apart from the earliest 'primitive' communities, every human society is stratified in some sense. Early tribal societies typically involved an elementary division of labour (see **differentiation**), incorporating the roles of the chief and the shaman. Early European medieval society formed a triangular hierarchy of three estates differentiated by the social functions of *laboratores* (labourers), *bellatores* (warriors) and *oratores* (ecclesiastics). In modern complex forms of **division of labour**, social hierarchy is determined by occupational differentiation. According to the **functionalist** theory of stratification formulated by Talcott **Parsons** (1954) and Davis and Moore ([1945] 1966), based on a modern industrial and achievement-based society, status and standing of individuals depend upon occupation, income and prestige. The focus of this theory is not on the emergence of social **inequality** but on its meaning and importance. Two questions predominate: Why do social positions differ in the prestige they attract? How are individuals allocated to positions? A number of responses are given to these questions. Every society must allocate individuals to positions and must motivate them to fulfil the obligations that go along with these positions. Furthermore, the most talented and qualified individuals must fill the most important positions. Since talents are scarce, and education is expensive and onerous, individuals must be motivated to invest in their qualification. Therefore the best system of incentives involves high remuneration tied to the most important positions. The more positions differ in the division of labour according to their functional importance for the survival of society, the more pressing the need for talent and the greater the gap between agreeable and disagreeable jobs.

This theory has been heavily criticized for its obvious ideological underpinnings (Bendix and Lipset 1966). However, it has since given rise to a notable tradition of status attainment research and mobility studies, among the best-known representatives of which are Blau and Duncan (1967). These authors ask 'how the status individuals achieve in their careers is affected by the statuses ascribed to them earlier in life, such as their social origin, **ethnic** status, region of birth, **community**, and parental **family**' (ibid.: 19). Although Blau and Duncan acknowledge that their model accounts for only 50 per cent of variance in status attainment, they conclude that achieved status is more important for society than ascribed status. This may be an overly optimistic conclusion. However, their research does indicate that even in the most perfectly open society, stratification is likely to occur in the form of meritocracy. Thus stratification appears to be a universal feature of human societies.

References and further reading

Bendix, R. and Lipset, S. M. (eds) (1966) *Class, Status and Power: Social Stratification in Comparative Perspective*. New York: Free Press.

Blau, P. M. and Duncan, O. D. (1967) *The American Occupational Structure*. New York: Wiley.

Davis, K. and Moore, W. E. ([1945]1966) 'Some Principles of Stratification', in R. Bendix and S. M. Lipset (eds) *Class, Status and Power: Social Stratification in Comparative Perspective*. New York: Free Press.

Duby, G. (1978) *Les trois ordres ou l'imaginaire du féodalisme*. Paris: Gallimard.

Kerbo, H. R. (1991) *Social Stratification and Inequality*. New York: McGraw-Hill.

Lenski, G. E. (1966) *Power and Privilege: A Theory of Social Stratification*. New York: McGraw-Hill.

Müller, H.-P. (1993) *Sozialstruktur und Lebensstile*. Frankfurt am Main: Suhrkamp.

Parsons, T. (1954) *Essays in Sociological Theory*. Glencoe, IL: Free Press.

Turner, J. H. (1984) *Societal Stratification: A Theoretical Analysis*. New York: Columbia University Press.

Young, M. (1961) *The Rise of Meritocracy 1870–2033: An Essay on Education and Equality*. London: Penguin.

HANS-PETER MÜLLER

STRUCTURAL FUNCTIONALISM

See: functionalism

STRUCTURALISM

'Structuralism' references a range of approaches and schools of thought in various fields including linguistics, **semiotics**, psychology, sociology and anthropology. In the social sciences, these emphasize structural features of social relations and symbolic **culture**, rather than human agency, subjectivity or historical evolution. Structuralists seek to understand the organization of phenomena in terms of the interrelation of their basic elements. They tend to oppose the use of general presuppositions to explain the organization of one set of phenomena by reference to a broad range of others, or to apply ideas developed in one context to other, different contexts. Similarly, structuralists often (but not always) tend to reject broad **evolutionary theories** in favour of specific studies of the organization of particular classes of phenomena. Such organization is seen as a complex of relations which determine or define their elements. For example, a structuralist approach to **social relations** would emphasize the ways in which such relations define and structure persons, groups or institutions, rather than focusing on the motives or purposes of the agents (people, organizations, etc.) who engage in those relations. Thus, structuralism is often said to emphasize form over content. Structuralists also often reject forms of study which stick mainly to observable detail, proposing instead that the surface diversity of language, social organization, or culture constitutes a set of variations in the organization of basic elements (hence, comparative studies distinguishing between classes of phenomena organized in terms of different elementary forms or 'deep structures,' or showing how apparent differences are only variations of the same basic structural relations). Applied to cultural or linguistic phenomena, structuralism has at times involved attempts to posit certain defining structural features of the human mind or consciousness, as for example, in the structural anthropology of Claude **Lévi-Strauss**.

Structuralism is often contrasted to forms of inquiry which emphasize historical development, function and process. However, structural and functionalist approaches have at times been allied, as American **structuralist-functionalist** sociology, or in 'genetic structuralism', which posits the idea that basic organizing features of societies, cultures or **languages** develop, shift or are otherwise transformed over time.

Structuralism in the social sciences traces its lineage to the structuralist linguistics of Saussure and Jakobson, to the philosophy of C. S. Peirce, and especially to the emphasis by **Durkheim** and his school on structural features to be found in symbolic culture and in 'elementary' social **forms**. A structuralist emphasis was especially evident in subsequent semiotic theory, in analyses of **myth** and **ritual** by Propp, Dumézil and others, and in anthropological studies of cultural classification systems by Lévi-Strauss.

In the work of Louis **Althusser**, and later, Nicos Poulantzas, a structuralist emphasis was deployed to combat **historicist** and 'humanist' tendencies in Marxism. Althusser stressed the structural qualities of relations of production, arguing that these relations constitute members of societies as particular ideological **subjects**. Thus to understand the human condition in **capitalism**, one should not try to identify some 'alienated' human essence, but rather should seek to specify the social relations in terms of which consciousness and social organization are constituted in given instances. Althusser thereby 'decentred' the human subject as an effect of relations of which it is not the source. Althusser also stressed the relative autonomy of various social, cultural and political structures, maintaining a Marxist emphasis on economic determination by arguing that these are 'determined in the last instance' by material relations of production. He was influenced by the work of Lévi-Strauss as well as the by the **psychoanalysis** of Jacques **Lacan**, who characterized the **unconscious** as analogous to linguistic structures.

The work of Michel **Foucault** has occasionally been called 'structuralist', despite Foucault's vehement objections. Like Althusser, Foucault rejected evolutionist historiography and the centrality of the human subject, turning instead to an analysis of specific 'epistemes' or later, 'discursive formations', suggesting that these succeeded each other not in terms of some evolutionary continuity, but in a series of ruptures and discontinuities. Foucault's objection to structuralism stemmed from his emphasis on the contingency of the practices by which discursive formations and institutions are constructed. He rejected any notion that these were determined by 'deep structures'. refusing any distinction between surface phenomena and their supposed underlying determinants.

Some features of contemporary **exchange theory**, **game theory** and **cybernetics** can be said to exhibit elements of a structuralist approach, but structuralism as a self-conscious theoretical movement fell out of favour in the 1980s. Nonetheless, the structuration theory (see **structuration school**) of Anthony **Giddens**, the analyses of fields and of forms of capital by Pierre **Bourdieu**, and Peter **Berger**'s discussions of the creation and experience of social structures, all constitute responses to issues raised by structuralism. Further, the **postmodern** emphasis on the social construction of reality and the contingency of 'universal' or 'essential' categories owes much to the decentring tendency of structuralism, and to its emphasis on the production of social realities, subjectivities and cultural distinctions as effects of organized relations which form their conditions of existence but continually escape their comprehension.

References and further reading

Althusser, L. (1990) *For Marx*. London: Verso.
Badcock, C. R. (1975) *Lévi-Strauss: Structuralism and Social Theory*. London: Hutchinson.

Bottomore, T. and Nisbet, R. (1978) 'Structuralism', in T. Bottomore and R. Nisbet (eds) *A History of Sociological Analysis*. New York: Basic Books.

Boudon, R. (1971) *The Uses of Structuralism*. London: Heinemann.

DeGeorge, R. and DeGeorge, F. (eds) (1972) *The Structuralists: From Marx to Lévi-Strauss*. New York: Doubleday.

Lévi-Strauss, C. (1967) *Structural Anthropology*. New York: Doubleday.

Piaget, J. (1970) *Structuralism*. New York: Basic Books.

Rabinow, P. and Dreyfus, H. L. (1983) *Michel Foucault: Beyond Structuralism and Hermeneutics*. Chicago: University of Chicago Press.

Sturrock, J. (ed.) (1979) *Structuralism and Since: From Lévi-Strauss to Derrida*. Oxford: Oxford University Press.

WILLIAM RAMP

STRUCTURATION SCHOOL

The term 'structuration' (deriving from **Piaget** and Gurvitch) has acquired a particular sociological meaning largely as the result of the work of the British theorist Anthony **Giddens**. Structuration refers to 'the structuring of social relations across time and space' (Giddens 1984). As such, it is the outcome of the interaction of pre-existing **structure** and individual or collective **agency**, in which neither agency nor structure is accorded primacy. A particular definition of 'structure' is employed by Giddens, in which structure is – as it were – *virtual* and refers to the 'rules and resources' that do not exist apart from actors. Social relations are then seen as the outcome of the operation of a 'duality of structure' in which structure is the both medium and outcome of the **action** it recursively organizes. For Giddens, structures can always in principle be examined in terms of their structuration 'as a series of reproduced practices', in which structures must also be seen as enabling as well as constraining.

Rather than existing as a unified 'school' involving an explicitly stated collective view, a number of theorists can be identified

as embracing a broadly structurationist approach involving an emphasis on the process of reproduction and transformation of society via the operation of both agency and structure and an opposition to a dualism of action (or agency) and structure, which characterizes much previous sociological theory. Other contemporary theorists who can be seen to adopt such an approach include Bhaskar, **Bourdieu** and **Elias**. However, there is a noticeable lack of agreement on how 'structure' should be conceptualized. In the case of Bhaskar there is an insistence on a more concrete 'macro' conception of structure than Giddens's and a clearer 'analytical' distinction between structure and agency (see also Layder 1994).

In practice, the distinctiveness claimed for a structurationist approach may have been exaggerated, its proponents tending to caricature earlier approaches as over emphasizing either action or structure. In such caricatures, two main general positions are typically identified: (1) theorists (e.g. **Durkheim**) and approaches (e.g. **structuralism**, structural **functionalism**, Althusserian Marxism) are seen to represent social life as largely determined by social structure, with individual action mainly explained as the outcome of structure; (2) theorists (e.g. **Weber**) and approaches (e.g. **symbolic interactionism**, **ethnomethodology**, social **phenomenology**) that reverse the emphasis, stressing the capacity of individuals – of 'individual agents' – to construct and reconstruct their worlds. The latter approaches often couch social explanations in actors' terms.

It can, in fact, be argued that most forms of sociological theory are implicitly structurationist, acknowledging the force of both individual agency and structural determinacy. Nonetheless, crucial issues in conceptualizing the relationship between agency and structure have been illuminated by the explicit formulations and debates that have taken place in relation to Giddens's structuration theory.

It is the comprehensiveness and conceptual innovation of Giddens's structuration theory that perhaps explains its wide influence. Responding to the **linguistic turn** in social theory, his conception of 'structure' as 'rules and resources' draws directly on structuralism. Specific sets of rules and resources become the identifiable structural properties and principles of particular societal collectivities and systems. Taking a cue from phenomenology and ethnomethodology, the **self** (possessing 'discursive' as well as 'practical' consciousness) is framed as 'competent', and 'knowledgeable' about his/her own action. Here the concept of the 'double hermeneutic' is also important: the ever present interaction of the meaningful worlds of lay actors and sociologists. Drawing on **Heidegger** and the work of the *Annales* historians, and avoiding any hard-and-fast distinction between synchrony and diachrony, a structurationist approach 'grasps the time-space relations inherent in the constitution of all social interaction' as a central aspect of the 'duality of structure'.

Giddens advances structuration theory as a 'social ontology' to aid analysis and as an orientation to social research. However, it is clear that 'structurationist' reformulations of the relations between structure and agency as mutually implicated and mutually independent have not ended debates about the finer details of the relations between the two, or the prior, or interrelated, question of how agency and structure should be defined in the first place. Thus, Layder (1994) regards Giddens's conception of structure as depriving this concept of any 'autonomous properties or pre-given facticity', while Bryant and Jary (1991) among others detect a persistent bias towards agency. Moreover, whatever sophistication **ontological** formulations of the structure-agency relations may achieve, issues are likely to remain in the application of such notions to concrete cases.

For Peter Berger and his associates (see **Berger and Luckmann**), the relation between society and the individual is one in which society forms the individuals who create society in a continuous dialectic: 'social structure is not characterizable as a thing able to stand on its own, apart from the human activity that produced it'. However, once created, it can be 'encountered by the individual as an alien facticity (and) a coercive instrumentality' (Berger and Pullberg 1966), even if a humanly constructed reality only comes to take on the *appearance* of having been constructed by some external, non-human, force.

Roy Bhaskar (1979), although sympathetic to much of Giddens's approach and unhappy about the dialectical emphasis in Berger's approach (which he sees as wrongly presenting action and structure as 'separate moments'), nevertheless contends that a 'transformational' view of the individual/society relation such as Giddens's requires a much stronger emphasis on **society** as 'both the ever present *condition* and the continually reproduced *outcome* of human agency'. As a critical realist, he also wants to insist on the 'reality' rather than the virtuality of structures, even if within a transcendental **realism**, where 'causal powers' are apparent only via their outcomes.

Alongside a shared opposition to antinomies (including objectivism and subjectivism), affinities exist between Bourdieu's theories and Giddens's structuration theory; for example, between the latter's view of structure and Bourdieu's concept of **habitus**. However, Bourdieu's viewpoint on human action – while recognizing that actors are purposive and reflexive beings – seems to give far greater emphasis to structural determination.

The case for Elias to be seen as structurationist rests upon his use of the term structuration, an emphasis on 'process' within his 'figurational theory' (see **figuration**), and his denial of the 'so-called' problem of the 'individual and society'. There are claims that in his early career Giddens was directly influenced by Elias.

605

However, it is Giddens who is by far the more systematic and front-ranking of the structurationist theorists.

Questions continue to be widely raised concerning the conception of structure used by Giddens. John B. Thompson, for example, repeats that this loses the substantive, institutional and constraining aspects uppermost in most other senses of social structure (Thompson and Held 1990). However, in defence of Giddens, this sense of social structure is retained when Giddens refers to *particular* social institutions, 'structural properties' and **social systems**. He also concurs with the view that actors reproduce and transform rather than create social institutions. Giddens (1993) meets Mouzelis's further charge that his approach neglects collective action and the macro level by responding that there are multiple levels of collective activity and that collective action with macro implications can arise from small groups of individuals.

One final criticism of importance in relation to Giddens's structurationism is that, despite its reference to the **unconscious**, it is over cognitivist and over-rationalist in its framing of agency, failing to do justice to the fragmentary nature of the self or to the **emotions**, (e.g. as portrayed by **Lacan**). As such, Giddens has been described as the 'last **modernist**'. However, this is not a label which Giddens or other structurationists would resist. While drawing on a range of post-structuralist and psychoanalytic theories, the structuration approach remains thoroughly sociological and recognizably continuous with the classical sociological tradition.

References and further reading

Berger, P. and Luckmann, T. (1967) *The Social Construction of Reality*. London: Allen Lane.

Berger, P. and Pullberg, S. (1966) 'Reification and the Sociological Critique of Consciousness', *New Left Review*, 35.

Bhaskar, R. (1979) *The Possibility of Naturalism*. Brighton: Harvester.

Bourdieu, P. ([1980] 1990) *The Logic of Practice*. Cambridge: Polity.

Bryant, C. and Jary, D. (eds) (1991) *Giddens' Theory of Structuration*. London: Routledge.

Bryant, C. and Jary, D. (eds) (2001) *The Contemporary Giddens*. London: Palgrave.

Elias, N. ([1970] 1978) *What Is Sociology?* London: Hutchinson.

Giddens, A. (1984) *The Constitution of Society*. Cambridge: Polity.

Giddens, A. (1993) *New Rules of Sociological Method*, 2nd edn. Cambridge: Polity.

Layder, D. (1994) *Understanding Social Theory*. London: Sage.

Mouzelis, N. (1991) *Back to Sociological Theory*. London: Macmillan.

Thompson, J. and Held, D. (eds) (1990) *Social Theory of Modern Societies*. Cambridge: Cambridge University Press.

DAVID JARY

STRUCTURE

Because the concept of structure, and especially social structure, evokes the conception of an objective, collective level of social reality with resilience and determinant force, it is at once a central concept in sociology, a loosely arrayed range of conceptual tools, and also a site of very considerable analytical contestation.

Structure concerns the relationships among the parts of some social phenomenon, and further, how those parts are constituted and the nature of the boundary that mediates between the structure and its environment. Structural approaches tend to agree that there are two foci of analysis: that individual attitudes and behaviors are shaped (in varying ways, and to varying extents) by the position that a person holds in a social structure, and that the properties and trajectories of social structures themselves need to be analyzed.

Different structural approaches provide alternative perspectives on what the parts are and what the nature of the relationships binding them are. They vary from implicit use of structural models through to formal **structuralism**. Claims are made that structure can be found at different levels of abstraction: at its simplest, structure merely means the patterns that can be discerned in the flux of **everyday** life, but more often structure means deeper relationships, which underlie these patterns. Claims are also made that structure can be found at different scales: structures have been unearthed at the micro-level of social **interaction**, in small groups, within and among broader **organizations** and groupings, at a societal level and on the **world-systems** level (see also **micro-, meso-, and macro-levels**).

'Structure' (from Latin, *structura*) is a term derived in medieval times from the construction industry to mean the framework of building, but also the activity of construction, and has since spread more widely across many realms of activity. According to the *Oxford English Dictionary*, **Tocqueville** (1835) was the first to use the term 'social structure' followed by **Spencer** (1872) and then by references in the 1940s (Fortes) and 1960s (**Lévi-Strauss**).

There is a range of fairly straightforward synonyms: social order, arrangement, composition, fabric, **form**, organization, pattern, system, web, etc. 'Social order' may imply rather more consensus than other terms, and 'social system' may imply a more definitely closed-system of interactive interrelationships. 'Society' can have a rather more differentiated meaning since it is often used to refer to that particular form of higher-level social structure which is largely (at least potentially) self-sufficient and self-contained (e.g. **tribes** or **nation–states**) (see **society**).

Structure is often absent in appropriate discussions. Nevertheless, it is often evoked as a boundary-marker of sociology, as opposed to anthropology's central concept of **culture** (although that distinction is not very viable). Since the reception of a concept will depend on its fit with the cultural ambiance of the times, the popularity of the concept has waxed and waned. Sewell (1992) has suggested that the difficulties

engendered in contemporary times by the term's connotations, which imply a vision which is too hard and reified, too impervious to change, and too contradictory, may limit its use.

Structural analyses have long been conducted by historians and other social commentators, especially from the onset of modernity. C. Wright **Mills** identified (and collected in his 1960 anthology) many examples of broad structural analyses. While none of the now recognized founding fathers of sociology had a well-developed and explicit model of social structure, a concern with social structure was central within their work. For **Marx** in particular, and **Weber** to a lesser extent, structural analyses particularly focused on **class**. Weber's analysis of **bureaucracy** is also important. Both emphasized the interplay with **action** and **agency**, although their philosophical bases were quite different. **Durkheim** was the one most seriously concerned with social structure, providing an aggressive statement of an anti-reductionist, collectivist approach in sociology. However, even for Durkheim, the precise term is used only in passing, and references are usually made more generally to society and to the social bonds constituting society. At a more descriptive level, Durkheim developed a conception of 'social morphology' involving accounts of the nature (e.g. size, functions), number, arrangement (e.g. spatial distribution) and interrelations (e.g. modes of communication, movement and mutual obligation) among the social parts (individual or collective) of a society. The structural analytical contributions of **Simmel** have proved to be of lasting significance. At a more micro-level, Simmel developed a 'formal' sociology in which the properties of small groups and social situations were seen to affect behaviour across a range of social contents.

Beginning in the late 1920s, and maturing in the immediate post-war period, a particular and self-conscious analytical approach to structural analysis was developed by the British school of **structural functionalists** – Malinowski, Radcliffe-Brown, and a later slew of texts culminating in Nadel's theoretical treatise (1957). Earlier approaches in which emphasis was placed on the evolution and diffusion of cultural traits were rejected. Instead, the functionalists' emphasis lay in understanding the current operation of small-scale societies (and later rather larger African ones). Apparently 'strange' tribal practices could be 'mapped' onto more commonly-understood Western concepts.

During the 1950s and 1960s, American sociology was dominated by an approach generally labelled as 'structural-functionalist', involving translation and adaptation of British anthropology into a more modern and larger-scale American context. One path of this work lay in the development of research tools (such as surveys) for investigating social structures. While much of this structural sociology retained a strong interest in the patterns among the characteristics of individuals, surveys were also employed to study characteristics of various types of social units such as **groups**, **families and households**, organizations, suburbs, **regions** and **nations**. Another path lay in the development of concepts such as '**role** theory', 'reference groups' and 'social system', and a range of other concepts relating to social structure that were widely deployed by a range of theorists, including **Merton** and **Parsons**.

American sociology of the 1950s was later criticized for being overly concerned with **consensus** and insufficiently attentive to **conflict**. However, a sharp distinction between consensus and conflict models proved difficult to sustain as it came to be realized that the two approaches could be seen for the most part as complementary and as sharing essentially similar underlying views of social structure.

In 1975, Peter Blau organized a group of eminent American social theorists to directly confront the concept of 'social structure'. These included several sociologists involved in historically orientated or comparative studies. As well attempting integration of the work of other structural theorists, Blau pursued his own programme of structural analysis, which he termed a 'primitive theory of social structure'. Others pursued a programme of 'radical structuralism', deliberately ignoring the sources of social meaningfulness in favour of a strongly objectivist approach.

During the late 1960s, there were two forms of structural analysis that captured much attention, both drawing inspiration partly from Marxism and both emanating from Paris (Glucksmann 1974). For Claude Lévi-Strauss social structure involved underlying symbolic linguistic models through which people experience the social world (see **symbol**). The other development was Louis **Althusser**'s 'structural Marxism', which reinterpreted Marx to fit a highly determinist understanding of social development. Althusser promulgated a three-fold distinction between the **economy**, the **polity** and the '**ideological** state apparatus'. The functional role of the latter two sectors was to repress the population by force, and through the manufacturing of consent, into supporting the continuing operation of the current mode of economic organization.

Other more recent theorists have also sought to expound a concept of social structure. In a series of works since the mid-1970s, Anthony **Giddens** has developed a theory under the banner of 'structuration' (see **structuration school**). The theory of structuration is a synthesis of (1) functionalism and structuralism, on the one hand, compromised by a deterministic emphasis on collectivities; and (2) theories stressing meaningful action on the other hand, compromised by an excessively voluntaristic emphasis on individuals and their agency. Giddens writes that structure refers to 'the structuring properties allowing the "binding" of time-space in social systems, the properties which make it possible for discernibly similar social practices to exist across varying spans of time and space and which lend them "systemic" form' (1984: 17). While Pierre **Bourdieu**'s terminology is different from Giddens's, there is some similarity in his approach. Yet the picture of social structure presented by these 'structurationist' theorists has many difficulties (Mouzelis 1995; Parker 2000).

Blau (1981) argued that structures have 'emergent effects'. These include the idea that structures: (1) have a degree of 'systemness' and interdependence; (2) persist over time, especially over generations of members; (3) consist of a set of (empty) places not dependent on the peculiarities of the particular people filling them; (4) are usually experienced as hard and factual, external to the individual and with a 'coercive force' which is sometimes quite direct, as in the application of direct physical force; and (5) continue to work 'behind their backs' of the people involved in them, irrespective of their consciousness or wilful involvement.

Conceptualizations of the nature of social structure are shaped by how they are related to various of the antimonies against which structure is usually ranged: especially the oppositions of the objective/subjective, the collective/individual, and the static/dynamic. The illustrative cross-tabulation in Table 2 shows two axes of the interrelations between objective/subjective, social/cultural, macro/micro, and collective/individual. It can be used to categorize different varieties of social structural theory, each of which seems best located in a different

Table 2. Two axes of different views of structure

	Objective/social	Subjective/cultural
Macro/collective	1 Macro-structural models	2 Cultural functionalism
Micro/ individual	3 Rational choice theory	4 Negotiated social orders

'home' cell. Some are 'purely' structural (e.g. Blau, in Cell 1) while others require considerable interdependence between the cultural and the social (e.g. Parsons, in Cell 2). Rational choice theorists (in Cell 3) see structure as arising out of individual patterns of action and interaction. The most fluid conceptions of social structure have their home in Cell 4 in the idea of 'negotiated social order' that some **symbolic interactionists** see as arising from the foundations of a micro-level 'interactional order'.

Most early conceptualizations of structure emphasize its hard, objective, collective nature against the softer cultural aspects and also against the reductionist individualism of micro-level perspectives. More recent conceptualizations emphasize ways in which the 'social' and the 'cultural' are closely intertwined: the very categories into which social realities are 'poured' are socially constructed and culturally defined. Similarly, a structural sociology that does not recognize its underpinning in the agency of its own members is clearly difficult to sustain (see **reflexivity**). Many recent theories also emphasize the 'rise and fall' of social structures as phenomena that are at once static and processual in character.

References and further reading

Blau, P. (ed.) (1975) *Approaches to the Study of Social Structure*. New York: Free Press.

Chew, Sing and Knottnerus, D. (eds) (2002) *Structure, Culture and History: Recent Issues in Social Theory*. Lanham, MD: Rowman and Littlefield.

Crothers, C. (1996) *Social Structure*. London: Routledge.

Kontopoulos, K. (1993) *The Logics of Social Structure*. Cambridge: Cambridge University Press.

Lévi-Strauss, C. (1952) 'Social Structure', in A. L. Kroeber (ed.) *Anthropology Today*. Chicago: University of Chicago Press.

López, J. and Scott, J. (2000) *Social Structure*. Buckingham: Open University Press.

Mills, C. W. (ed.) (1960) *Images of Man: The Classical Tradition in Sociological Thinking*. New York: Braziller.

609

Murdock, G. (1949) *Social Structure*. New York: Macmillan.

Nadel, S. F. (1957) *The Theory of Social Structure*. Melbourne: Melbourne University Press.

Parker, J. (2000) *Structuration*. Buckingham: Open University Press.

Porpora, D. (1987) *The Concept of Social Structure*. Westport, CT: Greenwood.

Rubenstein, D. (2001) *Culture Structure and Agency*. Thousand Oaks, CA: Pine Forge.

Sewell, W. H., Jr. (1992) 'A Theory of Structure: Duality, Agency and Transformation', *American Journal of Sociology*, 98(1): 1–29.

Smelser, N. (1988) 'Social Structure', in N. Smelser (ed.) *Handbook of Sociology*. Newbury Park, CA: Sage.

CHARLES CROTHERS

SUBCULTURE

Even in an apparently unified national culture there are subcultural differences. No society, and no 'national society' or nation–state, encompasses the **cultures** of its people uniformly. Such an issue was especially important historically for the United States of **America**, made up of various ethnic groups through migration including, for instance, Asian, Chinese, English, French, German, Hispanic, Irish, Italian, Russian, Scandinavian and Scots, not to mention the descendants of slaves from Africa as well as Native Americans themselves. In **structural-functionalist** social theory American society was seen as held together by a common **value** system, yet it was debatable to what extent the USA had a common culture. It certainly had many diverse cultures, latterly hyphenated as African-American, and so forth. Ethnic communities hosted criminal subcultures, such as the Italian Cosa Nostra. The phenomenon of subcultural **crime** and **deviance** was of prime concern to US sociology. Structural functionalism acknowledged the existence of subcultures and gave rise to much thinking and research, particularly in the work of **Merton** and Albert K. Cohen. There was also the tradition of **Chicago School** social ecology that examined the various **identities** and **community** relations in the city. This entailed a special attention to youth and an ethnographic style of enquiry.

Robert Merton's **anomie** paradigm, first formulated towards the end of the 1930s, postulated a disjunction between the cultural goals of the American dream and unequal access and blockages in the institutional means to achieving them. Disadvantaged **groups** might thus seek alternative and possibly illegitimate means of achievement. This was particularly true of **working class** males drawn into criminality. In the 1950s, Albert K. Cohen studied gang culture, which, while not a reliable means of achieving legitimate success, nevertheless provided a subcultural solution in terms of alternative criteria of accomplishment. This was a reaction formation in which young working-class males were, in effect, rewarded for their wayward behaviour by the gang's subcultural values, thus constituting a sense of belonging and an outlaw identity.

In Merton's theoretical framework and Cohen's empirical application, the formation of deviant and criminal subcultures was explained structurally, as based on responses to societal **inequality**. Another strand of subcultural analysis proffered not so much structural explanation but appreciation of exotic ways of life, such as Howard Becker's drug-taking Jazz world. Such work sought to understand deviant subcultures and, to a great extent, wound up romanticizing them. The question of juvenile delinquency, especially from the 1950s and 1960s, in effect celebrated youth rebellion. This was an enduring strand of subcultural theory and research. It became very popular in Britain from the 1970s.

British subcultural research inherited American sociological **romanticism** and combined it with a **Marxist** critique of society and the **semiotic** reading of style. Dick Hebdige's *Subculture: The Meanings of Style* (1979) was the exemplary text. It was forged in the theoretical cauldron of the

University of Birmingham's Centre for Contemporary Cultural Studies. For this school of thought, spectacular subcultures – Mods, Rockers, Rastas, Punks, and so on – were said to be issuing messages of resistance to the dominant culture in their dress, deportment, rituals and tastes constructed out of a **bricolage** of disparate elements.

Resistant subculture was not just a feature of 'the generation gap', as it was mainly considered in American research on youth culture. Instead, it was a matter of **class**. Spectacular subcultures usually had working-class roots, though not exclusively so (as in the case of the hippies). There were also issues of ethnic subordination, as was evidently so for the Rastas and their successors in Hip-hop culture (see **ethnicity**). More generally, the adoption of black culture was a salient characteristic of white youth subcultures as well. Within the mix of subcultural analysis, complaints were raised by **feminist** sociologists, notably Angela McRobbie and others, who argued that the celebration of spectacular subculture was masculine biased. Girls hardly figured. Their bedroom cultures, their interest in magazines and their feminine relation to style and sexuality were ignored. These absences were rectified in numerous studies and increasing emphasis was placed on 'race' as well as **gender** and **sexuality**.

The classical subcultural analysis of the 1970s Birmingham School was carried on up to and including Paul Willis's 1990 study, *Common Culture*, and beyond. However, the approach fragmented with the fragmentation of youth culture, recycling, picking and mixing, and ever quickening commercialization and incorporation of cultures of resistance. While marketeers are obsessed by 'lifestyle' groupings, especially the youth groups, the very idea of distinctive subcultures rising and falling in succession is no longer much of a preoccupation for sociology. This is unfortunate because there has been little attempt to make sense of older generation cultures in a comparable manner, in particular, the elderly. As well as a general concern with identity and **difference** superseding subcultural analysis, there is more interest now in ethnic cultures and especially multiple and **hybrid** identities. That youth culture has become in several respects more conformist than in the heydays of the 1960s and 1970s has made it less attractive to sociologists (see also **popular culture**).

References and further reading

Gelder, K. and Thornton, S. (eds) (1997) *The Subcultures Reader*. London: Routledge.
Hebdige, D. (1979) *Subculture: The Meanings of Style*. London: Methuen.
Jenks, C. (2005) *Subculture: The Fragmentation of the Social*. London: Sage.
Willis, P. (1990) *Common Culture: Symbolic Work at Play in the Everyday Cultures of the Young*. Boulder, CO: Westview.

JIM MCGUIGAN

SUBJECT AND SUBJECTIVITY

The term 'subject' refers to beings capable of consciousness and self-consciousness, or reflection and reflexivity, including the ability to relate to other beings and the capacity of **differentiation** from others. Somewhat paradoxically, and as the contemporary philosopher Judith **Butler** (1997) has made clear, a subject becomes a subject when it is able to treat itself as an object. Within both classical and contemporary sociological discourse, the properties of consciousness and self-consciousness have typically been assigned to *human* beings. Indeed, these properties are not only designated to humans, but these very capacities are understood to mean that human action qualitatively differs from forms of action associated with other entities. Thus, within sociological discourse, capacities towards consciousness and self-consciousness are broadly (either explicitly or implicitly) understood to be peculiarly human capacities, meaning that human action has specific characteristics, designating it as specifically *social* action. Within contemporary social theory, for example, Anthony **Giddens** (1976) argues that one of the defining characteristics of human action is **reflexivity** – that is, consciousness and self-consciousness – which allows for a recursive nature of human action and conduct. That is, human action is not mechanically reproduced but is affected and mediated by actors' **knowledge** of the world. Crucially, this formulation of action and the human subject introduces (and allows for) the idea that human conduct is subject to change, and this articulates the notion of social change at the heart of the sociological enterprise. In addition – and against positivistic notions of science – this formulation allows for the recognition that science (including the social science enterprise) is a social activity mediated by human reflexivity. In his contemporary social theory, Jürgen **Habermas** (1989) also conceives the subject as a thinking subject. Here the human subject is defined (and differentiated from other entities) via its capacities to engage in communicative action with other human beings, a form of action characterized by its linguistic properties, and especially by intersubjective dialogue.

While the sociological enterprise has certainly described the human subject as being capable of self-consciousness and reflection (and this has been central to the designation of human beings as social), mainstream social theorists have often fallen short of theorizing and elaborating this self-consciousness, and in particular of elaborating a fully fledged theorization of subjectivity. Social theory has generally glossed over the theorization of interiority in favour of the theorization of exteriority (for example, the theorization of social **collectivity** and social **structure**). For the theorization of subjectivity and its dynamic interface with exteriority, we must look beyond the mainstream of social theory and turn to those who have worked and are

working on the boundaries of social theory and psychoanalytic theory (see for example Elliot 1992) and especially to post-structuralist theory (see **psychoanalysis**; **post-structuralism**). **Freud** is a key player here, for he argued that human being-ness, and especially human drives and motivations, are driven by deep psychic structures which are for the most part unconscious. The Oedipal complex (an unconscious psychic law), for example, regulates and puts in check the free expression of **sexuality**, and in particular regulates against incest. Freud's theorization of psychic life and especially his understanding of how psychic processes regulate human conduct have been taken up in some very interesting ways by social theorists. For example, fascinating fusions of forms of Marxism with psychoanalytic theory have sought to illuminate the dynamic interface between internal psychic worlds and social structures. Herbert **Marcuse** (1969), for example, elaborated how the psychic repression of sexuality relates to broad power structures in Western societies while Juliet Mitchell (1975) elaborated how psychically mediated formations of masculinity and femininity easily lend themselves over to forms of social **organization** in **capitalist** societies, and in particular to the gendered organization of social life into **private and public** spheres.

However, for many sociologists and social theorists psychoanalytic explanation does not pass one key test central to sociological thinking, that of historicism. Psychoanalytic theories of the subject and of subjectivity are often critiqued by sociologists and social theorists for positing psychic structures in a rather universalist, ahistorical fashion that does not attend to the historicity of these structures. A key figure who has helped to rescue psychoanalytic theory from this line of critique is Jacques **Lacan**. Reinterpreting Freud's work, Lacan argues that rather than conceiving the unconscious as operating in line with universal **laws** or principles, it is better understood linguistically or symbolically, as a structure which is open to change. From this perspective, humans achieve subjectivity (the capacities of **communication**, reflection and reflexivity) when they enter into language. Lacan's rewriting of Freud has been particularly influential and significant in the theorization of **gender** and sexual difference since Lacan posited the symbolic order as a gendered order. Thus in the theorizations of sexual difference posited by writers such as Luce Irigaray, Lacanian theory is central even as it is criticized for its normalization of masculine sexuality.

While psychoanalytic theory has been central to the theorization of subjectivity, many social theorists want to avoid a focus on both the subject and subjectivity, and in particular would want to avoid unproblematic use of notions of interiority. The French post-structuralist thinker, Michel **Foucault** (1977, 1979), is foremost here in his insistence that subjectivity is a product of history, and in particular must be recognized as a key instrument of government in disciplinary society. Foucault maintained that modern societies are characterized by systems of power/knowledge (see **discourse**) which incite or evoke an elaboration of subjectivity, or a sense of 'depth' or interiority *vis-à-vis* the **person**. The birth of expert knowledges, especially those related to the emergence of administrative professions and **bureaucracies** played a key role in this elaboration of subjectivity. The techniques of psychoanalysis, for example, encouraged people to think of themselves as possessing (and brought into being the idea of) a dramatic inner psychic life, establishing subjectivity as both an object of professional and self-knowledge. Yet at the same time as inciting or bringing into being self-knowledge, such techniques encouraged a particular form of regulation, namely self-regulation. The practice of confession for example, brings particular areas of life into being, yet at the same time encourages their (self) regulation. In Foucault's view

the elaboration of subjectivity must be understood as tied into (and inseparable from) the operation of a specifically modern form of **power**, biopower, which both creates and administers forms of life. To know oneself (the process of the becoming of the subject) therefore always involves subjection to power. From this perspective, rather than an explanation of subjectivity, psychoanalysis should be conceived as a form of expert knowledge which has worked (along with other knowledges) to bring modern forms of subjectivity and power into being.

Further important work in the understanding of modern subjectivity is found in the work of contemporary feminist philosopher Judith Butler (1993, 1997). Butler explores the limits of and exclusions from subjectivity by considering the significance of psychic processes of the abjection and repudiation of desire in subject formation. Her argument is not simply that subjectivity acts as a norm from which there are certain exclusions, but rather that subjectivity and the subject can only come into being (can only be achieved) through the very processes of repudiation and abjection. Butler explores these processes particularly in regard to the formation of heterosexuality, outlining their significance for the operation of what she terms the heterosexual matrix. Along with a range of other post-structuralist thinkers such as Foucault, Butler therefore demonstrates that subjectivity can in no way be taken for granted, and in particular cannot be posited as a universal.

References and further reading

Beechey, V. and Donald, J. (eds) (1985) *Subjectivity and Social Relations*. Milton Keynes: Open University Press.

Butler, J. (1993) *Bodies That Matter: On the Discursive Limits of 'Sex'*. London: Routledge.

Butler, J. (1997) *The Psychic Life of Power: Theories in Subjection*. Stanford, CA: Stanford University Press.

Elliot, A. (1992) *Social Theory and Psychoanalysis in Transition: Self and Society from Freud to Kristeva*. Oxford: Blackwell.

Foucault, M. (1977) *Discipline and Punish: The Birth of the Prison*. Trans. A. Sheriden. London: Allen Lane.

Foucault, M. (1979) *The History of Sexuality*, vol. 1: *An Introduction*. Trans. R. Hurley. London: Allen Lane.

Giddens, A. (1976) *New Rules of Sociological Method*. London: Hutchinson.

Habermas, J. (1989) *The Theory of Communicative Action*, vol. 2: *Lifeworld and System*. Trans. T. McCarthy. Cambridge: Polity.

Henriques, J., Hollway, W., Urwin, C., Venn, C. and Walkerdine, V. (1984) *Changing the Subject: Psychology, Social Regulation and Subjectivity*. London: Methuen.

Irigaray, L. (1985) *The Sex Which Is Not One*. Trans. C. Porter with C. Burke. Ithaca, NY: Cornell University Press.

Marcuse, H. (1969) *Eros and Civilization: A Philosophical Inquiry into Freud*. London: Allen Lane.

Mitchell, J. (1975) *Psychoanalysis and Feminism*. Harmondsworth: Penguin.

LISA ADKINS

SUICIDE

See: deviance

SURVEILLANCE

See: social control

SYMBOL

Symbol derives from the Greek verb *symballein*, 'to throw together', and its noun *symbolon*, 'mark', 'emblem', 'token' or 'sign'. While the word 'symbol' is often used as a synonym of 'sign', something that stands for something else, symbols are generally regarded as a sub-species of signs, having only a functional value, and being open to interpretation, variable and equivocal, and essential prerequisites of a normative order. For some thinkers symbols simultaneously manifest the cognitive code that culture provides for all mental activity and an imaginative divergence from reality. A typical proponent of this understanding is the German idealist philosopher Ernst Cassirer, for whom symbols are the means by which synthesis is created in the perceptual manifold, although 'physical reality seems to recede in proportion to man's symbolic advances' (Cassirer 1945: 43). Most social theorists contend that symbolization has preconditions rooted in social institutions 'common-sense' experience or in social **interaction**.

According to **Durkheim**, society can form itself only through the creation of collective ideals, and these in turn can be manifested only when objects are selected, invested with a unique **prestige** and embedded in **ritual** practices. Objects become symbols, and the world is transformed: 'collective thought substitutes for the world revealed to us by the senses, a quite different world which is nothing other than the projection of the ideals it constructs' (quoted in Lukes 1973: 424). While such symbolism is necessary for all social life and for **society** to become conscious of itself, social science needs to penetrate beneath the symbol 'to the reality which it represents and which gives it true meaning'. That reality is society itself (Lukes 1973: 460–1). Symbols are the site of sociality, products of society; but, once produced, they influence the structure of society.

A contrary orientation was developed in the **phenomenological** and **ethnomethodological** strands of social theory. Developing the phenomenology of Edmund Husserl and Max Scheler, the Austrian-born philosopher and social theorist Alfred **Schutz** argued that agents produce 'finite provinces of meaning' in order to remember connections between phenomena, recording the structures of the common sense world, and then develop **intersubjective** 'signs' in order to communicate meanings. In this way, social actors transcend what they encounter in everyday life. Symbols act as a conduit between the so-called 'quotidian realm' of everyday life and the 'transcendence' represented by these 'provinces' (see **everyday**). When symbols are produced within groups, a given object represents a reality belonging to an entirely different province of meaning (Schutz 1964). We thus have the same progression away from the immediately given as was noted by Cassirer and Durkheim. This mode of thought is continued in the work of Peter **Berger and** Thomas **Luckmann** (1973).

The **symbolic interactionist** school of sociology and social psychology developed from the work of the American philosopher and sociologist George Herbert **Mead**, who argued that the mind and self emerge from the social process of significant communication. According to Mead, 'mind' is based on the exchange of mutually recognized vocal gestures or 'significant symbols' in social interaction: 'only in terms of gestures which are significant symbols can thinking – which is simply an internalized or implicit conversation of the individual with himself by means of such gestures – take place' (1934: 47). Mind emerges from interaction between the human organism and its social environment. This takes place through the development of significant symbols. Research into symbolic (inter-)action was further stimulated in the United States by the literary theorist Kenneth Burke, who stressed the contextual meanings of symbols. According to Anselm Strauss, the progenitor of **grounded theory** symbols are products of social interaction, which constitute the fabric of interaction and thus condition interaction (Strauss 1991).

In the **structuralist** tradition, often inspired by the French anthropologist Claude **Lévi-Strauss**, culture is viewed as a symbolic system based around **binary** oppositions, which structure the basic characteristics of mind. In the work of Roland **Barthes**, the **methodology** arising from this perspective was applied to contemporary society, with particular reference

to the mass **media** (Barthes 1972). In the work of such figures as the American anthropologist Clifford **Geertz** the analysis of symbolic systems highlighted the specificities of individual cultures, while the Romanian-born historian of religions Mircea **Eliade** contended that it was possible to identify a panhuman mythical paradigm.

The question of symbols is also a crucial dimension of **psychoanalysis**, in which the fanciful, subconscious resemblances between symbol and the thing symbolized are stressed. This position was especially developed by the Swiss psychologist Carl Gustav Jung, who proposed a theory in which mythological themes become widespread not only because of the spread of a particular culture but also because archetypal images or symbols make up a 'collective **unconscious**'.

These trends, although different, are certainly not mutually exclusive. Jürgen **Habermas**, for instance, has combined the principles of social interactionism with research into the strategies that agents employ in order to achieve certain ends: agents aim for certain perlocutionary effects through the manipulation of symbolic structures. Pierre **Bourdieu** has combined the ideas of, among others, Cassirer, Durkheim, **Weber** and **Marx** to argue that such strategies have institutional preconditions. Thus, questions connected with symbolism are brought under the heading of 'symbolic capital', that is, 'economic capital when it is known and recognised'. 'Symbolic relations of power' impose categories of perception and thereby 'tend to reinforce the power relations that structure social space' (Bourdieu 1989: 21).

References and further reading

Barthes, R. (1972) *Mythologies*. London: Cape.
Berger, P. and Luckmann, T. (1973) *The Social Construction of Reality*. Harmondsworth: Penguin.
Bourdieu, P. (1989) 'Social Space and Symbolic Power', *Sociological Theory*, 7(1): 14–25.

Cassirer, E. (1945) *An Essay on Man*. New York: Doubleday.

Durkheim, E. (1976) *The Elementary Forms of Religious Life*. London: Allen and Unwin.

Habermas, J. (2001) *The Liberating Power of Symbols: Philosophical Essays*. Cambridge: Polity.

Lukes, S. (1973) *Emile Durkheim: His Life and Work*. Harmondsworth: Penguin.

Mead, G. H. (1934) *Mind, Self and Society from the Standpoint of a Social Behaviorist*. Chicago: University of Chicago Press.

Schutz, A. (1964) 'On Multiple Realities', in *Collected Papers I*. The Hague: Martinus Nijhoff, pp. 340–56.

Strauss, A. (1991) *Creating Sociological Awareness: Collective Images and Symbolic Representations*. New Brunswick, NJ: Transaction.

CRAIG BRANDIST

SYMBOLIC INTERACTIONISM

The title 'symbolic interactionism' was adopted by Herbert **Blumer** as a name for the sociological position that he partially drew and partially extrapolated from the 'social behaviorist' thought of the philosopher George Herbert **Mead**. The central concern of the approach is the study of social **interaction** and the mediation of such interaction by **symbols** or symbolizing systems of **meaning**. The title was coined to name a distinctive approach to sociology but has been used also as the name for a school, the **Chicago School**, involving (loosely) affiliated researchers who began or spent their careers there. The unity and coherence of the supposed school has always been subject to reservations from those who have been attributed membership, and the heterogeneity of views within it is a matter of scholarly debate even today. Everett Hughes was as significant a figure in influencing the school as Blumer, primarily through his approach to empirical investigation of the world of **work** in particular – though Hughes was reluctant to engage in explicit theoretical argument. Among the most prominent names subsequently associated with the school are Howard S. Becker, Erving **Goffman** and Anselm Strauss, while leading contemporary advocates include Gary Allen Fine and David Maines.

Blumer elaborated Mead's view into a conception of 'society as symbolic interaction', retaining Mead's principal objective of overcoming needless opposition between the individual and society, treating these as reciprocally formed. An individual's nature and behaviour can be understood in the context of **social relations**, being formed in and through participation in those relations. The nature of those social relations must themselves be understood as a resultant of the **actions** of those individuals as they address, reproduce and modify social arrangements even as they participate in them.

The first premise of Blumer's approach was that individuals respond to an environment to which they attribute meaning. It is not the intrinsic nature of situations that gives rise to their actions but their perceived character. (This idea received one of its most explicit and controversial applications in the 'labelling theory of **deviance**', holding that deviance is not intrinsic to an action, but is bestowed upon it by the 'societal reaction'.) The fundamental relationship between individuals and their environment is fundamentally one of 'interpretation', of deciding how a situation is to be identified, understood, and responded to. However, the point for Blumer was to avoid exclusive concentration on the individual and to emphasize that the materials and means through which interpretation is undertaken are social and collective. The understandings that the individual brings to bear in interpretation are those that have been initially formed within the social setting and acquired from it by the individual, and the interpretation of situations is something that individuals commonly do together, arriving at shared understandings and responding through joint projects of action. This encouraged a conception of social phenomena as emergent: individuals do not just act out understandings they have inherited; rather, they modify, revise and elaborate these understandings in their response to and interpretation of situations. In this sense, they are both participants in and reconstructors of the social relations that have been handed down to them. Interpretation is thus fundamental to social life as a whole, applying in principle to all levels of activity, regardless of scale and complexity.

The approach was first articulated by Blumer in the 1930s, but became most influential during the 1950s and 1960s when it offered opposition to the ambitions of the then predominant structural **functionalism** of Talcott **Parsons** as well as the 'variable analysis' methodology associated with Paul Lazarsfeld. The adherents of interactionism regarded the dominant functionalist approach as involving an excessively generalizing and uncritical acceptance of **authority**, including the authority of the **profession** of sociology itself. A more sceptical view of authority was recommended and pursued in terms of sociological conceptualization and practical implementations. Yet symbolic interactionism's critical role was soon eclipsed by more militant political critiques of the status quo that saw the dominant sociological orthodoxy as providing a merely ameliorative gloss on a society in need of radical change. The most notable partisan of this view was Alvin Gouldner (1970).

While the major conceptual contributions of symbolic interactionism had been outlined by the late 1960s, work has continued within the tradition and innumerable studies have been made under its aegis. There have been many attempts to update the approach in ways that suggest a rapprochement with developments such as **social constructionism**, **semiotics** and **postmodernism**.

Critics of symbolic interactionism tend to regard it as being unable to deal adequately with large scale or systemic social phenomena; but such criticisms have invited counter-responses of various kinds. To a significant extent, many of the leading themes of the symbolic interactionists have been incorporated into general sociological self-understanding today. There is an important sense in which it can be said that we are 'all interactionists now' (Akinson and Housley 2003).

References and further reading

Atkinson, P. and Housley, W. (2003) *Interactionism*. London: Sage.
Blumer, H. (1986) *Symbolic Interactionism*. Berkeley, CA: University of California Press.
Bulmer, M. (1984) *The Chicago School of Sociology*. Chicago: University of Chicago Press.
Charon, J. (2004) *Symbolic Interactionism*. 8th edn. Upper Saddle River: Pearson Prenctice Hall.
Denzin, N. (1992) *Symbolic Interactionism and Cultural Studies*. Oxford: Blackwell.
Gouldner, A. (1970) *The Coming Crisis of Western Sociology*. London: Heinemann.

WES SHARROCK

SYSTEMS THEORY

The importance of comprehending systems pre-dates 'systems theory' as a branch of technical theorizing in the social sciences. In German idealist philosophy, conceptions of the 'system of knowledge' suggested that a particular phenomenon can only be understood as a part of a whole. This is the case, for example, in Fichte's idea of the subsumption of all differences within a wholeness or in Hegel's (see **Hegelianism and neo-Hegelianism**) 'system of reason' in *The Phenomenology of Spirit*. In this milieu of philosophical and **metaphysical** thinking, the term 'system' refers to a holistic structure which controls all constituent phenomena. Each particular element is subordinate to the general structure of a more encompassing system characterized by a high degree of order. In general, systems suggest the idea of structures in which degrees of freedom are limited and in which a special kind of total **rationality** is enacted (see also '**totality**').

For many sociologists, the concept of a *systemic* approach or a *systemic level* emphasizes the effect of a general structure of rationality operating above the heads of individual actors. The central concept is that of the **social system**. The regulating power of a system is associated with a top-down hierarchy of control. However, what has technically come to be called 'systems theory' since the first half of the twentieth century has rather less to do with this common-sense understanding. Contemporary systems theory argues that particular phenomena can be understood neither as the result of a deduction from general principles, nor as the result of isolated actions. Instead, it advocates a model thematizing interrelationships between of phenomena. 'Control' is admittedly the fundamental subject of systems theory, but not control in the sense of a top-down process or a one-way street. In a narrower and stricter sense, systems theory begins with the insight in **cybernetics** that control in dynamic structures is a *mutual* process. Together with cybernetics, systems theory addresses the question of how systems become self-steering and regulating, and how feedback loops enable special forms of reactions and practices in complex systems to emerge. Systems theory has its roots in **communication** theory, in chaos theory, and in what Bertalanffy in the 1950s termed theories of 'organized complexity' (1956: 2) (see **complexity**).

Organized complexity is implied if particular phenomena exhibit mutual interaction and recursive relations to one another but not linear dependence on one another. Systems theory in this sense deals with phenomena in which the interaction between parts or individuals brings forth the structure which afterwards is the starting point for new interactions. Here seven basic ideas of systems theory can be noted:

1. A system is the result of interactions of its parts, not the other way round (the parts are not outcomes of the system).

2. These interactions have a temporal dimension, insofar as the operations of a system have to reproduce themselves by connecting individual events in succession.

3. The present state of a system is the result of its past operations.

4. The system's dependency on its own processing and the operational connectedness of its interactions constitute a boundary between the system and its environment.

5. The relation between system and environment is an asymmetric relation, insofar as changes in the environment do not bring about linear effects inside a system; rather, a system can adapt to changes in its environment only by its own operations.

6. Systems are areas of reduced and enforced complexity: on the one hand, a system reduces the possibilities of its operations; on the other hand, this reduction of possibilities is the precondition of its ability to develop a special kind of complexity.

7. Systems theory is concerned with mechanisms of possible order in the face of an improbability of order.

The emergence of systems theory can be seen as a reaction to experiences of **modernity**, insofar as modernity stands for the idea that order is primarily a *result*, rather than a precondition, of practice and practices (see **praxis and practices**). In this regard one of the basic aims of systems theoretical thinking is criticism of the Newtonian conception of linear relationships and one-to-one causation as basic principles of empirical reality. However, systems theory does not describe the world as a system in explicitly ontological terms. Rather, its conception of the wholeness or 'totality' of the world is more adequately understood in terms of an idea of *noise*. Noise in the relevant systems-theoretic sense is a space in which order is both *possible* and *improbable*. All areas of order are thus spaces with limited possibilities and degrees of lowered improbability. The functional meaning of systems thus refers to the appropriation of reduced degrees of freedom that can only be controlled by the systems themselves.

Systems theory introduces the concept of *self-referential processes* to resolve problems posed by the absence of external control mechanisms and the absence of one-to-one causal and hierarchical relations. Systems theory begins at the level of practices understood as operations, and with the dynamics of self-enforcing and self-energizing processes that bring about order against the background of the noise of the world. In this sense, a system is not an algorithm of practice or a general logical scheme from which a practice or practices can be deduced. Rather, the system *is* the practice itself. In the same sense, a system is not a mechanical device that controls everything happening inside it. Rather, it *is* what happens inside it.

In sociology, systems theory has been especially connected with the work of Talcott **Parsons** and Niklas **Luhmann**. Parsons adapted systems theoretical elements from theories of living systems to answer the question how **social systems** maintain their stability through cybernetic control processes and homeostatic mechanisms. His analysis focused on interaction between different subsystems on behalf of a more global and encompassing system of **integration**. Parsons posited a general four-function scheme, consisting of functions that must be fulfilled if the system's structure is to be stable.

Parsons's work needs to be understood in the context of a strong desire among mid-twentieth-century social scientists to find solutions to societal plurality and to unify different scientific disciplines in a well-ordered system. For today's purposes, however, Parsons's approach is too inflexible in many of its analytical assumptions. 'Neo-**functionalist**' exponents of Parsons such as Jeffrey **Alexander** (1985) have sought to avoid the impression of an over-emphasis on stability, cohesion and hierarchical control in theories about systems in sociology and have sought to respond to criticisms of Parsons's work since the 1960s. But it is the German theorist Niklas Luhmann who has contributed the most notable recent advances in sociological systems theory. In the 1960s, Luhmann emphasized the problem of beginning an analysis with an idea of a fixed set of functions or stable structures in mind. Against this, Luhmann proposes starting with functional *processes*. Thus, Luhmann's focus lies on the dynamics of emerging orders, not on the mechanisms that serve to maintain a presupposed structure. In his later work, Luhmann adapted the idea of 'autopoietic', 'self-referential' and 'operationally closed' forms of self-reproduction of social systems.

References and further reading

Alexander, J. (ed.) (1985) *Neofunctionalism*. London: Sage.

Ashby, W. R. (1956) *An Introduction to Cybernetics*. London: Wiley.

Baecker, D. (2001) 'Why Systems?' *Theory, Culture & Society*, 18(1): 59–74.

Bertalanffy, L. v. (1956) 'General System Theory', *General Systems, Yearbook of the Society for the Advancement of General Systems Theory*, 1: 1–10.

Buckley, W. (1967) *Sociology and Modern Systems Theory*. Englewood Cliffs, NJ: Prentice Hall.

Foerster, H. von (1981) *Observing Systems*. Seaside, CA: Intersystems.

Luhmann, N. ([1984] 1995) *Social Systems*. Stanford, CA: Stanford University Press.

Parsons, T. (1977) *Social Systems and the Evolution of Action Theory*. New York: Free Press.

Shannon, C. E. and Weaver, W. ([1949] 1963) *The Mathematical Theory of Communication*. Urbana, IL: Illinois University Press.

ARMIN NASSEHI

T

TABOO

The term 'taboo' is of Polynesian origin and entered the English language through Captain Cook, who heard the word used by Tahitians to describe forbidden or 'wrong' behaviour. In ordinary speech, taboos are often referred to as irrational, outdated **prohibitions**. But taboos may point towards fundamental rules or **sacred values** within a **society**. Breaking a taboo is dangerous, and will often be followed by punishment or ritual purification. Why human societies create taboos has remained a crucial question within comparative **religion**, anthropology and psychology. **Freud** developed his theory in *Totem and Taboo* ([1913] 1965), where he focused on two particular sets of restrained behaviour among the Australian Aborigines, the taboo against eating the totem animal, and the taboo against clan endogamy: a cultural elaboration of the Oedipus complex, according to Freud. Freudian-inspired theories suggest that taboos are created around acts of behaviour or objects for which we have a natural desire (hence the **incest** taboo).

From an idealist approach, Mary **Douglas** argues that taboos should be understood from within cultural schemes of categorization: objects or acts that fall outside the category are considered 'matter out of place' (Douglas 1966). It is not the intrinsic quality of an object that makes it 'dirty' and tabooe, nor repressed desires towards it, but its place within a larger **classification** system. Arguing from a materialist point of view, Harris (1985) suggests that taboos are useful cultural instruments for deleting types of behaviour that might be damaging to a given ecosystem. By investing the prohibition with sacredness, individuals are more likely to obey them, whereas the real cause of the taboo remains **materialistic**.

References and further reading

Douglas, M. (1966) *Purity and Danger: An Analysis of the Concepts of Pollution and Taboo*. London: Routledge.
Freud, S. ([1913] 1965) *Totem and Taboo: Some Points of Agreement between the Mental Lives of Savages and Neurotics*. London: Routledge.
Harris, M. (1985) *The Sacred Cow and the Abominable Pig*. New York: Touchstone.

BJØRN THOMASSEN

TAYLOR, CHARLES (1931–)
Canadian philosopher

Taylor's work in philosophy and social theory centres on the historical genesis and current state of the modern idea of the **self**. Drawing on classical thinkers like **Hegel**, **Heidegger** and **Wittgenstein** and engaging in debates with contemporaries such as **Foucault** and **Habermas**, Taylor developed original approaches in a variety of fields including a hermeneutic **methodology** of the social sciences, an expressivist account of **language**, a genealogy of the modern conception of the **self** and a history of the privatization of the good in modern moral philosophy. Taylor's analyses explicate the social and historical conditions of individual and collective identities and **practices**. His work aims at opening up alternative ways of understanding ourselves by means of a historical reconstruction of modern concepts, practices and self-understandings. Due to his critique of individualist **liberalism** and his emphasis on **community** and on **recognition**, Taylor has been regarded as a supporter of **communitarianism**. Taylor makes clear, however, that his objective is a broader self-understanding, not an abandonment of values of **freedom** and **autonomy** of the individual.

Major works

(1985) *Philosophical Papers*, 2 vols. Cambridge: Cambridge University Press.
(1989) *Sources of the Self*. Cambridge, MA: Harvard University Press.
(1991) *The Ethics of Authenticity*. Cambridge, MA: Harvard University Press.
(1995) *Philosophical Arguments*. Cambridge, MA: Harvard University Press.
(2004) *Modern Social Imaginaries*. Durham, NC: Duke University Press.

Further reading

Abbey, R. (2000) *Charles Taylor*. Teddington: Acumen.
Abbey, R. (ed.) (2004) *Charles Taylor*. Cambridge: Cambridge University Press.
Smith, N. (2002) *Charles Taylor*. Cambridge: Polity.
Tully, J. (ed.) (1994) *Philosophy in an Age of Pluralism*. Cambridge: Cambridge University Press.

ROBIN CELIKATES

TECHNOLOGY AND TECHNOCRACY

A first-order conception of technology is machinery and tools used to carry out tasks. In this sense it is usually defined as referring to physical objects such as a washing machine, a computer or a drill. A second-order conception includes the range of technical procedures involved in the operation of affairs (e.g. the arrangements of a factory assembly line, the rules governing the operation of a computer network). A third-order definition includes the expertise necessary for the operation of machines and procedures, and this is frequently a matter of human beings with specialist **knowledge** (e.g. the knowledge of water engineers controlling sewerage systems). A fourth-order definition points to the practical application of abstract knowledge, thereby including important elements of **science** (often referred to as 'technoscience'). Analyses of technology tend to be sociologically naïve when they restrict themselves to the first-order conception (technology as machinery and tools). Analyses that include some or all of conceptions two to four may lose in clarity and focus what they gain in sophistication.

Many sociologists have studied the impacts of technology on society. They may do this from a narrow perspective (e.g. the effects on particular employees of a new machine) or from a much wider point of view (e.g. the consequences for war of the introduction of the stirrup). They may also undertake this from a position of more or less hard technological **determinism**, taking the view that technology is autonomous from **society** yet capable of exercising an influence on society. Conceptually technological determinist approaches have been criticized from two positions. The first, the social shaping approach, contends that society can influence the **development** of technology itself (e.g. military budgets may skew technological innovation for defence reasons). The second, more radical intellectually if not politically, adopts a social construction approach, insisting that technology and the social are indivisible. Constructivism rejects the view that technology is autonomous from society and insists that it is imbued with social **values** and relationships.

Since the mid-1990s this has become the orthodoxy in **social studies of science** and technology, with the **actor-network theory** of Bruno **Latour** commanding much assent (see also **constructivism** and **social constructionism**).

Despite the emergence of social constructivism, much influential sociological thought has argued that technology is the major dynamic in **social change**. In the work of many classical social thinkers after **Marx**, major epochs such as the transition from Agricultural to Industrial Society are designated by technological advance, and technology is awarded a privileged role in bringing about social change. Technology is seen as representing increases in output, new products and processes (the railway engine, electricity, the microchip), and resolutions to problems (e.g. pharmaceuticals such as penicillin, birth control technologies). In these terms, technology is the application of **rationality** and reason to the social world, and advances in living conditions are the consequence. Results are evident in mortality and morbidity figures, in standards of living, and conditions of **labour** today.

It was conventional among sociologists in the 1950s and 1960s to emphasize the confluence of **modernization**, **industrialization** and technological innovation. Raymond **Aron** (1967), Walt Rostow (1960), and Talcott **Parsons** (1966) charted stages of development that put technology at the centre of their analyses. They did so because, in the words of Daniel **Bell** (1973), technology increased productivity, providing 'more for less', and thereby brought about change. The presumption here was that a technological society was a superior form and that the wealth it generated was to be welcomed. Accordingly, leading thinkers expressed a convergence theory of development, with an explicit model of **progress** forwarded on the basis of the 'logic of industrialization' (Kerr *et al.* 1960). During the late 1960s and early 1970s this

view was attacked as either hubristic or conservative, but it is noteworthy that the view of a progressive and evolutionary direction to change, one which runs along a technological route, has returned in the influential theories of the 'end of history' (Fukuyama 1992) and **post-industrial society** (Bell 1973).

This way of thinking finds an echo in much scientific **Marxist** (Gouldner 1980) analysis where the metaphor of base and superstructure pervades. Here social relationships are presumed to be founded upon forces of **production** and these are readily conceived in technological terms: material forces on which **culture**, **politics** and social life are premised come easily to be seen as technical arrangements. Because of this consonance, critics have often observed an affinity between Marxism and post-industrial society theorizations. Indeed, during the Soviet era (1919–89), the idea of a Scientific Technological Revolution (STR) emerged in post-war Eastern and Central Europe and had much in accord with post-industrial and convergence theory (Webster and Robins 1986).

Manifest problems associated with technology (e.g. global warming, oil spillages, desertification) have led some to stress unanticipated consequences of its development (e.g. congestion from increased access to the motor car, care for the very elderly and frail) and others, notably Ulrich **Beck** (1992) creating the notion of a '**risk** society' to stress the ambiguities and uncertainties of technological innovation.

The concept of technocracy is closely associated with these views. Technocrats are those who manage, operate and initiate complex technological systems. The reach of technocrats extends from research and development of advanced machinery, administering welfare organizations, to commanding political affairs. They occupy leading positions because the 'imperatives of technology' (Galbraith 1967) require their specialist knowledge and capabilities. Technocracy as a term was coined in 1919 by an engineer, William Henry Smyth, for his proposed 'rule by technicians'. It was introduced into social science thinking by the maverick critic Thorstein Veblen in his *The Engineers and the Price System* (1921). Its roots, however, can be traced to Henri de Saint-Simon who celebrated the emerging rule by scientists and engineers (the 'administration of things') that would replace militarist and monarchist authority. This legacy is evident also in Emile **Durkheim**'s account of *The Division of Labour in Society* (1893).

Technocracy is open to a variety of interpretations. During the 1930s it was generally regarded positively as a sign of the superiority of planning in politics and economic affairs. Its appeal owed much to dissatisfaction with *laissez-faire* **capitalism** that seemed incapable of controlling inflation and providing employment, and to the expansion of the modern **state**. The notion is present in James Burnham's influential tract, *The Managerial Revolution* (1941) which foresaw in **communism**, **fascism** and state intervention elsewhere the emergence of technocratic **elites**. Others have interpreted technocracy as the anti-**democratic** usurpation of power or as the result of pervasive **instrumental reason** (Habermas 1971). In this area, apprehension regarding the development of nuclear power, agribusiness and large-scale welfare organizations, with little political accountability or debate, has fuelled concern. Elsewhere, technocrats have been presented as 'servants of the powerful' as well as an inevitable feature of advanced societies (Galbraith 1967).

References and further reading

Aron, R. (1967) *The Industrial Society*. London: Weidenfeld & Nicolson.
Beck, U. (1992) *Risk Society: Towards a New Modernity*. London: Sage.
Bell, D. (1973) *The Coming of Post-Industrial Society: A Venture in Social Forecasting*. London: Peregrine.
Fukuyama, F. (1992) *The End of History and the Last Man*. Harmondsworh: Penguin.
Galbraith, J. K. (1967) *The New Industrial State*. Harmondsworth: Penguin.
Gouldner, A. (1980) *The Two Marxisms: Contradictions and Anomalies in the Development of Theory*. London: Macmillan.
Habermas, J. (1971) *Towards a Rational Society: Student Protest, Science, Politics*. Boston: Beacon.
Kerr, C. *et al.* (1960) *Industrialism and Industrial Man*. Cambridge, MA: Harvard University Press.
Parsons, T. (1966) *Societies: Evolutionary and Comparative Perspectives*. Englewood Cliffs, NJ: Prentice Hall.
Rostow, W. (1960) *The Stages of Economic Growth: A Non-Communist Manifesto*. Cambridge: Cambridge University Press.
Webster, F. and Robins, K. (1986) *Information Technology: A Luddite Analysis*. Norwood, NJ: Ablex.

FRANK WEBSTER

TERRORISM

Terrorism is a specific form of **violence**. When first used as a political concept during the French **Revolution**, the word had a positive connotation: terror was understood as a radical and necessary means of establishing social order (Robespierre). Today, after a long history of terrorist attacks and in the shadow of a huge number of victims, terrorism is held to be an odious form of attack against the social order, provoking governments to stern measures of counter-attack. But there is, at least in liberal democracies, a permanent political dispute concerning the question of what kind of violence should be understood as terrorism (Laqueur 1999) and what kind of response is appropriate (Wilkinson 2000).

Most researchers focus on terrorism as an organized system of violent attacks, undertaken by non-**state groups** against people or material objects in order to delegitimize state **power** and the ruling **class** (Hoffman 1998). Some widen this definition to include examples of 'state terrorism', but this neglects elementary characteristics of what can be described as an **ideal type** of 'terrorist strategy' (Waldmann 1998). This strategy is based on the assumption that terrorism is the weapon of relatively weak groups being unable to win open battles and **wars**. They therefore prefer sudden attacks out of the underground that function as provocations to the dominant powers. Terrorist attacks are not meant primarily to weaken the enemy by destroying its armies and the social and material infrastructure of its power. They are calculated to horrify the population so that governments, being responsible for the security of their territory, are forced to react. Their under-reaction as well as their over-reaction might destabilize the political system by turning people against their governments and motivating rising numbers of them to engage in political resistance, perhaps even guerrilla war.

In their efforts to explain the phenomenon of terrorism, social scientists refer to the fact that most terrorist groups appear to be factions of broader **protest** groups and **social movements**. That parts of them turn militant and vanish into the underground is best understood sociologically as an outcome of a complex interplay of conflicting actors. To analyze their **interaction** system, one must take into account several reference groups. The nucleus of the field of conflict is constituted by the terrorist groups themselves. Usually, the operating groups are rather small and only loosely connected in a **network**-style of organization. Not only the personal lives of terrorists, but also their strategies and actions, seem to be strongly influenced and radicalized by their persecuted and isolated existence in the underground. It is relevant for the operational strategies of terrorists as well as for the reactions and interpretations of the public that the attacks hurt and/or kill people with whom the terrorists have no prior or ongoing interaction. The **actions** of terrorists are clandestinely prepared, socially one-sided, and usually their victims are innocent bystanders. The different types of terrorism, however, vary with regard to the specification and quantification of their victims. Distinguishing between left and right extremist terrorism and, furthermore, ethnoseparatist and **fundamentalist-religious** terrorism, researchers find the latter groups characteristically unconcerned about the kind and number of people they kill (Rapoport 1992). Not only the Islamic groups of Al Qaeda demonstrate this; Jewish and Christian terror groups have historically been indiscriminate, too.

Terrorists cannot be understood without referring to the social environments they come from and refer to as their source of material, **ideological**, and **symbolic** means – their supporters and sympathizers. It is, therefore, not enough to make war against the terrorists in order to overcome terrorism. One has to obstruct their supporters and understand the motives of the sympathizers. Sympathizers are a variable part of the general public that observes and evaluates what is going on between terrorists and the so-called security forces of the state or – in the case of international terrorism – state-coalitions. The public and its demand for **security** and **social justice** are the decisive reference points for all actors in the conflict field. Of course, the opinions of the diverse parts of the general public are largely influenced by the mass **media**. Since both meet in their common search for the attention of mass publics, a kind of symbiotic relationship between terrorism and the media can be observed (Hoffmann 1998). The media tend to turn terrorists into celebrities.

Under such conditions governments cannot afford not to react to terrorism. But it is very difficult for them to react in a balanced way. **Democracies**, being humiliated by terrorist attacks, cannot maximize the militancy of their security strategies without colliding with the ideals of liberty they are obliged to respect. In addition, the opaqueness of the social structure of terrorism and the non-institutionalized nature of the conflict make it impossible to reliably calculate the effects of alternative strategies. Interactions in the field of terrorism, therefore, are full of misunderstandings and miscalculations on both sides, and the probability of unintended side-effects and paradoxical outcomes of all actions is high.

References and further reading

Habermas, J. (2003) *Philosophy in a Time of Terror: Dialogues with Jürgen Habermas and Jacques Derrida*, ed. G. Borradori. Chicago: Chicago University Press.

Kavoori, A. P. and Fraley, T. (eds) (2005) *Media, Terrorism, and Theory: A Reader*. Lanham: Rowman and Littlefield.

Hoffman, B. (1998) *Inside Terrorism*. London: Gollancz.

Laqueur, W. (1999) *The New Terrorism*. Boston: Little, Brown.

Rapoport, D. (1992) 'Terrorism', in M. Hawkesworth and M. Kogan (eds) *Routledge Encyclopedia of Government and Politics*, vol. 2. London: Routledge.

Waldmann, P. (1998) *Terrorismus*. Munich: Gerling Akademie.

Wilkinson, P. (2000) *Terrorism versus Democracy*. London: Frank Cass.

FRIEDHELM NEIDHARDT

TILLY, CHARLES (1929–)

US historian and sociologist

Concentrating on large-scale historical processes in European history since 1500, Tilly is recognized for his accounts of trajectories of **social change** focusing on **revolution**, economic **rationalization**, **urbanization** and the formation of **nation–states**. Inspired by Barrington **Moore**, and at odds with deterministic approaches like **Marxism** or evolutionary accounts as well as culturalist programs, Tilly argues for conceptual flexibility in the service of empirical investigation. In his *European Revolutions, 1492–1992* (1993), he comparatively accounted for a diversity of contingencies that preceded **revolutionary** outbreaks in various regions of **Europe**, eschewing broad general-izations. Conceiving of history as a contingent process comprehensible by neither individual **actions** nor immanent rules alone, Tilly's explanation of revolutions is sensitive to the unique pre-existing social mechanisms which shape revolutionary struggles and their results. In *Coercion, Capital and European States, AD 990–1990* (1990), he focuses on infrastructural and economical aspects connected with **warfare** and **conflict** resolution within territorial settings to illustrate the development of European nation–states, thereby intentionally downplaying ideological factors. In several works he has elaborated on phenomena associated with social change such as urban culture in *An Urban World* (1974), the politics of contention in *Dynamics of Contention* (2001), and collective **violence** in *The Politics of Collective Violence* (2003).

Major works

(1974) *An Urban World*. Boston: Little, Brown.

(1990) *Coercion, Capital and European States, AD 990–1990*. Oxford: Blackwell.

(1993) *European Revolutions, 1492–1992*. Oxford: Blackwell.

(2001) (with D. McAdam and S. Tarrow) *Dynamics of Contention*. Cambridge: Cambridge University Press.

(2003) *The Politics of Collective Violence*. New York: Cambridge University Press.

Further reading

Hunt, L. (†1984) 'Charles Tilly's Collective Action', in T. Skocpol (ed.) *Vision and Method in Historical Sociology*. Cambridge: Cambridge University Press.

Tilly, C. (1997) *Roads from Past to Future*. Lanham, MD: Rowman & Littlefield.

Tilly, C. (2002) *Stories, Identities, and Political Change*. Lanham, MD: Rowman & Littlefield.

BERNHARD GIESEN
DANIEL ŠUBER

TIME

It is commonly believed that until the 1980s social theorists neglected the concept

625

of time. This view is misleading. Previous theorists discussed various topics involving temporality, but without explicitly using temporal **language**. Furthermore, temporality can enter theory formation in different ways, and it is important to distinguish between these different aspects of time.

The first dimension of time distinguishes between 'diachrony' and 'synchrony'. While diachronic analyses investigate social phenomena across time, synchronic analyses take snapshots of society. **Structuralist** approaches, for instance, favour synchronic analysis: the meaning of a cultural item or artefact can be identified by tracing relationships of difference with other items that are currently in usage. By contrast, **evolutionary** perspectives investigate mechanisms of change across time; recent versions include complexity and chaos theory (Baert 2000). However, not every diachronic analysis searches for change. **Giddens**'s structuration theory, for instance, studies the way in which people, across time, unintentionally contribute to the reproduction of the social structures that they employ (Giddens 1984).

The second temporal dimension concerns the relationship between different temporal modes (past, present and future). Several early nineteenth-century social theorists portrayed the future as a given, with past and present directed towards this *telos*. Karl **Popper** called this view 'historicist': a theoretical outlook according to which history is governed by a set of immutable laws, the uncovering of which allows for prophecies (see **historicism**). Twentieth-century **positivism** questioned the validity of prophecies, but believed in the possibility of predictions ('if A, then B'), which, within the social sciences, were of a probabilistic nature. By contrast, some theorists emphasized the relative openness of the future. For G. H. **Mead** and Niklas **Luhmann**, for instance, the future is not a given because it is partly accomplished in the present (Baert 1992; Mead 1959; Luhmann 1976, 1982).

'Novelty' and 'emergence' are central to both Mead's 'philosophy of the present' and Luhmann's functional structuralism. Likewise, **Lyotard**'s postmodern 'incredulity towards metanarratives' and its focus on discontinuity indicate a similar uneasiness with all-embracing theories that incorporate past, present and future (Lyotard 1979).

The third dimension of time refers to the relationship between the temporal flux and the invariant. Some sociological notions focus on **social change** (for instance, social dynamics, process and social transformation); some refer to the invariant (for instance, social statics, order and **social structure**). Theories differ in the importance they attach to either side of the dichotomy. Structuralist approaches, for example, search for stable structures beneath the flux, e.g. Ferdinand de Saussure's *langue* or Fernand Braudel's *longue durée*. From a different theoretical angle, a-temporal models such as **game theory** bracket out **culture** and history. Other theories delve into the changing features of the social realm. Norbert **Elias**, for instance, argued that conventional sociological language fails to capture change, and his **figuration** sociology was a conscious attempt to investigate *processes* – not social structures. Likewise, Herbert **Blumer** reacted against Durkheim's view that structures are imposed on people. Blumer's **symbolic interactionism** emphasized how social life is a creative process by which people make sense of, not bow to, their surroundings. Institutions are alterable, as they are contingent on individuals' interpretations. More recently, theorists used chaos and **complexity** theory to deal with the unprecedented change which characterizes contemporary **social life** (Urry 2003).

A number of theorists use temporal language to characterize contemporary society. For Giddens, social life today is most distinctive in its increasing 'space–time distantiation' (1990, 1992): not only can events in faraway places now affect us instantly, we also operate with media of exchange (like money) that transcend time and space. Barbara Adam, Ulrich **Beck** and Giddens argue that the shift towards a **risk** society has consequences at a temporal level. We live in a 'runaway world', constantly dealing with the negative effects of previous attempts to control **nature**. We can no longer rely on **knowledge** of the past in order to deal with problems; any solutions must move beyond the 'short-termism' that characterizes current policy making (Adam 1995, 1999). Finally, Zygmund **Bauman** and John Urry emphasize the fluid nature of the contemporary world. Institutions and loyalties are eroding, as if we live in a 'liquid' or fluid **modernity** (Bauman 2000; Urry 2003).

References and further reading

Abbott, A. (2001) *Time Matters*. Chicago: University of Chicago Press.

Adam, B. (1990) *Time and Social Theory*. Cambridge: Polity Press.

Adam, B. (1995) *Timewatch: The Social Analysis of Time*. Cambridge: Polity Press.

Adam, B. (1999) *Timescapes of Modernity: The Environment and Invisible Hazards*. London: Routledge.

Baert, P. (1992) *Time, Self and Society*. Aldershot: Ashgate.

Baert, P. (2000) 'Social Theory, Complexity and Time', in P. Baert (ed.) *Time in Contemporary Intellectual Thought*. Amsterdam: Elsevier, pp. 205–32.

Bauman, Z. (2000) *Liquid Modernity*. Cambridge: Polity Press.

Giddens, A. (1984) *The Constitution of Society: Outline of the Theory of Structuration*. Cambridge: Polity Press.

Giddens, A. (1990) *The Consequences of Modernity*. Cambridge: Polity Press.

Giddens, A. (1992) *Modernity and Self-Identity: Self and Society in the Late Modern Age*. Cambridge: Polity Press.

Lyotard, J.-F. (1979) *The Postmodern Condition: A Report on Knowledge*. Manchester: Manchester University Press.

Luhmann, N. (1976) 'The Future Cannot Begin: Temporal Structures in Modern Society', *Social Research*, 43: 130–52.

Luhmann, N. (1982) *The Differentiation of Society*. New York: Columbia University Press.

Mead, G. H. (1959) *The Philosophy of the Present*. Chicago: University of Chicago Press.

Urry, J. (2003) *Global Complexity*. Cambridge: Polity Press.

PATRICK BAERT

TOCQUEVILLE, ALEXIS DE (1805–1859)
French political critic and statesman

Tocqueville developed a 'new science of politics' in order to study the modern phenomenon of **democracy** in his celebrated work *Democracy in America* (1835). In the spirit of Montesquieu, he can be regarded as one of the founders of comparative political sociology. *Democracy in America* has since risen to the status of 'Bible of American studies'. In his analysis he combined lucid empirical observation based on archival sources with theoretical reasoning. Convinced that equality of **status** was on the rise in the modern world, Tocqueville considered democracy not only as a type of political regime but also as the general form of modern life. Consequently, he examined political and social **institutions**, the horizontal division of powers between government, parliament and law as well as the vertical division of powers between the federal level, the states and the **communities**. As a grass-roots phenomenon the democratic form of life is nourished by political and social engagement in the community, by **voluntarism** and voluntary **associations** and embeddedness in **religion**. The danger of despotism resulting from the striving for material well-being and the risk of excessive 'individualism' (a term he coined) was countered by the frugal combination of **freedom** and **equality** in the USA.

In his second great work, *The Old Regime and the Revolution* (1856), Tocqueville attacks the idea of a historical watershed caused by the French Revolution instead stressing rather the continuity between the old **state** and the new **society**. This was due to French centralization in which France is governed from and by Paris and by abstract and general ideas designed by the French *philosophes* or **intellectuals**. De Tocqueville was not a thinker of systems, nor did he form a school, but his ideas remain fresh and fruitful to this very day.

Major works

(1951) *Œuvres complètes*. Paris: Gallimard.

Further reading

Aron, R. (1967) *Les Etapes de la pensée sociologique*. Paris: Gallimard.

Bellah, R. N. *et al.* (1985) *Habits of the Heart*. Berkeley: University of California Press.

Birnbaum, P. (1970) *Sociologie de Tocqueville*. Paris: Presses Universitaires de France.

Drescher, S. (1968) *Dilemmas of Democracy: Tocqueville and Modernization*. Pittsburgh, PA: University of Pittsburgh Press.

Jardin, A. (1984) *Alexis de Tocqueville 1805–1859*. Paris: Hachette.

Schleifer, J. T. (1980) *The Making of Tocqueville's Democracy in America*. Chapel Hill, NC: University of North Carolina Press.

Zunz, O. and Kahan, A. (eds) (2002) *The Tocqueville Reader*. Oxford: Blackwell.

HANS-PETER MÜLLER

TÖNNIES, FERDINAND (1855–1935)

Together with George **Simmel** and Max **Weber**, Tönnies belongs to the founders of modern sociology in Germany. He was co-founder of the German Sociological Association and president of the Association from 1909 to 1933.

Tönnies first became well known in 1912 with the second edition of his main work *Gemeinschaft und Gesellschaft* (**Community** and **Society**) ([1887] 1979). Tönnies's main interest concerned the development of sociological categories, of which he considered these the most basic. With the help of these terms, the emergence of **capitalism** from the social forms of the Middle Ages was to be made 'thinkable and describable'. Tönnies created a complex system of terms based on the categories of

Gemeinschaft and Gesellschaft with the aim of enabling a sociological analysis of the different areas of the social and of the social world as a whole.

Tönnies's sociology drew on the political philosophy of Thomas Hobbes, the ethics of Baruch Spinoza, the philosophy of the will of Arthur Schopenhauer, the **evolutionary theory** of Charles Darwin, the theory of ancient law of Henry Maine, the theory of associations of Otto Gierke, and the political and economic theories of Karl **Marx**. Social forms were, for Tönnies, **associations** based on human will, for which the model was legal conditions. These, in turn, were the 'certified terms' of social **forms**. Human expressions of will were nothing but 'effects of the spirit'. His sociology shows no connection with social **metaphysics** nor with biologism.

Major works

([1887] 1979) *Gemeinschaft und Gesellschaft*. Darmstadt: Wissenschaftliche Buchgesellschaft.

([1896] 1971) *Thomas Hobbes*. Stuttgart-Bad Cannstatt: Fromman (Holzboog).

([1922] 1981) *Kritik der öffentlichen Meinung*. Aalen: Scientia.

(1925, 1926, 1929) *Soziologische Studien und Kritiken I-III*. Jena: Fischer.

([1931] 1981) *Einführung in die Soziologie*. Stuttgart: Enke.

Further reading

Bickel, C. (1991) *Ferdinand Tönnies*. Opladen: Westdeutscher Verlag.

Merz-Benz, P.-U. (1995) *Tiefsinn und Scharfsinn*. Frankfurt am Main: Suhrkamp.

PETER-ULRICH MERZ-BENZ

TOTALITARIANISM

The Italian philosopher, Giovanni Gentile, coined the term 'totalitarianism' in the 1920s to express the unity of 'total **freedom**' and 'total **domination**' which occur when individual self-realization is identified with the universality of the state and the state is all-embracing and total. Later the idea of totalitarianism was appropriated in a deeply unsympathetic vein by writers such as Arthur Koestler, George Orwell and even Leon Trotsky to identify what Stalinist Russia and Nazi Germany had in common and to express their fear that these regimes were marking out the future of the world (Trotsky 1937). In the post-war period, the concept of totalitarianism was taken up in the academic discipline of political science to denote an essentially anti-liberal political system which annihilates all boundaries between the state, **civil society** and the individual. Totalitarianism was taken to be a modern form of dictatorship in which state power is concentrated in a single party and exercised over all areas of social life (see **state and nation–state**). Terror is employed by the secret police, while the rule of **law** and human rights are suppressed, and an irrefutable official **ideology** is disseminated among the masses. During the Cold War totalitarianism was often employed polemically as an epithet to indict **Marxism** and Marxist regimes (Linz 2000; Talmon 1986; **Aron** 1968).

A more reflexive approach to totalitarianism was developed by German critical theorists who argued that totalitarianism was the culmination of certain tendencies inherent within liberal polities, notably intensified **class** antagonism and the dominance of **instrumental reason**, and stressed the implication of **liberalism** in the origins of totalitarianism (**Marcuse** 1979; Neumann 1942). Hannah **Arendt**'s (1979) monumental study of *The Origins of Totalitarianism* has been the single most important work on the subject. Among the origins of twentieth-century totalitarianism she counted the following factors: the rise of modern political anti-Semitism; the collapse of legal inhibitions on state **violence** associated with the imperialist grab for colonies; the upsurge of ethnic **nationalist** movements

in the former territories of the Austro-Hungarian, Prussian, Russian and Ottoman Empires; the displacement of millions of pariah peoples who were excluded from any national belonging; and finally the nihilism of the Front generation for whom the First World War signified the devaluation of all values and who expressed contempt for the falseness of liberal principles.

Arendt counted the failure of liberalism to live up to its own ideals as a crucial reason why it was incapable of stopping the rise of totalitarianism and even helped to spawn it. She also argued that the elements of twentieth-century political life which were once reconfigured into totalitarianism are still present and capable of re-emerging. Arendt saw totalitarianism less as a 'type' of political system than as an unstable 'movement', committed to the idea of total power and rooted in the destruction of civil society and atomization of the masses. She argued it was organized on 'leadership' principles quite distinct from the rational architectonic of the modern state. It was composed of multiple and competing authorities, all of whom owed loyalty directly to the leader. It was contemptuous of both national parochialism and state **sovereignty**. It had global ambitions to change the world which it translated into the principle that everything can be destroyed. Death camps were its pivotal institution.

The concept of totalitarianism has been criticized by Marxist scholars who refuse to accept totalitarianism as the identity of the Soviet Union and Nazi Germany. They argue that one was based on class and the other on a racial **myth**, one on the overcoming of private property and the other on the raw rule of capital. Claude Lefort (1986) has demonstrated, however, that this objection remains on the surface of political life and that different forms of totalitarian ideology are less important than the comparable functions they perform. Those Marxists in the post-war period who faced up to the facts of Soviet totalitarianism, some associated with the journal *The New International*, tended to drift away from Marxism.

More recently, **postmodern** social theories have recovered the idea of totalitarianism only to emphasize its affinity to modernity as such. At the limit they present modernity as inherently totalitarian because it elevates society over the individual, subjects all aspects of social life to surveillance and discipline, sacrifices moral principles at the altar of **instrumental reason**, and in the name of humanity eliminates what it sees as 'inhuman'. This viewpoint raises the question both of whether the idea of totalitarianism has been overstretched and whether the modernist conditions that produced it have now changed (**Žižek** 2001).

References and further reading

Arendt, H. (1979) *The Origins of Totalitarianism*. New York: Harcourt Brace.

Aron, R. (1968) *Democracy and Totalitarianism*. London: Weidenfeld & Nicolson.

Lefort, C. (1986) *The Political Forms of Modern Society: Bureaucracy, Democracy, Totalitarianism*. Cambridge: Polity.

Linz, J. (2000) *Totalitarian and Authoritarian Regimes*. Boulder, CO: Lynne Rienner.

Marcuse, H. (1979) *Reason and Revolution: Hegel and the Rise of Social Theory*. Boston: Beacon Press.

Neumann, F. (1942) *Behemoth: The Structure and Practice of National Socialism*. London: Gollancz.

Talmon, J. L. (1986) *The Origins of Totalitarian Democracy*. Harmondsworth: Penguin.

Trotsky, L. (1937) *The Revolution Betrayed: What Is the Soviet Union and Where Is It Going?* London: Faber.

Žižek, S. (2001) *Did Somebody Say Totalitarianism? Five Interventions in the (Mis)use of a Notion*. New York: Verso.

ROBERT FINE

TOTALITY

Totality is a category in Hegel's (see **Hegelianism and neo-Hegelianism**) philosophy, denoting the experience of history which itself is inwardly differentiated and fractured. According to Hegel, the unity of modern science and classical philosophy is restored in the totality of 'mind' or 'spirit' (*Geist*). In Hegel's **dialectical** conception of reason, the true and the good are always a 'Whole' that is more encompassing than its individual empirical historical parts.

Rejecting Hegel, **Marx** abandoned the category of totality on grounds of suspicion of **ideology**, seeing greater scientific amenability in the concept of '**society**' (*Gesellschaft*) than that of 'spirit'. 'Everything' for Marx is thematized from the standpoint of material social relations. After Marx, the classical idea of sociology as it developed after **Spencer** and **Durkheim** essentially regarded Marx's privileged perspective of material social relations only as one perspective among other perspectives, and in this sense constituted itself only as one science among other single sciences. The sum of these sciences was no longer seen as releasing a whole or a totality. According to Georg **Lukács**, the 'totality of spirit' was now fragmented into many different, each individually totalizing perspectives. 'Everything' and 'anything' could now be the theme or object of sociology or psychology or any other discipline, so long as the **ontological** or **metaphysical** question of what this thing *is*, in itself, is left open.

This state of affairs was the principal target of Lukács's philosophical rehabilitation of the idealist concept of totality in his early Marxist text, *History and Class Consciousness*. For Lukács, the Whole is already divided between the totality of all previous history – which is the Untrue – and the totality of all future history after the communist **revolution**, which is the only true Whole. Yet from the perspective of historical **materialism** – which must dispense with all notion of a divine or messianic **agency** – reconciliation between the Goodness of this future and the Evil of past history is not yet conceivable.

The theme of the irreconcilability of the future with past suffering was to become an intellectual thorn in the flesh for all the advocates of **critical theory** among the **Frankfurt School** – from **Benjamin** to **Horkheimer** and **Adorno**. In *Negative Dialectics* and *Minima Moralia*, Adorno turned Hegel on his head by asserting that 'the Whole is the Untrue' (Adorno 1973, 1974).

References and further reading

Adorno, T. W. (1973) *Negative Dialectics*. London: Routledge.
Adorno, T. W. (1974) *Minima Moralia: Reflections from Damaged Life*. London: Verso.
Jay, M. (1984) *Marxism and Totality: The Adventures of a Concept from Lukács to Habermas*. Berkeley, CA: University of California Press.
Lukács, G. (1971) *History and Class Consciousness*. London: Merlin Press.
Lukács, G. (1971) *The Theory of the Novel*. London: Merlin Press.

HAUKE BRUNKHORST

TOURAINE, ALAIN (1925–)

French theorist

Touraine's writing covers a variety of topics from **work**, **post-industrial society**, **democracy** and **inequality**. He is best known, however, for his work on **social movements**, together with the theory of action and the methodological innovations that came out of this research. In the 1970s Touraine completed studies of the movement of May 1968 in Paris, the workers' movement and the **peace** movement. This latter movement, as an archetypal 'new social movement', is particularly significant as much of Touraine's work, including *The Voice and the Eye* (1981), centres on the claim that lines of division have shifted in modern Western societies, leading to the eruption of new types of **conflict**. Touraine argues that the shift to 'post-industrialism' and the rise of the **welfare state** have displaced the structure and conflicts of **capitalism**, at least as defined by **Marxism**. This gives rise to what he calls 'the programmed society'. New social movements, such as the peace and environmental movements, respond to the problems and issues thrown up by this new type of 'historicity' (see **ecology and environmentalism**).

Writing against the grain of **structuralism**, Touraine puts great emphasis on **agency**, change and history. Much of his concern is focused on the way that agents make movements that, in turn, provide a crucial motor for historical change. However, he also holds that movements are not always fully transparent to themselves. For this reason he advocates what he calls 'sociological interventionism'. This is a form of engaged social research which involves working with social movements in an effort to allow them to clarify more fully their own nature and purpose.

Major works

(1971) *The May Movement: Revolt and Reform*. New York: Random House.
(1974) *The Post-Industrial Society*. London: Wildwood House.
(1977) *The Self-Production of Society*. Chicago: University of Chicago Press.
(1981) *The Voice and the Eye: An Analysis of Social Movements*. Cambridge: Cambridge University Press.
(1983) *Solidarity*. Cambridge: Cambridge University Press.
(1988) *Return of the Actor*. Minneapolis, MN: University of Minnesota Press.
(1994) *Critique of Modernity*. Oxford: Blackwell.
(1997) *What is Democracy?* Boulder, CO: Westview.
(2000) *Can We Live Together?* Stanford, CA: Stanford University Press.
(2001) *Beyond Neoliberalism*. Cambridge: Polity.

Further reading

Scott, A. (1991) 'Action, Movement and Intervention: Reflections on the Sociology of Alain Touraine', *Canadian Review of Sociology and Anthropology*, 28(1): 29–46.

NICK CROSSLEY

TRADE UNIONS

Trade unions are **interest organizations** that aim to promote the interests of employees in relation to employers and **governments**. The structure and function of trade unions differ between countries, sectors, professions and over time. According to Beatrice and Sidney Webb, the three main functions of trade unions are the mutual insurance of employees against social **risks**, **collective** bargaining with employers, and the legal enactment of individual and collective **rights** (Webb and Webb 1894).

Trade unions may organize either cohesive groups of employees with high skills and strong bargaining positions, or large numbers of unskilled workers. *Craft unions* representing small groups of skilled employees aim to control **production** arrangements, the local **labour** market, and the provision of vocational training. Due to their privileged position, craft unions attempt to exercise control over the production process. *General unions*, which emerged alongside the rising number of unskilled labourers at the end of the nineteenth century, are open to all employees, regardless of skill or trade. They draw strength from mobilizing large numbers and from political in addition to industrial action.

The evolution of trade unions took place in close interaction with state regulation of employment conditions. As **class conflict** subsided during the twentieth century, trade unions were increasingly incorporated into the political systems of modern **democracies**. Legal recognition of trade unions often turned into active support for collective organization by governments. This took the form of monopoly of representation (such as in Germany and Austria), the ability to enforce compulsory membership in closed shops (as in Anglo-Saxon countries) or union involvement in social policy (in Scandinavia).

Three types of organizational problems have characterized the study of trade unions. As *voluntary organizations*, trade unions face a problem of collective action due to rational behaviour of individuals. The achievements of trade unions tend to be public goods for a wider group of employees which cannot be withheld from those members who have not contributed to their production. When the number of potential beneficiaries is large, and the contribution of any individual group member is therefore marginal, there may be a strong incentive for rational actors not to contribute to the costs of organized collective action. Trade unions typically try to close the gap between individual and collective **rationality** by offering their clients so-called 'outside inducements' (Olson 1971). Unlike public goods, outside inducements are selectively reserved for members of the organization. They consist of special economic rewards.

As *intermediary organizations*, trade unions interact with their membership, on the one hand, and employers and the **state**, on the other (Streeck and Schmitter 1985). The interaction between an intermediary organization and its constituents is governed by the interest perceptions and demands of their members; by the willingness of the members to comply with decisions made on their behalf; by the means available to the organization for controlling its members; and by the collective benefits and outside inducements the organization has to offer. The political exchanges between a trade union organization and its political environment depend on the degree of control the union has over its constituency and the concessions that are offered to it, such as the degree to which the union is granted privileged access and status within its institutional context.

In those cases where unions are able to develop sufficient organizational properties as corporate actors, they become part of a corporatist system of political intermediation. In these settings, trade unions can draw on state support, given official interest in stable, reliable and above all moderate representation of the **groups** in question. To generate member compliance and ensure moderation of demands and adherence to negotiated agreements, they often rely on organizational privileges granted to them by the state, in exchange for delivering the **discipline** of their members. In the process they may cease to be just 'pressure groups', or 'lobbies', and turn into private interest governments, or agents of collective self-regulation.

As *interest organizations* trade unions have to mediate between *representativeness* and *effectiveness* (Child *et al.* 1973). On the one hand, a large and broad membership base might enhance an interest organization's political influence; on the other, a small and homogeneous group can be represented more accurately. When translating individual into collective interests and collective interests into organizational goals, unions face the challenge of aggregating and operationally defining the interests they represent. The closer the goal of a trade union to what its members perceive to be their interests, the easier it should be for the organization to rely on the intrinsic attraction of its primary objectives to motivate contributions from members. Unions representing large heterogeneous groups have to aggregate a wide range of special interests into a common collective interest and have to bridge different interests by other means, often with support from employers and the state.

Further reading

Child, J., Loveridge, A. and Warner, M. (1973) 'Towards an Organizational Study of Trade Unions', *Sociology*, 7: 71–91.

Ebbinghaus, B. and Visser, J. (2000) *Trade Unions in Western Europe since 1945*. Basingstoke: Macmillan.

Olson, M. (1971) *The Logic of Collective Action: Public Goods and the Theory of Groups*. Cambridge, MA: Harvard University Press.

Streeck, W. and Schmitter, P. C. (eds) (1985) *Private Interest Government: Beyond Market and State*. London: Sage.

Webb, S. and Webb, B. (1894) *The History of Trade Unionism*. London: Longman.

ANKE HASSEL

TRADITION

From the Latin *traditum* – meaning that which is passed on – the word tradition can be understood only in relation to *tradere*, 'to pass on', or in other words, 'to translate'. Tradition is thus the passing on of something and as such concerns a process of transmission involving a sender and a receiver. The nature of this process of tradition has been the subject of very different interpretations. In some accounts the process of translation involved is what is important, while in others the salient issue is the survival of the past in the present. Clearly, the critical question concerns the definition of the past and whether tradition signals resistance to change.

The controversy over tradition goes back to at least the seventeenth-century French 'Quarrel of the Ancients and the Moderns' over the authority of the **classics** as against modern thought. In this dispute, the debate concerned the status of classic texts or the authority of a canon as the received wisdom handed down from the past. The French **Enlightenment** continued this critique of tradition with a view of science as the means of emancipation from tradition. Within the social sciences, the debate on tradition began with Ferdinand **Tönnies**'s *Gemeinschaft und Gesellschaft* ([1887] 1979) which drew a sharp distinction between traditional **communities** and modern society, whereby tradition is equated with a pre-modern condition defined by custom, **conventions**, and continuity with the past. Tradition in the sense of 'traditional society' was the subject of Daniel Lerner's *The Passing of Traditional Society* which describes the transition from tradition to **modernity** in a way that did not question the linear logic that was also central to Tönnies (Lerner [1958] 1964). In this sense, Max **Weber** was different in his treatment of the three types of **legitimacy** or **authority** on which political orders are based: legal rational authority, charismatic authority and traditional authority. While Weber saw the latter being replaced by the former, he did not see these as exclusive forms of legitimation and noted that they are often found together.

In the late 1960s sociologists began to question the tradition – modernity divide. Works by Reinhard **Bendix** (1967), Edward Shils (1981) and S. N. **Eisenstadt** (1983) drew attention to the ways tradition survives in modernity and takes different forms. This required a shift in perspective, away from Western modernization as the key reference point. Although Lerner's book was a study of modernization in the Middle East, he did not question the Eurocentric perspective. As against the view that tradition and modernity are two quite different kinds of social orders, it has become more accepted to see aspects of tradition and modernity in all kinds of societies.

Nevertheless, the view has persisted that modernity is replacing tradition more and more and that tradition is about resistance to change and the conservation of the past. This has been reflected in works by Laslett (1965), Gross (1992) and the more recently proposed theory of reflexive moderniza tion, which, as argued by Ulrich **Beck** and Anthony **Giddens**, claims contemporary societies are 'post-traditional' and based on the reflexive critique of tradition (Beck *et al.* 1994). This notion of modernity as the critique of tradition is also central to the social theory of **Habermas**, who has argued that modernity entails post-traditional morality. This modernist conception of tradition has been hotly contested from three very different perspectives.

First, the notion of 'invented traditions' questions the idea that modernity replaces tradition. Eric Hobsbawn and Terence Ranger argued in *The Invention of Tradition* that many traditions are not handed down from the past but are created by the present (Hobsbawm and Ranger 1983). Much of what is often considered traditional, in the sense of old or customary, is quite literally recent invention. This is particularly the case with national traditions and public **rituals** which do not simply reproduce that which is traditional but create it anew (see **rationalism**). Tradition thus can be seen as socially constructed. Second, the assumption implicit in the older conception of tradition as the voice of custom and stability has been criticized by Craig Calhoun, who has proposed the thesis of 'the radicality of tradition' (Calhoun 1983). This is the argument that tradition has often been the basis for many kinds of popular protest and that, far from maintaining the status quo, traditional communities supplied the moral and political energy for collective action. Third, with **hermeneutics**, a conception of tradition as a model of cultural interpretation suggests a view of tradition as a basic feature of communication. Thus **Gadamer** ([1960] 1979) outlined a philosophical conception of tradition as a framework of understanding which is capable of change since it is the nature of communication to require interpretation. In this sense, the term tradition can be used to refer to the ways people translate meaning through interpretative understanding.

References and further reading

Beck, U., Giddens, A. and Lash, S. (1994) *Reflexive Modernization: Politics, Tradition and Aesthetics in the Modern Social Order*. Cambridge: Polity Press.

Bendix, R. (1967) 'Tradition and Modernity Reconsidered', *Comparative Studies in Society and History*, 9(3): 292–346.

Calhoun, C. (1983) 'The Radicalness of Tradition: Community Strength or Venerable Disguise and Borrowed Language', *American Journal of Sociology*, 88(5): 886–914.

Eisenstadt, S. N. (1983) *Tradition, Change and Modernity*. New York: Wiley.

Gadamer, H.-G. ([1960] 1979) *Truth and Method*. London: Ward and Steed.

Gross, D. (1992) *The Past in Ruins: Tradition and the Critique of Modernity*. Amherst, MA: University of Massachusetts Press.

Hobsbawn, E. J. and Ranger, T. (eds) (1983) *The Invention of Tradition*. Cambridge: Cambridge University Press.

Laslett, P. (1965) *The World We Have Lost.* London: Methuen.
Lerner, D. ([1958] 1964) *The Passing of Traditional Society.* New York: Free Press.
Shils, E. (1981) *Tradition.* London: Faber and Faber.
Tönnies, F. ([1887] 1979) *Gemeinschaft und Gesellschaft.* Darmstadt: Wissenschaftliche Buchgesellschaft.

GERARD DELANTY

TRANSCENDENTAL

Although there are many different philosophical uses of the term 'transcendental', its chief modern usage stems from **Kant**, who provided analysis of **knowledge** through the conditions of possibility of experience and thought ([1781] 1929). In this way, transcendental arguments aim at establishing 'the necessary conditions of possibility' of something, whether it is experience, thought, interpretation or judgment. 'Weak' transcendental arguments only rely on 'necessary conditions', while 'strong' transcendental arguments establish conditions that are both necessary and sufficient, often uniquely so. A strong transcendental argument might, following Kant, refute sceptical relativism by arguing that certain necessary, universal and invariant concepts are necessary conditions for knowledge and experience as such. An example of a weak transcendental argument is P. F. Strawson's argument that the ability to attribute mental states to ourselves presupposes that we are at the same time able to do so to others (1966).

Weak transcendental arguments emerge in social science in the context of discussions of **rationality, relativism**, and interpretation. Davidson (1984) put transcendental arguments at the center of these debates when he claimed that we could not interpret the beliefs of others unless we assume that they are largely true. This does not rule out the sceptical possibility, however, that some beliefs are for the interpreter neither true nor false. Often current transcendental arguments refer to implicit knowledge, as

when Searle (1995) argues that much social activity presupposes a holistic background of 'stances'. **Habermas**'s claim that 'all **language** use is oriented to consensus' works by showing that nonconsensual uses are parasitic on consensual ones.

References and further reading

Davidson, D. (1984) *Inquiries into Truth and Interpretation.* Oxford: Oxford University Press.
Kant. I. ([1781] 1929) *The Critique of Pure Reason.* London: Macmillan.
Searle, J. (1995) *The Social Construction of Social Reality.* London: Penguin.
Strawson, P. F. (1966) *The Bounds of Sense.* London: Methuen.

JAMES BOHMAN

TRANSEXUALISM

See: sex/gender distinction

TRIBE

The Romans described the Latins, the Sabines and the Etruscans each as a *tribus.* Westerners have since used the concept of tribe to denote many different forms of non-**state** social and political **organization**. Colonial rulers applied the term to indigenous **groups**, making little distinction between smaller bands of loosely organized hunter–gatherers and larger kingdoms. In most popular and administrative usages today the 'tribes' of a country refer to the indigenous inhabitants within a nation–state, who were never fully modernized and who preserve some of their original (pre-colonial or pre-civilizational) culture. Connoting cultural authenticity and pre-**modernity**, the tribal adjective has since the 1980s been domesticated in Western, urban environments (e.g. references to 'tribal' as a rock genre), arguably in connection with **postmodernism** and its taste for primitivism.

Most anthropologists reserve the term to classify one of four major types of political organization: bands, tribes, chiefdoms and states. The differences are based on population size and degree of complexity in economic and political life. *Band* organization (a number of families living together) has mostly been found among peoples with foraging economies, with low population density and seasonal mobility. Decisions are made informally with no formalized leadership. *Tribes* possess domesticated plants and/or animals and are larger in size (which means anything from 1,000 to 100,000 members). Tribes also typically possess institutions that may unite sometimes scattered communities. Leadership is more articulated and might involve some degree of coercion. However, political organization remains essentially egalitarian and uncentralized. There tends to be little **division of labour**, little social **stratification**, and leadership is normally dependent on the persuasive abilities of the leader(s). *Chiefdoms*, on the other hand, have hereditary leadership and a higher degree of social stratification (people being divided into 'nobles' and 'commoners'), while *states* are characterized by a highly developed division of labour and a permanent, centralized government run by professional bureaucrats. Tribes, therefore, lie between bands, on the one hand, and centralized political systems, on the other.

Tribes are most often thought of as territorial and cultural-linguistic groups, organized around **kinship** and descent. How descent groups become activated in political organization was always central to political anthropology (Fortes and Evans-Pritchard 1940; Gluckman 1965). Membership is based on descent and in-**marriage**, but often with an in-built flexibility: membership can be arranged through fictive kinship or by reinterpretation of the mythic continuum.

These shorthand definitions form the basis for a series of disputes concerning the concept of tribe (see, for example, Helm 1968; Gutkind 1970; Godelier 1973). One

proposal is that tribe is primarily a 'unit of subsistence', i.e. a form of organization created to arrange control of territory and adaptation to the environment, political organization being secondary (Marx 1977). The understanding of tribe representing an intermediate level in terms of size and level of social complexity was crucial to **evolutionary theories** as these developed from the 19th century, but evolutionary schemes are far from being accepted by all anthropologists. The **value** judgment, often made by Western rulers, of tribes being prior and 'inferior' to states is arbitrary and ethno-centric, and often served to legitimize destruction. Theoretically, it is far from obvious that all societies *must* move towards more centralized political organization. Anthropologists have also documented cases of devolution (centralized societies developing into smaller groups). Moreover, tribes need not disappear with state organization. Tribes often came into being simultaneously *with* states, specializing in certain labour tasks at the periphery of larger systems. Finally, not only do tribes 'survive' state organization: they can become the vehicle of state organization.

Since the 1980s, there has been much focus on the creation of tribes through Western, colonial **discourse**. It can be argued that the very idea of human beings falling into neatly defined cultural groups was a product of the Western mind of the nineteenth century, projecting the **epistemology** of the nation–state onto non-Western populations. In 'The Invention of Tradition' (1983), Terence Ranger analyzed the **reification** of 'traditional' African culture, 'tribe' being a central organizing concept. As he showed, many tribes were in fact not part of a supposedly non-changing pre-colonial world. **Colonialism** also influenced local populations concretely by provoking stronger forms of political organization in response to the exercise of Western power. This happened in North America as Native Americans organized to meet the military challenge of the colonizers. Many tribes and tribal leaders were created in this situation, sometimes even put in place by colonial rulers, in order to facilitate control over territory. Arguably, this reification of tribes has continued in the postcolonial competition between groups fighting for control of the state apparatus, Rwanda being a dramatic example.

The dividing line between tribes and **ethnic** groups is often not clear. Ethnic groups in complex societies are sometimes referred to as 'urban tribes', while tribes in Africa and Asia are sometimes called 'ethnic groups'. In Africa, there has from the 1990s been much talk of a 'return to tribal politics'. Many political parties and state administrations in Africa are based on tribal affiliations, resembling 'ethnic politics' in the West. 'Tribal politics' may refer to a situation where party or state politics are actually organized by tribes, or to social and political organization taking place outside the official political system (see also **party**). For example, conflict resolution is sometimes dealt with within the tribal system, and in some states this parallel legal system is officially recognized. The notion of tribal politics is also used in much political science research in the Middle East and the Arab World. While tribal affiliations continue to play a major role in some Arab states, such as Saudi Arabia and Morocco, in others, such as Libya or Egypt, the ruling **elites** have consciously tried to downplay the **role** of tribal identities. In Iraq and Afghanistan, tribes have had a role to play in the local political organization emerging after the US-led military interventions. Therefore, whatever the origins of present-day tribes, their existence and role today must be analyzed against recent socio–political transformations and contemporary forms of power and territorial administration.

References and further reading

Fortes, M. and Evans-Pritchard, E. E. (1940) *African Political Systems*. Oxford: Oxford University Press.

Gluckman, M. (1965) *Politics, Law and Ritual in Tribal Society*. Oxford: Oxford University Press.

Godelier, M. (1973) 'Le concept de tribu: crise d'un concept ou crise des fondements empiriques de l'anthropologie?', *Diogene*, 81: 3–28.

Gutkind, P. (ed.) (1970) *The Passing of Tribal Man in Africa*. Leiden: Brill.

Helm, J. (ed.) (1968) *Essays on the Problem of Tribe*. Seattle: University of Washington Press.

Marx, E. (1977) 'Tribe as a Unit of Subsistence', *American Anthropologist*, 79(2): 343–63.

Ranger, T. (1983) 'The Invention of Tradition in Colonial Africa', in E. Hobsbawm and T. Ranger (eds) *The Invention of Tradition*. Cambridge: Cambridge University Press.

BJØRN THOMASSEN

TRUST

Trust is a highly problematic but beneficial feature of social relationships characterized by **risk**. The majority of analysts of its nature, causes and consequences define trust as the confidence that partners will not exploit each other's vulnerability (Misztal 1996; Sztompka 1999). The concept of trust, seen as a form of reliance on other people which involves beliefs about the likelihood of their behaving in a certain way, has only recently started to attract the attention of sociologists. This growth in popularity of the concept, conceptualized as a precaution against uncertainty and vulnerability, reflects not only the omnipresence of trust in **social relations** and its essential role in the stability of democratic societies but also the re-conceptualization of **modernity** in terms of high levels of risk and uncertainty which create a demand for trust. The visibility and importance of the issue of trust are also underlined by the erosion of the old bases for social **cooperation** and **solidarity** as well as the current deficit of trust in the working of **democracy** and the new challenges posed by the operation of electronic **communication**.

Notwithstanding the recent proliferation of middle-range theories about trust, its definition and understanding have proved elusive as definitions are always embedded in particular theoretical frameworks that determine what it can actually explain. While there is an emerging **consensus** that any conceptualization must refer to the notions of vulnerability, uncertainty and risk, there is still a lack of agreed definition and an absence of precise understanding of the factors responsible for trust production. As the number of definitions and approaches increases, research becomes more specialized and definitions more specific. Today writers no longer talk about trust in general, but rather about various categories of trust or about trust in different contexts; for instance, trust in organizations, political systems or in **families**. The sociological literature, which discusses both psychological and institutional sources of trust, conceptualizes trust as either the property of individuals or the property of social relationships and **social systems**. The first socio–psychological approach puts emphasis on **emotion** and **values** and identifies familiarity as the main mechanism by which trust is generated. In the second case, trust is taken to be a valuable **public** good – a resource that need not circulate only between members of a familiar **group** but may also be generalized to **strangers**. The categories of trust can also be broken down into trust in **persons**, which – as confidence in others – is connected with the genesis and maintenance of what Giddens calls 'ontological security', and trust in abstract systems, or trust in the correctness of impersonal principles, which is unique to modernity (**Giddens** 1990).

Although the literature is united in its main focus on how one may set about creating and fostering trust in the context of various recent changes, there is a lack of an integrative theory of trust. Several theoretical approaches can be identified. The **functionalist** perspective, which introduces a conceptual and substantive set of distinctions between familiarity, confidence and trust, takes trust to be a means of reducing **complexity** and a vital element in increasing tolerance of necessary uncertainties (**Luhmann** 1979). The **rational choice** approach sees trust as a means of economizing on transaction costs (Gambetta 1988). Rational individuals are prepared to grant trust only when the potential gains from granting it are larger than the potential losses and the relationship is underwritten by sanctions against violations. As a means of mutually reinforcing expectations about reciprocity, trust serves as a lubricant for cooperation. Theorists of **democracy** therefore conceptualize trust as the key to democratic participation. They argue that the functioning of any civic order must depend upon a certain type of generalized trust and seek to identify the kinds of trust that are necessary for democracy (Warren 1999).

The **social capital** perspective assumes both that trust is the key to democratic participation and that it is the essential ingredient in economic success. This approach, recently popularized by Putnam (1993), has its roots in **Coleman**'s (1990) argument that mutual trust reduces the costs of monitoring and sanctioning activities and can thus be characterized as a form of social capital. Putnam, who follows this utility model and equates trust with social capital, identifies norms of reciprocity and **networks** of civic engagement as the two primary sources of social trust. A high level of social capital within a **community** is the basis for cooperation, an improved democracy and an innovative economy.

Notwithstanding its interest, the social capital approach fails to answer some specific questions about the nature of the linkage between trust and democracy and about the conversion of interpersonal trust into the generalized trust of social capital. Interpersonal trust, which is specific to face-to-face relationships, cannot simply be equated with a more general social trust, since the forms of trust generated in small groups cannot be assumed to be directly extended to the societal level. Offe (1999) thus argues that such a solution to the deficit of trust which assumes that trust can be generated on the basis of personal knowledge and mutual obligation in communities and **associations** must be supplemented by the strategy which presumes that trust can be increased by an institutional order which is characterized by high levels of truth telling, promise-keeping, fairness and solidarity.

References and further reading

Coleman, J. S. (1990) *Foundation of Social Theory.* Cambridge, MA: Belknap Press.

Cook, K. (ed.) (2001) *Trust in Society.* New York: Sage.

Gambetta, D. (ed.) (1988) *Trust: Making and Breaking Cooperative Relations.* Oxford: Blackwell.

Giddens, A. (1990) *The Consequence of Modernity.* Cambridge: Polity.

Luhmann, N. (1979) *Trust and Power.* Chichester: John Wiley & Sons Ltd.

Misztal, B. A. (1996) *Trust in Modern Societies.* Cambridge: Polity.

Offe, C. (1999) 'How We Can Trust Our Fellow Citizens', in M. E. Warren (ed.) *Democracy and Trust.* Cambridge: Cambridge University Press.

Putnam, R. (1993) *Making Democracy Work: Civic Tradition in Modern Italy.* Princeton, NJ: Princeton University Press.

Seligman, A. (1997) *The Problem of Trust.* Princeton, NJ: Princeton University Press.

Sztompka, P. (1999) *Trust: A Sociological Theory.* Cambridge: Cambridge University Press.

Warren, M. E. (ed.) (1999) *Democracy and Trust.* Cambridge: Cambridge University Press.

BARBARA A. MISZTAL

TYPE AND TYPIFICATION

In social science, the concepts of type and typification have two meanings. They are used to describe a special mode of perception that underlies the construction and reconstruction of social reality. They are also used as analytical categories to explain social reality.

Type and typification are the most evident concepts for characterizing the **everyday** logic of the construction and reconstruction of social reality. To fully grasp this logic, it is essential to read Georg **Simmel**'s essay, 'Sociology of the Senses' together with his short masterpiece 'How is Society Possible?' (both in Simmel 1908).

Simmel points out that our visual perception – far more than our acoustic perception – gives us what we have in common with other people. He notes the truism that the act of seeing generally produces imperfect results. Very few people can specify with certitude the color of a friend's eyes or describe the shape of his or her mouth. We see another person in a generalized manner. The contours of a person's face become blurred, and his or her individuality is connected with other people who look like him or her. Even though every **person** is an individual, our visual perception subsumes persons under a general conception.

Simmel infers that it is easier to form general concepts if we merely see people. His example is the large nineteenth-century factories in which one could see hundreds of people without a chance to talk to them. These circumstances, which were unknown to people who had worked in guild crafts and the small manufactures of pre-industrial societies, led to the formation of the general concept of the modern 'worker', which Simmel understands as a type. Comparable types function in every society as a 'social *a priori*'. One perceives the other not as an individual, but as a worker, a Muslim, a Yankee, etc. This veil of generalization lies over every case of individuality. But it is important to note that typification is a special way of generalization. On the one hand, the type is general, and the content of the type is unique. But, on the other, in a **dialectical** sense, the type as such is unique (a Muslim is unique in relation to a Yankee or a **Christian**, and vice versa). The type as such is unique, whereas the content of the concept type is general, i.e. applicable to a multitude of people.

Following Simmel, **Berger and Luckmann** in their book *The Social Construction of Reality* (1966) claim that in any face-to-face situation one person perceives the other by means of such given types. The construction and reconstruction of social reality begin with typification. The next steps are **habituation** and **institutionalization**; the latter occurs as soon as habitual actions are reciprocally typified by types of actors.

Type and typification are also analytical categories for explaining social reality. Although the French philosopher Montesquieu did not explicitly use the concept of type, he was the first to develop a typology of social phenomena. Ernst Cassirer even claimed that Montesquieu's famous forms of government constituted the first cases of ideal types (Cassirer 1932).

It was the Austrian economist Carl Menger who introduced the concept of type – which had been in use in ancient Greek philosophy and Christian theology (*typus*, *typologia*) – to social science to express a periodically recurring individuality. He also coined the term 'real type' to refer to an elementary form of real phenomena whose typical sketch includes more or less latitude for peculiarities (Menger 1883). Later Ferdinand **Tönnies** not only used the concept of type to represent the common attributes of a group's members, but also to denote the idea of the group itself (Tönnies 1979).

Borrowing the term **ideal type** from the German jurist Georg Jellinek – and in accordance with Heinrich Rickert's **neo-Kantian** philosophy (Merz-[Benz] 1990) – Max **Weber** developed a theory of ideal types that became one the most prominent analytical categories of twentieth-century social science (Weber 1949). The Weberian ideal type is a pure conceptual construct; it is a special kind of typification created by social scientists to express an absolutely rational vision of social action. This cognitive utopia then functions as a measure against which real social action is compared. The ideas of handicraft and **capitalist culture**, for example, are ideal types.

Types are still important today. It was Simmel who not only conceived the **stranger** as a social type but stimulated a discussion that outlasted the twentieth century, creating types like the marginal man (Robert E. Park), the homecomer (Alfred **Schutz**), the cosmopolitan (Ulf Hannerz), and the tourist (Zygmunt **Bauman**) that have proved to be valuable in explaining social reality in an era of **globalization** (cf. Merz-Benz and Wagner 2002).

References and further reading

Berger, P. L. and Luckmann, T. (1966) *The Social Construction of Reality*. Garden City, NY: Doubleday.

Cassirer, E. (1932) *Die Philosophie der Aufklärung*. Tübingen: J. C. B. Mohr.

Menger, C. (1883) *Untersuchungen über die Methode der Socialwissenschaften und der Politischen Ökonomie insbesondere*. Leipzig: Duncker & Humblot.

Merz-[Benz], P.-U. (1990) *Max Weber and Heinrich Rickert*. Würzburg: Königshausen & Neumann.

Merz-Benz, P.-U. and Wagner, G. (2002) *Der Fremde als sozialer Typus*. Konstanz: UVK.

Simmel, G. (1908) *Soziologie*. Berlin: Duncker & Humblot.

Tönnies, F. (1979) *Gemeinschaft und Gesellschaft*. Darmstadt: Wissenschaftliche Buchgesellschaft.

Weber, M. (1949) '"Objectivity" in Social Science and Social Policy', in *The Methodology of the Social Sciences*. New York: Free Press, pp. 49–112.

PETER-ULRICH MERZ-BENZ
GERHARD WAGNER

U

UNCONSCIOUS

In modern thinking the unconscious is a key concept in psychoanalytical theory (see **psychoanalysis**), but has also entered and is widely accepted in Western thought. It refers to mental processes and outcomes that are in some sense beyond consciousness.

A notion of the unconscious had an important place in the thought of nineteenth-century philosophers such as G. W. Leibniz, Arthur Schopenhauer and Friedrich **Nietzsche**; but it is **Freud** who brought the notion into close technical relation with problems of psychological explanation. Freud's interpretation of the unconscious removed the ego from the position where Western philosophy since Descartes had assigned it.

Used by Freud as an adjective, the term 'unconscious' describes mental processes or issues that are not available to consciousness at a particular moment. As a noun, it refers to one system of the psychic topical apparatus, appropriate to Freud's first theory of mental structure (composed of conscious, preconscious and unconscious systems). The unconscious system contains representations of instinctual and repressed material, which only gain access to the system of the conscious and preconscious through distortion and through censorship. Freud theorized the most important psychic mechanisms of the unconscious in terms of 'displacement', 'condensation' and 'symbolization'. These were the principles of his

analysis of the dream, the 'royal road to the unconscious' as he called it in *The Interpretation of Dreams* (Freud 1900). Here, the unconscious in Freud's conception is determined by the pleasure principle and there is in it no sense of negation, nor of time and space, nor of doubt and contradiction. In Freud's second *structural* theory of mental processes, which distinguishes between the three agencies of the ego, the id and the superego, the unconscious is not the same as any one of these agencies; rather, all three have unconscious elements. In contrast to Freud, Georg Groddeck, from whom Freud borrowed the term 'id', identified this term with unconscious forces, by which 'we are "lived"' (Groddeck 1949). Freud's concept of the 'dynamic' unconscious is at the centre of his meta-psychology. The dimension of the unconscious that he describes as 'dynamic' can influence and subvert conscious thought and **action** from no fixed place and from any direction.

One of the more controversial aspects of Freud's conception of the unconscious, however, is his idea of unconscious contents that can be transmitted from generation to generation. Similar problems compromise C. G. Jung's notion of collective unconscious contents and original psychological archetypes. The French psychoanalyst Jacques **Lacan** argued against any assumption of a primordial unconscious, as well as against the equation of the unconscious with the repressed or its reduction to the instincts. Lacan famously states that the 'unconscious is structured like a language' (1977). He also describes it as **discourse**, the 'discourse of the **Other**' (1955). In Lacan's linguistic terminology, the unconscious refers to 'the effects of speech on the subject' (1977), and is therefore located in the order of the *symbolic*. In opposition to a notion that the unconscious is located deep inside the subject, Lacan also conceives it as a kind of memory, which externally determines the subject as symbolic or 'unknown **knowledge**'.

The unconscious is also central to many interpretations of Freud and Lacan in social theories associated with **post-structuralism**. Fredric **Jameson** combines Marxist ideas of class struggle with a psychoanalytic concept of the unconscious. His 'political unconscious' is formed from narrative sediments of this struggle in a similar fashion to Lacan's 'absent real' (Jameson 1981).

The definition of the unconscious proposed by Gilles **Deleuze** and Félix Guattari is pitted directly against standard psychoanalytic ideas of 'lack'. They conceptualize the unconscious through different formations built up from the social field, including what they describe as the '**body** without organs'. Jacques **Derrida** interprets Freud's unconscious in terms of radical otherness, as a non-rational intended thinking, which is not present to itself, but is always deferred, similar to Derrida's conception of the *différance* of meaning (see **difference**).

References and further reading

Deleuze, G. and Guattari, F. ([1972] 1983) *Anti-Oedipus: Capitalism and Schizophrenia*. Minneapolis, MN: University of Minnesota Press.

Derrida, J. ([1976] 1982) *Margins of Philosophy*. Chicago: University of Chicago Press.

Ellenberger, H. (1970) *The Discovery of the Unconscious*. New York: Basic Books.

Freud, S. ([1915] 1958) 'The Unconscious', in J. Breuer and S. Freud (eds) *The Standard Edition of the Complete Psychological Works of Sigmund Freud*. London: Hogarth.

Groddeck, G. ([1923] 1949] *The Book of the Id*. London: Vision.

Jameson, F. (1981) *The Political Unconscious: Narrative as a Socially Symbolic Act*. Ithaca, NY: Cornell University Press.

Lacan, J. ([1955] 1988) 'Seminar on "The Purloined Letter"', in J. Muller and W. Richardson (eds) *The Purloined Poe: Lacan, Derrida and Psychoanalytic Reading*. Baltimore, MD: Johns Hopkins University Press.

Lacan, J. ([1964] 1977) *The Seminar*, Book XI: *The Four Fundamental Concepts of Psychoanalysis*. London: Hogarth.

MICHAELA WÜNSCH

UNDERCLASS

The concept of underclass is used to identify a sub-stratum, or **subculture**, of the poorest sections of **society** that fails to subscribe to society's **values and norms**. The underclass is one of the most hotly contested terms in the social sciences. In virtually every country there are social commentators who claim to have identified an underclass and other social scientists who fiercely reject these claims. It is generally accepted that the term was first used in the USA in the 1960s by those on the political Left in order to highlight social isolation and economic exclusion within an increasingly affluent society. Consequently early advocates suggested that eradicating **discrimination**, gross income **inequality** and social divisions would prevent an underclass developing (see **social inclusion and social exclusion**). Although used occasionally in the 1970s, the term came to prominence in the mid-1980s in the USA and the UK as observers sought to explain the combined effects of economic and **labour market** restructuring, increasing expenditure on public **welfare** programmes, the spatial/geographical segregation of poorer **communities**, and changes in social attitudes to divorce and lone motherhood (see also **marriage and divorce**).

However, the features used to identify the underclass can vary enormously. For some, the underclass is young, homeless or rootless. Others see an underclass which is black, Hispanic, North African or whatever the poorest minority **ethnic** community consists of in specific countries. Importantly most advocates of the term emphasize the behaviour of the underclass as contributing to their place in society. The idea of an underclass therefore replays an older debate regarding the degree to which human **agency** is constrained by **social structures**. Welfare dependency, **crime**, a low labour force participation rate, drug dependency, lone motherhood, alcohol abuse, physical or mental **disability**, begging or promiscuity are some of the key indicators used by different advocates of the term.

For some, the underclass consists of those who are politically marginalized, superfluous to the economy and excluded from the **consumption** patterns available to the majority, and in this context the concept engages with debates about social exclusion, **poverty** and deprivation (**Bauman** 1998). For American conservatives like Murray (1984) it is the values of the underclass that threaten to demoralize the rest of society. As crime becomes more worthwhile than paid **work** and lone mothers provide inadequate male sex **role** models, a culture of welfare dependency grows among the poorest sections of society and the values of self-help and restraint associated with the respectable poor are undermined. In contrast the liberal William J. Wilson considers the behaviour of *The Truly Disadvantaged* (1987) in the USA to be a response to structural social forces beyond their immediate control. Urban degeneration, the decline of manufacturing industry and the flight of the black **middle class** to the suburbs are some of the factors he stressed in the 1980s (see **urbanism and urbanization**). The underclass concept is most contentious when crime, **race**, IQ, **unemployment**, spatial segregation and 'illegitimacy rates' are correlated (Herrnstein and Murray 1994)

In response Left/liberal critics assert that it is those who use the term who are potentially dangerous, rather than the people assigned to the underclass. Indeed, crit-

ics of the term point to a long history of similar ideas; e.g. the nineteenth century pauper class, **Marx**'s lumpen-proletariat, and the residuum of London in the 1880s (see **proletariat**). Each of these sub-strata disappeared when enlisted for war or the economy recovered. There are also questions asked of the empirical data and methods used by the advocates, with a common criticism being that they confuse causation and correlation (see **causality**). That is to say, different data sets (e.g. unemployment, lone motherhood, crime) may correlate but this does not demonstrate any causal relationship between them. Critics have also suggested that the underclass concept is **ideologically** driven, a useful label to brand the poorest and to define groups who are social failures, misfits and/or a drain on public welfare services. Others acknowledge the social changes that have occurred and the social divisions these have generated but regard these more dispassionately as marking a transition from **patriarchal** and traditional male breadwinner/female career **family** forms to more diverse households within a service economy and a consumerist society. A further difficulty sociologists have with the idea of an underclass is whether it is a real **class**, a part of the **stratification** pattern of society, or simply a label for the poorest. Given that the term offends those identified with it, that journalists bandy the term around and that politicians have employed it to promote their particular agendas, it needs to be used with caution, if at all.

References and further reading

Bagguley, P. and Mann, K. (1992) 'Idle Thieving Bastards: Scholarly Representations of the Underclass', *Work, Employment and Society*, 6(1): 113–26.
Bauman, Z. (1998) *Work, Consumerism and the New Poor*. London: Routledge.
Dean, H. and Taylor-Gooby, P. (1992) *Dependency Culture*. Hemel Hempstead: Wheatsheaf.

Herrnstein, R. J. and Murray, C. (1994) *The Bell Curve: Intelligence and Class Structure in American Life*. New York: Free Press.

Katz, M. B. (ed.) (1993) *The 'Underclass' Debate: Views from History*. Princeton, NJ: Princeton University Press.

MacDonald, R. (ed.) (1997) *Youth, the 'Underclass' and Social Exclusion*. London: Routledge.

Murray, C. (1984) *Losing Ground*. New York: Basic Books.

Wilson, W. J. (1987) *The Truly Disadvantaged*. Chicago: University of Chicago Press.

Wilson, W. J. (ed.) (1989) 'The Ghetto Underclass', special edition of *Annals of the American Academy of Political and Social Science*, 501(January). London: Sage.

KIRK MANN

UNEMPLOYMENT

The study of unemployment involves questions of definition and **measurement** which relate to its status as a phenomenon associated with **modernity**. Substantive perspectives fall into two categories: those which emphasize economic factors, and those which emphasize socio-psychological factors. Unemployment has been of interest to social scientists since **Marx** ([1887] 1970) who recognized the advantages to employers of having a reserve army of **labour** which would be available to **work** as and when they were required. Unemployment is an economic category which has developed alongside processes of **industrialization** and **urbanization** throughout the developed world over the past two centuries. As people increasingly became involved in **capitalist** relations as an employee, selling their labour to an employer, the possibility of seeking but not finding employment emerged. Unemployment, therefore, is a product of the formalization of working relations within a society that places **value** on being in employment. Hence many people who are classified as unemployed are in fact working, only this work is unpaid, for example, those looking after a **family and household** are not in employment but would not be categorized as unemployed

because they have an alternative economic **status**. This has given rise to a **feminist** critique of both employment and **unemployment** (Oakley 1974).

Measuring unemployment is notoriously difficult. Sources of data are varied and give rise to different estimates. The most widely recognized measure is that used by the International Labour Office (ILO). The ILO definition includes those over the age of compulsory schooling not in paid employment who have looked for paid employment over a particular time period and who are not institutionalized. This definition is generally operationalized using a national sample survey of the working-age population. This measure is regarded as the most accurate way of counting unemployment in relation to the extent to which people are actually looking for work but it overestimates unemployment by counting people who are not eligible for state unemployment welfare payments (benefit). Another measure of unemployment involves counting people who register as unemployed with a **governmental** agency in order to qualify for unemployment benefit. This measure tends to underestimate the ILO measure of unemployment as there is a significant proportion of people who do not claim unemployment benefit but who are nonetheless looking for work.

Economic perspectives on unemployment concentrate on causes: there are those related to decisions made by an individual (leaving a job to look for another), and those related to the workings of the **economy** (being made redundant due to a changing economic situation). Rates of unemployment are measured regularly and are regarded as a key indicator of national economic performance. As economies transform as in the decline of manufacturing and the rise in service sector employment since the 1970s, there are always flows of people into unemployment from industrial sectors which are in decline (see **post-industrial society**). Of particular interest is the extent to which there is a flow of people out of unemployment back into the labour force. The dynamics of the flows into and out of unemployment are therefore important in establishing not only the general way in which an economy is changing, but also the extent to which some people are better able to cope with unemployment than others.

Unemployment was a key social issue in the development of the **welfare state** during the twentieth century. Welfare benefits systems that involve the transfer of taxes from the employed to the unemployed have developed to varying degrees throughout the industrialized world since the end of the Second World War. State intervention has taken a variety of forms over the years and in different countries, reflecting different political and ideological contexts (Esping-Andersen 1990). There is a debate over the level of unemployment benefit and over the extent to which state payments to unemployed people are said to either encourage or discourage them from seeking further employment by alleviating their **poverty**. This is part of a wider debate about the threshold where a range of state benefits on offer to unemployed people is economically the same or higher than if a low-paid job were taken.

Socio-psychological perspectives are rooted in the tradition begun by Jahoda *et al.* ([1933] 1972) in the 1930s where the psychological stresses of unemployment over a period of time were studied. They developed a stage model whereby the length of time in unemployment was said to determine particular phases of attitudes towards being unemployed: optimism, resignation, despair and finally, apathy. Different models have since been suggested. One common feature in them is that the longer one spends in unemployment, the greater the psychological distress it causes and that this affects the vigour with which further employment is sought. This perspective resonates with the discourse regarding the **individualization** of modern life.

References and further reading

Burnett, J. (1994) *Idle Hands*. London: Routledge.

Esping-Andersen, G. (1990) *The Three Worlds of Welfare Capitalism*. Cambridge: Polity.

Gallie, D., Marsh, C. and Vogler, C. (eds) (1993) *Social Change and the Experience of Unemployment*. Oxford: Oxford University Press.

Jahoda, M., Lazarsfeld, P. and Zeizel, H. ([1933] 1972) *Marienthal: The Sociology of an Unemployed Community*. London: Tavistock.

Marx, K. ([1887] 1970) *Capital*. London: Lawrence and Wishart.

McLaughlin, E. (ed.) (1992) *Understanding Unemployment*. London: Routledge.

Oakley, A. (1974) *The Sociology of Housework*. Oxford: Martin Robertson.

Warr, P. B. (1987) *Work, Unemployment and Mental Health*. Oxford: Clarendon.

GARY POLLOCK

UNIVERSALISM

The meaning of universalism in social theory is elusive and controversial. Universalism can more easily be defined in a negative way, as standing in opposition to at least three other ideas: (1) 'particularism', defined as the claim that only the particular and local have moral relevance; (2) **relativism**, defined as the claim that different theoretical and moral systems of belief cannot be judged according to any neutral, objective or higher-order criterion; and (3) 'contextualism', defined as the claim that these belief systems can only be understood in their specific social and historical context. The idea of universalism is closely related to the concepts of universality (e.g. of truth or human rights) and universal validity (e.g. of claims to truth or rightness). Depending on area and subject – sociology of science, social theory, political philosophy – universalism takes on different meanings. Today, however, the most prominent debates about universalism take place in normative political theory.

Methodological universalism in the sociology of **science** and in **epistemology** claims that scientific statements and theories aspire to universal validity, i.e. to be true not only here and now. It is closely linked to the ideals of **objectivity**, **rationality** and the overcoming of particularity and partiality. A specific variant, **positivism**, holds that social science should follow natural science in discovering universal laws. However, the idea that science delivers universal truths has been challenged, among others, by **standpoint epistemology** which claims that there are only particular perspectives whose **hegemony** in the discursive field produces the effect of universality.

The debate about universals which dates back to medieval scholasticism is closely related to questions of **methodology**. While nominalism holds that the universal (an idea or a concept) is secondary to its particular instantiation in concrete phenomena, realists or Platonists believe that the universal is more real than the individual. In social theory this dispute appears in relation to the implications of such abstract notions as '**society**', '**class**' and '**gender**'. Another much debated methodological problem concerns the validity of inferring universal statements (all Xs are Y) from a limited number of singular observational statements.

In the sociology of **culture** and **religion** the debate about universalism has focused on anthropological universals and on structures underlying all cultural phenomena. Claude **Lévi-Strauss**'s structuralist anthropology and Noam **Chomsky**'s theory of universal grammar can be seen as paradigmatic approaches in this field. In **historical sociology** Max **Weber** (1905) argued that the process of rationalization represents a cultural development of apparently universal significance and value. He also emphasized the doctrinal universalism of some religions. And Karl Jaspers's notion of the 'axial age', a historical period in the first millenium BCE in which universalist worldviews emerged in different civilizations, has been developed by Shmuel **Eisenstadt**.

In social theory, universalism has been explicitly held as a position in the early 'universal **functionalism**' of Bronislaw Malinowski who claimed that every cultural object, activity or attitude fulfills a specific function. In Talcott **Parsons**'s version of functionalism, the dichotomy 'particularism v. universalism' is one of the 'pattern variables' that represent alternative basic values and types of action orientation. These can be interpreted as a specification of the distinction between **Gemeinschaft and Gesellschaft**: whereas particularism describes the primary orientations of actors in traditional societies (family or social group), actors in modern societies are more frequently oriented towards general rules (e.g. universal **values and norms** such as human **rights**). Parsons identified 'evolutionary universals', defined as patterns of interaction that emerge in societies as complexity increases. These include **language**, social organization through **kinship**, procedures for conflict resolution. In modern societies they include a legal system and **money**. Parsons claimed that universalistic norms – norms that are ever more inclusive – emerge in all social fields (1967: Chapter 15).

Universalism in moral philosophy and normative political theory has its roots in the **Enlightenment**, especially in Kant's 'categorical imperative' ('Act only according to that maxim whereby you can at the same time will that it should become a universal law' ([1785] 1964: 421). This form of universalism, which links universal validity to rational acceptability, has found more recent expressions in John **Rawls**'s constructivist theory of justice (1971) and Jürgen **Habermas**'s 'discourse ethics' (1992). Universalization is regarded as the criterion for justifying the validity of normative claims, for their being binding for everyone anywhere and anytime. Both assume that there are formal procedures that can serve to test the universality and impartiality of norms, namely unconstrained argumentation between rational, free and equal persons.

646

Habermas starts from the basic thesis that agreement is the telos of communication (in contrast to strategic action) and that all communicative action (implicitly) raises validity claims that transcend the concrete context and aspire to an unforced **consensus**. Habermas here claims to identify a form of universality that lies beyond historical and cultural particularity. This idea is further spelled out in his conception of post-conventional **morality** whose basic principles can be institutionalized in a legal order with universal rights. Against such an understanding of universalism as the normative core of the project of **modernity**, **postmodernism** emphasizes **pluralism, difference** and particularity. Furthermore, it is still contested whether the process of modernization leads to a harmonization and generalization of values or to increasing fragmentation and conflict.

An especially sensitive case is the universality of human rights. Although they are historically rooted in the **Christian** tradition of natural law, universalists claim that human rights possess universal validity as moral standards which can serve to criticize every existing social, political and legal order irrespective of time and place. There are numerous critiques of universalism, many of them directed at the notion of universal human rights, from **communitarianism** to **post-colonial theory**. All of them claim that the rhetoric of universality and neutrality simply masks the fact that universalisms usually turn out to be rather particularistic – **bourgeois**, Eurocentric, sexist and even imperialist. It should be acknowledged, however, that this critique, when it is not driven by **power** interests, is often put forward in the name of a more *inclusive* universalism. Furthermore, actual political claims to **social inclusion** often mobilize universal principles and values. Still, what universalism means and which principles and values count as universal will most likely continue to be – theoretically as well as politically – contested, since the **dialectic** of universality and particularity seems to be constitutive for modernity itself.

References and further reading

Butler, J., Laclau, E. and Žižek, S. (2000) *Contingency, Hegemony, Universality*. London: Verso.

Donnelly, J. (2003) *Universal Human Rights in Theory and Practice*. Ithaca, NY: Cornell University Press.

Habermas, J. ([1992] 1995) *Between Facts and Norms*. Cambridge, MA: MIT Press.

Kant, I. ([1785] 1964) *Grounding for the Metaphysics of Morals*. Indianapolis, IN: Hackett.

Parsons, T. (1967) *Sociological Theory and Modern Society*. New York: Free Press.

Rawls, J. (1971) *A Theory of Justice*. Cambridge, MA: Harvard University Press.

Weber, M. (1905) *The Protestant Ethic and the Spirit of Capitalism*. New York: Scribner.

ROBIN CELIKATES

URBANISM AND URBANIZATION

An urban settlement might be a 'city', a 'town', a 'metropolis', a 'suburb', a 'conurbation' or possibly a 'village' or a 'hamlet'. Typically, the term 'city' is taken to evoke the essence of urban life; but cities are elusive objects of definition. (While a 'town' in English usually denotes a smaller unit than a 'city', words in other languages such as *ville* and *Stadt* in French and German usually encompass both magnitudes.) Among an array of criteria, at least five features can be mentioned as contributing towards a definition of the city. Cities usually presuppose: (1) a high degree of demographic density based on a settled population residing within a delimited area; (2) concentration of institutions of economic **production**, exchange and **consumption** or **markets** located in a physically delimited place; (3) political, administrative or **governmental** institutions relevant to an associated territorial space; (4) **communication** functions of interconnection between pathways of transit, often facilitated by naturally occurring topographical features such as rivers, coastlines or valley nexuses; and (5) distinct **cultural** institutions arising out of the transformation of practices of land cultivation into practices of human moral cultivation or civic, civil or civilized conduct of life, vested in schooling and apprenticeship, in places of **religious** worship, and in places of organized **leisure**, sociability and public **association** (see **civilization**). A few disparate themes can be singled out as characterizing central foci of research on the city in social theory.

Many Western social and political thinkers underline the normative significance of the classical Greek idea of the *polis* as the place of the collective political self-determination of the people. In this 'classical republican' sense, the *polis* is the centre of the *politeia*, the **republic** or *res publica*, in which a people comes to define itself as a **polity** and debates the decisions pertaining to its public life. All modern Western norms of **citizenship** and **civil society** owe a part of their inception to the Greek idea of the *polis* and its dissemination through the legal institutions of the Roman world and these institutions' subsequent Christianization in the Middle Ages.

One among many modern champions of this ancient normative image of the city was the nineteenth-century French historian, Fustel de Coulanges. Fustel distinguished significantly between the Latin words *civitas* and *urbs*, regarding the former as pertaining to the religious and political association of **families** and **tribes** and the latter as referring to the place of dwelling and sanctuary (Fustel de Coulanges 1864: 126ff.). Fustel emphasized that rather than reducing *civitas* to *urbs*, the ancients maintained a belief in the existence of the city as an association even if it did not have a corresponding spatial form. Modern ways of thinking were misguided in inferring the essence of the city purely from its spatial characteristics such as concentration, arrangements, and elements of its buildings, bridges, and walls. Rather, the essence of the city was revealed in its nature as association. Fustel thus considered the city to be 'religious' in the sense that historically when various tribes agreed to 'unite' and to practise the same worship, they founded the city as a religious sanctuary for common worship.

Many other images compete for attention in our ideas of the essence of urban life. The city has been characterized variously as the 'space of citizenship', 'cradle of democracy', '**war** machine', 'dense and heterogeneous settlement', 'space of accumulation', or conglomeration of 'texts' and 'signs'. At the minimum a broadly cross-cultural account of the city applicable to both Western and non-Western contexts, of both ancient and modern heritage, would seem to need to refer to the emergence of relatively specialized systems of division of labour involving not only cultivation of surrounding land but also functions of trading, food storage and administrative centralization. On this definition, the ancient settlements of Mesopotamia, the Nile, and Anatolia, as well as the Indus Valley and valley settlements of ancient China count among the first cities of the world.

Yet it should be emphasized that all such projects of definition represent a will to impose order and unity on an object that is inherently diffuse and essentially contested. Any attempt to define the ancient Greek city of Athens, for example, is problematized by the fact that the symbolic identity of the city was itself an object of struggle for a long period of time between oligarchs, warriors, tyrants, and peasants (Lévêque and Vidal-Naquet 1964). The accounts we have inherited themselves bear all the marks of these struggles. In China, Bianzhou during the T'ang Dynasty was an object of struggle at least between **aristocrats** and **bureaucrats** and the accounts we have inherited bear the marks of that struggle (Heng 1999; Southall 1998).

In early modern European history, the decisive watershed in the crystallization of cities as politico-economic centres is the emergence in the Middle Ages of autonomous city charters and other legal **freedoms** protecting against interference by larger surrounding territorial **powers**, states and empires, including the Papacy. The exemplary cases are the Italian city–states – Florence, Pisa, Venice, Genoa – and the northern trading ports of the Low Countries. Max **Weber** here reiterated Fustel de Coulanges's distinction between the *civitas* and *urbs*, emphasizing the ways in which medieval European cities are not only centres of economic association but also expressions of collective political identity embodied in citizenship (Weber [1909] 1976; [1921]: 1978). Urban settlements are only truly cities insofar as they develop, cultivate, and make possible a legal and political status of belonging. It is in this sense that Weber argued that only the **occidental** city could be called the city: oriental cities were not truly cities because in his view they lacked a corporate identity embodied in citizenship. While Weber can be criticized for this distinction (Isin 2002), his theoretical innovation is unmistakable. Weber pointed out that specific qualities such as the presence of the wall, or the autonomous administration of autonomous law-making cannot be taken as qualities that determine the essence of the city. While developing various typologies of the city such as the 'consumer city', the 'producer city', Weber insisted that these do not define the city but merely provide heuristic concepts with which to develop interpretations.

The industrial expansion of European cities in the eighteenth and nineteenth centuries was a key concern for classical social theorists of the later nineteenth century. These writers were centrally concerned with the link between economic **differentiation**, **industrialization**, technological modernization and population growth, on the one hand, and key socio-cultural transformations, on the other. Central to their narratives was the rise of an econom-

ically, politically and culturally powerful class of city-dwelling, property-owning burghers or **bourgeoisie** or **middle class** with interests in the maintenance of an open, pluralistic, tolerant and in some sense **cosmopolitan** civil society. In varying ways the commercially minded townspeople were pitted against the traditional political and cultural hegemony of the landowning rentier aristocracy and other carriers or locations of agrarian power, including the **peasantry**, the **church** and the **monarchy**.

In his essay 'The Metropolis and Mental life' ([1903] 1997), as well as in his larger magnum opus, *The Philosophy of Money* ([1900] 1990), Georg Simmel portrayed the city as the distinctive social **space** in which **form and forms** of social interaction come to be mediated more and more by **money** as the most abstract, efficient and anonymous medium of exchange. Cities witness ever more complex patterns of stylization of life based on commerce, consumption and melting of immigrant ethnicities and **intellectuals**, precipitating revolutions in cultural manners and morality, including attitudes to **sexuality**, **authority** and **gender**. Studying Berlin, Vienna and Paris at the *fin de siècle*, Simmel observed how urban experience is at once more aestheticized, insofar as it is displays sensory plenitude, movement and intensity, and *an*aestheticized insofar as it necessitates a 'blasé attitude' among individuals who must protect themselves from nervous exhaustion by maintaining an indifferent exterior. The city in this sense reveals the strongest possible divisions between the **public and private** dimensions of life, between professionalized routines of work and bureaucratic office, on the one hand, and the inner secreted side of **intimacy**, on the other, often triggering pathological phenomena of voyeurism and distinctive kinds of **crime** and **deviance**.

Simmel's studies are closely paralleled by those of Walter **Benjamin** and Siegfried **Kracauer** on urban avant-garde movements in **art and aesthetics**, on the role of bohemian subculture, and struggles over access to public space and public display in the face of privatized capital interests, sites of mass consumption and agencies of centralized imperial state power mediated through city architecture, street construction, **policing** and municipal **social control**.

Simmel's influence also stands behind the wide-ranging studies of the early twentieth-century **Chicago School** of sociologists in the USA, represented by Louis Wirth, Albion Small, Robert Park and others. In parallel with a tradition of surveys of urban **poverty** by European socialists and social reformers at the end of the nineteenth century – notably beginning with Engels's study of the industrial cities of northern England – the Chicago sociologists inaugurated a long-standing agenda in urban sociology focused on urban mafia organization and the informal economy, on immigrant ghettoization, inner-city ethnic conflict and gang **violence**, and the spatial distribution of socio-economic inequalities. Wirth (1938) in particular emphasized the diminution of neighbourly kinship bonds and their replacement by new logics of spatial segregation. City dwellers gain a degree of freedom from the personal and **emotional** controls of intimate groups' but lose 'the spontaneous self-expression, the morale, and the sense of participation that comes with living in an integrated society'. Key social **stratification** functions come to be played by density, land values, rentals, accessibility, healthfulness, prestige, aesthetic consideration, absence of nuisances such as noise, smoke, and dirt…Diverse population elements inhabiting a compact settlement thus become segregated from one another in the degree in which their requirements and modes of life are incompatible and in the measure in which they are antagonistic. Similarly, persons of homogeneous status and needs unwittingly drift into, consciously select, or are forced by circumstances into the same area. The different parts of the city acquire specialized functions, and the city consequently comes to resemble a mosaic of social worlds in which the transition from one to the other is abrupt (Wirth 1938).

In a different vein, the mid-century US urban historian and theorist Lewis Mumford (1961) maintained a more Weberian understanding of the essence of the city as citizenship. Mumford was critical of Wirth, who in his view, attempted to deduce *civitas* from *urbs*. Implicitly endorsing Weber's distinction between the occidental and oriental city, and associating the latter with oriental despotism, Mumford argued that the modern occidental city had resuscitated the despotic and oriental city by reducing citizens to subjects.

Among central issues of research on contemporary Western cities have been the social transformations brought about by the decline of industrial manufacturing bases and their replacement by a large preponderance of **post-industrial** services-based sectors. Bound up with this have been the emergence of problematic inner-city social voids marked by poverty, **unemployment**, and rising crime rates, on the one hand, and movements of affluence away from undesirable zones in the wake of gentrification processes turning formerly industrial spaces and infrastructures into spaces of fashionable leisure and consumption, on the other. Many urban theorists and researchers since the 1980s such as Davis (1990), Soja (1989) and Harvey (1990) examine the phenomenon of the uncontained, unstructured **'postmodern'** city, exposing a profound crisis in the ability of municipal authorities to protect against destructive market-driven logics of spatial polarization of the life chances of urban populations. In several respects the paradigmatic case of Los Angeles reveals ways in which wealthy commuting **elites** enjoy privileges of living and working behind secure air-conditioned and policed façades while vast sectors of the remaining population toil under the effects of pollution, poor

educational opportunities, substandard housing, inadequate public transportation, **crime** and highly depressed or casualized employment conditions. Almost always, the most disadvantaged **demographic** sectors are here represented by immigrant communities and non-white-majority **ethnic** groups, sometimes regarded as composing an **underclass**.

The 'postmodern' city is paralleled by the so-called 'global city' (Sassen 1991) represented by centres of global financial commerce such as New York, London, Frankfurt and Tokyo, tightly linked to one another through mobile flows and **networks** of professionals, capital, expertise and **information**. Members of global urban business networks appear to live in what Manuel Castells (1996) calls a 'virtualized' or 'deterritorialized' space–time manifold, unperturbed by the life of the mass of the population on the streets, among the garbage cans at the feet of the skyscrapers and the ever-expanding slums of the cities of the global South.

References and further reading

Davis, M. (1990) *City of Quartz*. London: Verso.

Fustel de Coulanges, N. D. ([1864] 1978) *The Ancient City: A Study on the Religion, Laws, and Institutions of Greece and Rome*. New York: Doubleday.

Harvey, D. (1990) *The Condition of Postmodernity*. Oxford: Blackwell.

Heng, C. K. (1999) *Cities of Aristocrats and Bureaucrats: The Development of Medieval Chinese Cities*. Honolulu, HI: University of Hawaii Press.

Isin, E. F. (2002) *Being Political: Genealogies of Citizenship*. Minneapolis, MN: University of Minnesota Press.

Lévêque, P. and Vidal-Naquet, P. ([1964] 1996) *Cleisthenes the Athenian: An Essay on the Representation of Space and Time in Greek Political Thought from the End of the Sixth Century to the Death of Plato*. Trans. D. A. Curtis. Atlantic Highlands, NJ: Humanities Press.

Mumford, L. (1938) *The Culture of Cities*. New York: Harcourt, Brace and World.

Mumford, L. (1961) *The City in History: Its Origins, its Transformations, and its Prospects*. London: Harcourt Brace Jovanovich.

Sassen, S. (1991) *The Global City*. Princeton: Princeton University Press.

Sennett, R. (1994) *Flesh and Stone: The Body and the City in Western Civilization*. New York: W. W. Norton.

Simmel, G. ([1903] 1997) 'The Metropolis and Mental Life', in *Simmel on Culture*. Ed. M. Featherstone and D. Frisby. London: Sage.

Simmel, G. ([1900] 1990) *The Philosophy of Money*. New York: Routledge.

Soja, E. (1989) *Postmodern Geographies*. London: Verso.

Southall, A. W. (1998) *The City in Time and Space*. Cambridge: Cambridge University Press.

Weber, M. ([1909] 1976) *The Agrarian Sociology of Ancient Civilizations*. Trans. R. I. Frank. London: New Left Books.

Weber, M. ([1921a] 1958) *The City*. New York: Free Press.

Weber, M. ([1921b] 1978) *Economy and Society: An Outline of Interpretive Sociology*. Trans. G. Roth and C. Wittich, 2 vols. Berkeley, CA: University of California Press.

Wirth, L. (1938) 'Urbanism as a Way of Life', *American Journal of Sociology*, 44(1): 1–24.

ENGIN F. ISIN
AUSTIN HARRINGTON

UTILITARIANISM

Utilitarianism is a comprehensive program both in sociological theory and in normative political theory, originating from the intellectual movement that emerged in eighteenth-century Britain. The core utilitarian idea is that **society** and its **institutions** can be explained by what Jeremy Bentham called 'principle of utility'. Normative utilitarianism is a consequentialist approach: an act or a rule ought to be followed if its consequences are good.

Utilitarian social thought was elaborated by Bentham, J. S. **Mill** and other thinkers, working under the influence of Hume, **Smith**, Hutcheson and other British moralists. Bentham describes classical utilitarianism with the famous words: 'Nature has placed mankind under the **governance** of two sovereign masters, *pain* and *pleasure*. It is for them alone to point out what we ought to do, as well as to determine what we shall do' (1823: 358). This means that the principle of utility should be used as an empirical law in order to explain human **action** and behaviour. Utility theory in this sense is a theory of motivation and action ('psychological hedonism'). It assumes that an individual chooses an action if it has more pleasant and less painful consequences than its alternatives. Predominantly, utilitarianism is also a theory in normative ethics, which argues that it is morally right to choose among alternative social states, institutions, rules or acts so that the sum of interests or utilities of the members of a society is maximized.

Classical sociologists reacted critically to utilitarian thinking. **Parsons** (1937: 60) pointed to atomism (**individualism**), **rationality**, **empiricism** and 'randomness of ends' as the core features of what he called 'the utilitarian system of social theory'. Today, this set of ideas or its more recent elaborations is generally termed **rational choice** theory. **Durkheim**, Parsons and others argued that the utility principle cannot explain how social order or **solidarity** emerges from a society of egoists. The basic reason is that social order requires that the individuals categorically or unconditionally commit themselves to certain values of solidarity. Max **Weber**'s conception of value rationality implies a similar **Kantian** conception of normative obligation.

In normative social and political theory, utilitarianism implies that a social state s should be evaluated by a social welfare function $W(s)$ which is a sum of the utilities $u_i(s)$ of the n individuals who live in a society:

$$W(s) = u_1(s) + u_2(s) + \ldots + u_n(s).$$

This means that every individual's **interests** are equally included into society's welfare function. But utilitarianism as a normative program has to solve some obvious problems: constructing an additive welfare function from individuals' interests (utilities) requires cardinally measurable utilities and their interpersonal comparability. Modern decision and utility theory imply that an individual's **preferences** can be measured by a cardinal utility scale. However, there is no clear foundation for interpersonal comparisons of utilities in utility theory (see Roemer 1996 for a discussion of some solutions).

In normative utilitarianism, there has been a discussion about the merits of so-called act-utilitarianism versus rule-utilitarianism. According to rule-utilitarianism, moral judgments focus on the consequences of general rules ('a rule with good consequences ought to be followed') but not on individual acts ('an act with good consequences ought to be performed'). Act-utilitarianism sometimes yields moral judgments that do not match moral intuitions. To illustrate, consider a person P who can participate in a national political election. On the day of the election, P recognizes that the weather is fine and that she will have a lot of fun if she goes to a swimming-pool. In a large electorate, the chance that P's vote will be pivotal is extremely small. Act-utilitarianism therefore may recommend that P ought to go swimming. In contrast, rule-utilitarianism may be understood as the postulate that an act is morally wrong if bad consequences occur if *everybody* follows the act. For instance, it will be bad for the functioning of democracy if every **citizen** abstains from voting. Consequently, P ought to vote. Another variant of rule-utilitarianism requires that a rule must *in general* have positive factual consequences. Although rule-utilitarianism seems *prima facie* more appealing to many people's moral intuitions, it has been argued that certain types of rule-utilitarianism are practically equivalent to act-utilitarianism.

In relation to rational choice theory or to any empiricist conception of **morality**, utilitarianism is confronted with a central difficulty. It requires that moral decisions be made so that the interests of *all* members of a society (and possibly future generations) are equally represented. Provided individual actors are motivated by their own personal self-interested preferences, why should they adopt the moral point of view of utilitarian ethics? In an intriguing argument that originally was published in the 1950s, Harsanyi (1977) asserts that rational agents who act under the **role** of an 'impartial observer' and decide with a lack of **knowledge** about their personal social position (that is, behind a kind of pre-**Rawlsian** 'veil of ignorance') will necessarily choose utilitarian social rules. However, why should an egoist decide behind a 'veil of ignorance'? Modern **game-theoretic** ideas are appropriate intellectual tools to discuss such questions (Binmore 1994).

References and further reading

Bentham, J. (1823) *An Introduction to the Principles of Morals and Legislation*. London: Pickering.

Binmore, K. (1994) *Game Theory and the Social Contract*, vol. 1: *Playing Fair*. Cambridge, MA: MIT Press.

Hardin, R. (1988) *Morality within the Limits of Reason*. Chicago: University of Chicago Press.

Harsanyi, J. C. (1977) *Rational Behavior and Bargaining Equilibrium in Games and Social Situations*. Cambridge: Cambridge University Press.

Parsons, T. (1937) *The Structure of Social Action*. New York: Free Press.

Roemer, J. (1996) *Theories of Distributive Justice*. Cambridge, MA: Harvard University Press.

Smart, J. J. C. and Williams, B. (eds) (1973) *Utilitarianism: For and Against*. Cambridge: Cambridge University Press.

THOMAS VOSS

UTOPIA

The word 'utopia' derives from the Greek *outopos*, meaning 'no-place', but also carries the meaning of *eutopos* or 'good-place'. The term was coined by Thomas More in his treatise *Utopia* of 1516. There he portrayed an ideal society in which **money** is banned, the **work**-day shortened, **violence** eradi-

cated and substantial **equality** between inhabitants guaranteed by a series of measures such as compulsory **education**. While depictions of utopian cities or ages (like the sunken city of Atlantis, or Plato's Republic) can be found in earlier times, More's text presents the first truly modern utopia. Written from the perspective of Renaissance **humanism**, it launches a critique of the disintegrating medieval order of **feudalism**, of social hierarchy and **poverty**. With this work, the whole genre of utopian novels was inaugurated. The most prominent early utopias include Tommaso Campanella's *The City of the Sun* (1623) which depicts a tightly organized and '**collectivized**' society without **private** property, Francis Bacon's *New Atlantis* (1627) where experimental science plays a leading role, and James Harrington's republican utopia *Oceania* (1656) which is established on the basis of land redistribution.

A common characteristic of these utopias is that they are located at a remote place, quite often an island, to be reached only with difficulties. Only with Louis-Sébastien Mercier's *The Year 2440* (1770) is utopia is located in the *future*. This alteration is part of a larger development called by the German historian Koselleck (2000) the 'temporalization of space', which started in the second half of the eighteenth century. In this 'age of **progress**', utopia is no longer to be found at the horizon of geographical space, as it was in the former 'age of discoveries'. It is the future itself which becomes the new horizon of social and political imagination. Mercier's portrayal of Paris in the year 2440 presents an enlightened and rational time in which the Bastille will be destroyed, the estates abolished and **religion** turned into **morality**. After the French Revolution of 1789 demonstrated the potential to realize such a future within the present, utopians became more and more concerned in the nineteenth century with the practical realization of their programs. Utopian socialists like Robert Owen and

Charles Fourier not only devised programs for communal living but also organized or inspired utopian colonies in the United States (see **socialism**). What many of these utopias exhibit is a belief in the power of social engineering and the organizability of all aspects of communal and private life. As a result, **egalitarianism** is often accompanied by extreme uniformity. In More's utopia, people are clothed identically, get up (and go to bed) all at the same time of the day and take their meals in common dining halls while improving literature is read to them. The most notorious example is Campanella's *The City of the Sun* where everything, including sexual reproduction, is subject to rational communal **organization**. Not surprisingly, one encounters a subgenre of satirical utopias or 'anti-utopias' (so-called dystopias), of which Samuel Butler's *Erewhon* (1872) is one of the first, and Aldous Huxley's *Brave New World* (1932) is one of the best-known examples.

From a political point of view, the utopian socialists were criticized by **Marx** and Engels for offering imaginary solutions to real problems. In contrast, Marx and Engels sought to develop a scientific form of **socialism** which, however, shared with social utopianism an optimistic view of progress and the blessings of social engineering. From today's perspective, utopian thought can be criticized for aiming at a state of harmony in which all internal conflict is suppressed and supplanted by administrative procedures, leading to what we would now perceive as profoundly depoliticized societies. Moreover, **Jameson** (1988) has argued, following Louis Marin's seminal work ([1973] 1984), that utopian models do not work by solving problems but by expelling

them beyond their boundaries. In More's peaceful utopia, for instance, the business of war is left to foreign mercenaries, and while money is not tolerated within the community, it is still used in the foreign trade. Utopias then turn out to be founded on the constitutive exclusion of all seemingly disturbing elements. Nevertheless, the utopian spirit was held high in twentieth-century thought by the single most important philosopher of utopianism, Ernst **Bloch**. In his *The Principle of Hope* ([1954–59] 1986) Bloch develops a philosophy of the 'not yet', according to which visions of a better world can be found in emancipatory politics as much as in fairy tales, **popular culture**, art or daydreams. Critical of the idea of an imaginary perfect state of society in the far future, Bloch coined the term *concrete utopia* in order to designate the 'latent' but realistic possibilities of social change in the present.

References and further reading

Bauman, Z. (1976) *Socialism: The Active Utopia*. London: George Allen & Unwin.

Bloch, E. ([1954–59] 1986) *The Principle of Hope*, 3 vols. Cambridge, MA: MIT Press.

Jameson, F. (1988) 'Of Islands and Trenches: Neutralization and Production of Utopian Discourse', in *The Ideologies of Theory*, vol. 2. Minneapolis, MN: University of Minnesota.

Koselleck, R. (2000) 'Die Verzeitlichung der Utopie', in *Zeitschichten*. Frankfurt am Main: Suhrkamp.

Mannheim, K. ([1929] 1991) *Ideology and Utopia*. London: Routledge.

Marin, L. ([1973] 1984) *Utopics: Spatial Play*. New Jersey: Humanities.

Mumford, L. (1922) *The Story of Utopias*. New York: Boni & Liveright.

OLIVER MARCHART

V

VALUES AND NORMS

The word values indicates the principles and standards that are identified with 'the good', while the word norms indicates the practical guidance that enables 'good' action to be carried out, and 'wrong' action to be condemned. The distinction between them is clearer in theory than in **practice**, and in social theory the distinction was formalized by Talcott **Parsons**.

Parsons argued that **society** can be understood as a **social system** of **action**. Actors are motivated by values and norms that give action meaning. For Parsons, values are the beliefs of actors about what the world ought to be like and what fundamental meanings it possesses, and norms are the socially accepted rules which actors use in order to decide upon and carry out appropriate courses of action. Of these, the most deep-rooted are values. Parsons identified three different value systems: (1) the *cultural value system* deals with questions of 'ultimate concern' (such as life and death); (2) the *social value system*, establishes what society ought to be like; and (3) the *personal value system*, establishes why actors do what they do.

Parsons argued that the value system of the USA in the 1950s was based on secularized Protestantism. Here, Parsons owed a debt to **Weber**'s analysis of the **Protestant Ethic** (Weber 1930). These were the values that permeate all aspects of American life and which provide ultimate meanings (see **America**). To this extent, Parsons saw

Protestantism as a *cultural value system*. But it is also a *social value system* because it gives social roles a meaning and establishes how they ought to be carried out. In particular, Parsons stressed that Protestantism leads to an emphasis on ambition and success, and that this results in a vision of society that rewards hard work. In addition, Protestantism underpins the *personal value system* insofar as individuals are socialized through **education** into the belief that what actors achieve in this world is the measure of their social standing. In this way, values are the foundation of norms, and these norms are communicated to actors through socialization and the maintenance of social **roles**. Parsons saw these norms as institutionalized, leading to a system of 'status roles' to which are attached expectations of action (for example, norms of professionalism). Actors accept and practice the norms of these status roles because they wish to be socially rewarded and not condemned. There is, then, a normative social order that is both individually meaningful and socially systematic.

Where values and norms are unclear or have lost their relevance, a condition of **anomie** emerges. According to Parsons, in the 1960s this was the situation of youth in America. Parsons argued that dominant social and personal value systems emphasized individual achievement and success, and in so doing hastened processes of social change that made traditional values and norms obsolete. This insight is often reflected in sociological studies of moral life in contemporary America, as in the work of Bellah (Parsons 1964; Bellah 1985).

Parsons can be considered to be trying to provide a sociological resolution of a philosophical dispute about values and norms. The *subjectivist* position argues that values are expressions of **subjective interests**; something is 'good' if it serves interests, and not because of any intrinsic merit it might have. According to the subjectivist argument, hard work is good within the American value system because it enables actors to achieve their interests in success. A clear statement of the subjectivist position in social theoretical approaches to values and norms is provided by **rational choice** theory. By contrast, the *objectivist* position contends that values are expressions of intrinsic qualities independent of human interests. According to the objectivist argument, work is good because it glorifies God, irrespective of individual achievement. These two positions can be found in the social theory that Parsons sought to synthesize. Weber's position can be understood as a sociological variant of subjectivism insofar as he was concerned with the actions of individuals in the pursuit of subjectively meaningful goals. By contrastz, **Durkheim** represents a more objectivist approach in that he thought that values have a meaning over and above individuals, and together constitute the 'collective conscience' that is the basis of the norms that guide action, and into which actors are required to be socialized. Where the **division of labour** undermines the unity and stability of the collective conscience, the force of values and norms is weakened, resulting in anomie. Durkheim (1957) argued that a resolution of this situation is the institutionalization of codes of professional ethics and the development of civic morals.

References and further reading

Bellah, R. *et al.* (1985) *Habits of the Heart: Individualism and Commitment in American Life.* New York: Harper & Row.

Durkheim, E. (1957) *Professional Ethics and Civic Morals.* London: Routledge & Kegan Paul.

Durkheim, E. (1984) *The Division of Labour in Society.* London: Macmillan.

Inglehart, R. (2003) *Human Values and Social Change: Findings from the Values Surveys.* Boston: Brill.

Joas, H. (2000) *The Genesis of Values.* Cambridge: Polity Press.

Parsons, T. (1937) *The Structure of Social Action.* New York: Free Press.

Parsons, T. (1964) *Social Structure and Personality.* New York: Free Press.

Parsons, T. (1969) *Politics and Social Structure.* New York: Free Press.

Weber, M. (1930) *The Protestant Ethic and the Spirit of Capitalism.* London: George Allen & Unwin.

Weber, M. (1948) *From Max Weber: Essays in Sociology.* London: Routledge & Kegan Paul.

KEITH TESTER

VERSTEHEN

Verstehen is the German word for 'understanding' with an associated meaning of 'empathy'. Its **epistemological** significance for interpretative sociology lies in the role it originally acquired in the hands of **Dilthey**, ([1923] 1988) and **Weber** ([1922] 1970).

As a **methodological** concept, it distinguishes the social or human sciences from the natural sciences. Natural scientists are faced by phenomena that are perceived as 'given' and existing in the world 'outside' them. Any connections between different phenomena have to be deduced secondarily, through the testing of hypotheses. In contrast, sociologists can only understand the **meaning** of social phenomena from the 'inside', in terms of how such phenomena resonate with lived experience; connections between phenomena are given with this lived experience.

The idea that *Verstehen* is an inner, psychological method requiring the imaginative recreation of others' motives is problematic and has led to dispute. Weber argued that motives could be treated as causes of **action** and this has led authors such as Abel and Rudner (see Dallmayr and

McCarthy 1977) to claim that *Verstehen* is no more than a way of identifying hunches in need of testing as hypotheses. However, others, such as Apel, **Taylor** and Winch (see Dallmayr and McCarthy 1977), dispute this **positivist** interpretation, arguing that it is the **hermeneutic** adequacy of the interpretation that matters, not the observed regularity between cause and effect.

References and further reading

Dallmayr, F. and McCarthy, T. (eds) (1977) *Understanding and Social Inquiry*. Indianapolis, IN: Notre Dame University Press.
Dilthey, W. ([1923] 1988) *Introduction to the Human Sciences*. Detroit, MI: Wayne State University Press.
McCarthy, T. (1973) 'On Misunderstanding Understanding', *Theory and Decision*, 3: 351–70.
Outhwaite, W. (1975) *Understanding Social Life: The Method called Verstehen*. London: Allen & Unwin.
Weber, M. ([1922] 1978) *Economy and Society*, vol. 1. Berkeley, CA: University of California Press.

ALAN HOW

VIOLENCE

Defining and explaining violence is a scientific challenge of the highest order. Its ambiguity, the ubiquity of its occurrence, its immediate availability as a resource, and the cognitive indistinctness of the human understanding of violence, mark some of the fundamental difficulties.

We draw on the term 'violence' to characterize widely differing phenomena: the nuclear bomb dropped on Hiroshima, the massacres in ex-Yugoslavia, **terrorism**, child abuse, **police** operations against demonstrators, rape, murder. The range of meaning encompasses complexes of action that are aimed at destroying order and endangering or ending life, as well as those designed to create order and protect life. Herein lies the essential ambivalence of violence. When it is branded as illegitimate, it is regarded as destructive and is outlawed; when its applica-

tion is seen as legitimate, it is regarded as a force for order and is felt to be necessary. The struggle over **legitimacy**, however, does not resolve the ambivalence.

Specific forms of violence must also be taken into consideration. *Physical* violence is the unchallenged primary phenomenon, while *psychological* and *structural* forms of violence are contentious (Galtung 1975). One must also distinguish between 'violence' and **power**, 'force' and 'coercion'. Thus empirical analyses and theories of violence must be able to deal with different forms, agents, and levels. That is why for many variants the current state of theory development is unsatisfactory. One reason for this is that the phenomena of violence are themselves subject to transformation.

For a long time analyses of violence played no special role in sociology. The **civilization** theory of Norbert **Elias** and the theories of functionally differentiated societies proposed by Talcott **Parsons** and his colleagues fostered an optimistic expectation of successive reductions in violence. For example, inter-**ethnic** violence was held to be absent in modern societies, but bitter reality has shaken these assumptions.

As a result, the relevance of analytical paradigms has been questioned, with claims that analysis of the causes of violence has failed, and that violence itself should be analyzed instead. The focus shifts from explaining the deed, the perpetrators, and the causes to a description of the suffering of the victims. This, it is claimed, is the innovative perspective in the sociology of violence (von Trotha 1997). 'Thick description' in this sense becomes the method of choice. Yet this too is open to an obvious criticism: analyses of violence degenerate into literary descriptions.

An **agent**-oriented sociological approach focusing on direct violence elicits a range of variants:

- *Individual violence*: The central questions concerning individual violence, whose most drastic form is homicide,

concentrate on the causes of this violence and its increase *or* decrease. A
long development trend shows that
the homicide rate in Western Europe
fell from the fifteenth to the mid-
twentieth centuries. The question of
whether the rise since 1960–65 is a
temporary deviation, or a reversal of the
trend, is still unresolved.

- *Collective violence*: Uprisings, pogroms,
and non-peaceful mass protests are
typical examples of this type of violence, which inherently implies a
certain degree of guidance and leadership. It has a political character in that
it involves an intention to exercise
power and maintain or challenge control. The dynamics of violence and
processes of escalation deserve particular close attention here.
- *Institutional state violence*: The heterogeneous forms of state violence extend
from a state's legitimate monopoly on
violence to state terrorism and **war**. A
central problem for the internal order
function arises when – for example,
under the pressure of terrorism – the
boundaries of legality and legitimacy
become blurred or legal and legitimate state action degenerates into
preventive wars or even state terrorism.
In the twentieth century as a whole,
the violence applied by the state was
many times greater than the extent of
individual and collective violence.

Violence occurs in different contexts of
interaction. If we are to obtain clarity about
the dynamics of escalation and de-escalation,
we need to consider the consequences of
socio-structural relations and the role of
violence **discourses**, **ideologies** and patterns
of justification (an overview is given in
O'Toole and Schiffman 1997; Heitmeyer
and Hagan 2003).

The repertoire of sociological explanations is broad, and can be placed in the
macro/micro paradigm (**Coleman** 1990):

- **Socialization** theory draws primarily
on learning theories by way of
explanation.
- Criminological theories focus on
individual violence and demonstrate
a broad spectrum of explanations
(ethiological approaches, interactionist approaches, control theories,
life-course theory) which operate at
different levels (an overview is given
in Albrecht 2003).
- **Deprivation** theory accentuates
absolute and relative disadvantages in
its explanations (Gurr 1972).
- **Social movement** theory attempts to
explain the origins of collective action
and the dynamics of collective violence
(Smelser 1963). Structural strains,
collective identity, **framing**, resource
mobilization, and political opportunity
structures represent competing explanations, as well as providing a potential
framework for an integrated concept.
- **Modernization** explanations start
from social transformation and its
effects on problems of integration and
disintegration (Heitmeyer 2003).

The theories differ in their significance
depending on the type of violence being
explained. Socialization theories might
particularly explain the attitudes acquired at
an early age, while **subculture** theories can
elucidate the habitualization of specific
behaviour in groups; social movement theory
focuses on mobilizations; and modernization approaches tend to stress the structural
discontinuities.

Because they have different strengths, the
theories also differ in scope. For example,
structural theories that are based on social
tensions and crises (Joas 1999) suffer the
drawback of an unsatisfactory explanation
of situative dynamics of action. Conflict
theory approaches, in turn, are greatly
restricted when it comes to explaining
long-term trends (see **conflict**). This means
that we have to develop combinations of

theories and integrative theory models, which comprise several levels and relate to different settings, to short-term events as well as long-term trends.

Many interpreters of modernity have interpreted this epoch as a leap forward for civilization that relegated violence to a merely pre-modern phenomenon. The relationship between modernity and barbarism is, however, a matter of controversy (Offe 1996). Four basic positions can be identified (Imbusch 1999: 150ff.). The first position interprets violence as a temporary aberration that can be 'offset' against the benefits of civilization (such as **security**) to give the overall development equation a positive outcome. A second, diametrically opposed, position focuses on the 'instrumental character' of modernity, arguing that the civilizing process of modernity is barbaric at its core, because it is itself the prerequisite for certain forms of violence. A third position emphasizes the ambivalence of the progress of modernity and of the potential for violence. It assumes that the potentials for humanism and destruction are both increased. The fourth position denies any connection between civilization and the eruptions of violence in the twentieth century. Instead, from an anthropological point of view, violence appears to be the immutable fate of the human race.

It is not difficult to see that all four approaches have to deal with problems in their core assumptions. So we have a wealth of well-known fundamental analytical problems, which can only be tackled in concise analyses, and a number of new phenomena of violence on which hypotheses could be tested.

The idea of a non-violent society was never a realistic one. It feeds on an idea of controllability of violence, but forgets that control is a highly ambivalent category, because it can itself be a source of violence. This is the case, for example, when individual or collective behaviour deviates from the norm (of the powerful) in the eyes of

the controllers of violence. If we consider phenomena such as ethnic and religious terror, the privatization of collective terror in dysfunctional states, and preventive wars, we must contrast controllability with loss of control.

References and further reading

Albrecht, G. (2003) 'Sociological Approaches to Individual Violence and their Empirical Evaluation', in W. Heitmeyer and J. Hagan (eds) *International Handbook of Violence Research*. Dordrecht: Kluwer Academic Publishers.

Coleman, J. S. (1990) *Foundations of Social Theory*. Cambridge, MA: Harvard University Press.

Galtung, J. (1975) *Strukturelle Gewalt: Beiträge zur Friedens-und Konfliktforschung*. Reinbek: Rowohlt.

Gurr, T. R. (1972) *Why Men Rebel*. Princeton, NJ: Princeton University Press.

Heitmeyer, W. (2003) 'Right-Wing Extremist Violence', in W. Heitmeyer and J. Hagan (eds) *International Handbook of Violence Research*. Dordrecht: Kluwer Academic Publishers.

Heitmeyer, W. and Hagan, J. (eds) (2003) *International Handbook of Violence Research*. Dordrecht: Kluwer Academic Publishers.

Imbusch, P. ([1999] 2003) 'Moderne und postmoderne Perspektiven der Gewalt', in S. Neckel and M. Schwab-Trapp (eds) *Ordnungen der Gewalt*. Opladen: Leske & Budrich.

Joas, H. (1999) 'Social Theorizing about War and Peace', in L. Kurtz (ed.) *Violence, Peace, Conflict*. San Diego, CA: Academic Publishers.

Offe, C. (1996) 'Moderne Barbarei: Der Naturzustand im Kleinformat', in M. Miller and H.-G. Soeffner (eds) *Modernität und Barbarei*. Frankfurt am Main: Suhrkamp.

O'Toole, L. L. and Schiffman, J. R. (eds) (1997) *Gender Violence: Interdisciplinary Perspectives*. New York: New York University Press.

Smelser, N. J. (1963) *Theory of Collective Behavior*. New York: Free Press.

von Trotha, T. (ed.) (1997) 'Soziologie der Gewalt', special issue of *Kölner Zeitschrift für Soziologie und Sozialpsychologie*, 37.

WILHELM HEITMEYER

659

VITALISM

Vitalism is a philosophy of life with an ancient pedigree in the world **religions** and Greek philosophy, most notably in Aristotle's theory of form. In the modern sciences it has an elective affinity with biology. In popular consciousness it expresses a rebellion against the dualism of mind and body, or spirit and matter. In the late eighteenth-century dialectic of **Enlightenment** and **romanticism**, vitalism was often a monist doctrine of immanent spirit, as in the German *Naturphilosophie* of Goethe through to Schelling and Novalis. This was appropriated into Anglophone discussions, poetically by William Blake (energy force), philosophically by Samuel Coleridge, and in cultural-political terms by Thomas Carlyle ('Force'; 'natural supernaturalism'). By the late nineteenth century, vitalism was re-energized by the social and aesthetic 'triumph of life' polemics of **Nietzsche** by the discovery of the two laws of thermodynamics in physics which shifted scientific focus from matter to that of energy as process and flow. This latter focus – combined with the Darwinian turn in biological theories of **evolution**, and the emergence of a 'new science' of consciousness (psychology) – was synthesized by the French philosopher, Henri Bergson into a philosophy of intuition, time and lived experience. These interests were renewed in the last two decades of the twentieth century by a popular turn to deep ecology and New Age physics (the 'Gaia' hypothesis). Most notably, Bergson and Nietzsche were re-appropriated by **Deleuze** into a philosophy of multiplicity, **complexity**, **differentiation** and **individuation**.

References and further reading

Bergson, H. ([1907] 1983) *Creative Evolution*. Lanham, MD: University Press of America.

Burwick, F. and Douglass, P. (eds) (1992) *The Crisis in Modernism: Bergson and the Vitalist Controversy*. Cambridge: Cambridge University Press.

Deleuze, G. ([1966] 1988) *Bergsonism*. New York: Zone Books.

TREVOR HOGAN

VOCATION

Sometimes used as a synonym for occupation, vocation means an official and regular **work** position, job activity or employment. In particular, vocation involves personal engagement, a strong feeling of fitness or suitability to pursue a particular career, a function to which a **person** is called and a dedicated mode of life. While everyone might have a work position, not everyone has a vocation. In this sense, vocation comes close to the notion of **profession**. Primordially, vocation refers to a feeling of being called by God to perform a specific (especially religious) task or function. To have a sense of vocation means to have a mission in life, working with submission and devotion (Cochran 1990). The **religious** background of the term is closely connected with the concept of calling that Max Weber analyzed in his **Protestant ethic**. According to Weber, the word 'calling' is a historical innovation that first appeared in Luther's German translation of the Bible (in German, *Berufung* means calling, while *Beruf* means vocation or occupation). Calling requires **discipline** of the **self**. Weber was convinced of the significant historical role played by the Puritan concept of calling. He introduced a secular version of that concept into social theory referring to an ethos and a discipline for **action**. For Weber, calling became a distinctive, crucial trait for coping with modern **rationalization**, for leadership in **economy**, policy, and **science**, for mastering modern politics and economy.

References and further reading

Cochran, L. (1990) *The Sense of Vocation: A Study of Career and Life Development*. New York: State University Press.

Weber, M. (1989) 'Science as a Vocation', in P. Lassman and I. Velody (eds) *Max Weber's 'Science as a Vocation'*. London: Unwin Hyman, pp. 3–31.

GÜNTER BURKART

VOEGELIN, ERIC (1901–1985)
Austro-German theorist

A life-long friend of Alfred **Schutz**, Voegelin's encounter with the legacy of Max **Weber** was a decisive formative experience in his work. After emigration to the USA, Vogelin embarked on a major study of the history of political ideas. Its guiding thought, paralleling Weber's concern with the impact of inner-worldly asceticism on the rise of modern **capitalism**, was the diagnosis of intramundane eschatology at the heart of modern politics, especially the national state. The undertaking remained unfinished and unpublished until the 1990s, as Voegelin was unable to revise the 4,500-page long manuscript on the basis of insights gained during the writing process.

In 1951 he published *The New Science of Politics* (1952), his best-known work, presenting the thesis of **modernity** as a 'Gnostic revolt'. His project then turned to *Order and History* (1956–87), focusing on building bridges between philosophy and revelation, especially Plato and **Christianity**, in order to understand the emergence of modernity and diagnose its shortcomings.

Voegelin's most important work is *The Ecumenic Age* (1974, vol. 4 of *Order and History*, 1956–87), which amplifies the ideas of the previous volumes, identifying the age of world-conquering empires as the 'ecumenic age', revisiting the 'Gnosticism' thesis, and revising the central ideas of *Anamnesis*, especially the crucial term 'experience'.

Major works

(1952) *The New Science of Politics*. Chicago: University of Chicago Press.
(1956–87) *Order and History*, 5 vols. Baton Rouge, LA: Louisiana State University Press.

([1966] 2002) *Anamnesis*. Columbia, MO: University of Missouri Press.
(1997–99) *The History of Political Ideas*, 8 vols. Columbia, MO: University of Missouri Press.

Further reading

Cooper, B. (1999) *Eric Voegelin and the Foundations of Modern Political Science*. Columbia, MO: University of Missouri Press.
Rossbach, S. (1999) *Gnostic Wars*. Edinburgh: Edinburgh University Press.
Sandoz, E. (ed.) (1999) *Eric Voegelin's Thought: A Critical Appraisal*. Durham, NC: Duke University Press.
Szakolczai, A. (2000) *Reflexive Historical Sociology*. London: Routledge.

ARPAD SZAKOLCZAI

VOLUNTARISM

Voluntarism marks the specific feature of Talcott **Parsons**'s theory of action (Parsons [1937] 1968) compared with other theories of **rational** or **symbolic action**. Parsons sees action made up of four essential elements: (1) actor; (2) situation; (3) end (*telos*); and (4) a mode of relation between the situation and the end of action, which is normative in character (Parsons [1937] 1968: 43–7). In effectively pursuing his/her end the actor changes the way the situation would develop without his/her interference. The relation between situation and end is characterized by symbolic reference to **values**. The efficient use of means for achieving an end rests upon the distinction of means and conditions in the situation which is due to the symbolic reference to the value of **cognitive** rationality. Rational action in terms of an efficient use of means for an end is therefore not just successful action, it is a symbolic exemplification of the value of cognitive rationality. Voluntarism means choice between values that normatively regulate action.

Being situated implies that action is embedded in an order of other actions. To achieve an end means that the respective action will be added as another unit to that order. In this conceptualization of the relation between action and order Parsons relies on the philosophy of Alfred North Whitehead ([1929] 1978). Parsons develops his voluntaristic conception of action against both, the notion of an unbound free will that realizes itself without taking into account obstacles of the situation, and against the **determinism** of ideas of situational forces that make free will to achieve ends redundant. Both notions pervert the idea of free will by eliminating its precarious character, being exercised in a fallible manner, troubled by error and delusion, or by insufficient effort and motivation.

References and further reading

Parsons, T. ([1937] 1968) *The Structure of Social Action*. New York: Free Press.

Whitehead, A. N. ([1929] 1978) *Process and Reality: An Essay in Cosmology*. New York: Free Press.

HARALD WENZEL

W

WALLERSTEIN, IMMANUEL (1930–)

US sociologist

One of the founders of **world systems theory**, Wallerstein is primarily interested in three domains: (1) the historical development of the modern world-system; (2) the contemporary crisis of global **capitalism**; and (3) the social structure of **knowledge**. Based upon the Marxist tradition of **imperialism** and Latin American dependency theory, he takes the globe as the methodological unit and capitalism as the driving force of the 'system'. The core countries, which are developed and rich exploit countries at the fringe, the periphery of underdeveloped countries (see **centre and periphery**). In between are semi-peripheral countries which can be regarded as the global **middle class** between the core ('the top') and the periphery ('the bottom') of the world hierarchy. Much of Asia and Africa, however, formed the external arena and were not even part and parcel of the world-system. But after the end of **colonialism** and due to the activities of large corporations, these regions were more and more drawn into the world economy. As the pioneer of world-system analysis, Wallerstein not only pointed out the patterns of global **inequality** but began to study the world as a social system. His work can be seen as an important forerunner of **globalization** analysis.

Major works

(1974) *The Modern World System*. New York: Academic Press.
(1979) *The Capitalist World Economy*. Cambridge: Cambridge University Press.
(2000) *The Essential Wallerstein*. New York: Academic Press.

Further reading

Bairoch, P. (1993) *Economics and World History: Myths and Paradoxes*. Chicago: University of Chicago Press.
Chase-Dunn, C. K. (1989) *Global Formation: Structures of the World-Economy*. Oxford: Blackwell.
Evans, P. B. (1995) *Embedded Autonomy: States and Industrial Transformation*. Princeton, NJ: Princeton University Press.
Smelser, N. J. and Swedberg, R. (eds) (1994) *The Handbook of Economic Sociology*. Princeton, NJ: Princeton University Press.

HANS-PETER MÜLLER

WALZER, MICHAEL (1935–)

US political philosopher

Walzer's work in political theory and moral philosophy on such diverse topics as political obligation, **nationalism** and **religion**, **civil society** and democratic **citizenship** is marked by his engagement with concrete political and historical issues. Situated between established intellectual traditions from **soci-**

alism, to **liberalism** and **communitarianism**, his thought is deeply pluralistic and opposed to all forms of dogmatism. In addition to his work on just **war** theory, Walzer is best known for his account of complex **equality** which holds that there is no one universal principle of justice. Rather, according to the shared understandings of particular political communities, different social spheres are legitimately governed by their own **norms**.

Walzer has also developed a **hermeneutic** conception of social criticism as the critical interpretation of the values shared in a **community**, thereby rejecting what he regards as the vain claims of radically detached critics who do not speak as members of their communities. Walzer's contextualism leaves open the possibility of both a universal minimal morality and criticism of economic and political **domination**.

Major works

([1977] 2000) *Just and Unjust Wars*. New York: Basic Books.
(1983) *Spheres of Justice*. New York: Basic Books.
(1987) *Interpretation and Social Criticism*. Cambridge, MA: Harvard University Press.
(1988) *The Company of Critics*. New York: Basic Books.
(1994) *Thick and Thin*. Notre Dame, IN: University of Notre Dame.

Further reading

Miller, D. and Walzer, M. (eds) (1995) *Pluralism, Justice, and Equality*. Oxford: Oxford University Press.
Orend, B. (2000) *Michael Walzer on War and Justice*. Montreal: McGill-Queen's University Press.

ROBIN CELIKATES

WAR AND MILITARISM

War is one of the oldest, most ubiquitous and dominant forms of **collective** social **action**. However, until recently it was rarely treated as such in the mainstream of social theory, and sociological textbooks gave it only a cursory treatment. Only in the last two decades of the twentieth century have social theorists given war a central place in the understanding of **society** – extraordinary given the often determining role of war in modern society.

This entry first defines war and shows its centrality to the sociology of political **violence**. It then discusses the relationships between war and the **state** and between warfare, **economy** and society.

War can be defined as *armed conflict between two or more collective actors that use organized violence to compel each other to submit to their wills*. War is therefore a fundamental type both of social action and of social **conflict** in complex societies. As action, war involves the conscious **organization** of large numbers of people to inflict violence, so as to destroy the power of an enemy and its will to resist. As conflict, it is distinguished from other forms by the clash of organized violent actions. The classic modern military theorist, Carl von Clausewitz, elaborated this understanding in his *On War* ([1831] 1976), and should be considered one of the principal classical social theorists alongside Auguste **Comte** and Karl **Marx**.

As a category of social action and conflict, war is fundamental because of its extreme character. Its core activities are ones that would be illegitimate in all other social circumstances. The killing of other human beings is the subject of fundamental **taboos** in all societies, and in modern societies has become increasingly illegitimate even for states (for example, most advanced societies have abolished the death penalty). In war, however, killing is not only allowed but – even if constrained by social norms and legal rules – is the goal of action. It is chiefly through killing the enemy that actors aim to prevail.

War's centrality to the sociology of political violence is underlined by the fact that it can be seen as the ultimate form that other types of political action can take.

Revolution, for example, may be generally defined as social and political mobilization that aims to overthrow existing forms of state power and **social relations**. Revolutionary activity is not necessarily violent, but when it reaches the point of actually overthrowing existing centres of power, it passes into violent insurrection, which in turn leads to civil war.

War's centrality is also underlined by the way that it tends to spawn other forms of violence. Genocide, for example, is the most extreme violent extension of more common forms of coercion and **discrimination** against social **groups**. Carried out by states and other armed bodies, it is an illegitimate form of war, in which violence is directed at destroying the social **power** – the **wealth**, **institutions** and **culture** – of an unarmed social group (rather than an armed enemy as in legitimate warfare). Although genocide has occurred outside conventional war situations, mostly it has been carried out during or as an extension of international or civil wars. Indeed, genocide, as a sociological category, derives from its development within the laws of war in the mid-twentieth century.

States, actors and ways of war

These examples suggest that while war is typically thought of as conflict between **states**, organized violent conflict between any collective actors can be considered war. *Interstate or international war* is only one form, a relatively uncommon form today since most armed conflicts today are either civil wars or hybrid international-cum-civil wars (in which genocide is often an element).

Thus, while the organized collective actors, between which wars are fought, are typically thought of as recognized states, many wars involve different kinds of protagonist – for example, movements, **parties**, warlords and **networks**. What these actors have in common is that they all use organized violence to achieve a degree of

control over social life within a given social **space**, usually territorially conceived. The motives for achieving this sort of control vary greatly, and are conditioned by different national, political and religious **ideologies** as well as by more material **interests** in seizing or exploiting commercial assets.

Thus, not all actors in wars are states, but they all want to take over or change the forms of state power, by controlling territory. This means that there is an intrinsic connection between war and the state, as major sociologists have recognized. Thus Marx saw the state as constituted by bodies of armed men, while Max **Weber** saw it as an organization aiming to monopolize violence within a given territory, although later sociologists such as Michael **Mann** (1993) have refined this definition.

Because of the variety of armed actors, many wars are 'asymmetric' (a buzzword of twenty-first-century strategy), not just in the sense of involving combatants of unequal power, but also in the more fundamental sense of involving protagonists who mobilize different types of power. And because actors vary so much in their socio-political bases and military strengths, they develop distinctive ways of fighting and different kinds of forces. Thus major states fight with high-technology weapons and formal standing armies that are bureaucratically organized. Insurgent movements often rely on less powerful weapons and irregular forces to fight *guerrilla* and terrorist campaigns (see **terrorism**).

Militarism and militarization

Sociological interest in war has often been less concerned with wars than with the embedding of war-preparation and military institutions in society. Some nineteenth-century theorists like Auguste Comte saw industrial society, with its rational, scientifically based organization, as inherently pacific. Even Marx saw modern society as constituted by its mode of **production** and assigned no analytically important role to war (although with his collaborator Friedrich Engels he produced some interesting accounts of particular wars: see Semmel 1981). Later, Marx's followers – notably Rosa Luxemburg and Lenin – argued, however, that modern **capitalism**, as **imperialism** was necessarily militaristic.

Mann (1988) has challenged both the pacific and militaristic theories, arguing that there was only a contingent relationship between capitalism and militarism. In his view, while the comprehensive *industrialization of warfare* (laid out by MacNeill 1982) had greatly increased war's destructiveness, it had not affected war's causes, which lay in geopolitical relations between states. This argument reflected the general position of the influential 'neo-Weberian' school of **historical sociology**, which produced the most developed social theories of warfare. For Mann (1986, 1993), warfare is one of the four major sources of social power, alongside economy, **polity** and ideology. Likewise Anthony **Giddens** (1985) identified warfare as one of the four 1to the role of nation–states as 'bordered power-containers'. A Marxisant version of these theories is the argument of Kaldor (1982) that there was a *mode of warfare* in which war is produced. Building on Clausewitz's insight that battle in warfare is the moment of 'realization' comparable to exchange in commerce, she argues that there is a cycle of war-preparation (arms production, mobilization) leading to the deployment of armies in actual wars and finally to battle.

All these writers insist, in contrast to the economic determinism of Marxism and other schools of social science, on the non-reducibility of warfare and its contingent, changing relations to capitalism, **industrialism** and other dimensions of social power. Shaw (1988) takes this case further and argues that in twentieth-century society, warfare actually comes to dominate capitalism.

Most kinds of armed actor mobilize bases in society to support their campaigns. Historically, the emergence of distinct warrior classes was linked to the development of agrarian civilizations, which produced the surpluses that allowed large-scale states (empires) to develop. Warriors were usually **elites** socially distant from local peasant (see **peasantry**) populations, but war often required the recruitment of larger armies from among the mass of society. In feudal societies (see **feudalism**), this relationship was institutionalized, as peasants owed the duty of military service to their lords who in turn owed allegiance to kings and emperors.

In modern industrial society, *mass armies* were recruited from the formally free **working** and peasant **classes**. Typically, in late nineteenth- and twentieth-century Europe, this involved conscription, through national schemes of universal military service. Today, as warfare is more capital-intensive, there has been a 'decline of mass armies' (van Doorn 1975); armies are relatively small and military organization is based more on professional, all-volunteer forces. The specialist field of *military sociology* has produced an extensive literature on the implications of these changes.

The nineteenth-century extension of military organization into society was the classic form of militarism, a new concept developed to describe these new developments. Although it is sometimes seen as primarily ideological, as a sociological category it is broader and describes the extensive influence of military organizations and culture on society.

Nevertheless the influence of militarist ideology, glorifying military power through newspapers, cinema, parties and the commercial reproduction of military images, was an important component of classic militarism. However, militarisms have varied considerably in ideological terms, for example between the **authoritarian** militarisms of fascist regimes (see **fascism**), with their extreme glorifications of war and armies, and the democratic (see **democracy**) militarisms of liberal states, which represent wars as unfortunate necessities.

Militarisms also vary in the intensity of their influence of military organization and culture on society. It is possible to talk about *militarization* when military influences on society are increasing, and *demilitarization* when these influences are weakening. The abolition of conscription in many Western societies means that the structural dimension of militarism has declined, leading to the description of these societies as post-military, or more accurately, post-militarist (Shaw 1991). However, in some societies, the ideological dimensions of militarism remain strong despite the end of mass participation in the military.

Scholars have attempted to capture the characteristics of this new post-military militarism. There has been a developing armament culture as the focus of militarism has switched from soldiers to weapons systems. Mann (1988) has influentially distinguished the spectator-sport militarism of the masses, watching wars on television, from the deterrence-science militarism of the elites. Much contemporary sociological study of war focuses on the mediation of warfare in the **mass media** such as the press, television and (in the twenty-first century) the Internet. The media have become increasingly a central arena of warfare, as wars are fought out not just on the battlefield but in other battlespaces.

Participation, civilians and war

The extensive influence of war, militaries and military values on society has long led scholars to focus on social participation in war. Stanislav Andreski (1968), who produced an ambitious sociology of war, developed the concept of the military participation ratio: the proportion of a society that is mobilized into the armed forces. His thesis was that the higher the military participation ratio, the greater the degree of resulting social change. The social historian, Arthur Marwick (1974), qualified this, arguing that general wartime participation by civilians as well as soldiers determined the scope of social change. He highlighted the advancement of women through their wartime participation, although this relatively optimistic interpretation was challenged by feminist scholars who pointed out the limited nature of the resulting improvements in women's lives (see **women's movement**).

This work has contributed to a developing sociology of *total war*. Mann (1988) interprets the world wars as citizen wars leading towards greater democracy in Western societies. Shaw (1988) points out, however, the unevenness of wartime experiences and democratic change and the dangers of generalizing from relatively positive cases like Britain. Total war involved not only total mobilization but also total destruction, and many societies experienced far more of the latter than the former. Total war was inherently degenerate war, with systematic targeting of non-combatants, and leading in some cases to genocide (Shaw 2003).

This discussion highlighted the growing importance of civilians as a social category. Growing wartime participation had led to the targeting of non-fighters and a general blurring of the distinction between combatants and non-combatants. In the aftermath of the Second World War, however, a growing body of international **law** reaffirmed the difference, underlining its significance in expanded concepts of war **crimes**, crimes against humanity and (a completely new term) genocide. In the 1990s, these ideas became even more critical in the 'new wars' in the Balkans, Africa and elsewhere. With the spread of so-called ethnic 'cleansing', the question of protecting civilian society became central to the international politics of war. Sociologists were, however, slow to recognize the significance of the civilian as a social category.

667

The decline of major interstate war and the prevalence of hybrid and genocidal conflicts have led to arguments about 'new wars' and even the claim that war is now 'post-Clausewitzian' (Kaldor 1999). Since most wars today occur in the non-Western world, there has been a new convergence of security and development in studying war. Social theory has begun to focus on the emergence of a 'global surveillance' mode of warfare, in which war is fought out in the gaze of global media, publics, non-governmental organizations and international institutions. While governments seek to conceal from television screens the dead bodies that wars produce, terrorists increasingly kill in spectacular ways in order to achieve media-driven political effects. Western governments claim to have developed, through a technologically based 'revolution in military affairs', new 'precision' weapons that enable them to avoid civilian deaths. In practice, however, sociologists have argued that the new Western way of waging war centres on containing risk to soldiers, even at the cost of transferring it to civilians.

References and further reading

Andreski, S. (1968) *Military Organization and Society*. Berkeley, CA: University of California Press.

Clausewitz, C. von ([1831] 1976) *On War*. Princeton, NJ: Princeton University Press.

Doorn, J. van (1975) *The Soldier and Social Change*. London: Sage.

Giddens, A. (1985) *The Nation-State and Violence*. Cambridge: Polity.

Joas, H. (2003) *War and Modernity*. Cambridge: Polity.

Kaldor, M. (1982) 'Warfare and Capitalism', in E. P. Thompson *et al.* (eds) *Exterminism and Cold War*. London: New Left Books.

Kaldor, M. (1999) *New and Old Wars*. Cambridge: Polity.

MacNeill, W. H. (1982) *The Pursuit of Power*. Oxford: Blackwell.

Mann, M. (1986, 1993) *The Sources of Social Power*, vols I, II. Cambridge: Cambridge University Press.

Mann, M. (1988) *States, War and Capitalism*. Oxford: Blackwell.

Marwick, A. (1974) *War and Social Change in the Twentieth Century*. London: Macmillan.

Semmel, B. (1981) *Marxism and the Science of War*. Oxford: Oxford University Press.

Shaw, M. (1988) *Dialectics of War*. London: Pluto.

Shaw, M. (1991) *Post-Military Society*. Cambridge: Polity.

Shaw, M. (2003) *War and Genocide*. Cambridge: Polity.

MARTIN SHAW

WEALTH

'Wealth' is a stock; 'income' is a flow. In any normal economic system, the former is the origin of the latter, so that **inequality** in the distribution of wealth tends to be associated with income inequalities. But how far such inequalities in the distribution of income are directly linked to inequalities in the distribution of wealth has been a matter of dispute for centuries. Since the seventeenth century, arguments for greater political **equality** have been linked to criticism of the concentration of wealth in the hands of a privileged few. During the nineteenth century, **socialist** and **communist** thinkers proposed that an egalitarian society would be one where such concentrations would be transferred into common property, severing the linkage between personal and national wealth (see **egalitarianism**). In response, critics of this **socialization** of **private** property argued that the increase of national wealth depended upon the institution of private property and the consequent inequities involved (see **property and property rights**). Redistribution of wealth, they suggested, would instead make everyone poorer, robbing individuals of the motivation and initiative upon which the growth of the national economy depended.

This argument continues today. Progressive taxes on income and wealth are everywhere in advanced industrial economies the norm, and much central and local government expenditure – on **health**, **education**, social **security** and pensions – is redistributive from the richer sections of the population to the poorer. This tends to equalize the financial resources available to the broad mass of the population, independent of their ownership of financial and non-financial assets. Consequently, for any given country, inequalities in the distribution of income tend to be less marked than inequalities in the distribution of wealth. However, conservative governments typically argue that high levels of taxation represent a disincentive to effort. The 'reductions' in taxation that they propose, or introduce, generally turn out to be regressive, reducing taxation on the assets and incomes of the wealthy, handing larger marginal gains in income to the rich rather than middle or lower income groupings. This is sometimes supported by the argument that tax reductions of this kind provide incentives and hence increase the level of economic activity. But the truly 'wealthy' in any given society make up much less than 5 per cent of taxpayers, and around two-thirds of the adult population generally receive incomes at or below the arithmetic mean. Such policies have therefore little detectable economic impact. It is the marginal changes in the incomes of middle and lower income groups that have the greatest impact upon aggregate consumption.

'Income' is not only a flow; it is usually in cash of one form or another. It is therefore relatively easy to compare inequalities in income – even if the spending patterns of social groups differ (see **consumption**). Thorstein Veblen's phrase 'conspicuous consumption' in lifestyle – the acquisition of high-profile consumer goods – is not to be confused with 'wealth', which is a more complex matter. **Money** that is saved from income will be held in interest-bearing bank accounts and various financial instruments designed to preserve value and increase it over time. The more sophisticated the financial instruments, the more

likely they will be tied to the movements of financial markets and exposed to the risk of absolute losses in value. Such investments are, however, made in the expectation that, over a long period, the general rate of return on such investments will be higher, the greater the exposure to risk. Valuation of such assets in terms of personal wealth therefore fluctuate.

Wealth can be inherited, while incomes generally cannot. Inequities in the distribution of wealth are thus perpetuated over time, although it should also be noted that historically wealth has often been passed on through a family line in the expectation that future generations should benefit. Legal impediments often prevent the present holder of 'wealth' from converting it directly into a cash income. Where such wealth is tied up in land, it is quite possible that a 'wealthy' person will have a relatively modest disposable income. Wealth might be in the form of financial assets, but it is more usually in land, property, works of art, and precious metals. These can also be acquired by the newly-wealthy as investments for the future. Given the length of time during which such assets are held, their nominal value will vary. Land values may rise; they can also fall, as for instance in late nineteenth-century Britain as a consequence of agricultural depression and the decline of rental income, on which rural estates had typically depended. The value of works of art will vary according to cultural fashions and changes in taste. Precious metals are a store of value, but one not subject to great changes. In Britain, most housing is owner-occupied and a proportion of such assets are debt-free, so that many households occupy their greatest asset. Rises in nominal housing values will increase the 'wealth' of home-owners, but this increase cannot for most people be converted into income since they live in it. It is consequently more appropriate to treat house ownership as a form of lifetime saving, rather than as inter-generational accumulated wealth. With increased longevity the accumulated lifetime assets of lower and middle income **groups** will increasingly be used to finance care in old age, the education of children, and healthcare for **family** members, running down funds built up in an earlier working life. The physical nature of 'wealth' therefore varies across social classes, as does its degree of liquidity.

The preceding remarks are directed primarily to the idea of personal wealth, based on financial and non-financial assets held by an individual person. The characteristics which make a country 'wealthy' are, however, only indirectly related to this, for such 'wealth' is typically be held in the name of institutions and enterprises, if not that of governments. Why one country is 'wealthier' than another, and to what degree, then becomes a matter of debate. In seventeenth- and eighteenth-century Europe, for instance, it was often thought that the larger the population, the wealthier the country. Hence countries with a large population (like France) were wealthier than countries with a small population (like the Netherlands). It became obvious, however, that the average Dutchman enjoyed a higher level of welfare than the average Frenchman, and so attention was directed to the circumstances that brought this about. Once the 'welfare of a population' displaces sheer numbers, or the size of army or navy, or the treasure of a sovereign, as the criterion of 'national wealth', the measurement of national wealth becomes an issue.

Economic growth, the bedrock of modern economies, means growth of the national income, which in turn depends on constant investment in the physical and human capital from which national income flows. Measurement of growth, and therefore of national income, dates back only to the 1930s when, in Britain and the United States, economists sought to determine the relationship between national income and economic growth. Typically national accounts record flows of income and expenditure,

and do not seek to provide a general representation of 'national wealth', since valuation is so difficult. Since the late 1990s, however, social scientists have become increasingly critical of national income accounting as a reliable representation of 'national welfare', pointing out, for example, that the pollution that results from high levels of economic activity is a social cost not added into the equation of national welfare. Furthermore, some economists have sought to compile 'happiness' indices, which demonstrate that there is no clear relationship between high levels of economic growth and the general welfare of a population. With Ruskin (1862), perhaps, some social scientists are rediscovering that 'there is no wealth but life'.

References and further reading

Edey, H. C. and Peacock, A. T. (1954) *National Income and Social Accounting*. London: Hutchinson.

Joseph Rowntree Foundation (1995) *Income and Wealth*, 2 vols. York: Joseph Rowntree Foundation.

Phelps Brown, E. H. (1988) *Egalitarianism and the Generation of Inequality*. Oxford: Oxford University Press.

Ruskin, J. (1862) *Until This Last*. London: Penguin.

Smith, A. (1776) *An Inquiry into the Nature and Causes of the Wealth of Nations*. Oxford: Oxford University Press.

KEITH TRIBE

WEBER, MAX (1864–1920)
German sociologist

Concerned that **bureaucratization** and instrumental **rationality** threatened to eradicate societal dynamism, individual **autonomy**, ethical responsibility, and compassion, Weber undertook sweeping comparative-historical analyses in order to comprehend the modern West or **Occident** and its dilemmas. He first sought to demonstrate how a constellation of religious **values** – a **Protestant ethic** ([1904–5,

1920] 2002) – 'co-participated' in the birth
of a 'spirit of **capitalism**' that played a causal role in calling forth modern capitalism.
To him, the economic interests of the
bourgeoisie, human greed, or a general
evolutionary process never fully explained
the broad expansion in the West of the
market economy. Through wide-ranging
comparisons with Hinduism, Buddhism,
Jainism, Confucianism, Taoism, and
ancient **Judaism**, Weber undertook to iso-
late, in the series 'Economic Ethics of the
World Religions', the particularity of the
Protestant ethic's 'inner-worldly asceticism'.
This massive project also aimed to describe,
by reference to economic **ethics** as well as
political forces and **stratification**, the
uniqueness of the modern West and the
causes behind its singular historical pathway.

Throughout his investigations Weber
sought, in keeping with his ideal of impartial
analysis ('value-freedom') and his 'interpretive
understanding' methodology (see **Verstehen**),
to reconstruct the *subjective meaning* of persons
in groups. His work was guided by a focus
on encompassing 'spheres of life', the
economy, authority, religion, status groups,
and the **family** and their singular juxtapo-
sitions in different social contexts. Weber's
central methodological tool was the **ideal
type**. The aim of this heuristic construct
was to enable rigorous comparisons across
groupings and ultimately causal analysis
(Kalberg 1994: 98–191). Weber's magnum
opus was *Economy and Society* ([1921] 1976).
Its chapters influence to this day the sociology of religion, **urban** sociology, political
sociology, stratification, comparative **historical sociology**, and sociological theory.

Major works

([1904–5, 1920] 2002) *The Protestant Ethic and
the Spirit of Capitalism.* Oxford: Blackwell.
([1921] 1976) *Economy and Society.* Berkeley,
CA: University of California Press.
(1948) *From Max Weber: Essays in Sociology*, ed.
H. H. Gerth and C. Wright Mills. London:
Routledge.

Further reading

Kalberg, S. (1994) *Max Weber's Comparative
Historical Sociology.* Chicago: University of
Chicago Press.
Sica, A. (2004) *Max Weber: A Comprehensive
Bibliography.* New Brunswick, NJ: Transac-
tion.

STEPHEN KALBERG

WELFARE STATE

The welfare state is typically defined as a set
of **state** interventions that provide for life
contingencies and redress **market**-pro-
duced **inequality**. In general, welfare state
institutions are those statutory arrangements that contribute to the provision for
life risks such as illness, unemployment, old
age and **poverty**, as well as state policies in
areas such as housing, **education**, personal
social services and social care. The term
'welfare state' became popularized after the
Second World War, referring to the
responsibility of the state for the well-being
of its citizens and the promotion of the
'common good'. In theoretical conceptualizations of the welfare state, **citizenship**
appears to be its most salient dimension.
Following T. H. Marshall's (1964) evolutionary scheme of the successive establishment of civic, political and social **rights**,
scholars concur that the welfare state is the
key institutional mechanism for rendering
social rights to citizens. In contrast to phi-
lanthropic or discretionary forms of social
provision, the welfare state establishes legal
entitlements *vis-à-vis* the state. The overarching claim in Marshall's account is that
the establishment of citizenship rights has
fundamentally transformed inequality patterns within **society**.

Since Marshall's theory drew mainly on
the British experience, and hence tended to
stylize a particular historical trajectory,
subsequent research has analyzed in a comparative frame the forces driving welfare
state development. The answers proffered
differ quite significantly. **Functionalism** and

671

industrialization theories view the welfare state as a response to growing socio-economic pressures faced by all modernizing societies as a result of **urbanization**, population growth and economic development. As welfare gaps and inequalities threatened to undermine social peace and the process of economic accumulation, a state apparatus stepped in to provide remedies in the form of social provision. The emergence of the welfare state, therefore, has been viewed as a product of the 'logic of industrialization', with the state responding to society's 'objective **need**' for a healthy and reliable workforce. Conventionally, the impact of economic development on welfare growth has been analyzed by examining the relationship between GDP and social security spending. On this basis, a landmark study by Wilensky (1975) found that economic growth – more so than political or **ideological** factors – drives welfare state development. However, the 'politicized version' of the industrialization thesis highlights that **modernization** is a multidimensional societal process entailing economic growth, social and political mobilization, and the transformation of the political order through **democratization** and bureaucratization (Flora and Heidenheimer 1981).

The **power** resource approach has criticized such approaches for their tendency to neglect **class conflict** surrounding welfare state development (Korpi 1983; Esping-Andersen 1990). Rather than assuming the participation of the masses as the main determinant of welfare state expansion, they see the growing political influence of leftist **parties** and **trade unions** as driving welfare state expansion. The argument fundamentally questions, first, whether one can assume an equal distribution of power between various **groups** and collectivities in **capitalist** democracies, and, second, whether all social classes and groups are interested in collective provision. Alternatively, they conceptualize the welfare state as the outcome of class conflicts whereby different social

groups try to influence the distributive process within society to their advantage. The sizable variation in welfare state scope and redistributional generosity is found to be a function of the strength of the **working class**. Social democratic parties and trade unions attempt to bring public policies closer to wage-earners' interests and therefore promote **egalitarian** measures. According to this theory, welfare states tend to be universal and generous in countries in which social democratic parties were able to gain political power, whereas they are residual and less redistributive where working-class **organizations** remained weak and politically fragmented.

The power resources approach leaves no conceptual space, however, for other important factors shaping the welfare state. There is now considerable evidence that the welfare state cannot be fully understood merely as the pinnacle triumph of the working class, for other forces played a decisive role in its development. Studies have drawn attention to the crucial role of the **middle class** in calling for collective arrangements for the reapportionment of **risk** (Baldwin 1990), the role of social **elites**, white-collar workers and state employees with vested interests in public welfare provision (De Swaan 1988), or the interest of employers in externalizing the social costs of production via state welfare provision. Since the 1980s, explanations of the welfare state have accorded greater importance to the impact of the nature and timing of state formation and state institutional structure on social **security** schemes (Weir *et al.* 1988).

In recent decades, scholars have invested great effort into the development of comprehensive welfare state typologies. In the most prominent example, Gosta Esping-Andersen (1990) distinguishes three welfare regime types, namely liberal, conservative-continental and social democratic. Building on Richard Titmuss's (1958) **classification** of welfare states into residual, institutional and industrial-achievement types, on the one hand, and on **Marshall**'s suggestion that social citizenship constitutes the core principle of the welfare state, on the other, Esping-Andersen clusters welfare states according to their state-market relations, their impact on **stratification**, and the degree of de-commodification they realize. De-commodification refers to the state enabling citizens to make ends meet outside the scope of labour market relations, i.e. independent of market wages. Liberal welfare regimes entail minimal state interference with the market, place priority on self-help and provide only residual, and often means-tested benefits. Conservative regimes, in contrast, are based heavily on social insurance schemes linked to citizens' labour-market **status** and, therefore, tend to preserve status differentials. The social democratic model, finally, provides universal benefits on the basis of citizenship status, is largely financed out of general revenues and promotes social **equality**. Critics of the Esping-Andersen typology have noted that most countries represent composites of his different regime types, or that certain countries fit rather poorly. Others have proposed additional welfare state types such as that constituted by the Latin rim countries of Italy, Spain and Greece, or by the 'Antipodean' countries of Australia and New Zealand. **Feminist** scholars have criticized the typology's failure to theorize the roles of **gender** relations and families, which are fundamental to welfare production.

A contemporary strand of research examines the 'new politics' of the welfare state. Rather than focusing on welfare expansion they have begun to map the new terrain of welfare retrenchment (Pierson 2001). In contrast to welfare state expansion, retrenchment requires governments to pursue unpopular politics that often work against the **interests** of both voters and well-entrenched interest groups. As a consequence, elected officials have to pursue policies that minimize the loss of political support by directing cuts to politically weak groups or making cut-backs less visible. Research on the new politics of the welfare state focuses on its institutional and programmatic structures, for these shape the entrenched constituencies of interest and support. In addition, scholars have demonstrated a renewed interest in the relationship between welfare institutions and capitalist systems. One branch of research examines institutional affinities between types of social security systems and types of employment regimes (Hall and Soskice 2001), while another investigates whether social policies hinder or enhance international competitiveness (Scharpf and Schmidt 2000).

References and further reading

Baldwin, P. (1990) *The Politics of Social Solidarity*. Cambridge: Cambridge University Press.

Castles, F. (1985) *The Working Class and Welfare*. Sydney: Allen & Unwin.

De Swaan, A. (1988) *In Care of the State*. New York: Oxford University Press.

Esping-Andersen, G. (1985) *Politics against Markets*. Princeton, NJ: Princeton University Press.

Esping-Andersen, G. (1990) *The Three Worlds of Welfare Capitalism*. Oxford: Polity.

Flora, P. and Heidenheimer, A. (eds) (1981) *The Development of Welfare States in Europe and America*. New Brunswick, NJ: Transaction.

Hall, P. and Soskice, D. (eds) (2001) *Varieties of Capitalism*. Oxford: Oxford University Press.

Heclo, H. (1974) *Modern Social Politics in Britain and Sweden*. New Haven, CT: Yale University Press.

Korpi, W. (1983) *The Democratic Class Struggle*. London: Routledge & Kegan Paul.

Marshall, T. H. (1964) *Class, Citizenship and Social Development*. New York: Doubleday.

Pierson, P. (ed.) (2001) *The New Politics of the Welfare State*. Oxford: Oxford University Press.

Rimlinger, G. (1971) *Welfare Policy and Industrialization in Europe, America, and Russia*. New York: Wiley.

Rueschemeyer, D. and Skocpol, T. (1996) *States, Social Knowledge and the Origins of Modern Social Policies*. Princeton, NJ: Princeton University Press.

Scharpf, F. and Schmidt, V. (eds) (2000) *Welfare and Work in the Open Economy*. Oxford: Oxford University Press.

Timuss, R. (1958) *Essays on the Welfare State.* London: Allen & Unwin.

Weir, M., Orloff, A. and Skocpol, T. (eds) (1988) *The Politics of Social Policy in the United States.* Princeton, NJ: Princeton University Press.

Wilensky, H. (1975) *The Welfare State and Equality.* Los Angeles: University of California Press.

STEFFEN MAU

WEST

See: Occident

WITTGENSTEIN, LUDWIG (1892–1953)

Austrian philosopher

Influenced by his studies with the philosopher, Bertrand Russell, Wittgenstein published his *Tractatus Logico-Philosophicus* ([1921] 1961). The overt theme of the book was the construction of a perfect language to describe the world, the grammar of which was logic, a set of rules for manipulating **symbols**, the **meaning** of which was fixed by reference to the objects denoted. The covert theme was moral, that the language of science had nothing to offer for the expression of religious longings, moral principles, or **aesthetic** intuitions.

By the end of the 1920s, he had come see that the principles on which the perfect language of the *Tractatus* was based were unrealistic. Many philosophical errors came from subtle misunderstanding of the grammar of the vernacular. The main themes of the later philosophy, published after his death in the *Philosophical Investigations* (1953), included the idea of meaning as use, a broader picture of grammar as the norms of all kinds of correct and proper **discourse**, and a new method for resolving problems. If problems arose by mistakes in grammar – for example, the mistake of assuming adjectives were always used to ascribe properties to substances – an overview of the way language was actually used would reveal the hidden misunderstanding. The 'Private Language Argument' showed that language was essentially a social phenomenon. Wittgenstein's analysis of the kinds and uses of rules was linked to criticisms of linguistic **essentialism** and to the idea of meanings as patterns of **family** resemblances in the uses of verbal and written signs.

Major works

([1921] 1961) *Tractatus Logico-Philosophicus.* London: Routledge & Kegan Paul.

(1953) *Philosophical Investigations.* Oxford: Blackwell.

Further reading

Glock, H.-G. (1996) *A Wittgenstein Dictionary.* Oxford: Blackwell.

Hacker, P. M. S. (1996) *Wittgenstein's Place in 20th Century Analytical Philosophy.* Oxford: Blackwell.

Monk, R. (1990) *The Duty of Genius.* Oxford: Blackwell.

ROM HARRÉ

WOMEN'S MOVEMENT

The term 'women's movement' refers to all collectively organized efforts to accord women equal **rights**, **recognition**, political **power** and social resources in all aspects of **society** and **culture**. The term 'feminism' was introduced at end of the nineteenth century, but has only become common with the 'newer' women's movements. As a social, cultural and political movement, its agenda includes a broad range of issues entailing nothing less than a total transformation of society (Katzenstein 1987). Because of the plurality of its forms, phases of emergence, objectives, **frames**, social bases, and **meanings** to its participants, it is appropriate to use the plural form women's movements/feminisms.

Women's movements illustrate how modern **social movements** are both 'product and producer' of social change. For over 200 years, women's movements have been given impetus by the contradiction between the promise of **freedom** and **equality** for all humans and the various forms of structural **discrimination** which have limited women's social participation and life chances. The considerable achievements of women's movements have had consequences for their subsequent forms. The metaphor of 'waves' applied to periods of particularly vigorous periods of women's activism in the nineteenth and twentieth centuries (in English, termed 'first' and 'second' wave feminisms) aptly signals that protest movements originate from still unsolved problems, and that movements have 'doldrums' (Rupp and Taylor 1990) or 'times of breathing space' (Gerhard 1996). However, the continued emergence and development of initiatives globally provide evidence of the still unsolved concerns of women's movements throughout the world.

For a long time, theories of social movements ignored or underestimated women's movements. Compared to the prototype of the 'old' social movements, the workers' movement, the concerns of women's movements were often considered 'particularistic', organized around only limited **needs** and **interests**, and thus not politically or historically important. This is a misjudgement which has since been reversed.

The analysis of women's movements has especially benefited from the recent integration of the theory-based European research on new social movements with the more empirically orientated American research (della Porta and Diani 1999). The latter was less interested in a new **paradigm** of acting politically than in the political and institutional environment in which social movements operate. From this perspective, women's movements in the nineteenth and twentieth centuries are a paradigmatic example of the various concepts of social movements that are of interest to theorists of both historic and contemporary movements.

That experiences of injustice and of discrimination do not automatically create readiness for protest and collective **action** can be seen by the history of women's movements. **Gender inequality** had to be understood not as arising from individual shortcomings or fate, but as socially constructed and hence amenable to social change. To effect this understanding required political action. Especially since women – differing on the basis of **class**, **race** and sexual orientation among other dimensions – often live in a dependent and intimate way with those against whom they stand, their 'natural' alliance on the basis of common experience cannot be assumed (Buechler 1990).

The emergence of the European and American women's movements were each embedded in specific *political opportunity structures*. Women first organized in political associations in Europe in the context of the democratic uprisings around the revolution of 1848 (Offen 2000). In the USA, women were radicalized by their experiences in the anti-**slavery** movement, passing 'The Declaration of Sentiments' in their first convention at Seneca Falls in 1848. The rise of women's movements and their peak at the turn of the twentieth century, characterized by a variety of initiatives and a great number of international organizations (Rupp 1997), coincided with a new push of **modernization** which highlighted the crises of the **industrial-capitalist** development (Gerhard 2004). Similarly, the world-wide emergence of a 'new' women's movement at the end of the 1960s was closely connected to fundamental political and **social change** initiated by civil rights and students' movements in many countries of the West, as well as by liberation and independence movements in the countries of the South. The increased participation of women in paid labour and improved **educational** opportunities also fuelled the higher demands and expectations which accompanied an atmosphere of social reform.

American social movement research emphasized access to new resources, such as **work**, **money**, education and avenues of **communication**, as creating improved

675

conditions for political action. Feminists have criticized this resource mobilization approach, arguing that it relies too heavily on a model of **rational choice**, which treats people as abstract individuals, thus universalizing the experience of white, western middle-class men, and not taking the role of **emotions**, grievances, and **values** into account.

The creation of collective action and awareness of common experiences of injustice need more than rational strategies. Also required is a sense of belonging, a shared set of beliefs and **solidarity** – an emergence of *collective identities*. Mobilization of followers works by forming **groups** and informal **networks** which become a movement only in the form of 'mobilized networks of networks'. The importance of **friendship** and **kin** relations among women – symbolically expressed by the term 'sisterhood' – and thus of a 'female culture' as a basis of women's politicization and empowerment must be recognized (Wiesen-Cook 1979), particularly also in international co-operation. Friendship, emotions, social and **intellectual** networks can be of the same importance for mobilizing as organized campaigns and lobby work. Also in the case of the new women's movement, the concept of a 'We' and the formation of a collective **identity** were supported by social practices, rituals, symbols like the women's symbol, certain colours and fashions, and by gender-sensitive speech. The formation of consciousness-raising groups was a new and effective method for mobilizing and was, at the same time, a collective learning process. But the politics of personal identity may also be conflictual and exclusionary Thus, black feminists' criticism of white, Western feminism, focusing on the differences among women and intersection with other social classifications such as race, class, religion and sexual orientation, triggered off a process of fracturing feminist theory and de-constructing the idea of gender, which contributed to the de-stabilizing of

any idea of a unified women's movement. For younger women, not coming from active participation in a women's movement, 'the generation of a new intellectual tradition of feminist theory' may be 'one major form of action for creating solidarity' (Jenson 1995) via gender studies programs.

The objectives and reasons for mobilizing to form a movement are captured in social movement research by the concept of framing. Framing includes the interpretations and explanatory patterns, and the staging of subjects of protest, which set the goals of mobilization as well as convince and unite followers. The struggles and factional conflicts within the various wings of the women's movements in past and present reflect not only their historically different conditions but different frames. There are many examples here: at the turn of the twentieth century, the ideological conflicts between liberal (or **bourgeois**), **radical**, and **socialist** feminists; in the inter-war period, differences between representatives of a 'welfare feminism', the so-called maternalists, and egalitarians (Danks 1986), in the 1970s and after, the international debates of feminists about **patriarchy** and/or **capitalism**, about equal rights versus autonomy, about the priority of eco-feminism, pacifism, or anti-racism. Just as varied were the issues which were put onto the political agenda: women's legal and political rights, **violence** against women, reproductive choice and abortion, sexual freedom, employment opportunities, and women's political participation and representation. In retrospect, the debate which dominated theoretical controversy at the end of the twentieth century about the dualism of equality and difference proved to be a 'false dichotomy' – in Joan Scott's words 'the antithesis itself hides the interdependence of the two terms, for equality is not the elimination of **difference**, and difference does not preclude equality' (Scott 1990). The central theme which has connected the fights for equal rights and recognition since Olympe de Gouges's (1791) *Declaration of the Rights of Women and Citizen* with the challenges of the twenty-first century is the unrealized promise of full citizenship, with political, civil, and social rights for all people, including women, thus exposing the women's movement as one of the key features of **civil society**.

References and further reading

Banks, O. (1986) *Faces of Feminism: A Study of Feminism as a Social Movement*. Oxford: Blackwell.

Buechler, S. M. (1990) *Women's Movement in the United States: Women's Suffrage, Equal Rights and Beyond*. New Brunswick, NJ: Rutgers University Press.

Della Porta, D. and Diani, M. (1999) *Social Movements: An Introduction*. Oxford: Blackwell.

Gerhard, U. (1996) 'Atempause: Die aktuelle Bedeutung der Frauenbewegung für eine zivile Gesellschaft', in *Aus Politik und Zeitgeschichte. Beilage zur Wochenzeitung Das Parlament*, B 21–2, 3–14.

Gerhard, U. (2004) 'Illegitimate Daughters: The Relationship between Feminism and Sociology', in B. L. Marshall and A. Witz (eds) *Engendering the Social: Feminist Encounters with Sociological Theory*. Maidenhead: Open University Press, pp. 114–35.

Jenson, J. (1995) 'Extending the Boundaries of Citizenship: Women's Movements of Western Europe', in A. Basu (ed.) *The Challenge of Local Feminisms: Women's Movements in Global Perspective*. Boulder, CO: Westview, pp. 405–34.

Katzenstein, M. F. (1987) 'Comparing the Feminist Movements of the United States and Western Europe: An Overview', in M. F. Katzenstein and C. McClurg Mueller (eds) *The Women's Movement of the United States and Western Europe: Consciousness, Political Opportunity and Public Policy*. Philadelphia, PA: University of Pennsylvania Press, pp. 3–43.

Offen, K. (2000) *European Feminisms 1700–1950: A Political History*. Stanford, CA: Stanford University Press.

Rupp, L. J. (1997) *Worlds of Women: The Making of an International Women's Movement*. Princeton, NJ: Princeton University Press.

Rupp, L. and Taylor, V. (1990) *Survival in the Doldrums: The American Women's Rights Movements 1945 to the 1960's*. Columbus, OH: Ohio State University Press.

Scott, J. W. (1990) 'Deconstructing Equality-versus-Difference', in M. Hirsch and E. Fox Keller (eds) *Conflicts in Feminism*. New York: Routledge, pp. 134–48.

Wiesen-Cook, B. (1979) *Female Support Networks and Political Activism: Women Support Networks*. New York: Out & Out.

UTE GERHARD

WORK

Social theory and philosophy has been perplexed by the subject of work since Aristotle. What counts as work? Does work fulfil us or damage us and is it possible to talk of good work and bad work? Have men and women freely chosen work or have they succumbed to an **ideology** of work? How are the rewards of work determined and distributed and what are the costs of doing more work? How does work change?

'Work' is often synonymous with paid employment but, in the second half of the twentieth century, feminist writers pointed out that much of the work of the world received no payment at all. Most of this unpaid work – housework, child-care, caring for the aged and infirm, volunteering – was performed by women (see **women's movement**). This rediscovery of unpaid work occurred just as it was becoming clear that much of it was being converted into paid work. More and more people were being drawn into paid employment and many were now earning enough to be able to buy machines that would do their unpaid work for them or to pay other people to do that work instead. All forms of unpaid work diminished as they were squeezed between paid employment and **leisure** time.

Theorists and philosophers from Aristotle to **Keynes** had imagined that work of all kinds, not just unpaid work, would diminish over time as the need for work diminished. **Marcuse** and subsequently Gorz (1989) suggested that the reason why work had not become a scarce good must be that a great deal of paid work was not actually necessary. The obsessive pursuit of growth prevented people from scrutinizing the criteria used to determine what counted as work and how much work there should be. Others argued that reducing the amount of work, or even halting its growth, would send the **economy** into a deflationary spiral. Gorz's answer was to have the state pay people to reduce their working hours, although this was not to be seen as payment for domestic work such as child-care. Gorz insisted that society should seek to resist the tide of economic **rationality** that turned all our free time into money and that use of quasi-servants for domestic work was morally questionable.

Other theorists have focused on changes in the way work gives opportunities for self-expression and social interaction. Marx put the disappearance of such opportunities in the capitalist workplace at the centre of his theory of **alienation**, but **Freud** and **Durkheim** thought that work remained of value for the opportunities it afforded for social interaction and cohesion. A popularized synthesis of their ideas was propagated by the Human Relations School in the middle of the twentieth century. In the second half of the century, however, theorists began to worry about the effect of the changing character of work on individuals and **society**. Thus, Sennett (1998) suggested that the kind of insecure work that he thought was growing was leading to the devaluing of resolution and commitment, a process he summarized as the 'corrosion of character'.

The young Engels ([1845] 1958) was less worried about alienation than about the damage that particular kinds of work could do, especially to workers' **health**. In the second half of the twentieth century, it was the developing countries which seemed to have more than their fair share of dangerous and damaging work. Theorists since Max **Weber** had often suggested that such work disappeared as development pro-

ceeded since such work was necessarily of low productivity, and therefore incompatible with **modernization**. Yet very large pockets of such work have persisted even in the most developed economies.

From the 1950s social theory began to pay attention to the rather less obvious damage that might be caused by white-collar work. C. Wright **Mills** (1953) drew attention to the way white-collar workers had to give of their very selves – in a way that blue-collar workers were spared – in pursuit of organizational ends. Whyte (1956) described an ideology which rationalized the business **organization**'s demand for loyalty from its employees and legitimated the abandonment of American **individualism**. According to this 'social ethic', the **group** was the source of creativity. Individuals' most pressing need (particularly where they were geographically mobile) was to belong to groups. The human sciences were therefore to be trusted to untangle those misunderstandings that made it seem as if there was **conflict** between the individual and the organization. This social ethic fostered an assumption that **morality** necessarily coincided with the ends of the organization.

Nearly 30 years later, Hochschild (1983) examined the ways in which flight attendants on airplanes were meant to change the way they allowed their moral judgement to influence their behaviour to meet the ends of economic rationality. Morality for Hochschild was being domesticated for commercial purposes. In her subsequent research, the more general emphasis on human resources in modern corporations was taken as a sign that employers wanted to train their staff in attributes that might once have been identified with everyday civility but were now packaged as customer care (Hochschild 1997).

Morality also makes an appearance in arguments about whether people *want* to work or not. Weber ([1904–5] 1958) famously discussed the way, at a point in the history of **capitalism**, that individuals developed an attachment to work best understood as a moral compulsion: the **Protestant ethic**. But this compulsion was succeeded in time by the economic rationality of 'the spirit of capitalism' and the moral element apparently withered away, so that it was now only the idea of accumulating possessions that drove people to work. Today, there is a widespread **public discourse**, closely associated with neo-**liberalism**, that work makes possible both autonomy and social worth, together with the resources to live well. Whyte (1956), however, thought that 'organization man' had submitted to a new ideology of work.

The relationship between work and morality has also been central to thinking about the way workers, especially manual workers, set limits on the amount of work they perform. By the 1970s the idea of a fair day's work for a fair day's pay had developed with the absorption of men and women into the capitalist workplace. The desire to counter, or manipulate, the collective enforcement of socially inspired, and sanctioned, output norms was a major stimulus to management thinking and the spread of a new ideology of work, as described by Anthony (1977).

Despite the evidence that successive generations of managers have drawn on their ingenuity in order to extract more work from their employees, the ideas that employees themselves entertain about the value of their work have rarely counted in procedures establishing the rewards that different kinds of work should receive. According to Hannah **Arendt** (1967), although the re-evaluation of all **values** that had occurred after the **Enlightenment** seemed to celebrate labour for the first time, it was only the productive kind of labour that was moved up to the top of the hierarchy of values. Arendt found clear continuity with the values of antiquity in which the activities through which people could make their mark on the world were seen as the

ones that mattered. In contrast to *work* which made a mark, *labour* was made necessary by the permanent treadmill of producing what must be consumed to stay alive. **Labour** produced goods which were immediately consumed and made no lasting ethical contribution. Therefore, this labour remained at the bottom of the hierarchy of values and was rewarded accordingly.

Arendt's analysis of the downgrading of 'labour' in relation to 'work' appears to be confirmed by a variety of theoretical positions and empirical observations in sociology. For example, there are those who share with **structural functionalism** the belief that differentials in pay reflect the differentiated nature of work. In this view, the **market** ensures that work that is more valuable to society is better rewarded. Since the market is the measure, the skills of the workers undertaking the most valuable work must be naturally scarce or hard to learn. These limitations on the supply of such workers guarantee that demand will exceed supply and, therefore, that such skills will be rewarded differently. From within the hierarchy of values Arendt describes, this equation of value and scarcity makes sense. Arendt's *labour* may be vitally necessary to the continuation of life but it has the lowest value. **Intellectual** and moral discomfort about the taken-for-granted nature of the hierarchy may be reduced with the introduction of the idea that the people who are capable of more valuable work must undertake more **education** and training in order to be acquire the necessary skills and therefore deserve greater rewards. But this 'human capital' theory begs the question of whether such education and training really do make people more productive or whether they simply provide them with credentials which legitimate their greater rewards (Collins 1979).

It is possible to be more critical of this hierarchy of values while still retaining a prominent role for the **market**. This is particularly common in theories where differential rewards are thought to have something to do with **class** and **status**. The idea that social groups have a hand in shaping the distribution of the rewards for work has a long pedigree. Galbraith (1958) described a 'new class' of mental labourers as the natural replacement for the old leisure class. Collins (1979) and Parkin (1979) followed Weber in arguing that groups accomplished the 'social closure' which helped them to achieve a degree of monopoly which created the necessary excess of demand over supply from which greater rewards would follow. In the theory of social closure, scarcity becomes a product of **agency**, but the market still dictates the level of rewards.

Yet the theoretical opportunities opened up by stepping outside the hierarchy of values described by Arendt have not been fully explored. To begin this process we must consider whether social groups may be the agents who devise and reproduce the hierarchy itself. **Bourdieu** (1986) proposed that in order to understand differential rewards for work we need to understand the way that social **groups** construct the frameworks within which competition takes place. From such a viewpoint, the values given to various kinds of work do not reflect scarcity, or even contrived scarcity, or people's propensity to invest in themselves. Rather, they reflect *culture* and *power*.

Two concluding points can be made in these connections. The first concerns the unpaid labour which tends to disappear from view. The view of work in the home as unpaid drudgery which destroys the soul – a view notably associated with the thought of Simone de **Beauvoir** – now commands a wide following. As Hochschild points out, in these circumstances it is not surprising that people do not want to do unpaid work, including child-care. The key agency in respect of this cultural change has not been class but **gender**. We must not think that the hierarchy of values described by Arendt actually refers to the value attached by everyone to this kind of labour, since gender was the key implicit dimension in Arendt's distinction between *work* and *labour*. The values attached to *work*, as distinct from *labour*, had always been male: men undertook the productive activity in Arendt's sense (for example, they produced use-values), whereas labour, and particularly any labour connected with children, was not only of very little value but was undertaken by women. Where women had once held to a rather different hierarchy of values, the intensification of feminist battles in the 1960s made more and more women attracted to this 'male' view of work. They no longer valued child-care or home-making enough to want to do it themselves. With women joining men in the same hierarchy of values, with labour at the bottom and productive work at the top, the seeds were sown for battles between partners who were now equally determined to avoid doing the low value labour and to prioritize their engagement with real, productive work.

A final point concerns the way in which work is created and what the future of work may be. It makes little sense to think about this hierarchy of values without also thinking about the way work is created. The constitution of places in the **division of labour** should not be taken for granted or assumed to be inevitably determined by imperatives of **technology**, efficiency or profit. The distribution of tasks in the division of labour, just as much as the distribution of income, is a function of the distribution of **power**, which can be challenged. Social groups create the work of the future in a way that suits their interests and their values. They may be able to recreate an existing monopoly of the sort described by social closure theory and thereby transfer their privileged status. But this process can also be subverted, by **social movements**. There is no certainty that men and women will always adhere to the hierarchy of values they have inherited from **tradition**.

References and further reading

Anthony, P. (1977) *The Ideology of Work*. London: Tavistock.

Arendt, H. (1967a) *Vita activa: oder Vom tätigen Leben*. Munich: Piper.

Arendt, H. (1967b) *Der Begriff der Arbeit bei Hannah Arendt*. Hamburg: Druckerei Lüdke.

Bourdieu, P. (1986) *Distinction: A Social Critique of the Judgement of Taste*. London: Routledge.

Collins, R. (1979) *The Credential Society*. New York: Academic Press.

Durkheim, E. ([1893] 1964) *The Division of Labor in Society*. New York: Free Press.

Engels, F. ([1845] 1958) *The Condition of the Working Class in England*. Oxford: Blackwell.

Galbraith, J. K. (1958) *The Affluent Society*. Boston: Houghton Mifflin.

Gorz, A. (1989) *Critique of Economic Reason*. London: Verso.

Hochschild, A. (1983) *The Managed Heart*. Berkeley, CA: University of California Press.

Hochschild, A. (1997) *The Time Bind*. New York: Metropolitan.

Mercure, D. and Spurk, J. (2003) *Le Travail dans l'histoire de la pensée occidentale*. Saint-Nicholas, Québec: Les Presses de l'Université Laval.

Mills, C. W. (1953) *White Collar*. Oxford: Oxford University Press.

Parkin, F. (1979) *Marxism and Class Theory*. London: Tavistock.

Sennett, R. (1998) *The Corrosion of Character*. New York: W. W. Norton.

Weber, M. ([1904–5] 1958) *The Protestant Ethic and the Spirit of Capitalism*. New York: Charles Scribner's Sons.

Whyte, W. H. (1956) *The Organization Man*. New York: Doubleday.

RALPH FEVRE

WORKING CLASS

The working class, composed of formally free, propertyless wage labour, formed in European social history as a comprehensive **class** during capitalist **industrialization** after the eighteenth century. Agrarian and craft populations migrated to growing manufacturing regions, dominated by insecure life and work conditions and massified experiences of urban housing, factories and institutions. This process did not, however, lead immediately to class unity or solidarity. Class links grew within regional communities but were marked initially and recurrently by strong differences of occupational skills and ethnicity and religion and by the effects of periodic migration. In many regions and nations, wage labourers remained embedded in small ownership milieus. Sociologists and historians discuss how such a 'class in itself' historically became, or becomes, a 'class for itself', with a distinct social and political identity. For a long while since the nineteenth century, the working class was distinguished in popular discourse from disreputable and precarious *Lumpenproletariat*. **Marxism** expected rising class antagonisms to transforming the workers into a revolutionary **proletariat**, homogenized by de-skilling and expropriation. The term 'proletariat' became widely used in popular Marxism, which expected capitalism to dissolve the middle classes into the factory proletariat, being deskilled, exploited, and demoralized. United by factory discipline, it would overthrow capitalism, instructed by communist theory and parties. In reality, however, historians such as E.P. Thompson (1963) found that among industrial workers – especially among Irish immigrants – 'immiseration' produced fatalism, while other data disproved general wage decreases. In the British case, class consciousness came to be formed among the skilled working classes and their traditions of dissent, opposing not so much machinery as political repression. Conflicts were antagonistic mainly only as exceptions. After 1848, movements turned to more institutionalized struggles for civil and economic rights. By the turn of the nineteenth century, class homogeneity did develop, but less as a class than as a segregated world of neighbourhoods, associations, **trade unions** and political parties. This latter movement was at first led by the ethos and worldview of the skilled labourers, based on a practical reformism that strove for respectability, better social conditions, for **education** and for a democratic redistribution of power *within* the capitalist system.

In Russia, where social and economic rights had been denied, Lenin revived the revolutionary model. Where Rosa Luxemburg ([1906] 1971) argued that skilled workers, participating in power conflicts, could develop autonomous political competences, Lenin held trade union consciousness was insufficient: workers needed leadership from party **intellectuals**. The Russian revolution followed Lenin, and the vision of proletarian abolition of domination became the legitimating ideology for **domination** over the working class.

In Western Europe by the 1920s, all these processes of class integration were challenged by a new contrary movement, caused by extended capitalist accumulation and by significant growth in service employment in clerical positions. Here the debate was whether the 'old middle estate' became proletarianized or just reconverted to a new middle estate. Mooser (1984), analyzing the case of West German workers since 1900, states that classic proletarization marked by urbanization, industrialization and de-skilling belongs to a phase ending in the 1920s. Thereafter occupational upward mobility continued and life chances were consolidated 'beyond proletarity' (see also Blauner 1964).

In the 1960s, the combination of increased wage labour and further processes of deproletarianization converged in a differentiated employee class in many countries. On the one hand, interrupted by fascist periods, manual workers lost their precarious standards through skill-upgrading, institutionalized collective bargaining, through the **welfare state** and through the achievement of greater of employment rights. Even Marxist commentators such as **Marcuse** predicted the end of the working class at this time, due to embourgeoisement, consumerism and ideological manipulation. Marcuse also modified the model for rebellious intellectuals: as workers were 'integrated', fundamental opposition could only come from marginalized groups or from the Third World. For others, such as **Dahrendorf** and

Geiger, class conflict had become 'institutionalized' and in this sense domesticated. Recent research has confirmed, however, that against a background of continued domination from employers, a working class identity persisted in this period, although the continuous sense of identity and solidarity was less of an 'emotional' character and more of a rational, instrumental nature based around efforts of labour organizations (Goldthorpe *et al.* 1968; Vester 1998). By the end of the 1960s, service employees, growing to a majority, had converged with workers in a largely common 'employee mentality', based on similar experiences and common attitudes towards employers and state authorities (Vester 2005). By 1970, two thirds of the working population worked in small and medium-sized enterprises, while four fifths owned their housing. 'Affluence' remained modest, as rising incomes and savings were mainly used for consumer needs, including housing, equipments, cars and vacations, paid by intensified labour and increasingly female employment. In Germany the skilled working class became more homogeneous, as new Turkish immigrants and former east German migrants took their places *below* skilled labour. At the better end, children left for qualified service jobs which often remained functional for industry, still employing around 35 per cent of the active population.

After 1970, these developments continued, but unemployment, skill polarization, immigration and welfare state deregulations increased, in competition with developing countries and their rising classical working classes. Sustained re-skilling (Blauner 1964; Piore and Sabel 1984) produced new differentiations of employee milieus, increasingly turning white collar workers into a 'new employee milieu', distinguished from the more traditional employee class factions and the precarious underclass milieus. Indeed their sense of difference from the bourgeois classes did not diminish in the 1970s and 1980s (Vester 1998). Class culture was not lost in the face of the rise of what many sociologists now call 'post-materalist values', but rather was modified and modernized (Hall and Jefferson 1977). Indeed it can be argued that political camps since the 1980s have eroded less than expected (Vester 1998, 2005). Class alliances are still predominantly aligned with conservative, social-democratic and liberal attitudes to the **welfare state**. But public questioning of the meaning of **social justice** has risen considerably since the last years of the twentieth century, as welfare state concepts move into crisis and standards of social **security** stagnate and become precarious even for members of the large employee middle class.

References and further reading

Blauner, R. (1964) *Alienation and Freedom: The Factory Worker and His Industry*. Chicago: University of Chicago Press.

Bourdieu, P. and Accardo, A. *et al.* (1999) *The Weight of the World*. Stanford: Stanford University Press.

Briefs, G. ([1926] 1975) *The Proletariat*. New York: Arno.

Goldthorpe, J. H., Lockwood, D., Bechhofer, F. and Platt, J. (1968) *The Affluent Worker in the Class Structure*. Cambridge: Cambridge University Press.

Hall, J. R. (ed.) *Reworking Class*. Ithaca, NY: Cornell University Press.

Hall, S. and Jefferson, T. (1977) *Resistance through Rituals: Youth Subcultures in Post-War Britain*. London: Hutchinson.

Lamont, M. (2000) *The Dignity of Working Men: Morality and the Boundaries of Race, Class and Immigration*. Cambridge, MA: Harvard University Press.

Mooser, J. (1984) *Arbeiterleben in Deutschland 1900–1970*. Frankfurt am Main: Suhrkamp.

Piore, M. J. and Sabel, C. F. (1984) *The Second Industrial Divide*. New York: Basic Books.

Thompson, E. P. (1963) *The Making of the English Working Class*. London: Penguin.

Vester, M. (1998) 'Was wurde aus dem Proletariat?' in J. Friedrichs, M. R. Lepsius and K. U. Mayer (eds) *Die Diagnosefähigkeit der Soziologie*. Opladen: Westdeutscher Verlag.

Vester, M. (2005) 'Class and Culture in Germany', in F. Devine, M. Savage, J. Scott and R. Crompton, *Rethinking Class*. Basingstoke: Palgrave Macmillan.

MICHAEL VESTER

WORLD SYSTEMS THEORY

World systems theory is an approach which takes the world as a whole as its unit of analysis. World systems theory in its early manifestations is certainly of Marxist origin because it was **Marx** and Engels who developed the first intrinsically global account of **capitalism** in their seminal *Communist Manifesto* of 1848. In their picture, capitalism's key feature was its inherent restlessness due to competition on an ever higher scale. Consequently, entrepreneurs are driven to technological improvement and the cutting of prices in order to stay in the **market** or to tap new markets. In turn, Lenin portrayed the consequences of this competitive mechanism on the international level. Where Marx remained still primarily interested in domestic class struggle between the **bourgeoisie** and the **proletariat**, Lenin envisioned an international class struggle resulting from the 'laws of capitalist production'. This inherent tendency for capitalist expansion would eventually drive capitalism to conquer the globe. Thus Lenin and Rosa Luxemburg saw **imperialism** as the latest stage of developed capitalism, with the First World War as the logical outcome of the competition among capitalist nation-states for colonies and for new dependent markets.

After the Second World War, it was above all Latin American thinkers who took up this theoretical legacy in order to make sense of economic underdevelopment in Latin America. In this perspective, economic backwardness in South America was a direct effect of the exploitation by core capitalist economies of the West, mainly Europe and the USA. 'Dependency theory', as this type of reasoning came to be called, became increasingly popular among the Left in the West, although Cardoso, one of its creators, abandoned this theory long before eventually becoming president of Brazil.

In contemporary social theory, world systems theory has developed along three basic lines of thought. First and foremost, Immanuel **Wallerstein** distinguished between

(1) core countries, making up the eco-nomically developed centre, (2) the semi-periphery, and (3) the periphery and the external arena (see **centre and periphery**). In this view, it is the capitalist world econ-omy emerging in the sixteenth century in Europe which has shaped the world. The countries of the core comprising England, the Netherlands, France and – somewhat later – Germany created modern capitalistic enterprises in the process of **industrializa-tion**. By contrast, southern Europe, the semi-periphery, remained comparatively stag-nant and dependent upon the core. The periphery consisted of Eastern Europe and the rest of the world. But here too, at the outer fringes, Wallerstein distinguishes between the periphery and what he calls the 'external arena'. During the time of Eur-opean take-off, the external arena consisted of Africa and large parts of Asia which remained isolated from world exchange and trade. This was then followed by the era of colonialism and later by the intervention of large corporations, drawing these con-tinents into the world economy. At the same time, the core was extended from Europe to Japan and the USA by the sec-ond half of the twentieth century. What never changed throughout this process, however, was the same basic pattern of exploitation whereby First world countries profit from the less developed world.

Despite the advantage of treating the world as system dominated by global capit-alism, however, one weakness of Waller-stein's approach is his exclusive concentration on the capitalist economy to the detriment of political and cultural factors. This is the line of reasoning taken among others by John W. Meyer (see Meyer *et al.* 1997) and Niklas **Luhmann**. What Meyer and his collaborators observe is a striking degree of political and cultural *conformity* toward glo-bal models at the level of institutions such as education and political constitutions. Throughout the world after the Second World War, more and more independent nation-states exhibit similar patterns as to what it means to be a 'good nation-state', to serve one's people, and to create 'good schooling'. For Meyer, the challenge is how to explain this surprising pattern of convergence in an economically and ideo-logically divided world. On the one hand, **associations**, **professions** and academics set up new standards in different domains of social life, only to see them established on a world-wide scale. On the other hand, establishment 'on paper' does not necessarily mean establishment in practice. The 'brave new world' creates new forms of strife, particularly if the differences between the ideal on paper and practical reality are addressed by non-governmental actors and social movements as unjust inequality.

Another approach is developed by Niklas Luhmann. From an early stage in his work, Luhmann sought to make sense of the glo-bal interconnectedness of the world. Mod-ern society is characterized by functional **differentiation** with social systems specia-lised in different areas such as the economy, polity, education and science. Yet this domestic process in one modern society needs a common reference point which is not necessarily a system. Luhmann calls this entity the 'world society' – a kind of global imaginary whose smallest common denomi-nator is 'communicative reachability'. Being within communicative reach thus marks the limits of world society for Luhmann.

All three of these types of world systems theory are far from satisfactory: Wallerstein is too economistic, Meyer too idealistic, and Luhmann perhaps too abstract. But all three approaches demonstrate the fruitful-ness of conceptualizing the world as a social unit. In this respect, world systems theory is part and parcel of **globalization** studies.

References and further reading

Arrighi, G. (1994) *The Long Twentieth Century: Money, Power, and the Origins of our Times.* London: Verso.

Bairoch, P. (1993) *Economics and World History: Myths and Paradoxes*. Chicago: University of Chicago Press.

Cardoso, F. H. and Faletto, E. (1979) *Dependency and Development in Latin America*. Berkeley, CA: University of California Press.

Chase-Dunn, C. K. (1989) *Global Formation: Structures of the World-Economy*. Cambridge, MA: Blackwell.

Lenin, V. I. (1939) *Imperialism, the Highest Stage of Capitalism: A Popular Outline*. New York: International Publishers.

Luhmann, N. (1997) *Die Gesellschaft der Gesellschaft*. Frankfurt am Main: Suhrkamp.

Meyer, J. W., Boli, J., Thomas, G. and Ramirez, F. (1997) 'World Society and the Nation-State', *American Journal of Sociology*, 103(1): 144–81.

Wallerstein, I. M. (1974) *The Modern World System*. New York: Academic Publishers.

Wallerstein, I. M. (1979) *The Capitalist World System*. Cambridge: Cambridge University Press.

HANS-PETER MÜLLER

WORLD-VIEW

A 'world-view' is the total set of beliefs, values and basic background assumptions held in common by a group of people or culture, either self-consciously (as in an **ideology**, **discourse** or **paradigm**) or unconsciously (as intuition, faith or **myth**). The modern roots of reflection on world-views lie in late eighteenth and early nineteenth century German-language debates about culture and language (Hamann and Herder) and about universal reason and world history (Kant and Hegel). A century later Wilhelm **Dilthey** developed an explicit theory of world-views (*Weltanschauungslehre*) as part of his broader theory of the human sciences (*Geisteswissenschaften*). Dilthey's project was extended, criticized, and modified across the century in **Weber**'s interpretive sociology, in Husserl's **phenomenology**, and in **Mannheim**'s sociology of knowledge. Discussion of world-views in twentieth-century social theory has been animated by three kinds of concerns: anxieties about cultural difference and **relativism**; an ideological concern to convert others to one's own world-view (most notably by the world **religions** and ideological sects of social and political movements); and attempts to preserve the free agency and creativity of humans and of culture over and against structural logics and systems. The most important interlocutors on notions of world-view as reflections of socio-economic location have absorbed Weber as much as Marx in their work. They include **Lukács** on **reification** and **Gramsci** on **hegemony** and counter-hegemonic culture. In England, William Hoggart's 'uses of literacy', E.P. Thompson's 'moral economy' and Raymond Williams's 'structures of feeling' provided a conceptual template for two decades of cultural studies. In the sociology of religion, there have been attempts to differentiate world-view from ideology, church-sect-mysticism (after Troeltsch), enculturation and belief. Today, the world-religions, Americanism, anti-Americanism, and the **globalization** of the world-system all appear as contenders to replace the world-views that previously dominated 'the age of ideologies' as Samuel Huntingdon (1996) has controversially stated.

References and further reading

Dilthey, W. (1957) *Philosophy of Existence: Introduction to Weltanschauungslehre*. New York: Bookman Associates

Huntingdon, S. (1996) *The Clash of Civilizations and the Remaking of the World Order*. New York: Simon and Schuster.

Jaspers, K. (1919) *Psychologie der Weltanschauungen*. Berlin: Springer.

Mannheim, K. ([1929] 1976) *Ideology and Utopia*. London: Routledge & Kegan Paul.

Mannheim, K. (1952) 'The Problem of "Weltanschauung"' in id., *Essays in the Sociology of Knowledge*. London: Routledge.

Morrow, R. A. (1996) 'Weltanschauung', in M. Payne (ed.) *A Dictionary of Cultural and Critical Theory*. Oxford: Blackwell.

Scheler, M. (1963) *Schriften zur Soziologie und Weltanschauungslehre*. Bern: Francke.

TREVOR HOGAN

Z

ŽIŽEK, SLAVOJ (1949–)
Slovenian theorist

Žižek is today's most prominent exponent of the **psychoanalytical** approach to **cultural** and social phenomena. He extends the insights of the psychoanalyst Jacques **Lacan** from the clinical field to many other areas, including **popular culture**, opera, literature, philosophy and politics. Žižek employs Lacanian categories such as 'enjoyment', 'fantasy', 'the **imaginary**', 'the real', and 'the **symbolic**' as tools for social analysis. These allow him to re-invigorate the theory of **ideology**, arguing that ideology does not consist in forms of 'distorted representation', as stated by **Marxism**, but in the very obliteration or imaginary concealment of the inherent limit of all social **objectivity**. This limit, which Lacan calls 'the real', shows itself in the social field in the form of antagonism and class struggle. Similarly, Žižek argues that the **subject** must be conceptualized along Lacanian lines as a lack in the symbolic **structure** of the social, rather than being determined by the latter – as **classical structuralist** theorists claimed. Žižek's work, together with those of other members of the so-called Slovenian Lacanian school, has made a considerable impact on current **post-structuralist** theorizing and cultural studies.

Major works

(1989) *The Sublime Object of Ideology*. London: Verso.
(1991) *For They Know Not What They Do*. London: Verso.
(1999) *The Ticklish Subject*. London: Verso.
(2000) (with Judith Butler and Ernesto Laclau) *Contingency, Hegemony, University*. London: Verso.

Further reading

Stavrakakis, Y. (1999) *Lacan and the Political*. London: Routledge.
Torfing, J. (1999) *New Theories of Discourse: Laclau, Mouffe and Žižek*. Oxford: Blackwell.
Žižek, S., Wright, E. and Wright, E. (1999) *The Žižek Reader*. Oxford: Blackwell.

OLIVER MARCHART

index

Bold numbers indicate a main entry

action(s) **1–4**, 33, 38, 74, 103, 106; collective 127; complexity 89; conception of 117; cooperation 287; emotion 167; functionalism 211; game theory 215; greatest amount of happiness 563; hermeneutics 246; Homans 254; human 51, 188, 371, 553; human and play 433; imperialism , unilateral political 268; individuals and 134; interactions between and actors 571; interpretations of agents' 359; language or language-like symbolic systems 323; Luhmann 329; markets 333; meaning 346; mediated and self 540; microsocial units such as 361; model of intentional 50; modernity 371; morality 380; needs 393; networks 395; outcome and structuration school 604; overcoming dualism of mind and body 217; Pareto and theory of 415; persons are responsible for their 425; police and uses of force 436; political 86, 439; polity 440; preferences 465; principle of utility and human 652; products of 467; property rights 473; protest 475–6; public 482; rational choice theorists 493; Ricoeur 517; rights 518; ritual 522; scientists and rational 430; Smith and distinct orientations 552; social 389; social and rationality 495; social relations 567; society 580; states and Skocpol 549; structuration school 604; symbolic interactionism 616; teaching and professional 470; theory of 78; Tilly on in revolutions 625; two fundamental modes 114; typifications which structure 429; the unconscious can subvert conscious thought 641; *Verstehen* 656; vocation and a discipline for 660; women's movement 675

actor-network theory **4–5**, 154, 258, 312, 377, 505–6, 534

actor(s), identity formed through shifting network of relations 4; inequality between two or more 275; institutions 280; working through forms of society 342

Adorno, Theodor Wiesengrund **5**, 22, 101, 113, 170, 193, 205; Frankfurt School 342, 481; friend of Horkheimer 255; Gehlen and 218; 'mass culture' 341; myth 386; 'positivism dispute' 444; power of the media 350; rationalization 495; science, concern over 533; totality 631; World analysis of 'total administration' 340

aesthetic 445, 510, 674

age **5–8**, 68, 123, 130–31, 143, 165, 223–5; generation 6–8; groups 237; leisure 318; marriage 335; medical involvement 354; old and individualization 271; old and welfare state 671; poverty 456

agency **8–10**, 190, 201, 354; active and prestige 466; agent-oriented and range of variants 567; and agents in rational choice 493; audience membership in mass media 352; culture leaves little room for 576; education 432; functionalism 211; Giddens 226; habitus 240; human 149, 257, 393, 643; lacking through poverty 456; liminality 323; masculine forms as normative 223; media and mass media 350; messianic and totality 630; neglect of collective social under post-Fordism 448; neglect in functionalism and related theories 525; Nietzsche 397; political economy 438; positivism 444; pre-existing structure 604; products of 467; public sphere 485; Queer theory 489; or rationality in philosophy of social science 431; reflexivity in 501; revolutionary process 515; role 524; scarcity becomes a product of 680; slaves 550; state and its agencies to exercise sovereignty 306; structure and 1, 39, 160; Touraine's emphasis on 631

Alexander, Jeffrey, C. **10–11**, 14, 119, 209, 371; critical relism 444; differentiation 141;

311, 344, 518; subjectivity 613; trust in 638; vocation 660

person and personality 8, 67, 173, **425–7**

personality 114, 304

petty bourgeoise *see* bourgeoisie; middle class

phallocentrism 309, 327, 421, **427**, 506

phenomenological analysis, measurement 349

phenomenological sense 81, 281, 299, 332

phenomenological sociology, social constructionism 556

phenomenology 3, 28, 31, 77, 118, 180, 290, 315, 322, **427–9**; Bourdieu and 38; classical and Schutz 36; empiricism 169; Heidegger 246; hermeneutics 247; humanism 257; Husserl's 329, 685; Mannheim 332; master-slave dialectic 342; Merleau-Ponty 165, 357; philosophical traditions and space and place 586; realism 498; Ricoeur 517; social constructionism 556; social studies of science 570; socialization 576; structuration school 604; symbols and social theory 614

philosophy 38, 498, 513, 542, 545, 547, 569

philosophy of social science 87, 218, 239, 391, **429–32**, 443, 463, 495

Piaget, Jean 33–4, 80, 99, 203, **432**, 604

planning *see* governance and governmentality

play and game 183, 200, 202, 311, **433–4**, 469, 523

pluralism 14, 85, 173, 321, 351, **434–6**; balance of power 458; debates about legal pluralism 313; instead of religious monopolies 511; modern 115; philosophy of social science 431; postmodernism 647; Reisman 518; relativism 506; value and multiculturalism 383; Western society and parties 418

police 343, 378, **436–7**, 557, 650, 657

Polish Peasant in Europe and America, The 55

political economists, French and mode of production 468

political economy 3, 7, 57, 104, 154, 164, 301, 304, 322, 329, 365, 370, **437–40**; capitalist and organization 408; effect of reduction of work 678; explaining of the *polis* 437; fascism 192; gender 220; globalization 228; Islam 295; media 351; mixed 34; new and rational choice 494; power and elite 458; problems of 45; reflexivity 501; relationship to war 664; Smelser and sociological approach 551; Smith and 338; social capital 552; of space 316; structure 608; unemployment 644; vocation and leadership 660; wage 420; Weber 671

politics, modernity 371, 570, 577, 622

polity 97, 105, 123, 173, 207, 276, **440–41**; reflexivity 501; structure 608; urbanization 648; warfare 666

Popper, Karl Raimund 78, 139, 169, 218, 362, 406, **441**; falsification criterion 430;

historicism 251, 626; 'open society' 408; rationalism 444, 495

popular culture 29, 37, 40, **441–3**; intimacy 291; leisure 318; Riesman 518; utopia 654

populations 7

positivism 2, 5, 36, 73, 76, 114, 240, 255, 300, 326, **443–5**; anti- 260; Comte is founder of term 'sociology' and 90, 256; dispute with 'interpretivism' 360; dispute and rationality 495; empiricism 169; essentialism 174; legal 313; naturalism 391; (neo-), comparative methods 87; ontology 407; Pareto 415; philosophy of social science 430; Popper 441; realism 498; scientific and relativism 506; state of in Comte 553; time 626; universalism 646; upward reductionism explanatory ideal of 500

positivist, interpretation of *Verstehen* 657

positivist thinking, British 104; 'irrational' or 'non-rational' factors 3

post-colonial theory 13–14, 40, 79, 118, 135, 139, 150, 164–5, 406, **445–7**; *Black Skin White Masks* 192; critical theory 246; critique of universal human rights 647; de-colonization 574; ethnicity 175; Fanon's discussion 414; globalization 228; hybridity 257; Islam 295; monies imposed by colonizing power 378; Orientalism 413; perspective of psychoanalysis 481; relativism 507; Said 530; science and global colonization 533; standpoint epistemology 590

post-colonialism 117, 121, 569

post-colonialist critics 179

post-Fordism 101, 228, 342, 410, **447–9**, 468

post-industrial society 34, 46, 71, 152, 274, 296, 420, **449–51**, 467, 497; 'end of history' 622; services-based sectors in the city 650; Soviet era and Scientific Technological Revolution 622; Touraine 631; unemployment 644

post-Marxist, analysis of political struggle 487

post-materialist, values and social movements 565

postmodern, architecture 40; city and crises 650; deviance 135–6; domination, thinkers on 148; embodiment 164; identities 80; and modern theories of psychoanalysis 479; patriarchy 420; social theories and ideal of totalitarianism 630; societies and police 436; structuration 603; theories of restructuring or destructuring of class 71; theory of leisure 318; thinkers and myth 286

postmodernism 22, 30–31, 80, 86, 135, 163, 369; emphasizes pluralism, difference and particularity 647; end to idea of progress 472; Gehlen 218; Giddens 227; Habermas 239; Jameson 296; in organization studies 409; positivism 444; post-colonial theory 445;

post-structuralism 454; 'production
paradigm' 467; relativism embraced under
heading of 506; representation 376; social
constructionism 556; socialization 575, 576;
speculation about simulacra 548; symbolic
interactionism 617; tribe 635
postmodernism and postmodernity 30–31, 100,
137, 221, 330, 340, 350, **451–3**, 576
postmodernist, attitude to communication 80;
critiques 257; militant relativist positions 401;
perspective and play 434; tendencies 163;
theories 376
postmodernity 116, 120, 263
'postpositivist' theory 10
post-structuralism 116, 133, 135, 145, 163, 175,
195, 221, **453–5**; and criticisms of
Enlightenment project 581; French and
psychoanalysis 481; Heidegger 246; identity
263; Jameson 296; methods 360;
organizational studies 412; post-colonial
theory 445; racism 492; reality 499;
relativism 506; Rorty 527; sex/gender
distinction 544; social constructionism 556;
social control 559; socialization 575; and the
subject 612; and theory of sexuality 546; the
unconscious 642; variants of downward
reductionism 500
post-structuralist 125; approaches to space and
place 586; arguments of Derrida and
Foucault 257; psychoanalysts 404; queer
theory 487; theories 112, 245; theory and
social studies of science 570; thought and
myths 386
poverty **455–7**; concept of 131; culture of and
exclusion 561; debate on unemployment
benefit 645; eradicated under communism
82; freedom from indispensable to equality
321; migration 365; social justice 564;
socialism a reaction to new forms of 572;
space and place in 586; underclass 643;
unpaid portion of labour 338–9; urban 650;
utopia 653; variations in UK under different
welfare regimes 51; welfare state 671;
working classes and 45
power 9, 14, 24, 31, 36, 43, 115, 203, 316, **457–
62**; -knowledge 203; -knowledge relations
506; actors striving for produce social
practices 554; alien 442; another's and
security 538; archaeologists 124; Aristotle
and *politeia* 440; asymmetry between centre
and periphery 52; balance between spouses
189; balances 200; class and 68; coercive 284;
communicative media 326; consumers and
popular culture 443; corporate 108; of
counter-revolutionary forces 332; crime and
110; cultural productions of gender and
sexuality 487; death 123; democracy 127–8;

determines what is deviant 135; difference
101; differences between men and women
165; discourses and social 118, 146;
distinction between violence and 657;
distribution of power and work 680;
dynamics and Mills 368; early socialists 573;
economic and regionalism 502;
egalitarianism 158; elites 161; embodiment
165; emotion 167; European societies 123;
exchange theory and networks 186;
exclusion 561; feudalism 198; form and
forms 202; Foucault and 'technologies of the
self' 540; Foucault 233; functionalism 209;
game theory 215; gender and social 219;
group 237; hermeneutics 248; Homans 255;
identity 263; ideology 265; imbalances in
marriage 336; imperialism 269;
individualization 272; industrialization 274;
inequality 275; knowledge is 305; labour 79;
legitimation of 313; macro-structural variable
362; Mann 331; markets 333; mass media
350; media 345; medical 354;
'misrecognized' in schooling system 567;
needs 393; Nietzsche on 397; parental abuse
of and society 482; patriarchal in post-
industrial society 420; pluralism 434; political
economy and political 437; political in mid-
nineteenth-century Europe 157; political and
public sphere 483; positivism and 444; post-
industrial society 450; in poverty 456;
productive of psychological categories 399;
of professions 470–71; property 473;
Protestant ethic 477; in public sphere 484;
reflexivity on amounts of social 501; relations
and 'ordinary' spaces 587; relations in pre-
colonial society and caste 49; relationship
between and ritual 523; relationships shaped
by governance of property 475; religion 511;
republic fortified by citizens' civic virtue
514; role of 524; royal explained 374; 'sacred
ideals' retain 529; sexuality 546; in social
control 558; social structures 102; Spencer as
theorist of 587; standpoint epistemology 590;
state and legitimation of money 378; status
597–8; stratification 601; struggles between
social groups 75; struggles in post-
structuralism 454; subjectivity 613; territorial
and urbanism 649; terrorism to delegitimize
state and ruling class 623; universalism 647;
upper classes and marriage 335; war and
destroying social 665; in welfare state 672;
Western and Islam 295; 'Western' science
533; women and political 674
powers, separation of 96
practice(s) 165, 217, 262, 540, 556, 559, 621;
Chicago School codes and 55; consuming
342; distinction between values and norms

167; employment 644; ethnicity 177; groups 69, 671; health and illness 243; Homans 255; *karma* and caste in next life 49; labour-market and welfare 673; leisure 318; liminality 322; macro-structural variable 362; markets and 333–4; networks 396; prestige 466; recognition 499; rewards for work 680; role 524; security 538; social reproduction 568; social and social capital 552; socialization 575; Tocqueville on 627

stranger 61, 367, 389, **599–600**, 638, 640

stratification 470, **601–2**; age 5; American society and Mills 368; archaeologists 124; Bourdieu and 39; Coleman 77; development 134; elites 160; exclusion 561; functions in the city 650; harmonized theories of 71; hierarchy 15; impact of welfare state 673; industrialization 19; inequality 276; little in tribes 636; Marshall 337; poverty 455; question of underclass 643; social 52, 361; social of the electorate 418; status 597; theories that emphasize order in society 466; Weber on 92, 671

structural functionalism *see* functionalism

structural functionalist, school 281, 608

structural-functionalist thinking, 'consensus model' 93

structuralism 8, 23, 29, 75, 116, 118, 143, 195, 350, **602–4**; affinity for binary conceptual pairs 399; Althusser 340, 504; Durkheim 151; French and post-structuralism 453; Giddens 227; Jameson 296; Lacan 319; Lévi-Strauss 319; meaning 347; Merleau-Ponty 357; methods 360; myth 386; organized activity 409; Piaget 432; racism 492; Ricoeur 517; and structuration school 605; and structure 606; synchronic analysis 626; Touraine writing aginst grain of 631

structuralism and network theory 24, 145

structuration 1, 77, 216, 357, 460

structuration school 1, 9, 201, 211, 226, 507, 554, 603, **604–6**, 608

structure 34, 77, 117, 124, 168, 199, 344, **569**, **606–10**; action in social theory 1; basic 128, 361; consciousness has intentional 428; debates about human agency 8; degree of uniformity 94; domination 147; of economy and the state or social system 322; Elias 160; evolutionary mechanisms 185; family and kinship 304; gender and 220; groups 236; habitus 240; industrialization 273; inequality 275; interaction 288; internal and influence of inequality 587; kinship 303; markets as relating roles 333; myths 385; networks 394; outcome of conduct or agency 226; parties 417; post industrial society 449; post-structuralism neglects analysis of 455; practice

464; reductionism 500; reflexivity between agency and 501; relationship with agency and culture 10; ritual 523; role of mass media 350; social 33, 128, 413, 599, 612; time 626; underclass 643; untouchables at bottom of 48; versus agency and realism in organization 409

subculture **610–11**; exclusion and deviant 111, 137, 156, 236; poorest sections of society 642; specific behaviour of groups 658

subject and subjectivity 118, 225, 233, 251, 291, 372, 397, 399, **611–14**; person and personality 426; psychoanlysis 479; ritual 523; romanticism 526; social constructionism 556; socialization 576

subjective, definitions of social relations 567

subjective interests, values expressions of 656

subjectivism, anti-objective positions 402

subjectivity 57, 175, 203, 267, 272, 319, 357, 487; disciplined 448; race and racism 492; vulnerable to effects of the unconscious 575

subject(s) 115, 165, 173, 183, 317, 454, 546, 599; as agents 399; ambiguity between active agency and passive subjection 8; divided as effect of language 309; individual 107; other 414; relationship with object 428; social being 482; solidarity 583; structuralism 603; turned into objects with money 375; who engage in common activity 384

suicide *see* deviance

surveillance *see* social control

Sweden, Church of 58

Switzerland, church and state 58

symbol 64, 80, 103, 116, 159, 202, 217, 310, 351, **614–16**; destruction of power and protest 475; emotion 167; framing 204; group 237; hegemony 245; knowledge 278; Lacan 309; measurement 348; phallocentric position of phallus 427; postmodern of consumerism 453; ritual 522; role and personal identity 280–81; solidarity 583; structure 608; use of in living in society 463; Wittgenstein 674

symbolic, 'culture' determining belief in race 491; means of terrorists 624

symbolic content 217

symbolic forms, knowledge and 305; structures of meaning and 117

symbolic identity 13

symbolic interactionism 8, 33, 38, 55, 77, 111, 136, 149, **616–17**; Blumer and 183, 281, 463; Goffman 232; groups 236; identity 262; Mead 346; methods and methodology 359; micro-level 362; play and game 433; role of the other 525; social constructionism 556; social control 558; social studies of science